INSTRUCTORS...

Would you like your **students** to show up for class **more prepared**?
(Let's face it, class is much more fun if everyone is engaged and prepared...)

Want an **easy way to assign** homework online and track student **progress**?
(Less time grading means more time teaching...)

Want an **instant view** of student or class performance? *(No more wondering if students understand...)*

Need to **collect data and generate reports** required for administration or accreditation? *(Say goodbye to manually tracking student learning outcomes...)*

Want to **record and post your lectures** for students to view online?

 With **McGraw-Hill's *Connect*™ *Plus Business Law*,**

INSTRUCTORS GET:

- Simple **assignment management**, allowing you to spend more time teaching.

- **Auto-graded** assignments, quizzes, and tests.

- **Detailed Visual Reporting** where student and section results can be viewed and analyzed.

- Sophisticated **online testing** capability.

- A **filtering and reporting** function that allows you to easily assign and report on materials that are correlated to accreditation standards, learning outcomes, and Bloom's taxonomy.

- An easy-to-use **lecture capture** tool.

- The option to **upload course documents** for student access.

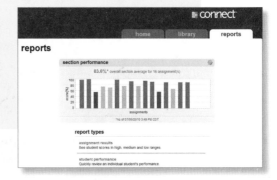

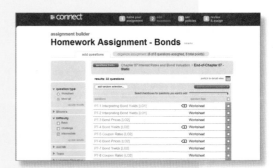

Want an online, **searchable version** of your textbook?

Wish your textbook could be **available online** while you're doing your assignments?

 ### *Connect™ Plus Business Law* eBook

If you choose to use *Connect™ Plus Business Law*, you have an affordable and searchable online version of your book integrated with your other online tools.

Connect™ Plus Business Law eBook offers features like:

- Topic search
- Direct links from assignments
- Adjustable text size
- Jump to page number
- Print by section

 Want to get more **value** from your textbook purchase?

Think learning business law should be a bit more **interesting**?

 ### Check out the STUDENT RESOURCES section under the *Connect™* Library tab.

Here you'll find a wealth of resources designed to help you achieve your goals in the course. Every student has different needs, so explore the STUDENT RESOURCES to find the materials best suited to you.

THE LEGAL ENVIRONMENT *of* BUSINESS

A MANAGERIAL APPROACH

Theory to Practice

SEAN P. MELVIN

Elizabethtown College

THE LEGAL ENVIRONMENT OF BUSINESS: A MANAGERIAL APPROACH: THEORY TO PRACTICE

Published by McGraw-Hill/Irwin, a business unit of The McGraw-Hill Companies, Inc., 1221 Avenue of the Americas, New York, NY, 10020. Copyright © 2011 by The McGraw-Hill Companies, Inc. All rights reserved. No part of this publication may be reproduced or distributed in any form or by any means, or stored in a database or retrieval system, without the prior written consent of The McGraw-Hill Companies, Inc., including, but not limited to, in any network or other electronic storage or transmission, or broadcast for distance learning.

Some ancillaries, including electronic and print components, may not be available to customers outside the United States.

This book is printed on acid-free paper.

1 2 3 4 5 6 7 8 9 0 DOW/DOW 1 0 9 8 7 6 5 4 3 2 1 0

ISBN 978-0-07-337769-8
MHID 0-07-337769-4

Vice president and editor-in-chief: *Brent Gordon*
Editorial director: *Paul Ducham*
Publisher: *Doug Hughes*
Executive editor: *John Weimeister*
Director of development: *Ann Torbert*
Senior development editor: *Trina Hauger*
Vice president and director of marketing: *Robin J. Zwettler*
Senior marketing manager: *Sarah Schuessler*
Vice president of editing, design, and production: *Sesha Bolisetty*
Lead project manager: *Christine A. Vaughan*
Senior buyer: *Carol A. Bielski*
Senior designer: *Mary Kazak Sander*
Senior photo research coordinator: *Jeremy Cheshareck*
Photo researcher: *Ira C. Roberts*
Senior media project manager: *Greg Bates*
Typeface: *10/12 Times Roman*
Compositor: *Laserwords Private Limited*
Printer: *R. R. Donnelley*

Library of Congress Cataloging-in-Publication Data

Melvin, Sean P.
    Legal environment of business : a managerial approach : theory to practice / Sean P. Melvin.
        p.   cm.
    Includes index.
    ISBN-13: 978-0-07-337769-8 (alk. paper)
    ISBN-10: 0-07-337769-4 (alk. paper)
      1. Businesspeople—United States—Handbooks, manuals, etc. 2. Law—United States—
    3. Business law—United States. I. Title.
    KF390.B84M45 2011
    346.7307—dc22
                                                                                          2010029961

This book is dedicated to my students:
past, present, and future.

Sean P. Melvin is an associate professor of business law at Elizabethtown College (PA) where he has taught since 2000 and served as department chair for eight years. Prior to his appointment at Elizabethtown, he was an assistant professor of business at West Chester University of Pennsylvania, where he taught in both the undergraduate and MBA program. Before his academic career, Professor Melvin was a corporate lawyer in a large Philadelphia-based law firm and went on to become vice president and general counsel at a publicly traded technology company. He is the author of five books (including two textbooks), has contributed over a dozen scholarly and professional articles and case studies to various publications, and is a member of the Academy of Legal Studies in Business.

preface

Think of this textbook as a roadmap that guides you through the twists and turns of the laws that impact business entities, owners, and managers. This roadmap will help you understand ways in which business owners and managers can add value to their companies by using legal insight for business planning and limiting liability. I have tailored the text, examples, cases, and teaching features to the needs of business students by providing concise explanations of law (theory), then supplying the tools necessary to apply their knowledge in the business environment (practice).

MASTERING THE MATERIAL

The first step in mastering the material is to recognize that you must *internalize* the concepts presented in your courses. This requires more than a casual reading of assignments. For many years, I have asked students who earned an "A" in my courses to write a few sentences of advice to future students on how to internalize the material and achieve a top grade in the course. I offer you some of their collective wisdom:

- At the beginning of the course, match the syllabus with the textbook. Note the areas that the instructor is focused on by comparing the amount of coverage between topics. For example, if it appears from the syllabus that you will be spending several classes on constitutional law, that is an area that will undoubtedly be assessed (through an examination, project, etc.) and requires more intense study and review.

- The day before a class, study the assignment as follows: (1) read the major and minor headings in the textbook to get a general sense as to what the material covers; (2) go back and read the text carefully using a highlighter and pencil to mark important text and make notes in the margins; and (3) review the concept summaries, flow charts, and self-checks to be sure you understand the material and put question marks next to any concept you do not understand.

- The day of your class, if possible, take 15 minutes before your class and review the highlighted text, margin notes, and concept summaries.

- During class, be sure that your text is open and that your notes are tied to any assignments in the text. For example, suppose your instructor has taken time to go over the concept of jurisdiction in some detail during class, drew a flowchart on the board, and went over the self-check answers. This is a clear sign that jurisdiction will be assessed in some form (most commonly through an examination or quiz). In your notes on jurisdiction, indicate that the concept is important (and requires more intense study) and cross-reference it with page numbers in your textbook.

- As soon as possible after class (ideally, immediately after class but no later than that same evening), take 15 minutes to write out 10 note cards. First, write out five of the most important concepts covered in class that day. Second, write out five terms (words or short phrases) that were used by the instructor during class. This will give you a convenient and portable resource for reviewing.

Finally, I offer you the same advice for success in your course that I have offered my own students for more than a decade: the secret is that there is no secret. No methodology, advice, or review cards substitute for sustained and diligent study of the material.

A NOTE TO THE INSTRUCTOR

The instructor's materials are based on a turnkey approach that provides a comprehensive set of course materials along with the textbook. These materials have been developed with an eye toward minimizing instructor preparation time, while still allowing the instructor to tailor the course in way that meets the unique needs of instructors and students alike. In addition to the traditional supplementary materials package that includes an *Instructor's Manual* (written by the author), test bank, and PowerPoint slides, the instructor's version of the textbook package is also integrated with a robust package of online content including McGraw-Hill's unique interactive exercises via Connect, quizzes, links to streaming videos, case updates, sample text-specific syllabi with alternatives for a variety of classroom circumstances, multiple formats, teaching notes, sample questions, and assignment sheets tied to the simulation materials and the capstone case studies.

Contact Information   I invite you to contact me with any comments, suggestions, or updates. A special link to my e-mail address may be located on this textbook's Web site www.mhhe.com/melvin.

Sean P. Melvin

walkthrough

Beginning of Chapter Features

Each chapter begins with a *Learning Outcomes Checklist* and a short overview that provides students with a map of the chapter. The *Learning Outcomes Checklist* is a point-by-point checklist of the skills and learning objectives, which gives students a convenient study guide for previewing and reviewing material in the chapter.

learning outcomes checklist

After studying this chapter, students who have mastered the material will be able to:

3-1 Explain the role of the judiciary in the context of the American legal system.

3-2 Distinguish between the role of federal courts and state courts.

3-3 Identify the responsibilities of trial courts versus appellate courts.

3-4 Articulate how the law develops via adjudication of cases.

3-5 Differentiate between subject matter jurisdiction and personal jurisdiction.

3-6 List the types of controversies over which federal courts have subject matter jurisdiction.

CASE 3.1   Estate of Weingeroff v. Pilatus Aircraft, 566 F.3d 94 (3rd Cir. 2009)

FACT SUMMARY   The legal representative of the estate of Weingeroff ("Weingeroff"), a passenger on a turboprop plane who was killed when the plane crashed near State College, Pennsylvania, brought a negligence and product liability lawsuit against Pilatus Air ("Pilatus"), the manufacturer of the plane. The plane crashed when approaching a small airport in Pennsylvania on a planned stop en route between Florida and Rhode Island. Weingeroff sued Pilatus in a federal district court situated in the Eastern District of Pennsylvania. Pilatus, a Swiss company, asked the court to dismiss the case for lack of personal jurisdiction. Pilatus claimed that they had no offices, no agents, no commercial transactions with Pennsylvania residents, and no physical presence in the state that constitutes purposeful availment. Weingeroff pointed to evidence that (1) Pilatus had conducted a nationwide marketing campaign in the United States

$1,030,139 in products, equipment, or services from suppliers in Pennsylvania, this amount represented less than 1 percent of Pilatus's total annual purchases for an approximately five-year period.

WORDS OF THE COURT: Purposeful Availment   "We acknowledge that there is a certain reasonableness to an argument that a manufacturer should be subject to suit in a jurisdiction in which its plane crashes if the suit charges that a manufacturing defect caused the crash. Yet it is clear that the critical finding that the defendant purposefully availed itself of the privilege of conducting activities within the forum [state] requires contacts that amount to a deliberate reaching into the forum state to target its citizens. Pilatus's efforts to exploit a national market necessarily included Pennsylvania as a target, but those efforts simply do not constitute the type of deliberate contacts within Pennsylvania

Cases

The textbook uses a *hybrid* format to report case law rather than including lengthy excerpts from judicial opinions. Students are provided with (1) a summary of the facts, (2) a decision and opinion synopsis, (3) short excerpts from the actual opinion called "Words of the Court" that helps students understand a key point in the case, and (4) several case questions to facilitate discussion. Students will find this format useful for understanding legal cases in a business context.

Business Ethics Discussion

The coverage of business ethics continues its increasingly important place in the business world. In addition to Chapter 5, "Business, Societal, and Ethical Contexts of Law," the textbook features logically placed boxes with discussion questions intended to help students understand ethical decision making in contemporary contexts. *Business Ethics Discussion* topics include a wide variety of topics, including an examination of the practices of AIG, Countrywide Mortgage, and others involved in the financial crisis that began in 2008.

BUSINESS ETHICS *perspective*

Ethical Issues Involved in Abusive Litigation

While commercial litigation typically involves two parties attempting to resolve a legitimate dispute in good faith, the costs, burdens, and uncontrollable risks of litigation render it subject to potential abuse. Although federal and state courts have strict procedural rules intended to curb abusive litigation, it is sometimes difficult to enforce those rules because of the inherent vagueness in defining what constitutes abusive. Abusive litigation may be defined as *vexatious* litigation or abuse of the litigation *process*.

Vexatious litigation may be defined as lawsuits that are filed for reasons other than legitimate damages being suffered by the plaintiff. These illegitimate reasons include using a lawsuit to harass, annoy, intimidate, or cause the opposite party to expend unnecessary costs. Reread the *Alston v. Advance Brands and Importing Company* case featured earlier in this chapter (Case 4.1), and as you read consider the plight of the alcoholic beverage manufacturers in facing this lawsuit. The parents in Alston's group were members of a consumer advocacy group with the objective of curbing underage alcohol consumption. The plaintiffs' theory and proposed remedy was so speculative that it could conceivably fall within the vexatious category.

Self-Checks

Self-Check exercises offer students an opportunity to reinforce and apply the material being studied in the textbook. Students use black letter law and cases to answer short hypothetical questions on a specific topic. *Self-Check*s appear in the textbook after important legal concepts and are always keyed to problems faced by business managers and owners. *Answers to the Self-Checks* are provided at the end of the chapter.

Self-Check

Does a federal district court located in New Jersey have *subject matter* jurisdiction?

1. A New Jersey businessperson sues her in-state business partner for breach of contract that resulted in $40,000 in losses.

2. The U.S. Environmental Protection Agency sues a New Jersey corporation for cleanup costs under a federal statute that regulates local waste disposal.

3. A Pennsylvania resident sues a New Jersey corporation for an injury caused by the corporation's product resulting in $90,000 of unpaid medical bills.

4. A New Jersey corporation is sued by a New Jersey resident under the federal employment discrimination statutes.

5. A New Jersey resident sues the U.S. government in an appeal from the ruling of the U.S. Copyright Office.

Answers to this Self-Check are provided at the end of the chapter.

Solutions for Managers

In keeping with the text's managerial focus, *Solutions for Managers* provides practical answers for legal problems faced by managers and business owners. *Solutions for Managers* is structured in a problem and solution format that allows students to understand how a particular section's legal concepts may be used to solve real-world business problems.

SOLUTIONS FOR MANAGERS   LO4-8

Online Dispute Resolution

PROBLEM *In situations involving small amounts of money, is there a way for a business to resolve such relatively minor disputes in a cost-effective manner?*

A business may be engaged in hundreds of relatively low-cost transactions per year with various out-of-state vendors such as suppliers, shipping companies, office supply stores, contractors, and the like. When disputes arise, a business may be at a distinct disadvantage and bargaining position because the amount in controversy is too low to justify even the least expensive form of alternative dispute resolution. However, over an extended period of time these small losses add up to unnecessary liabilities leaving managers with a difficult choice when faced with a dispute over a relatively low amount of money with an out-of-state vendor: (1) invest in a dispute resolution method despite the fact that the costs may very well exceed the benefits in that particular

Another form of ODR is more geared toward complex transactions. For example, Square Trade proposes prewritten resolutions. For example, if you received a damaged shipment of goods, Square Trade offers a standard menu of solutions such as (1) replacement with an undamaged good, (2) return for a full refund, or (3) keep the merchandise with a partial refund. The parties may also fill in their own solution, but this guided approach helps the parties focus on a resolution to the dispute.

If direct negotiation fails to resolve the issue, Square Trade users can request a mediator for a $20 fee per participant plus a percentage fee if the dispute exceeds $1,000. At OnlineResolution.com, mediation fees range between $15 and $25. For disputes of more than $500, participants each pay $50 per party per hour scaling up to $150 per party per hour, based on the value under

Concept Summaries and Flowcharts

To help students with *reinforcing* and *reviewing* the application of the law in a business context, each major section within each chapter features a summary of the section. When a legal procedure is involved, flowcharts are used to summarize the process.

CONCEPT SUMMARY   Jurisdiction

	Federal Trial Courts	State Trial Courts
Personal Jurisdiction	1. Residents and business entities located in the state where the federal trial court sits; or 2. Nonresidents with *minimum contacts* with the state in which the federal trial court sits; or 3. Nonresidents owning property in the state in which the federal trial court sits; or 4. Voluntary	1. Residents and business entities located in state; or 2. Nonresidents owning property in the state; or 3. Nonresidents with *minimum contacts* with the state according to state long-arm statutes; or 4. Voluntary
Subject Matter Jurisdiction	1. Federal question; or 2. U.S. is a party; or 3. Diversity of citizenship *and* amount in controversy is more than $75,000 (amount required only in diversity cases)	State law matters (statutes, common law, state constitutional issues).

End of Chapter Features

Each chapter ends with several features crafted to help students review and connect the different sections of the chapter by applying the material learned in the text in a practical way.

Theory to Practice: Each chapter features a hypothetical legal problem faced by a manager that is related to specific material in that chapter. The hypothetical problem is followed by 6–8 questions that connect the problem to several different sections in the chapter.

Manager's Challenge: This feature allows students to engage in writing or a group work assignment that sets forth a manager's task relating to the material in the chapter. Some challenges are designed for teams, others for individuals.

Key Terms: Key terms for students are boldfaced in the text, and listed as a group at the end of the chapter with a definition and reference to the page number in the chapter where the term was first mentioned.

Case Summaries: Four brief case summaries are included along with a heading for each that indicates its general topic reference to the chapter as well as questions about the case summary. These are intended to reinforce students' knowledge of how laws apply in different fact circumstances.

Other Textbook Features

Key Points (briefly reinforces an important concept); *Web Checks* (various Web sites related to the material in the textbook); *Legal Implications in Cyberspace* (applying traditional legal concepts in the context of the Internet); *Legal Speak* (instant definitions of important legal terms provided in the margins of the text).

Business Law Simulation Exercises for Managers

The textbook features three business law simulation exercises. In a simulation exercise, students are provided with facts, law, and cases related to a hypothetical business dispute, and are assigned to analyze the material, understand the legal and ethical issues presented, and then work toward a resolution. The simulations are also excellent for review and reinforcement because the materials involve cases directly related to one or more topics covered in a particular unit of the textbook.

BUSINESS LAW SIMULATION EXERCISE 1

Restrictive Covenants in Contracts: Neurology Associates, LLP v. Elizabeth Blackwell, M.D.

learning outcomes checklist

After studying this simulation, students who have mastered the material will be able to:

1. Explain the legal doctrines that govern the use of restrictive covenants.
2. Interpret and apply the rules set forth in current case law.
3. Articulate a cogent argument for each party/side in the dispute.
4. Negotiate a tenable solution as an alternative to a judicial forum.

Chapters 6 and 7 provided you with a variety of legal doctrines and rules governing contract formation and performance, and then illustrated how these doctrines and rules apply in the corporate sector context. This simulation is designed

The simulation is structured in three parts:
- Part 1 is a hypothetical fact pattern describing events leading up to a legal dispute in the hypothetical U.S. state of Longville.

CAPSTONE CASE STUDY 1
The Odwalla Juice Company Crisis

Overview and Objectives

In 1996, a deadly strain of bacteria broke out among residents of some West Coast states and eventually spread into western Canada. When the bacteria was traced to juice products made by the Odwalla Juice Company in California, the company's loyal customers and market analysts were shocked in disbelief. Odwalla had prided itself on being a socially responsible company that was passionate about producing the healthiest juice on the market.

The events that followed the outbreak provide an example of how vastly different areas of the law impact corporate strategy during a corporate crisis and how business ethics principles help drive the decision-making process. The objective of this case study[1] is to attempt to understand legal and ethical implications using a comprehensive and practical approach. In analyzing this case, students hone skills in constructing a business strategy for handing a crisis by (1) spotting the multifaceted legal and ethical challenges of the crisis, (2) recognizing the strengths and weaknesses in Odwalla's responses, and (3) using legal insight and ethical decision-making models to craft a response.

organic food consumption. Odwalla's founders held the belief that pasteurization, the process of heating the juice to a certain temperature for purposes of killing any bacteria that had developed during growing, picking, or processing, affected the taste of the juice and was unnecessary. Instead, Odwalla used an acid-based rinsing process to kill bacteria. Producing fresh organic fruit juice as a central component of its business model, Odwalla developed a loyal following of consumers that desired the freshest juice possible and its sales grew exponentially. By the mid-1990s, Odwalla was selling nearly $90 million worth of juice per year.

"SOIL TO SOUL"

Odwalla's founders were at the forefront of the corporate social responsibility movement that can be traced to the mid-1980s. Indeed, as one of their founders was fond of saying, they embraced a "Zen-like philosophy" in all of their dealings, where community was an important factor in the equation. The company employed a *soil to soul* metaphor to describe its commitment to using fresh organic fruit (soil) to nurture the "body whole" (soul) of its consumer. Odwalla's repu-

Capstone Case Studies

Capstone case studies center on the dilemmas of actual corporations that were faced with a corporate crisis involving legal and ethical issues. It is intended to help students connect several different legal and ethical concepts in a single case study. First, students reread concept summaries from specific chapters to reinforce their knowledge of specific legal issues. Second, students study a narrative of facts of the case, dynamics of the marketplace, and important trends of the time. Discussion questions are grouped by topical subject matter such as negligence, product liability, administrative agency regulation, criminal law, and so forth. Ethical decision-making questions are integrated into each case. The *Capstone Case Study* feature also provides a short exercise designed for use as a writing assignments, small group work, or class discussion.

support materials

Instructor's Manual

The instructor's manual, developed by the author, is designed to be an effective course management tool and an integral part of the turn-key approach used throughout the supplementary material package. The features and format are intended to give instructors maximum flexibility to determine and produce high-quality course content. The IM also has a special "Day One" section addressing important fundamental course decisions for instructors who are new to the course.

Test Bank

The test bank, created by Michael Katz of Delaware State University, allows instructors to custom design, save, and generate tests. The test bank includes multiple-choice, true-false, fill-in-the-blank, and essay questions for every chapter in the text. To help instructors meet the requirements of AACSB, each question is tagged with the corresponding chapter learning objective and applicable AACSB categories.

EZ Test

McGraw-Hill's flexible and easy-to-use electronic testing program allows instructors to create tests from book-specific items. It accommodates a wide range of question types, and instructors may add their own questions. Multiple versions of the test can be created, and any test can be exported for use with online course management systems. EZ Test Online allows you to administer EZ Test-created exams and quizzes online.

PowerPoint Presentation

The PowerPoint presentation, created by Kurt Stanberry of the University of Houston—Downtown, offers additional support by providing detailed teaching notes, particularly for more complex topics.

Online Learning Center, www.mhhe.com/melvin

The Online Learning Center includes study materials for students. Use the site to access the chapter review quizzes, key term review, legal resources, additional cases for discussion, online access to the UCC and US Constitution, and other news updates and resources.

You Be the Judge Online

This interactive product features case videos that showcase courtroom arguments of business law cases. These case videos give students the opportunity to watch profile interviews of the plaintiff and defendant, read background information, hear each case, review the evidence, make their decisions, and then access an actual, unscripted judge's decision and reasoning. There are also instructor's notes available with each video to help prepare you for classroom discussion.

MCGRAW-HILL *CONNECT BUSINESS LAW*

 Less Managing. More Teaching. Greater Learning.

McGraw-Hill *Connect Business Law* is an online assignment and assessment solution that connects students with the tools and resources they'll need to achieve success.

McGraw-Hill *Connect Business Law* helps prepare students for their future by enabling faster learning, more efficient studying, and higher retention of knowledge.

McGraw-Hill *Connect Business Law* Features

Connect Business Law offers a number of powerful tools and features to make managing assignments easier, so faculty can spend more time teaching. With *Connect Business Law,* students can engage with their coursework anytime and anywhere, making the learning process more accessible and efficient. *Connect Business Law* offers you the features described below.

Simple Assignment Management With *Connect Business Law,* creating assignments is easier than ever, so you can spend more time teaching and less time managing. The assignment management function enables you to:

- Create and deliver assignments easily with selectable end-of-chapter questions and test bank items.
- Streamline lesson planning, student progress reporting, and assignment grading to make classroom management more efficient than ever.
- Go paperless with the eBook and online submission and grading of student assignments.

Smart Grading When it comes to studying, time is precious. *Connect Business Law* helps students learn more efficiently by providing feedback and practice material when they need it, where they need it. When it comes to teaching, your time also is precious. The grading function enables you to:

- Have assignments scored automatically, giving students immediate feedback on their work and side-by-side comparisons with correct answers.
- Access and review each response; manually change grades or leave comments for students to review.
- Reinforce classroom concepts with practice tests and instant quizzes.

McGraw-Hill *Connect Plus Business Law* McGraw-Hill reinvents the textbook learning experience for the modern student with *Connect Plus Business Law.* A seamless integration of an eBook and *Connect Business Law, Connect Plus Business Law* provides all of the *Connect Business Law* features plus the following:

- An integrated eBook, allowing for anytime, anywhere access to the textbook.
- Dynamic links between the problems or questions you assign to your students and the location in the eBook where that problem or question is covered.
- A powerful search function to pinpoint and connect key concepts in a snap.

In short, *Connect Business Law* offers you and your students powerful tools and features that optimize your time and energies, enabling you to focus on course content, teaching, and student learning. *Connect Business Law* also offers a wealth of content resources for both instructors and students. This state-of-the-art, thoroughly tested system supports you in preparing students for the world that awaits.

For more information about Connect, go to **www.mcgrawhillconnect.com,** or contact your local McGraw-Hill sales representative.

TEGRITY CAMPUS: LECTURES 24/7

Tegrity Campus is a service that makes class time available 24/7 by automatically capturing every lecture in a searchable format for students to review when they study and complete assignments. With a simple one-click start-and-stop process, you capture all computer screens and corresponding audio. Students can replay any part of any class with easy-to-use browser-based viewing on a PC or Mac.

Educators know that the more students can see, hear, and experience class resources, the better they learn. In fact, studies prove it. With Tegrity Campus, students quickly recall key moments by using Tegrity Campus's unique search feature. This search helps students efficiently find what they need, when they need it, across an entire semester of class recordings. Help turn all your students' study time into learning moments immediately supported by your lecture.

To learn more about Tegrity watch a 2-minute Flash demo at **http://tegritycampus. mhhe.com.**

ASSURANCE OF LEARNING READY

Many educational institutions today are focused on the notion of *assurance of learning,* an important element of some accreditation standards. *The Legal Environment of Business* is designed specifically to support your assurance of learning initiatives with a simple, yet powerful solution.

Each test bank question for *The Legal Environment of Business* maps to a specific chapter learning outcome/objective listed in the text. You can use our test bank software, EZ Test and EZ Test Online, or in *Connect Business Law,* to easily query for learning outcomes/objectives that directly relate to the learning objectives for your course. You can then use the reporting features of EZ Test to aggregate student results in similar fashion, making the collection and presentation of assurance of learning data simple and easy.

AACSB STATEMENT

The McGraw-Hill Companies is a proud corporate member of AACSB International. Understanding the importance and value of AACSB accreditation, *The Legal Environment of Business* recognizes the curricula guidelines detailed in the AACSB standards for business accreditation by connecting selected questions in the text and the test bank to the six general knowledge and skill guidelines in the AACSB standards.

The statements contained in *The Legal Environment of Business* are provided only as a guide for the users of this textbook. The AACSB leaves content coverage and assessment within the purview of individual schools, the mission of the school, and the faculty. While *The Legal Environment of Business* and the teaching package make no claim of any specific AACSB qualification or evaluation, we have within the text and the test bank of

The Legal Environment of Business labeled selected questions according to the six general knowledge and skills areas.

MCGRAW-HILL CUSTOMER CARE CONTACT INFORMATION

At McGraw-Hill, we understand that getting the most from new technology can be challenging. That's why our services don't stop after you purchase our products. You can e-mail our Product Specialists 24 hours a day to get product-training online. Or you can search our knowledge bank of Frequently Asked Questions on our support website. For Customer Support, call **800-331-5094,** e-mail **hmsupport@mcgraw-hill.com**, or visit **www.mhhe. com/support**. One of our Technical Support Analysts will be able to assist you in a timely fashion.

acknowledgments

I have the great fortune of having a team of professionals at McGraw-Hill/Irwin as my partners in this venture. These men and women worked assiduously on this textbook with a balance of humor and efficiency, and always with an eye toward excellence. They are: Paul Ducham, John Weimeister, Sarah Schuessler, Trina Hauger, Christine Vaughan, and Sarah Hunter. A special note of thanks goes to Dana Woo and Christine Scheid who, in the very early stages, guided me in turning a good idea into a high-quality textbook. Many other McGraw-Hill/Irwin team members also contributed to the book during its production and I am thankful to them all.

I am also grateful for the backing of my colleagues at Elizabethtown College, especially President Theodore Long, who supported faculty sabbatical leaves in the face of uncertain economics in higher education. My colleagues, Dr. Ed Chung and Dr. Sanjay Paul, are owed thanks for providing me with their expertise in business ethics and economics respectively, My research assistants, Thomas Melvin, Joseph Swartz, and Jeffrey Mullen, were a key part of the project and often labored under very tight deadlines. They are a talented group of young lawyers and I am most appreciative of their efforts.

My wife Joanna, and my children, Sean and Ally, are owed my deepest gratitude. For more than three years, they have sacrificed their time and rearranged their lives around the development of this textbook. Without their love, support, smiles, and Sunday dinners, it would not have been possible to write it.

Throughout the development of this book, I was privileged to have the candid and valuable advice of our reviewers and focus group. These reviewers provided me with priceless suggestions, feedback, and constructive criticism. The depth and sincerity of their reviews indicate that they are a devoted group of teacher-scholars. The content of the book was greatly enhanced because of their efforts.

Wayne Anderson
Missouri State University

Linda Axelrod
Metropolitan State University

David Berkowitz
Chapman University

Perry Binder
Georgia State University

Andrea Boggio
Bryant University

Eli Bortman
Babson College

Michael Bryant
Bryant University

Gretchen Carroll
Owens Community College

Anita Cava
University of Miami

Robert Cherry
Appalachian State University

Tracy Cole
Arkansas Tech University

Angelo Corpora
Palomar College

Glenn Doolittle
Santa Ana College

Craig Ehrlich
Babson College

Teressa Elliott
Northern Kentucky University

Tim Fogarty
Case Western Reserve University

John Geary
Appalachian State University

Wendy Gelman
Florida International University–Miami

John Gergacz
University of Kansas

Jeane Gohl-Noice
Parkland College

Marc Hall
Auburn University–Montgomery

Eloise Hassell
University of North Carolina–Greensboro

Diane Hathaway
University of Cincinnati

Arlene Hibschweiler
State University of New York–Buffalo

Frederick Jones
Kennesaw State University

Susan Kendall
Arapahoe Community College

Cheryl Kirschner
Babson College

Stan Leasure
Missouri State University

Christine Lewis
Auburn University–Montgomery

Mark Lewis
Arkansas State University

Janice Loutzenhiser
*California State University–
San Bernardino*

Nancy Mansfield
Georgia State University

Ernest Mayo
Johnson & Wales University

Martha Novy-Broderick
University of Maine

Les Nunn
University of Southern Indiana

Tom Parrish
Liberty University

Steven Popejoy
University of Central Missouri

Brenda Rice
Ozarks Technical Community College

Alan Roline
University of Minnesota–Duluth

Steven Schamber
St. Louis Community College

Randy Skalberg
University of Minnesota–Duluth

Cheryl Staley
Lake Land College

Kurt Stanberry
University of Houston–Downtown

Connie Strain
Arapahoe Community College

Frank Sullivan
University of Nevada–Las Vagas

Greg Swan
Chandler-Gilbert Community College

Mary Torma
Lorain County Community College

Michael Vasilou
DeVry University–Chicago

Ronald Washburn
Bryant University

Mark Whitaker
Hampton University

Susan Willey
Georgia State University

LeVon Wilson
Georgia Southern University

John Wrieden
Florida International University–Miami

brief table of contents

table of contents

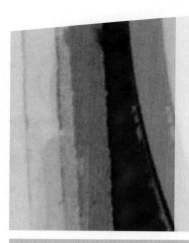

Fundamentals of the Legal Environment of Business

1 CHAPTER

Legal Foundations

learning outcomes checklist

After studying this chapter, students who have mastered the material will be able to:

1-1 Understand the broad definition and origins of law.

1-2 List and explain the purposes of law.

1-3 Explain the importance and benefits of legal awareness for business owners and managers in creating strategy and adding value to a company.

1-4 Articulate the role of counsel in legal decision making in a business context.

1-5 Recognize, explain, and give examples of sources of American law.

1-6 Differentiate between the concepts of law and equity.

1-7 Identify and apply important equitable maxims.

1-8 Understand the legal doctrine of stare decisis.

1-9 Classify the law into several broad categories.

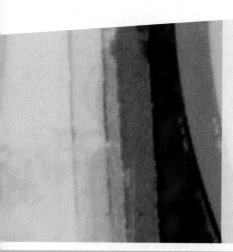

Undertaking the study of law may seem overwhelming. Legal doctrines and rules can be complex and difficult to navigate. Yet the law impacts many facets of our daily life both at home and at work. This textbook is designed to make studying the law more *manageable* by examining legal issues that are most commonly encountered in the business environment. In fact, studies have shown that business owners and managers who have a high level of legal insight create *value* for their business and recognize legal challenges as business planning opportunities. This legal awareness may only be gained by understanding important legal doctrines and processes. Applying this knowledge allows managers to limit risk and incorporate the law into their business strategies. This chapter introduces students to the foundations of the law and why the application of legal doctrines is an important part of the business environment. Specifically, in this chapter students will learn:

- How legal issues impact business planning and strategy.
- The foundations, definitions, and scope of various primary and secondary sources of law.
- Categories of law.

LO1-1 INTRODUCTION TO LAW

The term **law** has been defined in a variety of ways throughout recorded history. A generally accepted generic definition of the law is a *body of rules of action or conduct prescribed by controlling authority, and having legal binding force.*[1] When studying law in any context, it is important to think of the law in broad terms. While many equate the law with stacks of neatly bound volumes of codes in a library, this is only one component of a much larger body of law. Law may be set down in a written code as prescribed by an elected legislative body, but also takes the form of judicial decisions and actions of government agencies. While there are many sources of American law, the common characteristic of the current state of law is that it creates *duties, obligations,* and *rights* that reflect accepted views of a given society. Much of the origins of the law dealt with issues related to ownership of property, but modern legal doctrines have evolved into a relatively complex system of principles and protections. Most importantly, the law also provides a mechanism to resolve disputes arising from those duties and rights and allows parties to enforce promises in a court of law. Law is often classified by subject matter so that one refers to certain rules regarding agreements as *contract law* or certain laws that regulate certain rights of employees as *employment law.*

Jurisprudence

Jurisprudence, roughly defined as the science and philosophy of law, defines several schools of thought that are used to describe various approaches to the appropriate function of law and how legal doctrines should be developed and applied. Most schools of jurisprudential thought center on how legal rights are recognized. *Natural law* proponents argue that a system of moral values, that are inherent in humankind, form the basis for all law and those certain principles are of a *higher* authority than national laws (laws defined by a governing body).[2] *Positivists* believe in a specific set of agreed-upon laws that are enforced *uniformly* and strictly unless the law is changed expressly via the government. They reject the natural law notion of a higher authority that surpasses national law. *Legal realism* began to take shape in the United States after World War I and is based on the concept that law is a *social institution* that should be used to promote fairness by taking into account social and economic realities when arriving at legal conclusions. Perhaps the most dramatic example of the legal realism school of thought in practice was the U.S. Supreme Court's formal recognition during the civil rights era of its role in achieving equality for all Americans by interpreting the Constitution as protecting certain rights that previous Courts had never recognized.

LO1-2 Purposes of Law

Although the most visible function of the law on a day-to-day basis is to provide for some system of order that defines crimes and levies punishment for violation of the crimes, there are many other purposes of recognizing a uniform system of laws. The origins of recorded law were initially a collection of rules of powerful tribal chieftains intended to perpetuate domination and power of their authority with little consideration for rights of individuals. However, over the better part of three millennia, the purpose of law evolved substantially into ensuring consistency and fairness. In the United States, lawmakers have increasingly embraced legal mechanisms, such as antidiscrimination laws, to help promote equality and justice in society and especially in education and in the workplace. The law also sets out a system for resolving disputes by providing a basis for deciding the legal interests and rights of the parties. For purposes of studying the impact of law on business, it is important to recognize that the law also serves as an important catalyst for commerce by promoting

---

[1] *Black's Law Dictionary.*

[2] Aristotle was perhaps the most famous advocate of the natural law theory.

good faith dealing among merchants and consumers and giving some degree of *reliability* that can be considered in business planning and commercial transactions.

LEGAL DECISIONS IN A BUSINESS ENVIRONMENT: THEORY TO PRACTICE

LO1-3

While an in-depth understanding of the various areas of law is a vast undertaking requiring years of intensive study, the primary objective of this textbook is to cover a variety of legal topics that are most commonly encountered in the business environment. However, developing legal insight by understanding the fundamentals of legal theory and how they may impact business is only a first step in learning how legal decisions should be made in a business context. The second step involves learning to *apply* legal theories in practice and recognizing that having legal awareness may present opportunities for proactive business planning and empowering business owners and managers to limit liability, gain a competitive edge, and add value to the business. Relying exclusively on attorneys to drive the legal decision-making process in the context of business is both expensive and involves the significant risk that a decision will be made without sufficient knowledge of business operations, objectives, and current economic realities. Instead, studies and research indicates that when managers work *cooperatively* with their attorney, the results contribute to better strategic business decisions that add value to the business. Later in this chapter, we will discuss a mechanism that business owners and managers may use to spot legal issues, apply an appropriate analysis, decide on alternative solutions, and plan a legal and ethical course of action that limits liability and maximizes business opportunities.

> **KEY POINT**
> Learning to apply legal awareness in practice involves recognizing opportunities for proactive business planning, limiting liability, gaining a competitive edge, and adding value to the business.

Management teams with legal insight add value to their company by limiting liability and identifying opportunities.

Legal Insight and Business Strategy

To understand how various areas of the law impact business and the importance of having legal insight in a business context, let's examine a typical business planning process. Suppose that the management team at Indiana Printing Company (IPC) is planning to expand their existing business into new markets. The team considers several options and will have to have a sufficient understanding of the legal risks and business opportunities associated with each option. Table 1.1 sets out possible options for IPC's expansion and some of the potential legal impact for each option.

TABLE 1.1 Expansion Options and Potential Legal Impacts

Option	Area of Law	Potential Legal Impact
Expansion through acquisition of another company. One common way to expand is to purchase an existing business entity through an acquisition of assets or of stock.	■ Contracts	■ Governs negotiations and agreements for the acquisition.
	■ Property/Environmental	■ If acquisition involves any land purchase, real estate law (such as zoning) and environmental law.
	■ Employment and labor	■ The hiring of employees by IPC (even former employees of the target company) must be done in conformance with state and federal employment and labor laws.
	■ Tax	■ The transaction may create tax liability under local, state, and/or federal laws.
	■ Antitrust	■ If the acquisition results in IPC's gaining too much market share, federal antitrust laws must be considered and preacquisition approvals may be needed from the government.
Expansion through introducing and aggressively marketing a new product line. Expanding through marketing of a new product line generally involves raising sufficient capital to properly develop, manufacture, and go to market.	■ Securities law	■ Any solicitation by IPC to sell shares of its business to the public is highly regulated by securities laws.
	■ Intellectual property	■ In order to maintain its competitive edge, IPC will need to put measures in place to help guarantee protection of ideas and processes by trade secret law; the final design may be protected by patent law.
	■ Administrative law	■ Federal regulatory agencies have guidelines for advertising and labeling of products.
Expansion through aggressive integration of a highly interactive Web site and e-marketing campaigns including international markets. In light of the growth in e-commerce, some companies find this to be the most cost-efficient method of expansion.	■ Jurisdiction	■ Web site expansion may result in IPC being subject to the jurisdiction of more out-of-state courts than the previous business model.
	■ International law	■ IPC may be subject to international agreements and treaties regarding sales and intellectual property.

The list of legal issues in Table 1.1 is meant to be illustrative and not exhaustive. Indeed, issues regarding negligence, criminal law, administrative law, bankruptcy, consumer protection, agency, and many others may present themselves before, during, or after the transaction is complete.

Role of Counsel

LO1-4

Although this textbook emphasizes understanding legal issues in the context of business decision making, this is not to suggest that an attorney's role in this process is diminished—quite the opposite. The content, features, and exercises contained in this textbook emphasize that working closely with a business attorney results in business opportunities, reduced costs, and limitation of risk and liability. Attorneys, particularly in a business context, may also be referred to as **counsel.** Business owners and managers work with counsel in one of two formats. For larger companies or companies that have extraordinary regulatory burdens (such as complying with securities or patent laws), counsel may very well be a part of the executive or mid-level management team. These attorneys are referred to as *in-house counsel* and usually have the title of general counsel at the executive management level (e.g., vice president and general counsel). Depending on the size and complexity of the company, the general counsel may also supervise one or more attorneys, usually with the title associate counsel. Additionally, the general counsel may also serve as a corporate officer of the company, called the secretary, who is responsible for record keeping and complying with notice and voting requirements for the board of directors.[3] The general counsel is also responsible for selecting and supervising lawyers from outside law firms when a particular field of expertise is needed such as a trial lawyer (also called a *litigator*).

The majority of companies, however, rely on attorneys employed by *law firms* for their legal needs. These attorneys devote a significant amount of their professional time to advising businesses on issues such as formation, governance, labor and employment laws, regulatory agency compliance, legal transactions (such as an acquisition), intellectual property (such as trademarks or patents), and other legal issues important to business operations. These attorneys (known as *business lawyers* or *corporate lawyers*), rarely if ever appear in court or perform other tasks that are associated with lawyers in the minds of the general public. Indeed, the law has become increasingly complex and specialized. Therefore, it is not unusual that more than one attorney's advice is needed when facing a significant legal issue such as an employment discrimination lawsuit or when obtaining financing for a corporation from the general public through the sale of stock. Law firms vary greatly in size from one or just a few lawyers in a local or regional practice, to those firms that have hundreds of lawyers spread throughout the globe. In a business context, law firms bill clients based on an hourly rate that is tied to an individual lawyer's experience, her reputation in the field, and the market being served (with large cities that are the center of business operations having higher rates).

Language of the Law

In order to maximize the value of interaction between business owners/managers and attorneys, a basic understanding of legal terminology is useful. Students studying business law face the task of learning legal syntax at the same time as they learn

> **web**check **dictionary.law.com**
> This is a useful online law dictionary. This textbook's Web site, www.mhhe.com/Melvin, contains several links to other law dictionaries as well.

how to apply the legal doctrines in a business context. This is analogous to learning a complicated subject matter in a foreign language, yet it is manageable with careful study. Legal terms are sometimes referred to as jargon or legalese, but having a working knowledge of

---

[3]The legal structure of corporations and other business entities is discussed in detail in Unit Three.

some common legal terminology is an important step to mastering the material. Although much of the language of the law has Latin roots, the terminology is primarily a combination of Latin, early and modern English, and French. The vocabulary of American law is drawn from the various cultures and events that shaped American history. To facilitate your understanding of legal expression, important legal terms are highlighted throughout the text, summarized at the end of each chapter, and are also featured alphabetically in the glossary. The authoritative source for legal terms is **Black's Law Dictionary,** first published in 1891. There are also several Web sites that provide definitions and examples for legal terms.

LO1-5   SOURCES AND LEVELS OF AMERICAN LAW

American law is composed of a unique blend from various sources based on U.S. historical roots. Fundamentally, much of American law is derived from English legal doctrines that came with the English settlers of the colonies. Modern law in the United States regulating businesses and individuals is generally a combination of **constitutional law, statutory law, common law,** and **administrative** (regulatory) **law** at the federal, state, and local levels. These sources of law are known as *primary sources* of law and may sometimes work in conjunction with one another or independently. For example, law related to the protection of trade secrets[4] is composed from a variety of sources of law. Perhaps the most famous and profitable example of a trade secret is the recipe and process for making Coca-Cola. While most states have specific trade secret statutes that give legal recourse to a party who has suffered a loss as a result of the unlawful use of trade secrets, some do not. Does this mean that the company that owns the Coca-Cola recipe has no legal recourse against someone who steals their trade secret in those states where no *specific statutes* exist? The answer is no because even absent a specific statute, the law still provides the damaged party some recourse against the violator. This recourse is provided through court case history (called *common law,* discussed later) that provides guidance to the trial courts deciding trade secret disputes. Even in states that *do* have statutes related to trade secrets protection, there is case law that helps courts apply the statute consistently.

Constitutional Law

Constitutional law is the foundation for all other law in the United States and is the supreme law of the land. It functions in tandem with other sources of law in three broad areas: (1) establishing a *structure* for federal and state governments (including qualifications of certain offices and positions) and rules for amending the constitution; (2) granting specific *powers* for the different branches of government; and (3) providing *procedural protections* for U.S. citizens from wrongful government actions.

Constitutional law is different from other sources of law primarily in terms of *permanence* and *preemption.* In terms of permanence, a constitution is thought to reflect the basic principles of a particular society and should be amended only in extraordinary cases and only when a majority of its constituents agree over a certain period of time. Preemption in this context means that constitutional law is supreme over other sources of law such as statutes.

Constitutional law exists at both the federal and state level because each state has its own constitution that is the highest source of law within the state's borders (so long as it is not inconsistent with federal law). States tend to amend their constitutions more frequently than is the case with the U.S. Constitution. Constitutional issues that impact businesses include Congress's powers to regulate interstate commerce; creation of legal protections for intellectual property (such as patents and copyrights); protection of certain forms of

---

[4]Trade secret law, which is covered in detail in Chapter 24, "Intellectual Property," is the legal protection of certain confidential business information.

commercial speech from unwarranted government regulation; limitations on a state's authority to tax products and services in commerce; and powers of the executive, legislative, and judicial branches to regulate business activity. Constitutional law is discussed in detail in Chapter 2, "Business and the Constitution."

Statutory Law

Statutory law is created by a legislative body and approved or disapproved by the executive branch of government. The U.S. Congress, for example, is the exclusive legislative body for the passage of federal law. When Congress is drafting a federal statute, but has not yet passed it or had the executive's concurrence, it is known as a *bill.* On the *federal level,* the president is the executive and may either sign a bill into law (thereby adopting it as a statute), or the president may veto (reject) the bill subject to the Congress's right to override the veto and make the bill into a statute with a two-thirds majority vote.

At the *state level,* the state legislature (called by different names in different states such as the *General Assembly*) passes statutes that regulate

webcheck **www.mhhe.com/melvin**
Go to this textbook's Web site to see an example of (1) a federal statute (Employment Discrimination), (2) a state statute (Pennsylvania Business Corporation Law), and (3) a local zoning ordinance.

such areas as motor vehicle laws, business corporation and partnership laws, and other traditional state matters. The governor (as executive) has authority to sign a state bill into law or to exercise other rights as laid out in the state constitution. Statutes at the *local* level are called **ordinances** (sometimes referred to as local regulations). Ordinances generally regulate issues such as zoning (regulating where certain businesses, such as factories, may be located) or impose health and safety regulations on local merchants such as restaurants.

Statutory Scheme and Legislative History When interpreting statutes, courts look to two sources for guidance. The structure of the statute itself generally provides some indication of how the legislature intended for it to be applied. The structure of the statute and the format of its mandates in a law are referred as its **statutory scheme.** When interpreting statutes, courts also look to the records kept by the legislature including the debates, committee and conference reports, and legislative findings of fact. These records are known as the statute's **legislative history** and may provide some indication of the intent of the legislative body that passed the statute. For example, in Chapter 12, "Employment Discrimination," we will discuss federal employment discrimination laws. After the primary federal employment antidiscrimination statute was passed by Congress in 1964 (known as Title VII[5]), the U.S. Supreme Court used that law's statutory scheme and legislative history to develop several theories of discrimination and various tests and applications currently used by courts to determine if a violation of the statute has occurred.

The U.S. Congress is the exclusive legislative body for the passage of federal law.

---

[5]Derived from Title VII of the Civil Rights Act of 1964.

Finding Statutory Law   The official publication of federal statutory law is the United States Code (U.S.C.), which arranges all existing federal laws in a system organized by title and divided into chapters and sections. The legal community uses a special format to express where a statutory law can be found known as a **citation.** You'll note citations in the footnotes of each chapter of this text that identify a specific reference for the statutes being covered in the chapter. For example, later in this textbook, students will study a federal law called the Fair Labor Standards Act (also known as the "minimum wage" law) in detail. The citation for the law (listed in the footnote) is 29 U.S.C. § 201. This indicates that in order to find the Fair Labor Standards Act, we need to consult Title 29 of the United States Code and turn to section (abbreviated § in singular or §§ in plural) 201 for the first chapter of the statute. Although attorneys and judges often use specialized software and legal research services to find and understand statutes, an increasing amount of information about statutory resources and statutes themselves are available online for free. Note also that Appendix A of this textbook ("A Business Student's Guide to Understanding Cases and Finding the Law") provides further information on using the Internet to find and apply statutory law.

State statutes have the same fundamental format and purpose of the U.S.C., but the actual term used to refer to state statutes varies from state to state. *Codes* or *consolidated statutes* are two common terms.

Commercial services also sell print and online versions of federal and state statutes in a unique format that includes annotations and short comments used to interpret the statutes correctly. Attorneys use these commercial services in performing legal research important to properly counseling their clients on the law.

Administrative Law

While statutory law stems from the authority of the legislature and common law is derived from the courts, administrative law is the source of law that authorizes the exercise of authority by *executive branch* agencies and *independent* government agencies. Federal administrative law is largely authorized by statutes and the Constitution, and rules for applying the law are articulated and carried out by *administrative agencies.* Pursuant to congressional mandates, these agencies are empowered to administer the details of federal statutes and have broad powers to impose regulations, make policy, and enforce the law in their designated area of jurisdiction. For example, the U.S. Environmental Protection Agency (EPA) is charged with drafting regulations that carry out the broad mandates set out by Congress in the Clean Air Act (among many others) to reduce air pollution. The EPA sets out regulations and imposes restrictions on some industries to help accomplish that goal. The EPA is also empowered to enforce those regulations. Courts are highly deferential to agency decisions involving how and when an agency enforces a regulation. Detailed coverage of this source of law and administrative agencies is featured in Chapter 17, "Administrative Law."

Common Law

Common law is essentially law made by courts; that is, law that has not specifically been passed by the legislature, but rather law that is based on the fundamentals of previous cases that had similar facts. The notion of applying the law of previous cases to current cases with substantially similar circumstances is called **precedent.** The common law is composed of established principles of law based on a just resolution of disputes between parties, which also sets a specific standard for other courts to follow when the same dispute arises again.

Origins   The U.S. system of common law is deep-seated in British common law that has developed over several centuries beginning around 1066 when the Norman kings established uniform methods for resolving (mostly land) disputes in England. King Henry II established King's Bench courts around 1178. English courts have always ruled that English people carried English law with them wherever they settled, and therefore English law applied to the people living in the American colonies. However, the American colonists had some flexibility in establishing laws that were fit for life in the colonies. Although English law was a starting point, the colonists supplemented the laws with rules prepared by landowners in the individual colonies to create a unique American common law.

The largest industrialized nations using the common law in some form include the United States, the United Kingdom, Canada, Australia, and generally former colonies of Britain. Other countries, such as Japan, use a *civil law* system that requires courts to adhere to a strict interpretation of a legislatively established code or regulation. While civil law still recognizes the general notion of precedent, its role is substantially reduced in a civil law system. The power of courts to establish law in matters not specifically addressed by the code is very limited in civil law countries. Legal systems and sources of law of foreign countries are covered in Chapter 25 "International Law and Global Commerce."

Law versus Equity

Early English courts were classified under the king's authority as either *courts of law,* applying existing laws and rules strictly, or *courts of equity* that applied the rule of fairness when application of technical rules resulted in an injustice. Most modern American courts are combined courts of law and equity. However, we still use the terms law and equity when describing the appropriate *measure of judicial action* intended to compensate an injured party in a civil lawsuit. These measures are known as **remedies.** Remedies at law generally take the form of *money damages* whereby a court orders the wrongdoer to pay another party a certain sum of money to compensate for any losses suffered as a result of the wrongdoer's conduct. However, in some cases, a party will not necessarily be fully or even partially compensated through money damages. In such a case, a court may award **equitable relief** instead of (or in addition to) a remedy at law. Most commonly, equitable relief can include an *injunction* or *restraining order* (a judicial order requiring a party to cease a certain activity), and *specific performance* (an order requiring a party to carry out her obligations as specified in a contract).

To understand this concept in a business context, suppose that Maxwell enters into a valid written agreement with Book Barn to purchase a first edition of *The Old Man and the Sea,* autographed by Ernest Hemingway, for $25,000. Maxwell leaves the store to obtain a certified check from his bank. When he returns one hour later, the owner of Book Barn refuses to sell him the book because he had received a phone call from another buyer offering $30,000. In this case, Maxwell may file a lawsuit for Book Barn's failure to live up

Henry II established English common law courts, called "King's Bench" courts, around 1178.

> **KEY** POINT
> Where a remedy at law is inadequate, an injured party may also obtain a remedy at equity.

LO1-6

to the agreement (known as *breach of contract*[6]), but he has not suffered an out-of-pocket loss because he never had the opportunity to present Book Barn with the check. However, Maxwell could seek a *remedy at equity* from a court where he would request an injunction to prevent Book Barn from selling the book to another buyer until the court can hear the case. If Maxwell wins the case, he may seek an order of *specific performance* whereby the court orders Book Barn to transfer ownership of the book to Maxwell in exchange for the $25,000 price as specified in the agreement between the parties. Maxwell would likely be awarded these equitable remedies because the legal remedies available to him are not adequate to address his injury.

LO1-7   Important Equitable Maxims

The term *equity* is also used in the context of common laws rules that guide courts in deciding cases and controversies before them. These equity rules are called **equitable maxims** and are intended to be broad statements of rules that are based on notions of fairness and justice in applying the law. These maxims have been developed by early American courts (primarily based on English common law) and continue to be refined and applied by modern courts. The most commonly applied maxims are "equity aids the vigilant," "substance over form," and the "clean hands doctrine."

Equity Aids the Vigilant   Perhaps the most universal of the maxims is the notion that the law favors those who exercise *vigilance* in pursuing their claims and disfavors those who rest on their legal rights by failing to act to protect their rights in a reasonable period of time. In many areas of the law, a time period is fixed for which to assert legal rights. These timelines are called the *statute of limitations*. For example, suppose that Roscoe is fired from his job and believes that he was the victim of employment discrimination. However, Roscoe is too busy trying to find another job to file a complaint with an appropriate agency. One year later, Roscoe decides to file the complaint. Roscoe's claim is likely barred because too much time has passed between the incident and the complaint. In fact, federal statutes require that a claim of discrimination must be filed within 180 days from the time of the event of discrimination. There are similar statutes of limitation for breach of contract disputes. For instance, in Michigan a party has a maximum of six years to file suit for breach of contract claims.[7]

Substance over Form   When applying the law, courts look to the intent of parties involved and adhere to a standard of good faith and fair play instead of applying the letter of the law in a way that would violate fundamental principles of fairness and consistency. For example, later in this textbook we'll discuss the various requirements and legal impact of choosing certain types of business entities. Suppose that Fitzgerald wishes to start a partnership with Anderson but wants to protect his personal assets from any liabilities associated with the partnership. They draft a partnership agreement that states that Fitzgerald will be a limited partner (inactive partner with no personal liability for the partnership's debts) and not a general partner (active partner with personal liability for partnership debts). However, Fitzgerald is fully involved in the business operations to the same extent as general partner Anderson. When a creditor attempts to sue Fitzgerald to recover a partnership debt, Fitzgerald argues that he has no legal obligation, citing the partnership agreement that made it clear he was a *limited partner*. In this case, a court may very well disregard the document labeling Fitzgerald as a limited partner because *in practice* Fitzgerald was participating as a general partner. Despite the form (the partnership agreement),

---

[6]Breach of contract is covered in detail in Chapter 7, "Contract Performance."

[7]*See* Mich. Comp. Laws §600.5807 (2009).

FACT SUMMARY   Kauffman created a corporation to hold certain assets in a manner intended to minimize tax liability. After creation of the corporation, a judgment was entered against Kauffman as a result of a lawsuit against him. In order to avoid paying the judgment, Kauffman transferred all of his stock into his spouse's name. His spouse eventually transferred ownership of the stock to several Kauffman children. Several years later, a dispute developed between the children concerning the stock and Kauffman intervened by filing a claim with the trial court requesting that all stock be transferred back to him on the basis that he was the rightful owner of the stock and that the transfer was nothing more than a temporary trust. The children contended that Kauffman is not the equitable owner of the stock and is not entitled to relief due to the clean hands doctrine.

SYNOPSIS OF DECISION AND OPINION   The Supreme Court of Montana ruled in favor of the Kauffman children holding that Kauffman was not entitled to relief. Because Kauffman's transfer was in perpetrating an exchange of stock only to avoid paying the judgment legally entered against him, the transaction was a bad-faith action that bordered on a fraudulent transaction. The court reasoned that the rightful owner of the stock was the Kauffman children and that Kauffman's claims were barred by the clean hands doctrine. The court concluded that recognizing his claim would result in a gross wrong being done to the children and the shareholders of the corporation.

WORDS OF THE COURT: Clean Hands Doctrine "The doctrine of clean hands provides that parties must not expect relief in equity, unless they come into court with clean hands. [. . .] Thus, no one can take advantage of his own wrong. [. . .] Court['s] will not aid a party whose claim had its inception in the party's wrongdoing whether the victim of the wrongdoing is the other party or a third party."

Case Questions

1. Would the court's ruling be the same if the children had also participated in the transactions and were accused of wrongdoing? Why or why not?

2. Given the court's reasoning, would the result of this case be the same if the transfer of stock was for a legitimate purpose and the only wrongdoing Kauffman had committed involved a third party in an unrelated matter? Why or why not?

---

courts prefer substance in applying legal doctrines. It would not be fair to allow Fitzgerald the protection of a limited partner when he remained active in the partnership.

Clean Hands Doctrine   Commentators sometimes describe loopholes in the law as responsible for creating injustice and protecting wrongdoers. However, more often than not courts are not inclined to decide disputes based on technicalities that benefited a party who acted dishonestly. Courts are guided in their decisions not only by the letter of the law, but also on the basis that one seeking the aid of a court must come to the court with clean hands that are unstained by bad faith, misrepresentations, or deceit. In Case 1.1, a state appellate court applies the clean hands doctrine.

Stare Decisis and Precedent

The **doctrine of stare decisis,** one of the most important concepts in American law, is the principle that similar cases with similar facts and issues should have the same judicial outcome. This allows individuals and business to have some degree of confidence that the law will remain reasonably constant from year to year and court to court. Once an appellate court has decided a particular case, the decision becomes a **case precedent.** The principle of stare decisis requires all *lower courts,* such as a trial court, from that point in time onward, to follow the case precedent so that any similar case would be decided according to the precedent. Trial courts apply precedent by making use of key statements from earlier

Legal Speak ›))
Appellate courts
Courts that review the decision of trial courts and have the authority to overturn decisions if they are inconsistent with the current state of the law. Trial courts, appellate courts, and other types of dispute resolution forums are covered in detail in Chapter 3 "The American Judicial System, Jurisdiction, and Venue."

LO1-8

FACT SUMMARY   Flagiello, a patient at Pennsylvania Hospital ("the Hospital"), sued the Hospital claiming they were negligent in maintaining certain conditions on hospital property that resulted in her injuring her ankle. The ankle injury was unrelated to the original reason for Flagiello's admission to the hospital. A Pennsylvania state trial court dismissed the lawsuit without trial because established state common law clearly exempted charitable institutions, such as the Hospital, from any liability related to its negligence (called the charitable immunity doctrine). Flagiello appealed on the basis that (1) she was a paying patient, and (2) the charitable immunity doctrine was outdated given the fact that most charity hospitals now received funding from state and local governments.

SYNOPSIS OF DECISION AND OPINION   The Pennsylvania Supreme Court ruled in favor of Flagiello. Although the court acknowledged the important role of stare decisis, they also pointed out that the doctrine is not intended to apply when societal norms dictate otherwise. In this case, the court noted that other states had abandoned the charitable immunity doctrine as no longer necessary and that public benefit and fairness demanded that injured parties who are entitled to recover for their losses be allowed to pursue a negligence action against a charitable institution.

WORDS OF THE COURT: Limits of Stare Decisis
"Stare decisis channels the law. It erects lighthouses and [flies] the signals of safety. The ships of jurisprudence must follow that well-defined channel which, over the years, has been proved to be secure and trustworthy. But it would not comport with wisdom to insist that, should shoals rise in a heretofore safe course and rocks emerge to encumber the passage, the ship should nonetheless pursue the original course, merely because it presented no hazard in the past. The principle of stare decisis does not demand that we follow precedents which shipwreck justice."

"Stare decisis is not an iron mold into which every utterance by a court, regardless of circumstances, parties, economic barometer and sociological climate, must be poured, and, where, like wet concrete, it must acquire an unyielding rigidity which nothing later can change."

Case Questions
1. If Flagiello had been a burglar who was breaking into the medical supply cabinet instead of a patient when she injured her ankle, would the court have been willing to abandon the charitable immunity doctrine? Why or why not?
2. Does this case mean that stare decisis may be discarded whenever a judge perceives that following precedent will "shipwreck justice"?

---

judicial opinions, known as the *holding* of the case. Note that the court system and how appellate courts form precedent is covered in detail in Chapter 3, "The American Judicial System, Jurisdiction, and Venue."

Stare Decisis and Business   To understand the importance of stare decisis in the business environment, consider the opportunities for business planning that may benefit the company by understanding the legal impact of a certain course of action. Suppose that Jackson is a manager in charge of managing the acquisition of certain assets from another company. One important aspect of such a transaction is how the acquisition will be *taxed.* If Jackson's company enters into an agreement with Main Street Industries (MSI) to acquire certain assets from MSI, how will the transaction be treated by the Internal Revenue Service (IRS)?[8] This, of course, is a very important fact in determining the price of the transaction and planning for allocation of the tax burden between buyer and seller. How can the parties structure the transaction to be sure that the taxation represents the parties' intent? Ultimately, because stare decisis is a deeply rooted concept that applies to all laws, Jackson need only learn how the IRS has treated similar transactions in the past and how courts have ruled on the IRS's interpretation and actions in applying the law. If a

---

[8]The IRS is the federal government's tax agency.

certain transaction has been taxed in a certain way in the past, the doctrine of stare decisis dictates that if Jackson structures her transaction in a similar fashion, that her transaction will be taxed in the same way. The parties may now proceed with negotiations and structuring a mutually acceptable agreement with sufficient legal certainty about its taxation impact.

However, strict adherence to precedent and the doctrine of stare decisis has a significant drawback: it doesn't allow for evolving societal standards of behavior or expectations. On a case-by-case basis, courts sometimes justify departing from precedent on the basis that technological or societal changes render a particular precedent unworkable. In the Landmark Case 1.1, a state appellate court considered the question of when to abandon standing precedent.

Some of the specific laws that impact business owners and managers covered in this textbook are featured in Table 1.2.

Primary sources of law are applied consistent with a hierarchy where one source may trump another source if the two sources conflict. Figure 1.1 illustrates the hierarchy of primary sources of federal and state law.

LO1-5 SECONDARY SOURCES OF LAW

When interpreting statutory law or applying judicially created law, courts also look to **secondary sources** of law. In the business context, the most important secondary sources of law are (1) a collection of uniform legal principles focused in a particular area of traditionally state law called *Restatements of the Law,* and (2) various sets of **model state statutes** drafted by legal experts as a model for state legislatures to adopt in their individual jurisdictions. The purpose behind these secondary sources of law is to increase the level of uniformity and fairness across courts in all 50 states. The secondary sources of law

TABLE 1.2 Laws That Impact Business

Type of Law	Source(s)	Level(s)
Negligence (tort)	Statutory and common law	Primarily state
Employment discrimination	Primarily statutory and administrative	Primarily state and federal, some local
Copyright	Statutory and administrative	Federal
Contracts for sale of goods	Statutory	State
Contracts for services	Primarily common law	State
Bankruptcy	Statutory and administrative	Federal
Securities law (selling company stock to the public)	Statutory and administrative	Federal and state
Zoning ordinances	Statutory	Local
Taxes	Statutory and administrative	Federal, state, and local

FIGURE 1.1 Hierarchy of Primary Sources of Federal and State Law

also feature commentary and examples to help guide courts in applying the law. However, secondary sources of law have *no independent authority* or legally binding effect. State legislatures and courts are free to adopt all, part of, or to reject secondary sources of law.

Uniform Model Laws

In 1892, the National Conference of Commissioners on Uniform State Laws (NCCUSL) was formed by the American Bar Association for the purpose of establishing uniform standards in areas of the law where national interests would be achieved through use of uniform laws. The primary focus of the model laws was commerce and the NCCUSL drafted the Uniform Commercial Code (UCC), which has been adopted in some form by every state except Louisiana. The UCC provides a comprehensive set of rules and principles intended to increase reliability and predictability in business transactions. Although this textbook refers to several different sections of the UCC, extensive coverage is given to Article 2 of the UCC, which governs contracts for the sale of goods. The NCCUSL also created several uniform codes related to the formation and structure of business entities such as the Uniform Partnership Act and the Model Business Corporation Act. The NCCUSL will from time to time revise these model acts and the new model laws are referred to, for example, as the *Revised* Uniform Partnership Act.

Restatements of the Law

In the 1920s, the American Legal Institute (ALI) was formed to reduce the undue complexity and growing uncertainty of judicial decisions by systematically publishing a *statement* of common law legal principles and rules in a given area of the law, such as torts. The ALI is composed of law professors, judges, and lawyers and they developed the *Restatements of the Law* in various legal categories. Explanatory notes and applicable examples accompany the Restatements. Restatements are continuously revised and when the ALI publishes a revision, the new version is referred to by the name and edition so that the second edition of the contracts restatements is called *Restatements (Second) of Contracts*. The areas covered by the Restatements that are included in this textbook are: contracts, property, agency, torts, and foreign relations law.

CONCEPT SUMMARY   Sources of Law

Primary:

■ Primary sources of law include constitutional law, statutory law, administrative law, and common law at both the federal and state levels.

■ Constitutions have two primary functions: (1) to prescribe the basic structure and powers of a particular government body and (2) to protect certain rights of individuals and businesses from government encroachment.

■ Statutory law is created by a legislative body and approved or disapproved by the executive branch.

■ When interpreting statutes, courts often look to two sources for guidance: (1) the structure of the statute itself, called the *statutory scheme,* and (2) the records of the legislative history behind the statute.

■ The official publication of federal statutory law is in the United States Code (U.S.C.).

■ Common law is law made by appellate courts and is based on the fundamentals of previous cases that had similar facts.

■ Appellate courts create precedent and under the doctrine of stare decisis, lower courts apply the precedent to new cases with similar facts.

■ Administrative law is the source of law that regulates the exercise of authority by administrative agencies.

■ Pursuant to congressional mandates, administrative agencies are empowered to administer the details of federal statutes and have broad powers to impose regulations, make policy, and enforce the law in their designated area of jurisdiction.

Secondary:

■ Secondary sources of law include the *Restatements of the Law* and sets of model statutes such as the Uniform Commercial Code (UCC).

■ Secondary sources have no independent authority, nor are they legally binding.

■ The *Restatements of the Law* are collections of uniform legal principles in a specific area of law that are designed to reduce the complexity of judicial decisions.

■ Model statutes are drafted by legal experts, in hopes that they will be used or adopted by state legislatures so as to provide uniformity in laws between the states.

 Self-Check

What is/are the source(s) and level(s) of law that govern the following business transactions?

1. American Hardware Supply enters into an agreement with a retail home improvement chain to supply them with certain inventory.

2. Whitney wishes to apply for a patent for a device he invented.

3. Marshall is considering raising money for his business by selling stock in the company.

4. Bio-Tech Inc. ran out of cash and cannot pay its debts as they become due. Management seeks protection from creditors.

5. Barnum wishes to bring his famous horse show into town and plans to stage it in a residential area of the city.

Answers to this Self-Check are provided at the end of the chapter.

CATEGORIES OF LAW

Because the body of American law is so vast and diverse, it is sometimes helpful to break down the law into broad categories based on classifications related to a particular legal function or a right afforded by law. It is important to note that these classifications are not mutually exclusive. One particular act or transaction may be classified in more than one legal category. For example, suppose that a party to a contract breaks her promise to the other party (known as a breach of contract). The remedy for the breach may depend its the legal classification of contracts as *civil law*. At the same time, one party may have rights classified as *substantive law*, which are derived from a source of *statutory law*.

Criminal Law versus Civil Law

Laws, primarily statutes, are either *criminal* or *civil* in nature. **Civil laws** are designed to compensate parties (including businesses) for losses as a result of another's conduct. These losses are known as **damages. Criminal laws** are a protection of society, and the violation of criminal laws results in penalties to the violator such as fines or imprisonment. Remember that these categories are not mutually exclusive. For instance, a driver who is intoxicated and injures a pedestrian in an accident has committed both a criminal act (driving while intoxicated) for which he can be prosecuted by authorities, and committed a civil wrong (negligence) for which the driver can be sued by the injured party to recover for any losses suffered as a result of the injury (medical bills, etc.).

Substantive Law versus Procedural Law

Substantive laws provide individuals with rights and create certain duties. **Procedural laws** provide a structure and set out rules for pursuing substantive rights. For example, while state common law may provide an individual who has suffered losses due to the negligence of another the right to obtain restitution from the wrongdoer (substantive law), a state statute will prescribe the procedure for using legal apparatus to actually collect the restitution (procedural law). This includes rules that govern court procedures such as how and when to file a lawsuit as well as the process for obtaining the restitution once a court has given the injured party a certain money award.

Public Law versus Private Law

Public laws are those derived from some government entity. Examples include statutes (legislature/executive) and administrative regulations (state or federal administrative agencies). **Private laws** are recognized as binding between two parties even though no specific statute or regulation provides for the rights of the parties. The most common example is a contract for services. For example, suppose Claude hires Pablo to paint a portrait of Claude's wife. After it is complete, Claude thinks Pablo's painting is too abstract and refuses to pay for it. Although no specific public law exists that regulates this relationship, the agreement is still legally binding and the rules of the transaction are governed by the common law of contracts.

Legal Decisions in Business: An Analytical Model

PROBLEM *Legal decision making by managers is reactionary, uneven, and sometimes uninformed.*

SOLUTION *Use a systematic analytical model designed to identify legal issues, and understand those issues as business planning opportunities that enable the management team to add value to the company.*

Understanding the theories and applications of law in a business context is important to meeting legal challenges, but incorporating this knowledge via the use of an analytical model helps to convert legal challenges into astute business planning and potential opportunities. This model may be used for any legal challenge, but a fundamental understanding of applicable legal doctrines and applications are necessary to take full advantage of its use. Keep this model in mind while you are studying the material in this textbook. You'll find that it will become more valuable as your knowledge of substantive law increases. When confronted with a legal challenge, managers with a high level of legal awareness should follow a seven step model: *Identify → Assess → Analyze → Examine Alternatives → Compare* with business mission, objectives, and ethical considerations → *Implement,* monitor, and revise → *Review* for business planning opportunities.

Step 1: *Identify potential legal issues.* One of the objectives of this textbook is to provide students with essential legal doctrines and examples of how the law impacts business operations and planning. Legal awareness is the primary tool for identifying legal issues and responding appropriately. Businesses should be both proactive and reactive in identifying potential legal issues. Proactive measures include having apparatus in place that limits liability exposures (such as standardized hiring and promotion procedures), while reactive measures require that business owners and managers follow a legally sound course of action once they become aware of a potential legal issue.

Step 2: *Assess the imminence and level of any legal challenge and decide whether to confer with counsel.* While legally adept managers have the ultimate goal of understanding legal challenges as potential planning opportunities, the primary consideration when confronted with a legal challenge is to assess how much potential liability may be involved and to understand the posture of the parties. For example, if a manager of a wholesaling company receives a complaint from a customer about the quality of goods purchased, that is a legal challenge (essentially an allegation of breaking a contract) with potential for litigation in the future, but the level and immediacy of the threat is low. The matter may be worked out amicably, ethically, and legally without counsel. If, during negotiations, the customer begins to indicate that he will be pursuing legal alternatives, the threat level has increased and counsel should be consulted immediately. Although there is no need for counsel to intervene at this point, she should be briefed on the matter in the event that the customer takes more formal action. On the other hand, if a company manager receives a complaint from an employee about being sexually harassed by her co-workers, the *potential* threat is high and it is an imminent threat because the business's liability will continue to accrue rapidly unless immediate action is taken. The costs of this type of legal challenge may be very high and alternatives become more limited. Thus, counsel should be consulted immediately.

Step 3: *Analyze the legal implications of the legal challenge using the* worst-case scenario *and include an estimate of costs including legal fees and courts costs, a losing judgment, and potential draws on human resources required to meet the challenge.* Using the worse-case scenario gives a manager context, which is helpful to understanding the potential liability faced because of the legal challenge. For example, if a customer is threatening to sue his supplier for breach of contract based on a $50,000 loss that he suffered, the worst-case scenario for the *supplier* is if the case goes to trial and the customer wins the judgment. Thus, the expenditure is $50,000 plus legal fees (which vary greatly from case to case and from attorney to attorney, but one could reasonably expect the legal fees and costs to be $25,000 to $100,000 based on the complexity of the case), plus the time and expenses that will be required for officers and employees to participate in the pretrial and trial process. An appeal will be even more costly. The scenario essentially sets the baseline for what a certain course of action could cost the company.

(continued)

Step 4: *Evaluate alternatives by developing a list of various approaches that could be used to meet the legal challenge. While considering advantages and disadvantages of alternatives, estimate the costs and potential return on expenditures made to meet the legal challenge.* Once a baseline potential for costs has been set, a variety of approaches should be considered. However, it is important that each approach also be subjected to a *cost-benefit analysis* (e.g., what will it cost to invest in this approach and what benefit will the business reap through the investment?). For example, suppose that TechCo enters into a contract with Big Insurance Company (BIC) to provide installation and maintenance of BIC's computer network based on "industry standards." After the installation, BIC is unhappy with the work and threatens to sue TechCo on the basis that their work was below industry standards and therefore violates the terms of their agreement. BIC demands that TechCo rewire its entire office (which will cost TechCo $60,000) or they will file a lawsuit. When examining alternatives, TechCo managers will almost certainly consider aggressive litigation as one approach.

TechCo could simply refuse to act any further, wait for the lawsuit to be filed, and then hire a law firm that promises to be hard-nosed and refuses to concede even the smallest point or to entertain any settlement offers. If indeed TechCo is within their legal rights to refuse BIC's demand, they will emerge from the trial victorious. However, the cost-benefit analysis is more problematic. Even if TechCo wins, the legal fees[9] for pretrial activities, trial work, and a possible appeal may very well end up being close to or even exceed the amount in dispute. Add the costs of human resources necessary to support this alternative and the possible damage to TechCo's reputation in the market that is inherent in litigation, and this approach begins to look less attractive. The following table lists alternatives along with sample costs, risks, and benefits to meet TechCo's legal challenge.

[9] Note that in the American legal system, the general rule regarding legal fees is that each side bears their own legal fees and costs of litigation. However, some exceptions exist to this general rule such as when a statute specifically provides that a successful litigant may recover attorneys' fees from the losing party (e.g., employment discrimination statutes).

Alternative	Costs/Risk/Impact	Benefit to the Corporation
Aggressive litigation	**Costs:** *Monetary*—high *Human resources*—high **Risks:** (1) Uncertainty about outcome; (2) irreparable client relations; (3) long-term distractions (3–8 yrs); and (4) potential damage to reputation in the marketplace.	Winning the lawsuit will settle the matter (subject to appeal).
Alternative dispute resolution such as arbitration or mediation.	**Costs:** *Monetary*—medium *Human resources*—medium to high **Risks:** (1) Damage to client relations; (2) potential failure to obtain a satisfactory outcome.	Dispute is settled without costly litigation or (usually) uncertainty of appeal. Potential to repair client relations or reputation in the business community.
Amend existing contract to provide for limited additional services by TechCo that will satisfy the parties (e.g., TechCo will be willing to renetwork any computer system that impairs its functionality according to industry standards to a maximum of $30,000).	**Costs:** *Monetary*—low *Human resources*—medium **Risks:** Potential that BIC may still not be satisfied and a lawsuit will still be filed.	Potential to repair client relations and/or increase reputation in the business community as a company that is highly committed to quality and customer service.

(continued)

Step 5: *Compare the alternatives with the business's mission, objectives, and ethical codes of conduct. Which alternatives are consistent with ethical decision-making standards and any statement of corporate social responsibility?*[10] *May any of the alternatives be turned into a business opportunity?* Once various strategies have been tested in terms of cost-benefit and risks, an equally important comparison should be done in the context of the company's mission, objectives, and ethical codes of conduct. If the company has developed certain statements concerning ethics and/or corporate social responsibility, what alternative is most consistent with those statements? In the TechCo–BIC case above, suppose that TechCo's internal policies provided that "TechCo believes that each client must be 100 percent satisfied with our services, or we will work at our own expense until the client is fully satisfied." While TechCo has no legal duty to comply with that internal standard, doesn't this maxim help TechCo's management in selecting an approach to legal challenges by its clients? Also, perhaps this dispute can be turned into an opportunity whereby BIC will potentially spread the word in the business community that TechCo is highly committed to customer service rather than to fighting its clients in a courtroom. Even if TechCo does not make a profit on the BIC agreement, isn't the long-term view more compelling?

Step 6: *Implement the chosen alternative and adjust the solution based on your monitoring of the costs, values, and opportunities. Be ready to revise and seek more opportunities as more information about the challenge becomes available.* Once a course of action has been determined, the model then shifts toward implementation and monitoring. As more information becomes available or as costs rise unexpectedly, if may be necessary to adjust the alternatives to accommodate the new information. For example, assume that in the TechCo–BIC case, the parties agreed on private arbitration.[11] Just before the arbitration, a TechCo internal investigation concludes that one of its installers incorrectly wired a small segment of the BIC network, but that the entire network was not corrupted. At this point, given TechCo's business values, its potential for liability and the costs of arbitration, TechCo may now be willing to enter into a settlement agreement with BIC rather than risk a loss at arbitration. On the other hand, if BIC continues to demand a total re-wiring costing $60,000, TechCo may opt to take its chances at arbitration.

Step 7: *During monitoring and after the legal challenge has been met, evaluate how the challenge could have been prevented or handled better. Devise a system or process that will help to limit future legal challenges.* While it is natural for managers to move onto other pressing matters after having met a legal challenge, a significant business opportunity may be lost in failing to analyze the dispute with the benefit of hindsight. For example, after resolving the BIC dispute, TechCo could confer with their counsel on possible revisions to future installment contracts to make it more clear what installation standards apply instead of using the term "industry" standards. There may also be an opportunity to revise future contracts to ensure that any lawsuit filed as a result of a dispute related to the agreement takes place close to TechCo's headquarters. That will help contain TechCo's costs in the event of litigation or arbitration (known as a *forum selection clause*). Other opportunities may include designing a quality control system for future installation, rethinking its risk in that particular market segment, and other business planning opportunities unique to their industry and practices.

[10]Business ethics and corporate social responsibility are discussed in detail in Chapter 5, "Business, Societal, and Ethical Contexts of Law."

[11]Private arbitration is a nonjudicial method for resolving legal disputes. Its costs tend to be much lower than litigation. Arbitration is discussed in detail in Chapter 4, "Resolving Disputes: Litigation and Alternative Dispute Resolution Options."

KEY TERMS

Law p. 4   A body of rules of action or conduct prescribed by controlling authority, and having legal binding force.

Jurisprudence p. 4   The science and philosophy of law that defines various approaches to the appropriate function of law and how legal doctrines should be developed and applied.

Counsel p. 7 Another name for an attorney.

Black's Law Dictionary p. 8 The leading legal dictionary.

Constitutional law p. 8 The body of law interpreting state and federal constitutions.

Statutory law p. 8 The body of law created by the legislature and approved by the executive branch of state and federal governments.

Common law p. 8 Law that has not been passed by the legislature, but rather is made by the courts and is based on the fundamentals of previous cases with similar facts.

Administrative law p. 8 Law made by government administrative agencies.

Ordinances p. 9 local statutes passed by local legislatures.

Statutory scheme p. 9 The structure of a statute and the format of its mandates.

Legislative history p. 9 The records kept by the legislature including the debates, committee and conference reports, and legislative findings of fact used when creating a law, which can be used to show the legislature's intent.

Citation p. 10 The special format used by the legal community to express where a statute or case law can be found.

Precedent p. 10 When courts apply the law of a previous case to current cases with similar facts.

Remedies p. 11 Judicial actions, which can be monetary or equitable, taken by courts that are intended to compensate an injured party in a civil lawsuit.

Equitable relief p. 11 A type of remedy, including injunctions and restraining orders, that is designed to compensate a party when money alone will not do, but instead forces the other party to do (or not do) something.

Equitable maxims p. 12 Common laws rules that guide courts in deciding cases and controversies and are intended to be broad statements of rules based on notions of fairness and justice.

Doctrine of stare decisis p. 13 The principle that similar cases with similar facts under similar circumstances should have a similar outcome.

Case precedent p. 13 The opinion of an appellate court, which is binding on all trial courts from that point in time onward so that any similar case would be decided according to the precedent.

Secondary sources p. 15 Sources of law that have no independent authority or legally binding effect, but can be used to illustrate a point or clarify a legal issue.

Restatements of the Law p. 15 A collection of uniform legal principles focused in a particular area of the law, which contains statements of common law legal principles and rules in a given area of law.

Model state statutes p. 15 Statutes drafted by legal experts to be used as a model for state legislatures to adopt in their individual jurisdictions in order to increase the level of uniformity and fairness across courts in all states.

Civil laws p. 18 Laws designed to compensate parties for money lost as a result of another's conduct.

Damages p. 18 Money lost as a result of another's conduct.

Criminal laws p. 18 Laws designed to protect society, which results in penalties to the violator such as fines or imprisonment.

Substantive laws p. 18 Laws that provide individuals with rights and create certain duties.

Procedural laws p. 18 Laws that provide a structure and set out rules for pursuing substantive rights.

Public laws p. 18 Laws derived from a government entity.

Private laws p. 18 Laws recognized as binding between two parties even though no specific statute or regulation provides for the rights of the parties.

THEORY TO PRACTICE

Galaxy Inc. is a supplier of greeting cards, small gifts, tokens, and games appropriate for special occasions such as holidays and birthdays. Galaxy distributes their products primarily through large supermarket and drug-store chains. Increasingly, Galaxy has lost revenue due to supermarkets that prefer to enter into the supplier market by manufacturing these products in a foreign country at a steep discount (instead of buying

Galaxy's products) and selling them in their stores at a higher profit. In response to this, Galaxy's management team begins to roll out a new business model where Galaxy will begin to retail its own products through newly created Galaxy retail stores. Jackson is a senior manager charged with overseeing the expansion efforts.

1. Suppose that Jackson intends to lease (rent) these new spaces for the Galaxy stores and hire new employees to staff them. What areas of the law may impact Jackson's planning process?

2. What options does Jackson have for legal advice to guide his efforts? What is the role that counsel might play in these transactions?

3. What sources and levels of law would Jackson need to have a fundamental knowledge of to help him protect his company from liability and meet any legal challenges? Give specific examples.

4. Assume that Jackson also plans to acquire the assets of a smaller retail company in order to carry out this expansion. Jackson is concerned about the potential tax impact that may be triggered by the transaction. How can Jackson plan with certainty for a particular type of tax treatment? What legal doctrine allows him to rely on the law in the planning process?

5. Assume that Jackson enters into a contract with Holmes for Holmes to act as store manager in one location. After two weeks, Jackson fires Holmes for incompetence. Holmes believes that Jackson fired him in violation of an anti-discrimination law, but he keeps forgetting to file the appropriate paperwork and eight months passes by. Finally, Holmes gets around to filing a complaint. What equitable maxim would apply to Holmes's complaint? Does this maxim favor Holmes or Jackson?

MANAGER'S CHALLENGE

Mid-level managers are frequently involved with vendors, competitors, customers, and employees on a daily basis and this makes them invaluable tools for spotting and meeting legal challenges in the early stages. Suppose that in the Theory to Practice example above, Jackson, a senior manager, receives an e-mail from a competing company.

> "Galaxy: You have stolen our trademark. We have the trademark rights for the Hobgoblin Necklace and you don't have our permission to use it. Yet, on a recent visit to one of your stores, you have Hobgoblin Necklaces for sale. Cease and desist or we will turn this matter over to our attorney.
> Signed,
> Necklace Emporium

Assume that you are a mid-level manager and that Jackson hands you the memorandum and informs you that, to his knowledge, Galaxy followed all proper legal procedures for the trademark. Using the Solutions for Managers: Legal Decisions in Business: An Analytical Model on page 19 of this chapter, compose a two- to three-page memorandum addressed to Jackson that gives guidance on handling this legal challenge. A sample answer may be found on this textbook's Web site at www.mhhe.com/melvin.

CASE SUMMARY 1.1 :: Sokoloff v. Harriman Estate Development Corp., 754 N.E.2d 184 (N.Y. 2001)

EQUITY AND FAIRNESS

Sokoloff purchased land in the Village of Sands Point and, in anticipation of building a home, he hired Harriman to provide preconstruction services, including the creation of architectural and landscaping plans. Sokoloff paid Harriman a $10,000 retainer fee and a total of $55,000 for creating and filing the architectural plans with the village. However, when it came time to build the home, Harriman estimated the cost to be over $1.8 million. Sokoloff, finding this amount to be exorbitant,

decided to get quotes from other builders, based on the plans he had Harriman design. However, Harriman said that the plans could not be used to construct the home unless he was the builder.

CASE QUESTIONS

1. Can Harriman withhold the plans from Sokoloff?
2. What legal theories or maxims would a court consider in deciding this case?
3. How should the court rule and why?

STATUTE OF LIMITATIONS

The U.S. Congress enacted a statute providing for a four-year statute of limitations for any cause of action arising out of an act of Congress enacted after 1990. Jones, an African American employee of R. R. Donnelley & Sons Co. (Donnelley), was denied a transfer to one of Donnelley's other plants when his plant closed. Moreover, while an employee for Donnelley, Jones was subject to a hostile work environment and various acts of discrimination. Jones, an Illinois citizen, wishes to sue Donnelley for violating federal antidiscrimination statutes. It has been three years since Jones worked for Donnelley, and Illinois has a two-year statute of limitations.

CASE QUESTIONS

1. Which statute of limitation governs and why?
2. Will Jones be able to sue Donnelley?

CLEAN HANDS DOCTRINE

Case Credit Corp. (Case) finances the sale of farm equipment to farmers. Day bought farm equipment financed by Case, yet Day never actually signed the sales contract. Instead, an employee of Case forged Day's signature on the sales contract with higher prices in an effort to pocket the difference for himself. Case was aware of the forgery, but did not make any effort to stop him or inform Day. When Day could not pay the loans back, Case filed suit to recover the farm equipment or compel payment.

CASE QUESTIONS

1. If the Court applies the clean hands doctrine, will Case be able to recover the farm equipment because Day is unable to make the payments? Why or why not?
2. Are Case's hands clean? Why or why not?

EQUITABLE RELIEF

Monfort, the nation's fifth largest beef packer, is concerned about a merger of the nation's second largest packer, Cargill, with the nation's third largest packer. Monfort believes that the merger will give Cargill almost 21 percent of the market leaving Monfort with only 5 percent. Monfort believes this merger may result in a violation of federal antitrust laws and wishes to file suit to prevent it.

CASE QUESTION

1. If Monfort files suit and the merger is deemed to violate antitrust laws what type of remedy will Monfort want to receive and why?

✓ Self-Check ANSWERS

1. A contract issue governed by statutory (UCC) law at the state level.
2. A patent issue governed by statutory law at the federal level.
3. A securities issue governed by statutory and administrative law at the federal and state level.
4. A bankruptcy issue governed by statutory and administrative law at the federal level.
5. A zoning issue governed by statutory law at the local level.

2
CHAPTER

Business and the Constitution

learning outcomes checklist

After studying this chapter, students who have mastered the material will be able to:

2-1 Explain the federal system in the context of the U.S. Constitution.

2-2 Describe the purpose and structure of the Constitution.

2-3 List the major provisions of the first three articles of the Constitution and explain the underlying assumptions of coequal branches of government.

2-4 Identify the powers of Congress that impact individuals and businesses.

2-5 Recognize the role of judicial review in interpreting the Constitution.

2-6 Understand the various applications and limits of congressional power under the Commerce Clause.

2-7 Apply Constitutional restrictions on state regulation of commerce in the business environment.

2-8 Explain how the tax and spend powers impact business.

2-9 List the major protections in the Constitution's Bill of Rights and explain how they apply in the business environment.

2-10 Understand limits imposed on government overreaching by virtue of the Due Process Clause and Equal Protection Clause.

2-11 Explain the right of privacy that has been recognized by the U.S. Supreme Court and Congress.

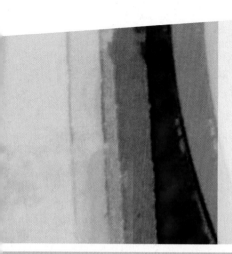

A fundamental knowledge of constitutional law is an important step in understanding the source and application of federal statutory law as well as the power and limits of government agencies enforcing regulations. Business managers and owners should also be aware of the impact of constitutional law and protections of individuals and business entities across a broad spectrum of sectors. In this chapter students will learn:

- The structure of the U.S. Constitution and individual state constitutions, and their respective roles in the American legal system.
- The specific powers granted to the government in the Constitution.
- The protections afforded by the Constitution in the Bill of Rights and the Fourteenth Amendment.

STRUCTURE AND NATURE OF THE CONSTITUTION: FEDERAL POWERS

The United States uses a **federal system** in which a national government coexists with the government of each state. An important concept underlying the federal system is that the federal government has only *limited powers* to regulate individuals and businesses. States are thought of as having more inherent powers to protect the general welfare of their citizenry with only general constitutional authorization.[1] In contrast, the federal government's power to regulate must be *specifically* granted by the U.S. Constitution. For example, the Constitution grants Congress the explicit power to collect taxes and to control the issuance of patents and copyrights.

LO2-2, 2-3   From a broad perspective, the Constitution may be thought of as having three general functions: (1) establishing a *structure* for the federal government (including qualifications for certain government offices) and rules for amending the Constitution; (2) granting specific *powers* for the different branches of government; and (3) providing *procedural protections* for U.S. citizens from wrongful government actions.

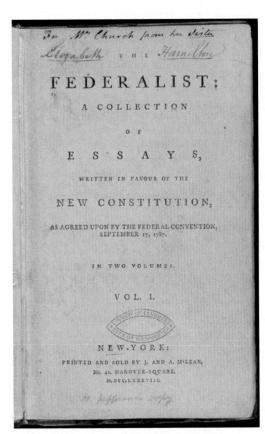

The *Federalist Papers,* written in 1789 by Alexander Hamilton and John Jay as an advocacy publication for ratification of the Constitution, is still cited in modern cases when courts interpret the Constitution.

Structure of the Constitution

The U.S. Constitution is composed of a **preamble,** seven **articles,** and 27 **amendments.** The first three articles establish a three-part system of government with three coequal branches: the **legislative branch,** the **executive branch,** and the **judicial branch.** The underlying rationale for this structure is that each of the branches exercises its respective powers to ensure that one branch does not exceed its authority under the Constitution.

Specifically, the Constitution begins with a preamble stating the Constitution's broad objectives (e.g., justice, liberty, tranquility, common defense). The articles then set out structure, powers, and procedures. From a business perspective, it is also important to note that Congress's powers to directly and exclusively regulate *bankruptcy, patents,* and *copyrights* are set out in Article I. Table 2.1 is a brief synopsis of the provisions in each article.

In addition to the creation of federal courts, the Constitution also establishes boundaries of **jurisdiction.** Jurisdiction is the legal authority that a court must have before it can hear a case. Both the U.S. Constitution and individual state constitutions contain language that establishes jurisdiction for certain matters to be heard by certain courts. The concept of jurisdiction is discussed in detail in Chapter 3, "The American Judicial System, Jurisdiction, and Venue."

Amendments

The Constitution has been *amended* (added to or changed) on several occasions since its ratification. These amendments are an important part of the Constitution's function as a protection of the citizenry from unlawful or repressive acts of the

---

[1]This inherent power of the state to protect its citizenry's health, safety, and general welfare is also referred to as the state's "police powers."

TABLE 2.1	Overview of Articles in the U.S. Constitution
Article I	Establishes the legislative branch (a Congress composed of the House of Representatives and the Senate); sets qualifications for members; grants congressional powers (lawmaking).
Article II	Establishes the executive branch (president); sets qualifications for the presidency; grants executive powers (enforcement of laws).
Article III	Establishes the judicial branch with a federal system of courts, including a Supreme Court; grants certain judicial powers.
Article IV	Establishes the relationship between the states and the federal government; describes how to admit new states to the Union.
Article V	Describes the process for amending the Constitution.
Article VI	Establishes the Constitution and federal law as the supreme law of the United States over any conflicting state law; authorizes the national debt (Congress may borrow money); public officials must take an oath to support the Constitution.
Article VII	Lists the requirements for ratification of the Constitution.

government. The first ten amendments, called the **Bill of Rights,** were added in 1791. The Bill of Rights preserves the rights of the individual U.S. citizens, and in some cases U.S.–based businesses, from unlawful acts of government officials, freedom of speech and religion, prohibition on random searches, and others. In all, there have been 27 amendments to the Constitution. The applicability of the Bill of Rights in the specific context of business is discussed in detail later in this chapter.

OVERVIEW OF FEDERAL POWERS

LO2-4

Powers granted to the three branches of government in the Constitution are known as **enumerated powers** and are typically *limited in scope.* This means that each act of federal legislation or regulation must come from within one of the very specific, enumerated powers. The primary authorization of Constitutional powers is given to Congress under Article I.[2] Congress has enumerated powers in 18 different clauses. The powers that generally impact business owners and managers include (1) the power to *regulate commerce* (**Commerce Clause**); (2) *taxing* the citizenry and commercial entities and *spending* government funds (tax and spend provisions); (3) *bankruptcy, patents, and copyrights;* and (4) a more *general implied authority* to make all laws necessary for carrying out its enumerated powers (**Necessary and Proper Clause**).

Separation of Powers

Enumerated powers are also granted to the executive and judicial branches. For example, the president is granted the power to (1) carry out laws made by Congress; (2) be the commander in chief

> **KEY** POINT
> Federal legislation or regulation must be authorized by a specific, enumerated power in the Constitution.

---

[2]§ 8.

TABLE 2.2 Example of Constitutional Checks and Balances

Branch	Power	Power Checked
Executive	Veto	Congress's lawmaking authority
Legislative	Override veto with supermajority	President's veto authority
Legislative	Impeachment and removal	President and federal judiciary's general powers
Judicial	Invalidate a law as unconstitutional	Congress's authority to make laws; the president's authority to enforce laws

of the armed forces; (3) enter into a treaty (subject to approval by the Senate) and to carry out foreign policy; and (4) appoint federal officers and judges (also subject to Senate approval). The judiciary is authorized to decide cases and controversies falling within federal jurisdiction. In addition, the three branches also have powers that are part of an overall scheme to provide a system to resolve conflicts among the branches and ensure that no one branch exceeds its constitutional authority. This system of checks and balances is called the **separation of powers.**

Table 2.2 sets out some of the various powers each branch has that acts as a check on the other branches.

LO2-5 Judicial Review

One of the central concepts in federal Constitutional law is the notion that federal courts have the right to invalidate state or federal laws that are inconsistent with the U.S. Constitution in some way. The U.S. Supreme Court is the ultimate judge of federal constitutional law. This authority was established by the Court in the landmark case of *Marbury v. Madison* in 1803. In *Marbury,* the Court explicitly ruled that (1) the Constitution was superior to federal and state statutes, and (2) when there is a conflict between the Constitution and state or federal law, the Court has the authority to strike down the law as unconstitutional. The Court based these conclusions on the judiciary branch's enumerated powers found in Article III, § 2 which includes authority of matters arising under the Constitution or "laws of the United States."[3] *Marbury,* although decided over two hundred years ago, is still considered valid precedent, and federal courts regularly cite the case as a source of authority for the power to invalidate a law that is in conflict with the Constitution. Over the better part of two centuries, the Court further defined its judicial review authority, including the power of federal courts to review state court decisions to the extent that the decisions involve federal law or federal constitutional issues.

---

[3]Because of its sweeping importance, *Marbury* has been subject to intense analysis, justification, and criticism. Some critics argue that the Supreme Court, in essence, gave the power of judicial review to themselves. Most of the criticism of the *Marbury* opinion is derived from the fact that the Constitution does not expressly authorize the courts to invalidate congressional statutes and that such a power is not contemplated in any preratification debates or in advocacy publications such as the *Federalist Papers.*

Applying the Constitution: Standards of Review

The U.S. Supreme Court has established three standards of review for applying Constitutional law. These standards appear in a broad range of constitutional law cases, and the Court has fashioned these standards for use by lower courts in applying the provisions of the Constitution as uniformly as possible. When reviewing a government action for constitutional soundness (such as passage or enforcement of a federal or state law), the Court classifies the action into one of three categories of scrutiny: (1) the **rational basis** category, (2) **intermediate-level scrutiny,** or (3) **strict scrutiny.**

Rational Basis   Government actions that are in this category are subject to the *least* amount of scrutiny. In order for the court to uphold the action, the government need only show that their action advanced a *legitimate* government objective (such as public welfare, health, or safety) and the action was minimally related to the government's objective. Government actions that fall into this category include those that do not involve any fundamental constitutional rights. Fundamental rights are generally limited to voting, access to criminal appeals, and interstate travel. Therefore, almost every economic- and tax-related law is reviewed using this undemanding threshold and ultimately the law is found to be constitutional. For example, suppose that, in response to pressure by consumer advocacy groups to regulate Internet access, pricing, and service, Congress passes a law requiring all Internet service providers (ISPs) to be directly regulated by a new federal administrative agency. The law imposes a tax on the ISPs to fund the agency. MegaSearch is an ISP subject to the law and files suit contending the law is an unconstitutional exercise of congressional powers. Because the regulation is purely economic, a court will likely rule against MegaSearch and uphold the law as constitutional using the rational basis category so long as the government provides evidence that the law advanced some legitimate government objective (such as consumer protection).

Intermediate-Level Scrutiny   Some actions are categorized as subject to intermediate-level scrutiny. Courts will uphold government actions as constitutional so long as the government can prove that their action advanced an *important government objective* (a higher level than "legitimate" used in the rational basis test) and that the action is *substantially related* (a higher level than "minimally") to the government's objective. A relatively small number of cases fall into this category. For example, courts have used this category in cases involving government action related to regulating time, place, and manner of a political demonstration that is protected under the First Amendment. For example, suppose in the MegaSearch case, above, that the management at MegaSearch organizes a protest against the law and applies for permits to stage demonstrations opposing the law in several cities across the country. One city, Silicone Village, rejects the permit application because MegaSearch's proposed demonstration would block a high-volume traffic area and endanger both pedestrians and drivers. The village also points out that a public park located in the village would be a more appropriate venue. If MegaSearch sues the village for denying them their First Amendment right to protest, a court would likely find the village's actions permissible under the intermediate-level scrutiny standard because the government's denial of the permit is substantially related to an important government objective (protection of drivers and pedestrians).

Strict Scrutiny   When the government action is related to a fundamental right or is based on a "suspect" classification (i.e., race, national origin, or alienage) courts apply a *strict scrutiny* standard when deciding whether to uphold the government action. Courts will only uphold the law if (1) the government's objective is *compelling,* (2) the means chosen by the government to advance that objective is necessary to achieve that compelling end, and (3) no *less-restrictive alternatives* existed. In the strict scrutiny category, the government has the burden of persuasion. As a practical matter, when courts classify government actions as belonging in the strict scrutiny category, they are signaling that the government action is likely to be ruled unconstitutional. For example, suppose that in the MegaSearch case above, that the government passes a law that imposes a higher level of tax on ISPs who catered to Latino users by assessing the tax based on the number of searches conducted using words and phrases in Spanish. Such a law would be a clear example of the government's use of a suspect classification (national origin) and would clearly be struck down under a strict scrutiny analysis.

The Supremacy Clause and Preemption

Because our federal system of government contemplates the coexistence of federal law with the various laws of the states, there is sometimes a conflict between federal law and state law. Article VI of the U.S. Constitution provides that valid federal laws (those made pursuant to Congress's constitutional authority and that are constitutionally sound) are always *supreme* to any conflicting state law. This is known as the **Supremacy Clause** and it invalidates any state law that is in direct conflict with federal law. The power granted by the supremacy clause to override a state law is called **preemption.** In order for preemption to occur, the federal law must be directly in conflict with the state law to the point where the two laws cannot coexist. For example, in *Geier v. American Honda Motor Company,*[4] the U.S. Supreme Court held that a federal regulation giving auto manufacturers the choice between airbags or alternative methods of passenger safety restraints preempted a claim by an injured party against an auto manufacturer under a state common law doctrine based on failing to install airbags. The Court ruled that, because the injured party's case depended upon a claim that auto manufacturers had a legal duty to install airbags and the violation of that duty resulted in the injury, the state common law could not coexist with federal law that specifically allowed auto manufacturers to opt not to install airbags in favor of another type of restraint system.

In Case 2.1, a famous dispute involving the early tobacco product liability litigation, the U.S. Supreme Court applied the doctrine of preemption.

LO2-6   COMMERCE POWERS

Congress's broadest power is derived from the Commerce Clause whereby Congress is given the power to "regulate Commerce among the several states."[5] Under the modern trend, federal courts have been largely deferential to legislative decisions under Congress's commerce powers. Despite some limits placed by the U.S. Supreme Court in the relatively recent past, Congress still exercises very broad powers to pass laws where the activity being regulated affects interstate commerce in any way.

Application of Commerce Powers

Congress exercises its commerce powers in various forms. However, the direct and broad power to regulate all persons and products related to the flow of interstate commerce is the fundamental source of its authority.

Interstate versus Intrastate Commercial Activity   Congress has the express constitutional authority to regulate (1) channels of interstate commerce such as railways and highways, (2) the instrumentalities of interstate commerce such as vehicles used in shipping, and (3) the articles moving in interstate commerce. Even for commercial activity that is purely *intrastate* (takes place within one state's borders), Congress has the power to regulate the activity so long as it has a *substantial economic effect* on interstate commerce. For example, suppose that Congress passes the Whistleblower Act, a statute that prohibits any business

---

[4]529 U.S. 861 (2000).

[5]Article I, § 8.

FACT SUMMARY   Cipollone brought suit against Liggett for violation of several New Jersey consumer protection statutes alleging that Liggett (and other cigarette manufacturers) were liable for his mother's death because they engaged in a course of conduct including false advertising, fraudulently misrepresenting the hazards of smoking, and conspiracy to deprive the public of medical and scientific information about smoking. Liggett urged the court to dismiss the state law claims contending that the claims related to the manufacturer's advertising and promotional activities were preempted by two federal laws: (1) the Federal Cigarette Labeling and Advertising Act of 1965, and (2) the Public Health Cigarette Smoking Act of 1969.

SYNOPSIS OF DECISION AND OPINION   The U.S. Supreme Court ruled against Cipollone, holding that his claims relying on state law were preempted by federal law. The Court cited both the text of the statute and the legislative history in concluding that Congress's intent in enactment of the laws was to preempt state laws regulating the advertising and promotion of tobacco products. Because Congress chose specifically to regulate a certain type of advertising (tobacco), federal law is supreme to any state law that attempts to regulate that same category of advertising.

WORDS OF THE COURT: Preemption   "Article VI of the Constitution provides that the laws of the United States shall be the supreme Law of the Land. Thus,

[. . .] it has been settled that state law that conflicts with federal law is 'without effect.' [. . .] Accordingly, 'the purpose of Congress is the ultimate touchstone' of pre-emption analysis. Congress's intent may be 'explicitly stated in the statute's language or implicitly contained in its structure and purpose.' In the absence of an express congressional command, state law is preempted if that law actually conflicts with federal law, [. . .], or if federal law so thoroughly occupies a legislative field 'as to make reasonable the inference that Congress left no room for the States to supplement it.' [. . .] [Cipollone's] claims are preempted to the extent that they rely on a state-law 'requirement or prohibition . . . with respect to . . . advertising or promotion.'"

Case Questions

1. Given the Supreme Court's language and the result of this case, is Congress's preemption power broad or narrow? Explain your answer.

2. Does the Supreme Court's ruling bar all residents of New Jersey, or any other state, from bringing suit against a tobacco company for false advertising or promotion? Why or why not?

3. Why would Congress want to preempt state law regarding the advertising and promotion of tobacco products? Do you agree with their decision to do so? Why or why not?

---

engaged in interstate commerce from firing their employees for reporting safety violations. Steel Co., a West Virginia company, begins to engage in a pattern of firing all employees who report safety violations. When a government agency files a civil lawsuit against Steel Co. to enforce the Whistleblower Act, Steel Co. defends that the act is unconstitutional because the activity of firing their employees is *purely within* the state of West Virginia and not related to interstate commerce. A court would likely find that if Steel Co. had any commercial activity at all (such as shipping, warehouses, equipment, advertising, or importing) that is outside of West Virginia, Congress has the authority to regulate Steel Co.'s workplace policies.[6] In the dynamics of the modern-day commercial world, a large amount of seemingly intrastate activity has some degree of economic effect on interstate commerce.

The U.S. Supreme Court has even deferred to congressional regulation of a product that is cultivated for noncommercial purposes solely in one state as sufficiently related to

---

[6]Based on the landmark Supreme Court case of *NLRB v. Jones & Laughlin Steel Corp.,* 301 U.S. 1 (1937). This was the first modern case where the Supreme Court began to broaden its interpretation of Congress's commerce powers. The groundwork for this expansion was laid out in *Gibbons v. Ogden,* 9 Wheat. 1 (1824) in which the Court recognized a more wide-ranging view of congressional power to regulate commerce.

interstate commerce. In *Gonzalez v. Raich*,[7] the Court ruled that Congress had the power to criminalize the possession of marijuana even if it was noncommercially cultivated and consumed by medical prescription all in the same state. The case involved a challenge by two California residents to the enforcement by federal officials of the federal Controlled Substances Act after California passed a state law via voter ballot proposition to exempt anyone involved in the cultivating, prescribing, and consuming marijuana for medical purposes from prosecution. The plaintiffs were each arrested by federal officials for possession of marijuana that had been grown at home. Each had a prescription from a licensed physician. In refusing to invalidate the Controlled Substances Act, the Court noted that Congress could have rationally believed that the noncommercially grown marijuana would be drawn into the *interstate market* and, therefore, the banning of the substance was sufficiently related to interstate commercial activity.

Civil Rights Legislation   A key use of the federal commerce power has been in the area of civil rights legislation. Indeed, the Supreme Court's level of deference for use of congressional commerce powers reached its peak during and directly after the civil rights era. In the 1964 Civil Rights Act, Congress used its commerce power to ban discrimination in places of public accommodation such as restaurants and hotels. In two important civil rights cases decided by the U.S. Supreme Court, the Court ruled that the Civil Rights Act was a permissible application of Congress's commerce powers. In *Heart of Atlanta Motel v. U.S.*,[8] the Court made clear that a federal ban on racial discrimination was a constitutionally permitted use of congressional commerce powers because the hotel was open

Legal Speak ›))
Ballot proposition A question put to the voters during a state election to decide (usually controversial) issues such as imposing a new income tax or whether the state should allow marijuana to be used for medicinal purposes. In some states, this is known as a ballot *initiative* or a *referendum*.

President Johnson, seen here with Dr. Martin Luther King, Jr., signed the Civil Rights Act in 1964.

[7]545 U.S. 1 (2005).
[8]379 U.S. 241 (1964).

to *interstate* travelers. Additionally, the Court deferred to a congressional finding of fact that racial discrimination in accommodations discouraged travel by limiting a substantial portion of the black community's ability to find suitable lodging. In a companion case,[9] *Katzenbach v. McClung,*[10] the Court held that a local restaurant that was located far from any interstate highway, and with no appreciable business from interstate travelers, was nevertheless subject to the reach of the federal statute because the restaurant purchased *some* food and paper supplies from out-of-state vendors. Since these purchases were of items that had moved in commerce, Congress could properly exercise their power to regulate a restaurant whose business interests were primarily local.

Noncommercial Activity   In 1995, the U.S. Supreme Court signaled that some limits on Congress's commerce power still exist. In cases where the activity is purely *noncommercial* (such as when Congress passes a criminal statute that is seemingly unrelated to commerce), the Court has used increased levels of scrutiny to be sure that the activity that Congress seeks to regulate has a sufficient nexus (connection) to some legitimate economic interest. In *U.S. v. Lopez,*[11] the Court invalidated a federal statute on the basis that it was beyond Congress's commerce powers. In *Lopez,* the Court struck down the Gun-Free School Zones Act of 1990, which made it a federal crime to possess a gun within a certain distance from a school. The Court rejected the government's argument that gun possession in schools affected economic productivity (by making it more difficult for students to obtain an education) and thus was within the purview of congressional commerce power. The Court held that such a broad interpretation of the commerce power would mean that congressional power was virtually unlimited, and that such an expansive authority was directly contrary to the express limits imposed by the Constitution. The court reasoned that the banning of firearms in local schools was a government police power and, therefore, more appropriately handled by the state government. Five years later, in *U.S. v. Morrison,* the Court invalidated another statute on the same grounds. In that case, the Court struck down the Violence Against Women Act, which gave victims of gender-motivated violence the right to sue their attacker for money damages in a federal court. In light of the *Lopez* decision, Congress made exhaustive findings of fact that detailed the cumulative economic affect of gender-motivated crimes. Nonetheless, the Court held that the congressional findings were too broad to justify use of the commerce power and that virtually any local crime could become a federal offense under a similar justification. As a general rule, the further that Congress strays from regulating commercial activity, the more likely the Court will be to give the law intense constitutional scrutiny.

> **KEY POINT**
> Congress's broadest powers are derived from the Commerce Clause. Courts are highly deferential to congressional action in areas that affect interstate commerce.

Constitutional Restrictions on State Regulation of Commerce   LO2-7

The U.S. Supreme Court has ruled that the mere existence of congressional commerce powers restricts the states from *discriminating* against or *unduly burdening* interstate commerce. States often wish to regulate commerce that crosses into their state borders. States are free to regulate commerce so long as (1) it does not impose a discriminatory law (such as a tax) on out-of-state businesses, and (2) the state law is a *legitimate* effort to regulate health, safety, and welfare. For example, suppose that in order to protect its own economic

> **web**check **www.mhhe.com/melvin**
> Visit this textbook's Web site for additional information and case summaries related to constitutional limitations on a state's imposing a tax on out-of-state vendors (including Internet vendors).

---

[9]Two cases that have similar issues where the Court publishes its opinion at the same time.
[10]379 U.S. 294 (1964).
[11]514 U.S. 549 (1995).

interests, the Idaho state legislature imposes an inspection requirement and fee on all non-Idaho grown potatoes sold within Idaho state borders. The state legislature justifies this process and fee on the basis that it is protecting its citizens from rotten potatoes. A court would likely strike down the law because it discriminates against out-of-state producers, and its explanation could be seen as a pretext (not the actual reason) since the law presumes that in-state potatoes are safe. Moreover, the inspection fee and the inspection process itself could be viewed as unreasonably burdening interstate commerce.

In Case 2.2, a federal appellate court considers whether a state law infringes on congressional rights to regulate interstate commerce.

CASE 2.2   Cavel International, Inc. v. Madigan, 500 F.3d 551 (7th Cir. 2007)

FACT SUMMARY   Cavel, an Illinois–based business, owned the one and only facility in the United States for slaughtering horses where the meat was shipped to Europe for human consumption. The state of Illinois passed a statute banning the practice of slaughtering horses if the primary reason for the slaughter was to produce horse meat for sale. Cavel sued to have the law invalidated as an unconstitutional act of the state government. Cavel contended that the state legislature had improperly encroached on Congress's exclusive jurisdiction over interstate commerce because enforcement of the law meant (1) a loss of $20 million in revenue for Cavel, (2) dozens of jobs would be lost in the local economy, and (3) the act effectively banned the exporting of meat to Europe and affected interstate commerce.

SYNOPSIS OF DECISION AND OPINION   The Seventh Circuit Court of Appeals ruled against Cavel. The court held that the effect on foreign commerce was minimal and that the state had a legitimate interest in enacting the law. The court determined that the law was not discriminatory in nature because Cavel, a foreign-owned firm, was not subject to selected discrimination because all businesses in the state were prohibited from slaughtering horses. The Court also held that the Illinois state legislature had a legitimate interest in prolonging the lives of certain animals and in doing so through this statute they were not substantially affecting interstate or foreign commerce. Although the court did express a reluctance to validate the statute because of the effect that it would have on Cavel and its shareholders, it upheld the statute as a permissible regulation of commerce by the state legislature because, on balance, the regulation was constitutionally sound.

WORDS OF THE COURT: State Regulation of Commerce   "The clearest case of a state law that violates the commerce clause is a law that discriminates in favor of local firms. [. . .] [However,] [t]he absence of outright discrimination does not terminate inquiry into a possible violation of the commerce clause. [. . .] There are situations in which states, by ostensibly local regulations, distort the operation of interstate markets. Such cases present more difficult factual issues than cases of outright discrimination. Plaintiffs have sometimes prevailed, at least if the impact on commerce is evident. [. . .] [But,] [w]here the statute regulates evenhandedly to effectuate a legitimate local public interest, and its effects on interstate commerce are only incidental, it will be upheld unless the burden imposed on such commerce is clearly excessive in relation to the putative local benefits. [. . .] Quite apart from economic consequences, an interference by a state with foreign commerce can complicate the nation's foreign relations, which are a monopoly of the federal government; [. . .] [However,] [t]he curtailment of foreign commerce by the amendment is slight and we are naturally reluctant to condemn a state law, supported if somewhat tenuously by a legitimate state interest, on grounds as slight as presented by Cavel."

Case Questions

1. Do you agree with the Court's decision or do you think that Cavel's business affects interstate or foreign commerce? Why or why not? Explain your answer.

2. In the opinion, Justice Posner notes: "Cavel, [. . .] did not tell the district court and has not told us what percentage of the horse meat consumed by Europeans it supplies and thus whether its being closed down is likely to have an impact on the price of horse meat in Europe." Had Cavel showed that it produced 20 percent of all horse meat consumed by Europeans, would the result have been different? Why or why not? What if it was 50 percent or 70 percent?

TAX AND SPEND POWER[12]

Congress has a far-reaching power to tax the citizenry and to spend the federal government's money in any way that promotes the common defense and general welfare. The power to tax is an independent source of federal authority. That is, Congress may tax activities or property that it might not be authorized to regulate directly under any of the enumerated regulatory powers. The power to spend is linked to the power to tax in that the money may be raised by taxation and then spent on the general welfare of the United States. The U.S. Supreme Court has been highly deferential to Congress in terms of what constitutes general welfare and under what circumstances Congress may exercise its authority to tax its citizenry and its decision-making power on how to allocate government money.

Necessary and Proper Clause

Congress may also place *conditions* on the use of federal money in order to achieve some public policy objective. Congress generally cites the Necessary and Proper Clause as authorization to set conditions on the spending. This ability to set conditions on the use of federal money has been a somewhat controversial method of congressional regulation because it falls outside the areas of *traditional* regulation. However, the U.S. Supreme Court has upheld federal spending conditions that are tied to individual states passing certain laws that carry out a congressionally set ambition. State legislatures have objected to this type of regulation, characterizing it as a backdoor method for imposing laws on states that are outside Congress's enumerated powers.

In *South Dakota v. Dole*,[13] the Court deferred to Congress's right to attach certain spending conditions related to the legal drinking age (a state law issue)[14] on federal funds distributed to the states for use in repairing and building highways. Unless a state passed a law to raise the legal drinking age to 21 by a certain date, they would lose a certain percentage of their allotted highway funding from the federal government. South Dakota and other states challenged the law as an unconstitutional intrusion by Congress into state affairs and an overreaching use of its spending power to regulate. The Court sided with Congress and ruled the drinking-age condition is constitutionally permissible under Congress's spending authority so long as the condition itself is not a violation of individual constitutional rights. This case signaled an important victory for Congress and it now regularly uses spending conditions as a form of regulation for individuals and businesses.

 Self-Check

What is the constitutional source of authority for each of the following laws?

1. A federal statute that makes it more difficult for businesses to qualify for protection under bankruptcy laws.

2. An increase in the federal corporate income tax.

3. A federal statute that adds criminal penalties for patent infringement.

4. A federal statute creating an agency to regulate ground shipping between states.

5. A federal statute that requires that 25 percent of federal government construction contracts be awarded to companies that are women- or minority-owned enterprises.

Answers to this Self-Check are provided at the end of the chapter.

---

[12]Article I, § 8. "The Congress shall have the Power To lay and collect Taxes, Duties, Imposts and Excises . . . to pay the Debts and provide for the common Defence and general Welfare of the United States. . . ."

[13]483 U.S. 203 (1987).

[14]At that time, 19 states permitted consumption of some or all alcoholic beverages before the age of 21.

CONCEPT SUMMARY   Structure and Nature of the Constitution: Federal Powers

- Under the federal system used by the United States, the federal government has only limited powers to regulate individuals and businesses.
- These powers are specifically enumerated in the Constitution and are limited in scope.
- The limited powers of the legislative branch, which are specifically enumerated in the Constitution, include (1) the power to regulate commerce; (2) the power to tax and spend; (3) the power to regulate bankruptcy, patents, and copyrights; and (4) a general implied authority to make all laws necessary for carrying out its enumerated powers. Similarly, the president is granted the power to (1) carry out laws made by Congress; (2) be the commander in chief of the armed forces; (3) enter into a treaty and carry out foreign policy; and (4) appoint federal officers and judges. Finally, the judiciary is authorized to decide cases and controversies falling within federal jurisdiction.
- Congress's broadest power is derived from the Commerce Clause.
- Under the Commerce Clause, Congress has the authority to regulate (1) channels of interstate commerce such as railways and highways; (2) the instrumentalities of interstate commerce such as vehicles used in shipping; (3) the articles moving in interstate commerce; and (4) any activity that has substantial economic effect on interstate commerce, including activities that are not commercial in nature.
- The U.S. Constitution is composed of a preamble, seven articles, and 27 amendments, the first ten of which are called the Bill of Rights.
- The first three articles of the Constitution establish a three-part system of government with three coequal branches: the legislative branch, the executive branch, and the judicial branch.
- This structure is designed so that each of the branches exercises its respective powers to ensure that one branch does not exceed its authority under the Constitution (referred to as a separation of powers or checks and balances).
- Under the Supremacy Clause, federal laws preempt (override) any conflicting state laws.
- Congress has the power to tax the citizenry and to spend the federal government's money in any way that promotes the common defense and general welfare.
- Under the Necessary and Proper Clause, Congress may also place conditions on the use of federal money in order to achieve some public policy objective.

LO2-9 CONSTITUTIONAL PROTECTIONS

In addition to the Constitution prescribing the structure of government and granting the government certain powers, it also provides protection for the citizenry from unlawful or repressive acts by the government. These protections are contained primarily in the Bill of Rights (the first ten amendments) and in other amendments that guarantee the right of **due process.** From a business perspective, however, it is important to note that corporations and other business entities *do not* always receive the same level of constitutional protections as individuals.

The Bill of Rights and Business

The Bill of Rights contains many of the rights common in the American vernacular. Among them are freedom of speech, the press, religion, and expression (First Amendment); freedom from government-conducted searches without cause or warrant (Fourth Amendment); rights against self-incrimination and to a speedy jury trial by our peers (Fifth and Sixth Amendments); and freedom from cruel and unusual punishments (Eighth Amendment).

While each amendment carries it own significance in a historical and public policy context, the coverage of this textbook is primarily concerned with the Bill of Rights provisions that relate directly to business and management issues.

First Amendment

The First Amendment contains the important introductory phrase "Congress shall make no law" and then articulates several specific protections against government encroachment in the areas of religion, press, speech, assembly, and petition of grievances. The introductory phrase demonstrates that the framers intended the Constitution to function as a *limit* on government actions. Although certain First Amendment rights for individuals do not extend to business owners, courts have increasingly broadened protections for business owners in the area of free speech.

Limits on Free Speech   Although the U.S. Supreme Court has given broad protections to speech that involves political expression, the First Amendment is by no means absolute. Justice Oliver Wendell Holmes famously wrote that the First Amendment was not without limits by giving an example that the Constitution did not protect one that falsely yells "fire" in a crowded theatre. Courts have ruled that the government may place reasonable restrictions related to time and place of political expression in cases, for example, where public safety may be threatened.

Commercial Speech   The most common form of commercial speech (ways in which business entities communicate with the public) is *advertising* through print, television, radio, and Web-based sources. Traditionally, advertising had little or no First Amendment protection, but the Supreme Court has gradually increased the constitutional protections related to advertising. In *Virginia State Board of Pharmacy v. Virginia Citizens Consumer Council,*[15] the Supreme Court held that purely commercial speech (speech with no political implications whatsoever) was entitled to partial First Amendment protection so long as the speech was truthful and concerned a lawful activity. In the *Virginia* case, the Court struck down Virginia state laws that prohibited a pharmacist from advertising prices for prescription drugs. The Court rejected the state's contention that it has a substantial interest in ensuring that cut-rate prices that may be created by competition among pharmacies doesn't result in substandard service. Given that the information banned by the statute was limiting the free flow of information to consumers, the Court held that such regulation violated the First Amendment.

Four years after the *Virginia* case, the Court expanded the analytical framework for deciding whether certain regulations were constitutional in *Central Hudson Gas v. Public Service Commission.*[16] The *Central Hudson* case created a framework for a four-part test that subjects government restrictions on commercial speech to a form of intermediate-level scrutiny.

- *Part One.* So long as the commercial speech concerns lawful activities and is not misleading, the speech qualifies for protection under the First Amendment. If the speech is entitled to protection, then the government's regulation must pass the final three parts of the *Central Hudson* test in order for the restriction to be constitutionally sound.
- *Part Two.* A *substantial government interest* in regulating the speech must exist.
- *Part Three.* The government must demonstrate that the restriction *directly advances* the claimed government interest.
- *Part Four.* The government's restriction must be *not more extensive* than necessary (not too broad) to achieve the government's asserted interest.

---

[15]425 U.S. 748 (1976).
[16]447 U.S. 557 (1980).

FACT SUMMARY   The Village of Glendale, Ohio, passed an ordinance that prohibited parking a vehicle on a public road for the purposes of displaying it for sale. Pagan, a resident of Glendale, parked his car on the public street and posted a "For Sale" sign on the vehicle. A Glendale police officer warned Pagan to take the down the sign or face a citation for violating the ordinance. Pagan corresponded with several Glendale officials but was unable to satisfactorily resolve his complaints. Pagan then filed suit against the Village of Glendale and Fruchey, Glendale's Chief of Police (collectively "Glendale"), claiming that the ordinance was an unconstitutional infringement of his commercial speech rights under the First Amendment. Glendale contended that its ordinance satisfied the requirements under *Central Hudson* because the government has a substantial regulatory interest in traffic and pedestrian safety. The trial court dismissed Pagan's claim and he appealed.

SYNOPSIS OF DECISION AND OPINION   The Court of Appeals for the Sixth Circuit reversed the trial court's decision and ruled in favor of Pagan. The court held that Glendale had not met the third part of the *Central Hudson* test because there was not a sufficient connection between Glendale's asserted interest (traffic safety) and government regulation. Glendale's asserted interest of traffic safety was not necessarily met by the ordinance. Given that Glendale did not offer any data, rather only the opinion of the police chief to support

their contention, it failed to meet its burden in showing that the ordinance actually advances its claimed interest in traffic safety.

WORDS OF THE COURT: Applying the *Central Hudson* Test   "[Glendale's attempt to justify its ordinance] amounts to nothing more than a conclusory articulation of governmental interests. While it suffices for the second part of the *Central Hudson* test by identifying two substantial government interests, it fails to address the third prong at all: that is, how the particular restriction chosen by Glendale directly and materially advances those interests. Its reference to people in the roadway looking at cars displaying 'For Sale' signs is most accurately characterized as simple conjecture by the police chief about something that might occur. Certainly, it is not evidence that 'For Sale' signs on cars in streets pose any concrete harm to traffic or aesthetics or that the ordinance has any connection to the interests Glendale asserts."

Case Questions

1. Could the ordinance itself be modified to meet the third part of the *Central Hudson* test?

2. What types of data do you suppose the court wanted from Glendale to support their claim that the ordinance advanced their traffic safety interest? Why didn't the court give more weight to the police chief's opinion?

In Case 2.3, a federal appellate court applies the *Central Hudson* framework to a municipal ordinance that prohibits displaying of a car for sale on a public road.

Advertising and Obscenity Regulation   Sometimes commercial speech runs afoul of government's attempt to ban or regulate materials it deems obscene. However, obscenity regulation of commercial speech is subject to the same scrutiny as any other government regulation of commercial speech. For example, a federal appellate court has ruled that a state agency's decision to effectively prohibit a corporation's use of a certain label on its beer products, which the agency deemed offensive, violated the business owner's right under commercial speech protections. In that case, *Bad Frog Brewery, Inc. v. N.Y. State Liquor Authority,*[17] the U.S. Court of Appeals for the Second Circuit held that labels on the company's beer products, which depicted a frog with his unwebbed "fingers" extended in a manner evocative of a well-known human gesture of insult, were protected commercial speech under the First Amendment. The court ruled that when the New York State Liquor Authority denied Bad Frog's application to use the labels in New York on the basis that the labels were offensive, the state agency failed to show that their ruling achieved their asserted interest

---

[17]134 F.3d 87 (2nd Cir., 1998).

of protecting children from vulgarity. Because the labels were not misleading and did not concern an unlawful activity, the labels were a protected form of commercial speech and any government regulation must conform with the requirements set out in the *Central Hudson* case. Ruling in favor of Bad Frog, the court remarked that a state must demonstrate that its commercial speech

webcheck **www.mhhe.com/melvin**
Visit this textbook's Web site to see the Bad Frog label.

limitation is part of a substantial effort to advance a valid state interest, "not merely the removal of a few grains of offensive sand from the beach of vulgarity."

Political Speech by Corporations   Another form of commercial speech, broadly speaking, is when corporations and other business entities fund political speech or engage in corporate advocacy of a particular candidate or political issue. May the government regulate such commercial speech under the same standards as the *Central Hudson* case? Generally, the answer depends of the specific form and content of the speech—but typically political speech by corporations is fully protected by the First Amendment.

In *First National Bank of Boston v. Bellotti*,[18] the Supreme Court created a new level of First Amendment protection for corporations engaged in *politically* oriented speech when it struck down a Massachusetts state statute that prohibited corporations from using corporate assets to fund expenditures related to "influencing or affecting the vote on any question submitted to the voters" (known as a *ballot proposition*).[19] In *Bellotti*, the Court held that that while some constitutional rights are not afforded to corporations, freedom of corporate political speech is fully protected. As such, any attempt to regulate politically oriented speech by corporations is subject to *strict scrutiny*. The Court also held that a corporation's freedom of speech is not limited to matters materially affecting its business. Rather, a business has a constitutionally protected right to communicate about any political matter that is consistent with the goal of the First Amendment: societal interest in the free flow of information and debate. For the first time, the Court recognized that speech that otherwise would be within the protection of the First Amendment does not lose protection simply because its source is a corporation.

Political Spending and Corporations

In a 2010 case that attracted significant media attention, the U.S. Supreme Court ruled that the government may not ban all political spending by corporations in *candidate elections*.

In *Citizens United v. Federal Election Commission*,[20] the Court held that the provisions of the Bipartisan Campaign Reform Act of 2002 (commonly referred to as the McCain-Feingold Act), which prohibited corporations and labor unions from using general funds to sponsor "electioneering communications," were unconstitutional. It is important to note that the ruling did not involve a challenge to limits imposed by the law on campaign contributions, or with the prohibition of

> **KEY POINT**
> Commercial speech in the form of advertising has partial First Amendment protection (subject to intermediate-level scrutiny) under *Central Hudson*. Corporate *political* speech has full First Amendment protection (subject to strict scrutiny) under *Bellotti* and *Citizens United*.

corporate contributions to a candidate. These limits remain intact. Rather, the Supreme Court's ruling applies only to *independent expenditures* on speech. Independent expenditures mean speech (such as advertisements) engaged in by an organization on its own behalf, and not with coordination with any candidate.

The case originated when Citizens United, a conservative nonprofit corporation, produced a 90-minute documentary called "Hillary: The Movie" which criticized then-Senator Hillary

---

[18]435 U.S. 765 (1978).

[19]Also known in certain states as a *referendum* or *ballot initiative*.

[20]558 U.S. 50 (2010).

Clinton and questioned her fitness for office. The group planned to release it during the 2008 Democratic presidential primaries. Fearful that uncertainties in the law would result in enforcement action by the government upon release of the movie, Citizens United filed suit against the Federal Elections Commission (FEC) in federal court challenging the act. After they lost that case, Citizens United scrapped its plans to release the movie, but continued to appeal the trial court's decision. The U.S. Supreme Court ruled in favor of Citizens United, striking down the provisions of the law that banned Citizens United from releasing the movie. Justice Anthony Kennedy wrote the majority opinion:

> When the government seeks to use its full power, including criminal law, to command where a person may get his or her information or what distrusted source he or she may not hear, it uses censorship to control thought. This is unlawful. The First Amendment confirms the freedom to think for ourselves.

Political speech by corporations, such as the non-profit California Nurses Association's advertising campaign opposing Governor Arnold Schwarzenegger, is protected under the First Amendment.

OTHER AMENDMENTS

In addition to the First Amendment, certain other protections afforded by the Constitution may be important to business owners and managers. The **Fourth Amendment** protects individual citizens' rights to be secure in their "persons, houses, papers and effects." The U.S. Supreme Court has systematically applied a *reasonableness test* to define the limits of when the government may search without a warrant based on probable cause that criminal activity is afoot. From a business perspective, it is important to understand that the law recognizes two basic types of searches. First, when the government wishes to obtain a warrant to search particular premises while investigating a *criminal offense,* they must demonstrate that they have sufficient information, called *probable cause,* that justifies the issuance of a search warrant by a court.[21] Second, the government also investigates noncriminal *administrative violations.* The standard for the issuance of a warrant for a search in an administrative violation investigation is lower than for investigating a criminal offense. Administrative warrants may be used by government regulatory agencies (such as the Environmental Protection Agency) to gain access to worksites for compliance inspections. Administrative agencies and administrative warrants are discussed in detail in Chapter 17, "Administrative Law."

The **Fifth Amendment** provides that no person "shall be compelled in any criminal case to be a witness against himself." Simply put, this amendment guarantees individuals the right to remain silent both during the investigation and during any subsequent judicial proceedings. Although it is clear that this amendment does not apply to corporate *entities* when the government is seeking certain business records, individual corporate officers and employees are entitled to Fifth Amendment protection when facing a criminal investigation by the

---

[21]Criminal offenses and probable cause are discussed in detail in Chapter 22, "Criminal Law and Procedure in a Business Context."

police, or more commonly in a business context, administrative agencies investigating a possible criminal offense (e.g., the Internal Revenue Service investigating tax fraud). This right is a central and fundamental part of the Supreme Court's famous decision in *Miranda v. Arizona.*[22] The Miranda case set out specific procedures to be used by the government when interrogating possible suspects of criminal wrongdoings. The *Miranda* case is covered in detail in Chapter 22, "Criminal Law and Procedure in a Business Context."

DUE PROCESS PROTECTIONS

In addition to protection afforded by the Bill of Rights, the law provides protections to individuals and businesses from government overreaching through constitutional guarantees contained in the **Due Process Clause** of the Fifth and Fourteenth Amendments. These clauses protect individuals from being deprived of "life, liberty, or property" without due process of law. Fundamentally, due process rights require the government to provide some type of *hearing* and *procedure* whenever the government has taken some action that deprives an individual or business of some liberty or property interest.

Fourteenth Amendment

Perhaps the most important role of the Fourteenth Amendment is that it makes the Bill of Rights applicable to the states. Note, for example, that the First Amendment begins with the explicit restriction that "Congress shall make no law . . ." Originally, the framers intended the Bill of Rights to be a protection against certain acts of the *federal* government, and therefore states were not bound by the Bill of Rights. However, in the post-Civil War reconstruction period (mid-1860s), the Fourteenth Amendment was passed, which effectively expanded the protections under the Bill of Rights to include restrictions and actions by *state governments.*

The Due Process Clause has two primary functions. First, it imposes certain *procedural* requirements on federal and state governments when they impair life, liberty, or property. The U.S. Supreme Court has held that procedural due process requires the government to give appropriate notice, a neutral hearing, and an opportunity to present evidence before any government action may be taken that would affect the life, liberty, or property of an individual. The Due Process Clause also limits the *substantive* power of the states to regulate certain areas related to individual liberty. These substantive due process rights require that laws passed by the government be published for public inspection and to be specific enough so that a reasonable person would understand how the law applies. Laws that are vague or overly broad are unconstitutional under the substantive due process doctrine.

In Case 2.4, the U.S. Supreme Court applied the Due Process Clause in the context of a state statute that regulated certain jury awards.

Equal Protection   The Equal Protection Clause is the part of the Fourteenth Amendment that prohibits the government from denying citizens' equal protection of the laws.[23] Fundamentally, the clause guarantees that the government will treat people who are similarly situated equally. Recall from our discussion earlier in this chapter that courts use a variety of levels of review when applying constitutional law. This is especially important in equal protection cases where courts apply one of the three categories of review that are classified by their level of scrutiny (strict, intermediate-level, or rational basis).

When a government action (such as passage of a statute or enforcing a law or regulation) is based on a suspect classification, or if the action impairs a fundamental right, the *strict scrutiny* standard is applied. Courts have held that any government action based on

---

[22]384 U.S. 436 (1966).

[23]Although the direct text of the clause applies to state governments, the federal government is also bound by the same rules of equal protection via the Fifth Amendment.

FACT SUMMARY Campbell was involved in an accident where one party was killed and another was severely injured. State Farm was Campbell's insurer and despite their own investigation's conclusion that Campbell had acted negligently, they refused to settle a case brought by the injured parties for the $50,000 policy limit. Prior to trial, State Farm gave Campbell assurances that (1) he did not have liability in the case, and (2) that their mutual interests were closely aligned, therefore hiring his own counsel was an unnecessary expense. Given State Farm's assurances, Campbell did not consult an attorney. Nonetheless, a jury found against both Campbell and State Farm and concluded that no other parties were at fault. They awarded the plaintiffs $185,849, far more than the amount offered during pretrial settlement discussions. After the verdict, State Farm refused to pay any amount beyond the $50,000 policy limit, and their general counsel went so far as to advise Campbell to sell his house in order to cover the excess award owed to the plaintiffs.

Campbell sued State Farm for bad faith, fraud, and intentional infliction of emotional distress. The jury found against State Farm and awarded Campbell $2.6 million in damages to compensate him for losses (called compensatory damages) and $145 million in punitive damages. Consistent with a state statute limiting certain damage awards, the trial court reduced the awards to $1 million in compensatory damages and $25 million in punitive damages. An appellate court reinstated the original $145 million punitive damage award on the basis that the state's punitive damages statute allowed larger damage awards if the defendant acted in a particularly reprehensible manner. State Farm appealed the punitive damages award arguing that such a disproportionately large punitive damages award amounted to a violation of the Due Process Clause.

SYNOPSIS OF DECISION AND OPINION The U.S. Supreme Court ruled in favor of State Farm and held that the damages awarded were excessive and, therefore, violated the Constitution's Due Process Clause. The Court noted that there are constitutional limits to the amount of damages that are recoverable and when damages are excessive it constitutes an arbitrary deprivation of property. The Court laid out a three-part analysis for determining the constitutionality of a statute regulating punitive damages. The statute must include considerations of (1) the degree of reprehensibility of the defendant's misconduct, (2) the disparity between the actual or potential harm suffered by the plaintiff and the punitive damages award, and (3) the difference between the punitive damages awarded by the jury and the civil penalties authorized or imposed in comparable cases. In this case, the Court concluded that the $145 million award was constitutionally impermissible because the statute did not incorporate these factors.

WORDS OF THE COURT: Due Process and Punitive Damages "While States possess discretion over the imposition of punitive damages, it is well established that there are procedural and substantive constitutional limitations on these awards. The Due Process Clause of the Fourteenth Amendment prohibits the imposition of grossly excessive or arbitrary punishments on a [party committing the wrong]. To the extent an award is grossly excessive, it furthers no legitimate purpose and constitutes an arbitrary deprivation of property. [. . .] Although these awards serve the same purposes as criminal penalties, defendants subjected to punitive damages in civil cases have not been accorded the protections applicable in a criminal proceeding. This increases our concerns over the imprecise manner in which punitive damages systems are administered. We have admonished that 'punitive damages pose an acute danger of arbitrary deprivation of property. Jury instructions typically leave the jury with wide discretion in choosing amounts, and the presentation of evidence of a defendant's net worth creates the potential that juries will use their verdicts to express biases against big businesses, particularly those without strong local presences.'"

Case Questions

1. Do you agree with the Court that the damages awarded in this case were arbitrary? Applying the factors outlined by the Court, describe why or why not.

2. Using these factors, how can one determine what constitutes an excessive award of damages that violates a defendant's due process compared to one that does not violate the Due Process Clause? Is this distinction clear?

race, national origin, and alienage are automatically *suspect* classifications. The Court has held that government actions related to the right to vote, to have access to the courts, and the right to migrate from state to state are subject to strict scrutiny standards as well.

Note also that *semi-suspect* (also called *quasi-suspect*) classifications trigger *intermediate-level* scrutiny. Courts have used this standard of review when government actions were based on gender or illegitimacy. Recall from earlier in this chapter that economic or tax regulations are judged under the rational basis category.

Legal **Speak** »)
Punitive damages
Money awarded in addition to actual damages of an injured party that is intended to punish the wrongdoer and deter unlawful conduct in the future.

CONCEPT SUMMARY   Constitutional Protections

- The Bill of Rights contains protection for citizens from unlawful or repressive acts by the government.
- Corporations and other business entities do not always receive the same level of constitutional protections as individuals.
- Traditionally, advertising had little or no First Amendment protection, but the Supreme Court has gradually increased the constitutional protections related to advertising allowing purely commercial speech to have partial First Amendment protection so long as it is truthful. Commercial political speech has full First Amendment protection.
- The Due Process Clause of the Fifth and Fourteenth Amendments protect individuals from being deprived of "life, liberty, or property" without due process of law.
- The Fourteenth Amendment makes the Bill of Rights applicable to the states.
- The Due Process Clause serves two purposes. First, it imposes procedural requirements on federal and state governments. Second, it limits the substantive power of the states to regulate certain areas affecting individual liberties.

PRIVACY

LO2-11

Although not explicitly mentioned in the Constitution, privacy rights play a central role in constitutional law. The U.S. Supreme Court struggled with the notions of individual rights of privacy during the early 1900s, but did not formally recognize the right to privacy until 1965 in the landmark case of *Griswold v. Connecticut.*[24] The case involved a challenge to a Connecticut statute that criminalized (1) the use of contraceptives, and (2) aiding or counseling others in their use. Griswold and others were convicted under the statute for counseling married couples in the use of contraceptives at a local Planned Parenthood office.[25] The U.S. Supreme Court struck down the statute as unconstitutional. They held that the right of privacy was implied by language in the First, Third, Fourth, Fifth, and Ninth Amendments, which created a constitutionally protected zone of privacy. The right of privacy recognized in *Griswold* was extended to abortion rights in *Roe v. Wade,*[26] one of the most famous U.S. Supreme Court decisions in American history. The *Roe* Court struck down a state statute, which banned all abortions under any circumstances, as unconstitutional. The Court recognized that a woman's right to privacy is fundamental under the Fourteenth Amendment. Thus, the government has only a limited right to regulate, and could not completely outlaw, abortion procedures and providers. Although the existence of a constitutional right of privacy has generated intense and emotional debate, the

---

[24]381 U.S. 479 (1965).

[25]Note that no users of contraceptives, married or single, were ever charged with violating the statute.

[26]410 U.S. 113 (1973).

U.S. Supreme Court has reaffirmed the central tenants of the privacy rights recognized in *Griswold* and *Roe* over several decades and it has become settled law.

Federal Statutes

In addition to privacy rights afforded by the Constitution, Congress has legislated specific privacy rights such as the Health Insurance Portability and Accountability Act (HIPPA),[27] which regulates health-care providers, plans, and plan administrators in gathering, storing, and disclosing medical information about individuals. The law requires specific policies and record-keeping practices to be used in order to assure privacy of any medical information such as diagnosis, tests, medications, and so forth. Congress has also sought to assure certain privacy protections by mandating that government agencies allow appropriate public and media access to agency records and reports under the Freedom of Information Act.

One of the more controversial federal statutes that deal with modern privacy issues was the Uniting and Strengthening America by Providing Appropriate Tools Required to Intercept and Obstruct Terrorism Act (called the *USA Patriot Act*). The USA Patriot Act was passed immediately after the terrorist attacks of September 11, 2001, and provides increased authority for government officials to surreptitiously access and/or monitor individual and corporate financial records, e-mail, telephone conversations, and Internet activity when investigating possible terrorism-related activity. Although the law does create an infrastructure that is designed to prevent government overreaching and protect individual privacy (e.g., the government must provide evidence that the investigation is related to terrorism and not being used for investigating other matters), critics have derided the law as lacking appropriate safeguards to prevent invasion of privacy.

Workplace Privacy

Most privacy rights afforded by the U.S. Constitution do not extend to the workplace. Nonetheless, privacy rights have become increasingly important to business owners and managers as Congress and state legislatures seek to clarify workplace privacy rights by statute in areas such as employee drug testing, searches of employee areas (such as lockers or desks) by employers, and electronic monitoring of e-mail and Internet usage. Statutes that regulate the workplace are covered in detail in Chapter 11, "Employment Regulation and Labor Law."

---

[27] 29 U.S.C. Section 1181.

Jurisdiction p. 28　The legal authority that a court must have before it can hear a case.

Bill of Rights p. 29　The first ten amendments to the Constitution that preserve the rights of the people from unlawful acts of government officials, freedom of speech and religion, and so on.

Enumerated powers p. 29　Those powers that are explicitly granted to the three branches of government in the Constitution.

Commerce Clause p. 29　The constitutional clause giving Congress the power to regulate commerce.

Necessary and Proper Clause p. 29　The constitutional clause giving Congress the general implied authority to make laws necessary to carry out its other enumerated powers.

Separation of powers p. 30　The system of checks and balances created by the Constitution whereby the three branches have unique powers that allow them to resolve conflicts among themselves, thus ensuring no one branch exceeds its constitutional authority.

Rational basis p. 31　The lowest level of scrutiny applied by courts deciding constitutional issues through judicial review, upheld if the government shows that the law has a reasonable connection to achieving a legitimate and constitutional objective.

Intermediate-level scrutiny p. 31　The middle level of scrutiny applied by courts deciding constitutional issues through judicial review, upheld if the government shows that a regulation involves an important governmental objective that is furthered by substantially related means.

Strict scrutiny p. 31　The most stringent standard of scrutiny applied by Courts deciding constitutional issues through judicial review when the government action is related to a fundamental right or is based on a suspect classification, upheld if the government shows a compelling need that justifies the law being enacted and no less restrictive alternatives existed.

Supremacy Clause p. 32　The constitutional clause that makes clear that federal law is always supreme to any state law that is in direct conflict.

Preemption p. 32　The power to override state law that is granted by the Supremacy Clause.

Due process p. 38　Principle that the government must respect all of the legal rights that are owed to a person according to the law.

Fourth Amendment p. 42　Protects individual citizens' rights to be secure in their "persons, houses, papers and effects."

Fifth Amendment p. 42　Provides that no person "shall be compelled in any criminal case to be a witness against himself," guaranteeing individuals the right to remain silent both during the investigation and during any subsequent judicial proceedings.

Due Process Clause p. 43　The constitutional clause protecting individuals from being deprived of "life, liberty, or property" without due process of law.

THEORY TO PRACTICE

Quick Courier Services ("Quick") is a company with 25 employees located in the hypothetical state of Longville. Quick provides services to businesses that require documents or packages to be delivered on a same day basis. While most of these deliveries are made by car or van, Quick also employs several bicycle couriers to accommodate customers in large cities.

1. After a rash of bicycle courier accidents in several cities, Congress passed a federal statute that banned bicycle couriers. The statute is intended to protect the safety of the public at large. Congress justifies the statute on the basis that couriers are inherently involved in commercial activity. What enumerated power is Congress using as the basis of its authority to pass this statute? If Quick challenges the constitutionality of the statute, what would be their probable legal theory?

2. Suppose that, instead of an outright ban on bicycle couriers, Congress passed a law that banned any companies that used bicycle couriers from receiving any money from federal grant programs or federal contracts. How does that impact your analysis relating to congressional authority?

3. Assume that Quick also does business in the adjoining state of Holmestown. Holmestown's state legislature passes a state law that imposes a registration requirement on all couriers that are headquartered outside of Holmestown's state borders. The registration requirement also includes an annual fee that is not required of in-state couriers. Has Holmestown infringed on Congress's constitutional authority? What is the standard used by courts to analyze such a law?

4. Assume further that the Occupational Safety and Health Administration (OSHA), a government agency, issues a fine to Quick without giving its officers adequate notice to provide evidence that no violation occurred. How would the Due Process Clause protect Quick from OSHA's actions?

5. If OSHA wishes to search Quick's premises for evidence of an administrative violation, what amendment(s) would govern the process? If the purpose of the search was investigation of a criminal conspiracy involving Quick's officers, how would that change your answer?

MANAGER'S CHALLENGE

Assume you are a manager at Quick (in the Theory to Practice example above) and you receive an e-mail from your senior manager:

> Quick is considering paying for full-page advertisements in local newspapers that encouraged people to vote for certain Holmestown politicians based on their opposition to the out-of-state courier registration law [in the Theory to Practice example above]. However, I recently read about the Holmestown legislature considering a law that bans such advertisements if funded by a corporation.

> Before I contact our counsel, I would like a two-to three-page background memorandum addressing the question: May Holmestown ban the advertisement on the basis that it is funded by corporate money and not by individual voters or political committees? Why or why not? Is there any important case law to support your answer to this question?

A sample answer may be found on this textbook's Web site at www.mhhe.com/melvin.

CASE SUMMARY 2.1 :: Buckman Company v. Plaintiff's Legal Committee, 531 U.S. 341 (2001)

PREEMPTION

Buckman Co. is a consulting company that assists companies in getting their products approved for medical use by the Food and Drug Administration (FDA). Tara, a resident of Pennsylvania, filed a lawsuit based on a Pennsylvania antifraud law against Buckman in state court for injuries she received from the use of AcroMed brand screws during her spinal surgery. The lawsuit contended that Buckman made fraudulent representations to the FDA in their attempt to have the AcroMed screws approved for use in spinal surgeries.

Buckman sought to have the suit dismissed on the grounds that the Food, Drug, and Cosmetics Act and Medical Devices Act regulate the advertising and promotion of medical devices and thus preempted Tara's lawsuit.

CASE QUESTIONS

1. Can Tara file a lawsuit against Buckman that uses state law as its cause of action?
2. Why or why not?

CASE SUMMARY 2.2 :: State v. DeAngelo, 930 A.2d 1236 (N.J. Super. 2007)

COMMERCIAL SPEECH

During a labor dispute, a local labor union engaged in a protest of what they claimed were unfair labor practices of a local business. As part of this protest, the union displayed a 10-foot inflatable rat-shaped balloon on a public sidewalk in front of a business involved in the dispute. A municipal ordinance banned all public displays of "balloon or inflated" signs except in cases of a

grand opening. The union challenged the ordinance as an unconstitutional ban on commercial speech.

CASE QUESTIONS

1. Is the ordinance constitutionally sound?
2. What level of scrutiny will a court apply to the ordinance?

COMMERCE CLAUSE

In 2002, Congress passed the Body Armor Act that made it illegal for anyone who has been convicted of a violent felony to possess body armor. Alderman was convicted of violating the statute and challenged the law's constitutionality during appeal. Alderman contended that Congress had exceeded its authority because the law was not sufficiently related to interstate commerce.

CASE QUESTIONS

1. Is the law constitutionally sound?
2. If Alderman purchased the body armor in the same state as it was manufactured, how does that affect "interstate" commerce?

NECESSARY AND PROPER CLAUSE

In an effort to increase Internet access for the public, Congress passed a law creating the E-Rate program (providing for discounted Internet rates), and the Library Services and Technology Act (LSTA), which provides financial grants to libraries. At the same time, Congress also passed the Children's Internet Protection Act (CIPA). CIPA conditions the receipt of federal funds under the E-rate program and LSTA on libraries purchasing and installing expensive software that blocks obscene or pornographic material. A group of libraries and citizens filed suit claiming connecting LSTA grant funds to CIPA compliance is unconstitutional.

CASE QUESTIONS

1. Is the plan constitutional?
2. Is the First Amendment at issue? Explain your answer.

 Self-Check **ANSWERS**

Source of Constitutional Authority

1. Article 1 § 8: Congress's power to regulate bankruptcy laws.

2. Article 1 § 8: Tax and spend powers

3. Article 1 § 8: Careful! This answer appears to be Congress's power to grant and regulate patents. But the fact that Congress is passing a criminal law would be outside the scope of the narrow patent power. Rather, this law is best thought of as Congress's authority to legislate under the Necessary and Proper Clause because the law was directly ancillary to the enumerated power (patents).

4. Article 1 § 8: Congress's power to regulate interstate commerce.

5. Tax and spending power.

3
CHAPTER

The American Judicial System, Jurisdiction, and Venue

learning outcomes checklist

After studying this chapter, students who have mastered the material will be able to:

3-1 Explain the role of the judiciary in the context of the American legal system.

3-2 Distinguish between the role of federal courts and state courts.

3-3 Identify the responsibilities of trial courts versus appellate courts.

3-4 Articulate how the law develops via adjudication of cases.

3-5 Differentiate between subject matter jurisdiction and personal jurisdiction.

3-6 List the types of controversies over which federal courts have subject matter jurisdiction.

3-7 Explain the role of long-arm statutes in determining personal jurisdiction.

3-8 Apply the minimum contacts test in both a traditional and cyber setting and describe the importance of the *Zippo* sliding scale.

3-9 Articulate the special problems posed by different international jurisdiction standards.

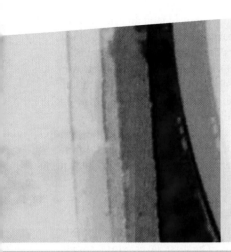

Courts play a crucial role in the interpretation and development of legal doctrines. An important premise of the American legal system is the notion that a certain judicial process guides the operation of courts in determination of the legal disputes between two or more parties. A fundamental knowledge of the structure and operation of the court system is important because business managers and owners encounter lawsuits in the normal course of business operations. In this chapter students will learn:

■ The role and structure of the American judicial system.

■ The function and authority of state and federal courts.

■ How the law develops through court decisions.

Not all courts have the authority to hear all cases. In order for a court to render a binding decision, a court must have authority over both the dispute and the parties in each case that it hears. Specifically, students will learn:

■ The circumstances when a court has the authority to hear a certain case.

■ The appropriate location to resolve disputes.

ROLE AND STRUCTURE OF THE JUDICIARY

The American legal system is primarily structured around a set of federal and state **courts** that are collectively known as the **judiciary.** The judiciary has two primary roles. First, courts *adjudicate* disputes. This means that many courts are responsible for interpreting and applying the rules of law and principles of equity to settle legal cases and controversies. Second, certain courts are charged with the responsibility of *judicial review.*[1] In this role, these courts review decisions of lower courts and the actions of other branches of the government to be sure that these decisions and actions are consistent with existing law and that they comply with constitutional requirements.

Which courts are authorized to hear which cases is determined by a set of legal principles collectively called **jurisdiction** and **venue.** These principles are discussed later in this chapter.

LO3-2, 3-3 ### State versus Federal Courts

The U.S. system of government recognizes two distinct levels of government and, therefore, there are two levels of courts aligned to that structure. The first level, **state courts,** adjudicates matters dealing primarily with cases arising from state statutory, common, or state constitutional law. In some cases, state courts also apply federal constitutional provisions. **Federal courts** are courts concerned primarily with national laws, federal constitutional issues, and other cases that are outside the purview of state courts. It is important to note that not all courts have the *authority* to hear all cases. In order for a court, state or federal, to hear a case, the court must have legal authority, called *jurisdiction,* over the dispute and parties in the case. The concept of jurisdiction is discussed in detail later in this chapter.

The American judiciary is a system of state and federal courts working in tandem.

---

[1]Recall from Chapter 2, "Business and the Constitution," that the U.S. Supreme Court, in the landmark case of *Marbury v. Madison,* 2 L.Ed. 60 (1803), established the concept of judicial review, now a stalwart power of the judiciary.

State Courts   The majority of court cases filed in the United States are filed in state courts. All states have two types of courts: **state trial courts** and **state appellate courts.**

State Trial Courts   When one party alleges a violation of some legal right or standard, the aggrieved party, called the **plaintiff,** may bring a lawsuit against the alleged violator, called the **defendant,** in a trial court. Trial courts are where cases are originally brought and heard. They are structured to adjudicate matters through an established procedure in which both parties present evidence, question witnesses, and articulate legal arguments about the case.[2]

The names of the courts vary widely from state to state. However, all state trial courts have either *general authority* to hear a case or *limited authority* to hear a particular type of case. Courts of general authority are organized into geographic districts (often divided by county or a set of contiguous counties) and hear many types of cases, including breach of contract, employment discrimination, personal injury, criminal cases, property disputes, and so forth. Courts of limited authority are often confined to a particular type of dispute such as family law matters (e.g., divorce or adoption cases) or probate courts (dealing with issues related to wills and trusts). Some states, notably Delaware, have courts devoted solely to issues relating to commercial law matters. Delaware calls these forums *chancery courts.* It is important to remember that state trial court decisions are binding *only* on the parties involved in the dispute. Trial court decisions do not set precedent for future disputes or parties. Only appellate level courts set precedent.

For minor matters and cases with a dollar value that is relatively low, typically less than $10,000 depending on the state, states provide local courts known alternatively as municipal courts, small-claims courts, justice-of-the-peace courts, or district justices. Such courts provide local access to a court for the purpose of resolving relatively simple disputes on an expedited basis. These courts are sometimes referred to as *inferior* trial courts because states provide an automatic appeal for the losing party, usually to the state trial court, for decisions from local judges.

Trial courts are often divided into those that hear civil matters where one party seeks redress for a wrong committed by another party (such as a lawsuit for breach of contract), and those that hear criminal matters where a party accused of a crime (such as theft) is put on trial.

State Appellate Courts   After a trial court has rendered a decision, the losing party must decide whether to file an appeal in the appellate court. These courts are primarily concerned with reviewing the decisions of trial courts. Most states also have an intermediate appellate court, which is where the first appeal is filed. In some states, appeals to any appellate-level courts are *discretionary.* That is, the party requesting the appeal (known as the *petitioning* party or the *appellant*) files a document with the court petitioning for an appeal. Based on a variety of factors, the appellate court then decides whether to allow the appeal to be heard by the court. In other states, the losing party has an automatic right of appeal to the intermediate-level court, but only a discretionary appeal to the highest court. If the appellate court denies an appeal, the trial court ruling is *binding* on the parties in that case.[3] If the court grants an appeal, the appellate judges engage in the process of determining whether the trial was conducted in accordance with the legal rules and doctrines of that state. Appellate courts assess the lower court's decision by (1) reviewing lower court transcripts and rulings, (2) reading documents written by attorneys for each side articulating legal reasons why their side should prevail (known as *briefs*), and

---

[2]Note that the role of trial courts is examined in the context of a civil lawsuit, known as *litigation,* in the next chapter.

[3]In extraordinary cases, a petitioning party sometimes has the right to appeal to a higher court if the intermediate appellate court denies the appeal.

(3) sometimes allowing the attorneys to engage in *oral argument,* which requires the attorneys for the parties to appear in front of the appellate panel of judges to participate in an oral question and answer session on the legal issues in the case. The court focuses on such issues as the rulings of the trial judges, the admission of evidence, jury selection, and other factors that may have been a factor in the original trial's outcome. Note that appellate courts, except in some rare cases, do *not* consider new evidence in their review. Using these methods, appellate courts determine whether an error was made at the trial level. In cases where the error is substantial enough, a court may reverse the decision of the trial court and *remand* the case back to the trial court.

Legal Speak ›))
Remand To send a case back to the lower court from which it came for further action consistent with the opinion and instructions of the higher court.

The major distinction between state trial courts and state appellate courts is that appellate courts decisions set *precedent* that is binding on all lower courts.[4] Because one of the primary purposes of the law is to provide some degree of reliability and uniformity in adjudicating cases, trial courts are required to follow the rulings of appellate courts. In states where there is an intermediate level of appellate court, the highest court is often (although not always) called the *state supreme court.* A state supreme court's decision is final and binding on *all* courts situated in that state (including federal courts located in that state) so long as the decision does *not* involve a federal constitutional issue.

States vary as to how state trial court judges are selected. Some states elect all trial and appellate judges as part of their general elections, while others use an appointment process whereby the governor appoints a judge, but is subject to review and rejection by the state legislature (typically the state senate). Some states use a hybrid method where local judges are elected and appellate court judges go through an appointment process.

KEY POINT
Only appellate courts are considered courts of authority that have the right to set precedent.

Federal Courts   The federal government also operates a system of courts. The principal trial courts are the **U.S. district courts.** Federal appellate courts are called the **U.S. courts of appeal.** Because these courts are divided into circuits, federal appellate courts are frequently referred to as the *circuit courts of appeal.* Finally, the **U.S. Supreme Court,** the ultimate arbiter of federal law, reviews not only decisions of the federal courts but also reviews decisions of state courts that involve some issue of federal law such as applying a provision of the U.S. Constitution.

U.S. District Courts   District courts serve the same primary trial function as state trial courts, but for issues involving federal matters such as federal statutes, regulations, or constitutional issues. There is at least one federal district court in every state and one for the District of Columbia. U.S. district courts also may decide certain matters involving *state law* when the parties are from different states and meet other jurisdictional requirements. These federal trial courts hear a variety of matters and render decisions that are binding only on the parties involved in the dispute. Some federal courts are specialized for certain areas of law. They include the Bankruptcy Court, the Tax Court, and the Court of International Trade.

KEY POINT
When the parties are from different states and meet other jurisdictional requirements, federal courts may decide state law matters (e.g., a contract dispute).

Circuit Courts of Appeal   The thirteen U.S. courts of appeal, each of which reviews the decisions of federal district courts in the state or several states within its circuit, are the intermediate appellate courts in the federal system. Two exceptions are the Court of Appeals for the District of Columbia, which decides cases originating in Washington, D.C., and the Federal Circuit Court of Appeals, which decides a variety of exclusively federal issues such as patent, copyright, and trademark cases or cases where the

---

[4]Recall from Chapter 1, "Legal Foundations" that the concept of *precedent* springs from the doctrine of *stare decisis.*

FIGURE 3.1 Map of the U.S. Circuits

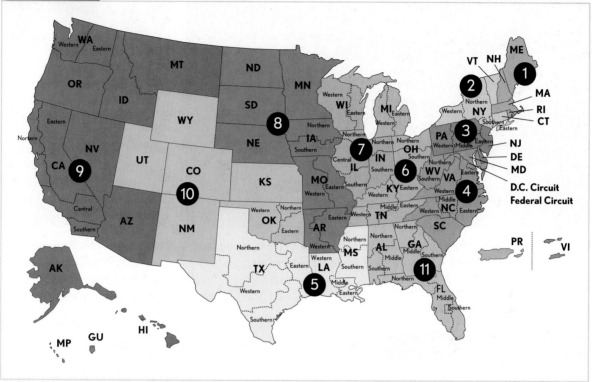

Source: www.uscourts.gov/courtlinks

United States is named as a defendant. The Federal Circuit is said to have national jurisdiction since its authority is not confined to one particular circuit. Just as with state appellate courts, federal circuit courts of appeal set precedent and their decisions are binding on all the states in that circuit. Appeals to the federal circuit courts of appeal are discretionary.

The circuits are divided geographically. Figure 3.1 illustrates how circuits are broken down.

U.S. Supreme Court   The ultimate arbiters of federal law are the nine justices of the U.S. Supreme Court (the "Court"). Although the Court has both original[5] and appellate jurisdiction, the primary role of the Court is to finalize a legal decision on any given case. In addition to the Court's authority to decide any appeal from the U.S. circuit courts of appeal, the Court may also exercise its appellate authority over state courts when a federal issue is involved. Finally, the Court has the final authority on matters of interpretation of all federal law and the U.S. Constitution.

While the Court is known to most of the citizenry as the court that decides highly publicized and politically charged constitutional issues, more often cases are decided by the Court when conflicting opinions among the appellate courts are issued (referred to by the Court as a *conflict among the circuits*) and relatively complex commercial matters such as cases involving patents, antitrust regulation, or securities laws. Of course, the Court's review is discretionary and, in fact, the odds of getting a case to the Court are very low. Typically, the Court grants only about 1 percent of the requests it receives to hear a case. An aggrieved party may petition the Court for an appeal using a petition for

---

[5]The Court's original jurisdiction is limited to cases involving ambassadors and selected other public officials and those cases where the disputing parties are two states.

The Supreme Court of the United States, pictured here on the opening day of their October 2009 term, is the ultimate arbiter of federal law.

Former U.S. Solicitor General Elena Kagan was chosen by President Obama in 2010 to replace retiring justice John Paul Stevens.

Legal Speak »))
Writ of certiorari
A discretionary order issued by the Supreme Court (and federal appellate courts) granting a request to argue an appeal. A party filing for an appeal must file a petition for a writ of certiorari.

TABLE 3.1 Supreme Court Case Acceptance Rate

Term	Number of Petitions (requests) for a Writ of Certiorari	Number Granted	Acceptance Rate
2006	8,857	78	Approx. .9%
2007	8,241	75	Approx. .9%
2008	7738	87	Approx. 1.1%

writ of certiorari that explains the basis for the appeal. Upon review, if four of the nine justices vote to hear the case, the parties in the case are then permitted to pursue the appeal. Table 3.1 sets out the rate of requests versus cases that are actually heard in recent years.

webcheck **www.oyez.org/oyez/frontpage**
Go to this Web site for a multimedia reference to the Supreme Court and a virtual tour of the Court's building, or connect via the link on this textbook's Web site at www.mhhe.com/melvin.

All federal judges are selected via the appointment process. The president nominates candidates for federal trial and appellate courts. The nominees are subject to the review of the Senate. The Senate may either confirm or reject the judicial nominee. If the nominee is rejected, the president nominates candidates until one is confirmed. Once confirmed, the nominee is sworn in as a federal judge and may only be removed from office by impeachment.

LO3-4 HOW THE LAW DEVELOPS

It can be a somewhat daunting task to figure out how a case works its way through the court system and the role that precedent plays in how the law develops. Fundamentally, state trial courts rule on certain points of state law and render a decision. That decision is

FIGURE 3.2 Understanding State and Federal Courts

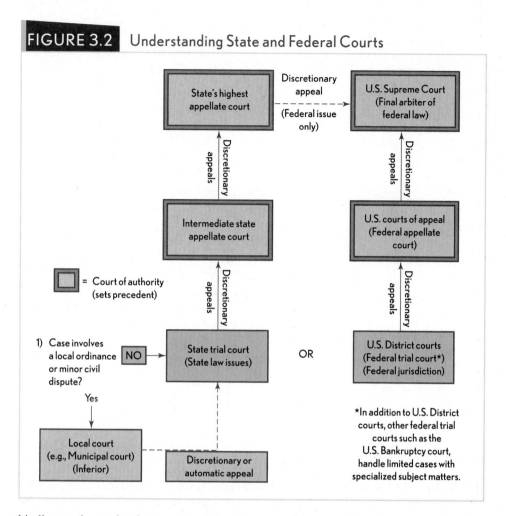

binding on the parties, but on no one else. If an appellate court affirms or reverses the findings of the trial court, then from that point on, the appellate court's ruling on that point of law is applied to all future cases. Remember also that federal trial courts within a certain state may rule on *state law* issues in some cases where the federal court has jurisdiction. Figure 3.2 sets out the structure of state and federal courts.

Consider the following case to illustrate how law develops. Assume that in the hypothetical U.S. state of Longville, no precedent exists for the following issue of state law: *Does an e-mail constitute a signed writing sufficient to satisfy the Longville state statute that requires certain contracts to be in writing?*

Case Number	Court	Date	Ruling on Issue	Effect on Parties and Future Cases
Case #1	Longville state trial court	Jan. 10	*E-mail is sufficient*	Binding only on parties in Case #1
Case #2	Federal district court (federal trial) located in Longville	Jan. 15	*E-mail not sufficient*	Binding only on the parties in this case (Case #2). No effect on the parties in Case #1.

(continued)

Case Number	Court	Date	Ruling on Issue	Effect on Parties and Future Cases
Case #3	Longville state appellate court	Feb. 1	*E-mail is sufficient*	Binding on all Longville state and federal trial courts in Longville. Case #1 decision is upheld and its ruling is now applied in Longville state trial courts / federal trial courts in Longville from Feb. 1 onward.
Case #4	Federal court of appeals that includes Longville in its circuit	March 1	Must follow Longville state appellate court's precedent set in Case #3 because it's an issue of state law: *E-mail is sufficient.*	If there are no federal issues, the court applies Longville state law as interpreted by Longville state appellate courts in Case #3. The court's decision is only binding on Longville, not on other states in the circuit.
Case #5	State supreme court of Longville	June 1	Denies appeal from losing party in Longville appellate court decision (Case #3).	Law as decided by the appellate court in Case #3 is settled and binding on all Longville courts. Precedent is undisturbed.

CONCEPT SUMMARY   Role and Structure of the Judiciary

- The roles of the judiciary are to (1) apply rules of law and principles of equity equally to settle cases and controversies, and (2) review the decisions of trial courts and the actions of the other branches of government to ensure they comply with existing legal and constitutional requirements.
- State courts generally handle matters dealing with state statutory, common, and state constitutional law. The majority of cases filed in the United States are filed in state courts.
- There are two types of state courts: trial courts, where parties present their cases and evidence; and appellate courts, which review the decisions of lower courts.
- Only appellate courts set precedent. The decisions of trial courts are binding only on the parties in that particular matter.
- Federal trial courts are called U.S. district courts. Federal appellate courts are called the U.S. courts of appeal and often referred to as the circuit courts of appeal.
- Courts with general authority hear a wide variety of cases. Courts with limited authority hear specific types of cases such as family law matters.
- The ultimate arbiter of federal law is the U.S. Supreme Court. It has both original and appellate jurisdiction.

LO3-5 JURISDICTION AND VENUE

As noted earlier, it is important to understand that not all courts have the authority to hear all cases. The law sets out certain rules that govern which courts may decide certain cases. *Jurisdiction* is a court's authority to decide a particular case based on (1) who the parties are, and (2) the subject matter of the dispute. *Venue* is a determination of the most appropriate court *location* for litigating a dispute.

Jurisdiction and Business Strategy

The increasing integration of advanced technology in product and service delivery has made jurisdiction and venue an important part of business planning for business managers and owners. As with all legal decisions that business owners and managers make, jurisdiction must be considered in a cost-benefit context. For example, consider a dispute between two hypothetical companies, Ultimate Widget Corporation (UWC) and Knock Off Stores Inc. (Knock Off). Suppose UWC, a New York company, is considering suing Knock Off, a California company, over a trademark dispute. UWC management should consider the costs involved in pursuing the suit in a business context. In considering their strategy, UWC's management must consider (1) the total amount of the possible recovery from Knock Off; (2) the actual benefits UWC will reap from the prevention of Knock Off's use of the trademark; and (3) any alternate dispute resolution methods available. If Knock Off is a small company and not likely to dilute the trademark in any of UWC's markets, it may not be worth the costs of litigation to sue UWC in their home state. Pursuing the infringement action would involve UWC's expense of traveling to California, hiring local counsel in California, and the lost hours of managers and other witnesses who would be required to travel to testify and be deposed for the case. However, if a New York court could possibly have jurisdiction over the dispute, that fact will change the dynamics of the cost-benefit analysis because the expenses of the suit would be markedly lower.

Legal Speak »)
Jurisdiction An English word derived through the combination of two Latin words combining *juris* (of law or of right) and *dictio* (speaking). Thus, the combination of the words refers to a specific court's right to *speak the law* or render a decision in a legal dispute.

> **KEY POINT**
> The cost-benefit analysis involving jurisdictional restrictions may affect the managerial decision-making process when a company or individual contemplates filing a lawsuit. Litigating disputes in out-of-state courts increases the costs of litigation.

Overview of Jurisdiction

LO3-6

The origins of federal jurisdiction law are found in the U.S. Constitution, specifically, the Due Process Clause of the Fifth and the Fourteenth Amendments. In essence, the Constitution prohibits the deprivation of a property interest (usually money damages) without a legal process being applied. While origins of jurisdiction lie in the Constitution, appellate courts and legislatures have shaped the framework and rules used by modern courts to analyze jurisdiction questions.

Two-Part Analysis Jurisdiction requires a two-part analysis: a court must have both (1) **subject matter jurisdiction** and (2) **personal jurisdiction** (also known as *in personam jurisdiction*). Subject matter jurisdiction is the court's authority over the *dispute* between the parties, while personal jurisdiction is the court's authority over the *parties* involved in the dispute. For example, suppose that Baker is employed by Auto Parts Company (APC) to drive a delivery vehicle. One morning, Baker is on a delivery and due to his lack of care (called *negligence*),[6] hits Cain, a pedestrian who is crossing the street in a designated public crosswalk located directly in front of the hotel where she was staying. Cain is severely injured and she considers filing a lawsuit against Baker to reimburse her for losses she suffered as a result of the incident. However, Cain discovers that Baker is without assets and, in the state where the incident took place, the law provides that APC is responsible for Baker's actions. Consequently, Cain decides to pursue a lawsuit against APC.

Initially, Cain must decide in *which* court to file the lawsuit. She probably will have some choice, but it will be a limited one. This is true because the court selected must have jurisdiction over the case of this type of dispute (a negligence case) and over the

---

[6]The legal term for such a lack of care is *negligence*. Negligence is discussed extensively in Chapter 9, "Torts and Product Liability."

defendant (APC). Cain will likely bring this suit in a *state* trial court because the jurisdiction of federal courts is limited in this type of case. Be sure to remember the basic facts of the APC–Cain hypothetical as it will be used throughout this section to illustrate various aspects of jurisdiction and venue.

Subject Matter Jurisdiction: Authority over the Dispute

Recall from the discussion at the beginning of this chapter that state and federal statutes define which courts have *general* jurisdiction and which have *limited* jurisdiction. State statutes give state trial courts subject matter jurisdiction on virtually all matters involving a state statute, state common law, or a state constitutional issue.

Federal district courts are limited by the Constitution and by federal statutes as to what types of cases they have authority to hear. In order for a federal court to have subject matter jurisdiction in a case, the issue must generally involve a **federal question** (e.g., some issue arising from the U.S Constitution, a federal statute or regulation, or federal common law). Federal courts also have *exclusive* jurisdiction over all cases where the United States is a **party** in the litigation. For example, a business that sues the Internal Revenue Service for a federal tax refund must pursue the matter in federal court since it involves the United States as a party named in the lawsuit.

Even if there is no federal question and the United States is not a party to the litigation, federal courts may have subject matter jurisdiction over cases involving parties from *two different states* (or if one party is from outside the United States), known as **diversity of citizenship.** An additional requirement in diversity of citizenship cases (only) is that the amount in controversy must be more than $75,000. For example, if a dispute arises in which a business in New York sues a business in California for breach of contract for $80,000, the parties are said to be *diverse* and a federal court sitting in New York or California would have subject matter jurisdiction in the case. Note that the amount in controversy requirement applies *only* when a court has jurisdiction via the diversity of citizenship requirement. In a diversity case, a federal court will be applying *state law* because the dispute is likely to involve issues governed by state statutes or common law.

 Self-Check

Does a federal district court located in New Jersey have *subject matter* jurisdiction?

1. A New Jersey businessperson sues her in-state business partner for breach of contract that resulted in $40,000 in losses.

2. The U.S. Environmental Protection Agency sues a New Jersey corporation for cleanup costs under a federal statute that regulates local waste disposal.

3. A Pennsylvania resident sues a New Jersey corporation for an injury caused by the corporation's product resulting in $90,000 of unpaid medical bills.

4. A New Jersey corporation is sued by a New Jersey resident under the federal employment discrimination statutes.

5. A New Jersey resident sues the U.S. government in an appeal from the ruling of the U.S. Copyright Office.

Answers to this Self-Check are provided at the end of the chapter.

Recall the Cain–APC hypothetical from the beginning of this section. Assume that Cain was a resident of Massachusetts who was visiting Texas, where APC is headquartered, when the incident occurred. Cain would likely prefer to file the lawsuit in her home state so that she doesn't have to spend time and resources in traveling to Texas several times for pretrial and trial tasks. Assuming that Cain's injuries were sufficiently severe to warrant damages exceeding $75,000, Cain may consider filing suit in the federal district court in Massachusetts. That court has subject matter jurisdiction because the parties are diverse and the amount in controversy has been satisfied. However, that is only the first part of the jurisdiction analysis. Once it has been determined that the federal district court in Massachusetts has subject matter jurisdiction, Cain must also clear another substantial jurisdictional requirement: *personal jurisdiction.*

Personal Jurisdiction

Personal jurisdiction is a court's authority over the *parties* in a legal dispute. In this context, a party may be either an individual or a business entity such as a corporation. Since 1877, in the landmark case *Pennoyer v. Neff,*[7] the U.S. Supreme Court has articulated a framework for the exercise of personal jurisdiction by lower courts with the objective of providing *fairness* to the parties and complying with federal constitutional requirements related to due process. Of course, courts have modified this framework as necessary based on the realities of industrial and technological advances in society. This framework is used to determine jurisdiction over the defendant by both that state's courts *and* federal district courts within that state. Typically, the focus of a jurisdiction analysis focuses on the *conditions* of the controversy and *actions* of the defendant.

Out-of-State Defendants   Courts use a two-prong test to determine whether it has personal jurisdiction over a party who does not live in the same state in which the court is located. First, the court's jurisdiction must be authorized by a **state long-arm statute** that grants the court specific authorization over the defendant due to the defendant's conduct or other circumstances. As its name implies, these statutes are intended to allow a court to "reach" into another state and exercise jurisdiction over a nonresident defendant. Typically, these long-arm statutes[8] provide for jurisdiction if an out-of-state defendant (1) transacts business within that state's borders, or (2) commits a negligent act in that state that results in a loss to another party, or (3) owns property in the state.[9] The second prong requires a court to ensure that exercising jurisdiction over an out-of-state defendant meets the constitutional requirements of *fairness* and *due process.* This means that courts must consider the plight of the defendant who has been forced to defend a lawsuit in another state by taking into account the burden on the defendant. Courts examine two questions in this analysis: First, does the defendant have some level of **minimum contacts**[10] with the state such as regularly shipping products to that state? If a defendant has continuous and systematic contact with a particular state, this will be sufficient to satisfy the minimum contacts requirement. Second, has the defendant *purposefully availed*[11] themselves by some affirmative act such as advertising directed to that specific state?

In Case 3.1, an appellate court applies the purposeful availment standard in determining the contacts of an out-of-state vendor.

Injurious Effects   Another important consideration that courts explore in a personal jurisdiction analysis is whether it was reasonably *foreseeable* that the defendant's actions would have an *injurious effect* on a resident of that state. This question is usually in the

LO3-7, 3-8

---

[7]95 U.S. 714 (1877).

[8]Many states base their long-arm statute on a model act called the Uniform Interstate and International Procedure Act.

[9]A court's authority over parties that own property within state borders is known in common law terms as *in rem jurisdiction.*

[10]*International Shoe v. Washington,* 326 U.S. 310 (1945).

[11]*Asahi Metal Industrial Company v. Superior Court of California,* 480 U.S. 102 (1987).

FACT SUMMARY The legal representative of the estate of Weingeroff ("Weingeroff"), a passenger on a turboprop plane who was killed when the plane crashed near State College, Pennsylvania, brought a negligence and product liability lawsuit against Pilatus Air ("Pilatus"), the manufacturer of the plane. The plane crashed when approaching a small airport in Pennsylvania on a planned stop en route between Florida and Rhode Island. Weingeroff sued Pilatus in a federal district court situated in the Eastern District of Pennsylvania. Pilatus, a Swiss company, asked the court to dismiss the case for lack of personal jurisdiction. Pilatus claimed that they had no offices, no agents, no commercial transactions with Pennsylvania residents, and no physical presence in the state that constitutes purposeful availment. Weingeroff pointed to evidence that (1) Pilatus had conducted a nationwide marketing campaign in the United States to sell its planes, which included Pennsylvania; and (2) Pilatus has purchased over $1 million in products, services, and equipment from Pennsylvania suppliers. The trial court ruled in favor of Pilatus and dismissed the suit for lack of personal jurisdiction.

SYNOPSIS OF DECISION AND OPINION The Court of Appeals for the Third Circuit upheld the trial court's decision in favor of Pilatus. The court pointed out that Pilatus had not sold any aircraft to purchasers in Pennsylvania or shipped anything directly to persons or entities in Pennsylvania. Moreover, Pilatus has not advertised or marketed its products in Pennsylvania and did not design the plane for the Pennsylvania market specifically, although it did target the U.S. market generally by designing the plane to ensure its compliance with FAA requirements. Although Pilatus purchased $1,030,139 in products, equipment, or services from suppliers in Pennsylvania, this amount represented less than 1 percent of Pilatus's total annual purchases for an approximately five-year period.

WORDS OF THE COURT: Purposeful Availment "We acknowledge that there is a certain reasonableness to an argument that a manufacturer should be subject to suit in a jurisdiction in which its plane crashes if the suit charges that a manufacturing defect caused the crash. Yet it is clear that the critical finding that the defendant purposefully availed itself of the privilege of conducting activities within the forum [state] requires contacts that amount to a deliberate reaching into the forum state to target its citizens. Pilatus's efforts to exploit a national market necessarily included Pennsylvania as a target, but those efforts simply do not constitute the type of deliberate contacts within Pennsylvania that could amount to purposeful availment of the privilege of conducting activities in that state. Rather, any connection of Pilatus to Pennsylvania merely was a derivative benefit of its successful attempt to exploit the United States as a national market."

Case Questions

1. What facts could you change that may sway the court's judgment in analyzing personal jurisdiction over Pilatus in this case?

2. Does this decision mean that Weingeroff is without any legal recourse against Pilatus unless the case is brought in Swiss courts?

3. Suppose the plane has crashed and injured a pedestrian on the ground. Given the court's reasoning, would the victim be able to bring a case against Pilatus in a Pennsylvania (state or federal) court?

---

context of a dispute involving some *intentional* act by the defendant that results in an injury to an individual or business entity resident of that state. For example, in *Calder v. Jones,*[12] the Supreme Court ruled that a California court had jurisdiction over a Florida corporation in a defamation case filed by an actress against a tabloid newspaper. Despite the fact that the defendant had no physical presence or other traditional minimum contacts with California, the Court reasoned that jurisdiction was proper because the defendant knew, or should have known, that the defamation would have an injurious effect on the actress in California where she lived and worked. This became known as the *effects test* and is now an important part of a personal jurisdiction analysis. Note, however, that courts

---

[12]465 U.S. 783 (1984).

apply the effects test narrowly and, thus far, only to cases involving intentional injurious acts (such as defamation).[13]

Legal Speak »))
Defamation
Discussed in detail in Chapter 9, "Torts and Product Liability," defamation is an intentional act of making an untrue public statement about a party that caused some loss to be suffered by the defamed party.

Physical Presence   The physical presence of an out-of-state party in a particular state is generally an automatic basis for jurisdiction over the defendant by both that state's courts *and* federal trial courts within that state. In a business context, physical presence may include having an office, agent, or personnel (such as a sales team located within the court's jurisdiction). Many states have also passed specific statutes that give state courts personal jurisdiction over out-of-state residents that operate motor vehicles within the state for the narrow purposes of allowing a victim of an auto accident to pursue a claim against an out-of-state driver.

Voluntary   A court has personal jurisdiction if the parties agree to litigate in a specific court. Voluntary personal jurisdiction applies when a nonresident party agrees to the jurisdiction of a particular court in a certain state. This voluntary jurisdiction is often done through a *forum selection clause* written in a contract between the parties. A forum selection clause is a contractual agreement that obligates the parties to litigate any dispute arising out of the contract in a particular court named in the clause. Essentially, the parties are agreeing to a forum *ahead of time* so that if any litigation involving that particular contract is instituted, both parties are obligated to litigate the dispute in a predetermined court.

In *Shute v. Carnival Cruise Lines*,[14] a federal court in Washington dismissed a personal injury claim by the passenger of a Carnival Cruise Lines ship who fell during a guided tour of the ship. The court ruled that the passenger ticket was a contract between the passenger and Carnival Cruise Lines and that the ticket contained a forum selection clause whereby the parties agreed to litigate any disputes in Miami, Florida (where Carnival's headquarters was located).

Figure 3.3 is a sample of a typical forum selection clause in a contract.

FIGURE 3.3   Sample Forum Selection Clause

"In the event of any dispute that arises from the performance, breach or any obligations under this contract, the parties agree and expressly consent to litigate any such disputes in the State Court of Common Pleas, located in Philadelphia, Pennsylvania, as the exclusive venue and both parties hereby voluntarily submit to their exclusive jurisdiction over the matter."

Recall our Cain versus APC hypothetical. Suppose that Cain files her lawsuit in a federal district court in Massachusetts. In addition to establishing subject matter jurisdiction, she must also meet the court's standards for personal jurisdiction over APC. In this case, given the fact that the incident took place in Texas, it may be difficult for Cain to demonstrate APC's connection with Massachusetts unless APC owns property, maintains an office, regularly sent personnel to Massachusetts, or has some other regular and systematic connection with the state. In its jurisdiction analysis of the Cain versus APC matter, a federal court would first look to the Massachusetts long-arm statute and then to the constitutional requirements of due process and fairness, including APC's level of minimum contacts and purposeful availment in Massachusetts.

---

[13]The Court also applied the test used to justify jurisdiction in *Keeton v. Hustler Magazine,* 465 U.S. 770 (1984). The case involved a libel claim filed by Keeton in federal district court in New Hampshire. Keeton chose New Hampshire believing it to be a forum favorable to her case. Hustler's only contact with the state was the circulation of copies of its magazine in New Hampshire. The Supreme Court held that a "regular circulation of magazines in the forum State is sufficient to support an assertion of jurisdiction in this case because of the potential for the injurious effect to be felt in New Hampshire."

[14] 499 U.S. 585 (1991).

	Federal Trial Courts	State Trial Courts
Personal Jurisdiction	1. Residents and business entities located in the state where the federal trial court sits; or 2. Nonresidents with *minimum contacts* with the state in which the federal trial court sits; or 3. Nonresidents owning property in the state in which the federal trial court sits; or 4. Voluntary	1. Residents and business entities located in state; or 2. Nonresidents owning property in the state; or 3. Nonresidents with *minimum contacts* with the state according to state long-arm statutes; or 4. Voluntary
Subject Matter Jurisdiction	1. Federal question; or 2. U.S. is a party; or 3. Diversity of citizenship *and* amount in controversy is more than $75,000 (amount required only in diversity cases)	State law matters (statutes, common law, state constitutional issues).

Venue

While jurisdiction requires an analysis of whether a court has authority over a particular case, venue is the legal concept that defines the most appropriate *location* for the trial. Two or more courts will sometimes have jurisdiction over the very same matter, but it would be more appropriate from a fairness perspective to hear the case in a particular location. Many states have venue rules to determine where a case may be heard. Typically, state statutes provide that venue in a civil case is where the defendant resides or is headquartered, while in a criminal case the venue is ordinarily where the crime is committed. If a crime (or a criminal defendant) is very high profile, a defense attorney will ask for a *change of venue* to help select a jury from outside of the area where the crime was committed, under the theory that the out-of-area jury will be more impartial and less influenced by the media.

To understand how venue may be important in a business context, suppose two Florida–based companies are involved in a breach of contract dispute and Beta sues Alpha. The transaction involved an order that took place over a Web site based in Florida and the order was shipped from Alpha's warehouse in Georgia to Beta's branch office in South Carolina. Although a number of state and federal courts may have jurisdiction over a dispute in this case given the contacts, a Florida court may decide that Florida is the best *venue* for the dispute to be litigated, because both parties have their principal office located there and assumedly it is the most convenient forum for the parties. It is likely that the witnesses and records are in Florida as well. Note however, that a state court cannot unilaterally declare that venue exists in *another* jurisdiction. Courts apply venue statutes to determine whether or not *their* court is the most appropriate venue.

Minimum Contacts over the Internet

The technology boom of the 1990s brought new challenges for courts grappling with the concept of minimum contacts in cyberspace. For example, suppose that Copperfield is the principal owner of an advertising firm headquartered in New London, Connecticut. Hoping to attract new clients and generate new leads, Copperfield decides to develop a Web site with tips on running an effective marketing campaign that was free to all Internet users so long as they filled out a brief form with the user's contact information. Does that subject Copperfield to the jurisdiction of all 50 states simply because users from across the country could access the Web site? Because courts have held that advertising in a particular state may be a factor in determining whether minimum contacts exist, couldn't a *Web site* be the basis for those contacts as well? How does that square with the purposeful availment standard? Suppose that Copperfield decided to start a subscription-based service and charged users to access the site? Or if Copperfield made downloads available for users for a fee, would that change your analysis? Is there any way that Copperfield can limit a court's authority over his firm's minimum contacts? Although the Supreme Court has yet to directly rule on minimum contacts in the context of cyberspace, the law developed thus far gives business owners and managers a relatively clear framework in answering the questions posed in the Copperfield hypothetical.

The *Zippo* Standard

In 1997, a federal district court in Pennsylvania generated the first comprehensive scheme for testing a minimum contacts analysis of personal jurisdiction based on one party's use of the Internet in its business. Named after the parties in the case, this analytical model became known as the **Zippo standard.** Recall from the earlier discussion in this chapter that federal district courts are trial courts and thus do not set precedent. However, since the case was decided, at least six federal circuit courts of appeal have adopted the *Zippo* standard as the legal framework to be used by trial courts in determining personal jurisdiction when one party is asserting minimum contacts based on a certain level of Internet activity by the defendant.

The *Zippo* standard was established in *Zippo Manufacturing Company v. Zippo Dot Com, Inc.*[15] As one may imagine from its name, the case centers on a trademark infringement dispute between Zippo Manufacturing Company (Zippo), the famous lighter manufacturing company, and Zippo Dot Com (ZDC), an Internet news subscription service.[16] When Zippo sued ZDC, ZDC asked the court to dismiss the case claiming a federal court in Pennsylvania did not have personal jurisdiction over them because ZDC had no offices, agents, or property in Pennsylvania. Zippo argued that ZDC's sale of approximately 3,000 subscription-based memberships to residents of Pennsylvania satisfied both the state's long-arm statute and the constitutional fairness and due process requirements of minimum contacts.

In developing a framework for deciding the case, the court adopted a *continuum*, also called a *sliding scale*, approach for measuring the number of minimum contacts based on the interactivity of a Web site owner vis-à-vis the user. The court focused this test on the *level* and *nature* of interactivity between source and user that an individual or business transacted over the Internet. The court explained the continuum by using an illustration of three points along the scale: passive, interactive, and integral to the business model.

Passive On one far end of the continuum, a party with a passive Web site that provided information that could be accessed by any Internet user cannot be the *sole basis* for personal jurisdiction. The court analogized this type of Web site to a billboard advertisement and reasoned that such Web sites could not meet the purposeful availment standard and, thus, could not satisfy the minimum contacts requirement.

Interactive The middle of the continuum applies when a Web site provides users with some interactive function where users may exchange information, purchase products, download or upload material via the Web site, or other uses that involve the user activity beyond merely viewing the content of the Web site. For cases that fall into this category, the court would be required to examine the interactivity more closely on a case-by-case

[15]952 F. Supp. 1119 (W.D. Pa. 1997).
[16]ZDC is now defunct.

(continued)

basis with a focus on the *level* of interactivity and *commercial* nature of the Web site. For example, was the level of interactivity simply a product order form that could be downloaded, filled out, and faxed to the vendor? If so, the case may fall on the passive side of the scale and no minimum contacts exist. On the other hand, if the interactivity involved credit card purchases from a significant number of users in one particular state via the Web site or some subscription-based service provided by the Web site's owner, the case may fall on the active side of the scale indicating that minimum contacts exist to the extent necessary for personal jurisdiction over the Web site's owner.

Integral to Business Model   The other far end of the scale is a business where the use of the Web site is an *integral part* of a business model and is used to accomplish commercial transactions with residents in the state of the court's jurisdiction. For example, Internet vendors such as Amazon.com or NetFlix.com regularly transact business with residents of all fifty states (and beyond), and their business model depends almost exclusively on consumers interacting with their Web site, including financial transactions. In this case, the minimum contacts and purposeful availment standards are met and personal jurisdiction is appropriate.

Ultimately, the court ruled that since ZDC contracted with 3,000 residents and seven Internet access providers all located in Pennsylvania, the purposeful availment standard was met, minimum contacts existed, and thus the federal court in Pennsylvania had personal jurisdiction over the case.

Figure 3.4 is an illustration of the *Zippo* sliding scale used by many courts to analyze minimum contacts via the Internet.

FIGURE 3.4   *Zippo* Sliding Scale Test

Passive/Billboard	Interactive	Integral to Business Model
← ------------------------------------]		[--------------------------------------→
No personal jurisdiction	Case-by-case	Minimum contacts established

Courts in many jurisdictions have adopted the *Zippo* standard when determining personal jurisdiction based on Internet activity.

Adoption of the *Zippo* Standard

Soon after *Zippo* was decided, several other courts began to use the same type of analytical framework. In *Cybersell, Inc. v. Cybersell, Inc.,*[17] a trademark infringement dispute between businesses located in two different states, the Ninth Circuit Court of Appeals used a *Zippo*-like analysis in concluding that the defendant's Web site, which did little more than advertise the defendant's business services, was essentially passive and did not meet the requisite level of interactivity required to constitute minimum contacts.

In Case 3.2, the Fifth Circuit Court of Appeals became the first federal *appellate* court to expressly adopt the *Zippo* standard and also provided a useful application of the standard when the defendant had a Web site that involved some degree of interactivity.

[17]130 F.3d 414 (9th Cir. 1997).

 Self-Check

Would the court have personal jurisdiction under the *Zippo* standard?

1. Scanner Corp., a Maryland-based corporation with its principal place of business in Baltimore, creates and markets copyrighted photos of models that are used as background material on product packaging and picture frames. AP Picture Co. (AP) wrongfully appropriated hundreds of Scanner's photos and published them on its Web site where members could pay to download them. AP received advertisement fees based on the amount of consumer traffic generated by the Web site. Scanner files suit in a Maryland court against AP and AP's Internet Service Provider, Megabites, a Georgia corporation with its principal place of business in Atlanta. Does the court have jurisdiction over Megabites?

2. Kristin, a resident of Hawaii, maintains a not-for-profit Web site from her home that offers information and opinions on commercial household movers. While the Web site does not charge for its usage, it does accept donations. Last summer, Kristin posted various derogatory and unflattering comments about Moving – U Inc. (MU) a New York corporation, one of which was in response to a user's question. Kristin asserted that Moving – U was operating without the requisite legal authorization and insurance. If MU wishes to sue Kristin in a federal court in New York, does the court have personal jurisdiction?

3. Natural Foods Inc. (Natural) is a Nevada-based firm that sells organic beef. Although it originally did business exclusively in Nevada through a small retail stand, Natural eventually created a Web site whereby customers throughout the United States could order beef to be shipped from Natural's ranch in Nevada to any city in the United States. When ordering, customers provided their billing and shipping addresses as well as credit card information and could sign up to receive newsletters. Johanna, a resident of Florida, ordered beef via Natural's Web site and became sick after eating the product. Johanna sues Natural in a federal district court in Florida under a variety of theories. Does Natural have sufficient contact for the Florida court to have personal jurisdiction over them?

4. Big Bank Securities Inc. (BBS) is a Delaware corporation, with its principal place of business in New York. BBS trades various securities for its own benefit and for its clients. Cheyenne Securities Investors Inc. (CSI) is a Wyoming corporation providing portfolio management for various clients. A trader for CSI contacted BBS through an instant messaging program used by investors. CSI offered to sell $15 million in bonds to BBS in response to an earlier inquiry. BBS agreed to buy the bonds and set a price and time for delivery of the bond instruments. The entire transaction was completed via the instant messaging system. The next day CSI reneged on the sale claiming it believed BBS had insider information. CSI has no offices or agents in New York. Would New York state courts have personal jurisdiction over a BBS versus CSI lawsuit for breach of contract?

Answers to this Self-Check are provided at the end of the chapter.

FACT SUMMARY   Mink, a Texas resident, had experience and expertise in the retail furniture business. He developed a computer program called the Opportunity Tracking Computer System ("OTCS") that was designed to analyze information regarding retail furniture sales to pinpoint potential new leads for use in the furniture industry. Mink submitted an application for a patent for OTCS. While the patent application was pending, Stark approached Mink to gauge interest in the possibility of marketing the OTCS software bundled with Stark's existing software through the use of Stark's marketing company called AAAA Development ("AAAA"). Although Mink declined the offer to market the software together, he later approached Stark to discuss the possibility of AAAA marketing OTCS as a separate product. During the discussions, Stark allegedly shared Mink's ideas and information on the OTCS with Stark's AAAA business partner. AAAA was a Vermont corporation.

Eventually, Mink filed suit in a federal district court in Texas against AAAA Development and its principals, alleging that they conspired to copy Mink's patent-pending OTCS system for their own financial gain. None of the defendants owned property or had any other contact in Texas. In the course of its business, AAAA maintained a Web site advertising its software products on the Internet. The site was available to all users, including residents of Texas, and Mink argued that the Web site alone was sufficient contact to warrant jurisdiction in Texas. The federal district court in Texas dismissed the case for lack of personal jurisdiction and Mink appealed.

SYNOPSIS OF DECISION AND OPINION   The Fifth Circuit Court of Appeals ruled in favor of AAAA, holding that the federal district court in Texas did *not* have personal jurisdiction over AAAA by virtue of the Web site alone. In expressly adopting the *Zippo* standard, the court reasoned that although the Web site did have some level of interactivity, it was not sufficient to satisfy the minimum contacts requirement. Further, the court ruled that the district court could not exercise personal jurisdiction over AAAA simply because its Web site is *accessible* by Texas residents. Courts addressing the issue of whether personal jurisdiction can be constitutionally exercised over a defendant look to the *nature* and *quality* of commercial activity that an entity conducts over the Internet. The court also pointed out that it was not reasonably foreseeable, nor particularly fair, that AAAA would be subject to personal jurisdiction in Texas.

WORDS OF THE COURT: *Zippo* Standard   "We find that the reasoning of *Zippo* is persuasive and adopt it in this Circuit. [. . .] Applying these principles to this case, we conclude that AAAA's website is insufficient to subject it to personal jurisdiction. Essentially, AAAA maintains a website that posts information about its products and services. While the website provides users with a printable mail-in order form, AAAA's toll-free telephone number, a mailing address and an electronic mail ("e-mail") address, orders are not taken through AAAA's website, this does not classify the website as anything more than passive advertisement [and] is not grounds for the exercise of personal jurisdiction.

There was no evidence that AAAA conducted business over the Internet by engaging in business transactions with forum residents or by entering into contracts over the Internet.

We note that AAAA's website provides an e-mail address that permits consumers to interact with the company. There is no evidence, however, that the website allows AAAA to do anything but reply to e-mail initiated by website visitors. In addition, AAAA's website lacks other forms of interactivity cited by courts as factors to consider in determining questions of personal jurisdiction. For example, AAAA's website does not allow consumers to order or purchase products and services on-line.

[T]he presence of an electronic mail access, a printable order form, and a toll-free phone number on a website, without more, is insufficient to establish personal jurisdiction. Absent a defendant doing business over the Internet or sufficient interactivity with residents of the forum state, we cannot conclude that personal jurisdiction is appropriate."

Case Questions

1. Where did AAAA Web site fall on the sliding scale of the *Zippo* standard?

2. As a practical matter, what happens to Mink's case now? May he refile it in another court?

E-MAIL AND MINIMUM CONTACTS

In a 2002 case, a federal trial court ruled that e-mail communications between parties who had an ongoing business relationship with a party in the forum state had *sufficient* minimum contacts with the state to justify an exercise of jurisdiction.[18] In reaching its decision, the court took note that it has become the general rule in modern commercial relationships for parties to communicate by electronic means rather than face-to-face. Jurisdiction in this case was justified by an ongoing relationship that included regular interstate communications by e-mail in the forum state.

The court ruled that the defendant's physical presence or agents in the forum state was not necessary when continuous communications were conducted between the parties using electronic and nonelectronic means and the out-of-state party engaged in ongoing business transactions with parties located in the forum state.

Legal Speak ›))
Principal The term used to denote those persons with ownership interest in a business venture.

INTERNATIONAL JURISDICTION FOR INTERNET TRANSACTIONS[19]

LO3-9

The advances in technology and logistical efficiency make the prospect for engaging in international trade more opportune than ever. While international commerce presents a substantial opportunity for a business's product or service to be advertised and sold to hundreds of millions of potential consumers worldwide, there are attendant legal risks that business owners and managers need to understand. Even with the rapid movement toward global harmonization of laws and regulations, individual countries still have their own political challenges, culture, and identity that impact the way a country applies its laws and legal systems. For example, suppose that Snow Sports Equipment (SSE) decides to expand its business to the European markets. The owners of SSE set up an export chain where the equipment is sold via a Web site with computers and servers from an office in Boulder, Colorado, then shipped from leased warehouse space in Prague, Czech Republic, to a retail store in Geneva, Switzerland. Who has jurisdiction over any disputes involving the product? Must a U.S. court apply European Union law? Swiss law? Czech law? Can a European consumer sue SSE in Europe under Swiss law or European law? (Note that the Czech Republic is an EU member state, but Switzerland is not.) This uncertainty and the inherent difficulty in determining what nation's law to apply in an Internet transaction creates challenges for business owners and managers. Some degree of cost-benefit analysis is necessary to measure the risks of international trade versus the return on investment.

Country of Origin Standard

The United States, Canada, and the European Union governments have generally agreed to apply the law of the country where the defendant's servers are *located*. This so-called **country of origin principle** allows courts an easy rule of thumb to determine choice of law. Yet, some countries have adopted a *country of reception* approach that increases the risk to a business because, in theory, one would need to have a fundamental knowledge of the laws of each individual country in order to reduce risk of noncompliance.

---

[18]*Johnson v. King Media Inc.*, 2002 U.S. Dist. LEXIS 12311. Although several other trial courts have subsequently adopted the reasoning in this case, this particular point of law is still developing in the appellate courts.

[19]Note that commercial jurisdiction in the general context of International Law is discussed in detail in Chapter 25 "International Law and Global Commerce."

Other Theories of Jurisdiction in Electronic Commerce

Consider a decision by Australia's highest court issued in December 2002. The court ruled that American–based publisher Dow Jones could be sued in Australia for defamation based on an article that appeared on its Web site, even though Dow Jones has no presence in Australia and its Web site and infrastructure (such as the mainframe servers) are located in New Jersey. The plaintiff in the case, Joseph Gutnick, a wealthy Australian businessman, likely chose the forum because of its convenience and Australia's relatively proplaintiff defamation laws. Dow Jones contended that the case should take place in the United States because that is where the article was uploaded to their computer servers in New Jersey and that is the closest location to where the article was published. The Australian court ruled against Dow Jones, reasoning that the article is actually published where and when the article appeared on the user's computer screen.

CONCEPT SUMMARY   Minimum Contacts on the Internet

- The *Zippo* standard is a sliding scale approach for measuring the amount of minimum contacts a party has based on the interactivity of a Web site.

- Under the *Zippo* standard, passive Web sites that provide information that can be accessed by any Internet user alone do not provide a basis for personal jurisdiction. On the other hand, Web sites that are integral to the business model and used consistently for transactions constitute minimum contacts.

- Web sites used with some degree of interactivity are evaluated on a case-by-case basis, with those simply exchanging information generally not being grounds for jurisdiction, but those involving subscription services and other purposeful contact may provide the basis for minimum contacts and purposeful availment.

- E-mail communication between parties with ongoing business relationships has been found to be sufficient minimum contact by a limited number of courts.

- In international Web transactions, generally the courts in the location of the Web site's servers will have jurisdiction over any disputes arising out of the use of the Web site. This is known as the country of origin approach.

KEY TERMS

Court p. 52   A judicial tribunal duly constituted for the hearing and determination of cases.

Judiciary p. 52   A collection of federal and state courts existing primarily to adjudicate disputes and charged with the responsibility of judicial review.

Jurisdiction p. 52   The legal authority that a court must have before it can hear a case.

Venue p. 52   A determination of the most appropriate court location for litigating a dispute.

State courts p. 52   Adjudicate matters dealing primarily with cases arising from state statutory, state common, or state constitutional law.

Federal courts p. 52   Adjudicate matters dealing primarily with national laws, federal constitutional issues, and other cases that are outside the purview of state courts.

State trial courts p. 53   The first courts at the state level before which the facts of a case are decided.

State appellate courts p. 53 State-level courts of precedent, concerned primarily with reviewing the decisions of trial courts.

Plaintiff p. 53 The party initiating a lawsuit who believes the conduct of another party has caused the plaintiff to suffer damages.

Defendant p. 53 The party alleged by the plaintiff to have caused the plaintiff to suffer damages.

Remand p. 54 To send a case back to the lower court from which it came for further action consistent with the opinion and instructions of the higher court.

U.S. district courts p. 54 Serve the same primary trial function as state trial courts, but for issues involving federal matters.

U.S. courts of appeal p. 54 The intermediate appellate courts in the federal system frequently referred to as the *circuit courts of appeal,* consisting of thirteen courts, each of which reviews the decisions of federal district courts in the state or several states within its circuit.

U.S. Supreme Court p. 54 The ultimate arbiter of federal law that reviews not only decisions of the federal courts but also reviews decisions of state courts that involve some issue of federal law.

Subject matter jurisdiction p. 59 The court's authority over the dispute between the parties.

Personal jurisdiction p. 59 The court's authority over the parties involved in the dispute.

Federal question p. 60 Some issue arising from the constitution, federal statute or regulation, or federal common law.

Party p. 60 A person or entity making or responding to a claim in a court.

Diversity of citizenship p. 60 When opposing parties in a lawsuit are citizens of different states or if one party is a citizen of a foreign country, the case is placed under federal court jurisdiction if the amount in controversy exceeds $75,000.

State long-arm statutes p. 61 State statutes intended to allow a court to reach into another state and exercise jurisdiction over a nonresident defendant due to the defendant's conduct or other circumstances.

Minimum contacts p. 61 A defendant's activities within or affecting the state in which a lawsuit is brought that are considered legally sufficient to support jurisdiction in that state's courts.

***Zippo* standard** p. 65 The legal framework used by trial courts in determining personal jurisdiction when one party is asserting minimum contacts based on a certain level of Internet activity by the defendant.

Country of origin principle p. 69 General agreement between the United States, Canada, and the European Union governments to apply the law of the country where the defendant's servers are located.

THEORY TO PRACTICE

Santiago Information Systems ("Santiago") is a business based in Baltimore, Maryland, that purchases old computers, refurbishes them with new software and hardware parts, and sells them in bulk for about half the price of a new PC. For the past three years, Santiago shipped approximately 40 percent of its inventory to the same client. The client was the Wilmington, Delaware, school system ("Wilmington") and the school paid approximately $80,000 to Santiago for the computers per year. Santiago would also visit each school to be sure that the computers were installed correctly and that the school district was satisfied with the order. Santiago has a Web site that gives contact information for the company, but is not interactive because users cannot transact business except for sending Santiago e-mail via the Web site.

Recently, Wilmington has discovered that large shipments of Santiago's products were defective and they have been unable to come to a resolution with Santiago over the matter.

1. If Wilmington wishes to sue Santiago, what court(s) would have jurisdiction over this matter?
2. What would be the best venue and why?
3. If a Delaware court decides that it does not have jurisdiction, how may that affect Wilmington's decision on whether or not to file a lawsuit?

Assume that one of Santiago's suppliers, Parts R Us ("Parts") is headquartered in Union, New Jersey, and has been shipping Santiago parts for approximately four years in a row. Last year Parts sold approximately $7,000 in hardware to Santiago. In the past 10 years, Parts R Us shipped to businesses in Maryland, New York, New Jersey, and Connecticut. Parts also e-mailed advertisements to potential leads in each of the 50 states. Wilmington determines that Parts provided the defective parts used in the Wilmington computer order.

4. If Wilmington decides to file suit against Parts in Delaware, would a Delaware court have personal jurisdiction over Parts? Why or why not?

5. If Parts had a Web site where customers may order products, pay for them via credit card, and have parts delivered via a delivery service to any U.S. city, how would that affect your jurisdiction analysis?

6. If the only contact that Parts had with Delaware was via their Web site, what standard would the trial court apply to determine jurisdiction?

Managers are frequently involved in various aspects of business planning and have to be alert to current trends that affect their industry as well as being alert to potential liability during the planning process. Assume that you are a mid-level manager at Santiago Information Systems (see Theory to Practice, above). After settling with Wilmington in an out-of-court agreement, Santiago embarks on an expansion plan, and you receive the following e-mail from your senior manager:

> We are planning a very aggressive marketing campaign and extending our reach beyond institutions such as Wilmington by targeting individual consumers as

well. This will include revamping and expanding the functionality of the Web site to include online ordering and the use of e-mail advertisements to selected consumer groups. Write a two- to three page memorandum advising me of any potential liability associated with the Web site in terms of out-of-state clients and make recommendations on how to limit any liability from the marketing plan related to revamping the Web site and use of mass e-mail advertisements to selected consumers. Be sure to include any cost-benefits issues that may be applicable.

A sample answer may be found on this textbook's Web site at www.mhhe.com/melvin.

CASE SUMMARY 3.1 :: Bickford v. Onslow Memorial Hospital Foundation, 855 A.2d 1150 (Me 2004)

PERSONAL JURISDICTION

Bickford, a resident of Maine, received hospital bills over a period of several months from Onslow Memorial Hospital, which had treated a relative of Bickford's ex-wife. Although Onslow eventually acknowledged that Bickford was not legally responsible for the bills, Onslow continued to pursue the debt through collection and reported the debt as delinquent to Bickford's credit agencies. Bickford filed suit against Onslow in a Maine state court alleging a violation of several consumer protection laws. Onslow is located in North Carolina and does not own property or have any agents in Maine.

CASE QUESTION

1. Does the Maine court have jurisdiction over Onslow?

JURISDICTION: FORUM SELECTION CLAUSE

Zapata, a Texas corporation, hired Unterweser, a German corporation, to provide a tugboat for pulling Zapata's oil rig. Unterweser prepared a contract and Zapata signed the contract after having made several changes. The contract contained a forum selection clause requiring any disputes be litigated in an International Commercial Court in London. Zapata had not altered that part of the contract. Unterweser's tugboat departed from Louisiana pulling Zapata's oil rig, but while in international waters off the Gulf of Mexico a storm arose that resulted in severe damage to the oil rig. Zapata instructed Unterweser to tow the rig to the nearest port in Tampa, Florida. Zapata then filed a lawsuit in the federal district court in Tampa for $3.5 million against Unterweser.

CASE QUESTIONS

1. Does the court in Tampa have jurisdiction? Why or why not?
2. Will the forum selection clause be enforced? Why or why not?

PURPOSEFUL AVAILMENT

Colelli & Associates (Colelli) is a firm with its principal place of business in Ohio. Colelli was engaged in the manufacture and sale of a specialized oil well solvent to several oil producers based in Ohio. Sixty percent of the oil produced by the Ohio producers was shipped to refineries in Pennsylvania, including a refinery owned and operated by Pennzoil Products Company (Pennzoil). Pennzoil, a corporation based in Nevada with refineries around the world, sued Colelli in a federal district court located in Pennsylvania on a product liability claim, contending that Colelli's solvent had damaged its Pennsylvania refinery. Colelli contested the court's jurisdiction because they had no *direct* contact with Pennsylvania business owners and had no other contacts within Pennsylvania. Pennzoil argued that Colelli knew that their product was being used by Pennsylvania companies and had gained a substantial benefit by virtue of their product being used by Pennsylvania oil refineries such as Pennzoil's.

CASE QUESTION

1. Has Colelli purposefully availed itself to Pennsylvania to warrant personal jurisdiction?

MINIMUM CONTACTS

The Robinsons, residents of New York, purchased a new Audi car from Seaway, a car dealership in New York. Seaway obtained this car from World-Wide Volkswagen, a New York corporation that is a regional distributor for Audi serving the New York, New Jersey, and Connecticut markets. While driving the car through Oklahoma, the Robinsons were severely injured in a car accident. The Robinsons brought a product liability lawsuit against both Seaway and World-Wide Volkswagen in a federal trial court in Oklahoma. World-Wide contended that the Oklahoma court did not have personal jurisdiction because World-Wide had no property, presence, or agents in Oklahoma.

CASE QUESTIONS

1. Who prevails and why?
2. Are the minimum contacts requirements being met? Why or why not?
3. Since the car is inherently mobile, does that mean that jurisdiction is appropriate in any state where the car has traveled?

MINIMUM CONTACTS VIA THE WEB AND THE *ZIPPO* STANDARD

Toys "R" Us is a Delaware corporation headquartered in New Jersey that owns and operates retail stores worldwide. In 1999, they acquired Imaginarium Toy Centers, including the rights to various trademarks held by Imaginarium. Step Two, a corporation based in Spain, owns franchised toy stores operating under the Imaginarium name in several Spanish cities, but does not maintain any offices or stores outside of Spain. Each corporation registered multiple e-mail addresses under the Imaginarium name. Step Two's sites were interactive and allowed users to purchase toys online, but the company would ship only within Spain. If a user signed up for Step Two's electronic newsletter, they were prompted to enter personal information and were provided with a drop-down menu of various Spanish provinces where the users were located. This menu did not accommodate mailing addresses within the United States, and

Step Two maintains that it has never made a sale in the United States. Toys "R" Us claimed that it had evidence that a resident of New Jersey made two purchases via the Web site, but conceded that these purchases were delivered to a Toys "R" Us employee in Spain, who then forwarded the items to the purchaser in New Jersey. Toys "R" Us filed a trademark infringement suit in federal district court in New Jersey.

CASE QUESTIONS

1. Does the federal court in New Jersey have subject matter jurisdiction over this case?
2. Has Step Two purposefully availed themselves in New Jersey and, thus, have the requisite minimum contacts? Why or why not?
3. Analyze this case under both the *Zippo* and *Asahi* frameworks. Describe the analysis and potential outcome under each. Which one is the correct test to use and why?

✓ Self-Check **ANSWERS**

Subject Matter Jurisdiction

1. No. No diversity, or federal question.

2. Yes. U.S. government agency is a party to the litigation.

3. Yes. Diversity of citizenship with amount exceeding $75,000.

4. Yes. Federal issue involving a federal statute.

5. Yes. U.S. is a party to the litigation and federal statute at issue.

Zippo Standard

1. No. The court cannot exercise personal jurisdiction over Megabites. Their conduct is strictly passive and, thus, not sufficient for an exercise of jurisdiction. See generally *ALS Scan, Inc. v. Digital Serv. Consultants, Inc.*, 293 F.3d 707 (4th Cir. 2002).

2. No. Regardless of the acceptance of donations or response to user questions, New York courts would not have jurisdiction for defamatory comments made outside of New York. The Web site in question here can be accessed by anyone in the world, and there is no evidence that Kristin was availing herself of the opportunity to directly conduct business in New York. See generally *Best Van Lines, Inc. v. Walker*, 490 F.3d 239 (2d Cir. 2007).

3. Yes. Considering the interactivity of its Web site and the fact consumers can purchase product from it, courts in Florida could exercise jurisdiction over Natural Foods Inc.

4. Yes. A New York court would have jurisdiction because CSI was clearly attempting to do business in New York with BBS through the instant messaging system. CSI had knowingly contacted BBS in order to initiate the transaction, which culminated in the sale of $15 million in bonds; thus, CSI had entered into New York to conduct business. See generally *Deutsche Bank Sec., Inc. v. Montana Bd. of Invs.*, 850 N.E.2d 1140 (N.Y. 2006).

4 CHAPTER

Resolving Disputes: Litigation and Alternative Dispute Resolution Options

learning outcomes checklist

After studying this chapter, students who have mastered the material will be able to:

4-1 Identify the ways in which dispute resolution can be used in business planning.

4-2 Explain the meaning and purpose of civil litigation as a method of resolving disputes.

4-3 Name the stages of litigation and identify the characteristics of each stage.

4-4 Articulate the concept of standing.

4-5 List the methods of alternative dispute resolution (ADR) and potential advantages of using ADR.

4-6 Distinguish between arbitration and mediation and explain both processes.

4-7 Apply the legal standards for when an arbitration clause may be held invalid.

4-8 Explain how online dispute resolution can be used to solve small claim disputes.

4-9 Provide an example of a hybrid form of alternative dispute resolution.

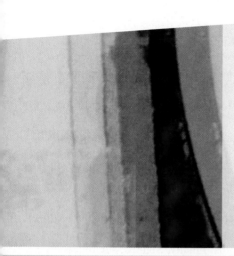

Litigation and dispute resolution are an important part of business planning and strategy. Because the chance of being involved in a lawsuit or alternative dispute resolution is relatively high, business owners and managers must be knowledgeable of the relative advantages and disadvantages of litigation and also have a firm grasp on the options for various methods of dispute resolution. In this chapter students will learn:

- The role of dispute resolution in business planning.
- The process of using civil litigation to resolve disputes.
- Methods of alternative dispute resolution (ADR).

LO4-1 DISPUTE RESOLUTION AND BUSINESS PLANNING

In a business context, dispute resolution is not simply a matter to be delegated to attorneys. While legal counsel is a primary and important source of information and advice, the decisions regarding how to resolve a dispute are decisions for business managers and owners. Dispute resolution can be a crucial part of business planning and strategy that requires a thoughtful cost-benefit analysis. Business managers and owners have an ever-increasing number of options to resolve disputes within and outside of the legal system and each come with its attendant advantages and disadvantages.

To illustrate how dispute resolution may be used in business planning, suppose that Classic Retail Outlets (CRO) enters into a contract with Sign Designs Company (SignCo.). The contract calls for SignCo. to design, manufacture, and install signage for several CRO locations. The parties agreed on certain specifications and a payment of 50 percent at the time of signing the contract and 50 percent at the time of delivery. SignCo. delivered a prototype of the new sign, but CRO management was unhappy with the design and claimed SignCo. had not followed the specifications in the contract. SignCo. agreed to work on a new prototype, but delayed the process for several months. Finally, SignCo. submitted a new prototype, but CRO again rejected the prototype citing additional flaws in its design. In addition, so much time passed that CRO had to go through the expense of installing temporary signs.

In this hypothetical, a legal dispute is brewing between CRO and SignCo. Yet the fact remains that at least two business problems still exist: (1) despite that 50 percent of the contract price has been paid to Sign Co., CRO still needs a sign and has now expended more money than anticipated due to the temporary signs; and (2) SignCo. has devoted significant time and some materials to the project and may believe that CRO is being unreasonable in its expectations. Business owners and managers have a host of options to resolve this dispute. Therefore, CRO should consider the alternatives presented in Table 4.1 to resolve the dispute in the context of a cost-benefit analysis and business planning.

LO4-2 CIVIL LITIGATION

Civil litigation is the term used to describe a dispute resolution process where the parties and their counsel argue their view of a civil (noncriminal) controversy in a court of law. While sometimes the term *litigation* is used as synonymous with the word *trial,* the scope of litigation is much broader and includes *pretrial* events as well. There are many varieties of business litigation, including contract disputes, and lawsuits related to employment, negligence, collection actions, and bankruptcy. The odds of a business organization becoming involved in litigation have increased precipitously in recent years. From 1980 to 2005, the number of civil cases filed in federal courts more than doubled. The American Bar Association reported that, for the first time in the history of the court system, the total number of civil cases filed in state and federal courts in 2008 combined exceeded 20 million cases per year.

LO4-3 STAGES OF LITIGATION

Litigation is most easily understood when broken down into stages. However, it is important to note that the timing of these stages may sometimes overlap.

Prelawsuit: Demand and Prelitigation Settlement Negotiations

When a dispute arises between two parties, one party will typically make an informal demand of the other party in which the principals (or their attorneys) lay out the basics of the dispute and demand a certain action. This usually leads to informal discussions. In some states it is necessary to make a formal demand before filing suit. The demand is often

Action	Potential Benefit(s)	Potential Costs	Threats
Lawsuit	Court-ordered resolution to have the deposit refunded and have SignCo. pay additional damages to compensate for the temporary signage.	Significant expenditures: Legal fees; hard costs (such as travel and fees for experts); human resources costs when time must be devoted to litigation procedures; appellate costs.	1. Loss at trial or loss upon appeal. 2. Legal fees may be higher than the final judgment amount awarded. 3. Possible countersuit by SignCo. 4. Permanent damage to business relationship. 5. Potential for bad publicity.
Nonjudicial dispute resolution Arbitration, mediation, or hybrid form.	Enforceable resolution to have the deposit refunded and have SignCo. pay additional damages to compensate for the temporary signage.	Moderate range in legal fees, arbitration/mediation fees; limited human resource expenditures; no chance of appellate fees (if binding).	1. Loss at arbitration that is not appealable (if binding). 2. Win in arbitration, but still have to go to trial (if non-binding). 3. Potential damage to business relationship.
Informal settlement Cancel the contract, agree not to sue each other and agree to a figure that (1) compensates CRO for the temporary signage and; (2) allows a percentage of the total fee to compensate SignCo. for time invested in the project.	1. Parties agree not to sue each other. 2. Potential to preserve the business relationship. 3. Time and talent are not used to prepare for dispute resolution methods.	Low range of legal fees; moderate human resources investment; no threat of litigation by SignCo.	Settlement negotiations may drag on and CRO must find a new vendor.
Revise contract, continue relationship Make contract expectations clearer and revise payments that compensate both parties for the loss.	Transaction is completed (perhaps even at a profit) and business relationship is preserved.	Low range of legal fees; Moderate human resources;	Potential litigation by SignCo. and potential for the new contract to generate yet another dispute.

followed by an informal prelitigation settlement discussion involving the parties and their lawyers. If the issues are relatively simple, this can be a cost-effective method to resolve a dispute fairly. However, if the legal issues are more complex or the parties are antagonistic toward each other, the prelitigation discussion will simply act as notice that a party intends to file a lawsuit if an agreement cannot be reached.

Standing   In order for one party to maintain a lawsuit against another party, she must **LO**4-4 have **standing** to sue. This means that the party asserting the claim: (1) must have suffered

The parties may attempt to resolve a dispute through informal negotiations in order to avoid litigation.

Legal Speak ›))

Plaintiff The party who initiates a lawsuit by filing a complaint with the clerk of the court against the defendant(s) demanding damages, performance, and/or court determination of rights.

Defendant The party sued in a civil lawsuit or the party charged with a crime in a criminal prosecution. In some types of cases (such as divorce), a defendant may be called a *respondent*.

an *injury in fact;* (2) suffered harm that is *direct, concrete,* and *individualized;* and (3) articulates what *legal redress* exists to compensate for the injury. In a business context, most lawsuits involve economic interests and, therefore, most parties in commercial litigation have no trouble meeting the requirements for standing. However, businesses and industries can sometimes be the target of consumer advocacy organizations and other groups that use litigation to advance their group's policy objectives. In Case 4.1, a federal court of appeals applies the rules of standing to a lawsuit filed against several businesses in the same industry.

Pleadings Stage

Complaint and Summons   If informal attempts at resolution fail, formal action begins when the plaintiff initiates a lawsuit by filing a **complaint** with the local clerk of courts.[1] This sets the pleadings stage in motion with both sides filing documents that set out the facts of the case, theories of liability, and any available defenses. At the same time, the plaintiff is typically required to arrange for service of the defendant with a **summons** along with a copy of the plaintiff's complaint. The summons is formal notification to the defendant that she has been named in the lawsuit and informs her that an answer must be filed within a certain period of time. In some cases, the summons and complaint may be served by certified mail to the defendant. In other cases, a deputy sheriff or process server must deliver the documents in person. Statutes and court rules impose time limits on the *litigants* (the adverse parties involved in litigation) requiring pleadings to be initiated within a set time frame. Failing to adhere to the timelines may result in the loss of any legal rights or defenses. The complaint sets out the plaintiff's version of the facts of the case, the damages that have been suffered, and why the plaintiff believes that the defendant is legally

---

[1]Although clerk of courts is a common title for the official designated to receive civil complaints, the actual title varies widely among the states.

FACT SUMMARY   Alston and a group of other plaintiffs in the case ("Alston") are the parents of minor children. Alston filed a lawsuit against several domestic manufacturers and importers of alcoholic beverages and the Beer Institute, a trade association, ("Manufacturers") alleging that their advertising is responsible for the illegal purchase of alcoholic beverages by minor children. Alston contended that their own minor children have been subject to the Manufacturers' advertising campaigns, but conceded that no facts demonstrated that their own minor children, or any particular minor children, have actually purchased any such alcohol. Alston sought to recover money allegedly spent on purchases of alcoholic beverages by minor children and to prevent any further advertising. The Manufacturers moved to have the suit dismissed on the basis that Alston lacked standing.

SYNOPSIS OF DECISION AND OPINION   The Sixth Circuit Court of Appeals ruled in favor of the Manufacturers, holding that Alston did not have standing. The court reasoned that Alston did not allege any *actual injury* involving parental rights. While parents had a right to make fundamental decisions about a child's upbringing, they had no legal right to prevent other private parties from attempting to influence their children. Moreover, Alston did not show any economic injury, as the parents did not allege that their children had purchased any alcohol. The court went even further and ruled that even if Alston could show an economic injury, the injury was not direct because any

connection between Manufacturers' advertising and Alston's alleged injury was broken by the intervening criminal acts of the third-party sellers and the third-party, underage purchasers.

WORDS OF THE COURT: No Standing When No Remedy Is Available   "[Alston] [. . .] cannot articulate a viable remedy. [Alston's] most obvious remedy would be to recover from their children the money those children converted from the parents in order to violate the law prohibiting underage purchase of alcohol. A second obvious remedy would be to recover money from the retailers who sold alcohol to minors in violation of the law. [. . .] The plaintiffs, of course, cannot obtain these remedies through this litigation against these named defendants.

In any event, if outlawing the actual sale and purchase is insufficient to remedy the alleged injuries (which is the premise underlying the [Alston's] theories), then outlawing mere advertising must be insufficient as well."

Case Questions

1. Given the court's reference to the rights of parents, is there any alternative theory that Alston could have used to allege injury?

2. If Alston had been the parent of a smoker who suffered a smoking-related illness, could Alston have alleged an injury despite the fact that several different brands of the cigarettes contributed to the injury? Why or why not?

---

responsible for those damages. Court procedures prescribe how the complaint should be served upon the defendant to ensure timely notice of the claims asserted by the plaintiff. Figure 4.1 sets out a sample complaint for the hypothetical *CRO v. SignCo.* dispute.

Answer   Once the defendant is served with the complaint, she must provide a formal **answer** within a prescribed time frame (normally within 20 days). The answer responds to each paragraph of the complaint. Often, the answer is simply a device for the parties to understand what issues they agree on and what issues will be in dispute at trial. If the defendant does not answer on time, she is said to *default* and generally will automatically lose the case without the benefit of trial. This is known as a *default judgment.* Figure 4.2 sets out to answer CRO's complaint.

Counterclaim   If the defendant believes that the plaintiff has caused her damages arising out of the *very same* set of facts as articulated in the complaint, the defendant files both an answer and a **counterclaim** (in some states, this is called a *counter-suit*). The counterclaim is similar to a complaint in that the defendant's allegations and

Daniel J. Webster, Esquire
ID# 70665
1120 Liberty Place
Philadelphia, Pennsylvania 19124
Attorney for Plaintiffs

In the Pennsylvania Court of Common Pleas

Philadelphia County

CLASSIC RETAIL OUTLETS, INC.   :

          Plaintiff,   :

                 :

          v.   :   **Complaint**

                 :   Civil Docket 09-2100

SIGN DESIGNS COMPANY   :

          Defendant,   :

                 :

_____ :

In this complaint, the plaintiff alleges as follows:

1. Plaintiff and defendant are both Pennsylvania business entities headquartered in Philadelphia, Pennsylvania.

2. Jurisdiction over the subject matter is proper under the Pennsylvania Code.

3. On July 1, 2008, plaintiff contracted with defendant for services related to the design and installation of exterior signage for several of plaintiff's retail outlet sites. The contract specified the appearance and features of the signs.

4. The contract called for plaintiff to pay $25,000 at the execution of the contract and $25,000 at the completion of defendant's services.

5. Plaintiff fulfilled their obligation under the contract by paying $25,000 to defendant on July 1, 2008.

6. On July 30, 2008, Troy Machir, a principal in the plaintiff company, met with Matthew Diller, a principal in the defendant company, to review a preliminary version of the designs that defendant had completed.

7. During that meeting, Machir expressed his dissatisfaction with the work done and pointed out several errors where defendant had failed to follow the specifications detailed in the original contract.

8. As a result of that meeting, Diller promised to begin the design process anew and adhere more closely to the specifications of the contract.

9. Over the next two months, Machir attempted to obtain another preliminary design from defendant by contacting Diller and others at the defendant company via telephone and e-mail.

10. Diller, nor anyone else at the defendant company, responded to these calls or e-mails.

11. On October 1, 2008, Machir met with Diller once again and Diller presented a revised version of the design.

12. At that meeting, Machir expressed continued dissatisfaction with the design and again pointed out that the design was not consistent with the specifications in the contract.

13. In addition, Machir pointed out several instances where the problems identified at their July meeting were not remedied. Diller again promised to fix the problems.

14. On October 15, 2008, Diller informed Machir that the defendant company could not follow the specifications in the contract at the price agreed to and that an additional fee of $20,000 would be necessary to complete the work.

15. Because of the delay caused by the defendant, plaintiff has had to expend $10,000 to erect temporary signage at its retail outlet sites.

16. The failure of Defendant Company to design a sign according to the specifications of the contract is a failure to perform its obligations under their agreement and constitutes a breach of contract.

    WHEREFORE, plaintiffs request judgment in the amount of $25,000 as refund of the deposit, plus $20,000 for the necessary temporary signage, plus statutory interest, and any other damages the court deems appropriate.

Dated: 1st day of October, 2010.

By:_____

Daniel J. Webster, Esquire
Attorney for the Plaintiff

Oliver W. Holmes, Esquire
ID# 40016
One Alpha Drive
Elizabethtown, Pennsylvania 17022
Attorney for Defendants

In the Pennsylvania Court of Common Pleas

of

Philadelphia County

CLASSIC RETAIL OUTLETS, INC.   :
          Plaintiff,   :
                  :
          v.   :   **Answer**
                  :   Civil Docket 09-2100
SIGN DESIGNS COMPANY   :
          Defendant, :
                  :
_____ :

In this answer, the defendant responds to plaintiff's complaint as follows:

1. Admitted.
2. Admitted.
3. Admitted.
4. Admitted.
5. Admitted.
6. Defendant has insufficient information to admit or deny.
7. Defendant has insufficient information to admit or deny.
8. Defendant has insufficient information to admit or deny.
9. Defendant has insufficient information to admit or deny.
10. Denied. Diller contacted Plaintiff Company several times during this period.
11. Defendant has insufficient information to admit or deny.
12. Defendant has insufficient information to admit or deny.
13. Defendant has insufficient information to admit or deny.
14. Defendant has insufficient information to admit or deny.
15. Defendant has insufficient information to admit or deny.
16. Paragraph 16 is a conclusion of law to which no answer is required.

    Defendant also denies any and all parts of the plaintiff's complaint not specifically mentioned in this Answer.

Dated: 20th day of October, 2010.
By:_____

Oliver W. Holmes, Esquire
Attorney for the Defendant

theory of liability against the plaintiff are set out in the pleading. The plaintiff must now answer the counterclaim allegations by the defendant within a prescribed time period.

Cross-Claim   The defendant can also file a **cross-claim** to bring in a third party to the litigation. A cross-claim is filed when the defendant believes that a third party is either partially or fully liable for the damages that the plaintiff has suffered and, therefore, should be involved as an indispensable party in the trial.

Motions

From the time that the pleadings are filed, through discovery, trial, and even after the trial, parties to the litigation may file **motions.** A motion is a document filed by one party that requests court action in a matter pertaining to the litigation. Some of the more common motions are described in Table 4.2.

Discovery Stage

Once the initial pleadings are filed, most lawsuits move into the **discovery** stage in which the parties attempt to collect more evidence for trial. While it may make television shows and movies more interesting, surprise evidence may not be introduced at an actual trial. Discovery is the legal process for the orderly exchange of evidence. Each side has the right to know and examine the evidence that the other side has, including evidence that is both *inculpatory* and *exculpatory.*

Everything relevant to the dispute is discoverable. Unless the information is protected by a legal privilege, such as certain conversations between attorney and client, it must be produced in discovery if the information is relevant or could be useful in any way for resolving the dispute.

Methods of Discovery   The rules for exchanging information during discovery are set out in court procedures (called the *Rules of Civil Procedure*) and accomplished primarily by four methods: depositions, interrogatories, requests for production, and request for admissions.

Depositions   **Depositions** are oral questions asked of a witness in the case. A deposition can be taken at a courthouse, but is more commonly taken in the setting of a conference room at a law firm. Although there is a court reporter present to create a written record and the witnesses are under oath, no judge is present. Depositions can be taken from the plaintiff, the defendant, or any other witness in the case.

Interrogatories   **Interrogatories** are written questions to be answered by one of the litigants (plaintiffs or defendants) involved the case. Generally, interrogatories involve questions to which the litigant does not have readily available knowledge. The litigant may have to review files, memoranda, transcripts, and so forth in order to properly answer the questions.

Requests for production   These requests are aimed at producing specific items to help one party discover some important fact in the case. **Requests for production** are usually very wide in scope so that a request would cover all documents, memoranda, reports, notes, calendars, videotape, audiotape, e-mail, computer hard drives, and so on. In a complex securities or banking fraud case or one where many documents are involved, it is not uncommon for the parties to send a truckload of boxes containing materials that were requested by the other side.

KEY POINT
Unless protected by a legal privilege, all information relative to the case is subject to methods of discovery.

TABLE 4.2 Motions Used during Litigation

Stage of Litigation	Motion	Request
Pretrial	To Dismiss	To dismiss the case because of a procedural defect such as a court's lack of jurisdiction, or failure to state a recognized legal theory in the complaint.
Pretrial	For Summary Judgment	To enter judgment in the requesting party's favor without a trial because no issues of fact are presented in the case and, thus, no jury trial is needed. The requesting party believes that they win as a matter of law.
Pretrial	To Compel Discovery	To issue a court order demanding that a party comply with a lawful discovery request.
Trial	To Dismiss for Mistrial	To stop the trial in progress and dismiss it because of some extraordinary circumstance resulting in prejudice against one side or the other (rare in civil litigation).
Posttrial	For Judgment as a Matter of Law*	To reverse the verdict of the jury because no reasonable jury could have heard the evidence presented at trial and rendered such a verdict.

* Also called by some state courts a judgment *non obstante veredicto* (not withstanding the verdict).

Discovery does have some important limits however. One key issue for business owners and managers that arises in the context of litigation involving one or more business entities is when discovery includes an attempt by the opposing party to obtain legally protected business information (known as *trade secrets*[2]). In Case 4.2, a state appellate court considers a request by an injured party for access to information about a tire company's trade secret: the process for making its products.

Request for Admissions While the first attempt to narrow the issues in dispute is through the defendant's answer, a **request for admissions** furthers the objective of determining what facts are in dispute (and, thus, must be proved at trial) and which facts both parties accept as true. For example, one party may request that they admit the existence and date of a certain contract. If the other party refuses to admit those facts, witnesses must be called at trial to prove the existence and date of the contract.

 Self-Check

A customer is injured after slipping on a wet floor in a retail store. What discovery technique(s) could he use to obtain the following evidence:

1. Photographs of the site that were taken by the store manager immediately after the fall.
2. Request from the plaintiffs for the defendants to concede that an employee had spilled water on the floor on the morning of the accident.
3. Statement of an employee as a witness who was in charge of keeping the floors clean.
4. Questions that will require the store's manager to look up calendars and logs in order to answer it accurately.

Answers to this Self-Check are provided at the end of the chapter.

---

[2]Trade secrets are covered extensively in Chapter 24, "Intellectual Property."

CASE 4.2 Bridgestone Americas Holding, Inc. v. Mayberry, 854 N.E.2d 355 (In. 2006)

FACT SUMMARY Mayberry filed a product liability action against Bridgestone alleging that tire tread separation caused a car accident that killed her son. During pretrial discovery, Mayberry sought the formula for the steel belt skim stock* on the tire in question. Bridgestone objected to these requests and moved for a court order to prevent disclosure of all trade secrets used to produce the tires, including the skim stock formula. The trial court directed the companies to disclose the formula for the steel belt skim stock on the tire in question, and Bridgestone appealed.

SYNOPSIS OF DECISION AND OPINION The Indiana Supreme Court ruled in favor of Bridgestone. The court found that Mayberry had not demonstrated the necessity of disclosing the formula and that the record demonstrated that the skim stock formula is a trade secret. Bridgestone demonstrated that the skim stock formula qualified as a trade secret because (1) it frequently took several years to arrive at the detailed formula for a new rubber compound; (2) the steel belt skim stock formula represented one of the tire companies' most valuable assets and most closely guarded secrets; and (3) access to the recipes was very narrowly limited. The court reasoned that although

_____
* Skim stock is a specially formulated rubber component designed to provide adhesion between the rubber and steel cord, and between the belts and surrounding components in a radial tire.

Mayberry successfully demonstrated the general relevance of the skim stock formula, she failed to show that it was necessary to the presentation of her case. An inspection of the failed tire's appearance was a more than adequate substitute for examining the skim stock formula.

WORDS OF THE COURT: Protecting Trade Secrets from Misappropriation during Discovery "For over a quarter century, courts have consistently applied a three-part balancing test when a party seeks an order protecting trade secrets from discovery. [. . .] First, the party opposing discovery must show that the information sought is a 'trade secret or other confidential research, development, or commercial information' and that disclosure would be harmful. Then the burden shifts to the party seeking discovery to show that the information is relevant and necessary to bring the matter to trial. If both parties satisfy their burden, the court must weigh the potential harm of disclosure against the need for the information in reaching a decision."

Case Questions

1. If Bridgestone's formula for the tire were already known to its competitors, would they have been able to protect it from discovery? Why or why not?

2. Under what circumstances would potential harm of disclosure outweigh the need for the information in a trial using the three-part test?

Pretrial Conference

Several weeks before a trial, the parties will typically attend a **pretrial conference** with the judge. The conference is generally held between the attorneys for the parties and the judge in the case and no court reporter is present. The purpose of the conference is to accomplish two primary objectives. The primary reason is to encourage _settlement_. A judge can often give a neutral face value view of the case and facilitate some negotiations between the two sides or eliminate any obstacles that have blocked negotiations such as one party's refusal to discuss settlement. Second, the court will resolve any outstanding motions, confirm that discovery is proceeding smoothly, and dispose of any procedural issues that arose during the pleadings or discovery stages.

Trial

If the case cannot be settled, the parties will eventually go to **trial.** The trial generally takes place in front of a judge as the _finder of law_ and with a jury as a _finder of fact._ As the finder of law, the judge determines such important rulings as what evidence will be admitted, what witnesses may testify, what the jury will hear and not hear, and even what

Attorneys first present their theory of the case to the jury during opening statements.

legal arguments the attorneys may present to the jury. Juries, as a finder of fact, determine whose version of the facts is more believable by examining the evidence and listening to the testimony of witnesses. In some cases, the judge will act as both the finder of fact and the finder of law at the same time. This is known as a **bench trial.**

Jury Selection and Opening   The actual trial begins with **jury selection.** This is the process of asking potential jurors questions to reveal any prejudices that may affect their judgment of the facts. The questioning process is known as *voir dire.*[3] For a criminal trial, voir dire can be extensive and last for days or even weeks depending on the case. However, in civil litigation the voir dire process is not as extensive and the jury will be seated (selected) in relatively short order. After the jury is selected, the attorneys present their theory of the case and what they hope to prove to the jury in **opening statements.**

Testimony and Submission of Evidence   After the opening statement, the plaintiff's attorney then asks questions, known as **direct examination,** of the witnesses on the plaintiff's list. The defendant's attorney may then conduct **cross-examination** of the witness. The cross-examination is composed of questions limited to issues that were brought out on direct examination. The same process is repeated for the defendant's witnesses. Each side also uses its witnesses to introduce relevant evidence. Witnesses may be called upon to authenticate documents, to verify physical evidence, or to provide expert testimony accompanied by charts or graphs shown to the jury.

Closing Arguments and Charging the Jury   Once the testimony is completed and the evidence has been submitted to the jury, the attorneys sum up the case and try to convince the jury that their version of the case is more compelling. This is known as a **closing argument.** The judge then proceeds with the **charging of the jury,** by giving them instructions on how

Legal Speak ›))
Preponderance of the evidence A standard used to decide a civil case whereby the jury is to favor one party when the evidence is of greater weight and more convincing than the evidence that is offered in opposition to it (i.e., more likely than not). It is a substantially lower standard of proof than that used in a criminal case.[4]

---

[3]Pronounced vwar deer, this is a permutation of a Latin word and a French word meaning "to speak the truth."

[4]The standard used in a criminal case is "beyond a reasonable doubt," and is discussed in detail in Chapter 22, "Criminal Law and Procedure in a Business Context."

to work through the process of coming to a factual decision in the case. The judge will also inform the jury that the standard of proof in a civil case is a **preponderance of the evidence.**

Deliberations and Verdict   After receiving the charge, jurors move to a private room and engage in **deliberations.** Although the jury is permitted to send questions to the judge or make other requests (such as a request to reexamine evidence), the jurors are alone in their deliberations and the jury returns a decision known as the **verdict.** If, however, the jury cannot agree on a verdict, this is known as a **hung jury** and the litigants must start the process all over again with a new jury. Rules in state courts for civil litigation frequently do not require a unanimous verdict, so hung juries are rare in a commercial dispute.

Posttrial Motions and Appeals   As discussed earlier in this section, there may be post-trial motions in which the losing party tries to convince the original judge that the verdict was flawed. Finally, the losing party may appeal to a higher court. Appellate courts engage in judicial review to decide whether any errors were committed during the trial and also have the power to *reverse* or *modify* the decisions of trial courts.

Collecting the Judgment   Although the prevailing party may have received a court judgment stating what she is entitled to recover from the defendant, collecting judgments may sometimes be difficult, especially if the defendant's assets are tied up in nonliquid forms such as real estate, or are exempt from claims of creditors through a bankruptcy filing. However, the law does afford the prevailing party some tools to collect the judgment. For example, some states allow a judgment to be collected through the garnishment of wages whereby the defendant's employer is ordered by the court to pay part of the defendant's wages directly to the holder of the judgment. The holder of a judgment also becomes a creditor (typically called a *judgment creditor*) and has the right to pursue the defendant's assets to satisfy the debt owed. Rights and regulation of creditors and debtors are discussed in detail in Chapter 20 "Creditors' Rights and Bankruptcy."

CONCEPT SUMMARY   Stages of Litigation

Prelawsuit: Demand and Prelitigation Settlement Negotiations
  Standing

Pleadings Stage
  Complaint and Summons
  Answer
  Counterclaim
  Cross-Claim

Motions

Discovery Stage
  Methods of Discovery

Pretrial Conference

Trial
  Jury Selection and Opening
  Testimony and Submission of Evidence
  Closing Arguments and Charging the Jury
  Deliberations and Verdict
  Posttrial Motions and Appeals
  Collecting the Judgment

Ethical Issues Involved in Abusive Litigation

While commercial litigation typically involves two parties attempting to resolve a legitimate dispute in good faith, the costs, burdens, and uncontrollable risks of litigation render it subject to potential abuse. Although federal and state courts have strict procedural rules intended to curb abusive litigation, it is sometimes difficult to enforce those rules because of the inherent vagueness in defining what constitutes abusive. Abusive litigation may be defined as *vexatious* litigation or abuse of the litigation *process*.

Vexatious litigation may be defined as lawsuits that are filed for reasons other than legitimate damages being suffered by the plaintiff. These illegitimate reasons include using a lawsuit to harass, annoy, intimidate, or cause the opposite party to expend unnecessary costs. Reread the *Alston v. Advance Brands and Importing Company* case featured earlier in this chapter (Case 4.1), and as you read consider the plight of the alcoholic beverage manufacturers in facing this lawsuit. The parents in Alston's group were members of a consumer advocacy group with the objective of curbing underage alcohol consumption. The plaintiffs' theory and proposed remedy was so speculative that it could conceivably fall within the vexatious category.

In the next chapter, the topics of business ethics and corporate social responsibility are covered in detail. For the moment, one need simply understand that a working definition of business ethics is a *consciousness* or awareness of what is right or wrong in the workplace and taking responsibility for an ethical course of action given its impact on the business and its constituents. Given that definition, consider the following ethical dilemmas in the *Alston* case:

1. Once they were threatened with a lawsuit, what ethical obligation did the management of Advance Brands have to its stockholders?* Should they have settled the case for a small sum to avoid legal costs even if they were convinced the suit had no merit?

2. Does Advance have an ethical obligation to the community and public? Would that duty include fighting vexatious litigation to prevent future abuses of the legal system?

3. Does management's ethical duty to stockholders to settle this case for minimal costs override any ethical duty owed to the community?

4. Are there any circumstances under which a business could ethically use litigation as a legitimate business strategy?

Abuse of the litigation process occurs when, after the lawsuit is filed, one party engages in a course of conduct that is contrary to the good faith requirements underlying all litigation. Destruction of documents, refusing to hand over evidence during discovery, stalling, and overly broad discovery requests can all be categorized as abuse of the process.

5. Suppose you were a manager that was ordered by your senior manager to shred certain documents. Do you have an ethical obligation to find out if those documents may be relevant to threatened or pending litigation?

6. Assume that in Question 5 above, you had knowledge that litigation was pending and that the document may be relevant to the case. How does that affect your analysis?

*A stockholder (also called *shareholder*) has a legal ownership interest in the company based on the amount of stock owned.

LO4-5 ALTERNATIVE DISPUTE RESOLUTION

Alternative Dispute Resolution (ADR) is the process (usually in a private setting) by which disputes involving individuals or businesses are resolved outside of the federal or state court system through the help of third parties. According to the American Arbitration Association, an increasing number of businesses and individuals have turned to ADR and use of certain forms of alternative dispute resolution methods has increased between 20 percent and 31 percent each year for the past five years.

Recall the Classic Retail Outlets' (CRO) hypothetical dispute with SignCo. from the beginning of this chapter. In that example, several forms of informal and formal dispute resolution offered benefits to CRO and SignCo. If CRO decides to file a lawsuit, the company's management has committed to significant expenditure in terms of legal fees and expenses of litigation. Equally as important, CRO assumes several risks, including (1) they may lose at trial, or (2) even if they prevail, they will pay more in overall costs than CRO was awarded or could collect from SignCo. Moreover, any litigation process will result in a dissolution of the business relationship between CRO and SignCo. Aside from those costs, time is wasted that could be spent on more productive activities such as securing new business or executing existing business. Some of the potential advantages of ADR over litigation are:

- *Costs:* ADR could potentially cost a fraction of the normal legal costs. Depending on the location of the trial, trial attorneys may charge anywhere between $200 per hour (in smaller markets) to as much as $1,000 per hour in, for example, New York City. Although some of the more mundane work in litigation may be done by non-lawyer professionals (such as legal assistants or paralegals) at lower rates, the legal fees accumulate quickly once a lawsuit is commenced and accelerate once discovery begins.

- *Preserving the business relationship:* Litigation is, by its nature, adversarial. Allegations and defenses may turn antagonistic and result in termination of any business relationship. ADR, particularly informal ADR (discussed next), is focused on preserving the business relationship as part of the dispute resolution process. Business owners and managers work carefully to build alliances among vendors, suppliers, retailers, advertisers, and many other businesses that add value. ADR can help preserve alliances and avoid unnecessary antagonism over a dispute.

- *Time:* The time spent in ADR is a small percentage of the normal two to three year (or more) period normally associated with discovery, a civil jury trial, and possible appeal.

- *Expertise:* In some cases the parties may choose their own party to help resolve the dispute and this party may be an expert in the industry in question. When a case is before a jury, there is an uncontrollable risk that the jury may have a difficult time grasping the details of a complex case.

- *Privacy:* ADR may be held in private with no public record required. This ensures that any confidential business information is not at risk of accidental disclosure in the public eye (including competitors) of the court system. The privacy factor is also helpful in avoiding any unwanted publicity in the matter.

Informal ADR

Informal ADR often involves the parties negotiating face to face or through intermediaries to arrive at a mutually agreeable solution without the use of a formal process. It can take the form of (1) a *settlement agreement* whereby one party agrees to a payment in exchange for the other party's promise not to sue, or (2) an agreement to cancel a contract or to revise an existing contract to better reflect the parties' obligations and needs.

Formal ADR

The most common formal ADR techniques are: *arbitration, mediation, expert evaluation,* or some hybrid of those methods. Although sometimes state or federal courts will require mediation and/or nonbinding arbitration prior to allowing certain civil lawsuits to go to trial, typically, in a business context, ADR is invoked either via *contract* (including a union contract) or by mutual agreement. In a contractual arrangement, the parties have entered into a contract that contains a clause requiring the parties to submit any disputes to a specific alternative dispute resolution process (usually arbitration or mediation). These ADR clauses are commonly contained in contracts relating to employment, sale of goods, brokerage agreements (such as a stockbroker or online trading account), financing, and licenses to use software. In a mutual agreement, the parties mutually and voluntarily agree to resolve their dispute via alternative dispute resolution procedures.

When the agreement is by contract, sometimes the parties argue that the clause is not valid because it is too burdensome on one of the parties. In Case 4.3, which has been cited by a variety of federal and state courts, a New York appellate court considers the enforceability of a contractual clause requiring the parties to submit to alternative dispute resolution.

Legal Speak ⟩⟩
Breach of warranty Legal violation that occurs when a product fails to perform as promised by the seller.

CASE 4.3   Brower v. Gateway 2000, Inc., 246 A.2d 246 (N.Y. App. Div. 1998)

FACT SUMMARY Brower purchased a computer from Gateway 2000 through a retail outlet. The computer box contained appropriate manuals and a document titled "Standard Terms and Conditions Agreement," which provided that the terms and conditions in the agreement would become binding if the consumer retained the computer for 30 days. Brower retained the product for more than 30 days. The Gateway agreement contained an arbitration clause mandating that any disputes arising out of the purchase be arbitrated before the International Chamber of Commerce (ICC). The ICC is situated in Europe and its procedures require arbitration parties to pay an advance fee of $4,000, of which $2,000 is nonrefundable regardless of which party prevails.

Brower filed suit against Gateway alleging breach of warranty. Gateway sought to have the suit dismissed from the court and to compel ICC arbitration in accordance with the terms of the Gateway agreement. Brower argued that the arbitration clause was unenforceable because, among other reasons, the ICC rules were too burdensome on the parties and prevented them from protecting their rights

SYNOPSIS OF DECISION AND OPINION The New York Appellate Division court ruled in favor of Brower and held that the arbitration clause was invalid. The court reasoned that the ICC rules unreasonably favored Gateway and posed a substantial burden on the consumer. Citing an example of this unreasonable burden,

the court pointed to the ICC's rules that mandate any party seeking to arbitrate a dispute under $50,000 must deposit a $4,000 fee as a prerequisite to filing a dispute, and that 50 percent of that fee is nonrefundable even if the consumer prevailed. Because most of Gateway's products sold for less than $2,000, this clause could be used by Gateway to extinguish virtually every warranty claim that arose and halted consumers from asserting their legal rights.

WORDS OF THE COURT: Unreasonably Burdensome Arbitration Clauses "We do find [. . .] that the excessive cost factor that is necessarily entailed in arbitrating before the ICC is unreasonable and surely serves to deter the individual consumer from invoking the process. Barred from resorting to the courts by the arbitration clause in the first instance, the designation of a financially prohibitive forum effectively bars consumers from this forum as well; consumers are thus left with no forum at all in which to resolve a dispute."

Case Questions

1. How would you rewrite Gateway's clause to be sure that it would be judged reasonable by the New York court?

2. In this case, Brower was the named plaintiff in a potential class action against Gateway. What are the practical implications of Gateway's loss in this case? If Gateway had prevailed, would that change the cost-benefit analysis involved in deciding whether to settle the case?

LO4-6 Arbitration

One of the most common forms of ADR is **arbitration.** During arbitration, an individual *arbitrator* (or group of arbitrators) conducts a hearing between the parties in the dispute. The hearing is similar to a court setting, but is less formal. Parties seeking arbitration typically apply for an arbitrator through an ADR agency. The largest provider in the United States is the American Arbitration Association (AAA). The AAA receives the application and first appoints a *tribunal administrator* who coordinates the case and prepares the parties by informing them of procedures and rules of arbitration. Next, an arbitrator who is mutually agreed upon by the parties is appointed to the case. The arbitrator functions much like a judge would in a standard trial, and in some states even has the power of subpoena (the ability to demand certain documents or witnesses). For arbitration cases, although an attorney is not required, parties in a business dispute often opt to be represented by counsel. An arbitration hearing resembles a trial in that there are opening statements, both parties present limited evidence and calls a predetermined number of witnesses, each party has the right of cross-examination, and both parties make closing arguments. At the beginning of the arbitration both parties agree to either binding or nonbinding arbitration. If binding, the arbitrator's decision is final unless both parties agree to have the case reopened.

Legally Mandated Arbitration   When the parties agree to arbitrate, this is known as a *private* arbitration. Additionally, most states and the federal judiciary have a requirement (either by statute or a court-imposed procedure) that certain civil lawsuits go through an arbitration hearing before the case proceeds to trial. In this type of arbitration, the arbitrators are typically attorneys from that jurisdiction who are fulfilling a duty to serve on an arbitration panel imposed by the professional rules that govern attorneys. Although the arbitration is nonbinding (the losing party has the right of automatic appeal to the

An arbitration panel is a common form of Alternative Dispute Resolution.

trial court), the idea is to encourage the parties to settle before trial. The key advantage of legally mandated arbitration is that each side is able to present the case to a neutral party and the arbitrator's decision can be used as a starting point for settlement negotiations.

Federal Arbitration Act   The Federal Arbitration Act[5] (FAA) is a statute in which Congress endorsed the use of arbitration as the preferred dispute resolution method in matters governed by federal law. Congress took this action because of incidents in which state and federal courts invalidated arbitration clauses or overturned arbitration awards. Courts would usually base their decision on the notion that an individual could not effectively pursue their legal rights in an arbitration forum. This hostile view of arbitration caused Congress to pass the FAA in order to make clear that arbitration was preferred over litigation as a method of dispute resolution so long as the parties agreed to an arbitration clause. Specifically, the FAA requires that "a written provision of [. . .] a contract evidencing a transaction involving commerce to settle by arbitration a controversy thereafter arising out of such a contract . . . shall be valid, irrevocable, and enforceable, save upon such grounds as exists at law . . . for the revocation of any contract."[6] However, it is also important to note that the FAA provides four grounds when courts may *set aside* the award of an arbitrator: (1) the arbitration involved some degree of corruption or fraud, (2) the arbitrator exhibited inappropriate bias, (3) the arbitrator committed some gross procedural error (such as refusing to hear relevant evidence) that prejudiced the rights of one party, and (4) the arbitrator exceeded her explicit powers or failed to use them to make an appropriate final award. Note that some states have passed similar proarbitration statutes that define additional rights and responsibilities of the parties.

LO4-7

Although the FAA does not spell out any specific procedure or format for the arbitration, it does provide a means for enforcing both arbitration agreements and the decisions of arbitrators through use of federal courts. In *Gilmer v. Interstate/Johnson Lane Corporation,*[7] the Supreme Court held that the FAA applied to arbitration clauses contained in employment contracts even when an employee brought suit against an employer for violating federal antidiscrimination laws.

In Case 4.4, the U.S. Supreme Court applied the FAA in the context of a lawsuit brought by a consumer alleging that a lending institution violated federal consumer disclosure law.

Mediation

Another common form of ADR is **mediation.** Mediation is becoming increasingly common as a cost-efficient form of dispute resolution primarily because mediation is relatively informal and does not require as much time or preparation as arbitration. A mediator is typically appointed in much the same manner as an arbitrator and, in fact, the American Arbitration Association provides mediation services as well. A mediator is often, but not required to be, an attorney that is specially trained in negotiations and dispute resolution, and is paid by a set hourly rate or fixed fee for a certain period of time (usually per day). The mediator's task is to listen to the grievances and the arguments of both sides and communicate each party's concerns to the other. The mediator defuses some of the

> **KEY** POINT
>
> The primary difference between arbitration and other methods of ADR is that it provides the parties with a decision on who prevails in the dispute and any monetary award.

---

[5]9 U.S.C. § 1–15.
[6]9 U.S.C. § 2.
[7]500 U.S. 20 (1991).

FACT SUMMARY Randolph financed the purchase of a mobile home through Green Tree Financial Corporation (Green Tree). The finance contract contained an arbitration clause whereby both parties waived any right to a trial and agreed to arbitrate any disputes, but the clause was silent on the location of the arbitration. Randolph, as lead plaintiff, filed a class action lawsuit against Green Tree in a federal district court alleging a violation of a federal statute that regulates consumer lending. Green Tree moved to have the matter dismissed based on the arbitration clause in the financing contract. Randolph sought to have the clause invalidated because it was too costly for Randolph to arbitrate and this effectively resulted in Randolph's rights under the federal consumer protection statutes being severely curtailed.

SYNOPSIS OF DECISION AND OPINION The U.S. Supreme Court ruled in favor of Green Tree, holding that the arbitration clause was valid. The Court reasoned that the Federal Arbitration Act's purpose was to favor the use of arbitration over litigation and that any party to an arbitration agreement that was resisting arbitration had the burden of proving that the claims at issue are not suitable for arbitration. The Court held that while high arbitration costs could *potentially*

preclude a consumer from exercising her rights under federal statutes and would thus be invalid, Randolph had not proved that such prohibitively expensive costs would be incurred in her case.

WORDS OF THE COURT: Purpose of the FAA "In considering whether [Randolph's] argument to arbitrate is unenforceable, we are mindful of the FAA's purpose 'to reverse the longstanding judicial hostility to arbitration agreements [. . .] and to place arbitration agreements upon the same footing as other contracts.' [W]e have recognized that federal statutory claims can be appropriately resolved through arbitration, and we have enforced agreements to arbitrate that involve such claims."

Case Questions

1. The Court held that Randolph's theory was viable, but she didn't prove it. What evidence could she have shown that would have bolstered her case?

2. Recall the Court's explanation of the purpose behind the FAA. Why do you suppose that the Court had traditionally been "hostile" to arbitration agreements to the extent where it would be necessary to pass legislation to reverse it?

---

antagonism between the two parties and focuses the parties on working toward a solution. Note, however, that in mediation no decision is rendered and if the parties do not reach an agreement, they must attempt to resolve their dispute using another method.

Mediation is sometimes required by statute or court procedure before bringing a dispute to trial. As with legally mandated arbitration, the goal of required mediation is to allow the parties the opportunity to settle the case. Because much of the antagonism that surrounds a legal dispute is dissipated by the mediator's efforts, the process can help parties to see the dispute in a more even-tempered fashion. The ultimate goal is to work toward a mutually satisfactory resolution.

Expert Evaluation

For parties involved in a business dispute where the issues are somewhat complex and related to the intricacies of a certain industry or profession, **expert evaluation** (neutral fact-finding) by an independent expert who recommends a settlement is an attractive alternative. The **expert evaluator** reviews documents and evidence provided by each party that gives a full description of the events and circumstances leading to the claim and the resulting loss. The evaluator follows up with questions and will sometimes take statements from witnesses if necessary. Drawing on her range of experience and expertise in the industry, the evaluator gives her opinion on the merits and value of the claim and recommends a settlement amount. The goal of this process is to facilitate a negotiated settlement without the expense and time of a trial or other methods of ADR.

Online Dispute Resolution

PROBLEM *In situations involving small amounts of money, is there a way for a business to resolve such relatively minor disputes in a cost-effective manner?*

A business may be engaged in hundreds of relatively low-cost transactions per year with various out-of-state vendors such as suppliers, shipping companies, office supply stores, contractors, and the like. When disputes arise, a business may be at a distinct disadvantage and bargaining position because the amount in controversy is too low to justify even the least expensive form of alternative dispute resolution. However, over an extended period of time these small losses add up to unnecessary liabilities leaving managers with a difficult choice when faced with a dispute over a relatively low amount of money with an out-of-state vendor: (1) invest in a dispute resolution method despite the fact that the costs may very well exceed the benefits in that particular dispute; or (2) allow the losses to accumulate and potentially seek favorable tax treatment for writing off bad debt.

SOLUTION *Attempt to use Online Dispute Resolution* (ODR).

Businesses are now capable of making small purchases from vendors across the globe and can do so quickly and conveniently. This renders traditional forms of ADR impracticable, given the reluctance to pay for an arbitrator or attorney and the fact that traveling to another location to settle a dispute often returns a sum less than the costs of travel. ODR has all of the advantages of traditional forms of ADR: The parties in question can avoid the expense and publicity of trial plus an agreement is usually reached much faster.

Online technology is ideal for low-cost transactional disputes such as a party seeking a refund for a defective product. Often these types of issues can be resolved using the technology alone. For example, blind-bidding sites like ClickandSettle.com and Cybersettle.com offer an automated service where parties individually enter the price they're willing to pay or receive. The software evaluates these numbers and then sends each party a fair price based on their initial demand.

Another form of ODR is more geared toward complex transactions. For example, Square Trade proposes prewritten resolutions. For example, if you received a damaged shipment of goods, Square Trade offers a standard menu of solutions such as (1) replacement with an undamaged good, (2) return for a full refund, or (3) keep the merchandise with a partial refund. The parties may also fill in their own solution, but this guided approach helps the parties focus on a resolution to the dispute.

If direct negotiation fails to resolve the issue, Square Trade users can request a mediator for a $20 fee per participant plus a percentage fee if the dispute exceeds $1,000. At OnlineResolution.com, mediation fees range between $15 and $25. For disputes of more than $500, participants each pay $50 per party per hour scaling up to $150 per party per hour, based on the value under dispute.

Option 1: Online Mediation. Online mediation is a logical first step to settling disputes. Like traditional forms of mediation, online mediation is generally nonbinding. Parties present their positions to a mediator who considers their arguments and attempts to negotiate a settlement. An advantage to online mediation is that dialogue is carried out via e-mail so participants can submit responses at their convenience and can think out their replies rather than engage in what may be an antagonistic live hearing.

Option 2: Online Arbitration. Online arbitration is similar to traditional arbitration, except that all communications take place using the Internet. The arbitrator convenes the arbitration via live Web cast and issues a decision based on the evidence presented. In an online setting, all communications, including the presentation of evidence, is supplied in electronic form: text, image, audio, or video. Participants in online arbitration agree in advance to abide by the arbitrator's decision, and that the award may be enforced by an appropriate court. Following completion of the online arbitration, each participant typically completes a brief evaluation of the arbitrator and the process.

LO4-9   Hybrid Form of ADR

In some cases, parties to a dispute want to have the opportunity to settle the case through mediation, but want some degree of certainty in the event that mediation fails. In those circumstances, parties may use a hybrid of mediation and arbitration. Sometimes known as **med-arb,** both parties first submit to mediation for a set period of time (perhaps two business days). If the mediation fails, the process then moves to binding arbitration. The goal is to reach an agreement with the least amount of formality possible. The hope is that the dispute can be settled during mediation, but since both parties are determined to conclude the matter, arbitration is available as an automatic fallback method should mediation fail.

CONCEPT SUMMARY   Alternative Dispute Resolution (ADR)

- The primary advantages of ADR are reductions in costs and time and preserving business relationships and privacy.
- ADR usually arises as a result of a contract between two parties that have agreed ahead of time to resolve any disputes using a certain ADR method such as arbitration.
- The primary methods of ADR are arbitration, mediation, expert evaluation, or some hybrid of those three methods.
- In arbitration, the parties submit their dispute to one or more arbitrators, present evidence and limited witness testimony, and then a decision is made.
- Mediation is the attempt by a trained third party to bring the parties to an agreement on the dispute by proposing possible solutions.
- The primary difference between arbitration and other methods of ADR is that arbitration provides the parties with a decision.
- Online dispute resolution is an attractive alternative for resolving disputes where the amount in controversy is relatively low.

KEY TERMS

Civil litigation p. 78   The term used to describe a dispute resolution process where the parties and their counsel argue their view of a civil controversy in a court of law.

Standing p. 79   Requirement for any party to maintain a lawsuit against another party, necessitating that the party asserting the claim must have suffered an injury in fact and that harm must be direct, concrete, and individualized.

Complaint p. 80   The first formal document filed with the local clerk of courts when the plaintiff initiates a lawsuit claiming legal rights against another.

Summons p. 80   Formal notification to the defendant that she has been named in the lawsuit and informs her that an answer must be filed within a certain period of time.

Answer p. 81   Defendant's formal response to each paragraph of the complaint.

Counterclaim p. 81   Filed when the defendant believes that the plaintiff has caused her damages arising out of the very same set of facts as articulated in the complaint.

Cross-claim p. 84   Filed when the defendant believes that a third party is either partially or fully liable for the damages that the plaintiff has suffered and, therefore, should be involved as an indispensable party in the trial.

Motions p. 84 A request by one party to the court asking it to issue a certain order (such as a "motion for summary judgment"). Motions may be made by either party before, during, and after the trial.

Discovery p. 84 Process for the orderly exchange of information and evidence between the parties involved in litigation (or in some cases arbitration) prior to trial.

Depositions p. 84 Method of discovery where a witness gives sworn testimony to provide evidence prior to trial.

Interrogatories p. 84 Method of discovery where one party submits written questions to the opposing party attempting to gather evidence prior to trial.

Requests for production p. 84 Requests aimed at producing specific items to help one party discover some important fact in the case.

Request for admissions p. 85 A set of statements sent from one litigant to an adversary, for the purpose of determining what facts are in dispute and which facts both parties accept as true.

Pretrial conference p. 86 A meeting between the attorneys for the parties and the judge in the case several weeks prior to trial, with the objectives of encouraging settlement and resolving any outstanding motions or procedural issues that arose during the pleadings or discovery stages.

Trial p. 86 Stage of litigation occurring when the case cannot be settled, generally taking place in front of a judge as the finder of law and with a jury as a finder of fact.

Bench trial p. 87 Trial without a jury where the judge is both the finder of law and the finder of fact.

Jury selection p. 87 The process of asking potential jurors questions to reveal any prejudices that may affect their judgment of the facts.

Opening statements p. 87 Attorneys' presentation of their theory of the case and what they hope to prove to the jury at the onset of the trial.

Direct examination p. 88 The first questioning of a witness during a trial in which the plaintiff's attorney first asks questions of the witnesses on the plaintiff's list.

Cross-examination p. 88 The opportunity for the attorney to ask questions in court, limited to issues that were brought out on direct examination, of a witness who has testified in a trial on behalf of the opposing party.

Closing arguments p. 88 Attorneys' summation of the case with the objective of convincing the jury of what theory to decide the case upon, occurring after testimony is completed and evidence has been submitted.

Charging of the jury p. 88 Instructions given from judge to the jury on how to work through the process of coming to a factual decision in the case.

Preponderance of the evidence p. 89 A standard used to decide a civil case whereby the jury is to favor one party when the evidence is of greater weight and more convincing than the evidence that is offered in opposition to it.

Deliberations p. 88 The process in which a jury in a trial discusses in private the findings of the court and decides by vote with which argument of either opposing side to agree.

Verdict p. 88 The final decision of a jury in a case.

Hung jury p. 88 Term used to describe a jury that cannot come to a consensus decision on which party should prevail in a case.

Arbitration p. 92 Method of alternative dispute resolution where the parties present their side of the dispute to one or more neutral parties who then render a decision. Arbitration often involves a set of rules designed to move from dispute to decision quickly.

Mediation p. 93 Method of alternative dispute resolution where a mediator attempts to settle a dispute by learning the facts of a dispute and then negotiating a settlement between two adverse parties.

Expert evaluation p. 94 Method of alternative dispute resolution where an independent expert acts as the neutral fact-finder; particularly useful for parties involved in a business dispute where the issues are somewhat complex and related to the intricacies of a certain industry or profession.

Expert evaluator p. 94 The neutral fact-finder in expert evaluation who reviews documents and evidence provided by each party and draws on her range of experience and expertise in the industry to offer an opinion on the merits and value of the claim and recommend a settlement amount.

Med-arb p. 96 Method of alternative dispute resolution whereby the parties begin with mediation and if mediation fails in a fixed time period, the parties agree to submit to arbitration.

Medical Instruments Inc. (MII) required a larger warehouse for its facilities. MII located a 10,000 square foot building in New Hampshire and signed a lease with Commercial Properties (CP) for one year with a right to renew for five, one-year terms upon 60 days notice. After the first renewal, CP sent back a new lease with substantially the same terms, except that the new lease had a mandatory arbitration clause that requires any tenant to go through arbitration in CP's home state of California. MII signed the lease without objection. One month after they took occupancy, MII complained that a leak in the warehouse roof was allowing water to drip into a corner of the warehouse and that MII had to move its hardware equipment out of the warehouse to protect it from water damage. CP did not fix the leak until one month later, and MII suffered losses because their hardware was partially destroyed by the leak and additional out-of-pocket losses related to expenses of having the equipment moved to another location.

1. If MII sues CP in a state trial court for the losses it incurred, what would CP's likely defense be?

2. Discuss the significance of the fact that the original lease did not have an arbitration clause, but the new one did. Also, is it significant that the place of arbitration would require MII to travel to California? Do these facts give a court any reason to invalidate the arbitration clause?

3. What cases that you studied in this chapter help to support your arguments in Question 2.

4. Assume that *no* arbitration clause existed in the new lease. What would be MII's options to pursue damages if CP refused to compensate MII for the losses it incurred?

5. Assume that MII files a lawsuit against CP. As part of their case, they wish to show that CP had notice of the leak and failed to fix it for one month. What methods of discovery would be useful to obtain this information from CP?

6. Suppose that CP refused to turn over all phone records and repair request forms to MII based on the fact that the information is confidential and cannot be disclosed in litigation. What standard will a court use to judge whether the information is a trade secret and therefore not subject to disclosure? What case supports your answer?

Managers are sometimes the first line of opportunity in resolving a dispute before it turns into litigation. Assume that you are an MII manager in charge of the property in New Hampshire described in Theory to Practice above. Write a two- to three-page memorandum to your senior manager that describes the relative advantages of ADR over litigation in the MII–CP dispute. Using Table 4.1, make suggestions on how this particular dispute may be resolved.

A sample answer may be found on this textbook's Web site at www.mhhe.com/melvin.

ARBITRATION PROVISION IN CONTRACT

Doctor's Associates Inc. (DAI), the national franchisor for Subway sandwich shops, entered into a franchise contract with Casarotto to open a Subway shop in Great Falls, Montana. Although the franchise was not in Casarotto's preferred location, he agreed to open the shop in a less desirable location based on a verbal agreement that if his preferred location became available he would have the exclusive rights to that location. Subsequently the location became available but DAI awarded it to another franchisee. Casarotto claimed his business was irreparably harmed and as a result withheld his franchise fee from DAI. The contract executed between Casarotto and DAI did not indicate on the first page that the contract was subject to arbitration.

However, page nine of the agreement contained an arbitration clause using American Arbitration Association rules at a hearing to be held in Bridgeport, Connecticut, the cost of which is to be born equally by both parties. Casarotto filed suit in a Montana court against DAI for breach of contract. DAI moved to have the case dismissed and moved to arbitration.

CASE QUESTIONS

1. Is the arbitration provision enforceable? Why or why not?
2. Suppose Montana state law required that an arbitration provision be underlined in the text of the contract and also noted on the first page of the contract. In such instances, would the arbitration provision still be enforceable? Why or why not?

REQUEST FOR PRODUCTION

Chang was terminated from his employment at Infinite Energy, Inc., for allegedly leaking confidential information to competitors. Litigation ensued and during discovery Infinite requested access to all of Chang's e-mail accounts. Although Chang turned over e-mails from his work account, he refused to turn over e-mails from his private account with Yahoo! Infinite claimed that the e-mails were essential to their case, and Chang contended that the e-mails were confidential and unrelated to his employment and, therefore, not within the scope of discovery.

CASE QUESTIONS

1. Who prevails and why?
2. Is this information necessary for Infinite's case? Why or why not?

ARBITRATION CLAUSES AND PUBLIC POLICY

After the Exxon *Valdez* disaster, Exxon implemented a strict policy of testing its employees who served on tankers for drug and alcohol use and allowed a manager to immediately discharge any employee who was intoxicated at the time of their duty aboard the ship. Fris was an employee who boarded the ship while intoxicated and was discharged when his manager determined that he was unfit for work. However, Fris's union contract allowed him to appeal the discharge through an arbitration procedure. The arbitration panel ordered Fris reinstated and Exxon filed suit in a federal court to have the arbitration set aside on the basis that the arbitration order violated public policy and subjected Exxon to liability in the event Fris may act negligently while intoxicated. The Union argued that the court should give deference to the arbitration system articulated in the union contract.

CASE QUESTION

1. Who prevails and why?

ADR IN CONSUMER CONTRACTS

Leroy purchased a used car from AutoNation, a used-car dealer chain. All buyers entered into a purchase agreement and those who financed their vehicles through AutoNation also signed a retail installment contract. The purchase agreement included an arbitration agreement, but the retail installment contract did not. Leroy alleged that he and all other customers that signed installment contracts were overcharged as a result of a computer error committed by AutoNation. He filed a motion in a trial court to have his lawsuit certified as a class action. Although AutoNation argued that the arbitration clause in the purchase agreement controlled the case, the trial court certified the class action ruling that because the installment contract had no arbitration agreement, the plaintiffs were free to pursue their remedy in court.

CASE QUESTION

1. Did the trial court rule correctly? Explain.

Self-Check **ANSWERS**

Discovery Techniques

1. Request for production
2. Request for admissions
3. Deposition
4. Interrogatories

5

CHAPTER

Business, Societal, and Ethical Contexts of Law

learning outcomes checklist

After studying this chapter, students who have mastered the material will be able to:

5-1 Articulate a working definition of business ethics.

5-2 Differentiate between primary and secondary stakeholders.

5-3 Categorize alternate approaches to ethical decision making based on different theories of moral philosophy.

5-4 Identify the challenges to business ethics management and articulate a response to each challenge.

5-5 Define values management and articulate several reasons why values management is important in business operations.

5-6 List the common traits of an ethical organization.

5-7 Demonstrate an understanding of how to develop a code of ethics and conduct.

5-8 Employ an ethical decision-making paradigm used by managers for resolving ethical dilemmas.

5-9 Give examples of ethical lapses using historical case studies of businesses facing ethical dilemmas.

5-10 Articulate the various views on corporate social responsibility and defend a particular view.

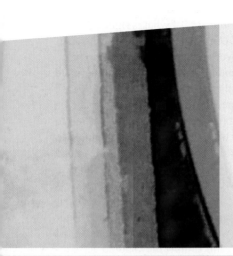

Although the law provides one set of guideposts for business operations, a concurrent set of guideposts, business ethics and principles of corporate social responsibility are equally important to business owners and managers. While some critics argue that business ethics is a recent phenomenon meant simply to fill popular and management literature, one need not look too far back in economic history to discover instances of when breaches in ethical behavior (whether legal or not) have resulted in direct harm to business owners, investors, employees, customers, and wider constituencies such as the community.[1] In this chapter, students will learn:

- The definition of business ethics, systems of ethical reasoning, and goals of values management.

- Ethical decision making in the business environment.

- Fundamentals of corporate social responsibility.

---

[1]Business ethics actually has an ancient history, including commentary by Cicero in *On Duties*.

LO5-1 BUSINESS ETHICS DEFINED

A useful working definition of business ethics is a *consciousness* of what is right or wrong in the workplace and taking responsibility for an ethical course of action in business operations given its impact on its owners, investors, employees, customers, and the community at large (collectively known as *stakeholders*). Attention to business ethics is critical during times of fundamental change such as the financial crisis that began in late 2008. In such volatile times, unethical and/or illegal practices are often highlighted as the media and public become aware of the internal strife within preeminent companies that led to their near or total collapse. Some of the practices that were deemed to be acceptable in various areas of the financial services and corporate sectors are now deemed dubious and even immoral. Practices that were sanctioned as ethical, such as corporate jets, bonuses, and corporate sponsorship of stadiums and events, have become a symbol of reckless corporate spending. Consequently, companies that fail to be committed to managing business ethics as part of their business model have no clear moral compass to guide leaders through complex dilemmas about what is right or wrong. Attention to ethics in the workplace sensitizes business owners and managers in terms of how they should act. Perhaps most important, attention to ethics in the workplace helps ensure that when leaders and managers are struggling in times of crises and confusion, they retain a strong moral compass. Attention to business ethics provides numerous other business and community benefits as well. Ethics is also a useful tool for managers in preventing legal liability for the company.

LO5-2 Primary and Secondary Stakeholders

Business ethics embraces a broader constituency than just its owners and managers. In their planning and operations, many business entities have replaced the word *stockholder* with *stakeholder.* **Stakeholder** is an expansive term that includes a business entity's owners, investors, employees, customers, suppliers, and the wider community. In planning and decision making, many companies now consider both *primary stakeholders* and *secondary stakeholders*. Although various commentators have given a wide variety of definitions for stakeholders, primary stakeholders are generally those who will feel a direct impact based on the decision. Secondary stakeholders are those without any direct connection to the business, but may suffer some adverse consequences in an indirect way. For example, suppose that AirCo. is a manufacturer of private and commercial aircraft. AirCo.'s management is under pressure to cut costs due to a decreased demand for aircraft. In considering how to best cut costs, AirCo. considers demolishing one of its older plants in the hypothetical city of Urbanville. If AirCo. embraces the notion of considering its stakeholders, it will include an analysis not only of the impact on primary stakeholders (such as investors, owners, and employees of the company) but also on secondary stakeholders such as Urbanville merchants who depend on business generated from employees at AirCo.'s plant or Urbanville residents that live near the plant who may be affected by the safety or environmental impact of the demolition. Business ethicists also identify certain *key stakeholders* who can significantly influence a project (such as a manager). Primary and secondary stakeholders are also an important part of the social responsibility of a corporation, which is discussed in more detail later in this chapter.

Ethical Culture in Which Managers Operate

Managerial misconduct includes illegal, unethical, or questionable practices of individual managers or organizations. There has been a great deal written about managerial misconduct, yet certain attitudes and myths about creating an ethical culture in the workplace still remain. Inevitably, some managers believe that business ethics is merely a matter of preaching the basics of what is right and wrong. More often though, business ethics is a matter of dealing with dilemmas that have no clear indication of what is right or wrong. That is, ethical decision making often involves resolution of moral mazes. Managers are frequently faced with such mazes when dealing with potential conflicts of interest, wrongful use of resources, or mismanagement of assets, contracts, and agreements.

Moral Philosophy and Ethical Decision Making **LO**5-3

Certain moral philosophies may influence moral judgments such as one's assessment of whether a given situation is viewed as ethical or unethical. This assessment, in turn, then dictates one's reaction and subsequent behavior when confronted with an ethical dilemma. **Morals** refer to generally accepted *standards* of right and wrong in a given society. These standards may be based on the law and/or religious and personal belief systems. **Ethics** is the term used to describe having a *conscious system* in use for deciding moral dilemmas. Individual approaches to thinking ethically may be based on several broad sources of ethical standards that stem from certain historical theories of morality. Although a close examination of moral philosophy is outside the scope of this textbook, it is important to understand two major approaches and how they apply in a business context.

Principles-Based Approach

Ethical decisions that are made according to a set of established principles or standards such as religious tenets or codes such as the Koran (Islamic canonical law) or the Old Testament (Judeo-Christian tradition) employ a principles-based approach. These religious-based principles are the source of individual decision making and not subject to exceptions, but are tempered by other religious principles such as mercy and justice.

In addition to religious-based principles, some philosophers and ethicists also use the notion that humans have certain *inherent* moral rights that spring from their ability to reason and choose freely what they do with their lives. Famed Prussian-born philosopher Immanuel Kant's (1724–1804) work on a form of principle-based ethics, which he called *duty-based* ethics in his famous essays *Critique of Practical Reason,* is based on an inherent notion that humans act in accordance with and from a sense of duty to human dignity. Kant theorized that rights imply *duties* and the duty to respect other's rights was paramount in acting morally.

The notion of *categorical imperatives* is a central theme in Kant's work. This school of thought is centered on the belief that ethical dilemmas must be resolved through a categorical imperative test whereby individuals make ethical decisions with an eye toward the potential consequences if everyone in society acted the same way. In other words, when considering how to prevent people from acting in a certain way, the question posed is "What if everybody took those same actions?" This question is sometimes called a *universalization* test. If one can consistently act in accordance with the notion that society benefits from everyone acting the same way, then the action is moral.

Consequences-Based Approach

This approach emphasizes that the ethical course of action is the one that provides the most good (happiness) for the greatest number of people, and has the least harmful consequences for the majority of the community. The approach stems from the **utilitarian** stream of moral philosophy[2] and method for evaluating ethical dilemmas. Under this model, an action is ethically sound if it produces positive results for the most people. Simply put, the course of action that results in the most benefits for the most individuals is the most ethical. If the action impacts the majority of community members in a negative way, it is inherently unethical. Critics of utilitarianism argue that it amounts to using a mathematical formula to decide how decisions impact individuals. Business owners and managers that employ a consequences-based approach

---

[2]The founder of utilitarianism is the famous 18th-century philosopher Jeremy Bentham.

seek to produce the greatest balance of good over harm for all who are affected including owners, employees, customers, investors, and the community at large.

Business ethics is concerned chiefly with ethics and morality that will help the company grapple with moral issues confronting the business. For example, suppose that a manager is charged with cutting personnel costs by 10 percent. The two logical choices are: Option 1, reduce the workforce by 10 percent; or Option 2, reduce the wages for the entire workforce by 10 percent.

A principles-based approach may result in a conclusion that Option 2 is most ethical because, although all of employees will suffer some pay cut, no employees will have the severe impact of losing a job. If the manager concludes that the categorical imperative is that everyone keep his or her job, but with a slight reduction in pay, then Option 2 is most consistent with an ethical moral decision. A consequences-based approach (utilitarianism) may conclude that Option 1 is most ethical because, while 10 percent of people would lose their job, the majority would not lose their job nor have their pay cut back. The utilitarian-based standard requires that the majority good be placed ahead of the individual good when faced with a moral dilemma.

LO5-4 VALUES MANAGEMENT AND CHALLENGES TO BUSINESS ETHICS

Business ethics in the workplace context emphasizes prioritizing moral values for the organization and ensuring behaviors are aligned with those values. This is known as **values management.** Yet despite evidence that embracing business ethics promotes profitability and contributes to sound public policy, a resistance to values management programs exists in some business cultures. Some of the resistance arises from challenges based on general confusion about the notion of ethics. Other challenges arise from narrow or simplistic views of ethical dilemmas. Table 5.1 lists common challenges and appropriate responses to business ethics and values management.

LO5-5 STRATEGIC ADVANTAGES OF VALUES MANAGEMENT

Managing ethics in the workplace involves identifying and prioritizing values to guide behaviors in the organization, and establishing associated policies and procedures to ensure those behaviors are conducted. Values management is also crucial in other management practices such as managing a diverse workforce, total quality management, and strategic planning.

This means that values management has strategic importance on par with other types of managerial systems. There are both business and public policy benefits to values management. Managing values in the workplace legitimizes managerial actions, strengthens the coherence and balance of the organization's culture, improves trust in relationships between individuals and groups, supports greater consistency in standards and qualities of products, and cultivates greater sensitivity to the impact of the enterprise's values and messages. Indeed, companies that have embraced a values management system often report that it has strategic advantages.

Cultivation of Strong Teamwork and Productivity

Values management may help align employee behaviors with the top priority ethical values preferred by organization's top-level management. Sometimes an organization finds surprising disparity between its preferred values and the values actually reflected by behaviors in the workplace. Ongoing attention and dialogue regarding values in the workplace builds openness, integrity, and community, which are critical ingredients of strong teams in

TABLE 5.1 Challenges and Realities in Business Ethics

Challenge	Reality
Business ethics cannot be taught. It is religion and not management.	Altering people's values isn't the objective of an organizational ethics program. Managing values and *conflict* among them is the primary objective.
Business ethics is unnecessary because it asserts the obvious: act ethically.	The value of a code of ethics to an organization is its priority and focus with respect to certain ethical values in the company. Dishonesty takes a variety of forms. If an organization is confronting varying degrees of dishonesty (including more common examples such as office supply theft) or deceit in the workplace, a priority on honesty is very timely—and honesty should be listed in that organization's code of ethics.
Complying with the law is an organization's sole guide for ethical conduct.	While the law may operate as a baseline for ethical decision making, unethical acts may operate within the limits of the law (e.g., withholding information from superiors, casting revenue in favorable terms with a dubious basis for the projection, spreading rumors). Illegal conduct sometimes has its genesis in unethical behavior that has gone unnoticed.
Ethics can't be managed.	Management inherently incorporates a value system. Strategic priorities (profit maximization, expanding market share, cutting costs, etc.) can be very strong influences on ethical decision making. Workplace regulations and rules directly influence behaviors in a manner that improves the general good and/or minimizes potential harm to stakeholders.
Business ethics is a philosophical debate that has little to do with the day-to-day realities of running an organization.	Business ethics is a management discipline with a programmatic approach that includes several practical tools. Ethics management programs have practical applications in other areas of management as well.

the workplace. Employees who feel strong alignment between their values and those of the organization tend to react with strong motivation and performance.

Clarity in Business Operations

Setting ethical standards gives an organization's employees context for executing business operations. This gives more clarity to strategic planning by identifying preferred values and ensuring organizational behaviors are aligned with those values. This effort includes identifying the values, developing written policies and procedures to align behaviors with preferred values, and then training all personnel about the policies and procedures. These standards can be the framework for performance, reliability, measurement, and feedback. Business ethicists promote the notion that management techniques are highly useful for managing strategic values, for example, expanding market share, reducing costs, and so forth. A comprehensive values management program may also be used in managing diversity (considering different values and perspectives among stakeholders).

Strong Public Image

Devoting consistent and serious attention to values management also allows a business organization to portray a strong positive image to the public. People see those organizations as valuing people more than profit and as striving to operate with the utmost integrity. Aligning behavior with values is critical to effective marketing and public relations programs.

Ongoing attention and dialogue on values management helps to cultivate teamwork and stimulates productivity.

Staying the Ethical Course in Turbulent Times

The financial crisis that began in 2008 is the most recent example of turbulent times in the corporate and financial sectors. Strong leadership in values management is critical during times of fundamental change. Continuing attention to ethics in the workplace sensitizes leaders and staff to how they want to act in a consistent manner.

> **KEY POINT**
> Values management should have strategic parity with other management priorities.

LO5-6, 5-7 COMMON TRAITS OF EFFECTIVE ETHICAL PROGRAMS IN BUSINESS

Typically, ethics programs convey corporate values, often using codes and policies to guide decisions and behavior, and can include extensive training and evaluation depending on the organizational structure. At a very minimum, ethics programs provide guidance in ethical dilemmas. Business ethicists have various views on how an ideal ethical organization operates, but there are certain common traits:

■ Management has articulated a clear vision of integrity throughout the organization.

■ Reward systems are aligned with the vision of integrity.

■ Responsibility is seen as individual rather than collective in that individuals are willing to assume personal responsibility for actions of the organization.

Developing Codes of Ethics and Conduct

PROBLEM *While many organizations have a set of informal values and standards to which they adhere, effectiveness can be limited if the values are not articulated in a fixed medium or if the code is a management directive rather than a product of the entire organization. Informal value systems may be too vague and not helpful in a practical context.*

SOLUTION *Develop a Code of Ethics and Conduct for your organization.*

These codes should be developed in cooperation with (and not exclusively by) the human resources manager and legal counsel. Codes are insufficient if intended *only* to ensure that policies are legal. The entire organization must see the ethics program being driven by top management and carried out by management and the workforce.

Depending on the organization, a Code of Ethics and Code of Conduct may be in the same writing. They are examined here separately.

For a Code of Ethics, consider the following guidelines:

- Review any values needed to adhere to relevant laws and regulations.
- Review which values produce the top three or four traits of a highly ethical and successful product or service in each area. For example, the chief financial officer may identify objectivity and accuracy as important values. Identify which values produce behaviors that exhibit these traits.
- Identify values needed to address current issues in your workplace. Consider which of these issues is ethical in nature, for example, issues in regard to respect, fairness, and honesty.
- Consider any top ethical values that might be important to primary and secondary stakeholders (expectations of employees, clients/customers,

suppliers, lenders, members of the local community).

Examples of ethical values may include:
- *Trustworthiness:* honesty, integrity, promise-keeping, loyalty.
- *Respect:* autonomy, privacy, dignity, courtesy, tolerance, acceptance.
- *Responsibility:* accountability, pursuit of excellence.
- *Caring:* compassion, consideration, giving, sharing, kindness.
- *Justice and fairness:* procedural fairness, impartiality, consistency, equity, equality, due process.
- *Civic virtue and citizenship:* law abiding, community service, protection of the environment.

Codes of conduct specify actions in the workplace and *codes of ethics* are general guides to decisions about those actions. An effective code of conduct contains examples of appropriate behavior. Examples of topics typically addressed by codes of conduct include: preferred style of dress, avoiding illegal drugs, following instructions of superiors, being reliable and prompt, maintaining confidentiality, not accepting personal gifts from third parties as a result of a company role or action, avoiding conflict of interest, complying with laws and regulations, not using organization's property for personal use, conducting business without discrimination, and reporting illegal or questionable activity. Managers should also think beyond these traditional legalistic expectations. It is important to identify what's ethically sensitive in your particular organization as well. Codes of conduct should be integrated into the various areas of the organization, including personnel matters such as job descriptions and performance appraisal forms, management-by-objectives expectations, standard forms, checklists, budget reports format, and other relevant control instruments to ensure conformance with the code of conduct.

- Policies and practices of the organization are aligned with the vision.
- The vision of integrity is well integrated into the decision-making process so that any significant management decision has ethical value dimensions.

As with any management practice, the most important outcome is behavior that is consistent with the organization's value system. The best of ethical values and intentions are relatively meaningless unless they generate fair and just behaviors in the workplace.

That's why practices that generate lists of ethical values, or codes of ethics, must also generate policies, procedures, and training that translate those values into appropriate behaviors.

LO5-8 ETHICAL DECISION MAKING: A MANAGER'S PARADIGM

It is not uncommon for business ethics to be portrayed as a matter of resolving conflicts in which one option appears to be the clear choice. Case studies that present situations where an employee is faced with whether or not to lie, steal, cheat, abuse another, break terms of a contract, and so on are too simplistic. Ethical dilemmas faced by managers are often complex, with no clear ethical choice. The use of a paradigm in the following flowchart (see Figure 5.1) can help business owners and managers apply ethical decision making more consistently.

FIGURE 5.1 Ethical Decision Making

1. Define the dilemma →
How and when did the dilemma occur?
What were the underlying reasons for the conflict?

2. Identify impact →
Which and in what way will primary and secondary stakeholders be affected?

3. Apply standards →
What is the legal impact of the dilemma?
What values and ethical principles has the organization set out for guidance?
What are the consequences of action or inaction?

4. Develop choices →
and discuss impact with various constituencies
Which choice results in the most benefit to stakeholders?
Will any of the choices result in harm to stakeholders?
What are the level and severity of the harms?
Which choice upholds the values of the organization?

5. Implement, evaluate, and monitor
How can this decision be implemented with greatest attention to all stakeholders?
Under what circumstances are you willing to make an exception to your decision?
How could this company avoid this dilemma in the future?

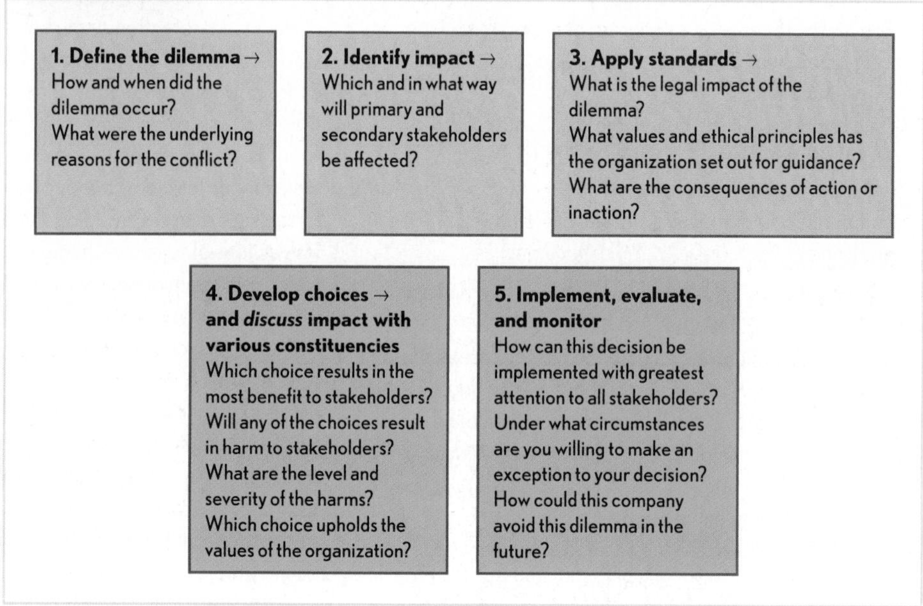

LO5-9 ETHICAL DECISION-MAKING CASE STUDIES

Business ethics cannot be studied in a vacuum. The principles and theories that are discussed in this chapter are only useful if they can be understood in a business context. Study these two well-known cases in some detail, and apply the concepts that have been covered thus far. Use the ethical decision-making flowchart in Figure 5.1 to assess and discuss the ethical challenges presented in the cases. Several questions for discussion are included at the end of each case study. The first case involves a company that touted a strong values statement, but that engaged in illegal and unethical conduct that caused direct harm to stakeholders. The second case involves a legally permissible transaction that poses several ethical dilemmas.

Enron, once a hundred billion dollar company, collapsed under the weight of ethical lapses by its management team who ignored their company's own values management policies.

The Enron Scandal

Of the high-profile corporate scandals that erupted at major public companies[3] in 2000 and 2001, Enron is perhaps the most notorious. The systematic looting of a corporation by its executives and the massive fraud and subsequent cover-ups that culminated in a public crash made Enron the symbol of corporate greed and arrogance. After a meteoric rise to the top, Enron's shareholders lost about $62 billion of value over a period of about two years. Employees, believing in Enron's vision and leadership, filled their retirement portfolios with Enron stock only to have their savings wiped out when the company sank into bankruptcy.

Enron's Business Model

Enron Corporation was a multinational conglomerate[4] with a core business of energy trading. When Congress deregulated the energy markets in the mid-1990s, Enron positioned itself to be a market share leader in the practice of acting as a sort of **energy bank** by purchasing energy from one source at a discount rate and selling it to markets where demand was greatest for energy. This business model depended on Enron contracting with producers of natural gas while also contracting to sell the gas with regional natural gas suppliers (companies supplying natural gas to the general public). Enron would capture the profits between the price at which it acquired the gas and the price at which it had promised to the sell the gas. Enron's executives devised this plan using the model of a bank earning the spread between what it pays depositors and what it collects from borrowers paying interest on a loan.

---

[3]A publicly held company is one whose stock is bought and sold in public markets. Regulation of public companies and markets is discussed in detail in Chapter 16, "Regulation of Securities, Corporate Governance, and Financial Markets."

[4]A conglomerate is a business entity that has a variety of industries that operate under a common corporate structure.

Rise to the Top   Although they initially struggled, by the 1990s, Enron was in position to benefit from the energy deregulation efforts in Congress. Enron hired Washington's top lobbyists and spread heavy campaign cash to both political parties in a successful effort to pass the California Deregulation Act. Virtually overnight Enron's business model became highly profitable. Its first quarter revenues went from $12 billon in 2000 to $84 billion in 2001. Employees, many of whom held the rising stock as part of their retirement savings, became fiercely loyal to the company. Using their profits and a talented employee pool, Enron began to add on additional business ventures that complemented their energy trading business, such as operating power plants. While some of these ventures were successful in terms of revenue, they also provided a convenient hiding place to disguise losses incurred by other Enron entities. Enron continued its growth at a rapid pace by expanding its business holdings into emerging (and risky) technology companies, including major holdings in the new technology of fiber optics.

Wall Street commentators, politicians, and investors alike all acclaimed Enron as the most innovative company since Microsoft. Analysts rated Enron's stock risk as "staggeringly low" and called it the last great technology stock in the new economy. The stock soared, and Enron's executive management's compensation shot up into the tens of millions of dollars based on stock options in the company. The top-level management team all received generous bonus compensation packages that were tied to the performance of Enron's stock. Enron's board of directors, who were in charge of oversight of the company, were equally exuberant because their compensation also included generous stock options and expensive perks.

Key Enron Players   The founder and first CEO of Enron was Kenneth Lay. Observers described Lay as an affable man from humble beginnings who was seen to be the epitome of the American dream. All through Enron's history, Lay was Enron's public face and Wall Street investors hailed him as one of the greatest innovators of all time. But the real mastermind of Enron was its Harvard Business School educated and former McKinsey consultant Jeffrey Skilling. Skilling, Enron's chief operating officer, was the architect of Enron's energy trading business model. Andrew Fastow, Enron's young chief financial officer, was a Skilling protégé who oversaw Enron's transactions and was known to browbeat anyone who questioned Enron's accounting or business practices. Rick Causey, Enron's chief accounting officer, deviated from established accounting standards and then pressured auditors to sign off on dubious financial statements that were presented to the board and shareholders.

Vision and Values   Enron's meteoric rise was even more impressive because, according to Lay, Enron was a prime example of a company that could be profitable and ethical. He proclaimed himself the keeper of the company's vision and values, which he defined as "respect, just treating other people the way we want to be treated, we're sincere, we mean what we say, we say what we do." Enron's code of business ethics articulated a philosophy of honesty and transparency. Lay also embraced the concept of community stakeholders and Enron's responsibility to groups beyond its shareholders, including its neighbors and employees.

*web*check **www.mhhe.com/melvin**
Go to this textbook's Web site to see a complete version of Enron's actual Code of Ethics.

The Fall   So what went wrong? As Enron's stock price climbed, a sort of fervor developed in Enron's executive office suite. The entire company focused its efforts on showing revenue streams and keeping its stock price high and pushing it even higher. The only way to continue this trend was to keep Wall Street investors enthusiastic about the company and to downplay any bad news. However, as the overall economy began to slow and the technology bubble deflated, Enron's boils began to show. Enron had kept its operations afloat through the use of credit that was now in short supply. By March 2001, the financial news media began to scrutinize Enron's financial transactions, the use of offshore partnerships, questionable accounting practices, and self-dealing by Fastow. Enron's board issued flat denials and pointed out that all of its financial transactions and business operations had been endorsed as proper by Arthur Andersen, one of the world's leading accounting firms.

Yet the media continued its investigative reporting of the company, and investors became increasingly skeptical about Enron's numbers. The stock continued to drop as Enron's various entities ran out of cash to cover expenses. Over the next few months, Enron suffered a barrage of embarrassing publicity that implied that its executives had looted the company to support an opulent lifestyle while the company was suffering billions in losses. Government investigators began several probes into the company's dealings and discovered that Skilling, Fastow, and others had fraudulently hidden Enron's losses from the investor community in an effort to manipulate the stock. Questions were also raised about why Andersen auditors had signed off on the fraud. Amid the allegations, Skilling resigned his position. As Enron's lenders pressured the company to pay back loans and with Enron's stock in free fall with no end in sight, the company finally filed for bankruptcy on December 2, 2001. It was, at the time, the largest bankruptcy in the history of the United States.[5] Loyal employees and stockholders who had ridden Enron's rising stock as a primary retirement vehicle were wiped out. Nearly 5,000 employees lost their jobs, and the American public was outraged. Enron, its executives, brokers, lenders, auditors, and attorneys were all now the subject of a massive fraud investigation by the Securities and Exchange Commission and the Federal Bureau of Investigation. Congress issued subpoenas to Enron's executives calling them to Capitol Hill in order to explain their conduct, but the only one who testified was Skilling. All of the others had followed their counsel's advice to invoke their constitutional right not to testify. Skilling was combative in his testimony, stating that he "absolutely unequivocally thought the company was in good shape" when he resigned.

Arthur Andersen   Enron's long-time auditing firm, Arthur Andersen, was one of the largest and most prestigious professional service firms in the world. After revelations about Enron's fraud surfaced, Andersen became the object of great scrutiny as well. How could the venerable firm, founded in 1913 by an accounting professor who built its reputation on honesty and integrity, have missed the fraud? Because it was inconceivable that such a massive fraudulent cover up of billions in losses could escape auditing detection, there was only one explanation: Andersen had turned a blind eye and gone along with it. Enron was a very profitable client for the firm, netting nearly $100 million in fees annually at a time when Andersen was seeing its share of the overall auditing market drop. David Duncan, Andersen's lead auditor in charge of Enron, became one of Andersen's top-paid employees primarily due to the massive fees he was collecting from Enron. Duncan, though, became more of an Enron advocate within Andersen rather than an auditor. Any time top-level managers at Andersen questioned the propriety of a transaction or financial report, it was Duncan who argued Enron's case to convince the others in the firm that, although aggressive and pushing the envelope, the structures were perfectly legal. When one senior Andersen manager objected to certain Enron accounting practices, Enron's chief accounting officer demanded that he be removed from the auditing team. Enron kept Andersen in tow by threatening to leave the firm and taking their substantial fees to Andersen competitors.

Aftermath   After an intensive investigation, federal prosecutors brought charges of wire fraud, securities fraud, conspiracy, insider trading, falsifying financial reports and tax returns, and obstruction of justice against Skilling, Fastow, Lay, and a host of other Enron

---

[5]The 2008 bankruptcy of investment banking firm Lehman Brothers eclipsed Enron as the largest bankruptcy in U.S. history (in terms of total debt owed).

FACT SUMMARY As Enron Corporation's financial difficulties became public, Andersen, Enron's auditor, instructed its employees to destroy documents pursuant to its established document retention policy. Andersen was indicted under a federal statute that makes it a crime to "knowingly . . . corruptly persuad[e] another person . . . with intent to . . . cause" that person to "withhold" documents from, or "alter" documents for use in, an "official proceeding." The jury returned a guilty verdict, and the Fifth Circuit Court of Appeals affirmed, holding that the district court's jury instructions properly conveyed the meaning of "corruptly persuades" and that the jury need not find any consciousness of wrongdoing in order to convict.

SYNOPSIS OF DECISION AND OPINION In a unanimous decision by the Supreme Court, Andersen's conviction was overturned. The Court reasoned that the instructions allowed the jury to convict Andersen without proving that the firm knew it had broken the law or that there had been a link to any official proceeding that prohibited the destruction of documents.

The Court specifically held that the jury's instruction, which stated that, even if Andersen honestly and sincerely believed its conduct was lawful, the jury could still convict them, was a serious error. The statute under which Andersen was charged used the language "knowingly . . . corruptly persuade." Andersen managers did instruct their employees to delete Enron-related files, but those actions were within their document retention policy. If the document retention policy was constructed to keep certain information private, even from the government, Andersen was still not corruptly persuading their employees to keep the information private.

WORDS OF THE COURT: Improper Jury Instruction "The jury instructions failed to convey properly the elements of a 'corrup[t] persuas[ion]' conviction. [. . .] The jury instructions failed to convey the requisite consciousness of wrongdoing. Indeed, it is striking how little culpability the instructions required. For example, the jury was told that, even if petitioner honestly and sincerely believed its conduct was lawful, the jury could convict. The instructions also diluted the meaning of "corruptly" such that it covered innocent conduct.

executives. In all, 34 people either pled guilty or were convicted on charges stemming from the Enron scandal. Skilling is currently serving a 24-year prison sentence. Fastow was sentenced to 6 years in prison. Kenneth Lay was convicted of fraud, but died of a heart attack before he could be sentenced. Other Enron-related defendants received sentences ranging from probation to 5-years incarceration.

The public outcry over the scandal and waning public confidence in the oversight of financial frauds in the market led Congress to pass several laws to improve the quality of the financial disclosure by public corporations. Most famously, Congress passed the Sarbanes-Oxley Act that dramatically increased the responsibilities of people in charge of running the finances of public companies including officers, directors, and outsiders such as attorneys and accountants.[6] The law imposes criminal penalties of up to 20 years for willful violations.

The government also indicted the entire firm of Arthur Andersen on charges of obstruction of justice. The charges stemmed from the government's allegations that Andersen insiders, led by Duncan, engaged in a pattern of cover-up by ordering massive shredding of documents once it suspected that the Securities and Exchange Commission would investigate Enron. In June 2002, the firm was convicted of the obstruction charges, sentenced to

---

[6]The Sarbanes-Oxley Act is discussed in detail in Chapter 16 "Regulation of Securities, Corporate Governance, and Financial Markets."

pay a $500,000 fine, and was banned from performing audits for publicly traded companies. It was, in essence, a death sentence as the firm's clients and key employees defected to competitors. The firm that had once employed 28,000 people around the globe was nearly defunct.

However, in a stunning reversal that could aptly described as too little too late, the U.S. Supreme Court reversed Andersen's conviction in 2005 and ordered a retrial. The decision is featured in Case 5.1. Shortly after the Court's decision, the government announced that they would not retry the case.

Enron Scandal: Questions for Discussion

1. Consider Kenneth Lay's statements about Enron's values and visions. Is it possible to reconcile these statements with Enron's business practices? What were the factors that corrupted these values? Is it possible that Lay actually believed that these values were being followed by the company, but had been duped by Skilling and Fastow? What steps could Lay have taken to be sure that Enron's business practices were consistent with the values?

2. Lay also instituted a bonus structure based on Enron's revenues and stock price instead of actual profitability. Are such bonuses inherently corrupting?

3. During an interview with *The New York Times* just 10 months after Enron's bankruptcy, Skilling argued that every transaction and report was scrutinized and approved by Enron's auditors and attorneys. In essence, he claimed that so long as Enron had met the technical aspects of the existing law, that they had no further obligations. What's the difference between technical compliance with the law and ethical obligations to stakeholders? Is it ethical to exploit gray areas of the law (areas that are not clearly defined) in the name of profit? What should be the drivers behind decision making at this level?

4. Given the complexity of the transactions and the assurances of auditors, what steps could the board of directors have taken to be sure these transactions were not only legal, but consistent with the company's stated ethical values?

5. Recall Andersen's decision to remove an auditor who refused to go along with Enron's schemes. What pressures was Andersen facing when Enron demanded the removal? Andersen had every legal right to remove the auditor, but doing so ignored their own system of ethics. What should Andersen have done when faced with Enron's demands?

6. Consider the government's actions in this case. When the Supreme Court reversed Andersen's conviction, famed defense lawyer Daniel Petrocelli, who had represented Skilling, gave a press statement that lambasted the Justice Department for conducting witch hunts and attempting to criminalize innocent conduct. Defense attorneys argued that the government consistently used scare tactics, pushed the limits of the law, and had indicted Andersen in order to use criminal charges as leverage to garner government witnesses who would testify against the Enron defendants. Did the government act ethically in this case? Were their actions justified or was it more about politics than justice? Was it good public policy to destroy the world's largest professional service firm for the actions of a handful of employees? Why do you think the government chose not to retry the case?

AIG Bonusgate: Legal, Managerial, and Ethical Perspectives

When *The New York Times* reported that insurance giant American International Group (AIG) had distributed $165 million in performance bonuses to some of its executives, it lit a public and political firestorm. AIG was in the center of the financial crisis of 2008 that culminated in massive government bailouts for financial institutions and others who were considered too important to the financial infrastructure to be allowed to fail. Just months before the bonuses were distributed, AIG had received $173 billion in taxpayer money in exchange for an 80 percent stake in AIG for the U.S. government.

Political Reaction   After the news of the bonuses broke, President Obama immediately denounced the bonuses and castigated AIG for using funds from one the federal government's original bailout packages in November 2008. He promised the outraged American populace that the government would pursue all "legal means to prevent the bonuses from being paid." Yet, the White House subsequently revealed that Treasury Secretary Geitner had knowledge of the bonuses and did not move to stop them from being paid because they were contractual obligations between a private company and an employee.

Congress reacted to the increasing public outrage by holding press conferences and subpoenaing witnesses for hearings on the bonuses. Representative Barney Frank called a special press conference to express his outrage at the bonuses and announced his plan to introduce a law to *tax* the entire amount of the bonuses retroactively so as to effectively place the bonus money in the U.S. Treasury. The attorney general of New York (where AIG is headquartered) launched an immediate investigation into the bonuses. During a congressional hearing, Edward Libby, the CEO appointed to revitalize the sagging company, called on AIG executives to return a portion of their bonuses. The public's anger continued to rise. A poll conducted by Gartner Group showed that 8 out of 10 Americans thought that distributing and taking the bonus was immoral. AIG was forced to hire security for the bonus recipients because of death threats. Pickets were organized in front of AIG's headquarters in New York City.

Mounting Pressures   Initially, most AIG bonus recipients were reluctant to consider the idea of returning their bonuses. These were highly skilled employees who negotiated specific performance goals and agreed to bonus compensation based on their individual goals. Those individual goals, they argued, were met despite the collapse of AIG. Moreover, such bonuses are crucial to retaining top talent that is necessary to AIG's emerging from insolvency. Yet, as the N.Y. attorney general continued to pressure bonus recipients with the threat of investigation, and Congress threatened to tax 100 percent of the bonus amounts, many recipients returned all or a portion of their bonus money totaling nearly $50 million.

Cooler Heads   As the weeks passed and network commentators moved on to other pressing issues, the rage dampened down. Despite the rush through the House of Representatives, the more cautious Senate halted the bonus taxation bill. The Obama administration, apparently after a change of heart, urged Congress not to pass any special taxation on bonuses, arguing that such action may make private investors, a key part of the economic recovery plan, reluctant to engage in the investment community. Although congressional leaders continued to hold hearings on what the media had dubbed *bonusgate,* no official action was taken either by Congress or the Obama administration. Yet, bonusgate took its toll on AIG. Several key executives defected, and AIG leaders were left picking up the pieces. Even AIG employees who had not received the bonus were scorned and demoralized.

AIG Bonusgate: Questions for Discussion

1. Consider President Obama's initial promise to use any means necessary to recoup the bonus money. It was clear that these recipients were contractually entitled to the bonuses. We'll learn later in this textbook that some contracts can be voided because they are inconsistent with public policy or the public good. It is a very high bar to reach, but courts have recognized this argument as valid. Could the AIG bonuses be categorized as bad public policy? Does paying the bonuses result in harm to the public in a tangible or intangible way? How? Could it be argued that these bonuses actually benefited the public?

2. Who are the primary and secondary stakeholders in the AIG decision to pay the bonuses?

3. If there was no legal basis for voiding the bonus contract, what ethical dilemmas are posed by accepting the bonuses? If you agreed to give the bonus back, how would that square with utilitarian notions of ethical conduct? If you decided to keep the bonus, would that mean that you followed a principles-based philosophy?

4. Much of AIG's executive management argued that the bonuses were a commonly used method of incentive and that the recipients were high achievers that were necessary to retain if AIG was to avoid insolvency even with the bailout money. Do you believe that bonuses should be banned if the company received government money? Is it ethical to pay out bonuses even when the company, overall, performs poorly?

5. Consider Congress's movement to tax the bonuses retroactively. Setting aside the possibility that the tax may be unconstitutional, is it ethical for the government to attempt to interfere in a private contract between an individual and her employer? Was this a political reaction to an ethical dilemma? Is it good public policy?

6. In general, is it ethical for a country's government to own 80 percent (a controlling stake) of a private business enterprise?

CORPORATE SOCIAL RESPONSIBILITY

LO5-10

While business ethics may be thought of as an application of ethics to the corporate sector and useful as a paradigm for determining responsibility in business dealings, corporate social responsibility (CSR) involves a broader-based identification of important business and social issues, and a critique of business organizations and practices. The fundamental notion underlying CSR is that *conscience* resides not just in individuals but also in a corporation. Thus, business organizations committed to CSR aim to achieve commercial success in ways that honor ethical values and respect people, communities, and the natural

Corporate social responsibility includes the notion of recognizing the importance of good corporate citizenship and partnering with the community.

environment in a sustainable manner while recognizing the interests of its stakeholders. Stakeholders include investors, customers, employees, business partners, local communities, the environment, and society at large. This involves corporate citizenship, which is the adoption by a business of a strategic focus for fulfilling the economic, legal, ethical, and philanthropic social responsibilities expected of it by its stakeholders. There are essentially three schools of thought that define CSR in practice.

The Narrow View: Invisible Hand

In his classic condemnation of the corporate social responsibility movement, Nobel Prize-winning economist Milton Friedman offered that the only responsibility a business has is to maximize shareholder wealth. Indeed, an implicit perspective underwriting much of the free enterprise persuasion is that businesses are amoral, and as Friedman would suggest, managers who pursue social initiatives with corporate funds are violating their fiduciary duties to the owners of the corporation. While individuals are free to act morally and behave in a socially responsible manner on their own time and with their own resources, managers are responsible solely to the shareholders and to make as much profit as legally possible. As for society's well being, the argument goes, Adam Smith's invisible hand will provide. Smith's invisible hand theory is that a deliberate amorality in corporate decision making is encouraged in the name of a new morality: the common good is best served when each of us and our economic institutions pursue not the common good or moral purpose, but rather society is best served when we pursue a competitive advantage.[7] Hence, what is good for business is good for America because the market's efficiencies provide an invisible hand that guides morality and responsibility. Corporations acting unethically would inevitable suffer.

The Moderate View: Government's Hand

Advocates of a more moderate view argue that the government provides the exclusive view of corporate responsibility. The government is seen as the most valuable source of setting guidelines because it represents the moral views of the general public. Under this view, corporations have the responsibility to pursue objectives that are rational, legal, and purely economic. The regulatory hands of the law and the political process, rather than Smith's invisible hand, provide the basis for ethical decision making. Neither the invisible hand view nor the government's hand view trusts corporate leaders with any stewardship over noneconomic values.

The Broad View: Management's Hand

An underlying tenet of the broadest view of CSR is that corporations have a social responsibility and that profitability is secondary. Indeed, in the broadest terms, some business ethicists argue that corporations are only allowed to exist because they can serve some public good. It is not necessary to justify the need for a greater corporate role in social responsibility. Thus, these groups often invoke a set of societal expectations with the idea that corporations conduct their business on such terms. The starting point is not business objectives, but socially defined goals.

---

[7]While the overwhelming majority of scholars and commentators use Smith's invisible hand metaphor in the same context as it is used in this textbook, there are some persuasive articles that argue that Smith did not intend the invisible hand metaphor to be a significant part of his economic theories. To read an excellent discussion on the controversy, see Professor Gavin Kennedy's article in *Economic Journal Watch* titled "Adam Smith and the Invisible Hand: From Metaphor to Myth." A link to the article may be found on this textbook's Web site at www.mhhe.com/melvin.

Within the broad view, the majority is not willing to buy into such a radical notion that business prosperity should be an afterthought. Instead they argue that CSR is in the public's interest and a company's self-interest, *and* a company does well by employing socially responsible principles in their business operations. In this way, CSR may be thought of a form of enlightened self-interest because the long-term prosperity of a firm depends not on short-term profits but societal well being.

An integral part of the broad CSR perspective is the focus on what some ethicists call the *triple bottom line*. Essentially, the triple bottom line emphasizes not only the conventional creation of economic value (profits), but also a company's creation (or destruction) of environmental and social value. This naturally places a great deal more pressure on managers to perform, as it is not uncommon when these three sets of bottom line issues conflict. It is not enough, then, for managers to aggressively pursue a social agenda, but she/he must not lose sight of financial and environmental performance as well. Yet, this may be difficult to do in practice. It is easy for managers to underestimate the linkage between enterprise sustainability and the creation of shareholder value. Rather than looking at the three bottom lines as being offsetting, it is more preferable to view them as possessing a cumulative strategic value to a company.

In Landmark Case 5.1, a state appellate court decides a product liability issue in the context of a dangerous design flaw. But this dangerous flaw was known to management and was ignored because the costs of repair were thought to be significantly more than the costs of compensating injured victims. It is a case frequently cited by CSR advocates as an example of the failing of the invisible hand and government's hand approaches.

LANDMARK CASE 5.1 Grimshaw v. Ford Motor Company, 119 Cal. App. 3d 757 (1981)

FACT SUMMARY In an effort to add a more fuel-efficient car to its offerings, Ford designed the Pinto. During design, Ford engineers became concerned that the placement of the gas tank was unsafe and subject to puncturing and rupturing at low-impact speeds. Crash tests confirmed the dangerous design flaw, and engineers recommended halting production until a solution to the product was developed. However, Ford's management overruled the engineers and pushed the Pinto into the manufacturing phase. There was evidence that Ford considered the alternatives too expensive and decided that the proposed fix would have a higher overall cost than the risk of liability from lawsuits as a result of injuries to its customers. Grimshaw purchased a Pinto and was injured when the gas tank erupted in a low-speed crash. The jury found Ford liable for Grimshaw's injuries and awarded him $125 million. The trial court reduced the award to $3.5 million pursuant to a California state statute.

SYNOPSIS OF DECISION AND OPINION The California appellate court upheld the jury's verdict and the $3.5 million award. The court pointed out that the dangerous design flaw carried with it the severe risk of injury and that the evidence showed that Ford would need to spend only $15.30 per car to have made it safer.

WORDS OF THE COURT: Corporate Malice "[T]here was substantial evidence that Ford's management decided to proceed with the production of the Pinto with knowledge of test results revealing design defects which rendered the fuel tank extremely vulnerable on rear impact at low speeds and endangered the safety and lives of the occupants. Such conduct constitutes corporate malice."

Case Questions

1. Which view of CSR do you believe Ford's managers were aligned to when making this decision?

2. Suppose that the changes would cause Ford to expend $1,000 per car rather than $15.80. Would that have changed the outcome of the case? Could it be argued that, given the fact that Ford's sales plummeted after this lawsuit was filed, Smith's invisible hand actually worked here?

Stakeholder p. 104   An expansive term that includes a business entity's owners, investors, employees, customers, suppliers, and the wider community.

Morals p. 105   Term referring to generally accepted standards of right and wrong in a given society.

Ethics p. 105   Term used to describe having a conscious system in use for deciding moral dilemmas.

Utilitarian p. 105   Model of moral philosophy stating that an action is ethically sound if it produces positive results for the most people.

Values management p. 106   The prioritizing of moral values for an organization and ensuring behaviors are aligned with those values.

Energy bank p. 111   Business model adopted by Enron Corporation in which they purchased energy from one source at a discount rate and sold it to markets where demand was greatest for energy following deregulation of the energy markets.

THEORY TO PRACTICE

Java Road (Java) is a corporation that retails high-quality coffee products through coffee carts in conveniently placed locations such as malls and office complexes. Java owns 10 such carts and employs a workforce of 40 to maintain business operations. The owner, Miguel, founded the company 10 years ago with the idea that a high-quality coffee product could be sold at a profit because his overhead was limited to product, employee compensation, and the cart. Although he has always stressed honesty with his employees, he never developed a written code of ethics.

1. Suppose that an employee that works at one of the most profitable carts, Jacob, has one or two cups of free coffee a day. He justifies it based on the fact that the cart is so profitable, no one will notice. Given the lack of a written code of ethics or conduct, is it OK for Jacob to drink a free cup of coffee from the cart?

2. Suppose that one customer consistently buys coffee from Jacob and leaves a small tip. In an effort to increase the size of the tip, Jacob gives the customer a free coffee every Friday. Is it ethical for Jacob to do this? Is it ethical for the customer to take the free coffee?

3. What theories of moral philosophy help your decision-making answer in Questions 1 and 2 above?

4. Suppose that Miguel's general manager suggests that he develop a code of ethics for Java Road. Miguel bristles at the idea because he said business ethics "cannot be managed—people are either ethical or not." What responses could the general manager use to persuade Miguel to employ a values management system?

5. Assume that Miguel finds a vendor that will sell him coffee beans at a discounted price. However, Miguel reads an article about the fact that the vendor uses child labor in Asia to produce the products. The vendor argues that the beans are high quality and that their practices of employing child labor are perfectly legal in Asia. Which view of CSR would result in Miguel's refusing to buy the beans? What is the vendor's view of CSR?

MANAGER'S CHALLENGE

Assume that you are Miguel's general manager in the Theory to Practice above. In groups (or individually) draft a two- to three-page Code of Ethics and/or Code of Conduct that would be appropriate for Java Road. Use the Solutions for Managers feature in this chapter for guidance.

A sample answer may be found on this textbook's Web site at www.mhhe.com/melvin.

ETHICS IN DEBT COLLECTION

American Collections Enterprise, Inc. (ACEI) is a debt collection company that contracted with Capital One bank to provide debt collection services. Under the terms of the collection agreement, Capital One assigned delinquent accounts to ACEI for collection, and ACEI collected these debts on a contingent fee basis. Under the collection agreement, Capital One gave ACEI the authority to settle any of its accounts at a discount according to a set formula. Goswami owed approximately $900 on her Capital One credit card and failed to pay. Capital One referred that debt to ACEI for collection on March 20, 2001, and ACEI pursued Goswami's delinquent account. The debt collection letter offered to settle the outstanding balance due with a 30 percent discount off of the balance owed and stated that no other offers would be forthcoming. Unbeknownst to Goswami, ACEI actually had authority to settle for up to a 50 percent discount according to ACEI's agreement with Capital One. The Fair Debt Collection Act prohibits misleading statements by debt collectors.

CASE QUESTIONS

1. Is the letter misleading?
2. Is it ethical to tell a partial truth as ACEI did here?
3. Do private debt collection agencies serve any public policy functions?

PROFESSIONAL ETHICS

Greenen was a Certified Public Accountant (CPA) licensed by the state of Washington. During the course of her employment as a CPA, Greenen violated a workplace rule by failing to inform her employer's health care plan administrator that she and her spouse had divorced. The effect of her failing to disclose the divorce was that Greenen's ex-husband continued to receive health care benefits that Greenen's employer afforded to its employees' spouses even though he was no longer eligible under the rules of the plan. After her employer discovered the discrepancy, Greenen was charged by the State Board of Accountancy with a breach of the CPA's ethical code for professional misrepresentation. Greenen countered that the CPA ethical code governed accounting-related transactions and practices only and that she should not be subject to sanction for failing to disclose her divorce.

CASE QUESTIONS

1. Should ethical codes apply to employees outside their scope of employment?
2. If Greenen were accused of a violent crime, would she have been charged by the State Board of Accountancy for an ethical violation?
3. What is the purpose of having mandatory ethical codes for professionals such as CPAs?

CORPORATE SOCIAL RESPONSIBILITY

In 2007, Countrywide was the largest provider of home mortgage loans in the world. Countrywide specialized in so-called subprime mortgage loans that allowed homebuyers with relatively low credit scores the opportunity to qualify for a mortgage by paying a higher interest rate along with a monthly premium to insure the loan in case of a default. One of Countrywide's mortgages featured "teaser rates" that made initial payments artificially low. Nearly 50 percent of Countrywide's customers ended up defaulting within one year of when the teaser rate adjusted upward. Several customers filed complaints with regulatory authorities contending that Countrywide never disclosed

that the payments would increase so dramatically and applicants relied on Countrywide's judgment that they could afford the loan.

CASE QUESTIONS

1. Does Countrywide have an ethical obligation to refuse making risky loans to consumers?
2. Is there an ethical obligation for Countrywide to verify the income of its applicants?
3. What ethical duty does an applicant have when applying for a loan?
4. Could Countrywide's program to offer mortgages to those that otherwise could not buy a home be construed as being socially responsible? Why or why not?

ETHICS

A group of parties injured by the oil tanker Exxon *Valdez*'s crash in 1989 brought suit against Exxon charging, among other things, that Exxon was negligent for allowing the oil tanker to be captained by an employee who had a known history of alcohol abuse. The captain was, in fact, intoxicated at the time of the crash that spilled 11 million gallons of crude oil in Prince William Sound, Alaska. Commercial fisheries were temporarily disabled and permanently damaged as a result of the spill. The jury awarded $5 billion in punitive damages against Exxon. Exxon appealed the judgment

on the basis that the damages were grossly excessive. The appellate court upheld the jury's finding, but reduced the punitive damage award by 50 percent.

CASE QUESTIONS

1. What are the ethics of punitive damages awards?
2. Is it ethical to try and bankrupt a company using a lawsuit?
3. Should courts be able to reduce punitive damage awards?
4. Is $5 billion excessive against a company as large as Exxon?

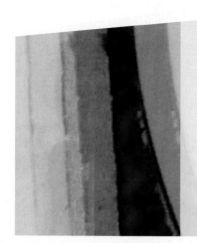

Law and Commerce

6
CHAPTER

Overview and Formation of Contracts

learning outcomes checklist

After studying this chapter, students who have mastered the material will be able to:

6-1 Distinguish between contracts based on categories and apply the correct source of law to specific contracts.

6-2 Explain the concept of mutual assent by defining the legal requirement of agreement.

6-3 Identify and explain the other requirements for the formation of a valid contract.

6-4 List the events that terminate the power of acceptance and distinguish between termination through action of the parties versus operation of law.

6-5 Apply the mailbox rule to resolve a question of when acceptance is effective.

6-6 Articulate the legal requirement of consideration and identify which contracts do not require consideration.

6-7 Give examples of circumstances where the legal requirements of capacity or legality are at issue.

6-8 Explain the concept of enforceability and geniune assent.

6-9 Categorize what contracts must be in writing to be enforceable and explain the minimum required terms that satisfy the law.

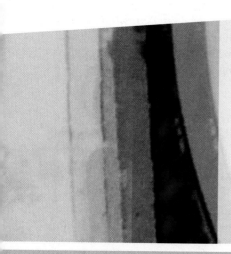

The law of contracts is one of the most common and important areas of the law that business owners and managers deal with on a day-to-day basis. Everyone working in a business environment will, in one form or another, deal with contracts throughout their career. Employment contracts, leases, and agreements of sale for assets or land or merchandise are just a few examples of contracts commonly used in business transactions. The simple act of purchasing office supplies from a local merchant is a form of agreement governed by contract law.

Formation and legal enforcement of agreements have been recognized since ancient times. As early as 1780 BC, contracts were being enforced by the Babylonians by virtue of the authority of the Code of Hammurabi. During much of the rule of the Roman Empire, the Justinian Code included the rule *pacta sunt servanda* (agreements shall be kept). Many legal scholars, notably Dean Roscoe Pound, have written extensively on the importance of society recognizing legally enforceable promises and providing remedies for those who suffered losses. Consider the consequences of failing to provide for legal enforceability of a promise and its impact on the very fabric of civilized societies.

Since business owners and managers are often involved in day-to-day oversight of various agreements and transactions, understanding contract law reduces risk by limiting liability through the recognition of potential legal issues, crafting an appropriate response, and implementing a system to ensure compliance. Contract law is also essential to structuring business transactions in strategic ways to achieve business objectives without excessive risk.

In this chapter, students will learn:

- Definitions and categories of various contracts.
- The legal requirements for forming an enforceable contract.
- Writing requirements that apply to certain contracts.
- Use of contracts to reduce legal risk.

DEFINITION AND CATEGORIES OF CONTRACTS

One generally accepted definition of a contract is a *promise or a set of promises enforceable by law.*[1] Put another way, a contract is simply an **agreement** that a court of law will recognize and enforce. Contract law also defines certain circumstances that excuse one or both parties from performing their obligation or enforcing the agreement's promise.

Categories of Contracts

Because the subject of contracts is so vast, it is useful to categorize the different types of contracts in order to understand various forms of promises and agreements. This is *not* to say that these categories are mutually exclusive. In fact, all contracts will fit into more than one category.

Written versus Oral Contracts
While the word *contract* is often used to describe a written document, many contracts are not in writing and yet are enforceable. Any agreement, oral or written, may result in a binding contract so long as it meets certain requirements. Some contracts, however, are *required* to be in writing in order to be enforceable. These contracts are defined by the statute of frauds, which is covered later in this chapter.

Bilateral Contracts versus Unilateral Contracts
A **bilateral contract** involves two promises and two performances. Most contracts are bilateral contracts. To take a simple example, suppose Ginny says to Harry: "I offer to pay you $5,000 for your delivery van." Harry responds, "I accept." On the following day, Ginny shows up with a check for $5,000. Harry signs over title to the delivery van to Ginny. Ginny's promise was to pay $5,000 for the delivery van. Harry's promise was to sell the delivery van for $5,000. Ginny performance was to pay Harry via check for $5,000. Harry's performance was to turn over title of the delivery van to Ginny.

A **unilateral contract** involves one promise, followed by one performance, which then triggers a *second* performance from the offeror (the party making the offer). Perhaps the best example of a unilateral contract is when the offer is in the form of a reward. For example, if Jonah places several reward posters in his neighborhood and offers to pay $500 to anyone who finds his missing dog, this is an example of a unilateral offer. Jonah has made one promise, but there has been no second promise made by any of the neighbors. Therefore, the only way that a neighbor may accept the offer made by Jonah is to *perform* by finding the dog and delivering him to Jonah as specified in the promise (via the reward posters). Once a neighbor has performed, Jonah is now obligated to perform his promise (to pay a $500 reward). Of course, if no one performs, Jonah may not sue his neighbors for recovery because no return promise was ever made.

Express Contracts versus Implied Contracts versus Quasi-Contracts
An **express contract** is created when the parties have expressly agreed on the promises and performances. An **implied contract** is one in which the agreement is reached by the parties' *actions* rather than their words. The classic example of an implied contract is when a party seeks care from a physician. The patient does not typically negotiate terms of the transaction (e.g., the patient will not ask for a 15 percent frequent visitor discount), yet a contract is formed and enforceable by the doctor who is owed a reasonable fee for services rendered even though the patient has not expressly agreed to payment terms. This contract was formed as an implied contract *in fact.* In some cases where no express or implied contract exists, a party may still be able to recover losses based on a **quasi-contract.** The law permits quasi-contracts to be enforceable where one party suffers losses as a result of another party's unjust enrichment. This theory of contract is based on an implied by law recovery whereby one party does

---

[1]For exact wording of the definition, see *Restatement (Second) of Contracts* § 2.

not actually request a certain service, but still benefits from the services rendered. Suppose that in the physician–patient example above, that the physician has instead stopped at an automobile accident and renders the unconscious patient emergency care. Although there is no express contract or implied contract (because the patient never agreed to or requested physician services), the physician may still recover a reasonable fee for her services to the patient under a quasi-contract theory because the patient received a benefit.[2] Recovery under a quasi-contract theory is also possible when an express contract is unenforceable for some legal reason, but one of parties has gained a benefit. For example, Contractor is hired to install a new floor in ManufactureCo.'s warehouse. Contractor rips out the old floor, pours the concrete, and waits overnight for the concrete to dry. Before Contractor can install the new floor, a fire destroys the warehouse. Although the contract is now unenforceable due to impossibility (discussed in the next chapter), Contractor may still recover for services of demolition to the old floor since this work directly benefited ManufactureCo.

Valid versus Void Contracts

When a contract has the necessary elements, it is said to be a **valid contract. Void contracts** are those agreements that have not been formed in conformance with the law from the *outset* of the agreement and, thus, cannot be enforced by either party. For example, a contract for the sale of an illegal narcotic is void as prohibited by statute and against public policy despite the fact that two parties may have agreed to the sale.

FIGURE 6.1   Is a Contract Valid, Void, Voidable, or Unenforceable?

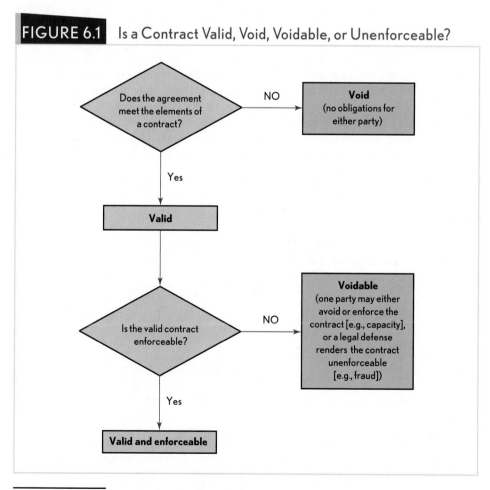

---

[2]Based on *Cotnam v. Wisdom,* 83 Ark. 601 (1907).

Voidable versus Unenforceable Contracts   Even when two parties have formed a valid contract, sometimes the agreement may still *not* be fully enforceable. A **voidable contract** is one in which one party may at its option either disaffirm the contract or enforce it. For example, suppose that Ally, a minor,[3] purchases a used car from a local car dealer. Because the law allows minors (and guardians) the right to cancel the contract up until the time that the minor turns 18, Ally may choose to disaffirm the transaction and return the car, or to enforce it by keeping the car until she turns 18. When a party chooses to legally disaffirm a contract that was voidable, this is known as *avoiding* the contract. An **unenforceable contract,** on the other hand, is one that meets the elements required by law for an otherwise binding agreement, but is subject to a legal defense such as the statutory requirement that certain contracts be in writing in order to be enforceable.

SOURCES OF LAW

In general, contracts for *services* (e.g., legal, accounting, or engineering) or *real estate* (such as an agreement of sale for an office building or a lease for a commercial retail space) are governed by **state common law.** Contracts for *goods* or products (defined as something that is moveable at the time of identification in the contract) are governed by **state statutory law** based on the Uniform Commercial Code (UCC).[4] The UCC also covers transactions related to leasing of equipment. Note that the UCC provisions for sales and leases are covered extensively in Chapter 8 "Contracts for the Sale of Goods."

Some contracts involve terms for both goods *and* services. These are known as **hybrid contracts.** In a hybrid contract, the source of law is established by determining the *predominant thrust* of the contract subject matter. If the contract is predominantly for services, and the goods are incidental, then the contract is governed by the common law. If, on the other hand, goods are the main feature of the contract, and the services come incidentally, then the contract is governed by statutory law. For example, Huxley is a manager charged with the task of hiring a portrait artist to paint the portrait of the founder of the company to be displayed in the lobby. Huxley hires Pablo, and Pablo paints the portrait. This is a hybrid contract because it involves services (of the artist) and goods (Huxley gets the canvas, paint, etc.) at the conclusion of the services. However, in this case the goods are *incidental* to the

---

 Self-Check

Which source of law governs this contract?

1. A contract for the sale of an office building from Abel to NewCo.

2. A contract providing for installation of networking cable in an office facility where the materials are $5,000 and the labor is $20,000.

3. A consulting contract between a management consulting firm and a software development company.

4. The sale of several completed sculptures from an artist to a retail art dealer for a total of $10,000.

5. A contract between the owner of a building and a painting company to paint the building's lobby over a holiday weekend for $5,000. The owner agrees to supply all of the paint.

---

[3]In the context of contract law, almost all states define a minor as one who not yet reached their 18th birthday.

[4]Recall from Chapter 1 that the UCC is a "model" statute drafted by a group called the National Conference of Commissioners of Uniform State Laws (NCCUSL). Each state legislature makes its own decisions about whether to adopt the UCC in total, partially, or not at all. Louisiana is the only state to have rejected the UCC in its entirety.

The Uniform Electronic Transactions Act (UETA) is best thought of as a *procedural* model law that applies to transactions as long as the parties to a contract agree to use electronic commerce for that transaction. This means that the UETA does not create substantive rights or protections (such as providing consumers with a right to sue), but rather gives legal recognition to certain electronic media. Whether the parties agreed to conduct a transaction by electronic means is determined from the context and surrounding circumstances, including the parties' conduct. The UETA essentially elevates electronic signatures and records to the same legal status as are accorded to traditional signatures and paper records, memoranda, notices, and so forth. The law covers both e-commerce sale of goods transactions *and* the use of electronic communication alongside paper contracts.

The UETA gives formal legal recognition of electronic records, signatures, and contracts by providing that (1) a record or signature may not be denied legal effect or enforceability solely because it is in electronic form; (2) a contract may not be denied legal effect or enforceability solely because an electronic record was used in its information; (3) if a law requires a record to be in writing, an electronic record satisfies the law; and (4) if a law requires a signature, an electronic signature satisfies the law. Currently, 47 states have adopted the UETA in some form.

services; thus, it is primarily a contract for services and governed by the common law. In determining the source of law governing a hybrid contract, courts will examine (1) *allocation of price* in the contract (value of goods versus value of services), and (2) *uniqueness* of the services (did it require special talent, such as the portrait artist above?). The more unique the service, the more likely the contract is covered by the common law.

OVERVIEW OF A CONTRACT TRANSACTION

Before learning the individual components required to form a contract and the rules that govern the parties, it is helpful to consider a typical contract transaction from a macro perspective. First, a contract is formed when two or more parties agree to a particular set of terms. One party typically agrees to provide services, real estate, or goods in exchange for something of value (usually money). An agreement is recognized as legally binding so long as it meets certain *formation* requirements. Second, after the formation requirements are met, the contract is governed by laws that set out requirements for *enforceability* of the agreement. Finally, assuming that the contract was properly formed and is legally enforceable, the law sets out rules and consequences related to how the parties fulfill their obligations to one another. This is known as *performance* (or nonperformance) of the agreement.

For example, suppose that Ahab agrees to provide ship repair services to White Whale Industries. Using e-mail exchanges, the parties negotiate a monthly fee and specify that

TABLE 6.1   Overview of a Contract Transaction

Formation	Enforceability	Performance
Parties reached mutual agreement on terms. All formation elements are met.	Contract meets legal requirements to enforce terms.	Governs parties performing (or not performing) the terms of the agreement and provides compensation if one party fails to perform.

Ahab is to repair and maintain White Whale's fleet of ships as necessary for two years. At this point, a contract is likely to have been *formed* assuming that all of the required elements for mutual agreement are met. However, suppose that one month into the agreement Ahab notifies White Whale that he has a better opportunity in another city and cannot perform the services in the agreement. After White Whale objects, Ahab claims the contract is not enforceable because the law requires this contract to be in writing. White Whale counters that the e-mail exchanges were sufficient to meet the legal requirements. The resolution of this issue depends on the *enforceability* of this contract. Alternatively, assume that parties had a written contract, but that White Whale began having financial difficulty one year into the contract. They notify Ahab that they will be reducing his monthly fee by 30 percent. Can Ahab sue White Whale immediately? Does White Whale have any defense? What can Ahab expect to recover to compensate for losses? These are issues of *performance*. Formation and enforceability are covered in this chapter. Performance is covered in Chapter 7 "Contract Performance: Conditions, Breach, and Remedies." Table 6.1 provides an overview of a contract transaction.

Understanding contract law helps business owners limit their company's liability and manage risk.

CONTRACT FORMATION: MUTUAL ASSENT

LO6-2, 6-3

The broad underlying requirement to form an enforceable contract is the notion of **mutual assent.** Mutual assent means that in order for a contract to be valid, the parties must reach an agreement using a combination of **offer** and **acceptance.** The *offeror* must make a valid offer to the *offeree,* who in turn must accept the offer in order for the parties to be bound by the agreement's terms. However, this mutual assent requirement does *not* mean that both parties *actually* intended in their minds (subjective standard) to enter into an agreement. Rather, the law requires only that the parties' acts or words lead the other party to reasonably believe (objective standard) that an agreement has been reached.

In addition to agreement, there are *three* other requirements for the formation of a valid contract. First, the agreement must be supported by **consideration.** Second, the parties entering into the agreement must have **capacity.** Third, the subject matter and performance of the contract must have **legality** and be consistent with **public policy.**

Moreover, in order for the contract to be *enforceable,* the agreement must also be the product of **genuine assent** and, in some cases, certain terms must be in *writing* as required by the **statute of frauds.**

Agreement Part 1: Offer

An offer is a promise or commitment to do (or refrain from doing) a specified activity such as selling a good at a certain price or offering to provide services at a given rate. An offer also is the expression of a willingness to enter into a contract by the offeror promising an offeree that she will perform certain obligations in exchange for the offeree's counterpromise to perform. To take a simple example, suppose that Lewis offers to sell Williams a rare book for $1,000. In this case, Lewis is the *offeror* and is promising to perform through a transfer of ownership rights to the book so long as Williams, as the *offeree,* counterpromises to perform by paying $1,000.

> ## KEY POINT
> The elements of a contract are (1) agreement (offer and acceptance) that indicates mutual assent, (2) consideration, (3) capacity, and (4) legality/public policy. To enforce a contract, it must be a product of genuine assent and in writing (in certain cases).

In order for an offer to have legal effect, the offeror must have an **objective intent** to contract when making the offer. Generally, the offeror must have a *serious intention* to become bound by the offer and the terms of the offer must be *reasonably certain.* Courts look to the *language* of the offer and *actions* of the offeror to determine how a reasonable person would interpret that language. Does the language indicate a *serious intent to form* a contract? Or perhaps the language indicates intent to negotiate rather than agree. Or is the language so innocuous that a reasonable person would conclude that there was no intent at all (for example, an offer made in jest)? Note that it does not matter what the offeror *actually* intended. Rather, the objective test is what a reasonable person would ordinarily believe the language and conduct (collectively referred to as *manifestations* of intent) to mean in those circumstances. Otherwise, the offer is considered simply an offer to discuss or negotiate the terms of an agreement. For example, an e-mail from the owner of a computer retail store to a computer hardware wholesaler may contain the following language: "I am interested in purchasing ten new personal computers. Please contact me about the price and delivery terms regarding the computers." This message does not express an immediate objective intention to contract. Rather, a reasonable person would look at this language as an invitation to negotiate.

Under modern case law, the importance of the parties' intention, or lack of intention, to form a contract depends largely upon the context of the agreement. When an agreement is in the context of a business transaction, there is a strong presumption that the parties intended the agreement to be legally enforceable.

In Landmark Case 6.1, one of the most famous in American contract law, a state supreme court considers the circumstances of a transaction and language of the parties in determining whether an offer involved a serious intent to contract.

> ## KEY POINT
> The objective test for intent to form a contract is: Given the language and circumstances of the offer, would a reasonable person in the position of the offeree conclude that the offer was an objective manifestation of serious intent to contract?

Advertisements as an Offer   Most advertisements appearing in the mass media, in store windows, or in display cases are *not* offers. Rather, the law recognizes mass advertisements as an invitation for the consumer to make an offer to the seller to purchase the goods at a specified price. Frequently, these advertisements do not constitute an offer because they do not contain a specific commitment to sell. For example, Big Time Appliances runs an advertisement in a local paper which misprinted the ad as "46-inch plasma screen TV for $10" instead of $1,000. Ernest shows up at Big Time Appliance with a $10 bill and excitedly hands over the bill to a cashier saying "I accept your offer to sell me this television for $10." Big Time Appliance is not obligated to perform (i.e., sell the television for $10).[5]

---

[5]*Restatement (Second) of Contracts* § 26, Comment b. Also note that this example is a contracts analysis. In the case of advertising, certain state consumer laws may apply to protect buyers against merchants acting in bad faith using advertising as a "bait and switch" method discussed in Chapter 21, "Consumer Protection Laws."

FACT SUMMARY   Lucy was a farmer who knew Zehmer for a period of 15–20 years. At one point during their relationship, Lucy offered to buy Zehmer's farm for $20,000, but Zehmer rejected the offer outright. Seven years later, Lucy met Zehmer at a restaurant and had a conversation over a period of hours while the two drank whiskey together. During this conversation, Lucy again offered to purchase Zehmer's farm. According to the testimony at trial, the following exchange of words took place:

Lucy:	"I bet you wouldn't take $50,000 for that farm."
Zehmer:	"You haven't got $50,000 cash."
Lucy:	"I can get it."
Zehmer:	"But you haven't got $50,000 cash to pay me tonight."

Eventually, Lucy persuaded Zehmer to put in writing that he would sell Lucy the farm for $50,000. Zehmer handwrote the following on the back of the pad, "I agree to sell the Ferguson Place [Zehmer's farm property] to W.O. Lucy for $50,000 cash." The parties then modified this writing several times and discussed terms over a period of 30–40 minutes. At the end of the evening, each party had signed the modified document that agreed to a sale of Zehmer's farm to Lucy for $50,000. The next day, Lucy believed that the contract was valid and proceeded to act accordingly by seeking financing for the purchase and checking title. However, Zehmer notified Lucy that he would not transfer title since no contract was formed. Rather, Zehmer had understood the whole transaction as a joke. At trial Zehmer testified that he "was high as a Georgia pine," while modifying and discussing the contract and that he was just "needling" Lucy because he believed Lucy could never come up with the money. Zehmer claimed that before he left the restaurant that night, he told Lucy that it was all a big joke, that the negotiations were just the "liquor talking." Zehmer claimed that he

had not actually intended to sell the property, thus the contract lacked serious intent and was void.

SYNOPSIS OF DECISION AND OPINION   The court ruled that Zehmer was bound by the contract even if he had no *actual* (subjective) intent to sell the farm and may have been joking. The court used the objective standard in determining that a reasonable person would have construed Zehmer's actions and words as a serious intent to contract. The court held that evidence from the trial indicated that Zehmer took the transaction seriously, and that Lucy was not unreasonable in believing that a contract was formed under the circumstances. The court made clear that actual mental intent is not required for formation of a contract.

WORDS OF THE COURT: Manifestation of Intent to Contract   "The appearance of a contract; the fact that it was under discussion for forty minutes or more before it was signed; Lucy's objection to the first draft; [. . .] the discussion of what was to be included in the sale [. . .] are facts which furnish persuasive evidence that the execution of the contract was a serious business transaction rather than a casual, jesting matter as the defendant now contends.

An agreement or mutual assent is of course essential to a valid contract but the law imputes to a person an intention corresponding to the reasonable meaning of his words and acts. If his words and acts, judged by a reasonable standard, manifest an intention to agree, it is immaterial what may be the real but unexpressed state of his mind."

Case Questions

1. What factors does the court focus on when deciding whether Lucy's understanding of the contract formation was reasonable?

2. What facts could you change in this case that would result in the court determining that no contract existed?

The law recognizes Ernest's actions not as an acceptance of Big Time's offer, but rather an offer by Ernest to buy the television—which Big Time may accept or reject.

The primary exception to this rule is when the advertisement is *specific* enough to constitute a unilateral contract. Advertisements that offer to sell a particular number of certain products at a certain price may constitute an offer. In the previous example, if the advertisement offered 46-inch plasma televisions for $10 to the first 50 buyers on Friday, then the advertisement would be specific enough to constitute a valid offer requiring Big Time Appliance to sell as promised. Or, if the advertisement invites the other party to accept in a *particular manner,* courts will treat these types of advertisements as a valid offer for a unilateral contract. For example, Anti-Flu Inc. sells an herbal inhaler device they claim will work effectively to prevent the flu as well as any flu shot vaccine. They advertise "We will pay $1,000 to anyone who uses the Anti-Flu herbal inhaler for two consecutive weeks and still contracts the flu." Pauline uses the device for two weeks (thereby accepting Anti-Flu's offer), and contracts the flu one day later. Anti-Flu would be obligated to perform their promise by paying the $1,000 sum because Anti-Flu's advertisement invited any party to accept their offer in a particular manner (by using the device).[6]

In Case 6.1, an appellate court considers a claim that a famous company created an offer through a television advertisement.

Agreement Part 2: Acceptance

A valid offer creates the power of *acceptance* for the offeree. An acceptance is the offeree's expression of agreement to the terms of the offer. An offeree typically communicates the acceptance in writing or orally, but in some cases may also accept via some action or conduct (such as in a unilateral contract). So long as the offer is still in force (has not yet been terminated) the offeree may accept the terms of the offer thereby forming an agreement. The party that the offeror intended to create a power of acceptance is the only party that may accept. In order for agreement to exist though, the offer has to be *properly* accepted by the offeree.[7] Note that the offeror is considered the "master" of the offer and, therefore, has the power to terminate, modify its terms, or prescribe the method of acceptance of the offer *up and until the offer has been accepted* by the offeree. Once the offer has been terminated, the offeree has lost the power to accept and form an agreement.

Events of Termination of the Power of Acceptance: Action of the Parties versus **LO**6-4
Operation of Law   An offer may be terminated by action of the parties in one of three ways: (1) **revocation,** where the offeror revokes (withdraws) the offer; (2) **rejection,** where the offeree rejects the offer; and (3) **counteroffer,** where the offeree rejects the original offer and proposes a new offer with different terms. Offers may also be terminated by **operation of law.**

Revocation   When the offeror decides to revoke (withdraw) the offer by expressly communicating the revocation to the offeree prior to acceptance, the offer is terminated by revocation. Revocation is consummated through an express repudiation of the offer (e.g., "I revoke my offer of May 1 to paint your office building for $1,000") or by some *inconsistent act* that would give reasonable notice from the offeror to the offeree that the offer no longer existed. For example, on Monday, Owner offers WidgetCo. the nonexclusive opportunity to purchase a parcel of land for $100,000 with a deadline of Friday to respond. On Wednesday, WidgetCo. learns that Owner has entered into a contract with ServiceCo. for the land. On Thursday, WidgetCo. calls Owner with an acceptance. No contract exists between Owner and WidgetCo. because Owner's inconsistent acts were sufficient to give WidgetCo. notice of the transaction.[8]

One important issue with revocation is the timing of the revocation. Most states follow the rule that revocation is only effective *upon receipt* by offeree or the offeree's agent.[9]

---

[6]Based on the landmark case *Carlill v. Carbolic Smoke Ball Co.,* 1 Q.B. 256 (1893).

[7]*Restatements (Second) of Contracts* (§§ 29, 50, 54).

[8]Based on *Restatement (Second) of Contracts* § 42, Illustration 1.

[9]Note that a few states, notably California, do not follow the "receipt" rule, opting instead to make revocation effective upon dispatch of the revocation notice.

FACT SUMMARY Pepsi ran an advertisement on national television promoting its Pepsi Points program whereby consumers could obtain points by purchasing Pepsi products and then redeem the points for certain apparel and other items. An alternate way to accumulate points was to purchase them for a certain dollar figure. The Pepsi advertisement opened with the morning routine of a high school student. The commercial was based on a *Top Gun* movie theme and depicted the student wearing apparel such as a leather bomber jacket, a Pepsi T-shirt, and aviator sunglasses. For each item, the advertisement would flash the corresponding number of Pepsi points required to obtain the item. For example, when showing the actor with the aviator sunglasses, the advertisement featured the subtitle "Shades 175 Pepsi Points." The advertisement then showed a view of the cover of a Pepsi Stuff Catalog with a narration of "Introducing the new Pepsi Stuff Catalog" and the subtitle "See details on specially marked packages." Finally, the advertisement shows the student arriving at his high school in a Harrier Fighter Jet to the amazement of his friends and teachers. The student hops out of the jet and says, "Sure beats the bus." At this point, the subtitle flashes "Harrier Jet 7,000,000 Pepsi points."

Leonard filled out the Pepsi Stuff order form (located in the catalog produced by Pepsi), but since there was no mention of the Harrier Jet, Leonard simply wrote in the item on the order form and sent the order to Pepsi with a check for $700,000, the amount necessary to purchase the requisite points as stated in the advertisement. Pepsi refused to transfer title on the basis that no contract existed. The trial court ruled in favor of Pepsi. Leonard appealed, among other reasons, on the basis that the Pepsi advertisement was specific enough to constitute a valid offer of a unilateral contract through their advertisement.

SYNOPSIS OF DECISION AND OPINION The court ruled against Leonard. While acknowledging that certain advertisements could be an offer if the promise is clear, definite, and explicit, such was not the case here. The advertisement was not sufficiently definite because it reserves the details of the offer to a separate writing (the catalog).*

WORDS OF THE COURT: Requirements for Advertisements as a Unilateral Offer "In the present case, the Harrier Jet commercial did not direct that anyone who appeared at Pepsi headquarters with 7,000,000 Pepsi Points on the Fourth of July would receive the Harrier Jet. Instead, the commercial urged consumers to accumulate Pepsi Points and refer to the catalog to determine how they could receive their Pepsi Points. The commercial sought a reciprocal promise, expressed through the acceptance of, and in compliance with, the terms of the Order Form. [. . .] [T]he catalog contains no mention of the Harrier Jet."

Case Questions

1. What facts would support Leonard's primary argument as to why this commercial was a unilateral offer to contract?

2. If the wording on the catalog order form had allowed a consumer to write in the item (rather than check a box next to the item), would that change the outcome of this case?

To see video of the actual Pepsi advertisement, go to this textbook's Web site at www.mhhe.com/melvin.

---

*The court also rejected Leonard's other primary argument that the advertisement constituted an objective intent by Pepsi to sell a $23 million Harrier Jet for $700,000. The court ruled "In light of the obvious absurdity of the commercial, the court rejects plaintiff's argument that the commercial was not clearly in jest."

For example, on Monday, Adams sends, via same-day courier, a letter of revocation to Bell's office. Bell's administrative assistant receives the revocation on that same day, but Bell is traveling in Japan and never actually sees the letter. On Wednesday, from his hotel room in Tokyo, Bell calls Adams and accepts Adams's initial offer. No contract exists because the revocation would be deemed effective upon receipt by Bell's administrative assistant. At that point, despite that Bell had no *actual* knowledge of the revocation by Adams, the offer is revoked and Bell may no longer accept the offer.

Note that some offers are **irrevocable:** (1) offers in the form of an option contract; (2) offers where the offeree partly performed or detrimentally relied on the offer; and (3) so-called firm offers by a merchant under the UCC (firm offers under the UCC are discussed in Chapter 8 "Contracts for the Sale of Goods").

Option Contracts   One way to make an offer irrevocable is for the offeror to grant the offeree an *option* to enter a contract. Typically, the offeror agrees to hold an offer open (not enter into a contract with another party) for a certain period of time in exchange for something of value (known as *consideration,* discussed later). For example, Coleridge is interested in a parcel of real estate owned by Shelley for his company's warehouse. Coleridge is traveling for a week, but doesn't wish to lose the property to another party even though he hasn't firmly decided to lease the real estate. Coleridge pays Shelley $1,000 to keep the offer open for two weeks to lease the parcel. Shelley is now obliged to keep the offer open and not to entertain offers by third parties. However, if, at the end of the two weeks Coleridge hasn't leased the property, Shelley keeps the $1,000 and is now permitted to lease or sell the property to another party.

Partial Performance and Detrimental Reliance   There are certain offers whereby the offeree may, prior to actual formation of the contract, take some action that *relies* on the offer; for example, if the offeree begins to perform based on a unilateral offer. Recall that a unilateral offer is one in which the offer makes clear that acceptance can occur only through performance, and not through a prom-

Option contracts are sometimes used to provide flexibility in commercial real estate transactions.

ise. This is known as partial performance and can render an offer temporarily irrevocable. For example, Burns offers Realtor a commission of 10 percent of the sales price if Realtor can find a buyer for the Burns Building for $500,000. Realtor spends funds to research and obtain potential buyer contact information and locates Walters, who is willing to accept the $500,000 offer to sell from Burns. Before any transaction takes place, Burns revokes his offer to Realtor and refuses to sell the property to Walters. Burns's revocation is *not effective.* Burns's promise to pay for a particular performance (a unilateral contract) was rendered irrevocable once Realtor performed by finding a buyer for the building.[10] Also, an offer may be rendered irrevocable if the offeree makes preparations prior to acceptance based on a reasonable reliance on the offer. This is known as **detrimental reliance.** For example, SubCo. is a subcontractor for GeneralCo. GeneralCo. relies on SubCo.'s bid in preparing to make an offer to renovate a commercial office complex. After GeneralCo. is awarded the renovation contract, SubCo. notifies them that its bid was too low due to the poor business forecasting of one of SubCo.'s partners. Because they are no longer interested in the job, SubCo. attempts to revoke their offer/bid. In this case, SubCo. is *still required to perform* even at a loss. GeneralCo. reasonably relied on SubCo.'s bid and would suffer a significant detriment based on this reliance. SubCo.'s offer became irrevocable once GeneralCo. exercised reasonable reliance on the offer.[11]

---

[10]Based on *Restatement (Second) of Contracts,* § 45, Illustration 5.

[11]Based on *Restatement (Second) of Contracts,* § 87(2), Illustration 6 [*Drennan v. Star Paving,* 51 Cal. 2d 409 (1958)].

Rejection and Counteroffer   An offer is also terminated once the offeree has either rejected the offer outright or makes a counteroffer by rejecting the original offer and making a new offer. Under the common law,[12] the offeree's response operates as an acceptance only if it is the *precise mirror image* of the offer. If the response conflicts with the original offer even slightly, the original offer is terminated and the new offer is substituted. This principle is called the **mirror image rule.** Once the offeree has rejected or made a counteroffer, her power of acceptance is terminated. For example, apply the mirror image rule to the following conversation:

Franz: "I will pay you $1,000 to paint the interior of our office building."

Josef: "I've seen your office; it is going to cost you more than that."

Franz: "How much more?"

Josef: "I'll do it for $2,000."

Franz: "Ah, yes. Well, let's split it down the middle. I'll pay you $1,500."

Josef: "OK. I agree to do it for $1,500, but you must also supply the paint, brushes, ladder, tarps, cleaner, and other equipment I need."

Does a contract exist between Josef and Franz? Carefully examine the language of the parties. Josef made an outright rejection of Franz's first offer to paint the office for $1,000. Then Josef made an offer to paint the office for $2,000. Franz then rejected the offer via *counteroffer* and now has made a new offer for Josef to accept or reject his offer to pay $1,500 for the services. Although Josef starts out his response with "OK," he adds additional terms (Franz must supply the paint, etc.) and, therefore, Josef has rejected the offer because his acceptance was *not the mirror image* of Franz's offer. Thus, despite the "OK" language, the law treats Josef's response as a counteroffer (and therefore a rejection). Franz's offer is now terminated, and *no* contract exists at this point. Of course, Franz is now free to accept or reject Josef's counteroffer.

> ## KEY POINT
> The mirror image rule, which applies to common law contracts (not UCC contracts), requires that any acceptance by the offeree must be the mirror image of the original offer. Any deviation from the original offer results in a rejection and counteroffer.

Operation of Law   An offer may also be terminated by certain happenings or events covered by operation of law. Generally, these include (1) lapse of time, (2) death or incapacity of the offeror or offeree, and (3) destruction of the subject matter of the contract before acceptance.

Lapse of Time   Following the "offeror is the master of his offer" rule, the offeror will frequently attach some time limit on the offeree's power of acceptance. Once the time limit has expired, the offer is considered to have terminated via **lapse of time.** If, however, the offeror has not set a time limit, the offer will still expire after a *reasonable time*. Courts determine the "reasonable time period" for an acceptance by analyzing the circumstances when the offer and attempted acceptance are made. When the offer involves a speculative transaction where the subject matter is subject to sharp fluctuations in value, a reasonable time period will be considerably shorter. For example, Milton sends Dryden an e-mail: "I offer to sell you my private stock in Local Oil Company for $500 per share." Dryden waits one week, and the price of oil skyrockets in the week making stock in Local Oil rise to $700 per share. He responds to Milton's e-mail: "I accept your offer of last week." In this case, Dryden would likely not be obligated to perform because the subject matter of the offer was so speculative that it dictated a short time

---

[12]Note that the UCC rules are different regarding counteroffers. The UCC rules for counteroffers are discussed in Chapter 8 "Contracts for the Sale of Goods."

period for expiration. On the other hand, if Milton wishes to sell Dryden a used lawn mower for $100, the weeklong time period may still be a reasonable time in which to accept the offer.

Death, Incapacity, or Destruction In the event that the offeror or the offeree either dies or becomes incapacitated before acceptance, the offer automatically terminates. Similarly, if the subject matter of the contract is destroyed before acceptance, the offer is considered terminated by operation of law.

When Acceptance Is Effective: The Mailbox Rule   The **mailbox rule** governs common law contracts and provides a rule for when a contract is considered to be deemed accepted by the offeree, thus depriving the offeror of the right to revoke the offer. In essence, the mailbox rule provides that the acceptance of an offer is generally effective upon dispatch using a commercially reasonable manner (e.g., when the offeree places the acceptance in the mailbox, overnight mail, or faxes) and not when the acceptance is received by the offeror. The time of acceptance depends on whether the offeror specified a method of acceptance or not. Figure 6.2 sets out a flowchart to help understand the rules that govern when acceptance is effective.   **LO**6-5

 Self-Check   Mailbox Rule

For each transaction, does a contract exist? If yes, why, and what is the date of the contract. If no, why not?

PROBLEM #1

Day 1: Connelly sent a fax to Raleigh's office: "We offer to provide you with widget-covering services for $1,000 per month for six months starting January 1."

Day 2: Raleigh sends a letter via U.S. mail to Connelly: "I accept your offer of Day 1."

Day 3: Connelly telephones Raleigh and tells him: "I revoke my widget-covering offer of Day 1." Upon hearing this, Raleigh states "too late, I already put my acceptance in the mailbox!"

Day 4: Connelly receives Raleigh's letter of acceptance on Thursday.

PROBLEM #2

Day 1: BookCo.'s manager e-mails an offer to sell a rare first-edition of *For Whom the Bell Tolls* signed by Hemingway for $50,000 to Rare Book Retailer (RBR).

Day 2: RBR receives the offer, prints out the e-mail, writes "ACCEPTED, 1 Hemingway Book for $50,000. RBR Manager" and faxes BookCo. the acceptance.

Day 3 (9:00 a.m.): BookCo.'s receptionist receives RBR's fax.

Day 3 (12:00 p.m.): BookCo.'s manager calls RBR to revoke her offer.

Day 3 (1:30 p.m.): The RBR acceptance fax is delivered to BookCo.'s manager.

CONCEPT SUMMARY   Agreement

■ The formation of a contract requires mutual assent whereby the parties reach an agreement.

■ An agreement results from the offeror making a valid offer (had objective intent to contract) and the offeree accepting the terms of the offer and agreeing to be bound by its terms.

■ Advertisements are generally not considered an offer. Rather, they are an invitation for the consumer to make an offer to a seller of goods or services.

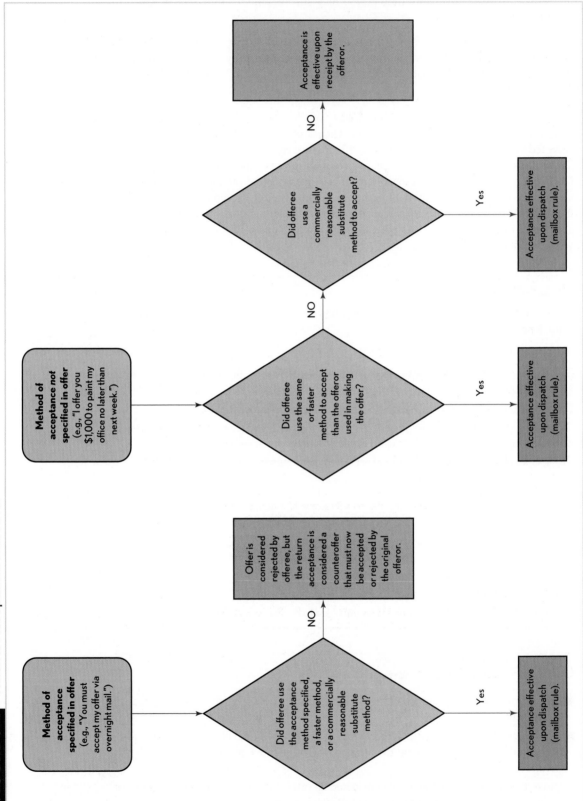

FIGURE 6.2 When Is Acceptance Effective?

Method of acceptance specified in offer (e.g., "You must accept my offer via overnight mail.")

Did offeree use the acceptance method specified, a faster method, or a commercially reasonable substitute method?

NO → Offer is considered rejected by offeree, but the return acceptance is considered a counteroffer that must now be accepted or rejected by the original offeror.

Yes → Acceptance effective upon dispatch (mailbox rule).

Method of acceptance *not* specified in offer (e.g., "I offer you $1,000 to paint my office no later than next week.")

Did offeree use the same or faster method to accept than the offeror used in making the offer?

Yes → Acceptance effective upon dispatch (mailbox rule).

NO → Did offeree use a commercially reasonable substitute method to accept?

Yes → Acceptance effective upon dispatch (mailbox rule).

NO → Acceptance is effective upon receipt by the offeror.

- In order for an offer to be valid, the parties must reach agreement on all of the essential terms of the agreement. An offer that is too vague or indefinite cannot be the basis for an agreement.
- Most offers may be terminated either by the actions of the parties or by operation of law. However, certain offers are considered irrevocable.
- The time acceptance becomes effective is governed by the mailbox rule.

Insufficient Agreement

In some cases the parties may actually have satisfied the elements of offer and acceptance, but the agreement still lacks *mutual assent* and the agreement is insufficient to constitute a properly formed contract. Some common circumstances where parties lack mutual assent are in cases when the agreement's terms are too indefinite, or one or both parties are mistaken about an important term.

Indefinite Terms   For an offer to be valid, the parties must reach mutual assent on all of the *essential terms* of the agreement. Even though two parties who are negotiating with each other may have an objective intent to contract, there is no valid contract if the terms are too vague to be performed. Typically, these terms must either be expressly agreed upon or capable of being reasonably inferred. These essential terms are: (1) parties to the contract, (2) subject matter of the contract, (3) time for performance or delivery, (4) price or other consideration to be exchanged.

Note, however, that courts have become increasingly tolerant of uncertainty in terms before allowing a contract to be voided for indefiniteness. The *Restatement* test requires a court to examine the terms of the agreement to determine whether "they provide a basis for determining the existence of a breach and for giving an appropriate remedy."[13] Thus, even though an agreement does not contain all of the required terms, courts have held that missing terms may be supplied by the court when the term may be implied as "reasonable" or by the course of past dealing. So long as the agreement is definite enough to allow the court to determine whether one party failed to fulfill the obligations of the agreement, and to award some kind of reasonable damages to the wronged party, the contract is not void for indefiniteness.

Agreements to Agree   In certain circumstances in the business environment, the parties enter into an agreement with an essential term unfilled, intending to agree upon the term in the future. Although historically courts were reluctant to enforce such agreements, the modern trend is to allow such agreements to be enforced with the court supplying the missing term according to industry standards and market values. So long as the court determines that the parties themselves intended to make a binding contract, the agreement is enforceable and a court may supply the missing term. For example, suppose that Ernest offers to purchase an office building from Whitehead for $100,000 in 30 days. At the time of the agreement, Ernest was unsure of the method that he would use to pay the purchase price, so the parties leave that term unfilled. On the day of the purchase, Ernest pays Whitehead $10 in cash and signs a promissory note for $99,990. Whitehead refuses to complete the transaction and demands a check or cash for the full $100,000. In this case, a court would likely hold that (1) the agreement to agree on the payment terms was enforceable because it is clear the parties intended to enter into a contractual relationship, and (2) the court can supply the missing term with a degree of reasonableness based on pattern of past practices and/or industry standards (e.g., requiring that Ernest obtain a mortgage or pay in cash for the property).

---

[13] *Restatement (Second) of Contracts,* § 33(2).

FACT SUMMARY Wichelhaus contracted to purchase a shipment of expensive cotton from Raffles. The contract required the goods to arrive in England aboard the *Peerless,* a freighter ship from Bombay. Wichelhaus had intended for the contract to require the goods to be shipped on the *Peerless* from Bombay in *October.* Raffles believed that the cotton was to be shipped on a different freighter (also called *Peerless*) that left from Bombay in *December.* When the goods arrived in December, Wichelhaus refused to accept them contending that he had already purchased the cotton from the *Peerless* ship that arrived in October. Raffles sued to recover the damages suffered due to Wichelhaus's refusal to accept delivery of the cotton aboard the December *Peerless* ship.

SYNOPSIS OF DECISION AND OPINION The court ruled in favor of Wichelhaus on the basis that each party believed the ship *Peerless* to mean two different ships. The court determined that the misunderstanding resulted in a lack of mutual assent because the parties attached materially different meanings to an essential term of the contract. Therefore, the parties are discharged from any obligations.

WORDS OF THE COURT: Mistake by Ambiguity "There is nothing on the face of the contract to show that any particular ship called the *Peerless* was meant; but the moment it appears that two ships called *Peerless* were about to sail from Bombay there is a latent ambiguity . . . showing that the defendant meant one *Peerless,* and the plaintiff another. That being so, there was no consensus . . . and therefore no binding contract."

Case Questions

1. If there were some evidence that one party was unreasonable in their understanding of what *Peerless* meant, would that affect the mistake analysis?

2. What made this mistake one that qualifies as an essential term that required "consensus"?

Mistake   Over the course of a business life cycle, it is inevitable that a manager involved in a contract will make a **mistake** (or contract with a mistaken party). The law recognizes certain mistakes and provides a remedy intended to make the parties whole again. One famous legal commentator wrote that "mistake is one of the most difficult [doctrines] in the law, because so many men make so many mistakes, of so many different kinds, with so many varying effects."[14]

Generally, a mistake is defined in contract law as a *belief that is not in accord with the facts.*[15] It is important to note that not *all* erroneous beliefs are classified as a mistake. A mistake refers to an erroneous belief about an *existing* fact, not an erroneous belief as to what will happen in the future. Erroneous beliefs about the future are covered by doctrines of impossibility and impracticability, which are discussed in the next chapter. Mistakes are classified as either *mutual* (both parties) or *unilateral* (one party).

A **mutual mistake** may be the basis for *canceling* a contract (also called *avoiding* the contract) when both parties hold an erroneous belief. In order for the adversely affected party to cancel the contract, the mistake must concern a *basic assumption* on which the contract was made. Landmark Case 6.1, known as the *Peerless* ship case, is a historically famous analysis of the mutual mistake doctrine. It is still cited by modern courts as framework for deciding whether the parties attached materially different meanings to the terms of a contract.

Other examples of mutual mistakes include mistakes as to the existence of the subject matter (parties agree to the sale of goods, but the goods were already destroyed by fire at the

---

[14] *Corbin on Contracts,* Section 103.

[15] *Restatement (Second) of Contracts,* § 151.

time of the contract) and quality of the subject matter (parties agreed to sale of a rare first edition book that turns out to be a second edition and not nearly as valuable). Courts will *not* generally consider market conditions (such as the fair market value of a piece of real estate) or financial ability (such as relying on one party's representation that she can receive adequate credit to purchase the real estate) as a mistake that allows a contract to be avoided.

A **unilateral mistake** is when only one party had an erroneous belief about a basic assumption in the terms of the agreement. Courts are much less willing to allow a mistaken party to cancel a contract for a unilateral mistake than in the case of a mutual mistake. In fact, the general rule is that a unilateral mistake is not a valid reason to avoid a contract. However, if the nonmistaken party had reason to *know* of the mistake or his actions *caused* the mistake, a court will allow the mistaken party to avoid the contract. For example, General Contractor solicits bids from Cement Inc. in order to calculate a bid for a new construction project. Cement Inc. sends a letter offer with a clerical error that promises to provide $20,000 worth of cement for $2,000. General Contractor sends an e-mail accepting the $2,000 bid. A court would likely allow Cement Inc. to cancel the cement contract based on unilateral mistake.[16] Note that courts are much less willing to allow a party to cancel a contract if the unilateral mistake is essentially an error in business judgment rather than a clerical error.

Consideration

LO6-6

Not all promises are legally enforceable. A promise to pay a cash gift for graduation is not an enforceable promise. For a binding contract to exist there must be not only agreement (i.e., offer and acceptance) but the agreement must be supported by *consideration*. The function of consideration is to distinguish between those promises that are *binding* on the promisor and those that are not. For most contracts, a court will not enforce a promise unless the promisee has been given consideration for the promise. If either party to a contract has not given consideration, the agreement is unenforceable, unless it falls under one of the exceptions (discussed later). Generally, a promise is supported by consideration if (1) the promisee suffers a *legal detriment* by giving up something of *value* or some *legal right,* and (2) the promisor makes his promise as part of a *bargained for exchange.*

Legal Detriment   Proper consideration requires that the parties suffer some type of detriment that the law recognizes as adequate. This is satisfied if the party promises to perform something that the party is not legally obligated to do (such as promising to sell your car for $5,000) or refrain from doing something that party had a right to do (such as waiving your rights to pursue a lawsuit when you have been injured). In one famous decision from 1891, an appellate court in New York held that one party's promise to abstain from the then-legal practices of drinking, smoking, and gambling until age 21, in exchange for a promise by his uncle to pay him $5,000,[17] was sufficient legal detriment for both parties and thus was an enforceable contract.[18] The nephew had given up a legal right that was sufficient to satisfy the legal detriment required.

Preexisting Duty Rule   If a party does or promises to do what she is already legally obligated to do, the law generally *does not* recognize this as a legal detriment and, thus, the contract is unenforceable. The classic example is that a police officer cannot collect the reward for arresting a fugitive because the officer had a **preexisting duty** to find and arrest fugitives. More often, however, the preexisting duty rule applies in circumstances where

---

[16]Based on *Restatement (Second) of Contracts,* § 154, Illustration 6.

[17]Using the Consumer Price Index rate to calculate the time value of money, this sum would be approximately $104,000 in today's dollars.

[18]*Hammer v. Sidway,* 124 N.Y. 538 (1891).

one party claims they wish to modify an existing contract because of unforeseen difficulties in performing their obligations. For example, Helsel contracts with Mullen to renovate Helsel's office building. During the renovation, Mullen discovers the costs of renovation will be more than he anticipated. Mullen threatens to walk off the job unless Helsel agrees to pay an amount higher than stated in the contract. Because Helsel's choices would be limited to either agreeing or hiring a new contractor and then suing Mullen, he consents to the price increase. Most courts would *not* enforce Helsel's promise to pay the additional amount because Mullen already had a preexisting contractual duty to perform for the original price.

There is a modern trend in most courts that has fashioned a number of exceptions to the preexisting duty rule.[19] For example, if a party who promises to do what she is already bound to do assumes additional duties, her undertaking of these duties is considered sufficient legal detriment.[20] Also, courts may allow an exception in a case where certain circumstances were not reasonably *anticipated* by either party when the original contract was formed. For example, Waste Disposal Company (WDC) contracts with ManufactureCo. to collect garbage from ManufacturerCo.'s warehouse for one year. Six months into the agreement, WDC requests an additional $5,000 per month to provide this service because the ManfactureCo. warehouse is now unexpectedly producing some hazardous material waste that must be removed by specifically designed equipment. The parties then execute a modification to the contract agreeing to the increase. One month later, ManufactureCo. changes managers and the new manager refuses to pay the additional sum, citing the preexisting duty rule. In this case, most courts would *enforce* the modification as an exception to the preexisting duty rule.[21]

Bargained for Exchange   Even if a legal detriment is suffered by one party, that alone does not satisfy the consideration requirement. The **bargain for exchange** aspect of consideration is primarily to distinguish contracts from gifts. Since gift promises are not enforceable and contract promises are, it is important to understand the precise difference. A performance or return promise is "bargained for" only if it was exchanged for another promise.

Past Consideration   Another type of contract that is not considered to meet the bargained for exchange requirement is when a promise is made in return for a detriment previously made by the promisee. This is known as **past consideration** and it is not sufficient to meet the consideration requirement. Let's suppose that Winston enters into an agreement with Neville to provide Winston's company with same-day courier services for a period of six months. Neville is so happy about the contract that he calls Winston and says: "Thanks for your business. I'll deliver a bottle of rare Napoleon brandy to your office today." Winston replies: "I accept your generous offer." The brandy never arrives and Winston sues claiming that the fee paid for the same-day courier contract is sufficient consideration to cover the brandy contract. Although the brandy contract has both offer and acceptance it is *unenforceable* because it lacks consideration. Winston's contention that the courier contract consideration was sufficient is false because it is past consideration for another contract. Thus, the brandy is a gift offer and not enforceable as a contract.

Amount and Type of Consideration   Although the consideration does not need to be of equal value, gift promises and moral obligations are usually not considered valid. Ordinarily, courts will not look to the *amount* or *type* of consideration, or the relative bargaining power of the parties (except in the rare case when the contract is so burdensome on one

---

[19]In fact, some states (such as New York) have repudiated the preexisting duty rule altogether and allow a good-faith modification made in writing to be enforceable.

[20]*Restatement (Second) of Contracts,* § 73.

[21]Based on *Angel v. Murray*, 332 A.2d 630 (R.I. 1974).

party as to indicate unconscionability, discussed later) in deciding the validity of consideration. So long as some bargained for exchange is contemplated, the contract will be deemed enforceable.

Contracts may be based on **nominal consideration** (i.e., consideration that is stated in a written contract even though it is not actually exchanged). Most courts have held that the consideration requirement is still met even if the nominal amount is never actually paid so long as the amount is truly nominal (such as $1.00). In *Bennett v. American Electric Power Services Corp.,*[22] a state appellate court ruled against an employee who had signed an employment agreement that assigned all of his rights for any invention made in the scope of employment to his employer "in consideration of the sum of One Dollar" even though the actual dollar was never paid. The court reasoned that the offer of employment to the employee in the contract was a sufficient bargained for exchange.[23]

Promissory Estoppel   If one party justifiably relies on the promise of another, under certain circumstances, the relying party may recover costs of the reliance from the promisor even though the original promise agreement lacked consideration. Under the theory of **promissory estoppel,** a relying party may recover damages if (1) the promisee *actually* relied on the promise (the promise must have induced the act); (2) the promisee's reliance was *reasonably foreseeable* to the promisor (what an objectively reasonable person would have foreseen under the same circumstances); and (3) principles of *equity and justice* (did each party act in good faith and fair dealing) are served by providing compensation to the reliant party.

One particularly important domain of promissory estoppel for managers is in dealing with promises of employment. Most commonly, this arises in a situation where an employer has made a promise of employment to an at-will[24] employee candidate, and then revokes the promise before the employee's start date (or soon thereafter). Typically, the employee would have left her previous position and potentially incurred moving expenses. In those cases, courts have held that the revocation of the employment at-will promise before any consideration was exchanged triggers the doctrine of promissory estoppel whereby the innocent party is entitled to damages. In promissory estoppel cases, courts frequently award damages equal to the out-of-pocket costs plus what the employee lost in quitting her job and declining employment elsewhere.[25] For example, suppose that Donatello is given a written offer of employment to go to work for Renaissance Architect Firm (RAF) for an annual salary of $50,000 to begin in 30 days. Donatello gives his current employer notice of his resignation, then moves his home 100 miles in order to be closer to RAF's headquarters. The day before Donatello shows up for work, RAF informs him that due to financial difficulties they can no longer honor their offer of employment. When Donatello attempts to regain his old employment, he is told that his position was filled and there is no chance of rehiring him. Donatello cannot prevail on a breach of contract claim because no consideration was actually ever exchanged and, therefore, the promise is not supported by consideration and not enforceable as a contract. However, a court would likely award Donatello damages based on promissory estoppel. RAF may be liable for damages related to Donatello's actions in

---

[22] 2001 WL 1136150 (Ohio Ct. App. 2001).

[23] In its opinion, the court wrote "[a]lthough ancient, the best authorities on the issue hold that nonpayment of such nominal consideration will not constitute breach, at least in instances where the actual value of the subject of the contract does not, in fact, correspond to the nominal consideration."

[24] At-will employees are those that may be fired with or without cause because the employee is not covered by a contract or any other promises of continued employment. Employees-at-will are discussed in detail in Chapter 10 "Agency and Employment Relationships."

[25] Note that generally courts do *not* measure damages by looking at what the employee would have earned from the defendant in a certain time period.

reliance of RAF's promise, such as the moving expenses and compensation in connection with Donatello's resignation from his previous employer.[26]

LO6-7 Capacity

In addition to meeting the requirements for agreement and consideration, courts will only enforce contracts where each party had the legal *capacity* to enter into a contract. Certain classes of persons have only limited power to contract: **minors** and those with **mental incapacity.** In these cases, parties may seek to *avoid* (cancel) the contract immediately or they may enforce the contract with the option of avoiding it at any time up until the time they regain capacity. Once the party has regained capacity, the contract becomes binding on both parties.

Minors   Until a person reaches her majority age, any contract that she may enter into is *voidable* at the minor's option. Minors (referred to as *infants* in legal terminology) are defined by most states as those who are younger than 18. For example, Junior is 17 and enters into to an agreement to purchase a pickup truck from Roscoe's Dealership. Junior later changes his mind and decides not to go through with the transaction. Roscoe may not enforce the agreement against Junior. However, Junior may still enforce the contract against Roscoe if he so desires.[27]

A minor may avoid a contract even before she reaches the age of majority.[28] It is important to remember that a contract made by a minor is not *automatically* void. Rather, the minor either avoids the contract or may enforce the contract. While a minor may avoid a contract up until the age of majority, the minor may also *ratify* the contract upon reaching the age of 18. Note that a minor is assumed to have ratified the contract upon reaching the age of 18 if she fails to *disaffirm* (avoid) the contract in a reasonable time period.[29] In the case where the minor has disaffirmed and avoided the contract, the other party may be entitled to an economic adjustment if the minor received some economic benefit from the contract. Generally, this means that the minor will have to return any goods or make restitution for any damages that affected the value of the good or service. In the example above, suppose that Junior goes through with the truck purchase, and avoids the contract on his 18th birthday. Roscoe is entitled to claim the truck back and may be entitled to compensation for the loss of the truck's market value from the previous year.

Virtually all jurisdictions recognize an *exception* to the minor capacity rule for necessities such as food, clothing, and shelter. Thus, a 16-year-old customer at a restaurant may not disaffirm a contract to purchase french fries when presented with the bill.

Mental Incompetents   Like minors, mental incompetents are treated as having limited capacity to contract. This category covers not just obvious cases (such as mental retardation or dementia) but also temporary incompetence such as parties who are highly intoxicated.

In general, a person lacks capacity because of mental illness or defect if either (1) she is *unable to understand* the nature and consequences of the contract, or (2) she is *unable to act in a reasonable manner* in relation to the transaction and the other party has *reason*

---

[26] Based on *Grouse v. Group Health Plan, Inc.,* 306 N.W.d 114 (Minn. 1981).

[27] In cases where the minor misrepresents her age, courts differ in their treatment of the transactions. In some cases, courts place a greater burden of restitution for any misrepresentations. In other cases, courts have allowed either party to avoid the contract. A minority of states allow the nonminor party to be sued for the tort of misrepresentation.

[28] Michigan is the only state with an exception to this rule.

[29] There is no definitive test for determining what is a "reasonable time" because the time period may be case specific depending on individual industry standards and practices.

to know of her condition.[30] For example, Oliver has Alzheimer's disease and enters into a contract with Wendell to sell 100 widgets for $1 per widget (the widget's fair market value). Oliver may avoid the contract even though the contract terms were fair and Wendell had no notice of Oliver's condition. This is true because Oliver has met the "unable to understand" criteria. On the other hand, suppose that Oliver and Wendell were at a bar drinking heavily. Wendell writes on a cocktail napkin: Because you bought me so many pints of beer, I will sell you 100 widgets for only five cents per widget. The next day Wendell sobers up and realizes what he did. Wendell may avoid the contract because he was so intoxicated he was unable to act in a reasonable manner *and* because Oliver had *reason to know* of Wendell's condition.

In most states contracts made by an incompetent are *voidable,* not void. If the incompetent party regains her mental capacity, or has a guardian appointed, she may ratify the contract. Note that the other party does *not* have the power to avoid the contract. However, many states classify a contract as *void per se* (not valid from the outset) if one party has been legally declared to be incompetent prior to entering into the contract.

Legality

In order for a contract to be enforceable, both the subject matter and performance of the contract must be legal. Some contracts are specifically barred by statute (e.g., a contract related to illegal gambling such as betting on sports events[31] or a contract for the sale of goods that is banned by a trade embargo), while other contracts are illegal because the terms violate some public policy objective (such as an overly broad restriction on employment possibilities known as a *restrictive covenant*). As a general rule, illegal contracts are *void automatically* and neither party may enforce it against the other. This is true even when only one party's performance is illegal. For example, if Holmes promises to paint Cardozo's home in exchange for Cardozo's promise to smuggle 500 Cuban cigars into the United States in violation of federal law, then neither Holmes nor Cardozo may enforce the contract.

CONCEPT SUMMARY Contract Formation

Agreement	Mutual Assent	Consideration	Capacity	Legality
The offer must represent a serious, objective intent to contract; proper acceptance of the offer must occur prior to termination by the parties or operation of law.	The terms must be sufficiently definite, and there must be no mistake (belief by one or both parties not in accord with the facts).	There must be the possibility of legal detriment to the promisee and a bargained for exchange on the part of the promisor.	If one of the parties is a minor, the contract is voidable by the minor or the minor's guardian. If one of the parties is mentally incapacitated, and the other party had reason to know of the incapacity, the contact may be avoided.	The subject matter of the contract and transaction must be legal.

---

[30]*Restatement (Second) of Contracts,* § 15(2).

[31]Many states do allow "small games of chance" such as church-sponsored Bingo or an office football pool.

Enforcing Contracts with Covenants not to Compete

PROBLEM *How do you protect the company's interests from employees who depart the company in order to directly compete with their ex-employer?*

One type of special contract that managers are increasingly encountering at a variety of levels in the corporate sector are contracts where one party agrees not to compete with another party for a specified period of time. Known as **covenants not to compete** (also called a *restrictive covenant*), courts have historically subjected these contracts to close judicial scrutiny. This is not to say that covenants not to compete are unenforceable; rather, courts use a "reasonableness" approach in determining the extent to which the covenant is enforceable. Even if a court finds that the terms of the covenant were unreasonable, most courts will opt to enforce the covenant to the extent required to protect the legitimate interests of the business. For example, Jordan signs a noncompete agreement with Robert, her employer, whereby Jordan agrees not to contact any of Robert's clients anywhere in the United States for two years after she has left Robert's company. After Jordan quits and starts her own firm, Robert finds out Jordan has been contacting Robert's clients. Robert sues to enforce the covenant. If a court finds the covenant to be too broad, the covenant may be pared back by the court to, say, one year and a more limited geographic region. This is an alternative to striking down the covenant completely.*

SOLUTION *Be sure that your company's restrictive covenant agreements are narrowly tailored keeping the following requirements and standards in mind:*

- *Source* Covenants not to compete most often arise out of either (1) the sale of a business whereby the buyer is purchasing business assets, goodwill, and promises by the seller's principals not to compete with the buyer; or (2) as part of an employment contract.
- *Sale of a Business* In the context of a sale of a business, courts are willing to enforce such covenants, but are often focused on the geographic area

*Based on *Restatements (Second) of Contracts,* § 184(2), Comment b, Illustration 2.

involved. If the covenant restriction is substantially broader than that where the buyer and seller are currently doing business, courts are unwilling to enforce such an overly broad restriction.

- *Employment Agreements* Covenants that are part of an employment contract (or an employment relationship) are subjected to a higher degree of scrutiny. Courts will generally permit the employment covenant to stand so long as it is designed to cover a recognized legitimate interest of the employer. Courts recognize an employer's interest in guarding *trade secrets* from being disclosed or used by an ex-employee.[†] Employers also have a legitimate interest in ensuring that former employees do not act in a way that could *damage relationships* with their existing customers. Therefore, courts have permitted contracts that prevent ex-employees from soliciting (or even contacting) customers of the ex-employer for a certain period of time. However, these types of covenants must be *reasonable* in duration, subject matter scope, and geographic scope. Although these standards vary from industry to industry, some general guidance regarding reasonableness are helpful.
- *Duration.* The higher the position of the employee, the longer the employer can restrict the employee. A sales staffer who quit after only one year would likely not be bound any more than one or two years. The CEO of a corporation may be bound in the range of five years or more. In any case, the duration must be no greater than is required for the protection of the employer while still considering the potential for undue hardship on the employee.
- *Scope of Subject Matter.* The restriction must be directly tied to the employee's work responsibilities. For example, if Foley works 10 years as an insurance agent for Garvey's Insurance Agency, the restrictive covenant may only cover a competing interest of insurance sales. Thus, if Foley quits Garvey Insurance, starts a career as a

[†] Generally, a trade secret is a process, data, or system that gives a company a competitive edge over another (e.g., customer lists, formulas, etc.). Trade secrets are covered in depth in Chapter 24, "Intellectual Property."

(continued)

golf instructor and contacts customers he met while employed by Garvey, a court would not enforce a covenant to prevent this contact because any such restriction is too broad in terms of the scope of the subject matter.

• *Geographic Scope.* Employers must limit the geographic area in which the employer conducts business *and* the geographic region must not impose an undue hardship on the employee. While some companies may legitimately claim that they do business in all 50 states, courts are still reluctant to allow a restriction to be effective countrywide because that would require ex-employees to move abroad in order to comply with the covenant. On the other hand, a small manufacturing company in Philadelphia may wish to restrict its ex-engineering employees from competing within a radius of several miles of the city. This would likely be seen as a protection of legitimate business interests without an undue burden to the employee.

ENFORCEABILITY

LO 6-8

Once it is determined that the parties have properly formed a contract, the analysis turns to **enforceability.** A contract is of little use if it is not enforceable in a court of law, and business owners and managers can reduce risk and unnecessarily exposing their company to liability by ensuring that contracts are not only properly formed, but legally enforceable. Even if the elements of a contract are met, the contract must still be (1) the product of genuine assent, and (2) in writing under certain circumstances.

Genuineness of Assent

Recall from the discussion in the previous section of this chapter that an agreement must reflect mutual assent (sufficiently definite terms, lack of mistake, etc.) in order to legally form a contract. In order for a contract to be enforceable, the contract must *also* be the result of *genuine assent.* This means that in order for a contract to be valid and enforceable, the law requires the parties to have given genuine consent on the terms of the contract. A lack of genuine assent occurs in cases of (1) misrepresentation and fraudulent misrepresentation, (2) duress, (3) undue influence, and (4) unconscionability.

> **Legal Speak** ›))
> **Goodwill** Intangible assets that represent value to the business such as its reputation for quality and/or service.

> **KEY** POINT
>
> Contracts that include restrictive covenants must protect a legitimate business interest of an employer and be reasonable in terms of scope and duration.

Misrepresentation   When one party to an agreement makes a promise or representation about a material fact that is not true, the other party may avoid the contract on the basis of **misrepresentation.** This is true even if the misrepresenting party doesn't actually know that the promise or representation was false. Consequentially, the defense is sometimes called *innocent misrepresentation,* which distinguishes it from *fraudulent misrepresentation* (discussed later). In order for one party to avoid the contract on the basis of misrepresentation, she must prove (1) the misrepresented fact was *material* (i.e., it concerns a basic assumption in the agreement or the false representation somehow changed the value of the contract); (2) that she *justifiably relied* on the misstatement when forming an agreement (such as determining the price to be paid for a commercial office building); and (3) the misrepresentation was one of *fact* and not just someone's opinion or mere puffing (e.g., "this building's roof is only 5 years old" is a verifiable fact versus "the roof is in great shape," which is puffing).

Sometimes it is difficult to distinguish between fact and opinion. In one famous case, a dance student sued her dancing school on the basis of misrepresentations by her instructor who had frequently assured her that she had "excellent potential" for dance so long as she kept purchasing pricey lessons from the dancing school. Eventually, the student sought another teacher who informed her that she had minimal dance aptitude and could barely detect a musical beat. The dance school argued that the advice was merely opinion and, therefore, could not be the basis for a misrepresentation claim. Nonetheless, the court ruled in favor of the student and reasoned that because the dancing school had "superior knowledge" on the subject that it had a duty to act in good faith in their contract transactions.[32]

Fraudulent Misrepresentation   When one party has engaged in conduct that meets the standards for misrepresentation, but that party has actual *knowledge* that the representation is not true, this is known as **fraudulent misrepresentation** (sometimes referred to simply as *fraud*). That is, misrepresentation plus knowledge (also known as *guilty knowledge*[33]) equals fraudulent misrepresentation. The primary difference between misrepresentation and fraudulent misrepresentation, from a manager's perspective, is the relief available to the innocent party. In both cases, the innocent party may *avoid* the contract and be released from any obligations. In cases of misrepresentation, the innocent party has only limited relief in terms of money damages because recovery in many states is limited to any actual out-of-pocket damages. In cases of fraudulent misrepresentation, most states classify the contract as void and the innocent party is generally entitled to recover money damages for any losses incurred, plus more for speculative damages such as loss of future profits.

> ## KEY POINT
>
> The elements of misrepresentation (materiality, justifiable reliance, and fact) *plus* the element of actual knowledge of the misrepresented fact is considered fraudulent misrepresentation, and the innocent party may be entitled to additional recovery.

To better understand the difference between innocent misrepresentation and fraudulent misrepresentation, suppose Marshall negotiated to purchase Nino's office building. During the negotiations, Marshall asked Nino if the building had any radon[34] in the underground storage basements. Nino replied that he has owned the building for 10 years and there was no radon. Marshall then agreed to buy the property for $100,000, but before the closing date he finds out that radon is present in the basements and it will cost $15,000 for a radon evacuation system to be installed. In this case, the radon was a material fact (changes the value of the contract by $15,000), Marshall relied on that fact in calculating the price, and Nino's representation was of a fact that turned out to be false. Marshall may, therefore, avoid the contract based on *innocent misrepresentation*.

However, suppose that after Marshall cancels the contract, Nino finds another party to buy the building (New Buyer). When New Buyer asks Nino about the radon, Nino gets nervous about the sale falling through, so he lies saying that "as far as I know" there is no radon. New Buyer may avoid the contract on the basis of fraudulent misrepresentation because Nino's statements fit the requirements for misrepresentation, but in this case he had knowledge that his statements were false. Thus, the new buyer would also be entitled to additional money damages from Nino for any losses that New Buyer suffered as a result of the *fraudulent misrepresentation*.

In Case 6.2, a court analyzes a fraudulent misrepresentation claim in the context of promises made as part of a franchise contract.

Concealment of Material Fact   Although many fraudulent misrepresentations stem from affirmative promises (such as the age of a roof), sometimes a fraudulent misrepresentation occurs when one party *conceals* a material fact. While parties do *not* have a general duty to disclose all information to each other, courts have allowed the use of misrepresentation in

---

[32]*Vokes v. Arthur Murray, Inc.,* 212 So. 2d 906 (Fla. Dist. Ct. App. 1968).

[33]The legal term for this type of guilty knowledge is *scienter.*

[34]Radon is an invisible, naturally occurring gas that the EPA has determined to be a risk factor for cancer.

FACT SUMMARY   PowerSports applied for a franchise license from Harley-Davidson ("Harley") to sell Harley products in Seminole County, Florida. During Harley's interview of PowerSports, officers of PowerSports made certain representations and promises about PowerSports' business practices and procedures. This was an important part of the negotiations because Harley had strict standards of quality and customer service with which all of its dealers had to comply. Based on these representations, Harley granted the franchise license and PowerSports became an authorized dealer. Just days after they signed the franchise agreement, Harley became aware that PowerSports had taken significant steps toward plans to take their company public (sell company stock on the public market). This was inconsistent with Harley's requirements and conditions for owning a franchise. Harley alleged that the representations made by PowerSports were false and sued PowerSports for fraudulent misrepresentation, demanding a rescission of the contract plus additional damages.

SYNOPSIS OF DECISION AND OPINION   The Seventh Circuit Court of Appeals held in favor of Harley, citing PowerSports' statements and representations made during the preliminary phase of the agreement. The evidence showed that Harley would only grant the license to a business venture that met certain criteria. Chief among them was that the franchise would only be awarded to a privately owned company that had no intention of becoming a company with stock that was traded publicly. In order to induce Harley to approve the franchise, PowerSports either concealed or misrepresented their desire to become a publicly held company immediately after acquiring the franchise license. The misrepresentations were (1) knowing, (2) concerned material facts, and (3) were justifiably relied on by Harley in approving the franchise agreement. Thus, PowerSport potentially engaged in fraudulent misrepresentation and rescission plus damages are appropriate.

WORDS OF THE COURT: Rescission in Cases of Fraudulent Misrepresentation   "Under contract law, when seeking rescission all that is required is that a party's manifestation of assent is induced by fraudulent misrepresentation. Harley-Davidson explained its expectations for how dealers should run Harley-Davidson dealerships and repeatedly asked for information concerning PowerSports' plans for [their dealership] and for going public. From these facts, it could be inferred that PowerSports knew that its representations that it would operate a community-oriented, exclusive Harley-Davidson dealership, owned by a company that was not going public, would induce Harley-Davidson to approve the transfer and thus were fraudulent misrepresentations."

Case Questions

1. Why were PowerSports misrepresentations "material"?

2. Suppose PowerSports went public two years after the awarding of the franchise agreement. Could Harley still sue for recession? How about 10 years?

cases where a party has asserted a half-truth that led to an overall misrepresentation, where one party takes affirmative action to conceal truth from the other, and when one party fails to correct a past statement that the other party subsequently discovers is untrue.

Duress   If one party to a contract uses any form of unfair coercion to induce another party to enter into or modify a contract, the coerced party may avoid the contract on the basis of **duress.** Generally, the law recognizes three categories of duress: (1) violence or threats of a violent act;[35] (2) economic threats such as wrongful termination or threats to

---

[35]Note that duress is one of the few areas of contract law based on the subjective belief of one of the parties in the agreement. That is, regardless of the form and content of the threats, if the coerced party shows that he was, for example, unusually timid or in an unusually vulnerable state of mind, he may use the duress defense even if an ordinarily reasonable person would not have been intimidated by such threats. *See generally,* J. D. Calamari, J. M. Perillo, and H. H. Bender, *Cases and Problems on Contracts,* 4th ed. (St. Paul, MN: West/Thomson, 2004), p. 309.

breach a contract; and (3) threats of extortion or other threats where the other party has no meaningful choice. One important point to consider is that if one party threatens another with a certain act, it is *irrelevant* that he would have the legal right to perform that act. This becomes a central principle in a case where some economic duress is at issue. For example, Bloom works for Joyce as an employee at-will (that is, either party may terminate the employment with or without cause).[36] Joyce threatens Bloom that he will be fired unless he agrees to sell his stock to Joyce for $5 per share. Bloom has no choice, so he sells the stock. A court will allow Bloom to avoid the contract based on this threat even though Joyce had a legitimate right to fire Bloom with or without just cause.

Undue Influence   The defense of **undue influence** gives legal relief to a party that was induced to enter into a contract through the improper pressure of a trusted relationship. Undue influence allows the influenced party to avoid a contract where the court determines that the terms of the contract are *unfair* and the parties had some type of relationship that involved a *fiduciary duty* or some duty to *care* for the influenced party. For example, Edna is a caregiver for June, a wealthy widow who is confined to a wheelchair. Edna informs June that she can longer be her caregiver unless June signs a contract to assign to Edna $50,000 worth of Microsoft stock. June cannot imagine the thought of being alone or finding another caregiver, so she goes ahead with the contract. In this case, a court would likely allow June to avoid the contract based on the undue influence that Edna had asserted over her.

Unconscionability   When an agreement is reached between two parties that have met the required elements and are not subject to the defenses discussed previously, the contract may still potentially be avoided on the grounds that one party suffered a grossly unfair burden that shocks the objective conscience. Recall from our discussion of consideration that courts will generally not be inclined to weigh the amount and type of consideration to determine whether the exchange is objectively fair. While this doctrine remains true, the defense of **unconscionability** gives the court the tools to refuse to enforce a contract where the consideration is grossly unequal. For example, in *Waters v. Min Ltd.,*[37] an appellate court allowed one party to avoid a contract in which she signed over an annuity insurance contract with an immediate value in excess of $150,000 in exchange for a check for $50,000. The fully annuitized value of the contract would have been over $530,000. The court ruled that although there was a written contract that met the elements required under the law, the disparity of value in the exchange along with other circumstances such as drug dependency and lack of legal advice was "too hard of a bargain for a court [to enforce]." While courts apply this defense *very* narrowly, it remains a viable defense when one party was induced to enter the contract through oppressive terms where no bargaining is possible. Thus, high-pressure sales tactics that mislead illiterate consumers may be one case in which a court would likely allow a party to avoid the contract.[38] Courts have also been suspicious of standardized preprinted contracts, known as *adhesion contracts,* because there is an assumption that the nondrafter has not genuinely bargained for the terms of the agreement. For example, in *Henningsen v. Bloomfield Motors, Inc.,*[39] an appellate court held that a disclaimer of a warranty that was buried in small print in a preprinted agreement to purchase a used car was *void* because the drafter had "gross inequity of bargaining

---

[36]Employment at will is discussed in detail in Chapter 10, "Agency and Employment Relationships."

[37]587 N.E.2d 231 (Mass. 1992).

[38]In the landmark case of *Frostifresh Corp. v. Reynoso,* 274 N.Y.S.2d 757 (1966), the court held that a contract where one party sold a freezer to another party who spoke very little English was unconscionable because of unethical sales practices, an oppressive credit installment agreement, and little benefit to the buyer.

[39]161 A.2d 69 (N.J. 1960).

position" and that an ordinary person would not be able to fully comprehend what legal rights he was giving up. Therefore, the court held that enforcement of the disclaimer was against public policy. In some cases, courts have held that arbitration clauses contained in contracts are unconscionable.[40] The enforceability of arbitration clauses in contracts is discussed in detail in Chapter 4, "Resolving Disputes: Litigation and Alternative Dispute Resolution Options."

Statute of Frauds

LO 6-9

The statute of frauds is the law governing which contracts must be *in writing* in order to be enforceable. As its title suggests, the statute's purpose is to prevent fraud by requiring that certain contracts have written evidence of their existence and terms in order to be enforceable. This is not to say, however, that the statute requires all contracts to be in writing. Nor does it require that the contract writing be in a prescribed format. Courts have even held that an agreement on a brown piece of wrapping paper written in crayon between an art buyer and an artist was acceptable as an enforceable writing because it contained a signature, quantity, and was supported by circumstances that indicated a contract with the artist for the sale of paintings.[41] The one element that is uniformly required is a signature of the party against whom enforcement of the contract is sought.

For common law contracts, in general, the statute of frauds applies to (1) contracts that involve the sale of an interest of *land;* (2) contracts that cannot (that is, *not able,* by its terms) to be performed in *under one year;* (3) contracts to pay the *debt of another* (such as a loan surety); and (4) contracts made in consideration of *marriage* (such as a prenuptial agreement).[42]

Under the Uniform Commercial Code, the statute of frauds applies to any contract for the sale of goods for $500 or more, and any lease transaction for goods amounting to $1,000 or more.

✓ Self-Check   Statute of Frauds

Which of the following contracts would need to be in writing to be enforceable?

1. A contract whereby the president of NewCo. gives a personal guarantee (i.e., uses personal assets as collateral) for a $150,000 revolving line of credit loan to NewCo. from First National Bank.

2. An agreement of sale for a piece of real estate for a corporation to build a new warehouse for $500,000.

3. A contract for consulting services for $10,000 over the next 90 days.

4. A two-year advertising contract between a retail store and a local newspaper.

E-mail and the Statute of Frauds   One question that continues to work its way through various state courts is to what extent that e-mail transmissions can be used to satisfy the statute of frauds. In Case 6.2, a New York Appellate court uses an "intent to authenticate" standard to determine whether an e-mail satisfies the statute of frauds.

---

[40]*Brower v. Gateway 2000, Inc.,* 246 A.D.2d 246 (N.Y. App. Div. 1998).

[41]*Rosenfeld v. Basquit,* 78 F.3d 184 (2d Cir. 1996).

[42]Note that some states have added additional types of contracts to the traditional statute of fraudulent misrepresentations categories. For example, almost all states require insurance policies and contracts to be in writing.

FACT SUMMARY In a transaction to sell Stevens's public relations firm to Publicis, the parties entered into two agreements. The first was a stock purchase agreement transferring all of Stevens's stock to Publicis for a certain price. The second was an employment agreement whereby Stevens would be employed by Publicis as the CEO of a newly formed subsidiary entity, Publicis-Dialog Public Relations (PDPR), created by virtue of the stock acquisition. The employment agreement required that any modification to the agreement had to be in writing signed by both parties. The agreement defined Stevens's duties as the "customary duties of a Chief Executive Officer." When PDPR failed to reach certain financial targets, Publicis removed Stevens as CEO. Subsequently, an executive from Publicis and Stevens had an e-mail exchange regarding a new role for Stevens at PDPR whereby Stevens would now be cultivating new clients. The e-mail exchanges contained unambiguous terms of acceptance by Stevens to the modification to his terms of employment. Additionally, each e-mail transmission bore the typed name of the sender at the foot of the message. Eventually, Stevens and Publicis had a breach of contract dispute and Stevens claimed that the modification was not effective because it failed to meet the requirements of the statute of frauds because the e-mails did not constitute a "writing" and did not contain any signatures.

SYNOPSIS OF DECISION AND OPINION The appellate court held in favor of Publicis and ruled that the series of e-mails amounted to signed writings that could be used to modify the employment agreement and met the statute of frauds requirement. The court focused on the fact that the e-mails contained the name at the end of each message that signaled the author's intent to validate its contents.

WORDS OF THE COURT: Satisfying the Statute of Frauds "The e-mails from Stevens constitute 'signed writings' within the meaning of the statute of frauds, since Stevens name at the end of his e-mail signified his intent to authenticate the contents. Similarly, Bloom's (the Publicis executive) name at the end of his e-mail constituted 'signed writing' and satisfied the requirement of the employment agreement that any modification be signed by all the parties."

Case Questions

1. If the parties did not wish to allow e-mail to serve as an appropriate method to modify the contract, what wording could have been used in Stevens's employment agreement?

2. Could the principle that the court articulates apply in a negotiation via e-mail for the sale of goods? That is, if two parties are negotiating a price via e-mail and there is language of agreement by the parties, does that alone satisfy the statute of frauds even if no actual written contract with the parties' signatures exists?

Interpretation Rules for Written Contracts In adjudicating disputes concerning the contents of a contract, courts use interpretation rules to guide their analysis. Before signing a written agreement, the parties typically engage in preliminary negotiations that involve discussions and perhaps documents during the negotiation, such as letters or memos, which are intended to help the parties come to an agreement. The **parole evidence rule** provides that any writing intended by the parties to be the *final* expression of their agreement may not be *contradicted* by any oral or written agreements made prior to the writing. Note the parole evidence rule does not bar admission of the preliminary documents when they are being used to determine the meaning that the parties intended concerning a particular term in the contract.

Sometimes contracts contain **ambiguous terms.** In such cases, these terms are construed by the court *against the interest* of the side that drafted the agreement. Courts may also *supply* a reasonable term in a situation where the contract is silent and has **omitted terms.**

Agreement p. 126 Any meeting of the minds resulting in mutual assent to do or refrain from doing something.

Bilateral contract p. 126 A contract involving two promises and two performances.

Unilateral contract p. 126 A contract involving one promise, followed by one performance, which then triggers a second performance from the offeror.

Express contract p. 126 A contract created when the parties have specifically agreed on the promises and performances.

Implied contract p. 126 A contract in which the agreement is reached by the parties' actions rather than their words.

Quasi-contract p. 126 A classification that permits a contract to be enforceable in cases where no express or implied contract exists, where one party suffers losses as a result of another party's unjust enrichment.

Valid contract p. 127 A contract that has the necessary elements and, thus, can be enforceable.

Void contract p. 127 A contract where the agreements have not been formed in conformance with the law from the outset of the agreement and, thus, cannot be enforced by either party.

Voidable contract p. 128 A contract where one party may, at its option, either disaffirm the contract or enforce it.

Unenforceable contract p. 128 A contract that meets the elements required by law for an otherwise binding agreement, but is subject to a legal defense.

State common law p. 128 The governing body of law of contracts for services or real estate.

State statutory law p. 128 The governing body of law of contracts for goods or products based on the Uniform Commercial Code.

Hybrid contracts p. 128 Contracts that involve terms for both goods and services, where the source of law is established by determining the predominant thrust of the subject matter.

Mutual assent p. 130 The broad underlying requirement to form an enforceable contract necessitating that the parties must reach an agreement using a combination of offer and acceptance and that the assent must be genuine.

Offer p. 130 A promise or commitment to do (or refrain from doing) a specified activity. In contract law, the expression of a willingness to enter into a contract by the offeror promising an offeree that she will perform certain obligations in exchange for the offeree's counterpromise to perform.

Acceptance p. 130 The offeree's expression of agreement to the terms of the offer. The power of acceptance is created by a valid offer.

Consideration p. 130 Requirement for an enforceable contract in addition to agreement in which there is a benefit that must be bargained for between the parties. Generally, a promise is supported by consideration if the promisee suffers a legal detriment by giving up something of value or some legal right and the promisor makes her promise as part of a bargained for exchange.

Capacity p. 130 Requirement for a valid contract necessitating that both parties have the power to contract. Certain classes of persons have only limited powers to contract, including minors and those with mental incapacity.

Legality p. 130 Requirement for an enforceable contract necessitating that both the subject matter and performance of the contract must be legal.

Public policy p. 130 Requirement for an enforceable contract necessitating that the terms are consistent with public policy objectives.

Genuine assent p. 130 Requirement for a contract to be enforceable necessitating the knowing, voluntary and mutual approval of the terms of a contract by each party.

Statute of frauds p. 130 The law governing which contracts must be in writing in order to be enforceable.

Objective intent p. 131 Requirement for an offer to have legal effect necessitating that generally, the offeror must have a serious intention to become bound by the offer and the terms of the offer must be reasonably certain.

Revocation p. 133 An action terminating an offer whereby the offeror decides to withdraw the offer by expressly communicating the revocation to the offeree prior to acceptance.

Rejection p. 133 An action terminating an offer whereby the offeree rejects the offer outright prior to acceptance.

Counteroffer p. 133 An action terminating an offer whereby the offeree rejects the original offer and proposes a new offer with different terms.

Operation of law p. 133   Another way in which an offer may be terminated by certain happenings or events. Generally, these include lapse of time, death or incapacity of the offeror or offeree, and destruction of the subject matter of the contract prior to acceptance.

Irrevocable offers p. 135   Classification of offers that cannot be withdrawn by the offeror. These include offers in the form of an option contract, offers where the offeree partly performed or detrimentally relied on the offer, and firm offers by a merchant under the Uniform Commercial Code.

Detrimental reliance p. 135   When the offeree makes preparations prior to acceptance based on a reasonable reliance on the offer.

Mirror image rule p. 136   Principle stating that the offeree's response operates as an acceptance only if it is the precise mirror image of the offer.

Lapse of time p. 136   Term used to describe an event covered under operation of law in which a contract may be terminated once either the offeror's expressed time limit has expired or reasonable time has passed.

Mailbox rule p. 137   Governs common law contracts and provides a rule for when a contract is considered to be deemed accepted by the offeree, thus depriving the offeror of the right to revoke the offer. Generally, the mailbox rule provides that the acceptance of an offer is effective upon dispatch and not when the acceptance is received by the offeree.

Mistake p. 140   In contract law, an erroneous belief that is not in accord with the existing facts.

Mutual mistake p. 140   When both parties hold an erroneous belief concerning a basic assumption on which a contract was made.

Unilateral mistake p. 141   When only one party had an erroneous belief about a basic assumption in the terms of an agreement.

Preexisting duty p. 141   A duty that one is already legally obligated to do and, thus, generally not recognized as a legal detriment.

Bargained for exchange p. 142   Aspect of consideration differentiating contracts from gifts by holding that a performance or return promise is bargained for only if it was exchanged for another promise.

Past consideration p. 142   Type of contract that is not considered to meet the bargained for exchange requirement when the promise is made in return for a detriment previously made by the promisee.

Nominal consideration p. 143   Consideration that is stated in a written contract even though it is not actually exchanged.

Promissory estoppel p. 143   Theory allowing for the recovery of damages by the relying party if the promisee actually relied on the promise and the promisee's reliance was reasonably foreseeable to the promisor.

Minors p. 144   Category of individuals who have limited capacity to contract, covering those younger than the majority age of 18. Until a person reaches her majority age, any contract that she may enter into is voidable at the minor's option.

Mental incapacity p. 144   Category of individuals who have limited capacity to contract, covering those who are unable to understand the nature and consequences of the contract, or are unable to act in a reasonable manner in relation to the transaction and the other party has reason to know of her condition.

Covenants not to compete p. 146   Type of contract where one party agrees not to compete with another party for a specified period of time.

Enforceability p. 147   A term used to determine whether a properly formed contract can be imposed by examining whether it is a product of genuine assent and is in writing (under certain circumstances).

Misrepresentation p. 147   When one party to an agreement makes a promise or representation about a material fact that is not true.

Fraudulent misrepresentation p. 148   When one party has engaged in conduct that meets the standards for misrepresentation, but that party has actual knowledge that the representation is not true.

Duress p. 149   Basis for avoiding a contract when one party uses any form of unfair coercion to induce another party to enter into or modify a contract.

Undue influence p. 150   A defense that gives legal relief to a party that was induced to enter into a contract through the improper pressure of a trusted relationship.

Unconscionability p. 150   A defense that may allow a party to potentially avoid a contract on the grounds that they suffered a grossly unfair burden that shocks the objective conscience.

Parole evidence rule p. 152   Provides that any writing intended by the parties to be the final expression of their agreement may not be contradicted by any oral or written agreements made prior to the writing.

Ambiguous terms p. 152   Contract terms that are vague and indefinite. In contract law, these terms are construed by the court against the interest of the side that drafted the agreement.

Omitted terms p. 152   Contract terms that are left out or absent. In contract law, courts may supply a reasonable term in a situation where the contract is silent.

THEORY TO PRACTICE

Big Time Toymaker (BTT) develops, manufactures, and distributes board games and other toys to the United States, Mexico, and Canada. Chou is the inventor of a new strategy game he named *Strat*. BTT was interested in distributing Strat and entered into an agreement with Chou whereby BTT paid him $25,000 in exchange for *exclusive negotiation* rights for a 90-day period. The exclusive negotiation agreement stipulated that no *distribution* contract existed unless it was in writing. Just three days before the expiration of the 90-day period, the parties reached an oral distribution agreement at a meeting. Chou offered to draft the contract that would memorialize their agreement. Before Chou drafted the agreement, a BTT manager sent Chou an e-mail with the subject line "Strat Deal" that repeated the key terms of the distribution agreement including price, time frames, and obligations of both parties. Although the e-mail never used the word *contract*, it stated that all of the terms had been agreed upon. Chou believed that this e-mail was meant to replace the earlier notion that he should draft a contract, and one month passed. BTT then sent Chou a fax requesting that he send a draft for a distribution agreement contract. Despite the fact that Chou did so immediately after receiving the BTT fax, several more months passed without response from BTT. BTT had a change in management and informed Chou they were not interested in distributing Strat.

1. At what point, if ever, did the parties have a contract?
2. What facts may weigh in favor of or against Chou in terms of the parties' objective intent to contract?
3. Does the fact that the parties were communicating by e-mail have any impact on your analysis in Questions 1 and 2 (above)?
4. What role does the statute of frauds play in this contract?
5. Could BTT avoid this contract under the doctrine of mistake? Explain. Would either party have any other defenses that would allow the contract to be avoided?
6. Assuming, *arguendo,* that this e-mail does constitute an agreement, what consideration supports this agreement?

MANAGER'S CHALLENGE

Managers are frequently on the front lines when ambiguous preliminary agreements are involved and must have a relatively sophisticated knowledge of what constitutes a contract and what rules govern those contracts. In Theory to Practice, above, the BTT manager has done a very poor job protecting BTT from potential liability due to the ambiguity in the e-mails and his actions. Draft an e-mail that a BTT manager could send to Chou after their first meeting that outlines some preliminary working terms. However, your objective is to draft the e-mail in a way that no reasonable person would believe it to be an offer; rather, the e-mail should be thought of as a preliminary attempt to settle terms after a negotiation meeting. For instance, would the subject line be the same as the one the BTT manager used ("Strat Deal")? Also, focus on language in your e-mail that clearly outlines what the parties must do next in order to enter into a formal agreement and time frames. A sample answer may be found on this textbook's Web site at www.mhhe.com/melvin.

MUTUAL ASSENT/ACCEPTANCE

Lexmark is a manufacturer and distributor of ink cartridges for computer printers. They introduced a rebate plan called Return Program Cartridges whereby a consumer could receive a "prebate" (i.e., a discount upon purchase) on ink cartridges. This price product discount was given in exchange for an agreement by the consumer not to tamper with the cartridge. The consumer simply agrees to return the empty cartridge to Lexmark. The agreement is printed on the ink cartridge box and, Lexmark claims, by opening the box,

the consumer has agreed to the terms of the Return Program Cartridge program. A consumer group challenged Lexmark's program contending, among other things, that Lexmark could not enforce an agreement on the box because the consumer had never formally accepted the terms of Lexmark's offer.

CASE QUESTION

1. Can one party be deemed to accept an offer simply by opening a product box even if there is no evidence that the party *actually* read the terms?

LEGALITY

GE Marquette Medical Systems ("GE") contracted with Biomedical Systems Corp. to manufacture a new medical instrument based on technology owned by Biomedical. The contract required GE to obtain clearance from the Food and Drug Administration (the federal regulatory agency that covers such medical devices) within 90 days in order to move ahead on the project. After this contract was signed, GE determined that obtaining this clearance was not a prudent path to reach their ultimate objective of having the product approved for selling to the public. Rather than seek the clearance required by the Biomedical contract, GE decided to pursue a different

strategy with the FDA that took several years to complete. When Biomedical sued GE for breach of contract, GE defended on the basis that the clearance provision in the contract was a violation of FDA procedure and, thus, the term was illegal and the contract was void.

CASE QUESTIONS

1. Can a party make a unilateral judgment as to illegality on a term of the contract when there is no affirmative finding from a regulatory authority?
2. If GE had gone ahead with the clearance process and the FDA had told them it was not the proper procedure, would the contract be void for illegality?

MISTAKE

Reed owned a small photography store and purchased his price label products from Monarch. Over a period of years, Reed ordered no more than 4,000 labels at a time from Monarch. While preparing a new order form for labels, Reed was interrupted by a customer and wrote "4MM" on the order form instead of "4M." In the industry, 4M means 4,000 labels, while 4MM means four million labels. Reed sent the mistaken order to Monarch. Despite the course of past dealings

and the fact that the maximum order that Monarch had ever received from a single customer was one million labels, they proceeded to produce and deliver four million labels to Reed. Reed refused delivery and defended on the basis of mistake.

CASE QUESTIONS

1. Who prevails and why?
2. Is this a unilateral or mutual mistake? What's the difference?

STATUTE OF FRAUDS

McCarthey sold controlling stock interests of his newspaper publishing company to TCI in 1997. During that sale transaction (which involved a detailed contract covering all aspects of the sale), McCarthey allegedly articulated a "side-agreement" with TCI that provided McCarthey with the right to repurchase the stock from TCI on the five-year anniversary of the sale (in 2002). The side-agreement was never memorialized. Before the five-year anniversary, TCI sold its interest in the newspaper to MediaNews. When McCarthey sued for breach of the oral agreement, TCI asserted that the statute of frauds barred his claim.

CASE QUESTIONS

1. Is the oral agreement enforceable? Why or why not?
2. Could the parole evidence rule apply here?

 Self-Check ANSWERS

Source of Law

Which source of law governs this contract?

1. Common law (real estate).
2. Hybrid contract governed by common law based on (1) price allocation weighted to services and (2) uniqueness of services.
3. Common law (services).
4. Statutory law (sale of goods).
5. Common law (services) because no goods were sold (owner supplied the paint).

Mailbox Rule

For each transaction, does a contract exist? If yes, why, and what is the date of the contract? If no, why not?

PROBLEM #1

No contract. Connelly still had the power to revoke the offer on Day 3 because Raleigh used a slower method (U.S. mail) to accept than Connelly used to make the offer (fax). Therefore, Raleigh's acceptance could only take effect upon receipt of the acceptance by Connelly. Because Connelly did not receive the acceptance until Day 4 his revocation of Day 3 is effective and no contract exists.

PROBLEM #2

Contract exists on Day 2 upon dispatch (mailbox rule) because RBR used a reasonable method to accept (using fax to accept an e-mail offer is reasonable because they are similar in that they are relatively instantaneous when sending). When the offeror actually received the acceptance is irrelevant.

Statute of Frauds

Which of the following contracts would need to be in writing to be enforceable?

1. Writing required. Promise to pay the debt of another.
2. Writing required. Real estate/land.
3. Careful! No writing required. Despite the high fee, the services can be performed in less than one year and, thus, the contract is not subject to statute of frauds requirements.
4. Writing required. A two-year contract for services that cannot be performed in less than one year.

7

CHAPTER

Contract Performance: Conditions, Breach, and Remedies

learning outcomes checklist

After studying this chapter, students who have mastered the material will be able to:

7-1 Define what a condition is used for in a contract and distinguish conditions precedent from conditions subsequent.

7-2 Apply the doctrines related to good faith performance, discharge of a contract, and substantial performance.

7-3 Identify the ethical dilemmas that a manager faces in the context of good faith performance.

7-4 Articulate circumstances that give rise to events of discharge via mutual consent and operation of law.

7-5 Recognize events that result in breach of contract and explain anticipatory repudiation.

7-6 Identify the appropriate remedy available to nonbreaching parties and understand the responsibilities of an injured party to avoid and mitigate damages.

7-7 Explain the rights of third parties who have rights in a contract through assignment or delegation and third-party beneficiaries.

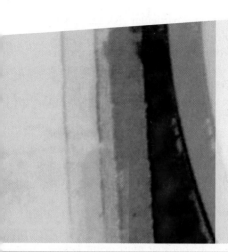

Once it has been determined that a valid and enforceable contract exists, the inquiry then necessarily focuses on whether contract obligations were faithfully met through performance by the parties. Most contracts are fully performed by the parties as contemplated, but what happens if contractual commitments are not met? This chapter continues the survey of contract law with attention to rules that govern performance and consequences of nonperformance. In this chapter, students will learn:

- How conditions are used in a contract to allocate risk between parties.
- Requirements to meet the standard of good faith performance, substantial performance, and events that discharge a party from having to perform.
- The consequences of failing to perform as promised, known as a *breach of contract,* and the options of the damaged party after a breach.

LO7-1 NATURE AND EFFECT OF CONDITIONS

Parties to an agreement sometimes wish to allocate or adjust a particular risk associated with performing a contract. This risk allocation is typically accomplished by attaching some event, known as a **condition**, which must occur before a particular performance obligation is triggered. Ordinarily, the parties express these conditions using language such as "on the condition that" or "provided that" or "unless." For example, suppose that Graham hires Frost as a sales representative. The parties agree to a base salary and other basic employment terms. In addition, Graham offers to pay Frost a $1,000 bonus *provided that* Frost secures 10 new accounts during his first 30 days as an employee. Frost was only able to secure nine new accounts in that time period. Graham has no duty to perform (pay Frost $1,000) because his duty to pay was conditional on the achievement of the 10 new account requirements. Because Frost did not meet the condition set in the agreement, Graham is discharged from his obligation to pay the bonus.

Categories of Conditions

A condition is categorized as either a *condition precedent* (event that must occur *before* performance under a contract is due, as in the Graham–Frost example above), or a *condition subsequent* (event occurs after the performance under the contract and discharges the parties' obligations). Although a condition subsequent is rare in modern commercial transactions, business owners and managers are most likely to encounter such a condition in an insurance context. For example, NewCo. enters into a fire insurance contract with Big Carrier Inc. that provides:

> No lawsuit for recovery under this contract shall be valid unless the lawsuit is commenced within 12 months of the fire.

A fire destroys NewCo.'s office and they file an immediate claim; however, Big Carrier refuses to pay based on an exclusion in the policy. NewCo. takes no further action until 14 months after the fire, and then files a lawsuit to recover damages under the policy. A court will dismiss NewCo.'s claim because Big Carrier is discharged from their obligation to pay (or even to litigate the dispute) by virtue of the time period condition in the policy.[1]

The parties may also agree to *concurrent conditions* whereby each party is required to render performance simultaneously. If Abel contracts with Baker to paint Abel's portrait, the parties may agree that Abel will pay the full price of the contract at the same time as Baker delivers the portrait painting to him. If Baker fails to perform, Abel is no longer obligated to meet his obligation and he may seek legal redress for any losses suffered as a result.

Modern contract law does not recognize any substantive difference between these categories of conditions.[2] In fact, today most courts do not make any distinction between them. Rather, the law defines a condition as "an event, not certain to occur, which must occur, [. . .] before the performance under a contract becomes due."[3] Generally, courts do enforce a strict compliance standard for conditions. In *Luttinger v. Rosen,*[4] an appellate court ruled that a condition, namely that a real estate buyer being able to obtain financing at a certain rate before going through with the purchase, must be strictly applied.

---

[1]Based on *Abolin v. Farmers American Mutual Life Insurance,* 100 Pa. Super. 433 (1931).

[2]Note, however, that the two differ *procedurally* with respect to who bears the burden of proof.

[3]*Restatement (Second) of Contracts,* § 230.

[4]316 A.2d 757 (Conn. 1972). The contract in question was conditional upon the buyer obtaining a mortgage at a rate not to exceed 8.5 percent. The only lending institutions in the area that would lend to the buyer charged 8.75 percent. Even after the seller offered to subsidize the loan so that the effective rate was 8.5 percent for the buyer, the court held that the buyer's duty to perform was discharged by failure of a condition.

CONCEPT SUMMARY   Conditions

- A condition is an event that triggers a particular performance in order to allocate the risk that some part of a contract may not be completed.
- Conditions are normally signaled by phrases such as "only if," "unless," or "provided that."
- A condition is categorized as a condition precedent (*before* performance is due), a condition subsequent (*after* performance of one party), or a concurrent condition (simultaneous performance).

GOOD FAITH PERFORMANCE AND DISCHARGE   LO7-2, 7-3

If the promises to perform in an agreement are not conditional, the duty to perform is absolute. Most commonly, the parties agree on terms and the parties perform the contractual obligations in **good faith** in order to complete the contract. This completion is

BUSINESS ETHICS *perspective*

Good Faith and the Nuclear Condition Option

Note that while the law imposes a good faith requirement on all contracting parties, as a practical matter, the law may also protect those who are ostensibly acting in good faith, but may have unethical motives. In some contracts, the parties agree to a conditional clause sometimes known as a *nuclear condition;* that is, a clause where one party may cancel the contract completely if a condition is not met to that party's subjective satisfaction. Consider a case whereby the president of WidgetCo. assigns Manager to purchase a piece of real estate. Manager enters into a contract with Owner for the sale of a piece of commercial real estate. Manager insists that the contract contain an "acceptable financing" clause as follows: "As a specific condition precedent to WidgetCo.'s obligation to close, the parties agree that WidgetCo. must obtain financing for the transaction on terms and conditions acceptable to WidgetCo. in WidgetCo.'s sole discretion."

After entering into the agreement with Owner, the president notifies Manager that WidgetCo. is no longer interested in the property and that Manager is to use all "legal means" necessary to break the contract with Owner. Assume that Manager also learns that WidgetCo. is able to obtain financing on extremely favorable terms according to industry standards.

1. Given that the contract requires that any financing terms must be acceptable to WidgetCo., what are Manager's legal obligations to go through with the transaction? Does this differ from Manager's ethical obligations?

2. Is it possible for Manager to comply with the good faith requirement and still avoid the contract with Owner?

3. Recall the discussion for ethics decision-making models in Chapter 5. How could these models help guide Manager's course of action?

4. Assume that the president orders Manager to lie on the loan application thereby ensuring that any financial institution would reject the loan application. Note that lying on a loan application to a bank is a crime. What are Manager's options at that point?

5. Is this a case where using the nuclear option is simply a good hard-nosed business practice? Are there any circumstances you could articulate where Manager has no legal obligation, but does have an ethical obligation to Owner?

known as **discharge,** because both parties have now "discharged" their obligation to the other by performing the agreed upon duties. Performance may also be accomplished by delivering products to an agreed upon location (such as a warehouse). This is known as *tendering goods* (discussed in detail in Chapter 8, "Contracts for the Sale of Goods"). The law also imposes an affirmative duty of good faith in performing obligations. In every contract, the parties have the duty of good faith and fair dealing in performance and enforcement.[5] Although the good faith requirement is ordinarily met by the parties simply performing their obligations completely, known as *perfect performance,* the law recognizes that there are some cases in which one party does *not* perform completely, yet has still acted in good faith and is entitled to enforce the remaining obligations in the contract against the other party.

Substantial Performance

In some situations, the parties agree to terms of a contract and pursue a good faith performance, but one party cannot give perfect performance. The law recognizes a party's good faith effort to *substantially perform* her obligations by allowing the **substantial performance** to satisfy the requirements of the agreement and trigger the other party's obligation to perform. In order to prevail in a substantial performance case, the party trying to enforce the contract must show good faith and that any deviation from the required performance was not *material.* In this context, material means some deviation from the contract that resulted in a substantial change in value of the contract or changes a fundamental basis of the agreement.

Note that although the doctrine of substantial performance allows a party to meet her obligations in a contract through less-than-perfect performance, the innocent party is still entitled to collect *damages* to compensate for the imperfect performance. Generally, courts allow the substantially performing party to be paid the full amount of the contract price (or other performance due) *less* any costs suffered. In Landmark Case 7.1, known as the *Reading Pipe* case, has been used for decades as a guidepost for applying the doctrine of substantial performance.

 Self Check   Substantial Performance

Which of the following constitute substantial performance?

1. Wholesaler contracts with Delicatessen to deliver 50 cases of bottled beverages each week in exchange for a $3,000 monthly payment. Due to heavy holiday volume, the December shipment contains only 45 cases.

2. The Yellow Pages agrees to publish a half-page advertisement for Local Dry Cleaner in exchange for $2,000. The advertisement is published, but one digit in the telephone number is incorrect.

3. A vegetable cannery contracts with Farmer to buy 54 units of "fancy grade" spinach, defined as "dark green in color, firm in texture, and with a leaf/stem ratio of less than 15 percent stem." Farmer delivers spinach with a leaf/stem ratio of 25 percent stem.

4. Widower contracts with Artist to paint a portrait of his late wife. The portrait is done on time and professionally but the likeness, while resembling her, does not look exactly like the woman.

Answers to this Self-Check are provided at the end of the chapter.

---

[5]*Restatement (Second) of Contracts,* § 205.

FACT SUMMARY   Kent contracted with Jacob and Youngs ("JY") for the construction of Kent's vacation home in upstate New York. The contract required JY to use "standard pipe of Reading manufacture." During the construction, one of the JY subcontractors mistakenly used some pipe made by other manufacturers. Just before the construction was complete, Kent's architect discovered the mistake and directed JY to remove the non-Reading pipe. However, the pipe was already sealed off and encased within the walls and, thus, costly demolition would have been necessary to repair the mistake. JY claimed that the substitute pipe was the same in terms of quality, appearance, market value, and cost as the Reading pipe. Thus, JY completed construction but refused to fix the pipe mistake. Kent refused to pay the remaining balance on the contract and JY sued to recover the amount due.

SYNOPSIS OF DECISION AND OPINION   The court ruled in favor of JY under the doctrine of substantial performance. In its opinion, the court focused on practical application to obtain fairness rather than a strict application of performance requirements and pointed out that trivial and innocent omissions may not always be a breach of a condition. Although there are limits to the substantial performance doctrine, in this case, the omission of the Reading pipe was not as a result of fraud or willfulness. Moreover, there was no evidence of substantial change in the value of the contract.

WORDS OF THE COURT: Applying Substantial Performance   "Where the line is to be drawn between important and trivial cannot be settled by formula. [. . .] Nowhere will change be tolerated, however, if it is so dominant or pervasive as in any real or substantial measure to frustrate the purpose of the contract. [. . .] We must weigh the purpose to be served, the desire to be gratified, and the excuse for the deviation by the letter, and the cruelty of enforced adherence."

Case Questions

1. A dissenting opinion in this case pointed out that JY's failing to use the correct pipe was grossly negligent and, thus, JY should bear the costs of reinstalling the Reading pipe. Does that strike you as convincing? Why or why not?

2. If Kent had a vested interest in the use of Reading pipe (suppose Kent was the heir to the Reading pipe fortune), what condition could he have inserted in the agreement that ensured the use of Reading brand pipe?

In the *Jacob and Youngs v. Kent* case, the court ruled that a contractor's substitution of non-Reading brand pipe during construction of a home constituted substantial performance.

LO7-4 OTHER EVENTS OF DISCHARGE

As discussed earlier in this chapter, the most common way for the parties' obligations under a contract to be discharged is by good faith performance. However, there are other circumstances under which the parties may be discharged from obligations. Parties may be discharged via **mutual consent** or **operation of law.**

Mutual Consent

If neither party has fully performed, the parties may agree to cancel the contract. This cancellation is known as a **rescission** and each party gives up rights under the contract in exchange for the release by the other party from performing. For example, Earl hires Peter to paint his office lobby for $1,000. The fee was to be paid in a lump sum upon Peter completing the entire lobby. After beginning work and painting one wall, Peter realizes that he vastly underestimated the time and supplies to make the job profitable and he now has another customer across town where he could make a profit. So long as Peter offers to rescind the contract and Earl accepts, the contract is cancelled and Peter no longer has to perform. At the same time, despite the fact that Earl's lobby was partially painted, Earl does not have to pay any sums due under the original contract.[6]

In some cases, the parties to a contract agree to accept performance that is different from the originally promised performance. Under the doctrine of **accord and satisfaction,** one party agrees to render a *substitute performance* in the future (known as *accord*), and the party promises to accept that substitute performance in discharge of the existing performance obligation. Once the substitute performance has been rendered, this acts as a satisfaction of the obligation. Note that discharge of the obligation only occurs once the terms of the accord are actually performed. If the accord performance is *not* rendered, the other party has the option to recover damages either under the original contract or under the accord contact. For example, in the Earl and Peter painting contract example above, suppose that Peter finished the job, but that Earl did not have the $1,000 fee to pay Peter in one lump sum. Therefore, Earl offers to pay Peter $1,100 in 60 days. Peter accepts. The new agreement on payment terms is an *accord*. Once Earl has paid the $1,100 in 60 days, his accord has been *satisfied* and Peter will not be able to sue for any damages that he may have suffered as a result of Earl's failing to pay as originally agreed in the contract.[7]

The parties to a contract may also discharge their obligations by replacing the original contract with a **substitute agreement,** also known as **modification.** The substitute agreement is generally used to compromise when two parties have a dispute as to performance of the contract and wish to amend its terms. The substituted agreement, unlike the accord agreement discussed previously, *immediately* discharges any obligations under the original contract. Therefore, in the Earl–Peter painting contract above, suppose that Earl and Peter enter into a substitute agreement whereby Earl agrees to pay $1,100 in 60 days so long as Peter agrees to extinguish the $1,000 debt immediately. If Earl does not perform (by paying), then Peter now has only one option: recover for damages under the *substitute agreement.* He cannot recover damages under the original agreement. Earl's obligation to pay the $1,000 sum at conclusion of the work was immediately discharged by the substitute agreement.

When the parties agree to substitute a third party for one of the original parties to the contract, the agreement may be discharged through **novation.** Essentially, a novation is a kind of substitute agreement that involves a substitute third *party* rather than a substitute promise. A novation revokes and *discharges* all obligations under the old contract. For

---

[6]Based on *Restatement (Second) of Contracts,* § 283, Illustration 1.

[7]Since an accord does not discharge the previous contractual duty as soon as the accord is made, if Earl does not perform the accord agreement, Peter may recover damages from Earl under either the original contract obligation ($1,000 lump sum due upon completion) or under the accord agreement ($1,100 in 60 days from completion).

Understanding Check Deposits as Accord and Satisfaction

PROBLEM *In some cases, a business depositing the check of a customer may be an accord and satisfaction without the depositing business fully realizing the impact of depositing the check.*

Managers must have a fundamental understanding of this concept and businesses should have mechanisms in place to avoid an accidental accord and satisfaction claim. For example, General Contractor Inc. (GCI) contracts with Windows R Us (WRU) to install specially designed windows in a new office building constructed by GCI for a total of $100,000 to be paid after services are completed. After WRU installs the windows, GCI notifies them that they are dissatisfied with the installation work. WRU claims that the windows were installed to industry standards and demands payment. GCI then sends a check for $50,000 (half of what is owed to WRU under the contract) to WRU's office. The check contains the endorsement "Payment in Full for Installation Services at the Office Center Site."

SOLUTION *Consider WRU's options and the consequences of each option.*

- *Deposit the check as is.* In most states, this option would result in an accord and satisfaction. When GCI sent the check with a restrictive endorsement, in effect they offered to render a substitute performance in the future (pay $50,000 instead of $100,000) as an accord agreement. Most courts view depositing a check as an affirmative acceptance of that accord offer and, thus, when the check has cleared the bank's processing it

is considered a satisfaction of the accord agreement. WRU cannot sue for damages.

- *Write "Under Protest" under the check and deposit it.* In most states, this option would result in an accord and satisfaction. Just as in the previous example, when GCI sends the check with a restrictive endorsement, in effect they have offered to render a substitute performance in the future (pay $50,000 instead of $100,000) as an accord agreement. Most courts view depositing a check as an affirmative acceptance of an accord offer regardless of any attempt by the receiving party to unilaterally alter the check. Thus, writing the words "in protest" ordinarily has no effect. When the check has cleared the bank's process it is considered a satisfaction of the accord agreement and WRU cannot sue for damages.

- *Strike out the "payment in full language" with a black marker, and then deposit the check.* Same result as above. Unilateral attempts by the offeree to alter the substitute offer check will not bar GCI's discharge through accord and satisfaction.

- *Return the check to GCI with a letter from WRU that the offer is rejected and demand full payment.* This is the only method that will fully protect WRU from accepting the accord via satisfaction. By returning the check with an affirmative statement that the substitute accord is rejected, WRU has made clear that no satisfaction could occur and may then sue for damages if appropriate.

example, in the Earl and Peter painting contract above, suppose that Peter starts work and the next day receives an offer from another customer for a major painting job. Peter proposes to Earl that Pablo (another painter that Peter knows does excellent work) complete the painting work under the original contract. If Earl then agrees to allow Peter to substitute Pablo for the performance of the lobby painting duties articulated in the original Earl–Peter contract, then a novation has occurred and Peter is now discharged from his obligation to perform the Earl–Peter contract. Earl is bound only by the new novation terms with Pablo.

Operation of Law

Contract obligations may also be discharged through *operation of law*. Despite the fact that the parties have fulfilled the requirements to form a valid contract, the law provides a discharge under certain circumstances where fairness demands it.

In some cases, after the parties have formed a contract, unexpected events occur that affect the probability of one party's ability to perform. In such cases, the law allows the parties to be excused from performance under the contract. Courts analyze these special circumstances according to three separate doctrines: **impossibility, impracticability, and frustration of purpose.**

Impossibility   After the parties have entered an agreement, the contemplated performance of the obligations may become impossible and, therefore, may be subject to discharge. When encountering a situation where one party is claiming impossibility, it is important for managers to understand that the impossibility must be *objective* (a reasonable person would consider the obligation impossible to perform) rather than subjective (one party decides unilaterally that performance is impossible) in order for the obligation to be discharged.[8] This can sometimes be a tricky distinction, and the modern trend of courts is against allow-

In some cases, depositing a payment check from a customer may be an event of discharge via accord and satisfaction.

ing impossibility as a defense unless it fits into one of four intervening events: (1) *destruction* of the subject matter (A promises to sell B 1,000 widgets to be delivered on Tuesday. On Monday, a fire destroys the widgets. A is discharged from her obligation to provide the widgets); or (2) *death or incapacitation* of one of the parties to the contract[9] (A promises to paint B's portrait. Prior to the sitting date for the portrait, A becomes incapacitated. A is discharged from his obligation to paint the portrait); or (3) the *means of performance* contemplated in the contract cannot be performed (W, a wholesaler, agrees to sell R, a retailer, 5,000 widgets. Prior to the W–R contract, W contracted with M, a manufacturer, to supply him with 10,000 widgets. M halts production and cannot produce the widgets for W. W may be discharged from performance [unless the parties agreed otherwise about risk allocation]); or (4) performance of the obligation has *become illegal* subsequent to the contract but prior to performance (Importer promises to buy 1,000 cigars from Producer, a manufacturer in the Dominican Republic. Subsequent to the agreement, but before Producer ships the cigars, Congress passes a federal statute imposing a complete trade embargo with the Dominican Republic. Importer and Producer are discharged from performance based on impossibility).

Sometimes performance is *temporarily impossible* for one or both parties. The illness of a party who is to perform unique personal services may prevent her from performing on a timeline contemplated by the parties. However, in most cases, an illness will not prevent the performance forever. The doctrine of impossibility operates to *suspend* (not discharge)

---

[8]The *Restatements,* § 261, Comment c, distinguish between the two standards by giving an example of objective impossibility ("the thing cannot be done") versus subjective impossibility ("I cannot do it").

[9]Note that unless a contract for services calls for *unique personal* services, it cannot be discharged via impossibility. The law contemplates that nonunique personal services should simply be delegated to another appropriate substitute party.

the obligation to perform until the impossibility ceases. Note that an exception to this general rule is when, after the temporary impossibility ends, the performance is considerably more burdensome than if the parties had performed on time (i.e., the lapse of time affected the parties' abilities to perform). Courts then will allow the obligation of the burdened party to be discharged.

Impracticability   There are certain agreements where, although performance is not objectively impossible (as defined above), performance becomes extremely burdensome due to some unforeseen circumstance occurring in between the time of agreement and the time of performance. If the burden is both *unforeseeable and extreme,* courts may allow the burdened parties obligations to be discharged before performance. For example, GravelCo. contracts with Builder to "provide all necessary gravel for Builder's project on Main Street at a rate of $10,000 per ton. Estimated need: 10 tons." Builder then purchases 10 tons, but due to an unforeseeable landscape design problem, Builder needed five more tons than originally anticipated. However, GravelCo. refused to deliver the additional five tons because to do so would require GravelCo. to mine the additional gravel in a way that would require expensive mining techniques costing nearly double the price of the first 10 tons of gravel. So long as the court determines that the additional gravel delivery burden was *unforeseeable and extreme* in nature, Gravel Co. may be discharged from its obligation to provide "all necessary gravel."[10]

> **KEY POINT**
>
> In order for a contract to be discharged under impracticability, the burden must be *unforeseeable* and be *extreme* in terms of cost burden.

Frustration of Purpose   In some cases, events may occur that destroy a party's *purpose* in entering into the contract even though performance of the contract itself is not objectively impossible. Where one party's purpose is completely or almost completely frustrated by such supervening events, courts will discharge her from performance.[11] Frustration of purpose may be used to discharge an obligation if, after the parties enter into an agreement, (1) a party's *principal purpose* is substantially frustrated without her fault; (2) some event occurred, when the *nonoccurrence* of the event was a central assumption of both parties when entering into the contract; and (3) the parties have not otherwise agreed to who bears the risk of such an occurrence. Just as with impracticability, frustration requires the burdened party to show that the event was unforeseeable and extreme. For example, Padraig contracts with White Hall Inn to rent a room that faces Main Street for a period of two days. Padraig's intent is to have a balcony view of the street to see the St. Patrick's Day parade. One week before the parade is scheduled, White Hall sends Padraig a confirmation of the agreement:

> Confirmed: Balcony Room at White Hall Inn (Guaranteed view of Main Street) for Padraig. $200 per night (St. Patrick's Day Parade Special). Two days. $100 deposit due in 5 days—Balance due upon check out.

Padraig signs the letter and sends it back with a $100 bill. Much to Padraig's dismay, the St. Patrick's Day Committee cancels the parade due to a last-minute regulatory problem in obtaining a permit. Padraig cancels his reservation. If Padraig sues for his $100 to be refunded (contending that his obligation has been discharged by virtue of frustration of purpose) and White Hall countersues for the $300 balance owed (contending that Padraig could still use the room even if there was not a parade), who would prevail? It is likely that Padraig would prevail because the letter sent by White Hall *acknowledges* that the primary purpose of the contract was to have the balcony view of the parade. Assuming a court finds that the parade cancellation was reasonably unforeseeable, was not the fault

---

[10]Based on the oft-cited case *Mineral Park Land Co. v. Howard,* 172 Cal. 289 (1916).

[11]*Restatement (Second) of Contracts,* § 265.

of Padraig, and was a basic assumption of the agreement, Padraig would prevail due to frustration of purpose.[12]

Consider, alternatively, if the parties had agreed on risk allocation through the use of language in the letter such as: "In the event that the St. Patrick's Day parade does not take place for any reason, the parties agree that Padraig will pay only 50 percent of the full price for the room whether he uses the room or not. Such amount shall be due on the checkout date." In that event, a court will very likely consider the parties to have bargained away any notion of frustration (or impossibility for that matter) as an event of discharge and, thus, enforce the agreed upon terms.

The parties may also be discharged through operation of law when (1) a contract is **unilaterally altered** by a party (the other party is discharged from performing); (2) a contract is subject to relief of the **bankruptcy** code (debtor is entitled to complete discharge from any contract once the bankruptcy filing has been approved by a court); (3) expiration of the **statute of limitations** (also known as the *statute of repose* in certain states) where state law imposes a time limit on enforcement of contract obligations.

CONCEPT SUMMARY Performance and Discharge

- If two parties to a contract complete performances faithful to the mutual goals of the contract, and in good faith, it will result in discharge for both.
- If a party substantially performs only essential duties of the contract, a court will enforce the agreement though the party remains liable for anything left undone.
- A party may be discharged from the original terms of the contract by a mutual consent to rescission, a substitute performance, or a modification to the original agreement.
- A party may be discharged from the original terms of the contract by the operation of law if the contract has become impossible (no one can do it), impracticable (I can't do it), or its purpose has been frustrated (why would I want to do it now).

LO7-5 BREACH OF CONTRACT AND ANTICIPATORY REPUDIATION

Recall from the previous chapter that, if a party to an agreement owes a duty to perform and fails to fulfill her obligation, she is said to have **breached** the contract. In cases where the breach is material (i.e., relates to a fundamental term of the contract or has an effect on the value of the contract), this is called a *total* breach, and the nonbreaching party will be entitled to either suspend performance or to be discharged from her obligations completely. The party that suffered the breach is also entitled to sue the breaching party in an attempt to recover *money damages*. Money damage awards are one of the ways in which the law provides a method to compensate the nonbreaching party for losses suffered. These methods are known as **remedies.** Remedies are discussed later in this chapter.

There are some cases where the breach is not material, sometimes referred to as a *partial* breach,[13] where the nonbreaching party may not be relieved from performing. However, the nonbreaching party may still recover damages related to the breach from the breaching party. Recall the *Jacob and Youngs v. Kent (Reading Pipe)* case from earlier in the chapter.

---

[12]Based on the landmark case *Krell v. Henry,* 2 K.B. 740 (1903). This is commonly known as the *coronation case* because it involved room reservations to view a parade in connection with the coronation of the King of England. When the King fell ill, Henry refused to use the premises or make payment. When the landlord Krell sued, the court ruled in favor of Henry and the doctrine of frustration of purpose had its modern-day launch.

[13]*Corbin on Contracts,* § 1374 (1963).

In that case the court decided that because the deviation from expected performance was not material, it was only a partial breach. Because the breach was partial, the court awarded the nonbreaching party damages equal to the difference in price between Reading brand pipe and the pipe actually used.

Anticipatory Repudiation

After the parties have entered into an agreement but before performance has occurred, it sometimes becomes apparent that one party does not intend to perform as agreed. This may be apparent through the party's words or conduct. Under certain circumstances, the law provides an avenue of recovery for the nonbreaching party even *before* the nonperforming party actually breaches the contract or even before the performance is due. For example, on December 15, Manager enters into an agreement with Consultant to provide operation-consulting services for a period of six months to commence January 2. On December 20, Manager is told to cut costs, so Manager contacts Consultant in an e-mail: "Dear Consultant: We don't require your services. Sorry. —Manager." At this point, Manager has not technically breached the contract because performance is not due until January 2. However, Consultant would still be entitled to sue for damages (or other remedies if appropriate) under the doctrine of **anticipatory repudiation** immediately without waiting for the actual breach to occur on January 2.

When one party uses unequivocal language (such as in the Manager–Consultant contract above) to repudiate, there is no question that the other may file suit immediately.

CASE 7.1 Mobil Oil Exploration & Producing Southeast, Inc. v. United States, 530 U.S. 604 (2000)

FACT SUMMARY In 1981, Mobil Oil bought a lease contract for land owned by the U.S. government at the price of $156 million. The contract gave Mobil exclusive rights to explore and drill for oil off the coast of North Carolina. As a condition of the contract, the U.S. government required that Mobil submit a plan for the oil exploration that demonstrated compliance with existing environmental statutes including the Outer Continental Shelf Lands Act (OCSLA). After the contract was executed, Mobil submitted a plan to the appropriate government agency and was informed that the plan was satisfactory and that a permit would be issued when Mobil formally filed the plan with the agency. However, two days before Mobil officially filed the plan and applied for the permit, Congress passed a new law, the Outer Banks Protection Act (OBPA), which severely curtailed drilling in the region where Mobil owned the leases. The OBPA also prevented approval of any exploration or drilling plans (including Mobil's) indefinitely. Based on representations made by the government, Mobil alleged that the government actions were a repudiation and sued to recover the fee paid for the leases.

SYNOPSIS OF DECISION AND OPINION The U.S. Supreme Court held for Mobil, ruling that the original contract did not subject Mobil to regulations enacted under new law. The enforcement of the new law's standards substantially changed the terms of the contract, and that amounted to repudiation. The Court reasoned that the government had breached their contractual promise and that the breach was so substantial as to deprive Mobil of the benefit of the bargain. Mobil need not wait for the government to actually reject its plan before pursuing a remedy for breach of contract because the government's actions were sufficient to make a reasonable person believe they did not intend to honor their contractual obligation.

WORDS OF THE COURT: Anticipatory Repudiation "Repudiation of contract is a statement by the obligor to the obligee indicating that obligor will commit a breach that would itself give the obligee a claim for damages. . . . We find that the oil companies gave the United States $156 million in return for a contractual promise to follow the terms of pre-existing statutes and regulations. The new statute prevented the Government from keeping that promise. The breach substantially impair[ed] the value of the contract."

Case Questions

1. What was the actual event of breach in this case?
2. How could the government have avoided an anticipatory repudiation claim in this case?

However, in cases where the language is more ambiguous or when conduct is the basis for determining the repudiation, the analysis is more complex. Modern courts have held that repudiation occurs in one of three ways:

- A *statement* by one party of her intent not to perform. Note that the statement must be such that a reasonable person would have believed that the promisor is *quite unlikely* to perform. Vague doubts about the statements are insufficient.[14]
- An *action* by the promisor that rendered her performance impossible. For example, A agrees to sell an office building to B with conveyance in 30 days. Several days later B learns that A subsequently sold and conveyed the building to C. B may sue immediately for A's breach and need not wait the full 30-day period in the contract.
- Knowledge by the parties that one party may be *unable* to perform despite both parties best efforts.

It is also important to understand that any threatened breach must be for a material breach (or total breach, discussed above) for the nonbreaching party to use anticipatory repudiation. In Case 7.1, the U.S. Supreme Court applied the anticipatory repudiation dectrine.

CONCEPT SUMMARY   Breach of Contract

- Total breach occurs when one party fails to perform its duties under the contract; partial breach is a failure to perform that is not substantial enough to discharge the nonbreaching party.
- Repudiation occurs by a statement that, reasonably interpreted, communicates nonperformance; an action making performance impossible; or knowledge by the parties that one party will be unable to perform.
- The doctrine of anticipatory repudiation allows a nonbreaching party to suspend performance and recover damages before performance is due if the other party has made an unequivocal statement or action suggesting that performance will not occur.

In 2000, the U.S. Supreme Court ruled that passing a federal law limiting Mobil's contractual right to drill on property owned by the government amounted to anticipatory repudiation.

---

[14]Note that under a UCC sales contract, a potentially aggrieved party may ask for "assurances" of performance even for doubts. A right to assurances is covered in Chapter 8, "Contracts for the Sale of Goods."

REMEDIES

The law provides certain relief for aggrieved parties that suffer losses as a result of another party's breach of contract. These relief mechanisms are collectively referred to as *remedies*. Recall the distinction discussed in Chapter 1 between *remedies at law* and *remedies in equity*. For many contracts, the remedy at law will be **money damages** awarded by the court to the nonbreaching party. This is simply a legal mechanism for compelling the breaching party to compensate the innocent party for losses related to the breach. In a contract claim, money damages are primarily limited to (1) *compensatory* (also called *direct*) *damages,* (2) *consequential damages,* (3) *restitution,* and (4) *liquidated damages.*[15]

Compensatory Damages

Compensatory damages cover a broad spectrum of losses for recovery of *actual damages* suffered by the nonbreaching party. These damages are an attempt to put the nonbreaching party in the same position she would have been in if the other party had performed as agreed. This includes such sums as out-of-pocket damages and even potential profits that would have been earned if performance had occurred. For example, BigCo. hires LowPrice to prepare BigCo.'s tax returns and financial statements in time for BigCo.'s shareholders meeting on March 1 for a fee of $5,000. On February 15, the principal of LowPrice notifies BigCo. that she cannot prepare the returns because she decided to switch careers and shut down the tax practice. BigCo. must then hire HighPrice to prepare the documents. Because of the short time line, HighPrice charged a fee of $12,000. BigCo. is entitled to recover the difference between the price actually paid ($12,000) and the price that would have been paid if LowPrice had performed ($5,000) as originally agreed. Thus, BigCo. is entitled to $7,000 as compensatory damages (plus any additional out-of-pocket costs related to locating and hiring a new accounting firm).

Consequential Damages

Consequential damages compensate the nonbreaching party for *foreseeable indirect* losses not covered by compensatory damages. An aggrieved party is entitled to recover consequential damages if the damages are caused by unique and foreseeable circumstances beyond the contract itself. In order to recover consequential damages, the damages must flow from the breach (i.e., the damages were a consequence of the breach). For example, in the BigCo.–LowPrice case above, suppose that LowPrice had breached on the day before the tax returns were due and that BigCo. needed the tax returns as documentation for a bank loan on that day. Because the tax returns were not ready until one month after the due date, the bank charged BankCo. a delay fee and then raised the interest rate on the loan. These costs to BankCo. are related to the unique circumstances (tax returns needed on a certain date) and are foreseeable (assuming LowPrice had reason to know of the bank loan).

The rules that limit damages for which a nonbreaching party may recover were set out in *Hadley v. Baxendale,*[16] a landmark case on consequential damages that has been followed almost universally by U.S. courts. The case involved Hadley, a 19th-century mill owner, who was forced to cease operations due to a broken crankshaft. The mill owner sent the shaft out for repairs by hiring Baxendale to deliver the shaft to a repair shop in another city. Baxendale had no reason to know that the mill was shut down and, in fact, it was common practice in the industry for mill owners to have a back up shaft for just such

---

[15]Two other forms of civil damages recognized as a remedy at law are punitive damages (intended to deter conduct and/or punish a wrongdoer) and nominal damages (a breach exists, but no actually damages were suffered). However, these forms of damages are rare in contracts cases.

[16]156 Eng. Rep. 145 (1854).

an occasion. Baxendale delayed delivery of the shaft and this resulted in additional days of shutdown for the mill and, thus, lost profits for Hadley. Hadley sued Baxendale for the lost profits as consequential damages. The court ruled in favor of Baxendale because Hadley had not shown that a reasonable person could have *foreseen* Hadley's ongoing damages. Because Hadley had not actually communicated the unique circumstances, Baxendale was not liable for the damages related to the delay.

Restitution

Restitution is a remedy designed to prevent *unjust enrichment* of one party in an agreement. In the event that one party is in the process of performing the contract and the other party commits a material breach, the nonbreaching party is entitled to rescind (cancel) the contract and receive fair market value for any services rendered. For example, BuildCo. contracts with WidgetCo. to build a new warehouse for WidgetCo.'s inventory. One-third through the construction, WidgetCo. fails to make its payments on time and, therefore, materially breaches the contract. BuildCo. rescinds the contract and in a lawsuit against WidgetCo., BuildCo. may recover restitution equal to the fair market value of the work performed.

Liquidated Damages

Liquidated damages are damages that the parties agree to ahead of time. In some cases it may be very difficult to determine actual damages, so parties may agree at the time of the contract that a breach would result in a fixed damage amount. Liquidated damages provisions are commonly used in license agreements (such as a software-user's license) whereby the parties agree, for example, that a breaching party will pay $10,000 in the event of a breach caused by one party making unauthorized copies of the software. In order to be enforceable, courts have held that liquidated damage clauses must be directly related to the breach and be a reasonable estimate of the actual damages incurred (i.e., damages cannot be excessive so as to penalize the breaching party).

EQUITABLE REMEDIES

Although the usual remedy for a breach of contract is money damages, there are some instances where money damages are insufficient to compensate the nonbreaching party or when one party was unjustly enriched at the other party's expense. In these cases, a court may grant **equitable relief.** This relief comes primarily in the form of (1) *specific performance,* (2) *injunctive relief,* or (3) *reformation.*

Specific Performance

Specific performance is a remedy whereby a court orders the breaching party to render the promised performance by ordering the party to take a specific action. This remedy is only available when the subject matter of the contract is sufficiently *unique* so that money damages are inadequate.[17] Therefore, specific performance is rarely available in a sale of goods case unless the goods are rare (such as a coin collection) or distinctive (such as a sculpture) where the buyer cannot reasonably be expected to locate the goods anywhere else.

One of the most common circumstances where specific performance is awarded is in a real estate contract. Most courts consider each parcel of land to be sufficiently unique to trigger specific performance as a remedy. For example, Andrews agrees to sell Baker an office building in 30 days. At the closing where conveyance of the title is to take place, Andrews breaches the agreement by refusing to sell the building. In this case, Baker cannot be completely compensated for the breach because Baker chose that building for its location, convenience, accessibility, appearance, and other important factors. Baker contracted

---

[17]*Restatement (Second) of Contracts,* § 359.

for a unique parcel of real estate and is entitled to the benefit of the agreement for the same parcel. The court will require Andrews to *perform as promised* by conveying the property to Baker. If, however, Andrews has already sold the property to a good faith buyer, then Baker may only be awarded money damages as a remedy.

Specific performance is also an appropriate remedy in a narrow category of personal services contract where the parties agree that a *specific individual* will perform the services, and the individual possesses a *unique quality* or expertise central to the contract. For example, if Marcel contracts with Constantine to paint Marcel's office lobby in whitewash and Constantine breaches, a court would not consider specific performance as an option because the work is not specialized enough. On the other hand, if the Marcel–Constantine contract requires that Constantine paint a special mural on the wall, that would be sufficiently unique as to qualify for specific performance.

Injunctive Relief

A court order to refrain from performing a particular act is known as **injunctive relief.**[18] In the Andrews–Baker office building contract, suppose that Andrews promises to sell the building to Baker in 30 days. Baker learns that Andrews is intending to breach the contract and sell the building to Dominguez for a higher price. In this case, both money damages and specific performance are inadequate because Baker still wants the building instead of compensation for the breach. Baker will ask the court to issue an injunction that would prevent the sale of the building to Dominguez as an equitable remedy consistent with the notion of putting the aggrieved party in the same position as if the other party had performed as agreed.

Reformation

When the parties have imperfectly expressed their agreement and this imperfection results in a dispute, a court may change the contract by rewriting it to conform to the parties' actual intentions. This contract modification is called **reformation.** For example, suppose in the Andrews–Baker building contract above, that Andrews' real estate broker mistakenly placed the decimal in the price making it $10,000 instead of the parties agreed upon price of $100,000. At the closing, Baker gives Andrews the check for $10,000 and refuses to pay any more, citing the price on the contract. So long as there was a sufficient basis for believing the parties intended the price to be $100,000, a court may simply reform the contract. Andrews may then show that Baker breached the contract and request specific performance as an additional remedy.

AVOIDANCE AND MITIGATION OF DAMAGES

The law imposes an obligation on the parties in a contract to take appropriate steps in order to avoid incurring damages and losses. So long as a party can avoid the damages with reasonable effort, without undue risk or expense, she may be barred from recovery through a lawsuit. The rule preventing recovery for reasonably avoidable damages is often called the *duty to mitigate.*[19] For example, Leonardo contracts with NewCo. to design a new office building for NewCo. Midway through the design planning process, NewCo. changed its management, notified Leonardo that it believes that the design contract is invalid, and ordered them to stop work. Despite this, Leonardo continues the design process, submits the final work product to NewCo., and demands payment in full. In this case, it is likely that a court will not allow Leonardo to recover for any damages occurring after the NewCo. stop order. Once Leonardo learned of NewCo.'s claim, he had an obligation to avoid any further damages incurred by his failure to stop the work even if NewCo.'s stop order breached the contract.

---

[18]The concept of injunctive relief is covered in more detail in Chapter 4, "Resolving Disputes: Litigation and Alternative Dispute Resolution."

[19]*Restatements (Second) of Contracts,* § 350.

Managers may encounter a mitigation of damages issue when dealing with employees who claim that their employer breached an employment contract. If an employee has been wrongfully terminated, for example, that employee has a duty to seek new employment (of similar type and rank) if available in order to avoid damages resulting from the alleged breach by the employer.

CONCEPT SUMMARY Damages

- For a breach of contract, courts will award monetary damages to the nonbreaching party to remedy the loss suffered by nonperformance.
- Monetary damages can be (1) *compensatory*—direct losses from nonperformance; (2) *consequential*—indirect but foreseeable losses from nonperformance; (3) *restitution*—losses equal to the amount that the breaching party has been unjustly enriched by the nonbreaching party; or (4) *liquidated*—losses of a predetermined value according to the contract.
- Equitable relief is given when the monetary damages are insufficient; it takes the form of (1) injunctive relief, (2) specific performance, or (3) reformation.
- The duty to mitigate is the nonbreaching party's obligation to avoid excessive or unnecessary damages through reasonable efforts or else be barred from recovery for those avoidable costs of nonperformance.

LO7-7 CONTRACTS INVOLVING RIGHTS OF A THIRD PARTY

In some cases, a party to an existing contract wishes to substitute another party in her place. Because these contracts involve more than two parties, the law recognizes a special set of rules to govern such a substitution. One party may wish to do this by transferring to a third party her own rights in the contract, known as an *assignment,* or by appointing another to perform her duties, known as a *delegation.* Another form of a contract that involves rights of a third party occurs when a person who is not a party to the contract at the time of formation becomes a *third-party beneficiary* because the parties to the contract intended to confer a benefit on that person.

Assignment

An **assignment** is a transfer of current rights (not future rights) under a contract by one party in a contract to a third party. The party making the assignment is known as the *assignor* and the third party receiving the rights is the *assignee.* Once a valid assignment occurs, the assignor's rights under the contract are extinguished and the rights may then only be exercised by the assignee. The assignee then has the right to demand performance from the other party and to legally enforce the obligations. For example, Abel contracts to sell Baker 10,000 gallons of gasoline at $3.00 per gallon for Baker's fleet of delivery vehicles. Cain's research reveals that the price of gasoline may jump as high as $10.00 per gallon over the next year, so Cain contracts to pay Baker $70,000 for an assignment of Baker's rights under the Abel–Baker contract. Baker's rights (the assignor) are now extinguished, and Abel is compelled to perform his obligations by providing the gasoline to Cain (the assignee) at $3.00 per gallon. If Abel refuses to perform, Cain (but not Baker) may enforce the contract against Abel.

Generally, all rights in a contract are assignable at the sole discretion of the assigning party. Mutual consent is not required. However, in some instances, an assignment would be unfair to the nonassigning party. Therefore, some rights are not assignable:[20]

---

[20]*Restatement (Second) of Contracts,* § 322.

- Assignment is not permitted when the parties have included an *antiassignment clause* using such language as "No rights under this contract may be assigned."
- Assignments are invalid when the assignment *materially alters the duty* of the other party or by increasing a *burden or risk.* For example, an insurance contract that insures risk of one building against a flood may not be assigned to another building owner who owns a property in a flood plain. The obligor's (insurance company's) risk for the premium paid is materially altered. Thus, this assignment is prohibited.
- Some states have added additional assignment prohibition statutes related to general *public policy* matters (e.g., states that prohibit assignment of alimony payments before they become due).[21]

Delegation

Parties to a contract may also substitute another party to perform any *duties* owed under the agreement. A **delegation** is a transfer of current duties owed by one party under a contract to a third party. The party making the delegation is known as the *delegator* and the third party receiving the rights is the *delegatee.* One major difference between assignment and delegation is that when a party delegates duty, the delegator remains liable for the obligation. Thus, if the delegatee fails to perform, the delegator must either perform or suffer liability for the breach of contract.

Although duties may generally be delegated without mutual consent of the parties, certain duties are nondelegable:

- *Special personal skills,* such as those of an attorney, physician, portrait artist, or actor, may not be delegated.
- When a contract contains an *antidelegation clause.*
- When the delegatee is a *competitor* of the obligee (the nondelegating party).[22]

Third-Party Beneficiaries   In an assignment or delegation, the third party's rights occur *after* the formation of the contract. However, sometimes a party may form a contract to benefit not her, but a third person. In this case, the party, called the **third-party beneficiary,** becomes a party to the contract and certain rights arise to protect the third party. The key to understanding whether these rights arise or not is to examine whether or not the parties *intended to confer a benefit* on the third party. Such a third party is known as the *intended beneficiary* and has rights to enforce the contract as appropriate. For example, Ernest borrows money from Scott to pay his living expenses while Ernest writes a novel. When Ernest is negotiating a contract for the novel with Scribner's Publishing, Ernest asks that 50 percent of the royalties be paid to Scott in payment of the debt Ernest owes him. Because Scott is an intended beneficiary of this contract, he may sue Scribner's if they fail to perform by paying the royalty as agreed.

By contrast, third parties who are not contemplated as beneficiaries by the original contracting parties are known as *incidental beneficiaries.* Incidental beneficiaries may not sue to enforce contractual rights. For example, Perkins owns a retail bookstore in the Main Street Mall (MSM). MSM contracts with Big Buy Appliances for the space next to the Perkins bookstore. Perkins is ecstatic upon learning of this because Big Buy is a major retail chain with high customer drawing power. After the lease is signed, Big Buy backs out. Although Perkins did benefit from the MSM–Big Buy contract, he cannot sue any of the parties in that contract because he is an incidental beneficiary.[23]

---

[21]J. D. Calamari, J. M. Perillo, and H. H. Bender, *Cases and Problems on Contracts,* 4th ed. (St. Paul, MN: West/Thomson, 2004,) pp. 683–84.

[22]See *Sally Beauty Company v. Nexxus Products Co.,* 801 F.2d 1001 (7th Cir. 1986).

[23]Based on *Restatement (Second) of Contracts,* § 302, Illustration 16.

CONCEPT SUMMARY   Third-Party Rights

- Assignment is the unilateral shifting of rights under a contract from one party to a third party and is permitted only in the absence of an antiassignment clause, material change to the burden, or legal prohibition.
- Delegation is the assignment of contractual duties to a third party when the original party still remains liable for nonperformance and is permitted except in cases of special personal skills, a nondelegation clause, or where the delegatee is a competitor of the nondelegating party.
- A third party who benefits from a contractual promise between two other parties may only seek damages if she is an intended beneficiary as opposed to an incidental beneficiary.

KEY TERMS

Condition p. 160   An event that must occur before a contract obligation is triggered.

Good faith p. 161   The obligation to act in good faith is the duty to honestly adhere to the contract's common purpose. Under this obligation neither party can do anything to prevent the other party from enjoying the "fruits of the contract." Instead, both must try and make the deal work as written.

Discharge p. 162   In contract law, discharge is the removal of all legal obligations under the agreement and occurs only after full performance of the party.

Substantial performance p. 162   Performance of the essential terms of the contract such that performance can be considered complete less damages for anything still unperformed.

Mutual consent p. 164   Circumstance under which contracting parties may be discharged from obligation where neither party has fully performed and they agree to cancel the contract.

Operation of law p. 164   Circumstances in which contract obligations may be discharged where fairness demands it through the doctrines of impossibility, impracticability, and frustration of purpose.

Rescission p. 164   A contract is rescinded when both parties agree to discharge each other from all duties under that contract and end the agreement, no matter what has been done or left undone.

Accord and satisfaction p. 164   A doctrine that allows one party to create an agreement, or *accord,* with the other party to accept a substitute performance in order to *satisfy* the original performance; the completion of the new duty discharges the old one.

Substitute agreement (modification) p. 164   A modification occurs when two parties agree to different duties under the contract; these new duties then replace and dissolve the original obligations of that agreement.

Novation p. 164   Novation occurs when the duties of the contract remain the same but a new third party assumes the duties of an original party, discharging the original party from further obligations. (Note that many courts use *novation* for new parties and new terms or substitute agreements.)

Impossibility p. 166   Impossibility excuses performance when an essential part of the contract has become impossible because a crucial, irreplaceable thing has been destroyed; a crucial person has died; a crucial means of performance no longer exists; or a crucial action has become illegal.

Impracticability p. 166   Impracticability excuses performance when an extreme circumstance occurs or reveals itself that destroys the value of the performance to the party, when that circumstance was the fault of either party and was not reasonably foreseeable.

Frustration of purpose p. 166   A party is excused from performance if, before a breach, a state of things that was the basis for forming the contract no longer exists, by no fault of either party.

Unilaterally altered p. 168   A contract is unilaterally altered when one party changes a term of the offer or acceptance after the contract has been made and without the consent of the other party, who is then discharged from performing.

Bankruptcy p. 168   A procedure by which a debtor's assets are reorganized and liquidated by a court in order to pay off creditors and free the debtor from obligations under existing contracts.

Statute of limitations p. 168   A statute that places a time limit on the enforcement of certain contracts in order to ensure diligent enforcement.

Breach p. 168   A party is in breach when she has failed to perform its obligation under the contract such that the nonbreaching party is excused from its performance and can recover monetary damages.

Remedies p. 168   Remedies are the relief mechanisms by which courts compensate nonbreaching parties for the losses that result from the other party's breach of contract.

Anticipatory repudiation p. 169   When one party makes clear that he has no intention to perform as agreed, the nonbreaching party is entitled to recover damages in anticipation of the breach rather than waiting until performance is due.

Money damages p. 171   Money damages are sums levied on the breaching party(ies) and awarded to the nonbreaching party(ies) to remedy a loss from breach of contract.

Compensatory damages p. 171   Compensatory damages are meant to make the injured person whole again. In contract law, they seek to place the nonbreaching party in the position he would have been in had the contract been executed as agreed.

Consequential damages p. 171   Consequential damages repay the injured party for any foreseeable but indirect losses that flow from the breach of contract.

Restitution p. 172   Restitution restores to the plaintiff the value of the performance that he has already rendered to the breaching party, and by which the breaching party has been unjustly enriched.

Liquidated damages p. 172   Liquidated damages are reasonable estimates of the actual damages resulting if the contract is breached, which is agreed to by the parties ahead of time.

Equitable relief p. 172   A court grants equitable relief in the form of either specific performance ("do it") or an injunction ("stop doing it") when monetary damages are insufficient due to the unique or irreversible consequence of the breach.

Specific performance p. 172   A remedy whereby a court orders the breaching party to render the promised performance by ordering the party to take a specific action.

Injunctive relief p. 173   A court order to refrain from performing a particular act.

Reformation p. 173   Rewritten contract by the court to conform to the parties' actual intentions when the parties have imperfectly expressed their agreement and this imperfection results in a dispute.

Assignment p. 174   The transfer of one party's current rights under a contract to a third party such that the original party's rights are extinguished.

Delegation p. 175   One party's appointment of a third party to perform her duties under a contract, while still holding the original party liable for any breach.

Third-party beneficiary p. 175   Someone who, while not party to a contract, stands to benefit from the existence of that contract.

THEORY TO PRACTICE

After a 30-year career as a shipping logistics executive, Ishmael retired and began to offer his services as a logistics consultant. Ishmael entered into a consulting contract with the general manager at ExportCo. to provide logistical advice to the company for 12 months. The parties agree in the contract that Export will pay Ishmael $5,000 per month on the last day of each month. Ishmael promised to devote "100 percent of his professional time" to Export for a period of at least eight consecutive weeks.

1. After one week on the work site, Ishmael finds that he is devoting more time then he initially believed was necessary to Export, so he attempts to convince Export to pay him $6,000 per month for his consulting

services. Export does not agree to any change, so Ishmael begins to cut down his hours so that he is spending only 80 percent of his professional time at Export. If Export sues Ishmael for breach of contract, are there any circumstances where Ishmael may use the doctrine of substantial performance to complete his performance obligation? Why or why not?

2. Two months after the Ishmael–Export contract, Export loses a large client. They send Ishmael a letter explaining the financial emergency has caused them to consider rescinding Ishmael's contract under the theory that they were discharged from the remaining months of the contract based on the doctrine of impractability. Will a court support Export's theory?

3. In Question 2 above, if a manager from Export notifies Ishmael on March 1 that they do not intend to pay him for the month of March, must Ishmael wait to sue Export until the date performance is actually due (recall he is paid his fee on the last day of each month)? What doctrine may help Ishmael recover compensation without incurring further damages by waiting until performance is due?

4. What type of remedies would be most appropriate for Ishmael if a court were to find that Export breached the contract as in Question 2 above?

Would specific performance be appropriate? Why or why not?

5. Suppose that Ishmael meets with another potential client, but the needs of the client are such that Ishmael's immediate services are required and he cannot complete the work for Export. Because there is no antiassignment clause in the contract, he assigns the contract to his brother, who is also familiar with importing logistics. Export objects. Must Ishmael perform or must Export accept Ishmael's brother? What legal doctrines apply?

MANAGER'S CHALLENGE

Although at the beginning of a contract the parties may have a certain understanding, managers are sometimes be in a position where a change in the agreement becomes necessary. Clearly in Theory to Practice above, the parties need to retool their agreement to reflect (1) Ishmael's concern that the assignment is more work than originally anticipated, (2) Export's weakened financial position, and (3) Ishmael's desire to substitute his brother to complete the assignment. Draft a memorandum to your senior manager outlining specific options and consequences for altering these agreements through rescission, accord and satisfaction, substituted agreement, and/or novation. A sample answer may be found on this textbook's Web site at www.mhhe.com/melvin.

CASE SUMMARY 7.1 :: Dalton v. Educational Testing Service, 87 N.Y.2d 384 (N.Y. 1995)

GOOD FAITH AND SPECIFIC PERFORMANCE

Dalton took the SAT exam in May 1991. He retook the exam in November 1992 and scored 410 points higher. The Educational Testing Service (ETS), which administers the exam, has a policy of flagging score differentials greater than 350 points. After analyzing handwriting on the two tests, ETS concluded that someone else may have taken the exam for Dalton. Before the exam Dalton signed a contract with ETS stating that if he was flagged for cheating he had five options: cancel the score, have a third party review it, go to an arbitrator, retake the test, or send in information relevant to whether or not he had cheated. Dalton sent in information showing he had mononucleosis during the first test, that he had taken a prep course,

and provided affidavits from people who saw him at the test site. Testimony from the ETS showed that officials were convinced that the handwriting issue meant that Dalton had only the option to retake the test and, thus, they failed to consider the information he sent to them unless it dealt directly with the handwriting analysis.

Dalton sued for specific performance to have the scores reported as official by ETS. He argued that by giving him the contractual option of sending in information relevant to his cheating accusation, the ETS had a good faith obligation under the contract to examine and fully consider what he had sent in.

CASE QUESTIONS

1. Who prevails and why?
2. Why is specific performance an option here as a remedy?

CASE SUMMARY 7.2 :: Pepsi-Cola Co. v. Steak 'n Shake, Inc., 981 F. Supp. 1149 (S.D. Ind. 1997)

REMEDIES

The Steak 'n Shake restaurant chain entered a contract with Pepsi to replace King Cola with Pepsi in all its

stores. Several issues surrounding the contract's execution strained the agreement, and Steak 'n Shake cancelled the contract and refused to perform. Pepsi sued, and in court Steak 'n Shake insisted that Pepsi had no "legally cognizable" damages because all potential profits were purely speculative. Pepsi argued that it stood to gain from the contract and that they should be compensated for the breach even though damages could not be calculated exactly. The damages could be equal to what it reasonably stood to gain from the contract if not for Steak 'n Shake's breach.

CASE QUESTIONS

1. Will a court award damages to Pepsi even though they admitted the damages could not be calculated exactly?
2. What other types of damages or relief could Pepsi seek?

CASE SUMMARY 7.3 :: Sechrest v. Forest Furniture Co., 264 N.C. 216 (N.C. 1965)

IMPOSSIBILITY

Sechrest Plywood Company contracted with Forest Furniture Company to sell them plywood bottoms for drawers that Forest would manufacture. After the contract, Forest's warehouse, where it intended to make the drawers, was completely destroyed by a fire. Forest asserted that the contract was void for impossibility. Sechrest argued that while the fire prevented Forest from manufacturing drawers it did not prevent them from purchasing the plywood bottoms it had contracted with them for and, therefore, the doctrine of impossibility does not apply.

CASE QUESTIONS

1. What are the standards for being discharged through impossibility?
2. Does it apply here? Why or why not?

CASE SUMMARY 7.4 :: Taylor v. Palmer, 31 Cal. 240 (Cal. 1966)

ASSIGNMENT TO A THIRD PARTY

The City of San Francisco contracted with a builder to do several tasks associated with roadwork and refurbishment. The contractor assigned the work to another contractor. The city sought breach of contract for, among other things, inappropriate assignment in that the service was of a personal nature, which under common law cannot be unilaterally assigned to a third party. The contractor argued that the roadwork in the contract was not of a personal nature and thus could lawfully be assigned by the original contractor to the third-party contractor.

CASE QUESTIONS

1. Who prevails and why?
2. Is the task specialized?

 Self-Check **ANSWERS**

Substantial Performance

1. Wholesaler has substantially performed, but Delicatessen is entitled to a reduction in price.

2. No substantial performance. The most important term in the contract (the phone number) was not met by Yellow Pages and the value of the contract to Dry Cleaner is now zero. Based on *Georges v. Pacific Tel. & Tel. Co.,* 184 F. Supp. 571 (D.C. Or. 1960).

3. No substantial performance. The industry standard is such that the difference between a 15 percent leaf/stem ratio is substantially more valuable than the 25 percent leaf/stem ratio. See *Del Monte Corp. v. Martin,* 574 S.W.2d 597 (Tex. Civ. App. 1978).

4. Substantial performance or perfect performance depending on whether the portrait objectively meets the criteria for a professional painting of that type.

8
CHAPTER

Contracts for the Sale of Goods

learning outcomes checklist

After studying this chapter, students who have mastered the material will be able to:

8-1 Articulate the fundamental purpose and role of the UCC in commercial transactions and why it is important to business owners and managers.

8-2 Identify which contracts are governed by UCC Article 2.

8-3 Discuss the requirements for agreement in a sale of goods contract and what terms the UCC provides in a sales agreement with open or missing terms.

8-4 Classify which contracts must be in writing and understand what the writing must contain to be enforceable under the statute of frauds.

8-5 Express how risk of loss is allocated among the parties in a sales contract and identify steps managers take to limit risks and assure performance.

8-6 Convey UCC requirements on the obligations of both buyer and seller and the consequences of breaching a contract.

8-7 Identify the appropriate remedy and damages available to buyers and sellers.

8-8 Explain the risks of sales transactions with foreign companies and how to mitigate that risk by understanding international commercial laws.

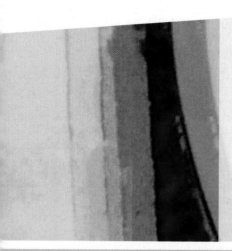

This chapter continues coverage from Chapters 6 and 7 of the challenges that managers face in the formation and performance of contracts, but with a focus on the role of Article 2 of the Uniform Commercial Code (UCC).[1] Article 2 of the UCC sets out rules that govern contracts involving the *sale of goods*. In this chapter, students will learn:

- The scope of Article 2 coverage.
- Formation of agreements for the sale of goods recognized under the UCC and how it differs from the common law.

- Legal rules regarding passing of ownership and allocation of risk for goods in a commercial transaction.
- UCC provisions governing the obligations of the parties in a sales agreement as well as UCC protections for innocent parties on occasions when the other party violates the agreement.
- The international commercial law principles governing sale of goods contracts with a company in a foreign nation.

---

[1]Note that the UCC also contains other articles pertaining to different aspects of commercial law. For example, Article 2A covers the *leasing* of goods. Leasing of goods in discussed in Chapter 23 "Real Property, Personal Property, and Land Use Law." This chapter focuses exclusively on Article 2: Sales of Goods.

INTRODUCTION TO ARTICLE 2 OF THE UCC

Recall from the previous chapters that contracts for the *sale of goods* are governed by statutory law in the form of the Uniform Commercial Code (UCC or sometimes referred to simply as the *Code*). The UCC is a model statute published by the National Conference of Commissioners of Uniform State Laws (NCCUSL).[2] Every state except Louisiana has adopted all (or substantially all) of Article 2 of the UCC. In 2003, the NCCUSL came out with a revised Code, but the revisions were substantial and have met opposition in state legislatures to the point where no state has adopted the revised Code.[3] Therefore, this textbook always references the pre-2003 Code.

UCC Coverage and Definitions

The UCC applies only to **sales contracts** that are agreements for the *sale of goods*. The UCC defines **goods**[4] as that which is (1) tangible (i.e., has a physical existence such as a laptop computer), and (2) moveable from place to place. Therefore real estate contracts or employment contracts are *not* covered by the UCC. While many sales contracts involve the sale of goods to a consumer, Article 2 also contains special provisions that apply only in transactions between *merchants*. A **merchant** is one that is *regularly engaged* in the sale of a particular good. The UCC imputes a certain level of knowledge and awareness to merchants and allows transactions to proceed in an expedited manner without the necessity for safeguards intended for average consumers. For example, suppose that Caesar's Equipment Co. sells a lawn tractor to Sanjay for $600. This sales agreement is subject to Article 2, but because Sanjay is not a merchant, certain UCC requirements exist primarily to protect Sanjay's interests in the sale. However if Caesar's is a wholesaler and Sanjay is the owner of a retail store, this is a *merchant* transaction and triggers special business standards that are intended to allow the parties to transact business unimpeded by any consumer protections.

Function of the UCC

The underlying policy of the UCC is to promote commercial efficiency by providing standardized procedures that merchants and consumers may rely upon. The provisions of the UCC were drafted with the goal of promoting the *completion* of a business transaction. Article 2 is intended to modify some of the stricter common law requirements and facilitate business transactions by providing merchants and consumers with a standard set of rules for the sale of goods.

In the context of sales contracts, the UCC should be thought of primarily as a *gap filler* in cases where the parties have not agreed otherwise. Typically, two parties will enter into a sales contract after negotiating certain terms. Terms of such a sales contract, assuming that they do not conflict with a UCC prohibition, are fully enforceable. The UCC principally comes into play when the parties to a sales transaction have *not* expressly agreed on certain terms. For example, suppose that on Monday, Hadley and Martha enter into an agreement for the sale of 1,000 Brand-A watches at $1 per Brand-A watch to be delivered to Martha's warehouse on Friday. However, the parties do not bother to negotiate any other terms except price and delivery date. Suppose that Hadley runs out of Brand-A watches and ships 1,000 Brand-B watches. Must Martha accept the

> ### KEY POINT
> Article 2 of the UCC acts to fill in only missing or open terms (where the parties have not expressly agreed otherwise) in a contract for the sale of goods.

---

[2]The NCCUSL and other similar organizations are discussed in more detail in Chapter 1.

[3]For an update on the status of the revised UCC, go to this textbook's Web site at www.mhhe.com/melvin.

[4]UCC § 2-103.

watches? What are her options under the law? Suppose that the watches are damaged in transit before they are delivered to Martha's warehouse. What are the parties' rights and responsibilities regarding the sale? Who will bear the risk of the loss? Because the parties have not specifically agreed on this contingency, they must turn to the UCC for the answers to those missing terms.

Contracts for the sale of goods are covered under Article 2 of the Uniform Commercial Code.

AGREEMENT IN A SALES CONTRACT: OFFER

LO8-3

Recall that the UCC generally aims to *promote* a sales transaction to be completed rather than shelter a party who doesn't complete the transaction. The formation elements for a sales contract, for example, are easier to meet and do not require the level of intent required for common law contracts. Article 2 lowers the bar for formation by allowing an enforceable contract to arise "in any manner sufficient to show agreement" between the parties.[5] Therefore, the UCC allows a contract to be enforced based on a larger picture that consists of (1) past commercial conduct, (2) correspondence or verbal exchanges between the parties, and (3) industry standards and norms. In fact, the parties need not even have a definite time of formation, so long as the conduct of the parties indicates some basis for a reasonable person to believe a sales contract *exists*. For example, Wholesaler delivers 1,000 digital music players to Retailer on the 15th of each month. Over a period of six months, Wholesaler has delivered the players on or about the 15th of the month and Retailer has sent Wholesaler a check within 10 days. Assume that in the digital music

---

[5]UCC § 2-204(1).

player industry, payment is generally made within 10 days after delivery. In month seven, Wholesaler delivers the product on the 15th, but Retailer never pays. Most courts would hold that the seventh month was an enforceable contract even if Retailer did not subjectively *intend* for the music player contract to linger into seven months. Under the UCC, the larger picture was that the parties' *conduct* indicated that they had an ongoing series of contracts with certain terms. Retailer must exercise some conduct that would indicate that the contract was at an end (a simple e-mail would suffice) before the delivery date in the seventh month in order for the contract to be considered at an end.

Offers with Open Terms

Sometimes merchants wish to engage in a sales transaction, but the parties overlook or are unsure about some key element of the contract such as quantity, delivery, payment terms, or even price of the goods. The missing provisions, known as **open terms,** are entirely acceptable under the UCC so long as there is evidence that the parties *intended* to enter into a contract and the other terms are sufficiently articulated to provide a basis for some appropriate *remedy* in case of breach. This is where the UCC provides gap filling. The UCC provides a variety of answers based on what term(s) is/are missing.

Quantity   While quantity is generally a *required* term necessary to create an enforceable contract, two important exceptions exist to this general rule. First, quantity *may* be an open term if the buyer agrees to purchase *all* of the goods that a seller produces (known as an **output contract**). In this case, the seller has given up the right to sell the goods elsewhere. Second, when the buyer agrees to purchase all or up to an agreed amount of what the buyer needs for a given period (known as a **requirements contract**), a court will generally enforce that agreement despite the missing quantity. For example, suppose that Builder wishes to purchase small pine trees from Grower for use at one of Builder's commercial office complex sites. If Builder agrees to purchase all of the pine trees grown by Grower over the period of one growing season, this is an output contract. If, on the other hand, Builder agrees with Grower to purchase all of the trees that are needed for this site only, the parties have agreed to a requirements contract. In both cases, an enforceable contract exists despite the missing quantity.[6]

Other Open Terms   When a sales contract is missing other terms and the parties have not had an established course of past conduct, the UCC provides the gap fillers as follows:[7]
- *Delivery:* Buyer takes delivery at the *seller*'s place of business (i.e., seller is not responsible for delivery). If no time of delivery is specified, the UCC provides for a reasonable time under the circumstances.
- *Payment:* Payment is due at the time and place where the seller is to make delivery and may be made in any commercially reasonable form (such as a business check).
- *Price:* The UCC requires the court to determine a reasonable price at the time of delivery. This is based on industry customs and market value.

Firm Offers by Merchants

Recall from Chapter 6, "Overview and Formation of Contracts," that the *offeror* has the right to revoke or modify an offer at any time prior to acceptance by the *offeree* (i.e., "offeror is the master of the offer"). There are certain exceptions to that principle under the common law, such as an option contract. The UCC creates its own brand of irrevocable offer known as a **merchant's firm offer** that applies only to transactions where the offeror is a *merchant.* A firm offer is created when a merchant offers to buy or sell goods with an

---

[6]UCC § 2-306(1).
[7]Delivery: UCC § 2-308(a); Payment: UCC § 2-310; Price: UCC § 2-305(1).

explicit promise, in writing, that the offer will be held open for a certain time period. In general, the UCC provides that the offer can be irrevocable for a maximum period of three months. This obligation is binding on the offeror even though the offeree has paid no consideration. Note that if the offeree has paid consideration tied to the offer, this constitutes an option contract and not a firm offer.

AGREEMENT IN SALES CONTRACTS: ACCEPTANCE

Article 2 provides its own rules for accepting an offer in a sales contract that are not as rigid as the common law rules. If the offeror does not clearly provide for a method of acceptance, the UCC allows the offeree to accept the offer in any "reasonable manner."[8] One important difference between acceptance standards in the UCC and the common law is that acceptance may still be effective even if the acceptance does *not* match the offer exactly (recall the common law mirror image rule from Chapter 6). Not only does the UCC recognize that a contract may in some cases be created where the acceptance does not match the offer, but it also fills in gaps to create certainty for the parties to the transaction.

Battle of the Preprinted Forms

As a practical matter, businesses frequently use preprinted forms to initiate or respond to an offer to sell a good. These forms usually have some blanks for the particular negotiated terms unique to that transaction. Normally, the offer takes the form of a **purchase order** from the buyer that contains preprinted clauses (that typically favor the buyer) with a purchase manager filling in terms such as shipment date, product information, quantity, and so forth. The seller's firm will then typically issue an **acknowledgment form,** which also has preprinted provisions (that typically favor the seller) and also has blanks to accommodate the specifics of that transaction.[9] The UCC provides guidelines on how to resolve a dispute when the terms in these forms conflict. This dilemma is known as the **battle of the forms.**

In a battle of the forms case, the UCC provides that (1) a document may constitute acceptance even though it states additional or different terms from those offered by the offeror, and (2) in certain transactions the additional terms proposed in the acceptance may become part of the contract.

Nonmerchant Transactions   If one of the parties in a sales contract is *not* a merchant, the contract is formed as *originally* offered. That is, the contract is considered accepted, but the additional terms are *not* part of the contract.

Merchant Transactions   If both parties are merchants, the rules are more complicated. Between merchants, in a sales contract acceptance with additional terms, the additional terms *automatically* become part of the enforceable contract unless (1) the offeror has expressly and clearly limited acceptance to the original terms such as "The terms of this Purchase Order may not be altered or changed and any alteration of the original terms are expressly rejected" (this is common language on a purchase order); or (2) the additional term was a *material* change that diverges significantly from those contained in the offer (i.e., one that changed the value of the contract or affected the parties' obligation to perform in a significant way);[10] or (3) the offeror raises an objection to the additional terms within a reasonable time period according to industry standards.

---

[8]UCC § 2-206.

[9]UCC § 2-207.

[10]For example, some courts have held that the insertion of an arbitration clause materially alters an offer. See *Dorton v. Collins & Aikman Corp.,* 453 F.2d 1161 (6th Cir. 1972).

Self-Check

Does a sales contract exist? If so, what are the terms of the contract?

1. Boston Hardware Co. agrees to buy all the snow shovels it needs from New England Shovel Co. In past years this has been around 5,000 shovels per year. The mild winter in 2009 caused Boston Hardware to need only 250 shovels, leaving New England Shovel Co. with over 4,000 unpurchased shovels.

2. New York High School agrees to purchase 200 desks for $100 each from Big Apple School Supply Inc. The desks are to be ready for September 1, 2008, but there are no delivery terms in the contract.

3. L.A. Outfitters offers to sell West Coast Burrito Co. 1,100 uniforms by sending them a letter with price, quantity, and delivery terms and an offer to keep the offer open for seven months. Six months later, West Coast Burrito responds with a standard acknowledgment and acceptance form. The standard form includes an agreement to arbitrate.

4. Chicago Toy Depot Inc. sends a purchase order to Midwest Dolls Inc. for 10,000 "Fancy Nancy" dolls by November 1, 2010, in time for the holiday season. Midwest Dolls returns an acknowledgment letter guaranteeing the dolls for January 1, 2011.

Answers to this Self-Check are provided at the end of the chapter.

Consideration

Recall from the coverage in Chapter 6, "Overview and Formation of Contracts," that most contracts must be supported by consideration. Remember also that that most cases involving a nongoods agreement (i.e., those governed by the common law) cannot be *modified* without some additional consideration. While the UCC follows a similar rule that consideration must support sales contracts, a major difference is that the UCC allows contracts to be modified even *without* any additional consideration. The UCC recognizes that market conditions are not static and that the parties may have good faith reasons for modifying a contract without having some additional burden to continue its enforceability. For example, suppose that Wargrave sells 2,000 golf balls to Owen on credit. Owen agrees to pay Wargrave $1,000 plus 6 percent interest on the principal still owed per month for a period of 24 months. After two months, Owen's cash flow is impaired by an unexpected downturn in Owen's business. Owen and Wargrave agree to modify the contract that will allow Owen to pay a smaller monthly payment ($500 per month) but at the same interest rate until the balance is paid off in full. Later, Wargrave runs into his own cash flow problems and demands that Owen honor the original Wargrave–Owen credit contract terms. Despite the fact that no additional consideration was given for the modification, the *modified* Wargrave–Owen contract is fully enforceable and the original contract is cancelled.

LO8-4 STATUTE OF FRAUDS

The statute of frauds is a legal requirement that certain contracts be in writing in order to be enforceable. The UCC contains a specific section detailing the writing requirements for sales transactions. Any sales contract for goods with a total value of *$500 or more* must be in writing.[11]

While common law contracts require several *specific* terms of a contract to be in the writing, the UCC has a much more liberal rule concerning what must be in the writing. The UCC's statute of frauds provisions are satisfied so long as the writing contains (1) quantity, (2) the signature of the party against whom enforcement is sought, and (3) language that would allow a reasonable person to conclude that the parties intended to form a contract.

---

[11]UCC § 2-201(1).

All other terms and conditions may be proved via testimony concerning oral agreements, past practices, and industry standards. In *Rosenfeld v. Basquiat,* a New York appellate court held that a brown piece of wrapping paper that had quantity, price, a deposit amount, the name of the goods, and the signature of both parties in crayon was more than sufficient to satisfy the UCC's statute of frauds.[12]

The statute of frauds section of the UCC also provides a relatively lenient rule for sales contracts between two merchants. A merchant who receives a signed **confirmation memorandum** from the other merchant will be bound by the memorandum just as if she had signed it, unless she promptly objects. Thus, if Abel telephones Cain to order 1,000 golf balls, then Cain sends a written confirmation of the agreement with the correct quantity and price, Abel will be bound by the contract and the statute of frauds is satisfied.

CONCEPT SUMMARY   Formation under the UCC

- In order to encourage the formation and execution of sales contracts, the UCC offers more lenient rules regarding offer, acceptance, consideration, breach, and the statute of frauds.

- An agreement is still valid despite the fact that delivery, pricing, or payment terms are left *open;* the UCC provides standards to fill the gaps left by the missing terms.

- A written offer by a merchant includes an implied promise to keep the offer open for a stated or unstated amount of time even absent consideration for the option.

- When two merchants submit standardized offer and acceptance forms with conflicting terms, the UCC will still consider the contract accepted unless (1) the offer stated explicitly the terms of acceptance, (2) the conflicting terms substantially change the duties of the contract or its value to one party, or (3) the new terms were rejected in a timely manner by the offeror.

- A sales contract can be modified without additional consideration.

- The UCC statute of frauds requires that contracts for sales of goods valued at more than $500 be written, but requires only that the document contain (1) quantity, (2) the signature of the party against whom enforcement is sought and, (3) language that reasonably shows the parties intended to form a contract.

TITLE AND ALLOCATION OF RISK   LO8-5

Business owners and managers must have a working knowledge of the UCC provisions regarding title and risk allocation because these rules play an important part in determining commercial risks at various stages of a business transaction. Once an agreement has been made between the parties, there is likely to be a lapse of time before the buyer actually comes into physical possession of the goods. For example, ManufactureCo. agrees to sell a new printing press to CopyCo. for $100,000 to be delivered within 30 calendar days. During the delivery process, the press is damaged in a trucking accident. Or suppose that the press is delivered to a port to be picked up by CopyCo., but a warehouse fire destroys

---

[12]*Rosenfeld v. Basquiat,* 78 F.3d 84 (2d Cir. 1996). The case involved the famous artist Basquiat who sold several paintings to Rosenfeld, an art dealer. Rosenfeld requested a receipt for a deposit and Basquiat, who one could justly call eccentric, found a brown piece of wrapping paper, and with crayon in hand, wrote the names of paintings, the amount paid, the names of the parties, and then signed the paper. Basquiat died soon after the sale of the paintings, but before the art dealer could take delivery. Basquiat's estate refused to honor the contract on the basis that the writing was not a formal enough contract because it never specified delivery terms. Rosenfeld sued and won, with the court holding that delivery terms were not required to satisfy the statute of frauds under the UCC Article 2.

the press before the buyer picked it up. Who bears the burden of the loss? In both cases, CopyCo. still needs a press, while ManufacturerCo. made good faith efforts to deliver the merchandise as agreed upon. The UCC provides answers to these types of questions in its provisions governing **risk of loss.**[13] Of course, as with other provisions of the UCC, the risk of loss rules apply *only* when the parties have not specifically agreed to risk allocation. If the buyer and seller negotiate and agree to provisions relating to the risk of loss and/or when the ownership of goods actually passes, the UCC provisions are not applicable.

Title

Title is the legal term for the right of ownership in a good. Thus, the UCC refers to *passing of title* to indicate the point in time when actual ownership of the goods is transferred from seller to buyer. A party holds title to a good when (1) the goods are actually in *existence* in tangible form, and (2) when the goods are *identified* to the contract.[14] Identification takes place when the seller has marked or designated the good in some fashion (such as by serial numbers or lot designations). Once the requirements for title have been met, the UCC provides that title passes to the buyer at the time and place the seller *completes performance* by making a physical delivery of the goods.

Risk of Loss

The UCC provides a delineation as to when the title actually passes between the seller and the buyer, and allocates *risk of loss* based on categorizing agreements as either **shipment contracts** or **destination contracts.**

- *Shipment contracts* require the seller to use a carrier (such as a delivery company) to deliver the goods. As a general rule, all contracts for goods are considered shipment contracts *unless* the parties have agreed otherwise. In this case, the seller needs only to deliver the goods to the "hands" of the carrier to achieve complete performance. Once the seller has accomplished this, title is deemed to have passed to the buyer.[15] Normally, the *risk of loss* is allocated to the seller until such time as the seller has delivered the goods to the carrier. If the goods are destroyed after that point, the loss is ordinarily borne by the buyer. Note that the buyer may have recourse against the *carrier,* but not against the seller. For example, Schubert agrees to sell Beatrice a specially designed grand piano for $50,000. Beatrice instructs Schubert to deliver the piano from his factory via a specific carrier, Piano Delivery Services (PDS), within 10 business days. On day one, Schubert delivers the piano to PDS in good condition. On day two, the PDS truck catches on fire and the goods are destroyed. The title and risk of loss passed to Beatrice at the point when Schubert delivered the good (piano) to the carrier (PDS) and Beatrice has no course of action against Schubert, but may have a claim against the carrier (PDS).

- *Destination contracts* require the seller to deliver the goods to a *specified* destination. Typically, the destination is the buyer's place of business or home, but it can also be a third party that the buyer designates. In this case, the UCC provides that complete performance occurs when the goods have been **tendered** at the specified destination. Tendering is the legal term for delivery of the *conforming* goods (i.e., the seller delivered what the buyer actually ordered) to the destination that would allow the buyer to take delivery.[16] Normally, so long as the goods were properly tendered as agreed, the risk of loss is allocated to the buyer at the time of tender. For example, in the Schubert–Beatrice contract above, suppose that the parties specifically designate their agreement

---

[13]UCC § 2-401.
[14]UCC § 2-401(1).
[15]UCC § 2-401(1)(a).
[16]UCC § 2-503(2)(b).

FACT SUMMARY Jamison purchased a set of encyclopedias from Encyclopedia Britannica for $1,652.08 plus a $95 shipping charge. Jamison paid a $100 deposit and the remainder was to be paid in 30 monthly installments of $57. Encyclopedia Britannica assigned the contract to Merchants Acceptance to complete the delivery and receive payment. The contract contained shipping instructions and specified Jamison's home address as the place of delivery. Jamison never received the encyclopedias because they were shipped via United Parcel Service (UPS) to her post office box, but never to her home. Jamison refused to pay the installments and cancelled the purchase. Merchants brought suit for nonpayment; Jamison counterclaimed for her $100 deposit to be returned.

SYNOPSIS OF DECISION AND OPINION The court ruled in favor of Jamison, reasoning that the contract's terms included delivery and specified a place for delivery and, therefore, title to the books could only be transferred to Jamison when they arrived at her home. Because nothing was tendered by Merchants at Jamison's home address, she could properly cancel the contract and owes nothing.

WORDS OF THE COURT: Risk of Loss "Merchants urges that the contract in the present case was a 'shipping' contract, as opposed to a 'destination' contract; thus, warranting a finding that Merchants fulfilled its obligation to Jamison once it delivered the encyclopedias to UPS. However, since the delivery term in the Contract was specified as Jamison's street address, we find that it is unnecessary to delve into the case law describing the differences between 'shipping' versus 'destination' contracts. . . . The risk of loss, therefore, remained with Merchants until the books were 'duly so tendered as to enable [Jamison] to take delivery.'"

Case Questions

1. Why would the law require Merchants to have title to something that was in Jamison's own post office box?

2. Why did the court find it unnecessary to "delve into" the differences between a shipment and a destination contract?

---

as a *destination contract* and that Schubert must deliver the piano to Beatrice's studio in New York City. Schubert selects his own carrier, Cheapo Trucks, and the truck catches on fire in transit. In this case, the loss must be borne by the seller (Schubert) because it had not yet arrived at its New York City location.[17]

Case 8.1 provides an example of a risk of loss analysis.

Goods Picked Up by the Buyer

In some cases, the goods are not to be delivered by the seller, but rather to be picked up by the buyer. In that case, the risk of loss generally depends on whether or not the seller was a *merchant*. Recall from our earlier discussion that a merchant is one who is regularly engaged in the sale of a particular good. If the seller is a merchant, the risk of loss to goods held by the seller passes to the buyer only when the buyer takes physical possession of the goods. If the seller is not a merchant, the risk of loss to goods held by the seller passes to the buyer on tender of the goods.[18] For example, suppose that on Monday, Gates agrees to purchase 20 computers from CompCo., a computer retail outlet. Gates tells CompCo. that he will pick up the computers on Friday. CompCo. marks each of the 20 computers with a tag "Sold to Gates." However, Gates cannot make it to CompCo.'s warehouse on Friday. On Saturday, a thief steals all of the 20 computers. In this case, CompCo. bears the loss because CompCo. is a merchant and Gates had not yet taken physical possession of the goods. On the other hand, let's suppose Gates agrees to buy 20 used computers from

---

[17]Note that, depending on the circumstances, Schubert may recover his losses from Cheapo.
[18]UCC § 2-509(3).

Local College (a nonmerchant) on Monday. Gates tells Local College he will pick them up on Friday. On Thursday, Local College tenders the goods by calling Gates and notifying him that they are ready to be picked up in the lobby of the college's Alpha Hall on Friday any time between the hours of 8 a.m. and 5 p.m. Gates fails to show up on Friday. During the weekend, a thief breaks into the building and steals them. In that case, Gates bears the burden of the loss because Local College is not a merchant under the UCC and Local College tendered the computers by giving Gates proper notice about the times pickup could occur and location of the goods.

Self-Check
Who bears the risk of loss?

1. Marshall Clothing entered a shipment contract with Chase Department Stores to send them 3,000 black robes via Mercury Shipping Co. The robes were irreparably damaged in Mercury's warehouse by moths.

2. Taney's Treats purchased 450 gallons of ice cream from Harlan Dairy Co. The contract states that payment is due upon receipt of the ice cream at Taney's store. All 450 gallons melt in transit on a broken truck owned by Hermes Food Delivery Service.

3. Holmes Hats enters a destination contract to deliver 1,000 top hats to Cardozo Men's Stores. The courier delivers 1,000 bowler hats to Cardozo. Before Cardozo can return the incorrect hats, a flood ruins the entire delivery.

4. White purchases a car from Brennan Motors. The contract states specifically that title is not transferred prior to the title document being signed by both parties. The clerk is out sick, so the title papers cannot be produced that day. White drives the car home with the contract signed only by him and crashes the car.

Answers to this Self-Check are provided at the end of the chapter.

CONCEPT SUMMARY Title and Allocation of Risk

- Any risk allocation provision in the UCC does not control if the contract specifically lays out terms for risk allocation or title transfer.
- Neither the seller nor the buyer can hold title to goods until the goods are in physical existence and have been identified.
- The risk of loss is borne by the party who has title to the goods.
- Tender of goods occurs when the seller produces conforming goods and provides adequate notice of their delivery to the buyer.
- In a shipping contract title is transferred from seller to buyer when the goods are given to the courier, while in a destination contract title passes when the goods are tendered to the buyer.

LO8-6 PERFORMANCE OF SALES CONTRACTS

Once the parties to a sales contract have agreed on its terms, the law imposes certain other duties and obligations in performing the contract. In addition to the express terms by the parties, the UCC imposes a requirement of *good faith* and spells out the standards for place, time, and acceptance of delivery. Additionally, courts may also look to the customary standards in that particular industry and the course of past dealing between the

CASE 8.2   Sons of Thunder, Inc. v. Borden, Inc., 148 N.J. 396 (1997)

FACT SUMMARY   Borden was a company that made clam chowder using clams purchased from commercial fishing boats. Borden had been buying clams from four boats run by their most competent captain, Capt. Donald DeMusz. The boats would deliver whole clams, which then had to be shucked (de-shelled) on land, causing increased costs of processing and shell disposal. To avoid these costs, Borden sought a "Shuck-at-Sea" project wherein all shucking could be done by adding extra equipment onto the boat. None of the four boats were large enough to sustain this project so DeMusz offered to buy two larger ones if Borden promised to buy a minimum amount of clams from the boats.

Based on Borden's promise to purchase the clams, DeMusz took out loans and bought the *Jessica Lori* and the *Sons of Thunder* that were equipped with "Shuck-at-Sea" technology. Soon thereafter, Borden came under new management who concluded that the "Shuck-at-Sea" project was not profitable and notified DeMusz that they did not intend to honor the old contract. Borden began to buy only a fraction of their clams from DeMusz's boats, and this significantly reduced the revenue produced by the boats. At the same time, Borden increased its clam buying from DeMusz's competitors. With diminished revenue from the clam boats, DeMusz could not pay off the loans and had to sell the boats at a loss. DeMusz and other owners of the *Sons of Thunder* brought suit for breach of good faith obligation under the UCC.

SYNOPSIS OF DECISION AND OPINION   The New Jersey court ruled in favor of *Sons of Thunder,* reasoning that Borden urged DeMusz to buy the boats and promised to buy the clams they needed from the *Sons of Thunder.* Instead, Borden's new management expressed that they had no intention of honoring the contract. In bad faith, knowing that without Borden's clam purchases the *Sons of Thunder* would suffer financially to the point of insolvency, Borden simply reduced their clam buying dramatically.

WORDS OF THE COURT: Honesty in Fact Requirement   "Borden knew that *Sons of Thunder* depended on the income from its contract with Borden to pay back the loan. Yet, Borden continuously breached that contract by never buying the required amount of clams from the *Sons of Thunder.* Furthermore, after [management changed, they] told DeMusz that [they] would not honor the contract with *Sons of Thunder.* . . . Accepting those facts and the reasonable inferences therefrom offered as true, we determine that the jury had sufficient evidence to find that Borden was not 'honest in fact' as required by the UCC."

Case Questions

1. How should the new manager have acted when he saw that his predecessor had entered a bad contract?
2. What would have been a proper remedy for *Sons of Thunder?*

---

parties in interpreting the parties' duties and obligations. Of course, the parties may always expressly agree to unique delivery, risk allocation, or payment terms. But if the terms are not expressed, the UCC helps to fill any gaps and the parties are bound by the UCC terms.

Obligations of All Parties

The UCC has a *good faith* provision (similar to the duty of good faith in a common law contract) that imposes a duty of good faith and commercial reasonableness as the bedrock of any sales contract.[19] Good faith is defined in the UCC as "honesty in fact in the conduct or transaction concerned."[20] Additionally, merchants also have the duty to act in a *commercially reasonable* manner. Generally, this means that merchants (merchants only) must observe industry standards and practices that may be unique to a particular industry or field. In Case 8.2, a state supreme court gives an example of a UCC good faith analysis.

---

[19]UCC § 1-203.
[20]UCC § 1-201(19).

Seller's Obligations and Rights

Fundamentally, the seller's primary obligation is to transfer and deliver *conforming goods* to the buyer. Conforming goods simply means that the goods must conform exactly to the agreed upon description of the goods. Referred to as **tender of delivery,** the UCC obligates the seller to have or tender the goods, give the buyer appropriate notice of the tender, and take any actions necessary to allow the buyer to take delivery.[21] Absent any specific agreement between the parties to the contrary, the UCC uses a general *reasonableness requirement* to govern the delivery process. That is, the goods must be delivered at a reasonable hour, in a reasonable manner, and in one shipment. In the case of goods that are to be picked up, the goods must be made available at a reasonable time so as to allow the buyer to take possession.

Perfect Tender
Under the UCC, the seller's obligation actually goes beyond just delivering conforming goods. The seller must tender the goods in a manner that matches the contract terms in every respect. This is known as the **perfect tender rule.**[22] If the seller fails to achieve perfect tender, the buyer has three options: (1) reject the entire shipment of goods within a reasonable time, (2) accept the shipment of goods as is, or (3) accept any number of commercial units and reject the rest of the goods in a reasonable time (e.g., accepting 100 nonconforming computer chips from a delivery of 500 nonconforming computer chips).

Although the perfect tender rule may sound oppressive, the UCC also gives the seller certain rights intended to promote the completion of the original contract.

Cure
If the seller has delivered goods and the buyer rejects them under the perfect tender rule, the seller has the right to repair or replace the rejected goods *so long as the time period for performance has not expired.* Once the time contemplated for performance has expired, the seller's right to cure also expires. If, however, the time for the seller's performance has not expired, the seller may cure by (1) giving notice of her intent to cure, and (2) tendering conforming goods in replacement of the rejected goods.[23] For example, on April 1, Lewis contracts with Clarke to provide Clarke with 100 type-A compasses at $10 per unit to be delivered no later than May 1. Lewis delivers 100 type-B compasses on April 15 and Clarke rejects the goods as nonconforming. At this point, Lewis has the option to cure because the date for performance is still two weeks away. So, if Lewis notifies Clarke that he intends to cure and then ships 100 Type-A compasses to Clarke on April 30, he has completed performance consistent with the UCC requirements and, assuming the new shipment of goods conform, Clarke must accept the goods.

In some instances, the right to cure may exist even *after* the time period for performance has come due. The UCC provides that if the seller reasonably believes that the nonconforming goods would be acceptable to the buyer (perhaps because the seller shipped a more expensive product or because of a course of past dealing between buyer and seller) with or without a money allowance, then the seller gets additional time to cure after the time under the contract has passed. The seller must seasonably notify the buyer of her intent to cure.[24]

In the Lewis–Clarke contract above, suppose that Lewis was out of stock in Type-A compasses and instead shipped Clarke Type-A1A compasses (a more expensive and newer model) on the last day for performance. If Lewis rejects the goods, most courts would allow Clarke, so long as he has given Lewis seasonable notice, to cure even though the time period for performance has passed. This is because Clarke was reasonable in his

Legal Speak ›))
Seasonable Notice
Notification to the other party either within an agreed upon time or a reasonable amount of time given the nature and goals of the contract.

---

[21]UCC § 2-503(1).

[22]UCC § 2-601.

[23]UCC § 2-508 (1) and (2).

[24]UCC § 2-508 (2).

Assuring Performance

PROBLEM *In ongoing relationships with vendors, there may be a time when a manager becomes wary about a provider's ability to sell or a buyer's ability to continue making regular payments.*

Perhaps this skepticism is based on conduct of certain parties or on conversations with the vendor. What legal methods will help reduce the risk that they won't be left fighting other creditors in bankruptcy or suffer any further losses? For example, two companies enter into an agreement for the sale of electronic components. Whiteside agrees to purchase 50 lots of components per month, from January through June, from Greenside and to pay Greenside $7,500 per lot *within 10 days* after the lots are delivered. On January 2, Greenside tenders a conforming delivery and Whiteside pays by check on January 6. In February, Greenside delivers a second lot, but Whiteside fails to make the payment as agreed. As the end of February approaches with Whiteside's monthly invoice still unpaid, Greenside's manager faces a dilemma. While she wishes to preserve the potentially lucrative contractual relation with Whiteside, she is also responsible for protecting Greenside's interests and inventory.

SOLUTION *Greenside's manager should seek assurances about the past due and future payments.*

The UCC provides both parties the right to demand **assurances** from the other party concerning performance. The Code provides that when one party has *reasonable grounds* to believe that another will not perform, she has the right to demand that the other party give her written assurances that performance will take place as agreed.* If that party does not provide adequate assurance of performance within 30 days, the demanding party may then suspend performance until she receives the requested assurance. In the Whiteside–Greenside contract, suppose that one week prior to the date when the March delivery is scheduled, Greenside requests that Whiteside provide her with *written assurances* that (1) Whiteside will pay the amount due immediately, and (2) that Whiteside will continue to pay Greenside within the 10-day period as stated in the original contract. If Whiteside ignores the request or does not provide the requested assurances, Greenside then has the right to suspend her performance and has no duty to deliver another lot until she receives assurances from Whiteside. By using this UCC protection, Greenside's manager minimizes losses without breaching the original agreement. She preserved the contractual relationship until such time as the payment problems may be worked out to Greenside's satisfaction and delivery may then resume and continue in accordance with the original contract. If, however, conditions are sufficient to allow Greenside to reasonably believe that Whiteside intends to *renege* on his obligations in the contract, Greenside may cancel the contract and pursue legal remedies (such as a lawsuit to recover money damages) under the UCC provisions governing *anticipatory repudiation* (discussed in the next section).

*UCC § 2-609 (1).

---

assumption that a newer and more expensive model would be an acceptable substitute for the ordered model.[25]

Commercial Impracticability

Recall from the previous chapter that the common law excuses performance when a contract becomes **commercially impracticable.** The UCC also adopts a commercial impracticability rule when a delay in delivery or nondelivery has been made impracticable by the occurrence of an unanticipated event, so long as the event directly affected a basic assumption of the contract. Commercial impractability is a *narrow doctrine.* For example, in *Maple Farms, Inc. v. City School District of Elmira,* a state appellate court in New York

---

[25]Based on *Bartus v. Riccardi*, 284 N.Y.S.2d 222 (1967).

ruled that an unexpected increase in prices was *not* sufficient to meet the standard of commercial impractability for a supplier to be excused from performance because a reasonable businessperson should have been aware that the general inflation at the time (early 1970s) may affect the price of the contract.[26]

Buyer's Rights and Obligations

The buyer's primary obligation is triggered when the seller tenders delivery. Once the buyer has accepted the goods, the buyer must pay for them in accordance with the contract. Payments may come in a variety of forms, and frequently the parties have negotiated and agreed on the details of payments (cash versus credit, terms of payment, etc.). In the absence of agreement, the UCC provides that the buyer must make full payment at the time and place that she has received the goods.[27] When the parties have agreed on credit for payment, the amount owed is paid out over a period of time at a certain rate of interest. Typically, the interest would begin accruing 30 days after shipment.[28]

Buyer's Right of Inspection: Acceptance or Rejection

Unless the parties agree otherwise, the buyer has a reasonable time period to inspect the goods to be sure they conform to the contract. After inspection, the buyer may (1) communicate to the seller that she has accepted the goods; (2) do nothing, and is presumed to have accepted the goods unless she gives prompt notice of a rejection (or partial rejection); or (3) notify the seller that she is rejecting the goods[29] (or part of the goods). If the buyer properly rejects the goods, the buyer may also cancel the balance of the contract and pursue any appropriate legal remedies against the seller (breach and remedies for sales contracts are discussed in the next section). The buyer has an obligation to affirmatively notify the seller of the rejection in a timely manner so that the seller still has some opportunity to cure or a reasonable amount of time to recover the goods.

If the seller has shipped conforming goods as agreed, the buyer has the *duty to accept* them and become the owner of the goods in accordance with concepts of title.[30] If the seller has shipped nonconforming goods, but the buyer is still willing to accept them, the UCC provides the buyer with the opportunity to later revoke acceptance *only* if the nonconformity substantially impairs the value of the goods. The acceptance of nonconforming goods by the buyer triggers the buyer's obligation to pay consistent with the terms of the agreement.

Buyers have a reasonable time to inspect the goods to be sure that they conform to the contract.

---

[26]352 N.Y.S. 2d 784. The case involved a supplier of milk who agreed to supply a school district with a certain quantity of milk for the school year 1973/74 at a price set in June 1973. By December, the price of raw milk increased by 23 percent and the supplier would lose over $7,000 if they continued providing milk at the June price.

[27]UCC § 2-310(a).

[28]UCC § 2-310(d) provides that the credit period begins on date of shipment from the seller—not on date of receipt.

[29]Recall the good faith requirement of the UCC. Note that the parties do not have an absolute right to reject the goods. The buyer must have a good faith and lawfully recognized reason to reject (such as where the seller has shipped nonconforming goods). UCC § 2-601 and § 2-602 allow for a rejection of goods on reasonable grounds only.

[30]UCC § 2-606 and § 2-607.

Self-Check Buyer's Rights and Obligations

Does the grocer have an obligation to pay? Why or why not?

1. Grocer orders 100 Grade A eggs from Farmer per month at market price for a period of three years. Farmer delivers Grade A eggs every month for one year, but Grocer then began rejecting the eggs claiming that the market price for eggs was too high and the egg contract was commercially impracticable.

2. Grocer receives 40 bushels of corn rather than the tomatoes he ordered, but he signs a receipt for the corn anyway. The next day Grocer changes his mind and sends back the rejected corn.

3. Grocer orders 50 gallons of whole milk from Dairy to be delivered December 23. On December 20 he receives 60 gallons of skim milk. He rejects the order but does not inform Dairy of his rejection. On January 2, Dairy demands full payment.

4. Two days day before Thanksgiving, Grocer orders 100 turkeys, but the delivery the next morning is of 200 chickens. Afraid of losing all his customers the day before Thanksgiving, Grocer accepts 100 chickens and notifies the seller that he is rejecting part of the delivery.

Answers to this Self-Check are provided at the end of the chapter.

Special Rules for Installment Contracts

Cash flow or other business reasons sometimes require delivery and billing in two or more separate lots. The UCC provides for such circumstances through use of an **installment contract.** In an installment contract, each lot must be accepted and paid for separately. This means that a buyer can accept one installment without giving up the right to reject any additional installments that are nonconforming. This is essentially an exception to the perfect tender rule because the standard for rejection is more restrictive and, thus, provides additional tender protection to the seller. In an installment contract, the buyer may reject an installment only if the nonconformity *substantially* impairs the value of that installment *and* the nonconformity cannot be cured. If a buyer subsequently accepts a nonconforming installment of the goods and does not notify the seller that she is canceling the contract, the UCC provides that the seller may assume the contract to be reinstated.

CONCEPT SUMMARY   Performance of Sales Contracts

- Under the UCC, parties to a sales contract have an implied good faith obligation to be "honest in fact in the conduct of the transaction concerned."

- Except in the case of commercial impracticability, the seller must fulfill an obligation to perfectly tender goods in accordance with the contract or the buyer may reject. If the time for performance has not ended after rejection, the seller may cure the breach.

- The buyer can accept the goods or reject them with seasonable notice, but if he accepts, his obligation to pay is then triggered.

- An installment contract permits delivery of goods in separate lots and payment at separate times, with the new right to accept or reject each time.

BREACH AND REMEDIES IN SALES AGREEMENTS   LO8-7

Although the UCC is grounded in the principle that the law should encourage the consummation of business transactions, it also defines what constitutes nonperformance, known as **breach,** and provides relief for parties that have acted in good faith and sustained damages through no fault of their own. These relief mechanisms are called **remedies**[31] in the UCC and are based on the goal of placing the innocent (nonbreaching) party back in the same position as if the contract *had been performed* by the parties as originally contemplated in the agreement.

Anticipatory Repudiation in the UCC

Recall that, under the common law, contracting parties have a right to cancel the contract even before any performance is due if it becomes clear that one party does not intend to perform as agreed. The UCC embraces that very same right by recognizing that if one party communicates either in writing, orally, or by some action inconsistent with performance, this is a *repudiation* of the agreement. The UCC treats that as a breach even if performance was *not yet due.* The nonbreaching party may then either (1) suspend her own performance, treating the breach as final, and pursue any remedies available (remedies are discussed in the next section); or (2) suspend her own performance, wait for a period of time for the breaching party to *retract* the repudiation, and promise to perform.

Remedies Available to the Seller

A buyer breaches a sales contract when she does any one of the following: (1) rejects the goods despite the fact the goods conformed to the contract specifications, (2) wrongfully revokes an acceptance, (3) fails to pay the seller in accordance with the contract, or (4) fails to meet her obligations under the contract. In the event of one or more of those instances, the UCC allows the seller to pursue certain remedies against the buyer to recover any losses and prevent future losses. Note that the UCC allows the seller more than one remedy as long as it is *necessary* to help the nonbreaching party recover damages. The choice of remedies depends on *when* the breach occurs relative to whether the goods have been delivered.

Goods in Hands of Seller   When the breach has occurred before the goods were actually received by the buyer, the seller may:

1. Cancel the contract outright or discontinue his own performance (such as withholding or stopping delivery).
2. Resell the goods at fair market value to another party or dispose of the goods for recycling in accordance with reasonable commercial standards of the industry.
3. Recover any incidental damages related to the exercise of the reselling remedy such as hard costs of resale (e.g., broker's commission, auction fees) and any difference in value between the original contract price and the resale price.[32]
4. If the seller is unable to sell the goods at fair market value, then he may recover the full value of the contract from the buyer. If the seller exercises this remedy, he may no longer resell the goods even if a new buyer is found.

Goods in Hands of Buyer   In the case of nonpayment after the buyer has accepted (or such time has passed that the buyer is assumed to have accepted) the goods, the seller may recover the *entire* contract price plus incidental damages. This is also true if the goods are damaged or destroyed assuming the risk of loss has been passed to the buyer via contract terms or by virtue of the UCC.

In the case of wrongful rejection (rejecting conforming goods) or wrongful revocation of acceptance, the seller may *reclaim* the goods and exercise the remedies provided for in the UCC when the goods are in the hands of the seller, including the recovery of costs related to the reclamation.

Legal Speak ›))
Incidental Damages Under the UCC Any commercially reasonable charges, expenses, or commissions incurred in stopping delivery, or in transportation, care, and custody of goods after a buyer's breach.

---

[31]UCC § 2-701, et seq.
[32]UCC § 2-207(1).

Remedies Available to the Buyer

The primary way that a seller breaches a contract is by delivering *nonconforming* goods to the buyer or if the seller fails to make timely delivery of all or part of the lot. A seller who has repudiated the contract prior to delivery of the goods (recall the doctrine of *anticipatory repudiation,* discussed previously in this chapter) is also deemed to have breached the contract, and the buyer is entitled to pursue remedies. The UCC provides remedies to protect the buyer from further damages and compensate her for any losses suffered due to the breach.

Remedies Following Rejection of Goods

The UCC provides buyers with the immediate remedy of **rightful rejection** of all or part of the lot when the seller delivers nonconforming goods. In the case of rejection due to nonconformity, the buyer must give the seller *seasonable notification* of the rejection. By exercising the right of rejection, the buyer has cancelled the contract and is thus discharged from performing (paying) under the agreement and may recover any money already paid (such as a deposit). Rejection also enables the buyer to pursue additional remedies to prevent any further losses and/or recover for losses incurred as a result of the breach.

Cover

Consider the dilemma of the buyer when the seller has not made a timely delivery or if the seller delivered defective goods. No matter what the legal impact of the seller's actions, the buyer who requires the goods in order to conduct business operations must act immediately to prevent her own losses. The UCC provides the buyer with an option to take immediate steps by canceling the contract and purchasing *substitute* goods from another vendor, known as **cover,** in order to continue business operations. The UCC requires the covering party to purchase the goods in good faith and without unreasonable delay.[33] The right of cover also allows the covering party to bring a lawsuit to recover from the seller the difference between the *cost of cover* and *original* contract costs. Covering parties may also recover incidental or consequential damages. However, if the buyer actually saved expenses because of the breach by seller, those costs are deducted.

For example, suppose that on June 1, PartCo. agrees to sell ToyCo. goods based on the following memorandum drafted by ToyCo.'s manager:

1. *Item and Quantity:* 1,000 Type-A toy parts.
2. *Price:* $5 per toy part.
3. *Delivery:* On or before June 30 by Swift Trucking Company to ToyCo. warehouse. Delivery charge of $500 to be paid by buyer.

On July 1, the parts do not arrive, but ToyCo. has invested substantial sums in preparing its manufacturing operations to be ready in anticipation of the June 30 shipment date. Thus, ToyCo.'s manager opts to cancel the contract and contacts a local company, NewCo., to order the substitute goods (toy parts). NewCo.'s price per part is $7. However, because NewCo. is a local company, the delivery charge will be only $100. The damages calculation is:

Cover damages:

$7 (reasonable price of substitute goods) less $5 (contract price) = $2 per part for 1,000 parts

Plus:

Incidental and consequential damages (if applicable)

Minus:

Costs saved by virtue of the seller's breach ($400 reduction on delivery charges)

---

[33]UCC § 2-712(1).
[34]UCC § 2-715(1).

Lawsuit for Money Damages   There may certain instances where the buyer properly rejects the goods, but does not think it prudent or necessary to use the right to cover. In this case, the UCC gives the buyer the right to sue the breaching party for damages sustained due to the breach. If the buyer chooses this option (not to cover), the measure of damages is different than the covering damage measure. The major difference is the *point in time* used to calculate any losses. In a no-cover case, the recovery is derived by taking the difference between the contract price and the market price at the *time when the buyer learned* of the breach.

Specific Performance   Sometimes it is simply not feasible for the buyer to use cover or a suit for money damages as a remedy. For example, if the goods in question are *unique* and cannot be obtained elsewhere in the market, such as in the case of a sales contract for a rare book, a particular work of art, or a unique coin collection. In these circumstances, the UCC provides the buyer with a remedy of **specific performance,** which allows the buyer to obtain a court order that compels the breaching party to perform his obligation under the contract.

Remedies Following Acceptance of Nonconforming Goods

Commercial conditions or special circumstances may sometimes make the buyer accept (knowing or unknowingly) nonconforming goods. The UCC recognizes certain situations where, even though the buyer has accepted the goods, there may still be a need to protect the buyer's rights by providing remedies for relief.

Revocation of Acceptance   Sometimes a buyer may not realize that the goods are *nonconforming* and, after a cursory inspection, the buyer may *unknowingly* accept the goods. The UCC provides protection for such buyers, so long as they act within a reasonable time after discovery of the nonconformance. Buyers who have accepted the goods that turn out to be defective or nonconforming may still recover for any losses by **revoking acceptance.** In order to effectively revoke acceptance, the UCC requires that the nonconformance must *substantially* impair the value of the goods and the buyer must notify the seller within a reasonable time after he discovers (or should have discovered) the breach.[35] Once a reasonable time (generally in accordance with industry standards) has passed after acceptance, the buyer is then barred from pursuing a remedy.

Lawsuit for Money Damages   The buyer may wish to accept the nonconforming goods with full knowledge that the tender of delivery was less than perfect. In this case, the UCC gives protection to the buyer by making it clear that the buyer *does not* give up the right to sue the seller for the buyer's damages resulting from the seller's delivery of nonconforming goods.[36] Just as in a revocation of acceptance (discussed above), in order to preserve the right to sue for damages, the buyer must *notify* the seller in a *reasonable time* after the defect was or should have been discovered.

CONCEPT SUMMARY   Breach and Remedies in Sales Agreements

- The UCC seeks to remedy breach by placing the nonbreaching party in the same situation as she would have been in had the contract been executed as written.
- Faced with anticipatory repudiation by the other party, a party under the UCC can either withdraw and sue for damages or halt performance until the repudiation is retracted.
- If a buyer breaches before delivery by rejection of or nonpayment for conforming goods, then the seller may stop further performance, resell the goods, or if unable to resell, seek damages. If the buyer's breach occurs after delivery, the seller may sue for full contract price or reclaim the goods and collect incidental damages.

[35]UCC § 2-607(3)(a).
[36]UCC § 2-714(1).

- If a seller breaches by delivering nonconforming goods, the buyer may reject the goods, seek cover and sue for damages incurred by the new purchase, not seek cover and sue for damages for the difference between contract and market price at the time of breach, or ask for specific performance. If the buyer accepts the nonconforming goods out of ignorance or necessity, he still retains the right to sue for damages incurred by the nonconformance.

CONTRACTS FOR INTERNATIONAL SALES OF GOODS   LO8-8

More than ever before in the history of commerce, business managers and owners are engaged in commercial transactions that reach beyond the borders of their own nation. Extraordinary advances over the last two decades in technology, shipping methods, and logistics control have lowered the global barrier to entry for many businesses. The focus of this chapter is on international transactions for the sale of goods by examining the international counterparts to the UCC: the U.N. Convention on Contracts for the International Sale of Goods (UNCISG) and International Chamber of Commerce (INCO) terms. In Chapter 25, "International Law and Global Commerce," international law is covered in broad strokes in order to understand sources of international law, foreign legal systems, trade protections, and public policy objectives of trading partners.

U.N. Convention on Contracts for the International Sale of Goods

In 1988, the United States became a signatory nation to a U.N. treaty that attempts to establish an international commercial code. The **U.N. Convention on Contracts for the International Sale of Goods (UNCISG)** governs sale of goods transactions between businesses in any of its 74 member countries. Much like the UCC, the UNCISG exists to fill in terms of a sale of goods contract when the parties haven't otherwise agreed. Parties are free to negotiate the allocation of risk, insurance requirements, delivery, payment terms, choice of law and the like to displace the UNCISG principles. It is particularly important for managers to understand *choice of law and forum* principles in international contracts, because risk and expense of enforcement become increasingly important factors that should be considered in arriving at appropriate pricing, delivery proposals, and insurance needs. If one party will have to travel significant distances or hire special counsel to enforce an agreement or recover for damages suffered, adjusting the price or delivery terms accordingly may sometimes help to reduce risk.

Legal Speak ›))
Choice of Law and Forum Clauses Terms of a contract that predetermine which nation's laws and court system will be used in a potential lawsuit under that contract.

Coverage and Major Provisions of UNCISG

The UNCISG operates on the same fundamental principle as many commercial codes around the world (including the UCC) in that the law favors the completion of a transaction as agreed upon, but also provides relief when one party has breached. The UNCISG covers parties that maintain a place of business in one of the signatory countries. Note that citizenship of shareholders, directors, or officers is not a factor under the UNCISG. The UNCISG covers contracts for the sale of goods between *merchants*. This is perhaps the biggest difference between the UCC and the UNCISG. The UNCISG provisions do *not* apply to transactions where one party is a nonmerchant. Other major important provisions are discussed below.

No Writing Required   The UNCISG has no formal writing requirement (such as the UCC's statute of frauds) and specifically provides that contracts are not subject to requirements as to format. A totality of the circumstances, such as course of past dealing, evidence of oral or written negotiations between the parties, and industry practice may be sufficient to prove that an enforceable contract exists.

Offer and Acceptance   A contract for the sale of goods between businesses located in different UNCISG signatory countries begins with offer and acceptance. As with the UCC, the offer need not have complete terms in order to be valid. The offer requires only

(1) a brief description of the goods, (2) quantity, and (3) price. Beyond those three terms, so long as there is some evidence that the parties intended to form a contract, nothing more is needed for a valid offer. Acceptance may be made within a reasonable time and is effective only when it is received by the offeror (thus, the offer may be withdrawn at any point prior to that time).

Remedies   The UNCISG provides for a party that has delivered nonconforming goods to be given an adequate opportunity to cure the problem. In general, the UNCISG gives sellers an absolute right and obligation to cure, and buyers must allow the seller the opportunity to cure even if the time for performance is past due. Of course, a buyer must give notice of the nonconformance in a timely manner in order to trigger the seller's cure obligations. If the seller does not cure, the UNCISG provides a right for the buyer to pursue remedies. Note that international dispute resolution is discussed in Chapter 4, "Resolving Disputes: Litigation and Alternative Dispute Resolution Options."

Many international sales transactions are governed by the U.N. Convention on Contracts for the Sale of Goods (UNCISG).

INCO: International Chamber of Commerce Terms

With respect to title, risk of loss, and delivery terms, sometimes the language barrier can lead to confusion among the parties and to disputes regarding a loss. The International Chamber of Commerce provides international abbreviations, known as **INCO terms,** to designate many of the responsibilities. INCO terms are generally used in conjunction with the UNCISG and are also used in domestic shipping contracts as well. For example, in the absence of any agreement between the parties, the UNCISG provides that risk passes at the point at which the seller has delivered the goods to a carrier. If the goods are not to be delivered, the risk of loss passes in accordance with the INCO term, EXW (Ex Works). The INCO term EXW has the universal meaning that the parties understand the goods will not be delivered or transported by the seller. Rather, the seller need only make the goods available to the buyer at the seller's place of business and provide the buyer with appropriate documentation of title. There are 11 INCO terms in all. The most common ones are:

- *FCA:* Free carrier means the seller provides transportation at the seller's expense only to the carrier named by the buyer.
- *FOB:* Free on board is always accompanied by the name of a port (e.g., FOB New York) and applies only when transportation is via freighter ship. It means that the seller's expense and risk of loss *end* when the seller delivers goods "over the ship's rail" to the freighter ship. The buyer is responsible for the freighter delivery charge and any losses occurring en route to delivery.

CONCEPT SUMMARY   Contracts for International Sales of Goods

- The UNCISG, the international counterpart to the UCC, is a treaty that governs sales contracts between businesses located in U.N. signatory countries.
- Four major differences between the UNCISG and the UCC are (1) it does not apply to nonmerchants, (2) it has no statute of frauds, (3) offers can be withdrawn at any point prior to the offeror receiving the acceptance, and (4) the right to cure exists even after the performance period is over.
- INCO terms are standardized contractual terms and designations used in international sales contracts to avoid confusion due to language barriers and differing legal systems.

KEY TERMS

Sales contracts p. 182   Agreements to transfer title to real property or tangible assets at a given price.

Goods p. 182   In contract law, goods are defined by the Uniform Commercial Code as that which is tangible and moveable from place to place.

Merchant p. 182   One that is regularly engaged in the sale of a particular good.

Open terms p. 184   Unspecified terms in a sales contract that do not detract from the validity of the contract so long as the parties intended to make the contract and other specified terms give a basis for remedy in case of breach.

Output contract p. 184   A contract in which the buyer agrees to buy all the goods that the seller produces for a set time and at a set price, and the seller may sell only to that one buyer. The quantity for the contract is the seller's output.

Requirements contract p. 184   A contract in which the buyer agrees to buy whatever he needs from the seller during a set period, and the buyer may buy only from that one seller. The quantity for the contract is what the buyer requires.

Merchant's firm offer p. 184   An offer in writing between merchants to buy or sell goods along with a promise without consideration to keep that offer for a stated amount of time, or if unstated no longer than three months.

Purchase order p. 185   A form commonly used in sales contracts as an offer from the buyer that contains preprinted clauses along with blanks to accommodate the specifics of that transaction.

Acknowledgment form p. 185   A form commonly used in sales contracts as an acceptance from the seller, responding to a purchase order that contains preprinted provisions and has blanks to accommodate the specifics of that transaction.

Battle of the forms p. 185   The conflict between the terms written into standardized purchase (offer) and acknowledgment (acceptance) forms, which differ in that one form favors the buyer and the other the seller. The Uniform Commercial Code attempts to broker a truce in this battle while keeping the contract of sale intact.

Confirmation memorandum p. 187   A written verification of an agreement. Under the statute of frauds section of the Uniform Commercial Code, a merchant who receives a signed confirmation memorandum from another merchant will be bound by the memorandum just as if she had signed it, unless she promptly objects.

Risk of loss p. 188   The risk of one party having to bear the loss due to damage, destruction, or loss of goods bargained for under a sales contract.

Title p. 188   Title is the legal right to ownership in a good and all the privileges and responsibilities it entails.

Shipment contract p. 188   A contract in which the seller is required to send the goods to the buyer via a carrier; when the carrier receives the goods the seller has fulfilled his duty and the buyer now has title and bears the risk of loss.

Destination contract p. 188   A contract in which the seller is required to deliver the goods to a chosen destination and not just to the carrier; only after the goods have been tendered at the destination has the seller fulfilled his duty and the buyer takes title and risk of loss.

Tender p. 188   An unconditional performance of the seller by delivering or making the purchased goods available to the buyer.

Tender of delivery p. 192   For delivery of goods, tender occurs when the seller produces goods conforming to the contract and provides adequate notice of their delivery to the buyer.

Perfect tender rule p. 192   This rule requires the seller to deliver her goods precisely as the contract requires in quantity, quality, and all other respects or risk the buyer's lawful rejection of the goods.

Assurances p. 193   A pledge or guarantee that gives confidence to one party that the other party is able to complete performance under a contract.

Commercially impracticable p. 193   Rule adopted by the Uniform Commercial Code when a delay in delivery or nondelivery has been made impracticable by the occurrence of an unanticipated event, so long as the event directly affected a basic assumption of the contract.

Installment contract p. 195   A contract allowing delivery of goods or payments for goods at separate times, to be accepted or rejected separately.

Breach p. 195   The failure to meet a contractual obligation.

Remedies p. 196   Either monetary, performance, or injunctive, the court-ordered means of enforcing rights and redressing wrongs after a breach.

Rightful rejection p. 197   The justified refusal to accept nonconforming goods under a sales contract.

Cover p. 197   A nonbreaching buyer's right to purchase substitute goods on the open market after a delivery of nonconforming goods from the original seller and to sue for the difference.

Specific performance p. 198   A court order to the breaching party to perform as the contract states when monetary damages would be an insufficient remedy.

Revoking acceptance p. 198   Even after accepting the goods, a buyer can still revoke acceptance if the goods are nonconforming in a way that substantially affects their value and he notifies the seller of the revocation in a timely fashion.

U.N. Convention on Contracts for the International Sale of Goods (UNCISG) p. 199   Treaty that governs the international sales contracts among businesses located in U.N. member countries.

INCO terms p. 200   Standardized contractual terms and designations used in international and some domestic sales contracts to avoid confusion due to language barriers and differing legal systems.

THEORY TO PRACTICE

Bentley is a manager at a high-end printing company called Graphic Communications Inc. (GCI). GCI designs and produces posters and other materials for advertising purposes for a variety of clients, including a local symphony orchestra and Main Street University. After GCI received a large order from the university that required a special press, Bentley was assigned to locate a suitable press, negotiate the purchase terms, and arrange for delivery no later than July 1. Bentley negotiated a price with Armstrong Press Manufacturing for the Armstrong Model 2000 printing press.

The press was sufficiently large as to require that it be delivered in three separate pieces, and then assembled on-site. One factor in choosing Armstrong as a vendor was that GCI had used Armstrong before for purchases of smaller presses and had been satisfied with their products and services. In those previous transactions, GCI had used their own standard preprinted purchase order, and no disputes developed.

Once the parties agreed on price, Bentley issued a preprinted purchase order. The purchase order was one page long and had very few terms. It contained only the price, description of the press, the date of the purchase order, a provision that agreed that all three pieces of the press would be delivered and operational by July 1, and Bentley's signature. After Armstrong received the purchase order, Armstrong's manager handwrote the phrase *"Acknowledged as a destination contract. To be delivered and assembled in three installments to GCI over the month of May"* in the delivery section of the purchase order. Armstrong's manager then signed the purchase order, faxed the purchase order back to Bentley, and began to process the order. Armstrong shipped the first part of the press using its own delivery service. Before delivery, the truck was involved in an accident, and the first part of the press was destroyed.

1. Is Armstrong's addition of the delivery term binding on GCI? Explain the UCC analysis governing the additional terms added by Armstrong.
2. Does the fact that the parties had a history of past dealings with each other impact your analysis in Question 1 above? Why or why not?

3. When did title to the goods pass in this contract? Who has the risk of loss? How is your answer related to your analysis of Question 1 above?
4. Is the purchase order sufficient to satisfy the statute of frauds? Why or why not?
5. Assume that Armstrong ships the first two parts of the press with no problem, but anticipates a significant delay for the third part. Knowing that GCI requires the press to be ready on July 1, Armstrong substitutes a newer and more expensive version of the final piece of the press by June 15. Has Armstrong breached the contract? When it is delivered, must GCI accept the final piece because it is newer and more expensive than the goods they had bargained for?
6. In Question 5 above, if GCI accepts the replaced good, but one week later discovers that the new press component is incompatible with the first two components, may GCI still reject the goods despite the fact they have accepted them and one week's time has passed? What UCC provision covers this situation?
7. If GCI rejects the final shipment of goods, what are GCI's options in terms of a remedy?

MANAGER'S CHALLENGE

Managers have a responsibility to protect their company from legal liability or disputes as much as possible through the use of various prevention measures. In Theory to Practice above, the crux of the potential disputes depends on the comprehensiveness of the purchase order. Even if ultimately the press is delivered, GCI could have avoided a number of potential liabilities through inclusion of basic language of agreement in the purchase

order. Assume that Bentley is required to submit a memorandum to her senior manager describing how the purchase order could be revised to provide protection for GCI to ensure that any future purchases anticipate potential problems with the vendor. Be sure to provide a potential solution for each problem posed in Theory to Practice above. A sample answer may be found on this textbook's Web site at www.mhhe.com/melvin.

CASE SUMMARY 8.1 :: Fisherman Surgical Instruments, LLC v. Tri-anim Health Services, Inc., 502 F. Supp. 2d 1170 (Kan. 2007)

REQUIREMENTS CONTRACTS AND GOOD FAITH

Fisherman makes high-end surgical instruments for use by medical professionals. Not long after the company opened, it contracted with a medical supply dealer, Tri-anim, to sell its instruments to doctors. The contract did not include quantity but did state that Tri-anim would buy from Fisherman based on "mutually agreed

upon sales goals." The parties also agreed that Tri-anim would not sell products that competed with Fisherman's instruments. Shortly after Tri-anim began selling the products, surgeons complained that the quality of Fisherman's instruments was substandard. Tri-anim then began selling a competitor's products. They also cancelled the contract with Fisherman saying it was void under the UCC because the agreement did not specify the quantity of goods.

1. Who prevails and why?
2. Is this a requirements contract or output contract?

3. If Tri-anim did not cancel the contract but instead bought nothing and sold nothing, would Fisherman have any cause of action against Tri-anim? If so, what would be the appropriate remedy?

CASE SUMMARY 8.2 :: General Motors Corp. v Acme Refining Co., 513 F. Supp. 2d 906 (E.D. Mich. 2007)

RIGHT OF REJECTION

Acme Refining collects, melts down, and resells scrap metal. In producing its cars, General Motors (GM) creates a massive of amount of scrap metal that must be removed. Acme contracted to purchase and pick up scrap metal from GM's plant. The contract provided that the metal was to be taken "as-is, where-is." After removing 850,000 tons of metal from the GM plant, Acme realized the metal was corrupted by nonmetal products and waste oils, making smelting much more costly. Instead of rejecting the metal, Acme e-mailed GM over several weeks in an attempt to negotiate a lower price. Unable to bring down the price, Acme then rejected all the scrap metal.

CASE QUESTIONS

1. Was Acme's rejection lawful?
2. Did Acme give seasonable notification of rejection?

CASE SUMMARY 8.3 :: Glenn Distributors Corp. v Carlisle Plastics, Inc., 297 F.3d 294 (3d Cir. 2002)

COVER

Glenn Distributors sells closeout merchandise to discount stores. These are goods that have been changed or discontinued so that large quantities can be bought at bargain prices. Carlisle Plastics makes "Ruffies" name-brand trash bags. Glenn contracted to buy $990,000 worth of Ruffies bags from Carlisle, but Carlisle only shipped Glenn $736,000 worth of the bags and sold the others to a different buyer. Glenn claimed they were unable to cover because the only name-brand bag for that price was Ruffies and only Carlisle made Ruffies. Unable to cover, Glenn sued for $230,000 in lost profits.

CASE QUESTIONS

1. Did Glenn make reasonable efforts to cover?
2. Should Glenn have to cover the lost profits by buying products other than trash bags? Why or why not?

CASE SUMMARY 8.4 :: S.W.B. New England, Inc. v. R.A.B. Food Group, LLC, 2008 WL 540091 (S.D.N.Y. 2008)

SPECIFIC PERFORMANCE

SWB is a distributor of kosher food products in New England. SWB's only substantial competitor is Millbrook. SWB entered a contract to buy kosher products from Rokeach. Rokeach is the dominant kosher food supplier in the region and has established a trusted brand name in New England for kosher products. After the SWB–Rokeach contract was in place, Food Group purchased Rokeach. Food Group refused to honor the SWB–Rokeach contract and began to sell only to Millbrook. SWB brought suit and asks for specific performance from Food Group and Rokeach.

CASE QUESTIONS

1. What are the specific requirements for a court to grant specific performance to SWB?
2. Do these requirements fit this case?

Existence of a Sales Contract

Does a sales contract exist? If so, what are the terms of the contract?

1. Yes. This is a requirements contract, so Boston Hardware is obligated to purchase only what they require (250 shovels).

2. Yes. The delivery terms would be supplied by the UCC because they are missing from the contract. Therefore, New York High School takes delivery at Big Apple's place of business. Big Apple needs only to have the desks available by September 1 for pick up by New York High School.

3. No contract. Careful! While this is a merchant's firm offer for seven months, the UCC restricts a merchants firm offer to no more than *three months* (see UCC § 2-205). Therefore, L.A.'s offer is no longer valid.

4. No contract. Midwest's return of the acknowledgement with the change in date of delivery would be considered a material change because the delivery date was such an important condition of the contract (holiday season).

Risk of Loss

Who bears the risk of loss?

1. Chase. In a shipment contract, the seller (Marshall) needs only to deliver the goods to the hands of the carrier. In this case, title passed to Chase when Marshall placed them in Mercury's hands. (*Note:* Of course Chase may be able sue Mercury for any losses, but Marshall is entitled to payment for the goods from Chase.)

2. Harlan Dairy Co. The fact that parties agreed to delivery and payment to be made at a specific destination indicates that this is a destination contract. In a destination contract, risk of loss is borne by the seller (Harlan) until the goods are tendered.

3. Holmes. Careful! Although this is a destination contract, Holmes delivered *nonconforming goods* (bowler hats instead of top hats). Therefore, Holmes did not complete performance and the risk of loss never passed to Cardozo.

4. White. The buyer, White, took physical possession of the good and, according to the UCC, risk of loss passed at that point so long as the seller is a merchant.

Buyer's Rights and Obligations

Does the grocer have an obligation to pay? Why or why not?

1. Grocer is obligated to buy eggs at market price from Farmer for the duration of the contract. Commercial impractability is a narrow doctrine and generally does not apply in cases where changing economic conditions impact the contract.

2. Grocer is obligated to pay for the corn. Grocer's knowing acceptance of the nonconforming goods triggered his obligation to pay.

3. Grocer is obligated to pay for the skim milk because he failed to affirmatively notify the seller of his rejection in a timely manner.

4. Grocer is obligated to pay the fair market value for 100 chickens (not turkeys). Because the seller didn't deliver a perfect tender, Grocer could have (1) rejected the entire shipment, (2) accepted the entire shipment, or (3) accepted part of the shipment and rejected the rest. He opted for the last choice and, thus, is only obligated for the goods accepted.

9
CHAPTER

Torts and Products Liability

learning outcomes checklist

After studying this chapter, students who have mastered the material will be able to:

9-1 Articulate a basic definition of a tort and identify the source of law governing various types of torts.

9-2 Determine the classification of tort based on the conduct of the wrongdoer.

9-3 Give specific examples of how tort law applies in the business environment.

9-4 Apply the elements and defenses of the torts of defamation, trade libel, and product disparagement, and discuss its applicability in the business environment.

9-5 Identify the differences in terms of liability for traditional print defamation and defamation in cyberspace.

9-6 Distinguish business competition torts from other intentional torts and understand their applicability in commercial relationships.

9-7 Recognize conduct that is classified as negligent and identify any potential defenses.

9-8 Provide alternate theories of liability and defenses when a product is the cause of an injury.

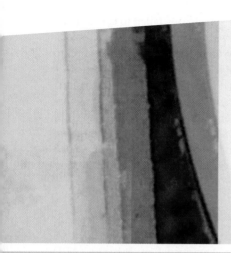

Learning to recognize situations where a business venture may have potential liability to another party is an important part of limiting risk in business operations. Tort and products liability law set out certain conduct and standards of reasonableness and provide legal recourse when a violation of those standards results in an injury causing losses. Because business owners are ordinarily responsible for the intentional or accidental conduct of their employees who cause another party harm, it is essential for managers to understand ways in which to control risk and reduce liability. In this chapter, students will learn:

- The fundamental principles of tort law, types of torts, and how each applies in a business context.
- Rules governing intentional and business competition torts.
- How liability arises for negligent acts and defenses to liability.
- Special rules governing products liability.

LO9-1 OVERVIEW OF TORT LAW

A **tort**[1] is a civil wrong where one party has acted, or in some cases failed to act, and that action or inaction causes a loss to be suffered by another party. The law provides a remedy for one who has suffered an injury by compelling the wrongdoer to pay compensation to the injured party. Tort law is best understood as intending to compensate injured parties for losses resulting in harm from some unreasonable conduct by another.[2] One who commits a tort is known as the **tortfeasor.** The tortfeasor's wrongful conduct is described as **tortious conduct.** Recall from Chapter 1, "Legal Foundations," that an individual may commit a criminal offense and a civil wrong in the very *same* act. While criminal statutes are intended to punish and deter the wrongdoer, the common law of torts is primarily intended to provide *compensation* for the victim. In some cases tort law also may be used to deter wrongful conduct in the future.

SOURCES OF LAW

For the most part, tort law is governed by state common law principles. Recall from Chapter 1 that courts look to rules articulated by the American Law Institute (ALI) for guidance on applying common law legal principles. Known as the **Restatement of Torts,** the ALI has amended the *Restatements* twice and, therefore, these sources of law are called the *Restatement (Second) of Torts* and the *Restatement (Third) of Torts.* Remember that courts are not bound by any of the *Restatements,* but they do recognize them as widely applied principles of law. The *Second Restatements* have the benefit of volumes of case law and wide acceptance, and therefore references to *Restatements* in this chapter refer to the *Second Restatements* unless otherwise noted.

*web*check **www.mhhe.com/melvin**
For a comprehensive index of hyperlinks about tort law, go to this textbook's Web site to access the Mercer Virtual Law Library.

Laws that cover individuals that are injured by a product, known as products liability laws, may take the form of state common law or state statutes that expressly impose liability for injuries that result from products. These statutes are based primarily on the *Restatements* and are relatively uniform from state to state.

LO9-2, 9-3 CATEGORIES OF TORTS

Legal Speak »))
Willful Conduct
Intentional behavior directed by the "will."

Torts fall into one of three general categories: *intentional, negligence,* and *strict liability.* An **intentional tort** is one where the tortfeasor was *willful* in bringing about a particular event that caused harm to another party. **Negligence** is an accidental (without willful intent) event that caused harm to another party. The difference between the two is the mind-set and intent of the tortfeasor. For example, suppose that Pangloss is the delivery van driver for Cultivate Your Garden Flowers Inc. One day while on a delivery he spots his archenemy crossing the street, so he accelerates his truck and hits him. In this case, Pangloss has committed an intentional tort (battery). If, on the other hand, Pangloss is late for his delivery and carelessly speeds around a turn accidentally hitting a pedestrian crossing the street, he has committed the tort of negligence.

Strict liability torts, where a tortfeasor may be held liable for an act regardless of intent or willfulness, applies primarily in cases of defective products and abnormally dangerous activities (such as major construction demolition).

---

[1]The term *tort* originally derives from the Latin root *tortus,* meaning twisted or wrested aside. As with many legal terms, Latin words were given a French twist in English common law via the Norman kings. Thus, the shortened term *tort* is a French root meaning "wrong."

[2]*Black's Law Dictionary.*

INTENTIONAL BUSINESS-RELATED TORTS

While the law provides relief for injured parties in a variety of circumstances, there are some intentional torts that are more important to business owners and managers because they have the potential to impact business relationships and operations.

Defamation

LO9-4

The law recognizes an individual's or a company's reputation as a valuable asset by imposing liability for any party that makes false and defamatory statements affecting another party's reputation. In this context, the term *party* means an individual, business, or product. Just as in all civil lawsuits, the *untrue statements* must have caused the victim to suffer *damages.* Generally, we think of written defamation as **libel,** and oral (spoken) defamation as **slander.** In order to recover for a defamation action, the plaintiff must prove four elements:

- *Defamatory statement.* A *false* and defamatory statement concerning a party's reputation or honesty, or a statement that subjected a party to hate, contempt, or ridicule. In order to qualify as defamatory, the statement must have a tendency to harm the reputation of the plaintiff.[3] Because many statements can be interpreted in more than one way, the law provides that the statement is defamatory so long as a defamatory interpretation is an objectively reasonable one, and the plaintiff shows that at least one of the recipients did in fact make that interpretation. Note that the statement must be false, not merely unkind. Moreover, if a statement was *pure opinion,* that statement is not defamatory. That is, a defamatory statement is one that must be *provable as false.*

- *Dissemination to a third party.* In the *Restatements,* this requirement is referred to as *publication,* but in this context it does not literally require the statement to be published. Rather, this element requires that the statement must somehow reach the ears or eyes of someone other than the tortfeasor and the victim. For example, suppose a manager telephones one of his employees and says, "You are the one who stole $100 in petty cash, so you're fired." Even if the accusatory statement is false, the manager has not defamed the employee based on that action alone. No third party heard the statement and, thus, the dissemination element is missing.

- *Specificity.* The statement must be about a particular party, business, or product. Thus, any general statement about a profession as a whole cannot constitute defamation, but a false statement about a company can be the basis of a reputation claim.

- *Damages.* The aggrieved party must be able to prove that he or she suffered some pecuniary harm. Examples of damages in a defamation suit include situations where the victim has lost a valuable client due to the tortfeasor's defamatory comment, or the inability of the victim to secure employment because of a tortfeasor's defamatory comment during a reference check.

Legal Speak ›))
Pecuniary Harm Lost revenue or profits, both actual and potential.

Public Figure Standard If the victim is a public figure, such as a candidate for political office, the defamation must have been committed with *malice* or reckless disregard for the truth. This "public figure" rule was based on the U.S. Supreme Court's landmark ruling in *New York Times v. Sullivan.*[4] The case involved a public official, a police commander, who sued *The New York Times* for defamation based on allegations printed in the newspaper that accused him of complicity in criminal activity. In announcing the public figure standard, the Court ruled that, in order for a public figure to prevail in a defamation case, the plaintiff must provide evidence that the defamer either had "actual knowledge" that the statement was false, or "reckless disregard for the truth."

Legal Speak ›))
Malice Typically defined as intentional doing of a wrongful act with intent to harm. However, in the context of defamation evidence of ill will is not required for the plaintiff to prevail.

---

[3] *Restatement (Second) of Torts,* § 559.
[4] 376 U.S. 254 (1964).

Privilege Defenses to Defamation   If the injured party meets all of the requirements of a defamation claim, the defendant may still avoid liability if the defamatory statement falls into a category of *privileged statements.* Privilege is a defense that recognizes either a legal or public policy-based immunity from a defamation claim. It is divided into two categories: **absolute privilege,** where the defendants need not offer any further evidence to assert the defense, and **qualified privilege,** where the defendants must offer evidence of good faith and be absent of malice to be shielded from liability.

Absolute Privilege   Courts generally recognize three categories of absolute privilege:

- *Government officials.* The framers recognized the need for free debate among members of Congress and gave immunity in the Constitution via the "speech and debate clause," which shields members of Congress from liability for any statement made during a congressional debate, hearing, and so on, while in office. The U.S. Supreme Court later extended that protection to all federal officials.[5]

- *Judicial officers/proceedings.* All states now recognize some protection of participants of a judicial proceeding for statements made during the proceeding. This includes judges, lawyers, and in some cases, witnesses.

- *State legislators.* Similar immunity has been extended by the states to protect state legislators for statements made in the course of carrying out their duties.

Qualified Privilege   Courts also recognize certain qualified privileges that are grounded in public policy.

- *Media.* Employees of media organizations (e.g., television, radio, periodicals) are afforded a qualified protection from defamation liability. So long as the media has acted in good faith, *absent of malice,* and without a reckless disregard for the truth, the media

Some states provide statutory immunity from defamation claims for employers providing references for ex-employees, so long as the information is factual.

---

[5]*Barr v. Matteo,* 360 U.S. 564 (1959).

is protected from liability through privilege as a defense for unintentional mistakes of fact in their reporting.

- *Employers.* An increasing number of states have extended some liability protection for employers who are providing a reference for an ex-employee. So long as the information is factual and the employer has not acted with malice, the employer's statement may be privileged.

In Case 9.1, the Connecticut supreme court applies a state employer reference privilege statute.

Trade Libel and Product Disparagement Laws

In cases where a competitor has made a false statement that disparaged a competing product, an injured party may sue for **trade libel.** This tort requires the statement to be (1) a clear and *specific* reference to the disparaged party or product (e.g., using the actual

---

CASE 9.1 Belanger v. Swift Transportation, Inc., 552 F. Supp. 2d 297 (Cn. 2008).

FACT SUMMARY Swift Transportation operates a trucking company and hired Belanger as a tractor-trailer driver. Swift has various safety policies, among them the "Forbidden Five," which are five infractions that can lead to immediate termination of its drivers. One such infraction is rear-ending another vehicle. In his third year of employment, Belanger was driving a Swift tractor-trailer on the Cross Bronx expressway when he crashed into the back of another tractor-trailer causing $40,000 in damage. Swift considers every accident preventable unless proven otherwise, so Belanger was immediately terminated for violating one of the Forbidden Five. Belanger claimed that the accident was not his fault, but a subsequent investigation by Swift's claims department concluded that the accident was preventable. Swift recorded the incident on a specialized database Web site (Data Website) that is operated by the U.S. government to promote highway safety through a readily available check on commercial driving records. When Belanger sought other truck-driving jobs, the companies looked on the Data Website and found out that, according to Swift, Belanger "did not meet the company's safety standards." Belanger sued Swift for defamation in the workplace. Swift defended that employer-to-employer references were privileged from liability for defamation unless Swift acted with malice. Belanger contended that (1) posting the information on the public Data Website resulted in a loss of the employer's reference privilege because it was not employer-to-employer, and (2) Swift acted maliciously by not acknowledging Belanger's side of the story in their investigation.

SYNOPSIS OF DECISION AND OPINION The Connecticut supreme court ruled in Swift's favor, citing

two reasons. First, there was no reason why employer candor regarding employee references should not be protected from defamation suits on the Web site since it was equally as important as in a one-on-one discussion. Second, Swift's following of company procedures of immediate termination, independent investigation, and recording the accident on Data Website did not indicate malice.

WORDS OF THE COURT: Defamation in an Employee Reference "Mr. Belanger offers no rationale for the distinction which he draws between a [Data Website]-type employer information clearinghouse and direct employer-to-employer contact addressing the candor concern underlying the [employer-to-employer reference] privilege. Here, employer forthrightness about employee driving records has obvious importance, as evidenced by the federal regulation compelling trucking companies to investigate applicant drivers' safety records before hiring." . . . **Malicious Defamation by the Employer** "the sparse record here contains no evidence capable of showing any improper motive in inputting the incident in the [Data Website] records. Mr. Belanger's evidence that he had received no contact from the defendant in response to his explanation of how the accident occurred provides no basis for a jury to reasonably find 'any improper or unjustifiable motive.'"

Case Questions

1. What is the public policy behind giving privilege to employer references?

2. Is it fair that Belanger has a permanent bad reference? Would you hire him?

---

brand name of the product), (2) made with either knowledge that the statement was false or reckless disregard for the truth, and (3) communicated to a third party (similar to defamation).

Some states have passed **product disparagement statutes** intended to protect the interest of a state's major industries such as agriculture, dairy, or beef.[6] Perhaps the most famous product disparagement case was when the Texas Cattle Ranchers Association sued Oprah Winfrey under a Texas law allowing recovery for any rancher who suffered damages as a result of false disparagement. On her television show, Winfrey agreed with statements made by one of her guests that alleged certain U.S. market hamburger meat could cause mad cow disease, which is fatal to humans. At the end of the segment, Winfrey took the position that she would cease eating any hamburgers. The ranchers showed evidence that beef sales dropped precipitously immediately after the broadcast and alleged that Winfrey's statements were false and caused the ranchers lost revenue. The jury rejected the cattle ranchers claim as too broad and without sufficient evidence that the remarks alone were the cause of the losses.[7]

Fraudulent Misrepresentation

Recall the discussion of misrepresentation and fraudulent misrepresentation in Chapter 6, "Overview and Formation of Contracts." It is important to note that there are some important overlapping legal principles of tort and contract law. For example, in some cases contract law allows a contract to be canceled if one party made false representations concerning a *material fact*. This means that the misrepresented fact must involve an important aspect of the basis of the contract such as a change in the value of the contract or increasing one party's risk. Fraudulent misrepresentation (sometimes referred to simply as fraud) is *also* recognized as a tort where the law provides a remedy to recover damages when the innocent party suffers a pecuniary loss as a result of the false representation. In cases of fraudulent misrepresentation, the law allows the innocent party to recover if (1) the misrepresentation was a material fact known to be false by the tortfeasor (or reckless disregard for the truth); (2) the tortfeasor intended to persuade the innocent party to rely on the statement and the innocent party did, in fact, rely on it; and (3) damages were suffered by the innocent party. For example, Buyer asks Seller about whether Seller's property is properly zoned for a manufacturing facility. In an effort to induce Buyer to purchase the property, Seller misrepresents that the property is zoned for manufacturing. Buyer then enters into a purchase agreement for the property with a 10 percent down payment, balance due in 30 days. Buyer then proceeds to spend money by hiring an architect to visit the site and draw plans for the new facility. The day after the agreement was signed Seller applies to the zoning board for a change in zoning, hoping that it will be changed before the Buyer completes the agreement by paying the balance owed. The zoning board does not change the status. In a case against Seller for fraud, Buyer would be entitled to cancel the contract *and* recover any losses in tort suffered as a result of Seller's fraudulent misrepresentations (such as the money spent on hiring the architect).

Courts will also allow recovery for misrepresentations that are not intentional but are rather *negligent* misrepresentations. In most cases, the parties have to have some type of

> ## KEY POINT
> Fraudulent misrepresentation (in both contracts and torts) must center on a *material fact*; that is, a fact that is significant or would impact the parties' rights or obligations in a transaction as opposed to a minor and inconsequential detail.

---

[6]For example, disparagement of Idaho potatoes is covered in Idaho Code § 6-2003. For a list of many such laws, see "Of Banana Bills and Veggie Hate Crimes: The Constitutionality of Agricultural Disparagement Statutes," 34 Harv. J. Legis. 135 (1997).

[7]Affirmed in *Texas Beef Group v. Winfrey,* 201 F.3d 680 (5th Cir. 2000).

Protections for Online Content Providers

Along with the actual tortfeasor in a defamation case, the law imposes certain liability upon the publisher of the libelous statements as well. However, the law does not impose liability on the *distributor* of the publication (such as a bookstore or newsstand). For example, suppose a famous movie star is the subject of a gossip feature in a hypothetical tabloid called the *American Tattler.* The feature implied that the movie star was seen at a local restaurant and was so intoxicated that she could not control her conduct. In a lawsuit for defamation, the movie star proves the story to be false and that it led to her being fired by her movie studio. In terms of liability, both the author of the defamatory feature and the publication (*American Tattler*) may be liable for damages.

However, the rules pertaining to publishers of online content in cyberspace are different. Suppose for example that, in the movie star example above, instead of the *American Tattler* publishing the defamatory feature that a gossip columnist hired by America Online (AOL) had written it for an AOL entertainment news board. There would be no doubt of the liability of the author, but would AOL be liable as the "publisher"?

As Internet accessibility increased rapidly, courts struggled with this question. In a 1991 case, *Cubby Inc. v. CompuServe, Inc.,*[*] plaintiffs filed a defamation action against CompuServe as a "publisher" of defamatory materials contained in an online publication called Rumorville, USA. Rumorville was composed, written, and edited by a third party who was not employed by CompuServe. The federal trial court in the southern district of New York held that CompuServe was *not* a publisher in the context of defamation law, but rather was more akin to a bookstore and thus Internet Service Providers (ISPs) such as CompuServe were to be treated as "distributors." Consequently, they were not subject to liability for any defamatory statements so long as CompuServe did not "edit, review or reformulate" the publication.

However, not all courts took that view. A few years later, as the number of Internet Service Providers grew, a New York state trial court issued a much different ruling. In *Stratton v. Prodigy Services Company*, decided in 1995, the court ruled that an ISP could be held liable as a publisher of defamatory material. The case involved a Prodigy-maintained electronic bulletin board available to its subscribers called "Money Talk." Although Prodigy did not formally edit these postings, they had a policy that reserved the right to eliminate postings if they were objectionable. The plaintiff filed suit against Prodigy as a publisher of material that was allegedly libelous. In stark contrast to the *Cubby* court, a state trial court in New York ruled that Prodigy was a publisher in the context of a defamation claim and, therefore, could be liable for damages resulting from defamatory comments in its electronic bulletin board. The court held that Prodigy's "conscious effort to maintain editorial control" over the content was sufficient to qualify it as a publisher as that term is understood in defamation law.

In an apparent effort to address the pleas of ISPs for a uniform standard, Congress enacted the **Communications Decency Act of 1996**[†] (CDA). This law extended immunity to the ISPs by protecting them from any defamation liability as a "publisher or speaker of any information provided by another information content provider." In effect, Congress made the policy choice that ISPs were to be treated as a newsstand-like distributor.

One of the first cases to interpret this law was *Blumenthal v. Drudge and America Online, Inc.*[‡] Although decided by a trial court, the reasoning is often cited by appellate courts when applying the ISP safe harbor. The case involved a defamation lawsuit filed by a high-profile White House adviser (Blumenthal) against a controversial political journalist (Drudge) and America Online (AOL) concerning spousal abuse and cover-up allegations in a column written by Drudge. The column was posted on an AOL news board as part of an agreement between Drudge and America Online. After Drudge posted a retraction and acknowledged that the allegations were false, Blumenthal sued Drudge and AOL for defamation. The trial court dismissed the case against AOL, citing the Communications Decency Act's safe harbor provisions for ISPs. The court noted that, even if AOL could conceivably be categorized as a *publisher* of defamatory material under previous cases, Congress specifically exempted ISPs such as AOL from civil suits for defamation.

*Cubby, Inc. v. CompuServe, Inc., 776 F. Supp. 135 (S.D.N.Y. 1991).
†18 U.S.C.A. § 1462. Note that some portions of the CDA, namely Congress's attempt to regulate Internet pornography, were struck down as unconstitutional by various federal courts. However, this section survived judicial scrutiny.
‡992 F. Supp. 44 (D.D.C. 1998).

business relationship for the innocent party to recover. Any statement made by a party that turns out not to be accurate may still allow the innocent party to recover if the tortfeasor's statement was negligent. In the Buyer–Seller case above, suppose that Seller had no actual knowledge of the zoning status for the property, but made a statement that it was zoned for manufacturing. Buyer would still be able to recover despite the fact that Seller did not know that the statement was false. Seller is still liable because he was negligent in his duty to know such an important fact (negligence is discussed in detail later in this chapter).

False Imprisonment

The tort of false imprisonment is defined by the *Restatements* as the "intentional infliction of a confinement upon another party." In the business context, a merchant most commonly encounters these circumstances in cases of suspected retail theft. While the merchant has the right to briefly detain a suspected shoplifter, she must be cautious about giving rise to a false imprisonment claim when detaining an individual or attempting to recover the merchandise. The *Restatements* provide for a **merchant's privilege**[8] to shield a merchant from liability for temporarily detaining a party who is *reasonably* suspected of stealing merchandise. This privilege, however, is very narrow. In order to gain protection under the privilege, the merchant must follow certain guidelines:

- *Limited detention.* The privilege only applies for a short period of time under the circumstances. Some courts have limited this time period to as few as 15 minutes. However, most courts follow a case-by-case analysis with the general framework that the detention may last the time duration necessary to confront the accused party, recover any goods stolen, and wait for the authorities to arrive (if necessary).
- *Limited to premises.* Generally, the privilege only applies if the suspected party is confronted on the merchant's premises or an immediately adjacent area (such as a parking lot).
- *Coercion.* The merchant or merchant's agent (such as a store security guard) may not attempt to coerce payment, or purport to officially arrest the detained party, nor attempt to obtain a confession.

Table 9.1 provides an overview of other types of intentional torts and examples of each.

LO9-6 Business Competition Torts

Tort law also provides for the promotion of fairness in business dealings and for the reimbursement of a party that has suffered some damages as a result of a competitor's tortious acts. These common law torts arise when a tortfeasor (typically a competitor to the harmed party) interferes with an existing contract or hinders a prospective contract between two parties.

Tortious Interference with Existing Contractual Relationship   When one party *induces* another party to break an existing contract with another party, the inducing party may be liable for any damages suffered by the innocent party as a result of breaking the contract. In order for the injured party to recover damages, the tortfeasor must have (1) had *specific knowledge* of the contract, (2) actively *interfered* with the contract, and (3) caused some identifiable damages (losses) to the injured party. Business owners and managers may encounter contract interference torts in the context of restrictions against working for competitors in an employment contract (known as a *restrictive covenant*[9]) or in defending

---

[8]Also known as "shopkeeper's privilege." See *Restatements (Second) of Torts,* § 120A.

[9]Restrictive covenants are covered in detail in Chapter 6 "Overview and Formation of Contracts."

TABLE 9.1 Other Intentional Torts

Tort	Definition	Example
Battery	Intentional infliction of harmful or offensive bodily contact.	One party strikes another causing injury. The injury requires payment for medical treatment.
Intentional Infliction of Emotional Distress	Extreme, outrageous, or reckless conduct that is intended to inflict emotional or mental distress (physical harm is not necessary).	A bill collector contacts a debtor's mother and threatens physical harm and imprisonment for the debtor/son, and to put a lien on the mother's house. The mother suffers two heart attacks after the threats persist.*
Trespass (land)	Trespass occurs when a party enters another's land or causes another person or object to enter land owned by a private party.	A survey crew mistakenly surveys the wrong property. While working, the crew damages landscaping. The landowner is entitled to compensation as a result of the crew's trespass.
Trespass (chattel†)	Trespass occurs when a party interferes with another's use or possession of chattel (such as personal property).	An employee takes home his employer's drill for personal use without the employer's permission and with the intent to return it the next morning. The drill is broken while under the employee's control. The employee is liable for costs of repair/replacement and any lost profits resulting from the down time.
Conversion	The civil counterpart to theft intended to reimburse a party who suffered damages as a result of theft or any other substantial interference with a party's ownership, where fairness requires that the tortfeasor reimburse the injured party for the full value of the property.	The controller of a corporation embezzles corporate funds and covers up discrepancies on the financial statements. In addition to criminal charges, the controller's employer may also sue her for conversion in an attempt to recover the embezzled funds.

*Based on *George v. Jordan Marsh Co.,* 268 N.E.2d 915 (Mass. 1971).
†Chattel is the English common law term for personal property or equipment that is moveable.

an allegation of interference in the process of hiring a new employee away from a competitor. For example, Lee is a talented software programmer and signs a contract with Computer Researchers Inc. (CRI) for three years. The contract stipulates that Lee will not work for any of CRI's competitors during that time even if he is terminated or voluntarily resigns from CRI. After one year, one of CRI's competitors, MultiCom, contacts Lee and attempts to convince him to leave CRI and work for MultiCom. During the negotiations, Lee shows MultiCom his contract with CRI, and MultiCom's manager then offers a higher salary and a $1,000 signing bonus to Lee. Lee resigns from CRI with two years left on his contract and goes to work for MultiCom. CRI must then spend several thousands of dollars recruiting and training a new programmer to finish Lee's projects. In this case, many courts would consider holding MultiCom liable for CRI's damages because CRI was injured as a result of MultiCom's tortious interference with the CRI–Lee contract. Of course, CRI would also be entitled to recover damages from Lee for breaking the contract.

FACT SUMMARY Mattison owned Hidden Hills Beauty Salon and hired Drowne as a hair stylist in 1982. In 1984, Drowne signed a contract agreeing not to work at any competing hair salon within one year of termination from Hidden Hills (known as a restrictive covenant contract). Over the next 10 months, Johnston, the owner of a competing beauty salon located one-half mile from Hidden Hills, actively solicited Drowne to leave Hidden Hills and work for his salon. Eventually, Drowne quit Hidden Hills and began working for Johnston. Mattison sued Johnston for intentional interference with the restrictive covenant contract. Johnston claimed he was simply engaging in standard business competition and that it was Drowne's individual choice to break her contract with Hidden Hills.

SYNOPSIS OF DECISION AND OPINION The Arizona state appellate court ruled in favor of Mattison. They reasoned that Johnston had known about the restriction and actively continued to induce Drowne to breach the restrictive covenant. Competition is not a valid excuse to break a restrictive covenant that was created to avoid just such practices.

WORDS OF THE COURT: Intentional Interference "Johnston [and his partner] also contend that when a defendant is a competitor regarding the business involved in the contract, his interference with the contract may not be improper since competition is a valid defense to such action. However, Johnston failed to recognize that Mattison is claiming that they induced Drowne to break the restrictive covenant [and] not the at-will employment relationship . . . [quoting the *Restatement*] 'Under these circumstances a defendant engaged in the same business might induce the employee to quit his job, but he would not be justified in engaging the employee to work for him in an activity that would mean violation of the contract not to compete.'"

Case Questions

1. What are the conflicting public policy concerns in this case?

2. Why would Mattison sue Johnston for interference rather than suing Drowne for breach?

In Case 9.2, a state appellate court analyzes the conduct of the parties in determining whether a competitor tortiously interfered with a contract between an employer and an employee.

Note that interference *does not* occur when a competitor merely offers a better price to a competitor's customer. For example, suppose that Chung is the owner of several self-service car washes and signs a two-year agreement with Mega Distributor for the supplying of snack vending machines in the lobby of each of Chung's car washes. Under the contract, Chung will receive 30 percent of the sales from the machines. Shortly thereafter, Chung is contacted by a sales rep from Start-Up Snacks and offered the same terms as the Mega contract, except that Chung will receive 60 percent of the sales from the machines. Chung crunches the numbers and concludes that the increase in revenue will more than make up for any penalties incurred for breaching the Chung–Mega contract, so he breaks his contract with Mega and enters into a new contract with Start-Up. Despite the fact that Start-Up knew of the Mega contract, the level of interference is *not* sufficient to constitute a tort. In this case, Chung decided on his own to break the contract with Mega and was not *induced* to do so by Start-Up. It is important to note, however, that Mega could still sue Chung for failing to perform his obligations as agreed in the contract.[10]

Legal Speak ›))
Induce To bring about or give rise to. In the context of tortuous interference liability is triggered if interference causes the harm.

Tortious Interference with Prospective Advantage   In addition to providing protection against interference from third parties in existing contracts, the law also protects interference with *potential* contract (prospects) or other business relationships. The protections

---

[10]Based on *Restatements (Second) of Torts*, § 766, Illustration 3.

and definition of interference are similar to the existing contractual interference rules discussed above. However, because no contract actually exists, courts only allow recovery for this tort under limited circumstances where the tortfeasor's conduct was highly anticompetitive. For example, assume that OldCo. intends to sabotage NewCo.'s efforts to obtain a new customer through a competitive bidding process. An OldCo. employee hacks into NewCo.'s computer and destroys the proposal forms. NewCo. cannot submit the bid before the deadline and, thus, doesn't get the contract. Assuming that NewCo. can prove it suffered damages, OldCo. could be held liable for interference with prospective advantage.

CONCEPT SUMMARY   Business-Related Intentional and Competition Torts

- A tort is a civil wrong and can be intentional, negligent, or strict liability.
- Defamation is a false statement directed specifically at a party, company, or product, aired to a third party, and resulting in pecuniary harm to the victim.
- A victim of fraud must show intentional misrepresentation by the tortfeasor of a material fact, reliance on that fact, and damages resulting from that reliance.
- False imprisonment is an intentional tort unless the tortfeasor is a merchant who temporarily and reasonably detains a suspected thief.
- Where actions exceed standard competitive practices, a company may be liable for intentional interference with a contract by a third party where they had specific knowledge of a contract and intentionally disrupted its proper execution.

NEGLIGENCE

LO9-7

Tort law also applies in circumstances when one party fails to act reasonably and, even though that party does not intend for harm to occur, the party is still liable for any injuries or damages suffered by another party as a result of the unreasonable conduct. This category of tort is called *negligence.* Recall from the first section of this chapter that the primary difference between intentional torts and negligence is the mind-set of the tortfeasor. Where a tortfeasor causes harm to an injured party by creating an *unreasonable risk of harm,* the law provides the injured party a remedy regardless of the tortfeasor's intent. The *Restatements* also recognize certain defenses that may be asserted in a negligence case.

Elements of Negligence

The law requires that specific elements be proven in order to recover in a lawsuit against a tortfeasor for negligence. The injured party must prove five fundamental elements by answering certain questions about the conduct in question:

- *Duty:* Did the tortfeasor owe a duty of care to the injured party?
- *Breach of duty:* Did the tortfeasor fail to exercise reasonable care?
- *Cause in fact:* Except for the breach of duty by the tortfeasor, would the injured party have suffered damages?
- *Proximate (legal) cause:* Was there a legally recognized and close-in-proximity link between the breach of duty and the damages suffered by the injured party?
- *Actual damages:* Did the injured party suffer some physical harm that resulted in identifiable losses?

Duty   The initial consideration in a negligence analysis is whether or not the tortfeasor owed the injured party a *legal* **duty.** The law imposes a general duty on all parties to act reasonably and not to impart unreasonable risk to others. In addition to this general duty, some parties owe a special (heightened) duty of conduct to avoid liability for negligence.

General Duty of Reasonable Conduct   The law imposes a general duty on every party to act as a *reasonably prudent person* would under the circumstances. That is, everyone owes a duty to everyone else to act in a manner so as not to impose unreasonable risk. The reasonably prudent person standard emphasizes that the conduct must be *objectively* reasonable. This means that a fact finder (such as the jury) at trial could conclude that a reasonably prudent person in the same circumstances should have realized that certain conduct would be risky or harmful to another person. In general, the scope of that duty is defined by *foreseeability.* In tort law, the term *person* in the reasonably prudent person standard is meant to be a generic term. The scope of duty is frequently defined by a particular industry or occupation. For example, the level of duty for a physician is defined by what a reasonably prudent *physician* would have done under the circumstances. It is important to understand that duty is an element that *expands* and *contracts* based upon whether or not it was foreseeable that the conduct in question would cause an unreasonable risk of harm. For example, Cain is a guest on a shock-host television show. The owners of the show arrange to have Abel surprise Cain on the show with an embarrassing secret. Cain is embarrassed and runs off stage, and no further incident ensues. Three days later, Abel persists in calling Cain and harassing him about this secret. Cain then shoots and kills Abel later that afternoon. Cain is sentenced to a life term, so Abel's heirs sue the owners of the shock-host television show for negligence, claiming they owed Abel a duty to protect him from Cain. In this case, a court will likely rule that due to the time period between the show and the shooting (three days), and the fact that no incident occurred on the show or immediately thereafter, the duty owed to Abel ended when the show ended and did not extend to the time of the incident. This is primarily because it was not reasonably foreseeable under the factual circumstances of this case that Cain would act in such a rash manner then or thereafter.[11]

No General Duty to Act   The duty of care, discussed above, does *not* include a general duty to act or to rescue another. Tort law allocates liability based on a fundamental difference between some *act* by one party that harms or endangers another party, known as **misfeasance,** and the failure to act or intervene in a certain situation, known as **nonfeasance.** While injured parties may generally recover for misfeasance, injured parties may not hold a defendant liable for failing to act *unless* the parties had a **special relationship** to each other. Special relationships that are set out in the *Restatements* include: a common carrier (such as a bus company) to its passengers; innkeepers to guests; employers to employees; a school to students; and a landlord to tenants.[12] One important special relationship of interest to business owners and managers is a business's duty to *warn* and *assist* any business visitors or patrons in terms of potential danger or harm (such as a slippery floor) on business premises. Therefore, businesses have a special relationship with its visitors and patrons that would allow recovery even in a case of nonfeasance.

Landowners   Landowners owe a general duty to parties off the land from any unreasonable risks to them caused by something on the land. Courts use a reasonableness standard to determine the point at which the landowner should have acted. For example, the owner of GreenAcre plants several trees on the edge of his property, which is adjacent to a busy

---

[11]Based on *Graves v. Warner Brothers,* 656 N.W.2d. 195 (Mich. App. 2002).

[12]*Restatements (Second) of Torts,* § 314A.

TABLE 9.2 Special Relationship Duties Owed by Landowners

Special Relationship To	Definition	Example	Duties Owed
Licensee	Party has owner's consent to be on property, but for a nonbusiness purpose.	Social guest	Warn licensee of any known dangerous conditions on or about the premises. *No duty owed to licensee to inspect for hidden dangers.*
Invitee	Party invited by owner for business purposes or when landowner holds the premises open to the public.	Customer in a retail store.	Warn invitee of any known dangerous conditions on or about the premises. Duty to inspect the premises for hidden dangers and take reasonable efforts to fix any defects.
Trespasser	Entry onto premises without owner's consent.	Landscaping crew accidentally mows wrong property.	No duty to warn, inspect, or repair. Exceptions are a general duty of care when (1) the owner has reason to know of regular trespass (such as a worn pathway), or (2) owner has reason to anticipate that young children might trespass on the property.

suburban street. One month later, one tree was dead with no green vegetation and with evidence of decaying bark and cracks in the roots. Eventually, the tree falls onto the road and injures a passerby. In this instance, a court may find that the landowner had a duty to inspect and remove the tree because it was foreseeable that the dead tree would be a risk to passersby if it fell.[13]

Landowners also owe a special duty to certain parties based on categories spelled out in the *Restatements*. It is important to understand that in a situation where a tenant is in possession of *leased space,* the tenant has the same special duties and level of liability that is imposed on landowners. Once a landlord/owner has given possession of the property to the tenant, the landlord is generally not held liable except for certain common areas (e.g., common stairwells, restrooms, or lobby).[14] The expected level of care varies by category. Table 9.2 sets out the categories of special relationship duties owed by landowners to licensees, invitees and trespassers.

Breach of Duty   Once it has been established that one party owed another party a general or special duty, the next factor is to assess whether or not that party fulfilled their obligations. Failing to meet these obligations is known as a **breach of duty.** As discussed above, duties include (1) general obligations to act in a reasonable manner so as not to put another in harm's way; and (2) special duties to certain parties, including the duty to inspect or duty to warn of defects. While the *Restatements* don't actually list events of breach, courts have traditionally looked to certain guideposts for determining whether a breach of duty has occurred.

---

[13]It should be noted that the *Restatements* do except "natural" conditions from the general duty. However, if a landowner planted the shrubs or excavated the land, this falls under the category of *artificial* and is not an exception to the landowner's general duty to persons off the property.

[14]There are exceptions to this rule such as when the landlord transferred possession knowing of a certain defect, but failed to warn the tenant about it.

Violation of Safety Statute   If the legislature has passed a statute intended to promote safety and one party violated the statute, there is a strong presumption that the party violating the statute has also breached her general duty to those that are protected by the law. Violations of these safety statutes are sometime referred to as *negligence per se.* For example, the state legislature passes a law requiring that construction companies provide hardhats for all workers and visitors on a construction site. One day a prospective tenant visits an office building construction site to check on its progress, but there are not a sufficient number of hardhats available. The site manager allows the visitor on the site without a hardhat. The visitor is then injured by falling debris. In this case, the construction company has violated the state safety statute and a court may find a breach of duty occurred without delving into a reasonably prudent person analysis.

States also pass statutes intended to establish specific liability standards in certain circumstances. For example, *dram shop laws* impose liability on the owners and employees of a public establishment where alcohol is being served. These laws allow a third party who has been injured or harmed by an intoxicated tortfeasor to recover damages against the owner or employee who served an obviously intoxicated patron.[15]

Common Law Standards of Behavior   Where the state legislature has been silent, appellate courts in each individual state have usually developed a fairly extensive body of cases in their common law so that certain standards of behavior may be used in judging whether or not a breach occurred. Standards related to maintenance of property (such as when ice must be cleared) and safety measures (such as keeping one's car in good repair if driving on public roads) are examples of nonstatutory standards for reasonable behavior.

Res Ipsa Loquiter   The doctrine of res ipsa loquiter (a Latin phrase meaning "the thing or matter speaks for itself") is deep-seated in American tort law. This doctrine allows an injured party to create a presumption that the tortfeasor was negligent by pointing to certain facts that infer negligent conduct without a showing of exactly how the tortfeasor behaved.[16] An English judge first used this Latin phrase over a century ago in a case where a pedestrian was struck by a flour barrel falling from a warehouse owned by the defendant. Although the injured party could not actually show how or why the barrel fell, the court held that the facts themselves were sufficient to impute a presumption of negligence.[17]

Cause in Fact   After establishing that a breach of duty has occurred, the injured party must also prove that the tortfeasor's conduct was the **cause in fact** of the damages suffered by the injured party. In other words, there must be a *link* between breach of duty and damages. The overwhelming majority of courts use a simple test, known as the *but for test,* to establish a link. Thus, the question that must be answered is *but for (except for) the breach of duty by the tortfeasor, would the injured party have suffered damages?* If the answer is no then there is a link between the tortfeasor's conduct and the harm suffered by the injured party. Another way to ask this question is: If the tortfeasor had complied with her legal duty, would the injured party have suffered damages? Again, a no answer indicates a link and, thus, cause in fact. For example, suppose that Donald checks into Hotel's twentieth-floor luxury suite. He watches a beautiful sunset while leaning on the balcony railing, but the railing snaps and Donald falls twenty stories. In a negligence analysis, one can reasonably conclude that Hotel owes Donald both a general duty and a special duty (innkeeper) and that the duty was breached because the rail was assumably

---

[15]Note that an increasing number of state legislatures have also imposed similar liability for all social hosts, including the serving of alcohol in a private home.

[16]*Restatement (Second) of Torts,* § 328(D).

[17]*Byrne v. Boadle,* 159 Eng. Rep. 299 (Eng. 1863). The court wrote, "a barrel could not roll out of a warehouse without some negligence, and to say the plaintiff who is injured by it must call witnesses . . . is preposterous."

defective in some way. For cause in fact, one asks: But for the breach of duty by Hotel, would Donald have suffered damages? The answer is clearly no because if Hotel hadn't breached their duty (e.g., had inspected and kept the railing in good repair), Donald would not have suffered damages. Thus, the breach of duty by Hotel was the *cause in fact* of Donald's injuries.

Scope of "But For Test"   One problem in applying the *but for test* is its overreaching broadness. Its application may result in holding a tortfeasor liable for injuries that occurred well beyond the foreseeable scope of the wrongdoing. For example, in the Donald–Hotel case, suppose that after Donald's balcony rail had snapped, Donald fell, but the broken balcony rail also fell and penetrated the windshield of a car on the street below injuring the driver. The injury causes the driver of the car to swerve, hit a pedestrian, and crash into an adjacent canal. A witness to the accident then attempts to rescue the driver of the car from the canal, but drowns doing so. Five blocks away, a shopkeeper is so startled by the noise from the accident that she drops a priceless vase on her foot. In this set of accidental chain reactions, using the *but for test* would impose liability on Hotel for each injury/damage, including Donald's fall, the driver of the car, the struck pedestrian, the drowned rescuer, and foot injuries from the destroyed vase. Yet, a sense of fairness demands that the law cannot reasonably impose *all* of this liability on Hotel. At what point, if any, is the tortfeasor relieved from liability? The broad sweep of the *but for test* requires a further step to establish liability. This step, known as **proximate (legal) cause,** is discussed next.

Proximate (Legal) Cause   In addition to showing that the tortfeasor's breach of duty was the cause in fact of the damages, the injured party must also prove that (1) the tortfeasor's conduct was also the closest-in-proximity cause of the damages, and (2) the tortfeasor's liability wasn't canceled due to a superseding cause. These *proximate cause* concepts protect tortfeasors from liability for far-reaching and out of the ordinary injuries resulting in damages from their tortious act.

Closest-in-Proximity   The majority of courts favor using *foreseeability* to define the scope of the risk. In the Donald–Hotel example above, the jury would be charged with determining the scope of Hotel's liability. Liability would hinge on whether or not it was foreseeable that a faulty balcony railing would result in damages to be suffered by Donald (probable liability), the driver of the car (possible liability), the pedestrian (possible liability), the drowned rescuer (improbable liability), and the owner of the vase (very improbable liability). The *Restatements* define proximate cause as that which helps draw the line that determines when a tortfeasor is "not liable for harm different from harms whose risk made the [tortfeasor's] conduct tortious." This proximate cause theme was first enunciated in Landmark Case 9.1, perhaps the most famous case in American tort law.

Superseding Cause   Sometimes an *intervening* event takes place after the tortfeasor's negligent act. This intervening act may also contribute to that negligence in producing additional damages to the injured party. Some (but not all) of these intervening acts may be the basis for limiting a tortfeasor's liability. These acts are called *superseding causes* (i.e., supersede the tortfeasor's liability) and are also defined by *foreseeability.* For example, in the Donald–Hotel case, suppose that Donald only fell one story and sustained a broken wrist. While being driven to the hospital, a freak tornado hits the car that Donald is in and the wrist injury is made worse. In a case for damages related to the injury, even though the *but for test* would impose liability on Hotel even for the aggravated broken wrist, Hotel's liability is discontinued (though not eliminated for the original injury) once the tornado hits as a superseding cause, and they are not liable for the aggravated injury. This limit applies because it was not reasonably foreseeable by Hotel that Donald would be injured by a tornado en route to the hospital.

FACT SUMMARY   Palsgraf bought a railroad ticket for Rockaway Beach, New York, and was waiting on the platform for her train. A different train arrived on a platform 100 yards away, allowed passengers to board, and began to depart from the station. Running to catch the departing train, two commuters grabbed onto the side and tried to hoist themselves up and into the moving car. To aid one of the men, the conductor on the train pulled him onto the train, but dislodged a package covered in newspaper that the passenger was carrying. The package, which turned out to be fireworks, fell to the platform and exploded. The blast shook the station with sufficient force so that large iron scales (used to weigh freight on various trains) hanging over Palsgraf fell on her resulting in a severe injury. Palsgraf sued the Long Island Railroad for the conductor's negligent conduct of pulling the commuter onto the train that eventually caused the explosion and her injury from the falling scales.

SYNOPSIS OF DECISION AND OPINION   In a famous opinion written by Judge Benjamin Cardozo (who would later serve on the the U.S. Supreme Court), the New York Court of Appeals ruled in favor of the Long Island Railroad. Cardozo reasoned that because the conductor *could not have known* the man he was helping onto the train had a box full of fireworks, the actions of the conductor was not a proximate enough cause to incur liability for Palsgraf's injuries.

WORDS OF THE COURT: Proximate Cause   "[T]he orbit of the danger as disclosed to the eye of reasonable vigilance would be the orbit of the duty. One who jostles one's neighbor in a crowd does not invade the rights of others standing at the outer fringe when the unintended contact casts a bomb upon the ground. The wrongdoer as to them is the man who carries the bomb, not the one who explodes it without suspicion of the danger. Life will have to be made over, and human nature transformed, before prevision so extravagant can be accepted as the norm of conduct, the customary standard to which behavior must conform. [. . .] The risk reasonably to be perceived defines the duty to be obeyed, and risk imports relation; it is risk to another or to others within the range of apprehension."

Case Questions

1. Are all the other elements of a negligence tort satisfied in this case?
2. Who else might Palsgraf have sued? For what?

 Self-Check   Proximate Cause

Is proximate cause met in these situations?

1. A truck driver crashes into a guardrail. During the accident, a defective steering wheel rapidly spins around breaking the driver's arm. The driver sues the maker of the steering mechanism.

2. A tenant hurts herself falling down defective steps. The tenant sues the landlord's insurance company, alleging that they knew the steps were defective but insured him anyway, thus discouraging him from fixing them.

3. An employer burns down his warehouse for the insurance money. An employee is arrested and falsely imprisoned by the police for the crime. The employee sues the employer for negligence.

4. A passenger is injured an automobile accident. The passenger sues the liquor store that sold alcohol to the driver of the car who was already visibly intoxicated.

Answers to this Self-Check are provided at the end of the chapter.

Actual Damages   In order to recover in a negligence case, the tortfeasor must have caused another party **actual damages.** This means that the party alleging injury must prove that she suffered some type of physical harm derived from an injury caused by the tortfeasor. An injured party may not prevail if the injuries were limited to mental/emotional harm alone. However, once a party has proved some *physical* harm, she is eligible for a variety of other types of damages, including out-of-pocket economic losses (such as medical bills), pain and suffering, lost time from employment, and similar categories. Punitive damages may be awarded, but are very rare because they can only be awarded where the tortfeasor's conduct was extremely reckless or willful and wanton.

Many states also allow a spouse or children of an injured party to recover damages related to the negligence. This includes loss of companionship or marital relations (known as *loss of consortium*). Moreover, if the injured party dies, her *estate* may sue for those damages that the injured party would have recovered if he had survived. Spouses and children may also recover damages for losses sustained by virtue of the death of an injured party.

Defenses to Negligence Claims

Once the elements of negligence are met, the analysis then shifts to potential defenses available to the tortfeasor. The two primary defenses to claims of negligence are *comparative negligence* and *assumption of the risk.*

Comparative Negligence In cases where the injured party's conduct has played a factor in the harm suffered, the *Restatements* allow the tortfeasor to assert the defense of **comparative negligence.** This defense requires a jury to divide up the proportion of negligence committed by the parties in terms of percentage (see Table 9.3). Ultimately, successfully asserting comparative negligence reduces (but does not eliminate) the final award to the plaintiff.

Note that comparative negligence is a cousin to the common law doctrine of *contributory negligence,* whereby even 1 percent of negligence on the part of the plaintiff was a complete bar to any plaintiff recovery. The overwhelming majority of states do not follow this standard because of its harshness on the injured party.

TABLE 9.3 Comparative Negligence Formula

Suppose Abel is injured by Baker's conduct and suffers damages totaling $100,000. A jury finds that Baker was 80 percent responsible the injury, but that Abel also contributed to his own injury and was 20 percent responsible for the harm. How much does Abel ultimately recover?

[Damages suffered] × [Percentage of Baker's negligence] = Recovery amount
$100,000 × 80% = $80,000

Assumption of the Risk When the injured party knows that a substantial and apparent risk was associated with certain conduct, and the party went ahead with the dangerous activity anyway, the *Restatements* allow the tortfeasor to assert the defense of **assumption of the risk** so long as (1) the injured party/plaintiff knew or should have known (by virtue of the circumstances or warning signs, etc.) that a risk of harm was inherent in the activity, and (2) the injured party/plaintiff voluntarily participated in the activity. Certain activities are considered to be "inherently dangerous" (such as bungee jumping or parachuting), and companies that are providers of these activities may have limited protection from liability if they acted reasonably in minimizing the dangers and made full disclosures of the risks to participants.

In Case 9.3, a state appellate court considers the assumption of the risk defense in the context of leisure sports.

Legal Speak »)
Estate In addition to land, assets, and personal property, a person's *estate* also consists of legal rights and entitlements after death. This includes the right to sue for the tortious conduct that caused the death.

FACT SUMMARY Zeidman and Fisher were participants in a golf foursome at a charity tournament. On one hole where the view of the fairway was partially blocked, the foursome became concerned that they may inadvertently hit into any players that may be hidden by the blind spots on the fairway ahead of them. The group agreed that Zeidman would take a golf cart and ride ahead to see if the course was clear for the group to hit. Zeidman made his observation and returned to his foursome in the cart. Because he intended on returning to his foursome to report that the group ahead was out of harm's way and because he never signaled to his group that it was safe to hit, Zeidman never entertained the possibility that one of his group would hit a shot. Before Zeidman returned, Fisher, becoming impatient, hit his shot while Zeidman was driving his cart back to the foursome. Fisher's shot was errant and the ball struck Zeidman in the face causing serious and permanent injuries. The trial court dismissed Zeidman's negligence lawsuit against Fisher on summary judgment, ruling that Zeidman had assumed the risk of participating in the golf match and this assumption of risk barred any recovery. Zeidman appealed.

SYNOPSIS OF DECISION AND OPINION The Pennsylvania Superior Court reversed the trial court's decision and ruled in favor of Zeidman. The court reasoned that the assumption of the risk doctrine requires that the evidence show that the injured party (1) fully understood the specific risk, (2) voluntarily chooses to encounter it, and (3) manifested a willingness to accept the known risk. In this case, an objectively reasonable person may have assumed that no risk existed because Zeidman's agreed upon task was to check if the fairway was clear and then report to his own foursome if it was safe to hit. Because he had not yet completed this task, Zeidman did not manifest a willingness to accept a known risk.

WORDS OF THE COURT: Assumption of the Risk Doctrine "In the circumstances of the present case, it is obvious that Zeidman, on returning from his forward observer mission, did not consciously assume the risk of friendly fire when, to the contrary, he had every right to anticipate none of his playing partners would attempt a tee shot until his return to the tee box. To grant summary judgment on the basis of assumption of the risk it must first be concluded, as a matter of law, that the party consciously appreciated the risk that attended a certain endeavor. . . . Accordingly, whether Zeidman is able to convince a jury that his version of events is true remains to be seen, he, in any event is entitled to his day in court."

Case Questions

1. If Zeidman had signaled to his partners that all was clear from the fairway and was then hit while returning in the cart, would Fisher be entitled to a summary judgment based on assumption of the risk?

2. What duty did Fisher owe Zeidman in the first place? Was it a special relationship duty?

CONCEPT SUMMARY   Negligence Analysis

- *Duty:* Did the tortfeasor owe a duty to the injured party?
- *Breach:* Did the tortfeasor breach the reasonably prudent person standard?
- *Causation:* Except for the tortfeasor's breach of duty, would the plaintiff have suffered the injury?
- *Proximate (legal) cause:* Was the breach the closest-in proximity? Were there any superseding causes? Was the harm foreseeable?
- *Damages:* Did the injury to person or property result in losses?
- *Defenses:* Did the injured party contribute to the injury (comparative negligence)? Was the injured party aware of the risk, but went ahead anyway (assumption of the risk)?

STRICT LIABILITY TORTS

The tort liability theories covered so far in this chapter were based on either intent or negligence. The *Restatements* also provide for liability in certain cases where neither intent nor negligence need be proven. This category of tort is known as *strict liability* and is recognized in the *Restatements* primarily for abnormally dangerous activities and for defective products (discussed in the next section).[18] Strict liability is a concept rooted in the notion that the general public benefits when liability is imposed on those who engaged in certain activities that result in harm to another party, even if the activities were undertaken in the most careful manner possible (without negligence).

Abnormally Dangerous Activities

The *Restatements* set out a six-factor test to determine whether abnormally dangerous activities trigger strict liability for any harm caused by the activity.

- Does activity involve a high degree of risk of some harm?
- Is there a likelihood that the harm that results will be great?
- Is it possible to eliminate the risk by exercising reasonable care?
- Is the activity relatively common?
- Is the location of the activity appropriate to the risk?
- Is there any community value that outweighs the dangerous attributes?

For example, suppose that ChemicalCo. produces 100 pounds of plastic explosives for use in the demolition of a building. They lease a railroad car and ship the explosives to their storage warehouse until the buyer can pick it up. Before the buyer picks it up, thieves break

Strict liability is imposed on businesses engaged in abnormally dangerous operations such as the use of explosives in building demolition.

---

[18]Strict liability is also imposed under the common law for the keepers of wild or dangerous animals.

in and inadvertently ignite the car. The explosion causes damage to several buildings and an injury to a party standing in the surrounding area. Using the six-factor test, a court will likely impose strict liability on ChemicalCo. due to the nature of the abnormally dangerous activity of the storage of explosives. Other strict liability cases involve storage and use of toxic chemicals, flammable liquids, nuclear power, and blasting for demolition or construction.

LO9-8 PRODUCTS LIABILITY

Products liability refers to the liability of any seller (including the manufacturer, retailer, and any intermediary seller such as a wholesaler) of a product that, because of a defect, causes harm to a consumer. Note that modern products liability law protects not only the actual purchaser, but also any ultimate users that were harmed by the product's defect. In a products liability case, the injured party may pursue a legal remedy against the seller under one of three theories: (1) negligence, (2) warranty, or (3) strict liability.

Negligence

The negligence analysis covered earlier in this chapter may also be applied to the seller of a product as well. Although historically negligence was severely limited as a remedy because the law protected only the actual purchaser, a revised rule announced in the landmark case of *MacPherson v. Buick*[19] has been adopted in every state. Under the *MacPherson* rule, one who negligently manufacturers a product is liable for *any injuries to persons* (and, in some limited cases, property) proximately caused by the negligence. For example, suppose that Holmes purchases a motorcycle from a dealer and gives it to his son Wendell. Wendell is injured on the motorcycle and sues the manufacturer for negligence. So long as Wendell can prove negligence, the manufacturer will be liable for Wendell's injuries despite the fact that Wendell was not the one who entered into the purchase agreement with the dealer or the manufacturer.

Courts have found that manufacturers have the duty of care regarding proper design, manufacturing, testing, inspection, and shipping. Retailers do not have as comprehensive of a duty as the manufacturer, but still have a duty to warn consumers of any product they know or suspect to be unreasonably dangerous.

Warranty

Historically, warranty laws were important protection for purchasers because they imposed liability even in the absence of negligence. Recall from Chapter 8, "Contracts for the Sale of Goods," that a warranty is particular representation and guarantee to the user about a product. When the seller makes a representation of fact about a product, this is known as an *express* warranty. If the seller has not made a specific representation about the product, the buyer may still be protected by a Uniform Commercial Code-imposed *implied* warranty. Because warranties are set out in Article 2 (Sales) of the UCC, they are discussed in detail in Chapter 8.

Strict Liability

The most appealing option for pursuing a products liability case is through the doctrine of strict liability, because the injured party need not prove the elements of negligence. In *Greenman v. Yuba Power Products, Inc.,*[20] the California supreme court decided a groundbreaking case that paved the way for adoption of a strict liability standard for product

---

[19]111 N.E. 1050 (N.Y. 1916). The historical requirement that negligence suits could only be brought by the direct purchaser was known as *privity of contract.*

[20]377 P.2d 897 (Cal. 1963).

defects by ruling that "a manufacturer is strictly liable in tort when an article he places on the market, knowing that it is to be used without inspection for defects, proves to have a defect which causes injury to a human being." Two years after the *Greenman* case was decided, a similar doctrine of strict liability tort for the sellers of products was included in the *Restatements (Second) of Torts* in § 402A. The *Restatements* specifically indicate that liability still exists even if the seller used all possible care. Note that the term *seller* means not only the product's manufacturer, but also all the parties through the chain of commerce, including the retailer.

§ 402A is a bedrock for strict products liability because a substantial majority of states have adopted the section that imposes special liability on the seller of a product that could harm the user. Specifically, § 402A imposes strict liability on the seller so long as the injured party can show that the product was in a *defective* condition, and that the defect rendered the product *unreasonably dangerous.* § 402A liability is triggered only when:

- The seller is engaged in the business of selling such a product, and
- The product is expected to and does reach the user or consumer without a substantial change in the condition in which it is sold.

§ 402A's strict liability is imposed on the seller even though:

- The seller has exercised all possible care in preparation and sale of the product, and
- The user or consumer has not bought the product from or entered into any contractual relationship with the seller.

Defining "Defect"   In order to recover for an injury caused by a product, it must have been defective and have created a danger that is outside of the reasonable consumer's expectations. Courts have recognized several theories of unreasonably dangerous defects.

Design or Manufacturing Defect   A product may become dangerous if it is *designed* improperly in that foreseeable risks of harm posed by the product could have been reduced or avoided by some *alternative* design. Even products that are designed properly may still be rendered dangerously defective by some mistake made during the *manufacturing* process. For example, suppose CarCo. designs a new car intended to have higher than average gas mileage. They achieve this by moving the gas tank to a different position on the car. The design, however, results in the gas tank rupturing during a rear-end crash. This is a classic design defect. However, if CarCo. designs the new car properly, but one of the factory workers improperly installs the brakes and this eventually results in an injury, the product has been rendered unreasonably dangerous via a manufacturing defect.

Inadequate Warning   Products that are ostensibly safe may also carry risks unknown to a reasonable consumer. In such cases, the law requires the product to carry sufficient warnings and instructions. Failure to warn may render the product unreasonably dangerous even absent any manufacturing or design defect. One common category of inadequate warning cases involves prescription drugs, but the theory of unreasonable danger applies to all products that carry some danger in use (such as a lawnmower or snow thrower).

Improper Packaging   A product can be rendered unreasonably dangerous by a defect in the packaging. Cases that have recognized this theory of defect are primarily asserted against manufacturers of products that require safety proof containers as well as food or beverage packages that clearly indicate whether the product has been tampered with (such as a seal on a bottle of juice). Perhaps the most famous case on improper packaging involved the well-publicized Tylenol scare in 1986. In *Elsroth v. Johnson & Johnson,*[21] a

---

[21]700 F. Supp. 151 (1988).

federal court in New York held that Johnson & Johnson, the manufacturer of Tylenol, was not liable for the death of a consumer who was the victim of tampering by an unknown third party. The estate of the consumer brought suit claiming that improper packaging had led to the tampering when an unknown third party removed a package of Tylenol from a supermarket shelf, laced it with cyanide, and then somehow resealed the container and box so the tampering was not readily detectable. However, the court pointed to the fact that the Tylenol bottle featured a foil seal glued to the mouth of the container, a shrink-wrap seal around the neck and cap of the bottle, and a box sealed with glue in which the bottle was placed. Because Johnson & Johnson went above and beyond existing standards by using three different methods to prevent consumption of a tampered product, they could not be held liable under § 402A.

Unavoidably Unsafe Some products are inherently dangerous. That is, some products are designed and manufactured correctly, and adequate warning has been given, but the product is still dangerous (such as a handgun). Most courts have been reluctant to impose strict liability for damages resulting from handgun use where the product was properly manufactured and designed. Until recently, cigarettes were in this same category, but some courts have recognized that depending on the circumstances, a cigarette manufacturer may be held liable for the damages suffered by a smoker.[22]

Causation and Damages Once it has been established that the product was unreasonably dangerous, the injured party need now prove only that the defective product was the cause of the injuries and that the product caused an actual injury that resulted in damages.

Seller's Defenses Although strict liability imposes a relatively onerous burden on the seller, the law recognizes several defenses for a seller even if the injured party has established all of the required elements for liability.

A court found that Tylenol's packaging was not defective and thus the company was not liable for any injuries resulting from third-party tampering.

[22]*Williams v. Phillip Morris, Inc.,* 2002 WL 1677722 (N.D. Cal. 2002).

Substantial Change   The *Restatements* draw a line of liability based on the condition of the product at the time it leaves the seller's control. In order for strict liability to apply, the product must reach the end user without substantial change. Thus, if a product leaves the manufacturing plant in a reasonable condition (not dangerous) and then is contaminated or damaged in the next stage of the commercial chain of delivery, any resulting harm is outside the strict liability model. Depending on the circumstances, of course, the manufacturer may still be liable for negligence, but not under strict liability.

Assumption of the Risk   Although courts apply this defense narrowly,[23] it is still recognized as a defense for sellers in a strict product liability case. An injured party has assumed the risk if the party knew or should have known about the risk and disregarded this risk by continuing with the activity at issue for her own benefit. For example, suppose that WidgetCo. owns a high-speed machine for producing widgets and a foreign object lodges in the machine while it is operating. The instructions warn to shut down the machine before removing the object, but the plant manager decides against a shutdown fearing it would cost money from lost production time. If the plant manager is injured while removing the object from the operating machinery and sues the machine's manufacturer under a strict product liability theory, the manufacturer may successfully assert the assumption of the risk defense.[24]

Misuse of Product   In a case where the injured party may have *not* known of a certain risk, but failed to use the product in a manner that an ordinarily prudent person would, then the seller may use product misuse as a defense. Courts have been reluctant to allow this defense unless that particular use of the product was so far from its ordinary use that it was not reasonably foreseeable by the seller.

FIGURE 9.1   § 402A Liability

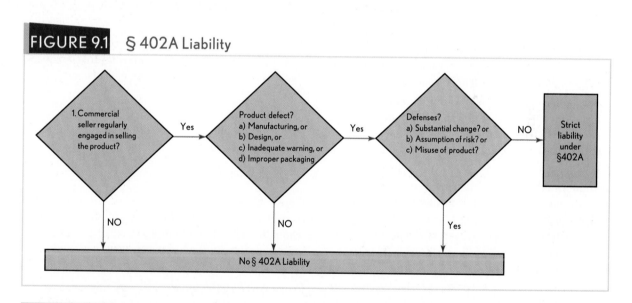

[23]See "Assumption of Risk and Strict Products Liability," 95 *Harv.L.Rev.* 872 (1982).

[24]Based on *Micallef v. Miehle Co.,* 348 N.E.2d 571 (N.Y. Ct. App. 1976).

Tort p. 208 A civil wrong where one party has acted, or in some cases failed to act, and that action or inaction causes a loss to be suffered by another party.

Tortfeasor p. 208 One who commits a civil wrong against another resulting in injury to person or property.

Tortious conduct p. 208 The wrongful action or inaction of a tortfeasor.

Restatement of Torts p. 208 An influential document issued by the American Law Institute (ALI) summarizing the general principles of U.S. tort law and recognized by the courts as widely applied principles of law. Note that ALI amended the *Restatements* twice and therefore these sources of law are called the *Restatement (Second) of Torts* and the *Restatement (Third) of Torts.*

Intentional torts p. 208 A category of torts where the tortfeasor was willful in bringing about a particular event that caused harm to another party.

Negligence p. 208 A category of torts where the tortfeasor was absent of willful intent in bringing about a particular event that caused harm to another party.

Strict liability p. 208 In tort law, where a tortfeasor may be held liable for an act regardless of intent or willfulness, applying primarily to cases of defective products and abnormally dangerous activities.

Libel p. 209 Written defamation, in which publishing in print (including pictures), writing, or broadcast through radio, television, or film, an untruth about another that will do harm to that person's reputation or honesty or subject a party to hate, contempt, or ridicule.

Slander p. 209 Oral defamation, in which someone tells one or more persons an untruth about another that will harm the reputation or honesty of the person defamed or subject a party to hate, contempt, or ridicule.

Absolute privilege p. 210 A defense to a defamation claim provided to government officials, judicial officers and proceedings, and state legislatures, where the defendants need not proffer any further evidence to assert the defense.

Qualified privilege p. 210 A defense to a defamation claim provided for the media and employers, where the defendants must offer evidence of good faith and be absent of malice to be shielded from liability.

Trade libel p. 211 A tort used to sue where a competitor has made a false statement that disparaged a competing product.

Product disparagement statutes p. 212 Statutes intended to protect the interest of a state's major industries such as agriculture, dairy, or beef.

Communications Decency Act of 1996 p. 213 Enacted by Congress to extend immunity to the ISPs by protecting them from any defamation liability as a "publisher or speaker of any information provided by another information content provider."

Merchant's privilege p. 214 A narrow privilege provided for under the *Restatements* to shield a merchant from liability for temporarily detaining a party who is reasonably suspected of stealing merchandise.

Duty p. 218 A fundamental element to recover a lawsuit against a tortfeasor for negligence where the injured party must prove that the tortfeasor owed them a duty of care.

Misfeasance p. 218 Some act by one party that harms or endangers another party.

Nonfeasance p. 218 The failure to act or intervene in certain situations.

Special relationship p. 218 In tort law, a heightened duty created between a common carrier to its passengers, innkeepers to guests, employers to employees, businesses to patrons, a school to students, and a landlord to tenants and landowners.

Breach of duty p. 219 A fundamental element to recover a lawsuit against a tortfeasor for negligence where the injured party must prove that the tortfeasor failed to exercise reasonable care in fulfilling its obligations.

Cause in fact p. 220 A fundamental element to recover a lawsuit against a tortfeasor for negligence where the injured party must prove that except for the breach of duty by the tortfeasor, they would not have suffered damages.

Proximate (legal) cause p. 221 A fundamental element to recover a lawsuit against a tortfeasor for negligence where the injured party must prove a legally recognized and close-in-proximity link between the breach of duty and the damages it suffered.

Actual damages p. 222 A fundamental element to recover a lawsuit against a tortfeasor for negligence where the injured party must prove that it suffered some physical harm that resulted in identifiable losses.

Comparative negligence p. 223 A defense to claims of negligence where the injured party's conduct has played a factor in the harm suffered and, thus, the proportion of negligence should be divided.

Assumption of the risk p. 223 A defense to claims of negligence where the injured party knows that a substantial and apparent risk was associated with certain conduct, and the party went ahead with the dangerous activity anyway.

Computer Installers Inc. (CI) is a company that sells, installs, and maintains computer networks for organizations that have large numbers of users. CI entered into a contract with Big Time Firm (BTF) to replace the firm's computer network. CI's contract included routine installation tasks such as laying network cable and wiring in the various offices to facilitate numerous network users simultaneously, installing new PCs in one-third of the network user stations, and setting up an appropriate network server with sufficient back-up capability. CI arrived on March 1 and began work on rewiring BTF's office to facilitate the new computer system. In the process of installing the new cabling for the network, a CI technician accidentally rewired the system that controlled the fire sprinklers and rendered the sprinklers inoperable.

Office Cleaners Inc. (OC) was cleaning BTF's offices at night on March 2. One of OC's employees left a lit cigarette in one of BTF's restrooms. That night, as a result of the lit cigarette, a small fire began in the restroom. Because the sprinklers were inoperable, the fire spread and caused damage to the entire office and equipment in the amount of $50,000.

1. What level of duty does CI owe to BTF and have they breached that duty?

2. To what extent is the concept of cause in fact versus proximate cause important when considering CI's liability?

3. At what point, if any, is CI's liability cut off? Does OC assume full liability for the fire?

4. Assume that BTF had fired their night security guard on February 1 and never replaced the position. Thus, no guard was present when the fire started. Articulate a possible defense for CI and OC based on this fact.

5. Suppose that after the incident the sales manager of Data Management Inc., one of CI's competitors, is having lunch with Sheldon, the chief information officer of City Hospital. City Hospital had an existing contract with CI to maintain City Hospital's network. During lunch, Data Management's sales manager tells Sheldon about the fire incident and also states that, based on his personal knowledge, CI was a shoddy outfit that had a poor reputation in the industry. The sales manager then proposed a new Data Management information system for City Hospital at a lower price than CI. When Sheldon was reluctant to consider the offer, Data Management's sales manager offered to pay out any penalty that City Hospital suffered as a result of canceling the CI contract. Sheldon cancels the contract with CI citing customer service problems. What possible torts were committed? What are the requirements for CI to recover damages?

Another context where managers encounter tort law is in the area of employment checks and references. Suppose that the technician/installer employed by CI in Theory to Practice (above) was suspended for incompetence. The installer was so enraged that he threatened his fellow employees with bodily harm and was subsequently fired. The installer sought new employment and listed several CI managers as references

for a new prospective employer. Consider the conundrum of the manager asked for a reference. How would you address the question? On the one hand, CI may be liable for any defamatory statements made by its managers in this situation. On the other hand, if CI simply refuses to say anything in a reference, and if it turns out that the installer is dangerous and assaults a colleague at a new employer, an injured party could possibly claim that CI was negligent in not providing a new employer with important information about the ex-employee installer's potential for danger.

In groups or individually, develop a policy for CI managers on giving references for ex-employees that balances the concern of defamation with that of negligence in failing to inform a prospective employer about a potentially dangerous employee. Assume that your state has the same laws as Connecticut and use

the *Belanger v. Swift Transportation, Inc.,* case found earlier in this chapter to help develop a legally sound policy. A more comprehensive briefing of the case is available on this textbook's Web site at www.mhhe.com/melvin. Be sure to address (a) a brief overview of the background and a summary of legal ramifications of not having a sound reference/defamation policy, and (b) how your policy fits into the privilege defense in the law. A sample answer may be found on this textbook's Web site at www.mhhe.com/melvin.

CASE SUMMARY 9.1 :: Maher v. Best Western Inn, 717 So. 2d 97 (Fla. App. 5th Dist. 1998)

SPECIAL RELATIONSHIPS

Maher is a blind woman who checked into a Best Western that welcomed pets like her Seeing Eye dog, Ina. Shortly after Maher checked in with her parents, another motel patron walked by with two unleashed dogs—one German shepard and one pit bull. The two unleashed dogs attacked Ina, Maher, and her parents. Maher sued Best Western for negligence.

CASE QUESTIONS

1. What duty did Best Western owe Maher?
2. Was it *reasonable* for Best Western to do more to prevent the attack?
3. Would a bystander have had a duty to prevent the attack if it occurred on the street?

CASE SUMMARY 9.2 :: Wurtzel v. Starbucks Coffee Co., 257 F. Supp. 2d 520 (E.D.N.Y. 2003)

RES IPSA LOQUITOR

Wurtzel bought a cup of coffee in her local Starbucks and placed it in her car's cup holder. Shortly after leaving the store and when making a turn, the lid came off the coffee and the liquid spilled over Wurtzel's right leg burning her severely. Wurtzel never looked to see if the lid was on correctly and did not see the coffee spill or the

clerk secure the lid to the cup. She sued Starbucks for negligence, invoking the doctrine of *res ipsa loquitor*.

CASE QUESTIONS

1. Was Starbucks clearly negligent without any need for witnesses?
2. Who else may have been negligent?

CASE SUMMARY 9.3 :: Coker v. Wal-Mart Stores, Inc., 642 So. 2d 774 (Fla. App. 1st Dist. 1994)

NEGLIGENCE PER SE

Bonifay and Fordham bought a box of .32 caliber bullets from a Wal-Mart in Florida. Four hours later, the two men robbed an auto-parts store and killed Coker with those same bullets. When they bought the ammunition both Bonifay and Fordham were under 21 years of age. The federal Gun Control Act makes it illegal to sell ammunition to anyone under 21. Coker's wife sued Wal-Mart for the wrongful death of her husband.

CASE QUESTIONS

1. Is Wal-Mart liable?
2. What if it was reasonable to assume that the two men were over 21?
3. Could Wal-Mart have foreseen the robbery any more than the train conductor could have foreseen the bag full of fireworks in Palsgraf?

STRICT PRODUCTS LIABILITY

Gorran suffered a heart attack after following the diet plan of *Dr. Atkins' New Diet Revolution*. Gorran claimed the heart attack was a result of the high-fat, high-protein diet advocated by Dr. Atkins. He sued the publisher for selling a defective product—a diet plan that causes a heart attack.

CASE QUESTIONS

1. Can a diet plan be considered a "product"?
2. Why would Gorran want to sue under products liability theory rather than just negligence?

 Self-Check **ANSWERS**

Proximate Cause

1. Yes. The injury (broken arm) was sufficiently proximate to the negligence (defective steering column). *McCown v. International Harvester Co.,* 342 A.2d 381.

2. No. Too many acts of intervening negligence on the part of the landlord. *Matthias v. United Pacific Ins. Co.,* 67 Cal. Rptr. 511, 514.

3. Yes. It was reasonably foreseeable that the employee would have been falsely arrested for the fire. The jury found that the employer had framed the employee. *Seidel v. Greenberg,* 260 A.2d 863, 871.

4. Yes. It was reasonably foreseeable and violated state dram shop laws. *Gonzales v. Krueger,* 799 P.2d 1318, 1321.

BUSINESS LAW SIMULATION EXERCISE 1

Restrictive Covenants in Contracts: Neurology Associates, LLP v. Elizabeth Blackwell, M.D.

learning outcomes **checklist**

After studying this simulation, students who have mastered the material will be able to:

1. Explain the legal doctrines that govern the use of restrictive covenants.

2. Interpret and apply the rules set forth in current case law.

3. Articulate a cogent argument for each party/side in the dispute.

4. Negotiate a tenable solution as an alternative to a judicial forum.

Chapters 6 and 7 provided you with a variety of legal doctrines and rules governing contract formation and performance, and then illustrated how these doctrines and rules apply in the corporate sector context. This simulation is designed to help students understand how the various topics covered in the contract law chapters connect through use of a simulated legal dispute. The simulation is intended to provide students with as close as possible real-world experience in applying legal doctrines and use of analytical and critical thinking skills. This simulation is a sequential decision-making exercise structured around a model in which the participants assume a role in managing tasks and work toward a tenable solution.

The simulation is structured in three parts:

- Part 1 is a hypothetical fact pattern describing events leading up to a legal dispute in the hypothetical U.S. state of Longville.

- Part 2 is a set of two hypothetical case summaries from Longville appellate courts that provide a brief set of facts, several legal points, and short excerpts from the opinion itself. While these cases are hypothetical, they are based on actual cases from appellate courts in various states and represent the view of the majority of state courts in the United States.

- Part 3 is an assignment sheet that will be provided to you by your instructor to be used in conjunction with this simulation.

PART 1: STIPULATED FACTS

1. In May 2005, Dr. Elizabeth Blackwell ("Blackwell") had earned her Medical Doctor degree and completed all necessary requirements to receive a license to practice medicine in the State of Longville. She specialized in neurological medicine. Although she was offered professional opportunities in several large hospitals, she pursued an employment offer with Neurological Associates, LLC ("NA"). NA is a two-physician practice located in a small town in the southwestern area of the state of Longville and located 20 miles north of the City of Galway, the largest city in Longville. Although the pay was lower than the larger hospitals, Blackwell wanted to be close to her family and did not wish to engage in a practice that required the strenuous schedules associated with larger medical providers.

2. NA was managed by the two partners, Dr. Richard Cohn ("Cohn") and Dr. Jean Valjean ("Valjean"). While negotiating Blackwell's Employment Agreement, Cohn was the primary contact and the parties agreed to compensation terms, vacation, on-call duties (after hours), and a fringe benefit package. The agreement included an arbitration clause requiring that the parties agree to nonbinding arbitration in the event of a dispute arising from the Employment Agreement. The Employment Agreement also provided for Blackwell to have paid time off to study for and take the examinations required to become board certified in neurology. NA agreed to a $1,000 payment to be used for a course intended to help prepare candidates for the test. Blackwell began her employment with NA on June 1, 2005.

3. Immediately after hiring Blackwell, NA paid for Blackwell to accompany them to a medical conference at which they were scheduled to speak. At the conference, Cohn and Valjean introduced her to a number of physicians in hopes of building the referral base for the practice.

4. In July 2005, Cohn approached Blackwell and told her that he needed her to sign an additional document that was supposed to be part of her contract, but that Cohn had neglected to mention during negotiations. He explained

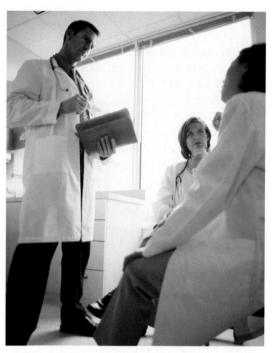

In this simulation exercise, a physician in a health care practice becomes involved in a dispute over a provision in her contract that restricted future employment.

that the document was standard procedure in medical practices and that he had been so busy during the negotiations period that he had forgotten to mention it to Blackwell. He went on to explain that Blackwell should sign the document by the end of the workday and that this would "make the lawyers happy."

5. The document was titled "Addendum to Contract—Restrictive Covenant and Noncompete Clause" and read in pertinent part:

Section 1: The parties hereby agree, in consideration of the exchange of good, valuable, and sufficient consideration, to be bound by the following provision:

For a period of three years after the date of her separation from NA, Blackwell agrees that she will not contract with any provider of neurological services, nor compete in any way with NA, within a radius of 50 miles of NA's practice location. It is acknowledged that this restriction covers the entirety of the southwestern region of Longville.

6. Blackwell felt that she should have a lawyer review the document, but Cohn insisted the addendum was normal procedure and that she needed to sign it quickly to make things "legal." He emphasized that he would have to have the document by the end of the day or that, as it was a condition of her employment, Blackwell's payroll check could not be processed until the document had been signed. Blackwell reluctantly signed the document and submitted it to Cohn.

7. In August 2009, Blackwell began to have conflicts with Cohn and, to a lesser extent, Valjean. While Cohn and Valjean took frequent vacations during the summer, Blackwell was left to staff the practice alone. She felt overwhelmed and met with Cohn to discuss a more equitable work schedule. Cohn refused any negotiation explaining that Blackwell was hired as a "workhorse" and that her salary was fair given the size of the practice and market. Cohn urged Blackwell to continue her hard work and not to complain about her work schedule. Eventually, explained Cohn, Blackwell would become a partner in the practice and would enjoy the fruits of her labor.

8. In September 2009, Blackwell continued to handle a very heavy caseload seeing almost twice as many patients as Cohn or Valjean. In response to Blackwell's plea for additional staff, NA hired a new physician to help manage the caseload. Although Blackwell was initially relieved, the situation at work continued to deteriorate. The workload was such that Cohn kept denying Blackwell's request for time off to prepare for the upcoming board certification exam advising her to put if off until the caseload lightened up a bit.

9. Blackwell began to receive phone calls from recruiters trying to lure her away from the practice to work at a new neurology clinic in Galway Hospital (located in the City of Galway). The recruiters offered a significant amount of money because there was a substantial shortage of neurologists in the southwest region of Longville. However, Blackwell never pursued these opportunities because she believed the restrictive covenant prevented her from working in Galway.

10. In January 2010, Blackwell was granted her paid leave to prepare for her board certification and she took the exam in February 2010. However, after she returned to the practice, she began to feel even more isolated from the other physicians.

11. On March 1, 2010, Blackwell, fed up with NA, announced that she was giving NA 60-days notice that she was leaving the practice to join Galway Hospital in the City of Galway and that her resignation was effective on May 1, 2010. She anticipated starting at Galway on June 1, 2010. Galway was forming a new neurology practice group and they had offered to employ Blackwell as one of the founding physicians in the group.

12. Cohn immediately sent Blackwell a letter informing her that he accepted her resignation, but that she had responsibilities under her contract that prevented her from accepting a new position with a competitor.

PART 2: STATE OF LONGVILLE CASE LAW

Wellspan Hospital and Medical Group v. Phillip Bayliss, M.D., Supreme Court of the State of Longville (2005)

Facts

■ This is the leading case on restrictive covenants/noncompete agreements in the context of medical practices in the state of Longville. It has not been modified or reversed since it was decided.

■ Wellspan is a not-for-profit health care system located in Columbus County in the southeastern portion of the state of Longville. Bayliss is a physician specializing in OB/GYN services.

■ Wellspan hired Bayliss as its medical director in 2000 at which time Bayliss signed an employment agreement that included a restrictive covenant under which Bayliss agreed not to engage in medical practice in Columbus County and five other contiguous counties (this covered the entire southeastern region of Longville) for a period of two years after the separation of employment between Wellspan and Bayliss.

■ Wellspan invested over $1 million in equipping Bayliss's practice, hiring additional physicians, and promotional strategies intended on marketing the practice and increasing the number of referrals.

■ Relations between Wellspan and Bayliss deteriorated when they disagreed over Wellspan's expansion strategy. In February 2004, Bayliss resigned his position at Wellspan and established his OB/GYN practice only 5 miles from the Wellspan practice. This was within the area covered under the restrictive covenant.

■ The state's highest court considered the enforceability of Wellspan's restrictive covenant against Bayliss.

POINTS OF LAW AND OPINION EXCERPTS

Point (a)

The state of Longville courts will enforce a restrictive covenant *only* if it is *reasonably necessary* to protect the legitimate interests of the employer and courts may either strike down a covenant altogether or may reform (known as *bluelining*) a covenant if it is overbroad in some way.

Excerpt (a)

"Courts in the State of Longville have historically been reluctant to enforce contracts that place restraints on trade or on the ability of an individual to earn a living; however, postemployment noncompetition covenants are *not* per se unreasonable or unenforceable."

Point (b)

The threshold requirement for enforceability of a covenant is that the employer must be protecting a *legitimate business interest*. The primary legitimate business interests that Longville courts have held to be protectible in a covenant are (1) trade secrets or confidential business information, (2) customer goodwill, and (3) investments in the employee.

Excerpt (b1)

"A *trade secret* is legitimate business interest because it may include a compilation of information which is used in one's business that gives one an opportunity to obtain an advantage over competitors. A trade secret does not include an employee's aptitude, skill, dexterity, manual and mental ability, or other subjective knowledge. In addition, if a competitor could obtain the information by legitimate means, it will not be given protection as a trade secret."

Excerpt (b2)

"The interest protected under the umbrella of *goodwill* is a business's positive reputation. Goodwill represents a preexisting relationship arising from a continuous course of business which is expected to continue indefinitely. A business's goodwill is considered

Legal Speak ›))
Threshold Requirement A requirement that must be met by the plaintiff prior to the court engaging in further legal analysis to determine the rights of the parties.

a protectible interest even when the goodwill has been acquired through the efforts of an employee. The concept of customer goodwill as a protectible interest has been applied to patient relationships when the noncompetition covenant at issue involves a health care professional. This court has cited the erosion of the ex-employer's patient relationships as one factor in the decision to enforce a restrictive covenant."

Excerpt (b3)

"A third protectible interest recognized by Longville courts is the *efforts and financial resources invested by an employer* to provide to its employees specialized training in the methods of the employer's business. In a past case, the defendant was a salesman of securities who had received extensive and continuous training from his employer, particularly with respect to methods and problems in the sale of mutual fund shares. He then voluntarily left his position with his employer and started his own business selling mutual fund shares. The court enforced the noncompetition covenant at issue, enjoining the defendant from engaging in the business of selling mutual fund shares in Pennsylvania. The court found merit in the argument that it would be inequitable for the defendant to start a new business in direct competition with his ex-employer after having received extensive, specialized training in the methods and problems of the business directly from his ex-employer."

Point (c)

A medical practice's patient referral base is a legitimate protectible business interest when a medical practice can demonstrate that they have invested in the production and generation of such a base.

Excerpt (c)

"Recognizing a patient referral base as a protected interest and of protecting the investments required to develop such a base is consistent with our holding in other employer–employee situations outside the health care field. In the context of a noncompetition covenant, we think that the referral bases of a specialized medical care institution are analogous to a physician's patient relationships or an employer's customer relationships. Viewed in such light, recognition of a patient referral base as a protected interest fits squarely within Longville case law."

Point (d)

If the threshold requirement of protectible interest is met, the next step in the analysis is to apply two *balancing tests:* (1) the employer's protectible interest balanced against the employee's interest in earning a living, and (2) the employee and employer interests with the interests of the public.

Excerpt (d1)

"In weighing the competing interests of employer and employee, the court must engage in an analysis of *reasonableness.* First, the covenant must be reasonably necessary for the protection of the employer. In addition, the temporal and geographical restrictions imposed on the ex-employee must be reasonably limited."

Excerpt (d2)

"Regarding the second balancing test, in the context of noncompete agreements among physicians, the *interests of the public* are defined as a function of the availability of appropriate medical services to the community. Since there is no evidence of a lack of availability of OB/GYN physicians within the restricted area, the interests of the public are served and, thus, enforcement of the covenant against Bayliss does not result in public harm."

Held

Because Wellspan has shown that they have a legitimate business interest in protecting their patient referral base, and that the court has determined that the restriction is tailored to those interests, and that no public harm will be suffered by enforcement of the restriction, the court finds *in favor of Wellspan.*

Regional General Hospital v. Anesthesiology Associates, Inc., Appellate Court of the State of Longville (2007)

Facts

- Anesthesiology Associates Inc. ("AAI") is a medical practice that employs physicians and certified registered nurse anesthetists ("Employees"). In January 2002, AAI entered into a contract with Regional General Hospital ("Regional") to provide mutually agreed upon services to Regional's patients.

- The employment agreements that AAI has with its Employees contained a postemployment restrictive covenant wherein Employees agreed to the following restrictions: (1) that for a period of two years from separation from AAI, ex-Employees would not contract with or compete against AAI at any facility where AAI was currently the provider of anesthesiology services, and (2) that for a period of one year from separation, ex-Employees agreed not to contract or compete against AAI at any facility where AAI has provided services for the last 12 months ending on the period of the Employee's departure date. Because AAI provided services to more than 35 hospitals in five different states, the geographic restrictions effectively covered a five-state region.

- Regional let the agreement with AAI expire and offered direct employment to several AAI Employees. Fearing that Employees of AAI would not accept these employment offers for fear of a lawsuit by AAI based on breach of the restrictive covenant, Regional filed suit against AAI seeking a declaratory judgment that the covenant was unenforceable because it was overly broad in scope and duration and unduly restricted the AAI Employees from accepting employment with Regional.

> **Legal Speak ⟩⟩**
> **Declaratory Judgment** A remedy used to determine the rights of the parties in a set of circumstances (such as the enforceability of a contract) and is binding on the litigants even though no damages were awarded.

POINTS OF LAW AND OPINION EXCERPTS

Point (a)

In accordance with the Supreme Court of Longville's decision in *Wellspan v. Bayliss,* this court will enforce a restrictive covenant *only* if it is *reasonably necessary* to protect the legitimate interests of the employer.

Point (b)

In addition to the legitimate business interest, the restriction must be narrowly enough tailored so that it is reasonably necessary to protect the interest of the employer. If an employer does not compete in a particular geographic area, enforcement of a covenant in that area is not reasonably necessary for the employer's protection. Any restriction that is *overly broad in geographic scope and duration* renders it unenforceable, and courts have the authority to either pare back the restriction or to set it aside entirely.

Except (b1)

"In determining reasonableness of scope and duration, we must balance the interest the employer seeks to protect against the important interest of the employee in being able to earn a living in her chosen profession. The court finds that neither the time limitations, nor the territorial scope of the agreement are overly broad or unreasonable. Furthermore, although the noncompete clause covers five states in scope, such restriction is reasonable given the *regional nature* of their current hospital clientele. In this case, the restrictions are narrowly tailored to be limited only to certain providers within that region."

Held

In favor of AAI. AAI's restrictive covenants in its employment agreements were reasonably related to AAI's business interests and were not overly broad.

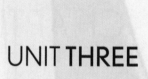

UNIT THREE

Regulation in the Workplace

10

CHAPTER

Agency and Employment Relationships

learning outcomes **checklist**

After studying this chapter, students who have mastered the material will be able to:

10-1   Recognize, define, and give examples of an agency relationship.

10-2   Classify agents as either employees or independent contractors by applying the direction and control tests.

10-3   Explain the process for creating an agency relationship and the impact of that relationship on the liability of the principal.

10-4   List the sources of an agent's authority to bind the principal in contract and give examples of each source.

10-5   Apply the doctrine of respondeat superior and identify its impact and limits.

10-6   Define the duties that collectively comprise a fiduciary obligation owed by the agent to the principal.

10-7   Articulate the duties owed by a principal to the agent and to third parties.

10-8   List the two primary methods used to terminate agency relationships and give examples of each method.

10-9   Recognize the dangers of the principal failing to notify third parties of an agent's termination.

10-10 Explain the employment-at-will doctrine, its primary exceptions, and give an example of each exception.

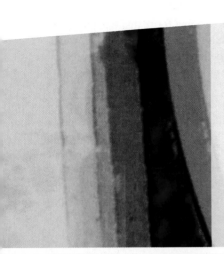

Agency relationships are fundamental to the business environment because they set out rules and standards for when one party hires another party to act on the hiring party's behalf. Business owners and managers that understand the obligations and liabilities of such a relationship are in a favorable position to limit their company's liability to both the hired party and third parties. Understanding **agency law** is also a crucial first step to understanding laws that govern rights, duties, and obligations between employers and employees.

In this chapter, students will learn:

- The definition, categories, and sources of law that govern agency relationships.

- Liabilities, duties, and obligations that are created by an agency relationship.

- Agency laws that govern certain aspects of employment relationships.

LO10-1 DEFINITIONS AND SOURCES OF AGENCY LAW

Agency is a legal relationship in which the parties agree, in some form, that one party will act as an **agent** for another party, called the **principal,** subject to the control of the principal. Agency relationships are common and essential in the business environment and exist in a variety of forms. A common form of agency is in an employer–employee relationship, but there are other important forms of agency as well.

In all agency relationships, the principal authorizes the agent to provide services or accomplish some task on behalf of the principal and under the principal's charge. Understanding agency law also requires one to be aware of (1) legal requirements for *creating* an agency, (2) *liability* of a principal for the agent's conduct, and (3) *duties* and obligations of the parties. The principal and agent may be either individuals or entities (such as a corporation). Agency law generally exists on the state statutory level and is based on the ***Restatements (Second) of Agency.***[1] Some states have also retained some common law doctrines of agency that operate in tandem with the statutes.

LO10-2 CLASSIFICATION OF AGENTS

Agents are classified into one of three broad categories: (1) *employee agents,* (2) *independent contractor agents,* or (3) *gratuitous agents.* Understanding these categories is important for business owners and managers primarily because the liability of the principal for acts of the agent depends on the agency relationship between the principal, the agent, and any relevant third parties.

Employee Agents

Individual employees who are authorized to transact business on behalf of the employer/principal are called **employee agents.** Principals are liable for the actions or omissions (such as negligence) of employee agents. However, it is important to understand that not every employee is an agent. In order to be classified as an employee agent, the employee must have some source of authority to represent the employer. The nonagent employee relationship is sometimes referred to as the *master/servant relationship* in order to distinguish it from an employer/employee agent relationship. For example, at the local branch of Mega Bank, the teller is an employee agent of Mega Bank who is authorized to conduct certain limited transactions (such as cashing a check) on Mega Bank's behalf. The branch manager at Mega Bank is also an employee agent, and her agency is likely wider in scope to include approval of small business loans and similar transactions. The security guard at the local branch is also an employee, but is not an employee agent in the sense that the guard does not have authority to transact business on Mega Bank's behalf. Therefore, the guard could be characterized as the servant in a master/servant relationship.

By contrast, an **independent contractor agent** is not considered an employee and has no legal protections of employees such as minimum wage and overtime compensation laws. An equally important factor is that the principal generally has no liability for actions and omissions of an independent contractor agent. In the business environment, professional service providers such as attorneys, outside accountants, and architects are all examples of independent contractors.

Agents who act on behalf of a principal without receiving any compensation are called **gratuitous agents.** To take a simple example, if you ask your roommate to pick up your laundry on your behalf as a favor, he is your gratuitous agent. In most respects, the rights and duties of a gratuitous agents are the same as those of paid agents except that the duty of

---

[1]Recall from Chapter 1 that the American Law Institute promulgates the *Restatements.* It should be noted that the ALI has published the *Restatements (Third) of Agency;* however, no state has adopted its provisions. Therefore, all references to the *Restatements* in this textbook are to *Restatements (Second) of Agency.*

Business owners and managers depend on their agents to help carry out business operations.

care applicable to the gratuitous agent is not as great (an agent's duty of care is discussed later in this chapter).

Employee Agents versus Independent Contractors: Direction and Control

Although the parties themselves may agree to a certain classification, the status of an agent is based not on what the parties agreed to, but is instead determined by the *actual* working relationship between principal and agent. Courts apply the *substance over form*[2] analysis to determine the classification of an agent. Fundamentally, the agent is classified based on the amount of *direction and control* that the principal has over the agent in terms of setting the agent's work schedule, pay rate, and the level of day-to-day supervision required. In an employer–employee agent relationship, the employer/principal typically sets work hours, decides what salary to pay, and exercises control over the employee agent's working conditions and responsibilities. Independent contractors usually work based on a deadline, but typically choose their own schedule to accomplish that deadline. In terms of payment, independent contractors usually send an invoice on a monthly basis (sometimes longer) for services rendered rather than drawing a weekly or biweekly paycheck. Courts also use other criteria for determining the status of an agent that focus on the nature of the agent's duties. For example, an *independent occupation/ profession* where the agent has more than one customer/client (e.g., accountants, attorneys, architects) indicates an independent contactor. On the other hand, if the principal

> ### KEY POINT
> The agent is classified based on the amount of *direction and control* that the principal has over the agent in terms of setting a work schedule, pay rate, and day-to-day supervision requirements.

---

[2]Recall that the substance over form standard is the equitable maxim discussed in Chapter 1, "Legal Foundations," whereby courts look to the intent of the parties involved and adhere to a standard of good faith and fair play instead of applying a technical and superficial standard or the parties' subjective intent.

provides tools or heavy equipment to the agent at the workplace, this generally indicates that the agent is an employee.

IRS's Three-Prong Test   Because so many questions regarding agency status occur in an employment tax context (e.g., is the employer liable to pay legally mandated employment taxes on a certain worker?), the Internal Revenue Service (IRS) has devised a three-prong test to determine an agent's status. While this test is not binding on courts, some appellate courts cite it as a useful tool in determining an agent's classification.[3] The IRS considers:

- *Behavioral* aspects of the agency. (Does the company control what the worker does and how the worker does the job assigned?)
- The *financial arrangements* between principal and agent. (Are the business aspects of the worker's job controlled by the payer?)
- The type of *working relationship* the parties had in terms of benefits and promises of continuing employment.

The consequences of a business owner or manager misclassifying an employee can be severe. For example, suppose that Computer Warehouse Corporation (CWC) classifies five computer programmers as independent contractors even though CWC sets their schedule and supervises the work product. This continues for one year until the IRS audits CWC and determines that the programmers were actually employees. The IRS will then assess CWC back employment taxes, plus a penalty for the wrongful classification, plus interest owed to the government for the one-year period. Depending on the salaries and the length of time the employees were misclassified, the amount due could exceed several hundred thousand dollars of unplanned tax liability. This would also likely be followed by a Department of Labor audit to determine compliance with federal labor and wage statutes.

In Case 10.1, a state appellate court applies a substance over form analysis to determine the classification of an agent. The case accentuates the importance of understanding these classifications because misclassification can be costly to businesses.

 Self-Check   Agency Classification

What is More's agency classification?

1. More, an author, is hired by Henry VIII Publications to write a book tentatively titled *Utopia*. The parties agree that More will be paid a lump sum of $50,000 when the book is complete and that the manuscript will be due in six months.

2. More is hired by Henry to work as a computer consultant. The parties agree that More will be on-site at Henry's office on Mondays from 9:00 a.m. to 5:00 p.m., for eight consecutive weeks and he will be paid each week upon a receipt of an invoice by Henry's bookkeeper. More has eight other clients.

3. More is hired by Henry to work as a sales associate for his retail-clothing store. The parties agree that More will work at the store Monday through Friday from 10:00 a.m. to 6:00 p.m. at a rate of $9.00 per hour plus a 15 percent commission on merchandise sold by More.

4. More is Henry's neighbor and agrees to do him a favor by transporting Henry's valuable rare coin collection to a local trade show.

5. More is hired by Henry to make telemarketing calls for Henry's media company. The parties enter into a written agreement named "Independent Contractor Agreement" in which both

---

[3]This three-prong approach replaced the IRS's notorious 20-point test in 1997. The IRS specifically disclaims the 20-point test and takes the position that there is "no magic or set number of factors that makes the worker an employee or an independent contractor."

parties agree that More will be an independent agent. Henry sets More's schedule and pays him $1,000 every other week plus a $500 bonus every year during the holiday season. More uses equipment owned by the media company.

6. More, a professional athlete, is hired by Henry, the owner of a major league baseball franchise, to play baseball at an annual salary of $1 million. More's contract requires that he show up for all off-season camps, practices, and games for the entire length of the event. If he fails to show up, he agrees to reduction in pay via a fine. More is paid every other week, and Henry pays for More's health and retirement benefits.

Answers to this Self-Check are provided at the end of the chapter.

CASE 10.1 Estrada v. FedEx Ground Package System, Inc., 64 Cal. Rptr. 3d 327 (2007)

FACT SUMMARY All employees who were hired by Federal Express (FedEx) as long-haul delivery drivers were required to sign an operating agreement that identified the driver as an independent contractor. Under the terms of the agreement, the driver would provide his own truck, mark the truck with the FedEx logo, pay all costs of operating and maintaining the truck, and use the truck exclusively in the service of FedEx along with other specific obligations. The drivers brought a class action suit contending that, for the purpose of their entitlement to reimbursement for work-related expenses, they were employees, not independent contractors. The trial court ruled in favor of the drivers, awarding $5.3 million to misclassified employees. FedEx appealed.

SYNOPSIS OF DECISION AND OPINION The Court of Appeals of California affirmed the judgment in favor of the drivers, holding that the trial court correctly determined that the drivers were FedEx employees, not independent contractors, and that their expenses should have been reimbursed. The court applied a substance-over-form test of employment versus independent contractor and noted that FedEx exercised extensive control over the drivers' work schedules and mandated a standard pay rate for all similarly situated drivers. Based on the level of direction and control, the drivers should have been classified as employees.

WORDS OF THE COURT: Direction and Control "Because the California Labor Code does not expressly define 'employee' . . . the common law test of employment applies. The essence of the test is the control of details—that is, whether the principal has

the right to control the manner and means by which the worker accomplishes the work—but there are a number of additional factors in the modern equation, including (1) whether the worker is engaged in a distinct occupation or business, (2) whether, considering the kind of occupation and locality, the work is usually done under the principal's direction or by a specialist without supervision, (3) the skill required, (4) whether the principal or worker supplies the instrumentalities, tools, and place of work, (5) the length of time for which the services are to be performed, (6) the method of payment, whether by time or by job, (7) whether the work is part of the principal's regular business, and (8) whether the parties believe they are creating an employer–employee relationship. The parties' label is not dispositive and will be ignored if their actual conduct establishes a different relationship [. . .] Because [FedEx] company's drivers worked full time, were paid weekly, had regular schedules and regular routes, received many standard employee benefits, wore uniforms, used company-specific scanners and forms, and were required to work exclusively for the company, substantial evidence supported the trial court's finding that the drivers were employees and not independent contractors."

Case Questions

1. Based on the court's opinion, is there any way for FedEx to change their practices so that the drivers would be classified as independent contractors?

2. What are the future implications for FedEx and other businesses based on the appellate court's ruling? What additional expenses may FedEx incur as a result? Explain.

Classification of Workers

PROBLEM *While some agent classifications are clear, as the global economy evolves and new positions and types of occupations are created, managers face the difficult choice of classification without the benefit of clear guidelines from previous court cases or IRS rulings. If misclassified, the tax liability incurred may be substantial.*

SOLUTION *File IRS Form SS-8.*

Form SS-8 was created by the IRS to assist business owners and managers in complying with tax regulations regarding independent contractor status. Filing the form gives the principal/employer assurances that either (1) the classification by the employer is correct, or (2) that the classification needs to be changed and that similar positions in the future should be classified in the same way. The other benefit to filing the form is that it may be evidence of good faith efforts to comply with the tax law. If the IRS determines that the principal/employer made a good faith mistake in classifying the agent, no penalty is imposed. If the IRS regards the principal/employer's classification as reckless or made without requisite good faith compliance efforts, penalties and interest are added to the assessment of back taxes.*

*Note that any intent, in any context, to purposefully (intentionally) evade tax due is also a criminal offense.

LO10-3 OVERVIEW OF AN AGENCY TRANSACTION

Before delving into the individual components of agency law, it is important to understand the function of an agency transaction from a larger perspective. Fundamentally, an agency transaction involves one party hiring another party to transact business on behalf of (or perform a task for) the hiring party. In a business context, this relationship is crucial because business owners and managers depend on agents to carry out the daily operations of the business.

Business owners and managers use agents to enter into contracts, perform necessary services, and advance its objectives in various ways. First, an agency relationship is typically created expressly by the parties with the duties of the agent being set out by the principal. Second, the parties perform their respective duties in accordance with their agreement and agency law. Finally, an agency transaction is ended by the termination of the agency by the parties. In some cases, the agency is terminated by operation of law (e.g., the principal hires the agent to paint a building, but the building is destroyed by fire before the agent begins to paint). Table 10.1 provides an overview of an agency transaction.

TABLE 10.1 Agency Transaction Overview

Creation of Agency	Performance of Obligations and Duties	Termination of Agency
Principal wishes to form agency and agent consents.	Agent performs as agreed and in accordance with fiduciary obligations. Principal's primary obligation is payment of the agent.	Express act of parties or operation of law.

Creation of an Agency Relationship

The *Restatements* define the creation of an agency relationship in terms of *consent* and *control*. Specifically, agency is described as a *fiduciary* relationship that results from manifestations of consent by the principal to the agent to act on the principal's behalf subject to her control. The agent must also give consent to perform the act.

Manifestations and Consent   The first step in creating an agency relationship is for the principal to **manifest** some offer to form an agency. **Consent** occurs when an agent agrees to act for the principal. In order to determine whether the parties have in fact manifested an offer of agency and acceptance by the agent, courts apply an objective standard. That is, given the parties *outward expressions,* actions, and words, would a reasonable person believe that the principal intended for an agency to be created and that the agent did in fact consent to the agency relationship? Courts do not look to the subjective intent of the parties as definitive. Rather, courts use the *objective* standard of what a reasonable person would have concluded about the manifestations and consent in the context of the relationship between the parties.

Control   In addition to consent, the parties must have an understanding that the principal is in control of the agency relationship. The control need not be total or continuous and need not extend to the way the agent performs, but there must be some sense that the principal is defining the tasks and objectives of the agency relationship.

Overlay of Agency Law with Other Areas of Law

Note that the law of agency often overlays and interacts with other areas of the law, especially contracts and torts. It is important to understand that several areas of law may all be operating in tandem during a given transaction, but that each area regulates a different aspect of the transaction. For example, although agency itself is not a contractual relationship, the parties to an agency often enter into contracts to accomplish a particular objective. While the contract governs the *terms* of performance for the parties, agency law governs the agent's authority to *bind* the principal to a third party. Contract law does not displace agency law. Rather, the two areas of the law operate together. This is also true concerning torts such as negligence. While negligence law guides us in defining what constitutes an act of negligence and provides defenses, agency law governs whether or not the *principal* is liable for any alleged negligence of the agent.

Legal Speak »))
Fiduciary Relationship
A broad term embracing the notion that two parties may agree that one will act for another party's benefit with a high level of integrity and good faith in carrying out the best interests of the represented party.

CONCEPT SUMMARY   Overview of Agency Law

- Agency is a legal relationship in which the parties agree, in some form, that one party will act as an agent for another party, called the principal, subject to the control of the principal.
- Agency law generally exists on the state statutory level and is based on the *Restatements (Second) of Agency.*
- The agent is classified, applying a substance-over-form analysis, as either an employee or an independent contractor based on the amount of direction and control that the principal has over the agent in terms of setting a work schedule, pay rate, and day-to-day supervision.
- Liability of a principal for any acts or omissions of the agent and regulation by federal and state labor laws are related to the relationship between the principal, the agent, and any relevant third party.
- The law of agency operates in tandem with other areas of the law, especially contracts and torts.

LO10-4 LIABILITY OF THE PRINCIPAL FOR ACTS OF THE AGENT

One of the most important aspects of agency law involves understanding the ways in which actions of an agent result in liability for the principal. For agency purposes, liability can arise either through a *contract* obligation or through vicarious liability (liability for another) in *tort.* Therefore, when a third party claims that the principal is liable for an agent's act, he is asserting that the principal is responsible for any legal consequences of that act (such as damages or losses suffered by the third party).

Authority

Creation of an agency relationship typically involves the agent's power to *bind* the principal to third parties (and third parties to the principal) in an agreement of some type. The power to bind the principal in a certain transaction is derived from the agent's *authority.* This authority arises primarily through one of three ways. The primary sources of an agent's power are (1) *actual authority,* (2) *apparent authority,* and (3) *ratification.*

Actual Authority   Typically, an agent's power to bind is through **actual authority** when the parties either expressly agree to create an agency relationship, or where the authority is *implied* based on custom or course of past dealings. For example, the president of a corporation is thought of as having implied powers to bind the corporation to virtually all contracts that she determines are in the best interest of the corporation. The president need not obtain express approval from the board of directors for day-to-day transactions (although the president may be required by statute or by virtue of the organization's bylaws to obtain approval from the board prior to entering into certain contracts, such as when signing a contract to sell all or most of the company's assets and other major decisions).[4]

Apparent Authority   An agent may also gain power to bind the principal from the *appearance* of legitimate authority to a third party, known as **apparent authority.** Determining whether an agent has apparent authority can be difficult because it is a source of power that is not expressly authorized by the principal. The key to understanding this power is to determine if a *third party* was objectively *reasonable* in her belief that the apparent agent is in fact authorized to act for the principal.[5] Apparent authority arises from the actions of a principal that lead a third party to believe that an agent has the authority to act on the principal's behalf. In Case 10.2, a state appellate court considered the creation of apparent authority in the context of settlement negotiations in a lawsuit.

Ratification   An agent can also have retroactive (after the fact) power to bind through **ratification.** Ratification occurs when the principal affirms a previously unauthorized act. That is, even though the agent did not have the authority to bind the principal initially, the principal may subsequently give after-the-fact authority by either (1) expressly ratifying the transactions, or (2) not *repudiating* the act by retaining the benefits while knowing that the benefits resulted from an unauthorized act by the agent. For example, suppose that Manager is the general manager of an apartment complex and is the agent of Owner. After a series of burglaries, Manager hires InstallCo. to install an expensive burglar alarm system in the complex. InstallCo. has never done business with Manager previously, but allowed him to sign an alarm services contract as Owner's agent. During the week-long installation, Owner notices the workers on the site and asks Manager to fill him in on the details. It is at this point where the authority is either ratified or disclaimed. Owner never expressly

---

[4]The authority of officers to bind a corporation is discussed in detail in Chapter 15, "Corporations."

[5]*Restatements (Second) of Agency,* § 27.

FACT SUMMARY Hannington, a graduate student at the University of Pennsylvania (Penn), brought suit against the university for breach of contract. Attorneys for both sides appeared to have reached a settlement when, just prior to trial, Hannington's attorney notified the court that a settlement had been reached and sent Penn a final draft of the settlement agreement. Penn agreed to the settlement terms and sent the settlement agreement back to Hannington's attorney with Penn's authorized signatures. However, Hannington refused to sign the settlement agreement, hired a new attorney, and opted to proceed to trial. The trial court refused to allow Hannington's case to go forward and held that Hannington's attorney had apparent authority to settle the case and Penn had reasonably relied on Hannington's attorney as being an agent authorized to settle the case. Hannington appealed.

SYNOPSIS OF DECISION AND OPINION The Superior Court of Pennsylvania affirmed the trial court's decision and ruled in favor of Penn. The court held that under the doctrine of apparent authority, the innocent party, Penn, was entitled to rely on counsel's representations where they reasonably believed that Hannington's attorney had the authority to settle the case. Negotiations were ongoing for six months, so Penn had reason to believe that Hannington's attorney was in fact authorized to act for Hannington. Any subsequent dispute about settlement terms was between Hannington and his attorney and should not affect Penn.

WORDS OF THE COURT: Apparent Authority "The doctrine of apparent authority permits a settlement agreement to be enforced where a third party reasonably believes that the principal's lawyer, the agent, has the authority to settle the case even though the lawyer fraudulently represents that he has such authority. [. . .] The fact that an agent has wronged his principal does not insulate the principal vis-à-vis an innocent third party who had no responsibility for the agent's conduct. [. . .] The doctrine of apparent authority applies to permit a settlement agreement to be enforced where a third party reasonably believes that the principal's lawyer, the agent, has the authority to settle the case, even where the lawyer does not have express authority to settle. [. . .] The Pennsylvania Superior Court will not presume that members of the Bar will disregard the requirement that they must obtain their clients' express consent prior to settling a case."

Case Questions

1. Suppose that in the middle of settlement negotiations, Hannington becomes frustrated with the impasse. He hires his neighbor, another attorney not yet involved in the case, to draft a settlement agreement and sends it to Penn. Is apparent authority created in this circumstance? Explain.

2. Since Hannington never actually signed the agreement, was it reasonable for Penn to assume that Hannington's attorney had obtained his express consent to the terms? Has the court effectively deprived Hannington of his right to proceed to trial?

---

gave Manager authority to contract with InstallCo. and, given the expense, nature of the contract, and a lack of past dealing, it is unlikely that any implied or apparent authority exists. Nonetheless, Owner may be pleased with the Manager's decision and *ratify* (affirm) the transaction. Owner also ratifies the transaction if he does *nothing to disaffirm* the transaction (such as stopping InstallCo. from continuing work), because Owner is still reaping the benefits of what he knows to have been an unauthorized transaction. Thus, if Owner learns of the transaction, says nothing, and receives the benefits, he may not now refuse to honor the contract on the basis that Manager lacked the agency power to bind Owner to a contract with InstallCo.

Contract Liability to Third Parties

An authorized agent who enters into a contract with a third party binds the principal to perform certain obligations and the third party may legally enforce the contract against the principal. However, there are also circumstances in which the *agent* may also be held liable to perform the contract in the event that the principal refuses to perform. An agent's liability to third parties in a contract hinges on whether the agency relationship is *fully disclosed, partially disclosed,* or *undisclosed.*

Fully Disclosed Agency

When the third party entering into the contract is aware of the identity of the principal and knows that the agent is acting on behalf of the principal in the transaction, then the agency relationship is a **fully disclosed agency.** In a fully disclosed agency relationship, only the principal is contractually obligated to the third party. Because the agent has no liability, third parties have no legal recourse against the agent if the principal fails to meet her obligations under the contract. For example, suppose that Abel is hired by Peters to locate and purchase a suitable piece of real estate for Peters's new warehouse. Abel locates the property and enters into a contract to purchase the property from Thompson. Abel signs the contract *"Abel, as agent for Peters."* In this case, if Peters changes his mind and decides not to complete the transaction, Abel has no liability because his agency was fully disclosed. Thompson's sole remedy is to pursue a breach of contract lawsuit against Peters.

Partially Disclosed Agency

If the third party knows that the agent is representing a principal, but does not know the *actual identity* of the principal, the agency relationship is a **partially disclosed agency.** In some cases, the agent may identify the principal only as an "interested real estate buyer" or by some other generic terminology. In a partially disclosed agency relationship, both the principal and the agent may be liable for the obligations under the contract.[6] Because the principal is not identified, the third party must rely on the agent's good faith dealings and credit. Therefore, the law imposes liability on the agent in the event that the principal does not perform her contractual obligations. For example, suppose in the Abel–Peters–Thompson transaction that Peters was a high profile real-estate developer and he hires Abel to purchase Thompson's land on Peters's behalf. Peters believes that Thompson may hold out for a higher price if he knows that the buyer is a wealthy land developer, so he instructs Abel not to make his identity known when entering into the real estate purchase contract with Thompson. Although Thompson is aware that Abel is an agent, he is not aware of the principal's identity. Abel signs the contract without any indication that Peters is the principal. If Peters later changes his mind and refuses to perform under the contract, Thompson may pursue remedies against Abel and/or Peters. If Thompson is successful in his case against Abel, Abel has the right of indemnification from Peters.

Legal Speak ›))
Indemnification Right of reimbursement from another for a loss suffered due to a third party's act or default.

Undisclosed Agency

When a third party is completely unaware that an agency relationship exists and believes that the agent is acting on her own behalf in entering a contract, this is called an **undisclosed agency.** In an undisclosed agency relationship, the agent is fully liable to perform the contract. Because the third party has no reason to know that an agency exists, he relies on the agent's good faith dealings and credit. Therefore, the law imposes liability on the agent in the event that the principal does not perform the contractual obligations. For example, suppose in the Abel–Peters–Thompson transaction that Peters was a high profile real-estate developer and he hires Abel to purchase Thompson's land on Peters's behalf. Peters believes that Thompson may hold out for a higher price if he knows that the buyer is a wealthy land developer. Moreover, Peters is sufficiently confident in his belief that his identity will drive up the price that he takes extraordinary efforts to keep his interest in the property confidential. He instructs Abel not to inform Thompson of his status as an agent and to enter into the real estate purchase

---

[6]*Restatements (Second) of Agency,* § 321.

contract with Thompson in Abel's individual name. Since Thompson is not aware that Abel is an agent, nor is he aware of the principal's identity, this is an *undisclosed agency* relationship. Therefore, if Peters later changes his mind and refuses to perform under the contract, Thompson may pursue remedies against Abel. In some states, if Thompson subsequently finds out that Peters is the actual principal, he may purse legal remedies against Peters as well. In any case, if Abel is made to pay, Abel has the right to indemnification from Peters.

Tort Liability to Third Parties

LO10-5

In some cases, a principal may be held liable for an agent's tort, most commonly the tort of negligence, even though the principal has not engaged in any wrongful conduct. This is particularly true when the agent is an employee. For example, suppose Pep's Pizza Parlor employs a driver to deliver their products. On the way to a delivery, the driver is negligent and injures a pedestrian. Pep's is held liable for damages suffered by the pedestrian even though they exercised all due care (checking the driver's record before hiring him, etc.). Liability for principals of agents that are classified as employees is derived from the doctrine of **respondeat superior.**[7] Note that respondeat superior also holds employer's liable for negligent acts of both employee-agents and nonagent employees. This is a form of *vicarious liability* because it involves one party's liability for the act of another party. However, principals are generally *not liable* for negligent acts of agents that are independent contractors. This question of liability is yet another reason why correct classification of agents by business owners and managers is crucial to controlling risk.

Scope of Employment

The doctrine of respondeat superior is limited by a requirement that in order for a principal (employer) to be liable for the employee's tort, the act must have occurred within the employee's *scope of employment.* Respondeat superior is a powerful tool for injured third parties because it allows the party to recover damages from the employer under the assumption that the employer's resources and insurance coverage are more abundant than those of the employee/agent that committed the negligence. The scope of employment rule is an attempt to place some limitations on the principal's liability. Thus, in order for the principal to be liable, the agent's tortious conduct must have (1) been related to her duties as an employee of the principal, (2) occurred substantially within the reasonable time and space limits, and (3) been motivated, in part, by a purpose to serve the principal.

In Case 10.3, a state appellate court applies the scope of employment rule in a case where an employee-agent committed an act of negligence while performing employment-related duties outside of the traditional workplace.

Frolics and Detours

The other exception to the respondeat superior doctrine is when an agent, during a normal workday, does something purely for her own reasons that are unrelated to employment. During this time, the employee's conduct is thought of as outside of the zone that is governed by respondeat superior. The law recognizes this activity, called a **frolic,** as a protection for the principal against any harm suffered as a result of an agent's negligence while on the frolic. The frolic exception is sometimes thorny to apply because

Legal Speak ›))
Vicarious liability
Liability that a supervisory party (typically an employer) bears for the actionable conduct of a subordinate or associate (such as an employee).

> **KEY POINT**
> The doctrine of respondeat superior stands for the proposition that a principal (employer) is liable for the servant/agent's (employee) tort when that act resulted in some physical harm or injury and occurred within the employee's *scope of employment.*

---

[7]Literal Latin translation, "let the master answer," *Collins Latin* (2008).

FACT SUMMARY Gatzke was employed as a district manager for Walgreen Company (Walgreen*) when he was assigned to supervise the opening and preliminary operations of a new Walgreen-owned restaurant in Duluth, Minnesota. This assignment required Walgreen to pay for Gatzke's temporary housing close to the new site. While on the Duluth assignment, Gatzke lived at the nearby Edgewater Motel for a period of several weeks. He used his motel room as a makeshift office and would use the desk in the room for routine paperwork including expense reports. Gatzke was a management-level salaried employee and, therefore, had no set work schedule.

On one workday, Gatzke and several employees had spent the entire day on-site at the new restaurant and then had a business dinner there until approximately midnight. Afterward, Gatzke and one of his colleagues went to a bar where they continued their discussion concerning the new restaurant over several cocktails in the span of one and one-half hours. Gatzke then returned to his motel room and began to fill out his expense report. The evidence showed that Gatzke accidentally dropped a lit cigarette in the trash can next to the desk in his room while filling out the reports. This started a fire, and although Gatzke escaped unharmed, the motel was severely damaged by the ensuing fire. Among other defendants, Edgewater sued Walgreen claiming that they were vicariously liable for the acts of Gatzke as its employee agent. Walgreen countered that Gatzke's negligent smoking was well outside the scope of his employment and they cannot be held liable for the damages he caused.

SYNOPSIS OF DECISION AND OPINION The Minnesota Supreme Court ruled in favor of Edgewater and held that Gatzke's act of smoking was within his scope of employment under the circumstances. The court pointed to the chain of events that led to the negligence and concluded that in this context, Gatzke's actions, including the dinner meeting, the discussions over cocktails, and the filling out of the expense report, were all in furtherance of Walgreen's business. Short personal interruptions, such as smoking, do not necessarily take the employee agent outside of his scope of employment.

WORDS OF THE COURT: Scope of Employment "The question of whether smoking can be within an employee's scope of employment is a close one, but after careful consideration of the issue we are persuaded by the reasoning of other courts which hold that smoking can be an act within an employee's scope of employment. It seems only logical to conclude that an employee does not abandon his employment as a matter of law while temporarily acting for his personal comfort when such activities involve only slight deviations from work that are reasonable under the circumstances, such as eating, drinking, or smoking.

A mere deviation by an employee from the strict course of his duty does not release his employer from liability. An employee does not cease to be acting within the course of his employment because of an incidental personal act, or by slight deflections for a personal or private purpose, if his main purpose is still to carry on the business of his employer."

Case Questions

1. If the evidence showed that Gratzke had intentionally tried to commit arson, how would that impact the court's analysis?

2. Suppose that Gratzke had been writing out personal postcards and not been filling out an expense report when he started the fire. Would Walgreen still be liable?

*No connection to the national drugstore chain Walgreens.

---

the precise time when the frolic began and when it ended can be a difficult determination. Moreover, if the conduct is a small-scale deviation that is normally expected in the workday, that is not considered a frolic, but rather a simple **detour.** Detours are still within the ambit of respondeat superior. Courts use a case-by-case approach to applying the frolic doctrine because the conduct is judged based on the degree to which it is or is not within the scope of employment. To understand the difference between frolic and detour, consider two alternative hypothetical cases.

Flash is employed by Apollo Messenger Service as the driver of their delivery van. During his workday, he is speeding in the delivery van and negligently injures a pedestrian. Suppose that at the time of the accident, Flash was on his lunch break and driving the van to the local stadium in order to purchase tickets for his family to a ball game to be played that night. In this case, a court will likely rule that Apollo is not liable under respondeat superior because of the frolic exception. Alternatively, suppose that Flash was on his way to pick up a cup of coffee at the local coffee shop and he struck the pedestrian in the parking lot. The coffee stop would likely be considered a detour. Although not acting for the employer, the negligence would likely be imputed to Apollo because Flash made only a short stop that constituted a small-scale deviation from employment duties. Because it can reasonably be expected that delivery van drivers will take short breaks during the workday, a court may find that Apollo is liable for Flash's conduct under respondeat superior.

Intentional Torts Generally, intentional torts by an agent (such as committing an assault in the workplace) are thought to be outside the scope of employment and, therefore, employers are not liable for such conduct unless the assault has a close connection to serving the principal. In a well-known decision on this topic, a state supreme court ruled that a sales associate employed by Nabisco who had assaulted the manager of a store in his territory was acting within his scope of employment because the original dispute involved shelf space at the store where the assault took place. The court held that because the agent/employee was in the store on Nabisco business, and the assault stemmed from his job as a sales associate, that even an intentional tort such as battery could be covered by respondeat superior.[8] Thus, even unauthorized acts by an agent do not necessarily exempt the conduct from liability for the principal.

Negligent Hiring Doctrine

A majority of states recognize a tort-based theory of liability for employers for negligent or intentional torts of employees when the employer had *reason to know* that the employee may cause harm within his scope of employment. This liability theory is called the **negligent hiring doctrine** and it requires employers to take reasonable steps (such as criminal background investigation and reference checks) in protecting third parties, particularly customers and other employees, from harm at the hands of an employee. Courts are especially inclined to hold employers liable under this doctrine in cases where (1) its employees are required to have a high level of public contact such as service and maintenance personnel, real estate agents, or delivery persons; or (2) employees are entrusted with caring for the sick, elderly, or other particularly vulnerable populations.

Negligent hiring occurs when, prior to the time the employee is actually hired, the employer knew or should have known of the employee's unfitness.[9] Liability generally focuses on the employer's methods for determining suitability for the position. For example, in *Abbot v. Payne*[10] a state appellate court in Florida held the owners of a pest control company liable for negligent hiring when the company's management failed to run a criminal background check on an employee who subsequently sexually assaulted a customer

---

[8]*Lange v. National Biscuit Company,* 211 N.W.2d 783 (Mn. 1973).

[9]*Restatements (Second) of Agency,* §§ 401–411.

[10]457 So. 2d 435 (Fla. App. 1984).

during a home service call. The employee had a record of multiple arrests for sexually related crimes, and the court found that the employer had a duty to screen the employee for any information that indicated that the employee should not have been placed in a position of trust with regular access to customer information and regular contact with the public on the employer's behalf. The doctrine also includes *negligent retention* if circumstances arose *after* the hiring process that should have given notice to the employer of a potential for an employee to cause harm.

Independent Contractors Recall from earlier in this chapter that, as a general rule, principals are not liable for the negligent acts or omissions of an independent contractor agent. One important exception to this rule is when the principal has been negligent in hiring and is based on the *peculiar risk doctrine* that is rooted in the *Restatements*. The doctrine requires a principal to take reasonable steps to determine the fitness of an independent contractor agent to perform an inherently dangerous task. For example, a land developer that hires a demolition company to take down a large old building with dynamite has a legal obligation to ensure that the demolition company has reasonable safety measures in place, experienced personnel, and proper safety licensing and permitting, and so on.

CONCEPT SUMMARY   Principal and Agent Liability to Third Parties

Contracts		
Agency Relationship	**Liability of Principal to Third Party**	**Liability of Agent to Third Party**
Fully disclosed (third party knew of agency relationship and identity of principal).	Full liability to perform contract obligations.	None (so long as agent did not exceed scope of authority).
Partially disclosed (third party knew of agency relationship, but not the identity of the principal).	Full liability to perform contract obligations.	Full liability to perform contract obligations if the principal fails to meet contractual obligations. If agent is made to pay, she is entitled to reimbursement (indemnification) from principal.
Undisclosed (third party had no reason to know that any agency relationship existed).	Full liability to perform contract obligations.	Full liability to perform contract obligations if the principal fails to meet contractual obligations. If agent is made to pay, she is entitled to reimbursement (indemnification) from principal.

Torts		
Type of Tort	Liability of Principal to Third Party	Liability of Agent to Third Party
Intentional torts of employees	No liability unless the act was directly tied to employee's responsibilities.	Fully liable to third party for damages or losses.
Intentional torts of independent contractor	No liability.	Fully liable to third party for damages or losses.
Negligence of employees	Vicariously liable under doctrine of respondeat superior for acts of all employees (including employee agents and employee servants) that resulted from harm within the employee's scope of employment.	Fully liable to third party for damages or losses.
Negligence of independent contractors	No liability (except in cases of negligent hiring; see below).	Fully liable to third party for damages or losses.
Negligent hiring of employees	Vicariously liable to third party for damages or losses if employer could have foreseen possible harm by the employee through a determination of fitness for the position.	N/A
Negligent hiring of independent contractor	None except for when the principal hires a contractor for an inherently dangerous job that poses a peculiar risk.	N/A

DUTIES, OBLIGATIONS, AND REMEDIES OF THE PRINCIPAL AND AGENT

LO10-6, 10-7

Inherent in an agency relationship are certain duties and obligations of the parties. Agents owe duties to principals, and principals owe duties to agents. If either party fails to fulfill their duties and obligations, the law provides a remedy for the party suffering an injury or loss.

Agent's Duties to the Principal

The very essence of an agency relationship involves the creation of a duty for the agent to act in good faith and in the principal's best interest at all times. These duties are automatic and need not be agreed upon by the parties specifically. The duties that define an agency relationship are collectively called a *fiduciary* duty, which requires the agent to act according to higher standards than nonfiduciaries in a transaction. Fiduciary duty consists of five subduties: *loyalty, obedience, care, disclosure,* and *accounting.*

Loyalty   The duty of loyalty is the centerpiece of fiduciary obligation. The law requires that the agent hold the principal's objectives paramount. Except when the principal has knowingly agreed to the contrary or when extraordinary circumstances exist, the agent is obliged to advance the principal's interest over her own interests. The *Restatements* require the agent to act *solely* for the benefit of the principal in all matters connected with the agency. This also includes obligations of the agent to refrain from *self-dealing,* or to engage in any *competition* or *other conflicts of interest,* and to keep information about the principal and transaction *confidential.* For example, suppose that Jingle, a real estate agent, is hired by Landis to market and sell a parcel of land. Landis expects to sell the land for $100,000, but Jingle knows the property's value to be higher. Unknown to Landis, Jingle forms a partnership with two friends and buys the land at the discounted price. Jingle has breached his duty of loyalty to Landis by engaging in self-dealing (benefiting from the undervalued property) and a conflict of interest. Jingle cannot represent both sides (taking a commission from both buyer and seller) without express permission from Landis.

The duty of loyalty applies universally to all agents irrespective of the scope of the agency. Therefore, all employees owe a duty of loyalty to their employers, but the specific implications of the duty vary with the position the employee occupies. If a clerk at a chain of retail stores mentions to a customer that "business is slow," it is unlikely that the employee violated the duty of loyalty to keep business information confidential. However, if the company's chief financial officer mentions to a friend at a neighborhood block party that "the company's revenues are dropping like a stone" this may constitute a breach of loyalty by discussing confidential business information.

> **KEY POINT**
>
> The duty of loyalty is the centerpiece of fiduciary obligation: the agent is obliged to advance the principal's interest over her own interests.

Obedience An agent also has the duty to obey *lawful instructions* from the principal and cannot substitute her own judgment for the judgment of the principal (unless specifically authorized). Instructions from the principal are considered to be manifestations of the principal's objectives. Note that agents who are instructed to conduct unlawful activities do not breach the duty of obedience by refusing to perform the illegal conduct.

Care An agent has the duty to act with **due care** when conducting business on behalf the principal. This requires the agent to act in the same careful manner when conducting the principal's affairs as a reasonable person would use in conducting her own personal affairs. The duty of care standard is similar to the standard discussed in Chapter 9, "Torts and Products Liability," in the context of negligence; that is, the duty expands and contracts based on the circumstances of the case and the position of the parties. Those agents with specialized knowledge are held to a standard of care that is higher than nonspecialists.

Gratuitous Agents Recall from the beginning of this chapter that gratuitous agents are agents that are not compensated for their work. A gratuitous agent is held to a lower duty of care than a paid agent. In order for a gratuitous agent to breach his duty of care to the principal, he must have acted so recklessly that a reasonable person would regard the conduct as *grossly* negligent.

Disclosure Agents have an ongoing duty to keep the principal informed and disclose any and all relevant facts to the principal. This duty is based on the notion that because agents may bind principals, it is essential that the agent provide as much information as possible to the principal. This includes all phases of the relationship such as keeping the principal informed during negotiations of a transaction. The duty also includes the obligation to disclose any pertinent negatives. This means that the agent must also disclose that he has a lack of information about an important fact. For example, suppose that Buyer is interested in purchasing the assets of BigCo. and hires Agent to investigate the possibility of an acquisition and to determine the value of the company. Agent has an obligation to inform Buyer of any contact and information he may have about the transaction. Agent

Agents owe principals a duty to account for any money the agent spends or receives on the principal's behalf.

must also disclose the fact that he cannot verify the actual value of the assets and that his estimates are best guesses. The fact that Agent cannot verify actual value is a pertinent negative and must be disclosed.

Accounting   Unless the parties agree otherwise, the agent must keep appropriate written records for any money that the agent spends or receives in the course of the agent's representation. Known as the duty to **account,** this includes keeping records such as reimbursable expenses, checks or cash received on behalf of the principal, and any liabilities incurred in the course of the agent's conduct. The duty to account includes a prohibition against intermingling the principal's funds (or property) with the agent's own funds or possessions. For example, suppose that Penelope gives her agent, Julia, a check for $100,000 and instructs her to use it for a deposit on a warehouse that Penelope wishes to purchase for her business. Julia has a large personal tax bill that must be paid that same day, so she deposits the $100,000 in her personal account and writes a personal check to pay her tax bill using Penelope's money. She knows that her employment check will be arriving the next day, so she is confident that she will be able to pay the money back without Penelope's knowledge. Julia has breached her fiduciary duty by failing to keep a proper accounting through commingling the funds.[11]

 Self-Check   Fiduciary Duty

Which fiduciary duty, if any, was breached?

1. Dorian is an employee of Gray Industries. His roommate works for a competitor to Gray. Dorian photocopies Gray's customer list and information and gives it to his roommate.

2. Dorian is a stockbroker for the Gray Family Trust with express authority to buy and sell stocks for the trust. Dorian knows that stock in High Flyers Inc. is overpriced and does not promise solid returns. However, he buys the stock in High Flyers because his commission will be higher than for other stocks.

---

[11]Julia has also committed the criminal offense of embezzlement, which is discussed in detail in Chapter 22, "Criminal Law and Procedure in Business."

3. Gray hires Dorian to represent his interests as his agent in a business transaction and expressly instructs him not to sign any contracts with Grendel. Dorian attends a meeting and decides that a contract with Grendel would be a good deal for Gray. Dorian signs the contract on Gray's behalf.

4. Gray hires Dorian to sell widgets on Gray's behalf. Dorian accepts cash payments from Gray's customers, but places the cash in his personal bank account for safekeeping and forgets to keep a record of the payments.

Answers to this Self-Check are provided at the end of the chapter.

Principal's Remedies for Breach

If an agent's breach of duty to the principal causes damages to the principal, the principal may recover those damages by suing the agent for the breach. If an agent's breach of duty resulted in the principal's becoming liable to a third party, then the agent must indemnify and hold harmless the principal from any losses as a result of the liability.

Rescission and Disgorgement   If the agent breaches the duty of loyalty, the principal's remedies also include the ability to *rescind* any transaction between the principal and agent. A court may also order the agent to return any funds earned as a result of the breaching conduct (known as *disgorgement*). For example, suppose that Coleridge hires Wordsworth as an employee in Coleridge's Investment Banking firm. Unknown to Coleridge, Wordsworth launches a competing firm and uses Coleridge's client lists to develop business for his own firm. In fact, in the first year of Wordsworth's new firm, $100,000 in fees was from client lists belonging to Coleridge. Because Wordsworth breached his duty of loyalty, Coleridge is entitled not only to out-of-pocket losses and damages, but a court will also order disgorgement of Wordsworth's profits by ordering him to pay Coleridge $100,000 in addition to any other damages suffered by Coleridge as a result of Wordsworth's breach.

Duties and Obligations of the Principal to the Agent

When an agent acts on behalf of its principal, the agent may incur expenses, make payments, suffer an injury, or cause damages to third parties. In such cases, the principal has a duty to *reimburse and indemnify* its agents. This duty applies in the following cases:

■ Payments made or expenses incurred within the agent's *actual authority.*

■ Payments made by the agent for the principal's benefit, but done *without authority,* so long as the agent acted under a mistaken good faith belief that he had the authority to act.

■ Claims made by third parties on contracts entered into by an *authorized* agent and on the principal's behalf.

■ Claims made by third parties for torts allegedly committed by the agent if the agent's conduct was within the agent's actual authority, or the agent was unaware that the conduct was tortious.

The principal must provide the *costs* of a legal defense including attorneys' fees and any resulting liability settlement payment. In order to obtain the principal's protection, the agent must give the principal *reasonable notice* of the claim and *cooperate* with the principal in managing the defense (e.g., by appearing as a witness).

However, a principal does *not* have a duty to reimburse or indemnify the agent if the payments made or expenses incurred were (1) *outside* the agent's actual authority, or (2) from losses resulting from the agent's negligence, or (3) from losses resulting from the agent's intentional tort or an illegal act.

Agent's Remedies for Breach

When a principal breaches a duty owed to an agent, the agent generally has the right to recover damages in court. The most common breach is when the principal refuses to reimburse or indemnify the agent. Assuming that the principal's obligation to do so is triggered by law, but she still refuses to properly compensate the agent, the agent's sole remedy is to file suit in order to collect any money owed to the agent and for reimbursement of out-of-pocket and incidental costs. As a practical matter, the principal and agent may have entered into some type of express agreement that spells out specific remedies the parties may exercise in the event of a breach. For example, suppose that Cardozo hires Holmes Inspection Company to perform an engineering inspection on a building Cardozo is considering buying. Cardozo agrees to pay Holmes $1,000 for services rendered, plus any out-of-pocket expenses, within 10 days of the inspection services. Although Holmes performs the services, Cardozo loses interest in the transaction, and fails to pay Holmes the fee. Cardozo has breached his duty as a principal by failing to pay Holmes. Holmes may sue for damages and is entitled to the agreed upon fee and reimbursement of the out-of-pocket expenses. However, suppose that Cardozo and Holmes signed a written agreement that also included a *penalty clause* whereby Cardozo agreed to pay a late fee and 10 percent interest per month for every month the invoice was outstanding. In this case, Holmes may recover not only the fee and expenses by virtue of Cardozo's breach of his duty as a principal, but may also recover the late fees and interest by virtue of their contractual agreement.

TERMINATION OF THE AGENCY RELATIONSHIP

LO10-8, 10-9

An agency relationship may be terminated in a variety of ways. Termination is an important issue for business owners and managers because the effect of a termination of the agency relationship also terminates the principal's *duties and obligations* to the agent and to third parties. It is equally important to understand the circumstances under which a third party must be notified of the termination in order to cut off the liability of the principal at a definite point. Failing to properly notify appropriate parties may result in *continued liability* of the principal for acts of the agent despite the termination. In general, an agency relationship is terminated either through **express acts** or through **operation of law.**

Express Acts

In a typical agency relationship, both the principal and the agent have the power to dissolve the agency at any time. Either party may end the agency through **termination** by simply communicating the desire to terminate the relationship. Termination by the principal is known as *revocation*. When the agent initiates the termination, this is known as *renunciation*. It is important to understand that the legal *power* of termination is not synonymous with the legal *right* of termination. Therefore, the principal may terminate the agreement (thereby revoking her authority for the agent to act in her place), but the termination may still be unlawful because the law did not give the principal the right to end the agreement before mutual performance. Thus, the agent may be entitled to damages as a result of the principal's conduct of wrongful termination. For example, suppose that Foley hires Paul to paint the lobby of Foley's office building. The parties agree that the Paul will paint the lobby over a period of two weeks and that Foley will pay him $1,000 upon completion. Halfway through the work, Foley learns that a major tenant has filed for bankruptcy, so he calls Paul up and tells him to stop work because he can no longer afford the costs of painting. In this case, Foley, as the principal, has the power to terminate the agency relationship by revocation. However, because Foley's actions are a breach of the

Eliminating Lingering Liability via Notification

PROBLEM *The effect of termination of an agency relationship is that the agent no longer has actual authority. However, agency law recognizes that in a case where a principal has terminated an agency by an express act, the agent may still have apparent authority to bind the principal to a contract with a third party. When the principal has acted in a way that would give a third party the belief that his agent has actual authority, then revokes the actual authority of the agent, the agent may still have lingering authority from the third party's perspective.*

For example, suppose that Sergio is employed as a buyer for High End Furniture Manufacturing Company (High End). One of Sergio's responsibilities is to order appropriate amounts of materials from Lumber Depot. Sergio would place the order by telephone with Lumber Depot and then he would pick up the materials in a rented truck for delivery to High End's workshop. Lumber Depot would issue an invoice and High End would pay within 30 days. This same transaction occurred approximately 10 times in six months. Assume that Sergio is terminated, but the next day he calls in an order to Lumber Depot from his home telephone. He then picks up the materials and absconds with them. This is a situation in which High End may still have liability to pay Lumber Depot based on Sergio's apparent authority. In order to terminate liability to a third party for the acts of Sergio, High End must notify the third party of the termination. This is especially true in cases where, as in the High End case, the pattern of repeated conduct (Sergio would order and pick up materials, Lumber Depot would issue an invoice, and then High End would pay) creates a reasonable belief that Sergio's authority was express and ongoing.

SOLUTION *Implement a third-party notification system to eliminate lingering authority and prevent liability based*

on apparent authority. *Whenever an agency relationship has been terminated by an express act, the principal must notify any third parties (such as vendors or suppliers) who may be affected by the termination. Without a systematic approach in place, an employer may still be liable for the acts of the former agent even without the agent having actual authority. Therefore, as part of its human resources management system, companies may put into a place a third-party notification system whenever an agent/employee has been terminated.*

In the High End–Sergio case above, High End could avoid liability by making third-party notifications part of their procedure when terminating an employee (or any agent). While typical employee termination checklists focus on return of company property, final paycheck, and other administrative tasks, a solution to lingering authority may be as simple as adding notification to the list. If High End had sent an e-mail to the manager of Lumber Depot notifying her of Sergio's status, that would eliminate any liability for High End for apparent authority actions of Sergio. The e-mail need not be lengthy or detailed[*]—but should be specific:

> **Dear Lumber Depot Manager: Please note that, effective immediately, Sergio is no longer employed by High End. Any purchases made on High End's behalf must be accompanied by a purchase order signed by me until further notice. Sincerely, Vice President of High End.**

This type of notice satisfies the termination notice required under agency law and, thus, eliminates any potential apparent authority claims by third parties based on Sergio's conduct.

[*]In order to avoid any potential liability for defamation, caution should be exercised in not giving any information about *why* the termination took place.

Foley–Paul contract,[12] Foley's termination is unlawful and Paul may recover any damages that he suffered as a result of the breach of contract.

More often than not, the parties in an agency relationship will have agreed to a fixed term for the representation. In that case, the agency relationship may be terminated by

---

[12]Recall from Chapter 6, "Overview and Formation of Contracts," that economic factors may generally not be used to excuse performance of a contract obligation (such as Foley's obligation to pay).

expiration. The expiration may be tied to a *time period* (principal hires agent for a one-year period) or an *event* (principal hires agent as a substitute worker only until an injured worker returns). Instead of setting a fixed time or event, the parties may agree to end the agency once the agency's *purpose* has been accomplished. For example, in the Foley–Paul agency relationship, above, suppose that Foley did not attempt to terminate the agency, but instead the painting services were finished on time. In this case, the agency ends automatically because the purpose of the agency, as originally contemplated by the parties, has been accomplished.

Operation of Law

Agency may also be terminated as provided for by statute or through certain common law doctrines. First, an agency relationship is terminated by the *destruction* of an essential subject matter of the relationship. So long as the agent's role is predicated on some particular property being at the disposal of the principal and the property is no longer practically or legally available, agency is automatically terminated. For example, Foley hires Paul to paint the lobby of Foley's office building. The day after the two agree, Foley's building burns down. The Paul–Foley agency relationship is terminated.

An agency relationship is also terminated automatically if either the principal or the agent *dies,* files for *bankruptcy,* or does not have the requisite *mental capacity* to continue the relationship. However, it is important to note that exceptions exist to these common law doctrines. Increasingly, various jurisdictions have prescribed statutory exceptions to certain events of termination. For example, in the case of the death of a principal, some state statutes permit the agent to continue to have actual authority until the agent learns of the death. Therefore, so long as the agent is acting in good faith, the agent may continue his duties until he actually receives notice of the death of the principal.

CONCEPT SUMMARY   Duties, Obligations, and Remedies of the Parties

- Agents owe a fiduciary duty to principals. This duty requires the agent to act according to higher standards than nonfiduciaries in a transaction, including the duty of loyalty, obedience, care, disclosure, and accounting.
- The duty of loyalty is the centerpiece of fiduciary obligation because the agent is obliged to advance the principal's interest over her own interest.
- If an agent's breach of duty to the principal causes damages to the principal, the principal may recover those damages from the agent.
- If an agent's breach of duty resulted in the principal's becoming liable to a third party, then the agent must indemnify and hold harmless the principal from any losses as a result of the liability.
- If an agent breaches the duty of loyalty, the principal may rescind any agreement between principal and agent and the agent may be liable to return profits earned as a result of the breach.
- Principals have a duty to reimburse and indemnify agents for expenses incurred, injuries suffered, or damages caused to third parties when the agent acted within actual authority or in good faith on behalf of the principal.
- A principal owes independent duties to third parties to use reasonable care in screening, hiring, informing, training, and supervising its agents.
- An agency relationship is terminated either through express acts (termination or expiration) or through operation of law (destruction of subject matter, death, bankruptcy, mental capacity).

EMPLOYMENT RELATIONSHIPS

Perhaps the most common form of agency relationship in the business environment is the relationship between employer and employee. The first part of this chapter focused on the how an agency relationship is classified and created, and the liability of the principal and agents to each other and to third parties. Equally important to business owners and managers are the agency-based legal doctrines that apply to the *interaction* between employer and employee, which is the focal point of this section of the chapter. This aspect of employment relationships is governed by a combination of state common law and statutory law at both the federal and state levels. While traditionally common law doctrines governed employer–employee relationships, state and federal lawmakers have increasingly displaced common law doctrines in favor of modern statutes with the objective of protecting workers through laws aimed at, for example, preventing workplace discrimination, banning children from hazardous work, ensuring workplace safety, and other important public policy objectives. Employment regulation and labor laws are discussed in detail in Chapter 11. Employment discrimination is covered in Chapter 12.

Employment-at-Will Doctrine

The **employment-at-will** doctrine is a deep-seated common law rule that exists in some form in every U.S. jurisdiction.[13] Fundamentally, the doctrine permits employers to terminate an employee with or without advance notice and with or without just cause, subject to certain exceptions. So long as it does not fall under one of the exceptions, the employer is insulated from a wrongful termination lawsuit. The employment-at-will doctrine reflects the principal's wide latitude in decision making when exercising the power and right to terminate an employee. However, several important exceptions limit the applicability to the rule. The employment-at-will doctrine does not apply in cases where the employee has (1) an express contract, (2) an implied contract, or (3) some specific statutory or public policy–based protection against job termination (such as anti-discrimination laws).

Express Contracts
One major exception to the employment-at-will rule is when an employee has an express contractual relationship with the employer that is intended to displace the employment-at-will rule. When the parties enter into a contract, the rights of the employee in the case of termination are spelled out in the contract. Typically, an employment contract will provide that employers may only terminate the employee for "good cause," such as a violation of a workplace rule or committing a criminal act in the course of his employment. The contract ordinarily lists the events of cause for termination and the parties agree as to any post-termination obligations. The parties may also formally agree to some type of severance pay in the event that the employer terminates the employee for any other reason than those causes listed in the contract.

Labor Contracts
While some employment agreements are contracts between managers and a business entity, some contracts give rights to nonmanagement employees as well. These contracts, called *collective bargaining agreements (CBAs)*, are negotiated by a labor union on behalf of a group of employees. CBAs often provide a protection by prescribing a process that must be used by the employer before terminating an employee. The process is designed to ensure that employees are being treated consistent with the standards in the CBA. CBAs and labor unions are covered in detail in Chapter 11, "Employment Regulation and Labor Law."

---

[13]One state, Montana, does not use the term employment-at-will, but a common law doctrine insulating employers from wrongful termination claims under certain circumstances does exist.

Implied Contracts   In addition to express contracts, an employment-at-will relationship may be converted to a contract relationship if the employer acted in a manner in which a reasonable person would believe that the employer intended to offer an employee protection from termination without cause. This protection, called an *implied contract,* arises in two circumstances. First, a manual or bulletin (such as an employee handbook) that is drafted and distributed by the employer may give rise to an implied contract theory if the manual extends some protections or process to the employee that she would not have under the employment-at-will doctrine. For example, if an employer designs a process where supervisors use a system of progressive discipline before a termination may occur (e.g., warning for the first violation of a workplace rule, suspension for the second violation, and termination for the third violation), this may be the basis for an implied contract that displaces the employment-at-will rule. Second, an oral promise made by an employer that a reasonable person would believe extends protection against termination without cause may constitute an implied contract. Suppose, for example, that Rousseau has worked for 20 years at World Industries. At a luncheon honoring Rousseau, the president of World Industries says "In honor of your excellent service, you have a job at this company until you wish to retire!" The next week, Rousseau is terminated. If a court determines that the language used by the president would lead a reasonable person to believe that Rousseau was more than just an employee-at-will, World Industries may be liable for a wrongful termination claim. Of course, any contract theory, express or implied, must be based on the standards in contract law for formation and performance of a contract that were covered in Chapters 6 and 7.

Statutory Prohibitions   Certain federal and state statutes also displace common law employment-at-will rules. Perhaps the best examples are the antidiscrimination laws that prohibit termination (and many other workplace actions) based on certain discriminatory motivations such as race or gender.[14] Other statutes prevent employers from terminating

Courts have ruled that certain language contained in an employee handbook may give rise to an implied employment contract.

---

[14]Employment discrimination is covered in detail in Chapter 12.

employees for specific reasons such as absence due to jury duty[15] or for attempting to form a union.

Whistle-Blowers   One important statutory prohibition for business owners and managers are federal and state statutory protections of **whistle-blowers.** Whistle-blower is a colloquial term used to describe an employee or agent who reports unlawful conduct or a statutory violation by their employer to the authorities. In general, employers may not terminate an employee on the basis of a report to the authorities (i.e., blowing the whistle) about the employer's conduct. Each state follows its own whistle-blowing statute, but most commonly, whistle-blowers are protected when they report the violation of a law or standard by their employer to the authorities. Some states only cover whistle-blowing by government employees or employees of government contractors. Although certain jurisdictions limit whistle-blower protection for employees whose disclosures involved conduct that could result in some harm to the employees or the public at large, a minority of states has extended that same protection to disclosures that involve *any* illegal or improper conduct. Some jurisdictions, such as the state of New York, have set a relatively high threshold for whistle-blowers to gain statutory protection. New York statutes require the disclosures be related to conduct "dangerous" to the public.

In any case, however, employers may terminate employees who are whistle-blowers if they can show that they terminated the employee for reasons that are *independent* of any whistle-blowing. For example, suppose that Padraig is an employee of Celtic Crystal Company (CCC). Over the past year, Padraig has been suspended twice for poor work and lateness. His manager warned him that any more instances of lateness would result in termination. On Monday, Padraig discovers that CCC has failed to take appropriate measures to remove a hazardous substance from the CCC warehouse. Padraig notifies the authorities that CCC is out of compliance. CCC learns of the complaint and its source on Tuesday. On Friday, Padraig is late for work and is terminated. Padraig is clearly protected as a whistle-blower in most jurisdictions. However, if CCC provides evidence that they intended to terminate Padraig prior to the whistle-blowing, or provides evidence that the decision, in light of Padraig's disciplinary record at CCC, was made independent of the whistle-blowing, CCC will most likely avoid liability for wrongful termination in violation of the whistle-blower statute.

In Case 10.4, a state appellate court considers whether a whistle-blower was subject to retaliation by her employer for reporting safety concerns in her workplace.

Federal Whistle-Blower Statutes   Federal employees are protected from retaliation for whistle-blowing by the Whistleblower Protection Act of 1989.[16] The law also covers employees of companies that contract with the government to provide goods or services (e.g., a construction company building a federal highway). Additionally, some federal statutes give specific antiretaliation protections for employees that disclose conduct that violates that law. For example, the False Claims Act protects employees who disclosed that their firm has committed fraud in dealing with contracts with the federal government. Similarly, the federal Fair Labor Standards Act and the Sarbanes-Oxley Act (regulation of corporations) both provide whistle-blowers with specific statutory protections for reporting or testifying against their employer in an investigation, hearing, or trial.

---

[15]For example, a statute in Pennsylvania prohibits employers from terminating, demoting, or depriving employees of seniority or other benefits because they have responded to a jury summons or have served as a juror. *See* 42 Pa. Cons. Stat., § 4563.

[16]5 U.S.C. § 1201.

FACT SUMMARY   Haynes, an animal keeper at the Zoological Society of Cincinnati (Zoo), was assigned to the bear and walrus area with responsibilities for feeding and general care of the animals. Haynes lodged several complaints with her supervisors about the unsafe conditions in her assigned areas, but the Zoo failed to address her concerns. One afternoon a co-worker, Stober, stopped in front of the den of a male polar bear and offered the bear a grape through the bars of the bear's cage. The bear pulled Stober's hand through the bars and bit off a portion of her arm. Haynes, who was with Stober when the attack occurred, gave a statement to authorities about the incident and blamed lack of personnel training and poor conditions inside the bear den as contributing factors to Stober's injuries. The next day Haynes was demoted to an entry-level position at the birdhouse and then, a few days later, suspended without pay for insubordination. Haynes sued the Zoo asserting that the Zoo had demoted and suspended her in retaliation for reporting alleged unsafe working conditions to authorities. The trial court ruled in favor of Haynes and the Zoo appealed.

SYNOPSIS OF DECISION AND OPINION   The Court of Appeals of Ohio affirmed the trial court decision, ruling in favor of Haynes. The court held that Haynes was entitled to the protections and remedies provided by Ohio's whistle-blower statute, because she reasonably believed that the Zoo violated safety standards that were a danger to other employees and the public. Therefore, her conduct was within the purview of whistle-blower statutory protection. She then sufficiently documented the safety violations so as to put the Zoo on notice of the alleged violations before reporting them to federal officials. The court pointed out that Haynes's reassignment to the birdhouse was a retaliatory action under the state statute and the Zoo failed to assert any credible independent reason for her demotion.

WORDS OF THE COURT: Scope of Whistle-Blower Protections   "If an employee becomes aware in the course of his employment of a violation of any state or federal statute or any ordinance or regulation of a political subdivision that his employer has authority to correct, and the employee reasonably believes that the violation either is a criminal offense that is likely to cause an imminent risk of physical harm to persons or a hazard to public health or safety or is a felony, the employee orally shall notify his supervisor or other responsible officer of his employer of the violation and subsequently shall file with that supervisor or officer a written report that provides sufficient detail to identify and describe the violation. The unsafe working conditions which Ms. Haynes reported orally and in writing to her supervisors violated [Ohio Codes on Safety in the Workplace], requiring all employers to furnish a safe place of employment. [. . .] Defendants violated the Ohio Whistleblower law by demoting Ms. Hanes to the birdhouse in retaliation for her reporting these unsafe working conditions to federal officials investigating the polar bear attack. [. . .] It is clear from the record that the trial court did not believe the Zoo's explanation of the reasons for Haynes's reassignment. We hold the record contains competent, credible evidence to support the trial court's determination and therefore it will not be reversed."

Case Questions

1. Suppose that over the past year, Haynes has been reprimanded for two safety violations of her own and after reporting the bear attack, she is suspended. Is Haynes still protected as a whistle-blower? Would the Zoo be liable for violation of the whistle-blower statute? Explain.

2. What could the Zoo management have done differently to prevent Haynes or other employees from filing similar whistle-blower suits?

Public Policy Exception   The final exception that displaces the employment-at-will rule recognizes that allowing employers to terminate an employee for certain reasons may contradict *public policy* (welfare of the general public). The public policy exception is a narrowly applied common law rule that places the public welfare ahead of the rights of an employer. This provision is best thought of as a backstop provision for situations when no specific statute is applicable, but the termination was inconsistent with the general public's well being. For example, in *Gardner v. Loomis Armored, Inc.,*[17] the Washington Supreme Court ruled that an armored car guard who was fired after he violated company rules by leaving his armored car to foil an armed robbery of a citizen occurring one block away was entitled to be reinstated in his job. The court explained that allowing the employer to terminate the armed guard for this particular conduct would deter similarly situated guards from prevention of a violent crime in the future.

However, it should be stressed that courts have been *reluctant* to expand the narrow public policy exception. In *Bammert v. Don's Super-Valu, Inc.,*[18] the Wisconsin Supreme Court refused to apply the public policy exception when the wife of a police officer alleged that she was fired in retaliation for her husband's arresting her employer's wife. The court held that the public policy exception was too narrow to include specific retaliatory conduct where there was a dubious connection to any public policy objectives.

The *Bammert* decision illustrates an important point in understanding the public policy exception to the employment-at-will doctrine: its limit in scope. Absent a specific statutory protection (such as a whistle-blower law) the threshold for relief using a public policy justification is very high. Some examples include refusal to commit an illegal act (such as filing a false tax return), exercising a legal right (such as refusal to take a polygraph test), or when an employee has performed an important act (such as the prevention of a violent crime as discussed in the *Gardner* case).

CONCEPT SUMMARY   Employment Relationships

- Agency-based legal doctrines that apply to the interaction between employer and employee are governed by a combination of state common law and statutory law at both the federal and state levels.

- The employment-at-will doctrine stands for the proposition that employers have the right to terminate an employee with or without advance notice and with or without just cause, subject to certain exceptions.

- An important exception to the employment-at-will rule is when an employee has an express contractual relationship with the employer.

- Employment-at-will relationships may be converted into an implied contract relationship if the employer acted in a manner where a reasonable person would believe the employer intended to offer an employee protection from termination without cause, through either a manual or bulletin, or an oral promise.

- Certain federal and state statutes also displace common law employment-at-will rules including protections of whistle-blowers.

- The public policy exception is a narrow common law rule that places the public welfare ahead of the rights of an employer and allows employers to terminate an employee for certain reasons that contradict public policy.

---

[17]913 P.2d 377 (Wa. 1996).

[18]646 N.W.2d 365 (Wi. 2002).

Agency law p. 243   Laws that govern the relationships created when one party hires another party to act on the hiring party's behalf.

Agent p. 244   One who agrees and is authorized to act on behalf of another, a *principal,* to legally bind an individual in particular business transactions with third parties pursuant to an agency relationship.

Principal p. 244   An agent's master; the person from whom an agent has received instruction and authorization and to whose benefit the agent is expected to perform and make decisions pursuant to an agency relationship.

Restatements (Second) of Agency p. 244   A set of principles, issued by the American Law Institute, intended to clarify the prevailing opinion of how the law of agency stands.

Employee agents p. 244   One of three broad categories in classifying agents; generally, anyone who performs services for a principal is considered an employee if the principal can control what will be done and how it will be done.

Independent contractor agents p. 244   One of three broad categories in classifying agents; generally, anyone who performs services for a principal is considered an independent contractor if the principal has the right to control or direct only the result of the work and not the means and methods of accomplishing the result.

Gratuitous agents p. 244   One of three broad categories in classifying agents; generally, anyone who acts on behalf of a principal without receiving any compensation.

Manifest p. 249   Apparent and evident to the senses; in the context of agency law, courts apply an objective standard to determine if the principal intended for an agency to be created.

Consent p. 249   When an agent agrees to act for the principal; in the context of agency law, courts apply an objective standard to determine if the agent did in fact agree to the agency relationship.

Actual authority p. 250   A source of the agent's authority occurring when the parties either expressly agree to create an agency relationship or where the authority is implied based on custom or the course of past dealings.

Apparent authority p. 250   A source of the agent's authority occurring when there is an appearance of legitimate authority to a third party rather than express authorization by the principal.

Ratification p. 250   A retroactive source of the agent's authority occurring when the principal affirms a previously unauthorized act by either (1) expressly ratifying the transactions, or (2) not repudiating the act via retaining the benefits while knowing that the benefits resulted from an unauthorized act by the agent.

Fully disclosed agency p. 252   A type of agency relationship created where the third party entering into the contract is aware of the identity of the principal and knows the agent is acting on behalf of the principal in the transaction.

Partially disclosed agency p. 252   A type of agency relationship created where the third party knows that the agent is representing a principal, but does not know the actual identity of the principal.

Undisclosed agency p. 252   A type of agency relationship created where a third party is completely unaware that an agency relationship exists and believes that the agent is acting on her own behalf in entering a contract.

Respondeat superior p. 253   [Latin for "let the master answer."] A common law doctrine that makes a principal (employer) liable for the actions of the servant/agent's (employee) tort when that act resulted in some physical harm or injury and occurred within the agent's scope of employment.

Frolic p. 253   An exception to the respondeat superior doctrine occurring when an agent, during a normal workday, does something purely for her own reasons that are unrelated to her employment.

Detour p. 254   Term used to describe conduct classified as a small-scale deviation that is normally expected in the workday and, therefore, within the ambit of respondeat superior.

Negligent hiring doctrine p. 255   A tort-based theory of liability for employers for negligent or intentional torts of employees when the employer had reason to know that the employee may cause harm within his scope of employment.

Due care p. 258   A subduty of fiduciary duty in which the agent is required to act in the same careful manner when conducting the principal's affairs as a reasonable person would use in conducting her own personal affairs.

Account p. 259   A subduty of fiduciary duty in which the agent is required to keep records such as a written list of transactions, noting money owed and money paid and other detailed statements of mutual demands.

Express acts p. 261 Acts in which an agency relationship is terminated through either simply communicating the desire to terminate the relationship, the expiration of a fixed term, or satisfaction of purpose.

Operation of law p. 261 Method in which an agency relationship is terminated as provided for a statute or through certain common law doctrines covering the destruction of an essential subject matter, or death, bankruptcy, or lack of requisite mental capacity.

Termination p. 261 Method in which either the principal (revocation) or the agent (renunciation) can end the agency relationship by simply communicating the desire to dissolve the relationship.

Expiration p. 263 Method in which an agency relationship is terminated by the parties agreeing to a fixed term for the representation.

Employment-at-will p. 264 Deep-seated common law rule that stands for the proposition that employers have the right to terminate an employee with or without advance notice and with or without just cause, subject to certain exceptions.

Whistle-blower p. 266 An employee or agent who reports some legal misconduct or statutory violation of their employer to the authorities.

THEORY TO PRACTICE

Cold Case Trucking (CCT) specializes in transportation of products that require refrigeration or freezing while being transported from the product's manufacturer to a wholesaler's warehouse. In an effort to improve its shipping logistics operations, CCT hired Crusoe, who had experience in operations logistics, as a consultant. CCT and Crusoe agree that Crusoe will study CCT's operations by conducting interviews with employees and customers, then design a new logistics plan and oversee its implementation. The parties agreed that Crusoe would give regular updates on his progress by attending weekly CCT management meetings. Because the CCT project was so time-intensive, Crusoe devoted 100 percent of his work time to CCT. The company also agreed to pay Crusoe $200 per documented hour for work on the project upon receiving an invoice from Crusoe and to make office space available at CCT's headquarters for Crusoe's exclusive use.

1. What is Crusoe's agent classification? What factors should CCT analyze in making this determination?

2. What is the source of Crusoe's authority to act as CCT's agent?

3. Assume that Crusoe is driving to interview one of CCT's customers for his study of CCT's logistical operations. While en route, he negligently hits a pedestrian. Is CCT liable for injuries to the pedestrian caused by their agent (Crusoe) under the doctrine of respondeat superior? Explain your analysis.

4. Suppose that Crusoe learns several important CCT trade secrets in the course of his agency and sells the information to a CCT competitor for $500,000. Which fiduciary duty has Crusoe breached? Explain your analysis. What are CCT's potential remedies against Crusoe?

5. Assume that part of Crusoe's agreement with CCT allowed Crusoe to use CCT's account at a local office supply store. Over a period of three months, Crusoe would order any office machinery or supplies he needed for his work directly from the store. The store billed CCT directly and was paid (along with any other charges by authorized CCT employees) within 30 days of receiving the bill. Suppose that a dispute arises between CCT and Crusoe about the quality of Crusoe's work and CCT terminates the consulting agreement. The next day Crusoe picks up a new computer from the office supply store, charges it to CCT's account, and absconds with it. Is CCT liable for payment to the office supply store for the computer? Explain your analysis.

6. What steps should have CCT taken to prevent possible liability in Question 5 above?

Legally astute managers are able to limit their company's risk by recognizing potential liability during business planning. Spotting potential legal issues and understanding when to contact counsel are important management skills. Suppose that in Theory to Practice, above, you are a CCT manager and that Crusoe presents his logistics and operations improvement plan at a management meeting. Part of Crusoe's plan involves converting the delivery truck drivers from employees to independent contractors. Crusoe claims that this will save employment taxes and limit CCT's liability for driver negligence. Crusoe recommends having the drivers sign Independent Contractor Agreements and paying them based on a monthly fee rather than as hourly employees. After the meeting, you receive the following e-mail from the vice president of operations:

To: All managers

Fr: VP/Operations

Re: Crusoe's plan

Please give me any feedback or concerns you have about Crusoe's recommendations presented at today's management meeting. I will be drafting a summary memorandum for top-level management next week and we will be moving to implementation of some or all of Crusoe's recommendations shortly.

Draft a three- to five-paragraph e-mail to your vice president concerning the proposal to convert drivers to independent contractors. Using your knowledge of agency law, be sure to raise any pertinent legal issues and discuss potential liability in explaining your concerns. Conclude the e-mail with a brief recommendation on how best to proceed.

RESPONDEAT SUPERIOR

A drama club at Texas A&M University (TAMU) performed *Dracula,* which was directed and supervised by a faculty adviser employed by TAMU. Bishop, a student at TAMU, was playing Vlad the Impaler in the performance when, during the final scene, a fellow student missed the stab pad attached to Bishop's chest and stabbed him with a Bowie knife. Bishop suffered a collapsed lung and brought suit against TAMU alleging that, under the doctrine of respondeat superior, TAMU was liable for the injuries he sustained as a result of the negligence of its faculty adviser employee. TAMU prohibited deadly weapons campus-wide and Bishop argued that the employee was negligent in using a real knife and in not ensuring that TAMU policies were being enforced.

CASE QUESTIONS

1. Do you believe TAMU should be held vicariously liable under the doctrine of respondeat superior in this case? Why or why not?
2. Assume that the directors were independent contractors rather than university-employed faculty. How does that affect your analysis? Explain.

PUBLIC POLICY

A crew of five pipe fitters was employed by a contractor and was ordered to put in a valve on a transfer pipe to a high-level nuclear waste tank. However, the crew had sufficient experience to realize that the wrong valve had been ordered. The valve to be used was rated at 1,975 pounds per square inch (psi) in a system of pipes that was to be tested at 2,235 psi. The crew was concerned that the underrated valve could cause nuclear contamination and injury to workers.

They refused the orders of their supervisor to install the underrated valve and stopped work at the site until management relented and ordered the sturdier valve to be installed. One month later the company terminated the whole crew, citing financial cutbacks in the company.

CASE QUESTIONS

1. What exceptions displacing the employment-at-will doctrine could the pipe fitters assert?
2. What theory would be best advanced by the pipe fitters? Explain.

CASE SUMMARY 10.3 :: Toms v. Links Sports Management Group, L.P., 2006 LEXIS 114677 (W.D.LA.)

FIDUCIARY DUTY

Parker, a sports agent, represented David Toms, a professional golfer. Parker also represented Shaun Micheel and other professional golfers. Parker received a 20 percent commission on any endorsement contracts signed by Toms, and a 25 percent commission on endorsement contracts signed by Micheel. In 2003, Parker was in the middle of negotiations with Cleveland Golf on Toms's behalf. After Micheel was the surprise winner at the PGA Championship, Parker convinced Toms that he should hold out for a more lucrative endorsement deal than was being offered by Cleveland and subsequently signed Micheel, instead of Toms, to the Cleveland Golf deal.

CASE QUESTIONS

1. What agency relationship exists between Toms and Parker?
2. If an agency relationship exists, when was a fiduciary duty created and what subduties apply to this case? Explain.
3. Is Parker's employer also liable for the actions of Parker? Why or why not?

CASE SUMMARY 10.4 :: Wal-Mart Stores, Inc. v. Guerra, 2009 LEXIS 4955 (Tex. Ct. App. 2009)

IMPLIED CONTRACTS

Guerra was hired to work as a cashier at a Wal-Mart store and signed an employment-at-will acknowledgment. Over the next eight years, Guerra held various positions at several different Wal-Mart stores before being promoted to store manager of the Rio Grande City Wal-Mart. Immediately after his promotion was announced, he was told by a Wal-Mart regional director and two Wal-Mart vice presidents that as long as the store met certain performance goals each year, the Rio Grande City Wal-Mart store would be "here for you for the rest of your life." Sixteen months later, after Wal-Mart received a complaint that Guerra was violating company policies and engaging in questionable practices with respect to store merchandise, he was terminated. Guerra filed suit alleging that Wal-Mart was bound by an oral agreement to employ him for the rest of his working life, as long as the store met certain performance goals each year.

CASE QUESTIONS

1. Is the employment-at-will relationship converted to a contractual relationship in this case? Why or why not?
2. Does the regional director or the vice presidents have authority to act on behalf of Wal-Mart as agents? Explain, and if so, what is the source of the agent's authority?

Self-Check **ANSWERS**

Agency Classification

1. Independent contractor. Factors: (a) a publisher has very little direction and control of an author in terms of time and schedule; (b) lump sum payment; and (c) no ongoing relationship.

2. Independent contractor. While this may appear at first glance to be an employee due to the schedule, consider that (a) More has eight such clients (he doesn't work exclusively for Henry); (b) More is paid through invoice; and (c) a short-term agreement exists with no promise of continuing employment.

3. Employee. Factors: (a) full direction and control over More's schedule; and (b) hourly wages (in addition to the commission).

4. Gratuitous agent.

5. Employee. While this may appear at first glance to be an independent contractor relationship because of the agreement, remember that courts apply a substance-over-form analysis in determining agency status. Consider that (a) More's schedule is set by Henry; (b) More is paid the same amount on a biweekly basis; (c) the annual holiday bonus may be evidence of a continuing employment; and (d) More uses Henry's equipment to do his job.

6. Employee. Level of salary is not determinative in an agency classification analysis. More's schedule is set, Henry provides his pay and benefits, and More predominantly uses Henry's equipment to perform his work.

Fiduciary Duty

1. Loyalty. Dorian's actions were a conflict of interest and violated a duty to keep business information confidential.

2. Loyalty. Dorian's actions constitute self-dealing because he put his interest ahead of Gray's interests.

3. Obedience. Gray's instructions were clear and lawful and Dorian violated his obligation to follow the instructions of the principal.

4. Accounting. Dorian's commingling of cash he accepted on Gray's behalf with his own cash violates his fiduciary duty.

11
CHAPTER

Employment Regulation and Labor Law

learning outcomes checklist

After studying this chapter, students who have mastered the material will be able to:

11-1 Assess the origins and impact of the labor movement on modern labor law.

11-2 Describe the main statutory protections for workers and regulations on employers in the areas of wages and hours, retirement, health care, sudden job loss, work-related injuries, and workplace safety.

11-3 List the benefits provided by federal law for workers who are in need of leave for medical purposes or a leave to care for an ill family member.

11-4 Identify federal statutes that impact labor—management relations and give examples of specific protections for workers that are set out in each law.

11-5 Explain the process for forming a certified labor union.

11-6 Describe the rights and limits of workers to engage in collective bargaining and to strike, and analyze the potential impact of a work stoppage.

11-7 Differentiate between an economic strike and an unfair labor practices strike.

11-8 Provide examples of illegal work stoppages.

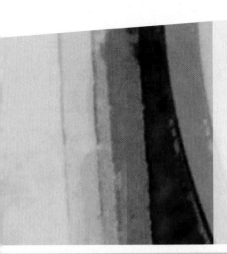

The nature and character of the relationship between employer and employee is continually evolving. Modern day employees enjoy protection primarily from an extensive array of federal and state statutes and administrative regulations that are intended to guard against abusive or oppressive actions or policies of employers. This chapter covers laws related to the *well being* of employees, and *labor law*, which governs the rights of workers to organize and operate labor unions. A working knowledge of employment regulation and labor law is fundamental for business owners and managers for reducing the risk of liability in hiring and managing their workforce. Note that employment discrimination law is covered in the next chapter. In this chapter, students will learn:

- Federal and state regulations related to employee wages and hours, retirement, health care, unemployment, workplace injuries/safety, and special laws and protections for employees who are minors.

- Laws that guarantee workers the right to unionize and the regulations that govern labor unions and practices.

LO11-1 ORIGINS OF EMPLOYMENT REGULATION AND LABOR LAW

As the American economy boomed with the dawn of the industrial age, employment opportunities shifted away from agriculture toward industrial production beginning in the mid-1880s. The industrial revolution was fueled in part by the availability of an abundant workforce comprised of immigrants and displaced farmers willing to work long hours for low wages. Conditions in the industrial plants were brutal and dangerous, and exploitation of unskilled labor was common and of little concern to politicians of that era. Workers who were injured on the job were terminated and given no compensation for medical care. Absent any compulsory education laws or financial alternatives, industrial labor families sent young children to work, including work in coal mines and slaughterhouses. Attempts by workers to organize or to bargain were met by industrialists with physical intimidation, assault, and job loss.

However, in the early 1900s, a growing labor movement, inspired by increased political power of immigrant groups and a growing intolerance of the public for corporate abuses,[1] forced the federal government to legislate federal protections for employees regarding working conditions, unionization, and child labor laws. Eventually, additional worker protections related to wages and hours, injuries on the job, workplace safety, and layoffs were added to the federal labor statutes.

LO11-2, 11-3, 11-4 EMPLOYMENT REGULATION

Congress and state legislatures have passed laws intended to protect employees from oppressive or unfair practices in the workplace.[2] These employment protection laws are intended to safeguard the welfare of individual workers who have little or no bargaining power in the employer–employee relationship. Federal law often works in tandem with state law in regulating employers with respect to minimum wages, overtime pay, use of child labor, sudden job loss, workplace injuries, workplace safety, and medical leaves.

Wages and Hours

The centerpiece of wage and hour law protections is the **Fair Labor Standards Act (FLSA)**[3] passed in 1938 and intended to cover all employers engaged in interstate commerce.[4] Although the statute is expansive, its primary provisions mandate (1) payment of a minimum wage,[5] (2) a maximum 40-hour workweek, (3) overtime pay, and (4) restrictions on children working in certain occupations and during certain hours. The FLSA and its regulations are administered and enforced by the U.S. Department of Labor.

Minimum Wage, Maximum Hours, and Overtime   The FLSA establishes a minimum wage to be paid to every employee covered under the act. Over the years Congress has raised the minimum wage to its current level of $7.25.[6] However, states are permitted

---

[1]Upton Sinclair's classic novel, *The Jungle,* which detailed employee abuses and described unthinkable sanitary conditions in the turn of the century Chicago meat factories, is cited in the legislative history for many worker protection statutes as a basis for the need for regulation. It is an example of how literature can influence the law.

[2]Note that although some municipalities have also passed worker protections that supplement the federal and state protections, the employer–employee relationship is typically considered the province of state and federal lawmakers.

[3]29 U.S.C. §201.

[4]Given the interpretation by modern courts, the statute covers virtually all employers.

[5]The FLSA is sometimes called the minimum wage law, but actually includes substantially more protections.

[6]For an update on the federal minimum wage, see this textbook's companion Web site at www.mhhe.com/melvin.

to set a higher minimum wage level for employees working within a state's jurisdictional boundaries. A more controversial provision of the FLSA is the requirement for employees to be compensated for commuting time if their employer requires the employee to perform a significant amount of work during the commute. However, courts have applied this provision relatively narrowly. For example, in *Singh v. City of New York*,[7] a federal appellate court ruled against a New York City fire inspector who claimed that he should have been compensated under the FLSA for commuting time from his home to individual inspection sites. The court held that the mere carrying of inspection documents without any other active employment-related responsibility while commuting was not counted as work as defined in the FLSA.

40-hour Workweek   In addition to setting the minimum wage, the FLSA sets a standard workweek at 40 hours in a seven-day period. Any hours worked by an employee over the standard workweek are entitled to **overtime compensation.** Overtime compensation is calculated by multiplying the hourly base rate of the employee times one and one-half. Thus, an employee making $10.00 per hour in her normal base pay is entitled to $15 per hour for overtime compensation. Note that all wage and hour laws under the FLSA assume a base unit of time as one week. Employees are not entitled to overtime pay based on an eight-hour workday. For example, suppose that Mikhail has morning childcare responsibilities and requests a schedule for seven hours a day on Monday through Friday and five hours on Saturday. Although Mikhail works six days per week, he is not entitled to overtime pay under the FLSA because his total hours did not exceed 40 in a one-week period.

Exempt Employees

Perhaps the most important concept that business owners and managers should understand about the FLSA is that the act does not cover all employees. Employers are not bound by the FLSA for employees classified as **exempt employees.** The underlying concept behind the FLSA is to level the playing field for employees who were in an untenable bargaining position with employers. Consistent with that concept, the law imputes a certain level of bargaining power for professional and management level employees and, therefore, exempts them from FLSA protections. When the FLSA was first enacted, the division between management and labor was relatively clear and classification was based on salary thresholds. However, as the lines between labor and management blurred during the rise of the information age and the general rise in the skill, education, and wages of workers, classification became increasingly problematic. In 2004, the Department of Labor overhauled the classification system and clarified the coverage of the FLSA, including a substantial increase in the base salary ceiling for coverage to $100,000 for white-collar employees.[8] Generally, exemptions include employees whose responsibilities are primarily executive, administrative, or professional. In classifying an employee as covered or exempt, employers must take into account multiple factors:

- Education or skill level or certifications required for the position, salary level, and compensation method (i.e., commission versus hourly).
- Amount of physical labor required.
- Amount of repetitive tasks (performing an unskilled task over and over again such as a clerk in a company mailroom).
- Degree of supervision required by the employer.

---

[7]524 F.3d 361 (2d Cir. 2008).

[8]Although this term is somewhat outdated, in the context of FLSA law, white-collar employees typically engage in employment that does not require physical labor, does not involve repetitive tasks, and are typically paid an annual salary and not on an hourly basis.

FACT SUMMARY Starbucks operates more than 6,500 retail coffee stores in the United States. Each store is staffed by "partners" including entry-level baristas, shift supervisors, assistant store managers (ASMs), and store managers. In October 2002, Starbucks changed the job description for ASMs to include routine tasks including service, cleaning, and other nonmanagement tasks, and reclassified them for purposes of the FLSA from "exempt" to "nonexempt." This made all ASMs throughout the country eligible for overtime. Although Starbucks anticipated that ASMs would continue to work more than 40 hours after the reclassification, it did not increase store labor budgets and store managers were discouraged from allowing workers overtime. Several ASMs contended that the new job responsibilities could not be completed in 40 hours and that Starbucks managers enforced an unwritten policy of encouraging or allowing ASMs to work "off-the-clock" (perform the job responsibilities without being compensated) in order to control overtime costs. One ASM testified that a district manager informed her that her job needs to get done, "regardless of how long it takes." Falcon and other ASMs filed suit claiming that Starbucks violated the FLSA. Starbucks contended that it had a written policy prohibiting off-the-clock work and filed a motion for summary judgment.

SYNOPSIS OF DECISION AND OPINION The Federal District Court ruled in favor of Falcon and denied Starbucks's motion for summary judgment. The court held that significant evidence showed ASMs either worked off-the-clock or that time was taken off if they attempted to record all of their hours. There

was a strong showing that (1) ASM job duties were not easily completed within 40 hours while overtime was strongly discouraged, (2) labor budgets were not increased, and (3) manager bonuses were based, in part, on limiting overtime hours. Despite an official "time worked is time paid" policy, Starbucks created an environment that encouraged FLSA violations. A policy of discouraging overtime, while not unlawful, could, together with other factors, lead to a consistent pattern of violations.

WORDS OF THE COURT: Motivation to Violate the FLSA "Plaintiffs have also provided significant evidence in support of their claim that [they] either worked off-the-clock or had time shaved off of their hours by Store Managers when they attempted to record all of the hours they actually worked. Finally, Plaintiffs have made a strong showing that Starbucks' general policy of requiring ASMs to perform job duties that could not easily be completed within 40 hours while, at the same time, strongly discouraging overtime after the reclassification, failing to increase labor budgets, and basing bonuses, at least in part, on labor hours created an environment that at least strongly motivated managers to commit the alleged FLSA violations."

Case Questions

1. What could Starbucks have done to be sure that its prohibition against off-the-clock work was enforced?

2. Why does the court consider it important that Starbucks did not increase store budgets when they reclassified the ASMs as nonexempt?

Examples of employees that are *not* covered by the FLSA include (1) professionals that require specialized study and certifications such as attorneys, physicians, and accountants; (2) management or supervisory employees; (3) computer programmers and engineers; and (4) employees subject to certain certification and regulatory requirements such as insurance adjustors or dental hygienists.

In Case 11.1, a federal trial court applies the FLSA to the workplace operations and practices of a well-known retail coffee shop chain.

The consequences of the misclassification may be severe. Unless an employee is clearly exempt from the FLSA coverage, she should be classified as *covered* under the FLSA provisions until such time as the employer has legal assurances that the employee is exempt. To understand the dilemma faced by employers over misclassification, suppose that Standish

FIGURE 11.1 FLSA Liability

1. Calculate Alden's approximate hourly base rate:	$26,000/52 weeks = $500 per week $500/40 hours = $12.50 per hour
2. Calculate Alden's overtime rate:	$12.50 × 1.5 = $18.75
3. Calculate overtime pay owed:	10 hrs/wk × 24 wks (6 mos) = 240 hrs $18.75 × 240 = $4,500

Because of the misclassification over six months, Standish owes Alden $4,500 in back pay, plus interest, set out by the FLSA regulations.

hires Alden as a customer service agent to handle complaints over the phone. Alden has a significant amount of practical experience and a diploma from a technical school. Standish agrees to pay Alden an annual base salary of $26,000. Because the work does not involve physical labor, Standish classifies Alden as exempt from the FLSA. Over the course of the next six months, due to an increase in customer complaints, Standish works an average of 50 hours per week on the phones trying to resolve complaints. Because Standish classified Alden as an employee with an annual salary and exempt from the FLSA, he does not pay Alden any overtime compensation.

Assume that the Department of Labor audits Standish and reclassifies Alden as being covered by the FLSA because of his relatively low salary level, the minimal educational requirements for the position, and the repetitive task of answering customer calls. In addition to any fine levied against Standish for violating the FLSA, the Department of Labor will order Standish to pay Alden back pay for any time worked by Alden over the 40-hour workweek. Figure 11.1 represents a sample calculation of Standish's potential liability.

 Self-Check   Exempt vs. Covered Employees

Which employees are exempt from the FLSA protections?

1. An employee hired as a computer programmer at a software manufacturing company for an annual salary of $50,000.

2. An architect hired to work for a design-build construction company at a rate of $85,000 per year.

3. A cashier at a supermarket who is paid $10 per hour.

4. An assistant store manager whose duties also include routine work such as stocking shelves during busy seasons.

5. An employee hired to sell life insurance for an insurance company who is paid a base salary of $15,000 plus a 10 percent commission on all insurance sold.

Answers to this Self-Check are provided at the end of the chapter.

Child Labor Laws

The FLSA outlaws the once common practice of sending school-aged children to work instead of to school by imposing restrictions on hiring workers under 18 years old. Table 11.1 sets out restrictions for the age requirements that have been issued by the Department of Labor pursuant to their FLSA authority. It is also important to note that

TABLE 11.1	Child Labor Restrictions

Age	Restriction
Under 14	No employment except newspaper sale and delivery.
14–15	Limited hours during school days in nonhazardous jobs (such as a busboy or dishwasher in a restaurant).
16–17	No limits on hours, but cannot work in dangerous jobs such as mining or heavy industry and other hazardous jobs as defined in FLSA regulations.

A federal court found that when Starbucks reclassified a group of employees from exempt to non-exempt, it triggered significant liability under the FLSA.

children in family agricultural jobs and child actors are not subject to the FLSA restrictions, but state statutes often require appropriate educational standards to be met through the use of tutors and home schooling.

Retirement

Employers are not required to establish retirement plans for their employees, although as a competitive matter many often do so to attract and retain high-quality employees. If an employer does offer retirement benefits, they are typically offered in the form of a **pension** or through a **tax-deferred retirement savings account** such as a 401(k)[9] plan. In a pension plan, the employer promises to pay a monthly sum to employees who retire from the company after a certain number of years of service. The amount is ordinarily based on the length of service and the employee's final salary rate as of the date of retirement. In a

---

[9]The name 401(k) is shorthand reference to the Internal Revenue Code regulation that regulates tax-deferred savings plans.

retirement savings account, the employee commits to saving a certain percentage of base pay in an account that is controlled directly by the employee and not the employer. The employee then has the ability to allocate her savings via various investment vehicles that range from very safe to high risk. Some employers match the employee's contribution by paying an extra amount into the account based on a certain percentage of the employee's base salary. The major benefit for the employee is that retirement savings grow without triggering any tax liability until the employee is ready to make retirement withdrawals from the account.

Regulation of Pensions and Retirement Accounts   If employers establish either a pension fund or a retirement savings plan, the employer is subject to the requirements of a federal statute called the **Employee Retirement Income Security Act (ERISA)**[10] of 1974. The ERISA is a comprehensive set of laws and regulations that require employers to make certain disclosures related to investment risk and provides transparency for plan beneficiaries. The ERISA establishes rules for conflict of interest (such as how much of a company's own stock can be held in a pension plan) and imposes certain fiduciary standards for investing and managing pension plans or administering retirement savings plans. Employers must adhere to record-keeping regulations and must treat all employees in accordance with a set of standardized vesting rules. The ERISA authorizes the Department of Labor to monitor pension and retirement savings plan administration. The department oversees the Labor Management Services Administration, in part, to implement, administer, and enforce the ERISA.

Legal Speak ›))
Vesting An ERISA guideline stipulating that employees are entitled to their benefits from various employer-contributed benefit plans, within a certain period of time, even if they no longer work for their employer.

Social Security

In addition to any pension or retirement plans offered by employers, workers are entitled to a retirement income from the federal government by virtue of the **Social Security Act of 1935 (SSA).** The SSA provides a broad set of benefits for workers that are funded by mandatory employment taxes paid by both employer and employee into a trust fund administered by the federal government. These employment taxes are mandated by the Federal Insurance Contributions Act (FICA).[11] Employees are entitled to retirement benefits based on how many credits they have earned during their working life. Credits are accrued as a worker progresses through her career no matter how many different employers the worker has over a lifetime. The SSA also provides for payments to be made when a worker becomes disabled and provides survivor benefits for spouses and children upon the death of a worker.

Health Care

Employers are not required to provide employees with health care insurance or plans. As a competitive matter, many companies do provide employees with a health care plan option whereby the employer and employee share the costs of the insurance plan. If the employer does provide a health care plan, two federal statutes regulate certain aspects of administering the plan. First, the Health Insurance Portability and Accountability Act (HIPPA)[12] sets administrative rules and standards designed to protect employee medical information and records from disclosure to a third party. Second, the Consolidated Omnibus Budget Reconciliation Act (COBRA)[13] mandates that employers provide continuous coverage to any employee who has been terminated even if the worker was terminated for cause.[14]

---

[10]29 U.S.C. § 1001, et seq.

[11]29 U.S.C. § 1001, et seq.

[12]29 U.S.C. § 1181, et seq.

[13]29 U.S.C. § 1161.

[14]In egregious cases, such as when an employee is terminated for theft from the company, COBRA benefits may not apply.

The COBRA requires that the employer provide the exact same health coverage for up to 18 months. It's important to note that the COBRA does not require employers to *pay* for the health plan premiums of a former employee. The employee has full responsibility for payment of all insurance premiums and administrative fees.

Health Care and Education Reconciliation Act of 2010   In March 2010, Congress passed the **Health Care and Education Reconciliation Act of 2010**[15] that overhauled the U.S. health care system. The legislation was the subject of intense debate and extended media coverage, but from a business manager's perspective, much of the law's mandate occurs in 2014. However, the law does offer small business owners (those employing fewer than 25 full-time workers) immediate tax incentives if they offer health care coverage to their employees, and pay at least 50 percent of the total costs for their employees' coverage. In 2014, individuals who are not covered through their employer's policy are legally required to purchase health care insurance from a health care "exchange" that is set up by individual states (or groups of states). By 2018, employers that offer high-end health care plans (plans which cost more than $27,500 per year) to its employees will be required to pay an additional tax based on the total cost of the plan.

For an update on federal regulation of health care, see this textbook's Web site at www.mhhe.com/melvin.

Sudden Job Loss

After the Great Depression sent unemployment rates soaring to 20 percent and higher, Congress responded with the **Federal Unemployment Tax Act (FUTA)**[16] of 1935, which provided limited payments to workers who had been temporarily or permanently terminated from employment thorough no fault of their own. The FUTA establishes a state-administered fund to provide payments to workers who have suffered sudden job loss. The FUTA is funded by employment taxes shared by employer and employee. In order to obtain unemployment benefits, the worker must actively seek out new employment and, if necessary, retraining in a different field. Unemployment compensation is intended to cover workers who lose their jobs because of economic difficulties and not intended to reward an employee who was terminated for cause. However, because states set their own standards and procedures, the exact eligibility requirements vary among different jurisdictions.

WARN Act   Employers that intend to either close down an entire facility or intend to lay off 50 or more workers are required to provide advance notice to employees in accordance with the **Worker Adjustment and Retraining Notification Act (WARN Act).**[17] However, the WARN Act applies only to employers with at least 100 full-time employees, and if the closing will affect 50 or more employees. The law's requirements are triggered when the intended closing will result in permanent terminations, layoffs for six months or longer, or when the company imposes a reduction in work time of 50 percent or more for six months or longer. The WARN Act requires the employer to provide each affected employee with at least 60-days written notice of the closing/layoff as well as notification of the local government where the facility is situated. Employers failing to comply with the WARN Act are subject to pay damages and attorneys' fees to displaced workers. A minority of states also provide additional statutory protections for workers displaced because of mass layoffs.

---

[15]Pub.L. No. 111-152

[16]26 U.S.C., § 3301, et seq.

[17]29 U.S.C., § 2101, et seq.

Workplace Injuries

While historically tort law was the only mechanism for compensating an employee who suffered an injury on the job or a job-related illness, all states now have **workers' compensation** statutes. These statutes establish a structure for an injured employee to be compensated through a statutorily mandated insurance program as the exclusive remedy for workplace injuries or illnesses. Employees with job-related injuries or illnesses are paid based on a percentage of the employee's salary at the time of the occurrence. Workers' compensation statutes typically require the establishment of a system for processing claims through the state workers' compensation board (or a similarly named agency) and the compensation is funded through employer-paid insurance policies. Companies may also be self-insured if they meet their individual state's requirements for establishing a fund that is sufficient to make payments to injured employees. The most important aspect of the workers' compensation system is that the employee is paid *regardless* of any issues related to fault or negligence of the employee, the employer, or any third party. This plan assures an injured worker a continuous income for an injury that requires her to stop working. In exchange for this compensation, the employee is barred from pursuing a negligence lawsuit related to the injury against the employer. The state statutes are often broad in terms of coverage, but most states exempt domestic workers and temporary or seasonal employees from protection.

Intentional Actions or Recklessness of Employer   Two important exceptions to the workers' compensation laws are (1) when an employer has engaged in actions that intentionally created conditions that resulted in harm, or (2) when an employer acts with a reckless disregard for the safety of its employees. In these cases, the injured or ill party may bypass the workers' compensation system and sue the employer for a full recovery including punitive damages. As a practical matter, however, although an injured employee may recover a higher amount through litigation, the prospect of immediate compensation and the uncertainties and delays inherent in litigation mean that many people will opt to file a workers' compensation claim rather than pursue litigation. In any case, once the injured party files a workers' compensation claim, she is barred from suing her employer in any suit related to the injury.

Course of Employment   In order to trigger protection under workers' compensation laws, the injury must meet two main criteria: (1) the injury was accidental, and (2) the injury occurred within the course of employment. Accidental injuries are injuries that occurred without any intent to cause harm or injure. The course of employment requirement varies by jurisdiction, but most state courts have interpreted the scope of employment requirement broadly and in favor of coverage of the injured worker. While cases where the employee is injured on the job at the worksite during regular business hours are clearly covered, off-premises activity is also covered so long as it is sufficiently related to the worker's employment. Even when the injury is indirectly related to the employee's job responsibilities, courts have been willing to extend workers' compensation coverage to the injured employee. Case 11.2 illustrates one state appellate court's willingness to extend workers' compensation rights to an employee who was injured during a criminal act.

Regulation of Workplace Safety

While workers' compensation laws are designed to protect workers who are injured, the federal statute intended to *prevent* workplace injuries is the **Occupational Safety and Health Act (OSHA)**[18] passed in 1970. The objective of OSHA statutes and regulation is to

---

[18] 29 U.S.C. § 553.

FACT SUMMARY   Sisco worked as a tow truck driver for Quicker Recovery, a towing company in Oregon that had a contract to provide towing services for a municipal police department. The contract required Quicker to provide a tow truck within 30 minutes of receiving the request for services. Sisco was dispatched to tow an impounded truck and was en route to the location when the police stopped him for speeding in the tow truck. Sisco refused to produce his driver's license or any other identification for the police and was arrested pursuant to a state statute allowing the police to arrest any traffic violator who cannot be identified sufficiently for purposes of issuing a citation. Sisco physically resisted arrest, but was eventually subdued by officers who used an electronic stun gun to take him into custody. The day after the arrest, Sisco complained of neck pain and recurring spasms caused by the altercation with the officers. He claimed that the pain prevented him from carrying out his job responsibilities as a tow truck driver and submitted a workers' compensation claim. The Oregon Workers' Compensation Board determined that his neck injury was not a compensable work-related injury. Sisco appealed.

SYNOPSIS OF DECISION AND OPINION   The Court of Appeals of Oregon reversed the board's decision and ruled in favor of Sisco. The court held that the risk of proximate interaction with the officers after being stopped for speeding while responding to a tow call was sufficiently related to his employment. Therefore, the employee's injury did "arise out of" his employment for purposes of the Oregon Workers' Compensation Law and, thus, the causal connection between the injury and the employment is sufficient to warrant compensation.

WORDS OF THE COURT: Work-Related Injury   "To be compensable under the Oregon Workers' Compensation Law, an injury must arise out of and in the course of employment. The 'arise out of' [part] of the compensability test requires that a causal link exist between the worker's injury and his or her employment. The

requirement that the injury occur in the course of the employment concerns the time, place, and circumstances of the injury. [. . .] Here, as the board acknowledged with respect to the 'time' and 'place' facets of that element, claimant was, in fact, responding to a tow call at the time that he was stopped, leading to the interaction that culminated in his injury. [. . .]

[The] claimant's work environment exposed him to numerous and diverse risks and dynamics associated with driving and involving interactions with third persons, such as other drivers and law enforcement personnel. One obvious example is the risk of a tow truck driver being involved in an accident with another motorist, while speeding in response to a tow call, and then being assaulted by that motorist because of anger and frustration over the accident. [. . .] Similarly, the risk of proximate interaction with law enforcement officers after being stopped for speeding, while responding to a tow call, is manifestly a risk related to claimant's employment. Further—albeit (fortunately) only rarely—such interactions can escalate, sometimes resulting in physical injury. In that regard, the assessment of the injury-producing risk here is qualitatively no different than that pertaining to an assault by an angry motorist—or, for that matter, an assault by a coworker. Each is extraordinary—for example, being assaulted by a coworker is hardly the 'norm' in most employment environments—but each is 'a risk to which the work environment exposed [the] claimant' [. . .]."

Case Questions

1. Suppose Sisco's altercation occurred while he was en route to his house during an unpaid one-hour lunch break. Would Sisco still be eligible for compensation? Why or why not?

2. Would Sisco have been better served trying to articulate a negligence claim? Explain.

3. Doesn't public policy prevent a worker from claiming compensation for an incident involving a criminal act? Should the court take public policy considerations into account?

make the workplace as safe as possible for workers engaged in business operations through (1) setting of national safety standards, (2) mandating information disclosure and warning of hazardous working areas/assignments, (3) record keeping and reporting requirements, and (4) imposing a general duty upon employers to keep a workplace reasonably safe. The

OSHA law has broad coverage encompassing virtually every private employer. Federal, state, and local government units are exempt.

Occupational Safety and Health Administration   The OSHA statute created the Occupational Safety and Health Administration ("Administration"), under the jurisdiction of the Department of Labor, to administer and enforce the statute. The Administration has expansive enforcement authority, including routine or unscheduled worksite inspections, in carrying out the provisions of the law. Industries that are ultrahazardous (such as mining) are highly regulated by OSHA administrative rules. The Administration also investigates complaints made by employees alleging that an employer violated safety standards. Employees making a complaint to the Administration are protected from retaliation by the employer via the OSHA's whistle-blowing provisions.[19]

OSHA Provisions   The OSHA regulations have evolved into a complex and lengthy set of rules and standards because so many of the regulations are industry specific. However, there are some provisions that apply to all employers. For example, employers with 11 or more employees are required to maintain records about the company's safety records and to document the investigation of any accidents. These reports must be kept current and prepared for inspection by the Administration without any subpoena or advanced notice required. If an employee is killed in a work-related accident or when three or more employees are hospitalized in one event, the employer is required to notify the Administration as soon as possible, but no later than eight business hours after the accident. Once notification is made, the Administration dispatches an inspector to investigate the accident. If the employer is found to have been in violation of a specific or general safety standard, then the Administration takes appropriate enforcement action including fines, cease and desist orders and, in egregious cases, pursuing criminal charges against the company and its officers. In the event of a workplace death, the Administration cooperates with local authorities that may also have jurisdiction, especially in criminal cases.

Under the OSHA rules, employees have a limited right to walk off the job when faced with a hazardous workplace condition. In *Whirlpool v. Marshall*,[20] the U.S. Supreme Court held that, despite the lack of any specific language in the OSHA statute that allows employees to walk off the job, the law permitted employees this right under the narrow circumstances when (1) the employee faces a condition which he reasonably believes will result in serious injury or death, and (2) the context makes it impractical for the employee to contact Administration inspectors.

Family Medical Leave Act

As American society has changed since the industrial revolution, so has society's need to provide for employees who are faced with choosing between caring for a loved one and losing a job, seniority, or a promotion. In response to pressures on the workforce to care for a family member, Congress passed the **Family Medical**

The OSHA statute was passed to prevent employee injuries in the workplace.

---

[19]Whistle-blowing protections were discussed in detail in Chapter 10, "Agency and Employment Relationships."
[20]445 U.S. 1 (1980).

Leave Act (FMLA),[21] which sets out the basic protections for workers who need a brief leave from work to care for themselves or an immediate family member. Some states have similar leave statutes that allow for additional time periods or provide additional medical leave protections to employees within its state's jurisdiction.

FMLA Scope and Coverage

The FMLA is administered by the Department of Labor and applies to employers who have 50 or more full-time employees and only full-time employees who have been employed for at least one year are protected. Both private and public employers are covered. The law mandates that those employers provide up to 12 weeks of unpaid leave to employees for the purposes of caring for family medical matters during any 12-month period. Eligible employees may take an FMLA leave to care for a newborn or newly adopted baby, or when a *serious health condition* affects the employee or the employee's spouse, child, or parent. In order to be eligible for an FMLA leave, the serious health condition must require continued treatments by a health care provider and must be of such severity as to render the person unable to care for herself for three consecutive days. All conditions that are covered under the FMLA must be properly documented by a physician and are subject to periodic reevaluation at the employer's request.

FMLA Protections

Although the FMLA does not require employers to pay employees on leave, it does require that the employer maintain the employee's health care benefits uninterrupted throughout the leave period. The FMLA also affords employees certain protections related to job security: (1) employers are restricted from taking or threatening any adverse job action against the employee because of an FMLA leave; (2) upon returning from the leave, employees are guaranteed employment in the same or a similar job at the same rate of pay; and (3) employers must reinstate an FMLA leave employee immediately upon the employee's notification that the leave is over. The FMLA does *not* require, however, that returning employees be credited with seniority that was accrued while on leave.

> **KEY POINT**
> The FMLA requires that an employee returning from a medical leave be reinstated at the same rate of pay.

Key Employees

If an employee's salary range is in the top 10 percent of all salaries in the company, the FMLA classifies him as a *key employee*. Although key employees are entitled to the FMLA protections, employers have a right not to reinstate the employee if reinstatement would cause a "substantial and grievous economic injury." However, courts apply this exception narrowly and employers must comply with required notifications and procedures set out by the statute, including the duty to notify an employee who is taking the leave that they are a key employee and the limits of the FMLA protections.

EMPLOYEE PRIVACY

The privacy of employees while in the workplace or performing work-related tasks is an issue of growing concern because many employers regularly monitor employee behavior in some form. A study coauthored by the American Management Association and the ePolicy Institute found that 73 percent of employers reported that they monitored employee e-mail messages and 48 percent regularly employed video surveillance. Ten percent even monitored social-networking sites.[22] Other issues related to employee privacy include telephone and voicemail monitoring, and drug and alcohol testing in various employment contexts.

---

[21] 29 U.S.C. § 2601, et seq.

[22] See *The 2007 Electronic Monitoring & Surveillance Survey* (New York: American Management Association, 2007).

As a general matter, an employee's right to privacy in the workplace is very limited. How-ever, employees may have some limited rights that are typically afforded by a statute.

CONCEPT SUMMARY   Employment Regulation Laws

Federal Statute	General Provisions	Coverage
Fair Labor Standards Act (FLSA)	Wages and hours/child labor	(1) payment of minimum wage, (2) maximum 40-hour workweek, (3) overtime pay rate, and (4) restriction on children working in certain occupations and during cer-tain hours.
Employee Retirement Income Security Act (ERISA)	Pensions and retire-ment funds	Employers that establish retirement benefits are subject to the requirements of ERISA laws and regulations that primarily require employers to (1) make certain disclo-sures related to investment risk, and (2) provide transpar-ency to plan beneficiaries.
Social Secu-rity Act	Retirement income	Workers are entitled to a retirement income from the fed-eral government and a broad set of benefits for workers that are funded by mandatory employment taxes paid by both employer and employee into a trust fund and admin-istered by the federal government.
Federal Unemploy-ment Tax Act (FUTA)	Temporary and perma-nent unem-ployment	Provides limited payments that are funded by employer–employee employment taxes to workers who have been temporarily or permanently terminated from employment through no fault of their own.
Workers' compensa-tion statutes (state level)	Workplace injuries	Mandatory alternative to negligence lawsuits by offering compensation to an employee who suffered an accidental injury (in the course of employment), which is funded through employer-paid insurance policies as the exclusive remedy for the injury.
Occupa-tional Safety and Health Act (OSHA)	Workplace safety	Sets workplace rules and regulations, administered and enforced by the Occupational Safety and Health Admin-istration, to promote the safety of workers and prevent workplace injuries.
Family Med-ical Leave Act (FMLA)	Medical leaves	Requires that an employee returning from a medical leave to care for himself or an immediate family member be reinstated at the same rate of pay.

Monitoring of E-mails and Internet Usage

An employee's activities while using an employer's computer system are not protected by any privacy laws. All computer use is ordinarily subject to employer monitoring including the right to:

- Track Web sites visited by their employees.
- Block employees from visiting specific Internet sites.
- Limit the amount of time an employee may spend on a specific Web site.

A company's information technology services may use filters, keystroke recording software, and other detection devices for determining whether the use of e-mail is inconsistent with company policy. At large companies, part of the management team may include compliance officers assigned to coordinate monitoring and ensure that employees are following all company e-mail and Internet policies.

Employer Liability   Employers are increasingly employing elaborate employee monitoring measures primarily to limit their risk of vicarious liability (liability for the act of an employee) in areas such as defamation and employment discrimination. For example, in the AMA/ePolicy Survey cited earlier, 15 percent of the companies surveyed had faced a lawsuit triggered by employee e-mail. Companies typically adopt specific guidelines and polices for e-mail and Internet use and inform employees that all Internet usage and e-mail is subject to monitoring.

Telephone and Voicemail

While the right of an employer to monitor e-mail and Internet usage of workplace computers for business reasons is very expansive, employees are afforded certain protections for telephone calls and voicemail by the **Electronic Communications Privacy Act (ECPA).**[23] The ECPA updated existing wiretap laws and restricts an employer from monitoring an employee's personal calls (even those from the workplace) without their consent. Nor may an employer access an employee's office voicemail without their consent. However, the ECPA has two exceptions that severely limit its protections for employees. First, the business-extension exception permits an employer to monitor employee electronic communications on company-owned devices so long as it is in the ordinary course of business. Second, the ECPA allows an employer to avoid liability if the employee consents to the monitoring. Some employers now routinely require employees to consent to monitoring as a condition of employment.

Drug and Alcohol Testing

Employee privacy protection from use of regular or random drug or alcohol tests in the workplace is governed primarily by state statutes, and these laws vary considerably. Some states permit employee testing so long as the employer follows certain procedural safeguards intended to ensure confidentiality, safety, and accuracy. Other states permit testing only in cases where the employee's job carries a great deal of risk to themselves or the public or when a worker has been involved in a work-related accident where drug use was suspected.

American with Disabilities Act Considerations   One important issue that arises with drug and alcohol testing is the rights of an employee under the Americans with Disabilities Act (ADA). The ADA, which is discussed in detail in Chapter 12, prohibits discrimination on the basis of a physical disability. If the testing uncovers a former drug addiction (or current alcoholism), under certain circumstances the employee is protected from discipline or termination under the ADA.

Polygraph Testing

In 1988, Congress passed the **Employee Polygraph Protection Act,**[24] which prohibits most private sector employers from requiring a polygraph (lie detector) test as a condition of employment. Additionally, employers are prohibited from taking or threatening action

---

[23]18 U.S.C. § 2510, et seq.

[24] 29 U.S.C. § 2001, et seq.

against current employees who refuse to take the test. However, the act permits employers to use polygraph tests when investigating losses attributable to theft or other economic loss, or the employee is in the security or pharmaceutical industry. The law does not apply if the employer is a federal, state, or local government entity. Note that some state statutes give employees added protections related to the use of a polygraph test such as limiting their use to preemployment screening only.

LABOR UNIONS AND COLLECTIVE BARGAINING

LO11-5

Another source of legal protections for workers is through labor unions. Although union membership peaked in the early 1950s when nearly one-third of American workers were unionized, in 2008 only 12.4 percent of employed workers belonged to a union.[25] Today most labor unions in America are members of one of the two larger umbrella organizations: the American Federation of Labor-Congress of Industrial Organizations (AFL-CIO), or the Changes to Win Federation, which split from the AFL-CIO in 2005.

Labor Law

The **National Labor Relations Act (NLRA),**[26] originally passed in 1935, is the centerpiece of labor-management regulation statutes. It provides general protections to the rights of workers to organize, engage in **collective bargaining,** and use economic weapons (such as a strike) in the collective bargaining process. Collective bargaining is the process of negotiating an agreement on behalf of an entire workforce instead of individuals negotiating privately on their own behalf (or not negotiating at all). The statute also contained an enabling provision that formed the **National Labor Relations Board (NLRB)** to administer, implement, and enforce the law's wide-sweeping provisions. In addition to the traditional administrative agency duties of implementation and enforcement, the NLRB monitors union elections for fraud and sets guidelines for employers and unions with respect to fair labor practices.

In general, the NLRA covers all employers whose business activity involves some aspect of interstate commerce. As a practical matter, under modern interpretation by the courts, this means that the NLRA coverage is practically universal. Some workers are specifically exempted by statute, including railroad and airline employees.[27] To be eligible for protection under the NLRA, the worker must be a *current* employee (not an applicant or retiree).

Labor-Management Relations

Through amendments to the NLRA since its enactment, Congress clarified and reformed the legal standards applicable to employers and unions intending to ensure fairness to both labor and management in resolving differences. These laws deemed certain labor practices as illegal, thus making them an *unfair* labor practice under the NLRA.

> **KEY POINT**
> The NLRA provides general protections to the rights of workers to organize and engage in collective bargaining.

Labor Management Relations Act   Passage of the NLRA brought about a wave of industrial strikes that impacted daily commercial activity across the United States. This created a backlash sufficient to cause Congress to limit certain union practices and rights

---

[25] See *Bureau of Labor Statistics Annual Report* for 2008. Note that in 2008 the number of unionized workers actually increased from 12.1 percent to 12.4 percent for the first time in four decades.

[26] 29 U.S.C. § 151, et seq. This law is also called the *Wagner Act* and it displaced an earlier attempt at labor regulation, the Norris-LaGuardia Act, which proved ineffective.

[27] Separate statutes govern railroad and airline labor management regulations.

by amending the NLRA with the **Labor Management Relations Act**[28] in 1947. The amendment prohibited employers and employees from agreeing that union membership is *required* as a condition for employment. The law also authorizes states to enact *right-to-work* laws, which make it illegal for employers to agree with unions that union membership be required for *continuing* employment. In sum, this permitted states to outlaw what had become a common part of labor-management agreements: forcing employees to join or continue membership in a union as a condition of employment. The law also made clear that employers had the right to voice their reasons for opposition to formation of a union and gave a specific authorization for the President of the United States to suspend a strike for up to 80 days in times of national emergency.[29]

Labor-Management Reporting and Disclosure Act   In response to increasing allegations of corruption in major trade unions, Congress enacted the **Labor-Management Reporting and Disclosure Act** in 1959,[30] which established a system of reporting and checks intended to uncover and prevent fraud and corruption among union officials. The law (1) regulates the internal operating procedures of a union including election processes, procedures, and rights of members at membership and officer meetings; (2) requires extensive financial disclosures by unions; and (3) gives the NLRB additional oversight jurisdiction for internal union governance.

Union Formation

While major labor unions such as the AFL-CIO are a well-known part of the American landscape, regional unions or even unions that have only one employer are recognized by the NLRA as well. If an employer has not already recognized a union, and a group of employees decides that they wish to form a **collective bargaining unit** to deal with labor-management matters such as negotiating a contract, the NLRA sets out a procedure for forming a union.

Authorization Cards   Typically, a group of employees organize an effort to have other workers sign **authorization cards** indicating that they wish to form a local union and/or to join an existing union. At least 30 percent of the authorization cards must be signed by employees in a certain bargaining unit. Employees may bargain collectively only if they have a mutuality of interests (similar, nonmanagement jobs, work sites, and conditions). Bargaining units may be recognized as employees of a single employer or those of an entire region or industry.

Election   Once the union organizers obtain authorization cards from at least 30 percent of the members of a bargaining unit, the authorization cards are filed with the NLRB. The formal union certification process begins when the NLRB sets a date for an **election** (vote to elect or reject unionization) by the entire bargaining unit. During the period of time prior to the election, union organizers are permitted to *campaign,* for example, by distributing flyers and leaflets to employees. However, employers still have a right to *limit* any union campaign activities that take place on the employer's property and/or during the regular workday so long as they can justify the limits based

---

[28]29 U.S.C. § 141 (also known as the *Taft-Hartley Act*).

[29]Labor unions waged an extensive lobbying campaign to oppose the bill, but the provision related to the right to suspend a strike in the event of national emergency was popular with the citizenry who still had Word War II in vivid memory. President Truman vetoed the law, but Congress overrode the veto.

[30]29 U.S.C. § 1154 (also known as the *Landrum-Griffin Act*).

on business reasons (such as safety or interference with business operations) and not simply an effort to stop unionization. One appellate court has held, for example, that employer restrictions on distribution of pro-union literature during an unpaid lunch hour in an employee cafeteria were overly restrictive and not sufficiently related to legitimate business objectives.[31] Although employers may not impose overly burdensome restrictions on employees engaging in pro-union campaigns, employees cannot use threats or coercion in their efforts to convince other bargaining unit employees to unionize. In a 1992 case, the Supreme Court ruled that nonemployee union organizers *may not* distribute pro-union flyers in a company owned parking lot without permission of the company.[32] Misconduct during a campaign constitutes an unfair labor practice and results in the NLRB or a court setting aside any election results as well as other enforcement action (and sometimes criminal charges).[33] Employers also have a right to campaign *against* unionization, but are subject to regulatory restrictions designed to prevent employers from using economic pressure to influence employee voting. The NLRA regulations prohibit employers from using threats of termination or demotions or incentives (such as a bonus) in exchange for a nonunion vote.

Certification   After a legally sound election is held, a simple majority of pro-union votes is required for the NLRB to **certify** the collective bargaining unit as a union. The employer must then recognize the union as the exclusive bargaining representative of the workers and is required to bargain in good faith with the union thereafter. Table 11.3 summarizes the union formation process.

Reform Efforts   Beginning in 2007, several efforts have been made to amend the NLRA with the Employee Free Choice Act (sometimes referred to by the media as the *Card Check Act*), which would provide workers an option of procedures for having a union certified as the legal representative of the bargaining unit. The most controversial provision of the law would authorize the NLRB to certify unions either through an NLRB supervised election or when the bargaining unit can show that over 50 percent of the employees in the bargaining unit have signed an authorization card. The later process is called *card check*. The proposed law is supported by labor unions on the basis that it protects the unionization process from employers that are resistant to collective bargaining. Employers are generally against the law on the basis that it puts undue pressure on employees to sign authorization cards. The law did not have the support necessary for passage in 2008 or 2009. However, given the current political climate, lawmakers may well attempt to pass a similar law during the current session. For an update on any amendments to the NLRA, check this textbook's Web site at www.mhhe.com/melvin.

Collective Bargaining   LO11-6

Collective bargaining is the process of negotiating terms and conditions of employment for employees in the collective bargaining unit. These terms are typically negotiated and, if a collective bargaining agreement is reached, the parties enter into a binding contract. The NLRA regulations set out certain guidelines for which terms must be negotiated and which terms are not subject to the bargaining requirements. Union contracts typically include terms related to wages, benefits (such as health care insurance and pension accounts), work hours, overtime procedures, promotion systems, as well as procedures for handing disciplinary violations, suspensions, terminations, and layoffs.

---

[31] *International Transportation Service v. NLRB*, 449 F.3d 160 (D.C. Cir. 2006).

[32] *Lechmere, Inc. v. NLRB*, 502 U.S. 527 (1992).

[33] *Associated Rubber Co. v. NLRB*, 296 F.3d 1055 (11th Cir. 2002).

Good Faith Bargaining Requirements   The NLRA requires that both parties engage in good faith negotiations. This is not a requirement that one side or the other concede a particular term. Rather, the parties are obligated to demonstrate that they are engaged in moving toward an agreement. Tactics by either side that are intended to delay, stall, or hinder the process, or to undermine the union through economic pressure on workers, constitute unfair labor practices and the NLRB may opt to intervene and conduct labor negotiations or pursue enforcement action for unfair labor practices if appropriate.

Grievances   Union contracts normally contain apparatus designed to arbitrate union **grievances** against an employer action or practice. Enforcement is initiated when an affected union member files an employee grievance. The union is given the exclusive authority to invoke the arbitration provisions of the agreement, and it conducts the proceedings before the arbitrator on behalf of the employee. The arbitrator's award is always subject to review by courts that are applying federal standards related to fairness and good faith. However, a court will not set aside an award by an arbitrator on the basis that the court disagrees with the decision. Courts give great deference to arbitrators and will only intervene in cases of fundamental unfairness in some procedural or substantive way.

If the union chooses not to bring a grievance to arbitration, the individual union member is normally *not authorized* to pursue a lawsuit against the employer to enforce contract provisions. The union has broad discretion in deciding when to seek arbitration on the basis of a union member grievance.

LO11-7, 11-8   Strikes and Other Work Stoppages

The NLRA specifically provides for union employees to commence a **strike** in order to induce the employer to concede certain contract terms during collective bargaining. Certain occupations, though, may be restricted from striking via statute if allowing a strike would significantly jeopardize public health or safety (such as air traffic controllers, law enforcement, or emergency services). Although the right to strike is protected, the NLRA also provides guidelines for when, where, and how a strike may be carried out. Most strikes are commenced when the employer-union negotiations have reached an impasse and the union membership has determined that extreme action is necessary to continue

TABLE 11.3   Forming a Union

Authorization Cards	Filing with NLRB	Campaign	Election	Certification or Rejection
A group of employees, with a mutuality of interests, organize an effort to have other workers sign authorization cards. 30 percent of collective bargaining unit must sign in order to proceed to next step.	Authorization cards are filed with the NLRB and a formal union certification process begins when the NLRB sets a date for an election.	Union organizers campaign according to fair labor practices. Management is also permitted to engage in certain practices to campaign against unionization.	Entire bargaining unit votes to either elect or reject unionization. A simple majority is required to certify the union.	Employer must recognize the union as the exclusive bargaining representative of the workers and is required to bargain in good faith with the union thereafter. If a simple majority voted *against* unionization, the union is rejected.

The NLRA provides unionized workers with the right to strike and picket in a peaceful manner in front of the employer's facilities.

the bargaining process. During an impasse, the union leadership will call for the members to vote for "strike authorization" to be given to leadership if the employer refuses to continue the bargaining process. Although most strikes occur in a collective bargaining context, unions may also commence a strike against an employer that is engaging in unfair labor practices.

Poststrike Rehiring   While a strike is a potent economic weapon of a union, its impact on striking union members can be harsh. Workers are cut off from any pay, medical benefits, and other compensation until the strike is over. Moreover, employers have no *legal* obligation to rehire striking workers or provide retroactive pay in cases of a strike for economic reasons. Although, as a practical matter, rehiring of striking workers and partial or full retroactive pay is frequently guaranteed by the poststrike contract agreement, it is still a risk for some workers. However, if a strike is commenced due to an *unfair labor practice* rather than for *economic* reasons the striking employees are entitled to immediate restatement with back pay once they unconditionally return to work. Economic strikes typically arise in the context of union members failing to agree with the employer on wages or benefits. In Case 11.3, a federal appeals court distinguishes between economic strikes and unfair labor practice strikes.

From the perspective of the union, however, a strike also has the potential to result in significant economic harm for the employer company. Because the NLRA also gives other employees the right to refuse to cross a picket line, a strike can be devastating to the revenue of the employer if the strike requires a full or partial shutdown of business operations.

Strikers have the right to engage in **picketing** at the employer's facilities, although there is no right to picket at the actual property site owned by the company. Picketing must be peaceful and not interfere with the operations of the employer. Picketing cannot be used to prevent or harass customers or nonstriking employees.

FACT SUMMARY Midwestern Personnel Services (MPS) provided cement and transport truck drivers to River City Holdings (River City), a construction materials company that serviced a variety of locations in different states. MPS contracted to supply drivers to River City for a project at a union job site. The contract for the project guaranteed that MPS would supply River City with unionized drivers. MPS obtained driver/employee signatures on union authorization cards by advising drivers that membership in an out-of-state union, which MPS had selected, was required to keep their job at MPS. Eventually, the drivers became dissatisfied with the out-of-state union and formed a local union for collective bargaining purposes. When MPS refused to recognize the local union on the basis that the agreement with the out-of-state union remained in effect, the drivers went on strike. MPS subsequently refused the employees' unconditional offer to return to work and hired replacement workers. The National Labor Relations Board (NLRB) concluded that the employees' strike at MPS was based on MPS's unfair labor practices, rather than an economic dispute, and ordered the drivers reinstated with back pay. MPS appealed.

SYNOPSIS OF DECISION AND OPINION The U.S. Court of Appeals for the Seventh Circuit ruled in favor of the employees and affirmed the NLRB's findings. The court held that the strike was clearly based on MPS's unfair labor practices and, thus, the employees were entitled to reinstatement with back pay. The court noted that MPS unlawfully assisted the out-of-state union by negotiating with and recognizing it without any indication of uncoerced majority support by the employees. Further, the union authorization cards were unlawfully obtained by threats of termination, and the refusal to reinstate the employees was itself an unfair labor practice.

WORDS OF THE COURT: Unfair Labor Practice Strikes "Under [the NLRA], unfair labor practices strikers are entitled to immediate reinstatement with back pay once they unconditionally offer to return to work, whereas economic strikers may be permanently replaced. An unfair labor practices strike does not lose its character as such if economic motives contribute to its cause, however; it remains an unfair labor practices strike so long as the employees are motivated in part by unfair labor practices. [. . .] In determining whether management–labor cooperation has crossed over from permissible cooperation to unlawful coercion, courts consider a confluence of factors, with no one factor being dispositive. This nonexclusive list of factors includes whether the employer solicited contact with the union; the rank and position of the company's solicitor; whether the employer silently acquiesced in the union's drive for membership; whether the employer shepherded its employees to meetings with a prospective union; whether management was present at meetings between its employees and a prospective union; whether the signing of union authorization cards was coerced; and whether the employer quickly recognized the assisted union after the employees signed authorization cards yet exhibited prejudice against another union selected by the employees. [. . .] Normally a court defers to the credibility determinations of the NLRB unless there is some extraordinary reason why the court should ignore them, for instance if those findings are inherently incredible or patently unreasonable. [. . .] We conclude that substantial evidence in the record as a whole supports the Board's conclusions that the strike was an unfair labor practices strike."

Case Questions

1. Why does the court criticize MPS for recognizing the out-of-state union as the exclusive bargaining representative of the workers?

2. Suppose that MPS did recognize the local union and, subsequently, MPS and the local union negotiations reached an impasse over wages. Does MPS have any legal obligations to rehire the striking workers? Explain.

Unions may also call for union members and public boycotts of the employer's product or services as a method of pressuring management to engage in negotiations or concede a disputed point in a collective bargaining contract. If other unions recognize the boycotts, the economic impact on the employer may be significant.

Illegal Work Stoppages and Boycotts

The term *strike* implies a statutorily authorized work stoppage under the NLRA. Other types of work stoppages (or slowdowns) are illegal and employers may terminate employees, unionized or not, for engaging in illegal work stoppages. Most importantly, if peaceful picketing turns violent, or union members threaten management, then the strike becomes an illegal work stoppage and union members engaged in that conduct are not protected under the NLRA. Other illegal work stoppages include:

- *Wildcat strikes.* When individual union members or small groups of union members go on strike for short bursts of time without union authorization, this is called a *wildcat strike*. Wildcat strikes are illegal, but sometimes the form of a wildcat strike is subtle, such as when a group of employees simultaneously uses sick time to perpetrate a work stoppage or slowdown.

- *Sit-in strikes.* Any occupation of an employer's facility for the purpose of a work stoppage is illegal.

- *Strike during cooling-off period.* The NLRA allows a federal court to enforce a strike prohibition for a period of 80 days if a strike threatens national public health or security. During this cooling-off period, the government facilitates negotiations between the parties and any strike during this time is illegal.

- *Secondary boycotts.* Efforts to increase the pressure on an employer involved in collective bargaining by directing a strike against a third party (such as a supplier or customer of the employer) is illegal. For example, suppose that Trade Union (TU) is at an impasse with BigCo. In addition to striking against BigCo., TU organizes a picket line in front of the headquarters of one of BigCo.'s main customers, SellerCo., with signs stating "Boycott SellerCo. They support unfair labor practices." TU's actions toward SellerCo. is a secondary boycott and constitutes an unfair labor practice.

Lockouts and Replacement Workers   Employers who are faced with the prospect of a strike have several options under the law. First, any employer that reasonably anticipates a strike by a group of employees may employ a **lockout** by shutting down the business and preventing employees from working, thus depriving them of their employment and putting economic pressure on the union's members before the union can do the same to the employer through a strike. For example, suppose that in the BigCo.–TU negotiations above the parties are at an impasse in contract negotiations in October. BigCo. is concerned that TU may be waiting until BigCo.'s busy holiday season in December before they commence a strike in order to exert maximum economic pressure on BigCo.[34] Under these circumstances, BigCo. is permitted to shut down its plant immediately, locking out union members, in hopes of driving the union to the bargaining table in an effort to reach an agreement well ahead of their busy season. Some lockouts are not permitted under the NLRA. Any time an employer lacks a *legitimate business reason* for employing a lockout, it may be an unfair labor practice. Additionally, any time a lockout is used for undermining the collective bargaining process or disrupting union organizing efforts, the practice is illegal.

> **KEY POINT**
> Lockouts are a permissible labor practice so long as a legitimate business reason underlies the lockout.

Second, employers who are subject to a strike may hire nonunion **replacement workers** in order to continue operations during the strike. When the strike is over, employers may either retain replacement workers or discharge them (without liability) in favor of returning workers.

---

[34]Based on the Supreme Court's decision in *American Shipbuilding Company v. NLRB*, 380 U.S. 300 (1965).

Which of these actions may constitute an unfair labor practice under the NLRA?

1. Management refuses to recognize a certified union on the basis that several employees in the union have presented a petition that indicates that 40 percent of the employees in the proposed bargaining unit oppose unionization.

2. During a union-vote campaign, management throws an antiunion dinner banquet party and invites all employees and their families to attend. During the banquet, management gives speeches and points out the benefits to working in a nonunionized workplace.

3. During a union-vote campaign, pro-union employees distribute leaflets to fellow employees in the employee locker room as they leave the plant at the end of their shift.

4. Management at a school supplies manufacturing company are at an impasse with a certified union over contract terms. Because they fear that the union will call a strike just before their fall busy season, they shut down the plant and lock out employees.

5. A certified union strikes over management's refusal to abide by the terms of an existing collective bargaining agreement. Once the dispute is resolved in arbitration, management refuses to rehire half of the striking workers.

Answers to this Self-Check are provided at the end of the chapter.

KEY TERMS

Fair Labor Standards Act (FLSA) p. 276 A federal law enacted in 1938 and intended to cover all employers engaged in interstate commerce in providing payment of a minimum wage, a maximum 40-hour workweek, overtime pay, and restrictions on children working in certain occupations and during certain hours.

Overtime compensation p. 277 A higher rate of pay, calculated at one and one-half times the employee's hourly base rate, for the hours nonexempt employees work in excess of 40 hours in one seven-day workweek.

Exempt employees p. 277 Classification of employees that are not included in FLSA protection, generally consisting of employees whose responsibilities are primarily executive, administrative, or professional.

Pension p. 280 A retirement benefit in which the employer promises to pay a monthly sum, ordinarily based on the length of service and the employee's final salary rate, to employees who retire from the company after a certain number of years of service.

Tax-deferred retirement savings account p. 280 A retirement savings plan where the employee commits to saving a certain percentage in an account that is controlled directly by the employee, and the funds grow tax-free until they are withdrawn.

Employee Retirement Income Security Act (ERISA) p. 281 A federal law enacted in 1974 creating a comprehensive set of laws and regulations that requires employers to make certain disclosures related to investment risk, providing transparency for plan beneficiaries.

Social Security Act of 1935 (SSA) p. 281 A federal law providing for a broad set of benefits for workers that are funded by mandatory employment taxes paid by both employer and employee into a trust fund administered by the federal government.

Federal Unemployment Tax Act (FUTA) p. 282 A federal law enacted in 1935 to provide limited payments, funded through employment taxes used to fund state workforce agencies, to workers who had been temporarily or permanently terminated from employment through no fault of their own.

Worker Adjustment and Retraining Notification Act (WARN Act) p. 282 A federal law enacted in 1989 to protect employees by requiring most employers with

100 or more employees to provide at least a 60-day written notification of facility closings and mass layoffs of employees.

Workers' compensation p. 283 Statutes that provide an employee, injured in the course of employment, with a partial payment funded through employer-paid insurance policies, in exchange for mandatory relinquishment of the employee's right to sue his or her employer for the tort of negligence.

Occupational Safety and Health Act (OSHA) p. 283 A federal law enacted in 1970 setting forth workplace rules and regulations to promote safety of workers and prevent workplace injuries.

Family Medical Leave Act (FMLA) p. 285 A federal law enacted in 1993 that requires certain employers to give time off to employees to take care of their own or a family member's illness, or to care for a newborn or adopted child.

Electronic Communications Privacy Act (ECPA) p. 288 A federal law enacted in 1986 extending legal protection against wiretapping and other forms of unauthorized interception and explicitly allowing employers to monitor communications by employees using the employers' equipment so long as it is in the ordinary course of business or if the employee consents to the monitoring.

Employee Polygraph Protection Act p. 288 An act that prohibits most private sector employers from requiring a polygraph test as a condition of employment.

National Labor Relations Act (NLRA) p. 289 A federal law enacted in 1935 providing general protections for the rights of workers to organize, engage in collective bargaining, and take part in strikes and other forms of concerted activity in support of their demands (also known as the *Wagner Act*).

Collective bargaining p. 289 The process of negotiating terms and conditions of employment for employees in the collective bargaining unit.

National Labor Relations Board (NLRB) p. 289 An independent federal agency created by the NLRA charged with administering, implementing, and enforcing NLRA provisions, as well as monitoring union elections for fraud and setting guidelines for employers and unions with respect to fair labor practices.

Labor Management Relations Act p. 290 A federal law enacted in 1947 as an amendment to the NLRA prohibiting the forcing of employees to join or continue membership in a union as a condition of employment (also known as the *Taft-Hartley Act*).

Labor-Management Reporting and Disclosure Act p. 290 A federal law enacted in 1959 to establish a system of reporting and checks intended to uncover and prevent fraud and corruption among union officials through regulating internal operating procedures and union matters (also known as the *Landrum-Griffin Act*).

Collective bargaining unit p. 290 An employee group that, on the basis of a mutuality of interests, is an appropriate unit for collective bargaining.

Authorization cards p. 290 Signed statements by employees indicating that they wish to unionize and/or are electing to be represented by an existing union.

Election p. 290 A vote to elect or reject unionization by the entire bargaining unit.

Certify p. 291 The process in which a collective bargaining unit is recognized as a union, occurring when a legally sound election reveals a simple majority of pro-union votes.

Grievances p. 292 In labor law, a complaint filed with or by a union to challenge an employer's treatment of one or more union members.

Strike p. 292 A concerted and sustained refusal by workers to perform some or all of the services for which they were hired in order to induce the employer to concede certain contract terms during collective bargaining or to engage in fair labor practices.

Picketing p. 293 A union's patrolling alongside the premises of a business to organize the workers, to gain recognition as a bargaining agent, or to publicize a labor dispute with the owner or with whomever the owner deals.

Lockout p. 295 The shutdown of a business by the employer to prevent employees from working, thus depriving them of their employment and putting economic pressure on the union's members before the union can do the same to the employer through a strike.

Replacement workers p. 295 A term that refers to nonunion employees hired in order to continue operations during a strike.

Collegiate Banner Company (CBC) is a manufacturer and distributor of flags and banners bearing the names, logos, mottos, and mascots of American colleges and universities. Their products are purchased for retail sale by college bookstores as well as large-scale retail outlet sports equipment chains. CBC's administrative headquarters and sole manufacturing facility are located in different buildings on the same site. Its total workforce is 121 employees, with 76 employees located in the plant and the remaining 45 employees working in the office. CBC classifies their employees into two broad classifications: administrative employees or trade employees. The breakdown is as follows:

Administrative Employees

Position	Primary Duty	Pay Range	Location	Number of Employees
Executive managers	Business planning and operations.	$150,000 and above	Office	5
General manager	Hiring, supervision, and evaluation of professional staff.	$75,000–$100,000	Office	10
Professional staff	Operational functions such as accounting, customer service, marketing, logistics, and human resources.	$50,000–$100,000	Office	15
Support staff	Support managers and professional staff with administrative tasks such as scheduling, document and report preparation, answering calls, and keeping track of expenses.	$20,000 (entry level) to $75,000 (president's administrative assistant)	Office	15

Trade Employees

Position	Primary Duty	Pay Range	Location	Number of Employees
Plant supervisor	Day-to-day supervision of line managers and employees in the manufacturing facility.	$30/hour	75% Plant 25% Office	1
Line manager	Supervision of line workers in various sections of the plant. Responsible for evaluation, efficiency reports, and ensuring quality control.	$25–$30/hour	90% Plant 10% Office	10
Skilled tradesperson	Uses specialized equipment for product designs and layouts.	$20–$25/hour	Plant	20
Tradesperson	Line work of repetitive tasks required to manufacture the product.	$12–$20/hour	Plant	30
Delivery truck driver	Load and deliver product to retailers or wholesalers.	$12–$25/hour	Plant	15

1. Name the FLSA classification (covered or exempt) for each position in the table above and give your analysis for each classification.

2. Suppose that Falstaff is a plant manager and exercises his right to take a leave under the FMLA. When Falstaff returns he is told that the replacement plant manager has increased efficiency in the plant by 30 percent and that he is being reassigned as a skilled tradesperson because no other jobs are available. Has CBC violated the FMLA? Could CBC limit its liability by informing Falstaff that he is a key employee? What is the impact of key employee classification in this case?

3. Assume that CBC management is concerned about productivity and hires a consultant to restrict its company computers from accessing certain Web sites in the month of March during the national college basketball playoffs. Has CBC violated the employees' rights to privacy?

4. Suppose that several employees were interested in forming a union. Which groups of people have sufficient mutuality of interests to form a collective bargaining unit under the NLRA? Can any administrative employees be recognized as a collective bargaining unit? Why or why not?

5. Assume that personnel employed as tradespersons obtained sufficient authorization cards and the NLRB schedules an election. One of the organizers of the union effort passes out union fliers in the plant cafeteria during an unpaid lunch hour. The plant manager halts the practice on the basis that no union solicitation is permitted on CBC's property. Has CBC committed an unfair labor practice by prohibiting the distribution of the fliers? Suppose that the pro-union organizer distributed the fliers while the tradespersons were on the line working. Could CBC ban that practice? Why or why not?

6. Assume a union for skilled tradespersons is certified, but CBC refuses to recognize the union. They strike and picket outside of CBC's headquarters. They also organize a picket line in front of several Sports Outlet stores because Sports Outlet is a major retail store customer of CBC. Are these two pickets (one in front of CBC and one in front of Sports Outlet) permitted under the NLRA? Why are they different? If the union workers cease the strike and offer unconditionally to come back to work, must CBC reinstate them? Is this an economic strike? Why or why not?

MANAGER'S CHALLENGE

Companies that have a unionized workforce must incorporate union considerations into their business planning. Managers may be faced with difficult choices if union members are threatening to strike. Assume that you are employed as a general manager at CBC in Theory to Practice above and that the delivery truck drivers are unionized. You receive a voicemail from an executive manager informing you that negotiations over a union contract for the delivery truck drivers have stalled and that the union has threatened to hold a strike vote. She requests that you (individually or in small groups) compose a two- to three-page memorandum that describes the advantages and disadvantages from CBC's perspective of (1) a lockout, (2) a strike where CBC hires replacement workers, or (3) continuing negotiations. Be sure to address legal, ethical, economic, and employee-relations implications. A sample answer may be found on this textbook's Web site at www.mhhe.com/melvin.

CASE SUMMARY 11.1 :: Bonilla v. Baker Concrete Construction, 487 F.3d 1340 (2007)

COMPENSATION FOR COMMUTING

Bonillo was one of several workers hired by Baker Concrete to work on construction at the Miami airport. During construction, airport security required the workers to pass through a security gate and ride in an airport-authorized bus to the site. Baker Concrete paid the workers for when they were at the site at 7:30 a.m. until they left at 4:00 p.m. Because of the security requirements, the workers had to arrive at the airport an hour early in order to get to the site on time, and their commute home was extended 15 additional minutes. The workers sued, contending that under the Fair Labor Standards Act they should have been compensated for time spent being transported to and from the employee parking area to the construction site.

CASE QUESTIONS

1. Who prevails and why?
2. Explain your analysis and construct a hypothetical situation in which the losing party may have prevailed.

CASE SUMMARY 11.2 :: Mitchell v. Abercrombie & Fitch Co., 428 F. Supp. 2d 725 (S. D. Ohio)

OVERTIME

Mitchell was employed by the retail clothing chain Abercrombie & Fitch as a manager-in-training (MIT). As an MIT, Mitchell was scheduled to work a fixed, preset, five-day, 40-hour workweek and was paid an annual salary. Other than a high school diploma and general retail experience, there are no specific requirements for the MIT position. Mitchell's daily tasks consisted of a general exposure to principles in retail management including human resource practices and operational tasks such as setting up displays. Mitchell's

hours fluctuated from week to week, sometimes well beyond 40 hours, and she argued that she was entitled to overtime compensation under the FLSA.

CASE QUESTIONS

1. Given the stipulated facts, could Mitchell be considered a nonexempt employee entitled to overtime compensation? Why or why not?
2. Would your answer change if Mitchell were promoted to the position of manager? Explain.

CASE SUMMARY 11.3 :: Waremart Foods v. NLRB, 354 F.3d 870 (9th Cir. 2004)

UNFAIR LABOR PRACTICES

WinCo operates a grocery store in California on a 10-acre lot. In accordance with company policy, WinCo allows no solicitors on its premises except for allowing scouts to sell cookies. When a local union was campaigning for the upcoming election, nonemployee union representatives came on the premises and passed out pro-union literature in the company parking lot and in the employee cafeteria during an unpaid

lunch hour. WinCo forced the organizers to vacate the premises and the union complained.

CASE QUESTIONS

1. Does WinCo have the right to limit the local union's campaign activities on their property? What would they have to prove in order to do so? Cite an example.
2. Would the union's actions have any impact on the upcoming election? Explain.

CASE SUMMARY 11.4 :: Childress v. Darby Lumber, Inc., 357 F.3d 1000 (3d Cir. 2004)

WARN ACT

Childress was one of 106 employees employed by Darby Lumber. When Darby was sold to a new company, the new company quickly ran into financial problems. As a result, the new employer informed employees that there would be a major layoff. The next day Darby shut down its mill and laid off 88 employees, including Childress. The other 18 employees

continued operations at the mill for several weeks until they, too, were laid off.

CASE QUESTIONS

1. Could the WARN Act apply to Darby given the stipulated facts? Why or why not?
2. Suppose the layoffs were for a period of 5 months. Are the law's requirements triggered? Explain.

Self-Check **ANSWERS**

Exempt vs. Covered

1. Exempt. Computer programmers are specifically exempted by statute (despite the lower than $100,000 salary).

2. Exempt. Professional with advanced study and certification.

3. Covered. Hourly wage earner with repetitive work tasks.

4. Covered. See *Falcon v. Starbacks* on page 279.

5. Exempt. White-collar employees are likely to be regulated by state insurance laws.

Unfair Labor Practices

1. Unfair labor practice. Once an election has taken place, if a simple majority (51 percent) of the bargaining unit vote to unionize, the union is certified and must be recognized even if 40 percent oppose unionization.

2. Probably not an unfair labor practice. Management is permitted to campaign against unionization in such a way—so long as there are no financial incentives (such as bonuses) offered. Management may not threaten employees with pay cuts, demotions, or the like during the campaign.

3. Given that the workers are leaving at the end of the shift and that the fliers are distributed in the employee locker room, this is likely a permissible labor practice even though it takes place on the employer's premises.

4. This is known as a lockout. So long as there is a legitimate business reason, lockouts are permitted by the NLRA.

5. Refusal to hire is an unfair labor practice because the workers were striking over an unfair labor practice (refusing to abide by an existing collective bargaining contract) rather than for economic reasons. See *NLRB v. Midwestern* on page 294.

12
CHAPTER

Employment Discrimination

learning outcomes **checklist**

After studying this chapter, students who have mastered the material will be able to:

12-1   Define the term employment discrimination and articulate the origins of antidiscrimination law.

12-2   Explain the role of the Equal Employment Opportunities Commission (EEOC).

12-3   List and describe the protections afforded under the major federal antidiscrimination statutes.

12-4   Identify the protected classes under Title VII and explain why membership in a protected class is essential in a employment discrimination claim.

12-5   Apply three theories of discrimination and name the U.S. Supreme Court cases used to establish the standards for each theory.

12-6   Explain the concepts of a prima facie case and shifting of the burden of proof.

12-7   Describe the provisions of the Americans with Disabilities Act (ADA) and its impact on business operations.

12-8   List and describe the major defenses available to employers.

12-9   Apply the U.S. Supreme Court's standards necessary for a lawful affirmative action program.

12-10   Explain the role of state law in employment discrimination cases.

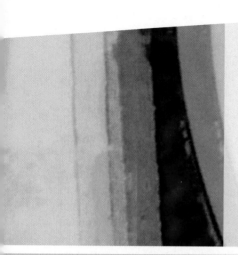

One of the most frequent legal challenges encountered by business owners and managers involves laws that prohibit *discrimination* in the workplace. Lawsuits related to employment discrimination have increased dramatically in the last 20 years, and managers frequently find themselves involved in employment discrimination claims as a witness, supervisor, defendant, or as a plaintiff/victim. This area of law has developed very rapidly over the last 50 years, and the assortment of statutes along with standards and tests developed by courts to apply the rules all combine to form a relatively complex body of law from a variety of sources. In this chapter, students will learn:

- The definition, source, and statutory framework of discrimination law.
- Theories of discrimination and employer defenses.
- The role of affirmative action in the workplace.
- Additional workplace antidiscrimination laws imposed by the states.

DEFINITION, SOURCE OF LAW, AND STATUTORY ORIGINS

Recall from previous chapters that one of the major exceptions to the employment-at-will doctrine, whereby employers may discharge employees with or without cause without triggering liability, is when a statute prohibits the employer's action. One of the major categories of statutes that prohibit employers from terminating employees are antidiscrimination statutes that bar any job action (such as termination) based on certain discriminatory motives. The term **employment discrimination** has a broad-based definition encompassing workplace-related discrimination that includes (1) the hiring process; (2) treatment of employees in terms of promotions/demotions, work schedules, working conditions, or assignments; and (3) disciplinary action such as reprimands, suspension, or termination. Historically, U.S. common law had recognized virtually no protections for employees from discrimination based on race, color, gender, religion, national origin, age, disabilities, and other characteristics. In fact, until the Equal Pay Act of 1963, employers were not prohibited from making job decisions that adversely impacted women in terms of pay disparity. One year later, Congress passed the most sweeping antidiscrimination protections for workers in U.S. history as part of the Civil Rights Act of 1964. In addition to federal statutes, some states have statutes that provide additional antidiscrimination protections in the workplace.

Equal Employment Opportunity Commission (EEOC)

An important part of the Civil Rights Act of 1964 is the creation of an agency to monitor employer compliance with the statute. The administrative agency[1] charged with carrying out federal workplace antidiscrimination laws is the **Equal Employment Opportunity Commission (EEOC).** The EEOC is a five-member commission whose members are appointed by the President with approval of the Senate. As an administrative agency, the EEOC uses its rulemaking authority, investigatory powers, and enforcement action as necessary to administer the statutory mandates established by Congress. The EEOC plays two important roles in assuring victims of discrimination protection under various statutes. First, filing a complaint with the EEOC is the first step for a party claiming unlawful employment discrimination (procedures for asserting a discrimination claim are discussed later in this chapter). Second, in certain cases the EEOC will sue on *behalf* of an aggrieved employee. This is a powerful method of enforcing antidiscrimination laws because it gives aggrieved employees the full resources of the federal government, which can be particularly crucial when bringing an individual claim of employment discrimination against a large employer.

However, as a practical matter EEOC can pursue only a fraction of claims that are made by employees. The agency often focuses on cases that have some important legal significance or where the employer's conduct was particularly egregious or in bad faith (e.g., attempting to prevent an employee's claim with a threat of termination or demotion).

FEDERAL WORKPLACE ANTIDISCRIMINATION STATUTES

The primary federal antidiscrimination statutes are (1) **Title VII** of the Civil Rights Act of 1964[2] and its subsequent amendments, especially the Civil Rights Act of 1991;[3] (2) the **Age Discrimination in Employment Act of 1967 (ADEA);**[4] and (3) the **Americans with**

---

[1] An administrative agency is a statutorily created body with responsibilities related to the formation, implementation, and enforcement of regulations intended to administer a federal law. Administrative agencies and law are covered in detail in Chapter 17, "Administrative Law."

[2] 42 U.S.C. § 2000e, et seq.

[3] 42 U.S.C. § 1981a, et seq.

[4] 29 U.S.C. § 620, et seq.

Disabilities Act of 1990 (ADA),[5] which was last amended in 2009. The **Equal Pay Act of 1963** is actually part of the Fair Labor Standards Act, but contains some antidiscrimination provisions as well.

These statutes may be categorized into two classes that are helpful to understanding their purpose: (1) laws that require the person in the protected class to receive *equal treatment* as nonclass members, and (2) laws that require the person in the protected class to receive *special treatment.* For example, Title VII of the Civil Rights Act of 1964 requires women to be treated equally with men. However, the Americans with Disabilities Act (discussed later in this chapter) requires that persons with certain disabilities be given special treatment via reasonable accommodations by their employer.

To illustrate the contours of the federal antidiscrimination statutes, suppose that Prescott is seeking employment as an internal accountant and provides a résumé and supporting application materials to WidgetCo., a manufacturing firm with 50 employees. This hypothetical is used throughout the chapter to discuss possible scenarios involving various employment discrimination theories and defenses.

TITLE VII

LO12-4, 12-5, 12-6

Title VII of the Civil Rights Act of 1964 and its amendments make up the centerpiece of antidiscrimination statutes. Even when interpreting antidiscrimination statutes that are not part of Title VII, courts often apply the antidiscrimination law using the Title VII statutory model and application procedures. Title VII applies to any private sector employer with 15 or more full-time employees as well as labor unions, employment agencies, state and local governments, and most federal government employees. The law covers a comprehensive set of job-related transactions including hiring/firing, promotion/demotion, disciplinary actions, work schedule, pay rate, job assignment, and other employer actions. Referred to simply as Title VII, the law prohibits discrimination in the workplace on the basis of an employee's race, color, national origin, gender, or religion. The classifications are known as **protected classes.** In 1978, Congress amended Title VII to specifically add pregnancy as a protected class as well.[6]

Antidiscrimination laws cover job-related transactions such as the hiring process.

Protected Classes

It is important to understand that one fundamental tenet of federal antidiscrimination laws is that not all discrimination is illegal. Under Title VII or any other antidiscrimination laws, statutory protection is only extended to those who have been discriminated against based on their membership in a protected class. For example, suppose that in our Prescott hypothetical, above, that Prescott was hired by WidgetCo. as an accountant. Prescott shows up on the first day wearing a T-shirt and blue jeans. His manager points out that his attire is not consistent with company dress policy and requests that he leave and return in more formal business attire.

---

[5]42 U.S.C. § 12002, et seq.

[6]Pregnancy Discrimination Act of 1978, 42 U.S.C. § 2000(e)k.

Prescott refused to comply with his manager's request, so he was terminated. For purposes of understanding employment discrimination statutes, there are two important questions. First, was Prescott discriminated against? The answer is clearly yes. Prescott was terminated not for his poor performance, but for wearing certain attire. Thus, it can be said that Prescott was the victim of anti-blue jeans discrimination. However, the second question is more important: Was Prescott discriminated against based on his membership in a *protected class?* In other words, did WidgetCo. terminate Prescott based on his color, race, national origin, religion, or gender? The answer is clearly no. Because this particular type of discrimination was not based on Prescott's association with a protected class, WidgetCo.'s discriminatory action (his termination) is not prohibited by Title VII.

It is also important to note that the plaintiff need not be in a *minority* of the protected classes in order to be covered by Title VII. While the majority of discrimination cases filed are based on discrimination related to a minority within a protected class, the statute protects against any discrimination based on association with a protected class and does not require that the plaintiff be a member of a certain ethnic category. For example, in *McDonald v. Santa Fe Train*,[7] the U.S. Supreme Court held that racial discrimination against white employees violates Title VII as well if the employer was motivated by race. However, there are certain instances when an employer's preference for certain minority class members in an employment decision is *permitted* by an affirmative action plan (discussed later in this chapter).

> ## KEY POINT
> In order to be protected under Title VII, the employer's discriminatory decision must have been based on the employee's membership in a *protected class*.

Theories of Discrimination

For several years following the passage of the Civil Rights Act of 1964, courts struggled with having to apply such a massive statutory scheme in the workplace with virtually no comparable protections in the history of labor law to use as precedent. The result was that federal courts applied the statutes unevenly and with varying application, which resulted in overly broad or overly narrow interpretations of the law. Beginning in 1971, the Supreme Court began to develop guidance for the courts on how to apply Title VII. In these landmark cases, the Court developed several theories of discrimination that plaintiffs may pursue based on the type of discrimination alleged. These cases also provided the lower courts with a system of tests used to apply the various theories of discrimination. Thus, the three most common theories and attendant tests are sometimes referred to by their case name. The theories are (1) **disparate treatment** (*McDonnell Douglas*[8] standard); (2) **mixed motives** (*Hopkins*[9] standard); and (3) **disparate impact** (*Griggs*[10] standard). Note that subsequent amendments to Title VII have added statutory language consistent with the case law on disparate treatment and disparate impact. Nonetheless, the theories are still commonly referred to by their case names.

Disparate Treatment   Disparate treatment is overt and intentional discrimination. Simply put, when an employer treats an employee (or potential employee) differently based on her membership in a protected class, it constitutes discrimination under Title VII. This theory of discrimination may be proved through the use of either *direct* or *indirect* evidence. Direct evidence is evidence that proves a fact without any further inference or presumption. For example,

---

[7]427 U.S. 273 (1976). The case involved a lawsuit brought by a white employee who was terminated for allegedly stealing from the company. The same incident involved a black employee who was also alleged to have stolen from the company, but was only given a reprimand.

[8]*McDonnell Douglas Corp. v. Green*, 411 U.S. 792 (1973).

[9]*PriceWaterhouse v. Hopkins*, 490 U.S. 228 (1989).

[10]*Griggs v. Duke Power Co.*, 401 U.S. 424 (1971).

suppose in our working hypothetical that Prescott is a woman who applied for the position at WidgetCo. After the interview, the manager informs her that she will not get the position and states: "I think you are the most qualified applicant, but we prefer a man in that role, because this job may involve night work and I would be concerned about a woman's safety." Here we have WidgetCo. treating Prescott differently based on a protected class—gender.

However, as one could imagine, direct evidence of discrimination became increasingly rare in favor of a more subtle form of discrimination. In *McDonnell Douglas Corp. v. Green,* the Supreme Court crafted an alternative method of disparate treatment proof that plaintiffs could use to obtain relief under Title VII. This method of proof is usually referred to as the *McDonnell Douglas* standard and it contemplates a burden-shifting analysis (explained below).

The *McDonnell Douglas* standard has *three stages.* In the first stage the plaintiff must establish a *prima facie*[11] case of discrimination.

To establish a claim of discrimination that satisfies the prima facie requirement under the *McDonnell Douglas* standard, the Supreme Court created a four-prong disparate treatment test that lower courts adapt to fit the type of discrimination at issue. The plaintiff must establish that:

- She is a member of a protected class.
- She applied for and was qualified for the job (or promotion, etc., depending on the factual circumstances of the controversy) and met the employer's legitimate expectations.
- She was rejected by the employer.
- The employer continued to seek applicants or filled the position with a person outside the protected class.

> **Legal Speak ›))**
> **Prima Facie Case**
> Establishing certain evidence that is sufficient to prevail in a discrimination claim without proving additional facts, unless disproved or rebutted by the opposing party.

In cases involving other types of discriminatory action unrelated to hiring or promotion, the appropriate prong is adjusted accordingly. For example, in a wrongful termination claim, the plaintiff would have to satisfy prongs two and three (candidate was qualified and rejected despite the qualification) by proving that she was terminated by her employer despite qualifications and performance and that, following the discharge, she was replaced by someone with comparable qualifications who was not in the same protected class.

Once the plaintiff makes out a prima facie case, the second stage of the *McDonnell Douglas* standard requires the **burden of proof** to *shift* to the employer who then must articulate a *legitimate, nondiscriminatory* reason for the discriminatory action. If the employer does provide a legitimate, nondiscriminatory reason for firing the plaintiff, the third stage of the standard con-

> **KEY POINT**
> *Burden of proof and presumptions.* As in all civil cases, the initial burden of proof rests upon the plaintiff to prove her case. Once the plaintiff establishes a prima facie case, a presumption is created that the employer discriminated against the employee. However, this presumption is rebuttable (refutable) because the burden of proof then shifts to the employer to provide a nondiscriminatory reason for the decision. If the nondiscriminatory reason is plausible and supported by the evidence, this creates a presumption that the employer is not liable for discrimination. The burden then shifts once again back to the employee who then has the opportunity to offer evidence that tends to prove that the reason offered by the employer is a pretext.

templates that the burden then *shifts back* to the employee to show that the reason given by the employer is not the actual reason for the employment action. A false reason under these circumstances is called a **pretext.** It should be noted that issues related to proving discrimination and pretext are *fact* questions for the jury to decide. In a disparate treatment case, the plaintiff is alleging intentional discrimination, the employer is asserting a legitimate reason for its action, and it is up to the jury as the finder of fact to decide which version of facts is more compelling and believable.

---

[11]A Latin phrase meaning "at a first view," which, according to the authoritative *Collins Latin Gem,* is sometimes mistakenly translated as "on its face."

Suppose that in the Prescott hypothetical case she was African American and was hired by WidgetCo. as a junior accountant. After three years, she was promoted to senior accountant and given a pay raise. When a manager's position was posted a year later, Prescott applied and was hopeful that with her four years of experience and other qualifications, she would get the promotion. However, she was passed over for this position and for several subsequent openings for management positions. Eventually, she learned that two managers who had been promoted ahead of her each had only one year of experience and that all of the managers promoted ahead of her were either white or Asian. Prescott's disparate treatment claim under the *McDonnell Douglas* standard's four-prong test would likely be sufficient to establish a prima facie case because (1) Prescott was in a protected class; (2) she had applied for and was qualified for the promotion; (3) she was not promoted; and (4) WidgetCo. promoted less-experienced individuals. At this point, the burden of proof *shifts* to WidgetCo. to provide a legitimate, nondiscriminatory reason for not promoting Prescott. Suppose that WidgetCo., submits employee records that indicate that Prescott was late for work three times in the last two years and they cite that as their legitimate reason. The burden of proof then *shifts back* to the employee/plaintiff to provide evidence that WidgetCo.'s reason is merely a pretext for discriminatory action. For example, Prescott could provide evidence of pretext by citing attendance records of others in the company to prove that a record of only three incidents of lateness did not disqualify other employees from bring promoted.

In Case 12.1, a federal appellate court applies the *McDonnell Douglas* standard for disparate treatment and provides an example of the burden-shifting analysis and when an employee must prove pretext.

Mixed Motives   Although the Supreme Court made it easier for plaintiffs to assert their Title VII rights under a disparate treatment theory, employers were being consistently insulated from liability from Title VII by asserting legitimate, subjective-based reasons (such as inability to work as a member of a team) to defeat a Title VII claim. Even when these cases involved unlawful discriminatory reasons for the employment action, so long as the employer could cite even one legitimate reason, the employee could *not* recover under a disparate treatment theory. To alleviate this problem, the Supreme Court articulated an alternative theory of protection under Title VII when the cause of the employment action was motivated by both legitimate *and* discriminatory motives. The mixed motives theory was articulated in *PriceWaterhouse v. Hopkins.*[12]

The case involved Hopkins, a woman employed as an associate at the global accounting and consulting firm of PriceWaterhouse (now PriceWaterhouseCoopers). Like many professional service firms, associates are eventually proposed for partnership in the firm after a certain length of time. Hopkins was proposed for partnership and, as part of the process, the firm's partners were asked to write evaluations of Hopkins and make a recommendation as to whether the firm should offer her partnership. In general, those that are not voted in as partners are either terminated or held over for reconsideration in the next year. Hopkins's evaluations were mostly positive, with partners praising her role in securing a large government client. They also evaluated her as extremely competent, bright, and hardworking. However, a significant number of partners were concerned about her interpersonal skills. She was abrasive, shouted at the staff, and used foul language in public. Several partners, though, went further into criticism and used gender-stereotypical, demeaning comments such as giving Hopkins advice to "act more like a lady" or "take a course in charm school." One partner even made a suggestion that Hopkins should "walk more femininely, talk more femininely, dress more femininely, and wear makeup" if she wanted to improve her chances for partnership. As a result of these negative comments, the

---
[12]490 U.S. 228 (1989).

FACT SUMMARY Aquino, a man of Chinese-Filipino origin, worked on a Honda assembly line. His time at Honda was tumultuous and he had been suspended on numerous occasions for disciplinary violations. Upon returning from a suspension in 2001, Aquino was assigned to an engine installation station. Concurrent with Aquino's assignment, Honda experienced a number of cases of vehicle tampering and vandalism. A Honda manager conducted an investigation and concluded that Aquino was the only person with access to the tools necessary to conduct the vandalism. Upon Honda's complaint, Aquino was arrested, but charges were eventually dropped due to insufficient evidence. Nonetheless, Honda terminated Aquino's employment after an internal investigation confirmed its initial conclusions on the matter. Aquino filed suit claiming his termination was based on the fact that he was the only nonwhite employee assigned to the unit.

SYNOPSIS OF DECISION AND OPINION The Sixth Circuit Court of Appeals ruled in Honda's favor and dismissed Aquino's claims. The court noted that during the second part of the *McDonnell Douglas* analysis the burden shifted to Honda to prove it had a legitimate, nondiscriminatory reason to dismiss Aquino. The court reasoned that Honda's reasonable belief that Aquino committed the vandalism met this burden. The court also pointed out that when the burden shifted back to Aquino to show this was pretextual, he could not offer any evidence of pretext. Therefore, Aquino did not meet his burden and, as a result, Honda was justified in terminating his employment.

WORDS OF THE COURT: Pretext "McDonnell Douglas's third step requires the plaintiff to introduce evidence to create a genuine issue of material fact that (1) the defendant's stated reasons had no basis in fact, (2) the stated reasons were not the actual reasons, or (3) the stated reasons were insufficient to explain the defendant's actions. [. . .] Aquino attempt[ed] to meet his burden by trying to discredit Honda's stated reason through innuendo and flat denial. [He asserted] (but d[id] not introduce evidence to corroborate the assertion) that Honda manipulated the evidence of the incidents. [. . .] Aquino may or may not have been the author of the vandalism, but that is essentially beside the point; what the court must assess here is whether Aquino has introduced evidence that Honda's accusation (and therefore its stated reason) was baseless, malicious, or pretextual."

Case Questions

1. Why did Aquino have the burden of proving that Honda's reason for discharging him was a pretext? Didn't he already prove a prima facie case?

2. Considering the criminal charges against him were dropped, what would Aquino need to have shown in order to meet his burden that Honda's reasons for dismissing him were pretextual?

---

firm initially opted to hold Hopkins over for one more year, but eventually notified her that she would not be placed for a partnership vote again. Hopkins sued under Title VII using a theory of disparate treatment, but the firm pointed to the documented legitimate reasons relating to Hopkins's inability to work as a team member. In essence, the case involved both legitimate reasons for the job action that were mixed with illegitimate discriminatory motives as evidenced by the evaluations written by the partners.

Ultimately, the Supreme Court adopted a new theory and framework for certain intentional discrimination: *mixed motives*. Under this theory, an employee was protected under Title VII in a case where legitimate motives were mixed with illegitimate motives if the employee proves the protected class membership was a *substantial factor in the decision-making process*. Once established, the burden then shifts to the employer to offer evidence that it would have made the same employment decision regardless of the protected characteristics. In the Hopkins case, the Court held that Hopkins had met her burden of proving that gender was a substantial factor in the firm's decision-making process because the language of the evaluations were so closely tied to gender discrimination. The Court also held that the employer's burden need only be proved by a preponderance of the evidence.

Legal Speak »))
Preponderance of the Evidence More likely than not. A lower standard of proof as compared to "clear and convincing evidence."

Disparate Impact   Even where an employer is not motivated by discriminatory intent, Title VII prohibits an employer from using a facially neutral practice (i.e., applies to all employees regardless of class membership) that has an unlawful *adverse impact* on members of a protected class. First announced in *Griggs v. Duke Power Co.,*[13] the Supreme Court recognized that *intent* was *not* always a necessary element to prove discrimination and that certain evaluation techniques for employee selection, promotion, and assignment such as written tests, height and weight requirements, educational requirements, or oral candidate interviews could be administered uniformly to all candidates yet still impact certain protected class members adversely. The Court ruled that some testing mechanisms operate as "built-in headwinds" for minority groups and are unrelated to measuring job capability.

The disparate impact framework is similar to that of intentional discrimination cases in that the plaintiff must first prove a prima facie case by showing that certain methods resulted in statistically significant differences that adversely impacted members of a protected class. To satisfy this requirement, the plaintiff frequently provides statistical data related to a testing measure. The EEOC has issued *Uniform Guidelines on Employee Selection Criteria* that defines adverse impact as occurring when members of a protected class are selected at a rate less than 80 percent of that of the highest scoring group.[14] For example, suppose that Prescott's mother is Cuban and, therefore, Prescott's national origin can be considered in the Latino class under Title VII. Prescott was required to take a test for the accounting position at WidgetCo. Of all candidates taking the exam, Asian candidates faired best with 10 of 20 candidates passing the test. Latino candidates as a group passed the test with only 3 out of 20 candidates passing. Because Latino candidates passed less than 80 percent of the highest scoring group (Asians), this would be important evidence in Prescott's disparate impact claim of discrimination. Once the prima facie elements are established, the burden of proof then shifts to the employer to provide evidence that the challenged practice is *job-related* for the position in question and is a *business necessity.* However, even if the employer shows a valid business necessity, the plaintiff may still prevail if he proves that the employer refused to adopt an alternative practice that would satisfy the employer's interests without having the adverse impact.

Despite the EEOC guidelines and federal court decisions, disparate impact is still a very thorny area of discrimination law. In Case 12.2, which received abundant media coverage, the U.S. Supreme Court weighed a disparate treatment claim by an employee when the discriminatory treatment was a based on an employer's concern over a disparate impact lawsuit based on promotion examinations given by the fire department in New Haven, Connecticut.

Sexual Harassment

Because Title VII includes sex as a protected class, federal law extends protection to employees who are being sexually harassed. Unwelcome sexual advances, requests for sexual favors, and other verbal or physical conduct of a sexual nature are considered violations of Title VII if the conduct is (1) in the context of explicit or implicit conditions of an individual's employment or as a basis for any employment decisions, or (2) unreasonably interfering with an individual's work performance or creating an offensive work environment. Generally, a victim of sexual harassment alleges one of two theories. In the *quid pro quo* theory (derived from the Latin phrase meaning "something for something else"), for example, the harasser demands sexual favors as a condition of continued employment or a prerequisite for promotion or pay raise. More commonly, sexual harassment takes the form of a *hostile work environment.* Under this theory, a violation of Title VII occurs when the harasser's (or group of harassers')

---

[13]401 U.S. 424 (1971).

[14]29 C.F.R. § 1607.4(D).

FACT SUMMARY   The City of New Haven, Connecticut, administered an objective written examination to any fire department employee who aspired to be promoted. The examination was designed and administered by a professional testing service company that specialized in race-neutral examinations for police and fire agencies. In fact, when designing the examination, the company deliberately oversampled* minority firefighters to ensure that the results would not unintentionally favor white candidates.

Nonetheless, the results of the exam were such that white candidates had outperformed minority candidates. After considerable debate, the city discarded the test results fearing that minority candidates who had underperformed in the exam would file a disparate impact–based lawsuit. Ricci was a white firefighter who placed highly on the promotion exam and he filed a Title VII lawsuit against the City based on a disparate treatment claim. The City defended on the basis that it acted on a good faith belief that canceling the examination results was necessary to comply with Title VII's *disparate impact* provisions. The trial court and the court of appeals ruled in favor of the City, and Ricci appealed to the U.S. Supreme Court.

SYNOPSIS OF DECISION AND OPINION   The U.S. Supreme Court reversed the lower courts and ruled in favor of Ricci. The Court held that the city's action in discarding the examination results violated Title VII's prohibition against disparate treatment because all of the evidence demonstrated that the city had rejected the test results solely on the basis that the higher-scoring candidates were white. According to the Court, if employers act in good faith to design a legitimate test to be race-neutral, the fact that the numbers come out differently than the employer expects is not, in and of itself, enough to discard the results of the test. Employers must provide some strong factual evidence that any discriminatory measures taken (such as discarding test results on the basis that higher-scoring candidates were of a particular race) were necessary to avoid liability. Such was not the case here and, therefore, the City's actions violated Title VII.

WORDS OF THE COURT: Discarding Test Results   "[Employers] may not take the . . . step of discarding the test altogether to achieve a more desirable racial distribution of promotion-eligible candidates—absent a strong basis in evidence that the test was deficient and that discarding the results is necessary to avoid violating the disparate impact provision. Restricting an employer's ability to discard test results (and thereby discriminate against qualified candidates on the basis of their race) also is in keeping with Title VII's express protection of bona fide promotional examinations."

Case Questions

1. The employer in this case is a municipal government agency. Does this case apply to private employers as well? Why or why not?

2. Given the Court's ruling, what's an example of circumstances where an employer *could* discard the results of a promotion test?

Sample is a term used in research studies meaning data from a cross-section profile of the population studied that represents the population as a whole.

---

conduct is of such a severe and crude nature that it interferes with the victim's ability to perform the job. Additionally, if the behavior is abusive and the abuse led the employee to quit, the employee is still permitted to bring an action against the harasser.[15] Note that this is different than a typical discrimination case where the employer must have actually taken some adverse action for a violation to occur. While there is no formula for determining a hostile work environment, courts have deemed certain behaviors as a violation of Title VII. These include (1) initiating a discussion of sexual acts, activities, or physical attributes in workplace areas (such as the employee cafeteria); (2) unnecessary or excessive physical contact; (3) crude, demeaning, or vulgar language; or (4) display of pornographic pictures or movies.

---

[15]*Harris v. Forklift Systems, Inc.,* 510 U.S. 17 (1993).

More recently, the U.S. Supreme Court has developed sexual harassment doctrines related to liability of an *employer* for harassment committed by the victim's coworker or supervisor, and has also made clear that sexual harassment prohibitions apply to same-sex harassment. In *Faragher v. City of Boca Raton,*[16] the Court held that an employer that (1) failed to make employees aware of its sexual harassment policy, (2) failed to have any system in place meant to deter harassment, or (3) failed to enforce an existing policy, could be liable for sexual harassment even when the employer had no *actual* knowledge of the illegal conduct. In that case, Faragher, a lifeguard employed by the city of Boca Raton, was subjected to a stream of harassment, sexual pranks, requests for sexual favors, and other crude behavior by her coworkers. Faragher made her supervisors aware of the harassment and, in fact, supervisory personnel themselves engaged in occasional verbal harassment of Faragher. However, Faragher never complained to the city manager, who supervised the Beach Safety Division where Faragher was employed. Nor did Faragher's immediate supervisor notify the city manager of the complaints. Nonetheless, the Court held that the city was liable under Title VII because it had failed to distribute its policy on or make any serious effort to deter sexual harassment. Moreover, the city had no system in place where Faragher could report the harassment and no other policy enforcement mechanisms. Thus, the Court held the city liable despite the fact that the city manager did not have actual knowledge of the harassment. In *Oncale v. Sundowner Offshore Services, Inc.,*[17] the Court held that an employee on an oil rig who was subject to homosexual advances by his coworkers was protected under Title VII. The Court made clear that Title VII was gender neutral and recognized sexual harassment as a form of discrimination regardless of the gender of the victim or the harasser.

> ## KEY POINT
> Although the *Ricci* case has many legal dimensions, its immediate impact on employers is that discarding results of a race-neutral employment or promotion test, even if done to avoid disparate impact liability, may give rise to a disparate treatment claim by affected employees or promotion candidates.

 Self-Check   Theories of Discrimination

What is the best potential theory of discrimination for the plaintiff to pursue?

1. Lian, an American of Chinese decent, is employed as an architect in a large regional firm. His evaluations by his superiors have been mostly positive for two years with the consistent exception that he arrived late for client meetings on a frequent basis. On one evaluation, his superior wrote, "I thought Asians were supposed to be efficient. What happened here?" One month later, Lian is denied a promotion based on his record of "tardiness and other general considerations."

2. Dothard applies for a position as a firefighter. She is excluded because she cannot lift the free-weight requirement mandated in the job description. Over the past five years, men have passed the test 50 percent of the time and women have passed 20 percent of the time.

3. Pettigrew is a woman insurance adjustor for a company that has a rule that no adjustors are allowed to enroll in law school because the employer perceives it as a conflict of interest. The company was aware of several adjustors who were in fact enrolled in law school, but did not act against them. Pettigrew enrolled in law school and when the company found out about it, she was terminated. The other adjustors were all male.

4. Bronte is employed as a bookkeeper at the nation's largest toy store where she works with Barnes. Barnes has a reputation as the office comedian and, over the course of several months, has made various jokes related to Bronte's figure and recommended that she come

[16]524 U.S. 775 (1998).
[17]523 U.S. 75 (1998).

on casual day dressed in sexy lingerie. Bronte tried to laugh at the jokes, but was in fact very upset about the remarks. When she confronted Barnes about the behavior, he advised her to "lighten up" and told her that he was equally sarcastic toward male employees. Bronte quit one day later.

Answers to this Self-Check are provided at the end of the chapter.

Figure 12.1 illustrates the steps in a Title VII analysis.

Remedies

Title VII provides aggrieved employees with a broad range of remedies to compensate for unlawful discrimination. These remedies include an injunction (a court order to cease from engaging in a particular unlawful practice or an order compelling a party to act), reinstatement, compensatory damages in the form of back pay, retroactive promotions, and requiring the employer to take certain actions in order to remedy patterns or practices resulting in discrimination. Punitive damages (intended to deter future conduct of employers) are available only when a plaintiff proves that a private employer acted maliciously, in retaliation, or with reckless disregard to the employment discrimination laws.

AGE DISCRIMINATION IN EMPLOYMENT ACT

One of the fastest growing varieties of employment discrimination claims are those based on age. Under the Age Discrimination in Employment Act (ADEA), employers are prohibited from discriminating against employees on the basis of their age once an employee has reached age 40. The ADEA is similar to Title VII in that the protected employees are not entitled to *special* treatment, but are included as a member of a protected class when employers discriminate against them in favor of a *substantially younger* employee. Courts also use a Title VII–based analysis for evaluating age claims. For example, *disparate treatment* under the ADEA requires proof that the employer intentionally discriminated against the employee based on the employee's age using a modified *McDonnell Douglas* standard for establishing a prima facie case. Therefore, plaintiffs may only make ADEA claims based on (1) protected class membership (40 or over), (2) satisfactory job performance (based on employer's legitimate expectations), (3) adverse job action such as termination or demotion, (4) replacement with someone substantially younger (or treated someone more favorably who is substantially younger), or (5) other evidence that indicates that it is *more likely than not* that an employee's age was the reason for the adverse employment action.[18]

In *Ricci v. DeStefano*, the Supreme Court ruled that the city of New Haven, Connecticut, violated Title VII when they discarded test results of a promotion examination for firefighters based on considerations related to race.

---

[18]*Robin v. Espo Engineering Corp.*, 210 F.3d 1081 (7th Cir. 2000).

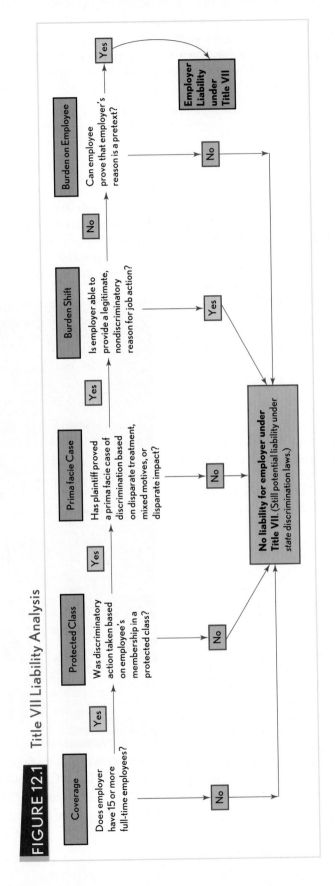

FIGURE 12.1 Title VII Liability Analysis

Coverage

Does employer have 15 or more full-time employees?

Protected Class

Was discriminatory action taken based on employee's membership in a protected class?

Prima facie Case

Has plaintiff proved a prima facie case of discrimination based on disparate treatment, mixed motives, or disparate impact?

Burden Shift

Is employer able to provide a legitimate, nondiscriminatory reason for job action?

Burden on Employee

Can employee prove that employer's reason is a pretext?

Employer Liability under Title VII

No liability for employer under Title VII. (Still potential liability under state discrimination laws.)

If the employee makes a prima facie case, then the employer must present a non-discriminatory reason for the adverse employment action. Once the employer presents the nondiscriminatory reason, then it is up to the employee to convince the fact finder that the reason the employer gave is false (pretextual) and the real reason is age discrimination.

Substantially Younger Requirement

If a plaintiff is attempting to prove age discrimination based upon the fact that younger employees are treated more favorably, then the plaintiff must prove that the younger employees are *substantially younger.* The federal courts vary greatly in their interpretation of what constitutes substantially younger, but many courts follow the general rule that the age difference must be at least 10 years in order to qualify as substantially younger.[19]

One important distinction of an ADEA claim is that it is irrelevant whether the younger employee is a member of the protected class or not. For example, let's assume Prescott is hired at WidgetCo. and is 50 years old. He is terminated and replaced by another employee who is 40 years old. Both employees are members of the protected class (40 years old and older), but because someone substantially younger has replaced the employee, Prescott may still pursue his claim by proving that the reason he was replaced was based on age discrimination. But assume that Prescott is a 69-year-old employee and is replaced by a 67-year-old employee. That age difference is not sufficient to make a claim of age discrimination.

Disparate impact claims under the ADEA that do not require proof of an intent to discriminate are rare, but disparate impact (similar to a *Griggs*-type standard based on statistical evidence of exclusion) was specifically recognized as an ADEA discrimination theory by the U.S. Supreme Court in *Smith v. City of Jackson, Miss.*[20] In that case, the Court held that the ADEA authorizes disparate impact claims, but the employer's burden to show the reasonableness of the business practice at issue is *minimal.* That is, the employer does *not* have to meet the higher standard of proof required in Title VII disparate impact cases that the practice at issue was a *business necessity.* Thus, it is easier for employers to prevail in an ADEA disparate impact action than in a disparate impact alleging (for example) race discrimination under Title VII.

AMERICANS WITH DISABILITIES ACT

LO12-7

One of the most significant federal antidiscrimination laws that impacts business owners and managers is the Americans with Disabilities Act (ADA).[21] The ADA was originally passed in 1990, but was amended in 2008 in order to settle some of the more controversial interpretations by courts related to the *definition* of a disability. Fundamentally, the ADA seeks to eliminate discriminatory employment practices against disabled persons that would prevent otherwise qualified employees from obtaining or continuing employment, being promoted, or obtaining benefits available to nondisabled employees. The ADA requires that employers with 15 or more employees to make **reasonable accommodations** for a disabled employee in the workplace so long as the accommodation does not cause the employer to suffer an undue hardship.

Documented Disability Requirement

In order to qualify for an accommodation, the employee must have a documented **disability.** The ADA defines disability in terms of individuals that have *physical* or *mental* impairments that substantially limit a person's ability to participate in *major life activities.* Courts

---

[19]*Pitasi v. Gartner Group, Inc.,* 184 F.3d 709 (7th Cir. 1999).

[20]125 S. Ct. 1536 (2005).

[21]42 U.S.C. § 1201.

have ruled that certain disabilities, such as blindness, cancer, heart disease, paraplegia, and acquired immune deficiency syndrome (AIDS), all fit squarely into the disability category. However, the definition and interpretation of the disability requirement has been the subject of considerable uncertainty since the passage of the original version of the ADA. Because Congress did not specify examples of major life activities in the original ADA statute, courts and the EEOC struggled to establish appropriate limits.

In a series of cases beginning in 1999, the Supreme Court narrowed the definition of what disabilities were covered under the ADA and ruled that any condition that could be corrected, such as severe myopia causing poor vision,[22] was not a disability covered by the act. In subsequent years, the Court ruled that carpal tunnel syndrome was also not covered because it could not be considered so debilitating as to interfere with any major life activity.[23]

ADA Amendments Act of 2008

As the narrow interpretation of ADA solidified in federal courts, Congress passed an amendment to the ADA that effectively reversed the Supreme Court's efforts to read the disabilities category as a narrow class of ailments. The ADA Amendment Act of 2008 (ADAAA) became effective for any ADA discrimination occurring on or after January 1, 2009. The ADAAA expanded the definition of disability with specific statutory definitions intended to urge courts to interpret the definition of disability "in favor of broad coverage of the individuals under this Act, to the maximum extent permitted by terms of the Act."[24]

Although the basic definition of a disability under the original ADA was left in place, the ADAAA expanded the statutory protections to specifically cover disabilities that had been excluded from coverage by virtue of the Supreme Court's ADA case law, including a requirement that courts make a determination of one's disability without regard for the ability to correct the condition with "medication, artificial aids" and other "assistive technology." Therefore, in order for an individual to be protected under the ADAAA, the plaintiff must still have a physical or mental impairment that substantially limits one or more major life activities.[25]

Regarded as Test

Even if an individual does not meet the definitional requirements of a disability under the ADA, employees may still be protected by the ADA under an alternative theory of the act known as the *regarded as* test. Like the definitional scope of the disability requirement in the ADAAA, the *regarded as* standard has been substantially broadened by Congress as well. The standard applies when an employee was *regarded as having impairment* by her employer (even if the impairment was not *actually* a disability). For example, Babak is diagnosed with a chronic medical condition, but the condition doesn't require any accommodation in the workplace. Babak applies for a promotion to supervisor, but is denied because his manager is fearful that Babak's condition will limit his energy level and impact his ability to fulfill his role. Under the ADAAA, Babak would be protected by the statute even though his condition was not a disability as defined in the ADA. This is true because Babak's employer *regarded him as* disabled by virtue of his condition.[26]

---

[22]*Sutton v. United Airlines*, 527 U.S. 471 (1999).

[23]*Toyota Motor Manufacturing v. Williams*, 534 U.S. 185 (2002).

[24]42 U.S.C. § 12002(4)(a).

[25]The statute also requires that there be "a record of" the disability. As one commentator has pointed out, this requirement is nearly obsolete and unaffected by the ADAAA. See A., Long, *Introducing the New and Improved Americans with Disabilities Act: Assessing the ADA Amendments Act of 2008,* 103 Nw. UL Rev. Colloquy 106 (2008).

[26]There is an ongoing debate as to the coverage of the *regarded as* test in light of the passage of the ADAAA. This explanation and example are based on EEOC guidance and public information contained on the Web site. For updates on how the ADAAA is being applied by the courts, see this textbook's Web site at www.mhhe.com/melvin.

Reasonable Accommodations

Once an employee has established that she has a covered disability, the ADA requires an employer to make *reasonable accommodations* that allows the employee to perform essential job functions. The ADA states that reasonable accommodations may include (1) making existing facilities readily available to individuals with disabilities, and (2) job restructuring, part-time or modified work schedules, reassignment to vacant positions, and the provision of readers or interpreters. Courts have held that accommodations such as wheelchair ramps, making training manuals or other materials available in oral form, modifying work assignments or a working schedule, and providing sound amplification are all reasonable.

However, the statute does not require the employer to provide accommodations that constitute an *undue hardship* on the employer. The statute defines an undue hardship as one that would result in significant difficulty or expense in the context of the overall resources of the employer, the number of persons employed, the effect on expenses or resources, or the impact of the accommodation upon the operation of the facility. For example, Gant is disabled and unable to walk stairs. He is employed as an accountant in a local real estate firm that occupies a converted Victorian house as its headquarters. Gant informs his employer that an elevator will need to be installed in the Victorian house, because he occasionally needs to visit the upstairs to collect documents necessary to perform his job. It is likely that Gant's employer could demonstrate an undue hardship for Gant's elevator request. However, if Gant requests that his employer assign an employee to regularly bring documents from the upper floors to Gant's desk, this would likely be a reasonable accommodation.

Federal courts continue to struggle to define the range of reasonable expectations and the limits of undue hardship in a variety of settings. In Case 12.3, the U.S. Supreme Court analyzed the reasonable accommodations request in the context of professional sports.

EQUAL PAY ACT

In 1963, President Kennedy signed the Equal Pay Act (EPA) into law, making it illegal for employers to pay unequal wages to men and women who perform substantially equal work. Technically, the EPA is an amendment to the Fair Labor Standards Act,[27] and is therefore not always categorized as an antidiscrimination statute. Nonetheless, the EPA does prevent discrimination by requiring an employer to provide equal pay for men and women who perform equal work, unless the difference is based on a factor other than gender.[28]

To establish a prima facie case, a plaintiff must demonstrate that (1) the employer pays different wages to employees of the opposite sex; (2) the employees perform equal work on jobs requiring equal skill, effort, and responsibility; and (3) the jobs are performed under similar working conditions.[29] If a prima facie case is established, the burden shifts to the employer to prove that the wage differential is justified by a preponderance of the evidence under one of four affirmative defenses: (1) a seniority system; (2) a merit system; (3) a system pegging earnings to quality or quantity of production; or (4) any factor other than sex. Equal Pay Act claims are often combined with Title VII claims of sex discrimination in compensation. Courts, however, have found separate essential elements and standards of proof for the two statutory claims.

---

[27]29 U.S.C. § 206(d).

[28]At the time of the EPA's passage in 1963, women earned only 59 cents for every dollar earned by men. Although enforcement of the EPA as well as other civil rights laws has helped to narrow the wage gap, disparities remain.

[29]*Corning Glass Works v. Brennan,* 417 U.S. 188 (1974).

FACT SUMMARY Martin is a professional golfer who is afflicted with a degenerative circulatory disorder recognized as a disability under the Americans with Disabilities Act (ADA). The disorder causes Martin severe pain due to an obstruction of blood flow between his legs and his heart. The Professional Golf Association (PGA) Tour* rules require that players in tournaments walk the course. However, because walking caused Martin pain, anxiety, and generally worsened his condition, he could not walk the course. As a collegiate athlete, Martin obtained a waiver for the walking rule from the National Collegiate Athletic Association. When Martin turned professional and tried to qualify for the PGA Tour, he requested that he be permitted to use a golf cart. Although PGA Tour rules prohibit players from using golf carts on the final two stages of the qualifying tournaments, Martin petitioned for a waiver on the basis that he was covered by the ADA. The PGA Tour rejected his request on the grounds that it was not a reasonable accommodation. The PGA Tour asserted that walking was a fundamental part of golf and waiving it for any reason would *fundamentally* alter the nature of the competition. They argued that the fatigue from walking is a critical factor in the outcome of tournaments. Martin countered by noting that even with the use of a cart he would be required to walk one mile during each round of golf and, because his disability causes him pain and fatigue, the use of the cart would not allow him an advantage over other players.

SYNOPSIS OF DECISION AND OPINION The U.S. Supreme Court ruled in Martin's favor and held that the PGA was required to accommodate Martin's disability under the ADA. The Court found that because nothing in the Official Rules of Golf expressly prohibits the use of carts, the PGA's walking rule was not an essential part of the game. The Court also reasoned that the actual fatigue from walking four rounds of golf was insignificant (noting expert testimony indicating that walking the golf course burns fewer calories than are contained in one Big Mac). Thus, the Court concluded that waiving the rule for Martin would not fundamentally alter the game.

WORDS OF THE COURT: Reasonable Accommodation "[The PGA Tour's] refusal to consider Martin's personal circumstances in deciding whether to accommodate his disability runs counter to the clear language and purpose of the ADA. [. . .] [T]he ADA was enacted to eliminate discrimination against 'individuals' with disabilities, and to that end, the Act requires without exception that any 'policies, practices, or procedures' [. . .] be reasonably modified for disabled 'individuals' as necessary to afford access unless doing so would fundamentally alter what is offered. To comply with this command, an individualized inquiry must be made to determine whether a specific modification for a particular person's disability would be reasonable under the circumstances as well as necessary for that person, and yet at the same time not work a fundamental alteration. [. . .] As we have demonstrated, however, the walking rule is at best peripheral to the nature of [golf], and thus it might be waived in individual cases without working a fundamental alteration. [. . .] Martin 'easily endures greater fatigue even with a cart than his able-bodied competitors do by walking.' The purpose of the walking rule is therefore not compromised in the slightest by allowing Martin to use a cart. A modification that provides an exception to a peripheral tournament rule without impairing its purpose cannot be said to 'fundamentally alter' the tournament. What it can be said to do, on the other hand, is to allow Martin the chance to qualify for and compete in the [PGA Tour.] [. . .] As a result, Martin's request for a waiver of the walking rule should have been granted."

Case Questions

1. Why was the PGA was so reluctant to allow Martin to use a golf cart, especially considering carts are allowed in other tournaments?

2. Do you agree with the Court's reasoning that allowing Martin to use a golf cart during tournaments does not give him an advantage? Why or why not? Are there any scenarios where it might, and as a result would alter the fundamental nature of the game?

3. Given the Court's reasoning, would a request to double the size of the hole so that a partially blind competitor could see it when putting fundamentally alter the game? Explain your answer.

*The PGA Tour is golf's most competitive and lucrative professional competition.

Lilly Ledbetter Fair Pay Act of 2009

The Lilly Ledbetter Fair Pay Act (Ledbetter Act) effectively reversed the U.S. Supreme Court's decision in *Ledbetter v. Goodyear Tire & Rubber Co.*[30] In the *Ledbetter* case, a 19-year-veteran of Goodyear Tire & Rubber Co. sued the company when she learned that for much of her career male counterparts had been paid more for doing the same work. Although the Supreme Court did not deny that Ledbetter had been discriminated against, they ruled that she should have filed suit within 180 days of *receiving* her first unfair paycheck, not 180 days from the time she *learned* of the difference in pay. The ruling upended long-standing practice in courts across the country that had held that the 180-day-period begins when an employee becomes *aware* of his or her plight. Under the Supreme Court's framework, any employer that could hide pay discrimination for six months could effectively avoid liability under the law and leave workers with no recourse. Because pay information is often confidential, pay discrimination is difficult to detect. Thus, if employers are insulated from liability after 180 days, they have little incentive to correct pay discrimination. The Ledbetter Act seeks to ensure that employees subject to discrimination on the basis of race, color, national origin, sex, religion, age, or disability have the opportunity to challenge *every* discriminatory paycheck that they receive.

CONCEPT SUMMARY   Federal Employment Discrimination Statutes

- Title VII of the Civil Rights Act of 1964 applies to any private sector employer with 15 or more full-time employees as well as labor unions, employment agencies, state and local governments, and most federal government employers.

- Title VII prohibits discrimination in the workplace on the basis of membership in a protected class. The protected classes are race, color, national origin, gender, pregnancy, and religion.

- There are three basic theories of discrimination: (1) disparate treatment (the *McDonnell Douglas* standard); (2) mixed motives (the *Hopkins* standard); and (3) disparate impact (the *Griggs* standard).

- Disparate treatment is overt and intentional discrimination and occurs when an employer treats an employee differently based on membership in a protected class.

- Under the *McDonnell Douglas* test a plaintiff must make out a prima facie case showing (1) membership of a protected class, (2) that the plaintiff was qualified for and applied for a job, (3) was rejected, and (4) the position was filled by a nonclass member. Second, the burden shifts to the employer to show a legitimate nondiscriminatory reason for the action. Finally, the burden shifts back to the individual to show the reason given by the employer was not the actual reason for their action.

- The mixed motives theory articulated in *Hopkins* protects employees when legitimate motives are mixed with illegitimate motives and an employee is discriminated against. Under this theory, the employee must prove that membership in a protected class was a substantial factor in the decision-making process. The burden then shifts to the employer to offer evidence that it would have made the same employment decision regardless of membership in a protected class.

- The disparate impact test articulated in *Griggs* prohibits an employer from using a facially neutral practice that has an adverse impact on members of a protected class.

---

[30]550 U.S. 618 (2007).

- Under the disparate impact theory a plaintiff must prove that the evaluation methods resulted in statistically significant differences that adversely impacted members of a protected class.

- Title VII provides for various remedies including injunctions, reinstatement, compensatory damages, retroactive promotions, and remedial actions by the employer.

- The Age Discrimination in Employment Act (ADEA) prohibits employers from discriminating against employees on the basis of their age if the employee is (1) 40 years old or over; (2) satisfactory in job performance; (3) adversely affected by the job action; and (4) better treatment is given to someone substantially younger.

- The Americans with Disabilities Act (ADA) seeks to eliminate discriminatory employment practices against disabled persons by requiring that employers with 15 or more employees make reasonable accommodations to allow the disabled employee to perform essential job functions, so long as the accommodation does not cause the employer to suffer an undue hardship.

- The Equal Pay Act (EPA) makes it illegal for employers to pay unequal wages to men and women who perform substantially equal work unless the difference is based on a factor other than sex.

PROCEDURES FOR ASSERTING A CLAIM

Federal antidiscrimination statutes prescribe a specific procedure for employees alleging employment discrimination. First, an aggrieved employee must file a **complaint** against the employer with the local office of the EEOC (generally within 180 days of the adverse job action). The EEOC then notifies the employer and commences a preliminary investigation. As an administrative agency, the EEOC may use its authority to obtain documents, statements from witnesses, and other evidence that will aid in the investigation. Courts have granted the EEOC wide latitude in investigating discrimination claims, including the authority to have access to confidential employer files.

During and immediately after the investigation, the EEOC is required by statute to engage in **conciliation negotiations.** This means that the EEOC has an affirmative statutory duty of good faith efforts in favor of settlement of the case instead of a lawsuit. In Case 12.4, a federal appellate court interprets the conciliation requirement.

If efforts at conciliation fail, the EEOC may choose to file suit against the employer on the employee's behalf or may decide not to take any action at all. After 180 days have passed from the time of the complaint, the employee may demand that the EEOC issue a *right to sue letter.* This letter entitles the employee to file a lawsuit in a federal court. Note that even though all employment discrimination claims must begin with the EEOC, ultimately the employee will have an

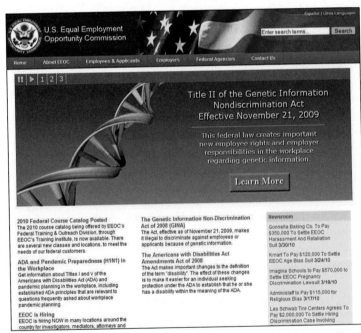

Employees alleging discrimination by their employer must first file a complaint with the EEOC, which then notifies the employer of the allegations and begins a preliminary investigation.

CASE 12.4   EEOC v. Asplundh Tree Expert Co., 340 F.3d 1256 (11th Cir. 2003)

FACT SUMMARY Lewis, an African American laborer working for Asplundh, alleged that he was subject to various racial comments in the workplace. After he complained, he was laid off. Lewis contacted the EEOC alleging he was a victim of discrimination by Asplundh. After a three-year investigation, the EEOC sent a settlement negotiation letter to Asplundh's primary attorney, who was based in Philadelphia, Pennsylvania, advising him of Lewis's complaint. Although the letter did not set out any specific theories of discrimination liability allegations that the EEOC was pursuing against Asplundh, it did require them to respond within 12 business days. Asplundh's attorney in Philadelphia contacted Sampo, a Florida-based attorney, to handle the matter because the incidents had occurred in Florida. Sampo attempted to contact the EEOC multiple times and left messages advising them he was handling the matter. However, the EEOC never responded to Sampo. Nonetheless, the EEOC notified Asplundh's Philadelphia attorney that because they did not respond to the settlement letter, the EEOC had filed a lawsuit in the matter. Asplundh defended on the basis that the EEOC violated its statutory obligation to attempt good faith settlement in a discrimination claim.

SYNOPSIS OF DECISION AND OPINION The Court of Appeals for the Third Circuit ruled in favor of Asplundh and held that the EEOC *did not* make a good faith effort to engage in conciliation negotiations with Asplundh as required by the statute. As a result of the EEOC's bad faith, the court dismissed the suit. The court noted that the EEOC spent three years investigating Lewis's claim and then only gave Asplundh 12 days to respond. Moreover, the EEOC's refusal to deal with Sampo and failure to set out a theory under which Asplundh was liable in the conciliation letter was sufficient evidence of a lack of fair dealing and

attempts at conciliation that is required by the statute. The EEOC's actions were so egregious as to cause the court to dismiss the suit against Asplundh.

WORDS OF THE COURT: Conciliation Required by Statute "To satisfy the statutory requirement of conciliation, the EEOC must (1) outline to the employer the reasonable cause for its belief that Title VII has been violated; (2) offer an opportunity for voluntary compliance; and (3) respond in a reasonable and flexible manner to the reasonable attitudes of the employer. In evaluating whether the EEOC has adequately fulfilled this statutory requirement, 'the fundamental question is the reasonableness and responsiveness of the EEOC's conduct under all the circumstances.' [I]t cannot be said that the EEOC acted in good faith. In fact, its conduct 'smacks more of coercion than of conciliation.' [. . .] As we have said [. . .] an 'all or nothing' approach on the part of a government agency, [especially] one of whose most essential functions is to attempt conciliation with the private party, will not do. The courts have interpreted the statute to mean precisely what it says. Nothing less than a 'reasonable' effort to resolve with the employer the issues raised by the complainant will do. This effort must, at a minimum, make clear to the employer the basis for the EEOC's charges against it. Otherwise, it cannot be said that the Commission has provided a meaningful conciliation opportunity."

Case Questions

1. What could the EEOC have done in this case in order to meet the statutory requirements?
2. Did Asplundh's counsel in Philadelphia act reasonably? Could their counsel have simply contacted the EEOC and either asked for an extension or for more information or notified them that Sampo was the proper contact in this case?

---

opportunity to present his case in court. This is true even if the EEOC decides that the case has no merit and declines to investigate.

EMPLOYER DEFENSES   LO12-8

Earlier in the chapter, we saw that the burden-shifting scheme in a discrimination case is subject to the employer offering either a nondiscriminatory motive for the action in question or asserting a legally recognized *defense*. Each antidiscrimination statute has its own set of defenses, but there is some level of commonality among employer defenses.

Business Necessity

Perhaps the broadest defense to employment discrimination is when a business can justify discrimination on the basis that it is *legitimately necessary* to the business operations of the company. This defense is used to rebut a *disparate impact* claim when a certain practice or procedure has impacted a particular protected class. For example, suppose MovingCo. requires all of its workers to be able to lift 100 pounds. During the application process, the applicants are required to pick up a 100 pound piece of furniture. After one year, the test resulted in more women than men being eliminated from job consideration. If sued under a disparate impact theory, MovingCo. has a strong business necessity defense so long as the standard was applied neutrally to all candidates. Another common business necessity is a particular level of education such as a requirement by an accounting firm that all of its professionals have at least a Bachelor of Science degree in accounting.

Bona Fide Occupation Qualification

Federal antidiscrimination statutes allow employers to hire and employ on the basis of religion, gender, or national origin in certain instances where the classification is a bona fide occupational qualification (BFOQ) that is reasonably necessary to the normal operation of that particular business or enterprise.[31] Note that the statute does not allow race to be used as a BFOQ. The ADEA has a similar BFOQ defense. Although the ADA does not have an express BFOQ provision, the statutory scheme allows exclusion of persons with disabilities if the person, with or without reasonable accommodation, cannot perform essential job functions (a similar concept to BFOQ).

Classic examples of BFOQ classifications are religion for the employment of clergy and the use of gender to hire a movie actor. On cases that are not as clear, the employer must prove that members of the excluded class cannot safely and effectively perform *essential* job duties. Courts have held that BFOQ cannot be based on paternalism (protecting women from work in potentially dangerous positions such as mining, construction, or law enforcement). It is also generally true that customer preference (such as passenger preferences for women flight attendants) is not a sufficient BFOQ, but that general rule is subject to the qualification that customer preference may ultimately deprive the worker of the ability to perform the essential job (e.g., a certain gender requirement based on the modesty of medical patients).

Seniority

Federal antidiscrimination statutes also provide a defense for employers using a seniority system as the basis for certain job decisions. In order to assert this defense, the seniority system must be based on objective elements of seniority (actual number of years on the job) and the employment decisions must have been made in good faith and pursuant to that established objective system. The employee/plaintiff has the burden of proving improper motivation behind the employer's adoption or use of the system.

Employee Misconduct

Employers are not required to overlook misconduct when complying with antidiscrimination statutes. When an employee commits an act of misconduct, so long as that act has been identified to the employee as misconduct, employers may discipline the employee in accordance with the company's general practices without liability for discrimination. If the employer's practices and procedures are set forth in a workplace publication (usually

---

[31]42 U.S.C. § 2000e-2(e).

in the employee handbook or a similar company document), misconduct is a powerful defense. The U.S. Supreme Court has even extended that protection to employers when the employer discovered the misconduct *after* the adverse employment action.[32] So long as the employer shows that the misconduct was sufficiently grave as to warrant the adverse employment action (such as termination for theft of a petty cash account), employers may use after-acquired evidence of misconduct as a defense.

AFFIRMATIVE ACTION PROGRAMS

LO12-9

Affirmative action as it is understood today includes, but goes beyond, outreach attempts to recruit minority applicants, special training programs, and the reevaluation of the effect of selection criteria. Affirmative action programs have their legal genesis in Executive Order 11246,[33] which was issued during Word War II and required that employers who have a contract with the federal government for services and supplies to initiate good faith efforts to implement an affirmative action plan in their company. Although most employers are not subject to the executive order, social pressures and/or threat of litigation has induced many employers to adopt voluntary affirmative action plans. Affirmative action may also be imposed on an employer by courts as a judicial remedy when finding that the employer acted in a pattern of egregious discrimination against employees.

Legality

Although federal antidiscrimination statutes do not require employers to give preferential treatment to minority employees, the Supreme Court has upheld the constitutionality of Executive Order 11246 and has allowed certain affirmative action plans to apply to private employers as a condition to a contract with the federal government. State and local governments soon followed suit with affirmative action plans aimed at addressing inequalities in the workplace and in education.[34] In *Adarand Constructors, Inc. v. Pena,*[35] the Supreme Court ruled that state and local government affirmative action plans in race-based or gender-based preferences for hiring contractors would be subject to the *strict scrutiny* standard. Recall from Chapter 2, "Business and the Constitution," that the strict scrutiny standard is the highest level of scrutiny and more often than not results in a finding of unconstitutionality. However, the Court's ruling made clear that a state and local government affirmative action program is constitutional so long as it (1) attempts to remedy an actual past practice of discrimination, and (2) does not employ a system of quotas (e.g., hiring according to a mathematical formula based on race).

STATE ANTIDISCRIMINATION STATUTES

LO12-10

In addition to federal antidiscrimination statutes, certain employers are also subject to regulation under a state law antidiscrimination statutory scheme. Each state has its own statutes that are often modeled after the federal statutes (although they have different titles such as the Human Relations Act). In addition, states also have their own administrative agencies (modeled after the EEOC) charged with enforcing and adjudicating discrimination cases.

---

[32]*McKennon v. Nashville Banner Publishing Co.,* 513 U.S. 352 (1995).

[33]41 C.F.R. § 60.1, § 60.2.

[34]The Supreme Court decided several cases specifically related to admissions by state-sponsored universities beginning in 1978. Most recently, in *Gruttinger v. Bollinger,* 539 U.S. 306 (2003), the Court held that affirmative action in admissions is constitutional so long as the minority status of the applicant is used as a plus factor and not in accordance with a rigid formula reserving certain seats for minority applicants.

[35]515 U.S. 200 (1995).

State antidiscrimination statutes sometimes differ substantially from federal laws in two ways that impact business owners and managers. First, state statutes tend to cover more employers, with some states imposing antidiscrimination statutes on small businesses with just *one* employee. Many federal statutes only cover employers (unions, etc.) with 15 or more employees. Second, while federal statutes are relatively conservative in exactly what constitutes a protected class, some states have expanded protected class membership, most notably, to discrimination based on sexual orientation or gender transformation. In Case 12.5, a state appellate court compares New Jersey's state statutory antidiscrimination protections with the protections under Title VII.

CASE 12.5   Enriquez v. West Jersey Health Systems, 777 A.2d 365 (N.J. Super. Ct. App. Div. 2001)

FACT SUMMARY   Enriquez, a biological male, was hired as a medical director for an outpatient treatment center operated by West Jersey Health Systems (Health Systems). Soon after his employment began, Enriquez began an external transformation from male to female. This transformation was a result of Enriquez's gender identity disorder. During the transformation, Enriquez was approached by coworkers and managers who voiced discomfort with her transformation. A Health Systems manager, citing Enriquez's obligation to contribute to a productive work atmosphere, requested that Enriquez halt the transformation process and go back to her prior appearance. When her contract came up for renewal, Enriquez was told that her contract would not be renewed unless she ceased the transformation. After Enriquez refused, her contract was not renewed and she was informed that the termination was permanent. After the termination, Enriquez completed the surgical portion of her transformation.

SYNOPSIS OF DECISION AND OPINION   The New Jersey Superior Court held that while Title VII does not bar discrimination based on sexual orientation or gender identity disorders, New Jersey's Law Against Discrimination (LAD) does. The court reasoned that since the LAD makes it unlawful to discriminate against someone based upon sex and affectional or sexual orientation, individuals who were transsexual or affected by a gender identity disorder were also considered to be members of a protected class and were protected from discrimination.

WORDS OF THE COURT: Coverage under LAD "Title VII of the Civil Rights Act of 1964 does not contain language barring discrimination based on one's affectional or sexual orientation. Moreover, the federal courts construing Title VII have unanimously concluded that discrimination on the basis of gender dysphoria is not sex discrimination. Basically, the federal courts conclude that discrimination on the basis of sex outlaws discrimination against women because they are women, and against men because they are men. [. . .] We disagree with [this] rationale [. . .]. A person who is discriminated against because he changes his gender from male to female is being discriminated against because he or she is a member of a very small minority whose condition remains incomprehensible to most individuals. [. . .] It is incomprehensible to us that our Legislature would ban discrimination against heterosexual men and women; against homosexual men and women; against bisexual men and women; against men and women who are perceived, presumed or identified by others as not conforming to the stereotypical notions of how men and women behave, but would condone discrimination against men or women who seek to change their anatomical sex because they suffer from a gender identity disorder. We conclude that sex discrimination under the LAD includes gender discrimination so as to protect plaintiff from gender stereotyping and discrimination for transforming herself from a man to a woman."

Case Questions

1. Why couldn't this case have been covered by Title VII on the basis of gender?

2. If Enriquez's employment with Health Systems were not terminated would she still have a claim for discrimination? Would the conduct of her coworkers and managers have been sufficient to prevail on a discrimination suit? Why or why not?

Employment discrimination p. 304 A broad term that includes workplace-related discrimination in the hiring process and treatment of employees. Employment discrimination encompasses everything from promotions or demotions to scheduling, working conditions, and disciplinary measures.

Equal Employment Opportunity Commission (EEOC) p. 304 A five-member federal administrative agency that enacts congressional mandates that assure victims of discrimination adequate protection. The EEOC accepts and investigates worker complaints and, in certain cases, will sue on behalf of employees.

Title VII p. 304 The centerpiece of antidiscrimination law. This section of the Civil Rights Act of 1964 applies to any private sector employer with 15 or more full-time employees, as well as unions, employment agencies, state and local governments, and most federal government employers. The law covers a comprehensive set of job-related transactions and is most known for its prohibition on discrimination in the workplace on the basis of an employee's race, color, national origin, gender, or religion.

Age Discrimination in Employment Act of 1967 (ADEA) p. 304 A statute prohibiting employers from discriminating against employees on the basis of their age once an employee has reached age 40.

Americans with Disabilities Act of 1990 (ADA) p. 304 A statute that seeks to eliminate discriminatory employment practices against disabled persons. The ADA requires that employers with 15 or more employees offer reasonable accommodations for a disabled employee in the workplace so long as the accommodation does not cause the employer to suffer an undue hardship.

Equal Pay Act of 1963 p. 305 Makes it illegal for employers to pay unequal wages to men and women who perform substantially equal work.

Protected classes p. 305 The classes of individuals laid out in Title VII including color, race, national origin, religion, gender, or pregnancy.

Disparate treatment p. 306 Theory of employment discrimination predicated on overt and intentional discrimination. This includes being treated differently because of one's membership in a protected class.

Mixed motives p. 306 Theory of employment discrimination where the cause of adverse employment action was motivated by both legitimate and discriminatory motives.

Disparate impact p. 306 Theory of employment discrimination where employee evaluation techniques that are not themselves discriminatory have a different, adverse, impact on members of a protected class.

Burden of proof p. 307 A party's duty to prove a disputed assertion or charge.

Pretext p. 307 A false reason offered to justify an action.

Reasonable accommodations p. 315 Accommodations, required under the Americans with Disabilities Act, which allow disabled individuals to adequately perform essential job functions.

Disability p. 315 A physical or mental impairment that substantially limits a person's ability to participate in major life activities.

Complaint p. 320 A form that an aggrieved employee files against their employer with the EEOC detailing how the employee was discriminated against.

Conciliation negotiations p. 320 The required attempts by the EEOC to settle a discrimination case instead of filing a lawsuit.

THEORY TO PRACTICE

Hudson runs a successful business operation called Cleaning Inc. and employs a workforce of over 100 people in various positions. The company has contracts with several companies to provide office-cleaning services. One employee, Curt, had been with the company for almost two years when he applied for a supervisory position. The position involved higher pay and better benefits. Although he was qualified to be a site supervisor, Curt was not promoted. Cleaning Inc. explained that *only* a woman could be hired because the position involved regular searches of the women employees' locker room to look for any items reported stolen from cleaning sites.

1. If Curt files suit against Cleaning Inc. for discrimination, what statute will he be relying on and what is his probable theory of discrimination?

2. What would Curt need to prove in order to shift the burden to Cleaning Inc.?

3. What is the company's best defense to a charge of discrimination?

4. In order to file the complaint against Cleaning Inc., what procedures must Curt follow? May he file a lawsuit immediately?

5. Assume that Curt was not promoted because he was undergoing a series of sex change procedures and that other employees were uncomfortable with him. Is Curtis protected under federal antidiscrimination statutes? Why or why not?

6. Same facts as in Question 5, but assume Curtis filed suit in a state that had a statute similar to New Jersey's antidiscrimination law (as seen in the *Enriquez v. West Jersey Health Systems* case). Would Curtis be covered under the state law? Why or why not?

MANAGER'S CHALLENGE

Recall that employers may be liable for sexual harassment under the *Faragher* case when the employer has not taken affirmative steps to deter harassment or failed to have a structure in place to enforce sexual harassment policies such as a system for deterring and reporting sexual harassment. Assume you are a manager at Cleaning Inc. (as in Theory to Practice, above) and you receive the following e-mail from the company's vice president of operations:

I just read an article about a company that was sued under the sexual harassment laws. I know we have a good policy, but we need a system in place for claims and compliance. Please draft a two- to three-page memorandum that outlines how to implement a system that will (1) help deter sexual harassment, (2) ensure that our policy is well known by the employees, and (3) provide a procedure for initiating and investigating complaints.

A sample answer may be found on this textbook's Web site at www.mhhe.com/melvin.

CASE SUMMARY 12.1 :: Dumas v. Union Pacific Railroad Co., 294 Fed. App. 822 (5th Cir. 2008)

MISCONDUCT

Dumas was an African American employee of UPRC, which employed him as a regional manager. UPRC, a rail freight company, was named in a discrimination claim by a coworker of Dumas. During the EEOC investigation, Dumas supported his co-worker's claims by offering statements verifying discriminatory practices at UPRC After the coworker's claim was settled, UPRC conducted a routine audit that found that Dumas had falsified his track inspection records over a period of time in the past. UPRC immediately terminated Dumas.

CASE QUESTIONS

1. Does Dumas have a valid employment discrimination claim?

2. If so, what theories would be best advanced by Dumas?

CASE SUMMARY 12.2 :: Harding v. Careerbuilder, Llc, 168 Fed. App. 535 (3d Cir. 2006)

ADEA

Harding was the CEO of Head Hunters International (HHI). After HHI was bought by MonsterCareers.com (MCC), the two firms were integrated. Soon after the merger, MCC informed Harding that his performance was lacking and he was terminated from his position. Harding later found out that Carey, a relative newcomer to MCC, was being promoted to his position.

Harding, who is 51, alleged discrimination on the basis of his age because Carey is 42.

CASE QUESTIONS

1. Does Harding have a claim for employment discrimination under ADEA? Why or why not?

2. Would your answer change if Carey was 24, 39, or 45? Explain.

ADA

Barnett, a baggage loader for U.S. Airways (USA), injured his back while loading an inordinately heavy suitcase. His doctor diagnosed him with a permanently slipped disc and recurring back spasms. Barnett's condition is permanent and he is considered to be disabled under the ADA. Upon returning to work, USA offered to reassign him from baggage loader to luggage deliverer, where he would drive the baggage carts from plane to plane. However, Barnett wanted a position in the mailroom sorting mail. USA denied Barnett's request because they operated on a strict seniority system for filling vacancies.

CASE QUESTIONS

1. Does Barnett have a cause of action under the ADA? Why or why not?
2. Has USA fulfilled their duty of reasonable accommodation?

STATE ANTIDISCRIMINATION PROTECTION

Hope, a homosexual who was infected with HIV, was hired as a cook in a youth correctional facility in California. While there, he was continually the subject of derogatory comments made by male guards and a supervising cook because of his sexual orientation. These comments were numerous in number and done in front of coworkers. Moreover, while other cooks received assistance in cleaning their stations, Hope received no such help and oftentimes his coworkers would throw their trash in his station. During his first five years of employment, Hope's medical condition never affected him. However, he eventually started to miss work because of the side effects of his medication, combined with the stress from the harassment he was subjected to. After informing his supervisors of his condition, he was put on administrative leave and later terminated for abusing sick leave policy.

CASE QUESTIONS

1. Is Hope a member of a protected class under Title VII?
2. Can he bring a federal claim for employment discrimination?
3. Suppose California has a state antidiscrimination statute that protects sexual orientation. Would Hope have a state claim for discrimination? Why or why not?
4. Had Hope not been terminated, would he have had a claim? Why or why not?

 Self-Check **ANSWERS**

Theories of Discrimination

1. Mixed motives. This is similar to the *Price Waterhouse* case. There are legitimate reasons for the denial of promotion (tardiness) mixed with potentially illegitimate reasons (based on national origin stereotyping).

2. Disparate impact. Based on the EEOC guidelines, a disparate impact claim could be made because women are impacted in a disparate manner. The fire department must show that the free-weight requirement is a business necessity in order for it to be valid.

3. Disparate treatment. A neutral workplace rule (prohibition) was applied (or not applied) differently to men than to women. The *McDonnell Douglas* framework applies here.

4. Sexual harassment via hostile work environment theory so long as there is evidence that the behavior was so crude as to interfere with the plaintiff's job function and led her to resign.

BUSINESS LAW SIMULATION EXERCISE 2

Employment Discrimination: John Falstaff v. Revere Furniture Company

learning outcomes **checklist**

After studying this simulation, students who have mastered the material will be able to:

1. Explain the legal doctrines that govern employers in the context of antidiscrimination statutes.

2. Interpret and apply the rules set forth in current case law.

3. Articulate a cogent argument for each party/side in the dispute.

4. Negotiate a tenable solution as an alternative to a judicial forum.

The chapters in this unit covered a variety of legal doctrines and rules governing labor and employment discrimination law as well as examples of how these doctrines and rules apply in the workplace. This simulation is designed to help students understand how the various topics covered in the employment discrimination chapter connect together through use of a simulated legal dispute. The simulation is intended to provide students with as close as possible real-world experience in applying legal doctrines and use of analytical and critical thinking skills. This simulation is a sequential decision-making exercise structured around a model in which the participants assume a role in managing tasks and work toward a tenable solution.

The simulation is structured in three parts:

■ Part 1 is a hypothetical fact pattern describing events leading up to a legal dispute in the hypothetical U.S. state of Longville, which is a state located in the jurisdiction of the fictitious U.S. Court of Appeals for the 14th Circuit.

■ Part 2 contains (a) a statutory excerpt based on the actual Americans with Disability Act Amendment Act (ADAAA) and (b) two case summaries from hypothetical appellate courts that provide a brief set of facts, several legal points, and short excerpts from the opinion itself. While these cases are hypothetical, they are based on actual cases from federal appellate courts and represent the view of the majority of federal courts.

■ Part 3 is an assignment sheet handout that will be provided to you by your instructor.

PART 1: STIPULATED FACTS

1. Paul Revere Furniture Company (Revere) is a manufacturer and retailer of high-end furniture based in Longville. Revere sells its products at its retail outlets across the United States and employs a workforce of approximately 800 employees in 30 states. Its largest retail outlet is adjacent to its headquarters in Longville.

2. On July 1, 2008, John Falstaff (Falstaff) applied for a position at Revere as a floor manager in Revere's Longville store. Falstaff applied for the position after finding out about the opportunity on Revere's Web site. The position description follows in Exhibit A.

3. After an interview with Constance Howe (Howe), Revere's regional vice president who supervised all floor managers in the retail stores in the Longville region, Falstaff was hired for the position on July 5, 2008. At the time of hire, Falstaff filled out a personnel form where he reported that he was in good general health with no injuries or conditions that would prevent him from performing his job, including the physical tasks; and that his weight was approximately 215 pounds and his height was approximately six feet tall.

4. From his start date through May 2009, Falstaff received favorable reviews for his performance as floor manager and no policy violations were noted in the file. In late June 2009, Falstaff called in sick for three consecutive days, complaining of a back injury. Revere's standard operating procedure required the regional vice president to contact any manager who called in sick more than two consecutive days. Howe telephoned Falstaff who explained that he had strained his back and was having severe back pain that prevented him from being able to stand or sit comfortably for more than one hour. Falstaff also acknowledged that the pain was subsiding and that he anticipated being able to return to work after one more day of rest. Howe wished Falstaff the best and advised him that he only had two more sick days left. Howe also informed Falstaff that he should consider filing a claim for disability insurance if his condition did not improve soon.

In this simulation exercise, an employee of a furniture company claims that he was terminated due to a disability.

5. Despite his assurances, Falstaff did not return to work as promised and called in sick for a sixth day. Howe then contacted Falstaff and directed him to see a company-hired physician for a determination as to whether Falstaff could return to work or whether he should be certified as disabled for purposes of filing a claim of disability with Revere's insurance carrier.

6. On July 1, Falstaff was examined by Dr. William Jefferson, a physician hired by the company. Dr. Jefferson concluded that Falstaff was not disabled and had suffered a mild sprain in his lower back region. Dr. Jefferson prescribed ice, over-the-counter pain relief, and a period of two weeks of light duty whereby Falstaff would not be required to lift anything over 10 pounds. After that, Dr. Jefferson

advised that Falstaff would be ready to return to his regular duties as floor manager.

7. On July 2, Falstaff returned to work on light duty status. Howe assigned Falstaff to desk duties only and instructed other floor managers that Falstaff was not to engage in any lifting of objects that weighed 10 or more pounds.

8. During the next three months, Falstaff's attendance at work was spotty. Although he never called in sick to work, he arrived late six times, took an extended lunch hour three times, and left work early nine times. On each occasion, Falstaff would explain his absence using the excuse that his back was causing him too much pain to sit up and that even the light lifting required on the floor was difficult for him. When Falstaff was at work, he would complain loudly to subordinates and customers that the company was making him work and that working was making his condition worse.

9. Falstaff's absences and workplace complaints also began to affect his performance. His monthly reports to Howe had been chronically late as were his payroll records. This resulted in several complaints by sales employees about Falstaff's performance. On September 1, 2009, Howe issued Falstaff a "Corrective Action" letter advising that Falstaff's performance was not satisfactory, outlining the specific violations including the late reports, his attendance problems, and his inappropriate workplace comments. The letter also warned Falstaff that failure to take correct action to improve would result in termination.

10. After receiving the letter, Falstaff sent an e-mail to Howe claiming that the poor performance was due to "increasing back pain" and that he had developed "shortness of breath" when exerting any physical labor such as moving the furniture displays as required.

11. During this same period of time (June–September), Falstaff's weight increased significantly from 215 pounds to 320 pounds. As Falstaff's weight increased, he was increasingly reluctant to perform any physical tasks and would order subordinates to move furniture, arrange "Manager's Special" displays, and other physical activities. During his shift, Falstaff would frequently stay in the manager's office without ever coming out to the showroom.

12. In October 2009, Falstaff sought help from his own physician. Falstaff's physician, Dr. Amanda King, examined Falstaff and diagnosed him with a strained lower back. However, in her report, she also made note that "the most significant factor in patient's health is his obesity. His weight increases the strain on his lower back, limits his range of motion, and leaves him short of breath after just a few steps. His weight severely impacts or eliminates his ability to stand for significant periods of time and to pick up anything over 5 lbs." Falstaff sent Dr. King's report to Howe.

13. In two phone conversations with Falstaff over several days after Dr. King's report, Howe indicated that she was concerned that Falstaff may not be able to fully perform the duties required. Falstaff indicated that he could still effectively manage the store so long as other employees were assigned to do any heavy lifting in Falstaff's store.

14. In December 2009, Revere terminated Falstaff. Revere cited a lower than expected revenue for the previous fiscal year as the primary reason for cutting back its workforce. On his discharge slip, Howe wrote that the reasons for Falstaff's termination were strategic need to cut costs and poor job performance.

15. Falstaff alleges that his termination violated the ADAAA.

Paul Revere Furniture Company—Employment Opportunity

Position: Store floor manager (Longville)

Pay Scale: Based upon experience

General Description: Floor managers are responsible for ensuring overall productive and efficient operations of a retail store location. This includes supervising a sales force of 4–6 people, keeping appropriate corporate records, resolving customer complaints, joining the sales team on the showroom floor during busy holiday seasons, tracking inventory, setting up "Manager's Special" displays and occasional physical work related to tracking and placing merchandise in showrooms in a fashion conducive to maximizing sales.

Physical Requirements: Applicants must be in good overall health sufficient to meet physical requirements of (1) long periods of standing without a break (1–2 hours); and (2) when necessary, occasional climbing, kneeling, bending, stooping, balancing, reaching, and occasional lifting of items (such as furniture) in excess of 50 pounds.

Qualifications:

■ High school diploma or G.E.D. required.

■ Two years of experience working as a supervisor in a large retail setting is preferred.

■ Ability to fulfill physical requirements.

■ No convictions for felonies or any theft-related offenses.

■ Reliable transportation to work.

Applications: Applications are available on our Web site at www.revere.com/employment

PART 2: STATUTORY AND CASE LAW

Statute: *United States Code* (Excerpt from American with Disabilities Act Amendments Act [ADAAA]) Passed April 2008

§ 1: This Act shall become effective January 1, 2009

§ 2: Definition of disability

As used in this Act:

(1) **Disability:** The term "disability" means, with respect to an individual—

   (A) a physical or mental impairment that substantially limits one or more major life activities of such individual;

   (B) a record of such an impairment; or

   (C) being regarded as having such an impairment on major life activities.

(2) **Major life activities:** In general, for purposes of paragraph (1), major life activities include, but are not limited to, caring for oneself, performing manual tasks, seeing, hearing, eating, sleeping, walking, standing, lifting, bending, speaking, breathing, learning, reading, concentrating, thinking, communicating, and working.

(3) **Major bodily functions:** For purposes of paragraph (1), a major life activity also includes the operation of a major bodily function such as brain, respiratory, circulatory, and endocrine.

(4) **Regarded as having such an impairment:** For purposes of paragraph (1)(C), an individual meets the requirement of "being regarded as having such an impairment" if the individual establishes that he or she has been subjected to an action prohibited under this Act because of an actual or perceived physical or mental impairment whether or not the

impairment limits or is perceived to limit a major life activity.

(5) **Exclusions:** Paragraph (1)(C) shall not apply to impairments that are transitory and minor. A transitory impairment is an impairment with an actual or expected duration of 6 months or less.

(6) **Rules of construction regarding the definition of disability:** The definition of "disability" in paragraph (1) shall be construed in favor of broad coverage of individuals under this Act, to the maximum extent permitted by the terms of this Act.

CASE LAW

Grindle v. Watkins Motor Lines
14th Circuit Court of Appeals (2007)

Facts

■ Grindle was hired as a dockworker by Watkins Motor Lines in 2005. The job description provided that applicants must be able to lift packages over 50 pounds on a repetitive basis and that the job involved daily loading and unloading of heavy freight, standing for eight hours at a time, and tolerance for outdoor weather on the loading dock. At the time of hire, Grindle weighed 345 pounds and he reported on his application that he had no medical conditions that he was aware of.

■ Over a period of one year, a supervisor at Watkins disciplined Grindle several times for failing to load his freight in a timely manner. Grindle had several written reprimands for this violation in his file and was placed on probation. Under the Watkins employee handbook, Grindle faced termination if his performance did not improve.

■ Grindle complained to his manager that Watkins's loading time goals were impossible to meet as Grindle was not physically able to perform the tasks in the time given. After a third letter of reprimand in April 2006, Grindle asked his manager for a different set of time goals, but Watkins management refused this option.

■ The day after his request for a time schedule adjustment was denied, Grindle saw a physician because he was unable to sleep due to the fear that he would lose his job. During the visit, Grindle's physician reported that Grindle's weight, which was now at 450 pounds, was classified as obese and that extended lifting and standing caused potential injury. The physician advised Grindle not to engage in these strenuous work activities until he had lost at least 75 pounds.

■ When Grindle returned to work, he again requested a time schedule adjustment citing his physician's report and recommendation. Again, Watkins refused any adjustment.

■ Shortly thereafter, Grindle was terminated due to his inability to perform the job duties for his position. After receiving a right-to-sue letter from the EEOC, Grindle filed suit against Watkins claiming they were required under the ADA to accommodate his obesity as a disability.

POINTS OF LAW AND OPINION EXCERPTS

Point (a)

A claim of disparate treatment under the ADA will be analyzed under the *McDonnell Douglas* standard.

Excerpt (a)

"We have held that claims under the ADA are analyzed under the framework set forth in *McDonnell Douglas v. Green.* In order to establish a prima facie case under the ADA, the plaintiff must prove that (1) the defendants are subject to the ADA; (2) the plaintiff is disabled within the meaning of the Act; (3) the plaintiff could have performed the job if accommodations had been provided; (4) the plaintiff was subject to an adverse employment action because of the disability."

Point (b)

The threshold requirement to qualify as an ADA-covered disability is that the disability must be physical or mental impairment that substantially limits one or more of the major life activities of the individual.

Excerpt (b1)

"An impairment, for purposes of the ADA, is any 'physiological disorder, or condition, cosmetic disfigurement, or anatomical loss affecting one or more of [various] body systems such as: musculoskeletal; special sense organs; respiratory, including speech organs; cardiovascular; reproductive, digestive, genito-urinary; hemic and lymphatic; skin; and endocrine.'"

Excerpt (b2)

"Examples of normal life activities in past cases in this circuit include seeing, walking, lifting a child, communicating with co-workers and sleeping."

Point (c)

Abnormal physical characteristics in height or weight that have no physiological cause are not considered disabilities under the ADA.

Excerpt (c1)

"We observed in previous cases that physical characteristics that are not the result of a physiological disorder are not considered impairments for the purposes of determining either actual or perceived disability."

Excerpt (c2)

"For example, in one previous case, we held that a plaintiff-firefighter's claim that he was disciplined because his weight did not meet a union standard failed because 'obesity, except in special cases where the obesity relates to a physiological disorder, is not a physical impairment within the meaning of the statutes.'"

Point (d)

This circuit declines to follow a minority of courts' rulings that adopts a medical-based formula (such as body mass index) to determine whether certain levels of obesity rises to the level of disability. Without any physiological cause, obesity is not covered as a disability.

Excerpt (d1)

"We specifically decline to follow some trial courts application of a body mass index or other height-weight calibrations because such calculations belie our previous holding in which we repeatedly emphasized that a physical characteristic must relate to a physiological disorder in order to qualify as an ADA impairment."

Held

Because Grindle has not shown that his obesity was as a result of some physiological condition or that it prevented him from engaging in normal life activities as required in the ADA, the court finds in favor of Watkins.

Adams v. Salt River Master Carvers
2nd Circuit Court of Appeals (2009)

Facts

- Adams was employed as a welding technician by Salt River Master Carvers (Salt River), an employer covered by the ADA. His position required strenuous physical activity.

- Approximately one year after his employment began, Adams was diagnosed by his family doctor as an insulin-dependent Type 2 diabetic. His doctor prescribed medication and a strict eating regiment requiring daily insulin injections and certain types of food at certain times of the day related to the time of the insulin injection.

- In January 2009, Adams informed his supervisor of his condition, submitted the doctor's report and recommendations, and requested that his schedule be adjusted to accommodate four to six breaks per day from his eight-hour work shift. He said this was necessary, or that he would become too dizzy and lightheaded and may pose a safety risk.

- Salt River then required Adams to see a company-hired physician. The company physician agreed with the diabetes diagnosis, but recommended that Adams have only one insulin injection per day and that he should be given two breaks for eating to balance the insulin. The doctor also recommended that Adams not be assigned any more than an eight-hour shift in any 24-hour period.

- A Salt River manager then met with Adams and told him that he was "concerned with Adams's ability to get the job done" and that diabetes had "slowed him down considerably." Salt River then implemented the company physician recommendations regarding Adams's work assignment.

- In March 2009, amid the continuing economic turbulences, Salt River announced that workforce reduction terminations were necessary. Adams, despite having more seniority than most of his coworkers, was terminated on March 31, 2009, with Salt River citing the work reduction plan as the reason.

POINTS OF LAW AND OPINION EXCERPTS

Point (a)

Because the alleged discrimination took place after January 1, 2009, the provisions of the ADA Amendments Act of 2008 (ADAAA) apply to this case.

Point (b)

The ADAAA significantly broadened the definition of disability necessary for protection under the ADA. Specifically, under the ADAA, a disability is any impairment that substantially limits a major life activity. That statute specifically adds several activities that have yet to be formally recognized. They include eating, sleeping, standing, lifting, bending, and reading.

Excerpt (b1)

"Under both the ADA and the ADAA, our analysis of whether the impairment is substantially limiting is based on the nature and severity of the impairment, the duration or expected duration of the impairment, as well as the permanent or long-term impact of the impairment."

Excerpt (b2)

"We conclude that Adams's diabetes substantially limits his life activity of eating. The record is replete with statements, both by Adams and his doctors, that to manage his disease Adams is required to strictly monitor what, and when, he eats. Adams stated that these restrictions constrain him every day, 'whether it's a workday, a weekend or a holiday.' He cannot eat large meals or skip meals, and must eat a snack every few hours. He must schedule each day's blood tests, medications, and food intake. He 'sometimes become[s] weak and dizzy without warning,' and only when he eats something do these sensations quickly subside. If he fails to follow his diet regimen for more than a meal or two, his blood sugar rises to a level that aggravates his disease. Adams's doctor testified that controlling diabetes is like being on a chemical roller coaster."

Point (c)

Even if the physical impairment was not actually a disability, Salt River's conduct indicates that they regarded Adams as disabled. The *regarded as* standards were also expanded under the ADAAA and would be applicable to this case.

Excerpt (c1)

"This court has held that an individual need not actually have a physical impairment to state a claim under the ADA . . . as long as that individual is 'regarded as having such an impairment.' To be 'regarded as' having a disability, a plaintiff must prove he is regarded as having an impairment that substantially limits one or more major life activities. A plaintiff must allege that the employer perceived that the employee suffered from an impairment that would be covered under the statute."

Excerpt (c2)

"Evidence in this case shows that Salt River management was 'concerned with Adams's ability to get the job done' and that they had concluded that the diabetes had 'slowed him down considerably.'"

Point (d)

The correlation of the discrimination and the termination may, coupled with other factors, constitute a pretextual reason for the discharge.

Excerpt (d1)

"When an employer offers inconsistent explanations for an adverse employment decision a genuine issue of material fact is raised with regard to the veracity of the nondiscriminatory reason. Here, the defendants have offered various explanations for Adams's termination including financial reasons, poor performance, and inappropriate conduct. The allegations regarding Adams's poor performance and inappropriate conduct is questionable in light of their failure to raise these issues prior to the proceedings in the trial court."

Held

In favor of Adams. The ADAAA covers Adams's disability under both the disparate treatment discrimination theory and under the *regarded as* theory.

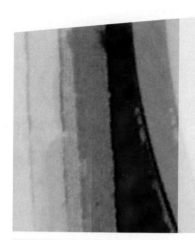

UNIT **FOUR**

Business Entities, Securities Regulation, and Corporate Governance

13 CHAPTER

Choice of Business Entity, Sole Proprietorships, and Partnerships

learning outcomes checklist

After studying this chapter, students who have mastered the material will be able to:

13-1 Articulate the factors that business owners should consider when selecting a business entity.

13-2 List the elements required to form a general partnership and the statutory requirements for forming a limited partnership.

13-3 Recognize the effect and role of the RUPA for general partnerships and the RULPA for limited partnerships.

13-4 Identify methods through which sole proprietorships and partnerships may be capitalized (funded).

13-5 Distinguish between personal liability for general partners and limited partners.

13-6 Explain the concept of pass-through taxation.

13-7 Articulate the consequences of partner separation and dissolution.

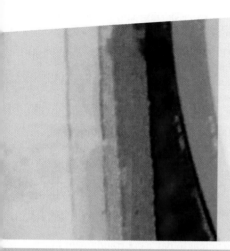

All business ventures operate as a legally recognized form of business entity.[1] Business owners and managers who have a fundamental knowledge of the structure, advantages, and risks associated with each form of business entity are more effective at focusing on business opportunities while limiting potential liability. Most states recognize at least six forms of business entities. In addition to providing an overview of the forms of business entities and factors used to determine the best choice of entity for a given business, this chapter focuses on the law governing two basic forms of entity: sole proprietorships and partnerships. Other forms of entities are covered in the next two chapters. In this chapter, students will learn:

- The factors to be considered in determining what business form fits which business type.

- Fundamental principles of the law governing sole proprietorships.

- Legal regulation for formation and governance of partnerships including personal liability of partners for business debts and other liabilities.

- Rules governing the separation of partners from the partnership and procedures for dissolving a partnership.

---

[1]Business entities are sometimes referred to as business organizations.

LO13-1 CHOOSING A BUSINESS ENTITY

The best choice of business entity is primarily driven by the risk, tax, and operational objectives of the owner(s) and the type of business operations contemplated. Choosing a business entity is an important part of business planning for both start-up entrepreneurs and the managers of a business supervising the launch of an additional venture that supplements an existing business. Each form of entity has its attendant advantages and drawbacks and a variety of legal consequences for the *owners,* known as **principals,** of the business. In choosing a business entity, principals should consider at least the following factors:

- *Formation.* How easy is the entity to form and maintain? Must there be more than one principal? What annual filings or fees are required and what formalities need be followed?
- *Liability.* To what extent are the principals *personally* liable for debts and other contract or tort liabilities of the business entity itself? To take a simple example, suppose Gardner owns a consulting business and rents office space from Landlord under a five-year lease agreement. After one year, Gardner loses a large client and can no longer afford the office space. He cancels his lease and moves his office to his the basement of his home. If the assets of the consulting business are insufficient to pay a court judgment in favor of the damaged party (Landlord) does Landlord, as the injured party, have a claim for the balance against Gardner's personal assets (such as a personal bank account or stock portfolio)?
- *Capitalization.* How will the business entity fund its operations? May the principal(s) sell ownership rights in the business to raise capital?
- *Taxation of Income.* How will tax authorities treat the entity? Will the entity itself pay taxes or are the taxes passed through to the principals?
- *Management and Operation.* How, and by whom, will the business venture be operated? Will the principals be involved in day-to-day operations of the business? What duties do the principals owe to the business and to each other? How will the profits and losses be split? If a principal decides to leave the business entity, may the remaining principals continue to operate?

Table 13.1 sets out the most common forms of business entities.

Principals in start-up business ventures have several alternatives when selecting a business entity.

TABLE 13.1 Common Forms of Business Entities

Name of Entity	Brief Description	Coverage in Text
Sole Proprietorship	One-person entity where debts and liabilities of the business are also personal debts and liabilities of the principal.	Chapter 13
Partnerships: General Limited	Two or more principals that agree to share profits and losses in an ongoing business venture. Debts and liabilities of the business are also personal debts and liabilities of the general partners. Limited partners have limited liability.	Chapter 13
Limited Liability Partnership	Two or more principals that agree to share profits and losses in an ongoing business venture. The principals have heightened liability protection from debts and liabilities of the partnership.	Chapter 14
Limited Liability Company	Two or more principals in an ongoing business venture with potentially favorable tax treatment and limited liability for its principals.	Chapter 14
Corporation	One or more principals that invest money in exchange for ownership (stock). Principals generally have no personal liability for debts and liabilities of the business.	Chapter 15

Sole Proprietorships

The easiest single-person ownership entity to form and maintain is a **sole proprietorship.** A sole proprietorship requires only a minimal fee and a straightforward filing requirement with the appropriate state government authority and typically requires no annual filings. Its ease of formation and maintenance makes this entity a top choice for start-up businesses with relatively low annual revenues and expenses. An individual planning to conduct a sole proprietorship business under a trade name, rather than her individual name (i.e., Gates IT Consulting rather than Joan Gates) will also file a D.B.A. certificate ("Doing Business As," sometimes known as a *fictitious name*) with a local or state office. There may be additional licenses required by the state and city where the business operates (sales tax licenses, etc.). These requirements vary by jurisdiction.

Sole proprietorships are typically capitalized using a proprietor's personal resources or through a private or commercial loan that is secured by the proprietor's personal assets.[2] A sole proprietorship business is not subject to corporate income taxation and no tax return is filed on behalf of the business. Rather, the principal reports business income and expenses on her own individual tax return and pays taxes on business income (or deducts business losses) based on her own individual tax rate. It is important to note that although most sole proprietorships are relatively small in terms of assets and revenues, sole proprietorships are not restricted in terms of the number of employees or operating in as many locations as the principal desires.

---

[2]A secured loan is one in which the borrower grants the lender legal rights to something of value until the loan is paid back in full (e.g., a car secures a car loan).

The chief drawback to this form of entity is a complete *lack of protection* of the principal's personal assets for unpaid debts and liabilities of the business. All debts and liabilities of the business are also *personal debts and liabilities* of the principal. For example, suppose Redfern is the principal of Redfern Catering, a sole proprietorship. Redfern Catering has approximately $5,000 in assets. One of Redfern's employees negligently uses spoiled ingredients in a soup that is served to customers. Marshall is a customer who develops food poisoning and obtains a court judgment against Redfern Catering to compensate him for damages that resulted from medical bills in the amount of $50,000. Assuming that Redfern Catering had no insurance coverage for this event, Marshall would have $45,000 of judgment unpaid after exhausting the business of its assets ($50,000 judgment minus $5,000 assets). Thus, Redfern would be *personally* liable to Marshall for the remaining unpaid judgment. This means that Marshall could execute the judgment against Redfern by using a judicially sanctioned process for seizing funds from Redfern's personal bank account, stock portfolio, and other assets. As a result of this lack of protection, sole proprietors often purchase comprehensive liability insurance for the business in amounts sufficient to cover potential tort liabilities such as the one described in the Redfern–Marshall example above.

Another drawback to a sole proprietor form of entity is that, by its very nature, the entity may not sell off ownership interests (known as equity) in the business in order to raise money to operate the proprietorship.

Legal Speak ›))
Execute the Judgment
If a winning plaintiff has obtained a court order for the defendant to pay the amount of the judgment, the plaintiff may take certain steps to collect the money owed from the defendant. In extreme cases, this may take the form of seizing the defendant's personal property for sale by the sheriff or garnishing the wages of the defendant.[3]

Partnerships

LO13-2, 13-3, 13-4, 13-5, 13-6

An entity with *more* than one principal has a number of additional choices. The simplest multiple-person business entity is a **partnership.** There are two traditional subcategories of partnerships: general partnerships and limited partnerships. Although most partnerships are **express partnerships,** where the principals agree to some ongoing business relationship, there are some cases when, even if the parties did not intend on being partners, the law recognizes the relationship as a partnership and imposes the same liability on the principals as if the parties had formed an express partnership. Two other related types of partnerships are limited liability partnerships (LLPs) and limited liability limited partnerships (LLLPs). These are a hybrid form of partnership (having characteristics common to several different entities) and are covered in detail in Chapter 14, "Limited Liability Partnerships, Limited Liability Companies, and Other Business Arrangements."

General Partnerships   Unlike most business entities, general partnerships are not created by filing a form with a government agency. Instead, the law recognizes two or more principals as being a general partnership if they have *demonstrated* an intent to carry on as co-owners of a business for profit. While some general partnerships have extensive written agreements detailing the internal operations of the business and the rights and responsibilities of the principals, others operate without any written agreement at all. In the absence of an agreement, the Revised Uniform Partnership Act (RUPA) governs a general partnership. Just like the Uniform Commercial Code, the RUPA is a *model statute* drafted and occasionally revised by the National Conference of Commissioners on Uniform State Laws. To date, approximately 40 states have adopted all or substantial portions of the RUPA. States that have not yet adopted the RUPA operate under the RUPA's predecessor, the Uniform Partnership Act (UPA).[4] The RUPA should be thought of as a default set of laws that only apply where the principals have not expressly agreed otherwise (similar to the UCC's gap filler function). The RUPA also contains certain agency principles including fiduciary

---

[3]Note that all states prohibit certain assets from being seized to satisfy a judgment such as the principal's home residence. Some states also exempt retirement portfolios as well.

[4]Louisiana is the only state not to adopt the UPA or the RUPA.

duties of partners to each other and to the partnership. In addition to the RUPA, the common law plays a role in general partnership law in certain cases where principles of general fairness must be applied and the RUPA doesn't contemplate that particular situation.[5]

Formation   No formal document or government filing is necessary to form a general partnership. In fact, it is important to note that the parties may not actually *intend* to be partners, but the law still recognizes their relationship as an **implied partnership.** For example, suppose that Carl and Jan are neighbors and during a block party Carl mentions that his family's secret salad dressing was popular with the neighbors and friends. Jan loves the dressing and offers to help Carl sell the dressing at local gourmet stores in exchange for 50 percent of the profits. Carl agrees so long as he is responsible for making the dressing and Jan is responsible for providing bottles and labels, transporting, and selling. Here, despite the fact that the parties may have intended to have an informal arrangement, legally they have created a general partnership. This is important because this arrangement gives rise to potential liability for both Carl and Jan even though they never intended to assume such risks.

Conversely, even if the parties *label* themselves as general partners and draft a partnership agreement, this does not, in and of itself, form a general partnership.[6] Fundamentally, a general partnership is thought of as (1) an association of two or more people or entities, (2) who are co-owners and co-managers of the business, and that (3) share in the profits of an ongoing business operation. These partnerships typically use the designation *GP* at the end of their business name to signify the general partnership as their form of entity.

Sometimes, the parties only wish to have a limited-in-time relationship instead of an ongoing business entity. This entity is generally referred to as a **joint venture** and is governed by the same legal principles as a general partnership.

An express partnership is created when two or more principals agree to share profits in an ongoing business relationship.

---

[5]The RUPA refers to this, stating, "Unless displaced by particular provisions of this [Act], the principles of law and equity supplement this act." RUPA § 104(a).

[6]Recall the equitable maxim from Chapter 1 relating to the law recognizing substance over form.

Liability of the Principals   Much like sole proprietors, general partners have no protection of their personal assets for unpaid debts and liabilities of the partnership. However, the RUPA imposes *additional* liability on general partners by making all general partners **jointly and severally liable** for unpaid debts and liabilities of the partnership. This means that general partners' personal assets are at risk both together (jointly) and separately (severally) for all debts and liabilities of the partnership regardless of the source of the debt or liability. In the Redfern Catering example above, suppose that Redfern and Colgate formed a general partnership to operate the catering business as Redfern-Colgate Catering, GP. Marshall obtains a judgment against the business for medical damages related to food poisoning. Marshall must first exhaust all of the assets of the partnership. If the assets are not enough to satisfy the judgment, Marshall may then attempt to collect the unpaid portion of the judgment from the personal assets of Redfern and Colgate together or separately because Redfern and Colgate have joint and several liability for the entire debt. Thus, Marshall may choose to collect 50 percent from Redfern and 50 percent from Colgate, or any combination thereof (60/40, 70/30, etc). Suppose that Redfern has no assets and moves to Key West to become a shrimper. In this case, Marshall may choose to collect the *entire* unpaid judgment from Colgate. However, because generally the partners share in losses as well as profits, Colgate could try to pursue Redfern through a civil suit for 50 percent of the loss he suffered in paying out the judgment to Marshall. This joint and several liability rule may *not* be altered by the parties' agreement, nor may the principals limit their liability based on the principals' agreement to split profits and losses based on a percentage. So, in the Redfern–Colgate partnership, suppose that they agreed at the start of the catering business that Colgate would receive 30 percent of the profits. Colgate *may not* assert that his liability to Marshall is limited to 30 percent of the total unpaid judgment.

The principals in the hypothetical Redfern-Colgate Catering, GP, have joint and several liability for all debts and liabilities of the partnership.

Capitalization General partnerships are generally funded through either debt (i.e., borrowing money from the principals, a commercial lender, or a private individual third party) or through selling of equity (selling a percentage of ownership rights in the partnership and any profits of the business). Partnerships may not, however, sell ownership rights through the public markets such as the New York Stock Exchange. Sometimes general partners hedge their financial investment through a combination of debt and equity. The concepts of debt and equity are discussed in detail in Chapter 16, "Regulation of Securities, Corporate Governance, and Financial Markets."

Taxation of Partnership and Principals Just as in the case of a sole proprietorship, a partnership is a **pass-through entity.** This means that the partnership entity pays no level of corporate tax. Rather, profits are taxed *after* they pass through the business and are distributed to the individual partners. The income is reported on the individual general partner's *personal tax return* (the familiar tax form 1040) and taxed based on the individual rate of the general partner. In fact, the partnership entity itself does not file a tax return, but does file an *information return* for purposes of providing the government with documentation regarding how much, when, and to whom profits were paid. Of course, partners also report business partnership losses on their individual tax returns and are permitted to deduct those losses to offset certain types of income. For example, assume that Redfern and Colgate operate R–C general partnership where the allocation of the profits is agreed upon at 40 percent for Redfern and 60 percent for Colgate. Colgate is a wealthy investor and, thus, has a higher tax bracket. In the first year of operations, R–C earns $10,000 in profits. Here is an example of the calculation:

	Redfern (40%)	Colgate (60%)
Profits paid	$4,000	$6,000
Partner's individual tax rate ("tax bracket")[7]	15%	35%
Net after tax	$3,400	$3,900

Operation and Management of the Partnership Absent an agreement by the parties, the RUPA also governs certain internal operations of the general partnership. For example, unless the parties agree otherwise, each partner receives an equal share of the partnership profit payments regardless of the partner's involvement in the success of the business. The same rule applies to losses. Absent an agreement to the contrary, general partners have the general power to *bind* the partnership to a contractual obligation (e.g., a lease for office space) even if the other general partners have no knowledge of the transaction.

Note that partners who provide labor to the partnership are not entitled to any compensation (other than a share of profits) for this work unless the principals have agreed ahead of time to certain compensation terms. For example, assume that in the Redfern–Colgate general partnership above, Redfern works in the kitchen 80 hours per week while Colgate spends no time working on behalf of the partnership. Absent any advance agreement between the partners, Redfern is not entitled to any compensation for the kitchen work.

---

[7]These tax brackets are for approximation purposes only. Income tax liability is actually determined using a series of calculations based on progressive tax brackets.

Fiduciary Obligations   General partners have a set of duties that ensure they are acting in the best interest of the partnership. These are known as **fiduciary duties.**[8] These duties are very similar to duties owed by an agent to a principal discussed in Chapter 10 "Agency and Employment Relationships." Fundamentally, the RUPA sets out these duties as threefold: (1) loyalty, (2) care, and (3) good faith. The loyalty standard prohibits a general partner from engaging in competition with the interests of the partnership and also prohibits other conflicts of interest with the partnership such as using the partnership property for personal gain at the expense of the interests of the entity. Partners must also exercise due care in handling the affairs of the partnership and treat business affairs with the same diligence as they would treat their own personal business affairs. The good faith standard requires that partners exercise appropriate discretion in dealing with other partners and third parties concerning the partnership's business enterprise operations. Case 13.1 illustrates that good faith is an underlying duty for all actions taken by the general partners in carrying out partnership interests and cannot be bargained away.

Limited Partnerships

A limited partnership is an entity that exists by virtue of a *state statute* that recognizes one or more principals as managing the business enterprise, while other principals participate only in terms of contributing capital or property. A limited partnership has at least one general partner (managing principal) and at least one limited partner (investing principal). In the absence of an agreement, the Revised Uniform Limited Partnership Act (RULPA) governs a limited partnership. However, the RULPA actually works in tandem with the RUPA. That is, when an issue of liability or operation arises, the written partnership agreement governs. If there is no agreement or the agreement is silent on this issue, then the RULPA resolves the issue. If the RULPA does not provide rules on a particular issue, courts may sometimes look to the RUPA for guidance.

Formation   A limited partnership is formed by the general partner filing a **certificate of limited partnership** with the state government authority[9] (usually in the secretary of state's office). Generally, the certificate is not overly complex. It requires routine information such as the names, addresses, and capital contribution of each partner. Although the RULPA does not formally require a partnership agreement, the vast majority of limited partnerships have one. The agreement details the rights, obligations, and relationships between partners. These partnerships typically use the designation *LP* at the end of their business name to signify the limited partnership as their form of entity. Figure 13.1 presents a sample certificate of limited partnership.

Personal Liability of Principals   Each general partner in a limited partnership is *personally liable* for all of the partnership's debts and liabilities, just as if the general partners were in a general partnership. However, limited partners do *not* have the same automatic personal liability of a general partner.[10] Rather, the limited partner's liability is limited to whatever the limited partner *contributed* to the partnership. For example, suppose that Redfern initially operates Redfern Catering as a sole proprietor, but decides to expand his business operations. He decides to raise capital through the selling of some ownership interest in his business. Redfern convinces Macduff to invest $20,000 in Redfern Catering. However, Macduff has substantial personal assets he wishes to protect and no interest in running the day-to-day operations of the business. The two form Redfern Catering LP, with Redfern as the general partner and Macduff as the limited partner. In an effort to cut costs, Redfern negligently uses spoiled ingredients and a customer, Marshall, is

---

[8]RUPA § 404.

[9]RULPA § 201.

[10]RULPA § 403(b).

FACT SUMMARY   In February 1992, author Thomas Clancy formed Jack Ryan Limited Partnership (JRLP) named after Clancy's fictional hero. Clancy's only partner in the venture was his wife, King. JRLP's purpose was to generate revenue related to the writing, publishing, and sale of certain novels. Each partner owned a half interest in JRLP. The partnership agreement had standard provisions imposing the duty of diligence, but also contained a specific provision that allowed each partner to compete freely on an individual basis with the interests of JRLP. Specifically, the partners gave up the right to claim that the other party breached the duty of care due to a partner's participation in a competing venture.

After formation of the partnership, JRLP entered into an agreement with a literary agency for Clancy to lend his name only to a series of novels written by an author who was using a "Clancy-esque" writing style. In this agreement, Clancy had the absolute right to withdraw the use of his name for the series at any time. Clancy apparently had very little to do with the venture, but his name had sufficient marketing power to propel the series to substantial financial success.

By 1996 Clancy and King were divorced but remained partners in the highly profitable JRLP entity. In 2001, Clancy announced that he was exercising his right to withdraw the right to use his name for the series starting in 2004. When Clancy did finally withdraw the right to use his name, King filed suit against him alleging that Clancy's withdrawal of the right to use his name was a breach of fiduciary duty that he owed to King and was done out of ill will toward her stemming from the divorce. Clancy countered that he had the right to conduct the partnership as he thought best and pointed to the partnership agreement's provision on insulation from liability for due care. The case eventually went to Maryland's highest court.

SYNOPSIS OF DECISION AND OPINION   The Maryland Court of Appeals ruled that Clancy's withdrawal of the use of his name constituted an act of bad faith that breaches the general duty of good faith and fair dealing owed to his partner King. No matter what the parties agreed to in terms of the duty of care, a duty of good faith and fair dealing underlie the actions of the partners. The court defined an act of bad faith as an act where a primary motivator of the partner's conduct is to injure either the firm's value or other partners. Under the doctrine of good faith, a partner impliedly promises to refrain from conduct that will harm the partnership and other partners.

WORDS OF THE COURT: Good Faith Requirement   "If a significant motive for Clancy exercising his right to withdraw his name from the [venture] series was to decrease the profitability of the series, thereby denying his JRLP partner and ex-wife revenue, because he desired to spite or punish King for or as a consequence of their divorce, it could reasonably be maintained that he acted in bad faith towards [them]. One certainly breaches the promise of good faith owed [. . .] as a fiduciary in a partnership by working actively to decrease the profits of the business venture."

Case Questions

1. Are there any circumstances under which there could be a *good faith* reason for Clancy to withdraw the right to use his name?

2. Why didn't the provision effectively waiving a breach of duty of care lawsuit by one partner against another govern this dispute?

---

sickened. Marshall obtains a judgment against Redfern Catering LP, but after the assets of the partnership are exhausted, Marshall is still owed a balance from the judgment. Because Redfern is a general partner, Marshall may recover the balance from Redfern's personal assets, but *not* from Macduff as a limited partner.

There are some exceptions to the liability rule spelled out in the RULPA. The primary exception is when a limited partner acts *illegally* or *negligently* within the scope of partnership duties. When a limited partner engages in wrongful conduct on behalf of the limited partnership and causes an injury resulting in damages, the limited partner is personally liable to pay damages to the injured party.

D

The Commonwealth of Massachusetts
William Francis Galvin
Secretary of the Commonwealth
One Ashburton Place - Room 1717, Boston, Massachusetts 02108-1512

Limited Partnership Certificate
(General Laws Chapter 109, Section 8)

(1) The exact name of the limited partnership:

Redfern Catering, L.P.

(2) The general character of the business of the limited partnership:

Catering services

(3) The street address of the limited partnership in the commonwealth at which it's records will be maintained:

1000 Restaurant Avenue
Boston, MA 02108

(4) The name and street address of the resident agent:

Francis Redfern   1000 Restaurant Avenue
                                      Boston, MA 02108

(5) The name and business address of each general partner:

Francis Redfern   Alexandra Macduff
1000 Restaurant Avenue   10 Flamingo Drive
Boston, MA 02108   Dania Beach, FL 33004

(6) The latest date on which the limited partnership is to dissolve: October 10, 2020

(7) Additional matters:

None

Signed *(by all general partners)*: _____

_____

Consent of resident agent:

I **Francis Redfern** _____,
resident agent of the above limited partnership, consent to my appointment as resident agent pursuant to G.L. c109
Section 8 (a) (3)*

or attach registered agents consent hereto.

Basic information including name, purpose, and address of the partnership. Note that Redfern Catering is using the L.P. (limited partnership) designation.

State statutes require that all business entities have a physical address within that state jurisdiction. Out-of-state entities use a resident agent to satisfy this requirement. Some commercial services offer resident agent services for a fee. Attorneys sometimes serve as resident agents for their business clients. A resident agent typically provides services such as accepting legal documents (such as a complaint in a lawsuit) for the partnership. In-state partnerships simply use a partner as their resident agent (such as in the case of Redfern Catering, LP).

Most states require the partners to select an ending date for the partnership, but allow the partners to continue the partnership after the ending date by simply filing an additional form extending the date.

The resident agent consents to serve in compliance with responsibilities set out by the state statute.

Capitalization   Limited partnerships are generally funded through either debt (i.e., borrowing money from the principals, a commercial lender, or private individual third parties) or through selling of equity (selling a percentage of ownership rights in the partnership and any profits of the business). Limited partnerships may not, however, sell ownership rights through the public markets such as the New York Stock Exchange (NYSE). Although not considered publicly traded equity, when limited partnership interests are sold to the public (usually through a broker-dealer with contacts in the investment community), they are subject to strict federal securities laws and state securities laws commonly known as *blue sky laws*. Securities law is discussed more extensively in Chapter 16, "Regulation of Securities, Corporate Governance, and Financial Markets."

Taxation of Partners and Partnership   Limited partnerships are pass-through entities just like general partnerships. The same rules apply for taxation as in a general partnership. That is, profits or losses are reported in the principal's personal tax return and tax is paid in accordance with the individual partner's individual tax rate. The general partner is responsible for filing an *information return* with taxing authorities, but limited partnerships do not pay corporate taxes. As in the case of general partnerships, this information return informs tax authorities of profits or losses of the partnership entity.

Management and Operation of the Partnership   One of the primary differences between general partners and limited partners is the extent to which they are permitted to be involved in day-to-day operations of the business. General partners manage the business and are permitted to bind the partnership. Limited partners *may not* participate in daily management of the business, do not have authority to bind the partnership, and remain primarily as investors. Limited partners that do engage in daily management and operations *jeopardize* their limited partnership status. Under the RULPA, limited partners may engage in consulting and contribute expertise, but may not engage in management activities such as supervision of employees.[11]

Although sometimes limited partners are referred to colloquially as *silent partners,* limited partners have the right to access partnership information (such as inspection of financial records) about the business and general information about the partnership's operations (such as contracts the partnership has executed). The partnership agreement may expand the limited partner's role in management (though not to the point where the limited partner's role constitutes day-to-day involvement in running the business) and may also expand her rights and prerogatives such as the right to remove a general

> **KEY POINT**
> Limited partners *may not* participate in daily management of the business, do not have authority to bind the partnership, and remain primarily as investors.

partner or the right to block admission of new partners. These provisions in a partnership agreement are relatively common because they allow the limited partner to better protect her investment.

Limited partnerships also differ from general partnerships in terms of the default rule for sharing profits and losses. Recall from our earlier discussion that the RUPA contemplates that partners, absent agreement to the contrary, share equally in profits and losses. However, in a limited partnership, the partners share in profits and losses in proportion to "the value of contributions made by each partner to the extent they have been received by the partnership and have not been returned."[12] For example, suppose Pablo, Vincent, and Frida form a limited partnership for the purpose of starting an art auction house. The partnership is initially structured as follows:

---

[11]RULPA § 303(b), (c).
[12]RULPA § 403(c).

Partner	Initial Capital Contribution	Role
Pablo	$20,000	General partner; salaried employee
Vincent	$45,000	Limited partner
Frida	$45,000	Limited partner

The partnership agreement provides for a salary for Pablo, but is silent on distribution of profits and losses. Frida has an immediate need for cash, so the parties agree to return $10,000 of her investment. Under the RULPA, profits and losses are now allocated with 20 percent to Pablo, 35 percent to Frida, and 45 percent to Vincent.

In some cases, the principals in a partnership make specific agreements and label themselves as limited partners. This labeling is not sufficient to maintain a limited partner status (and, thus, protection from certain liabilities). The focus of the inquiry is the principals' *conduct.* The question is not how did they *label* themselves or how did they sign certain documents or what they called themselves. Rather, the question is: did the principals *operate* as a limited partnership? Case 13.2 is an example of the substance over form analysis applied to partnership law.

Family Limited Partnerships   Another type of partnership is a family limited partnership. A family limited partnership is simply a limited partnership that is used for estate planning for families of considerable wealth. The actual process and legal procedures governing family limited partnership transactions are a very complex area of tax and estate law. The fundamental purpose of a family limited partnership is to allow wealthy members of one generation to distribute assets (in the form of an IRS recognized gift) to heirs using a method that allows the distributing generation to claim a much lower market value than the actual market value of the gift. It also allows the distributing generation to transfer assets out of their large estate into the smaller estates of their heirs and avoid estate taxes upon their death. Some states have amended their RULPA statutes to accommodate the special circumstances of a family limited partnership with respect to partner dissociation (discussed in the next section of this chapter).

LO13-7 Partner Dissociation and Dissolution of the Partnership

When a partner no longer wishes to be a principal in the partnership, she may choose to leave the partnership. The RUPA[13] uses the term **dissociation** to describe this act of separation while the RULPA uses the term **withdrawal.** Both the RUPA and RULPA give the partners substantial rights to govern withdrawal under the partnership agreement, but they differ significantly if the partners have not agreed to displace the RUPA and RULPA provisions.

Dissociation under the RUPA   The RUPA lists ten specific events that are events of dissociation, but the majority of dissociations are the result of one of the following three events: (1) voluntary separation from the partnership, whereby one partner gives specific

---

[13]The rules governing dissociation and dissolution are perhaps the biggest difference between the UPA and RUPA. Under the UPA, such events cause an automatic dissolution of the partnership. The RUPA allows the partnership to continue under certain circumstances.

FACT SUMMARY Dormilee Morton inherited the assets of her husband's construction company, consisting primarily of heavy equipment and building materials. Using these assets, her son, Steven Morton, began to run the day-to-day operations of the business, but the business failed in a period of five years. During that time, Steven Morton was responsible for all tax filings and signed the tax returns indicating that Morton Construction was a limited partnership. On Mrs. Morton's personal tax return, she indicated that she was a "silent partner" in Morton Construction. However, during these same years, Mrs. Morton signed for bank loans as "Dormilee Morton and Steven Morton d/b/a Morton Construction Company." She also provided additional capital for the business when needed. Her home phone number and home address were listed as the principal place of business for Morton Construction.

The IRS assessed Morton Construction over $40,000 in back taxes and penalties for failing to pay federal employment taxes during a four-year period. Because Steven Morton and the business were without assets, the IRS pursued Mrs. Morton as a general partner in the business. Morton defended on the basis that she has been nothing more than a limited partner, as indicated on the tax returns, and was thus insulated from liabilities of the partnership.

SYNOPSIS OF DECISION AND OPINION The court ruled against Mrs. Morton and upheld the judgment in favor of the IRS's tax assessment against Mrs. Morton's personal assets as a general partner. The court concluded that the notations on the tax returns in and of themselves are not determinative for the status of an entity. Mrs. Morton participated in the business in the same way as a general partner would and, thus, has no limited liability status. In coming to this conclusion, the court cited several factors that indicated the business was run as a general partnership: her contribution of all capital assets, her taking a 50 percent business loss on previous tax returns, her granting the bank a security interest in their equipment, and her willful ignorance of business mail that arrived at her own home.

WORDS OF THE COURT: Substance over Form "[T]he court concludes that she was not, in fact, a limited partner. The business was a general partnership or, at least, a joint venture. The mere marking on the tax returns of 'limited partner' has no effect when it is clear that there is no limited partnership, either *de facto* or *de jure*, exists. Thus, the reasons are twofold for denying Mrs. Morton's [emphatic declaration] that she was a limited partner in Morton Construction Company: (1) utter failure to comply with the [state] statutory requirements for establishing a limited partnership; and (2) her general involvement in the business."

Case Questions

1. What could Dormilee Morton have done to strengthen her status as a limited partner?

2. Both Mortons testified that Mrs. Morton was only involved in a very small part of the business and that Steven had taken charge over all financial and tax affairs. Do you think it is fair to hold a widow responsible for the misdealing or ineptness of her son in this case?

---

notice to withdraw from the partnership; or (2) expulsion by the *unanimous* vote of the other partners; or (3) the partner can no longer carry out her duties to the partnership (such as in the case of incapacity or death) or no longer has an economic stake in the business (such as in the case of an individual partner filing for bankruptcy protection). The RUPA makes a distinction between *rightful* and *wrongful* dissociation. When a partner exercises a rightful dissociation, she is no longer liable for the debts and liabilities incurred by the partnership. Although the partner is still liable for predissociation liability, she no longer owes any fiduciary duty to the partnership or the remaining principals. A wrongful dissociation occurs if a partner's withdrawal violates the partnership agreement or if a partner withdraws from a partnership before the expiration of a previously agreed upon time has elapsed. In the event of a wrongful termination, the wrongfully dissociated partner

Legal Speak »»
De Facto Existing in fact; having effect even though not formally recognized.
De Jure Existing in or by right of law.

CONCEPT SUMMARY   Sole Proprietorships vs. Partnerships

	Sole Proprietorships	Partnerships LP and GP
Formation	Low start-up costs and minimal filing. One-person entity.	Minimal filing requirements. Partnership agreement may result in some legal fees. GP has two or more partners. LP must have at least one GP and one or more LPs.
Liability of Principal(s)	All debts and liabilities of the business are the personal liabilities of the sole proprietor. All of proprietor's assets are at risk to satisfy business debts and liabilities.	GP: Each GP is jointly and severally liable for debts and liabilities of the partnership. All personal assets of the GP are at risk. LP: Personal assets of the LPs are not at risk for debts and liabilities of the entity.
Capital	Proprietor uses personal assets or bank loan secured by personal assets.	Partners each contribute capital as needed. The partnership agreement governs how and when additional calls for partners' contributions are made. Bank loans secured by partnership assets and/or personal guarantees.
Taxes	All income taxes of the business are paid at the proprietor's individual tax rate and reported on the proprietor's individual income tax return. Miscellaneous state and local taxes to operate business.	No taxation at the partnership entity level. All income tax of the business passes through the partnership, is distributed to the partners, and is paid at the individual tax rate of the receiving partner. Partnership files information return to inform IRS of profits or losses. Miscellaneous state and local taxes to operate business.
Management and Control	One-person entity.	Management and control as outlined in partnership agreements or under RUPA/UPA if not agreed upon. LP cannot have day-to-day involvement. Duty of good faith and fiduciary duty owed by partners.
Designation	John Doe d/b/a Doe Consulting Services	Doe Partners, GP Doe Partners, LP

"is liable to the partnership and to the other partners for damages caused by the dissociation."[14] For example, suppose that Abel, Baker, and Cain are general partners in ABC Landscape Design and have no written agreement about the partnership. Abel is knowledgeable in the operation of specific equipment crucial to the success of the business. ABC enters into a contract to provide services to several large office centers. After a few months, Abel withdraws from the partnership to pursue another career. As a result, the partnership cannot perform the services on time and breaches several agreements while attempting to locate a replacement to operate the equipment. Abel would be liable for damages suffered by the partnership.

When a partner dissociates herself (rightfully or wrongfully) from the partnership, the partnership *does not* automatically dissolve. In fact, the RUPA leans toward the notion that the partnership can continue.[15] If the remaining principals wish to continue operating the business partnership, they must purchase the partnership interest of the dissociating partner based on a formula contained in the RUPA. Again, it is important to note that these are RUPA default rules and that a partnership agreement often fixes the method or formula for determining the buyout price.

There may be certain cases where the remaining principals wish to dissolve the partnership after dissociation. The dissolution does not actually end the partnership, but rather triggers the process of **winding up.** Only after wind up is complete is the partnership officially considered terminated. Wind up is the period of time necessary to settle the affairs of the partnership such as discharging the partnership's liabilities, settling and closing the partnership's business, marshaling the assets of the partnership, and distributing any net proceeds to the partners.

Withdrawal under the RULPA   Because the overwhelming majority of limited partnerships operate under a partnership agreement that spells out detailed rules for withdrawal of a general or limited partner, the RULPA does not play as significant of a role as does the RUPA for general partnerships. However, the RULPA does set down default rules for withdrawal of partners in the event that the written agreement does not cover withdrawal or its consequences sufficiently. A *general partner* may withdraw at any time without causing dissolution of the partnership. The withdrawal does not result in automatic dissolution provided that (1) the partnership still has at least one remaining *general partner,* and (2) all of the partners (both general and limited) agree in writing to continue the partnership.

If the partner's withdrawal does not result in dissolution of the partnership, the partnership must pay the departing partner the fair market value of her interest in the limited partnership within a reasonable time after withdrawal.[16]

In contrast, *limited* partners are subject to restrictions on withdrawal. Absent an agreement in writing to the contrary, the general rule is that limited partners *may not* withdraw from a partnership before the time that the partners have agreed that the partnership will terminate. If the limited partnership agreement *does not* provide for a certain time before termination, limited partners may withdraw with at least six months' prior written notice to the other partners. Some states have passed additional restrictions, including an absolute prohibition of withdrawal, intended to address special circumstances in family limited partnerships.

> **KEY POINT**
>
> *Impact of a dissociation/withdrawal:* The dissociation (under the RUPA in a general partnership) or withdrawal (under the RULPA in a limited partnership) does not result in automatic dissolution so long as the remaining partners wish to continue.

---

[14]RUPA § 602(c).

[15]RUPA § 606(a).

[16]RULPA § 604.

Self-Check Rules for Withdrawal

Is there a basis for rightful dissociation?

1. Under RUPA, a general partnership that owns a diner has ten partners. One partner never works, only shows up to eat, and harasses servers. Seven partners vote to throw him out.

2. Under RUPA, a tax lawyer who is a partner in a small law firm wants to start a new career at the IRS. She informs her colleagues of her departure at the end of the year, just before the busy tax season.

3. Under RULPA, a limited partner in a partnership that owns a baseball team decides he no longer wants to be part of the steroid scandals, so he withdraws.

4. Under RULPA, a limited partner in a juice company wants to leave and get into the wind-powered energy business. The partnership agreement allows limited partners to leave so long as they do not invest in another beverage company for three years.

Answers to this Self-Check are provided at the end of the chapter.

Other Events of Dissolution Dissociation is not the only way that a partnership may be dissolved. Once a partnership has reached its agreed upon term (a certain date set out in the filings and/or partnership agreement), or by court order, or, in the case of a general partnership, by unanimous consent of the partners, the partnership may be *dissolved*. Note that dissolving a limited partnership does not require unanimous consent of all partners. Rather, unanimous consent of each general partner and consent of any limited partner that owns a majority of the rights to receive a distribution as a limited partner is sufficient to dissolve the partnership.

CONCEPT SUMMARY   Partner Dissociation/Withdrawal and Dissolution of the Partnership

- The RUPA lists a variety of events of dissociation, including voluntary separation, expulsion, incapacity, and death, that are termed *rightful* dissociations.

- In a rightful dissociation, the withdrawing partner is no longer liable for postdissociation liabilities of the partnership. In a *wrongful dissociation* (e.g., one that violates the partnership agreement), the withdrawing partner is liable for any damages the withdrawal caused.

- The RULPA plays a less significant role in a limited partnership context because so many limited partnerships operate under detailed agreements.

- Under the RULPA, a general partner may withdraw at any time without causing dissolution. Limited partners are subject to restrictions on withdrawal.

- Partnerships may also be dissolved if the partnership has reached its agreed upon term, by court order, or by unanimous consent of the parties.

Principals p. 340   Owners of a business entity.

Sole proprietorship p. 341   One-person business entity with minimal filing requirements.

Partnership p. 342   Multiple-person business entity where the partners conduct an ongoing business relationship in which profits and losses are shared.

Express partnerships p. 342   Partnerships formed when the parties have agreed to conduct a partnership on certain terms and conditions.

Implied partnerships p. 343   Partnerships formed when the parties have acted like general partners even if the parties did not agree or intend to form a partnership.

Joint venture p. 343   Business relationship between two or more parties for a limited-in-time venture.

Jointly and severally liable p. 344   Legal principle that imposes liability on partners both together (jointly) and separately (severally) for debts and liabilities of the partnership.

Pass-through entity p. 345   Business entity that does not pay corporate taxes, such as a partnership. Rather, any profits are taxed at individual rates when distributed to the partners.

Fiduciary duties p. 346   Under the Revised Uniform Partnership Act, general partners have the duties of loyalty, care, and good faith to ensure they are acting in the best interest of the partnership.

Certificate of limited partnership p. 346   The document filed with the state government authority by the general partner to form a limited partnership, requiring routine information such as the names, addresses, and capital contribution of each partner.

Dissociation p. 350   Term used by the RUPA to describe the act of separation of one partner from the partnership.

Withdrawal p. 350   Term used by the RULPA to describe the act of separation of one partner from the partnership.

Winding up p. 353   Period after dissolution where debts of the partnership are paid and remaining assets are liquidated/distributed.

THEORY TO PRACTICE

Demuth is a sole proprietor of a business that specializes in designing and manufacturing custom-made medical instruments for health care professionals. Several hospitals and physician practice groups approach Demuth and ask him to design and produce a highly specialized surgical instrument that is currently unavailable in the market from larger manufacturers. Demuth, unable to finance the research and development costs, convinces Warren, a private investor, to fund the project. Demuth also recruits Oakley, a physician, to lend her medical expertise. Demuth drafted a letter to Warren and Oakley thanking them for their confidence in the project and setting out certain terms for the venture. The letter was very brief and stated that the parties were equal participants in the business venture intending to develop and manufacture a certain surgical instrument. Demuth would contribute his expertise, laboratory workspace, and manufacturing facilities to the project.

Warren would contribute $100,000 as a capital contribution, and Oakley would contribute medical expertise, research knowledge, and $10,000 in capital. The letter ended with a statement that the business venture would last for five years unless the parties mutually agreed on extending the term. Profits or losses would be calculated annually and each party was to be paid in equal shares for any profits or bear equal losses. Warren and Oakley each wrote "Agreed" and signed the letter on the bottom along with the date. Demuth then went on to hire a top engineer and purchased equipment to work on the Demuth–Warren–Oakley project.

After a year of slow progress on the project, Demuth was concerned that the initial capital contribution was not going to be sufficient to carry the venture into its second year. Demuth approached Warren for an additional $100,000. Warren, who was disgruntled about the slow progress, refused. Demuth, now anxious about keeping the venture afloat, negotiates a *loan* on behalf of the business with Strand, another private investor. Without the knowledge of the other principals, Demuth signs the promissory note: *Demuth–Oakley–Warren Partnership, by Demuth, Partner.*

1. What form of entity has Demuth, Warren, and Oakley formed? What law governs the operation of the partnership and the rights of the partners?

2. If the venture becomes insolvent (runs out of money to pay its regular monthly bills), will Demuth, Warren, and/or Oakley be liable for any, some, or all of the debt owed to Strand? If, just after the venture becomes insolvent, Demuth files for personal bankruptcy, will Warren and Oakley now be liable 100 percent for the debt owed to Strand?

3. Assume that when Oakley found out about the loan to Strand, she was so angered that she gave notice to Demuth that she was withdrawing from the partnership before the agreed upon five-year period.

What is the legal impact of Oakley's dissociation on the partnership? Is the partnership automatically dissolved? Is Oakley still liable for the Strand debt and to any creditors to which the partnership owed money?

4. In Question 3 above, suppose that Demuth and Warren decide they cannot continue without Oakley's expertise and they dissolve the partnership. In the process, they are forced to breach several contracts with their vendors. What is Oakley's postdissociation liability to Demuth and Warren for any damages suffered by breaching the vendor contracts?

5. Suppose that instead of the conflict that developed, the parties ended up being profitable on the venture and they were eager to continue the business. What are the factors that the parties should consider when choosing a business entity that suits the company's needs now and in the future?

MANAGER'S CHALLENGE

A basic understanding of business entities is important when considering a start-up venture, such as the one contemplated in Theory to Practice above, or when a company wishes to start a new business, joint venture, or a partnership with another company or individual that leverages their existing business. Suppose you are a manager of Network Associates Corp., a company that retails, installs, and maintains computer networks for business clients. You receive the following e-mail from your senior manager:

> Our company has been approached by NewComp Inc. to form a business relationship that will involve our company being the exclusive supplier of NewComp computer networking products for the northeast

and mid-Atlantic regions of the United States. This could be a lucrative opportunity for us. To avoid any liability problems for Network Associates we are considering a new entity, separate and apart from the corporation. I will be consulting our counsel and analyzing whether the return will be worth the liability and investment risk. To assist me in my analysis, please write a two- to three-page memorandum that gives me some basic information on (a) what factors we should consider when selecting an entity, and (b) if we just begin doing business jointly without any formal agreement, are we exposing ourselves to liability unnecessarily?

A sample answer to this question may found on this textbook's Web site at http://www.mhhe.com/melvin.

CASE SUMMARY 13.1 :: Conklin v. Holland, 138 S.W.3d 215 (Tenn. Ct. App. 2003)

PARTNERSHIP LIABILITY

Lewis and Holland bought a rundown home in Memphis, Tennessee, to renovate and then sell for a profit. The two agreed that Lewis would live in the house during the

renovations. In this time period, twenty-year-old Amanda Conklin visited the house where Lewis provided her with alcohol and illicit drugs. As a result of the use of this combination, Conklin died. Lewis attempted to conceal the death by placing her in the car in the garage of the home under construction. Police discovered Conklin's body a month and half later and arrested Lewis. Conklin's estate sued Holland for civil damages related to Conklin's death under the theory that Holland and Lewis were partners in the co-ownership of the property and as Lewis's partner Holland is liable for whatever Lewis does upon the land they co-owned as general partners.

CASE QUESTIONS

1. Was there a partnership?
2. What was the partnership formed to do?
3. As a practical matter, why would the Conklins sue Holland instead of Lewis for partnership liability?

CASE SUMMARY 13.2 :: Meinhard v. Salmon, 249 N.Y. 458 (N.Y. 1928)

FIDUCIARY DUTY

Salmon and Meinhard were partners who entered into a 20-year leasing agreement to operate Hotel Bristol in midtown Manhattan. In exchange for his capital contribution, Meinhard would receive 40 percent of the profits for the first five years and 50 percent every year after until the twentieth year when the lease ended. All losses would be born equally. Salmon alone would "manage, lease, underlet and operate" the hotel. At first, the two lost money, but after twenty years the hotel was very profitable. Just before the lease was about to end, the owner of the hotel (who also owned the five lots surrounding the hotel) approached Salmon and encouraged him to lease the whole city block, including the hotel, for a term of 80 years. Salmon agreed to the expansion plan and drafted the agreements so that the new arrangement began they day after the Meinhard–Salmon lease ended. Under the new arrangement, Salmon had sole control of the hotel and the rest of the block. Meinhard sued Salmon for breach of fiduciary duty. Salmon asserted that their original partnership had ended when the 20-year lease expired and that he owed Meinhard no duty because they were not partners in the new venture. In their opinion, the court wrote: "Many forms of conduct permissible in a workaday world for those acting at arm's length, are forbidden to those bound by fiduciary ties. A trustee is held to something stricter than the morals of the market place. Not honesty alone, but the punctilio of an honor the most sensitive, is then the standard of behavior."

CASE QUESTIONS

1. Who did the court side with?
2. What duty did Meinhard claim was breached?
3. Does fiduciary duty end when the partnership expires?

CASE SUMMARY 13.3 :: Rahemtulla v. Hassam, 539 F. Supp. 2d 755 (M.D. Pa. 2008)

GOOD FAITH

Rahemtulla met Hassam at his religious congregation. Hassam visited Rahemtulla and his wife many times at their home before he pitched his idea to open a steak house restaurant in the Howard Johnson's Inn. Hassam owned the inn along with several other partners. Hassam told the Rahemtullas that revenues from the steak house could be over $2 million a year. Hassam knew that Rahemtulla had absolutely no experience in the food and beverage industry but offered to help him. Rahemtulla quit his job in the corporate sector and borrowed $100,000 using his house as collateral. The $100,000 was Rahemtulla's capital contribution in the partnership. The two entered into a partnership and signed a lease with the Howard Johnson's Inn partnership for the restaurant space. The restaurant opened and Rahemtulla began to co-operate it with Hassam. From the beginning, the restaurant was losing money and Hassam began to make unilateral decisions that would help cut expenses. The restaurant was dealt a serious financial setback when authorities refused to approve a liquor license for the restaurant, thus lowering revenue potential. After several months, Rahemtulla complained that he had been cheated by Hassam, whose financial reward came from the lease without any concern about the restaurant operations. Hassam blamed Rahemtulla for incompetence in managing the venture. Rahemtulla sued Hassam for breach of fiduciary duty and dealing in bad faith.

CASE QUESTIONS

1. What duties did Hassam owe Rahemtulla?
2. Does it matter that Rahemtulla made foolish decisions when he trusted his friend?
3. What is the potential conflict when Hassam creates a partnership to lease from another partnership he is part of?

CASE SUMMARY 13.4 :: In re Spree.com Corp., 2001 WL 1518242 (Bankr. E.D. Pa. 2001)

DUTY OF LOYALTY

Technology Crosser Ventures (TCV), LP, is a venture capital fund that invests as a limited partner in technology companies that require an infusion of capital. Among the partners are Testler, Hoag, and Kimball. One of the companies they invested in was Spree.com. The partnership was structured as to allow Spree, a corporation, to be the general partner with TCV as the limited partner. As part of the partnership agreement, Testler would represent TCV as a member of the board of directors on Spree.com. On August 24, 2000, *The Wall Street Journal* reported a story about TCV and its partners that depicted Testler, Hoag, and Kimball discussing their investments at Testler's office. The paper quoted Testler saying, "What do we want to do with this puppy? The cash runs out soon." Hoag then asked, "They're going to be looking at us for more capital, aren't they?" Kimball added, "I don't want to be supporting them until who knows when." The three men were talking about Spree.com. Spree.com became insolvent (unable to pay bills as they become due) not long after the article appeared. They sued TCV arguing that the article made it impossible for them to get more investors. Spree sued Testler for breach of loyalty and due care.

CASE QUESTIONS

1. Who prevails and why?
2. Does this case show potential problems with venture capital firms as limited partners?
3. Was TCV in "control" of Spree.com because they held the purse strings?

Self-Check ANSWERS

Rules for Withdrawal

1. No. In order to expel a partner, assuming the absence of a partnership agreement, the RUPA requires *all* partners to vote to expel.

2. Probably not. Her departure at the end of the year just before the busy tax season may result in the partnership being unable to perform the services on time and may breach agreements while attempting to locate a replacement. Under the RUPA, the departing lawyer may be liable for damages suffered by the partnership.

3. No. Under the RULPA *limited* partners are subject to restrictions on withdrawal. Absent an agreement in writing to the contrary, the general rule is that limited partners *may not* withdraw from a partnership before the time that the partners have agreed that the partnership will terminate. If the limited partnership agreement *does not* provide for a certain time before termination, limited partners may withdraw with at least six months prior written notice to the other partners. Some states have passed additional restrictions, including an absolute prohibit of withdrawal, intended to address special circumstances in family limited partnerships.

4. Yes, so long as the partner acts in good faith. Partnership agreements always displace any RUPA or RULPA rules.

14

CHAPTER

Limited Liability Partnerships, Limited Liability Companies, and Other Business Arrangements

learning outcomes checklist

After studying this chapter, students who have mastered the material will be able to:

14-1 Identify the sources and level of laws that govern LLP and LLC entities.

14-2 Explain the function of an operating agreement and the fundamental structure of an LLC.

14-3 Distinguish between the formation and management of an LLC and the formation and management of an LLP.

14-4 Determine the rights of principals upon withdrawal from an LLC.

14-5 Articulate the legal protections from personal liability afforded to the principals in an LLC and LLP.

14-6 Identify the tax treatment schemes of an LLC and LLP.

14-7 Provide the primary methods for capitalizing limited liability entities.

14-8 Recognize the utility of other business arrangements including franchise relationships and business trusts.

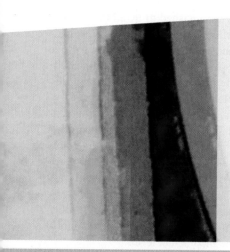

This chapter continues the discussion of forms of business entities and laws that govern business organizations by focusing on limited liability companies (LLCs) and limited liability partnerships (LLPs). The use of these entities has grown rapidly since states first began to recognize them in the late 1970s. They have become a common part of the modern business environment because they offer flexibility advantages for certain business ventures. This chapter also covers some business arrangements that fall outside of the entity categories, but are thought of as business arrangements. In this chapter students will learn:

■ Background and laws related to operation of a limited liability company (LLC) and a limited liability partnership (LLP).

■ Legal liability of principals in an LLC and LLP.

■ Use of franchises and business trusts to achieve business objectives.

OVERVIEW OF LLCs AND LLPs

Prior to the development of LLCs and LLPs, principals who wished to avoid the double taxation of a corporation, but still desired liability protection for their personal assets, had few choices. In 1977, the Wyoming legislature gave businesses the choice of new hybrid entities that were designed to have characteristics of a partnership, while providing full protections afforded to the principals of a corporation. The first hybrid entity was known as a **limited liability company (LLC)**. After the Internal Revenue Service began to classify the LLC as a partnership for tax purposes in 1988, many states followed suit and passed their own limited liability statutes primarily modeled on Wyoming's statute. The Uniform Limited Liability Company Act ("ULLCA") is the current model statute used by state legislatures. A subsequent IRS ruling in 1997 made the selection of the LLC even more attractive because the IRS eliminated strict operating requirements in order to qualify as a partnership for tax purposes. Now all states recognize and provide both procedural (formation) and internal default rules (in the event the parties do not agree otherwise) for the LLC. However, LLC statutes can vary considerably from state to state. Note that a minority of states do not permit partnership taxation at the *state* income tax level.

The growth in popularity of limited liability companies led state legislatures to consider the liability dilemma of general partners and they consequently expanded liability protection for general partners in a partnership. In 1991, Texas enacted the first **limited liability partnership (LLP)** statute, which provided limited protection to general partners. By 1996, many states adopted a more extensive shield for general partners from liability for LLP debts and other liabilities. Now, about half of all states provide the same level of liability protection to a general partner in an LLP as is provided to a limited partner in a limited partnership entity.

> ## KEY POINT
> States vary considerably in terms of how LLCs are taxed and operated.

Beginning in 1977, state legislatures began to authorize hybrid forms of business entities that afforded favorable tax treatment and limited liability for its principals.

While LLCs and LLPs are similar in many ways to corporations and partnerships, the legal terminology for describing procedural and governance aspects of these entities is different. It is important to understand these differences to avoid any confusion about the form of entity.

Limited Liability Companies (LLCs)

A limited liability company is an entity whose primary characteristics are that it offers its principals the same amount of liability protection afforded to principals of a corporate form of entity, and it offers pass-through tax treatment for its principals without the restrictions on ownership and scope required for other pass-through entities (such as an S corporation, discussed in detail in the next chapter). For example, suppose that Developer Inc. wants to start a land use project to build a commercial office building. They wish to partner with Garrett, the owner of several pieces of property in the area under consideration. Both the principals of Developer Inc. and Garrett wish to have pass-through tax treatment, but also wish to have as much protection as possible from liability of personal assets. Because Developer Inc. is a corporate principal, the parties cannot use an S corporation. They can, however, achieve these objectives by forming an LLC. In an LLC, owners are known as *members.*

Formation   An LLC is formed by filing **articles of organization** (also called **certificates of organization**) with the state public filing official in the secretary of state's corporation bureau. Although historically LLCs were required to file fairly extensive articles, modern day trends are akin to the same type of information as included on a corporation's articles of incorporation. Most states require only basic information such as the name of the entity, the location of its principal place of business, and the names of its members. A number of states also require a contemporaneous filing with tax authorities to notify them of the existence of the LLC. A sample certificate of organization for an LLC is presented in Figure 14.1.

Most importantly, LLCs are frequently governed by agreement of the parties in the form of an **operating agreement.**[1] If the parties do not execute an operating agreement, the state LLC statute sets out default rules. Operating agreements, similar to partnership agreements, cover much of the internal rules for the actual operation of the entity. One of the primary benefits of an LLC is that it affords its members a great deal of flexibility in terms of the rights and responsibilities of each member. This flexibility includes:

- *Structure of governance and responsibility of members.* The agreement will typically set forth a structure for managing the entity though a single or board of "managing members" (akin to a board of directors), and the agreement will define their responsibilities in terms of day-to-day operations of the entity. This provision will also spell out voting rights of members, procedures for voting, and transactions that require a vote of the general members (such as the sale of the LLC assets to another company, etc.), and procedures for admission of any new members.

- *Death, incapacity, and dissolution.* Members often agree to a series of "what ifs" of managing an LLC through their operating agreement. If a member can no longer perform the duties required by the agreement, this section details a procedure for handling the circumstance of a member's death or incapacity. The procedure is typically different for managing members and members, but in most cases the operating agreement allows the venture's remaining members to choose whether or not to continue. In the event the members choose not to continue, the procedure for dissolution (including preferences of members in terms of who gets paid first after liquidation) is typically outlined in the agreement.

---

[1]Some states call this document an "LLC agreement" or other similar names.

 **FIGURE 14.1** Sample LLC Certificate of Organization

PENNSYLVANIA DEPARTMENT OF STATE
CORPORATION BUREAU

Certificate of Organization
Domestic Limited Liability Company
(15 Pa.C.S. § 8913)

Name
Daniel J. Webster, Esquire
Address
1000 Professional Avenue, Suite 120
City   State   Zip Code
Philadelphia, PA 19130

Document will be returned to the name and address you enter to the left.
⇐

Typically, a business attorney will prepare this document for the LLC and assist the principals with administrative start-up.

Fee: $125

In compliance with the requirements of 15 Pa.C.S. § 8913 (relating to certificate of organization), the undersigned desiring to organize a limited liability company, hereby certifies that:

1. The name of the limited liability company (*designator is required, i.e., "company", "limited" or "limited liability company" or abbreviation*):

   Redfern Catering, LLC

Basic information about the LLC and its registered location. Note that an LLC may opt to use a commercial registered office provider (similar to resident agent services) for a fee. They typically provide services such as accepting legal documents (e.g., a complaint in a lawsuit) for the LLC.

2. The (a) address of the limited liability company's initial registered office in this Commonwealth or (b) name of its commercial registered office provider and the county of venue is:

(a) Number and Street	City	State	Zip	County
One Alpha Drive,	Elizabethtown,	PA	17022	Lancaster

   (b)   Name of Commercial Registered Office Provider   County
   c/o: None

3. The name and address, including street and number, if any; of each organizer is (*all Organizers must sign on page 2*):

Name	Address
Francis Redfern	One Alpha Drive, Elizabethtown, PA 17022
Alexander Colgate	10 Flamingo Drive, Dania Beach, FL 33004

Organizers are those who start up the LLC initially. Once the LLC is formed, they become *members*.

FIGURE 14.1 | Sample LLC Certificate of Organization

DSCB:15-8913-2

4. *Strike out if inapplicable term*
   A member's interest in the company is to be evidenced by a certificate of membership interest.

> These provisions allow the LLC's organizers to choose (1) whether the LLC actually has to issue a certificate to evidence a member's interest, and (2) whether the LLC is to be manager- managed or member-managed.

5. *Strike out if inapplicable:*
   Management of the company is vested in a manager or managers.

6. The specified effective date, if any is: **October 10, 2010**
   month   date   year   hour, if any

7. *Strike out if inapplicable:* The company is a restricted professional company organized to render the following restricted professional service(s):

Not applicable

> LLCs are sometimes used by professional service firms (such as a law firm or a group of architects). If the LLC wishes to restrict the business to members with professional licenses in a certain field, the profession is inserted here.

8. For additional provisions of the certificate, if any, attach an 8½ × 11 sheet.

> The organizers may add additional provisions of LLC management unique to the company by attaching a sheet to the certificate of organization.

IN TESTIMONY WHERE OF, the organizer(s) has (have) signed this Certificate of Organization this

_____ day of_____, _____.

_____
Signature

_____
Signature

_____
Signature

> Signature of all organizers.

Liability   Another important feature of an LLC is its limited liability of its members. LLC members are insulated from personal liability for any business debt or liability if the venture fails. For example, suppose that Phillips is the managing member of Active Wear LLC, and signs a five-year lease agreement with Landlord on behalf of Active Wear. One year into the lease, Active Wear has a downturn in business, is forced to breach the lease, and moves out hoping to convert to an online business model. Landlord's rights are against the LLC entity only. Landlord may not obtain a judgment against Phillips or collect back rent or other damages from Phillips's personal assets.

> **KEY POINT**
>
> Although LLC members are insulated from personal liability for any business debt or liability, creditors often require LLC members to sign personal guarantees and, in cases of fundamental unfairness, a court may disregard the LLC protections.

However, two important factors moderate this limited liability. First, landlords and other creditors will often require a **personal guarantee** from the members whereby the members pledge personal assets to guarantee payment obligations of the business venture.[2] Second, a court may discard the protection in the case where a court finds that fairness demands that the LLC members should compensate any damaged party when the entity is without resources to recover the full amount owed (such as where the members engaged in fraud).

Taxation   Another attractive advantage of an LLC is the various tax treatment alternatives. Although many LLCs are typically treated as a pass-through entity, the LLC's members may also elect to be taxed as a corporation if they consider the corporate tax structure more favorable. Recall from the discussion in previous chapters of pass-through entities that their advantages are primarily (1) the ability to flow through to the investors the tax deductions and losses that are typically generated by an emerging company or a company with significant up-front debt, and (2) the ability to distribute earnings without incurring double-level taxation (i.e., without having a tax imposed on both the entity and the member).

Capitalization   LLCs are capitalized primarily through debt via private lenders or commercial lenders, or by selling equity ownership in the LLC itself. The operating agreement of the LLC often controls the amount and methods of capitalizing the business.

Management and Operation   LLC statutes typically assume that the members will agree on the specifics of managing the venture through a management agreement. Some states require the entire agreement to be in writing, some require only certain parts of the agreement to be in writing, while other states have no writing requirement at all. Most states distinguish between a **member-managed LLC** and a **manager-managed LLC.** In a member-managed LLC, the management structure of the entity is similar to a general partnership with all the members having the authority to bind the business. In a manager-managed LLC, a named manager (or managers) generally has the day-to-day operational responsibilities while the nonmanaging members are typically investors with little input on the course of business taken by the entity except for major decisions (such as a merger). In a manager-managed LLC, nonmanaging members generally do not have the authority to act on behalf of the business venture. The choice of manager-managed or member-managed is generally made on the public filing of the articles of organization and is available to third parties for purposes of checking the authority of an individual to bind the LLC.

As in many business relationships, the managers of an LLC owe the *fiduciary duties* of care and loyalty to the LLC's other members. Controlling members (those with veto power or the ownership stake to block decisions by other members) also owe a duty of loyalty

---

[2]Personal guarantees are discussed in more detail in the next chapter.

to the other members. LLC statutes regarding fiduciary duties vary by state and can be strengthened or pared back by the operating agreement. In fact, the modern trend is to specifically eliminate any liability for a breach of the duty of care. However, managers and controlling members (i.e., members with ownership sufficient to decide or veto internal operational matters) must adhere to the duty of loyalty, are prohibited from self-dealing, and must act in good faith when dealing with the LLCs business matters.

> ## KEY POINT
> Managing members and controlling members owe a fiduciary duty to other members.

Dissolution of LLCs and Dissociation of Members

LO14-4

LLC laws define **dissolution** of an LLC as a liquidation process[3] triggered by an event that is specified in the operating agreement (such as the death of a key member) or the majority of membership interests (or the percentage called for in the operating agreement) deciding to dissolve the company. The members of an LLC may have also agreed to a maximum term for conducting business in its operating agreement. If the term expires, but the members want the LLC to continue, they must have a unanimous vote to fix an additional term *or* the majority of LLC member interests may vote to continue the LLC at-will (with no fixed term but subject to dissolution at any time). **Dissociation** occurs when an individual member decides to exercise the right to withdraw from the partnership. Generally, upon a dissociation the remaining members may either continue the LLC or decide to trigger dissolution. Of course, the parties may agree to their own unique set of rules through the operating agreement. Agreeing ahead of time what will happen if one member decides to withdraw and reducing the agreement to writing is a strategic way to avoid future disputes. Case 14.1 illustrates the dangers of failing to address an important issue in an operating agreement when a court takes up a dispute between the members of an LLC and a departing member.

Members of an LLC can prevent disputes from occurring by planning for events, such as death or dissociation of a member, in their operating agreement.

---

[3]Liquidation includes preserving assets of a business, paying creditors, and then distributing any remaining profits to the individual members.

FACT SUMMARY   Lieberman was a member and vice president of Wyoming.com, LLC (Wyoming), with a $20,000 ownership stake in the LLC at the time of formation in 1994. After a dispute between the parties in 1998, Lieberman was terminated as vice president by the other LLC members. Lieberman served Wyoming with a "notice of withdrawal" and demanded that Wyoming pay for Lieberman's "share of the company" in the amount of $400,000. Wyoming held a meeting of remaining members and voted to accept Lieberman's withdrawal and continue operating the LLC. Wyoming then notified Lieberman that they accepted his withdrawal, but offered him only $20,000 because that was his initial ownership stake. Lieberman rejected the $20,000 offer. Because the operating agreement was silent on the issue of dissociation, Wyoming filed suit asking for a declaratory judgment of its rights against Lieberman.

SYNOPSIS OF DECISION AND OPINION   The Wyoming Supreme Court ruled that Lieberman did not have the right to force Wyoming to buy his interest even after the notice of withdrawal. Lieberman's withdrawal is recognized as a dissociation under the state LLC statute, but there was no contractual provision (via the operating agreement) between the members related to a buyout of a dissociating member's financial interest in the venture. The operating agreement only provided a method for calculating member's interest in the case of *dissolution.* Nor does the state LLC statute provide for a buyout in the case of a dissociated member. Therefore, even though Lieberman is a dissociated member, he may not demand a buyout, nor may Wyoming force him to sell his interest. Lieberman continues to keep his interest in the LLC until dissolution.

WORDS OF THE COURT: Limited Rights   "Lieberman has withdrawn as a member of Wyoming.com and all remaining members unanimously accepted his withdrawal as a member. Lieberman is thus no longer a member of Wyoming.com. [. . .] Because the members of Wyoming.com failed to contractually provide for a buy-out, Lieberman remains a [financial interest] holder in Wyoming.com, LLC. There are no further rights or obligations of the parties for this court to construe with regards to this situation."

Case Questions

1. Based on the court's decision, what specific rights did Lieberman lose when he withdrew as a member of the LLC?

2. What kind of language and methodology could be included in an operating agreement that could have prevented this dispute?

LO14-5, 14-6, 14-7

Legal Speak ›))

Declaratory Judgment   A binding court judgment that establishes the rights and other legal relations of the parties without providing for ordering enforcement. In this case, Wyoming limited its legal risks and unknowns in relation to Lieberman by obtaining a court decision before taking any further action regarding Lieberman's rights in the LLC.

Limited Liability Partnerships (LLPs)

Most states recognize limited liability partnerships through their partnership statutes. Recall that the chief danger of being a general partner is the amount of potential liability for acts of other general partners or the debts and liabilities of the partnership itself. LLP statutes provide general partnerships with the right to convert their entity and gain the protective shield ordinarily only afforded to limited partners or corporate shareholders. Although the origins of LLP laws were rooted in protection of professional service firm partnerships (law, accounting, etc.), the use of LLPs is much more widespread now as some family businesses have also used the LLP form as a way to handle issues unique to the transition from one generation to another in a family business.

Formation   Limited liability partnerships are formed when a general partnership files a **statement of qualification** with the appropriate public official. The conversion of the partnership must be approved by a majority of ownership. The statement includes the name, street address, an affirmative statement electing to become an LLP, an effective date, and the signatures of at least two of the partners. Some states also require a filing to inform tax authorities of the existence of the entity. Once approved, the filing becomes part of the public record.

Liability   Of all of the business entities that we have discussed thus far, the LLP has the greatest variance of liability protection under state law. While the general idea behind being an LLP is that all partners have liability protection for debts and liabilities of the partnership, some states impose conditions on these limits. In cases except where a partner has engaged in some misconduct or tortious conduct (such as negligence), the LLP acts only to shield the personal of assets of *other* partners—never the partner who committed the misconduct or negligence.

Some states provide liability shields for LLP partners *only* when the liability arises from some *negligence* by another partner, but not for other types of liabilities such as those resulting from a breach of contract. For example, suppose that the LLP state statutes of New Chipperville provide for liability protection for partners when one partner acts negligently. Two accountants, Milton and Cowley, form a limited liability partnership called MC Tax Services LLP in New Chipperville. On behalf of the LLP, the partners sign a lease for space with Landlord and invest several thousand dollars from their own assets for start-up capital. One year later, Milton commits a serious error on a client's tax return, the client sues the firm for malpractice, and obtains a $50,000 judgment against the LLP. Because of the negative attention of this case, MC Tax Services loses several large clients, can no longer make its lease payments to Landlord, and the partnership dissolves. Assume that the judgment is not covered by insurance and exceeds the assets of the LLP. Under the law of New Chipperville, the client may pursue Milton's individual assets to pay the $50,000 judgment, but not Cowley's. The liability shield protects Cowley for any acts of his partner where the liability results from a *tort* (in this case professional malpractice, a form of negligence). However, Cowley is still liable to Landlord for defaulting on the lease because the liability resulted from a *contractual* obligation.

Consider the plight of someone who has suffered damages due to another's negligence, but cannot recover compensation because of the protection of an LLP. In the Milton–Cowley example above, suppose that the client who was damaged by Milton's error cannot actually recover the judgment awarded to him because Milton is without assets. Because Cowley is not liable, the client is left with a court order that is worthless. In order to be sure that parties have at least some ability to recover, an increasing number of states require that the LLP and individual partners carry and maintain a certain amount of *liability insurance* as a condition of LLP formation.

Taxation   LLPs are treated as pass-through entities. They are not subject to tax; any income is taxed only when it is distributed to it's partners. Because it is not a taxable entity, an LLP files an information return that informs federal and state tax authorities of the profits and losses of the LLP. All income or losses are reported on the partners' individual tax returns. Any losses are deductible and may sometimes help to reduce taxes on other sources of revenue in the individual's tax return.

Capitalization   LLPs are capitalized in the same way as a partnership: through debt via private or commercial lenders or by selling partnership equity for ownership in the LLP itself. The partnership agreement of the LLP often controls the amount and methods of capitalizing the business and the procedures for collecting additional contributions from partners as necessary (known as a *capital call*). Additional capital contribution requirements are frequently the subject of a partnership agreement. There are some cases in which the partnership has the right to "call" for more money contributions from each partner in order to keep the partnership afloat. Although terms vary, partners that are not in a position to make a call contribution may be forced to sell their interest in the partnership.

Management and Operation   Although not required by statute, limited liability partnerships will frequently have a partnership agreement that sets out the management and operational structure. LLPs are sometimes governed by one or more managing partners and/or some type of executive committee elected by the other partners. The day-to-day operations and powers of the partners and board of partners are spelled out in the partnership agreement as well. The election procedures, qualifications, compensation, meeting times, and other organizational matters are typically addressed in the partnership agreement. In most states, the default agreement is the governing RUPA/UPA provision.

CONCEPT SUMMARY   LLCs and LLPs

	Limited Liability Company (LLC)	Limited Liability Partnership (LLP)
Personal Liability of Principals	LLC members and managers are not personally liable for any debts or liabilities of the LLC so long as state law conditions are met.	LLP partners are generally not liable for the debts of the partnership, nor the liabilities of the other partners. Partners are personally liable for their own negligence.
Organization/ Start-Up Expenses	Articles of organization. Legal fees usually based on number of members and complexity of organization.	Statement of qualification. Legal fees usually based on number of members and complexity of organization.
Management and Control	Managed through managing member(s) (no officers, directors, or shareholders). Members abide by operating agreement for management and control issues.	Managed through managing partner(s) and/or executive committee (no officers, directors, or shareholders). Members abide by partnership agreement for management and control issues.
Capital	Typically sell shares of financial interest in the LLC and/or private or commercial loans.	Private/commercial loans. Personal financial contributions of partners may be required in partnership agreement.
Taxes	Option of being treated as a corporation or as a pass-through entity. May also have to pay miscellaneous state and local taxes to operate business.	Pass-through taxation treatment (no tax is paid on income to the entity, but when the entity distributes dividends, tax is paid at the individual partner's individual tax rate). May also have to pay miscellaneous state and local taxes to operate business.
Designation	Doe Group, LLC	Doe and Associates, LLP

OTHER BUSINESS ARRANGEMENTS

Some business arrangements do not fall squarely within one of the existing categories of business entity. However, these business arrangements are often intertwined in some way with an existing business entity and are often regulated through use of statutes that regulate business entities.

Franchises

An existing entity may wish to distribute its products to a broader market without the overhead costs of retail space, equipment, and employees through the use of a **franchise.** A franchise should be thought of as a *method* of conducting business that centers on a contractual relationship rather than a business entity. Federal statutes define a franchise as an arrangement of continuing commercial relationship for the right to operate a business pursuant to the franchisor's trade name or to sell the seller's branded goods. A franchise involves the **franchisor,** a business entity that has a proven track record of success, selling to a **franchisee** the right to operate the business and the business's trade secrets, trademarks, products, and so on. The franchisor assists the franchisee with financing, supplies, training and other aspects of running a successful operation.

Franchise Agreements

The parties are typically bound to each other via a franchise agreement. The franchise agreement covers some of the following terms that govern the relationship between franchisee and franchisor: (1) the term (time limit) of the agreement; (2) franchise fees, payment terms, and ongoing investment or buying requirements; (3) territory rights that usually provide the franchisee with an exclusive geographic area; (4) commitments from the franchisor for training, ongoing management support, and advertising; (5) commitments from the franchisee to follow operating protocol; (6) royalties and other fees that the franchisee must pay; and (7) franchisee termination/cancellation policies.

McDonald's worldwide market success was accomplished through franchising.

The FTC and Franchises

The Federal Trade Commission (FTC) is the federal regulatory authority that oversees the regulation of franchisors. The FTC regulations are primarily designed to ensure full disclosure of all information relating to a franchise company prior to a franchisee investment. The FTC regulations are very detailed, but almost all focus on mandatory disclosures about the financial condition of the franchise, success rates, and other important information used by potential franchisees faced with making the decision to invest in the franchise. The disclosure process is lengthy and complex and almost always requires the counsel of an attorney skilled in franchise law.

Federal Disclosure Requirements

Franchisors are required to provide written disclosures about the franchise at least 10 days before any contracts or letters of intent are signed and before any monetary investment takes place. Specifically, franchisors must disclose:

- *Internal legal data and facts.* The disclosure must contain information related to the rights of the franchise in terms of ownership of intellectual property (such as a patent or trademark) or any threats to the property (such as a trademark infringement suit) and, additionally, disclosure concerning the background of the board of directors or officers of the franchise corporation (such as fraud charges or bankruptcy).

- *Financial data.* Disclosures must also contain information concerning the financial status of the franchisor and particularly its record of financial stability and future earnings claims and/or forecasts. Franchisors must always provide audited documentation to provide a justifiable basis for the claims.

- *Registration not required.* The FTC rules do not require a registration statement or any approval from the FTC of the disclosure documents prior to publication and distribution.

State Franchise Regulations

Most states have implemented their own individual franchise rules and minimum disclosure requirements to supplement the federal legislation. These additional requirements are usually in the form of a registration statement filed with a state regulatory agency (the state-level equivalent of the FTC). The registration statements are public documents and often require more detailed disclosures and biographical information on the principals of the franchisor.

Small Business Franchise Act (SBFA)

The Small Business Franchise Act (SBFA) of 1999 was intended to deter franchisor abuse of franchisees. The law imposes certain safeguards designed to eliminate fraud and exploitation of franchisee investors by giving the franchisee additional bargaining power. Specifically, the law gave franchisees certain rights:

- *Antitermination restriction.* The law provides for a statutorily required 30-day period for the franchisee to cure any defaults prior to a notice of termination by the franchisor.

- *Freedom to work.* Even if the franchise agreement contained a restriction from working in certain businesses and in certain locations, this guarantees that a former franchisee cannot be unreasonably restricted from engaging in any business at any location by virtue of restrictions in the franchise agreements. However, in no case may a former franchisee use the franchisor's intellectual property, trademark, or trade secrets once the franchise agreement ends.

- *Franchisee options to buy certain products elsewhere.* Although typically the franchisee purchases trademark products (cups, bags, signs, etc.), other products need not be bought from the franchise as part of the franchise agreement. The law allows the franchisee to obtain goods and services from nonfranchisor sources at a lower price. However, these materials must meet reasonably uniform quality standards prescribed by the franchisor.

Despite the protections afforded by the SBFA, courts are still relatively strict about enforcing a franchisor's right to restrict franchisees from competing with the franchise after the franchise agreement has expired. These protections are usually in the franchise agreement and are known as a *restrictive covenant.* Case 14.2 considers the enforceability of such restrictions.

webcheck **franchise.org**

For a full description of the law and to see other information about franchises, connect to the American Franchise Association's Web site directly or via this textbook's Web site at www.mhhe.com/melvin.

CASE 14.2   Servpro Industries, Inc. v. Pizzillo, 2001 WL 120731 (Tenn. Ct. App. 2001)

FACT SUMMARY   Servpro is a well-established franchise engaged in the business of cleaning and restoring residential and commercial real estate after flooding or fire. Pizzillo entered into a franchise agreement to operate a Servpro franchise in Ft. Lauderdale, Florida. The franchise fee was $36,000 and franchisees also paid the franchisor a royalty fee based on the gross revenues of the business. Servpro trained Pizzillo and provided management support. The agreement also contained a clause whereby Pizzillo agreed not to work for a competing company in any capacity with 25 miles of his territory for two years after the termination of the franchise agreement. After four years, Servpro and Pizzillo mutually terminated the franchise agreement. At this point, Pizzillo owed Servpro $4,000 as a final royalty payment. Within the two-year restriction period, Pizzillo's wife set up a competing business within the franchise territory and he went to work for her in the same functional role that he played in Servpro. Pizzillo also actively solicited business from his former Servpro customers. Servpro filed suit to recover the money owed and to prevent Pizzillo from engaging in competition with them.

SYNOPSIS OF DECISION AND OPINION   The court held for Servpro. Despite the general resistance to enforcing restrictive covenants by courts, this was reasonable under the circumstances. The court focused on the fact that Servpro's franchise depended on such restrictions to add value to the franchise. Servpro had acted in good faith, trained Pizzillo, and allowed him exclusive territory. The fact that he was working for his wife, and not on his own, was irrelevant to the restriction. Moreover, the restriction was narrowly tailored and reasonable in terms of scope and duration.

WORDS OF THE COURT: Postfranchise Restrictions   "It is apparent that upon the termination of his franchise, Mr. Pizzillo continued to work in substantially the same business, but under a different name, and ostensibly under different ownership. Although he ceased using the Servpro name, his wife solicited and obtained business from some of the same customers that she dealt with as an unpaid employee of Servpro of Fort Lauderdale. Mr. Pizzillo attempted to distance himself from Servpro's core business of restoration by focusing on general contracting, but he could not, or would not, totally avoid restoration work. In any case, the franchise agreement prohibits him from working for any business that competes with Servpro, in any capacity whatsoever.

While we have no wish to unduly restrict Mr. Pizzillo in the exercise of his trade, we believe Servpro should be able to protect the value of its franchises by preventing its former franchisees from competing against it for a reasonable time and within a limited geographic area. By signing the franchise agreement, Mr. Pizzillo agreed to be bound by the non-compete covenant, and [. . .] it is enforceable against him."

Case Questions

1. Are there any circumstances under which Pizzillo could engage in the restoration business during the term of the restrictive covenant?

2. What factors did the court use to judge the reasonableness of the restriction?

Business Trusts

A **business trust,** also known as a common-law trust,[4] is a nonstatutory business arrangement. Although it is nonstatutory, most states recognize its existence under the common law or the state law regulating trusts. The use of a business trust is relatively rare, but is popular among businesses involved in development of very large commercial projects because a business trust has maximum flexibility in terms of management, provides its owners with liability protection (in most states), and provides important tax benefits for companies with significant amounts of passive income (e.g., income derived from investments such as interest).

Business trusts do not have officers or directors. Rather, a business trust has one or more trustees that are given legal title to the trust's assets. The trustee manages the trust for the benefit of the beneficiaries (owners) of the trust. Instead of stock, the beneficiaries are issued beneficiary interest certificates to evidence their ownership rights. In order to gain full protection of the law, the trustees and beneficiaries enter into a relatively complicated trust agreement that governs the powers and responsibilities of the trustee, the term of the trust, and other trust matters. However, generally no public filing is made.

A minority of states treat a business trust as a general partnership for purpose of liability. This, of course, means that beneficiaries may be personally liable for all debts and other liabilities of the partnership. In every state, trustees must use caution when entering into an agreement with a third party on behalf of the trust. Because there is no statutory protection of the entity, the trustee is acting as an individual from a legal perspective and, thus, may have personal liability under certain circumstances. It is for this reason that trustees will frequently wish all agreements to contain clear language that the business trust has primary liability for any debts and liabilities of the partnership.

In most states, the trustee(s) owes the same fiduciary duty to beneficiaries as that of a director's duty to a shareholder of a corporation. Beneficiaries are restricted from working in the day-to-day operations of the trust's business and can lose their liability protection by becoming too involved in the business. Business trusts are taxed differently by different states. Some treat them as a corporation and some treat them as a pass-through entity.

CONCEPT SUMMARY   Franchises and Business Trusts

- Franchises are a method of conducting business and not a business entity. Franchisors enter into a contractual agreement with franchisees that allow the use of the franchisor's business model, expertise, and trademarks in operating the business.
- A business trust is a nonstatutory entity that provides substantial operational flexibility for certain industries.

---

[4]This trust is also referred to as a *Massachusetts Trust,* named after the state where such trusts were first formed.

Limited liability company (LLC) p. 362   A multiperson form of business entity that offers liability protection for its principals with various tax options.

Limited liability partnership (LLP) p. 362   Form of business entity that provides the same level of liability protection to a general partner in an LLP as is provided to a limited partner in a limited partnership form of entity.

Articles of organization (also called certificate of organization) p. 363   Document used to create an LLC. Most states require only basic information such as the name of the entity, the location of its principal place of business, and the names of its members.

Operating agreements p. 363   Document used by an LLC to set out the structure and internal rules for operation of the entity.

Personal guarantee p. 366   Pledge from LLC members of personal assets to guarantee payment obligations of the business venture.

Member-managed LLC p. 366   LLC management structure similar to a general partnership with all the members having the authority to bind the business.

Manager-managed LLC p. 366   LLC members name a manager (or managers) who generally has the day-to-day operational responsibilities while the nonmanaging mem-

bers are typically investors with little input on the course of business taken by the entity except for major decisions.

Dissolution p. 367   In the context of an LLC, a liquidation process triggered by an event that is specified in the operating agreement (such as the death of a key member) or the majority of membership interests (or the percentage called for in the operating agreement) deciding to dissolve the company.

Dissociation p. 367   Individual members of an LLC exercise the right to withdraw from the partnership.

Statement of qualification p. 368   Document used to form a limited liability partnership by converting a general partnership.

Franchise p. 371   A business arrangement (not a form of business entity) of continuing commercial relationship for the right to operate a business pursuant to the franchisor's trade name or to sell the seller's branded goods.

Franchisor p. 371   A business entity that has a proven track record of success and ability to franchise its products.

Franchisee p. 371   Individual or business with the legal right to operate a franchised business and use the business's trademarks and trade secrets.

Business trust p. 374   Nonstatutory form of entity used in specialized circumstances where a certain type of flexibility is important to the principals.

THEORY TO PRACTICE

Beverly Hills Autos LLC (BHA) is a retail car dealership organized as a limited liability company and engaged in the business of selling various brands of luxury automobiles and SUVs in several dealership locations. The LLC was structured as a manager-managed LLC with two managing members and six other members who were primarily investors. The parties had an operating agreement that provided the structure and authority of managing members, included a provision eliminating liability for a breach of the duty of care, and stated that the members agreed to abide by the default LLC statute

in their state based on the Uniform Limited Liability Company Act (ULLCA) for terms not in the agreement. One of the nonmanaging members, Luciano, began a conversation with the owner of another car dealership and eventually negotiated a merger agreement. However, the managing members were out of town and Luciano signed the agreement on behalf of the partnership without the managers' knowledge. When the managing members learned of the merger, they immediately attempted to cancel the contract on behalf of BHA.

1. Will a court support BHA's attempt to cancel the contract? What will be BHA's likely theory of the case?

2. Assume that the managing members agreed with the transaction and signed on in agreement. Given BHA's choice of business entity, what are the options for financing this transaction?

3. Would an LLP be a better form than an LLC for BHA? Why or why not?

4. Assume that Luciano didn't bring the opportunity to the LLC members, but rather purchased the competing dealership with another partner outside the LLC. Subsequently, Luciano offers to sell the dealership to BHA at a premium over what he paid for it. Has Luciano breached his fiduciary duty? If so, which one? Do the operating agreement terms protect him from any liability to the other members? Why or why not?

5. Assume Luciano wants to bring a breach of fiduciary duty suit against the managing members, but his state does not provide a specific right to file a derivative suit. Could Luciano file a derivative suit in the absence of a specific right in the statute? What case supports your answer?

MANAGER'S CHALLENGE

Franchising can be a lucrative method of licensing out your business model, expertise, and intellectual property without actually incurring the expensive overhead of running several outlets of the business. Assume that you are the manager for BHA in Theory to Practice above, and you are approached by one of the managing members. She explains that the members are considering franchising a business catering to customers who need highly trained mechanics for the repair of specialized luxury cars. One aspect she is curious about is the level of regulation associated with selling a franchise. Write a memorandum that outlines the basic regulatory model that may be useful to the managing member in her consideration of franchising the luxury car repair operations. A sample answer may be found on this textbook's Web site at http://www.mhhe.com/melvin.

CASE SUMMARY 14.1 :: Kaycee Land and Livestock v. Flahive, 46 P.3d 323 (Wy. 2002)

LIABILITY OF LLC MEMBER

Flahive is the managing member of Flahive Oil and Gas, LLC. The LLC entered into an agreement with Kaycee to mine oil and gas from Kaycee's property. During the mining, Kaycee alleged that Flahive's process was flawed and resulted in contamination of Kaycee's property. After discovering that the LLC was without assets, Kaycee sued Flahive individually. Flahive defended on the basis that the contract was between the LLC and Kaycee and that he has no personal liability.

CASE QUESTIONS

1. Can the court disregard the LLC entity in this situation?

2. Does fairness demand that Flahive be personally responsible for the LLC's negligence?

CASE SUMMARY 14.2 :: Emprise v. Rumisek, ___ P.3d ___ (2009 WL 2633649, Kan. Ct. App. 2009)

PERSONAL GUARANTEES OF LLC MEMBERS

Four physicians formed an LLC to operate a medical practice. They capitalized the venture with a bank loan to the LLC. Each physician signed a personal guarantee to secure a proportionate part of the loan (25 percent each). A dispute developed that led two of the physicians to move to another practice ("Departing Physicians"). The bank became concerned that the loan was in jeopardy, so it brought suit against the remaining physicians in the practice to recover the amount due under the loan from them. While the bank sued the remaining physicians, the Departing Physicians were engaged in litigation with the remaining physicians over mismanagement of their former practice. The remaining physicians contended that the bank could not enforce the personal guarantees until disputes among the physicians were resolved because the LLC may still have assets if the litigation is successful.

CASE QUESTIONS

1. Does the bank have to wait until the litigation is complete to enforce the personal guarantees against the physicians? Why or why not?
2. What is the impact of the Departing Physicians' dissociation from the LLC?

CASE SUMMARY 14.3 :: Kawasaki Shop of Aurora, Inc. v. Kawasaki Motors Corporation, U.S.A., 544 N.E. 2d 457 (Ill. App. 1989)

TERMINATION OF FRANCHISE

Kawasaki Motors Corporation awarded a motorcycle franchise to the Kawasaki Shop of Aurora (Aurora Dealership) and signed an agreement that allowed Aurora Dealership to operate a multiproduct dealership (i.e., able to sell competing products side-by-side) and required Aurora Dealership to obtain Kawasaki's consent before moving the dealership to a new location. Over the beginning years of the franchise, Aurora Dealership aggressively added to its product line by securing other franchise agreements for its dealership with other motorcycle manufacturers. The evidence at trial showed that Kawasaki managers were displeased

with Aurora Dealership's business strategy. At that same time, Kawasaki learned that Aurora Dealership had moved its location without obtaining Kawasaki's consent. Even though this move was within Aurora Dealership's exclusive territory limits, Kawasaki terminated Aurora's Dealership's franchise rights.

CASE QUESTIONS

1. Does Kawasaki have a legal right to terminate the franchise?
2. Was it a coincidence that the termination happened during the same time frame as Kawasaki's uneasiness with Aurora's business methods?

CASE SUMMARY 14.4 :: Chrysler Corporation v. Kolosso Auto Sales, 148 F.3d 892 (7th Cir. 1998)

FRANCHISEE RIGHTS

Chrysler is a franchisor that entered into an agreement with Kolosso as franchisee. In the franchise agreement, the franchisor prohibited the franchisee from changing locations without the approval of Chrysler. Subsequent to the agreement, the state of Wisconsin passed a statute that allows a state agency to make a determination of fairness if a franchisee is prohibited from moving.

Kolosso requested that Chrysler allow them to move locations within the same city, but Chrysler refused.

CASE QUESTIONS

1. Does Chrysler, as franchisor, have the authority to block Kolosso's move?
2. Note that this case was litigated before the SBFA of 1999. Does that SBFA address this situation?

15

CHAPTER

Corporations

learning outcomes **checklist**

After studying this chapter, students who have mastered the material will be able to:

15-1　Articulate the concept of the corporation as a legally independent person.

15-2　Identify the sources and level of law governing formation and internal corporate matters.

15-3　Recognize the liability associated with improper formation by a promoter.

15-4　Understand the concept of a corporate veil and identify circumstances under which a court will pierce the veil and the impact on the principals.

15-5　Explain the primary methods for capitalizing a corporation.

15-6　Categorize corporate entities on the basis of how their income is taxed and understand the concept of flow-through taxation.

15-7　Describe the fundamental structure and roles for officers, directors, and shareholders in the corporate form of entity and understand the functions of each role and how the structure is governed.

15-8　Identify the major fiduciary duties owed by insiders of a corporation to its shareholders and give examples of each duty.

15-9　Apply the business judgment rule to an alleged breach of fiduciary duty by an insider.

15-10　Distinguish between a shareholder derivative suit and a direct action suit.

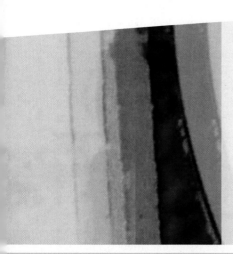

This chapter continues the discussion of business entities that provide liability protection for its principals. The principals of some business ventures form a *corporation* to achieve their objectives and provide flexibility not found in other entities. Although the corporate form is sometimes associated with large multinational corporations, in fact many corporations are relatively small with a limited number of principals (sometimes just a single owner). In this chapter, students will learn:

- The governing source of law and categories of corporations.
- Rules governing the formation of a corporation.
- Personal liability of the principals for corporate liabilities and debts.
- How corporations are capitalized, taxed, and structured.
- The duties of corporate managers, such as officers and directors, to the owners of the corporation.

CORPORATIONS

A **corporation** is a fictitious legal entity that exists as an independent "person" separate from its principals. Although this corporate "person" is a legally created fiction, it is a well-established and deeply seated principal of American law. Recall from Chapter 2, "Business and the Constitution," that the U.S. Supreme Court has ruled that corporations are entitled to full First Amendment protection for political speech. In a business context it is also important to note that a corporation, like an individual person, may file suit or be sued, or may form a contract or breach a contract. In contrast to sole proprietorships and partnerships, the obligations of corporations are separate and distinct from the personal obligations of their principals.

Corporations are created through a state law filing, and formation is governed through *state statutes.* State statutes vary in their corporate formation and governance rules, but each state has a specific law, often called the **Business Corporation Law** or something similar, that covers such matters as the structure of the corporation, oversight of the activity of the corporation's managers, rights of the principals in the case of the sale of assets or ownership interests, annual reporting requirements, and other issues that affect the internal rules of the business venture. Over half of the states have adopted all or substantial portions of a model act known as the **Revised Model Business Corporation Act (RMBCA)**[1] drafted by the American Law Institute. While state statutes regulate the internal governance of a corporation, federal laws regulate the offering or trading of ownership interests to the public and set certain standards for internal governance for some companies.[2]

Categories of Corporations

Corporations may be classified into one or more categories that reflect their overall purpose, capitalization (how they are funded), location, and structure. The two major categories are corporations that are owned exclusively by a group of private individuals (known as privately held), and corporations that sell their ownership interest via public stock exchanges (publicly held).

Privately Held versus Publicly Held   The most common category is a **privately held corporation.** Privately held corporations are those that do not sell ownership interests through sales via a broker to the general public or to financial institutions or public investors. Privately held corporations have substantial flexibility in terms of their internal operating procedures and do not generally have to comply with rigorous corporate structures or formalities. For example, in lieu of an actual meeting, privately held corporations often use a single document signed by each principal to dispose of necessary tasks such as elections of directors or issuing stock. This document is known as a *unanimous consent resolution.* Many states also give privately held corporations the option of electing to become a *closely held* or *family held* entity. This option further restricts the number or type of owners that a corporation may have, but gives even more flexibility on how the business venture may be organized and managed.

Note that even though many privately held corporations have a relatively small number of shareholders, there is no limit in terms of revenue. It is not uncommon for corporations with revenues in the eight-figure range to be privately held. Often, the flexibility of a privately held corporation outweighs any desire of the principals to be able to capitalize the business through a sale to the general public.

---

[1]The American Law Institute also issued *Principles of Corporate Governance* in 1994.

[2]Federal securities law is discussed in detail in Chapter 16, "Regulation of Securities, Corporate Governance, and Financial Markets."

When a privately held corporation wishes to fund capitalization through the sale of ownership interest to the general public and commercial investors, the principals pursue an Initial Public Offering (IPO) and then continue their corporate existence as a publicly held corporation. After the IPO, the corporation trades (buys and sells) stocks through a public stock exchange (the New York Stock Exchange [NYSE] is perhaps the most famous and influential, but many more exist). A publicly held corporation is subject to a substantial amount of federal and state regulation, primarily through securities laws and corporate governance statutes such as the Sarbanes-Oxley law. A publicly held corporation is subject to close scrutiny by a variety of regulatory agencies because investors across the globe depend on regulation to ensure integrity among the insiders managing the corporation. Regulation of publicly held corporations is discussed extensively in Chapter 16, "Regulation of Securities, Corporate Governance, and Financial Markets."

Other Categories   Besides being classified as publicly held or privately held, corporations may fall into one of the following categories:

- *Domestic.* In the state of its incorporation, a corporation is referred to as a *domestic* corporation.
- *Foreign.* A corporation that transacts business in a state other than its state of incorporation is known as a *foreign* corporation in the other state. For example, WidgetCo. is incorporated in Florida and sells its widgets in Florida and Georgia. In Florida, WidgetCo. is referred to as a domestic corporation. In Georgia, it is referred to as a foreign corporation.
- *Alien.* A corporation formed outside the United States that transacts business in the United States is referred to as an *alien* corporation.
- *Nonprofit. Nonprofit* corporations are those with no profit-seeking owners, but rather exist to perform some service to the public at large (e.g., charities, educational institutions, and certain hospitals).
- *Public corporation. Public* corporations are those formed by a government body to serve the public at large, such as public mass transit companies. Public corporations have a similar structure to a corporation, but have no owners. Be sure not to confuse *publicly held* corporations (discussed earlier) with a public corporation.
- *Professional corporations. Professional* corporations are those where the ownership is restricted to a particular profession licensed in that field. These corporations have a corporate structure, but are only open to members in good standing of a particular profession. For example, law firms that are organized as a professional corporation may only be owned by attorneys admitted to the practice of law who are currently active and in good standing.

Formation

Compared to other entities, a corporation has perhaps the most formal filing and reporting requirements. Principals that wish to form a corporation do so by filing a document with a state authority, usually the corporation bureau of the secretary of state's office, that sets out the corporation's name, purpose, number of shares issued, and address of the corporation's headquarters. This document, known as the **articles of incorporation**,[3] sets in motion the incorporation

> **web**check **www.mhhe.com/melvin**
> For examples of articles of incorporation from various states, check this textbook's Web site.

process. In addition to the articles of incorporation, state statutes often require additional filings with tax authorities to notify them of a corporation's existence.

---

[3]In a minority of states, this is known as the *corporate charter.*

State authorities then review the articles, and if in satisfactory form, the authorities register the document in public archives and the venture is considered formed. In most states, the date of incorporation is actually made retroactive to the date of filing with the state authorities.

Preincorporation Activity: Liability of Promoters

In most cases, an individual or group of individuals begin to carry out a business venture's activity before actually filing the articles of incorporation. These activities may include arranging for necessary capital through a loan, recruiting personnel, leasing property, and arranging to have the business incorporated. The individual who performs these activities is known as a *promoter*. If the promoter makes a contract on behalf of a not-yet-formed corporation, she may have some degree of *personal liability* to perform under the contract. Generally, the promoter is personally liable where she knows (and the other party has *no reason* to know) that the corporation is not in existence on the day of the signing. The RMBCA provides that anyone purporting to act on behalf of a corporation, knowing incorporation had not yet occurred, is jointly and severally liable for all liabilities created by the acts. For example, Edgar anticipates opening a private detective agency and enters into a one-year lease agreement for office space with Landlord signing on behalf of the yet-to-be-formed Edgar Detective Agency Inc. One month later, Edgar's financing falls through and he abandons the idea. Edgar would be a promoter and personally liable for the lease payments (or any penalty for breaching the lease contract) to Landlord.

However, a promoter's personal liability *ceases* at the moment that the corporation is formed and has adopted the contract. In the Edgar–Landlord contract above, suppose that Edgar signs on behalf of the corporation, incorporates the business venture the next day, and opens up a bank account. For the first month's rent, Edgar pays the rent via company check. Because the corporation has been formed and, by virtue of using a company check Landlord has adopted the contract, Edgar's personal liability has been extinguished. If Edgar abandons the business after six months, his personal assets are not subject to the Landlord's reach.

Choice of State of Incorporation

One of the first considerations for principals forming a corporation is choosing in what state to incorporate the business venture. Most corporations with a relatively small number of principals choose to incorporate in the state in which they will locate their principal office and operate the business venture. Some corporations choose the state of Delaware as the state of incorporation because of the advantages of that state's permissive rules on the flexibility of how its managers (in the form of officers and directors, discussed later) operate the business. For the most part, publicly held corporations decide that incorporation in Delaware is a wise choice because the Delaware statutes give officers and directors of those corporations wide latitude in decision making that does not require shareholder consent. Delaware has also adopted statutes that offer officers and directors strong protections from shareholder lawsuits that allege managerial negligence has resulted in damages to shareholder interest. This protection, known as the **business judgment rule,** is discussed in more detail later in this chapter. Moreover, Delaware has a well-established body of case law that allows more reliability in corporate planning. Note that despite some myths to the contrary, Delaware's tax structure is *not* favorable to out-of-state corporations that incorporate in Delaware. Although Delaware has no sales tax on retail merchandise, this rule applies to in-state sales only. Thus, an out-of-state business

> **KEY POINT** State of Incorporation
> Despite some significant advantageous for large publicly held corporations gained by incorporating in Delaware, most corporations are better served by incorporating in the state where they are headquartered.

that uses Delaware to incorporate, but does not sell any products or services in Delaware, has no tax advantage at all. In fact, in the big picture, corporations with a relatively small number of principals will end up paying more in taxes considering the assessment of business franchise taxes or fees in both Delaware and in the state where most of the business venture's activity takes place.

Initial Organizational Meeting

After filing the articles of incorporation, the principals typically hold an organizational meeting. This allows the principals to resolve any pending issues and to amend the articles of incorporation to reflect any changes in the principals' strategy since the time of formation. Specifically, the principals will address such issues as:

- *Bylaws.* Although state statutes govern some of the internal rules of a corporation, there are still some issues left to the principals. These rules are generally articulated in the corporation's bylaws. The bylaws typically specify the date, time, and place for the annual shareholders meetings, the number of officers and directors of the corporation, the process for electing the board of directors, and a listing of each officer along with a description of that officer's duties (responsibilities and liability of officers and directors are discussed later in this chapter). Note that the bylaws are not filed with the state filing official, and thus are not public, but are kept in the corporate records.

- *Board of directors and officers.* In some cases, the board of directors is reported on the articles of incorporation. If they are, the principals may make changes at this organizational meeting by holding another election for the board by the owners of the corporation. Officers are also identified at this meeting and, depending on the bylaws, the officers are appointed by the board or, in some special cases, elected by the board.

- *Issuance of shares.* The organizational meeting also often involves the official issuance of ownership interest consistent with the articles of incorporation filing. The ownership interests are referred to as *shares* and are evidenced by a stock certificate that indicates the owner's name and the number of shares issued. Therefore, owners of a corporation are referred to as **shareholders.** The issuance of shares is usually recorded in a stock register and kept by the secretary of the corporation along with other corporate records of the business (such as meeting minutes, resolutions, etc.). In a privately held corporation, the stock certificates and register are not public documents and are kept with the corporate records in the corporation's registered place of business.

Commencement of Business and Corporate Formalities

LO15-4

Once the corporation has been properly formed and postformation organizational matters have been attended to, the corporation's officers commence business operations. As a practical matter, the business entity may have already commenced operations under the promoter and, thus, the business operations are simply continued by the newly formed corporate entity. Even after commencement of business operations, officers and directors have a responsibility to comply with state statutory requirements regarding shareholders/directors meetings, filing annual reports, disclosures to shareholders, and must use their best efforts to keep corporate records and bylaws up to date. These responsibilities are examples of corporate formalities. Failing to attend to corporate formalities may have serious liability consequences (discussed in detail in the next section).

Liability   Perhaps the most attractive feature of a corporation is its limited liability for the personal assets of its owners and, with certain exceptions, for its officers and directors. In general, shareholders, directors, and officers of a corporation are insulated from personal

Preformation	Legal Formation	Postformation	Commence Business Operations	Corporate Formalities
1. Principal(s) decide(s) that corporate entity is advantageous to business objectives. 2. Promoter drafts articles of incorporation according to principal's (s') needs. 3. Promoter is personally liable for any preformation debts or activities on behalf of the future corporation.	1. Promoter files articles of incorporation with state agency. 2. Upon approval by state agency, the corporation is legally recognized as a business entity. 3. Promoter is no longer personally liable for debts or actions on behalf of the corporation.	1. Principals hold initial organizational meeting to approve bylaws, elect directors, and appoint officers. 2. Officers and directors formally issue stock certificates as evidence of shares in the corporation. 3. Shareholders typically sign a shareholders' agreement in which the parties agree to certain procedures for selling or transferring stock, etc.	Officers and directors oversee the start of business operations.	1. Officers and directors are responsible for complying with annual meeting, reporting, and filing requirements. 2. Ongoing review and adjustment of bylaws or shareholders' agreement when necessary.

liability in case the corporation runs up large debts or suffers some liability. This liability protection is often referred to as the **corporate veil.** For example, Roscoe and Pound are shareholders of Roscoe Corporation and obtain a credit card from Express Credit. They use it in good faith to make purchases to operate the business. For several years, Roscoe Corporation conducts business and pays its debts regularly. However, industry conditions worsen for Roscoe Corporation and it defaults on payment to Express Credit. Assuming that Roscoe Corporation has no assets, any attempt to collect the credit card debt from Roscoe or Pound individually will be thwarted by the protection of the corporate veil.

While this appears to be a boon for shareholders, officers, and directors at first glance, there are two important factors that temper the liability issue. First, most lenders, such as banks, will require a *personal guarantee* from the principals to back any loan given to a corporation. Second, in some cases courts will sometimes discard the corporate veil and allow parties to reach through the corporation to access the personal assets of one or more shareholders. This is known as **piercing the corporate veil.**

Personal Guarantees   As one would imagine, banks, landlords, and other creditors are fully aware of the limited liability provided by the corporate veil. Thus, if a corporation is a start-up or has limited assets, these creditors will almost always require that the shareholders give a personal guarantee. A personal guarantee allows the creditor to obtain a judgment against the personal assets of one or more shareholders in the event of a default by the corporation. These personal guarantees are frequently *in addition* to any collateral that is pledged by shareholders or the corporation itself. For example, suppose that Chef Perrier wishes to start up his own restaurant and forms Le Chef Inc. as the sole shareholder. In order to obtain a lease, his landlord will require a contract with Le

Chef Inc. and *also* with Perrier personally. In order to obtain a loan from the local bank to purchase equipment, inventory, and furniture, the local bank will require that (1) Le Chef Inc. agree to a loan repayment schedule; (2) Le Chef Inc. give the bank a right to claim the equipment and inventory as collateral; and (3) Chef Perrier provide a personal guarantee of the loan.

Piercing the Corporate Veil

A court will sometimes discard the corporate veil when it believes that fairness demands it. In these cases, which are relatively rare, courts may sometimes hold some or all of the shareholders personally liable. Most courts have used four factors to consider whether or not to pierce a corporation's protective veil. If at least two of these factors are present, a court is more likely to hold shareholders personally liable for corporate debts.

- *Inadequate capitalization.* One important factor courts examine in deciding whether to pierce the veil is whether or not a corporation has been adequately capitalized. When a corporation is merely a shell with nothing invested, courts are inclined to pierce the corporate veil as a matter of fairness. Similarly, if the corporation had initial capitalization, but the shareholders siphoned the profits and assets, a court will view this as an inadequately capitalized corporation.

- *Nature of the claim.* When the claim involves a voluntary creditor, such as a trade creditor who provides inventory for a corporation based on credit, courts are generally not inclined to pierce the corporate veil because these creditors had an opportunity to mitigate the risk of loss (such as requiring a personal guarantee). On the other hand, courts are more likely to pierce the corporate veil when the claim involves some sort of tort such as negligence by the corporation's employees or even the principals themselves. This is essentially because the victims of negligence (such as a pedestrian struck by a delivery truck operated by a corporate employee) have become *involuntary* creditors and have never had the opportunity to mitigate the risk of loss.

- *Evidence of fraud or wrongdoing.* If the shareholders, officers, or directors have committed fraud or have engaged in some type of serious and willful wrongdoing, this is an important factor in a court's decision to pierce the corporate veil. Misrepresentations to creditors regarding important facts about the financial condition of the company or lying to investors about potential liabilities of the corporation are both examples of fraud that could lead to a piercing of the veil.

- *Failing to follow corporate formalities.* Another important factor used by the courts in deciding whether piercing would be appropriate is to examine the corporation's adherence to the statutes, rules, and practices governing a corporation. For example, corporations that file articles of incorporation but never bother to follow up with required or standard practices are in danger of losing their corporate veil protection. Specifically, courts may look at whether there is a proper separation between the corporation and the individual shareholder(s), whether stock certificates were ever issued, if shareholders' meetings were ever held, and if proper corporate records (such as minutes of the meetings, resolutions, or stock register) were maintained. For example, suppose that two brothers, Abel and Cain, form AC Inc. by filing articles of incorporation. Because they are brothers, they decided to split the profits 50–50 and, wishing to save the expense of hiring an attorney, never kept up with corporate formalities after the articles were filed. In the event that a claim is made against AC Inc., Abel and Cain have potentially exposed their personal assets to claimants if AC Inc. does not have sufficient assets to pay the claim.

> **KEY POINT** Corporate Veil Protection
> The corporate veil that shields the personal assets of principals from corporate debts and liabilities may be pierced in certain cases of inadequate capitalization, fraud, or failing to follow corporate formalities.

Still, courts are reluctant to discard the corporate entity. In Case 15.1, a state appellate court considers whether to pierce the veil of a one-person corporation.

LO15-5 Capitalization

Corporations have perhaps the widest range of options when considering how to finance their operations. They may be funded through debt or through the selling of equity (ownership interests) in a variety of forms.

Debt Corporations often borrow money from either commercial lenders (such as banks) or private investors to fund day-to-day operations, usually evidenced by a loan agreement and a promissory note. For larger projects, corporations may also use more sophisticated forms of debt such as issuing bonds or debentures. Bonds are debt money issued by a corporation to the general public with promises to pay the bondholders back at a specified rate of interest for a specified length of time and to repay the entire loan upon the expiration of the bond (known as the *maturity date*). Note that bondholders are not shareholders but, rather, become creditors of the corporation. Bonds are secured through the corporation pledging certain assets. Debentures function essentially the same as bonds, but instead of pledging some specific piece of property, debentures are issued on the strength of the general credit of the corporation. Both privately held and publicly held corporations may issue bonds. Even relatively small corporations use bonds to finance expansion or the building of a new facility, and bonds can range in amount from several hundred million dollars to as little as $500,000 (referred to as *micro bonds*). The primary advantage of bonds and

---

CASE 15.1 Goldman v. Chapman and Region Associates, 44 A 3d 938 (N.Y. 2007)

FACT SUMMARY Chapman was the sole shareholder, officer, and director of Region Associates (Region). In 2001 Goldman obtained a judgment against Region in the amount of $209,320 as a result of Goldman's lawsuit against Region (but not Chapman individually). Goldman attempted to collect the judgment from Region but was unsuccessful because Region was without any substantial assets. After exhausting all efforts to collect the judgment from Region, Goldman filed suit asking the court to allow him to pierce Region's corporate veil and collect the judgment from Chapman's personal assets.

SYNOPSIS OF DECISION AND OPINION The Appellate Division of the New York Supreme Court ruled in favor of Chapman. The court held that in order to pierce the corporate veil, a judgment creditor such as Goldman must show that (1) the owner exercised complete control over the corporation, and (2) fraud or wrongdoing in the course of operating the business. Here, although it is undisputed that Chapman has sole control over the corporation, the court ruled that

Goldman had failed to provide any evidence of fraud or wrongdoing committed by Chapman.

WORDS OF THE COURT: Requirements to Pierce "One of the primary and completely legitimate purposes of incorporating is to limit or eliminate the personal liability of corporate principals. The mere claim that the corporation was completely dominated by the owners, or conclusory assertions that the corporation acted as their 'alter ego,' without more, will not suffice to support the equitable relief of piercing the corporate [veil]. The decision whether to pierce the corporate veil in a given instance depends on the particular facts and circumstances."

Case Questions

1. Did Chapman use the law to perpetrate an injustice? Is it fair that Goldman is stuck with a worthless judgment and that Chapman may simply start a new company for the next construction project?

2. What type of fraud or wrongdoing by Chapman would cause the court to pierce the corporate veil?

---

debentures is that the rate if interest is usually lower than a commercial bank loan. However, the process can be lengthy and is a more complex legal transaction than a conventional bank loan or a loan through a private individual.

Equity   Corporations also sell equity to capitalize their operations. For modest amounts of funding, corporations may turn to private investors or groups of investors. Sometimes a corporation will hire a registered broker-dealer that drafts a document describing the company and the intended use of the funds and distributes it to qualified individuals who are seeking investment opportunities that have relatively high risk in hopes of higher returns. This process constitutes the issuance of a security and, thus, is highly regulated. Securities law is discussed more extensively in Chapter 16, "Regulation of Securities, Corporate Governance, and Financial Markets."

Venture Capital Firms   When a corporation seeks a more significant amount of capital, the corporation may turn to a *venture capital* firm. Venture capital is funding provided by a group of professional investors for use in a developing business. These firms are frequently focused on one industry (e.g., health care or high-tech). The major advantage of venture capital is that these firms often have substantial resources and are also a source of expertise in operations and expansion of the corporation. However, in exchange for this, principals usually insist on substantial control over the corporation via its board of directors and even its officers. Venture capitalists are not thought of as long-term investors. They will usually require an "exit strategy" whereby the venture capital firm exits the corporation with a substantial return. This exit strategy may be to take the company public through an initial public offering or to get the company to grow to a point where a competitor would be willing to pay a substantial premium to purchase the corporation.

Public Offerings   Privately held corporations may also find that their expansion plans require even more capital than can be raised using private investors. In that case, some companies opt to proceed down a very complex and time-consuming process of converting the corporation from privately held to publicly held by engaging in an initial public offering (IPO). At that point, the corporation may raise equity by selling its shares to the general public and to financial institutions.

Taxation

LO15-6

For multiperson ventures, it is not uncommon for the tax-related needs of the individuals to differ. For example, Abel, Baker, and Cain wish to form NewCo.com. The corporate form may favor Abel, while the interests of Baker may favor a partnership. Before selecting an appropriate form of entity, the parties try to anticipate the best way to minimize taxes while maintaining an appropriate degree of liability protection.

C corporations are considered a separate legal, taxable entity from the owners for income tax purposes. Therefore, corporations pay tax on their earnings and then the tax is paid again if corporate earnings are distributed to shareholders in the form of dividends (known as double taxation). The taxation occurs at both the (1) corporate level when income is earned by the corporation, and (2) individual level when it is distributed as a dividend (profit) to the shareholder.

Corporations that qualify for and elect *Subchapter S* treatment offer flow-through (also known as pass-through) tax treatment. The term *Subchapter S* is simply a designation named after the section of the Internal Revenue Code that details requirements to qualify for flow-through tax treatment as a corporation. Subject to certain exceptions under the tax laws, these entities are not subject to tax at the entity level, and the taxable income or loss of the business operated by the entity flow through to the entity's shareholders. As a result, these sorts of entities can offer investors numerous tax benefits. Of particular importance are:

- *Use of losses to limit tax liability.* The ability to flow through to the investors the tax deductions and losses that are typically generated by an emerging company during its early years;

- *Avoiding double taxation.* The ability to distribute earnings without incurring double-level taxation (i.e., without having a tax imposed on both the entity and the equity holder).

The primary reason that some corporations do *not* choose an S election is because the tax code only allows certain types of corporations to have that status and, thus, the favorable tax treatment. However, only C corporations are entitled to certain tax deductions (amounts used to pay for employee benefits, for example). Thus, even small entities that qualify for S corporation status may opt to be a C corporation if it reduces their overall tax liability.

In order to qualify as an S corporation, the enterprise must meet the following criteria:

- *Limited classification.* S corporations must be a domestic corporation with no nonresident or alien shareholders.

- *Single class of stock.* An enterprise cannot be an S corporation if it has more than a single class of stock (except a differentiation of voting and nonvoting stock, explained later in this chapter).

- *No corporate shareholders.* An enterprise cannot be an S corporation if any of its shareholders is a corporation, a partnership, or a discretionary trust.

- *Limited scope of business.* Banks and insurance companies may not elect to be an S corporation.

- *Limited number and type of shareholders.* An enterprise cannot be an S corporation if it has more than 100 shareholders. Only individuals, estates, and certain trusts may be shareholders.

- *80 percent subsidiaries.* An enterprise cannot be an S corporation if it owns more than 80 percent of the stock of a subsidiary corporation.

- *Unanimous consent.* All shareholders must consent to S corporation status.

Figure 15.1 provides a comparison of the tax implications of C corporations versus S corporations.

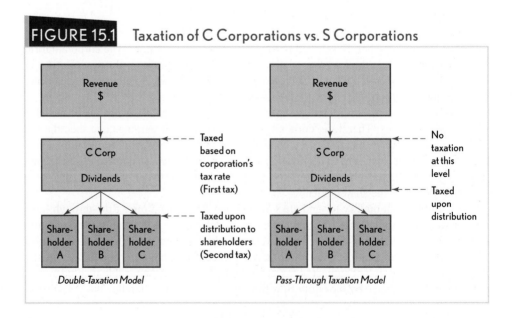

FIGURE 15.1 Taxation of C Corporations vs. S Corporations

STRUCTURE, MANAGEMENT, AND OPERATION

Fundamentally, corporations are structured around an allocation of power based on three categories: *shareholders, directors,* and *officers.* Shareholders are the owners of the corporation and act principally through electing and removing directors and approving or withholding approval of major corporate decisions. **Directors** are responsible for oversight and management of the corporation's course of direction. **Officers** carry out the directors' set course of direction through management of the day-to-day operations of the business. Although this allocation of power is based on the RMBCA, many states allow a corporation to alter the structure as necessary to meet the needs of the entity. Very large corporations and very small corporations often manage their operations using a modified form of this structure. For example, in some cases a corporation has only one or two shareholders, each of whom acts as director and an officer. The structure is essentially useless, so they may opt to adopt a slightly different structure through the bylaws and/or an agreement among the shareholders as to the rights and responsibilities of each shareholder.

Shareholders

Shareholders are the owners of the corporation. While shareholders do not directly manage the corporation, most states give shareholders certain rights to protect their ownership interests. Most importantly, shareholders, assuming a majority of ownership consent, have the power to elect and remove directors at the annual shareholders meetings. State statutes also give rights to shareholders to veto any fundamental changes to the corporation that are proposed by the directors and officers. Examples of fundamental changes are the sale of substantial assets, mergers, issuing more capital stock, pursuing venture capital financing, and issuing a bond. Shareholders also must approve any changes in the structure of the corporation through amending the articles of incorporation or bylaws. For example, Widget Manufacturing Inc. is structured as follows:

Name	Percentage of Total Stock Owned	Role
Abel	10	Officer, director, shareholder
Baker	10	Officer, director, shareholder
Cain	20	Director, shareholder
David	20	Shareholder
Elias	40	Shareholder

Suppose that Abel and Baker locate what they believe to be an excellent opportunity to merge with a larger competitor. They will need to convince either Cain and David or Elias to approve the transaction in order to move ahead. If they are only able to convince Cain or David, but Elias resists the transaction, Elias and the remaining shareholder would have the ability to block the merger from taking place. Note also that some corporations, particularly closely held corporations, issue *voting stock* to some shareholders and *nonvoting stock* to other shareholders. This is done to ensure that a certain shareholder or group of shareholders can control the corporation but still allows other shareholders the ability to receive payments from the corporation's profit (called *dividends*) and other benefits of ownership. For example, in the Widget Manufacturing Inc. example above, suppose that

Elias was the father of Abel, Baker, Cain, and David. He wishes to be sure that his heirs receive dividends in certain proportions, but does not yet wish to cede control of the corporation to them. Elias could issue nonvoting stock to Abel, Baker, Cain, and David, but still retain the power to elect/remove them as directors or to void any transaction. However, it is important to note that shareholders cannot bind the corporation, nor can shareholders demand that the directors take a certain action or adopt a certain policy.

Board of Directors

While shareholders have the power to veto transactions, it is the board of directors that actually sets the strategy and policies of the corporation. The board of directors also has an important oversight function, and state statutes contemplate that the body be *independent* from the shareholders and officers. Most planning initiatives that result in a change to the corporation, such as an acquisition of another corporation's assets or stock, are overseen by the board prior to submitting the plan to shareholders for approval.

Election of Directors

Shareholders elect directors. In most corporations directors hold that office for one year, but the bylaws can set any term. The bylaws also set the procedures and requirements for an election in terms of time and date, notification to shareholders, and how many shareholders must be present to hold a vote (known as the *quorum requirement*). Some states require at least three directors except in the case of a closely held corporation where the number of directors is equal to the number of shareholders. Therefore, a one-person corporation requires only one director. Other states (such as Delaware) have abolished any minimum number of directors. The number of directors is typically set out in the corporation's bylaws.

Removal of Directors

Directors may also be removed by a shareholder vote or, less frequently, by a court order. Absent a contrary provision in the articles of incorporation, shareholders may remove a director with or without cause.[4] The removal process is usually set out in the bylaws, but in almost all cases the shareholder vote must take place at a properly called shareholders meeting. Most states also allow a *court* to order a director to be removed, but only for *cause* (such as fraud). This is a rare event, but would be necessary in the event that the director at issue is also a shareholder with sufficient voting power to defeat removal votes by minority shareholders.

Meetings

Acts of the board of directors take place only at official meetings that occur at a regular annual or semiannual time as specified in the corporation's bylaws or by a statute. Special meetings to handle pressing matters may also be called so long as a notification procedure is followed in accordance with the bylaws. The votes of a majority of directors that are present at a meeting are required to take action. Most states allow board action to take place without a meeting if the directors act through unanimous written consent (all directors agree in writing to the action) or directors agree to meet by a communication means where all directors can hear and speak with one another at the same time (such as through videoconferencing or webcam). For routine matters such as approving the choice of the corporation's auditing firm or legal counsel, corporations often choose these alternate routes to board action.

Committees

Much of the board's work is done through its committees. These committees are a small group of board members who are charged with oversight or to perform a given task and make a recommendation to the full board. Examples of these committees are a compensation committee (investigates appropriate compensation for its officers, etc.,

---

[4]RMBCA § 8.08(a).

The board of directors typically makes use of committees to carry out its work and oversight responsibilities.

and makes a recommendation), an audit committee (oversight of the proper reporting of earnings and other audit functions), and an election committee (supervising the procedures for director elections).

Officers

The corporation's officers are appointed by, and may be removed by, the board of directors. The officers carry out the day-to-day operations of the corporation and execute the strategy and mandates set out by the board of directors. As a practical matter, officers work closely with the directors in setting the course of a corporation's path, but major changes in the corporation may not be taken through officer action alone. Although some states still require the traditional officer roles to be filled (president, vice president, secretary, and treasurer), the current trend is to allow the names and responsibilities of the officers to be set by the bylaws or through action of the board of directors.[5] Officers have both express and implied authority. Express authority comes from the bylaws or by a board of directors' resolution, which gives specific authority to a particular officer. For example, the board of directors may pass a resolution authorizing the treasurer of a corporation to open up a bank account or to start a money market account for surplus cash on hand. Officers may also have inherent authority, based on their position, to act on behalf of the corporation. Recall from Chapter 10, "Agency and Employment Relationships," that certain corporate officers have *implied authority* to be an agent of the corporation. This is an important concept in corporate law because it helps define the powers of corporate officers.

President   Traditionally, the president has the implied power to bind the corporation in ordinary business operation transactions and the oversight of nonofficer employees. Therefore, the president of a manufacturing corporation has the authority to enter into a distribution contract with wholesalers or to hire and fire a receptionist, for example.

---

[5]See *Delaware General Corporate Law* § 142(a).

Meg Whitman, former president and CEO of eBay, used annual shareholders meetings as an event to promote the company's future.

Vice President   Depending on the size and scope of the corporation, the vice president may have some limited implied authority. For example, a vice president for marketing would likely have implied authority to bind the corporation to a vendor of advertising. The implied authority of a vice president may also have additional powers to bind the corporation in ordinary business transactions if such authority is a routine practice in a certain industry.

Treasurer   Aside from the routine tasks of collecting the accounts receivable and paying the accounts payable, the treasurer has little or no other implied authority.

Secretary   The secretary has the implied authority to certify the records and resolutions of the company. When the board of directors passes a resolution, it is the secretary who affixes his signature to it, which confirms that the document is genuine. Third parties in a particular transaction may rely on this certification. For example, suppose that Antonin, the secretary of MusicCo., delivers a forged resolution to a bank that authorizes MusicCo. to borrow $50,000. The resolution has Antonin's signature affixed to it with a statement that the resolution was duly passed at a board of directors meeting. Bank loans the money to MusicCo. based on the resolution. MusicCo. then becomes financially insolvent and attempts to avoid repaying the loan on the basis that MusicCo.'s directors did not in fact authorize the loan. Bank would prevail, because, by virtue of Antonin's implied authority, it had the right to rely on Antonin's certification as secretary.[6]

Fiduciary Duties of Officers and Directors

Officers, directors, and controlling shareholders of a corporation (known as *insiders*) are in a unique position of trust to guide the corporation in a certain direction. Officers and directors owe the corporation's shareholders several well-defined fiduciary duties: the

---

[6]Based on *In re Drive-In Development Corporation*, 371 F.2d 217 (7th Cir. 1966).

CONCEPT SUMMARY Corporate Form of Entity

Personal Liability of Principals	Corporations exist as a separate legal "person."
	Officers, directors, and shareholders are not personally liable for any debts or liabilities of the corporation (absent fraud).
	Corporate veil protection.
Organization/ Start-Up Expenses	Formation procedures are relatively easy if the entity is privately held and has limited shareholders.
	Bylaws, shareholders' agreement, and resolutions are drafted by an attorney resulting in higher costs.
	Publicly held companies or "private offerings" involve extensive legal documentation and higher fees.
Management and Control	Shareholders elect directors. Directors appoint officers.
	Officers have day-to-day control over management with directors' oversight.
	Shareholders must vote on significant corporate decisions (merger, sale of significant assets, or stock issuance).
	Bylaws are the internal operating rules of the entity.
Capital	Capital may be raised by the sale of shares (equity) or by a loan from a bank (debt).
	Some corporations may also raise money by issuing bonds and other debt instruments.
Taxes	A C corporation pays taxes at the corporate rate for all income of the entity. When the entity distributes profits to shareholders (*dividends*), the income is taxed again at the shareholder's individual rate. This is known as *double taxation*.
	An S corporation has *pass-through* taxation treatment. No tax is paid on income to the entity, but when the entity distributes dividends, tax is paid at the individual shareholder's rate.
	May also have to pay miscellaneous state and local taxes to operate the business.
Designations	Doe, Inc.
	Doe Corporation
	Doe Company

duty of care and the **duty of loyalty.** Breaching these duties may result in *personal liability* for the officer or director. Officers and directors must act carefully when they act on behalf of the corporation and must also not put their *own* interests ahead of the corporation's interests. The duty of loyalty also applies to *controlling shareholders* in relation to other shareholders. The duty of care is tempered by a protection for officers and directors when they have acted in good faith, but still made an unwise decision that resulted in some loss to the corporation. This protection is known as the *business judgment rule.*

Duty of Care Fundamentally, officers and directors must exercise the degree of skill, diligence, and care that a reasonably prudent person would exercise under the same circumstances. Most states define the duty of care through a three-part test. First, the officer and director must always act in good faith. Second, they must also act with the care that an objectively prudent person in a like position would exercise under similar circumstances. Third, they must carry out their duties in a manner that is reasonably calculated to advance the best interests of the corporation. This duty applies to all directors and officers without regard to the size of the corporation or whether the directors are paid or unpaid. Courts have held that a director breaches her duty of care when she has failed to fulfill her role in oversight. This may occur in several ways:

- *Negligence.* When a director doesn't read reports, financial records, or other information provided by the corporation, or attend meetings, this weighs heavily in favor of a finding a breach of duty.

- *Failure to act with diligence.* Directors have the obligation to question any suspicious activity by the corporation or its officers. If the issue is outside of their field, they must investigate it by consulting outside experts (such as a CPA or an attorney). They must attempt to have more than just a cursory understanding of the inner workings of the corporation and must monitor the corporation and the business practices of its officers.

- *Rubber stamp.* Directors have the duty to be sure that any transaction proposed by the officers (or other directors for that matter) is, from the *best information* available to them at the time, in the best interest of the corporation and is not imprudent. They have a duty to determine if the proposed action will impact the corporation in a negative way and, thus, cannot act as a "rubber stamp." If they disagree with a decision being made by the other directors, they must register their dissent in the record of the meeting.

This is not to say that the directors cannot rely on the expertise and assurances of others. Under the RMBCA, directors still fulfill their duty of care even though they did not personally verify the records or other information provided to them by officers or outside experts. Directors may rely on opinions, reports, statements, and financial records if these were presented by the officers of a corporation whom the director "reasonably believes to be reliable and competent in these matters."[7] Directors may also rely on professionals such as attorneys and auditors or on board committees, so long as that reliance is reasonable in terms of the director's belief in their competence.

LO15-9 **Business Judgment Rule** At first glance, the duty of care looks onerous. When a corporation engages in a certain transaction or in a certain course of conduct that generates losses, some shareholders may inevitably believe it was the fault of the directors' lack of care. The business judgment rule protects officers and directors from liability for decisions that may have been unwise, but did not breach the duty of care. This rule insulates directors from liability when, based on reasonable information at the time, the transaction or course of action turns out badly from the standpoint of the corporation. Directors and officers often seek protection of this rule when an individual shareholder or group of shareholders files a lawsuit against them.

Although the RMBCA does not include a business judgment rule, every state has adopted the rule (either by including it in their statutes or recognizing its applicability in common law) as a defense to a breach of the duty of care claim against a director. Fundamentally, directors must have acted in *good faith* to insulate themselves from liability for breach of care. Most courts define good faith by requiring directors and officers to clear three hurdles in order to obtain the protection of the business judgment rule:

---

[7]RMBCA § 8.30(b).

- *No private interest.* In order to claim protection under the business judgment rule, the director must have had no financial self-interest in the disputed transactions or decision. Being a shareholder of a merging company or supplier to a corporation may be dangerous territory for a director because a transaction with the merger partner or supplier may have some degree of self-dealing contamination that will deprive the director of any business judgment rule protection.

- *Best information.* An important prerequisite to protection by the business judgment rule is the requirement that directors be active in keeping themselves informed on all material aspects of the decision or transaction at issue. Directors and officers have a duty to be diligent in investigating any proposal, decision, or transaction and this includes, when appropriate, consulting outside experts.

- *Rational belief.* The third requirement that directors and officers must meet in order to be protected under the rule is that the decision or approval of the transaction must have been the product of some reasoned decision-making based on rational beliefs. This rational belief requirement means that courts focus on the process of the decision-making. Directors and officers' decision-making procedures must be set up in a way that allows careful decisions to be made regarding the best interests of the corporation. Boards will often form committees to carry out their work, and often this committee structure itself is a significant step in establishing a procedure that helps preserve the business judgment rule protection.

> **KEY POINT** Business Judgment Rule
>
> In order for directors and officers to have protection under the business judgment rule, the director/officer must have exercised good faith, have no private financial self-interest, and must use diligence to acquire the best material information related to a proposed decision.

Despite the fact that Delaware is generally thought of as a state that has a fairly broad business judgment rule protection, Landmark Case 15.1, which sent shockwaves through corporate boardrooms nationwide, illustrates the importance of this duty to investigate all *material* facts of a proposed transaction before approving it.

Duty of Loyalty   An additional fiduciary duty owed to shareholders by officers, directors, and controlling shareholders is the *duty of loyalty.* Shareholders that have some degree of control over corporate decisions also owe this duty, and it is principally a duty intended to prevent oppression of minority shareholders. The duty of loyalty is primarily focused on providing protection to shareholders in cases where a transaction occurs where the possibility of self-dealing is present.

Prohibition against Certain Self-Dealing   Self-dealing in this context is where an officer, director, or controlling shareholder has some personal financial stake in a transaction that the corporation is engaged in and the officer, director, or shareholder helps to influence the advancement of the transaction. For example, recall our working hypothetical structure for Widget Manufacturing Inc.

Name	Percentage of Total Stock Owned	Role
Abel	10	Officer, director, shareholder
Baker	10	Officer, director, shareholder
Cain	20	Director, shareholder
David	20	Shareholder
Elias	40	Shareholder

FACT SUMMARY Van Gorkom was an officer, director, and shareholder of Trans Union Corporation. Trans Union's stock was traded on the New York Stock Exchange ("NYSE") and had never sold for higher than $39 per share. Prior to announcing his retirement, Van Gorkom sought to sell his shares to Pritzker, an individual investor, for $55 per share. Because Van Gorkhom's holdings in Trans Union were substantial, he was required to get the approval of Trans Union's board of directors for the sale to Pritzker. Van Gorkom proposed the sale to the board in an oral presentation. Most of the other officers opposed the sale on the basis that the price was too low given the value of the company. Indeed, the chief financial officer advised the directors that the price was in the "low range." The directors did not review the terms of the Van Gorkom–Pritzker agreement, did not perform any valuation analysis on the company, nor were any of the company's investment bankers consulted. After Van Gorkom pressured the directors by informing them that Pritzker would withdraw the offer within three days, the board deliberated for several hours and approved the transaction. A group of shareholders brought a lawsuit against the directors of Trans Union based on breach of the duty of care that resulted in the stock being sold at a value well under its actual worth. The directors sought protection under the business judgment rule, claiming they relied on Van Gorkom's representations and the NYSE stock price.

SYNOPSIS OF DECISION AND OPINION The Delaware Supreme Court ruled *against* the directors, holding that they could not be afforded the protection of the business judgment rule. Their decision was primarily based on the court's conclusion that the directors had failed to obtain all material information and the lack of any investigation about the transaction. The court pointed to the fact that the board never even reviewed the Van Gorkom–Pritzker agreement, nor had they undertaken anything more than a cursory inquiry into the actual value of the corporation.

WORDS OF THE COURT: Duty to Be Informed "We do not say that the Board of Directors was not entitled to give some credence to Van Gorkom's representation that $55 was an adequate or fair price. [T]he directors were entitled to rely upon their chairman's opinion of value and adequacy, provided that such opinion was reached on a sound basis. Here, the issue is whether the directors informed themselves as to all information that was reasonably available to them. Had they done so, they would have learned of the source and derivation of the $55 price and could not reasonably have relied thereupon in good faith.

None of the directors, management or outside, were investment bankers or financial analysts. Yet the Board did not consider recessing the meeting until a later hour that day (or requesting an extension of Pritzker's deadline) to give it time to elicit more information as to the sufficiency of the offer, either from inside management or from Trans Union's own investment banker, Salomon Brothers, whose Chicago specialist in merger and acquisitions was known to the Board and familiar with Trans Union's affairs. Thus, the record compels the conclusion that the Board lacked valuation information adequate to reach an informed business judgment as to the fairness of $55 per share for sale of the Company."

Case Questions

1. Assume that the directors were highly sophisticated business executives. Should they have to consult others about issues where they already have sufficient knowledge (such as a company's valuation)?

2. Note that, in light of Van Gorkom, many states (including Delaware) passed statutes that extended the scope of the business judgment defense. Should the business judgment rule protect directors even when they failed to verify the statements of internal management concerning a corporate transaction that is being touted to officers as advantageous to the corporation?

Suppose that Cain owns port properties and leases warehouse space to industries using the port. Abel, as president of the corporation, searches for a warehouse for Widget Manufacturing's storage needs and he identifies several potential properties. Abel writes a report for the board of directors describing the advantages and disadvantages of each property. Because Cain is an officer and director, this transaction has at the least the *potential* to conflict with the best financial interests of the corporation. This potential for conflict,

Self-Check Business Judgment Rule

Will these directors be protected by the business judgment rule?

1. Directors of a bank consult with legal, banking, and industry experts concerning a proposed merger. They set up a directors' subcommittee to investigate the merger and ultimately approve moving ahead after two months of deliberation. The day after the merger, a substantial drop in the stock price of the bank takes place and shareholders lose nearly 30 percent of the value of their investment.

2. The company president recommends to the board that NewCo. hire Dewey, Cheatham, and Howe as their auditing firm. In the same meeting as the recommendation, the directors approve the firm. One year later, it is revealed that the audits were fraudulent and that the president had been looting the company resulting in several millions of dollars in losses.

3. Shareholders of a major league baseball franchise corporation sue the directors because the team refuses to schedule night games. The shareholders argue that the revenue lost from night games is responsible for the poor financial performance of the company. The directors refuse to schedule night games because they believe it would have a deteriorating effect on the neighborhood.

4. The company vice president recommends that the directors of the corporation purchase a parcel of prime real estate on which to build a new office building for the company. Four of the six directors are members of a real estate partnership that owns that property. Without any disclosures, the directors vote unanimously to approve of the purchase and the decision is made the same day as the vice president's recommendation. One month later, it was revealed that the price paid by the corporation was 20 percent above fair market value for the property.

Answers to this Self-Check are provided at the end of the chapter.

however, is not a breach of the duty of loyalty automatically. The RMBCA provides that a self-dealing transaction is not a breach of the duty of loyalty so long as a majority of disinterested parties (those with no self-interest conflicts) approved it after *disclosure* of the conflict.[8] In the Widget Manufacturing example, Cain would simply need to disclose his interest in the property, and abstain from influencing other directors about the vote. After disclosure, the vote of Abel and Baker to approve the transaction insulates Cain from a charge of breaching his duty of loyalty to Widget's other shareholders.

Even if the transaction was not formally approved as provided in RMBCA, the modern trend has been for courts to allow such transactions so long as they are, under the circumstances, fair to the corporation and performed in good faith.

Corporate Opportunity Doctrine The duty of loyalty also requires disclosure and good faith when an insider (i.e., director, officer, or controlling shareholder) learns of a potentially lucrative business opportunity that could enrich her individually, but is related to the corporation's business. That is, an insider may not *usurp* for herself a business opportunity that belongs to the corporation or would benefit the corporation in some direct way.

Courts use several factors to determine when an opportunity belongs to a corporation and is therefore off-limits to insiders who are officers, directors, or controlling shareholders unless they have followed specific disclosure steps: (1) Did the corporation have a current interest or expected interest in the opportunity (such as an existing contract to purchase a piece of property)? (2) Is it fair to the corporation's shareholders to allow another to usurp a certain interest? (3) Is the opportunity closely related to the corporation's existing or

Legal Speak ›))
Usurp In the context of the corporate opportunity doctrine, *usurp* is to seize a particular opportunity for oneself when the opportunity rightfully belongs to the corporation.

[8]RMBCA § 8.60.

prospective business activities? In answering these questions, courts will take into consideration whether the officer, director, or controlling shareholder learned of the opportunity because of his role in the corporation and whether or not a party used corporate resources to take advantage of the opportunity.

Officers, directors, and controlling shareholders who become aware of a corporate opportunity belonging to the corporation must disclose the opportunity to the corporation in total. That is, all plans and relevant information on the opportunity must be presented to the board of directors. If the board, for whatever reasons, rejects the opportunity, the insider is then free to pursue the opportunity with no fear of liability.

For example, in our Widget Manufacturing Inc. example, suppose that the directors all discuss the need for a new warehouse facility and the directors authorize Abel to find a suitable lot on which to build. While Abel pursues this objective, Cain's neighbor makes him aware of a parcel of land that would fit Widget's needs in terms of space, zoning, workforce population, access, and price. Cain purchases the property for himself at a price of $100,000. He then tells a commercial real estate broker to contact Abel and advise him that the property is on the market for $200,000. In this case, because Cain was an insider who knew of a corporate opportunity that would benefit Widget Manufacturing, and knew that the corporation was in the market for a new warehouse, he had an obligation to disclose the opportunity to the corporation first rather than buying it.

However, suppose that, instead of buying the lot, Cain disclosed the opportunity to the corporation's board of directors. If the directors reject that opportunity to purchase, then Cain is free to make the purchase and even to sell it or lease it to Widget Manufacturing at a profit. Failing to follow the disclosure rules is a breach of the duty of loyalty.

CONCEPT SUMMARY   Fiduciary Duties of Officers, Directors, and Controlling Shareholders

- Officers, directors, and controlling shareholders (sometimes called *insiders*) owe corporate shareholders the fiduciary duties of care (use of skill, diligence, and care to advance the best interests of the corporation) and loyalty (prohibition against self-dealing or conflict of interests).

- The business judgment rule protects insiders from liability for breach of the duty of care so long as the insider acted in good faith, was diligent about making a well-informed decision, and had no financial self-interest in the decision.

LO15-10   ## Breach of Fiduciary Duty Lawsuits by Shareholders

One objective of this chapter is to focus on the rights of shareholders and the standards for fiduciary duties owed to shareholders by insiders such as officers, directors, and controlling shareholders. But how do shareholders actually enforce their rights in a corporation? Shareholders enforce their rights and fiduciary duties through the use of a lawsuit in the form of a shareholder's *derivative action* or a shareholder's *direct action.*

In a derivative suit, an individual shareholder (or a group of shareholders) brings a lawsuit against an insider in the name of the corporation itself. Most derivative lawsuits are brought because the shareholder alleges a breach of fiduciary duty of care or loyalty by an insider. There are several special procedural requirements for a derivative action, but the most important of these is that the shareholders must first make a formal demand on the board of directors to take corrective action and allow sufficient time for correction. Only if the board refuses to act may the shareholder commence a derivative suit.

FACT SUMMARY McCall and other investors are shareholders who brought a derivative lawsuit against Richard L. Scott as board chairman and all other officers and directors of Columbia/HCA Healthcare Corporation (Columbia) alleging various breach of fiduciary duty claims in connection with allegations of health care insurance fraud by Columbia executives and employees. The shareholders claimed that the board had intentionally and/or recklessly disregarded fraudulent activities of senior management. This included management's attempts to improperly boost revenue through systematic overbilling for a period of two years. The shareholders argued that given their experience in the industry, Columbia board members must have ignored red flags that would have indicated that questionable and/or fraudulent billing practices were being carried out by Columbia. The directors defended by citing a provision in the corporate charter that purported to limit the liability of the directors in the case of an allegation of the breach of duty of care so long as they did not act in bad faith.

SYNOPSIS OF DECISION AND OPINION The Sixth Circuit Court of Appeals ruled in favor of the shareholders, reasoning that the provision in the charter was unenforceable in the face of such gross, ongoing negligence by the directors to notice or investigate the illegal conduct of the corporation's officers. The board's gross negligence included willful ignorance to certain known risks that could have revealed the fraud.

This included: (1) failure to act in the face of unusual audit information, (2) failure to launch an inquiry after they were notified that Columbia was under federal investigation, and (3) inadequate response to a story printed in *The New York Times* about the questionable billing practices at several companies, including Columbia.

WORDS OF THE COURT: Director Liability for Illegal Corporate Activities "Liability on the part of a director for breach of the duty of care for failing to give appropriate attention to potentially illegal conduct may arise from an unconsidered failure of the board to act in circumstances in which due attention may have prevented the loss. Unconsidered action can form the basis for liability [. . .] and the magnitude and duration of the alleged wrongdoing is relevant in determining whether the failure of the directors to act constitutes bad faith."

Case Questions

1. If the corporation's officers have carefully covered up the wrongdoing, is it still fair to hold directors liable for failing to detect the illegal activities?

2. Is it ethical for directors to include a waiver of liability for shareholder suits in their corporate charter? Is it sound public policy for courts to recognize a limited liability provision in a charter? Why or why not?

*Modified in part by 250 F.3d 997 (6th Cir. 2001).

Shareholders may also file a direct action (where the shareholder is bringing suit on her own behalf) in cases where the shareholder alleges some oppression of minority shareholders or when a question of voting rights or shareholder inspection rights arises.

Limiting Director Liability A corporate board typically has several measures in place designed to limit their liability. This includes appointing oversight committees to monitor executive management, and consulting with outside professional firms to ensure validity of the information and data used by the board in their decision making. A more controversial method has been for directors to approve a *limited liability provision* in their corporate charter (articles of incorporation or bylaws) that eliminates any liability for ordinary negligence on the part of directors and officers. In Case 15.2, a group of shareholders sued the officers and directors of their corporation for breach of fiduciary duty. The court's analysis focuses on the validity of a limited liability provision.

During an investigation of a massive health care insurance fraud scheme, FBI agents confiscated hundreds of documents from various Columbia/HCA Healthcare Corporation locations.

Corporation p. 380   A fictitious legal entity that exists as an independent "person" separate from its principals.

Business Corporation Law p. 380   Often the title for a specific state law that covers such matters as the structure of the corporation, oversight of the activity of the corporation's managers, rights of the principals in the case of the sale of assets or ownership interests, annual reporting requirements, and other issues that affect the internal rules of the business venture.

Revised Model Business Corporation Act (RMBCA) p. 380   Model act drafted by the American Law Institute and adopted by over half of the states as a template for compiling their own statutes governing corporations.

Privately held corporation p. 380   A corporation that does not sell ownership interests through sales via a broker to the general public or to financial institutions or investors.

Articles of incorporation p. 381   The document filed with a state authority that sets in motion the incorporation process, including the corporation's name, purpose, number of shares issued, and address of the corporation's headquarters.

Business judgment rule p. 382   A protection for corporation officers and directors from their fiduciary duties when they have acted in good faith, have no private financial self-interest, and used diligence to acquire the best information related to a proposed decision, but still made an unwise decision that resulted in some loss to the corporation.

Shareholders p. 383   The owners of a corporation that act principally through electing and removing directors and approving or withholding approval of major corporate decisions.

Corporate veil p. 384   The liability protection shareholders, directors, and officers of a corporation have from personal liability in case the corporation runs up large debts or suffers some liability.

Piercing the corporate veil p. 384   When the court discards the corporate veil and holds some or all of the shareholders personally liable because fairness demands it in certain cases of inadequate capitalization, fraud, and failing to follow corporate formalities.

Directors p. 389   Those responsible for oversight and management of the corporation's course of direction.

Officers p. 389   Those appointed by the board of directors to carry out the directors' set course of direction through management of the day-to-day operation of the business.

Duty of care p. 393   A fiduciary duty owed to shareholders in which officers and directors must exercise that degree of skill, diligence, and care that a reasonably prudent person would exercise under the same circumstances, acting in good faith and in a manner that is reasonably calculated to advance the best interests of the corporation.

Duty of loyalty p. 393   A fiduciary duty owed to shareholders in which officers and directors must not engage in self-dealing or conflicts of interests, requiring fiduciaries to put the corporation's interests ahead of their own.

THEORY TO PRACTICE

Adams and Barker were two individual scientists engaged in research related to inventing a patentable pharmaceutical product. Once they had gained critical mass for the project, they convinced Barker's old college roommate, Cornelius, to invest $100,000 in exchange for an ownership share in a newly formed company called Pharma Corporation (Pharma). The parties agreed that Adams and Barker would continue product development until the company was ready to apply for a patent, then Cornelius would use his contacts to find a manufacturer to produce and market the patented drug. Pharma was structured as follows:

Name	Stock Owned (%)	Role
Adams	35	President, director
Barker	35	Vice president/ Secretary, director
Cornelius	30	Shareholder

The parties hired counsel to incorporate Pharma, issue stock certificates, and draft bylaws. The corporate records were then turned over to Barker and she filed them in her desk drawer. No additional formalities were followed and the records were not maintained, nor were any directors' or shareholders' meetings held.

In year 2, Pharma's application for a patent was rejected. The rejection required Adams and Barker to hire an additional expert to help with research and would put the project behind by approximately 16 months. Adams hired Elliot, a well-known scientist, to help with the project. At this point though, Pharma's financial resources were drying up and, trying to keep the company afloat, Adams began to pay certain Pharma bills with his personal credit card and

Baker would sometimes write out personal checks for lab equipment.

1. What category of corporation is Pharma and what are the options in terms of structure and raising capital?

2. Would Pharma be eligible to be an S corporation? If one of the shareholders objected, could the other two vote to become an S corporation without the third?

3. Did Adams have the right to hire Elliot without the others' consent? Suppose that Cornelius believes that Elliot is not a good hire for Pharma. Can he fire Elliot?

In year 3, the financial condition of Pharma continued to worsen. A representative of the dominant pharmaceutical company in the market, Multi-Drug (MD), approached Adams and Barker with an acquisition offer. MD offered to pay $50,000 to buy all of Pharma's assets and offered a five-year employment agreement with MD to both Adams and Barker. On the same day as the offer, Adams and Barker send a one-page e-mail to Cornelius informing him that they have voted to approve the sale of assets of Pharma to MD and the transaction would take place in one business day.

4. Suppose Cornelius is unhappy with the transaction. Does he have any say in the matter? Does he have the power to stop the sale?

5. Have Adams and Barker breached their fiduciary duties to Cornelius? If so, what duties, specifically, and how were they breached?

6. Are Adams and Barker protected by the business judgment rule? Why or why not?

7. What type of lawsuit, derivative or direct, would be filed by Cornelius to:

   a. Force Adams and Barker to have a shareholders' meeting and formal vote.

   b. Recover against Adams and Barker for damages Cornelius suffered as a result of an alleged breach of duty.

In Theory to Practice above, the principals have made a series of errors that could result in the piercing of the corporate veil. Corporations of all sizes can make similar mistakes if they are not diligent. Suppose that you have an e-mail from a senior manager who read an article in a newspaper about the liability for one company's principals where a court had pierced the corporate veil. She asks you to write her a two-page memorandum that recommends a standard operating procedure and policy aimed at preserving your company's corporate veil. Use the mistakes made by Pharma as one guide for avoiding potential liability.

A sample answer may be found on this textbook's Web site at www.mhhe.com/melvin.

CASE SUMMARY 15.1 :: Miner v. Fashion Enterprises, Inc., 794 N.E. 2d 902

PIERCING THE CORPORATE VEIL

Karen Lynn, Inc. (Lynn Corporation), is a wholly owned subsidiary of Fashion Enterprises, Inc. This meant that the sole shareholder of Lynn Corporation was the corporate entity of Fashion Enterprises, Inc. Lynn Corporation entered into a 10-year lease for retail space in Chicago with Miner with no personal guarantees or guarantee by Fashion Enterprises. The company defaulted on the lease by not making rental payments and Miner obtained a court judgment against Lynn Corporation. The corporation was without assets and Miner asked the court to pierce the corporate veil and allow the judgment to be enforced against its sole shareholder, Fashion Enterprises, Inc. The trial court dismissed the suit, holding that Miner was entitled only to the assets of Lynn Corporation. Miner appealed.

CASE QUESTIONS

1. Who prevails and why?
2. What factors would the court weigh in deciding whether to pierce the veil?

CASE SUMMARY 15.2 :: Morrison v. Gugle, 142 Ohio App. 3d 244 (2001)

SHAREHOLDER RIGHTS

Morrison and Gugle incorporated a company and opened a retail store together and agreed to a half ownership each. Each shareholder was an officer (Gugle as president, Morrison as secretary and treasurer), and each was a director. Additionally, each was an active employee of the business. Gugle and Morrison had a variety of business disputes and eventually Gugle, as president, fired Morrison. After the termination, Morrison demanded the right to inspect corporate records and financial documents, but Gugle refused to provide any information or access to the records citing her authority to do so as president of the corporation. Morrison sued Gugle for, among other counts, breach of fiduciary duty.

CASE QUESTIONS

1. Who prevails and why?
2. Does the president have the power to fire a fellow officer and director who is also half owner of the corporation?
3. What fiduciary duty, if any, was breached here?

BUSINESS JUDGMENT RULE

H. Ross Perot became the single largest shareholder and a director of General Motors as a result of GM's acquisition of Perot's highly successful company Electronic Data Systems (EDS). A rift grew between Perot and GM's other directors, and after appointing a subcommittee of directors to study possible alternatives, GM's directors offered to purchase back Perot's stock at a significant premium over market value. In exchange for the payment, Perot agreed to leave his director's seat, not compete with any GM subsidiary (particularly EDS), and cease any criticism of GM's directors. A group of GM shareholders sued the directors under a theory that the directors had breached their fiduciary duty by wasting corporate assets in buying Perot's silence. The directors asserted the business judgment rule as a defense.

CASE QUESTIONS

1. Who prevails and why?
2. What fiduciary duty is at issue?

LIABILITY OF DIRECTORS

Koerner, Inc., was found to have violated a copyright owned by Burdick. Burdick brought suit against each of Koerner's directors on the basis that the directors had financially benefited from the copyright infringement and, therefore, were liable for the copyright infringement damages by virtue of their membership on the board of directors. The directors argued that there was no evidence of day-to-day involvement, intent, or any specific knowledge of the infringement by the directors and, thus, they are not personally liable.

CASE QUESTIONS

1. Who prevails and why?
2. Does the corporate veil protect directors in these circumstances?

✓ Self-Check ANSWERS
Business Judgment Rule

1. Yes. The directors fulfilled their duties by consulting outside experts and appointing an oversight subcommittee. They acted in good faith and had a rational belief that the merger was in the interests of the company.

2. No. The directors have the obligation to investigate the auditing firm and not to rubber stamp the decision of the president. This is either gross negligence or willful ignorance. Either way, the directors violated their duty of care and were not acting with best information and, thus, cannot be shielded by the business judgment rule.

3. Yes. Even if the directors' explanation is a result of poor business judgment, it is not an act of bad faith and is done with a rational belief. Thus, the directors are protected by the business judgment rule.

4. No. The four directors violated the corporate opportunity doctrine by failing to disclose their financial interest in the real estate. This is an act of bad faith and, therefore, those four directors are not shielded by the business judgment rule.

16
CHAPTER

Regulation of Securities, Corporate Governance, and Financial Markets

learning outcomes **checklist**

After studying this chapter, students who have mastered the material will be able to:

16-1   Articulate factors that differentiate, and the laws that regulate, the primary and secondary securities markets.

16-2   Apply the legal test for what constitutes a security.

16-3   Distinguish between classifications of equity and debt instruments and give an example of each.

16-4   Recognize the fundamental reason behind securities regulation and have a working knowledge of the legal process leading to issuance of original securities.

16-5   Describe the role of the Securities and Exchange Commission (SEC) in securities law compliance and enforcement.

16-6   List the major categories of securities and transactions that are exempt from registration requirements.

16-7   Understand the ethical and legal duties of corporate insiders.

16-8   Identify the legal standard necessary to bring a securities fraud suit against directors and officers in light of the Private Securities Litigation Reform Act.

16-9   Explain the role of state blue-sky laws in securities regulation.

16-10   Show an awareness of the impact of the Sarbanes-Oxley Act on a corporation's officers and directors and its corporate governance.

16-11   Articulate key protections afforded by regulation of the financial markets.

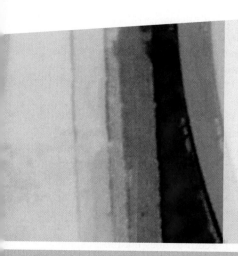

The options that various business entities have for funding operations were covered in the previous chapters in this unit. This chapter focuses on those entities that sell ownership of the venture, known as *equity,* to investors who are interested in receiving a return on their investment based on the success of the business. Other entities find it advantageous to raise money by issuing *debt* instruments to public investors who wish to receive a fixed rate of return regardless of the profitability of the business entity. The issuance and trading of equity and debt instruments to public investors is highly regulated by federal and state *securities law.* In addition to securities regulation, federal laws impose mandates on corporate governance procedures in certain corporations and regulate broad financial markets.

The actions of business owners and managers who are engaged in raising capital or operate in the financial markets, as well as corporate governance of publicly held entities, are subject to the scrutiny of regulatory authorities, and the consequences of noncompliance can be severe.

Specifically, students will learn:

- The background and scope of the primary and secondary securities markets and the role of regulatory agencies in enforcement.

- Classifications of securities and rules that regulate their issuance, sale, trading, and provide exemptions from certain securities laws for qualified ventures.

- Legal mandates associated with corporate governance and regulation of the broader financial market.

LO16-1 OVERVIEW OF THE SECURITIES MARKET

Securities transactions occur in two settings: (1) original and reissuance of securities by a business to raise capital (known as the *primary market*), and (2) the purchase and sale of issued securities between investors (known as the *secondary market*). Both of these markets are governed by federal and state **securities law,** and various securities regulations require registration and disclosures and prescribe certain procedures intended to give investors confidence in the value of a particular security.

In the primary market, issuers raise capital by selling securities in public markets (to the general investment community) or in private placements (to limited groups of investors, such as venture capitalists or institutional investors). Issuing securities to the public markets for the first time is known as an initial public offering (IPO). A company is said to "go public" when it decides to sell its voting common shares for the first time to outside investors through use of public markets such as the New York Stock Exchange (NYSE). The sale is made through the use of a mandatory registration statement that discloses important facts about the offering to potential investors.

In the secondary market, the trading of already-issued securities does not raise capital for the issuing business. Rather, investors sell to other investors in hopes of making a profit or preventing a loss. Once a company has sold shares to the public, it becomes subject to extensive reporting requirements to federal regulators. In theory, this secondary market provides cash flow for investors to continue their investments in primary markets.

Not all securities offerings and transactions are subject to the full burden of the federal and state regulatory schemes. Some securities transactions are exempt from full registration, and the law allows a fast-track system for securities that fall into the category of relatively small offerings or private placements. These exemptions are not automatic. The issuer or trader of a security must craft the security transaction to conform to the exemption requirements according to federal and state laws.

Companies may raise money through issuing securities to investors via a public exchange such as the New York Stock Exchange (NYSE). The NYSE is the world's largest stock exchange with almost $28.5 trillion in market capitalization.

Security Defined

Given the regulatory requirements that are triggered by a securities transaction, business owners and managers need a working knowledge of what instruments and transactions that federal and state laws define as a security and a securities offering. These regulations include registration and disclosure requirements, specific requirements to exempt a securities offering from the federal securities scheme, liability for misrepresentation or omissions in the offering materials, antifraud protections for buyers of securities, and criminal sanctions under certain circumstances for those engaged in fraud while selling or trading securities.

Federal Securities Law   Although stocks and bonds are well-known types of securities, partnership interests, stock options, warrants, agreements to invest, partnership interests, participation in a pool of assets, certain types of promissory notes, and many other arrangements that might commonly be considered an investment are regulated by securities laws.

Federal securities statutes define a security in two ways: (1) by recognizing specific forms of securities such as notes, stocks, treasury stocks, transferable shares, bonds, and debentures, and (2) by providing a catchall definition of other investment transactions in a more *generic* sense, including participation in profit sharing agreements; collateral trust certificates; preorganization certificates or subscriptions; investment contracts; and a fractional, undivided interest in gas, oil, or other mineral rights. Even some *business plans,* depending on the language and circumstances, may constitute a securities offering. Note that certain types of debt instruments, such as a promissory note secured by a home mortgage or a promissory note secured by accounts receivable or other business assets, are *not* securities.

Using these definitions, the general standard for determining whether an arrangement or offering is defined as a security is quite broad: a security is any *investment* where a person gives something with an *expectation of profit* through the efforts of a *third party.* In Landmark Case 16.1, the U.S. Supreme Court articulated a four-part test that helped to give lower courts a framework for defining a security and securities offering.

Modern Application of the *Howey* Test

Although the four parts of the *Howey* test remain intact, federal courts have added further clarification that has expanded the definition of what constitutes a securities offering. Courts now apply a sweeping standard including the investment itself, commonality, profit expectations, and the efforts of others.

Investment   The investment may be cash or a noncash instrument where the investing party receives only the speculative promise of a return and not any tangible commodity or assets.

Commonality   Courts have ruled that an investment scheme satisfies this requirement either through *horizontal commonality* (multiple investors have a common expectation of profit in the investment) or via *vertical commonality* (a single investor has common expectation of profit with the *promoter* of her investment).

Profit Expectations   The expectation of a return on investment (profitability) must be the primary reason for the investment.

Efforts of Others   The efforts of the promoter(s) or agents of the promoter(s) must be the primary sources of revenue that resulted in profits. Note that *Howey* actually required that the investor not be involved in any way with generating the profits. However, the modern trend is for courts to allow some *limited passive involvement* by the investor so long as the promoter/agent has been the primary source of the efforts.

FACT SUMMARY Howey owned a hundred acres of real estate that were used to grow citrus. In an attempt to raise capital for improvements in his citrus operations, Howey offered an investment opportunity to third-party investors. Investors could purchase a certain tract of the real estate and enter into a service agreement whereby Howey would provide services related to care and harvesting of the citrus crop on the real estate. Investors were not required to enter into the service agreement, but investors that did sign a service agreement were given a percentage of the profits from the harvest. Approximately 80 percent of the investors entered into the service contract. The Securities and Exchange Commission (SEC), the federal regulatory agency that enforces federal securities laws, charged Howey with several violations of federal securities law, alleging that the investment constituted an investment contract and was, therefore, required to be registered as a security. Howey argued that the investment opportunity was a contractual agreement and not a securities offering because the service agreement was not mandatory. Howey claimed that the transaction was simply a real estate purchase with an optional profit-sharing opportunity. The trial court and circuit court of appeals both ruled in favor of Howey. The SEC appealed to the U.S. Supreme Court.

SYNOPSIS OF DECISION AND OPINION The Court ruled in favor of the SEC and developed what has become a guidepost test for determining what constitutes a security subject to federal regulation. The so-called *Howey* test has a four-part analysis. Courts examine whether the investment opportunity at issue is (1) an investment of money; (2) which is invested in a common enterprise; (3) the investor did so with expectations of profits; and (4) the profits were generated *solely* by the efforts of persons other than the investor. In this case, the combination of the purchase of land along with the service contract satisfied the four requirements because the investors had no desire to occupy or develop the property themselves. Rather, the Court pointed out, the investors were attracted by the prospects of a return on their investment.

WORDS OF THE COURT: Investment Contracts as Securities "[A]n investment contract for the purposes of the Securities Act means a contract, transaction or scheme whereby a person invests his money in a common enterprise and is led to expect profits solely from the efforts of the promoter of a third party, it being immaterial whether the shares in the enterprise are evidenced by formal certificates or by nominal interests in the physical assets employed in that enterprise."

Case Questions

1. Could Howey adjust the business model and retool the opportunity without triggering securities regulation? How?

2. Recall from the facts that the service contract was optional and approximately 20 percent of the investors purchased the real estate only. Do those 20 percent of investors satisfy the four-part test? Was it enough to satisfy the test that all investors had the mere *opportunity* to enter into the service agreement?

CONCEPT SUMMARY   Modern *Howey* Test

Investment	Commonality	Promoter
Cash or noncash instrument.	Multiple investors in single transaction (horizontal).	Uses investor money to generate profits primarily by promoter's efforts.
Investor's primary motive is expectation of profit.	Single investor in single transaction (vertical).	Modern rule: limited passive action by investor OK.

Self-Check   The *Howey* Test

Do these opportunities constitute a securities offering under the *Howey* test?

1. Smith offers to sell earthworms to third-party investors. The investors entered into a contract whereby, after the purchase, Smith would raise the worms in such a way as to promote massive reproduction, and guaranteed to repurchase the worms from the investor at a certain rate based on the actual sale price to third-party farmers. Thus, an investor could purchase a certain dollar amount of worms, have Smith raise the worms and locate a farmer buyer, then have Smith repurchase the worms from the investor at a higher price than the investor's original price based on the sale price to the farmer.

2. Utley offered to sell one-half acre beachfront lots to the public at $50,000 per lot. After the completion of a sale, Utley offered to perform services as a general contractor for purposes of building a shore house on the lot. Twenty percent of the owners hired Utley to build the houses, but the other 80 percent either hired their own contractors or left the land undeveloped. Once the houses were built, Utley offered to find a buyer for a 10 percent commission on a complete sale.

3. Alliance was a leasing company that devised an opportunity for third-party investors in which the investors paid money to Alliance for the purchase of commercial or kitchen equipment. Alliance then acted as an agent to arrange an equipment lease with the business/lessee who needed the equipment. Alliance entered into a joint venture agreement with the investors to sell them the equipment and to broker a lease between the investor and a lessee. The lease agreement provided for lease payments to be paid by the lessees directly to the investor on a monthly basis over a two-year period, at the end of which a balloon payment (the entire principal) would be due. Alliance represented that the investors would earn a 14 percent rate of return on their investment and that risk was low.

Answers to this Self-Check are provided at the end of the chapter.

CATEGORIES OF SECURITIES

LO16-3

Securities fall into one of two general categories: **equity** or **debt.** Each category includes an inventory of *instruments* that are tangible representations of the security and that define the rights of the owner of the security. Some securities have restrictions on the ownership rights (such as the right to sell the security to another party).

Equity Instruments

Equity instruments represent an investor's ownership interests where financial return on the investment is based primarily on the performance of the venture that issued the securities. However, equity holders have no specific right or guarantee on the investment. Therefore, investors with equity interests may profit considerably from a company that is consistently profitable. However, if the company fails, the equity interest becomes worthless and the investor is without any legal recourse (assuming that no fraud or malfeasance occurred that lead to the company's demise) to recover her original investment. Two prevalent forms of equity instruments issued by corporations are *common stock* and *preferred stock.*

Common Stock   The most frequently used form of equity instrument is **common stock** (also called **common shares**) in which the equity owner is entitled to payments based on the current profitability of the company. The payments are known as *dividends,* and the decision to pay and how much to pay in dividends to equity owners rests with the company's board of directors. Common stock owners also have the right to payment in the event that the corporation is sold for a profit or if the company is dissolved (assuming any value is left in the company). In certain companies, common stock may be *voting* or *nonvoting*. A nonvoting common stockholder is entitled to all benefits of ownership except the right to vote for directors or in major corporate decisions. In any case, most common stockholders are typically entitled to full voting rights. Rights and duties of shareholders, directors, and officers were discussed in detail in Chapter 15, "Corporations." While common stockholders share in the profits, they also bear the greatest risk of loss because they are typically *subordinate* to all creditors and preferred stockholders if the corporation files for bankruptcy protection or simply dissolves with limited assets.

Legal Speak ›))
Subordinate In the context of stock ownership rights, a subordinate position is a lower or secondary position in terms of being entitled to profits or assets. For example, common stockholders are subordinate to preferred stockholders.

Preferred Stock   An alternative form of equity that has less risk than common stock because it has certain quasi-debt features is **preferred stock.** Perhaps the biggest advantage of preferred stock is that preferred stockholders have preference rights over common stockholders in receiving dividends from the corporation. In the event that the corporation fails or files for bankruptcy, preferred stockholders are ahead of common stockholders when trying to recover their losses from the liquidation proceeds. Preferred stock may be voting or nonvoting.

Debt Instruments

Debt is another common tool for raising capital. Debt instruments, which include promissory notes, bonds, and debentures, are generally entitled to receive payments that *are senior in priority* to preferred or common stockholders. *Promissory notes* are the most commonly used debt instrument. The note simply represents a promise to pay back a certain sum of money (principal) plus accrued interest over an agreed upon time period. The lender is paid back with principal and interest payments, typically monthly, in accordance with the terms of the note. *Bonds* are debt instruments issued by a corporation that are secured by certain assets of the company. *Debentures* are unsecured debt instruments issued by a corporation and are backed by the pledge of the corporation's general credit. Investors holding debt instruments are primarily interested in a fixed rate of return regardless of the profitability of the corporation and expect repayment of the debt after a certain period of years.

Legal Speak ›))
Senior in Priority When a business must liquidate assets because a venture fails and either dissolves or files for bankruptcy protection, payments to creditors and shareholders are made according to priority. Thus, those that are "senior" in priority get paid first.

Use of Bonds and Debentures   Bonds and debentures represent the borrowing of money from investors to raise capital for the corporate issuer of the debt instrument. Larger corporations prefer bonds as a method of splitting up its long-term debt, and blend the use of bonds with conventional borrower-lender (bank) loans for short-term debt. Because bonds are debt instruments, investors expect fixed payments at regular intervals until the bond *matures,* at which time the principal amount of the bond, known as its *face amount,* is paid to the investor.

Although bonds are thought of as capital-raising tools of major corporations, some newer bond issues, known as *micro bonds,* streamline paperwork, reduce fees, and are appealing to smaller business ventures who wish to take advantage of bond financing in the $500,000 to $1,000,000 range.

*web*check **www.mhhe.com/melvin**
To link to an article on how smaller companies use micro bonds, link to the article from *Entrepreneur* magazine via this textbook's Web site.

LO16-4, 16-5 SECURITIES REGULATION

Fundamentally, all securities regulation has the same rationale: protection of investors and assuring public confidence in the integrity of the securities market. Note that securities laws are not meant to provide insurance for losses or to punish a venture's principals simply because the business does not earn a profit. The underlying premise of all

The Securities and Exchange Commission (SEC) is an independent federal administrative agency that is charged with regulating the issuance and trading of securities.

securities regulation is **disclosure.** Much of the regulation concerning fraud or securities sales boils down to whether the seller or issuer has made truthful and sufficiently full disclosures about the security itself. Securities law is primarily a matter of federal statutes and regulations, but all states have similar disclosure and fraud laws within state borders.

Securities and Exchange Commission

The **Securities and Exchange Commission (SEC)** is the federal administrative agency charged with rulemaking, enforcement, and adjudication of federal securities laws. Unlike many administrative agencies, the SEC is an *independent agency* that does not have a seat in the president's cabinet and is not subject to direct control by the president. Five commissioners, appointed by the president and subject to advice and consent approval by the Senate, compose the SEC. Commissioners may be removed for misconduct, but no commissioner has been removed since the SEC was formed by Congress in 1934. In addition to being a source of expert information on securities laws, the SEC has wide-ranging executive, legislative, and judicial powers.

The SEC's executive powers include the power to investigate potential violations of securities laws and regulations. They also have a variety of administrative enforcement mechanisms such as issuing a cease and desist order.[1] In egregious cases, the SEC initiates criminal charges against an individual and/or company that has allegedly violated securities law. The SEC's legislative authority is granted by Congress and allows the SEC to draft and publish securities regulations and interpretations of statutes, rules, and court decisions. Pursuant to their legislative powers, the SEC also issues interpretative letters and no-action letters to advise the securities investment and trading community on how

---

[1]An administrative order requiring a certain party to halt unlawful activity.

the SEC will treat a proposed transaction. These letters are not binding on the SEC, but they do carry significant weight with courts and are crucial to the day-to-day operations of publicly held companies. The SEC's judicial powers are primarily rooted in its role as a hearing tribunal for enforcing certain securities violations, including alleged indiscretions of brokers in their business dealings. The SEC has the power to suspend or revoke professional licenses of brokers and others regulated by securities laws.

Though it is the primary regulatory authority of the securities markets, the SEC works closely with many other institutions, including Congress, other federal agencies, self-regulatory organizations (such as stock exchanges), state securities regulators, and various private sector organizations. The chair of the SEC is one of four members[2] of the President's Working Group on Financial Markets.

> **KEY** POINT
> The SEC is an independent regulatory agency with broad executive, legislative, and judicial authority over securities issuance, transactions, investors, and brokers.

The agency is composed of several divisions and departments. The highest profile divisions are Enforcement and Corporation Finance because they are primarily responsible for investigation and enforcement action against violators. Much of the SEC's day-to-day work is done through its 11 regional offices that are spread throughout the United States.

Figure 16.1 shows the SEC's organizational structure.

FIGURE 16.1   Structure of the Securities and Exchange Commission

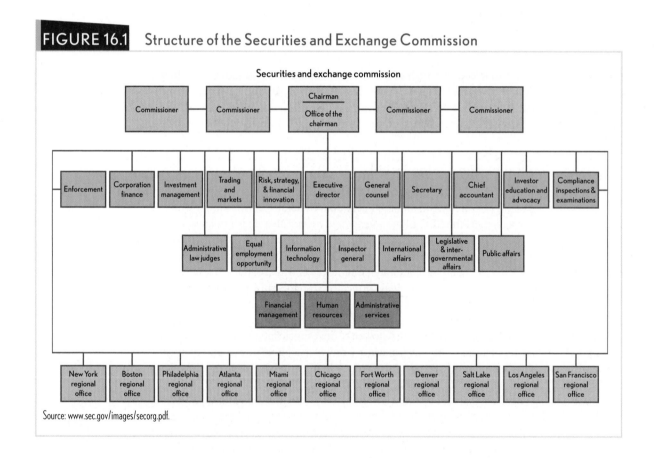

Source: www.sec.gov/images/secorg.pdf.

---

[2]The other members are the chair of the Federal Reserve, the chair of the Commodities Futures Trading Commission, and the Secretary of the Treasury.

EDGAR   An important function of the SEC is to maintain a national clearinghouse for public corporation disclosures and filing required by federal securities laws. This clearinghouse is made available to the public through the SEC's computer database known as EDGAR. In addition to EDGAR, the SEC's Web site also serves as a source of information to educate investors on risks and SEC procedures.

> **web**check   **sec.gov/edgar/quickedgar.htm**
> Check on the most recent filings and disclosures of any publicly held company on EDGAR. Before accessing the database, take a quick tutorial on using EDGAR at the SEC Web site or link to the page from this textbook's Web site at www.mhhe.com/melvin.

The Securities Act of 1933

LO16-6

The primary scope of the **Securities Act of 1933**[3] (the '33 Act) is the regulation of original issuance (and reissuance) of securities to investors by business venture issuers. The '33 Act mandates: (1) a registration filing for any venture selling securities to the public, (2) certain disclosures concerning the issuer's governance and financial condition, and (3) SEC oversight over the registration and issuance of securities. The system is designed to give potential investors a transparent view of the business entity's financial information, potential liabilities, management practices, and other pertinent information that a business venture is required to disclose in its registration materials. The '33 Act also provides defrauded investors with remedies against issuers that violate the statutory requirements. Congress has also provided *special exemptions* for issuance of securities to relatively small groups of qualified investors. These exemptions are discussed in the next section of this chapter.

> **KEY** POINT
> The Securities Act of 1933 covers the process of issuing or reissuing securities to the public. The law requires registration and certain disclosures and authorizes the SEC to oversee the transactions.

Preregistration Documentation   The '33 Act and the SEC regulations require extensive documentation even before the registration statement is filed. This documentation requires the expertise of a variety of professionals, but ultimately they are legal documents that are drafted by highly specialized attorneys skilled in securities law. Required documentation before registration includes a *letter of intent* (issuer indicates management and board approval of the issuing of shares); *comfort letters* (including an opinion of the issuer's corporate counsel verifying the business venture's adherence to corporate formalities and compliance and opinion of the business venture's accounting firm verifying the accuracy of the business's financial records); and an *underwriting agreement* where the issuer enters into an agreement with a syndicate of underwriters[4] specifying the amount of securities offered, the compensation for the underwriters, and terms related to representations and warranties of the issuer and underwriters.

Registration   Registering a security is a relatively complex process that is divided into four phases. First, as discussed above, the issuer assembles preregistration documents. Second, the issuer begins the prefiling period while the registration statement is being prepared. The form of the registration statement is prescribed by SEC regulations and is broken down into two parts. The first part is the **prospectus,** which is intended to give investors a realistic view of the issuer's business, risk factors, financial position, financial statements, and disclosures concerning directors, officers, and controlling shareholders.

---

[3]15 U.S.C. § 77a, et seq.

[4]In this context, an underwriter is a professional in the securities market that agrees to facilitate the sale of stock to the public for a fee.

The second part of the registration statement is *supplemental information* that documents and supports the prospectus. Once the prospectus is drafted, the next phase of registration is the *SEC review* of the statement. During these first two phases of the registration process, the securities may not be marketed or sold to the public. Once submitted, the SEC has 10 days to review the registration notice for incomplete or misleading disclosures. During this review period, the SEC may issue a *refusal order* that prevents the registration from taking effect. Even after the SEC's 10-day review period has expired, SEC can issue a *stop order* if it determines there was a defect in the disclosures. If the SEC does not act, the registration statement becomes effective 20 days after it was filed. During the SEC review phase, the security may not be sold, but it may be *marketed* to the public subject to strict SEC regulations. Once the registration statement has become effective, the securities are permitted to be sold to the public. The final phase is after the offering's contemplated registration statement expires. During this postregistration time, securities may still be sold and marketed to investors, but investors must receive a prospectus, and marketing materials are still subject to the SEC's oversight. Table 16.2 illustratates the phases of Securities Registration under the '33 Act.

Exemptions from Registration   While the SEC regulations pertaining to registering securities are intended to protect investors, the process itself is extremely onerous and expensive for issuers who are engaged in a relatively small offering. In order to assist business ventures seeking smaller amounts of capital from the public investment community, the securities laws allow a number of **exemptions** from registration for smaller issuers. For a number of economic, legal, and other practical reasons, *most businesses offer their securities on an exempt basis.* From a federal standpoint, the most common exemption is one for *nonpublic* offerings to a limited number of sophisticated investors who have prior business relationships with the issuer or who privately negotiate their securities purchases. Another common exemption, known as a regulatory *safe harbor,* involves offerings with specified dollar limitations and/or limitations on the number of *nonaccredited investors.* While the security may be exempt from the burdensome regulations of the '33 Act, as a condition to establishing an exemption a seller of securities is still required to make available or prepare and deliver *certain disclosures* to prospective investors. The breadth and

TABLE 16.2   Phases of Securities Registration

Phase 1 Pre-registration	Phase 2 Registration Statement	Phase 3 SEC Review	Phase 4 SEC Response
Proposed issuer assembles pre-registration documents such as letters of intent, comfort letters, and an underwriting agreement.	Proposed issuer drafts prospectus with disclosures and financial information and submits the statement to the SEC.	The SEC reviews the Registration Statement over a period of ten days.	The SEC may: (1) Issue a refusal order during the ten day review period or issue a stop order after the review period. Proposed issuer must revise and resubmit; or (2) Take no action and the registration becomes effective 20 days after the original SEC filing. The security may now be sold to the public.

content of these disclosures varies depending upon the particular requirements for registration or exemption imposed by law. The following securities are common examples of securities that are exempt from full registration requirements:

- Commercial paper (such as promissory notes that are purchased by sophisticated investors and investment banks) with a maturity date of less than nine months.
- Securities of charitable organizations.
- Annuities and other issues of insurance companies.
- Government-issued securities such as municipal bonds.
- Securities issued by banks and other institutions subject to government supervision.
- In certain cases under Regulation D (explained next), securities issues of up to $5 million in any 12-month period.

In addition to the exemption for some *types* of securities, the securities laws also exempt certain *transactions* that an issuer may use to sell the security. Some of the more common transaction exemptions fall under a securities law provision known as **Regulation D.** Regulation D exemptions are for *limited* offers of a relatively small amount of money or offers made in a limited manner. Within Regulation D, the exemptions are often referred to by their rule number.

- Rule 504 exempts a noninvestment company offering up to $1 million in any 12-month period.
- Rule 504a exempts offerings up to $500,000 in any 12-month period by certain companies.
- Rule 505 exempts a private noninvestment company offering up to $5 million in any 12-month period;
- Rule 506 exempts a private noninvestment company offerings in unlimited amounts that are not generally advertised or available to the general public.

Another commonly used exemption is known as a **private placement** where the issuer only accepts investments from those who meet the standards for *accredited investors.* Accredited investors are those who have sufficient experience, business savvy, and knowledge of the market so that the law imputes a certain cognizance of investment risk and the ability to protect their own interests. These investors must meet personal net worth or income requirements in order to qualify. Exempt private placement offers are still required to make important disclosures to potential investors about the business and its principals. In a private placement, these disclosures are made through the use of a *private placement memorandum.* The Securities Act of 1933 exempts these private placement transactions under Section 4(2). The most common are:

- Offerings up to $5 million made solely to accredited investors in any 12-month period that are not advertised.
- Purely local offerings; restricted to purchase by residents of the same state as the company; resale is barred to nonresidents for nine months.

Liability for Violations   The '33 Act, and its subsequent amendments, imposes both civil and criminal penalties on those offerors and sellers of securities who violate the act's provisions. The penalties include (1) rescission of the investment by the investor, (2) civil penalties and fines, and (3) incarceration for egregious cases. The SEC has broad authority to pursue civil and criminal sanctions when an offering is accomplished by false or misleading means. Table 16.3 provides specific remedies and penalties for noncompliance with securities issuance regulations.

> **KEY POINT**
> Exemption from registration does not exempt issuers from appropriate disclosures to investors and financial transparency.

TABLE 16.3   '33 Act Liabilities and Penalties

Violation	Remedy/Penalty
Noncompliance with registration requirements	Investors who purchased unregistered securities are entitled to rescind the investment and are entitled to be paid back in full.
Fraud in registration statement or offering	Investors may recover damages from issuer if they relied on the statements in considering the purchase.
Fraud in any transaction or offering	Subject to criminal penalties, including substantial fines and incarceration.

Defenses   If a corporation fails to comply with the '33 Act, it may avoid liability or penalties by successfully asserting one of two defenses: (1) the omission or misrepresentation in the registration or offering was not *material* (i.e., the omission or misrepresentation was so minor that it did not affect the value of the offering or injure an investor), or (2) the investor had *knowledge* about the omission or misrepresentation and proceeded with the investment *assuming the risk*. If the violator is not actually the issuer of the stock but a third party involved in the transaction (such as an underwriter), that party may avoid liability by proving she acted with *due diligence* in verifying the veracity and completeness of the required disclosures.

LO16-7   The Securities Act of 1934

While the '33 Act regulates the *issuance* of securities to the public by a corporation, the **Securities Act of 1934**[5] (the '34 Act) regulates the sale of securities between investors *after* an investor purchased it from a business entity issuer. Therefore, the '34 Act's authority is over brokers, dealers, securities associations, brokerage firms, and other business entities that are engaged in the sale of securities between investors. Similar to the structure of the '33 Act, this statute requires registration with the SEC for issuers who wish to have their securities offered on a *national exchange,* such as the New York Stock Exchange (NYSE), and compels all sellers of securities to fully disclose all pertinent details to potential investors. The '34 Act also regulates the relationship between existing stockholders and the corporation by requiring disclosure of information concerning (1) the financial performance of the company, (2) corporate governance procedures, and (3) any changes that increase or decrease risk that have occurred since the last report (such as the company being named as a defendant in a lawsuit).

Section 10(b)   Section 10(b) of the '34 Act is the primary *antifraud* provision covering the trading of securities. The section makes it a criminal offense to engage in any fraud, directly or indirectly, in connection with the purchase and sale of any security. Its scope is very broad, and the SEC enforces this section (often referred to as *rule 10(b)(5)*) strictly. Although the term *10(b)(5)* is perhaps best known for its use by the SEC in prosecuting insider-trading cases, in reality this section is a very expansive antifraud provision intended to cover all actions, conspiracies, or schemes that could potentially result in an investor being defrauded, damaged, or misled.

---

[5]15 U.S.C. § 78a, et seq.

Insider Trading   The SEC has become increasingly aggressive about the enforcement of rule 10(b)(5) with respect to **insider trading.** Essentially, when a corporate insider has access to certain information not available to the general investor public, the insider may not trade in their company's stock on the basis of the inside information. Insiders include executives, managers, corporate counsel, consultants, employees, brokers, accountants, vendors, partners, and even majority shareholders. In 1988, Congress passed the **Insider Trading and Securities Fraud Enforcement Act,** which raised the criminal and civil penalties for insider trading, increased the liability of brokerage firms for wrongful acts of their employees, and gave the SEC more power to pursue violations of rule 10(b)(5).

Tipper-Tippee Liability   Although rule 10(b)(5) clearly applies to insiders using internal corporate information to profit or prevent a loss in their own stock portfolios, the rule also extends specifically to outside parties who leak and who learn of the insider information and trade stock on the basis of the information. This is known as *tipper-tippee liability* (and can even be extended to other parties that the tippee told about the internal information) and is a criminal offense under the '34 Act. Rule 10(b)(5) is violated if (1) the information released by the tipper constituted a breach of the tipper's *fiduciary duty* to the company, (2) the tipper obtained some personal *benefit* by giving the tip, (3) the tippee knew or should have known that the information was *wrongfully disclosed,* and (4) the tippee *benefited* from the information. For example, suppose that Charles, the executive assistant to the chief financial officer at a public company, discovers information that is likely to adversely impact the price of the stock of the company. Because Charles owns no stock in the company, there is no possibility of direct 10(b)(5) liability for insider trading. However, suppose that Charles knows that his *neighbor* owns stock in the company and offers his neighbor the information in exchange for a fee. When the neighbor hears the insider information, he sells all of his stock in the company. The next day, the stock price falls by 50 percent. Both Charles (as tipper) and the neighbor (as tippee) are liable for violating rule 10(b)(5) under the tipper-tipee theory. Charles benefited by earning the fee, and the neighbor benefited by selling the stock on the basis of the inside information.

In Case 16.1, famous football coach Barry Switzer was charged with insider trading for inadvertently overhearing insider information while attending his son's sporting event. Although this case was decided by a trial court in 1984, the decision was never reversed and the reasoning has been adopted by other federal courts as late as 2005, including a U.S. Circuit Court of Appeal. It has also been cited in 53 law journal articles.

Section 16   While rule 10(b)(5) prohibits insider trading using information based on insider or tipper-tipee knowledge, **Section 16** of the '34 Act imposes restrictions and reporting requirements on ownership positions and stock trades made by certain corporate insiders named in the statute. It was most recently amended in 1991 to clarify certain provisions and extend its reporting requirements, but fundamentally Section 16 provides transparency of all stock trades by insiders and prohibits insiders from earning short-swing profits.

Section 16(a) classifies any person who is an executive officer, a director, or a shareholder with 10 percent or more of ownership of the total stock as an *insider* and requires these insiders to file regular reports with the SEC disclosing stock ownership and trading of their company's stock. This reporting requirement allows the SEC and the investment community to monitor unusual stock activity such as whether a company's chief executive officer sells substantial portions of his stock in the company during a short time frame. Although an insider's stock sale could be the result of outside influences unrelated to the

FACT SUMMARY   Although Barry Switzer is best known for his success as a professional and college football coach, he also had significant involvement in various business ventures in Oklahoma and Texas. While attending his son's track meet in 1982, Switzer was filling time in between events and laid down in the bleachers to sunbathe. Sitting in bleachers in front of Switzer was Platt, an executive at Texas International Corporation (TIC). Switzer and Platt knew each other and had greeted one another earlier in the track meet, but Platt was unaware of Switzer's presence in the bleachers at that time. Within earshot of Switzer, Platt discussed some of the challenges and troubles of TIC with his wife who was sitting next to him in the bleachers. The 20-minute conversation included highly confidential information about one of TIC's subsidiary companies named Phoenix.

The next day, Switzer, without expressly mentioning what he had overheard, convinced several investors to form a partnership for purposes of buying Phoenix stock. Switzer, both as an individual and as a partner with other investors, purchased large amounts of Phoenix stock. Before overhearing Platt's conversation, neither Switzer nor his partners ever heard of Phoenix. Ultimately, Switzer and his partners earned a substantial profit from the purchase and sale of the Phoenix stock.

After an investigation of Phoenix, the SEC filed a complaint alleging that Switzer was a tippee and tipped others on insider information. They charged that Switzer and his partners violated rule 10(b)(5) of the '34 Act by engaging in insider trading because Switzer had used the information that he overheard from Platt while lying in the bleachers. The SEC requested that the court order Switzer and his partners to return the profits realized in the Phoenix stock transactions.

SYNOPSIS OF DECISION AND OPINION   The U.S. District Court for the Western District of Oklahoma ruled in favor of Switzer and his partners. The court held that Switzer's conduct did not meet the requirements for rule 10(b)(5) liability under the tipper-tippee theory. The court pointed out that (1) it was not clear that Platt's casual conversation with his wife constituted a breach of duty, and (2) Switzer and his partners had no reason to know if the information they received was material or confidential.

WORDS OF THE COURT: Improper Purposes Requirement   "Platt did not breach a duty to the shareholders of Phoenix, and thus [SEC] failed to meet its burden of proof [required] to prove tipper/tippee liability. Moreover, even if SEC was able to prove this breach, Switzer's conduct does not rise to the level of a 10(b)(5) violation. Switzer [and his partners] could not have known that the information was material, non-public information disseminated by a corporate insider for an improper purpose, and thus are not liable as tippees under rule 10(b)(5)."

Case Questions

1. Although Platt did not intend on disclosing the information to Switzer, could Platt's choice to discuss confidential corporate matters with his spouse in a public place where one could easily overhear him constitute the requisite breach of duty required for a tipper-tippee case?

2. The SEC never appealed this case. Do you believe that the SEC prosecuted Switzer because of his high profile?

3. Did Switzer's partners have a legal and/or ethical duty to inquire about the source of Switzer's information?

---

company, many investors would see it as a sign of trouble. The SEC regularly investigates such activity as it may be indicative of stock manipulation.

Section 16(b) includes a clawback provision that allows a corporation to recapture any profits earned by an insider on the purchase and sale of the company's stock that occurred within a 6-month period. These earnings are called *short-swing profits,* and the prohibition against them is intended to deter insiders from profiting by manipulating the stock's short-term performance. Section 16(b) is a strict liability statute because it applies even if the insider did not use any insider information or intend any stock manipulation in realizing a short-swing profit.

ImClone Insider Tips: Ethical Dilemmas and Choices

ImClone Systems was a publicly traded biopharmaceutical company founded by Samuel Waksal who also served as the company's CEO and chairman of the board. In December 2001, ImClone and the public markets were anxiously awaiting FDA approval on an experimental cancer treatment drug called Erbitux that ImClone had developed. Because of his position at ImClone, Waksal had advance knowledge that the FDA would not be giving approval for the use of the drug. Before the public announcement by FDA, Waksal called his stockbroker, Peter Bacanovik from Merrill Lynch (now a subsidiary of Bank of America), and ordered him to sell substantial amounts of ImClone stock from his personal portfolio. Waksal also urged his immediate family to sell their ImClone stock as well.

Bacanovik had other brokerage clients that owned ImClone stock, including Martha Stewart, the star of her own media conglomerate and the CEO and chair of the board for the publicly traded holding company for her empire called Martha Stewart Living/Omnimedia. Bacanovik instructed his assistant to tip Stewart to the fact that Waksal had sold a substantial portion of ImClone stock. After the tip, Stewart instructed Bacanovic to sell all her ImClone shares. The next day, ImClone announced publicly that the FDA had not approved the use of Erbitux and ImClone's stock dropped by more than 20 percent. By selling when she did, Stewart avoided losses of over $45,000.

According to government documents, when the SEC launched an investigation of Waksal and ImClone, Bacanovic and Stewart fabricated an alibi for the sell orders and told investigators that Stewart had decided earlier that the stock should be sold once it reached a certain price. Stewart also told investigators that she did not recall anyone telling her about the Waksal sale. However, Bacanovic's assistant, Douglas Faneuil, faced with criminal charges, testified for the government against Stewart and Bacanovic. In 2004, Stewart and Baconovic were convicted of obstructing justice in a securities fraud investigation and were sentenced to prison and substantial fines. Stewart was barred from serving on any board of a publicly held company. Waksal and some of his family members were also convicted of securities fraud related to insider trading and sentenced to seven years in jail.*

*See SEC Release 2003-69 dated June 4, 2003.

Television personality and media conglomerate owner Martha Stewart, pictured here with her attorney outside of a federal courthouse, was convicted of obstruction of justice in connection with the SEC's investigation of insider trading at ImClone Systems.

(continued)

1. Stewart was not an insider of ImClone and she received the tip from her stockbroker. Does she have an ethical obligation to ask where the tip came from or why the broker was recommending selling the stock? Does the fact that Stewart was an officer and director of a publicly traded corporation require her to use higher ethical standards when buying and selling stock of other companies?

2. Given the relatively small amount of money involved, do you think that Stewart's sale manipulated the stock in a way that hurt other investors?

3. When Faneuil was ordered to commit an illegal act by tipping Stewart, what were his options as a practical matter? If he was told to tip Stewart or he would be fired from his job, does that affect the ethical decision-making model?

4. Some commentators have argued for the repeal of insider-trading laws because these laws impede economic efficiency. If insider-trading laws were repealed, how would that impact your analysis as to whether Waksal, Stewart, Bacanovic, and Faneuil acted ethically?

5. Ultimately, Stewart was convicted not for securities fraud, but for lying to investigators about the transaction. Given the nature of the transaction and the limited harm it caused other investors, did the government act ethically in pursuing her case? If she weren't a celebrity, would the government have acted in the same way?

Section 10(b)(5) and Section 16 in Tandem   To understand how the two primary regulations of insiders work in tandem, consider the following example. Suppose that RocketCo. is a publicly held corporation subject to the provision of the '34 Act. Armstrong is the company's chief financial officer and Shepard is on the board of directors. The company has invested several million dollars on a 10-year research project to produce an alternate fuel product that will result in substantially lower pollution. As of the end of the last year, Armstrong and Shepard each owned 10,000 shares of RocketCo.'s stock. This year, they traded as follows:

January 1	Armstrong purchases 1,000 shares at $10/share.
	Shepard purchases 5,000 shares at $10/share.
March 1	Shepard purchases 5,000 additional shares at $10/share.
May 1	Shepard purchases 1,000 additional shares at $20/share.
	Armstrong sells 1,000 shares at $20/share.
November 1	Shepard sells all of his shares of RocketCo. at $25/share.
December 1	RocketCo. stock drops to $2/share.

Assume further that on October 30, both Armstrong and Shepard learned in advance of public knowledge that the Environmental Protection Agency (EPA) failed to give regulatory approval to RocketCo.'s new alternative fuel and that improvements to the formula would likely take many more years of research and testing. After the public disclosure by the EPA of the adverse decision on November 30, RocketCo.'s stock price dropped precipitously.

■ *10(b)(5) liability.* Because Armstrong and Shepard are both unquestionably insiders, the information about the EPA's adverse decision cannot be used as the basis for selling RocketCo. stock. The timing of Shepard's sale of a substantial portion of RocketCo.'s stock gives rise to an inference that the insider information precipitated the sale of the stock. If he engaged in insider trading, Shepard faces potential civil liability to injured shareholders as well as possible criminal liability and SEC enforcement action under the '34 Act. Because there is no indication that Armstrong's May sale of the stock was related to the EPA's adverse decision, she does not face 10(b)(5) liability.

- *Section 16(a) coverage.* Armstrong and Shepard are both statutory insiders of RocketCo. and, therefore, are required to report each and every trade to the SEC. Indeed, Section 16(a) is designed to alert investors and the SEC to potential wrongdoing when an insider takes abrupt action in trading as in the case of Shepard's selling of all of his stock.

- *Section 16(b) liability.* Because Shepard did not profit from a short-swing (his last purchase was in May and he did not sell until November), he does not have Section 16(b) liability. Armstrong's sale of 1,000 shares in May would trigger liability under Section 16(b) because she reaped profits of $10 per share when selling within six months of her purchase. Therefore, the corporation would be entitled to recapture the $10,000 profit realized by Armstrong's short-swing. Note that it is irrelevant that Armstrong did not use insider information to make the profit. Section 16(b) short-swing liability is a *strict liability* provision.

Other Important Federal Statutes

LO16-8

Although the disclosure and registration requirements in the 1933 and 1934 acts are aimed at protecting investors, other federal statutes are focused on protecting publicly held companies from frivolous litigation by investors.

Private Securities Litigation Reform Act of 1995

In the early 1990s, the securities regulation community and publicly held companies became concerned about what they believed to be an increasingly unwarranted number of lawsuits that they characterized as abusive. Indeed, a number of law firms specialized in the initiation of litigation on behalf of alleged defrauded shareholders. While the shareholders recovered minimal amounts, sizable legal fees were awarded to law firms. The lawsuits were frequently based on glowing predictions of future growth and other such public comments by company executives. Congress, in an attempt to curtail this type of litigation, passed the **Private Securities Litigation Reform Act of 1995 (PSLRA).**[6] The PSLRA made it more difficult to pursue litigation under the securities laws based solely on commentary by the company's executives. The PSLRA provides *safe harbors* from lawsuits that shield the company and its officers and directors so long as the principals acted in *good faith* and *disclosed* all relevant facts. The law also requires that, in order for a shareholder to prevail in a suit based on statements of corporate executives that turned out to be incorrect or to be misrepresentations, the shareholder must prove **scienter** as an essential element of the case. Courts have traditionally required shareholder plaintiffs to *itemize* particular facts that give rise to a strong inference that the defendant acted with the required deceptive state of mind. The law defined suits as frivolous if the "shareholder derivative actions [are] begun with [the] hope of winning large attorney fees or private settlements, and with not intention of benefiting [the] corporation on behalf of which [the] suit is theoretically brought."

In Case 16.2, the U.S. Supreme Court made clear that shareholders have the substantial hurdle of scienter to pass in order to pursue their fraud claim against insiders.

Securities Litigation Uniform Standards Act of 1998

After the passage of the PSLRA, corporate concerns about shareholder litigation continued because shareholders could still engage in litigation by suing corporations for inadequate or overly optimistic

Legal Speak ›))
Scienter In the context of securities litigation scienter means evidence of specific intent to deceive, manipulate, or defraud.

---

[6]15 U.S.C. § 78u.

FACT SUMMARY   Tellabs, Inc., manufactures specialized equipment for fiber optic networks. The shareholders alleged that Notebaert, Tellabs' CEO, "falsely reassured public investors that Tellabs was continuing to enjoy strong demand for its products and earning record revenues," when, in fact, Notebaert knew the opposite was true. The shareholders of Tellabs alleged that Notebaert knowingly misled the public in several ways. First, he made statements indicating that demand for Tellabs' flagship networking device, the TITAN 5500, was continuing to grow, while demand for that product was actually dropping. Second, Notebaert made a series of overstated revenue projections when, in reality, demand for the TITAN 5500 was drying up and production of the TITAN 6500 was behind schedule. The shareholders alleged that, based on Notebaert's optimistic assessments, market analysts recommended that investors buy Tellabs' stock. Not long after these statements, Tellabs disclosed that demand for the TITAN 5500 had significantly dropped. Simultaneously, the company substantially lowered its revenue projections for the second quarter of 2001. The next day, the price of Tellabs stock, which had reached a high of $67, plunged to a low of $15.87. A group of shareholders filed a lawsuit alleging that Tellabs and Notebaert had engaged in securities fraud in violation of §10(b) of the '34 Act.

The trial court dismissed the complaint ruling that although the shareholders had alleged that Notebaert's statements were misleading, they had not provided specific instances of Notebaert's conduct that inferred *scienter.* The appellate court reversed, concluding that the shareholders had sufficiently alleged that Notebaert acted with the requisite state of mind. Tellabs and Notebaert appealed to the U.S. Supreme Court.

SYNOPSIS OF DECISION AND OPINION   The U.S. Supreme Court reversed the appellate court and ruled in favor of Tellabs/Notebaert. They reasoned that under the PSLRA, the complaint must allege a *strong* inference of scienter. To qualify as a "strong inference" within the meaning of the PSLRA, an inference of scienter must be more than merely plausible or reasonable—it must be cogent and at least as compelling as any opposing inference of nonfraudulent intent. Note that the Court *did not* rule on whether or not Notebaert's statements did or did not qualify as evidence of scienter. Rather, they vacated the lower court's judgment because the trial court had not used the correct standard to ascertain the inference of scienter.

WORDS OF THE COURT: Strong Inference of Scienter Required   "The strength of an inference cannot be decided in a vacuum. The inquiry is inherently comparative: How likely is it that one conclusion, as compared to others, follows from the underlying facts? To determine whether the plaintiff has alleged facts that give rise to the requisite 'strong inference' of scienter, a court must consider plausible nonculpable explanations for the defendant's conduct, as well as inferences favoring the plaintiff. The inference that the defendant acted with scienter need not be irrefutable, i.e., of the 'smoking-gun' genre, or even the 'most plausible of competing inferences,' yet the inference of scienter must be more than merely 'reasonable' or 'permissible'—it must be cogent and compelling, thus strong in light of other explanations. A complaint will survive, we hold, only if a reasonable person would deem the inference of scienter cogent and at least as compelling as any opposing inference one could draw from the facts alleged."

Case Questions

1. After reading this case, do you think that application of the PSLRA is consistent with balancing the rights of shareholders with curbing frivolous litigation?

2. Would you qualify Notebaert's statements as intentionally misleading or just overly optimistic? What's the difference?

---

statements in state courts under *state* securities statutes. Congress responded by enacting the **Securities Litigation Uniform Standards Act of 1998.**[7] The law, which took the form of an amendment to the '34 Act, is intended to prevent a private party from instituting certain lawsuits in federal *or* state court based on the statutory or common law of

---

[7]15 U.S.C. § 77z, et seq.

any state that punishes "a misrepresentation or omission of a material fact" or the use of "any manipulative device or contrivance" concerning the purchase or sale of a covered security.

Securities Regulation by States: Blue-Sky Laws

State securities laws are commonly known as **blue-sky laws,** named after the original state statutory protection of investors from unsavory issuers selling nothing more than blue sky. Blue-sky laws are frequently constructed to match federal securities statutes. In theory, these state statutes are intended to cover purely intrastate securities offerings (when the issuers and all potential investors are within one state's borders), but as a practical matter state securities regulators are an additional safeguard for investors when the federal government declines to exercise their jurisdiction over a particular securities offering. A majority of states have adopted all or substantially all of the Uniform Securities Act. Typical provisions include prohibition against fraud in the sale of securities, registration requirements for brokers and dealers, exemptions, civil liability for issuers failing to comply, and state court remedies for defrauded investors.

REGULATION OF CORPORATE GOVERNANCE AND FINANCIAL MARKETS

In addition to regulating the issuance and trading of securities, federal and state statutes also regulate certain internal governance procedures of publicly held corporations. **Corporate governance** is the procedure and system used by the officers and directors to establish lines of responsibility, approval, and oversight among the key stakeholders, and set out rules for making corporate decisions. While corporations have traditionally resisted any form of direct government regulation of internal corporate decision making, public scandals have caused Congress to impose certain mandates meant to ensure public confidence in the publicly traded markets and to protect investors. Professionals from outside firms that conduct services for publicly held corporations, notably accounting firms, are also subject to certain regulatory requirements when they conduct audits of public corporations. Most recently, the financial crisis that began in 2008 continues to spur regulatory reforms via Congress and through administrative agencies in the areas of corporate governance and, specifically, of firms and institutions involved in the financial markets.

The Sarbanes-Oxley Act of 2002

In the wake of the infamous corporate fraud and malfeasance scandals beginning in 2000—most memorably Enron,[8] MCI WorldCom, Global Crossing, HealthSouth, and Tyco—a public outcry and a growing lack of investor confidence in corporate financial disclosures caused Congress to overhaul the entire corporate governance regulatory structure by passing the **Sarbanes-Oxley Act (SOX Act) of 2002.**[9] Most commentators agree that the SOX Act provided the most sweeping and comprehensive amendments to the '33 and '34 Acts in securities law history. While substantial portions of SOX are aimed at solving specific mechanism failures in auditing and other accounting procedures, the law

> ### KEY POINT
> The Sarbanes-Oxley Act (SOX Act) of 2002 was passed in response to revelations of corporate fraud and malfeasance in publicly held companies. The law aims to solve specific mechanism failures in accounting methods and requires higher levels of fiduciary responsibilities for those involved in corporate governance.

---

[8]A business ethics case study on Enron is featured in Chapter 5, "Business, Societal, and Ethical Contexts of Law."

[9]15 U.S.C. § 7241.

also imposes higher levels of fiduciary responsibilities for those involved in corporate governance. It was widely believed that a lack of oversight by gatekeepers, such as auditors and federal regulators, was a leading factor in the fraud and malfeasance that caused the high-profile demise of these large, publicly held corporations.

The SOX Act was intended to impose stricter regulation and controls on how corporations do business through regulation of three broad areas: *auditing, financial reporting,* and internal *corporate governance.* The SOX Act also provided for additional enforcement apparatus and increased penalties for violation of existing securities laws.

Reforms in the Accounting Industry

As various corporate fraud and mismanagement scandals came to the public's attention, incidents of public corporations misreporting important financial information had spiked,[10] and Congress replaced the accounting industry's self-regulation of auditing with a new federal agency called the Public Company Accounting Oversight Board (PCAOB). The PCAOB implements, administers, and enforces the SOX Act mandates. Accounting firms that audit public companies accessing U.S. capital markets are required to register with the PCAOB and are subject to its oversight and enforcement authority. The PCAOB also establishes regulations that standardize certain auditing procedures and ethical parameters.

Former MCI WorldCom CEO Bernard Ebbers, seen here after his arrest on securities fraud charges, was a central figure in the corporate scandals that led to passage of the Sarbanes-Oxley Act of 2002.

Recall from Chapter 5, "Business, Societal, and Ethical Contexts of Law" in our discussion of Enron, that one major contributing factor to the collapse was questionable independence of the Andersen auditing partner assigned to Enron. The SOX Act seeks to increase auditor independence through setting mandatory rotation of auditing partners, banning accounting firms from providing nonauditing consulting services for public companies for which it provides auditing, and restricting accounting firm employees involved in auditing from leaving the auditing firm to go to work for an audit client.

Financial Reporting

The SOX Act makes key corporate officers more accountable for financial reporting by requiring that chief executive officers and chief financial officers personally certify the accuracy of all required SEC filings. These two corporate officers must also ensure that the certification is based on reliable and accurate information through the maintenance of internal financial fraud-detection controls that are subject to review by outside auditors. The SOX Act regulations set standardized financial reporting formats and restricts certain types of accounting methods that are not transparent to auditors such as using special off-shore tax entities to hold corporate assets.

Corporate Governance

The SOX Act requires that public companies maintain audit committees composed entirely of independent directors and the committee must contain at least one director with sufficient

---

[10]From 1990–1997, the number of publicly held corporations that misreported their revenue and had to restate earnings averaged 49 per year. In 2002, 330 corporations restated earnings.

financial acumen to probe audits in depth. Audit committees have substantial regulatory obligations under the SOX Act. These obligations include: (1) authority to engage, monitor, and terminate the company's outside auditing firm; (2) implementing a system of controls that involves a comprehensive examination of the audit reports and methods used by the company and outside auditors to properly report information that truly reflects the financial condition of the company; and (3) establishing a structure that facilitates communication directly between the audit committee and the auditors (not using corporate officers as a go-between).

The SOX Act also requires public companies to establish a code of ethics and conduct for its top financial officers as well as prohibiting certain practices such as a public corporation lending money to its officers and directors (with some narrow exceptions). In addition, officers and directors are obligated to disclose their own buying and selling of company stock within a certain time frame. To prevent the secret looting of a company by its officers, executive performance bonuses are required to be retroactively forfeited back (known as a *clawback provision*) to the company if the bonuses were tied to any financial reports that were later deemed false or issued without appropriate controls.

Enforcement under SOX

The SOX Act also greatly expanded the scope and methods of enforcing securities law. The SEC's jurisdiction, enforcement alternatives, and enforcement budget were substantially increased by the SOX Act.

Emergency Escrow   Recognizing that many of the remedies in the SOX Act are largely useless if the corporation's assets have been looted by insiders engaged in fraud, the law specifically gives the SEC the authority to intervene in any extraordinary payments made by a company that may be the subject of an SEC investigation. Upon approval by a federal court, the SOX Act allows the SEC to force any extraordinary corporate payouts into a government-controlled emergency escrow fund that is held pending further investigation by authorities. This is a powerful weapon in the SEC's enforcement arsenal because the SOX Act does not require any formal allegation of wrongdoing as a prerequisite for intervening in an extraordinary payment. For example, in a 2005 case, *SEC v. Gemstar-TV Guide International, Inc.,*[11] a federal appeals court held that the SEC was reasonable in intervening when a corporation's board of directors authorized multibillion dollar payments to its executives who were resigning under fire after the company had to revise its past earnings statements sharply downward. The court held that the payments to two executives, totaling $37 million, constituted an extraordinary payment and triggered the SEC's right to intervene and the court's right to approve the SEC's request for an emergency escrow. The court pointed out that, although the SEC had not launched a formal investigation, the substantial revision of earnings statements coupled with the fact that insiders were departing the company in wake of the scandal was sufficient to give the SEC intervention rights under the SOX Act.

Substantial Penalties   Violators of the SOX Act are subject to both civil penalties and criminal prosecution. For example, officers who certify required financial report filing knowing that the report is either inaccurate or knowing that the report was not subject to required controls before the certification are subject to criminal penalties of up to

---

[11]401 F.3d 1031 (9th Cir. 2005).

$1 million in fines and 10 years of incarceration. For cases in which the certification was used as part of a larger fraudulent scheme, the penalties increase to $5 million in fines and 20 years of incarceration. The SOX Act also specifically directs the U.S. Sentencing Commission to amend sentencing guidelines to provide for harsher penalties for those convicted of securities fraud statutes.

Whistle-blowers[12]   Parties that communicate information relating to any illegal conduct in financial reporting or corporate governance are protected against any retaliation by the company. Audit committees must have a structure in place to process and investigate any whistle-blower complaints and any party that engages in retaliation is subject to civil action and federal criminal prosecution.

Document Destruction Rules   The SOX Act creates new provisions to punish the destruction of evidence that might be relevant to the investigation of any violation of federal securities laws. Anyone who alters, destroys, or conceals relevant documents is subject to up to 20 years of incarceration. The law applies universally to any party who has control over the documents and covers any actions performed either before, during, or after any formal investigation is commenced.

Conspiracy to Commit Fraud   The definition of securities fraud was expanded by the SOX Act, and the creation of a new federal criminal law outlawing *conspiracy* to commit fraud has made pursuing criminal fraud charges against officers and directors substantially easier for government prosecutors. The law also extended the statute of limitations for civil lawsuits to be filed by defrauded investors attempting to recover lost money.

CONCEPT SUMMARY   Sarbanes-Oxley Act (SOX Act) of 2002

- The SOX Act imposes regulations on publicly held corporations in broad areas: auditing, financial reporting, and corporate governance.
- The PCAOB is the body created by the SOX Act as an oversight board for firms performing audits of public companies.
- Certain corporate officers are responsible for certifying the accuracy and completeness of financial reports and disclosures.
- The SOX Act requires a public corporation to form an audit committee, prescribes the composition of the committee, and imposes substantial responsibility on the committee to prevent and detect fraud.
- Enforcement provisions of the SOX Act include (1) establishment of an emergency escrow fund when the SEC intervenes into an extraordinary payment made by a company until further investigation is conducted; (2) enhanced criminal penalties for violations, especially for destruction of documents; (3) protection of whistle-blowers; and (4) expanding the definition of securities fraud by outlawing any conspiracy to commit fraud.

Troubled Assets Relief Program (TARP)

As the financial crisis that began in 2008 unfolded, increasing fears of a disastrous global financial meltdown and substantial public pressure caused Congress to provide direct loans to corporations most acutely impacted by the crisis. These loans were intended primarily

---

[12]*Whistle-blower,* a term used to describe an employee or agent who reports some legal misconduct or statutory violation to the authorities, is discussed in detail in Chapter 10, "Agency and Employment Relationships."

for large corporations in the financial services and insurance sectors (such as Citigroup and AIG), but federal loans were also extended to companies in other troubled industries such as auto manufacturers.[13] However, as a condition of the loan, recipients were required to abide by corporate governance and executive compensation mandates. The loan program and its mandates were created in the **American Recovery and Reinvestment Act of 2009**,[14] which established the **Troubled Assets Relief Program (TARP)** to administer the loans. In general, TARP loan recipients agreed to (1) impose restrictions on compensation (including bonuses) of officers, (2) form an independent compensation committee, and (3) give shareholders more say on compensation of officers and directors. The TARP provisions empower the Department of the Treasury to recover any bonuses paid that are inconsistent with the law's requirements.

Compensation   In general, the company's compensation plan for senior executive officers cannot encourage manipulation of the reported earnings of a TARP recipient in order to enhance the compensation of the officers (such as tying salary level to corporate earnings). Senior executive officers are defined by the statute based on the amount of TARP money received by their company. Table 16.4 sets out the standards for which executives are covered by the compensation mandates.

TARP recipients are restricted from paying or allowing the accrual of bonus, retention, or incentive pay for senior executives during the time when the recipient still owes any balance to the TARP fund. The law also bans golden parachute payments whereby a corporation pays a senior executive a certain sum in exchange for her departure from the company.

Corporate Governance   TARP recipients must establish a compensation committee within its board of directors that is composed entirely of independent directors (similar to the SOX Act audit committee requirement). The committee is responsible for evaluating executive compensation plans to be sure they are consistent with TARP regulations. Any compensation that is paid to senior executives of TARP recipients that is outside the regulatory requirements of the law are subject to a clawback provision that allows the U.S. Department of the Treasury to recoup the money. The chief executive officer and chief financial officer of a TARP recipient must provide written certifications of compliance by the company with the executive compensation standards.

TABLE 16.4	Senior Executives as Defined by TARP

TARP Funds Received	Definition of Senior Executives
$25 million or less	Highest paid employee only.
$25 million to $250 million	Five highest paid employees.
$250 million to $500 million	Chief executive officer, chief financial officer, three highest paid officers, and the next ten highest paid employees.
More than $500 million	Chief executive officer, chief financial officer, three highest paid officers, and the next twenty highest paid employees.

---

[13]These loans were dubbed by the media as "bailouts."

[14]Pub. L. No. 111-5, 123 Stat. 115 (2009).

The law also requires that TARP recipients hold a shareholder vote on the approval of any compensation plan recommended by the compensation committee. However, the shareholder vote is purely *advisory*. The vote is *not* binding on the company and the law makes clear that compensation plan approval is a board decision that cannot be overruled by a shareholder vote. Nor may shareholders claim that failing to follow a shareholders' vote constitutes a breach of the directors' fiduciary duty.

Luxury Expenditures   The board of directors of any TARP recipient must implement a companywide policy regarding excessive or luxury expenditures, including entertainment of customers, posh office or facility renovations, and private aviation or luxury transportation. The Department of the Treasury is required to issue regulations that specify what constitutes a luxury expense, but the law generally prohibits TARP recipients from paying for any activity or event that is not reasonably connected to business operations.

Repayment of TARP Funds   The restrictions imposed by virtue of receiving TARP funds have led several recipients to repay the funds as soon as possible. TARP recipients are required to apply for release from the program after showing that their assets are sufficient to continue operations and lending programs. Within five months of the TARP law executive compensation mandates, approximately 34 banks were approved to pay back the TARP funds. By May 2009, investment banking firm JPMorgan Chase paid back $25 billion while Capital One Financial repaid a $3.6 billion TARP loan. In April 2010, both Citigroup and General Motors announced that they would be paying back their loans well ahead of schedule.

Financial Market Regulation

Companies that do business in the financial markets are regulated by a complex structure of federal regulatory schemes that are enforced through a variety of administrative agencies and regulatory bodies. The Securities and Exchange Commission, the Federal Reserve, the Office of the Comptroller of the Currency, and the Federal Trade Commission all have some degree of jurisdiction over various aspects of transactions in the global financial markets. The regulated financial transactions include commercial and consumer loans, investments, credit, insurance, and commodities exchange.

Regulator Shopping   As the financial crisis that began in 2008 became more serious, lawmakers became concerned that the complexity of the regulatory scheme for financial markets was contributing to undetected fraud and extreme risks by financial institutions. Moreover, it had become apparent that the patchwork of administrative agency and regulatory body jurisdiction enabled companies to hide losses and conceal fraudulent activity. The system even allowed for *regulator shopping* in certain sectors of the financial markets. For example, when mortgage company giant Countrywide Financial Corporation started its subprime mortgage program in 1996 it was jointly regulated by the Federal Reserve and the Office of the Comptroller of the Currency. Countrywide's subprime mortgage program allowed home buyers with a relatively low credit score the opportunity to qualify for a mortgage by paying a higher interest rate and paying a monthly premium to insure the loan in the case of a default. The program also featured "teaser rates" that made the initial payments artificially low, but substantially larger payments were required as the loan's interest rate increased after each reset period (typically one to five years after the loan was made). Defaults on these teaser rate loans are widely cited as a significant contributing factor to the financial crisis and the deepening of the 2008–2010 recession. Although Countrywide was the leading lender of subprime mortgages, similar practices were widespread in the lending industry at that time. When Countrywide's senior executives became frustrated with regulatory authorities that were pressuring Countrywide to reexamine its risk level for subprime loans, Countrywide's management decided to convert its corporate organizational structure in 2007 so that it could now fall under the jurisdiction of the Office of Thrift Supervision (OTS). The OTS was widely regarded in the industry as a weaker regulator that took a hands-off approach to questions on risk standards enforcement.[15] As subprime loan payments adjusted upward and the economy worsened, cash-strapped borrowers began defaulting on their mortgages in record proportions. When credit markets tightened in 2008, Countrywide quickly became insolvent and unable to fund its operations. Facing bankruptcy, the once mighty lender and market share leader in mortgage loans was forced to sell its assets to Bank of America at less than a quarter of its previous market value. It was reported in the financial press that the OTS had ignored warning signs about Countrywide's risky practices and gave far too much deference to the company's aggressive accounting practices. Several Countrywide executives, including its founder Angelo Mozilo, were charged with fraud and insider trading and other top-level employees are the subjects of a continuing federal investigation. In 2010, Congress eliminated the OTS and transferred its functions to other agencies.

Recent Regulatory Reform of Financial Markets

In 2010, at the urging of the Obama administration and chief government regulators, Congress passed a new law with sweeping reforms of the financial regulatory system intending to address the systemic failure of previous regulatory systems and agencies to detect or prevent a recurrence of the financial crisis that began in 2008 and sent global financial markets reeling. The law, named the **Wall Street Reform and Consumer Protection Act,** overhauled the regulation of U.S. financial services and markets.

Financial Stability Oversight Council   The law created a new independent body with a board of regulators to address dangerous risks to the global financial markets posed by risky investments or actions of large financial institutions. The Financial Stability Oversight Council also has the power to break up companies deemed to pose a threat to the nation's financial stability even if those companies are not insolvent. The Council is composed of nine members, eight of whom already direct various agencies involved in the financial system (e.g., the Chairman of the Federal Reserve), and one member who is independent. The Council also has the power to compel the Federal Reserve to assume an oversight position of certain institutions that pose global risks to the financial markets. These institutions have been dubbed by commentators as "too big to fail" and were a central issue in the financial crisis that began in 2008.

Bureau of Consumer Financial Protection   The law also created a federal administrative agency called the Bureau of Consumer Financial Protection with direct oversight of companies providing mortgages, credit cards, savings accounts, and annuities. The bureau also has the authority to write new regulations that add additional layers of protection for consumers regarding disclosures, fees, and restrictions on certain lending practices.

> **web**check **www.mhhe.com/melvin**
> For an update on the Wall Street Reform and Consumer Protection Act and other regulatory reforms of the financial markets, check this textbook's Web site.

Other Provisions   The law also (1) gives shareholders greater power to limit executive officer compensation, (2) increased the authority and budget of the SEC for more enhanced oversight of sophisticated investment vehicles such as hedge funds and derivatives, (3) increased the power and oversight jurisdiction of the Federal Reserve, and (4) created an Office of National Insurance.

---

[15]The OTS was also the regulatory authority that failed to prevent numerous institutions under its authority from failing, including Washington Mutual Bank.

Securities law p. 406   The body of federal and state laws governing the issuance and trading of equity and debt instruments to public investors.

Equity p. 409   Ownership interest in a corporation where financial return on the investment is based primarily on the performance of the venture.

Debt p. 409   A common tool for raising capital including promissory notes, bonds, and debentures that represent a fixed rate of return regardless of the profitability of the corporation with repayment expected after a certain period of years. Debt is senior in priority to equity instruments.

Common stock (common shares) p. 409   A form of equity instrument in which the equity owner is entitled to payments based on the current profitability of the company.

Preferred stock p. 410   A form of equity instrument that has less risk than common stock because it has certain quasi-debt features and whose holders have preference rights over common stockholders in receiving dividends from the corporation.

Disclosure p. 411   The underlying premise of all securities regulation in which companies are to release all information, positive or negative, that might bear on an investment decision, as required by the Securities and Exchange Commission to protect investors and assure public confidence in the integrity of the securities market.

Securities and Exchange Commission (SEC) p. 411   The independent federal administrative agency charged with rulemaking, enforcement, and adjudication of federal securities laws.

Securities Act of 1933 p. 413   The act that covers the process of issuing or reissuing securities to the public. The law requires registration and certain disclosures and authorizes the Securities and Exchange Commission to oversee the transactions.

Prospectus p. 413   The first part of the registration statement of a security prescribed by Securities and Exchange Commission regulations, which is intended to give investors a realistic view of the issuer's business, risk factors, financial position, financial statements, and disclosures concerning directors, officers, and controlling shareholders.

Exemptions p. 414   Types of securities or transactions that an issuer may use to sell a security that are not subject to certain Securities and Exchange Commission regulations pertaining to registering securities, in order to assist business ventures seeking smaller amounts of capital from the public investment community.

Regulation D p. 415   A securities law provision exempting an issuer from registration where the issuer is selling the security for limited offers of a relatively small amount of money or offers made in a limited manner.

Private placement p. 415   A securities law provision exempting an issuer from registration where the issuer only accepts investments from those who meet the standards for accredited investors.

Securities Act of 1934 p. 416   The act that regulates the sale of securities between investors after an investor purchased it from a business entity issuer.

Insider trading p. 417   When a corporate insider has access to certain information not available to the general investor public and the insider trades in their company's stock on the basis of the inside information.

Insider Trading and Securities Fraud Enforcement Act p. 417   Passed by Congress in 1988 to raise the criminal and civil penalties for insider trading, increase the liability of brokerage firms for wrongful acts of their employees, and give the Securities and Exchange Commission more power to pursue violations of insider trading.

Section 16 p. 417   Provision of the Securities Act of 1934 that imposes restrictions and reporting requirements on ownership positions and stock trades made by certain corporate insiders named in the statute.

Private Securities Litigation Reform Act of 1995 (PSLRA) p. 421   A law intended to protect publicly held companies from frivolous litigation by making it more difficult to pursue litigation under the securities laws based solely on commentary by the company executives.

Scienter p. 421   Evidence of specific intent to deceive, manipulate, or defraud.

Securities Litigation Uniform Standards Act of 1998 p. 422   An amendment to the Securities Act of 1934, intended to prevent a private party from instituting certain lawsuits in federal or state court based on the statutory or common law of any state that punishes "a misrepresentation or omission of a material fact" or the use of "any manipulative device or contrivance" concerning the purchase or sale of a covered security.

Blue-sky laws p. 423   State securities laws intended to cover purely intrastate securities offerings.

Corporate governance p. 423   The procedure and system used by the officers and directors to establish lines of responsibility, approval, and oversight among key stakeholders, and set out rules for making corporate decisions.

Sarbanes-Oxley Act (SOX Act) of 2002 p. 423 Amendments to the '33 and '34 Securities Acts intended to impose stricter regulation and controls on how corporations do business, through regulation of auditing, financial reporting, and internal corporate governance.

American Recovery and Reinvestment Act of 2009 p. 427 Created a loan program and underlying mandates for corporations most acutely impacted

by the financial crisis beginning in 1998 and established the Troubled Assets Relief Program (TARP) to administer the loans.

Troubled Assets Relief Program (TARP) p. 427 A program established by the American Recovery and Reinvestment Act of 2009 to purchase assets and equity from financial institutions to strengthen the U.S. financial sector.

Wall Street Reform and Consumer Protection Act p. 429 Recent legislation to overhaul the regulation of U.S. financial services and markets.

THEORY TO PRACTICE

Four individuals are the collective owners, directors, and shareholders ("principals") of Cool Runnings Manufacturing Company (CRMC), which designs and manufactures snow sports equipment such as snowboards, racing skis, and related products. The principals built the company over a 10-year period from start-up to over $20 million in annual revenue. Six months ago, the principals met and decided to embark on an aggressive expansion plan with the objective of doubling CRMC's production capacity in five years.

This plan required approximately $50 million to fund the purchase of real estate, equipment, expanded payroll, additional taxes, and marketing expenses. One reason for this expansion plan is to develop a new snowboard product, the Tectonic Board, which early marketing research indicated would become one of CRMC's best-selling products. The principals were under pressure to develop this new product because of an overall slump in sales. However, given their current facilities and budget, the product was currently only halfway through the design phase and not expected on the market for at least three more years. The demand for their existing brands of snowboards was slowly, but steadily, declining. In fact, the company's profits had been so stagnant that it could not reasonably afford to borrow the entire amount of the expansion cost given their recently diminishing cash flow. However, because of the development of the Tectonic Board, the principals are hopeful that they can attract capital by selling stock to investors.

1. What are the alternatives for financing this expansion plan? Should CRMC consider a bond? Why or why not? Would selling equity be more or less advantageous than issuing a bond?

2. Assume that the principals decide to issue stock to the public in order to raise money. They know of five investors that may be interested in this opportunity,

so they send a copy of the business plan for CRMC's expansion along with a cover letter explaining the price of the stock and giving instructions on how to buy the stock. Has CRMC committed a violation of securities laws by sending out the business plans and cover letters? Could that constitute the sale of a security?

3. Suppose that instead of sending the business plan as in Question 2 above, the principals consulted counsel and informed her that they wish to develop a prospectus and distribute it to a limited number of high net worth investors. Must these securities be registered before marketing or selling them? If not, what exemption(s) could they fall into?

Assume that the principals proceed as in Question 3 above and send the plan to 15 high net worth potential investors. During face-to-face and videoconference meetings with the investors, the CEO made the following statements in response to investor questions:

Question: Is CRMC's financial position currently sound or are there threats to your financial well-being?

CEO: CRMC's cash flow is expected to increase steadily because the Tectonic Board is the board for a new generation of boarders. Our research shows that it has potential to bring us a sizable return on our investment.

Question: What stage of development is the Tectonic Board in?

CEO: If all goes well, it will be on store shelves in less than one year.

Question: Is there a current demand for your existing snowboard products?

CEO: We have had very strong sales. However, like every product, it has its ups and downs. It's likely to be on the upside shortly.

4. Based on these statements, one investor purchases a substantial amount of stock. If the business venture fails before the Tectonic is released, will the investor have any recourse against CRMC and its CEO based on the statements made by the CEO (above)? Why or why not?

5. If an investor files a fraud suit against CRMC and its CEO, would the statements alone be sufficient to pass the PSLRA standards for scienter?

6. Do any of the statements themselves constitute the required elements under PSLRA? What type of conduct, if coupled with the statements, could meet the scienter standard?

MANAGER'S CHALLENGE

From the facts in Theory to Practice above, one can see the potential complications and hazards of selling equity as a form of raising capital. Assume that the principals approach you as their senior manager and ask that you devise a potential plan to raise money without actually issuing securities. Individually, or in a small group, draft an "Opportunity Plan" that describes a process by which CRMC could raise money without being subject to securities laws. The effectiveness of your Opportunity Plan will depend on your knowledge of the *Howey* test to be sure that the opportunity does not qualify as a security that is subject to registration. A sample answer may be found on this textbook's Web site at www.mhhe.com/melvin.

CASE SUMMARY 16.1 :: Nursing Home Pension Fund v. Oracle Corp., 380 F.3d 1226 (9th Cir. 2004)

SCIENTER

Software giant Oracle released their newest product, the 11i Suite, in 2000. The company issued press releases and disseminated other information to the public that touted the software as a significant achievement that would enhance its revenue. Over the next 12 months, executive management continued making overly optimistic forecasts about the software and earnings. During that same time period, Oracle's CEO Larry Ellison sold nearly $1 billion worth of his personal stock in Oracle. Shortly after Ellison's sale was completed, Oracle released negative news about earnings and it became obvious that the 11i Suite sales were substantially below expectations and the stock price dropped sharply.

CASE QUESTIONS

1. Does the timing of the insider sale and the release of the negative earnings statement constitute sufficient scienter to clear the PSLRA's scienter hurdle?

2. Who prevails and why?

CASE SUMMARY 16.2 :: In re the Vantive Corporation Securities Litigation, 110 F. Supp. 2d 1209 (N.D. Ca. 2000)

MATERIAL MISSTATEMENTS

Vantive is a manufacturer of client management software designed for use by sales representatives from various industries. Vantive is also a retailer and provides support services for the software. After a successful public offering in 1995, the company's stock sold for $6 per share and soon rose to as high as $35 per share. When the tech sector slumped in 1998, the stock dropped to less than $15 per share over an eight-month period. During this eight-month period, management forecasted strong gains in income by using a model that recognized millions of dollars in revenue based on software licenses that would *not* actually be realized unless the licensees were successful in selling *sublicenses* for the software. A group of shareholders brought suit under 10(b)(5).

CASE QUESTIONS

1. Were the forecasts sufficient to constitute a material misstatement of fact and an omission that violated securities laws? Explain.

2. Is Vantive protected by the PSLRA?

EXEMPT SECURITIES

FSC was a securities brokerage firm that sold limited partnership interests to Mark and 27 other investors. All investors executed a *subscription agreement* where each investor revealed his income, represented that he/she had the opportunity to review relevant information including risk factors, and that they were sufficiently knowledgeable and savvy to understand the implications of the investment. However, FSC managers never actually reviewed the completed subscription agreements, and all who applied to be investors were admitted. When the interests dropped in value, Mark sued to rescind the contract on the basis that the securities were not registered and that he was not a qualified investor. FSC defended that the offering qualified under the '33 Act safe-harbor provision of Regulation D.

CASE QUESTIONS

1. Should Mark prevail?
2. Is it relevant that FSC never reviewed the subscription agreement?

GOOD FAITH IN PSLRA

Fleming is a publicly held company involved in litigation with another company over a trade dispute. During the litigation, the officers of Fleming disclosed the litigation and the relevant factual basis for the litigation in its SEC–required disclosure materials. The litigation resulted in a $200 million jury verdict against Fleming, causing Fleming's stock to drop precipitously. After an appellate court reversed part of the verdict and Fleming settled the case for $20 million, the stock regained some of its previous value, but never returned to its prelitigation levels. A group of shareholders sued Fleming's officers and directors claiming that the disclosure of litigation was not detailed enough and did not disclose the potential downside risks of a losing jury verdict and, thus, constituted a misleading statement and omissions in violation of the 1934 Securities Act. Fleming's officers defended that they disclosed all known facts of the litigation and were protected by the Private Securities Litigation Reform Act safe-harbor provisions because they acted in good faith and disclosed all the facts they were privy to at the time.

CASE QUESTIONS

1. Who prevails and why?
2. Should Fleming's officers be protected by the PLSRA?

 Self-Check **ANSWERS**

Howey Test

1. This question is based on *Smith v. Gross*, 604 F.2d 639 (9th Cir. 1979), where the court decided that the earthworm scheme did constitute a securities offering. It fit all elements of the *Howey* test and had vertical commonality where the investor profited from the work of the promoter.

2. Careful! This question first appears to be a replica of the *Howey* case's facts, but there are substantial differences in the investment opportunities. Utley's plan would likely *not* constitute offering a security. He is offering developing and real estate services, but that was not a requirement for purchasing the property. Owners of the property may simply be purchasing it for their own vacation use and not as an investment with expectations of return. Utley's services did not have the required commonality, nor did investors necessarily benefit from Utley's efforts.

3. This question is based on *SEC v. Alliance Lease Corp.*, 2000 LEXIS 5227 (S.D. Cal. 2000), in which the court held that Alliance's leasing plan was a securities offering under the *Howey* standards. The investment opportunity had both vertical and horizontal commonality, and the investors profited primarily due to the efforts of Alliance in arranging the leases.

UNIT **FIVE**

Regulatory Environment of Business

17

CHAPTER

Administrative Law

learning outcomes checklist

After studying this chapter, students who have mastered the material will be able to:

17-1 Explain the purpose of administrative law.

17-2 List and articulate the primary functions of an administrative agency.

17-3 Give examples of several administrative agencies that regulate business.

17-4 Identify the primary sources of law that provide authority and set limits for administrative agencies.

17-5 Discuss how the Administrative Procedures Act (APA) and enabling statutes interrelate to provide an agency with its jurisdiction and scope of authority.

17-6 Identify and explain the steps used in administrative rulemaking.

17-7 Define the powers of administrative agencies in the areas of licensing, inspection, and adjudication.

17-8 Describe the limits on agency powers imposed by the legislative, executive, and judicial branches of the government.

17-9 Name two federal public disclosure statutes and describe how these statutes make administrative agencies more accountable to the public.

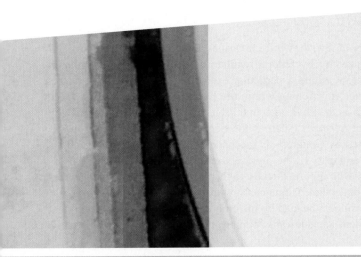

M uch of the law's reach over business occurs through federal and state agencies that create regulations based on legislatively set policy objectives, and then administer the policies through monitoring and enforcement actions. The various laws that prescribe or regulate this process are known *administrative laws.* The regulations are created and carried out by *administrative agencies,* and business owners and managers encounter these agencies at various levels. Although these agencies have broad powers, they are still limited by the Constitution, statutes, and judicial review. In this chapter, students will learn:

- The definition and role of administrative law in the U.S. legal system.
- The functions, scope, and limits on powers of administrative agencies.
- Ways in which administrative agencies are accountable to the public.
- The role of state administrative law.

LO17-1 DEFINITION, FUNCTION, AND SOURCES OF ADMINISTRATIVE LAW

Administrative law is a body of law, drawn from various sources, that defines, regulates and limits the exercise of authority by federal regulatory agencies. Federal regulatory agencies are bodies that function within a particular executive branch *department* (such as the Internal Revenue Service functioning within the Department of the Treasury) and *nondepartment* agencies (such as the Environmental Protection Agency). The federal government also has *independent agencies* (such as the Securities and Exchange Commission) that have been designated by Congress as independent of the executive branch and do not exist by virtue of the authority of the president or a department. Departments are headed by a *cabinet secretary* who reports directly to the president. Department agencies, nondepartment agencies, and independent agencies are headed by either *administrators* or they are composed of *commissioners* headed by the commission chair. These department, nondepartment, and independent agencies are collectively referred to as **administrative agencies.**

LO17-2, 17-3 Primary Functions of Administrative Agencies

Administrative agencies have a wide range of functions related to the formation, implementation, and enforcement of regulations intended to administer a federal law. Although the agencies are primarily thought of as a part of the executive branch and, therefore, exercise *executive powers* to enforce federal laws related to a particular agency's jurisdictional expertise, they also exercise important *legislative* and *judicial* functions as well.

Policymaking

One of the most important functions of an administrative agency is its responsibility to make policy that is consistent with implementation of federal law. When Congress passes a piece of legislation, it is often crafted in broad strokes that may include findings of fact and/or objectives of the law. However, the practical aspects of implementing the laws often require more complex and detailed policies. Administrative agencies are frequently charged by Congress to study potential solutions to a problem and then to exercise a legislative function by creating legally enforceable rules, known as *administrative regulations,* that purport to satisfy Congress's will by filling in the details of the statute. This policymaking function is known as **rulemaking.**

Administrative agencies also use a system of adjudicatory bodies established within the administrative agency to decide cases that involve an alleged violation of the agency's rules. These adjudicatory bodies are staffed with administrative law judges who are actually employees of that particular regulatory body. This judicial function is known as **adjudication.**

The rulemaking and adjudication powers and processes are discussed in detail later in the chapter.

Investigation and Enforcement

Many administrative agencies also have an agency enforcement division devoted to investigating alleged violations of the agency's administrative regulations and recommending enforcement actions such as fines and other sanctions. Agencies have a wide range of discretion as to when and how they enforce regulations against a violator. Administrative agencies also monitor compliance with regulatory requirements through inspection of facilities and grounds of business sites under their jurisdiction.

Licensing and Permitting

Some administrative agencies also are responsible for licensing and permitting in a wide variety of areas, including licenses for professionals and industries. Examples include the Securities and Exchange Commission issuing licenses to certain individuals involved in public trading of stocks, or the Federal Communications Commission's licensing of television and radio stations. Agencies also issue permits such as those issued by the Environmental Protection Agency to control air and water pollution.

Distribution of Federal Statutory Benefits to the Public When Congress confers a benefit to the citizenry at large, administrative agencies are the portal used by the law to actually distribute those benefits. Agencies are involved in the application process and distribute benefits according to law. These benefits include loan guarantees for students, medical care for the poor and elderly, compensation for workers laid off by their employers, and many other federal programs. For example, the Social Security Administration is responsible for distributing retirement and medical benefits to eligible citizens.

Figure 17.1 is an organizational chart that shows the major federal administrative agencies.

Sources of Administrative Law

LO17-4

Administrative law is not thought of as a *separate* body of statutes that govern administrative agencies. Rather, administrative law is a combination of four distinct sources of law that operate in tandem.

U.S. Constitution The U.S. Constitution places limits on the type of powers that agencies may exercise and also places limits on the methods that agencies may employ in carrying out their duties. Examples of provisions of the Constitution that limit agency powers include the Due Process clause, doctrines derived from the principle of separation of powers including the nondelegation doctrine, and the Fourth Amendment protections against certain warrantless searches by agency personnel.

Administrative Procedures Act (APA) The Administrative Procedures Act (APA)[1] of 1946 is a federal statute that imposes specific procedural structures and due process requirements on administrative agencies' duties of rulemaking, adjudication, and other agency functions. The APA also provides for judicial review of agency actions and determinations.

Enabling Statutes Congress will sometimes choose to create a new administrative agency to carry out the details of macro objectives set by the law. When Congress wishes to establish an administrative agency, it passes a federal law called an **enabling statute.** Enabling statutes are important because they are the source of an agency's authority and establish the agency's scope and jurisdiction over certain matters. For example, in 1970 Congress passed the Occupation Safety and Health Act,[2] which established the Occupational Safety and Health Administration (OSHA), and set this agency's mission as *prevention* of workplace injuries and providing employees with safe working conditions. The enabling act portion of the law placed OSHA under the authority of the Department of Labor and provided for jurisdiction necessary to study and develop workplace safety regulations as well as the agency's authority to investigate, enforce, and adjudicate matters involving those regulations. Enabling acts are also used by Congress to *charge* an agency with certain additional responsibilities or when providing additional authority for the agency in a particular area of need.

> **KEY POINT**
> *Administrative law* is a combination of several different sources of law. The primary sources are the Constitution, the Administrative Procedures Act (APA), and enabling statutes. Common law also plays a minor role.

---

[1] 5 U.S.C. §§ 551–706.

[2] 29 U.S.C, §§ 651–678.

FIGURE 17.1 Administrative Agencies in the Context of the U.S. Government Organizational Chart

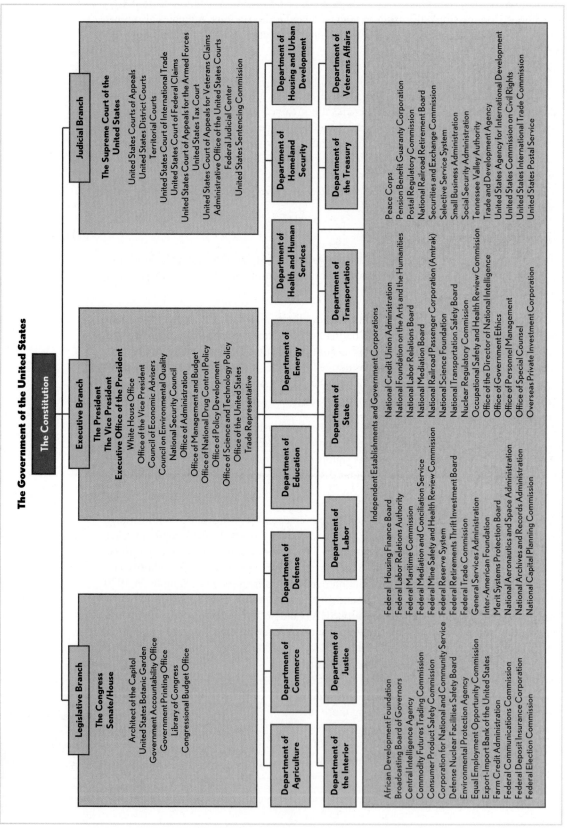

The Government of the United States

The Constitution

Legislative Branch

The Congress Senate/House

Architect of the Capitol
United States Botanic Garden
Government Accountability Office
Government Printing Office
Library of Congress
Congressional Budget Office

Executive Branch

The President
The Vice President
Executive Office of the President

White House Office
Office of the Vice President
Council of Economic Advisers
Council on Environmental Quality
National Security Council
Office of Administration
Office of Management and Budget
Office of National Drug Control Policy
Office of Policy Development
Office of Science and Technology Policy
Office of the United States
Trade Representative

Judicial Branch

The Supreme Court of the United States

United States Courts of Appeals
United States District Courts
Territorial Courts
United States Court of International Trade
United States Court of Federal Claims
United States Court of Appeals for the Armed Forces
United States Tax Court
United States Court of Appeals for Veterans Claims
Administrative Office of the United States Courts
Federal Judicial Center
United States Sentencing Commission

Department of Agriculture
Department of Commerce
Department of Defense
Department of Education
Department of Energy
Department of Health and Human Services
Department of Homeland Security
Department of Housing and Urban Development

Department of the Interior
Department of Justice
Department of Labor
Department of State
Department of Transportation
Department of the Treasury
Department of Veterans Affairs

Independent Establishments and Government Corporations

African Development Foundation
Broadcasting Board of Governors
Central Intelligence Agency
Commodity Futures Trading Commission
Consumer Product Safety Commission
Corporation for National and Community Service
Defense Nuclear Facilities Safety Board
Environmental Protection Agency
Equal Employment Opportunity Commission
Export-Import Bank of the United States
Farm Credit Administration
Federal Communications Commission
Federal Deposit Insurance Corporation
Federal Election Commission

Federal Housing Finance Board
Federal Labor Relations Authority
Federal Maritime Commission
Federal Mediation and Conciliation Service
Federal Mine Safety and Health Review Commission
Federal Reserve System
Federal Retirement Thrift Investment Board
Federal Trade Commission
General Services Administration
Inter-American Foundation
Merit Systems Protection Board
National Aeronautics and Space Administration
National Archives and Records Administration
National Capital Planning Commission

National Credit Union Administration
National Foundation on the Arts and the Humanities
National Labor Relations Board
National Mediation Board
National Railroad Passenger Corporation (Amtrak)
National Science Foundation
National Transportation Safety Board
Nuclear Regulatory Commission
Occupational Safety and Health Review Commission
Office of the Director of National Intelligence
Office of Government Ethics
Office of Personnel Management
Office of Special Counsel
Overseas Private Investment Corporation

Peace Corps
Pension Benefit Guaranty Corporation
Postal Regulatory Commission
National Railroad Retirement Board
Securities and Exchange Commission
Selective Service System
Small Business Administration
Social Security Administration
Tennessee Valley Authority
Trade and Development Agency
United States Agency for International Development
United States Commission on Civil Rights
United States International Trade Commission
United States Postal Service

Source: http://bensguide.gpo.gov/files/gov_chart.pdf.

Common Law   Prior to the establishment of the APA, a body of common law that regulated administrative agencies existed. While much of the common law has been codified through the APA, courts sometimes still refer to the common law in applying or interpreting the APA.

SCOPE OF ADMINISTRATIVE AGENCY POWER

LO17-5, 17-6

Administrative agencies are often granted broad powers by Congress to accomplish objectives set out in an enabling statute. These powers include policymaking through *rulemaking, enforcement/licensing/inspection,* and *adjudication.*

Rulemaking

Administrative agencies are charged with developing *rules* designed to facilitate the federal government's administration of the law and programs as set down in federal statutes. The rulemaking process is set out in the APA and is supplemented by the enabling statutes passed by Congress. In practice, much of an agency's rulemaking duties are carried out through *informal* rulemaking procedures that are permitted under the basic structure of the APA.[3] Despite its name, informal rulemaking actually involves a procedure set down in the APA that is centered on the concepts of notice, public comment, publication of a final rule, and the opportunity to challenge a rule in court. *Formal* rulemaking is only used when Congress has specifically indicated in the enabling statute that the agency rules must be made "on the record after a hearing." In the case of formal rulemaking, the agency is required to engage in an extensive hearing process outlined in the APA[4] to develop the rules. Formal rulemaking is very cumbersome and rarely used.

Agency Study and Research   Depending on the mandates in the enabling statute, the agency begins to study and research the various alternatives for achieving the goals set by Congress. In some cases, such as in environmental regulation, much of the study

Legal Speak ›))
Codified A common law doctrine that was previously not expressed in a code, but has now been arranged into an ordered, written code is referred to as being *codified.*

Many administrative agencies employ scientists to conduct research and provide data and conclusions to policymakers.

---

[3]APA § 553.

[4]APA §§ 556 and 557.

and research function is performed by government scientists or outside contractor experts who provide data and conclusions to regulatory policymakers in the agency. In addition to scientists, outside experts, and policymakers, regulatory agencies also typically employ a significant number of attorneys who ensure that the rulemaking process is compliant with various sources of administrative law. Agencies may also have separate divisions unrelated to rulemaking for enforcement, licensing, and other functions. These nonrulemaking functions are described later in this chapter.

Legal Speak ›))
Federal Register A daily publication distributed by the federal government (found in major libraries) primarily for announcing proposed agency rules, final agency regulations, and other administrative agency or executive branch announcements such as executive orders.

Notice: Publication of the Proposed Rule   After research and study, the agency drafts a proposed rule that purports to achieve one or more objectives set out in the enabling statute. The APA requires notice of proposed rulemaking to be published in the *Federal Register* and that the notice must include "actual terms, substance and description" of the proposed rule.[5] In theory, this requirement puts parties that have some stake in the rule on notice that the rule will become law unless the regulatory agency is persuaded otherwise or a court challenge is brought.

Agencies are also required to publicly disclose any studies, reports, data, or other pertinent material that the agency relied upon in creating the proposed rule. Figure 17.2 is a sample selection from the *Federal Register* that sets out a proposed rule under the Clean Air Act and seeks public comment.

Public Comment   Once the proposed rule has been published in the *Federal Register*, the agency must then give time for the public to comment. In fact, the APA requires that the affected parties be allowed to participate in the rulemaking through submission of their own research and findings and that the agency make a good faith effort to study anything submitted and to consider the arguments made in the comment period. In cases that impact a particular region of the country, agencies sometimes choose to meet public comment requirements by holding public hearings at strategic times and locations during the comment period. In practice, many of the comments and much of the evidence submitted on proposed rules are generally delivered by representatives from, among others, (1) various factions from business and industry (such as the National Manufacturers Association); (2) professional associations that represent large blocks of constituents (such as the National Association of Realtors); and (3) public advocacy groups (such as the National Resource Defense Council). For example, suppose the Securities and Exchange Commission proposes new rules relating to corporate reporting disclosure requirements for publicly held companies.[6] The SEC would likely expect various groups representing publicly held companies, as well as the executives of the affected companies, to comment urging the SEC to make the requirements the least burdensome possible. On the other hand, the SEC is also likely to receive comments from consumer advocacy and shareholder watchdog groups urging the agency to adopt even stricter disclosure requirements.

Protection of Small Business Owners   The Regulatory Flexibility Act of 1980 (RFA), as amended by the Small Business Regulatory Enforcement Fairness Act of 1996 (SBREFA), requires agencies to ask for and consider regulatory proposals that consider the size of the businesses or other organizations subject to regulation. When a proposed regulation will have a significant economic impact on a substantial number of small businesses, the RFA requires, among other things, that agencies analyze and take into consideration small business concerns. Under the RFA, when an agency issues a rule that will have a significant economic impact on a substantial number of small entities, the agency must

---

[5] APA § 553.

[6] A publicly held company's stock is sold to the general public via a public exchange such as the New York Stock Exchange. These companies are regulated by a variety of federal agencies and are discussed in detail in Chapter 16, "Regulation of Securities, Corporate Governance, and Financial Markets."

Federal Register / Vol. 75, No. 13 / Thursday, January 21, 2010 / Proposed Rules 3423

ENVIRONMENTAL PROTECTION AGENCY

40 CFR Part 55

[EPA–R10–OAR–2009–0799; FRL–9095–7]

Outer Continental Shelf Air Regulations Consistency Update for Alaska

AGENCY: Environmental Protection Agency (EPA).

ACTION: Proposed rule.

SUMMARY: EPA is proposing to include in the regulations the revised applicability dates in the emissions user fees provision in 18 AAC 50.410. Requirements applying to Outer Continental Shelf ("OCS") sources located within 25 miles of States' seaward boundaries must be updated periodically to remain consistent with the requirements of the corresponding onshore area ("COA"), as mandated by section 328(a)(1) of the Clean Air Act ("the Act"). The portion of the OCS air regulations that is being updated pertains to the emission user fee requirements for OCS sources operating off of the State of Alaska. The intended effect of approving the OCS requirements for the State of Alaska is to regulate emissions from OCS sources in a manner consistent with the requirements onshore. The change to the existing requirements discussed below is incorporated by reference into the regulations and is listed in the appendix to the OCS air regulations.

DATES : Written comments must be received on or before February 22, 2010.

ADDRESSES: Submit your comments, identified by Docket ID Number EPA– R10–OAR–2009–0799, by one of the following methods:

A. *Federal eRulemaking Portal: http://www.regulations.gov:* Follow the on-line instructions for submitting comments;

B. *E-Mail: greaves.natasha@epa.gov;*

C. *Mail:* Natasha Greaves, Federal and Delegated Air Programs Unit, U.S. Environmental Protection Agency, Region 10, 1200 Sixth Avenue, Suite 900, Mail Stop: AWT–107, Seattle, WA 98101;

D. *Hand Delivery:* U.S. Environmental Protection Agency, Region 10, Attn: Natasha Greaves (AWT–107), 1200 Sixth Avenue, Seattle, Washington 98101, 9th Floor. Such deliveries are only accepted during normal hours of operation, and special arrangements should be made for deliveries of boxed information.

Please see the direct final rule which is located in the Rules section of this **Federal Register** for detailed instructions on how to submit comments.

FOR FURTHER INFORMATION CONTACT: Natasha Greaves, Federal and Delegated Air Programs Unit, Office of Air, Waste, and Toxics, U.S. Environmental Protection Agency, Region 10,

1200 Sixth Avenue, Suite 900, Mail Stop: AWT–107, Seattle, WA 98101: telephone number: (206) 553–7079; e- mail address: *greaves.natasha@epa.gov.*

SUPPLEMENTARY INFORMATION: Forfurther information, please see the direct final action, of the same title, which is located in the Rules section of this **Federal Register**. EPA is incorporating 18 AAC 50.410 as amended through June 18, 2009 as a direct final rule without prior proposal because EPA views this as noncontroversial and anticipates no adverse comments. A detailed rationale for the approval is set forth in the preamble to the direct final rule. If EPA receives no adverse comments, EPA will not take further action on this proposed rule.If EPA receives adverse comments, EPA will withdraw the direct final rule and it will not take effect. EPA will address all public comments in a subsequent final rule based on this proposed rule. EPA will not institute a second comment period on this action. Any parties interested in commenting on this action should do so at this time. Please note that if we receive adverse comments on an amendment, paragraph, or section of this rule and if that provision may be severed from the remainder of the rule, EPA may adopt as final those provisions of the rule that are not the subject of an adverse comment.

Administrative Requirements

Under the Clean Air Act, the Administrator is required to establish requirements to control air pollution from OCS sources located within 25 miles of States' seaward boundaries that are the same as onshore air control requirements. To comply with this statutory mandate, EPA must incorporate applicable onshore rules into part 55 as they exist onshore. 42 U.S.C. 7627(a)(1); 40 CFR 55.12. Thus, in promulgating OCS consistency updates, EPA's role is to maintain consistency between OCS regulations and the regulations of onshore areas, provided that they meet the criteria of the Clean Air Act. Accordingly, this action simply updates the existing OCS requirements to make them consistent with requirements onshore, without the exercise of policy discretion by EPA. For that reason, this action:

• Is not a "significant regulatory action" subject to review by the Office of Management and Budget under Executive Order 12866 (58 FR 51735, October 4, 1993);

• Is certified as not having a significant economic impact on a substantial number of small entities under the Regulatory Flexibility Act (5 U.S.C. 601 *et seq.*);

• Does not contain any unfunded mandate or significantly or uniquely affect small governments, as described in the Unfunded Mandates Reform Act of 1995 (Pub. L. 104–4);

• Does not have Federalism implications as specified in Executive Order 13132 (64 FR 43255, August 10, 1999);

• Is not an economically significant regulatory action based on health or safety risks subject to Executive Order 13045 (62 FR 19885, April 23, 1997);

• Is not a significant regulatory action subject to Executive Order 13211 (66 FR 28355, May 22, 2001);

• Is not subject to requirements of Section 12(d) of the National Technology Transfer and Advancement Act of 1995 (15 U.S.C. 272 note) because application of those requirements would be inconsistent with the Clean Air Act; and

• Does not provide EPA with the discretionary authority to address, as appropriate, disproportionate human health or environmental effects, using practicable and legally permissible methods, under Executive Order 12898 (59 FR 7629, February 16, 1994).

In addition, this rule does not have tribal implications as specified by Executive Order 13175 (65 FR 67249, November 9, 2000), because it does not have a substantial direct effect on one or more Indian tribes, on the relationship between the Federal Government and Indian tribes, or on the distribution of power and responsibilities between the Federal Government and Indian tribes, nor does it impose substantial direct compliance costs on tribal governments, nor preempt tribal law.

Under the provisions of the Paperwork Reduction Act, 44 U.S.C. 3501*et seq.*, an agency may not conduct or sponsor, and a person is not required to respond to, a collection of information unless it displays a currently valid OMB control number. OMB has approved the information collection requirements contained in 40 CFR part 55 and, by extension, this update to the rules, and has assigned OMB control number 2060–0249. Notice of OMB's approval of EPA Information Collection Request ("ICR") No. 1601.07 was published in the **Federal Register** on February 17, 2009 (74 FR 7432). The approval expires January 31, 2012. As EPA previously indicated (70 FR 65897– 65898 (November 1, 2005)), the annual public reporting and recordkeeping burden for collection of information under 40 CFR part 55 is estimated to average 549 hours per response, using the definition of burden provided in 44 U.S.C. 3502(2).

List of Subjects in 40 CFR Part 55

Environmental protection, Administrative practice and procedures, Air pollution control, Hydrocarbons, Incorporation by reference, Intergovernmental relations, Nitrogen dioxide, Nitrogen oxides, Outer Continental Shelf, Ozone, Particulate matter, Permits, Reporting and recordkeeping requirements, Sulfur oxides.

Dated: December 14, 2009.

Michelle L. Pirzadeh,
Acting Regional Administrator, Region 10.
[FR Doc. 2010–1108 Filed 1–20–10; 8:45 am]
BILLING CODE 6560–50–P

Source: http://edocket.access.gpo.gov/2010/pdf/2010-1943.pdf.

provide small businesses the opportunity to participate in the rulemaking. Providing the opportunity to participate may include soliciting and receiving comments from small businesses. The participation of small businesses helps agencies fulfill their statutory objectives while reducing, as much as possible, the burden on small businesses.

Revision or Final Publication   After the comment period has ended, the agency may either revise the rule or simply publish the final rule in the *Federal Register*. If the agency revises the rule in between the time that it was originally proposed and the time when it was published as final, there is generally *no* legal obligation to provide an additional comment period. As a practical matter, agencies publishing controversial proposed rules may opt for a second comment period, but there is no legal mandate to do so. One exception to this rule is if the agency's revised rule is a *substantial* or *material alteration* of the originally proposed rule. Courts have given agencies broad latitude in publishing a revised final rule *without* an additional comment period so long as the revisions are a *logical outgrowth* of the originally proposed rule. Revisions that stay within the original scope of the proposed rule do not trigger the requirement of second comment period. In Case 17.1, a federal court of appeals applied the logical outgrowth test and the APA to the Internal Revenue Service's decision to revise a proposed rule and publish it as final without an additional comment period.

If the agency's view has not been swayed during the comment period, the agency will publish the proposed rule in the *Federal Register* as final.[7] When publishing the final rule, the APA requires the agency to include "a concise general statement of basis and purpose." This statement is used to meet legal requirements that the decision was based on *reasoned decision making* and not made arbitrarily or capriciously. The agency must also state their conclusions on major issues of fact or policy that were used in its decision making when issuing the final rule. Agencies also typically include an effective date in the final rule as well. Once effective, the rule is called a **regulation** and is published in the Code of Federal Regulations (CFR).

In 1990, Congress passed the Negotiated Rulemaking Act,[8] which provided an alternative to normal rulemaking policies in cases where it was possible that various cooperating parties could ultimately reach an *agreement* on the negotiated proposed rule. The law provides guidelines for administrative agencies to engage in a formal negotiation procedure intended to draft rules that have the support of affected parties even prior to publication. The negotiations are conducted through committees composed of representatives from the agency and parties that have an interest in the rule. However, the act does not relieve the agency of the responsibility to properly publish and establish a comment period for the negotiated proposed rule. Nor does the act require that the agency end up actually publishing the negotiated rule instead of an agency-made rule.

Legal Speak ⟩⟩
Arbitrary and Capricious Failure to exercise honest judgment instead of reasoned consideration of all relevant factors.

Judicial Challenges   After the final rule is published, the APA allows adversely affected parties to challenge the final rule in court.[9] Courts apply the *arbitrary and capricious* standard when reviewing a final rule. That is, in order to pass judicial muster, the evidence must show that the agency made its final decision based on a consideration of relevant factors without any clear errors of judgment and that its process was consistent with the APA procedural requirements. The right to judicial review of final rules is a relatively narrow one and courts give great *deference* to agency authority in the area of rulemaking. Judicial review as a limit on *nonrulemaking* agency action and authority is discussed in the next section.

---

[7]APA § 552(a)(1)(D).

[8]5 U.S.C. §§ 561–570.

[9]APA §§ 701–706.

FACT SUMMARY   The Internal Revenue Service (IRS) proposed a rule concerning the allocation of membership dues paid to nonprofit organizations under which certain nondues revenue was to be treated as taxable revenue. According to the proposed rule, the IRS intended to determine tax liability from this revenue using a seven-factor test. After the comment period, the IRS replaced the seven-factor test with a new allocation method that the IRS considered to be more fair and consistent. The new method carved down the factors used in the original rule and a new *three-factor test* was published as a final rule without any additional comment period.

The American Medical Association (AMA) is a nonprofit corporation that charges its members dues that cover a variety of services. The AMA also publishes several journals from which the AMA derives revenue. Under the IRS's three-factor test for allocation, the AMA's tax liability increased significantly. After the IRS assessed the AMA's tax liability under the three-factor test, the AMA brought a lawsuit claiming that the new three-factor allocation regulation was invalid because the IRS had never given the proper public notice required by the APA when they departed from their original seven-factor test.

SYNOPSIS OF DECISION AND OPINION   The Seventh Circuit Court of Appeals ruled in favor of the IRS, holding that the APA authorizes two types of notice for proposed rules: either a notice that specifies the "terms and substance" of the contemplated regulation, or a notice that merely identifies the "subject and issues involved" in the process. Because this language is used to clearly indicate that the notice need not identify every precise proposal the agency may ultimately adopt, the notice is adequate if it simply apprises interested parties of the issues to be addressed in the rulemaking process.

The court reasoned that the IRS's publication of the original proposed seven-factor rule was not binding on the agency and that the IRS's change in policy was a *logical outgrowth* of the original proposal and not a wholly new approach to the issue of proper allocation standards. In fact, the final three-factor test was contained within the original seven-factor test and, thus, the AMA and all other similarly situated organizations had adequate notice of the pending rule.

WORDS OF THE COURT: Logical Outgrowth Test   "[A] final rule is not invalid for lack of adequate notice if the rule finally adopted is a logical outgrowth of the original proposal. [. . .] [A] rule will be invalidated if no notice was given of an issue addressed by the final rules[,] [. . .] [if the] issue was only addressed in the most general terms in the initial proposal, or where a final rule changes a pre-existing agency practice. While an agency must explain and justify its departures from a proposed rule, it is not straitjacketed into the approach initially suggested on pain of triggering a further round of notice-and-comment. The AMA was given a meaningful opportunity to comment on the IRS's dues allocation rules, and those rules will not be invalidated for lack of proper notice."

Case Questions

1. Under the logical outgrowth test used by the court, would the outcome have been different if the IRS simply published a proposed rule saying that they were going to alter the calculation of membership dues by tax-exempt organizations and did not provide further details or methods? Why or why not?

2. Given the standard used by the court, can you think of an example of a change that would *not* be considered a logical outgrowth provided that the appropriate notice is initially given?

Enforcement, Licensing, and Inspection

LO17-7

In terms of **enforcement,** the U.S. Supreme Court has ruled that agencies have broad discretion in *when* and *whom* to regulate. This authority, known as the agency's *prosecutorial discretion,* has been held as practically unreviewable by the judiciary. While enabling statutes can sometimes narrow the agency's authority, courts are still highly deferential to an agency's decision on when and how to enforce its regulations. Absent a showing that the agency engaged in a patent abuse of discretion in enforcement, parties challenging

CONCEPT SUMMARY   Steps in the Rulemaking Process

1. Enabling statute	Congress passes a statute establishing an agency or charging an agency with new authority.
2. Agency study	Agency-selected experts research and review issues as set forth in the enabling statute.
3. Proposed rule published	Based on agency findings, the proposed rule is articulated and published in the *Federal Register* to give notice to those affected by the rule.
4. Public comment	Parties who have an interest in the rule may respond directly to the agency with comments.
5. Rule revised (if necessary)	Agency reconsiders the rule based on public comments and revises the rule if necessary. If revised, the rule need *not* be published unless it is radically different from the original.
6. Final rule published	Final version of the rule is published in the *Federal Register* and has the full force and effect of law. Becomes part of the Code of Federal Regulations (CFR).
7. Judicial challenges	Individual parties may challenge the rule in court under certain circumstances.

The American Medical Association ultimately failed in its claim that the IRS's rulemaking procedure was flawed.

administrative agency actions have a substantial obstacle to overcome in order to justify judicial interference. Agencies have a separate division (apart from rulemaking) that carries out enforcement responsibilities through the use of investigators and the agency's Office of General Counsel.

Administrative agencies also regulate and administer laws through **licensing.** Agencies are frequently delegated the statutory power to issue, renew, suspend, or revoke a license to conduct a certain business. Once a company is licensed, the agency may impose fines or impose restrictions upon the *licensee* for any violation of agency regulations. One of the more high-profile examples of an agency that regulates through licensing is the Federal Communications Commission (FCC), which issues licenses for use of broadcast frequencies. Administrative agencies at the state level often issue *occupational licenses* and regulate professionals such as attorneys and physicians, as well as occupations such as hair stylists and contractors. State administrative agencies are discussed in more detail later in this section.

Some agencies also monitor compliance with administrative regulations by conducting **inspections** of businesses and individuals within their jurisdiction. Recall from Chapter 2, "Business and the Constitution," that government agents are restricted from engaging in unreasonable searches without a search warrant. Administrative agencies are, of course, covered by that same requirement and ordinarily the agency must secure an *administrative warrant* before government agents may enter and inspect a business to monitor compliance with an administrative regulation. However, certain businesses are classified as *pervasively regulated* and, therefore, the Supreme Court has fashioned an exception to the warrant requirement where the agency is conducting regularly scheduled inspections pursuant to a rule. For example, MillCo. operates several mills that are subject to the hypothetical enabling statute called the Mill Control Act (MCA). The MCA provides that all mills must be maintained in a certain way and the administrative agency that has jurisdiction over the MCA should promulgate rules that include monthly inspections to assure compliance. Any inspections of MillCo.'s facilities pursuant to the rule would generally not require a warrant because MillCo. would qualify as a pervasively regulated business as defined in the MCA.

> **KEY POINT**
> Courts are highly deferential to agency decisions involving how and when an agency enforces a regulation.

Even in cases where courts have held that administrative agencies are required to obtain an administrative warrant to conduct an inspection of a business, the Supreme Court has held that agencies are held to a lower standard of probable cause to obtain the warrant than if the government were obtaining a criminal warrant. In Case 17.2, a federal appeals court considers the difference between an administrative warrant and a criminal warrant.

Also within the agencies' enforcement powers is the right to require businesses subject to the agency's jurisdiction to (1) keep certain records for inspection, (2) turn over relevant documents that may be useful in determining compliance with a particular rule, and (3) request statements or other information from the business's principals or managers.

Adjudication

Many (but not all) administrative agencies also have authority to *adjudicate* matters under their jurisdiction. Adjudication is a hearing where the government and the private party each presents evidence in a quasi-judicial setting. In most agencies, the presiding officer is an **administrative law judge (ALJ)** who is typically an attorney employed by the agency to adjudicate disputes.

Recall from Chapter 2, "Business and the Constitution," that federal adjudicatory powers are constitutionally vested exclusively in federal courts. However, federal courts have permitted agency adjudication when it occurs in the context of public rights disputes (a private party dispute with an agency over the agency's action or inaction) or when two private parties are disputing rights that arise out of an area of the agency's jurisdiction.[10]

Appeals   The losing party in an ALJ case generally has an automatic appeal to the administrative head of the agency who may overturn or affirm the ALJ's ruling. An adverse decision from the agency may also be challenged in a federal trial court. Court challenges are discussed in detail in the next section of this chapter.

---

[10]Some agencies use their adjudication power to actually set policy as an alternative method to their traditional rulemaking authority when they wish to take a particular course of action in a given case. This is a controversial method of making policy, but the U.S. Supreme Court has allowed agencies to use adjudication instead of rulemaking in instances where the adjudication promotes a fundamental fairness. However, the Court made clear that this was a relatively narrow power that may be exercised only when fundamental fairness to the parties requires it.

FACT SUMMARY Compliance officers from the Occupational Safety and Health Administration (OSHA)* arrived at the facilities of Trinity Marine Products (Trinity) to conduct an inspection pursuant to their authority under the Occupational Safety and Health Act. Trinity's managers turned OSHA inspectors away, so OSHA obtained an administrative warrant and returned with federal marshals. After the threat of arrest by the marshals, Trinity officials allowed the search under protest. Trinity later brought an action against OSHA, contending the warrant had been issued without probable cause and that administrative warrants could not be legally executed using force against nonconsenting parties. Trinity argued that refusal by a party to honor an administrative warrant should trigger a contempt of court proceeding to determine the validity of the warrant, but that the government may not use force or arrest to enforce an administrative warrant.

SYNOPSIS OF DECISION AND OPINION The Fifth Circuit Court of Appeals ruled in favor of OSHA reasoning that the standards for probable cause were lower for administrative warrants than for criminal warrants and that federal statutes and case law allowed administrative warrants to be executed using a reasonable degree of force. In this case, the government had shown that it had sufficient information to justify an inspection

and, because Trinity would not honor the warrant, that use of the marshals to gain entry was appropriate and consistent with the statutory intent that allows OSHA to "investigate and inspect without delay."

WORDS OF COURT: Probable Cause for Administrative Warrants "[A]dministrative warrants are distinguishable from traditional criminal warrants in a number of ways. They have, for instance, a different—linguistically idiosyncratic—'probable' cause standard: Probable cause may be based either on specific evidence of an existing violation, as in the traditional criminal context, or on a lesser showing that 'reasonable legislative or administrative standards for conducting an inspection are satisfied with respect to a particular establishment.'"

Case Questions

1. Would Trinity's case against OSHA have been stronger if the inspectors showed up with the marshals and forcibly searched the premises without first attempting to inspect without a warrant? Why or why not?

2. What are some examples of when the probable cause standard for administrative warrants would not be met?

*OSHA is an administrative agency under the auspices of the Department of Labor.

CONCEPT SUMMARY   Scope of Administrative Agency Power

- Administrative agencies have broad powers including rulemaking, enforcement, licensing, and adjudication.
- Agencies develop rules to be used in facilitating the government's administration of the law.
- The rulemaking process involves agency research, publication of a proposed rule in the *Federal Register,* a period for public comment on the proposed rule, and either revising the rule for additional comment or publishing a finalized rule.
- Agencies must use a reasoned decision-making process that was not arbitrary or capricious.
- After a final rule is published, the APA allows adversely affected parties to challenge the rule in court. However, courts give great deference to the agency's decisions.
- Agencies have prosecutorial discretion in deciding when and whom to regulate.
- Administrative agencies also regulate and administer laws through the licensing process where they issue, renew, suspend, or revoke a license to conduct certain types of business.

- Some agencies also monitor compliance with regulation by conducting inspections of businesses and individuals within their jurisdiction.
- Administrative agencies have the authority to adjudicate matters under their jurisdiction by holding a hearing between the government and private parties in front of an administrative law judge.

LIMITS ON ADMINISTRATIVE AGENCIES

LO17-8

Although the powers delegated to administrative agencies are broad, it is also important to remember that all administrative agencies, including independent agencies, are limited in their authority by the three-part system of the federal government. The legislative, executive, and judicial branches all have various means of power that limit the authority of administrative agencies.

Executive Branch

From a structural perspective, administrative agencies are extensions of the *executive branch's* authority to carry out the legislative mandates, and the Supreme Court has acknowledged that the President of the United States has some inherent general right to exercise power over administrative agencies in a variety of forms. Although this inherent power is notoriously vague, from an administrative law perspective, the president's power is derived from the Appointments Clause[11] and direct powers through executive orders and, to a lesser degree, through budgetary control.

Appointments Clause   The Constitution gives the president the power to appoint "officers of the United States" consistent with the Appointments Clause in Article II. Although subject to confirmation by the Senate, the president has the exclusive right to nominate principal officers such as *cabinet members* or *commissioners* of independent agencies that report directly to the president. Although not specifically articulated in the Constitution, the Supreme Court has held that the president also has the power to remove any principal officers at any time with or without cause and without any congressional approval. However, Congress sometimes passes an enablement act with a *restriction* on the president's power to remove a particular officer of the government. Federal courts have permitted this limiting type of statutory restriction as constitutional so long as the restrictions do not impair the president's ability to carry out his constitutional duty.[12] In fact, Congress has designated certain agencies, such as the Securities and Exchange Commission (SEC) and the Federal Trade Commission (FTC) as *independent* of the president's direct powers, and the heads and commissioners of independent agencies may only be removed for good cause (such as corruption) but not for mere differences in policy views between the agency and the president.

Direct Power   For the last several decades, presidents have exercised *direct power* over administrative agencies to accomplish the president's public policy objectives. For example, in 1982 in response to what President Reagan perceived as a regulatory system that was so burdensome on certain industries that it impacted the industrial output of the country, he issued an executive order that all federal administrative agencies submit to cost-benefit analysis along with any proposed regulation as part of a mandatory review process by the Office of Management and Budget (OMB). OMB was assigned to encourage agencies to be as cost-conscious as possible when imposing regulatory schemes on certain industries. This executive order is thought of as direct power over the agencies because the OMB reports directly to the president.

---

[11]U.S. Constitution, art. II, § 2, cl. 2.

[12]*Morrison v. Olsen,* 487 U.S. 654 (1988).

FIGURE 17.3 Typical Organizational Structure of an Administrative Agency: the Food and Drug Administration (FDA)

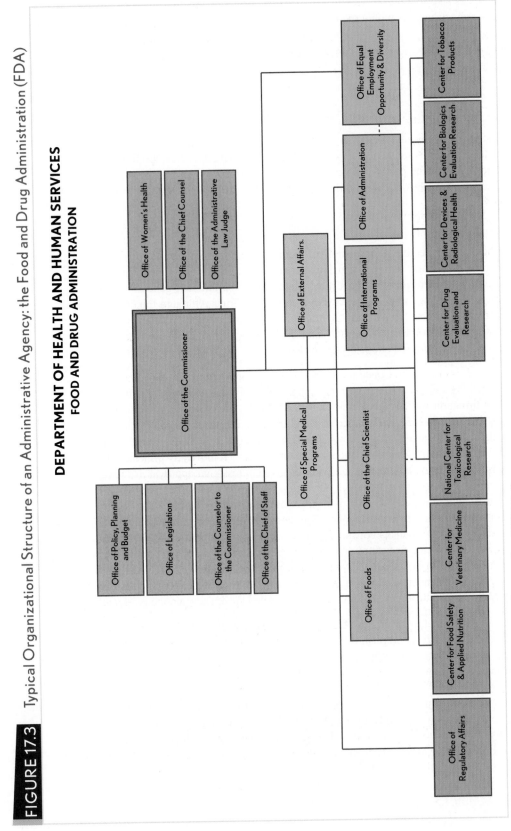

DEPARTMENT OF HEALTH AND HUMAN SERVICES
FOOD AND DRUG ADMINISTRATION

Source: http://www.fda.gov/downloads/AboutFDA/CentersOffices/OrganizationCharts/UCM181391.pdf.

Congress

Although the U.S. Supreme Court narrowed congressional review of agency actions in the famous 1983 case of *INS v. Chadha*,[13] Congress still retains significant power to influence, amend, or void actions of an administrative agency. For example, Congress may exercise their constitutionally granted *power of the purse* over government funding of particular agencies, or they may simply enact legislation that restricts an agency's authority, or pass a new law to overrule an administrative regulation. In 1996, Congress amended the APA[14] to restore their authority to cancel an agency's final rule if (1) both houses agree, (2) they pass a resolution to overrule within 60 days, and (3) the overruling resolution is presented to the president.

Congress also has oversight over administrative agencies by virtue of the Senate's power of *advice and consent*[15] to appoint certain high-ranking agency officers. Although Congress may not appoint administrative officials,[16] as a practical matter they still wield broad influence over appointments by virtue of political realities involved in agency head selection. Ultimately, Congress has the power to remove an administrative agency head via impeachment by the House of Representatives and removal by the Senate.

Judicial Review

The APA sets various standards of review for cases where administrative agency actions are challenged in a federal court.[17] Of course, courts will set aside any agency action that is inconsistent with the Constitution. But the APA also authorizes courts to void agency actions if the agency has exceeded their *statutory authority* or agency actions have been taken without adhering to the statutorily established *procedure*.

Statutory Interpretation by Agencies   Because Congress uses very broad objectives when they pass an enabling act and other laws, administrative agencies must sometimes interpret an ambiguous statute in order to carry out their duties or take administrative action. In 1984, the Supreme Court adopted the *Chevron* test[18] as the framework to analyze the validity of administrative agency statutory interpretation and action. First, courts look to the language of the statutory authority given to the agency by Congress. If the agency's interpretations or actions conflict with the plain language meaning of the statute, then a court may hold that the agency's interpretation or actions were unlawful. If, however, the statute is silent or ambiguous on the agency's authority, the court applies the **arbitrary and capricious standard** to determine whether the agency's actions were lawful. A heightened standard, known as the *substantial evidence test,* applies only in a relatively small number of cases where the formal rulemaking process was required by the enabling act.

Applying the Arbitrary and Capricious Standard   In order to meet the judicial review requirements, agencies must provide evidence that a *reasoned decision-making* process was used rather than an action that was *arbitrary and capricious*. This standard applies to all agency actions including rulemaking, adjudication, enforcement, inspection,

---

[13]462 U.S. 919 (1983). The Court held that a decades-old congressional procedure for overruling agency regulations, known as a *legislative veto,* violated the bicameralism and presentment requirements of the U.S. Constitution.

[14]The APA was amended by the Contract with America Advancement Act in 1996, which provides for congressional authority to review administrative regulations. The amendment was intended to reestablish congressional power to nullify agency regulations by addressing the constitutional problems with the legislative veto as outlined in *INS v. Chadha,* 5 U.S.C. §801, et. seq (2008).

[15]U.S. Constitution, art. II, § 2, cl. 2 (the Appointments clause).

[16]*Buckley v. Valeo,* 424 U.S. 1 (1976).

[17]APA § 706, et seq.

[18]*Chevron USA, Inc. v. NRDC,* 104 S. Ct. 2778 (1984).

and licensing. Arbitrariness and capriciousness is found when the agency has taken action that is not based on a consideration of relevant factors, including viable alternatives available to the regulatory agency, or a result of a clear error of judgment by the agency. The APA specifically requires that courts review only the information that the agency had available to it at the time it took the action in question.

Although the power of courts to set aside an administrative agency's action is clear, courts have traditionally been sparing in the use of this power. The U.S. Supreme Court has consistently held that judicial deference to administrative agencies is an important part of administrative law and that a court should not substitute its judgment for that of the agency.[19]

The Court provided guidance for lower courts in applying the arbitrary and capricious standard in *Motor Vehicle Manufacturing Association v. State Farm Mutual Automobile Association.*[20] In that case, the Court ruled that agency action was arbitrary and capricious if the agency had (1) relied on factors that Congress has not intended it to consider, or (2) failed to consider an important aspect of the problem, or (3) offered an explanation for its decision that runs counter to the evidence before the agency, or (4) is so implausible that it could not be ascribed to a difference in view or the product of agency expertise.

The arbitrary and capricious standard received significant media attention when it was the central issue in a case challenging the Department of Interior's six-month ban on deepwater drilling in wake of the Deepwater Horizon (BP) oil spill disaster. The government's drilling moratorium suspended drilling on 33 exploratory wells and halted any new permits from being issued. In a June 2010 ruling by the U.S. District Court in Louisiana, the government's drilling moratorium was found to be arbitrary and capricious and the court issued an injunction against the government's action. U.S. District Court Judge Martin Feldman wrote that "[t]he court is unable to divine or fathom a relationship between the findings [of the government agency] and the immense scope of the moratorium." The court invalidated the agency's actions based on its conclusion that the government failed to "cogently reflect the decision to issue a blanket, generic, indeed punitive, moratorium."[21] Note that the legal aspects of the Deepwater Horizon oil spill are covered in more detail in Chapter 18, "Environmental Law."

In Case 17.3, the U.S. Supreme Court applies the *Motor Vehicle Manufacturing* reasoning to a decision by the Federal Communication Commission (FCC) to change its view on the use of fleeting expletives on the public airwaves.

CASE 17.3 Federal Communications Commission v. Fox Television Stations, Inc., 129 S. Ct. 1800 (2009)

FACT SUMMARY The Federal Communications Commission (FCC) had traditionally followed a restrained enforcement policy for the use of profanity in broadcasts when the indecent material was of a fleeting and isolated nature. In 2001, the FCC further clarified its policy by acknowledging that although the First Amendment protects indecent speech, the government had a compelling interest in regulating profanity during certain hours when viewers were likely to include children. The FCC gave guidance to its media licensees (including Fox Television) that an indecency violation would be judged using a two-prong test: (1) whether the material describes or depicts sexual or excretory organs or activities, and (2) whether the broadcast is patently offensive (explicit or graphic description or depiction of sexual or excretory organs or activities). In 2003, the

continued

---

[19]*Citizens to Preserve Overton Park, Inc. v. Volpe,* 401 U.S. 402 (1971).

[20]463 U.S. 29 (1983).

[21]*Hornbeck Offshore Services, LLC v. Salazar,* U.S.D.C. Civil Action 10-1663 (E.D. Louisiana). For an update on any appeals on this case, see this textbook's website at www.mhhe.com/melvin.

FCC applied the test to an incident on an awards show where U2 lead singer Bono gave an acceptance speech that included the phrase "this is really, really, f---ing brilliant." The FCC ruled that the expletive did not constitute a violation of the FCC's indecency policy and reaffirmed their policy of enforcement restraint on fleeting expletives.

Five months after deciding the Bono incident was not indecent, the FCC abruptly changed its course and instituted a zero-tolerance rule for any use of certain words that were inherently indecent no matter what the context or brevity. In 2006, the FCC issued a decision that imposed fines on Fox Broadcasting for two incidents involving the use of fleeting expletives in two different broadcasts. The first was the *2002 Billboard Music Awards* when pop singer and actress Cher stated: "People have been telling me I'm on the way out every year, right? So f--- 'em." The second incident involved the *2003 Billboard Music Awards* where celebrity Nicole Richie, a presenter on the show, stated: "Have you ever tried to get cow s--- out of a Prada purse? It's not so f---ing simple."

Fox brought an action seeking to have the new standard invalidated on the basis that the agency had been arbitrary and capricious in their actions by adopting a new standard for the enforcement of profanity regulations involving the use of fleeting expletives. The Second Circuit Court of Appeals ruled in favor of Fox. The Court of Appeals held that although the arbitrary and capricious standard is a narrow one and agency decisions should be given deference by courts, the FCC had not supplied any reasoned analysis for the radical departure from its previous policies. The FCC appealed the case to the U.S. Supreme Court.

SYNOPSIS OF DECISION AND OPINION   In a 5-4 decision, the U.S. Supreme Court reversed the lower court's decision and ruled in favor of the FCC. The Court held that the FCC's actions were not arbitrary and capricious and that the Court of Appeals had misapplied the *State Farm* standard. The majority found that the FCC's reasoning for expanding the scope of its enforcement activity to be rational and the consistent with reasoned decision making. Moreover, the Court held that scientifically certain criteria were not required and that the FCC's repeated reliance on

context showed it had not adopted a presumption that all uses of the words were indecent.*

WORDS OF THE COURT: Empirical Data Not Always Required   "There are some propositions for which scant empirical evidence can be marshaled, and harmful effect of broadcast profanity on children is one of them. One cannot demand a multiyear controlled study, in which some children are intentionally exposed to indecent broadcast (and insulated from all other indecency), and others shielded from all indecency. It is one thing to set aside agency action under the Administrative Procedure Act because of failure to adduce empirical data that can readily be obtained [such as cost benefit analysis of mandatory restraints in autos at issue in the *State Farm* case]. It is something else to insist upon obtaining the unobtainable. Here it suffices to know that children mimic the behavior they observe—or at least the behavior is presented to them as normal and appropriate. Programming replete with one-word indecent expletives will tend to produce children who use (at least) one-word expletives. Congress has made the determination that indecent material is harmful to children, and has left enforcement of the ban to the Commission. If enforcement had to be supported by empirical data, the ban would effectively be a nullity."

Case Questions

1. Would the FCC have avoided this case if they published their intent to change policy in the *Federal Register*, solicited public comments and opinions on the matter, and then decided to make the reversal in policy? Why or why not?

2. Although the Court concludes that certain empirical data cannot be "marshaled", couldn't the FCC have provided studies, publications, etc., that examine the impact of indecent language on children? Shouldn't the FCC be required to attempt to obtain empirical data?

*Note that apart from its administrative law analysis, the Court was also concerned about potential First Amendment questions. They instructed the lower court to consider the issue on remand. The First Amendment is discussed in Chapter 2, Business and the Constitution.

Self Check Arbitrary and Capricious

Is the agency's action arbitrary and capricious?

1. After a series of deadly vehicle accidents on the nation's highways caused by underinflated tires, the National Highway Traffic Safety Administration (NHTSA), the administrative agency charged with regulating the nations highways with the objective of making them safer, proposed a rule requiring automobile manufacturers to include Tire Pressure Monitoring Systems (TPMS), which would warn drivers that they have underinflated tires, as standard equipment on all new cars. The rule states that manufacturers must provide a TPMS system that warns drivers when one tire is 30 percent or more underinflated. Despite the fact that a 20 percent standard proved to be more reliable and safer, the NHTSA settled on the 30 percent standard because of its slightly lower cost. A safety advocacy group challenged the rulemaking decision to adopt the 30 percent standard.

2. Pursuant to a congressionally set objective of improving and maintaining the quality of public bodies of water, the Clean Water Act authorizes the Environmental Protection Agency (EPA) to issue permits to and regulate any facility discharging pollutants into waters of the United States. OilCo. is a company specializing in refining pure Alaskan crude oil, which is found only in the town of Barren Ground, Alaska. Barren Ground is one of the few places in the United States that has a perfect, pollutant free, water quality due to its remote location. OilCo. wishes to build three new refining plants in Barren Ground that each use a state-of-the-art refining system. However, the system requires cooling via a saline-based solution. OilCo. applied for a permit to discharge its used coolant into Barren Ground Bay, but the EPA granted OilCo. a discharge permit with a maximum pollution level of 0. This meant OilCo. could not discharge any of their coolant without first treating it to the point where it is no longer a pollutant, but rather pure water. This process would be very expensive to implement and run for OilCo., so OilCo. challenged the EPA ruling on the permit.

3. The Federal Energy Regulatory Commission (FERC) is an administrative agency responsible for permitting new power plants. Under the Save the Waters Act, the FERC is responsible for establishing a permitting process and issuing permits to individuals and companies wishing to construct hydroelectric power plants. Under their established process, a company must obtain a permit in order to gather information, conduct feasibility studies, and create architectural plans. The information gathered can be used for subsequent applications for licenses to construct and operate the plants. Clean Green Electric Co. (CGEC) wants to build two hydroelectric power plants on the Raging Waters River in Colorado in an area outside of Small Town. CGEC applied for a permit to begin gathering information about the feasibility of locating the power plants outside of Small Town. However, the FERC denied their permit applications based in part on information from two prior permits CGEC had obtained for construction of the same power plants at the same site. CGEC challenged the ruling arguing that the FERC should consider only information in the most recent permit application.

Answers to this Self-Check are provided at the end of the chapter.

LO17-9

PUBLIC ACCOUNTABILITY

Because administrative agencies are granted broad powers and discretion, Congress has developed several safeguards to make agencies accountable to the public and to make their work as transparent as possible. This is accomplished through statutorily authorized citizen's suits as well as mandatory disclosure and open-meeting laws.

The U.S. Supreme Court ruled that the FCC's decision to institute a zero-tolerance rule for fleeting expletives in broadcasts was "entirely rational" and not arbitrary or capricious.

Private Citizen Suits

In addition to limits imposed on federal administrative agencies by the executive, legislative, and judicial branches, many enabling statutes contain provisions authorizing any member of the public at large who is directly affected by a particular agency action (or inaction) to bring a lawsuit against either violators of a particular regulation, and/or the administrative agency itself for failing to fulfill a duty imposed by statute. These suits are called **citizen suits** and are particularly prevalent in statutes related to protection of the environment.[22] As a practical matter, organized activist groups such as, in the case of environmental regulation, the Sierra Club or the Natural Resources Defense Council (NRDC), often file these citizen suits.

> **web**check **www.nrdc.org/policy/legislation.asp**
> For more information on the NRDC's legal efforts via citizen suits, go directly to the Taking Action and Legislative Analysis sections on their Web site or link to them via this textbook's Web site at www.mhhe.com/melvin.

In terms of suits against the government, it is important to realize that citizen suits cannot be used to attack the *substance* of a regulation that has been properly promulgated. Citizen suit provisions may only be used to compel the agency to act in a manner consistent with the enabling act or another federal statute. For example, suppose that Congress passed an enabling statute that required the Occupational Health and Safety Administration (OSHA) to promulgate regulations that provide a safe procedure for the removal of asbestos[23]-laden

---

[22] See, for example, *Bennett v. Spear,* 520 U.S. 154 (1997), interpreting the citizen suit provisions of the Endangered Species Act, 16 U.S.C. § 1540.

[23] Asbestos is a human-made material commonly used to make ceiling and floor tiles until the 1980s when governmental health agencies determined that asbestos dust was linked to cancer.

ceiling tiles within one year of the date of the law's passage. The OSHA properly promulgates a regulation pursuant to the statute, but an activist group, Friends of Workers (FOW), believes that the regulations do not do enough to protect employees of workplaces with asbestos. If FOW files a citizen suit against OSHA claiming that the OSHA failed to carry out the enabling act's objectives, most courts would dismiss a citizen suit because FOW is challenging the substance of the regulation. However, suppose that the OSHA fails to provide any regulations within the statutorily prescribed one-year period. In that case, FOW would be able to bring a citizen suit against the OSHA to compel the regulation to be promulgated.

> **KEY POINT**
>
> *Citizen suits* may be brought against a private party (as a violator) or against the administrative agency for failing to act consistent with the enabling statute's requirements.

Federal Disclosure Statutes

One way that administrative agencies are accountable to the public is through transparency via public access to informational records held by the government and through disclosure requirements concerning open hearings and other business conducted by federal agencies. Congress provides two primary mechanisms to achieve these transparency objectives: the *Freedom of Information Act (FOIA)*, which gives the public the right to examine a great many government documents, and the *Government in the Sunshine Act*, which requires that certain agency meetings be open to the public.

Freedom of Information Act (FOIA)   The Freedom of Information Act (FOIA—frequently pronounced *foy-a*), was originally passed by Congress in 1966 (expanded by amendments in 1974)[24] to open up certain agency records for public inspection. Fundamentally, the FOIA requires agencies to publish certain matters and to allow public inspection of all other records created or obtained by the agency in the course of doing the agency's work upon the request of an individual or agency (such as a media outlet). In order to assure agency cooperation in complying with the FOIA, the law allows private parties to sue the agency if the records are wrongfully withheld.

However, the FOIA also contains nine separate categories of exceptions designed to protect legitimate interests. The most commonly excluded records are documents that contain (1) sensitive national defense or foreign policy information; (2) agency personnel matters or agency policies on purely administrative issues such as schedules, performance reviews, or records related to personnel and medical files or other private matters; and (3) trade secrets and privileged commercial information such as a secret process or device submitted by a business under the agency of a certain jurisdiction. For example, assume that ProductCo. applies to the Environmental Protection Agency for a permit to discharge waste products into a stream after they were treated for pollution by a secret cleaning process designed by ProductCo.'s scientists. This process would likely need to be identified in ProductCo.'s permit application and, thus, within the orbit of the FOIA. However, this would fall into the trade secret exception and would be protected from disclosure to the public at large.

Government in the Sunshine Act   The Government in the Sunshine Act requires that agencies announce their meetings at least one week in advance and to open the meeting to the public unless the meeting falls within one of the Sunshine Act exceptions. However, the law does not apply to meetings that are purely consultative in character or when the meeting concerns investigatory or adjudication matters.

---

[24]5 U.S.C. § 552.

ADMINISTRATIVE LAW AT THE STATE LEVEL

Business owners and managers should also expect to encounter state administrative agencies as well as federal agencies. Although our discussion has focused primarily on federal administrative law, state agencies also have broad executive, legislative, and adjudication discretion in matters of state administrative law. Indeed, many state agencies exist to accomplish substantially the same objectives at a more micro level, where state administrative law is more tailored to the needs of their particular state. California, for example, supplements existing federal air pollution regulations with additional state regulations designed to reduce smog problems in its major cities.

States often haven their own versions of federal agencies. For example, all states have a Department of Revenue (or some similarly worded name) that is the state's version of the Internal Revenue Service. States frequently have agencies devoted to the regulation of parties within the state's borders for the sale of securities (selling a business entity's stock to the public), protection of the environment, regulation of banking and insurance companies, workplace safety, consumer protection, and labor and employee antidiscrimination regulations. Federal and state agencies also share information and work together on joint operations. State administrative law is very similar to the federal scheme in terms of how regulations are developed, implemented, and enforced.

KEY TERMS

Administrative law p. 438   A body of law and regulations that governs the organization and operation of administrative agencies.

Administrative agencies p. 438   Governmental bodies with the authority to implement and administer particular legislation. Administrative agencies include department, nondepartment, and independent agencies.

Rulemaking p. 438   The legislative function charged to administrative agencies, whereby they create legally enforceable rules in order to fill in the details of a statute.

Adjudication p. 438   The judicial function performed by administrative agencies, whereby the agencies make policy. Administrative law judges hear cases brought before the specific agency.

Enabling statute p. 439   A law passed when Congress establishes an administrative agency, which is the source of an agency's authority and describes the agency's scope and jurisdiction over certain matters.

Regulation p. 444   A rule that is effective and was published in the Code of Federal Regulations and has the force of a law.

Enforcement p. 445   Administrative agencies have prosecutorial discretion in deciding when and whom

to regulate, and this discretion is unreviewable by the judiciary. Administrative agencies generally carry out their enforcement responsibilities though their Office of General Counsel.

Licensing p. 446   The task of issuing a license authorizing a business or industry to do something.

Inspections: p. 446   The act of monitoring a business's compliance with administrative regulations whereby an administrative agency secures a warrant and then enters and inspects the business's premises.

Administrative law judge p. 447   An attorney employed by an agency to adjudicate disputes.

Arbitrary and capricious standard p. 451   The broad judicial benchmark used to determine if an agency's actions were a result of a reasoned decision-making process.

Citizen suits p. 455   Lawsuits brought by members of the public, who are directly affected by an agency action, against either violators of the regulation or the administrative agency itself for failing to fulfill a duty imposed upon it.

Main Line Restaurant Group (MLRG) is a company that owns and operates a national chain of Italian-themed restaurants. Each of their restaurants is equipped with a series of hoods that ventilate smoke from a wood-burning pizza oven to the outside via a roof vent.

In 2010, as part of a broader air pollution control law, Congress passed a statute authorizing the appropriate administrative agency to implement rules intended to decrease the amount of pollution caused by debris in the air from commercial use of wood-burning ovens.

1. What administrative agency would likely have jurisdiction under this statute?

2. When Congress passes a law such as the one articulated above, what is this type of statute called?

Assume that the appropriate administrative agency studies the issues presented in the pollution control law and proposes a rule that all wood-burning ovens used in a commercial establishment must either be replaced by gas ovens or be retrofitted with a certain pollution control device that will cost $15,200 per hood. Although a similar lower-cost device is available, the agency did not view costs as a barrier to implementation when proposing the rule. The proposed rule also requires the hoods to be installed within five years.

3. What options does MLRG have for affecting the proposed rule to include the lower-cost device as an option?

Assume that the agency published a revised final rule that includes an amendment to allow the use of the lower-cost device, but also added a provision that shortened the implementation deadline from the original five years to one year.

4. Is the administrative agency required to publish the amended rule again and allow a second comment period before they finalize it? What rule would govern this analysis?

5. Assuming, arguendo, that the administrative agency is not required to republish and allow an additional comment period, what are MLRG's options to challenge the rule at this point?

6. What standards will a court use to judge the validity of the final rule?

The following guide is excerpted from a federal administrative agency publication that sets out guidance for submitting public comments. Based on this guide, draft a two-page letter to the appropriate administrative agency on MLRG's behalf explaining why you would urge the agency to change the proposed rule in Theory to Practice above, concerning wood-burning ovens.

SUGGESTIONS FOR SUBMITTING COMMENTS

There are four general areas that you may wish to comment on concerning regulations:

1. *The need for the rule.*

2. *Other options.* If the agency has proposed or discussed requirements, you may be able to think of other things the agency could do that would solve the problem in a less costly way for your firm or industry. One option that has often been suggested is for the agency to give small firms more time to comply with a regulation, such as a change to a food label. Another option may be for the agency to identify a goal companies must meet, but to allow each firm to achieve the stated goal in its own way. Another option may be to request an exemption for certain types of businesses for which the requirements are not applicable. Because the quality and persuasiveness of your comment affects the agency's decision, including data, logical reasoning, and other information to support your comment always helps.

3. *Benefits of the rule.* You may want to explain (in detail if possible) whether you think a specific requirement would achieve the intended results. For example, you may want to provide detailed information documenting whether your industry has a particular problem. Furthermore, you may want to comment on the degree to which a proposed requirement is already common practice, and how much a federal rule would change practices in your industry.

4. *Costs of the rule.* In many cases, the regulatory options and costs of the rule will be the areas that you will know most about and may want to include in your submission. The chart below gives examples of costs that your company or industry may experience as a result of a regulation.

COST FACTOR CHART

The factors below can be used for commenting on each proposed requirement in the codified section. This chart is only a suggestion for submitting comments. You are free to comment in any manner you wish or not at all. You may also, for example, respond by plant, firm, industry group, or in any other manner.

A sample answer may be found on this textbook's Web site at www.mhhe.com/melvin.

Category	Explanation	Examples
1. What new capital equipment or materials will you have to buy to comply with the regulation?	Estimate the actual cost of new capital equipment or materials that you will have to purchase (one time or annually) and any loss of equipment that can no longer be used.	Chemicals for new tests will cost $40 per test for each of the 4 tests per week. The depreciated value of an extruder that will no longer be able to be used is $7,500.
2. What is the size of your firm?	Estimate the size of your firm either by number of employees or by annual sales. A range may be given.	Our firm has 200 full-time employees and 20 part-time employees. Annual sales are between $10 and $50 million.
3. What products do you make?	Describe the type of products that your firm makes that are covered by the potential regulation.	Our firm makes 2 varieties of herbal supplements in 3 sizes each. We make 4 flavors of Larry's Ice Cream in 2 sizes each.
4. What are your average annual profits?	Again, *do not report sensitive information* but you may wish to provide an approximate annual amount that you can use to finance new requirements.	My firm makes between $20,000 and $50,000 per year.
5. Who owns your firm? How many plants do you have?	Explain whether or not you are a subsidiary of a larger firm.	We are a solely owned firm with 2 plants.

CASE SUMMARY 17.1 :: Int'l Union, United Mine Workers of America v. Mine Safety and Health Admin, 407 F.3d 1250 (D.C. Cir. 2005)

LOGICAL OUTGROWTH TEST

The Secretary of the Mine Safety and Health Administration proposed a new rule intended to increase safety of workers by ensuring proper ventilation in the mines. The proposed rule required a minimum velocity of 300 feet per minute (fpm) to be kept through the ventilation regulator to ensure adequate mine ventilation. During the comment period, empirical data was submitted that suggested that requiring *minimum flow* was the safest alternative and, thus, the agency would not set a *maximum flow*. However, when the final rule was published it provided for a maximum airflow of 500 fpm. A mining company challenged the final rule because there was no comment period to discuss maximum airflows.

CASE QUESTIONS

1. Is the maximum airflow rule a logical outgrowth of the proposed rule? Why or why not?
2. Is the agency required to republish the rule?

ARBITRARY AND CAPRICIOUS

CBS Corp. (CBS) presented a live broadcast of the National Football League's Super Bowl XXXVIII on February 1, 2004. The broadcast included a 15-minute halftime program produced by MTV Networks, headlined by singer and actress Janet Jackson and singer Justin Timberlake. During the performance Mr. Timberlake, in an unscripted act, ripped off a piece of Ms. Jackson's bustier in what the network called a "wardrobe malfunction," which resulted in Ms. Jackson's bare breast being broadcast for nine-sixteenths of one second. While CBS had implemented a five-second audio delay to account for any profane language, they had no such video delay and the images were broadcast in real time. The FCC issued CBS a Notice of Liability for indecency and fined them $550,000 for the incident, claiming it was willful. CBS claimed that the ruling is arbitrary and capricious, based upon prior FCC decisions in similar circumstances. The FCC argued that they enforced a valid indecency rule even though prior rule changes failed to specifically address indecent *images*.

CASE QUESTIONS

1. Is the FCC's decision arbitrary and capricious? Why or why not?
2. Should CBS be found liable? Why or why not?

JUDICIAL REVIEW

Paul Holowecki was employed by Federal Express Corporation (FedEx) when FedEx implemented two new performance programs that tie employee compensation and continued employment to certain performance measures. Holowecki, along with other FedEx employees over the age of 40, claimed that the incentive programs unlawfully discriminate against older employees. Under the Age Discrimination in Employment Act (ADEA), claimants must file a *charge* with the Equal Employment Opportunity Commission (EEOC) and then wait a statutorily defined period of time before filing suit in federal court. However, the ADEA does not define what constitutes a charge. The EEOC used their authority to implement procedures necessary to carry out their objectives to promulgate a rule that states a "charge shall mean a statement filed with the Commission by or on behalf of an aggrieved person which alleges that the named prospective defendant has engaged in or is about to engage in actions in violation of the Act." Before filing suit, Holowecki submitted an Intake Questionnaire with EEOC and filed a six-page affidavit. FedEx claims that a questionnaire and affidavit do not constitute a formal charge against them because this was only one step in a formal complaint procedure. FedEx argued that EEOC's interpretation of the definition of "charge" was outside their statutory authority.

CASE QUESTIONS

1. Who prevails and why?
2. Will the court defer to the EEOC interpretation?
3. What is the standard used by the courts in this case?

ARBITARY AND CAPRICIOUS

In response to outbreaks of mad cow disease, the Food and Drug Administration and the U.S. Department of Agriculture (USDA) implemented a number of regulations to protect American consumers and cattle herds. Chief among them was a regulation banning cattle imports from countries where mad cow disease was known to exist. Shortly after the ban went into effect, the USDA partially reversed course and published a proposed rule allowing certain low-risk products into the United States. During the comment period, some groups objected to the proposed rule due to evidence of potential contamination even in low-risk products. The agency then published its final rule, which modified existing regulations to allow the import of low-risk products. The Ranchers Cattlemen Action Legal Fund United Stockgrowers of America challenged the agency's decision to allow low-risk products as arbitrary and capricious even though they held several comment periods.

CASE QUESTIONS

1. Is the decision arbitrary and capricious? Why or why not?
2. Does the fact that the agency held several comment periods impact your analysis?

 Self Check ANSWERS

Arbitrary and Capricious

1. The agency's decision is likely to be considered arbitrary and capricious. The NHTSA is charged with making the nation's highway's safer and by ignoring the fact that a four-tire, 20 percent TPMS is safer and more reliable and choosing a slightly cheaper, less safe alternative, they are not making a reasoned decision. See *Public Citizen, Inc. v. Mineta*, 340 F.3d 39 (2d Cir. 2003).

2. The EPA's decision is *not* arbitrary and capricious because they are tasked with improving or maintaining the nation's water quality under the CWA. Therefore, their decision to issue OilCo. a permit with an effluent limitation of 0 is perfectly reasonable because that is the level necessary to maintain water quality in that region. See *Texas Oil & Gas Ass'n v. United States EPA*, 161 F.3d 923 (5th Cir. 1998).

3. The FERC's decision is *not* arbitrary and capricious because there were no changed circumstances. The same power plants and the same sites were involved, therefore the FERC could rely on the prior permits and information from their review to determine whether or not to issue another permit for this site. See *Symbiotics, L.L.C. v. FERC*, 110 Fed. Appx. 76 (10th Cir. 2004).

18

CHAPTER

Environmental Law

learning outcomes **checklist**

After studying this chapter, students who have mastered the material will be able to:

18-1 Identify the origins and sources of environmental law.

18-2 Describe the role of the Environmental Protection Agency and other agencies in implementation and enforcement of environmental laws.

18-3 Understand the relationship between federal and state environmental agencies.

18-4 Explain the role of citizen suits in enforcing environmental regulations.

18-5 Describe the primary objectives and provisions of major federal statutes that protect the environment.

18-6 Provide examples of various industries regulated by the air and water pollution laws related to disposal of waste and hazardous materials.

18-7 Understand liability of parties under the federal environmental cleanup statutes.

18-8 Distinguish between removal and remedial cleanup efforts in the context of environmental regulation.

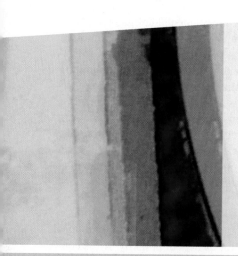

Environmental law is a collection of federal, state, and local laws that protect the natural resources and promote a healthier environment for the public at large. Whether it be the regulation of industrial plants or a city ordinance prohibiting the use of certain pesticides by landscapers within municipal limits, business owners and managers from across the spectrum of commercial sectors encounter environmental law and regulation in their daily operations and in their business planning. Specifically, students will learn:

- Environmental law's origins, sources, and enforcement mechanisms.

- Major federal environmental statutes that apply to business operations.

- Laws that impose liability on private individuals and businesses for environmental cleanup costs.

IMPACT OF ENVIRONMENTAL LAW ON BUSINESS

Business owners and managers all too often assume that environmental law and regulation is a concern only for large industrial plant owners who produce smokestack pollution or dump waste into rivers. Yet, it is clear that environmental laws must be thought of as having broad coverage and that an understanding of environmental law is important in limiting a company's liability and maintaining regulatory compliance. Any assumption that environmental laws are not pertinent to a particular business's operation may be costly in terms of liability and may forego opportunities for proactive business planning and risk control.

As the American public becomes increasingly concerned over threats to the environment and related issues such as oil spills and greenhouse gases, governments at the federal, state, and local level have broadened environmental regulation and liability for environmental cleanups. Local businesses such as dry cleaners, bakeries, mechanics, gas station owners, landscapers, contractors, and a host of others are subject to various environmental laws.

Liability for environmental cleanup is another concern for business owners and managers if their business operations involve ownership of land. Certain federal statutes (discussed in detail later in this chapter) create liability for owners of property that is contaminated even if the owner did not contribute to the contamination. This strict liability concept is an important factor when planning a land purchase.

LO18-1 ORIGINS AND SOURCES OF ENVIRONMENTAL LAW

The origins of environmental protections were primarily based on the common law doctrine of **nuisance.** In a suit for nuisance, an aggrieved party sues to compel a polluter to cease polluting based on the aggrieved party's right to enjoy her property without interference from a third party. Local zoning ordinances are generally designed to prevent nuisance by segmenting a municipality into industrial, residential, and so forth. However, this common law doctrine was a protection of a party's *individual property rights.* Historically, the federal government left regulation of the environment to state and local authorities. This resulted in a patchwork of standards with some areas of the country allowing heavy industrial pollution while other areas regulated or banned such pollution. Because pollution does not respect state boundaries, it became apparent that federal statutes would be necessary to achieve meaningful environmental protections.

Modern environmental protection statutes at both the federal and state level have largely supplanted any common law protections. In addition, local municipalities often have environmental ordinances standards related to safety and local public policy (such as proper disposal of engine oil or other hazardous waste by a local mechanic). Environmental protection statutes are wide-ranging, but federal and state statutes that impact business are primarily designed to (1) ensure that government agency decisions have as minimal as possible impact on the environment, (2) promote clean air and water through regulation and permitting, (3) regulate the use and disposal of solid and hazardous waste, (4) clean up property or waterways that are contaminated with hazardous waste, and (5) protect wildlife and endangered species.

LO18-2, 18-3 GOVERNMENT ENFORCEMENT

Federal environmental laws are primarily administered, implemented, and enforced by the U.S. Environmental Protection Agency (EPA). The EPA, created in 1970, works in tandem with other administrative agencies in handling a broad range of environmental concerns at the federal level. For example, the U.S. Fish and Wildlife Service primarily enforces statutes protecting endangered species. However, if the use of pesticides is responsible for depleting the population of certain endangered species, the EPA will work to use environmental regulation to halt the use of the pesticides. Other agencies that have certain environmental regulation jurisdiction include the Food and Drug Administration (FDA) and the Nuclear Regulatory Commission (NRC).

Like all administrative agencies, the EPA has broad powers to implement and enforce environmental laws through promulgation of rules,[1] permitting, issuing advisory opinions, investigating potential violations of federal environmental protections statutes, as well as traditional enforcement tools such as administrative fines and penalties, civil suits or, in egregious cases, criminal complaints.

In addition to the EPA and other federal agencies, each state has its own environmental agency to implement and enforce state environmental statutes. In certain municipalities, a local environmental agency may exist as well to enforce local ordinances such as illegal dumping. The names of the agency vary between jurisdictions, but titles such as Department of Environmental Protection or Department of Natural Resources or some variance of the two is common. An important feature to many federal environmental laws is that state governments are often mandated to work in conjunction with (or under the supervision of) the EPA when implementing and enforcing federal environmental statutes such as the Clean Water Act.

Citizen Suits Provisions and Watchdog Groups

LO18-4

Perhaps more than in any other area of the law, citizen interest organizations (also called watchdog groups) have contributed to the enforcement of environmental statutes and policy. These citizen interest organizations and individual citizens are statutorily authorized to file a lawsuit against either a polluter who is in violation of environmental statutes or regulations or a government agency or unit (such as the EPA or a municipality) that is not taking legally mandated steps to carry out environmental law enforcement. Individuals and groups derive this authority to file enforcement lawsuits by virtue of **citizen suits provisions** that are a part of many federal and state environmental statutes.

When an environmental statute authorizes citizen suits, it generally requires notice to the agency with jurisdiction over the matter and allows the agency to decide whether to initiate agency action instead of allowing the citizen suit to go forward. A private citizen or group cannot profit from an enforcement action, and frequently they seek only to have a court order preventing or requiring a certain action. Some of the more common initiators of environmental law citizen suits include the Sierra Club, the Natural Resources Defense Council, and the Environmental Defense Fund. Local environmental watchdog groups in different regions of the United States tend to focus on a particular concern unique to the region (e.g., the Spotted Owl Defense League of Oregon).

In Case 18.1, a local watchdog group sued New York City, claiming the city had violated the Clean Water Act.

NATIONAL ENVIRONMENTAL POLICY ACT

LO18-5

One the first attempts at comprehensive legislation to address environmental regulation was the **National Environmental Policy Act (NEPA)**[2] enacted in 1969. The law was intended to serve as a national charter for environmental regulation, but its focus is on planning and prevention rather than achieving a certain result (such as cleaner water) according to scientific standards. Instead, the NEPA establishes a process that must be followed by federal agencies in making decisions that have the potential to have a significant impact on the environment. The NEPA also created the Council on Environmental Quality to oversee the NEPA procedures and to make periodic progress reports to the Congress and the president.

---

[1] Recall from Chapter 17, "Administrative Law" that administrative agencies are authorized by statute to implement binding legal regulations after following a rulemaking process.

[2] 42 U.S.C. § 4321, et seq.

FACT SUMMARY   In the late 1990s, the city of New York (the City) confronted growing concerns surrounding the mosquito-borne West Nile Virus by implementing an aerial and ground spraying program. The program consisted of spray planes and trucks that would douse the city with Malathion, a controversial neurotoxin pesticide, in an attempt to eradicate mosquitoes carrying the potentially fatal virus. The plan was controversial because of the exposure of the general public to potentially hazardous pesticides. The No Spray Coalition (No Spray), a group of local organizations and individuals, filed suit to halt insecticide spraying, alleging that such spraying violated the Clean Water Act[*] (CWA) among others.

SYNOPSIS OF DECISION AND OPINION   The federal trial court ruled in favor of the City, holding that the spraying of insecticides in conformity with their labels as approved by the Environmental Protection Agency (EPA) did not violate the CWA. The court ruled that, although they were statutorily entitled to bring a lawsuit under the CWA's citizen suits provisions, No Spray failed to show that the City was spraying directly over navigable waters in violation of the CWA.[†]

WORDS OF THE COURT: Use of Pesticides and the Clean Water Act   "It is not the role of the Court to resolve the policy question of whether the benefits of the spraying program outweigh the danger that it poses for individuals or the environment. Fortunately, for the community, that question is to be decided by public health and environmental officials who are far better qualified to weigh the competing interests. The role of the Court is limited to determining whether in carrying out its mosquito control program, the City has violated any federal statute that Congress has authorized the plaintiffs to sue to enforce. No Spray contend[s] that the unintended drift of minuscule particles of the City's pesticide spray into the waters surrounding New York City violates the Clean Water Act. However, this is the natural consequence of the use of the pesticides for the very purpose for which they were approved by the EPA. [. . .] Given the broad definition of navigable waters in the Clean Water Act, any approved use of the pesticide, other than in a desert, will inevitably result in a drift of the spray into navigable waters. Because the EPA in registering the pesticide has made a determination that aerial use will not have 'unreasonable adverse effects on the environment,' it would frustrate the intent of the regulatory scheme to hold that such an approved use violates the Clean Water Act. [. . .] It is no doubt true that the use of pesticide for a purpose or in a manner well beyond that for which it was approved could result in a violation of the Clean Water Act. For example, if a pilot, who had finished spraying pesticide, dumped any pesticide remaining in the tank into a navigable stream, he could not defend an action under the Clean Water. [. . .] So long as the use is within the category of uses for which the EPA has approved the pesticide, Congress intended to leave it to the EPA to determine whether there has been compliance with the technical requirements of the label. [. . .]"

Case Questions

1. What would No Spray have to prove in order to have an actionable claim under the CWA?
2. Explain the significance of citizen suits provisions and watchdog groups in the context of the immediate case.

[*]33 U.S.C.S. § 1251 et seq.

[†]Note that an appellate court vacated the trial court's decision three years later for procedural reasons unrelated to the court's analysis of the City's liability under the CWA. However, since the City had ceased the spraying action, the litigation ended without any reconsideration of the case. 351 F.3d 602 (2nd Cir. 2003).

NEPA Coverage and Procedures

The NEPA procedures are triggered when a federal agency takes any action that may reasonably be considered to impact the environment. This action may be in the form of an agency issuing a permit or license, or when an agency is engaged in rulemaking. NEPA is also activated when Congress passes a law that requires federal funding (such as federal highway or bridge construction). Note that actions by private individuals, businesses,

Citizens suit provisions in many environmental laws permit watchdog groups such as the Sierra Club to file suit against alleged polluters or the government to enforce the statute.

and state and local governments are not regulated by the NEPA. However, all states have enacted parallel statutes (laws similar to the NEPA statute but covering a wider range of parties) to cover state and local government actions as well.

Procedural Steps

Federal agencies are required to incorporate the NEPA procedural steps into their decision-making process at the earliest possible opportunity by identifying the purpose and need for a promised project, possible alternatives, and environmental impact of certain actions. Once this step has been accomplished, the agency must categorize the action into one of three classifications based on its level of environmental impact:

■ *Categorical Exclusion (CE).* The CE category is for those actions that have little or no potential for significant environmental impact. A CE classification may also be mandated by a particular statute, which has the effect of exempting certain actions from any further environmental assessment.

■ *Environmental Assessment (EA).* Projects and actions in which the environmental impact is unknown are classified in the EA category. Actions classified as EA requires the agency to produce a public document setting forth the need for the proposed action, alternatives, the environmental impact of the proposed action and its alternatives, and a list of agencies and persons consulted. The EA is used to determine whether the action requires preparation of a more extensive report called an Environmental Impact Statement (EIS). If, however, based on the EA, the agency makes a finding of no significant impact, the agency may proceed with the proposed action.

■ *Environmental Impact Statement (EIS).* The EIS category is for actions classified as having the potential for *significant impact* on the environment. If an EA provides evidence that some significant environmental impact is at issue, the agency must prepare a draft of an EIS and publish it for public comment. The EIS is an expanded form of an EA that includes (1) a description of the proposed action, (2) a statement of significant issues and specific forecasting of what environmental risks are involved with the proposed action, (3) alternatives to the actions and an assessment of environmental risk of the alternatives, (4) financial assessments of the promised actions and alternatives, and (5) plans for reducing or preventing environmental harm. Once the public and interested constituencies have commented on the EIS, the agency revises the EIS as necessary and issues a final EIS. The final EIS also sets out the agency decision on environmental impact and its chosen alternative for pursuing the agency action.

As a practical matter, the NEPA process gives public notice and affords consumer interest groups, businesses, and private citizens a chance to influence the agency's decision. The NEPA contains a citizen suit provision whereby private individuals and organizations may sue a federal agency directly to force compliance with the NEPA procedures.

CONCEPT SUMMARY   National Environmental Policy Act

- The National Environmental Policy Act (NEPA) of 1969 established a process that must be followed by federal agencies in making decisions that may reasonably impact the environment or when Congress passes a law that requires federal funding.

- Federal agencies are required to incorporate NEPA procedural steps into their decision-making process by identifying the purpose and need for a promised project, possible alternatives, and environmental impact.

- Once the procedural steps are accomplished, the agency must categorize the action into one of three classifications based on its level of environmental impact: (1) Categorical Exclusion (little or no potential impact), or (2) Environmental Assessment [unknown impact], or (3) Environmental Impact Statements (potentially significant impact).

- The NEPA process gives public notice and affords consumer interest groups, businesses, and private citizens a chance to influence the agency's decision or directly force compliance via citizen suits provisions.

LO18-6   THE CLEAN AIR ACT

First enacted in 1963, the **Clean Air Act (CAA)**[3] is a considerably complex statute aimed at improving outdoor air quality in the United States. The CAA replaced earlier legislation that proved ineffective. The law has been amended several times since its original passage, most recently in 1997 to expand its coverage and provide a system of market-based incentives and enforcement options intended to encourage voluntary compliance with air standards. The starting point of the CAA was for the EPA to establish the National Ambient Air Quality Standards (NAAQS) that set permissible levels of certain air pollutants such as carbon monoxide, lead, and particulate matter (microscopic ash and dirt that are the ingredients for smog). Although the statute itself is multifaceted, its basic structure focuses on **stationary sources of air pollution** (such as an industrial manufacturing plant) and **mobile sources of air pollution** (motor vehicles).

Stationary Sources of Air Pollution

An important feature of the CAA is that *state legislatures* are required to determine the best way to achieve the NAAQS. State governments have a uniquely local understanding of state industries, geography, and demographics, and are usually in the best position to decide on a solution. Each state is required to develop a collection of regulations that help to achieve a reduction in each pollutant to below the maximum level set in the NAAQS. This plan takes the form of a mandated **State Implementation Plan (SIP),** and the SIP must be submitted to the EPA within certain time frames set out in the statute. If the SIP is not acceptable, the EPA may either impose sanctions on the state (such as withholding certain federal funding) or may step in to implement its own plan.

SIPs also feature a program for issuing **operating permits** to existing stationary sources that emit pollutants at special levels. Operating permits include information on which pollutants are being released, how much is being released, and steps the source is taking to

---

[3]42 U.S.C. §§ 7401–7671.

reduce pollution, including technological requirements and methods to monitor the pollution. SIPs also include the requirements to obtain a *preoperating permit* for any new source of pollutants being planned. Preoperating permits require the applicant to show that the construction of a stationary source has incorporated *state-of-the-art* technology to control the NAAQS pollutants. The CAA regulations also require a new source permit when a plant owner makes *substantial modifications* to an existing stationary source. Sometimes an issue arises as to what constitutes modification. This is an important factor in business planning because certain modifications may trigger additional regulatory measures and permit requirements.

Market-Based Approaches

One relatively controversial part of the CAA is the law's **market-based approach.** This approach was implemented by the 1990 amendments to the CAA and is accomplished through (1) *emission trading* via the permitting process, and (2) a *cap and trade* plan intended to achieve lower levels of pollutants that contribute to acid rain.[4] Although the plans have separate procedural systems, they are both considered market-based approaches. Under this approach, businesses have certain *choices* as to how they reach their pollution reduction goals and include pollution allowances that can be traded, bought, and sold. In that same vein, a business may be allowed to expand its pollution output in one area if it is able to offset the increase by reducing another pollutant in greater measure than the one being expanded. The emission-trading scheme embraces an economic incentive theory that overall pollution reduction will result if businesses have an economic and competitive incentive, rather than a mandate, to invest in modern equipment and plants. Proponents argue that this approach results in businesses investing in more efficient plants that will yield clean air units to sell or trade to an out-of-compliance buyer. As emitting pollution becomes more expensive, every company will be forced to modernize to stay competitive in the market. For example, suppose that Citadel Manufacturing Company (Citadel) and Guardian Operations Inc. (Guardian) operate manufacturing plants that emit pollutants regulated by the CAA. Each company obtains a permit to emit 50 units of Pollutant X and 50 units of Pollutant Y per year. Citadel decides to modernize its plant at a cost of $1 million. The modernization results in a significant reduction in Pollutant X so that now it emits only 10 units per year. Guardian, on the other hand, claims they do not have the resources to modernize, and its current plant will emit 80 units of Pollutant X. In a market-based approach, Guardian may chose to comply by either purchasing 30 units of Pollutant X emission credit from Citadel, or reducing its use of Pollutant Y to offset the additional units of Pollutant X. If using the offset method, Guardian would have to reduce its use of Pollutant Y at least 31 units (an amount greater than the exceeding pollutant). In this example, proponents of the market-based approach would point out that (1) this approach does not force burdensome mandates that may bankrupt a company, such as requirements to purchase expensive equipment; (2) eventually Guardian will likely begin to consider investing in new technology so as not to be dependent on sellers of pollution units; and (3) the overall pollution reduction is the same under this approach as it would be under a mandate approach.

> ## KEY POINT
>
> A market-based approach was instituted by the 1990 CAA amendments to give businesses alternative methods of complying with pollution standards.

Critics of this approach argue that it results in clean air being treated as a commodity rather than as a natural resource. Opponents of market-based solutions argue that the government could achieve greater reductions in pollution

---

[4]Acid rain is a broad term referring to a mixture of wet and dry components from the atmosphere that contains significant amounts of nitric and sulfuric acids. Governmental agencies have concluded that acid rain poses significant threats to the environment and specific ecosystems.

through the use of gradual statutory mandates to improve pollution control and government-backed loans to help companies purchase equipment.

Mobile Sources of Air Pollution

While substantial gains have been made in reducing pollution from motor vehicles over the past few decades, the internal combustion engine remains a significant source of hazardous pollutants. The EPA has issued standards intended to limit motor vehicle emissions through its Transport and Air Quality Program (TAQ Program). The TAQ Program regulates (1) tailpipe emissions, (2) fuel economy, (3) performance standards, and (4) the composition and distribution of fuels, particularly gasoline, used in motor vehicles.

Tailpipe Emissions
The CAA initially set the first federal tailpipe emissions standards, but granted California authority to set even tighter emission standards due to the state's higher-than-average levels of air pollution. The 1990 amendments gave states the choice between adopting the federal standards or using the California standards, but states may not adopt their own standards. Both the federal and California standards require an inspection and maintenance program to ensure that car manufacturers limit the exhaust emissions of five major pollutants that emit from tailpipes, including hydrocarbons and carbon monoxide. The difference between the two sets of standards is that the California standards have stricter miles per gallon requirements and lower levels of allowable pollution.

Fuel Economy Standards
Fuel economy standards set out average mile per gallon requirements for motor vehicles and are determined by the year of the motor vehicle's production and its classification (car versus light truck). These regulations are called Corporate Average Fuel Economy (CAFE) standards, and were enacted by Congress in 1975 with the purpose of reducing energy consumption by increasing the fuel economy of cars and light trucks. Regulating the CAFE standards is the responsibility of the National Highway Traffic Safety Administration (which sets the standards) and the EPA (which sets out a required standard calculation method for average fuel economy). The CAFE standards were overhauled in 2007 by the Energy Independence and Security Act,[5] which increased the mandated average for cars from 27.5 miles per gallon (mpg) to 35.5 mpg by 2020. However, in 2009, President Obama directed the regulatory agencies to explore a more rapid increase to the CAFE standards. Consequently, the National Highway Traffic Safety Administration issued a rule that the new 35.5 mpg standard must be instituted no later than 2016 instead of 2020.

Performance Standards
The TAQ program also requires that motor vehicle manufacturers obtain a Certificate of Conformity from the EPA that certifies a vehicle's useful life is at least 10 years or 100,000 miles for passenger cars and up to 365,000 miles for heavy trucks. The useful life standards are intended to make sure that manufacturers have designed the motor vehicle's emissions system to last a certain period of time. Performance standards also include requirements for certain in-vehicle diagnostic systems that would allow a mechanic to detect an otherwise hidden defect in the emission control systems.

Fuel Composition and Distribution
The manufacturing and transportation of gasoline, diesel fuel, or fuel additives is regulated by the EPA under authority of the CAA. The EPA uses a registration system to ensure that any fuel product is tested and certified as safe for public health and is used in compliance with CAA regulations. In addition to a complete ban on the use of lead-based gasoline in 1995, the law also includes a requirement that gasoline components contain certain detergents to reduce emissions.

---

[5]42 U.S.C. § 170001 et seq.

- The Clean Air Act is aimed at improving outdoor air quality based on National Ambient Air Quality Standards that set permissible levels of certain air pollutants.

- The basic structure of the statute focuses on pollution from either stationary sources (manufacturing plants) or mobile sources (motor vehicles).

- State legislatures are required to determine the best way to achieve the NAAQS for stationary sources in the form of a mandated State Implementation Plan (SIP) that must be submitted to the EPA.

- SIPs also feature a program for issuing operating permits to existing stationary sources that emit pollutants at special levels, preoperating permits for any new source of pollutants being planned, and new source permits required for substantial modifications to an existing source.

- A market-based approach embraces an economic incentive theory and was instituted by the 1990 CAA amendments to give businesses a choice of methods of complying with pollution standards.

- The EPA has issued standards intended to limit mobile source emissions through its Transport and Air Quality Program regulating (1) tailpipe emissions, (2) fuel economy standards, (3) performance standards, and (4) fuel composition and distribution.

WATER POLLUTION CONTROL

The pollution of waterways is one of the biggest challenges facing environmental policymakers. Waterways take the form of surface water (such as lakes or rivers) or ground water (subsurface water such as that used for wells). Because water travels through jurisdictional boundaries and may be subject to various legal property rights,[6] water pollution and conservation regulation is necessarily addressed by a combination of federal, state, and local statutes and rules.

The Clean Water Act

Water quality standards are set primarily by and regulated through the **Clean Water Act (CWA),**[7] a federal statute that is implemented and enforced by the EPA in tandem with the U.S. Army Corps of Engineers and state agencies. Much like the CAA, the CWA has been amended in significant ways to stem pollution from industrial, municipal, and agricultural sources.

Water Quality Regulation   States set water quality standards for the navigable waterways within their state's borders subject to the EPA review. State agencies set scientifically measurable standards consisting of several criteria intended to improve the quality of surface water. The standards are set according to the

Waterways are protected by an array of environmental regulation statutes including the Clean Water Act.

---

[6]The legal term for water ownership rights is *riparian rights.*
[7]33 U.S.C. § 1251, et seq.

designated use of the water source. Sources in which the designated uses are swimming or fishing must have the quality standards set high. Once the state has set its standards, it must monitor whether its water sources are meeting those standards and disclose the results through a mandatory reporting system. If progress toward achieving the standards is too slow or nonexistent, the state must propose a new strategy to meet the quality standards. The EPA must approve any new strategies and may step in and impose its own strategy if they determine the state to be out of compliance with the CWA.

Permitting   Pollution emission into the waterways from sources such as industrial plants is regulated through the EPA's National Pollution Discharge Elimination System (System). The System establishes permitting procedures for businesses and individuals that require discharge of some material into a water source in order to operate their facilities. A permit is required regardless of the quality of the receiving water or whether the discharge actually causes pollution. Permits are issued as either *individual* permits, which are specifically tailored to an individual facility, or *general* permits, which cover multiple facilities within a certain category. Individual permits are often issued to business facilities, while general permits are issued for all discharges in a specific geographic area (such as a city-designated development zone).

In order to obtain a permit, existing sources of pollution are required to install pollution control technology that is the best *practical* control technology. This means that the cost of implementation is given equal weight to effectiveness of pollution control. New applicants for permits are required to employ best *available* control technology, which requires the permit applicant to install the most technologically advanced control methods on the market regardless of cost. The EPA has established timetables for existing sources to adopt best *available* control technology as well.

Liability for Oil Spills

Largely in response to a ten million gallon oil spill resulting from the Exxon *Valdez* oil tanker running aground, Congress passed the **Oil Pollution Act[8](OPA)** in 1990. The OPA increased the EPA's authority to prevent and respond to disastrous oil spills in public water sources. The law also imposed a tax on oil freighters in order to fund the national Oil Spill Liability Trust Fund, which is available to fund up to $1 billion per spill. Energy companies are required to file environmental impact plans with the Minerals Management Service (MMS), an agency of the U.S. Department of Interior. MMS has oversight authority over all oil drilling. The OPA was intended to promote contingency planning between government and industry to prevent and respond to a spill event. The OPA also increased penalties for noncompliance and broadened the government's response and enforcement authority. The law caps the liability of responsible parties at $75 million per spill, plus removal costs. However, in case of gross negligence, the cap does not apply.

Deepwater Horizon (BP) Oil Spill   The largest off-shore oil spill in U.S. history began on April 20, 2010 after an explosion aboard the BP-controlled oil drilling platform *Deepwater Horizon*. The *Deepwater Horizon* is situated in the Gulf of Mexico approximately 40 miles southeast of the Louisiana coast. The explosion killed 11 people working on the platform and created an oil spill that the National Oceanic and Atmospheric Administration estimated was leaking almost 5,000 barrels (210,000 gallons) per day. BP tried several methods for controlling the leak, but the logistics of such a deep-sea operation resulted in a number of failed attempts to control the leaking.

*web*check **www.mhhe.com/melvin**
For an update on the legal aspects of the *Deepwater Horizon* oil spill, check this textbook's Website.

[8]33 U.S.C §§2702-2761

The spill's long-lasting impact on environment, economy, and culture of Americans living in the Gulf coastal communities in Louisiana, Mississippi, Alabama, Texas, and Florida are still too speculative to calculate with any degree of reliability. Although BP assured the U.S. government and public at large that they would pay for all of the liabilities related to the oil spill, including liabilities beyond the $75 million OPA cap,[9] as well as the cost related to loss of wild life, tourism, and other important coastal industries, the company came under intense scrutiny and criticism for failing to have an adequate emergency plan in place. In May 2010, the Justice Department announced that they were launching a criminal and civil investigation into the incident. Although BP acknowledged their liability in the accident, they alleged that other contractors on the oil rig were also negligent in the spill and announced their intention to seek reimbursement from the negligent parties. Within one month of the spill, over 100 lawsuits were filed against BP and other companies involved in the disaster.

Passed shortly after the Exxon *Valdez* oil spill, the Oil Pollution Act (OPA) imposes liability on responsible parties for cleanup costs and economic damages suffered by business owners and residents of affected areas.

Drinking Water

The **Safe Drinking Water Act (SDWA)**[10] is a federal statute that sets minimum quality and safety standards for every public water system and every source of drinking water in the United States. This includes rivers, lakes, reservoirs, springs, and subsurface water wells. The SDWA's standards vary based on the size and usage of the system. The statute requires the EPA to balance both *costs* and *health* benefits in setting the standards. Public water agencies are required to test and monitor water sources and systems at various points. A report of the results must be given to the state regulatory agency on a regular basis. The SDWA also requires states to oversee programs to certify that water system operators engage in safe practices and that they have the technical and financial capacity to ensure a consistent supply of safe drinking water as well as the ability to respond quickly to any defects in the water system.

CONCEPT SUMMARY   Water Pollution Control

- Water pollution and conservation regulation is addressed by a combination of federal, state, and local statutes and rules.
- Water quality standards are set and regulated through the Clean Water Act.
- States set and monitor water quality standards for the navigable waterways within their state's borders, subject to EPA review.
- Pollution emission into the waterways is regulated through the EPA's National Pollution Discharge Elimination System, which establishes permitting procedures issued as either individual permits or general permits, required regardless of the quality of the receiving water or actual pollution.

---

[9]As of July 2010, BP's cleanup costs were in excess of $3.2 billion.
[10]42 U.S.C. § 300.

- Existing sources of pollution are required to install the best practical control technology, whereas new applicants are required to employ the best available technology in order to obtain a permit.
- The Safe Drinking Water Act is a federal statute that sets minimum quality and safety standards for every public water system and every source of drinking water in the United States.
- Congress increased the EPA's authority to prevent and respond to disastrous oil spills in water sources through the Oil Pollution Act.

REGULATION OF SOLID WASTE AND HAZARDOUS MATERIALS DISPOSAL

Although hazardous waste was historically within the jurisdiction of state legislatures, several debacles in the early 1970s in which toxic waste was discovered to have polluted community water sources resulted in congressional action in the form of a comprehensive federal statute. Although the handling, proper disposal, and liability for cleanup of abandoned solid waste and hazardous materials is regulated by federal law, states still play a crucial role in enforcement. Solid waste generally means garbage, refuse, sludge from a waste treatment plant, and sewage. Hazardous materials are chemical compounds and other inherently toxic substances used primarily in industry, agriculture, and research facilities (such as cleaning fluids or pesticides).

Resource Conservation and Recovery Act

The **Resource Conservation and Recovery Act (RCRA)**[11] is intended to regulate *active and future facilities* that produce solid waste and/or hazardous materials. The RCRA created a "cradle-to-grave" procedure for handling waste from its origins, transportation, treatment, storage, and disposal. Like many other environmental laws, the RCRA established reporting requirements and procedures, and provides for civil penalties and citizen suits. In egregious cases, the RCRA also includes criminal provisions for prosecution of intentional violations.

The RCRA bans the open dumping of solid waste and authorizes the EPA to set standards for municipal waste landfill facilities. The law specifies special procedures that must be employed for disposal of certain types of municipal waste such as refrigerators (which often contain potentially toxic refrigerant solution). The regulations govern the location, design, operation, and closing of a landfill site and require regular testing for groundwater contamination.

Waste that is (or becomes) hazardous is also regulated by the RCRA. The statute regulates both those who generate the pollution and those transporting the waste. A generator is defined by the law as any facility whose processes create hazardous waste. A transporter is an entity that moves hazardous waste from one site to another via ground, water, or air transportation. These regulations include a mandatory tracking system using a standardized hazardous waste manifest form that establishes a chain of custody for the waste to ensure accountability. The RCRA also imposes a permit system for facilities that will treat, store, or dispose of hazardous waste.

Universal waste (batteries, florescent bulbs, and mercury-containing equipment such as thermostats) is included under the RCRA, but the EPA has issued federal rules that makes compliance easier for business owners who are disposing of universal waste in the ordinary course of operations. It allows for universal waste to be transported by

---

[11]42 U.S.C. § 6901, et seq.

common carrier rather than a more expensive hazardous waste carrier that has been certified by the EPA. Used tires, oil, and batteries are also covered by the RCRA, and the EPA has established special guidelines for disposal of motor vehicle waste products by repair and service facilities.

Toxic Substances Control Act

The **Toxic Substances Control Act (TSCA)**[12] is a federal statute that gives the EPA jurisdiction to control risks that may be posed by the manufacturing, processing, use, and disposal of chemical compounds. The TSCA's scope is very broad: it covers every chemical substance except pesticides, tobacco, nuclear material, and items already regulated under the Food, Drug and Cosmetic Act.[13]

The TSCA has both reporting and regulatory components. Specifically, the statute provides for (1) the EPA to maintain an inventory of every chemical substance that may be legally manufactured, processed, or imported into the United States; (2) the EPA authority to require companies to conduct specific screening tests that may reveal risks to public welfare; (3) the EPA regulation on use, labeling, and control measures of the substance; (4) record-keeping requirements; and (5) an obligation to report any potential adverse impact that the manufacturer, processor, or importer may become aware of in the course of operations.

CONCEPT SUMMARY   Regulation of Solid Waste and Hazardous Materials

- The Resource Conservation and Recovery Act is intended to regulate active and future facilities that produce solid waste and/or hazardous materials using a "cradle-to-grave" procedure for handling waste.

- The Toxic Substances Control Act is a federal statute that gives the EPA broad jurisdiction to control risks that may be posed by the manufacturing, processing, use, and disposal of chemical compounds.

- Although the handling, proper disposal, and liability for cleanup of abandoned solid waste and hazardous materials is regulated by federal law, states play a crucial role in enforcement.

COMPREHENSIVE ENVIRONMENTAL RESPONSE COMPENSATION AND LIABILITY ACT

LO18-7

While the environmental laws that we have discussed focus on controlling and reducing existing or new sources of pollution, toxic waste contamination that had been generated prior to the enactment of waste control statutes and then abandoned by the polluter became a major hurdle to achieving environmental safety for the public. To confront the problem, Congress passed the **Comprehensive Environmental Response Compensation and Liability Act (CERCLA)**[14] in 1980.

---

[12]15 U.S.C. § 2601.

[13]Includes food, food additives, pharmaceuticals, and cosmetics. This law is discussed in detail in Chapter 21, "Consumer Protection Law."

[14]42 U.S.C. § 9601.

Superfund

The CERCLA is commonly referred to as the **Superfund** because its main provisions center on the notion that cleanup operations for abandoned toxic waste sites (including both land and water sites) were to be funded by a self-sustaining quasi-escrow fund administered by the federal government. Superfund was initially funded by fees and taxes levied upon substances that contain hazardous components, primarily in the petroleum and chemical industries. However, the statutory scheme also replenishes the fund by allocating financial responsibility to parties that are statutorily responsible for all or part of the cleanup costs. Therefore, the cleanup of a particularly toxic site could be conducted, and then the EPA could sue a statutorily responsible party for cleanup costs. Critics of the law argue that the Superfund is consistently underfunded and that taxpayers bear a disproportionate amount of the cleanup costs. Proponents argue that the Superfund model is the most effective way to halt further damage from abandoned toxic waste sites while identifying polluters and assessing financial liability.

In 1986, the CERCLA was amended by the **Superfund Amendments and Reauthorization Act (SARA).**[15] Although SARA's provisions were primarily clarifications and technical definitional adjustments, the law contained a new requirement for states to establish emergency response commissions to draft and implement emergency procedures in the event of a hazardous chemical accident. All states must maintain and revise the plan as necessary, as well as funding a hazardous materials response unit. It also requires businesses to disclose the presence of certain chemicals within a community and imposes an affirmative obligation to notify authorities of any spills or discharges of hazardous materials. For continuity sake, this textbook refers to the term Superfund to mean all of the provisions of CERCLA and SARA *combined*.

LO18-8 Removal and Remedial Responses   The Superfund law established a two-front approach to handling hazardous substance cleanup: (1) **removal,** which authorizes actions to be taken to address releases or imminent releases of hazardous materials; and (2) **remedial,** which requires the EPA to identify the most hazardous waste sites and establish a National Priorities List (NPL) for cleanup. In determining what sites are eligible, the EPA considers the overall potential harm to public health. To date, the EPA has placed over 25,000 sites around the country on the NPL. Once on the NPL, the EPA begins the remedial enforcement process by investigating the site, identifying parties that may be liable for cleanup costs, assessing the toxicity of the site, and determining the best remedial measure to accomplish cleanup. Figure 18.1 provides a map of Superfund sites on the NPL.

> **KEY POINT**
>
> The Superfund law addresses hazardous substance cleanup in two ways: (1) removal (for imminent releases) and (2) remedial (long-term cleanup projects).

Liability of Principally Responsible Parties (PRPs)   The sharpest teeth of the Superfund law are (1) it is retroactive and, therefore, applies to any disposal made prior to its enactment in 1980, and (2) its statutory imposition of broad strict liability standards for cleanup costs on certain businesses and individuals that fit the statute's definition of a *principally responsible party* (*PRP*). The Superfund also specifically imposes *joint and several* liability on PRPs. There are three classes of PRPs:

- Current owners of the site.
- Any owner or operator of the site at the time when the hazardous substances were disposed at the site.
- Any business that accepts hazardous substances for transport to the site and selected the site (such as a waste hauler).

Legal Speak »))
Joint and Several Liability The legal principle that makes two or more parties liable for an entire debt either individually or jointly in any proportional combination.

---

[15]42 U.S.C. § 9601e.

FIGURE 18.1   Superfund Sites

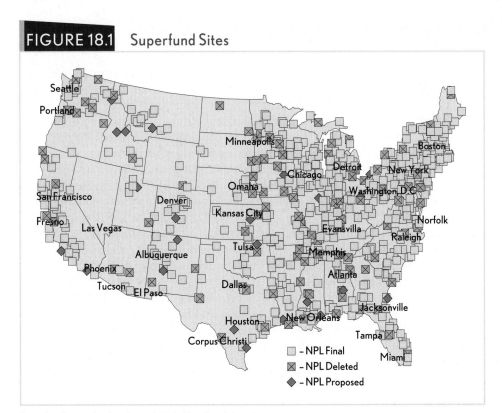

Source: http://toxmap.nlm.nih.gov/toxmap/superfund/mapControls.do.

For example, suppose that a parcel of commercial real estate is listed on the NPL because the groundwater is contaminated due to a leak in an underground storage tank. The EPA investigates the parcel and finds records of three previous owners: GasCo. (used it for a retail gasoline station), ChairCo. (used it for warehouse storage of furniture), and its current owner, DevelopCo. (using it for real estate development) who has plans to build a retail storefront. They also determine that hazardous materials were stored in underground tanks by GasCo. Subject to certain defenses (discussed next), both GasCo. and DevelopCo. have joint and several liability for cleanup costs. Suppose further that GasCo. has been dissolved or was liquidated under the bankruptcy law and it no longer exists as an entity. Under the Superfund law, the EPA can hold DevelopCo., as the parcel's current owner as of the NPL listing, liable for the *full* amount of the cleanup costs even though they never contributed to the contamination.

Consent Decrees   Once the EPA has contacted the PRPs, the agency begins negotiations centered on PRP liability and cleanup operations. The parties draft a series of nonbinding agreements in order to evidence their good faith in moving the cleanup process ahead. If negotiations result in a settlement being reached before cleanup efforts are commenced or are complete, the EPA and PRP enter into a binding agreement, called a *consent decree,* that lays out how the cleanup plan will be implemented and who bears which costs. If the EPA believes the PRP is not negotiating in good faith or is stalling, it may cease negotiations, implement a cleanup plan, and pursue a civil suit against the PRP to recover the entire amount of the cleanup costs. The EPA may also begin enforcement actions against the PRP that may result in civil fines or, in extreme cases, criminal prosecution.

Allocation of Liability   When the EPA enters into a consent decree with a PRP, the PRP now has the right to sue third parties such as transporters, other polluters, and municipalities to recover a portion of cleanup costs related to the polluter's action. However,

FACT SUMMARY   For decades, two public landfills in Connecticut accepted industrial waste, including municipal solid waste from various municipalities. The EPA declared the landfills to be Superfund sites because they were leaking chemicals and threatening the local water supply. The EPA began the remedial enforcement process by investigating and identifying various PRPs that contributed to the pollution and entered into consent decrees for them to contribute to the cost of cleanup. The PRPs, who were all corporations who had disposed of waste in the landfills, formed a coalition to represent their common interests and sued several municipalities for contribution to the cleanup costs. In a long, complicated litigation, a special master was appointed by the court to try to mediate a settlement. The special master came to certain conclusions about which parties contributed how much waste. At trial, the district court did not follow the conclusion of the special master and allocated much of the liability to the municipalities that ran the landfills. The municipalities appealed.

SYNOPSIS OF DECISION AND OPINION   The U.S. Court of Appeals for the Second Circuit affirmed the district court's ruling. Appellate courts will not overturn a district court's allocation of remediation costs in Superfund cases unless there is an abuse of discretion. It was within the right of the court not to follow all of the findings of the special master and to allocate more costs to the municipalities than recommended by the master. For the court to abuse its discretion, it would have to have committed an error of law or be clearly wrong in its finding of facts.

The allocation of costs in such complicated proceedings may produce varying results; the court chose a method of allocation that was proper based on the evidence.

WORDS OF THE COURT: Court's Discretion under CERCLA   "Because [CERCLA's] expansive language affords a district court broad discretion to balance the equities in the interests of justice, the appellate court will not overturn the district court's allocation of response costs absent an abuse of that discretion. A district court abuses or exceeds the discretion accorded to it when (1) its decision rests on an error of law (such as application of the wrong legal principle) or a clearly erroneous factual finding, or (2) its decision—though not necessarily the product of a legal error or a clearly erroneous factual finding—cannot be located within the range of permissible decisions. [. . .] A district court must give 'some deference' to a master's recommendation where the master has 'direct and extensive' knowledge about the particular circumstances of a given case. A district court that extends some deference to the master will consider his recommendation and the factors influencing it, but will not regard the recommendation as the alpha and omega of the analysis. [. . .] The Federal Rules of Civil Procedure expressly permit a district court to 'modify' a special master's report. [. . .] [A] plaintiff may recover any necessary costs of response incurred consistent with the national contingency plan. [. . .] [CERCLA] does not limit courts to any particular list of factors. The court may consider the state of mind of the parties, their economic status, any contracts between them bearing on the subject, any traditional equitable defenses as mitigating factors and any other factors deemed appropriate to balance the equities in the totality of the circumstances."

Case Questions

1. Suppose the coalition sues the companies that transported the waste? Are they liable as a PRP? Why or why not?

2. Do you think that courts should have broad discretion when engaging in a Superfund allocation analysis? Why or why not?

allocating liability among multiple polluters is a difficult process. In Case 18.2, an appellate court considers the scope of authority and discretion of courts engaged in a Superfund allocation analysis.

Defenses to Liability

As you may imagine, the Superfund law has come under fire by business advocacy groups for its potential to devastate innocent property owners and lenders. As a result, Congress carved out several defenses to liability for parties that meet certain criteria.

Secured Creditors   Suppose in the DevelopCo. case hypothetical that during EPA's investigation, DevelopCo. defaults on its mortgage payments and its financial lender foreclosed on the property. Because the lender is now the owner, does that subject the bank to liability under Superfund? Probably not. To protect lenders (such as banks) who have become owners of contaminated property through foreclosure, the Superfund law contains a provision that excludes any such lender from liability for cleanup costs. Lender/owners may avoid liability so long as the lender was (1) an owner by virtue of the contaminated property being used as collateral for a loan, and (2) not participating in the management of the facility prior to foreclosure. The EPA has issued specific guidelines to define what activities constitute participating in management.

Innocent Landowners   A current owner of a site that is listed on the NPL may avoid liability for cleanup costs so long as the owner establishes that she purchased the property without knowledge of the contamination. The owner must submit evidence that she

---

 Self-Check   PRP Liability
Who has PRP liability?

The EPA placed a parcel of land known as Noxious Flats on the NPL in 2009 due to contamination caused by chemicals from cleaning solvents and from lead paint. Determine whether each party has PRP liability from the following table:

Party	Relationship to Noxious Flats	Hazardous Substances Use
Richmond Industries	Owned property from 1970–1979 and operated an industrial plant.	After use of industrial cleaning solvents, the used solvents were stored in an underground tank.
Bright Paint Company	Leased the property from Richmond from 1979–1985.	Dumped paint production waste into hole in the ground and buried it.
Warehouse Storage Inc.	Purchased property from Richmond in 1986 without any environmental investigation. Installed concrete over the entire property and built warehouse spaces for lease.	No contamination by Warehouse Storage. Richmond underground tank ruptured in 1988 and caused groundwater contamination. Warehouse Storage had no knowledge of rupture.
The Factory Restaurant	Leased from Warehouse Storage from 1995 to 2008. Built an upscale restaurant as part of a community revitalization project to turn blighted industrial areas into retail and restaurant zones. Lessor hired an environmental service company to survey the property before signing a lease and no contamination was detected.	No contamination.
First Neighborhood Bank	Foreclosed on Warehouse Storage Inc. who defaulted on a loan in 2008.	None.

Answers to this Self-Check are provided at the end of the chapter.

conducted *all appropriate inquiries* into the previous ownership using a reasonable amount of investigation to determine if any contamination is present. So long as the owner complies with land use restrictions, takes reasonable steps to limit the impact of the hazardous substances on the general public, and cooperates with government agencies, she may avoid cleanup liability under the statute.

Prospective Purchasers   In 2002, Congress enacted the Small Business Liability Relief Act,[16] which provided a defense to Superfund liability for a party that purchased the property *with knowledge* of the contamination. The statute provides for limited liability so long as the owner agrees to take reasonable steps to limit the impact of the contamination, prevent further contamination, and to notify authorities of any imminent or actual pollutant release.

SOLUTIONS FOR MANAGERS

Avoiding Environmental Liability in Land Acquisitions

PROBLEM   *A land acquisition may result in Superfund liability for the purchasing business even if the acquirer did not contaminate the property.*

Suppose that Chef Kuo is looking for a new location for expanding her restaurant operations. She locates a potential property, but when visiting the site, Kuo notices that it is adjacent to inactive railroad tracks. In the past, Kuo recalls an article in the local newspaper that reported on some railroad yards in the area that were contaminated by a toxic substance called PCB that was buried beneath the tracks when they were put down many years ago. Kuo is convinced that this property is ideal for her newest restaurant, but is concerned about any potential environmental liability. Yet, at this early stage of the acquisition, she does not wish to invest in an expensive assessment.

SOLUTION   *Engage a qualified firm to perform an environmental transaction screen.*

When considering a property for acquisition or lease, a simple transaction screen can be conducted to provide the buyer with more data on potential environmental problems with the property. Prior to signing any agreement committing to the purchase, Kuo should engage an environmental services consulting firm to conduct a transaction screen. This screen (also called an *Environmental Phase I*) is a minimal, relatively inexpensive assessment that typically consists of (1) record checks for ownership,

code violations, or environmental agency actions; (2) an interview with the current site owner; and (3) a site visit for obvious signs of potential environmental liability (such as an aboveground port for an underground tank). In Kuo's case, if the transaction screen indicates potential contamination, Kuo may chose to either abandon the transaction entirely and continue her search, or may invest more money in further assessments (Phase II and Phase III) that include soil and groundwater testing to determine the presence of contamination and, if necessary, recommend a process for remediation of the contamination. These more advanced assessments are much more expensive, so Kuo will have to decide if the costs of assessment (and possible remediation) are sufficiently equal to the benefits of putting her restaurant on that site.

It is also important for business owners and managers to be sure that the firms they are hiring are *qualified* within the meaning of federal and state statutory definitions. In order to assert an innocent purchaser defense, the company must have relied on the report of a qualified environmental professional. Federal and state statutes lay out the standards for qualifications. The EPA standards include (1) certification by the federal government to perform environmental inspections, (2) the professional must be a licensed engineer or geologist, (3) with a minimum education of a bachelor's degree, and (4) 10 years of relevant work experience. To see the EPA's full set of guidelines, see this textbook's Web site at www.mhhe.com/melvin.

---

[16]42 U.S.C. § 9607(r).

CONCEPT SUMMARY   Superfund Response

- If there is an immediate threat of hazardous materials release, the Superfund law requires immediate *removal* efforts. Local authorities respond pursuant to their Superfund emergency plan.
- In cases of long-term contamination of a land or water site, the Superfund law requires the EPA to determine suitability for placement on the National Priority List (NPL).
- For sites listed on the NPL, government authorities then investigate the site's chain of ownership to determine any principally responsible parties (PRPs) and assess cleanup alternatives.
- Government officials negotiate with PRPs to determine contributions for cleanup. If an agreement is reached, the parties enter into a binding agreement called a Consent Decree. If the negotiations fail, the government typically files a Superfund lawsuit to collect cleanup costs from PRPs.

WILDLIFE PROTECTION

Wildlife and aquatic life are protected by a series of specialized federal statutes, including the Marine Mammal Protection Act and the Migratory Bird Conservation Act. These laws impact industries such as fisheries or logging because they restrict certain activities even on private lands with the objective of protecting wildlife. Perhaps the most important wildlife protection is the **Endangered Species Act (ESA).**[17] The ESA is administered jointly by agencies in the U.S. Department of Commerce and the U.S. Department of the Interior.

TABLE 18.1   Major Environmental Laws

National Environmental Policy Act (NEPA) of 1969	Establishes a process that must be followed by federal agencies in making decisions that may reasonably impact the environment or when federal funding is involved.
Clean Air Act (most recently amended in 1997)	Improves outdoor air quality based on National Ambient Air Quality Standards that set permissible levels of certain air pollutants. The law focuses on pollution from both stationary sources (manufacturing plants) and mobile sources (motor vehicles).
Clean Water Act	Sets standards and regulates disposal into public waterways.
Resource Conservation and Recovery Act (RCRA)	Regulates *active and future facilities* that produce solid waste and/or hazardous materials using a "cradle-to-grave" procedure, including handling regulations from its origins, transportation, treatment, storage, and disposal.
Comprehensive Environmental Response Compensation and Liability Act (CERCLA). CERCLA is commonly referred to as *Superfund.*	Addresses hazardous substance cleanup in two ways: (1) removal (for imminent releases) and (2) remedial (for long-term cleanup projects).

---

[17]16 U.S.C. § 1531.

Nuisance p. 464   A common law legal action to redress harm arising from the use of one's property based on the aggrieved party's right to enjoy his/her property without interference from a third party.

Citizen suits provisions p. 465   Laws that authorize private individuals or watchdog groups to file environmental enforcement lawsuits.

National Environmental Policy Act (NEPA) p. 465   Enacted in 1969 to serve as a national charter for environmental regulation by establishing a process that must be followed by federal agencies in making decisions that have the potential to have a significant impact on the environment.

Clean Air Act (CAA) p. 468   First enacted in 1963 to improve, strengthen, and accelerate programs for the prevention and abatement of air pollution, focusing on stationary and mobile sources in the United States.

Stationary sources of air pollution p. 468   Fixed-site emitters of air pollutants, such as fossil-fueled power plants, petroleum refineries, petrochemical plants, food processing plants, and other industrial sources.

Mobile sources of air pollution p. 468   Nonstationary sources of air pollutants, such as automobiles, buses, trucks, ships, trains, aircraft, and various other vehicles.

State Implementation Plan (SIP) p. 468   A mandated state plan for complying with the federal Clean Air Act, administered by the Environmental Protection Agency, which consists of a collection of regulations that help to achieve a reduction in pollution.

Operating permits p. 468   Licenses issued by authorities to existing stationary sources that permit pollution emission at certain levels.

Market-based approach p. 469   Instituted by the 1990 Clean Air Act amendments to give businesses a choice of methods embracing an economic incentive in complying with pollution standards.

Clean Water Act (CWA) p. 471   A federal statute that is implemented and enforced by the EPA to regulate water quality standards.

Oil Pollution Act (OPA) p. 472   A statute enacted in 1990 to streamline and strengthen the Environmental Protection Agency's ability to prevent and respond to catastrophic oil spills in water sources.

Safe Drinking Water Act (SDWA) p. 473   A federal statute that sets minimum quality and safety standards for every public water system and every source of drinking water in the United States.

Resource Conservation and Recovery Act (RCRA) p. 474   A federal law enacted in 1976 to regulate active and future facilities that produce solid waste and/or hazardous materials.

Toxic Substances Control Act (TSCA) p. 475   A federal statute that gives the Environmental Protection Agency jurisdiction to control risks that may be posed by the manufacturing, processing, use, and disposal of chemical compounds.

Comprehensive Environmental Response Compensation and Liability Act (CERCLA) p. 475   A statute enacted by Congress in 1980 to create a tax on the chemical and petroleum industries and provide broad federal authority to respond directly to releases or threatened releases of hazardous substances that may endanger public health or the environment.

Superfund p. 476   Another name for the CERCLA derived from its main provisions on the notion that cleanup operations for abandoned toxic waste sites were to be funded by a self-sustaining quasi-escrow fund to be administered by the federal government.

Superfund Amendments and Reauthorization Act (SARA) p. 476   An amendment to the CERCLA in 1986 containing a new requirement for states to establish emergency response commissions to draft and implement emergency procedures in the event of a hazardous chemical accident; for businesses to disclose the presence of certain chemicals within a community; and to impose an affirmative obligation on businesses to notify authorities of any spills or discharges of hazardous materials.

Removal p. 476   Authorizes actions to be taken to address releases or imminent releases of hazardous materials as established by the Superfund law.

Remedial p. 476   Requires the Environmental Protection Agency to identify the most hazardous waste sites and generate a National Priorities List as established by the Superfund law.

Endangered Species Act (ESA) p. 481   An environmental law passed in 1973 that lays out a procedure for identification and preservation from extinction of imperiled species.

Regional Cuisine Publications Corporation (RCPC) is the publisher of a monthly magazine that features recipes and features on culinary traditions from various geographic regions in the United States. RCPC began in the south and expanded into the mid-Atlantic and New England markets in the last 10 years. Part of RCPC's business model was that the actual name of the magazine distributed in a certain region took on that region's name (*Southern Cuisine, New England Cuisine,* etc.). Although RCPC began its business by contracting with outside vendors for supplying magazine-quality paper, as they expanded circulation RCPC sought to reduce rising paper costs by producing its own paper in-house. RCPC's management located a small production facility that was owned by Paper Production Inc. since 1950. RCPC begins to consider purchasing the facility and property.

1. In investigating the purchase of the facility, what environmental laws will RCPC need to be aware of? In what way could environmental regulation affect the costs of the transaction?

2. Assume that the facility emits certain pollutants in the air. RCPC wishes to partially reconstruct the facility after its purchase for purposes of being able to run the facility for longer periods of time. Does this trigger any regulatory concerns?

3. Suppose that the facility emits more of a certain pollutant than permitted by the EPA standards. What are RCPC's options under the CAA's market-based approach?

4. Assume that the facility discharges waste from the paper production process into an adjoining river and, because Paper Products was struggling financially, they never upgraded their technology. If RCPC purchases the facility, will they be required to upgrade the waste discharge technology under the Clean Water Act? What is the standard set by the CWA for upgrading technology?

5. What type of precautionary measures should RCPC's management take to be sure to limit potential Superfund liability prior to any purchase of the site?

Assume that in Theory to Practice above, RCPC wishes to pursue negotiations for the purchase of the facility and that you are a junior manager at RCPC. You receive the following e-mail from your senior manager.

We are pursuing the purchase of the paper facility, but we are concerned about environmental liability due to potential groundwater contamination. Please write a two- to three-page memorandum that recommends two environmental consulting firms in the area to conduct an assessment. We want to be sure that these firms are qualified as defined by the law. Research

(1) what qualifications are required by our state environmental agency or the EPA, (2) determine which firms in our area are qualified, and (3) provide a brief description in your memorandum of each firm based on their Web site.

After rereading the Solutions for Managers feature from earlier in this chapter, write a two- to three-page memorandum in response to your senior manager's request. Note that a link to EPA's standards (as well as a sample answer to this Manager's Challenge) may be found on this textbook's Web site at www.mhhe.com/melvin.

CLEAN WATER ACT

El Paso Gold Mines owns 100 acres of land bought in 1968 near Cripple Creek, Colorado. Though El Paso did not engage in mining activity on the land, the land contained a collapsed mine shaft built in 1910. The shaft is connected to a six-mile-long drainage tunnel that is connected to other old mines, draining into Cripple Creek. A citizens' watchdog group, the Sierra Club, brought suit alleging that El Paso violated the Clean Water Act by discharging pollutants (zinc and manganese) from a source, the mine shaft, into the creek without a discharge permit.

1. Does the Sierra Club have an actionable claim under the Clean Water Act? Why or why not?

2. If El Paso wanted to use the land for mining activity, would they be required to obtain a permit? If so, what would need to be done in order to obtain the permit?

CASE SUMMARY 18.2 :: U.S. v. Southeastern Pennsylvania Transportation Authority, 235 F.3d 817 (3rd Cir. 2000)

SUPERFUND

The Paoli Rail Yard covers about 30 acres in Paoli, Pennsylvania, and consists of an electric train repair facility owned by Amtrak and operated by Philadelphia-based Southeastern Pennsylvania Transportation Authority (SEPTA). Prior to Amtrak's acquisition of the property, the site was owned by the Pennsylvania Railroad Company from 1939 until 1967, Penn Central Transportation until 1976, and Conrail until 1982. All previous owners are now defunct. In 1979, a toxic chemical known as PCB was discovered in the rail yard and the EPA declared it a Superfund site. The EPA then began the remedial enforcement process and brought an action against potentially responsible parties.

CASE QUESTIONS

1. Do any of the prior owners of the rail yard have PRP liability?

2. Could SEPTA or Amtrak have taken action to avoid liability? Explain.

CASE SUMMARY 18.3 :: William Paxton v. Wal-Mart Stores, Inc., 176 Ohio App. 3d 364 (2008)

RESOURCE CONSERVATION AND RECOVERY ACT

Paxton, a proprietor, intended to set up a recycling facility on one of his properties. He then contracted with Wal-Mart to recycle or dispose of various lamps and bulbs that contained spent mercury, and other products that contained lead. Instead of recycling the items, Paxton crushed or shredded them and left them piled on the property. The state determined that there were hazardous waste violations, and it filed suit.

CASE QUESTIONS

1. What federal statute(s) could apply to this case? Explain.

2. Citing the RCRA "cradle-to-grave" procedure, do you think Wal-Mart was contributory in violation of the statute? Why or why not?

CLEAN AIR ACT

Black, a realtor, owned adjacent rental properties in a New York neighborhood. On the same block, Stroehmann Bakeries owned and operated a bakery. Black alleged that the bakery has emitted "noxious discharges," and that these emissions have coated his properties with mold and mold residue. As a result, Black's properties have been discolored, causing a loss of rental income and resale value. An investigation was conducted, and the agency concluded that the bakery is the source of the mold growth found on Black's properties.

CASE QUESTIONS

1. What standard is used to determine whether or not the discharges constitute a violation of the Clean Air Act?

2. What common law doctrine could Black have possibly pursued in an attempt to compel Stroehmann to cease polluting?

 Self-Check **ANSWERS**

PRP Liability

1. *Richmond Industries.* Liable as a PRP because it owned the plant at the time of disposal of the cleaning solvents in the tank. Note that, under Superfund, it is *irrelevant* that the disposal was made prior to the Superfund law's enactment (Superfund is retroactive) and that no actual *contamination* took place while they owned the parcel.

2. *Bright Paint.* Liable as a PRP. Same rationale as above.

3. *Warehouse Storage Inc.* Probably not liable as a PRP. No disposal took place under their ownership. The contamination occurred under their ownership, but they never disposed of any solid waste or hazardous materials.

4. *The Factory Restaurant.* No liability as a disposer of materials. If the EPA places Noxious Flats on the NPL while The Factory Restaurant was operating on the site, they are still shielded from liability under the Superfund as an innocent purchaser/lessor by performing environmental assessment prior to entering into a lease.

5. *First Neighborhood Bank.* No liability as a PRP. They are shielded because they are a secured creditor who did not actively participate in ownership or operation prior to the foreclosure.

19
CHAPTER

Antitrust and Regulation of Competition

learning outcomes checklist

After studying this chapter, students who have mastered the material will be able to:

19-1　Understand the fundamental purpose and source of law for antitrust regulation.

19-2　Identify the main federal statutes in antitrust law.

19-3　Distinguish and explain the differences between the per se standard and the rule of reason standard.

19-4　List and articulate the primary ways that businesses use horizontal and vertical restraints of trade.

19-5　Recognize when a business has achieved a monopoly and explain the restrictions on a monopoly business under antitrust law.

19-6　Explain why the *U.S. v. Microsoft* case is an important part of antitrust law.

19-7　Articulate the role of more modern antitrust statutes in regulating competition.

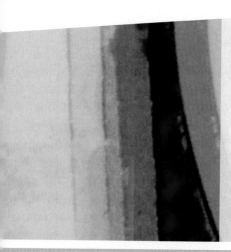

Even in a free market economy, business owners and managers depend on certain regulation of competition in the marketplace. This regulation allows for innovation and entrepreneurial effort to thrive without the threat of being eliminated from the marketplace by larger competitors who have already established a market share. The law also promotes competition among businesses that allows consumers to receive the benefits of competitive pricing. This chapter covers regulation of competition, which is primarily accomplished through antitrust laws enforced by the federal government. Specifically, students will learn:

■ The background, scope, and purpose of laws that regulate competition.

■ The statutory model for antitrust laws.

■ How antitrust laws are applied to various anti-competitive actions by business.

LO19-1 BACKGROUND, PURPOSE, AND SOURCE OF ANTITRUST LAW

The purposes of antitrust law are to prevent, punish, and deter certain anticompetitive conduct and unfair business practices. Original notions of antitrust law come from the shifting of the U.S. economy from predominantly family agriculture and small merchants into the industrial revolution era whereby the historically famous robber barons of the late 19th century accumulated and wielded such market power that other companies could not compete on a level playing field. These business entities were known as *trusts* (the most famous being Rockefeller's Standard Oil Trust) and ultimately resulted in one company being able to manipulate prices that resulted in limited choices and high prices for consumers. President Theodore Roosevelt, the renowned trustbuster, led a movement that resulted, eventually, in federal regulation of trusts that were engaged in anticompetitive behavior. Antitrust laws are exclusively federal statutes and the agencies charged with enforcement of these laws are the Department of Justice (U.S. Attorney's Office) and the Federal Trade Commission. Violators of antitrust laws are subject to both *civil penalties* and *criminal sanctions,* including incarceration.

Modern day antitrust enforcement is concerned primarily with protecting the *competitive process* rather than protecting individual competitor companies. The underlying theory is that protection of this process will ultimately benefit consumers.

LO19-2 FEDERAL STATUTES AND ENFORCEMENT

The statutory scheme of federal antitrust law is actually a combination of five different laws. The **Sherman Act**[1] (1890) is the centerpiece of the antitrust law and it prohibits contracts, combinations, and conspiracies in restraint of trade, and monopolization. The **Clayton Act,**[2] first enacted in 1914 and significantly amended in 1936 by the **Robinson-Patman Act** and in 1950 by the **Celler-Kefauver Antimerger Act,** deals with specific types of restraints, including exclusive dealing arrangements, tie-in sales, price discrimination, mergers and acquisitions, and interlocking directorates. These restraints are covered in detail later in this chapter.

Both the U.S. Department of Justice and the Federal Trade Commission (FTC) enforce various antitrust laws. The **Federal Trade Commission Act**[3] of 1914, administered solely by the FTC, is a catch-all enactment that has been construed to include all the prohibitions of the other antitrust laws.

In addition to government enforcement of antitrust statutes, the laws also permit an aggrieved party to file a private enforcement action against an alleged antitrust violator. Some antitrust statutes allow a party that suffered damages by virtue of any antitrust violation the right to a private suit in the federal courts for *triple* damages sustained plus reasonable attorneys' fees and a court order restraining future violations. These statutes are intended to provide a significant financial deterrent to antitrust infraction and to compensate parties injured through anticompetitive behavior.

> **KEY POINT**
>
> Antitrust matters are covered by federal law, with the Sherman Act as the primary governing statute.

LO19-3 SHERMAN ANTITRUST ACT

Thought of as the central piece of the federal antitrust law, the Sherman Act is divided into two parts. First, the act provides prohibitions against restraints of trade. The Sherman Act

---

[1] 15 U.S.C. §§ 1–7.
[2] 15 U.S.C. §§ 12–27.
[3] 15 U.S.C. §§ 41–58.

The Sherman Act was created to limit the ability of corporate giants such as Standard Oil Trust, founded by John Rockefeller (left), to monopolize markets and control major industries. President Theodore Roosevelt, depicted in an editorial cartoon of the era (right), became known as the nation's trustbuster.

prohibits "[e]very contract, combination in the form of trust or otherwise, or conspiracy, in restraint of trade or commerce."[4] The second part of the act covers monopolization. The Sherman Act provides a remedy against "[e]very person who shall monopolize, or attempt to monopolize . . . any part of the trade or commerce among the several States."[5] This prohibition does not make a monopoly illegal automatically. Only a monopoly that has been *acquired* or *maintained* through prohibited conduct is illegal. The Sherman Act has both civil and criminal penalties.

To understand the distinction between the sections, consider the difference between single-firm conduct (only one business engaged in a certain transaction or behavior) and multifirm conduct (more than one business engaged in a certain transaction or behavior). Multifirm conduct tends to be seen as more likely than single-firm conduct to have an anticompetitive effect, and is regulated under Section 1 of the act. Single-firm conduct is less likely to be considered as restraining trade, but under certain circumstances, for example, using market domination to eliminate a competitor, is covered by Section 2 of the act.

Per Se Standard versus Rule of Reason Standard

While the sweeping language of this section, taken literally, could reasonably be read as a blanket ban on virtually every commercial agreement, the U.S. Supreme Court has long held that the statute applies only to those parties who have acted in some *unreasonable*

---

[4]15 U.S.C. § 1.

[5]15 U.S.C. § 2.

manner that resulted in an identifiable anticompetitive behavior. The Court has developed two standards for use by federal courts in deciding whether or not a certain transaction or action violates the Sherman Act: the **per se standard** and the **rule of reason standard.** Some concerted activities are so blatantly anticompetitive that they are considered *per se* violations. Competitors that collude to set artificially high prices, known as *price fixing,* is a clear example of a per se violation. The per se standard has been developed into a comparatively complicated body of law and tests for federal courts to apply. But the case law still gives business owners and managers relatively clear guidance on what constitutes blatant violations of the Sherman Act that have no competitive justification. In effect, the per se rule means that if a company has committed a per se violation of the act, as articulated in the body of case law, the violator has no defense. The per se standard also promotes more consistent enforcement by regulatory authorities.

For example, suppose that SportCo. operates a chain of sporting goods stores in the southeastern United States. SportCo.'s president contacts the owner of Main Street Athletic Gear and the two agree not to undercut each other on the price of baseballs. They set the price at 30 percent higher than fair market value. These two have colluded against consumers by fixing an artificially high price for a product. Because the SportCo.–Main Street agreement is blatantly anticompetitive, it is a per se violation of the Sherman Act.

Rule of Reason

Despite the substantial body of case law that makes up the various rules used in applying the per se standard, the economic complexities of the global business community, technology and individual industry practices are too unique to be assessed using a strict per se standard. Recognizing the need to assess a certain transaction's impact on the broader marketplace, the Court developed a second standard known as the *rule of reason.* Even if a transaction is not considered a per se violation, the actions or transaction in question must also meet the alternate standard. The rule of reason requires that a fact finder (judge or jury) embark on an examination into market complexities and industry practices in order to determine whether or not the parties' actions violate the Sherman Act. Under this standard, a business alleged to have committed a violation may offer evidence that their actions were reasonable because they were justified and necessitated by economic conditions. In essence, the rule of reason contemplates a scale in which the court weighs any anticompetitive harm suffered against marketwide benefits of their actions. Through this examination, a court may determine whether or not such justification is merely a *pretext* for advancement of the violator's economic benefit or whether, in fact, the economic benefits outweigh the burdens.

For example, suppose that in our SportCo.–Main Street example above that instead of agreeing to set a price, that the president of SportCo. offered to lead efforts to form Retail Business Association (RBA) with Main Street and other area retailers for the purpose of sharing ideas, information, and data. Depending on the form and content of the information sharing, the RBA may be a violation of antitrust laws. However, RBA would argue that the rule of reason (not per se) should apply, and would have to offer legitimate business reasons and economic justifications. If a court finds that any anticompetitive harm caused by RBA is outweighed by marketwide *benefits* of their actions, RBA's formation does not violate the Sherman Act.

LO19-4   Per Se Sherman Act Violations: Restraints

The U.S. Supreme Court and other federal appellate courts have developed a body of case law that deems certain actions or transactions as a per se violation of the Sherman Act. Certain per se violations are through the use of **horizontal restraints;** that is, restraining trade through one company partnering with a *competing* company (thus located horizontally

FIGURE 19.1

Chain of Commercial Supply

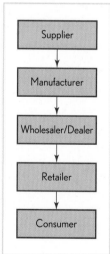

on the chain of commercial supply, such as competing retailers or competing manufacturers) to take action resulting in the elimination or reduction of competition from other competitors. Businesses may also commit a per se violation of the Sherman Act through use of a **vertical restraint.** This type of restraint of trade takes the form of one company colluding with another company (other than a competitor) along the chain of commercial supply (see Figure 19.1), such as a manufacturer colluding with a retailer on the price of a product.

Horizontal Restraints

Although any concerted agreement among competitors to reduce competition or attempt to manipulate the competitive market is a horizontal restraint and a per se violation of antitrust law, the most common types of prohibited horizontal restraints are horizontal price fixing, allocation of markets or customers, and boycotts.

Meeting of the Minds

One crucial component of a horizontal restraint is some meeting of the minds among the parties about the restraint. The statute requires the conspiring parties to *agree* to and then commit an *overt act.* As one would imagine, any illegal agreement is likely not to be explicit (or certainly not in writing), so courts have permitted proof of meeting of the minds to be satisfied through *circumstantial* evidence regarding the timing of any communication between the parties and their subsequent restraining actions.

In one of the most famous essays in the history of economic thought, Adam Smith wrote in *The Wealth of Nations* in 1766, that "people in the same trade seldom meet together even for merriment or diversity, but the conversation ends in a conspiracy against the public or in some contrivance to raise prices." This famous quote was used by prosecutors in a high-profile antitrust case against Alfred Taubman, the chairman of the well-known auction firm Sotheby's Holding, Inc., and Sir Anthony Tennant, chief executive of Christie's International. In the case, no direct evidence (such as a witness) of the agreement existed, but prosecutors used business calendars and other data to build a timeline and alleged that the two men met on twelve occasions, and then engaged in an unusual course of action concerning policies on commissions that each firm followed after the last of the twelve meetings. Both executives were convicted in December 2001.

Price-Fixing

Any agreement by competitors to fix the price for buying or selling a particular good, or an agreement by competitors to fix the quantity of goods to be produced, offered for sale, or bought are per se violations of the Sherman Act. For example, suppose NewCo. and OldCo. are competitors in the market selling computer chips. They may not agree to set the price at $250 per package of 50. Doing so would be a bald-faced attempt to increase their profits by leaving the consumer with no options. Nor may they agree to

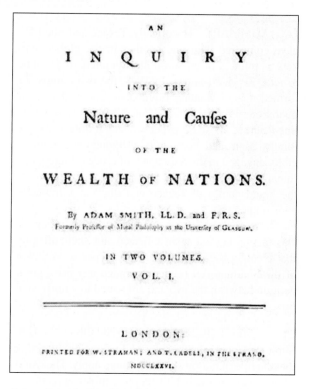

Adam Smith's *Wealth of Nations* is often cited in support of the notion that frequent meetings and conversations by competitors are circumstantial evidence of anticompetitive collusion.

limit the production or sale of computer chips to 100,000 per month in order to manipulate the supply and demand curve that is essential to a market economy.

There are, of course, some instances when conduct by competitors with respect to pricing policies does not constitute price-fixing. In some industries, price-leading (cutting or increasing prices based on the actions a competitor) is commonplace. Although this may appear to be price-fixing, the element of agreement is usually not satisfied, because the competitors are not taking these actions in concert. For example, suppose that Economy Jet begins to cut its airfare on the routes from Boston to New York City. It is almost inevitable that all other airlines would cut their fares on those routes as well. If Economy Jet cuts it price, there can be no legitimate conclusion that the parties intended to act to restrain competition.

In the past decade, the U.S. Supreme Court has narrowed the use of the per se standard and expanded the use of the rule of reason analysis in certain cases of horizontal price fixing. In Case 19.1, the Court used the rule of reason standard in evaluating a joint venture alleged to have engaged in price-fixing.

Market Allocation   Agreements among competitors dividing markets by territory or by customers are anticompetitive and illegal per se. Such arrangements are blatantly restrictive because they leave no room for competition of any kind. Thus, competing firms may not divide among themselves the geographical areas in which they sell, nor may they

CASE 19.1   Texaco, Inc. v. Dagher, et al., 547 U.S. 1 (2006)

FACT SUMMARY   Historically, Texaco and Shell Oil have competed with one another in the global markets as refiners of crude oil and suppliers of gasoline to retail service stations. In 1998, the two companies formed a joint venture, Equilon, to consolidate their operations in the western United States. Texaco and Shell agreed to share expenses and profits from the jointly controlled new entity. Although the Equilon entity engaged in the refinement of crude oil into gasoline, the actual end product was sold to retailers under the brand names of Texaco and Shell at a mutually agreed upon price.

The retailers of Texaco and Shell products brought a class action lawsuit against Texaco and Shell, alleging that creating the joint venture was a per se violation of the Sherman Act because it ended any price competition between the two and amounted to a horizontal price-fixing scheme.

SYNOPSIS OF DECISION AND OPINION   The U.S. Supreme Court ruled in favor of Texaco/Shell, holding that the rule of reason standard should apply. The Court reasoned that per se liability applies only to agreements that are so plainly anticompetitive that no study of the industry is needed to establish their illegality. In this case, the market analysis was relevant. The Court held

that the joint venture agreement was *not* horizontal price-fixing because the challenged pricing policy was simply price-setting by a single entity, Equilon, and not a pricing agreement between competing entities with respect to their competing products.

WORDS OF THE COURT: Narrow Per Se Rules   "[T]his Court has long recognized that Congress intended to outlaw only unreasonable restraints. Instead, this Court presumptively applies rule of a reason analysis, under which antitrust plaintiffs must demonstrate that a particular contract or combination is in fact unreasonable and anticompetitive before it will be found unlawful. Per se liability is reserved for only those agreements that are so plainly anticompetitive that no elaborate study of the industry is needed to establish their illegality. Accordingly, we have expressed reluctance to adopt per se rules where the economic impact of certain practices is not immediately obvious."

Case Questions

1. Does this case mean that competitors may simply create a joint venture to avoid any liability for price-fixing?

2. Why did the retailers allege that forming this joint venture was anticompetitive behavior?

distribute customers or allocate the available market. All such understandings, whether direct or indirect, are unlawful.

Boycotts   When competing firms agree to a *concerted* refusal to deal with a third party (whether it be buying from or selling to the party) this may be considered a per se Sherman Act violation. Although the U.S. Supreme Court has narrowed this doctrine and has applied the rule of reason in some limited cases, a concerted agreement to boycott a supplier or consumer group is still a very risky proposition. In *United States v. Colgate,* decided in 1919, the U.S. Supreme Court held that a *unilateral* boycott does not fall under the Sherman Act. However, even the so-called *Colgate* doctrine has been narrowed. In order to pass anticompetitive muster, the boycott must be truly unilateral with no other party having direct or indirect involvement.

 Self-Check   Horizontal Restraint

What type of horizontal restraint is at issue?

1. Two gasoline service stations are located on opposite sides of the same street. The two owners agree not to undercut each other on gas prices.

2. Two suppliers agree not to sell their product to a certain retailer because they believe that the retailer is undercutting other larger retailers in price and that has impacted the larger retailers' purchases from the two suppliers.

3. Two retailers of activewear clothing agree that one will sell only in the Miami market and the other only in the Atlanta market.

Answers to this Self-Check are provided at the end of the chapter.

Vertical Restraints

Vertical price-fixing occurs when a seller attempts to control the resale price of a product at a lower level in the supply chain. For example, any concerted action or agreement between a manufacturer and a retailer to fix the price at the retail level is a per se violation of the Sherman Act. Although a manufacturer may (and often does) suggest a resale price without running afoul of antitrust laws, any agreement between two business entities to establish a specific retail price is prohibited. Unlike horizontal agreements to fix a price, the per se rule does *not* apply to vertical agreements that only affect the price. The pivotal element to establish a per se vertical price fixing violation is an agreement to a specific retail price. This is why dealers and retailers will generally use the phrase "manufacturer's suggested retail price" (MSRP) in marketing literature, advertising, and so on.

Nonprice Restraints   The per se standard *does not* apply to nonprice vertical restraints. Rather, a court applies the rule of reason standard (discussed earlier in this section). Vertical restraints that do not involve price-fixing generally refer to some type of restraint on the distribution of a product in the marketplace. Although business entities have always had the right to *unilaterally* assign exclusive territories to its distributors, and to limit the number of distributors that are authorized to sell their product in a specific geographic area, certain agreements between sellers and distributors relating to sales of a product outside the exclusive territory may give rise to an allegation of an unlawful vertical restraint. These restraints are frequently an attempt to control *intrabrand competition* (i.e., the setting of different prices by different distributors for the same product) of a seller's products among various distributors with the intent of boosting the product's relative competitiveness with similar products made by other sellers (known as *interbrand competition*). For example, Raleigh is the manufacturer of expensive watches and sells the product through both Connelly and Sicius as exclusive distributors. Raleigh's interest is in making sure that Connelly and Sicius don't compete with each other in the same geographic market (intrabrand competition) because Raleigh wants to be sure that the pricing for the watches is in line with the pricing and the market share of Raleigh's competing companies (interbrand competition). Therefore, Raleigh attempts to impose a restriction that limits their distributors to specific geographic territories and prohibits them from selling outside those territories. These restraints on Connelly and Sicius help ensure that Raleigh watches will continue to thrive in the marketplace. Any arrangement Raleigh makes with Connelly and Sicius is considered a vertical restraint. Because courts use the rule of reason standard for vertical restraints, Raleigh's plan could still survive judicial scrutiny if it were justified on the grounds that it does not have a negative impact on competition in the watch-manufacturing industry.

Tying Agreements   Tying agreements occur when a seller refuses to sell a certain product (the tying product) unless the buyer also purchases a different product (the tied product) from the seller. Typically, this occurs where a seller has a substantial share of the market for the tying product, and is attempting to leverage the power of the tying product to gain market share for another of the seller's products. This tying arrangement model violates the Sherman Act. For example, Kahlo's firm has a substantial share of the cable modem market, but has recently introduced a new brand of Ethernet cable (used to connect the cable modem to a computer). If Kahlo requires her distributors to purchase the Ethernet cable as a condition of the sale of the cable modems, she has used her market share to tie the cable modems to the Ethernet cable. Note also that tying arrangements may be a violation of the Clayton Act (discussed later in this chapter).

The most difficult question in analyzing a tying agreement is where to draw the line between legitimate parallel product enhancements and anticompetitive market manipulation. A producer of shoes is clearly entitled to "tie" the right shoe with the left shoe, but what about products that have separate, albeit related, functions? This problem has resulted in courts developing a **soft per se analysis** for determining the legality of a tying arrangement. In *U.S. Steel v. Fortner Enterprises,*[6] the U.S. Supreme Court provided guidance for lower courts by setting out a four-part test. In order for a tying arrangement to be illegal, the government (or plaintiff) must show that (1) the agreement involves two separate and distinct items rather than integrated components of a larger product, service, or business system; (2) the tying product cannot be purchased unless the tied product is also purchased; (3) the seller has sufficient economic power in the market to appreciably restrain competition; and (4) a "not insubstantial" amount of commerce in the tied product is affected by the seller's tying agreement.

CONCEPT SUMMARY   Restraints of Trade

- Horizontal restraints (acting in concert with a competitor on same level of distribution) include
    - a. *Price-fixing.* Agreement between competitors to fix actual prices and agreements that affect prices are generally illegal per se.
    - b. *Market allocation.* Agreement between competitors to divide up markets or geographic regions is illegal per se.
    - c. *Boycotts.* Concerted refusal to sell or buy from an individual, firm, or group. May be illegal per se or by use of the rule of reason, depending on specific facts.

---

[6]429 U.S. 610 (1977).

- Vertical restraints (acting in concert with another party on a different distributional level) include
  a. *Vertical price-fixing.* Agreement between buyer and seller with respect to the price of resale of the product is illegal per se.
  b. *Exclusive selling, territorial, and dealing agreements.* Relationship between buyer and seller related to an exclusive franchise and/or a specified territory is governed by the rule of reason and the Clayton Act.
  c. *Tie-ins.* Sellers that tie a second product to the first product are acting illegally per se if the seller possesses sufficient market power as to render the tie-in as coercive.

ANTITRUST LAW AND PROFESSIONAL SPORTS

One particularly difficult question under antitrust law is whether professional sports leagues, such as the National Football League, are a legitimate joint venture or whether sports leagues are a conspiracy to restrain trade that is prohibited by the Sherman Act. In 2010, the U.S. Supreme Court gave its latest guidance on the topic in *American Needle, Inc. v. National Football League.*[7] The case involved the NFL's licensing contract for merchandising of its teams' logos for shirts, hats, sweatshirts and other attire and memorabilia. Although the NFL had previously extended nonexclusive merchandise rights to multiple companies, in December 2000 the NFL changed course and granted an exclusive contract to Reebok to produce and sell trademarked merchandise for *all* of the league's 32 teams. One of the company's frozen out by the new arrangement, American Needle, Inc., sued the NFL claiming that the Reebok agreement was a result of collusion between the 32 teams that amounted to an illegal conspiracy under the Sherman Act. The NFL argued that although the teams were separately owned and operated, the league itself was a single entity for purposes of merchandising and therefore was incapable of such a conspiracy effectively exempting them from Sherman Act liability. Although a federal appellate court ruled in favor of the NFL, the Supreme Court unanimously reversed the appellate court's decision and held in favor of American Needle. Using a rule of reason analysis, Justice John Paul Stevens, himself a former antitrust lawyer, wrote "[w]hen teams license such property, they are not pursuing the common interests of the whole league, but, instead, the interests of each 'corporation itself.'" The Court ruled that although the NFL teams did have some common objectives, that they were also competitors not only on the field, but as corporations. The teams compete to attract fans, increase gate receipts, and for contracts with management and player personnel. Therefore, the Court rejected the NFL's single-entity theory and held that they were subject to the Sherman Act.

MONOPOLIZATION

LO19-5

A monopoly holder has inherent power in setting prices without any chance of losing market share due to competition. Antitrust laws designed to combat this problem are known as **structural offenses** because they generally do not involve a behavioral aspect (such as price-fixing). Section 2 of the Sherman Act was designed to prevent business monopolies, but it does not *prohibit* a business entity from becoming a monopoly. Rather, the statute outlaws *affirmative action* toward monopolizing or attempting to monopolize a part of trade or commerce. The Sherman Act also prohibits the use of *monopoly power* to create an anticompetitive market in a particular industry. In the landmark monopoly case *U.S. v. Grinnell,*[8] the

> ### KEY POINT
> The Sherman Act does not prohibit a business entity from becoming a monopoly, but it does outlaw affirmative action toward monopolizing or attempting to monopolize a part of trade or commerce.

---

[7] 560 U.S. ____ (2010) [No. 08-661].
[8] 384 U.S. 563 (1966).

U.S. Supreme Court defined monopolization as "the willful acquisition or maintenance of power in a relevant market as opposed to growth as a consequence of superior product, business acumen or historical accident." Thus, in order for a business entity to violate Section 2 of the Sherman Act, they must have possessed not only monopoly power, but also must have an overt intent to monopolize.

Monopoly Power

A business entity that has the power to fix prices or to exclude competitors in a given market is said to have monopoly power. The focus for determining whether or not an entity has monopoly power is the entity's share of the relevant market. Although the Court has not laid down a bright-line test for what percentage of market share is required for determining whether a monopoly exists, firms that have had as low as 50 percent of the market have been found to have monopoly power. Courts may also look at other factors, such as the existence in the industry at issue of barriers to entry of new competitors, in their analysis.

LO19-6 The *Microsoft* Case

One of the most famous monopoly cases was *U.S. v. Microsoft,* in which the federal government sued Microsoft for anticompetitive behavior in development and distribution of its Internet browser software called Explorer. The government alleged that Microsoft used its monopoly in the computer operating systems market to eliminate competition from a more popular Internet browser, called Navigator, sold by Netscape. The trial court ruled against Microsoft and ordered the radical remedy of requiring Microsoft to reorganize its operating system entity separate and apart from its entity responsible for Explorer.

On appeal, the D.C. Circuit Court of Appeals issued an opinion that affirmed much of the trial court's decision, but reversed some key rulings as well. Most significantly, the appellate court vacated the order that required the company to break apart. While the court affirmed the finding by the trial court that Microsoft fundamentally employed illegal anticompetitive means to maintain and further their monopoly of the operating systems market, the court reversed and remanded for reconsideration on the findings that Microsoft illegally attempted to monopolize the browser market and ruled that the appropriate standard was the rule of reason analysis.[9]

The Consent Order   At the same time, a number of individual states and companies that had been damaged by Microsoft's actions, such as Sun Microsystems, were also suing Microsoft. However, before the new trial, the Department of Justice and many of the states came to terms and settled the case by entering into a consent order. The order required Microsoft to provide competitors with the detailed technical information to make competing products, such as e-mail and multimedia players, work seamlessly with its Windows operating system. Microsoft also agreed to make Windows available under a standard licensing agreement (without any tying product) to computer manufacturers.

In 2002, U.S. District Judge Colleen Kollar-Kotelly approved the settlement, ruling that the consent order was in the public interest and rejected arguments by some states that the order wasn't tough enough on Microsoft. This ruling was widely viewed as a victory for Microsoft and, once their appeal to a higher court failed, the states ended their legal battle against the software giant.

Intent to Monopolize

Once a court has determined that a particular business entity holds monopoly power, the next question centers on the entity's willful intent to acquire or maintain the monopoly. This analysis

Legal Speak »)
Consent Order An agreement between the government and a party that spells out detailed conditions and compliance measures that the party agrees to take in exchange for the government not pursuing a court action.

---

[9]*U.S. v. Microsoft,* 253 F.3d 34 (D.C. Cir. 2001).

requires a court to examine whether or not the alleged monopolizer has engaged in a course of conduct that would reasonably lead one to conclude that the entity has purposefully furthered or attempted to maintain monopoly power. It is a difficult standard to spell out because each case and each industry have their own complexities. However, it is important to note that the courts have not required a showing that the entity engaged in predatory practices against a competitor (although this would clearly be a sign of intent to maintain or expand a monopoly) in order to have liability under the Sherman Act. For example, an appellate court has held that a national aluminum manufacturer and distributor violated Section 2 of the Sherman Act simply by acquiring every new opportunity relating to the production or marketing of aluminum.

Attempted Monopolization

Because actual monopoly power is relatively rare, the Sherman Act also prohibits *attempts* by a business to gain monopoly power; that is, when a business entity that does not yet have monopoly power pursues an anticompetitive course of conduct designed to achieve it. The analysis of attempted monopolization focuses on a three-part test. First, the entity must have had a demonstrable and specific intent to achieve a monopoly. Second, the entity must have acted in an anticompetitive manner designed to injure its actual or potential competition. Third, a dangerous probability that monopoly power would in fact be achieved exists.

CLAYTON ACT

The Clayton Act (and its amendments) curb certain anticompetitive practices that are not specifically covered by the Sherman Act. Congress clearly intended the Clayton Act to be a vehicle for attacking practices that monopolists had historically used to create monopoly power. As a result, the act is designed as a preventative statute. Both the Department of Justice and the Federal Trade Commission (FTC) enforce the Clayton Act.

Tying Arrangements and Exclusive Dealing

One important provision of the Clayton Act prohibits tying arrangements and exclusive dealing agreements involving the sale or leasing of *commodities*. Any agreement that involves services, real estate, or intangible property must be attacked under the Sherman Act. The tying arrangement model discussed earlier in this chapter in the context of the Sherman Act is the same model that is covered by the Clayton Act. Any tying arrangement that requires a buyer to purchase one product (the tied product) as a condition of buying another product (the tying product) from the same seller is considered anticompetitive. Some courts have held that the standard for finding an antitrust violation under the Clayton Act is less rigorous than that required under the Sherman Act. These courts have held that the proof of the seller's economic power in the market, necessary to establish a Sherman Act violation, is *not* required for a Clayton Act tying violation.

Exclusive dealing agreements are also covered in Section 3 of the Clayton Act. As discussed earlier in this chapter, an exclusive dealing agreement (such as a franchise) is a form of vertical restraint. These agreements fall under the Clayton Act because they are arrangements between buyers and sellers where buyers agree to handle one seller's product exclusively, or to purchase their entire product line from the same seller. Not all such arrangements violate the Clayton Act (franchise agreements, for example, are exclusive dealing arrangements that don't violate antitrust laws). Only agreements that may "substantially lessen the competition or tend to create a monopoly" violate the act.

Mergers and Acquisitions

Historically, business entities could gain monopoly power by merging their company with a competitor or acquiring the competitor through a buyout. The Clayton Act was designed to prevent this monopoly strategy. The act prohibits business entities from acquiring the stock or assets of their competitors where the action will substantially lessen competition or tend to create a monopoly.

LO19-7 HART-SCOTT-RODINO ANTITRUST IMPROVEMENTS ACT OF 1976

The Hart-Scott-Rodino Act is a preventative statute that requires business entities that are contemplating mergers involving dollar amounts of a certain size to give advance notice to the FTC and the Department of Justice of their intention. This provides the Department of Justice with veto power on a proposed merger if the transaction would violate any of the antitrust laws (including the Sherman Act).

ROBINSON-PATMAN ACT

Although the Clayton Act covers the anticompetitive arrangement known as price discrimination, the Robinson-Patman Act, enacted in 1936, amended the Clayton Act provisions to provide for broader regulatory authority to curb price discrimination. As a practical matter, the Robinson-Patman Act is enforced almost exclusively by the FTC.

Price Discrimination

Section 2(a) of the act makes it illegal for a business entity to discriminate in price "between different purchasers of commodities of like quality or grade." This discrimination, however, is only illegal when the discrimination results in an effect that may substantially lessen competition or tend to create a monopoly, or injure, destroy, or prevent competition with any person who either grants or knowingly receives the benefit of such discrimination.

To violate Section 2(a), a business entity must have made two or more sales to different purchasers at different prices. This means that quoting a discriminatory price or refusal to sell except at a discriminatory price are not violations of the act.

KEY TERMS

Sherman Act p. 488 The centerpiece of the statutory scheme of federal antitrust law, prohibiting contracts, combinations, and conspiracies in restraint of trade, and monopolization.

Clayton Act p. 488 A federal antitrust law first enacted in 1914 as a preventative statute that deals with specific types of restraints, including exclusive dealing arrangements, tie-in sales, price discrimination, mergers and acquisitions, and interlocking directorates.

Robinson-Patman Act p. 488 A federal antitrust law enacted in 1936 amending the Clayton Act provisions to provide for a broader regulatory authority to curb price discrimination.

Celler-Kefauver Antimerger Act p. 488 A federal antitrust law enacted in 1950 amending the Clayton

Act provisions by severely restricting anticompetitive mergers resulting from the acquisition of assets.

Federal Trade Commission Act p. 488 Enacted in 1914, establishing the Federal Trade Commission to administer the act; intended as a catch-all enactment that has been construed to include the prohibitions of the other antitrust laws.

Per se standard p. 490 A Latin term literally meaning "of, in, or by itself," without any additional facts needed to prove a point; this is one standard used by federal courts in deciding whether or not a certain transaction or action violates the Sherman Act, occurring when concerted activities are blatantly anticompetitive.

Rule of reason standard p. 490 A second standard used by federal courts in deciding whether or not a certain transaction or action violates the Sherman Act, contemplating a scale in which the court weighs any anticompetitive harm suffered against marketwide benefits of their actions.

Horizontal restraints p. 490   Per se violations of the Sherman Act in which the restraining of trade involves agreements between competitors to take action resulting in the elimination or reduction of competition from other competitors.

Vertical restraints p. 491   Per se violations of the Sherman Act in which the restraining of trade involves agreements between noncompetitors acting in concert with another party on a different distributional level in the chain of commercial supply.

Vertical price-fixing p. 493   When a seller attempts to control the resale price of a product at a lower level in the supply chain.

Soft per se analysis p. 494   Developed by the courts for determining the legality of a tying arrangement. Under this analysis, sellers that tie a second product to the first product are illegal per se if the seller possesses sufficient market power as to render the tie-in as coercive.

Structural offenses p. 495   Antitrust laws designed to combat the problem of monopolization by outlawing affirmative action toward monopolizing or attempting to monopolize a part of trade or commerce.

THEORY TO PRACTICE

SurgiPro is a company engaged in the manufacturing and sale of surgical instruments to physician groups and hospitals. After several decades in the market, SurgiPro has a 75 percent market share in the surgical instrument industry. SurgiPro was approached by Medical Devices Corporation (MDC), a competitor of SurgiPro with only a 5 percent market share. MDC proposed that the two companies cease undercutting each other on the retail price of scalpels. Instead, MDC proposed that each company sell only 1,000 scalpels per month at a set price of no lower than $15 per scalpel. MDC reasoned that the sale of scalpels had such a low profit margin, that the only way either SurgiPro or MDC could make a profit on the product would be through this plan. An executive at SurgiPro agreed to consider the plan.

1. Have the parties committed a violation of any antitrust laws? What laws may apply in this situation, and is the fact that SurgiPro agreed to consider the plan significant?

2. How is the plan that MDC is proposing best characterized in the context of antitrust law?

Assume that SurgiPro has rejected MDC's proposal, but instead proposes that they agree that SurgiPro will sell its products only to customers in the mid-Atlantic states and that MDC will sell only in southern states.

3. Which, if any, antitrust laws does SurgiPro's proposal violate?

4. If SurgiPro and MDC are sued by a competitor, should the court use the per se standard or the rule of reasonableness? Why?

Suppose that both SurgiPro and MDC purchase raw materials for their products from SupplyCo. SurgiPro notifies SupplyCo. that they will no longer purchase their raw materials unless SupplyCo. ceases their sales to MDC. SupplyCo. agrees because they do not want to lose the substantial revenue from SurgiPro.

5. Which, if any, antitrust laws does this action violate?

6. Assume that SurgiPro wishes to merge with MDC. What antitrust laws will need to be considered before entering into a merger agreement?

Mid-level managers are sometimes required to prepare a memorandum for an executive manager that helps the executive manager prepare for a meeting (a "prep memo") with another company's principals. Assume you receive the following e-mail from your executive manager:

I will be meeting with a representative of MDC tomorrow. Please draft a two-page prep memo that provides information on entering into a joint venture with them for selling scalpels. We could share in expenses of manufacturing and distribution of scalpels, and split the profits equally. The memo should address how this venture could be structured and whether or not we could still use the brand names. I read an article in *The Wall Street Journal* about antitrust issues in a similar agreement between Texaco and Shell. Perhaps that will help you in preparing the memo.

Prepare a two-page prep memo for your executive manager. A sample answer may be found on this textbook's Web site at www.mhhe.com/melvin.

CASE SUMMARY 19.1 :: Covad Communications Co. v. BellSouth Corp., 299 F.3d 1272 (11th Cir. 2002)

PREDATORY PRICING

Covad is in the business of providing DSL Internet service to consumers in the southern region of the United States. BellSouth is the regional telephone company covering the area and also offers DSL Internet service. Covad and BellSouth entered into an agreement whereby Covad would lease BellSouth's phone lines used in Covad's DSL service. Covad alleged that, after the contract was executed, BellSouth engaged in predatory pricing. They sued BellSouth for violation of the Sherman Act, claiming that BellSouth's efforts were an attempt to further a monopoly and squeeze Covad out of the market.

CASE QUESTIONS

1. Who prevails and why?
2. What section of the Sherman Act is at issue here?
3. How should the court apply the statute to this case?

CASE SUMMARY 19.2 :: Data General Corporation, et al., v. Grumman Systems Support Corporation, 36 F.3d 1147 (1st Cir. 1994)

TYING

Grumman Systems accused Data General of violating the Sherman Act based on Data General tying the sale of their copyrighted software with a requirement that the buyer enter into an agreement to purchase Data General's support services for the software. Data General defended on the basis that the support services were an integral part of its software and not a separate product.

CASE QUESTIONS

1. Is this tying arrangement a violation of antitrust laws? Explain your answer.
2. Is this an example of a horizontal or vertical restraint?

ANTICOMPETITIVE ACTION

IBM manufacturers and sells computers and related equipment. It also has a leasing division. Greyhound was a leasing company that would purchase "second generation" computers from IBM at up to a 75 percent discount (depending on how old the equipment was) and then lease them to their customers at a relatively inexpensive price. In fact, because Greyhound could buy at such a high discount, they were able to undercut IBM's standard lease rates. Although IBM had about 82 percent of this leasing market, IBM became concerned when its leasing market share fell and determined that the main reason for their loss of the leasing market was due to companies like Greyhound being able to offer better terms to consumers. IBM phased in reduced discount rates so that the maximum discount was 12 percent. Greyhound sued IBM alleging monopolization in violation of the Sherman Act.

CASE QUESTIONS

1. Who prevails and why? Explain your answer.
2. Are there any similarities between this case and the Microsoft case?

HORIZONTAL RESTRAINTS

Tanka was a student-athlete attending the University of Southern California. When she decided to transfer to UCLA, the athletic director at USC invoked an NCAA rule that allowed USC to prevent Tanka for playing sports at UCLA for one year. The NCAA rule only applied to student-athlete transfers within a particular conference. Tanka sued USC and the NCAA claiming that the rule amounted to a horizontal restraint violating the Sherman Act.

CASE QUESTIONS

1. Who prevails and why?
2. Should the rule of reason be used in this analysis? Explain.

 Self-Check **ANSWERS**

Horizontal Restraint

1. Price-fixing.
2. Boycott.
3. Market allocation.

20
CHAPTER

Creditors' Rights and Bankruptcy

learning outcomes checklist

After studying this chapter, students who have mastered the material will be able to:

20-1 Distinguish between unsecured creditors and secured creditors and determine the rights of each set of creditors.

20-2 Apply the framework for a secured transaction for personal property under UCC Article 9 in a business context.

20-3 Articulate the process of obtaining a secured interest in real estate.

20-4 Explain the various nonstatutory options and legal ramifications for a business facing financial distress.

20-5 Determine the rights, protections, and obligations of both creditors and debtors under federal bankruptcy laws.

20-6 Distinguish and explain the various bankruptcy options for debtors under Chapter 7, Chapter 11, and Chapter 13 of the bankruptcy code.

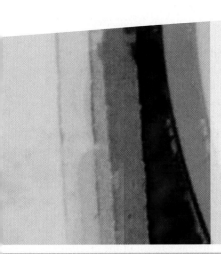

The financial crisis that drove the markets sharply downward in 2008 is perhaps the most prominent confirmation of the fact that global commerce depends on credit. Creditors are one of the most important components of the global economy because they provide merchants and consumers with the opportunity to purchase goods and inventory, acquire real estate/assets, and expand business operations without spending large sums of cash to fund current business operations. In order to encourage creditors to extend appropriate commercial credit to merchants and consumers, the law gives certain protection to creditors. At the same time, the law also provides statutory protections and other alternatives for borrowers in times of financial crisis. Business owners and managers frequently engage in extending or receiving credit, and understanding the legal ramifications in both circumstances is pivotal to protecting the interests of creditors and debtors. In this chapter, students will learn:

- Laws that govern the relationship between creditors and borrowers and how they apply in a business context.

- Legal ramifications of alternatives for a business facing a financial crisis.

- Fundamental principles of the federal bankruptcy code and its applicability to business.

CREDITORS' RIGHTS

Although people typically think of commercial lenders and banks as being creditors, the scope of creditors is much wider, including manufacturers, suppliers, and retailers. While most creditors have little problem collecting money owed to them, there are certain times the creditor must take legal action to recover the debt. Laws that protect creditors' rights come primarily from common law and statutory law at the state level. Bankruptcy laws, discussed later in this chapter, are primarily federal statutes. The level of protection varies in part based on whether or not the credit was secured by some type of collateral. Credit that is not collateralized is known as **unsecured debt.** When the borrower has pledged collateral in order to obtain credit, the creditor is known as a **secured creditor.**

Legal Speak »))
Collateral Property or land that a debtor promises to her creditor in case she fails to repay her debt.

Unsecured Creditors

Businesses often use unsecured debt in the form of a loan or line of credit primarily to help fund short-term operations. Examples include private loans from another party, loans from a bank or other commercial lender, and credit cards. In each of these cases, credit is extended based on the borrower's creditworthiness rather than as a result of the borrower's promise to pledge collateral. Unsecured creditors are offered very little protection if the borrower defaults on paying back the loan. Note that interest rates on unsecured loans tend to be higher than those based on secured credit.

When a borrower fails to pay back the loan or make payments toward the loan as agreed, the unsecured creditor's exclusive legal remedy is to bring a lawsuit against the borrower and obtain a judgment from the court. Essentially, the basis of such a debt collection lawsuit is breach of contract in that the borrower failed to fulfill his obligations under the contract (repayment). Once the creditor has obtained a judgment, the borrower must either pay the full amount of the judgment or the creditor may pursue court order. This allows the creditor to use a judicially created procedure to seize any property or assets of the borrower.[1] Certain assets, however, are exempt from seizure (such as the borrower's primary residence). Additionally, a creditor's lawsuit or execution of a judgment must be halted if the borrower files for protection under the bankruptcy code (discussed later). As a result, unsecured creditors have very little practical way to collect debts owed. Certain consumer loans and credit card debt are also subject to state and federal statutory regulation regarding late fees, interest rates, disclosures, and credit reporting practices. These regulations are discussed in greater detail in Chapter 21, "Consumer Protection Law."

A credit card is the most common form of unsecured credit used in consumer transactions.

Secured Creditors

When credit is secured by some pledge by the borrower of collateral, the creditor has more viable alternatives to collect the debt. The alternatives depend on the category of secured creditor.

---

[1] In most states, the judgment is executed through use of the Sheriff's Department and sold at auction (known as a *sheriff's sale*).

Secured Transactions under Article 9 of the UCC

One common way that a creditor attempts to ensure full payment by the borrower is by creating a *secured-party relationship* whereby the borrower pledges certain property of value to secure the debt owed. When personal property (such as goods or other assets such as cash) or fixtures to real estate (such as light fixtures or a built-in reception desk) are intended to serve as the collateral, Article 9 of the Uniform Commercial Code provides a uniform set of rules to govern the transaction. With some variations, Article 9 has been adopted in all states and it gives business owners and managers some degree of reliability in planning a loan transaction. Note that loans collateralized with real estate (also known as *real property*) are not governed by Article 9, but rather by statutes related to mortgages, discussed in the next section.

In essence, Article 9 provides a framework for secured transactions by recognizing the rights of the creditor, known as the **secured party,** against other creditors of the borrower and against the borrower himself in the event of a default in payment. In the UCC, a borrower is known as the **debtor.** Article 9 also provides a procedure for the secured party to establish priority in the collateral over other creditors, known as **perfecting** the interest in the collateral. The rights of the secured party are known as a **security interest.** There are several Article 9 requirements in order for a creditor to obtain the *full* benefit of a security interest:

Security Agreement Typically, the parties will enter into a security agreement that specifies the parties, describes the collateral, articulates the obligations of the debtor (primarily payment), and states the remedies available to the secured party in the event of default. In the event the agreement is silent on a particular matter, Article 9 acts to fill that void by providing a standard set of rules.

Perfection Perfection of security interest is the act of establishing the secured party's rights ahead of the rights of other creditors. Although Article 9 does not define the term *perfection,* it does describe an order of priority among creditors and actions that a secured party must take to establish these rights. Perfection occurs at the moment of (1) physical possession of the collateral, or (2) official filing of a statement of notice with a state and/or local government office, or (3) taking legal control of the collateral (such as establishing joint authority over a brokerage account where the account funds are being used to collateralize a loan).

Real Estate

When real estate (also called *real property*[2]) is being used to collateralize a loan, the creditor takes an interest in the collateral through use of a **mortgage.** A mortgage is a written document specifying the parties and the real estate that is filed with a state and/or local government agency and then becomes a public

> ### KEY POINT
> In a secured transaction a creditor must *perfect* her security interest in the collateral in order to be fully protected under UCC Article 9.

Secured credit transactions, such as when the debtor's inventory is used as collateral, are typically governed by a security agreement between the parties.

---

[2]Although some sources cite technical differences between these terms, according to *Black's Law Dictionary,* the term *real estate* is generally synonymous with *real property.*

record that others can look up. This filing is intended to give notice to the public and other creditors of the secured parties' interest in the real estate collateral. The creditor is known as the **mortgagee** and the borrower is the **mortgagor.** A mortgage is typically accompanied by a **promissory note.** The promissory note is a contract whereby the borrower promises to pay back the creditor at a certain rate of interest over a specified period of years (usually 15, 20, or 30 years). State statutes primarily govern the relationship between mortgagor and mortgagee. These statutes define the procedure that the creditor must follow in order to pursue certain remedies against the debtor. The most extreme measure is when a creditor declares the loan in default and institutes a **mortgage foreclosure** in an effort to take title and possession of the real estate in hopes of selling the property to pay off the debt owed. In the wake of the mortgage foreclosure crisis that began in 2007, Congress passed the Mortgage Forgiveness Debt Relief Act.[3] The intent of the law was to assist homeowners in avoiding foreclosure by offering certain guarantees and tax breaks from the government when refinancing a mortgage loan. Properties owned by business entities, or by individuals for business purposes (such as a seashore rental property), are not eligible for relief under this law.

Sureties and Guarantors

Another common method for helping to secure a loan is to require a *third party* to back up the promises made by the debtor regarding repayment of the loan. In some cases, a creditor may be willing to extend a loan to a borrower, but the borrower's creditworthiness may be either questionable or too brief to qualify for the credit required. In such a case, the creditor will usually require that a third party with sufficient creditworthiness and assets also sign the loan agreement and become jointly liable with the debtor for his promise to repay the loan (thus the commonly used term *cosigning*). When a party agrees to be *primarily* liable to pay the loan, she is known as a **surety.** When a party agrees *only* to be liable *if* the debtor actually defaults, she is known as a **guarantor.** For example, in order to secure a loan for the purchase of a new car, Bank requires Cain to have a cosigner because Cain's credit is insufficient to qualify for the loan. Cain convinces Abel to be his cosigner and Bank requires Abel to cosign as a surety. In the first year of the loan, Abel is late in making payments and eventually becomes 60 days past due. Bank now has the option of pursuing remedies against either Cain or Abel to pay the debt. Because Abel has more assets, he is likely the best party to pursue. However, suppose that Abel signed as a *guarantor* instead of a surety. In that case, the bank would have to pursue full remedies against Cain by obtaining a court judgment and attempting to collect as much as possible (such as repossessing the car for resale) before Bank could pursue Abel. In the event Bank cannot recover the full amount from remedies against Cain, *only then* is Cain liable for the balance owed.

Personal Guaranties for Business Loans

Business owners and managers often encounter suretyship and guaranty concepts in the context of a **personal guaranty** of a business loan. When a business borrows money, for example to expand operations or to fund an acquisition of some type, the creditor will often require that the owners (sometimes referred to as the *principals* of a business entity) of small and mid-sized companies give their personal guaranty to back up the business loan. This means that in the event of a default by the business entity/debtor, the principals have pledged their personal assets (such as individual bank accounts, equity in a property, or other assets) if the assets of the business are insufficient to repay the loan. Creditors realize

---

[3]Pub L. 110-142 (2007).

that without this guaranty, the principals of a debtor corporation can simply walk away from the debt without any personal liability for the loan. As a result, creditors often wish to make the principals more accountable by securing a business loan with both a security interest in certain collateral *and* the personal guarantees of the principals. For example, suppose that Caulfield is the principal of Rye Inc., a manufacturing firm specializing in production of high-quality baseball catcher's mitts with annual revenues of $25 million. Rye has been successful over the past 10 years. Now, Caulfield wishes to expand his operations to start to manufacture other baseball equipment and plans to fund the expansion with a loan from Big Bank. Although Rye's operations have been profitable in the past and it will likely have no problem in repaying the loan from existing revenues, in addition to granting Big Bank a security interest in any collateral owned by Rye, Big Bank will also likely require Caulfield to personally guaranty the loan as an additional measure of security. From Big Bank's perspective, the personal guaranty gives them maximum leverage over Caulfield in the event of a default by Rye.

 Self-Check Creditor Status

Determine the status of each creditor.

1. ExtremeCo., a manufacturer of a line of extreme gear such as snowboards, gives Retailer merchandise for her inventory on credit. ExtremeCo. requires Retailer to sign an agreement that describes the inventory as collateral and that Retailer will pay ExtremeCo. monthly based on sales of ExtremeCo.'s product. ExtremeCo. files a statement of interest in the collateral with the appropriate government agency.

2. Office Galaxy sells office supplies to a local insurance agency. Office Galaxy delivers the goods on the first of the month and sends an invoice on the 15th of each month to the manager of the insurance agency.

3. BigBank lends WidgetCo. $100,000 to purchase land in order to build a new warehouse. WidgetCo. uses the land itself as collateral.

4. BigBank lends WidgetCo. $50,000 to fund the hiring of seasonal employees during the holiday rush. BigBank requires the principals of WidgetCo. to sign a promissory note agreeing to pay the note from personal assets if WidgetCo. defaults on payments.

Answers to this Self-Check are provided at the end of the chapter.

CONCEPT SUMMARY   Creditors' Rights

- Unsecured creditors give loans based on creditworthiness without the security of collateral and must bring a lawsuit in the case of default.

- A secured creditor can retain the collateral given to secure his loan; no lawsuit is necessary under the UCC if there is a security agreement and the interest has been perfected.

- A creditor uses real estate as collateral with a mortgage. In the case of default, the debtor goes into foreclosure and the creditor sells the real estate to cover his losses.

- A debtor can obtain a loan with collateral or creditworthiness by getting a third party to pay off the loan for him (surety), or to pay off the loan if he defaults (guarantor). A business without credit can get a loan by using a creditworthy individual as a personal guaranty.

LO20-4 ALTERNATIVES FOR INSOLVENT BORROWERS

When a business venture no longer has adequate assets to maintain its operations and can no longer pay its bills as they become due in the usual course of trade and business they are considered **insolvent.** A company's specific response to insolvency is largely dependent on the type of financial crisis. For example, if the insolvency is a result of *temporary* poor cash flow but the receivables will likely provide enough cash to continue operations in the future, then bankruptcy may not be the best option (or even an option at all depending on the assets/debt ratio of the struggling venture). On the other hand, if the venture is cash-starved because of, for example, a particularly burdensome union contract and has no realistic way to recover from the financial crisis without some statutory protection from creditors, then the law provides the venture with the ability to hold creditors off while the business reorganizes and drafts a plan on how the venture intends to continue its operations in the future. This plan could include a reformation of the problematic union contract. When a business becomes insolvent, its principals have several choices in dealing with the venture's debt. Some of these options do not involve any statutory protections and, therefore, may have legal ramifications for the business and its principals.

Out of Existence

Out of existence (also known as the "lights-out option") is a nonstatutory option where the venture simply ceases operations without paying creditors. Usually the debtor company files an out-of-existence certificate or articles of dissolution with the state corporation bureau and simply ceases doing business. However, the debts are still valid obligations of the company, and a creditor may pursue a debt collection lawsuit in an attempt to collect any available cash or assets to satisfy the debt. In fact, some states require that all creditors be notified before the business is recognized as legally dissolved. Out of existence is a particularly dangerous option if the debt has been secured through a *personal guaranty* by principals of the business (discussed earlier). However, if the debtor has no assets, no personal guarantees exist, and the debt is not substantial enough to make legal methods to collect economically viable for creditors, the lights-out option is the quickest and least expensive option.

Workout: Accord and Satisfaction

When the principals of a business venture wish to continue operations of a business that is underperforming and in poor financial condition, they frequently hire a professional (sometimes called a *turnaround specialist*) to help revise its business model and to negotiate with commercial lenders with the objective of setting the company on sound financial footing. At the same time, in order to avoid collection lawsuits from certain suppliers and creditors, the business venture must also attempt to settle past debts. These various steps of turning around a business are often referred to by creditors as a **workout.**

Recall our discussion from Chapter 7, "Contract Performance: Conditions, Breach, and Remedies," concerning **accord and satisfaction.** When a company or individual is facing a financial crisis, the debtor may approach the creditor and offer to settle the debt for less than the amount owed. Thus, a legal contract is created between debtor and creditor whereby the creditor agrees to accept a sum less than owed in exchange for releasing the debtor from all legal liability. This may allow the debtor some additional time to seek an infusion of capital or collect a large receivable to continue its operations without the threat of a creditor's collection lawsuit or involuntary bankruptcy (discussed later). This option is sometimes used in conjunction with an *out of existence* strategy where the debtor's principals are seeking to have a personal guaranty discharged but have no intent to continue operations.

BANKRUPTCY

Of course, there are circumstances when the debtor's best option is protection from creditors via the bankruptcy code. The concept of forgiveness of debt and protection of borrowers from creditors has deep historical roots that some scholars have traced back to the Old Testament. The underlying concept and public policy objectives behind bankruptcy protection is to give a debtor a "fresh start" and to prevent creditors from gaining unfair advantage over each other in being paid. In the United States, the need for bankruptcy laws was recognized in Article I of the U.S. Constitution.[4] For the most part, bankruptcy proceedings are a matter of federal law. State courts can have some limited involvement in issues that involve the borrower, usually called the *debtor* in a bankruptcy context, in one way or another, but generally do not have any jurisdiction over bankruptcy proceedings. The law of bankruptcy is found within the federal statutes ("bankruptcy code"[5]). The starting place for all bankruptcy matters is the federal bankruptcy court.

The bankruptcy code is divided into chapters, and often the reference to someone filing for bankruptcy protection is known as "filing for Chapter 11." The most common forms of bankruptcy are Chapter 7 (liquidation of debtor's assets and discharge of debts), Chapter 11 (reorganization), and Chapter 13 (debt adjustment and repayment of consumer debt). Other chapters contain definitions, describe procedural aspects of bankruptcy, and contain special provisions for bankruptcies by municipalities, stockbrokers, and railroads. Congress amended the bankruptcy code in 2005 with the Bankruptcy Abuse Prevention and Consumer Protection Act, which imposed additional requirements on those seeking protection under the bankruptcy code. The specific provisions of the 2005 amendment are covered later in this chapter.

Insolvent business ventures have several alternatives for dealing with the business's debts including filing for protection from creditors under the bankruptcy code.

---

[4]Article I, § 8 gives Congress the responsibility to "[E]stablish . . . uniform Laws on the subject of Bankruptcies throughout the United States."

[5]See Title 11 of the United States Code.

Automatic Stay

Filing for bankruptcy protects the debtor through an immediate **automatic stay.** The automatic stay is a legal prohibition of creditors either initiating or continuing any debt collection action against the debtor or her property. The stay is a powerful legal tool because it stops all collection efforts, all harassment, and all foreclosure actions. It permits the debtor to attempt a repayment or reorganization plan or simply to be relieved of the financial pressures resulting from a financial crisis. The stay also allows the bankruptcy court to deal with the debtor's assets and creditors in a single forum where the rights of all concerned may be heard at once.

> **KEY** POINT
>
> An automatic stay halts creditors, including government agencies, from all collection efforts, including litigation.

Bankruptcy Trustee

Another important provision in the bankruptcy code provides for the appointment of a **bankruptcy trustee** in certain cases. A trustee is appointed in cases where the debtor seeks liquidation and discharge of debts (Chapter 7) or in cases where the debtor is a consumer attempting to repay much of the debt over a period of time (Chapter 13). The trustee, often an attorney highly skilled in bankruptcy law, is charged with the duty to collect the debtor's available assets, known as the **bankruptcy estate,** and reduce it to cash for distribution, preserving the interests of both the debtor and creditors. Federal law gives the trustee extensive authority and power to accomplish this objective. For example, the bankruptcy trustee may void certain transfers that are considered to be an unfair advantage of one creditor over another. These are known as **voidable transfers.**

The most common voidable transfer is a *preferential transfer.* A preferential transfer occurs when the debtor makes a payment to satisfy a *prebankruptcy petition* debt to a creditor within 90 days of the petition. If the creditor received more than it would have under the liquidation proceedings, the trustee may void the transfer and have the assets taken back from the creditor and placed back into the bankruptcy estate. Preferential transfers to *insiders* (including relatives, partners, officers, and directors of an individual or corporate debtor) are also voidable. Under certain circumstances, any insider transfers made within one year of the petition filing can be voided and placed back into the bankruptcy estate. Additionally, a transfer is voidable as *fraudulent transfer* if it occurs when a debtor transfers property to a third person within one year of the petition filing with intent to delay, hinder, or defraud creditors. For example, suppose that Eyre is the sole owner of Jane's Pretzel Company (JPC). After several years of reasonable success in business, JPC experiences financial difficulty and owes its creditors $100,000 with only $5,000 in assets. JPC files for Chapter 7 liquidation and discharge. After JPC files the petition, the trustee is appointed and discovers several transfers out of the ordinary course of business. First, two weeks before JPC's petition for bankruptcy, Eyre paid off the entire balance owed to an important vendor on a loan secured by Eyre's personal guaranty. If the trustee determines that the vendor obtained more than it would have from distributing JPC's assets under the bankruptcy code (which is likely in this situation given the assets versus the debts), the payment can be voided and the money would be put back into the bankruptcy estate. Second, Eyre had borrowed $20,000 from her brother-in-law and, despite the fact that the loan was to be paid over five years, Eyre paid back the entire amount one month before filing for bankruptcy. That

> **KEY** POINT
>
> The bankruptcy trustee has the legal power to void any transfer of money that the debtor made for the benefit of insiders.

transaction would be classified as an insider preferential transfer and the trustee would void the transfer and recover the payment from Eyre's brother-in-law on behalf of the bankruptcy estate.

Debtor's Options

When filing for protection under the bankruptcy code, the debtor chooses one of three main options under the code: Chapter 7, Chapter 11, or Chapter 13.

Chapter 7: Liquidation and Discharge

Chapter 7 bankruptcy is perhaps the most extreme measure a business or individual can take. In essence, the debtor agrees to have most of her property liquidated and then the cash distributed to creditors. In exchange, the bankruptcy court gives legal protection to the debtor by discharging any remaining debts. For example, suppose WidgetCo. has $50,000 in debts and only $10,000 in nonexempt assets. The bankruptcy court will distribute the $10,000 to creditors, and the remaining debt ($40,000) will be discharged. WidgetCo. will be out of business, but its principals will get a fresh start and will not have to pay any of the debts incurred. Chapter 7 outlines a very specific procedure for discharge of debt.

Legal Speak ›))
Exempt Assets The bankruptcy code (and some state laws) allows the debtor to keep certain assets even if he has filed for bankruptcy protection. These are known as *exempt assets*. An example is the *homestead exemption*, which allows a debtor to keep all or at least part of the equity in his home.

Bankruptcy Petition   The proceedings are started in the bankruptcy court by the filing of a bankruptcy petition. The petition can either be *voluntary* or *involuntary*. A **voluntary bankruptcy petition** is filed by the *debtor* and includes the names of creditors; a list of debts; and a list of the debtor's assets, income, and expenses. In order to qualify for protection under Chapter 7, the debtor's income must be less than the average income in her home state (known as the *means test*). An **involuntary bankruptcy petition** is one that is filed *against* a debtor by a group of three or more creditors with an unsecured aggregate claim of at least $11,625 who claim that the debtor is failing to pay the debt as it comes due. This is an extreme measure, and involuntary petitions are relatively rare. This option poses some risk for the creditors because the bankruptcy code allows a company to recover damages against creditors who attempt to drive a debtor into bankruptcy but are unsuccessful.

Automatic Stay   As discussed earlier, the filing of a petition gives protection to the debtor immediately. This means that creditors must suspend all collection activity as of the day the petition was filed. Note that the suspension is temporary and designed to give the bankruptcy court the time to decide the validity of the petition.

Order for Relief   Once the court determines the validity of the petition, an order for relief is granted, the automatic stay effectively becomes *permanent,* and the bankruptcy proceeds.

Appointment of Trustee   Once the order of relief is granted, the court appoints an interim bankruptcy trustee to oversee the case. A permanent trustee is elected at the first meeting of creditors. Once appointed, the trustee creates a bankruptcy estate. Note that the trustee is a representative of the court and *not* a representative of the debtor or of the creditors. The trustee has the responsibility to administer the bankruptcy proceedings in accordance with the law.

Meeting of Creditors and Administering the Estate   Within 30 days of the order of relief, the court calls for a meeting of creditors. The debtor (usually along with an attorney) must appear and submit to questioning by the creditors regarding the debtor's assets, financial affairs, and any attempt to conceal assets or income. After the meeting of creditors and election of the trustee, the trustee takes possession of the bankruptcy estate. The estate is comprised of the debtor's interest in real, personal, tangible, and intangible property no matter where that property is located at the time the petition is filed. Property acquired *after* the petition does not become part of the bankruptcy estate. The trustee's responsibility is to collect all assets that are legally required to be liquidated for the benefit of the creditors. Trustees separate exempt and nonexempt property, recover any improper transfers of funds before or during the filing of the petition, sell or otherwise dispose of the property, and finally distribute the proceeds to creditors.

In the case where the debtor is an individual, not all property is subject to liquidation. The debtor is entitled to hold onto certain assets. These assets are known as *exempt assets*.

Note that in a Chapter 7 bankruptcy of a business entity, there are no exempt assets. All assets must be liquidated. For individuals, some examples of exemptions are:

- Up to $18,450 in equity in the debtor's primary residence (homestead exemption).
- Interest in a motor vehicle up to $2,950.
- Interest up to $475 for a particular item, household goods, and furnishings (aggregate total limited to $9,850).
- Interest in jewelry up to $1,225.
- Right to receive Social Security and certain welfare benefits; alimony and child support; education savings accounts; and certain pension benefits.
- Right to receive certain personal injury and other awards up to $18,450.

Distribution and Discharge Once the trustee has administered the bankruptcy estate, the trustee then distributes the proceeds to creditors in an order of priority set by the bankruptcy code. Secured creditors are paid first and in full so long as the value of the collateral equals or exceeds the amount of their security interest. Unsecured creditors are paid from the remaining proceeds of the bankruptcy estate (if any). The order of payment for unsecured debtors is specified in the bankruptcy code (see Table 20.1).

Note that some debts are *nondischargeable.* These include:

- Claims for federal, state, and local taxes (including fines and penalties related to the taxes) within two years of the petition filing.
- Debts incurred within 60 days of the petition for luxury goods of more than $1,000 from a single creditor; or cash advances in excess of $1,000 obtained by a debtor using credit cards or revolving lines of credit.
- Alimony, maintenance, and child support.
- Debts related to willful or malicious injury to a person or property.
- Debts related to court-ordered punitive damages against the debtor.
- Student loan debts, unless the debtor can prove "undue hardship."

Under what circumstances can a debtor have a student loan debt discharged for hardship? In Case 20.1, a federal court gives some guidance on answering that question.

TABLE 20.1 Order of Priority for Unsecured Creditors

1. Administration expenses—court costs, trustee and attorney's fees.
2. Involuntary bankruptcy expenses incurred from date of filing to order of relief.
3. Unpaid wages and commissions earned within 90 days, limited to $4,300 per claimant.
4. Unsecured claims for contributions for employee benefits, 180 days prior to filing and $4,300 per employee.
5. Claims by farmers or fisherman up to $4,300.
6. Consumer deposits up to $1,950 before petition in connection with purchase, lease, or rental of property.
7. Paternity, alimony, maintenance, and support debts.
8. Certain taxes and penalties due to government units, such as income and property taxes.
9. Claims of general creditors.

CASE 20.1 In re Jones, 392 B.R. 116 (E.D. Pa. 2008)

FACT SUMMARY Jones graduated from a large university in Georgia with a degree in history and a minor in economics in the 1980s. Although Jones was supposed to enter the army upon graduation, he gained admission to law school and earned his law degree. However, Jones could not pass the bar examination after several attempts. He spent the next 14 years in various positions including the army, substitute teaching, writing, and social work. Jones then returned to school to get a Master of Education degree in the teaching of visual arts. Jones continued his education with yet another master's degree in divinity in 2005. At age 52, Jones held a bachelor's degree, a Juris Doctorate, and two master's degrees. He borrowed heavily for his education and, at the time of the bankruptcy petition, had defaulted on 18 student loans worth $140,000 of debt. Note that Jones's undergraduate and law school debts were discharged in a previous bankruptcy hearing. Jones argued that the debt was so high that to pay the debt would cause "undue hardship," and asked the court to discharge the loan. His creditor maintained that Jones does not meet the undue hardship standard.

SYNOPSIS OF DECISION AND OPINION The bankruptcy court ruled in favor of the creditor and refused to discharge Jones's student loans. The court reasoned that as a healthy, educated, employable man, paying the money back would not amount to "undue hardship."

WORDS OF THE COURT: Undue Hardship Standard "In order to demonstrate undue hardship, the Chapter 7 debtor must demonstrate: (1) that the debtor cannot maintain, based on current income and expenses, a "minimal" standard of living for herself and her dependents if forced to repay the loans; (2) that additional circumstances exist indicating that this state of affairs is likely to persist for a significant portion of the repayment period for student loans; and (3) that the debtor has made good faith efforts to repay the loans. . . . Mr. Jones is a relatively healthy, 52-year-old individual with no dependents. He has no medical or psychiatric condition that prevents him from employment. Although he is presently unemployed, he has not demonstrated that he has made diligent efforts to secure stable employment now or in the past. His present employment situation does not exist because he is unemployable. On the contrary, Mr. Jones is a highly educated individual who has marketable skills in a variety of areas: e.g., legal, managerial, correctional, religious, literary and artistic."

Case Questions

1. If Jones had been unable to work due to illness or injury, would that be sufficient to meet the "undue hardship" standard set out by the court?

2. Note that one court did not find undue hardship enough to discharge student loans for a "46-year-old part-time legal secretary, raising her 14-year-old child and living with her sister, and who had psychiatric problems and had twice attempted suicide" [*In re Brightful*, 267 F.3d 324 (3d Cir. 2001)]. Why would Congress and courts be reluctant to allow the discharge of student loans without meeting this difficult test?

Chapter 11: Reorganization Although located in the bankruptcy code, Chapter 11 differs greatly from a liquidation bankruptcy. Chapter 11 is best thought of as temporary protection for a corporation[6] from creditors while the corporation goes through a planning process to pay creditors and continue business without the need to terminate the entity completely. Chapter 11 is an acknowledgment that, as a matter of public policy, it is better to allow a business entity the opportunity to revise its business practices without the pressure of creditors who could halt the business operations and shut down the company with the consequential job costs and with some creditors not getting paid anything at all.

The fundamental proceedings of a Chapter 11 case are very similar to that of a Chapter 7 case as discussed earlier. A petition is filed either voluntarily or involuntarily, the automatic stay provision is triggered and, if the petition is proper, the order of relief then sets the reorganization process in motion. A creditor committee is appointed, and the committee can consult with the debtor and/or the trustee to formulate the repayment plan.

---

[6] Individual debtors are also eligible for relief under Chapter 11, but it is rare.

The major difference, however, is that unlike a Chapter 7 proceeding, the debtor generally continues to *operate the business* in a Chapter 11 case. The bankruptcy court may also opt to appoint a trustee to oversee the basic management of the business entity and report back to the court. This process, known as **debtor in possession (DIP),** gives great power to the debtor to rehabilitate the business entity.

DIP Powers　In many ways, the executives in a DIP business entity have an ideal situation from a workout perspective. While the stigma of Chapter 11 may cause difficulty in raising new capital, the bankruptcy code gives the DIP power to void prepetition preferential payments and to cancel or assume prepetition contracts (including leases, supplier contracts, and services contracts). The so-called **strong-arm clause** of the bankruptcy code allows the DIP to avoid any obligation or transfer of property that the debtor would otherwise be obligated to perform.

For larger companies, a DIP's power is most important in the context of *union contracts* known as collective bargaining agreements. The bankruptcy code sets forth standards and procedures under which a collective bargaining contract can be rejected if the debtor has first proposed necessary contractual modifications to the union and the union has rejected them without good cause.

Reorganization Plan　The centerpiece of a Chapter 11 case is the **reorganization plan.** It is a plan, generally filed by the debtor, which articulates a specific strategy and financial plan for emerging from financial distress. The DIP has the exclusive right to draft the plan within 120 days after the Chapter 11 petition. The court must approve the plan before it becomes binding on the creditors. The plan must be submitted to the creditors for a vote and generally must designate "classes" of claims and interests (such as secured vs. unsecured) and provide an adequate means for partial payment to creditors. Creditors are given the opportunity to accept or reject the plan, but if they reject the plan, the bankruptcy code allows the debtor to request that the court force the creditors to accept the plan (known as the **cram down provision**). So long as the plan is fair, equitable, and feasible from the court's perspective, the court will require creditors to accept the plan even over their objections. The plan is binding on all parties upon its approval by the court. It is important to note that Chapter 11 filings may be converted during any stage (even before the plan is submitted) to a Chapter 7 filing. Most financially distressed business entities will attempt a recovery using the generous provisions of Chapter 11 before deciding to liquidate. On the other hand, some companies do, in fact, turn around and emerge very strong from a Chapter 11 filing.

Chapter 13: Repayment Plan　Also known as the "wage-earner plan," this form of bankruptcy is limited to *individuals* who have a substantial debt, and it *cannot* be used to cover any business debt (even as a sole proprietor). Chapter 13 allows debtors with a regular source of income to catch up on mortgage, car, tax, and domestic support payments, to repay an adjusted debt to certain creditors over time (typically five years), and still keep all of their assets. It is less expensive and less complicated than reorganization or liquidation proceedings and can only be accomplished by filing a voluntary bankruptcy petition. Payments are typically made to the bankruptcy trustee, who distributes them to creditors. Unsecured creditors frequently are paid less than they are owed depending on the circumstances of the case.

Bankruptcy Abuse Prevention and Consumer Protection Act

In 2005, Congress passed legislation intended to curb perceived abuses of statutory bankruptcy protection by enacting the Bankruptcy Abuse Prevention and Consumer Protection Act (BAPCPA). While the congressional sponsors of the bill touted its public policy benefits of making the consuming public more responsible with debt, the law was widely

FACT SUMMARY   When Richie filed for Chapter 7 bankruptcy she had been making a living through odd jobs within the past year, yielding an income $22,608. The median income is $37,873 in her home state of Wisconsin. Just prior to her bankruptcy petition filing, Richie completed a master's degree in "outdoor therapeutic recreation administration," which qualified her to work as a therapist for the disabled in a camp or outdoor clinical setting. A job in this field would likely have brought Richie well above the median income and disqualify her for protection under a Chapter 7 bankruptcy. Additionally, Richie had been looking for jobs in her field, but only in the Racine/Kenosha area of Wisconsin where there were very few opportunities. She was qualified to work at many other jobs that would have brought her above the median income, but wanted employment only in her chosen field and in her home geographic area.

After her petition was filed, the bankruptcy trustee requested the court to reject the Chapter 7 petition and convert the case to a Chapter 13 petition, whereby Richie would have to pay all or much of her debt. The trustee alleged that Richie was abusing the Chapter 7 bankruptcy "means test" because she is *capable* of earning more money but does not. Moreover, Richie filed bankruptcy immediately after graduate school when her future earning potential was relatively high. Richie argued that moving elsewhere to work would be a burden and having a different full-time job would hurt her future prospects for getting a job in her chosen field.

SYNOPSIS OF DECISION AND OPINION   The bankruptcy court held that Richie was abusing Chapter 7 bankruptcy protection and should be required to refile for a Chapter 13 repayment plan. The court reasoned that just because she met the means requirement (i.e., her income fell below the average income of citizens of her home state) did *not* mean she was insulated from a claim of abuse. The court held that narrowing her job search in a small field to a small area while she was in reality capable of paying her debt with many other jobs amounted to a bad faith manipulation of the bankruptcy protections.

WORDS OF THE COURT: 2005 Means Test   "To assist courts in making the abuse determination, Congress created sub-parts to § 707(b). Sub-part (b)(2) is the infamous 'means test,' a mathematical calculation which, if it produces certain results, requires courts to presume that a debtor is too financially well-off to obtain an immediate discharge without making some attempt to repay creditors. . . . Thus, for a debtor who passes the means test, the court still may dismiss her Chapter 7 proceeding if either she filed the petition in bad faith or the totality of her financial circumstances demonstrates that it would constitute abuse to allow her to obtain an immediate discharge under Chapter 7.

[. . .] This debtor's circumstances do not pass the 'smell test.' . . . In light of the appearance that Congress intended that BAPCPA require debtors to make a good-faith effort to repay their debts, this Court concludes that a debtor who lacks the ability to pay because she has not engaged in a broad employment search, does not wish to work outside her chosen field, does not wish to work within her chosen field outside of southeastern Wisconsin, and takes this position at the expense of her creditors, abuses the provisions of Chapter 7 by seeking an immediate discharge."

Case Questions

1. Should Ms. Richie be forced to relocate or work in another field in order to use bankruptcy laws?

2. How might this case reinforce the point that calling the 2005 act the "Consumer Protection Act" is a misnomer? How might it detract from it?

criticized by bankruptcy attorneys and judges as unnecessarily burdening the debtor, the trustee, and the court with more paperwork and expenses while not curbing abuse.[7] The law overhauled the bankruptcy code for the first time since 1994 and, fundamentally, made it more difficult for debtors to seek protection under Chapter 7. The major provisions of

---

[7] See Judge Monroe's comment in *In re Sosa,* 336 B.R. 113 (Bankr. W.D. Tex. 2005); "the legislation's adoption in its title of the words 'consumer protection' is the grossest of misnomers."

the law are: 1) a *means test* for the debtor; 2) proof requirement of the debtor's income; 3) higher priority for alimony and support payments by the debtor; and 4) a credit counseling requirement for the debtor.

Means Test   The most important change was to increase the statutory requirements for eligibility under Chapter 7 straight liquidation by adding a "means test" that is determined by comparing the applicant's current monthly income to the median income for that state. If the applicant's income is more than the median, the applicant would not be eligible for Chapter 7. Thus, a substantial number of bankruptcy applicants who previously would have been eligible for a discharge of substantially all debts must now repay them under a Chapter 13 filing. For example, the state of Maryland's median family income for a family of one is $48,929 and $75,764 for a family of three. Therefore, if the debtor applies for a Chapter 7 bankruptcy seeking to discharge debts, but her income is above the median, the petition would be denied and the debtor would only have Chapter 13 (debt repayment) as an option. In Case 20.2, the bankruptcy applies the means test.

Proof of Income   Debtors must provide the bankruptcy trustee copies of recent tax returns and pay stubs or other income verification on a timely basis. If the debtor has failed to file a tax return for the previous year, she may be required to file a return as a condition of bankruptcy approval.

Alimony and Support   The BAPCPA gives alimony and support obligations a higher priority than certain other creditors.

Credit Counseling   Prior to filing for bankruptcy, the debtor must complete a short (approximately one hour) credit-counseling seminar and must also complete a longer course, known as Credit Education, prior to actually receiving a discharge of debts.

Table 20.2 is a summary and comparison of various bankruptcy options.

TABLE 20.2   Bankruptcy Options

Chapter 7 (Liquidation) Individuals and Businesses	Chapter 11 (Reorganization) Individuals and Businesses	Chapter 13 (Consumer Debt Adjustment) Individuals Only
1. Petition	1. Petition	1. Petition
2. Automatic stay	2. Automatic stay	2. Automatic stay
3. Order of relief or dismissal (apply means test)	3. Debtor in possession	3. Most debts paid back over five years
4. Creditor committee	4. File plan	4. Some unsecured debts reduced, some unsecured debts discharged
5. Trustee	5. Creditors approve a "cram down"	
6. Administration of bankruptcy estate	6. Emerge from Chapter 11 or convert to Chapter 7	
7. Distribution		
8. Discharge		

CONCEPT SUMMARY   Bankruptcy and Alternatives

- Upon filing for bankruptcy, a trustee is appointed by the bankruptcy court in most cases to protect the remaining bankruptcy assets, known as the estate.
- The trustee has the legal power to void fraudulent or preferential transfers made to certain creditors before filing bankruptcy.
- Once a business becomes insolvent, it can either file bankruptcy, dissolve itself out of existence or, if it wants to stay in business, work out terms of accord and satisfaction to pay creditors.
- A business debtor in Chapter 7 has its assets liquidated and debts discharged by the court.
- To avoid lost jobs and unpaid creditors some companies enter Chapter 11, wherein a debtor-in-possession (DIP) tries to rehabilitate the company and partially compensate creditors under a reorganization plan.
- An individual can development a repayment plan in Chapter 13 bankruptcy in order to use his income to slowly pay back debts while not having to liquidate assets.

KEY TERMS

Unsecured debt p. 504   Credit that is not collateralized.

Secured creditor p. 504   Title given to a creditor when the borrower has pledged collateral in order to obtain credit.

Secured party p. 505   The creditor in a secured transaction.

Debtor p. 505   The borrower in a secured transaction.

Perfecting p. 505   Procedure for the secured party to establish priority in the collateral over other creditors as provided by Article 9 of the Uniform Commercial Code.

Security interest p. 505   The rights of the secured party in a transaction.

Mortgage p. 505   A written document specifying the parties and the real estate that is filed with a state and/or local government agency when real estate is being used to collateralize a loan.

Mortgagee p. 506   The creditor when real estate is being used to collateralize a loan.

Mortgagor p. 506   The borrower when real estate is being used to collateralize a loan.

Promissory note p. 506   A contract whereby the borrower promises to pay back the creditor at a certain rate of interest over a specified period of years.

Mortgage foreclosure p. 506   When a creditor declares the loan in default and takes title and possession of the collateralized real estate in hopes of selling the property to pay off the debt owed.

Surety p. 506   A third party that agrees to be primarily liable to pay a loan.

Guarantor p. 506   A third party that agrees only to be liable to pay a loan *if* the debtor actually defaults.

Personal guaranty p. 506   Safeguard for creditors in a business loan where the principals of a business have pledged their personal assets if the assets of the business are insufficient to repay the loan in the event of a default by the business entity/debtor.

Insolvent p. 508   When a business venture no longer has adequate assets to maintain its operations and can no longer pay its bills as they become due in the usual course of trade and business.

Workout p. 508   The process of a debtor meeting a loan commitment by satisfying altered repayment terms to turn around a business when the principles wish to continue operations of a business that is underperforming and in poor financial condition.

Accord and satisfaction p. 508   A legal contract between debtor and creditor whereby the creditor agrees to accept a sum less than owed in exchange for releasing the debtor from all legal liability.

Automatic stay p. 510 A legal prohibition from creditors either initiating or continuing any debt collection action against the debtor or her property.

Bankruptcy trustee p. 510 An attorney highly skilled in bankruptcy law, appointed in Chapter 7 or Chapter 13 cases and charged with the duty to take control of the bankruptcy estate and reduce it to cash for distribution, preserving the interests of both the debtor and the creditors.

Bankruptcy estate p. 510 The debtor's available assets in a bankruptcy proceeding.

Voidable transfers p. 510 Certain transfers that are considered an unfair advantage of one creditor over another.

Voluntary bankruptcy petition p. 511 A petition filed in the bankruptcy court by the debtor that includes the names of creditors; list of debts; and a list of the debtor's assets, income, and expenses.

Involuntary bankruptcy petition p. 511 A petition filed in the bankruptcy court against a debtor by a group of three or more creditors with an unsecured aggregate claim of at least $11,625 who claim that the debtor is failing to pay the debt as it comes due.

Debtor in possession (DIP) p. 514 A Chapter 11 bankruptcy proceeding where the debtor generally remains in control of assets and business operations in an attempt to rehabilitate the business entity.

Strong-arm clause p. 514 Provision of the bankruptcy code that allows the debtor in possession to avoid any obligation or transfer of property that the debtor would otherwise be obligated to perform.

Reorganization plan p. 514 The keystone to a Chapter 11 case, generally filed by the debtor, which articulates a specific strategy and financial plan for emerging from financial distress.

Cram down provision p. 514 A term used in bankruptcy law to refer to the Chapter 11 provision that allows the debtor to request that the court force the creditors to accept a plan that is fair, equitable, and feasible.

THEORY TO PRACTICE

Yankee Export Company (YEC) is a purveyor of U.S. products for several European food market chains. YEC's annual revenue is approximately $10 million annually and they employ approximately 20 people, including YEC's only shareholders, directors, and officers: Moss and Whippany. Moss is the day-to-day manager of the venture, while Whippany is mostly an investor with no management duties other than giving consultation on business matters when asked by Moss. For several years, the venture was profitable, but due to a rapid increase in the value of the U.S. dollar against European currencies, YEC began to have cash flow problems. Its products were becoming more expensive for their European customers and their orders dropped slowly over a period of a year. When it appeared that YEC would be unable to generate enough cash to cover monthly expenses, Moss called for a meeting with Whippany and with YEC's accountants. The parties agreed that the rise of the dollar had a negative impact on all U.S. exports and that YEC was at the beginning of a financial challenge. The company's assets were approximately $200,000. The current major debts are set out in the YEC Creditor Table.

1. Identify the probable category of each creditor. What are the rights of each creditor in the event that YEC defaults on their obligation to that particular creditor?

2. If Moss and Whippany believe the financial crisis is temporary, what are their best nonstatutory options to continue the business if it becomes insolvent? What statutory option(s) do they have?

3. If Moss and Whippany do not believe the financial crisis is recoverable, what nonstatutory and statutory options does YEC have? What are the advantages and drawbacks of each option? If the building lease were not personally guaranteed by Moss and Whippany, how would this fact change your analysis?

4. Which creditors are bound by UCC Article 9's provisions?

5. Does that fact that YEC has 20 employees add any ethical obligations that should be considered in Moss and Whippany's decision making concerning the future of the company?

6. Suppose that the landlord begins to start eviction proceedings due to YEC's payment default. How could YEC stop the eviction?

7. If YEC files for Chapter 7, what debts are potentially dischargeable? Assuming any assets are left, in what order would the creditors be paid?

YEC Creditor Table

Creditor	Reason	Amount
IRS	Back taxes.	$35,000.
Ag Industries	U.S. trade creditor from which YEC buys its inventory.	$20,000 balance secured with a promissory note and perfected security interest in inventory.
Landlord	Five years left on the office building lease.	$50,000 per year (backed by personal guarantees of Moss and Whippany).
Office Leasing Company	Two years left on equipment lease.	$500 per month.
Company Credit Card	Office supplies and miscellaneous items.	$8,000 balance.
Whippany	Whippany gave YEC a $15,000 personal loan evidenced only by a promissory note.	$11,000 balance payable on a monthly basis for 36 more months at 8% interest.

MANAGER'S CHALLENGE

Sometimes managers and owners are one and the same, and playing both roles can be a difficult line to walk. Relationships between parties in a business entity are governed by legal duties (these duties were discussed in Unit Four) owed to one another. Yet the manager/owner must also be sure to be attuned to the other legal requirements and the relationships between the company and third-party creditors or vendors. Suppose that in Theory to Practice above that Moss and Whippany decide to try and maintain YEC's operations for one more month and then make a final decision on whether or not to seek bankruptcy. Whippany sends an e-mail to Moss requesting that Moss authorize immediately the full payment by YEC of Whippany's personal loan. Draft a two paragraph e-mail that Moss could send to Whippany that analyzes (1) the legal risks and consequences of honoring Whippany's request, (2) the potential harm to relationships with other creditors, and (3) the ethical implications of paying back the loan early. A sample answer may be found on this textbook's Web site at www.mhhe.com/melvin.

VOIDABLE TRANSFERS

In 2002, Fehrs met and began living with her boyfriend Murrietta. They also lived with her teenage son from another marriage, Jae. Fehrs bought a housing lot at 464 Second Street and another at 117 Terrill Loop, both in the city of Mullan, Idaho. Fehrs and Murrietta contracted with Peter Axtman to build them a house at 464 Second Street. As construction began, problems arose. Soon Murrietta and Fehrs broke up, and Axtman filed a lawsuit against Fehrs for what he was owed for his services. Two months after the suit was filed, Fehrs transferred her property at 117 Terrill Loop to her teenage son, Jae, in exchange for $1. Fehrs said the transfer was because Jae was always drinking and partying with friends at 117 Terrill Loop, so she did not want to be liable if anything should happen. Two months later Fehrs filed for bankruptcy.

CASE QUESTIONS

1. Why do you think Fehrs sold the lot to her son?
2. What can the trustee do to make sure Axtman gets all he is owed?

AUTOMATIC STAY

Ellison ran a small company and both he and his company filed for bankruptcy in 1994. The court issued an automatic stay to creditors. A month later the IRS contacted Ellison about unpaid taxes from 1993. Although Ellison consented to the tax being assessed, the IRS continued to pursue payment of the back taxes even after the bankruptcy petition was filed. Ellison filed suit against the IRS for the violation of her automatic stay rights under the bankruptcy code.

CASE QUESTIONS

1. Will Ellison not have to pay these taxes or can they be discharged?
2. Does the IRS have any defense to pursuing the debt during the automatic stay period?
3. If Ellison wins, what does that say about the power of an automatic stay?

NONDISCHARGEABLE DEBTS

Fedderson ran Big Al's restaurant, which was doing poorly. In a last-ditch effort to make more money, he bought a $2,000 ice cream machine for Big Al's on his personal credit card. Sixty days later Fedderson filed for bankruptcy. The credit card company argued that the ice cream machine debt should not be discharged because it is a luxury good that was bought too close to the bankruptcy petition.

CASE QUESTIONS

1. Should the ice cream machine debt be discharged?
2. Should it matter to the court that Fedderson should have known that he would be insolvent in two months and that trying to stop financial catastrophe with an ice cream machine was foolish?

CHAPTER 11 AND COLLECTIVE BARGAINING AGREEMENTS

In October, Northwest Airlines declared Chapter 11 bankruptcy and sought to renegotiate a collective bargaining agreement with the flight attendants' union. The contract would need to be changed for Northwest to reorganize and try to save the company. After several months of negotiations, the union finally rejected a March 1 proposal. Northwest's DIP asked the court to unilaterally enforce the terms of the rejected agreement because the union had failed to agree to reasonable terms.

CASE QUESTIONS

1. What is the name of the power that Northwest is asking the court to exercise?
2. What must the court find about the union's rejection to permit unilateral enforcement?
3. Should it matter that Northwest easily reached agreements with both the pilots' and mechanics' unions?

 Self-Check **ANSWERS**

Creditor Status

1. ExtremeCo. has a perfected (by filing) security interest in Retailer's inventory.
2. Office Galaxy is an unsecured creditor.
3. BigBank is a secured creditor as mortgagee with WidgetCo. as mortgagor.
4. BigBank is an unsecured creditor of WidgetCo., *but* the debt is collateralized through personal guarantees in the event of default.

21

CHAPTER

Consumer Protection Law

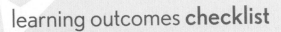

learning outcomes checklist

After studying this chapter, students who have mastered the material will be able to:

21-1 Explain the role of the Federal Trade Commission in terms of various statutory consumer protections.

21-2 Articulate the standards used to define false advertising and other deceptive practices and identify specific consumer protection laws applied to bulk e-mail.

21-3 Define and give an example of a warranty.

21-4 Distinguish between express warranties and implied warranties, explain the protections afforded by each type of warranty, and articulate the standards for disclaiming a warranty.

21-5 Name and explain the federal statutory protections afforded to consumers for faulty or unsafe products and for food and drug safety.

21-6 Identify the parties in a credit transaction and understand the role of federal statutory laws in consumer credit transactions.

21-7 List the various components of the Truth in Lending Act and give specific examples of regulatory requirements.

21-8 Explain the protections afforded to consumers by federal statutes regulating the collection of consumer debt.

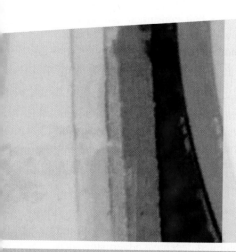

Since the height of the American industrial revolution, the body of law that protects consumers in transactions with merchants and creditors has grown dramatically. As the law becomes increasingly concerned with protecting consumers, statutes and administrative regulations that form a body known as **consumer law** has become progressively more important in its impact on business owners and managers.

Individuals and businesses are subject to regulation at the federal, state and local levels in a wide variety of consumer transactions. Specifically, students will learn how the law protects consumers in three areas:

- Unfair and deceptive trade practices.

- Product quality and functionality.

- Credit and collection of consumer debts.

UNFAIR OR DECEPTIVE SALES PRACTICES

Until the early twentieth century, the only legal protection that consumers had against unscrupulous sellers that engaged in deceit during a sale was a common law suit for fraud. In 1914, Congress passed the **Federal Trade Commission Act**[1] (FTCA), one of the very first statutory protections for American consumers. The FTCA established an administrative agency called the **Federal Trade Commission** (FTC) and charged the FTC with the broad mandate of preventing unfair and deceptive acts or practices in commercial transactions. Courts have been very deferential to the FTC's wide-ranging authority over advertising, price disclosures, and representations made during the sales process of consumer goods. Under this authority, the FTC has promulgated regulations that define a deceptive practice as one that is likely to *mislead* a reasonably prudent consumer, and where the conduct resulted in some sort of *detriment* to the consumer.

Advertising

Deceptive advertising is a significant source of consumer complaints. FTC regulations and memorandums provide several specific examples of prohibited deceptive advertising such as making *expressly false statements* in advertisement about a product's quality, ingredients, or effectiveness. Note that in addition to violating the FTC's regulations, expressly false advertisements may also give rise to a breach of warranty (discussed later in this chapter). The FTC rule also prohibits the use of fake testimonials or endorsements, or using fake pictures of the product performing in a manner that is inaccurate.

Bait and Switch   Regulatory authorities have become increasingly aggressive about investigation of complaints by consumers of bait and switch ploys. A bait and switch scheme involves a seller advertising an item for sale at a particularly good price (30 percent

The Federal Trade Commission (FTC) has broad authority to ensure that merchant advertising is not deceptive or misleading.

---

[1]15 U.S.C. § 41, et seq.

off retail) or favorable terms (zero down, zero interest), but the seller has no intention to actually sell that product at that price or on those terms. When the consumer comes to their business after seeing the advertisement, the seller discourages the purchase of the advertised item and instead tries to convince the buyer to purchase a different item for a higher price or on less favorable terms. The seller's techniques for discouraging the purchase of the product vary (such as lying about whether the product was sold out, or was ever available) but the end result is the same: the buyer walks out of the store with a more expensive product than the advertised product. For example, suppose that Widget Depot, a merchant, advertises a sale as follows: "Classic Widgets on sale: 40% off retail value! Clearance sale" (the bait). When Copperfield shows up a day later at Widget Depot and asks for a Classic Widget, he is referred to the manager. The manager gives a false explanation to Copperfield that the Classic Widget is out of stock, so more would have to be retrieved from an off-site facility. This means Copperfield would have to wait one week for a Classic Widget. However, the manager offers Copperfield an alternative: for his trouble and time, he will sell him the newly introduced Ultimate Widget, which is currently in stock at an introductory price of 5 percent off the normal retail price. The manager goes on to explain that although the Ultimate Widget is more expensive than the Classic Widget (especially given the 40 percent Classic Widget discount), the Ultimate Widget could be trusted to last longer than the Classic. Thus, the dishonest manager reasoned, the Ultimate was actually a better deal than the Classic. Copperfield relies on the manager's advice and buys the Ultimate Widget. Under most state statutes, the conduct of Widget Depot's manager was unlawful as a bait and switch scheme.

Pricing Pricing is an important component of advertising and is also subject to consumer protection regulations. Some of the more common examples of deceptive advertising via pricing are:

- Misrepresenting the prices of a competitor.
- Artificially inflating the original retail price of a product when featuring it as a sale item in order to make it appear that the original price was higher than it actually was.
- Using terms such as "clearance priced" or "marked down for sale" when the items are not being sold at reduced rates.

Financial Institutions

In addition to the FTC, the Office of the Comptroller of the Currency (OCC) also pursues violations of the Federal Trade Commission Act if the deceptive advertising involves a financial institution such as a bank. For example, in one case, California-based Providian National Bank agreed to pay fines and restitution totaling $300 million for deceptive advertising. The case centered on Providian's credit card "payment protection plan" program. The program involved an agreement for the credit card holder to pay a monthly fee for an insurance plan, which Providian advertised would cover the cardholder's monthly minimum amount due if the cardholder suffered involuntary unemployment, hospitalization, or disability. Providian's advertising materials promised that the cardholder would not have to pay monthly credit card payments for up to 18 months from the time of unemployment, hospitalization, or disability. However, Providian failed to adequately disclose that in the case of involuntary unemployment, consumers were covered under the plan *only* for the number of months in which the consumer paid credit protection fees, rather than the advertised 18 months. Authorities also took issue with Providian's claim that its credit card had no annual fee. In practice, Providian only waived the annual fee of $60 if the consumer signed up for the aforementioned credit protection plan—at a cost of $156 per year.[2]

---

[2]Comptroller of the Currency and Administrator of National Banks Press Release, NR 2000-49.

Telemarketing

Public concern about deceptive telemarketing practices targeting elderly victims in the 1990s resulted in Congress enacting several statutes regulating telemarketing firms and practices. The primary statutes are the **Telephone Consumer Protection Act**[3] and the **Telemarketing and Consumer Fraud and Abuse Prevention Act.**[4] These laws (1) allow consumers to *opt out* of receiving unwanted calls from telemarketers, (2) ban the use of unsolicited recorded calls and faxes, (3) regulate 900 number calls to prevent consumers from unknowingly generating charges, (4) prohibit telemarketers from making false representations, and (5) require disclosure of all the material terms of a proposed transaction. The laws prescribe *how* and *when* a telemarketer may obtain permission to obtain payment from the consumer's checking, savings, or credit accounts. It also prohibits any harassment, threats, or deceit by the telemarketer.

Do Not Call List   The FTC established a "do not call" registry where consumers may sign up to be on a list that protects them from certain unsolicited calls by telemarketers.

*web*check **donotcall.gov**
Consumers can register for the Do Not Call list at this Web site.

Some organizations are exempt from coverage of the do not call list prohibitions. They include calls from (1) charitable organizations, (2) certain political organizations, or (3) businesses with whom the consumer has had past commercial contacts.

Odometers

The U.S. Department of Transportation estimates that odometer rollback, the process of physically altering a vehicle's odometer in order to make it appear as if the vehicle had traveled fewer miles than it actually had, is a $3-billion-a-year enterprise.[5] Odometer fraud is perpetrated both easily and surreptitiously and it was often impossible for a consumer to detect. The **Federal Odometer Act**[6] makes it a crime to change vehicle odometers and requires that any faulty odometer be plainly disclosed in writing to potential buyers. The law sets out regulations that (1) define and prohibit odometer tampering, (2) prohibit buying or installing any device used for tampering, (3) prescribe procedures for odometer repair, (4) require certain disclosures related to the actual mileage of the vehicle when it is sold to a new owner, (5) give jurisdiction for the implementation and enforcement of the law to the secretary of transportation, and (6) impose a record-keeping requirement on vehicle dealers and distributors.

In addition to the secretary of transportation's authority to enforce the statute, the law provides victims of odometer tampering with a remedy of *triple* the actual damages suffered. However, the lawsuit must take place within two years from the date of purchase.

State Statutes

In addition to federal statutes, each state has adopted consumer protections by enacting state laws aimed at preventing unfair or deceptive trade practices within state borders. The statutes often empower the state attorney general to pursue violators using enforcement mechanisms such as civil lawsuits and, in extreme cases, criminal charges. Many states have created specific task forces to police merchants' and other sellers' compliance with consumer protection statutes where the transaction takes place primarily within its state borders. Enforcement powers are usually given to the state's law enforcement authorities: the state

---

[3]47 USC § 227.

[4]15 U.S.C. § 6101, *et seq.*

[5]See *Secretary of Transportation's Report to the Congress on the Federal Odometer Act* (2006).

[6]49 U.S.C. § 32701, et seq.

Regulation of Online Advertising

As use of the Internet by consumers increased in the late 1990s, *spam,* the term used as shorthand to refer to the use of unsolicited e-mails to advertise a product or service, became so increasingly problematic that state legislatures took the early lead in regulating spam, including tough criminal penalties for illegal spam suppliers. Thirty-three states passed some form of legislation that attempted to regulate unsolicited e-mails. California's law was one of the toughest because it required online marketers to obtain a consumer's permission *prior* to sending e-mail solicitations. Virginia went a step further and made sending certain unsolicited e-mails a felony and indicted two men for running a large illegal bulk e-mail operation. Some states, such as New York, passed antispam legislation as part of a larger package of identity theft laws. Then New York Attorney General Eliot Spitzer* grabbed headlines by indicting a man, dubbed the Buffalo Spammer, for sending 825 million spam messages.

However, there was no *federal* statute regulating unsolicited e-mail until Congress passed the **Controlling the Assault of Non-Solicited Pornography and Marketing Act of 2003,**[†] better known as the CAN-SPAM Act. The new law supplanted sometimes-tougher state statutes, but it still outlawed the dubious methods used by certain spam suppliers and provided for criminal sanctions in severe cases. The statute also prohibits online marketing providers from falsifying the "from" name and information in the subject line designed to fool consumers into opening an unsolicited e-mail message. It also requires the sender to provide a physical address of the producer of the e-mail and specifically label any pornographic links with adult-content warnings. The law imposes an affirmative obligation on the sender to notify the recipient of procedures to opt out of receiving any future e-mail from the sender. One controversial provision of the law required the FTC to start a "do-not-spam" list modeled on the "do-not-call" list. However, the FTC resisted the notion of creating such a list based on technology and privacy grounds and the list was never implemented.

The CAN-SPAM Act allows e-mail recipients the right to bring a lawsuit directly against the spammer as a compliance mechanism in egregious cases and when the plaintiff can prove that the spam produced actual damages (such as a shutdown of a retail store's computer server, which caused loss of profits or repair charges). The FTC has been aggressively enforcing the law against the most serious offenders and pursuing criminal charges where appropriate. For example, in June 2007, two spammers were convicted under the CAN-SPAM Act for sending out millions of e-mail messages with highly offensive pornographic images. The defendants were sentenced to five years in prison and ordered to pay $1.3 million from the profits of their front company.[‡] The FTC has also used its enforcement authority to file civil complaints against companies that are engaged in spamming as part of their marketing strategy. They are particularly strict in their enforcement of the CAN-SPAM Act when pursuing companies whose primary market is Internet pornography.[§]

In 2005, the FTC issued a report that indicated that the volume of spam leveled off since the law was enacted, with a marked decrease in sexually explicit e-mail reaching fewer mailboxes. Critics of the CAN-SPAM Act contend that the decrease is due primarily to enhanced technology improvements in e-mail filtering and that the act is ineffective and difficult to enforce. One report featured in *PC Magazine* concluded that less than 1 percent of spam complied with the CAN-SPAM Act. Responding to some industry criticism of the effectiveness of the law, the FTC revised its regulations in 2008 to widen its jurisdiction and specifically prohibit spam distributors from charging a consumer a fee in order to process an opt-out request.

---

*Mr. Spitzer was later elected governor of New York, but resigned in the wake of a prostitution scandal.
[†]15 U.S.C. § 7701, et seq.
[‡]*United States v. Schaffer* (U.S. District Court of Arizona 2007). The defendants were also convicted of mail fraud and racketeering.
[§]See "FTC Cracks Down on Illegal X-Rated Spam," *Federal Trade Commission Bulletin* 2005-07-20.

attorney general and local district attorneys. State statutes often give aggrieved consumers the right to bring a lawsuit directly against any violator to recover damages. Therefore, federal agencies and state authorities are thought of as having concurrent (overlapping) jurisdiction.

State statutory protections often fill gaps in federal protections. For example, the New Jersey Consumer Fraud Act covers certain transactions that would not be within the coverage of a federal statute. In Case 21.1, a New Jersey appellate court applies a state consumer fraud statute to a real estate transaction.

CONCEPT SUMMARY   Unfair and Deceptive Trade Practices

- The Federal Trade Commission (FTC) is charged with preventing unfair and deceptive acts or practices in commercial transactions. In doing so the FTC has wide-ranging authority over advertising, price disclosures, and representations made during the sales process of consumer goods.

- Bait and switch schemes involve a seller advertising an item for sale, but in reality the seller has no intention to actually sell that product at that price or on those terms. Instead, when the consumer comes to their business after seeing the advertisement, the seller discourages the purchase of the advertised item and instead tries to convince the buyer to purchase a different item for a higher price or on less favorable terms.

- Pricing is also subject to consumer protection regulations, including a ban on misrepresentations of the prices of a competitor, artificially inflating the original retail price of a product when featuring it as a sale item, and using terms such as "clearance priced" or "marked down for sale" when the items are not being sold at reduced prices.

- The FTC established a "do not call" registry in which consumers sign up to be on a list that protects them from certain unsolicited calls by telemarketers.

- The Federal Odometer Act makes it a crime to change vehicle odometers and requires that any faulty odometer be plainly disclosed in writing to potential buyers.

- The Controlling the Assault of Non-Solicited Pornography and Marketing Act of 2003 (CAN SPAM Act) regulates the sending of unsolicited e-mail (spam) by prohibiting certain online marketing practices, including falsifying the "from" name and information in the subject line and mandating that senders provide a physical address of the producer of the e-mail.

LO21-3, 21-4   # PRODUCT QUALITY AND FUNCTIONALITY

Consumers have certain statutory protections related to the quality and functionality of products sold by merchants. These protections are derived primarily from *product liability* statutes and *commercial law* statutes, which provide for *warranty* protection. Some of these statutes overlap with other consumer protection laws. Product liability statutes often operate in tandem with laws related to negligence; thus, product liability law is discussed in detail in Chapter 9, "Torts and Products Liability."

A **warranty** is a seller's (or lessor's) promise to a consumer concerning the quality and/or functionality of a product. Warranties are recognized as legally enforceable promises under state statutory laws that are based on Article 2 of the Uniform Commercial Code. Recall that in Chapter 8, "Contracts for the Sale of Goods," Article 2 was covered in the context of formation and performance of *sales contracts*. The focus of this chapter is the *warranty provisions* of Article 2 that protect consumers. When the seller makes a representation of *fact* about a product, this is known as an **express warranty.** If the seller has not made a specific representation about the product, the buyer may still be protected by a UCC-imposed **implied warranty.**

FACT SUMMARY   Vagias hired Dingle as his realtor and told her that he was in the market to buy a house in Montville Township, New Jersey. Vagias communicated to Dingle that he desired that particular municipality due to the favorable reputation of the township's schools. Dingle showed Vagias a house in a development called "Woodmont Court at Montville," and Vagias inquired as to whether this house was actually located within the jurisdictional limits of Montville Township. Dingle and a representative of the builder, neither of whom were familiar with the township boundaries, assured Vagias that the house was in Montville Township and Vagias purchased the home for $740,000. When Vagias attempted to enroll his son in the school system, he learned that his house was actually located outside of the Montville Township limits. Vagias sued to have the sale rescinded on the basis of Dingle's and the homebuilder's misrepresentation concerning location. Vagias argued that he had paid a premium for the house based on the reputation of the school system in a certain township. Woodmont argued that the misrepresentations were not intentional and that Vagias suffered no loss in the value of the home.

SYNOPSIS OF DECISION AND OPINION   The Superior Court of New Jersey ruled in favor of Vagias. The court held that Vagias specified that location in Montville Township was a prerequisite to purchasing a house at Woodmont and, therefore, that location became a part of the basis of the bargain. Under the New Jersey Consumer Fraud Act, Dingle's misrepresentation need not be an intentional misrepresentation. Dingle and Woodmont knew of Vagias's concerns and made an affirmative misrepresentation. That is all that is necessary to prevail in a New Jersey Consumer Fraud Act case.

WORDS OF THE COURT: No Intent Required   "[W]hen [the real estate agent] told [Vagias] that the house was in 'Montville' she made an affirmative misrepresentation. Her intent is not an issue for purposes of the Act. If she provided plaintiffs with affirmative misinformation on what she knew was a critical issue in their decision to purchase the house, she violated the Act. [. . .] Further, she was not an innocent bystander making a casual comment. She was assisting plaintiffs in choosing a house to buy, and she received a commission on the sale. [Thus] Dingle's statements were not idle comments or mere puffery."

Case Questions

1. Had Dingle not known that Vagias was specifically looking for a home in Montville Township, yet had still made her statements, would the outcome of the case have been different? Why or why not? Explain your answer.

2. If Vagias paid market value for his home, had still been able to send his son to a highly rated elementary school, and the only detriment imposed upon him was a lower social status due to the location of the home, how would that affect your analysis?

Express Warranty

In some cases a seller expressly represents that the goods have certain *qualities* or a certain level of *efficiency*. If the goods turn out not to have these qualities, the buyer may sue for a breach of the express warranty. As a practical matter, many of these seller representations are made through advertising. In one famous case,[7] the supreme court in the state of Washington held that a car manufacturer breached an express warranty when it advertised in its brochures that the car had "shatter proof glass" that would not fly or shatter even upon the "hardest impact." After a small pebble struck the windshield and resulted in the glass shattering and injuries to the driver, the court ruled in favor of the injured driver stating that the buyer had *reasonably relied* on those representations and had no reason to suspect they were false.

---

[7]*Baxter v. Ford Motor Co.,* 12 P.2d 409 (Wash. 1932).

Because many express warranties arise in the context of advertising, the UCC makes a distinction between factual promises and "puffery." Puffery is a *nonfactual*-based statement commonly used in advertising with such claims as "This car gets great gas mileage" or "Sweater made from finest wool." Of course, neither of these statements is fact-based because there is no method to verify words such as "great" or "finest." Thus, neither of these statements constitutes an express warranty. However, if the statements are changed slightly to "This car gets 35 miles per gallon when driven on the highway" or "Sweater is 100% Irish wool" then these statements may be considered factual promises to the buyer, which creates an express warranty from the seller.

 Self-Check   Express Warranty

Has an express warranty been created?

1. Randall has been the victim of several robberies in his store. He purchases a chemical weapon spray called Repel that was advertised to "instantly stop attackers" and "incapacitate groups of people instantly." Randall is robbed and attempts to use Repell to stop the crime, but the robber is not stopped. Rather, he becomes enraged and assaults Randall during the robbery.

2. Juliet sees a newspaper advertisement by a car manufacturer: "The sexiest convertible on the market."

3. Benjamin buys a watch that bears a sticker on the packaging, "100% waterproof".

4. Jenner watches a TV ad for running shoes that shows scenes of a jogger in a park then switches the scene to the same runner on a snow-covered hiking trail. The catch phrase "A sneaker for all seasons" flashes on the screen. No mention is made of the shoe's suitability for use on a particular surface. Jenner purchases the shoes and when he runs on a snowy trail, they fall apart and Jenner suffers foot injuries as a result.

Answers to this Self-Check are provided at the end of the chapter.

Implied Warranties

Even in cases where the seller makes no express promise about the goods, the UCC imposes several *implied warranties*. Implied warranties apply only in specific circumstances and have certain limits as to their protections of buyers.

Merchantability   The implied warranty of merchantability[8] applies to every sale of a product from a *merchant* to a buyer (note that the buyer may or may not be a merchant) and requires the seller to warrant that the product is fit for its ordinary use. For purposes of the UCC, a merchant is one who is regularly engaged in the sale of that product. Thus, if you purchase a new or used lawnmower from your neighbor (an accountant), no implied warranty exists. Merchants must also conform to the industry safety standards in packaging and labeling the goods in order for them to qualify as merchantable. This UCC requirement also applies to food and drink to be consumed either on the merchant's premises or somewhere else.

Fitness for a Particular Purpose   An implied warranty also arises when a seller promises that the product is fit for a particular purpose.[9] In order for this warranty to be created, the buyer must prove the seller knew of the buyer's desire to use the product in a specified way (not necessarily in its ordinary way) and the buyer relies on the seller's advice and recommendation. For example, suppose that Buyer consults with Salesperson and indicates that she requires a new set of boots for a hiking trip that will involve walking through small streams.

---

[8]UCC § 2-314(2).
[9]UCC § 2-315.

Salesperson recommends that Buyer purchase Brand A boots for the hiking trip. Buyer purchases the boots, but when hiking it turns out the boots are not waterproof and they fall apart on the first day of hiking through a small stream. Buyer's boots are destroyed and she suffers injuries to her feet that require medical care. Because no express promise was made concerning the boots, Buyer must turn to an implied warranty theory. In this case, Buyer will be able to recover based on a breach of *implied* warranty of fitness for a particular use.

Warranty Disclaimers and Limitations

The UCC allows a seller to **disclaim** both implied and express warranties under certain conditions. However, in order to disclaim a warranty, the seller must do so in a conspicuous writing such as capital letters, bold print, or a larger font that stands out from the rest of the writing. Although the UCC does not require specific language to disclaim warranties, courts have held phrases such as "with all faults" or "as is" as sufficient to disclaim a warranty. However, the UCC does require that any disclaimer of the warranty of merchantability actually use the word "merchantability" in the disclaimer.

Sellers may also, under certain circumstances, *limit the remedies* of a buyer who has suffered damages because of a seller's breach of warranty. This limitation of remedies is primarily used where the only harm suffered by the buyer was the loss of the use of the product. In those cases, the seller may attempt to limit the remedy to replacement or repair of the product and cut off any consequential damages (such as if the buyer suffered loss of profit due to the defective product). However, the UCC makes clear that any attempt to limit damages when a *personal injury* is involved will be automatically void. It is also important to note that the Magnuson-Moss Act, discussed later in this chapter, *restricts* certain disclaimers and limitations of remedies by sellers.

Case 21.2 illustrates the California Supreme Court's analysis of express warranties, implied warranties, and disclaimers for a product that caused an injury to the buyer.

In order to disclaim express or implied warranties, a seller must conspicuously use disclaimer language such as "with all faults" or "as is."

FACT SUMMARY Zogarts made the "Golfing Gizmo" that Hauter received as a gift from his mother for his thirteenth birthday. The Gizmo was billed as a "completely equipped backyard driving range" and consisted of a golf ball attached to a cord causing the ball to come back to the player after it is struck. The Gizmo's box read "COMPLETELY SAFE. BALL WILL NOT HIT PLAYER." Hauter read the safety manual and used the Gizmo a dozen times. In one hit, however, he hit too far under the ball, the cord tangled and the ball struck Hauter in the temple. Hauter suffered severe permanent injuries. Hauter sued Zogarts for breach of express and implied warranty. Zogarts defended by pointing out that the photos of the man using the Gizmo properly were a disclaimer that it was only "completely safe" when used in that way.

SYNOPSIS OF DECISION AND OPINION The Supreme Court of California found (1) that Zogarts breached their express warranty when the guarantee on the box that "ball will not hit player" proved false; (2) they breached the implied warranty of merchantability because the Gizmo cannot be used to practice golf without being dangerous (rendering the product inherently dangerous); and (3) an implied disclaimer in a photograph cannot disclaim a clear statement of safety on the box, which contradicts the statement.

WORDS OF THE COURT: Express Warranty "Any description of the goods which is made part of the basis of the bargain creates an express warranty that the good shall conform to the description . . . defendants expressly warranted the safety of their product and are liable for Hauter's injuries which resulted from a breach of that warranty."

Implied Warranty "The product must 'conform to the promises or affirmations of fact made on the container or label' and must be 'fit for the ordinary purposes for which such goods are used.' The Gizmo fails in both respects. As already explained, it does not live up to the statement on the carton that it's 'COMPLETELY SAFE. BALL WILL NOT HIT PLAYER.' Furthermore, as explained below, the evidence shows that the Gizmo is not fit for the ordinary purposes for which such goods are normally used . . . [D]efendants do not point to any language or conduct on their part negating their warranties. They refer only to a drawing on the box and to the notion that golf is a dangerous game; based on that meager foundation, they attempt to limit their explicit promise of safety."

Case Questions

1. What words on the box created the express warranty?
2. Is the phrase "completely safe" a verifiable fact or is it puffing? Is any product actually *completely* safe?

LO21-5   Magnuson-Moss Warranty–Federal Trade Commission Improvement Act[10]

Legal Speak »))
Federal Cause of Action A statutorily created right to sue a violator in federal court. Such statutes typically give federal courts specific subject matter jurisdiction over violations of a statute.

The Magnuson-Moss Warranty–Federal Trade Commission Improvement Act, generally referred to by its short title, the *Magnuson-Moss Act*, regulates warranties given by a seller or lessor to a consumer. As with other consumer protection statutes, the Magnuson-Moss Act does *not* apply to purely merchant transactions where the buyer and seller are regularly engaged in the sale of goods. A consumer is defined as one who purchases or leases goods with the intent to use it for *personal* reasons rather than resale or use in a business. The Magnuson-Moss Act does *not* mandate that sellers offer a warranty to a buyer. However, if the seller/lessor does offer a **written express warranty,** the transaction is subject to the provisions of the statute. It is important to note that the Magnuson-Moss Act did not create any *additional* implied warranties upon which consumers can sue; rather it created a *federal cause of action* for the breach of consumer warranties contained in state statutes. This is accomplished by permitting consumers to bring a lawsuit

---

[10]15 U.S.C.A. § 2301.

directly against the seller to recover damages as a result of a seller violating the statute. However, the statute does allow the seller to resolve disputes using an alternative dispute resolution (such as binding arbitration) system so long as the seller made appropriate disclosures about the dispute resolution requirement at the time of the transaction. The Federal Trade Commission is responsible for implementing and enforcing the Magnuson-Moss Act's requirements.

Labeling Requirements If the product being warranted costs $10 or more, the Magnuson-Moss Act requires the warranty itself to contain a label of the conditions of the warranty. Sellers and lessors of products that carry a full warranty label must honor a repair or replacement promise for defects. A full warranty must also carry a term of duration (e.g., full one-year warranty). A limited warranty label means only that the seller does not bind itself to promises of full warranty in some way (e.g., "limited warranty: engine transmission not covered by warranty").

> ## KEY POINT
> The Magnuson-Moss Act does not mandate that sellers offer a warranty to a consumer/buyer, nor does it create any additional implied warranties. If the seller does offer a warranty, the transaction is subject to the provisions of the statute.

The Magnuson-Moss Act also requires that warranties be written conspicuously and in plain and clear language. The language must be specific to the parts, products, characteristics, or functionality covered by the warranty.

Restrictions on Disclaimers and Limitations The Magnuson-Moss Act preempts state law and imposes a restriction on disclaimers made by sellers and lessors. The statute modifies rules on disclaimers that were allowed by state law with respect to the implied warranty of merchantability and the implied warranty of fitness for a particular use. If the transaction is covered by the Magnuson-Moss Act (because it involves a *written, express* agreement), sellers may *not* disclaim any implied warranties. Sellers are permitted to set a time frame on the implied warranties so long as this expiration date corresponds with the expiration of any express warranties. If the seller wishes to limit certain damages, the Magnuson-Moss Act requires that those limits be conspicuously featured in the warranty. Typically, the seller complies with this conspicuous disclosure requirement by featuring the limitation language in **bold** type or setting it apart in some other way in the document. Figure 21.1 provides an example of a warranty disclaimer and limitation of remedies.

FIGURE 21.1 Sample Disclaimer and Limitation of Remedies

Disclaimer of warranties
The buyer agrees to take the Widget Board with ***all faults*** and ***as is.*** The seller does not make any express warranties about the Widget Board and ***expressly disclaims the implied warranty of merchantability*** and ***disclaims*** any other ***implied warranty*** created by law including the ***implied warranty of fitness for a particular use.***

Limitation of remedies
Seller's sole obligation and Buyer's ***sole remedy*** for any damages related to the failure of the Widget Board to perform is ***limited to adjustment or replacement*** of any part causing the failure **or** at the ***Seller's option*** to refund the purchase amount to the Buyer.

Consumer Product Safety Act

Congress passed the **Consumer Product Safety Act**[11] (CPSA) in response to a growing number of injuries and deaths being caused by products, particularly toys, sold to consumers.[12] The statute created the Consumer Product Safety Commission as the federal regulatory agency and as a national information clearinghouse intended to achieve the statute's objective to make consumer products safer. The Commission researches, institutes, and enforces safety standards for consumer products that pose a potential risk of injury. If the Commission determines that a product defect poses an ongoing threat to consumer safety, the manufacturer may be required to institute a recall. As a practical matter, manufacturers that detect a potential problem with one of their consumer products will typically issue a recall order immediately without an order from the Commission in an effort to stem potential liability. The Commission also has traditional regulatory agency authority to enforce regulations and halt any action inconsistent with the CPSA's objectives. In 2001, the Commission instituted action against multinational manufacturer Cosco, Inc., a well-known maker of baby care products, when the company failed to report problems with its baby strollers, car seats, and cribs. After an investigation revealed that Cosco's products had resulted in more than 300 injuries and two deaths to infants and small children, the Commission levied a $1.3 million fine against Cosco—one of the largest in the agency's history. The CPSA also gives individual consumers the right to bring a lawsuit directly against a manufacturer who violates the statute.

Other CPSA Protections   Subsequent amendments to the CPSA expanded the Commission's jurisdiction to include more specific categories of consumer products. The agency now administers the Flammable Fabrics Act[13] (regulating material used in clothing, especially children's sleepwear), the Child Protection and Toy Safety Act[14] (standards for components used to make toys, such as a ban on lead paint), the Poison Prevention Packaging Act[15] (setting standards for disclosing use of poisons in consumer products such as detergents and cleansers), and the Refrigerator Safety Act (passed after several media reports of children who were suffocated after climbing in old refrigerators in refuse lots).

FOOD AND DRUG SAFETY

The **Food, Drug and Cosmetic Act** (FDCA) is the federal statute that created the **Food and Drug Administration** (FDA) to regulate testing, manufacturing, and distribution of foods, medications (including over-the-counter medication and prescription drugs), medical devices, and cosmetics. A major component of the FDCA is the requirement that makers of certain food ingredients, additives, drugs, or medical devices obtain formal FDA approval prior to selling the product to the general public. The application process is very rigorous and evaluates data supplied by the applicant as well as independent evidence from scientists in its agency or government contractors. When the FDA has approved a drug for public use, any advertising for the drug is subject to FDA regulation in terms of what representations may be made and what disclosures must be included. FDA regulations also govern *labeling* of food packages.

---

[11]15 U.S.C. § 2051, et seq.

[12]Just prior to enactment of the statute, the U.S. Department of Health, Education, and Welfare reported that consumer products were causing approximately 30,000 deaths, 110,000 permanent injuries, and 20 million injuries that required medical treatment per year. Familiar toys such as Etch-a-Sketch had caused serious lacerations due to broken glass from the toy's screen for dozens of children.

[13]15 U.S.C. § 1191.

[14]15 U.S.C. § 1262(e).

[15]15 U.S.C. § 2079.

FDA Regulations and Enforcement: Food Safety

The FDA regulations define specific *food safety* processes, procedures, and standards such as a requirement that employees handling food wear rubber gloves and hair netting. The statute also sets out a broader catchall standard by outlawing any generally *adulterated* food that has potential for public harm. The FDA defines adulterated food as that which contains a "filthy, putrid, or decomposed substance" or any food "unfit for consumption."

The FDA also investigates any public outbreaks of illness related to food contamination. During its investigation of such outbreaks, the FDA uses its broad enforcement powers to detect and prevent any further contamination. These powers include seizure of contaminated products, mandatory recalls, civil enforcement lawsuits, fines, and criminal prosecution for egregious cases. One of the largest fines ever levied by FDA was against Odwalla Juice Company in 1998. The Odwalla juice case is featured as a Capstone Case Study in the back of this textbook.

> ### KEY POINT
> The FDA enforces both specific and general standards for food safety. While certain regulations set out specific purity or safety standards, a catchall provision sets out a general standard banning all adulterated food.

CONCEPT SUMMARY   Product Quality and Functionality

- A warranty is a seller's legally enforceable promise to a consumer concerning the quality and/or functionality of a product.

- Express warranties are created (generally through advertising) when the seller promises that the goods have certain qualities or a certain level of efficiency.

- Puffery is a nonfactual-based statement used in advertising that does not create an express warranty.

- The implied warranty of merchantability applies to every sale of a product from a merchant to a buyer and requires the seller to warrant that the product is fit for its ordinary use.

- An implied warranty is created when a seller promises that the product is fit for a particular purpose. In order for the warranty to arise, the buyer must prove the seller knew of the buyer's desire to use the product in a specified way and the buyer relies on the seller's advice and recommendation.

- In order to disclaim a warranty, the seller must do so in a conspicuous writing such as capital letters, bold print, or a larger font that stands out from the rest of the writing.

- The Magnuson-Moss Act is a federal statute that regulates warranties given by a seller or lessor to a consumer. If the seller/lessor offers a written warranty, the transaction is subject to the provisions of the statute. If an express warranty is given, the seller may not disclaim implied warranties.

- Under the Magnuson-Moss Act, if the product being warranted costs $10 or more, the act requires that warranties be written conspicuously and in plain and clear language and be specific to the parts, products, characteristics, or functionality covered by the warranty.

- The Food, Drug and Cosmetic Act (FDCA) created the Food and Drug Administration (FDA) to regulate testing, manufacture, and distribution of foods, medications, and medical devices. A major component of the FDCA is the requirement that makers of certain food ingredients, additives, drugs, or medical devices obtain formal FDA approval before selling the product to the general public.

LO21-6 CREDIT TRANSACTIONS

As the financial crisis that began in 2008 illustrated, credit is one of the most important components of a stable economy.[16] The use of credit by consumers in the business environment is widespread and primarily exists in the form of loans and credit cards. A consumer credit transaction takes place between a **creditor**[17] (typically a financial institution, but any party regularly extending credit to consumers is considered a creditor) and a **borrower** (sometimes referred to as a *debtor*). Merchants are considered creditors when they regularly engage in extending credit terms to a patron. It is important for business owners and managers to be aware that establishing a credit relationship with a consumer borrower triggers protections for the borrower via federal and state statutes. There is a large body of administrative law that regulates credit transactions as well.

Consumer Credit Regulation

The centerpiece of federal statutory regulation of credit transactions is the **Consumer Credit Protection Act**[18] (CCPA). The CCPA has been amended several times so that it now has six components that regulate credit transactions between a creditor and a borrower. These include consumer protections in the areas of disclosure of credit terms, credit reporting, antidiscrimination laws for credit applicants, and collection of debts from consumers.

LO21-7 *Truth in Lending Act* **The Truth in Lending Act**[19] (TILA) is the part of the CCPA that requires lenders to disclose to borrower applicants certain information about the loan or terms of credit. It also mandates uniform methods of computation and explanation of the terms of the loan or credit arrangements. The primary objective behind the TILA is to allow consumers access to reliable information related to interest rates and other important terms and to provide a standardized reporting system for consumers to compare loan offers. The TILA's scope is limited to credit extensions to consumers used primarily for personal, family, or household purposes.

The TILA covers only creditors who are *regularly* engaged in extending credit for goods and services (such as banks, department stores, suppliers, wholesalers, and retailers) plus those who are regularly engaged in *arranging* credit that is for personal, family, or household goods (such as a mortgage broker). For example, suppose Armstrong wishes to renovate the kitchen in his home, which he plans to finance through a loan. If Armstrong applies for a home improvement loan from his local bank, the transaction is covered under the TILA and the bank would be required to strictly comply with its requirements. However, suppose Armstrong convinces his retired uncle, Rogers, to make a five-year loan instead. Rogers's attorney drafts a promissory note and sends it to Armstrong for signature. The Rogers-to-Armstrong loan transaction is *not* covered under the TILA and Armstrong is without any statutory disclosure protection.

> ## KEY POINT
> The TILA covers only creditors who are regularly engaged in extending (or arranging for) an extension of credit for goods and services that is for personal, family, or household goods.

---

[16]One major factor in the financial crisis that began in September 2008 was an extreme and abrupt tightening of the credit markets by financial institutions that were reeling from losses in a variety of industries, but especially from increasingly high default rates on home mortgage loans. This, in turn, made consumer credit (such as a mortgage or car loan) more difficult to obtain and contributed to a slowing in consumer spending. The inability of consumers and businesses to obtain credit is one of many factors that deepened the crisis and led to a precipitous rise in unemployment.

[17]In some contexts, the creditor is known as a *lender.*

[18]15 U.S.C. § 1601, et seq.

[19]15 U.S.C. § 1605.

The TILA also authorized the Federal Reserve Board to set regulations with procedures and protections that help achieve the objectives of the act. The most important regulation for business owners and managers is **Regulation Z,** which requires that certain written disclosures be made prior to the time that a credit transaction is consummated. The two most important terms in a TILA disclosure statement are the *finance charge* and the *annual percentage rate* (APR). These two terms are different ways of expressing the same disclosure: the total amount of interest that the consumer will pay over the life of the loan/credit extension. The finance charge must be stated in a dollar amount that represents the *sum* of interest charges that will be paid along with the required payment of principal to pay the loan back. The APR is written as a mathematical percentage that is used to determine the interest rate being paid by the consumer. Because the finance charge and APR are so important, Regulation Z requires that their disclosure must be *more conspicuous* that other disclosures. The regulation also requires that fees may not be hidden within a finance charge. Therefore, transaction charges, loan origination fees,[20] and charges for required life insurance (if the borrower dies, the policy pays off the creditor) must all be disclosed, if applicable. If a creditor fails to comply with the TILA's disclosure requirements

The Truth in Lending Act requires creditors to make certain disclosures about a loan transaction (such as fees), and allows consumers to cancel the loan contract for any reason within three business days of the transaction.

in any way, the debtor has the right to cancel any contract associated with the loan without any further obligation to the creditor. The creditor is also required to notify the debtor of her statutory right to cancel the contract for any reason within *three business days* of the transaction. Failing to provide proper notice of cancellation rights extends that right for up to three years from the date of the contract. As a practical matter, creditors can avoid liability by being sure that their notice of the right to cancel is consistent with the format authored by the Federal Reserve Board.

In Case 21.3, an appellate court considers a consumer's claim that the required cancellation notice was inadequate and, therefore, she was entitled to cancel the loan contract one year after signing it. Figure 21.2 and Figure 21.3 are sample TILA disclosure statements similar to the one that would have been used by the plaintiff in Case 21.3.

Other Federal Statutory Protections

The CCPA and the TILA have been amended several times to include additional protections for consumers related to credit discrimination, credit card issuers, and consumer leases.

Consumer Financial Protection Bureau   As part of a sweeping overhaul of the U.S. financial market regulatory system, Congress created the Consumer Financial Protection Bureau (CFPB) in 2010. The CFPB is an independent agency housed within the Federal Reserve. Fees paid by banks fund the agency, which is charged with setting rules to curb unfair practices in consumer loans and credit cards. Regulation of the financial markets is covered in detail in Chapter 16.

---

[20]Sometimes called points, loan origination fees are essentially prepaid interest. A loan at 7% with 1 point means that, upon receiving the loan, the borrower pays the creditor 1% (1 point) of interest based on the initial principal amount of the loan. Then the borrower repays the principal plus 7% in interest per year for the life of the loan.

FACT SUMMARY   In March 2003, Palmer obtained a debt-consolidation loan from Champion, which was secured by a second mortgage on her home (also known as a home equity loan). On the day the loan closing took place, she signed several loan documents as well as the required TILA disclosures. Several days later, Palmer received copies of these documents by mail along with the "notice of her right to cancel" disclosure required by the TILA. The notice of her right to cancel provided that Palmer could "cancel the transaction for any reason within three business days of (1) the date of the transaction, (2) the date she received her TILA disclosures, or (3) the date she received the notice of right to cancel." The notice also provided that if she was to cancel the transaction by mail or telegraph, the cancellation had to be postmarked no later than April 1, 2003. Palmer did not cancel the transaction within the allotted time period. However, in August 2004 she filed for cancellation of the transaction under the extended three-year statute of limitations under the TILA, claiming that Champion failed to make TILA disclosures because the times frames in the cancellation notice were too confusing.

SYNOPSIS OF DECISION AND OPINION   The United States Court of Appeals for the First Circuit affirmed the trial court's decision and dismissed Palmer's claim. The court reasoned that the notice of right to cancel provided by Champion complied with the TILA disclosure requirements, and that an objectively reasonable consumer would not find the notice confusing. Therefore, Palmer's right to rescind was not extended by a failure to follow TILA procedures.

WORDS OF THE COURT: Objectively Reasonable Notice   [I]n the TILA context [. . .] we, like other courts, have focused the lens of our inquiry on the text of the disclosures themselves rather than on plaintiffs' descriptions of their subjective understandings. [. . .] This emphasis on objective reasonableness, rather than subjective understanding, is also appropriate in light of the sound tenet that courts must evaluate the adequacy of TILA disclosures from the vantage point of a hypothetical average consumer—a consumer who is neither particularly sophisticated nor particularly dense. [. . .] Thus, we turn to the question of whether the average consumer, looking at the Notice objectively, would find it confusing. We conclude that she would not. [. . .] It clearly and conspicuously indicates that the debtor can rescind 'within three (3) business days from whichever of [three enumerated] events occurs last.' [. . .] We fail to see how any reasonably alert person—that is, the average consumer—reading the Notice would be drawn to the April 1 deadline without also grasping the twice-repeated alternative deadlines. [. . .] Because we find the Notice clear and adequate, and because the plaintiff otherwise concedes receiving all the required disclosures, her right of rescission under the TILA had long expired by the time she commenced this action."

Case Questions

1. Given the language of the time frame notice, do you agree with the court's statements that it was clear and objectively reasonable consumers would not be confused by it? Why or why not?

2. Examine Figure 21.3. This is a notice that is similar to the notice Palmer received. Does that affect your analysis?

Antidiscrimination   Denying an applicant credit based on discriminatory factors relating to the applicant's race, religion, national origin, color, gender, age, or marital status is unlawful under the **Equal Credit Opportunity Act,**[21] which was passed in 1974. The statute was driven primarily by the civil rights movement of the late 1960s and early 1970s to prevent what was then a relatively commonly practice of considering gender or race in credit decisions. The law also applies to charging higher interest rates based on discriminatory factors.

Credit Cards   In May 2009, Congress overhauled the statutory scheme governing consumer credit card transactions. The **Credit Card Accountability Responsibility and Disclosure Act of 2009** (CARD Act)[22] increases the power and oversight authority of the

---

[21]15 U.S.C. § 1691.

[22]Pub. L. No. 111-24, H.R. 627 (amending 15 U.S.C. § 1601, et seq.).

FIGURE 21.2 Sample Home Equity Loan TILA Disclosure

August 17, 2005
HOME EQUITY ("Account")
TRUTH IN LENDING DISCLOSURE
(Contract)

> **FIRST FINANCIAL BANK**
> **100 E LANCASTER AVE**
> **DOWNINGTOWN, PA 19335** ("Lender")

"you" and "your" means the recipient of this disclosure. "we", "us" and "our" means, the Lender listed above. "e" means an estimate.

IMPORTANT FACTS ABOUT OUR HOME EQUITY INTEREST ONLY LINE OF CREDIT

RETENTION OF INFORMATION. This disclosure contains important information about our home equity line of credit, Interest Only Line ("Account"). You should read it carefully and keep a copy for your records.

AVAILABILITY OF TERMS. All of the terms described below are subject to change. If these terms change (other than the annual percentage rate) and you decide, as a result, not to enter into an agreement with us, you are entitled to a refund of any fees you paid to us or anyone else in connection with your application.

SECURITY INTEREST. We will take a security interest in your home (collateral). You could lose your home if you do not meet the obligations in your agreement with us.

POSSIBLE ACTIONS. We can terminate your Account, and require you to pay us the entire outstanding balance in one payment if; you engage in fraud or material misrepresentation in connection with the Account; or, you do not meet the repayment terms; and/or, your action or inaction adversely affects the collateral or our rights in the collateral.

We can refuse to make additional extensions of credit or reduce your credit limit if: the value of the dwelling securing the Account declines significantly below its appraised value for purposes of the Account; or, we reasonably believe you will not be able to meet the repayment requirements due to a material change in your financial circumstances; or, you are in default of a material obligation in the agreement; or, government action prevents us from imposing the annual percentage rate provided for or impairs our security interest such that the value of the interest is less than 120 percent of the credit line; or, a regulatory agency has notified us that continued advances would constitute an unsafe and unsound practice; and/or, the maximum annual percentage rate is reached.

The initial agreement permits us to make certain changes to the terms of the agreement at specified times or upon the occurrence of specified events.

MINIMUM PAYMENT REQUIREMENTS. You can obtain advances of credit for 10 years (the "Draw Period"). During the Draw Period, payments will be due monthly. Your minimum periodic payment will be equal to the accrued interest as of the closing date of each billing statement. Although principal payments are not required, pay down on the unpaid principal balance can be made at any time without penalty.

BALLOON PAYMENT. After the Draw Period ends you will no longer be able to obtain credit advances. You will be required to pay the entire balance that you owe after the expiration of the Draw Period in a single balloon payment.

MINIMUM-PAYMENT EXAMPLE. As an example, the minimum interest only payment on a balance of $10,000 at an **ANNUAL PERCENTAGE RATE** of 8% would vary between 120 monthly payments of $61.37 and $67.95. This would be followed by one final payment of $10,067.95.

FEES AND CHARGES. To open and maintain your Account, you must carry insurance on the property securing your Account and pay us the following fees:

Mortgage or Trust Deed Preparation	$_____	Appraisal	$ _95.00 to $235.00 (Waived)_
Title Search	$ _35.00 (Waived)_	Abstract	$_____
Title Insurance	$_____	Recording Fees	$ _66.50 (Waived)_
Survey	$ _3.00 to $6.00 (Waived)_	Document Preparation Fee	$ _175.00_

*Payable at Application   **Payable at closing   ***Chargeable as a credit advance to your account   ****Based on a $10,000.00 representative amount of credit

If you tell us you have decided not to enter into the Account within three days of receiving this Disclosure in person, or within six days after the day we mail it to you, as the case might be, any fees or charges you might have already paid will be refunded.

TAX DEDUCTIBILITY. You should consult a tax advisor regarding the deductibility of interest and charges for the Account.

OTHER PRODUCTS. If you ask, we will provide you with information on our other available home equity Accounts.

MINIMUM TRANSACTION REQUIREMENTS. Credit advances must be in increments of $500.00.

VARIABLE RATE FEATURE. The Account has a variable rate feature. The annual percentage rate (corresponding to the periodic rate) and minimum payment can change as a result. The annual percentage rate includes only interest and no other costs. The annual percentage rate is based on the value of an index. The index is the Wall Street Journal published Prime Rate (if published in a range, the highest number in the range will be used) and is published in the Wall Street Journal.

RATE CHANGES. The annual percentage rate can change monthly. The maximum **ANNUAL PERCENTAGE RATE** that can apply is 18.000%. Apart from this rate cap, there is no limit on the amount by which the rate can change in any one-year period.

MAXIMUM-RATE AND PAYMENT EXAMPLE. If the **ANNUAL PERCENTAGE RATE** equaled the 18.000% maximum and you had an outstanding balance of $10,000.00, your minimum payment would be $152.88. This annual percentage rate could be reached the first time your interest rate changes, unless your initial rate is equal to the maximum, in which case it would be reached immediately.

HISTORICAL EXAMPLE. The following table shows how the annual percentage rate and the minimum payments for a single $10,000.00 credit advance would have changed based on changes in the index over the past 15 years. The index values are from July of each year. While only one payment amount per year is shown, payments would have varied during each year of the Draw Period.

The table assumes that no additional credit advances were taken, that only the minimum payments were made, and that the rate remained constant during each year. It does not necessarily indicate how the index or your payments will change in the future.

YEAR	INDEX (%)	MARGIN* (%)	ANNUAL PERCENTAGE RATE (%)	MINIMUM PERIODIC PAYMENTS ($)
1990	10.000%	00.50%	10.500%	$86.30
1991	8.500%	00.50%	9.000%	$73.97
1992	6.000%	00.50%	6.500%	$53.42
1993	6.000%	00.50%	6.500%	$53.42
1994	7.250%	00.50%	7.750%	$63.70
1995	8.750%	00.50%	9.250%	$76.03
1996	8.250%	00.50%	8.750%	$71.92
1997	8.500%	00.50%	9.000%	$73.97
1998	8.500%	00.50%	9.000%	$73.97
1999	8.000%	00.50%	8.500%	$69.86
2000	9.500%	00.50%	10.000%	$00.00
2001	6.750%	00.50%	7.250%	$00.00
2002	4.750%	00.50%	5.250%	$00.00
2003	4.000%	00.50%	4.500%	$00.00
2004	4.250%	00.50%	4.750%	$00.00

*This is a margin we have used recently

FIGURE 21.3   Sample Home Equity Loan Notice of Right to Cancel

HOME EQUITY LINE OF CREDIT
NOTICE OF RIGHT TO CANCEL

DATE 10/01/2010
LOAN NO. 5931569013
TYPE Equity Line

LENDER: Main Street Bank

BORROWERS/OWNERS Eva St. Clair

ADDRESS 123 Stowes Lane
CITY/STATE/ZIP New Town, MA
PROPERTY 10 Main Street, Unionville, MA

We have agreed to establish an open-end credit account for you, and you have agreed to give us a mortgage/lien/security interest on your home as security for the account. You have a legal right under federal law to cancel this account, without cost, within THREE BUSINESS DAYS after the latest of the following events:

      (1)   The opening date of the account, which is 02/20/2009   ; or
      (2)   The date you received your Truth in Lending disclosures; or
      (3)   The date you received this notice of your right to cancel the account.

If you cancel the account, the mortgage/lien/security interest on your home is also cancelled. Within TWENTY CALENDAR DAYS of receiving your notice, we must take the necessary steps to reflect the fact that the mortgage/lien/security interest on your home has been cancelled. We must return to you any money or property you have given to us or to anyone else in connection with this account.

You may keep any money or property we have given you until we have done the things mentioned above, but you must then offer to return the money or property. If it is impractical or unfair for you to return the property, you must offer its reasonable value. You may offer to return the property at your home or at the location of the property. Money must be returned to the address below. If we do not take possession of the money or property within TWENTY CALENDAR DAYS of your offer, you may keep it without further obligation.

HOW TO CANCEL

If you decide to cancel this account, you may do so by notifying us, in writing, at

Main Street Bank
Unionville, MA

You may use any written statement that is signed and dated by you and states your intention to cancel, or you may use this notice by dating and signing below. Keep one copy of this notice no matter how you notify us because it contains important information about your rights.

If you cancel by mail or telegram, you must send the notice no later than MIDNIGHT of October 5, 2010   (or MIDNIGHT of the THIRD BUSINESS DAY following the latest of the three events listed above). If you send or deliver your written notice to cancel some other way, it must be delivered to the above address no later than that time.

I WISH TO CANCEL

_____   _____
CONSUMER'S SIGNATURE   DATE

The undersigned each acknowledge receipt of two copies each of NOTICE OF RIGHT TO CANCEL.

Each borrower/owner in this transaction has the right to cancel. The exercise of this right by one borrower/owner shall be effective as to all borrowers/owners.

Eva St. Clair 10/1/10   _____
BORROWER/OWNER Eva St. Clair   DATE   BORROWER/OWNER   DATE

_____   _____
BORROWER/OWNER   DATE   BORROWER/OWNER   DATE

Federal Trade Commission over credit card issuers. The CARD Act was primarily intended to protect consumers from unreasonable surprises when interest rates increase and credit card fees are imposed, and to restrict marketing and card-issuing practices targeted to younger (18 to 21 years of age) consumers. Among other requirements, credit card issuers:

- Are prohibited from issuing a credit card to any consumer under the age of 21 unless the consumer submits either the signature of a cosigner over the age of 21 who has the means to repay debts incurred by the consumer, or financial information indicating an independent means (regular income) of repaying any debts. Special rules exist for credit cards issued to college students.

- Must comply with rules that require institutions of higher education (such as colleges and universities) to publicly disclose any contract of agreement made with a credit card issuer. Nor may credit card issuers offer college students tangible items (gifts) to induce them to apply for credit cards.

> **web**check **www.mhhe.com/melvin**
> For more information on how the CARD Act affects college students, check this textbook's Web site.

- Must give 45-days' advance notice of any impending raise in rates.

- Must mail credit statements at least 21 days before the bill's due date (extended from 14 days in the previous law).

Existing Regulations under the TILA   The CARD Act added to already existing disclosure and transaction regulations under the TILA. Those existing measures were left intact. The existing provisions of the TILA include:

- Protection of consumers when a card is used to buy what turns out to be a faulty product by requiring the card issuer to investigate and, depending on the results of the investigation, credit the consumer's account.

- A limitation of the consumer's liability for unauthorized charges to a total amount of $50. As a practical matter, consumers usually get even more favorable treatment than the law allows because many major credit card companies now have a policy of waiving any charges it determines to be fraudulent. If the card is reported stolen to the issuer *prior* to any unauthorized charge, the consumer has no liability for charges. Although credit card companies are permitted to send unsolicited cards to consumers, fraudulent or unauthorized use prior to the acceptance of the offer will not result in liability to the addressee/consumer.

- The TILA sets out a statutory procedure for consumers that are claiming a billing error[23] or disputing a charge on their account. The procedure includes a time frame and a requirement that the credit issuer attempt to investigate the dispute and resolve it in good faith. It also prohibits the credit issuer from charging the consumer interest on the charge while the dispute is being investigated.

Although the overwhelming majority of the cases featured in this textbook are appellate court decisions, Case 21.4 is a municipal court (local court) case, included here to illustrate the types of creditor abuses that spurred enactment of the CARD Act.

Identity Theft   In 2003, Congress gave some protections to consumers who were victims of *identity theft*. Identity theft occurs when a criminal assumes the identity of an individual for purposes of making fraudulent credit transactions in the victim's name. The **Fair and Accurate Credit Transactions Act** (FACT Act)[24] requires that credit bureaus stop reporting any fraudulent account information once a consumer alleges identity theft and during

---

[23]These protections were added to the TILA by the Fair Credit Billing Act (15 USCA § 1681, et seq.).

[24]Pub. L. No. 108-159, 117 Stat. 1952 (Dec. 4, 2003) (amending 15 U.S.C. § 1681).

FACT SUMMARY Discover brought a collection lawsuit in the amount of $5,564.28 against Owens after she defaulted on her credit card agreement. Owens had obtained the Discover card in 1996 with a credit limit of $1,900 and subsequently charged $1,460. However, her credit card agreement allowed Discover to add fees and increase her interest rate in certain circumstances, such as when she paid late or less than the minimum amount due. Owens became disabled and experienced severe financial difficulty. Although she stopped using the credit card and made payments regularly, Discover continued to assess fees consistent with the credit card agreement. In sum, despite never using the credit card and paying $3,492 toward an original debt of $1,900, with all of the fees and accrued charges, Owens nevertheless faced a $5,564.28 outstanding balance at the time of the collection suit.

SYNOPSIS OF DECISION AND OPINION The court ruled in favor of Owens, holding that the terms of Discover's credit card agreement provisions were unreasonable and the six-year accumulation of over-limit fees was manifestly unconscionable.* The court pointed out that this was not a case where a debtor recklessly used her credit card to purchase items beyond the agree-upon credit limit. Rather, the bulk of the balance owed was due to fees, charges, and substantial increases in the finance rate. Moreover, Discover had a duty to mitigate its damages once it became clear that Owens would never be in a position to make the required payments.

WORDS OF THE COURT: Credit Card Company Practices "This court is all too aware of the widespread financial exploitation of the urban poor by overbearing credit-card companies. Defendant has clearly been the victim of plaintiff's unreasonable, unconscionable, and unjust business practices. This court has broad legal and equitable powers, and now brings them to bear for the debtor in this case."

Case Questions

1. The court conceded that Discover had complied with existing federal regulations regarding disclosures of fees and so forth. Given this fact, is the court sacrificing legal principles in favor of a paternalistic approach? Is this good public policy?

2. Suppose that Owens had chosen to close the account and notified Discover that she was defaulting on the account and could not pay. Would she have been in a better position than if (as she actually did) she kept paying as much as she could afford (the minimum amount due or less) over a period of six years?

3. How could Discover have known that Owens, as the court said, would "never be in a position" to pay the full amount owed?

*Recall from Chapter 6, "Overview and Formation of Contracts," that unconscionability is a narrow doctrine used only when one party has used bargaining power to oppress the other party.

---

an investigation period. The FACT Act also contains provisions that established a national fraud alert system so that consumers have a timely way to guard their credit once they suspect identity fraud has occurred.

Consumer Leases   In addition to the regulation of debt incurred in purchasing products or services, the TILA regulates the *leasing relationship,* whereby a creditor/lessor typically gives the possession and use of equipment or a motor vehicle to a consumer/debtor in exchange for monthly payments over an agreed upon period of time. When the leasing period expires, the consumer either returns the goods or exercises an option to purchase the goods at a predetermined price. Consumer leasing is regulated by the **Consumer Leasing Act** (CLA), which covers lessors engaged in leasing or those arranging leases for consumers in the ordinary course of business. Many of the CLA's provisions mirror the statutory protections afforded to consumer debtors in a loan transaction such as APR disclosure requirements and standardizing certain information.

Credit Reports   Because creditors rely so heavily on credit bureaus (private companies that compile data about a consumer's credit history as well as current liabilities), Congress gave consumers federal statutory protection in the **Fair Credit Reporting Act**[25](FCRA). The FCRA sets privacy rights for consumer credit reports and requires that the credit bureaus give individual consumers complete and timely access to their own credit reports. In order to ensure that the credit report is accurate, the FCRA requires each of the credit bureaus to provide individual consumers with a copy of their own credit report, free of charge, once per year. Additionally, any time the report is used in a credit-making decision (such as a loan application), the consumer has the right to obtain a free copy of the credit report used in the decision-making. The FCRA also provides a dispute resolution system designed to allow consumers the right to challenge any information on their credit report if the information is incorrect. Further, the FCRA requires that credit bureaus remove any entry that is obsolete. The FCRA defines obsolete as any negative information (such as an account that was closed by the creditor and placed for collection) that is over seven years old and a bankruptcy filing that occurred more than 14 years prior to the date of the report.

CONSUMER DEBT COLLECTION

LO21-8

As discussed in the previous section, consumer credit transactions are heavily regulated in an effort to protect consumers and help level the playing field between creditors and debtor consumers. Similarly, when a creditor's agent is collecting a debt owed to them by virtue of an extension of consumer credit, the collection process is subject to regulation. Agents involved in debt collection for consumer debts are directly regulated by a federal statute called the **Fair Debt Collection Practices Act**[26] (FDCPA). The FDCPA applies only to *agents* of the debtor that are attempting to collect the debt from the consumer. These agents typically take the form of a collection agency, but others that are collecting consumer debts on behalf of the debtor (such as attorneys) may also be subject to the FDCPA under certain conditions.[27] A creditor that is attempting to collect her own debt is *not* subject to the act. However, both creditors and collection agencies are subject to additional state statutory and regulatory requirements as well.

FDCPA Requirements

The FDCPA requires that the collection agency make known certain rights of the debtor in a **validation disclosure** when making the initial contact to inquire about the debt. This disclosure notice must inform the debtor that he has 30 days to dispute the debt. The law also requires that the collection agency investigate any disputed debt and obtain written verification of the debt from the original creditor.

In addition to validation disclosure, the FDCPA also prohibits certain conduct in the course of attempting to collect a debt. First, the law limits the contact that a debt collector may have with third parties such as employers. Second, certain methods are unlawful. Specifically, the FDCPA prohibits collector contact (1) at inconvenient times, such as early morning or late night calls, or at inconvenient places, such as the debtor's place of employment or at social events; (2) once the collector is informed that the debtor is represented by an attorney; or (3) if the debtor gives written notice that she refuses to pay the debt and requests the agent to cease contact. The FDCPA also prohibits any harassing, intimidating, or misleading tactics by collection agents, such as threats of incarceration, posing as an attorney or law enforcement agent, or abusive, degrading language.

---

[25]15 U.S.C. § 1681, et seq.

[26]15 U.S.C. § 1692 (became Title VII of the Consumer Credit Protection Act).

[27]*Heintz v. Jenkins,* 514 U.S. 291 (1995).

Enforcement

Federal statutes that govern consumer debt collection are enforced primarily by the Federal Trade Commission (FTC). The FTC uses a system of penalties, cease-and-desist orders, and civil lawsuits to enforce the FDCPA. However, the law also provides individual consumers with a statutory cause of action so that a debtor may sue a collection agent directly for any damages suffered, plus attorneys' fees incurred in bringing suit. On the state level, state attorneys general often have authority to prosecute collection agents engaged in abusive collection tactics within their state's jurisdiction.

KEY TERMS

Consumer law p. 523   The statutory and administrative body of law that protects consumers engaging in transactions with merchants and creditors.

Federal Trade Commission Act p. 524   A statute that created the Federal Trade Commission and prohibited deceptive trade practices.

Federal Trade Commission p. 524   An agency charged with the broad mandate of preventing unfair and deceptive acts or practices in commercial transactions.

Telephone Consumer Protection Act and **Telemarketing and Consumer Fraud and Abuse Prevention Act** p. 526   Two statutes that regulate telemarketing firms and practices, including allowing consumers to opt out of unwanted calls from telemarketers, banning the use of unsolicited recorded calls and faxes, and prohibiting telemarketers from making false representations.

Federal Odometer Act p. 526   A law making it criminal to change vehicle odometers and requires that any faulty odometer be plainly disclosed in writing to potential buyers.

Controlling the Assault of Non-Solicited Pornography and Marketing Act of 2003 p. 527   Often called the CAN-SPAM Act, this statute regulates the sending of unsolicited e-mail (spam) by prohibiting certain practices such as falsifying the "from" name and information in the subject line and requires the sender to provide a physical address of the producer of the e-mail.

Warranty p. 528   A seller's (or lessor's) legally enforceable promise to a consumer concerning the quality and/or functionality of a product.

Express warranty p. 528   A warranty that occurs when a seller makes a representation of fact about a product.

Implied warranty p. 528   A warranty protecting consumers even when the seller does not make a specific representation about the product.

Disclaim p. 531   The act of renouncing one legal right or claim.

Written express warranty p. 532   A warranty whose terms are put into writing for the consumer.

Consumer Product Safety Act p. 534   The statute that created the Consumer Product Safety Commission, with the aim of making consumer products safer.

Food, Drug and Cosmetic Act p. 534   The statute that created the Food and Drug Administration.

Food and Drug Administration p. 534   The federal agency that regulates the testing, manufacture, and distribution of foods, medications, and medical devices and requires the makers of certain food ingredients, additives, drugs, or medical devices to obtain formal FDA approval before selling the product to the general public.

Creditor p. 536   Any party regularly extending credit and to whom a debt becomes owed.

Borrower p. 536   The individual to whom credit is extended and who owes the debt.

Consumer Credit Protection Act p. 536   The centerpiece of federal statutory regulation of credit transactions, which regulates credit transactions between a creditor and a borrower in the areas of disclosure of credit terms, credit reporting, antidiscrimination laws, and collection of debts from consumers.

Truth in Lending Act p. 536   A part of the Consumer Protection Act that requires lenders to disclose to borrower applicants certain information about the loan or terms of credit and mandates uniform methods of computation and explanation of the terms of the loan or credit arrangements.

Regulation Z p. 537   A part of the Truth in Lending Act requiring that certain written disclosures be made prior to the time that a credit transaction is consummated.

Equal Credit Opportunity Act p. 538   Passed in 1974, this statute prohibits discrimination of a credit applicant based on the applicant's race, religion, national origin, color, gender, age, or marital status.

Credit Card Accountability Responsibility and Disclosure Act of 2009 p. 538   Known as the CARD Act, this law protects consumers from unreasonable interest rate increases and credit card fees and requires card issuers to give a 45-day advance notice of any impending rate increase.

Fair and Accurate Credit Transactions Act p. 541   Often referred to as the FACT Act, this statute requires credit bureaus to stop reporting any fraudulent account information once a consumer alleges identity theft until an investigation is conducted.

Consumer Leasing Act p. 542   A statute that regulates lessors engaged in leasing or arranging leases for consumers in the ordinary course of business.

Fair Credit Reporting Act p. 543   A statute that sets privacy rights for consumer credit reports and requires that the credit bureaus give individual consumers complete and timely access to their own credit reports.

Fair Debt Collection Practices Act p. 543   A statute that regulates agents of the debtor involved in debt collection for consumer debts and that requires the collection agency to make known certain rights of the debtor.

Validation disclosure p. 543   A Fair Debt Collection Practices Act requirement that, when making initial contact with a debtor, a collection agency must make known certain rights of the debtor, including the fact that he has 30 days to dispute the debt.

THEORY TO PRACTICE

Outdoor World Inc. is a retailer of sporting goods gear, equipment, and accessories for use in outdoor sports and camping. Outdoor World carries two brands of tents, the Extreme Tent and the Tectonic Tent. The Extreme is more popular and less expensive, but the manufacturers of the Tectonic promised financial incentives to Outdoor World for selling a certain amount of Tectonics.

1. Suppose the manager of Outdoor World places an advertisement in the newspaper: "Extreme Tents 50% off—This week only." Willen, in the market for a tent, sees the advertisement and arrives at Outdoor World the next day. The manager explains to Willen that the Extreme is temporarily out of stock, and instead tries to sell him the Tectonic. Does the manager's conduct constitute a deceptive trade practice? What law governs unfair trade practices?

2. In Question 1 above, assume that Willen informs the manager that he is moving to Iceland and will require a tent that can maintain a certain degree of warmth. Although there is no specific reference to such a quality on the label, the manager assures Willen that he, himself, was an avid camper. The manager went on to say that he had used the Tectonic recently and that it will maintain warmth. Did the manager create a warranty? What kind of warranty?

3. In Question 2 above, assume that Willen purchased the Tectonic and the agreement of sale for the tent contains a provision: "All implied warranties are hereby excluded." Is Willen still protected by any warranty? Which warranty/warranties?

4. Assume that Outdoor World wishes to begin a marketing campaign by sending e-mail to its existing customers advertising sales and new items. Is that advertising subject to the provisions of the CAN-SPAM Act? Why or why not?

5. After a downturn in the economy and a tightening of consumer credit, Outdoor World decided to offer qualified customers credit for consumer purchases. What is the legal impact of that decision?

6. One year after starting Outdoor World credit accounts for its patrons, one customer defaults. The manager calls the customer to try and collect the debt owed. Is the manager subject to the provisions of the Fair Debt Collection Practices Act? Why or why not?

Managers are often involved in business planning discussions where having sufficient legal acumen enables them to limit the company's liability while maximizing opportunities. Assume that you are one of group of mid-level managers that receives an e-mail from the chief operating officer of Outdoor World.

Given the decline in customers who are buying new outdoor sports accessories, senior management is considering a plan to begin selling preowned sporting

equipment at discount prices. However, we want to make sure that we understand the liability exposure in tandem with the cost-benefit analysis. Lead a small group discussion among the mid-level managers about the opportunities and threats that such a plan would involve and write a two-page summary memorandum of your conclusions.

A sample answer may be found on this textbook's Web site at www.mhhe.com/melvin.

CASE SUMMARY 21.1 :: Barrer v. Chase Bank USA, 566 F.3d 883 (9th Cir. 2009)

TRUTH IN LENDING ACT

Barrer obtained a credit card with Chase in 2004 and accepted the Cardmember Agreement. In February 2005, Chase mailed a Change in Terms Notice to Barrer that notified him of a raise the annual percentage rate from 8.99 percent to 24.24 percent in certain events, including payment default and persistently late payments. The notice provided a right for Barrer to reject these terms in writing, but he did not. In April 2005, Barrer's APR jumped to 24.24 percent. Chase claimed that

they increased the rate because of information obtained from a credit agency about Barrer being an increased credit risk, even though that condition was not listed in the notice as an event qualifying for a rate increase.

CASE QUESTIONS

1. Do Chase's actions comply with TILA? Why or why not?
2. Shouldn't Barrer be liable for failing to reject the new terms?

CASE SUMMARY 21.2 :: Myers v. LHR, Inc., 543 F. Supp. 2d 1215 (S.D. Cal. 2008)

FAIR DEBT COLLECTION PRACTICES ACT

Myers owed over $11,000 to an automobile finance company in 2001. LHR was hired to collect the debt, and an LHR agent contacted her with threats of a lawsuit and garnishment of her wages. Myers negotiated a settlement whereby LHR accepted approximately $3,000 as complete payment for the debt. Myers wire-transferred the money to LHR to satisfy the debt, and later received a letter saying the debt was paid in full. However, Myers later found out that her settled

debt was still reported to the credit agencies by LHR and this adversely affected her credit rating. Despite the settlement, LHR agents continued to call Myers, threatening a lawsuit, wage garnishment, and reporting her to government authorities for tax evasion.

CASE QUESTIONS

1. Were LHR's actions lawful under the FDCPA? Why or why not?
2. If LHR's actions were not lawful, what could they have done to comply with the act?

CONSUMER FRAUD ACT

From 1995 to 2001, McDonald's, the famous fast-food chain, sponsored promotional games including "Monopoly Games at McDonald's," "The Deluxe Monopoly Game," and "Who Wants to be a Millionaire." For each of these promotional games, McDonald's conducted an extensive marketing and advertising campaign where they represented that all customers had a fair and equal chance to win, and specified the odds of winning. However, the FBI investigated McDonald's based upon claims that the game pieces required to win the high-value, "million dollar" prizes were compromised and being diverted to friends and family of personnel who had access to these pieces. Yet throughout this investigation, and even after individuals pled guilty to conspiracy charges related to these diversionary practices, McDonald's continued their advertising practices. Phoenix, a Burger King franchisee, sued under the CFA, claiming that the advertisements stating everyone has a fair and equal chance to win are false and deceptive.

CASE QUESTIONS

1. Does Phoenix have a claim under the Consumer Fraud Act? Why or why not?
2. Would there be any other factors affecting whether or not Phoenix had a claim?

IMPLIED WARRANTIES

Carney purchased a Suzuki Samurai SUV. Although Carney had never experienced any safety issues with his Suzuki, several SUV rollover incidents made him wary of continuing to drive the vehicle. Carney sued for a refund based on a theory of breach of implied warranty, citing an automotive expert who tested the Suzuki Samurai and concluded that it has a higher rollover risk because of its high center of gravity, narrow tread width, and light weight.

CASE QUESTIONS

1. Which implied warranty is Carney claiming here, and what is the legal standard for such warranties?
2. Can Suzuki disclaim this warranty? Why or why not?

✔ Self-Check **ANSWERS**

Express Warranty

1. Express warranty created by specific advertised promises such as *instantly stops* and *incapacitates.*
2. No express warranty. Puffing, not promises.
3. Express warranty created by verifiable promise of fact.
4. Although advertisements can create warranties by what they show, it is unlikely that any express warranty was created here because no express promise was made about quality.

22
CHAPTER

Criminal Law and Procedure in Business

learning outcomes checklist

After studying this chapter, students who have mastered the material will be able to:

22-1 Explain the origins and sources of criminal law and procedure.

22-2 Distinguish between criminal law and criminal procedure.

22-3 Compare criminal law with civil law.

22-4 Articulate the underlying tenets of criminal law and requirements for criminal liability.

22-5 Identify circumstances when business managers and owners may be liable for criminal violations by a corporation.

22-6 Give specific examples of white-collar crime laws that may impact a business entity and/or its owners/managers.

22-7 Explain the steps in the criminal justice system.

22-8 Name and explain the various constitutional procedural protections afforded to those accused of a crime.

22-9 Understand the exclusionary rule and how it applies to business.

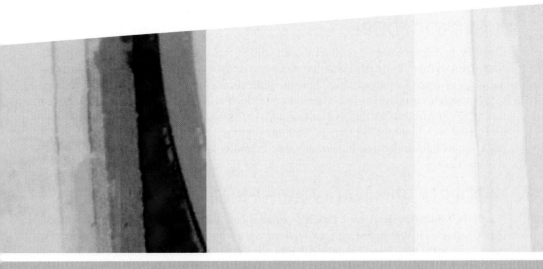

One way that the government regulates the practices and operations of business owners and managers is through **criminal law.** This chapter focuses on how criminal law, criminal procedure, and the criminal justice system's impact the legal environment of business. Specifically students will learn:

■ The origins and sources of criminal law.
■ Elements and examples of criminal acts.
■ Steps in the criminal justice system.
■ Legal protections for those accused of committing a crime.

LO22-1   ORIGINS AND SOURCES OF CRIMINAL LAW AND PROCEDURE

Legal Speak »))

Culpability The quality of being blameworthy in criminal law; it is used to assess the accused's guilt and determine whether he committed the crime purposefully, knowingly, recklessly, or negligently.

Crime in the United States is ordinarily dealt with by state authorities predominantly under state statutory law. While each state has its own system of criminal law, there is an increasing body of federal criminal law. Thus, the federal criminal justice system exists alongside (sometimes overlapping) the state systems. Much of American criminal law is derived from English criminal law that existed primarily as common law with some statutory mandates. However, in the 1960s, state legislatures began to assemble various statutes addressing criminal culpability and integrating state common law to form more comprehensive criminal codes.

MODERN CRIMINAL LAW: THE MODEL PENAL CODE

Nearly two-thirds of states have enacted criminal codes based on the **Model Penal Code (MPC)** adopted by the American Law Institute (ALI) in 1962.[1] The vocabulary and formation of the MPC has been very influential in shaping criminal law notions, even in states where the MPC has not been formally adopted. However, many states have retained certain portions of their common law within their criminal codes as well.

Legal Speak »))

Preempt A federal law that overrides a state law.

In 1971, the congressionally appointed National Commission on Reform of Federal Criminal Laws issued a model federal criminal code that consolidated and clarified existing statutory law. However, it has long been settled that there are no federal common law crimes.[2] Although a state criminal statute and a federal criminal statute may outlaw identical or substantially identical conduct, state law and federal law may coexist unless the federal statute contains specific language that preempts state law.[3]

LO22-2, 22-3   CRIMINAL LAW VERSUS CRIMINAL PROCEDURE

While *criminal law* defines the boundaries of behavior and sanctions for violating those boundaries, **criminal procedure** refers to the legal process and safeguards afforded to individuals (and in some cases business entities) during criminal investigations, arrest, trials, and sentencing. Criminal *law* consists of a body of law which, for the purposes of preventing harm to society, declares what conduct is criminal and prescribes the punishment to be imposed for such conduct. Criminal *procedure* sets limits on the government's authority in applying criminal law. Criminal procedure is covered in detail later in this chapter.

> ## KEY POINT
>
> Criminal *law* defines the boundaries of behavior and sanctions for violating those boundaries; criminal *procedure* refers to legal protections of citizens during criminal investigations, arrests, trials, and sentencing.

Criminal Law versus Civil Law

Recall the distinctions between civil law and criminal law covered in Chapter 1, "Legal Foundations." Civil laws are designed to compensate parties (including businesses) for damages as a result of another's conduct. Criminal statutes are a protection of *society*, and the violation of a criminal law results in a penalty to the violator such as a fine or imprisonment. It is important to remember that these categories are not mutually exclusive; one can violate a criminal law and commit a civil wrong in the very same act. For example, suppose that Mcduff is an accountant for Shakespeare Book Company (SBC) and steals $100,000

---

[1]Recall from Chapter 1, "Legal Foundations," that the ALI is an organization of attorneys, judges, and law professors that produces model statutes to promote consistency in the application of the law from state to state.

[2]*U.S. v. Hudson and Goodwin,* 11 U.S. 32 (1812).

[3]*Goldstein v. California,* 412 U.S. 546 (1973).

from the business by creating a fake employee on the company's books and secretly pays the fake employee's salary to himself. Upon discovery, SBC would notify the authorities and Mcduff would likely be charged with various criminal offenses such as grand theft and fraud. If he were convicted, he would likely be incarcerated for an extended period of time. Although sometimes courts order restitution as part of a criminal sentence, SBC may also choose to file a civil lawsuit against Mcduff individually in order to recover the losses due to Mcduff's commission of the tort[4] of conversion (the civil counterpart to theft). SBC may also be entitled to compensation from Mcduff for other incidental expenses it incurred as a result of the theft (such as costs of detecting the theft). If SBC is successful in obtaining a civil judgment against Mcduff, they may then attempt to recover their losses by tapping Mcduff's personal assets.

Burden of Proof   One significant difference between a criminal case and a civil case is the **burden of proof.** In a civil case, plaintiffs need only to prove that the defendant had committed a civil wrong by a **preponderance of the evidence.** This means that the fact finder need not be completely convinced that the plaintiff's arguments in the case should prevail. Rather, the fact finder need only be convinced that the defendant's liability was *more likely than not* for the plaintiff to meet her burden of proof. In criminal cases, where the stakes may involve an individual's liberty, the standard of proof is much higher. In a criminal case, the government must prove their case **beyond a reasonable doubt.** Thus, a fact finder must be convinced that the defendant's criminal liability is not in doubt to a reasonable person.

General Principles of Criminal Law

There are two important underlying tenets to criminal law: *legality* and *punishment.* The principle of **legality** is a protection of individuals from being charged with some unspecified general offense. Legality simply requires that crimes be specifically proscribed by law in advance of the conduct sought to be punished. This includes the notion that the Constitution bars both Congress and state legislatures from enacting retroactive criminal statutes (known as *ex post facto* laws). Statutes that fail to give fair warning that a particular conduct is unlawful may be struck down by the courts as too vague. The principle of **punishment** is based on the concepts that criminal law (1) acts as a *deterrent,* (2) *removes* dangerous criminals from the population, and (3) that *rehabilitation* is an important part of the criminal justice system. Punishments are applied using a sentencing system that follows a general range of years prescribed by the legislature. After conviction, a sentence is imposed by the court based on the individual trial judge's discretion and assessment of the severity of the crime and mitigating circumstances. However, starting in the 1980s, public dissatisfaction with an actual or perceived view that courts were not imposing sufficiently stiff penalties spurred federal and state legislatures to pass laws requiring courts to assess penalties based on statutorily prescribed **sentencing guidelines.** These guidelines have had the impact of severely restricting judicial discretion. This same movement is also responsible for a spate of statutes that include mandatory minimum sentences for certain offenses as well as minimum sentences for repeat offenders (some states adopted a "three strikes" law, which requires a 25-year sentence for a third felony conviction). Despite criticism by many prominent judges, attorneys, and legal scholars on various fronts, state and federal legislators continue to generally support the concept of sentencing guidelines and mandatory minimums.

---

[4]Torts were covered in detail in Chapter 9, "Torts and Products Liability."

Criminal Liability

From a legal perspective a crime has two parts: a physical part whereby the defendant committed an *act* or *omission,* and a mental part focusing on the defendant's subjective *state of mind.* Thus, an analysis of criminal liability involves three fundamental questions. First, did the defendant actually commit the prohibited act? Second, did the defendant have a culpable state of mind? Third, does the law give the defendant a palpable defense (such as a self-defense claim to a homicide charge)?

Act Requirement

The **act requirement,** also called by its Latin name, *actus reus,* requires the government to prove that a defendant's actions objectively satisfied the elements of a particular offense. The act requirement is based on the fundamental criminal law tenet that evil thoughts alone do not constitute a criminal act. Rather, there must be some overt conduct (either an act or an omission) and it must be voluntary. Courts generally follow the rule that an act is voluntary unless it is demonstrated that the defendant acted based on physical compulsion, reflex, or certain physiological or neurological diseases. An act by omission occurs when a crime is defined in terms of *failure* to act. For example, if the chief financial officer fails to disclose data required by federal securities law, she has committed an omission that satisfies the act requirement.

Mental Requirement

The mental element, also called by its Latin name, *mens rea,* which translates literally into "guilty mind," refers to the general requirement that the defendant have a requisite degree of culpability with regard to each element of a given crime. The fundamental underpinning is that an act does not make a person guilty unless his mind is guilty.[5] The words and phrases contained in a criminal statute to express the guilty mind requirement include *intentionally, knowingly, maliciously, willfully,* and *wantonly.* However, some criminal statutes set the intent requirement at mere recklessness or negligence and not actual intent as the level of culpability. Thus, an act or omission where the defendant's conduct so grossly deviated from the standard of conduct that a reasonable person would judge it as criminal, may also satisfy the mental element requirement.

Courts and legislatures have also established certain rules for applying the mental element requirement in cases of *mistake.* Certain statutes also impose *strict liability,* whereby the mental element is assumed by certain conduct so that the defendant's culpable state of mind need not be proved.

Figure 22.1 illustrates the typical language of act requirement and the intent requirement as set out in a Florida criminal statute prohibiting forgery.

FIGURE 22.1 Excerpt from a Florida Criminal Statute: F.S.A. § 831.02

Uttering forged instruments

"Whoever **utters** and **publishes** as true a false, forged or altered record, deed, instrument or other writing mentioned in § 831.01 (i.e., "letter of attorney, policy of insurance, bill of lading, bill of exchange or promissory note, or an order, acquittance, or discharge for money or other property") **knowing** the same to be false, altered, forged or counterfeited, with **intent** to injure or defraud any person, shall be guilty of a felony of the third degree."

---

[5]Expressed as the common law Latin maxim *actus not facit reum nisi mens sit rea* (*Collins Latin,* 2009).

Defenses Even when the requisite mental state and criminal act standards are proven, the law provides for certain defenses based on unique circumstances of the crime. **Self-defense** is an example of a defense to a criminal charge of homicide in that the law recognizes that certain cases necessitate the use of deadly force to repel an attack in which the defendant reasonably feared that death or substantial harm was about to occur either to the defendant or to a third party. The rules governing self-defense are complex and vary from state to state, especially on the question of whether the defendant is required to retreat before using deadly force. The defense afforded by the self-defense doctrine is at its height when it involves use of deadly force to repel an attack in the victim's home or place of business.

The other major category of defense is **mental incapacity.** As you may imagine, this defense is very controversial and is sometimes colloquially called the *insanity defense.* That term is potentially misleading because in certain jurisdictions incapacity covers a wider variety of conditions aside from insanity. Although mental incapacity has a variety of definitions depending on the jurisdiction, the MPC requires the defendant's actions to be related to some type of mental disease or defect.[6] The MPC also specifically rules out any sociopathic personality disorders as the basis for a mental incapacity case.

Less frequently asserted defenses include *duress,* in which a defendant committed a crime in response to another person's threat to inflict personal injury (threats to property or reputation are insufficient); and *intoxication,* which generally depends on whether the intoxication was voluntary or involuntary. If voluntary, the criminal act is only excused if the defendant was so intoxicated that he could not form the requisite mental intent (guilty mind) to have criminal culpability. If involuntary, the defense is broader, but still requires proof that the intoxication rendered the defendant unable to understand that his conduct constituted a crime.

Types of Crimes

Crimes may be classified in several different ways. **Felonies** are crimes that generally carry *one year or more* of incarceration as the penalty. **Misdemeanors** are crimes that carry *up to one year* of incarceration as the penalty. Frequently, states also have degrees (or grades) of crimes within each of those categories that further delineate the seriousness of the crime. Thus, a premeditated murder would be referred to as a first-degree felony, whereas shoplifting a shirt may be defined as a second- (or third-) degree misdemeanor. Many states also have a classification of crimes known as *summary offenses* or *infraction offenses* for minor crimes that carry no threat of jail (especially for first offenders) such as a charge of underage alcohol use.

Crimes are also sometimes classified based on the victim or result of the crime. Crimes where the prepretrator has used force or violence such as murder or sexual assault are classified as *violent crime.* Laws that prohibit offensive or disorderly conduct in public are referred to as *public order crimes.* This would also include crimes that have no direct victim, but that society has judged to be detrimental to public well-being such as crimes related to narcotics, prostitution, or obscenity. Crimes that involve damage or stealing property (such as theft, vandalism, or arson) are usually referred to as *property crimes.* When the crime takes place in the business environment, it is classified as *white-collar crime.*

CRIMINAL LAW AND BUSINESS ENTITIES

LO22-4

While any discussion of criminal law necessarily focuses on criminal culpability of individuals, business owners and managers should have a fundamental knowledge of how criminal law may be applied to business entities. This knowledge helps business owners and managers to reduce risk and add value to the business by taking affirmative steps to limit criminal culpability for the business and its principals.

---

[6]MPS § 4.01(1)

The modern trend in criminal law is to expand the scope of criminal statutes to include criminal culpability for corporations and their principals. Courts have allowed liability to exist for corporations so long as the prosecutor can prove that the corporation's agents (not just executive management) were engaged in criminal conduct on behalf of the company. Recall from Chapter 15, "Corporations" that courts have recognized that corporations exist as a separate legal "person." Criminal statutes have embraced the concept that a corporation may be charged with a crime along with, or apart from, its principals or agents. The Model Penal Code provides for criminal liability for business entities if (1) the criminal act by the business's agent is within the *scope of her employment*, and the statute imposes liability on the business for such an act (such as obstruction of justice for shredding documents related to potentially unlawful conduct); or (2) the criminal omission is the failure to perform a specific duty imposed by law (such as important disclosures on a report to investors); or (3) the crime was authorized by one of the corporation's top-level managers (such as a chief financial officer ordering an internal accountant to file a false corporate tax return). Congress has specifically included business entities in criminal statutes in areas that impact business, including fraud, obstruction of justice, health and safety requirements, selling of ownership interests (securities law), disclosure requirements, environmental regulations, and antitrust or other anticompetition laws.

Individual Liability for Business Crimes

Congress and state legislatures have also expanded criminal culpability for individual officers and directors (and sometimes majority owners) for corporate crimes committed within the scope of their employment. These principals are often included in criminal statutes that require officers and directors to act as responsible corporate officers in complying with statutes and being diligent about adhering to standards set out in statutes and regulations. Because of the inherent difficulties in terms of proof, most statutes do not require specific mental intent (guilty mind) that is required for other crimes. Since the mid-1970s, legislative bodies have begun to impose what amounts to strict liability statutes for corporate officers even when the officer in question did not have any actual knowledge that a crime had taken place.

In 2002, the Sarbanes-Oxley Act imposed significant criminal liability for officers, directors, and majority shareholders of corporations that falsify financial disclosures and provides up to 20 years of incarceration for any employee that destroys documents relevant to a government agency investigation. The Sarbanes-Oxley law is discussed in detail in Chapter 16, "Regulations of Securities, Corporate Governance, and Financial Markets." Case 22.1 provides an example of individual officer liability for business crimes.

CONCEPT SUMMARY Criminal Law

- Criminal law is based on state and federal laws that started as common law crimes but were codified into statutes based on the Model Penal Code.
- While some actions implicate both criminal and civil liability, civil laws protect individuals by redressing injuries, but criminal laws protect society as a whole by punishing wrongdoers.
- Criminal liability requires both a bad act (*actus reus*) *and* a guilty mind (*mens rea*).
- Even when a requisite mental state and bad act are proven, the accused can offer a defense such as mental incapacity, duress, and self-defense to avoid criminal liability.
- Corporations and their managers can be guilty of the crimes of their employees if the crime was committed for some corporate advantage or benefit of the company.

FACT SUMMARY   LaGrou's warehouse in Chicago stored frozen meat for various food companies in the region. Its cold storage facility held more than 20 million pounds of poultry, pork, and beef. That building also had a severe rodent problem as evidenced by rat droppings that could be found in every corner of the warehouse and nests found in boxes of meat. The company organized employee "rat patrols" that would catch up to 50 rats a day, but more would enter each night. Packing areas had puddles of beef blood mixed with rat hair and feces and meat boxes would show rat trails with teeth marks. According to government investigators, employees would mark rat-infested boxes with "MM" for Mickey Mouse, but the boxes were not discarded. The warehouse was referred to by employees as an "amusement park for rats" and a "house of horrors for the City of Chicago." Evidence indicated that Stewart, president of LaGrou, knew of the rat infestation for a period of three years. Stewart told the employees to keep catching rats but refused to perform a full extermination because he determined that it would be too expensive. After notification that the U.S. Department of Agriculture inspectors scheduled a visit, Stewart had the employees work through the night to throw away boxes of rat infested meat. Yet, the USDA inspectors still found the rats, the filth, and the discarded meat. Stewart was charged with violating federal criminal laws prohibiting the sale of adulterated meat. At trial, Stewart defended that he did not have the requisite knowledge for criminal liability because he had no actual knowledge of any specific meat contamination.

SYNOPSIS OF DECISION AND OPINION   The Seventh Circuit Court of Appeals ruled against Stewart

and LaGrou. The court held that knowledge of *any* rat problem was sufficient and that Stewart was liable for all the violations that he was in charge of preventing. The court ruled that the government need not prove that Stewart had actual knowledge of specific meats that were contaminated. Stewart had a responsibility to install systems to assure sanitation standards. The court affirmed the trial court's order that Stewart must contribute personal assets to the $8.2 million in fines and serve five years on probation.

WORDS OF THE COURT: Liability for Criminal Conduct of Others   "The conditions at LaGrou's cold storage warehouse at 2101 Pershing Road in Chicago were enough to turn even the most enthusiastic meat-loving carnivore into a vegetarian. . . . In this case, the government needed to prove that agents of the LaGrou corporation knowingly stored meat, poultry, and food products under unsanitary conditions. LaGrou's president, Jack Stewart, and the Pershing Road warehouse manager, David Smith, were both well aware of the rodent infestation problem and other insanitary conditions at the warehouse, yet persisted in storing and distributing meat, poultry, and food products there."

Case Questions

1. What if Stewart was never told about the rat problem. Did he have a responsibility to find out?

2. What about the workers who shipped the contaminated meat each day? Should they be guilty of some crime? What about the government inspectors who let the warehouse operate for three years? Who is most culpable?

WHITE-COLLAR CRIME

LO22-5

White-collar crimes usually signify criminal violations by corporations or individuals including fraud, bribery, theft, and conspiracy committed in the course of the offender's occupational duties. Typically, these crimes are set out in state and/or federal statutes.

Fraud

Perhaps the most common white-collar crime is fraud. Fraud is a broad general term used to describe a transaction in which one party made false representations of a matter of fact (either by words or conduct) that were intended to deceive another. In certain cases, active concealment of a material fact (versus an affirmative false representation) may also constitute fraud. The basic elements of criminal fraud are: (1) a false representation (or concealment) concerning a material fact and (2) another party relied on the false misrepresentation of the fact and suffered damages as a result. A material fact is one that is essential to the agreement or one that affects the value of the transaction. For example, suppose that Rasputin applies for a loan to start his business. Because his finances were in dire straights, Rasputin submitted a false set of tax returns to the bank loan officer. Based on this information, the bank lends Rasputin the money. Rasputin has committed a fraud upon the bank. Bank fraud of this nature is a felony punishable under state and, depending on the bank, federal criminal statutes.

In 1990, Congress passed the **Mail Fraud Act**[7] with the intent of giving federal prosecutors significant leverage in prosecuting white-collar criminals. The statute criminalizes any fraud where the defrauding party uses the mail or any wire, radio, or television in perpetrating fraud. This comprehensive approach to criminalizing fraud is based on Congress's authority to regulate mail and interstate commerce. It also covers any *organization* of a scheme to defraud by false pretenses. For example, in our Rasputin example above, suppose that Rasputin sets up an elaborate scheme to fool investors into thinking that he had invented a new product that would bring in several millions of dollars of revenue. He designs a brochure and mails it to several wealthy individuals. At this point, Rasputin has committed mail fraud even though he has not actually induced any investors. The ease of prosecution for mail fraud has made it a primary tool used by prosecutors in white-collar crime investigations.

Another form of fraud is *embezzlement*. Embezzlement is more appropriately categorized as a fraud (and not as theft) because it involves fraudulent concealment of financial records to perpetrate theft. Embezzlement occurs when someone in a position of trust creates fraudulent records to disguise the theft. For example, suppose that Rasputin is the controller of WidgetCo. Over the period of a month, Rasputin transfers small amounts of Widget's money to his personal checking account and adjusts the monthly financial statements to indicate that the money was in WidgetCo.'s account. This act constitutes embezzlement because of the cover-up aspect of the scheme. If Rasputin had come into his office one morning, stole cash from the safe and walked out never to return, this would likely constitute theft because no scheme was involved.

Ponzi Schemes

A Ponzi scheme is a fraudulent investment operation that pays returns to investors from their own money or money paid by subsequent investors rather than from any actual profit earned. The scheme is named after Charles Ponzi, who became notorious for using the technique in 1903. A Ponzi scheme usually offers returns that other investments cannot match in order to entice new investors. This is generally accomplished in the form of short-term returns that are either abnormally high or unusually consistent. The perpetuation of the returns that a Ponzi scheme advertises and pays requires an ever-increasing flow of money from investors in order to keep the scheme going. The system is destined to collapse because the earnings, if any, are less than the payments. The authorities uncover some schemes before they collapse if an investor suspects that she is a victim and reports the investments to authorities. As more investors become involved, the likelihood of the scheme coming to the attention of authorities increases.

For example, suppose that High Return Investments (HRI) prints advertising brochures that promise a 30 percent return on an investment in just one month—an extraordinary return by any measure. HRI represents that it uses a "complex off-shore

---

[7]10 U.S.C. § 1341.

investment strategy that is the result of years of study and testing." No matter how fancy the brochures are, it is difficult to attract any large initial investments without a track record. Thus, HRI convinces a few investors to take the risk with small amounts of money. Instead of investing the money, HRI then takes out a loan and repays the initial investors with the promised 30 percent return one month later. This is where HRI sets the trap: initial investors now invest larger sums and new investors want a piece of the action. It is no longer necessary to take out a loan because sufficient capital from eager new investors is flowing into HRI's hands. The cascading effect then allows HRI to pay back any loans used to perpetrate the scheme and take handsome bonus fees for managing the money. HRI covers its tracks by producing false investment statements for its investors showing high returns. When one or more investors would request a withdrawal, there was always sufficient cash to pay out. But HRI's scheme cannot last forever. Typically HRI's schemers will end up in one of two scenarios: (1) HRI disappears with the investment money or (2) the scheme collapses because too many investors demand their returns at the same time. The second scenario typically happens when investor confidence in the equities markets deteriorates and investors withdraw money from market-based investments in favor of cash and other safer forms. For example, when the financial crisis of 2008 began to shake investor confidence, it unraveled the largest Ponzi scheme ever operated by a single person. Federal prosecutors claim that a 20-year scheme, operated by well-known investment manager Bernard Madoff, cost his investors billions of dollars. Madoff's scheme is examined in detail in the Business Ethics Perspective.

Conspiracy

Conspiracy is an agreement by two or more persons to commit a criminal act. It is itself a punishable offense: all parties to the agreement are subject to prosecution. Because the crime is complete upon agreement, there is a very low threshold for satisfying the criminal act requirement. Conspiracy requires a specific *intent* to achieve the object of the conspiracy, but does not require that the act actually be carried out. The MPC contemplates conspiracy as a crime that requires two guilty minds. Therefore, both parties must actually *manifest* intent to commit the criminal act for a conspiracy to occur.

Racketeer Influenced and Corrupt Organizations Act (RICO)

The federal Racketeer Influenced and Corrupt Organizations Act[8] (RICO) was enacted in 1970 with the objective of providing the government with a powerful tool to fight the rising tide of organized crime. One purpose of the RICO law was to prevent the infiltration by organized crime into legitimate business operations. The statute makes it a criminal offense for anyone associated with an enterprise to conduct or participate in its affairs through a pattern of racketeering activity. Although racketeering is generally understood to mean an organized conspiracy to commit the crimes of extortion or coercion, state and federal legislatures have also added to the definition by including conduct such as engaging in illegal gambling, narcotics trafficking, and prostitution.

The modern trend is for authorities to use the RICO statute in an expansive manner, including criminal conduct that is not traditionally related to organized crime. Because RICO laws define racketeering in such broad terms, including crimes such as wire fraud, mail fraud, and securities fraud, prosecutors have been increasingly willing to bring RICO cases in white-collar crimes and political corruption cases. Although the penalties under RICO are stiff, the real teeth of the law are found in its forfeiture provisions. This allows

---

[8] 18 U.S.C. §§ 1961–1968.

Epic Fraud: Bernie Madoff's Multibillion-Dollar Ponzi Scheme

OVERVIEW Bernie Madoff founded Bernard L. Madoff Investment Securities firm in 1960 and was its chairman until his arrest in 2008. Madoff's firm originally thrived and he rose to become one of the chief figures in the financial markets. During the 1980s Madoff was a rising star in the investment community and eventually served as chairman of the Board of Directors of the National Association Securities Dealers (NASD), the self-regulating industry organization overseeing securities brokers and dealers. Madoff was also influential in Washington, D.C., and regularly donated hundreds of thousands of dollars to candidates and political committees including influential U.S. senators. During his rise, Madoff also gained a reputation as a generous philanthropist who donated significant sums of money to charities ranging from cancer research to the American Jewish Congress. In fact, it was his association with so many charities and nonprofits that allowed his Ponzi scheme to continue unabated for nearly 20 years.

MADOFF'S PONZI SCHEME Madoff began his scheme during the recessionary pressures of the early 1990s. His investors were defecting as Madoff's returns shrank and Madoff set on a course to reverse that trend. He designed a fake investment strategy, which he named "split-strike conversions," and marketed investment funds using this strategy with a promise of a 10–12 percent return per month on an investment no matter how volatile the stock market was. In reality, Madoff planned an elaborate hoax where he deposited all incoming investor money in a business account controlled exclusively by him, printed up bogus statements that were intended to dupe investors into having confidence that their investments were safe and returning high yields, developed an infrastructure of in-house analysts to convince investors of the firm's sophistication, and paid out strategically timed profits to certain investors designed to entice additional investment. The scheme was calculated to lure investors with consistent returns between 10–12 percent annually and increase investor confidence in Madoff's methods. The hoax worked. In a short period of time, investors were knocking down Madoff's door to get in. Madoff set up a screening system and was very selective in his choice of clients, giving his firm the air of inimitability, sophistication, and safety. A key part of Madoff's scheme depended on his emphasis on secrecy. He insisted that investment managers not list him on their own reports to individual investors. Madoff justified the secrecy requirements on the basis that his investment strategy was a valuable trade secret and he was simply being vigilant about protecting his investors.

PHILANTHROPY AS PART OF THE SCHEME Madoff's reputation in the philanthropic community allowed him access to large charity fund endowments and many of his clients were nonprofit institutions. These institutions were a crucial part of the scheme because Madoff knew that charities generally did not make withdrawals from their invested endowments even in times of financial strife. Nonprofits typically allow their endowments to grow and only withdraw funds in rare circumstances. This allowed Madoff the ability to funnel money where needed and when needed to continue perpetrating his fraud.

Madoff's scheme continued to grow because investors were more than willing to invest large sums of money, sometimes personal fortunes in the billion-dollar category, and he always had a plentiful supply of cash when investors would make periodic withdrawals. Of course, Madoff earned sizable commissions for his work and lived an opulent lifestyle with private jets, a Palm Beach mansion, and a yacht in the French Riviera.

FEEDER FUNDS As the pressure of the scheme demanded more cash to support the fraud, Madoff extended his fraud into Europe, Asia, and Latin America. A key component to the success of the scheme was a steady flow of new investor dollars from a group of super investors. Madoff depended on these super investors, who not only invested their own holdings but also funneled other wealthy investors to Madoff's firm. These super investors created what Madoff termed *feeder funds* to channel billions of dollars in investment cash into Madoff's fictitious investment fund. In return, the managers of the feeder funds were rewarded with handsome commissions. After the scheme collapsed, the government alleged that feeder fund investment managers Jeffery Picower and Stanley Chais were both involved in directing investor money to Madoff's firm and were paid both commission fees for bringing in investor cash and made extraordinary returns on their own personal investments with Madoff at rates much higher than other investors were paid. By early 2008, Madoff's firm had 4,800 clients—all clamoring to invest more money.

THE COLLAPSE In December 2008, the ongoing financial and credit crisis began to put pressure on Madoff's firm as clients demanded their investments be returned in order to cover their cash flow needs and to move their wealth into safer investments. As the demands mushroomed, Madoff quickly ran out of cash and could not turn to any financial institutions for credit. On December 10, when he could no longer stem the financial and legal catastrophes, Madoff confessed his scheme to his family and turned himself in to authorities the next day. The news of Madoff's arrest sent shock waves from Wall Street to Palm Beach as investors came to grips with the plot. Those who had invested all or substantially all of their assets with Madoff were wiped out overnight. Sophisticated money managers, wealthy investors, and large charities were all among Madoff's victims and the news shook investor confidence even more, contributing to further declines in the market. In perhaps the most tragic case of the Madoff scheme, French millionaire investor Terry Villochet, who had invested his family's substantial wealth with Madoff, lost billions in the scheme. Facing certain bankruptcy, Villochet committed suicide two weeks after learning of Madoff's arrest.

EARLY WARNINGS As early as 1999, a financial analyst named Harry Markopolos did an in-depth study of Madoff's investments at the request of a client. Markopolos was astonished at what he found and began to document at least two dozen red flags that indicated fraud. Markopolos was skeptical of the three-person accounting firm used by Madoff to verify the authenticity of the investments. Although Markopolos brought this information to government authorities, the subsequent investigations by the Securities and Exchange Commission (SEC) did not reveal any fraud. In the meantime, Madoff restructured his firm and agreed not to be involved in the actual sales of securities. However, Madoff was too deep into the scheme to halt it, and as volatility in market increased in 2000–2001, investors continued to seek Madoff's consistent returns.

AFTERMATH In March 2009, Madoff pled guilty to 11 felonies including fraud and perjury. He was given the maximum sentence of 150 years of incarceration. Madoff's accountant was also charged and cooperated with authorities in exchange for leniency. Prosecutors are still investigating allegations that certain investors had insider knowledge of the scheme. Hundreds of investors have filed lawsuits against a variety of banks, accounting firms, investment managers, and financial advisors.

The SEC was heavily criticized during a congressional hearing into the Madoff matter. Congress inquired why Markopolos had not been taken more seriously and how it was that

continue

Epic Fraud: Bernie Madoff's Multibillion-Dollar Ponzi Scheme

Bernie Madoff, seen here being escorted by U.S. Marshals after being sentenced to 150 years in jail, perpetrated the largest and longest Ponzi scheme in U.S. history.

the SEC did not have the expertise and system checks to discover the fraud earlier. Federal prosecutors froze all of Madoff's assets, and a federal court appointed a trustee to recover any funds that were unlawfully transferred before the collapse.

1. What factors caused Madoff to go from a legitimate and respected investor to a con man? Was it purely greed?

2. Madoff claimed that his scheme was simply a stopgap measure to bridge the 1990 recession and that he had intended to go back to legitimate methods once the economy improved. If this were true, would it remove the ethical taint from the scheme?

3. How was Madoff able to fool some of the most sophisticated investors for so long?

4. Consider the ethical decision-making of the investment managers that were funneling other investors to Madoff. Did they have an ethical obligation to inquire as to how Madoff was making these returns?

5. Madoff used the notion that his investment strategy was a trade secret to ward off any investor inquiries. If you were doubtful as to the strategy, but upon inquiry were denied any details of the strategy, would that affect your decision to invest?

6. Consider the ethics of self-regulation of brokers/dealers. Does self-regulation depend on adherence to high ethical standards? In the Madoff case, did he get the benefit of the doubt as a Wall Street insider? Why do you suppose that the SEC was not more aggressive with Madoff?

prosecutors to seize the defendant's personal assets if the government can prove that the assets were obtained using profits from criminal activity. This is a powerful tool because it has the effect of bankrupting the racketeering enterprise while an individual convicted under the statute is incarcerated.

Insider Trading

In the wake of the financial crisis that began in 2008, the government has become increasingly aggressive about the enforcement of **insider trading laws.** These laws are federal securities statutes that prohibit corporate insiders who have access to certain information that is not available to the general investment public from trading their company's stock based on the insider knowledge. Insiders can be executives, managers, corporate counsel, consultants, certain employees, brokers, and even majority shareholders. In 1988, Congress passed the Insider Trading and Securities Fraud Enforcement Act that raised the criminal and civil penalties for insider trading, increased the liability of brokerage houses for wrongful acts of their employees, and gave the government more authority to pursue insider-trading violations. Insider trading laws and other laws regulate the issuance and trading of certain business ownership interests (such as stocks) and are discussed in detail in Chapter 16 "Regulation of Securities, Corporate Governance, and Financial Markets."

Bribery

Bribery generally involves a scheme to pay government official money in order to obtain favorable treatment for a personal or business transaction. Bribery is covered in both federal and state statutes. Note that bribery is an offense that requires only the *offer* of a bribe. It is not necessary that the transaction actually took place. For example, suppose that Whitaker is the owner of a construction company and bids on a contract to build a firehouse in the city. Whitaker promises a city councilman that he will pay him 10 percent of the total profit in the contract if the councilman will vote to give Whitaker the contract. The offer itself is unlawful even if the councilman did not go along with the scheme. Of course, if the councilman had gone along with the bribe (known as a *kickback* in these circumstances), he would also be culpable for bribery (and perhaps several other *public trust* laws).

Obstruction of Justice

Prosecutors have been increasingly willing to prosecute white-collar criminals under federal laws prohibiting the obstruction of justice[9] for any conduct that is related to attempting to cover up evidence of wrongdoing. Cover-ups take many forms, including (1) lying to investigators, (2) altering documents, (3) shredding or concealing documents or any media such as videotape, and (4) inducing other witnesses to lie or influencing witnesses to refrain from cooperating with authorities. Note that an obstruction of justice charge may stand *independently,* and prosecutors need not charge or convict the defendant with the underlying crime. For example, suppose that prosecutors interview Rasputin during the criminal investigation of insider trading at Rasputin's firm. Rasputin lies about his involvement in the insider trading to the authorities. When it is found out that Rasputin lied, prosecutors charge Rasputin with obstruction of justice. Rasputin may be convicted of the obstruction charge even if prosecutors do not have sufficient evidence to charge Rasputin with the underlying crime (insider trading).

---

[9]18 U.S.C. § 1001 et seq.

One of the most famous cases of a company being charged with obstruction was when federal prosecutors charged the accounting firm Arthur Andersen with obstruction, alleging that individuals within the firm shredded documents related to the collapse and fraudulent practices of the Enron corporation. A federal grand jury also indicted individual employees of Arthur Andersen for obstruction. The Enron and Arthur Andersen cases are discussed in detail in Chapter 5, "Business, Societal, and Ethical Contexts of Law."

Foreign Corrupt Practices Act (FCPA)

The **Foreign Corrupt Practices Act**[10] **(FCPA)** of 1977 is a criminal statute that was enacted principally to prevent corporate bribery of *foreign officials* in business transactions. The law prohibits a company, its officers, employees, and agents from giving, offering, or promising anything of value to any foreign (non-U.S.) official, with the intent to obtain or retain business or any other competitive advantage. This prohibition is interpreted broadly in that companies may be held liable for violating the antibribery provisions of the FCPA whether or not they took any action within U.S. borders. Thus, a U.S. company can be liable for the conduct of its overseas employees or agents, even if no money was transferred from the United States and no U.S. citizen participated in any way in the foreign bribery.

A foreign official means any officer or employee of a foreign government, regardless of rank; employees of government-owned or government-controlled businesses; foreign political parties; party officials; candidates for political office; and employees of public international organizations (such as the United Nations or the World Bank). This can include owner/employees as well. Even if the improper payment is not accepted, just offering it violates the FCPA. Likewise, instructing, authorizing, or allowing a third party to make a prohibited payment on a company's behalf; ratifying a payment after the fact; or making a payment to a third party knowing or having reason to know that it will likely be given to a government official constitute FCPA violations. This includes not only cash and cash equivalents, but also gifts, entertainment, travel, and the like. The FCPA is discussed in greater detail in Chapter 25, "International Law and Global Commerce."

 Self-Check   White-Collar Crime

What white-collar crimes are at issue in the following circumstances?

1. WidgetCo. applies for a permit to do business in Venezuela. The government official denies the permit, and a WidgetCo. executive pays for a lavish meal at a four-star restaurant while discussing the permit application.

2. InvestCo. advertises a return of 15 percent on any investments in its Super Duper Fund. Even when the market drops dramatically, Super Duper continues to perform at this level for 18 consecutive months. In its disclosures, InvestCo. reports that its auditing firm is headed by an InvestCo. officer's son-in-law.

3. WidgetCo. and PlankCo. agree to illegally fix prices so that the lack of competition drives the prices of their products artificially high. The companies begin the process to set prices, but abandon the plan at the last moment.

4. Evidence exists that WidgetCo.'s CEO was funneling money from the corporation with the help of several other executive managers. The funds came from an investment fraud scheme where each executive played a part to perpetrate the scheme and use WidgetCo. as a front business to help bolster their scheme with investors.

Answers to this Self-Check are provided at the end of the chapter.

---

[10]28 U.S.C. § 1602, et seq.

THE CRIMINAL JUSTICE SYSTEM

The criminal justice system is best thought of as one process that operates in two phases: **investigation** and **adjudication.** This section describes the nuts and bolts of the criminal justice process. Procedural safeguards that are afforded to those suspected or accused of crimes, known as *criminal procedure,* are discussed in the next section of this chapter.

Investigation

During the investigation phase, the authorities become aware of an alleged criminal act and begin an investigation by gathering physical evidence and interviewing witnesses and potential suspects. Because most criminal acts are handled at the state level, most enforcement of criminal law is conducted by state or local police agencies. Violations of federal laws are investigated by various federal law enforcement agencies including the Federal Bureau of Investigation (FBI). In a business context, investigators from federal regulatory agencies such as the Securities and Exchange Commission (SEC) or the Internal Revenue Service (IRS) may also undertake specialized criminal investigation. During this initial stage, investigators may also ask a court to authorize a search warrant in an effort to obtain more evidence. A warrant may only be issued based on **probable cause.** Once the authorities believe that sufficient evidence creates enough probable cause to indicate the culpability of a suspect, they will, depending on the circumstances, either obtain an *arrest warrant* or, more commonly, *arrest* the suspect by taking him into physical custody. If the criminal violation is a minor one, the authorities may simply issue a *citation,* whereby the violator may resolve the charge by paying a fine or may contest the charge in court. If an actual arrest has taken place, the authorities may continue their investigation by gathering more physical evidence, interviewing new witnesses, and attempting to further interview the suspect. The investigators then file formal criminal charges against the suspect and prepare a brief report for a local magistrate and prosecutors. The suspect, now charged, is referred to as the *defendant* and is formally read the charges by a magistrate. The magistrate then sets bail (if appropriate) and, if necessary, appoints an attorney to represent the defendant. Frequently, the prosecutor will review the investigator's report (and sometimes conduct additional investigation) and then decide whether she can prove the charges in a court of law based on available evidence. The prosecutor decides whether to: (1) proceed with prosecuting the defendant on the original charge; or (2) amend the charges as necessary; or (3) drop the charges altogether due to lack of evidence. The actual title of the prosecutor varies between jurisdictions, but local prosecutors are typically employed by the district attorney, state prosecutors are employed by the state's attorney general, and federal prosecutors work for the U.S. Attorney General under the authority of the U.S. Department of Justice.

Legal Speak »»
Bail The security, in the form or cash or a bond, given to the court to assure the appearance of a defendant in court at a later date. If the defendant appears in court, the bail is returned. If he flees, the bail is forfeited.

Adjudication

If the prosecutor elects to proceed with the charges, the defendant is entitled to a **preliminary adjudication.** Some jurisdictions use the *grand jury* system, while others use a *preliminary hearing* in front of a local magistrate. In each case, the prosecutor presents evidence of the defendant's guilt and the decision maker (either the grand jurors or the magistrate) determines whether probable cause exists to hold the defendant over for trial. If the prosecutor cannot offer sufficient evidence of probable cause, the charges are dismissed. As a practical matter, very few cases are dismissed at this stage.

The defendant is notified that he is held over for trial through either an *indictment* (in the case of a grand jury) or formal filing of an *information* (in the case of a magistrate). The defendant is then entitled to be arraigned in a state trial court where he is informed of the final charges and is asked to enter a *plea* of guilty, not guilty, or no contest,[11]

---

[11]A plea of no contest, sometimes called by its Latin form *nolo contendere,* is when the defendant does not admit or deny the charges, but is willing to accept the sanctions as if guilty.

An overwhelming majority of defendants plead not guilty at this stage, even if they intend on negotiating an eventual guilty plea with the prosecutor. Following the arraignment, the prosecutor and defense counsel will typically enter into a plea bargaining negotiation. This involves the parties agreeing to concessions from each side that will avoid trial and result in a voluntary plea of guilty or no contest by the defendant. All states also have some type of pretrial intervention for first-time offenders of nonviolent crime, whereby the defendant typically agrees to fulfill certain conditions (community service, drug rehabilitation, etc.) in exchange for the charges being dismissed at a later date. If a plea agreement cannot be reached, the case proceeds to trial. In a trial, the finder of fact (usually a jury in a criminal trial)[12] weighs the evidence and determines whether the prosecutor has proven the charges against the defendant beyond a reasonable doubt. If the jury finds the defendant guilty, this results in a *conviction*. If the jury finds the defendant not guilty, this results in an *acquittal* and the defendant cannot be prosecuted for the same charges again. If the jury is deadlocked (unable to reach a consensus decision), this results in a *mistrial* and the prosecutor decides whether or not to refile charges against the defendant a second time. If the defendant is convicted, he may file an *appeal* setting out the basis for having the conviction reversed.

If the defendant is convicted, the judge sets a future date for *sentencing*. In the interim, the court considers requests and reports by authorities, victims of the defendant's crime, character witnesses for the defendant, and sentencing guidelines (or statutory mandatory minimum sentences) in determining the defendant's punishment.

CONCEPT SUMMARY   The Criminal Justice Process

Investigative Phase	Adjudicative Phase
1. Investigate possible crime.	1. Preliminary adjudication (via grand jury or magistrate depending on jurisdiction).
2. Interview witnesses.	2. File indictment (known as "information" depending on jurisdiction), *or* drop charges due to insufficient evidence.
3. Obtain search warrants if necessary.	3. Defendant enters plea and enters plea negotiations if necessary.
4. Arrest (warrant or taken into custody), *or* issued a citation for minor infractions.	4. If no plea agreement is reached, defendant goes to trial.
5. Defendant formally charged.	5. Conviction or acquittal of the defendant.
6. Local judicial authority sets bail and appoints defense counsel if necessary.	6. Sentencing (if convicted).

LO22-7   CRIMINAL PROCEDURE

Recall from the beginning of this chapter the differences between criminal law and *criminal procedure*. While criminal law defines the boundaries of behavior and sanctions for violating those boundaries, criminal procedure refers to legal safeguards to protect individual

---

[12]Recall from Chapter 3, "The American Judicial System, Jurisdiction, and Venue," that the finder of fact may be either a jury *or* a judge.

rights (and in some cases business entities) during investigation by the government, arrest, trial, and sentencing. The protections are primarily provided by the U.S. Constitution's Bill of Rights. For purposes of understanding criminal procedure in a business environment, our focus is on protections found in the Fourth, Fifth, and Sixth Amendments. While the Constitution regulates many aspects of criminal procedure, as a practical matter state and federal legislatures also enact statutes and rules setting forth certain procedures that authorities must follow during investigation, arrest, criminal trials, and sentencing. State constitutions may also provide *additional* criminal procedure protections for its citizens. For example, one state may be more apt to require a higher level of probable cause for arrest than is prescribed by the federal rules or courts. Of course, states may not repeal the federal constitutional rights of individuals.

Legal Speak ›))
Warrant A court order authorizing an official to do something she would otherwise be prohibited from; the most common are warrants for arrest, search, or seizure.

Searches and Arrest

The Fourth Amendment to the U.S. Constitution protects individuals (and sometimes businesses) from government agents performing an unreasonable search and seizure and permits warrants to be issued only if probable cause exists. The U.S. Supreme Court has developed a large body of law to guide courts in determining the appropriate boundaries of searches and arrests by the authorities. First, the Court has held that the Fourth Amendment applies to both *searches* and *arrests.* However, a warrant is usually required before a search takes place (with certain exceptions). A warrant for arrest is generally not required in order to take a suspect into custody. Second, the Constitution requires that an impartial magistrate issue a search or arrest warrant only if probable cause has been established. Third, whether or not a search or arrest warrant exists, the action taken by authorities must always be *reasonable* and consistent with constitutional protections. Fourth, the authorities may conduct *limited,* warrantless searches in certain cases. For example, police may conduct short, pat down searches even without probable cause so long as the officer has a reasonable suspicion[13] that criminal activity is taking place or for the officer's safety.

Expectation of Privacy A fundamental part of the protections provided by the Fourth Amendment is that its protections are based on whether an individual's *reasonable expectation of privacy* has been violated by government authorities. The courts have held that individuals have the highest expectations of privacy in their own homes. However, once an individual goes into the public (such as driving a car on a public highway) the privacy expectations are diminished and Fourth Amendment protections become more limited in scope. Examples of evidence that is *not* protected as reasonable expectations of privacy include trash that has been set out on the public curb for pick up, or any

Although the Fourth Amendment requires authorities to obtain a warrant before searching a citizen, the Supreme Court has allowed the police to conduct a limited pat down search when an officer has reasonable suspicion that criminal activity is taking place.

---

[13]Reasonable suspicion has been described as a standard that is lower than probable cause, but "more than just a hunch." *Terry v. Ohio,* 392 U.S. 1 (1968).

apparently abandoned property, and things a person says or does in public. In terms of the abandoned property example, note that if the evidence has been disposed of, but is still located on the real estate (land) of an individual, then the owner may still have a reasonable expectation of privacy. For example, Scofield is being investigated for tax fraud. The authorities observe Scofield putting large bags of paper for trash pickup. They wait until midnight, and then take the bags from the curbside outside of Scofield's residence. When Scofield is brought the trial, the prosecutor introduces the discarded papers as evidence of tax fraud. If Scofield claims his Fourth Amendment rights were violated, it is likely that he would lose that argument because courts have consistently held that public papers disposed of as garbage are abandoned property and not subject to reasonable expectations of privacy. Suppose, though, on the other hand, that the real estate at issue was a country home with a long driveway and that trash collectors actually traveled onto the property to collect the garbage. If the authorities entered the land without a warrant and confiscated the bag of discarded papers, a court may very well find the search to be illegal.

> **KEY POINT**
> Fourth Amendment protections apply only where an individual's reasonable expectation of privacy (such as the warrantless search of a house) has been violated by government authorities.

Plain View Doctrine   Courts have also held that the authorities generally do not commit a Fourth Amendment violation where they obtain evidence by virtue of seeing an object that is in plain view of a government agent who has the right to be in the position to have that view. This is called the **plain view doctrine.** For example, suppose that during a routine traffic violation stop, a police officer observes an illegal handgun lying on the seat next to the driver. The officer may then arrest the driver and confiscate the weapon without a warrant because the plain view search is not prohibited by the Fourth Amendment. The plain view doctrine also allows authorities to use simple mechanical devices that are available to the general public, such as a flashlight or a camera with telephoto lenses to enhance their view. However, courts have limited the authorities' ability to obtain information from special high-tech devices that are not available to the general public. For example, in a 2001 case, the U.S. Supreme Court held that the use of a thermal imager (a device used to produce images of relative amounts of heat escaping from a structure) by authorities on a public sidewalk outside a residence was *not* covered by the plain view doctrine and constituted an illegal search.[14] The Court reasoned that because the data could not be obtained through use of the naked eye or basic equipment available to the general public, the actions constituted a search even though government authorities had not physically entered the house.

The courts have adopted a similar position regarding aerial observations made by authorities. That is, so long as the plane/helicopter is in public navigable airspace, anything the police can see with the naked eye or basic equipment such as binoculars will be considered in plain view. In *Dow Chemical Co. v. U.S.,*[15] the Supreme Court ruled that the use of an airplane by government agents to fly over one of Dow's chemical plant complexes for purposes

---

[14]*Kyllo v. U.S.,* 553 U.S. 27 (2001). The case involved the use of a device by U.S. Drug Enforcement Agency officials to obtain information on a suspected marijuana growing operation in a residence. The agents obtained a warrant based on the fact that the thermal imager revealed that the garage of the residence was emitting extraordinary levels of heat. Indeed, Kyllo had been using heat lamps to grow marijuana in the garage and he was eventually convicted at trial. The Supreme Court reversed the conviction on the basis that the thermal search evidence was obtained in violation of the Fourth Amendment. Justice Scalia wrote famously that allowing the authorities to use advanced technology would "leave the homeowner at the mercy of advancing technology— including the technology that could discern all human activity in the home."

[15]476 U.S. 227 (1986).

of taking investigative photographs with a zoom lens fit into the plain view exception and did not require a warrant because a zoom lens was readily available for purchase by the public.

Searches of Business Premises   Courts have been very reluctant to extend reasonable expectation of privacy rights to the workplace. This is particularly true when the business is highly regulated. Recall from Chapter 17, "Administrative Law," that certain businesses are classified as *pervasively regulated* and, therefore, are not entitled to full Fourth Amendment protections. Instead, the U.S. Supreme Court has fashioned an exception to the Fourth Amendment warrant requirements where the agency is conducting regularly scheduled inspections pursuant to an administrative rule. Even in cases where courts have held that administrative agencies are required to obtain an *administrative warrant* to conduct an inspection of a business, the Court has held that agencies are held to a lower standard of probable cause to obtain the warrant than if the government were obtaining a criminal warrant.

Self-Incrimination

The Fifth Amendment provides that no person "shall be compelled in any criminal case to be a witness against himself." This means that individuals have the right not to offer any information or statements that may be used against them in a criminal prosecution. If an individual believes that any statement or testimony may incriminate her in a criminal case, she may decline to testify on Fifth Amendment grounds. Note that the right of self-incrimination also protects those called as witnesses in other types of matters. For example, suppose that in the tax fraud hypothetical case above, the government prosecutes Scofield for tax evasion. During the trial, the prosecutor issues a subpoena to Montgomery, Scofield's business partner. If Montgomery has a belief that any questions asked of him as a witness in Scofield's trial may uncover evidence of his own criminal culpability, he may refuse to testify at Scofield's trial even though Montgomery is not under investigation.

The Fifth Amendment right against self-incrimination also applies while authorities are *investigating* crimes as well. Generally, the context is when government authorities are interviewing an individual in the course of a criminal investigation. Although most case law surrounding this right deals with police interrogations of a suspect, in a business context, business owners and managers should realize that agents of regulatory agencies such as the Internal Revenue Service are bound by the same guidelines as police agencies when interviewing suspects during of a criminal investigation. An important element to this protection is that it is limited to *custodial* interrogations, where the interviewee has been taken into custody or deprived of his freedom in some significant way. In this event, the authorities are required to give affirmative preinterview warnings to the suspect that he has the right not to make any statements, and that any statement that is given may eventually be used as evidence against him in a criminal trial.

For example, suppose that an FBI agent telephones Barrabas and requests a meeting in Barrabas's office. The agent explains that he is investigating a fraud scheme involving government contracts. Barrabas agrees to the meeting and during the conversation, he admits to certain incriminating facts. The admission will likely be admissible as evidence despite the failure of the agent to provide the self-incrimination warning. Because the statement was made voluntarily, in a noncoercive setting (Barrabas's office) and because Barrabas could have stopped the interview at any time, the interview may not be considered custodial and Barrabas's Fifth Amendment protections are not triggered. Alternatively, if the agent had arrested Barrabas and transported him to a local FBI field office, the agent would be required to give the warnings about self-incrimination.

The warning requirements were set out in Landmark Case 22.1, perhaps the most famous case in criminal procedure.

FACT SUMMARY   Ernesto Miranda was a suspect in the knifepoint rape of an 18-year-old girl. Two police officers took Miranda into custody and detained him at a police station. They interviewed Miranda for two hours and obtained a full confession from him. The officers never told Miranda that he had the constitutional right to an attorney, the right to remain silent, or that whatever he said could be used against him later at his trial. Only after Miranda confessed did the police have him sign a statement that said the confession was made voluntarily and with full knowledge of his legal rights. After being convicted on the strength of the confession Miranda appealed, arguing that being interviewed in police custody is inherently coercive if the suspect is unaware of his rights. Thus, his confession was not, in fact, voluntary.

SYNOPSIS OF DECISION AND OPINION   The U.S. Supreme Court ruled in favor of Miranda. In a decision that sent shockwaves through the law enforcement community, the Court held that Miranda's confession was inherently involuntary and, thus, could not be used at his trial. They ordered a retrial. Even though the police did not physically force Miranda to confess, anything he said while trapped in a police interrogation room and not knowing that he could have a lawyer or just stay quiet, was inherently involuntary and violated the Fifth Amendment. The Court reasoned that because police always have inherent power in any custodial interrogation of a suspect that, unless the suspect is informed of his rights beforehand, any confession would be presumed involuntary and coerced and not admissible in court.

WORDS OF THE COURT: Coercive Environment
"It is obvious that such an interrogation environment is created for no purpose other than to subjugate the individual to the will of his examiner. This atmosphere carries its own badge of intimidation. To be sure, this is not physical intimidation, but it is equally destructive of human dignity. . . . Today, then, there can be no doubt that the Fifth Amendment privilege is available outside of criminal court proceedings and serves to protect persons in all settings in which their freedom of action is curtailed in any significant way from being compelled to incriminate themselves. We have concluded that without proper safeguards the process of in-custody interrogation of persons suspected or accused of crime contains inherently compelling pressures which work to undermine the individual's will to resist and to compel him to speak where he would not otherwise do so freely. In order to combat these pressures and to permit a full opportunity to exercise the privilege against self-incrimination, the accused must be adequately and effectively apprised of his rights and the exercise of those rights must be fully honored."*

Case Questions

1. Do the Miranda warnings really matter? If you ask for a lawyer or will not talk, doesn't that mean you have something to hide? What would you do if you were a suspect?

2. What if the suspect is not in the police station, but is he still in "custody" in a police car? Pulled over for speeding? Sitting in your office with the police in front of you? When do the police stop talking to you and start "interrogating" such that they need to give the Miranda warnings?

---

* What happened to Ernesto Miranda? On retrial he was found guilty based on other evidence. He spent over a decade behind bars. When he was paroled, he earned income selling police "Miranda cards" that he had autographed. In 1976, he was killed in a bar fight. See George C. Thomas, "Missing Miranda's Story," 2 *Ohio St. J. Crim. L.* 677, 683-4 (2005).

Production of Business Records

Business records such as letters, memoranda, e-mail exchanges, inventory, financial documents, and the like are often at the very crux of cases where government authorities are investigating potential criminal activity in the business environment. Although the U.S. Supreme Court has held that certain business records may be classified as private papers and are protected by the Fifth Amendment, this protection has been severely narrowed over the last several decades. In 1984, the Court ruled that certain business records of a sole proprietor could be considered private papers because a sole proprietor is a form of business

FACT SUMMARY   Braswell was the sole shareholder and officer in two companies engaged in brokering (buying and selling) timber, land, oil interests, and machinery. The only other directors in the companies were his wife and his mother. Federal authorities that were investigating Braswell's business subpoenaed his business records. Braswell refused to hand over the documents, claiming that he was asserting his Fifth Amendment right against self-incrimination. Braswell argued that when a business is so small that it is nothing more than a person's "alter ego," the Fifth Amendment safeguards should apply.

SYNOPSIS OF DECISION AND OPINION   The U.S. Supreme Court ruled against Braswell and compelled him to hand over the books and records. The Court held that a corporation can act only through its officers/employees and when an officer/employee acts as a records custodian for that company, then he is not entitled to Fifth Amendment protection because he is no longer acting as a private individual but as part of a corporation. The Fifth Amendment only protects private individuals.

WORDS OF THE COURT: Corporate Records   "Artificial entities such as corporations may act only through their agents, and a custodian's assumption of his representative capacity leads to certain obligations, including the duty to produce corporate records on proper demand by the Government. Under those circumstances, the custodian's act of production is not deemed a personal act, but rather an act of the corporation. Any claim of Fifth Amendment privilege asserted by the agent would be tantamount to a claim of privilege by the corporation—which of course possesses no such privilege."

Case Questions

1. If a corporation has been recognized as a legal "person" for First Amendment purposes, shouldn't the Fifth Amendment protect it too?

2. What if Braswell's company was a sole proprietorship rather than a corporation? What if he ran it alone out of his apartment? When should the Fifth Amendment start or stop protecting him?

---

entity that is essentially the alter ego of the individual.[16] The Court reasoned that because there was no legal separation between the business and the sole owner (unlike a corporation, which exists as a separate legal "person"), his records were considered personal and subject to Fifth Amendment protections. However, the Court has also made clear that records of a *corporation* are not subject to Fifth Amendment safeguards because that business entity is separate and distinct from its owners and does not qualify for self-incrimination protections.

In Case 22.2, the U.S. Supreme Court considers where to draw the line between personal and business records.

Trial

The Sixth Amendment provides that in all criminal prosecutions the accused shall enjoy the right to a *speedy trial.* Although the U.S. Supreme Court has not set out specific time periods when a trial must take place, they have given guideposts for state courts in applying the speedy trial guarantee. Courts apply a balancing test in which both the prosecutor's and the defendant's conduct are examined to determine reasons for delay. Ordinarily, a court weighs the length of the delay versus the severity of the crime. A general rule is that a delay of eight months or more is presumptively unconstitutional. The federal criminal justice system operates according to an infrastructure established by the **Speedy Trial Act,**[17] which sets out specific time periods in which an accused must be brought to trial. If the time limits are exceeded, the courts must dismiss the charges.

---

[16]*U.S. v. Doe,* 465 U.S. 605 (1984).
[17]18 U.S.C. 3161.

The Sixth Amendment also contains other important procedural rights such as a right to a jury trial for serious crimes (generally any offense that carries more than six months incarceration as a penalty), the right to a public trial, and the right to confront witnesses through cross-examination.[18]

Double Jeopardy   Although the role of the Fifth Amendment is usually thought of in the context of self-incrimination, it also protects a defendant from being subject to prosecution twice for the same offense. This guarantee is known as a prohibition of **double jeopardy.** In essence, the doctrine prevents prosecutors from retrying a defendant on the same charges after a jury has acquitted her.

LO22-8 Exclusionary Rule

Trial courts are required to exclude presentation of any evidence that is obtained as a result of a constitutional violation. This is known as the *exclusionary rule.* For example, if a law enforcement officer wrongfully searches a suspect's house without first obtaining a search warrant, any evidence obtained in that search may not be used against the suspect if he is arrested and brought to trial. One important exception in the business environment is that the exclusionary rule only applies to violations of the Constitution and not when a government agency has violated its own *internal procedures.* For example, suppose that a government agent secretly records a conversation with a suspected tax evader during a meeting in the agent's office. The suspect offers the agent a bribe. However, the agent violated internal agency rules because he had failed to obtain a supervisor's permission to record any conversations with taxpayers. When the suspect is tried, he asserts that the recording cannot be introduced at trial because it is barred by the exclusionary rule. The U.S. Supreme Court has *rejected* such an argument and held that the exclusionary rule only bars evidence obtained in violation of a constitutional provision. In this case, an agency rule was violated, but no constitutional violations took place and, thus, the exclusionary rule does not apply.[19]

Even evidence that is only indirectly obtained in violation of a defendant's rights is subject to the exclusionary rule because it is considered the *fruit of the poisonous tree.* This means that once original evidence is shown to have been unlawfully obtained, all evidence that stems from the original evidence (called *derivative evidence*) is also excluded. For example, suppose an agent of the Securities and Exchange Commission is investigating Falstaff for criminal fraud. The agent illegally searches the handbag of Falstaff's secretary and discovers evidence that Falstaff is concealing incriminating documents in his garage at home. Using the illegally obtained evidence, the agent then obtains a search warrant for Falstaff's home and discovers the incriminating documents. Because the agent's original evidence (obtained from Falstaff's secretary) was obtained in violation of the secretary's constitutional rights, a court would likely hold that the fruit of the poisonous

The exclusionary rule prohibits the use of evidence during a criminal trial that was obtained in violation of a defendant's constitutional rights.

---

[18]Cross-examination and other trial terminology are discussed in detail in Chapter 3, "The American Judicial System, Jurisdiction, and Venue."

[19]Based on *U.S. v. Caceres,* 440 U.S. 741 (1979).

FACT SUMMARY Police received information that Yenzer, a fugitive, would be at a local dentist the next day. The police arrived at the dentist's office in hopes of capturing Yenzer, but she was not there. The receptionist informed them that Yenzer's appointment had been rescheduled for the next week and when the police requested the exact date and time, the receptionist complied. The police arrived at the rescheduled appointment time and arrested Yenzer at her dentist's office. Subsequent to her arrest, the police discovered evidence of additional crimes committed by Yenzer and charged her with various felonies. The Health Insurance Portability and Accountability Act of 1996 (HIPAA) is a federal statute that prohibits dental offices from disclosing any information (including appointment times) about patients to third parties without the patient's permission. At trial, Yenzer argued that all evidence discovered after the dentist office arrest should be excluded because the arrest was made as a result of a HIPAA violation.

SYNOPSIS OF DECISION AND OPINION The Kansas state appellate court ruled against Yenzer reasoning that while a constitutional violation triggers the exclusionary rule, a violation of a federal statutory prohibition on disclosure of medical information did not.

WORDS OF THE COURT: Scope of Exclusionary Rule "[. . .], [I]n this case Yenzer has not made a constitutional claim warranting suppression. Nor has she presented any authority to support her assertion that suppression is a proper remedy for a HIPAA violation. While we do not condone the disclosure of information that occurred here, we must conclude that even if Yenzer could show a HIPAA violation, the district court did not err in denying Yenzer's motion to suppress."

Case Questions

1. Why isn't the time of the dentist's appointment protected by the Fourth Amendment in this case?

2. Did the police go too far in this case by requesting confidential information from the dentist's receptionist? Isn't the exclusionary rule intended to deter unlawful conduct by authorities?

---

tree doctrine rendered the warrant invalid and barred use of all evidence derived from the warrant (the incriminating documents) in a criminal trial against Falstaff.[20]

The exclusionary rule itself is controversial because it tends to benefit the guilty by excluding key evidence that would help convict them. Many legal commentators have filled volumes of journals and treatises on the topic, but ultimately the exclusionary rule is justified by its proponents on the basis that it acts as a deterrent to violations of the Constitution by government authorities and the integrity of the judiciary requires that courts not be made a party to lawless invasions of constitutional rights of citizens by permitting unhindered government use of unlawfully obtained evidence. Nonetheless, the Supreme Court has fashioned several exceptions to the exclusionary rule intended to differentiate between abuse by the authorities of an individual's constitutional rights and those cases where the government has made an innocent mistake in obtaining evidence. Perhaps the most important exception to the rule is when the government can show that authorities were acting in *good faith* in obtaining evidence based on a search warrant issued by an authorized judge that was later found to be unsupported by an appropriate level of probable cause. In that case, even though the evidence is derived from a warrant that was granted but that was later found to have been a constitutional violation, the prosecutor may still introduce the evidence yielded from the search so long as the authorities were acting in good faith and reasonable reliance on the search warrant.

The exclusionary rule does have its limits, however. In Case 22.3, a state appellate court considered the limits of the exclusionary rule when a federal statute that guarantees privacy in health care records is violated and leads to a criminal charge.

---

[20]See *Silverthorne Lumber Company v. U.S.*, 251 U.S. 385 (1920).

Computer Crimes and Internet Regulation

There are three major classes of criminal activity through use of a computer: (1) unauthorized use of a computer, which might involve stealing a username and password, or might involve accessing the victim's computer via the Internet through a backdoor created by a Trojan horse* program; (2) creating or releasing a malicious computer program (e.g., computer virus, worm, Trojan horse); and (3) harassment and stalking in cyberspace.

Congress responded to the continued growth of computer crime with the **Computer Fraud and Abuse Act,**† which was most recently amended in 2001 by the Patriot Act. In essence, the law prohibits unauthorized use of computers to commit seven different crimes: (1) espionage; (2) accessing unauthorized information; (3) accessing a nonpublic government computer; (4) fraud by computer; (5) damage to a computer; (6) trafficking in passwords; and (7) extortionate threats to damage a computer.

Obscenity in Cyberspace: The Communications Decency Act

The Internet has an element of entrepreneurial spirit associated with it, and many new companies and new business models were created to take advantage of the rapid growth of consumers in cyberspace. At the same time, it is clear that a significant number of business models benefiting from the boom are those associated with distribution of pornography. In the midst of some high-profile media stories involving the ease of access to online pornography by minors, Congress attempted to curb online content with the Communications Decency Act (CDA) in 1996. The CDA was intended to ban material that was "patently offensive" or "indecent" from being online if the content providers knew that children would have access to the material.

Challenges to the CDA

Shortly after the CDA was enacted, the American Civil Liberties Union (ACLU) filed a lawsuit challenging the act as an unconstitutional infringement on free speech.

The case, *ACLU v. Reno* (called *Reno I*), was decided by the Supreme Court in 1997. It was the first time that the U.S. Supreme Court had to apply existing obscenity standards in cyberspace. One important element of the case was the Court's recognition of cyberspace as a unique medium that cannot be equated to broadcast media (such as radio or television) or any printed media (such as magazines or newspapers). This distinction was a key part of the Court's analysis that government was not entitled to as much deference in regulation of the Internet as the government is entitled to with other media. That said, the Court went on to strike down much of the act's substance, reasoning that the CDA's prohibition against "patently offensive" material being distributed on the Web is too vague to pass constitutional muster.

Congressional Response to *Reno I*: Child Online Protection Act of 1998

Although the Court struck down much of the CDA, the opinion did set out, for the first time, the Court's view on the government's regulation of the Internet. The Court ruled that although the government had the right to regulate Internet traffic, the means employed by Congress was too broad of a sweep. Using *Reno I* as a roadmap on constitutionality, Congress passed a similar piece of legislation the next year with the Child Online Protection Act of 1998 (COPA).

The ACLU again filed a lawsuit challenging the COPA as unconstitutional. The new case, *ACLU v. Reno* (*Reno II*), was decided by the U.S. Court of Appeals for the Third Circuit in 2000. The court of appeals ruled in favor of the ACLU and struck the statute down as still too overly broad. In 2003, the Supreme Court upheld the court of appeals decision and adopted much of the court of appeals reasoning.

---

*A Trojan horse is a virus that appears to perform one function, yet it actually performs another, such as the unauthorized collection, exploitation, falsification, or destruction of data.

†18 U.S.C. § 1030.

CONCEPT SUMMARY   Criminal Procedure

- The Fourth Amendment requires the authorities to obtain a warrant before searching areas where a citizen has a reasonable expectation of privacy.
- The Fifth Amendment protects an individual from involuntary self-incrimination before, during, and after an investigation and trial, but does not protect a person from disclosing business records made in their capacity as corporate agent. The Fifth Amendment does not protect corporations.
- Anything said during custodial interrogation is presumed to be involuntary unless and until one has been read Miranda warnings.
- The exclusionary rule bans evidence obtained in violation of the Constitution from being used at trial.

KEY TERMS

Criminal law p. 549   Body of law that defines the boundaries of behavior and sanctions for violating those boundaries for the purpose of preventing harm to society.

Model Penal Code (MPC) p. 550   A statutory text adopted by the American Law Institute in 1962 in an effort to bring greater uniformity to the state laws by proffering certain legal standards and reforms.

Criminal procedure p. 550   Refers to Constitutional protections afforded to individuals or business entities during criminal investigations, arrests, trials, and sentencing.

Burden of proof p. 551   The responsibility of producing sufficient evidence necessary in support of a fact or issue and favorably convincing the fact finder of that fact or issue.

Preponderance of the evidence p. 551   Burden of proof used in civil cases in which the fact finder need only be convinced that the defendant's liability was more likely than not.

Beyond a reasonable doubt p. 551   Heightened burden of proof used in criminal cases in which a fact finder must be convinced that the defendant's criminal liability is not in doubt to a reasonable person.

Legality p. 551   A principle of criminal law that protects individuals from being charged with some unspecified general offense by requiring that crimes be specifically proscribed by law in advance of the conduct sought to be punished.

Punishment p. 551   A principle of criminal law imposing a hardship in response to misconduct based on the concepts that criminal law acts as a deterrent, removes dangerous criminals from the population, and that rehabilitation is an important part of the criminal justice system.

Sentencing guidelines p. 551   Statutorily prescribed standards for determining the punishment that a convicted criminal should receive based on the nature of the crime and the offender's criminal history.

Act requirement p. 552   Also called by its Latin name, *actus reus,* requires the government to prove that a defendant's actions objectively satisfied the elements of a particular offense.

Self-defense p. 553   A defense to avoid criminal liability whereby the law recognizes that certain cases require the use of deadly force to repel an attack in which the defendant reasonably feared that death or substantial harm was about to occur either to the defendant or to a third party.

Mental incapacity p. 553   A defense to avoid criminal liability whereby the defendant's actions are related to some type of mental disease or defect.

Felonies p. 553 Classification of crimes that generally carry one year or more of incarceration as the penalty.

Misdemeanors p. 553 Classification of crimes that carry up to one year of incarceration as the penalty.

Mail Fraud Act p. 556 Enacted by Congress in 1990 as a comprehensive approach to criminalizing any fraud where the defrauding party uses the mail or any wire, radio, or television in perpetrating fraud.

Insider trading laws p. 561 Federal securities statutes that prohibit corporate insiders who have access to certain information that is not available to the general investment public from trading their company's stock based on the insider knowledge.

Foreign Corrupt Practices Act (FCPA) p. 562 A criminal statute enacted principally to prevent corporate bribery of foreign officials in business transactions.

Investigation p. 563 The initial phase of the criminal justice system in which authorities become aware of an alleged criminal act and begin gathering physical evidence and interviewing witnesses and potential suspects.

Adjudication p. 563 A phase of the criminal justice system in which the prosecutor elects to proceed with the charges following an investigation.

Probable cause p. 563 A reasonable amount of suspicion supported by circumstances sufficiently strong to justify a belief that a person has committed a crime.

Preliminary adjudication p. 563 A hearing where the prosecutor presents evidence of the defendant's guilt and the decision maker (either the grand jurors or a magistrate) determines whether sufficient probable cause exists to hold the defendant over for trial.

Plain view doctrine p. 566 A doctrine stating that authorities generally do not commit a Fourth Amendment violation where they obtain evidence by virtue of seeing an object that is in plain view of a government agent.

Speedy Trial Act p. 569 A federal statute that sets out specific time periods in which an accused must be brought to trial.

Double jeopardy p. 570 The Fifth Amendment guarantee providing that a defendant cannot be subject to prosecution twice for the same offense.

Computer Fraud and Abuse Act p. 572 A law prohibiting unauthorized use of computers to commit seven different crimes: (1) espionage; (2) accessing unauthorized information; (3) accessing a nonpublic government computer; (4) fraud by computer; (5) damage to a computer; (6) trafficking in passwords; and (7) extortionate threats to damage a computer.

THEORY TO PRACTICE

Dania Beach Antique Supply Inc. (DBAS) is a wholesaler of antique merchandise. DBAS employs expert buyers that purchase antiques in Europe, then makes any cosmetic improvements necessary (such as cleaning), and resells the merchandise to retail antique shops in the United States. Grendel is a senior-level executive at the company in charge of its primary warehouse, located in Ft. Lauderdale, and a smaller facility at the Port of Miami. One of Grendel's responsibilities is to oversee worker safety in the facilities as the processing of the antiques sometimes involves use of industrial machinery and cleaning solvents.

It was well known among DBAS employees that the Ft. Lauderdale warehouse had less than ideal working conditions. The air-conditioning was often broken, and during the summer months the indoor temperature was in excess of 100 degrees. The cleaning solvents were left unattended, and the noxious fumes made working hazardous. When workers complained to Grendel, he purchased small fans to be placed in the facility but declined to overhaul the air-conditioning, claiming that the expense was too high and that the company was struggling financially. Grendel also ordered that the cleaning solvents be properly disposed of, but the on-site manager never carried out the order. In the meantime, several employees were hospitalized for heat exhaustion during their shift and several others were made sick by the fumes from the cleaning solvents.

1. Assume that one worker notifies the Occupational Safety and Health Administration (OSHA) and that an OSHA agent informs Grendel that an investigation will be undertaken into the allegations of workplace hazards. Grendel immediately hires an air-conditioning repair company to fix the air-conditioning system. He also tells the on-site manager to destroy any maintenance records of the warehouse air-conditioning

system history of inspections and repairs. What potential criminal culpability would DBAS, Grendel, and the on-site manager have at this point? Do Grendel's preinvestigation actions constitute a criminal act? Do Grendel's actions after OSHA's notification of an investigation constitute a crime in and of themselves? Is the on-site manager criminally liable for carrying out Grendel's orders?

2. Suppose that Grendel is charged with a crime related to the workplace hazards and he defends by showing evidence that he ordered subordinates to take care of the hazards, but his directions were never carried out. Is that a valid defense? If Grendel had second thoughts about his orders to destroy maintenance records and he calls the manager to reverse his previous directions, does he still have criminal liability for attempting the cover-up?

3. Assume that during the investigation, OSHA agents make a midnight visit to Grendel's residence and remove documents from Grendel's trash bin on the public curb in front of his house. The documents contain incriminating evidence. Was the OSHA search illegal? Does the exclusionary rule apply in this case?

4. If, during the criminal investigation of Grendel, OSHA issues a subpoena for Grendel's personal diary because they have information that Grendel wrote about having a guilty conscience about the working conditions in the warehouse, is Grendel's diary protected from inspection via the Fifth Amendment?

5. If OSHA investigators use cameras with telephoto lenses (that are available to the general public) to take pictures of the broken air-conditioning unit adjacent to the warehouse from the public sidewalk, does that require OSHA to obtain a search warrant?

MANAGER'S CHALLENGE

A common element in cases where corporate executives are found guilty of criminal charges related to corporate activity is a lack of a systematic compliance procedure in the company's infrastructure. Senior managers have the responsibility to have systematic, internal controls in place that will help assure compliance with federal and state statutes. Assume that you are a DBAS employee and that both Grendel and the on-site warehouse manager are fired. You receive the following e-mail from the new vice president of operations.

> Congratulations! You are being promoted to on-site manager at the Ft. Lauderdale warehouse. The

primary order of business is to develop a system of checks to be sure we are doing everything we can to avoid hazardous work conditions for our employees. Draft a two- to three-page memorandum that sets out a specific system for compliance. The system should address: (1) how complaints from workers will be handled; (2) procedures for inspecting the facility, reporting problems, and ensuring follow-up; (3) a clear chain of command; and (4) a response plan to handle hazards that require immediate response.

A sample answer may be found on this textbook's Web site at www.mhhe.com/melvin.

CASE SUMMARY 22.1 :: Bear Sterns & Co. v. Wyler, 182 F. Supp. 2d 679 (N.D. Ill. 2002)

PRODUCTION OF BUSINESS RECORDS

Bear Sterns had done business with Wyler, a Dutch businessman. A venture capitalist and resident of the Netherlands, Wyler kept offices in Toronto and Barbados. After the relationship soured, Bear Sterns sued Wyler for inducing one of their managing directors to make false statements and breach his fiduciary duties. In discovery, Bear Sterns requested that Wyler disclose any business records that related to that fraudulent

inducement. Wyler invoked his Fifth Amendment right against self-incrimination.

CASE QUESTIONS

1. Will the court force Wyler to disclose the documents? Are they business records?

2. Does the Fifth Amendment apply in civil suits?

CRIMINAL LAW AND BUSINESS ENTITIES

A harbor patrolman was hit by a bucket of garbage "consisting of cabbage, orange peel, celery, tea leaves, and water" thrown from a steamer named the *President Coolidge* in Honolulu harbor. Unable to find the actual sailor who had dumped the trash, the government charged the ship owner under a federal law making off-loading garbage into navigable waters illegal. The ship's owner, however, had taken measures to prevent such dumping such as issuing orders to the crew about its prohibition, hanging several warning signs in obvious places in both English and Chinese, and locking the "slop chutes" to prevent their use while in the harbor.

CASE QUESTIONS

1. Will the steamship company be criminally liable? Should they be even though they did everything to prevent the crime?
2. If they should not be liable, what is the best way to prevent this crime?

INSIDER TRADING

A wealthy businesswoman bought several thousand shares of a pharmaceutical company that was set to come out with a groundbreaking new cancer drug. She was a social friend of the company's CEO. On her way to vacation in Mexico, she received information from her broker that the CEO was selling all his shares. She eventually found out that the Food and Drug Administration was set to reject the cancer drug. She then sold all her shares and saved her own portfolio from devastation.

CASE QUESTIONS

1. Is the woman guilty of insider trading? Why?
2. Would you do what she did or just wait around to lose all your money?
3. Should the CEO get to sell his shares?

FOREIGN CORRUPT PRACTICES ACT

Phillip Morris buys tobacco for its cigarettes from all around the world, including South American growers in Venezuela. Phillip Morris entered a contract with La Fundacion Del Nino (the Children's Foundation) of Caracas, Venezuela, wherein the cigarette company would give the charity that helped poor Venezuelan children $12.5 million. In exchange, the Venezuelan government would put price controls on the country's tobacco crop.

CASE QUESTIONS

1. What criminal law did Phillip Morris possibly violate? Why?
2. Should the criminal law have a problem with money going to poor Venezuelan children and work for poor Venezuelan farmers?
3. Why would the Kentucky growers be upset if Phillip Morris kept buying the same amount of tobacco from them?

 Self-Check ANSWERS

White-Collar Crime

1. FCPA. Buying a lavish meal for foreign government officials is prohibited.
2. Fraud (Ponzi scheme).
3. Conspiracy.
4. RICO.

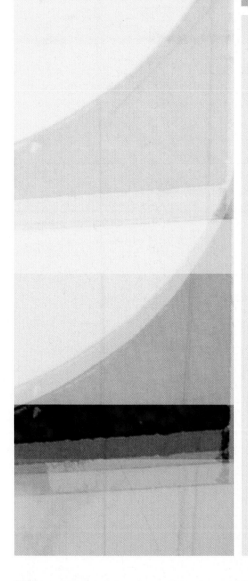

23
CHAPTER

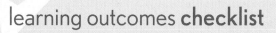

Personal Property, Real Property, and Land Use Law

learning outcomes checklist

After studying this chapter, students who have mastered the material will be able to:

23 - 1   Distinguish between tangible property and intellectual property.

23 - 2   Define and give examples of personal property used in business.

23 - 3   Explain the concepts of title, bundle of rights, and ownership by possession.

23 - 4   Identify the individual rights that landowners have in real property.

23 - 5   List and give examples of the three major forms of real estate ownership interests most commonly held by businesses and individuals.

23 - 6   Articulate and give examples of the duties, rights, and remedies of landlords and tenants in an agreement to lease real property.

23 - 7   Identify the differences between legal protections for tenants in commercial leases versus residential leases.

23 - 8   Distinguish between a sublease and an assignment and explain how each can be used in business planning objectives.

23 - 9   Give examples of two types of laws that regulate the use of real property by its owners.

23-10   Explain the government's rights and limits when exercising eminent domain.

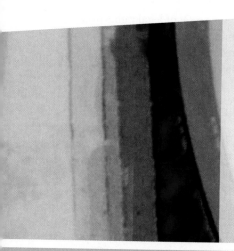

aws governing the ownership and use of property have deep historical roots and are an integral part of the American legal system. Business owners and managers regularly encounter property law issues in business planning and operations. Examples include deciding whether to own or lease certain property, rights of the property owners, landlord-tenant laws, and government restrictions on how property is used. Specifically, students will learn:

- Categories of various types of property that are important to conducting business operations.
- Various levels of property ownership rights, responsibilities, and restrictions.
- Specific laws governing legal relationships between landlords and tenants.
- Methods used by the government to regulate the use of certain property.

LO 23-1, 23-2 — DEFINITION AND CATEGORIES OF PROPERTY

The term property in a legal sense is defined broadly as having a set of legal rights over others to use the property exclusively. While the casual meaning of the word property is often used in connection with real estate, the law of property recognizes two distinct categories: tangible property (such as real estate or goods) and intellectual property (such as patents). Laws covering tangible property are discussed in this chapter, while intellectual property laws, also very important to business owners and managers, is covered in the next chapter.

TANGIBLE PROPERTY

Tangible property, of course, is property that can be touched and physically possessed. The two forms of tangible property are **personal property** and **real property.**

Personal Property

Personal property is both tangible and *moveable*. In a business context, goods, vehicles, inventory, and equipment for business operations such as computers are all examples of personal property. Personal property may be *owned* or *leased*. Leasing, which is governed by state statutory law modeled after the Uniform Commercial Code,[1] is discussed later in this section. Personal property rights of ownership, possession, and transfer are the subject of a blend of state statutes and common law principles.

LO 23-3 — Personal Property: Rights of Ownership and Ownership by Possession

The legal term for ownership rights in property is **title.** Normally, title is obtained by a grant of title by the current owner to a new owner, usually through a purchase or gift. Title is thought of as a *bundle of rights* related to the personal property. That is, the titleholder is permitted exclusive use and rights to sell, lease, or prohibit another from using the personal property.

There are some instances, however, when the law allows a party to take title solely on the basis of *possession.*

> **KEY POINT**
> Property ownership is fundamentally a bundle of rights whereby the titleholder has exclusive control, possession, and use of the property.

Found Articles The finder of lost property obtains title to the good by possession, except against the **actual owner.** Suppose that Commuter finds a gold wristwatch on a public sidewalk while walking to a commuter train station. She takes the watch to Station Manager who, after asking each passenger in the area if they are the owner of the watch, is unable to find the true owner. Station Manager then keeps the watch from Commuter on the basis that Commuter is not the original owner. Assuming the true owner is not found, a court would likely find that Commuter has title over Station Manager and everyone else except for the original owner.[2]

Adverse Possession Each state has a statute that applies to personal property held by a possessor who is not the true owner for an extended period of time. Once the statutory period has passed, the possessor of the goods is protected from any suit to recover

---

[1]Recall from Chapter 1 that the UCC is a "model" statute drafted by a group called the National Conference of Commissioners of Uniform State Laws (NCCUSL). Each state legislature makes its own decisions about whether to adopt the UCC in total, partially, or not at all (Louisiana is the only state to have rejected the UCC in its entirety).

[2]Based on the landmark English common law case *Armory v. Delamirie,* 1 Strange 505 (K.B. 1722).

the property except by its true owner. The rule of adverse possession is also applied in a real property context, and is explained in further detail later in this chapter.

Good Faith Purchasers   In some cases, a buyer will purchase a good or other personal property from someone who has physical possession of the property, but does not have title to the property (e.g., stolen goods). Under these circumstances, the buyer, even if the buyer had no reason to know the goods were stolen, does *not* acquire valid title. This situation is governed by the property law maxim that a seller cannot convey valid title unless she has valid title in the first place. Therefore, if the goods are stolen, the actual owner may recover the property even from a good faith buyer.

Bailments   In a bailment relationship, although a possessor does not gain title via possession, the nonowner is still a rightful possessor of the goods. A bailment relationship is created when the *bailor* (owner of the property) entrusts a *bailee* to temporarily hold the property, usually for the parties' mutual benefit. If the parties intend to create a bailment relationship, the bailee owes a duty of *care* and a duty to act reasonably in protecting the property. For example, suppose that Franz brings his gold pocket watch to Max, a jeweler, for repair. Leaving the watch with Max created a bailment relationship. That is, Franz entrusted Max with his watch for their mutual benefit (Franz gets his watch fixed; Max earns income). Assume that Max has to leave the store in a rush that night and accidentally leaves the door open. The store is burglarized and Franz's watch is stolen. Max would be liable for the cost of the watch due to his breach of the duty of care as bailee. On the other hand, suppose Max locked up the watch in a vault before he left, but a burglar with special skills broke into the vault and took the watch. In that case, most courts would find that Max had exercised due care and reasonableness and, therefore, is not liable for the theft.[3] Other common examples of a bailment relationship are coat check services, dry cleaning, or valet parking.[4]

CONCEPT SUMMARY   Personal Property

- Personal property is both tangible and moveable and can be owned or leased. Examples of personal property include inventory and business systems such as telephones or computers.

- Title is the legal form of ownership of property and provides the titleholder exclusive rights to sell, lease, or prohibit others from using the property.

- Finders of lost property obtain title to the good by possession, except against the actual owner.

- Sellers cannot convey better title than what they have; therefore, if a buyer purchases stolen goods the actual owner may still recover the property. It is irrelevant that the buyer who purchased the goods did so in good faith and did not know they were stolen.

- Bailments are created when the bailor (owner of the property) entrusts a bailee to temporarily hold the property. Common examples of bailments are coat checks and repair shops.

---

[3]Based on examples in Ray A. Brown, *The Law of Personal Property*, 3rd ed. (Chicago: Callaghan and Company, 1975).

[4]Note that courts distinguish between a "self-check" parking lot (no bailment) and a valet parking lot, where an agent of the lot actually takes physical possession of the car via keys, etc. (bailment).

A bailment relationship is created when the owner of the property (bailor) temporarily entrusts it to another party (bailee) usually for their mutual benefit such as when a customer gives shirts to a dry cleaner.

Leased Personal Property: UCC Article 2A

Businesses often choose to *lease* personal property, especially equipment, rather than purchase it outright. An *equipment lease* is when the lessor (owner of the property) allows the lessee (the party leasing the property) the exclusive right to possess and use the equipment for a fixed period of time. The lessee often makes a monthly payment to the lessor, but at the end of the lease term the equipment is returned to the lessor. As a business matter, leasing is often an attractive alternative because the business can still use the equipment on an exclusive basis without the investment required to purchase the equipment. There may also be tax advantages for the lessee in some cases. Examples of equipment that a business may lease are information systems equipment, telephones, furniture, and even heavy machinery used for manufacturing or construction. Note that leases fall into an area governed by both principles of property law and certain principles of commercial law. Lease agreements are a form of personal property contract and are governed by state statutory laws that are modeled after Article 2A of the Uniform Commercial Code. Article 2A covers many of the same subjects as the article governing the sale of goods, such as defining what constitutes a lease agreement, requirements for certain lease agreements to be in writing, and allocating the risk of loss (i.e., which party is responsible if the equipment is destroyed) to one party or other based on the circumstances of the transaction.

Real Property: Source of Law

The source of law that governs real property ownership is primarily state statutes, although some common law principles still exist. The statutes that regulate the legal relationship between residential landlord and tenant are based primarily on a model act known as the Uniform Residential Landlord-Tenant Act (URLTA). Note that when a landlord leases real property to a business, this is known as a *commercial* landlord-tenant agreement and is not governed by the URLTA. The landlord-tenant relationship is explored more fully later in this chapter.

Ownership Rights

LO23-4

The ownership right to a parcel (piece) of *real property,* also called *real estate,* includes land, any structures built upon it, as well as plant life and vegetation. The structures are known as the property's *improvements.* The ownership rights also extend to anything that is affixed, known as *fixtures,* to the structure such as plumbing or heating/cooling systems and the like. Similar to the ownership rights in personal property, the owner of a parcel of real property is also said to have a *bundle of rights* associated with ownership. This includes the right to sell, gift, lease, and control the property and its improvements. Ownership of real property is typically evidenced by a *deed.* Traditional property ownership rights are said to extend from "the soil upward into Heaven."[5] Generally, this means that certain rights are attached to the land that fit into four categories: (1) rights related to the *use and enjoyment* of the land; (2) *subsurface* rights; (3) *water* rights; and (4) *airspace* rights.

Use and Enjoyment of the Land   Generally, landowners have the right to use and enjoy the use of their property without interference from others. This interference is known as *nuisance* and occurs when one party creates *unreasonable conditions* that affect the landowner's use or enjoyment of the property. Many nuisance cases take the form of a residential or business property owner that sues a manufacturing company that owns a nearby plant for producing pollutants, making excessive noise, or emitting foul odors. Most courts apply the unreasonableness factor by examining the *nature* of the parcels of property at issue. In an area that is zoned for heavy industrial use, courts are reluctant to impose liability on a plant owner under the nuisance theory. Areas that are zoned for retail, office space, or residential are more likely to have legal protection from such nuisances.

Subsurface Rights   Landowners have rights to the soil, and most importantly to any mineral, oil, or natural gas among the soil. These subsurface rights may also be severed from the bundle of the rights owned by the landowner and sold to a third party.

Water Rights   Also known as *riparian* rights, landowners have the right to reasonable use of any streams, lakes, and groundwater (water contained in soil) that are fully or partially part of their real property. Reasonable use means that the landowner is entitled to only so much of the water as he can put to beneficial use upon her land while balancing the rights of others who have riparian rights in the same stream or lake (such as an adjacent landowner).

Airspace Rights   The law contemplates ownership of airspace by drawing an imaginary line emanating from the borders of the property into the sky. Perhaps the most significant exception to this rule is that courts have held that landowners may not use this right to prevent airplane flights over their property.[6] Most airspace rights cases involving businesses have taken the form of when one property owner builds a building that somehow interferes with the air rights of another. Consider the dilemma of a resort hotel when faced with a next-door neighbor that builds a building so tall that it blocks the sun from the resort's pool. In Case 23.1, the Florida supreme court considered the novel question of whether a famous Miami Beach resort's airspace rights included solar rights as well.

Real Property: Forms of Ownership Interests

LO23-5

In most cases, real estate owners are entitled to the same general bundle of rights that were discussed in the section on personal property. However, some forms of ownership limit those general rights and, therefore, it is also necessary to understand the various *forms of ownership.* These are known as **ownership interests.** There are seven legally recognized interests;

---

[5]From English common law cases that cite the Latin phrase *"cujus est solum, ejus usque ad coelum."*
[6]*U.S. v. Causby,* 328 U.S. 256 (1946).

FACT SUMMARY The Fontainebleau Hotel ("Fontainebleau") was in the process of constructing a 14-story addition to their resort hotel. After completion of eight stories, one of Fontainebleau's competitors, the Eden Roc Hotel ("Eden Roc"), which owns adjoining property to the Fontainebleau, filed suit asking a court to issue an order prohibiting further construction of the addition. Eden Roc alleged that in the winter months, beginning at two o'clock in the afternoon and continuing until sunset, the shadow caused by the new addition would extend over the Eden Roc's resort cabanas, a main swimming pool, and several designated sunbathing areas. They argued that this interference with sunlight and air violated the Eden Roc's air rights and was causing the Eden Roc to lose profits because the resort was now less desirable for guests wishing to use the pool facilities. Eden Roc also alleged the construction plan was based on ill will between the owners of the resorts.

SYNOPSIS OF DECISION AND OPINION The Florida Supreme Court ruled in favor of the Fontainebleau on the basis of the general property law rule that property owners may use their property in any reasonable and lawful manner. The court noted that landowners are not obliged to use their property in a way that would prevent injury to a neighbor. The court also pointed out that modern American courts have consistently rejected the historical English law doctrine of "ancient lights," which provides a right to the free flow of light and air from adjoining land, as unworkable in current commercial life. Therefore, the court held that there is no legal right to the flow of air or light, and that there is no cause of action so long as the structure serves a legitimately useful purpose.

WORDS OF THE COURT: Air and Solar Rights "[T]here [. . .] [is] no legal right to the free flow of light and air from the adjoining land, it is universally held that where a structure serves a useful and beneficial purpose, it does not give rise to a cause of action [. . .], even though it causes injury to another by cutting off the light and air and interfering with the view that would otherwise be available over adjoining land in its natural state, regardless of the fact that the structure may have been erected partly for spite."

Case Questions

1. If the Eden Roc could prove that the addition was completely out of spite, would this additional fact affect the court's decision?

2. The court also notes that individuals could build as high or in any way that they wanted provided that it does not violate any laws, restrictions, or regulations. If the Fontainebleau was in violation of any code or regulation would the outcome of the case have been different? Why or why not?

---

however, we will examine four common ownership interests that are important to business owners and managers: (1) *fee simple;* (2) *life estate;* (3) *leasehold estate;* and (4) *easements.*

Legal Speak ›))
Heirs Individuals who are legally entitled to inherit a decedent's property.

Legal Speak ›))
Defeasible Capable of being canceled.

Fee Simple   The term **fee simple** actually encompasses three distinct interests,[7] all centered on the basic concept that fee simple ownership interests are the highest level of general rights associated with real estate. *Fee simple absolute* means that the rights are *unrestricted* (of course always subject to the restrictions imposed by law, such as zoning), of an infinite duration, and inheritable by the owner's heirs. *Fee simple defeasible* is a fee simple right with certain restrictions. If one of these restrictions is violated, the property ownership automatically falls back (known as *reverting*) to the original owner. The right of reversion is why we think of the original owner as maintaining a partial ownership interest even after that owner has granted ownership interests to a third party. These restrictions primarily come in the form of restrictions as to a *particular use* (e.g., may be used only for certain charitable purposes) and the fulfillment of some *condition* or requirement related to the real estate (e.g., a

---

[7]A minority of states also recognize a fourth interest of *fee tail,* which ensures that certain real estate will remain within the current owner's family.

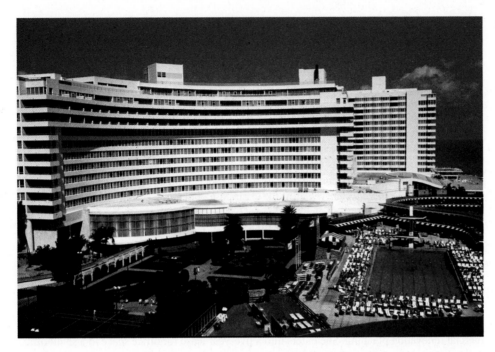

The Florida Supreme Court ruled that the famous Fontainebleau hotel in Miami Beach, seen here, had the right to construct an addition to their property despite the fact that the addition blocked the sunlight to an adjacent resort hotel.

municipality grants a contractor an interest in a 1,000 acre city-owned lot on the condition that the contractor build a landfill for public use on a 200-acre portion of the property).

Life Estate   A **life estate** is simply an ownership interest that lasts for the lifetime of a par- **LO**23-7
ticular person. The person who has a life estate interest is known as a *life tenant* because the life tenant may *not* sell, pledge, or convey the building in any way during ownership. However, life tenants do have day-to-day ownership duties such as paying taxes and repair/maintenance costs. A *life estate defeasible* is a life estate with a restriction attached in some way. Life estates are sometimes used as part of a business *succession* plan designed for the transition of ownership of a family-owned business from one generation to the next. For example, suppose that Blake has built a successful family business with assets that include a valuable piece of real estate, including a modern warehouse facility. Blake uses 75 percent of the warehouse for his business and leases

> **KEY** POINT
> *Fee simple absolute* is the highest level of ownership because it allows the titleholder unrestricted ownership rights.

the other 25 percent of the space to tenants. Blake Jr. is the sole heir and has helped run the business for many years. Blake wishes to pass the business and all of the business's property onto Blake Jr. upon his death. Blake also wishes to use the rental income from the warehouse lease to help support his spouse, for as long as she lives. To achieve both objectives, Blake may use the following language as part of his estate and business succession planning documents:

> If I die before my spouse, I, Blake, grant and convey my entire interest in Warehouse Real Estate to my spouse for her lifetime, on the condition that Blake Jr.'s business will pay no rent for use of the property; then to Blake Jr. in fee simple absolute.

In analyzing this language, we can determine that Blake intends to have his widowed spouse be the sole owner of the warehouse property during her lifetime, but only on the condition that Blake Jr. is not charged any rent (a *life estate defeasible*). After her death, Blake Jr. inherits the real estate with ownership rights in *fee simple absolute*. This ensures that the benefit flows to Blake's spouse without additional burden on Blake Jr.'s ability to run the family business. Blake's spouse could not sell her interest in the warehouse real estate and this ensures that Blake Jr. will eventually receive the property with no restrictions on use and the continuity between generations in the business has been preserved.

Leasehold Estate   A **leasehold estate** ownership interest affords the least amount of rights because it grants only a *qualified right* to use the real estate in an exclusive manner for a *limited* period of time. The most common form of leasehold estate is the *landlord-tenant agreement,* whereby the landlord gives the tenant a qualified right to possess and use the real estate for a specified period of years that is often spelled out in a written lease.[8] This is called a qualified right because the landlord retains the right to enter under certain circumstances. This leasehold estate is known as a *tenancy for years.* At the expiration of the time period, the leasehold estate expires automatically and the tenant no longer has any ownership interests. A landlord and tenant may also wish not to fix a specific time period, but rather to have a month-to-month[9] agreement that continues to renew automatically for that time period (in this case one month) until one party or the other gives advanced notice that she wishes to terminate the lease. Notice must be given at least one complete time period ahead (in this case, one month's notice would be required). This leasehold estate is known as a *periodic tenancy.* In a business context, it is not unusual for parties to use both types of leasehold estates to achieve certain business objectives. For example, suppose that Browning is an architect with a thriving practice in commercial renovation planning. She enters into a five-year lease for office space in a small office building owned by Gilbert. Toward the end of the lease's term, Gilbert approaches Browning about renewing the lease agreement for an additional five years. However, Browning informs Gilbert that she plans to expand her firm and anticipates hiring new employees over the next five years. This expansion will require Browning to move into larger office space in the future. Gilbert offers a solution by agreeing to lease on a month-to-month basis. This gives Gilbert the opportunity to locate a new suitable tenant and Browning the opportunity to find larger space without any legal commitment beyond a one-month notice period. Note that, typically, Browning would have to pay a higher monthly rental payment under the monthly agreement than if she signed another five-year lease. However, it is likely a valuable return on investment given the flexibility afforded to her in a monthly lease. Based on their business objectives, the parties shifted their leasehold estate interest from a tenancy for years (the five-year lease) to a periodic tenancy (a month-to-month) lease.

Easements   An **easement** is a privilege to use the real estate owned by another. A common example of an easement is the grant by property owners to utility companies for the privilege to install and maintain gas and water lines. Easements can arise by (1) an *express* grant (usually expressed in writing on the property deed); (2) *implication* or *necessity* when a property is landlocked in between other properties and the owner must cross through the property of another to gain access to her property; or (3) *prescription,* where the privilege is gained through adverse possession (discussed in the next section). Generally, easements are transferred with the property when the real estate is sold to another party so long as the new owner had reason to know of the easement (such as when the easement was expressly granted in a deed and has been publicly recorded with the appropriate government office).

A similar legal concept occurs when the landowner grants a *license.* A license is permission to use the property, but is revocable at any time at the owner's discretion. The owner's right of revocation is the difference between an easement and a license.

---

[8]A real estate lease is a form of contract and is, therefore, subject to the statute of frauds, which provides that certain contracts must be in writing to be enforceable. The statute of frauds is discussed in detail in Chapter 6, "Overview and Formation of Contracts."

[9]The parties will sometimes agree to even shorter time periods such as week-to-week.

Self-Check Ownership Interests

What is Swineburne's ownership interest?

1. Swineburne approaches Carroll with the idea of starting a charity soup kitchen. Carroll donates a parcel of real estate to Swineburne by providing an agreement: *"I convey this parcel to Swineburne in fee simple."* Swineburne uses the property to build a luxury resort hotel.

2. Swineburne approaches Carroll with the idea of starting a charity soup kitchen. Carroll donates a parcel of real estate to Swineburne by providing an agreement: *"I convey this parcel to Swineburne in fee simple provided that it be used for charitable purposes."* Swineburne uses the property to build a luxury resort hotel.

3. Swineburne approaches Carroll with the idea of starting a charity soup kitchen. Carroll agrees to rent a parcel of real estate to Swineburne for $1 a month on a month-to-month basis. The next day, Carroll gets an offer to purchase the real estate parcel for twice its market value on the condition that Carroll convey the real estate within five days. Carroll tells Swineburne to vacate the premises immediately.

4. Swineburne approaches Carroll with the idea of starting a charity soup kitchen. Carroll donates Swineburne a parcel of real estate by providing an agreement: *"I convey this parcel to Swineburne for his life, and then to Carroll Jr. in fee simple absolute."* Swineburne uses the property to start a soup kitchen, but dies shortly thereafter. Swineburne Jr. continues the soup kitchen. Carroll Jr. then informs Swineburne Jr. that she is selling the real estate and therefore Swineburne Jr. must vacate.

5. Swineburne approaches Carroll with a request that Carroll allow Swineburne the use of the driveway of a commercial office building owned by Carroll, which is on a parcel of property adjacent to Swineburne's charity soup kitchen. The driveway would allow easier access for trucks delivering supplies to the soup kitchen. Carroll executes and records a new deed with the statement: *"On the parcel of my commercial office building, I convey an easement for use of the driveway to Swineburne."* Carroll subsequently sells the property to Blago. Blago informs Swineburne that he may no longer use the driveway.

Answers to this Self-Check are provided at the end of the chapter.

Adverse Possession

In some cases, a party may gain title to real estate through the doctrine of adverse possession. In order to gain title to a parcel of property through adverse possession, the acquiring party must demonstrate that she has possessed it in a certain way for a certain period of time. These requirements are often spelled out in a particular state's statutory or common law. In general, the requirements are that the party must have met a three-prong test. Gaining title requires that the adverse possession must have been *open, notorious, and visible; exclusive and actual;* and *continuous.*

Open, Notorious, and Visible Possession   The true holder of title cannot be relieved of that title unless she could reasonably be expected to know that another person has taken possession of the real estate and that the adverse possessor *intended* to assert a claim to its ownership. Examples of cases where courts have held that this prong was satisfied include when the adverse possessor has (1) demonstrated that the true owner had actual or imputed knowledge that the adverse party had taken possession of the land; (2) erected a fence or other enclosure around the property; or (3) paid taxes or other maintenance fees in connection with the land.

Exclusive and Actual Possession   The adverse possessor must also show that she was in exclusive control of the property and did not share control or possession of the property with the true owner or the public generally. This also means that at least a reasonable percentage of the land claimed by the adverse possessor must be in actual use.

Continuous Possession   The adverse possession of the property must be continuous for a period of time set down by state statute or common law. About two-thirds of states require fifteen years or longer, but some states allow a shorter period when the adverse possessor pays the taxes on the property. This does not mean that the adverse possessor is required to spend every consecutive day on the property. Rather, it means that the adverse possessor cannot *abandon* the property for a period of time, or if the owner retakes possession within the prescribed time period, the adverse possessor's use stops and this prong cannot be satisfied unless the true owner abandons the property again in the future.

SALE OF REAL ESTATE

The most common way for commercial real estate to be transferred is through a sale.[10] Typically, the seller and buyer will agree on essential terms about the purchase and enter into an agreement of sale for the purchase of real estate. The agreement usually provides for a period of time devoted to due diligence and on a tentative settlement date (also called the *closing date*) and is supported by a cash deposit to be held by an escrow agent. The due diligence time period varies based on the complexity of the transaction. During this time the buyer will (1) arrange for financing through a financial institution or a private lender (such as a relative); (2) conduct an inspection of the property to be sure that the parties are aware of any physical defects, zoning issues, and other items that may affect the use or price of the property; and (3) have an attorney or title agent check to be sure that the seller has clear title to the property and will be able to convey the property without any legal obstacles. The agreement of sale spells out the time lines as well as the rights and obligations of the parties during the due diligence period. After the due diligence period has expired, the parties attend a settlement meeting where the buyer presents payment and the seller conveys title to the property via a deed.

Legal Speak »))
Escrow Agent A neutral third party designated to hold a sum of money while the parties fulfill conditions in a contract.

LO23-6, 23-7   ## LAWS GOVERNING LANDLORD-TENANT AGREEMENTS

An agreement between a landlord and a tenant for the rental of property is called a **lease** and is an example of the intersection between property law and contract law. As such, the sources of law governing leases range from state statutory protections of residential tenants to common law principles governing certain contracts. While the law of contracts is covered fully in Unit Two of this textbook, some references to contract law are necessary in the context of a discussion of property law. Additionally, while statutes that cover residential leases often feature protections for the tenants from arbitrary and wrongful acts of the landlord (such as a wrongful eviction), laws that govern the relationship between landlord-tenant agreements in a *commercial lease* (i.e., lease of a property that is to be used for commercial purposes such as a retail store in a shopping center) tend not to offer as much protection for business tenants. This is ordinarily because commercial leases are thought of as *negotiated* between the parties and, because both parties are engaged in business, a degree of sophistication is imputed to the tenant that is not present in a residential lease. Indeed, because many leases for property between landlords and businesses are documented in the form of a lease, most issues regarding landlord and tenant rights and duties are spelled out in the lease. However, in cases where the parties have not specifically agreed on certain terms, the common law provides a basic set of rules.

> ## KEY POINT
> The law tends to offer more protection to residential tenants than to commercial tenants because a certain level of business and legal acumen is imputed to business owners and managers.

---

[10]Other methods to transfer (mainly noncommercial) real estate are through a tax sale (for nonpayment of taxes), inheritance, gift, and adverse possession.

Because business managers and owners are frequently on the front lines in negotiating a lease, it is important to have an understanding of the basic legal framework governing landlord-tenant agreements.

Tenant Rights

Fundamentally, tenants have the rights of *possession, quiet enjoyment,* and *habitability.* The right to possession simply means that the landlord must deliver the legal right to possess the property to the tenant at the commencement of the lease agreement. In most states, the law requires the landlord to make reasonable efforts to give property access to the tenant by ensuring that any previous tenant has vacated and that the tenant has keys to the premises.[11] *Quiet enjoyment* is the tenant's right to use the premises without interference from the landlord. For example, Barclay leases a retail space to Jimenez. Barclay also owns the property next door to the leased property. One week after Jimenez takes possession of the space, Barclay begins to renovate the property next door and allows the contractor to place a construction dumpster in Jimenez's back lot. In this case Barclay has actually occupied a part of the property leased to Jimenez and, thus, has breached the tenant's right to quiet enjoyment.

Related to the right of quiet enjoyment is the tenant's right to have the leased space in a reasonable condition, known as the right to *habitability.* Note that the right of habitability is mostly applicable in the residential lease context. Essentially, this is a protection of the tenant's rights to occupy leased premises that are not in an unreasonably poor or unsafe condition so that a person cannot live there. Although an increasing number of courts are imposing this common law duty in a commercial context, some courts are still *reluctant* to protect this right for commercial tenants unless the circumstances are extreme (e.g., condition of the premises violates a state or local building safety code).[12]

Tenant Remedies

In the event that a landlord breaches a duty or promise to a tenant, the tenant has a variety of legal alternatives to compensate the tenant. These legal alternatives are known as **tenant remedies.** In the case of a violation of the tenant's right of possession, the tenant may either terminate the lease and sue the landlord for damages, or may continue the lease and recover damages after the landlord is able to give possession. In the case of violation of the right of either quiet enjoyment or habitability, the tenant generally may choose to either terminate the lease and/or to sue for damages (particularly if the violation occurs after possession has taken place). In some extreme cases under a violation of the right of habitability, tenants are permitted to withhold rent and pay the amounts due into escrow until any legal dispute is resolved. If the tenant cannot feasibly use the premises for its intended use because of landlord neglect or inaction, the tenant may claim to have been *constructively evicted* and may vacate the premises and terminate the lease without any further liability to the landlord.

Case 23.2 provides an example of the analytical framework used by a court to examine constructive eviction in the context of the right of quiet enjoyment and habitability in a commercial setting.

Tenant Duties

For the most part, in a commercial lease context, the tenant's duties under the common law are to pay the rent as agreed upon and to act reasonably in care and use of the property. This duty of reasonableness includes refraining from disturbing other tenants, obeying

Legal Speak »))
Escrow In a tenant remedy context, escrow is an amount of money delivered by the tenant to a third party (such as an attorney) to be held by the third party until the dispute between landlord and tenant is resolved.

---

[11]*Restatement (Second) of Property* § 6.2.

[12]*Restatement (Second) of Property* § 5.1.

FACT SUMMARY   Scene-In-Action ("Scene") rented a building from Automobile Supply Co. ("Auto") for Scene's business of manufacturing electrical advertising signs. The space was also used to house administrative offices of the business. Included in the lease was a provision requiring Auto to supply heat to the premises. The heat provision included language to the effect that efficient heat was necessary to keep the building comfortable in order to produce signs and carry on normal office tasks. Soon after the lease was signed, the building was without heat for several hours on numerous occasions throughout two months. Scene made repeated complaints about the situation to Auto, but Auto failed to fix the problem. The problems continued and, as the temperature dropped during the height of winter, there were many days when the temperature inside was below 50 degrees. As a result of the lack of heat, a number of Scene's employees would not return to work, claiming they were ill and unable to work in the cold conditions. Unable to carry on business, Scene terminated the lease, claiming they were constructively evicted because they were deprived of the beneficial use and enjoyment of the premises. Auto countersued for payments owed, claiming Scene could have vacated the premises earlier but instead stayed and maintained business operations without paying rent. Thus, Scene was not constructively evicted.

SYNOPSIS OF DECISION AND OPINION   The court ruled for Scene and held that, while not every act by a landlord that violates the tenant's right to quiet enjoyment of the premises amounts to a constructive eviction, acts that are of a grave and permanent character, which clearly indicate the intention of the landlord to deprive the tenant of the benefits of using the premises, constitute constructive eviction. The court also held that when a landlord engages in such a material breach of the lease, the tenant need not vacate the premises immediately. The affected tenant is entitled to vacate in a reasonable amount of time. Therefore, because the landlord breached the lease agreement in a way that deprived the tenant of the enjoyment of the premises, it constituted a constructive eviction and the tenant could terminate the lease and vacate the premises in a reasonable time without liability.

WORDS OF THE COURT: Constructive Eviction and Quiet Enjoyment   "The eviction of a tenant from the possession or enjoyment of the premises, or any part thereof, by the landlord releases the tenant from the further payment of rent. [. . .] [I]f the tenant is deprived of the premises by an agency of the landlord the obligation to pay rent ceases, because such obligation has force only from the consideration of the enjoyment of the premises. The eviction which will discharge the liability of the tenant to pay rent is not necessary and actual physical expulsion from the premises or some part of them, but any act of the landlord which renders the lease unavailing to the tenant or deprives him of the beneficial enjoyment of the premises constitutes a constructive eviction of the tenant, which exonerates him from the terms and conditions of the lease and he may abandon it."

Case Questions

1. Suppose that the landlord had made good faith efforts to fix the problem, but was unable to for a period of three months. Would that change the outcome of the case?

2. The court noted that tenants have a reasonable time to vacate the premises. What would you consider to be a reasonable time period in this case? Do multiple complaints to a landlord and not vacating the premises eviscerate any claims of constructive eviction?

---

reasonable landlord rules, complying with health and safety codes, and notifying the landlord when repairs are necessary on the premises.

Landlord Rights and Remedies

If a tenant violates the duty to pay rent (including when a tenant abandons the premises) or the duty to act reasonable in the use of the property, the common law allows several remedies to help the landlord recover damages. Depending on the circumstances, the landlord may keep any *security deposit* held by the landlord and/or *evict* (remove) the tenant from the premises. Most lease agreements typically call for the landlord to hold a certain amount of money to secure the landlord in the event that any damage is committed during the lease term and to give the landlord an option to recover part of any monies owed as a result of the tenant abandoning the premises (with or without notice) before the lease term ends. The right of the landlord to keep the security deposit is highly regulated by statute in both residential and commercial real estate leases. The landlord is typically required to return the security deposit to the tenant after subtracting any damages and giving an itemized list of the claimed damages to the tenant. The landlord must also act within a reasonable *time* after the end of the lease. The maximum period of time that the landlord may hold the deposit after the end of the lease is set by state statute and ranges between 15 and 45 days.[13] In addition to any action to recover damages via the security deposit, a landlord may also remove the tenant through *eviction.* This is an extreme remedy, and may only be used in cases when some significant violation of the tenant's duties has occurred. For example, a tenant that pays rent a few days late one month may *not* be evicted for violating the duty to pay. In order to evict a tenant, the landlord must follow statutorily prescribed procedures for eviction. This generally includes filing a lawsuit of eviction at a local court for a summary hearing on the issue. If the court agrees, the landlord is permitted to proceed with the eviction with assistance of the county authorities such as the sheriff's office.

Assignment and Subletting

LO23-8

Absent an agreement to the contrary, the parties in a lease agreement may transfer their interest to a third party. A landlord may sell her property to another party (who must honor the lease agreement) during the lease term and the tenant may *assign* or *sublet* the premises. If the tenant wishes to transfer their interests (right to possess and use the premises) to a third party for the *entire* remaining length of the term, this is called an **assignment.** The third party in an assignment is known as the *assignee.* If the tenant transfers anything less than the remaining term, this is known as a **sublease.** The third party in a sublease is called a *subleasee.* In both cases, the tenant remains bound to the original lease agreement and if the assignee or subleasee fails to pay rent, the original tenant is still liable for the payments. The only way that the original tenant's liability is extinguished is if the landlord has released the tenant from that particular obligation. The assignee/subleasee receives the full legal benefits of tenancy, including the right to sue the landlord if the landlord violates any of her duties such as the right to quiet possession (discussed earlier in this section). While landlords often insist that lease agreements contain *antiassignment clauses* that restrict a tenant's right to assign or sublet, there are certain cases where this right may be seen as a mutually beneficial way to achieve mutual business objectives.

CONCEPT SUMMARY   Landlord-Tenant Agreements

- A lease is an agreement between a landlord and a tenant for the rental of real estate.
- Generally, statutes are more protective of the tenant in residential leases than in commercial leases.

---

[13]For example, in Maryland landlords have 45 days to return security deposits to residential tenants. *See* Md. Real Property Code Ann. § 8-203. Conversely, in Florida landlords have 15 days to return a security deposit if they are not pursuing a damage claim against the tenant, but if they are going to impose a claim they have 30 days to notify the tenant. *See* Fla. Stat. § 83.49.

- Tenants have three basic rights: (1) possession, (2) quiet enjoyment, and (3) habitability. The right of possession is the tenant's right to possess and occupy the property, and the right of quiet enjoyment and habitability is the tenant's right to have the property be in safe, liveable condition.

- The duties of a tenant are to pay the rent and to act reasonably in care and use of the property. Acting reasonably includes not disturbing other tenants and notifying the landlord of any needed repairs so that the property remains safe.

- Both the tenant and landlord have remedies available to them in instances where the other parties breached the lease agreement or did not fulfill their duties. For example, tenants may be able to withhold rent or sue for damages and landlords may be able to evict the tenant and/or keep the security deposit.

- Tenants may also assign or sublease their interests in a property. Assignments are for the full term of the original lease and subleases are for any period of time less than the full term. Similarly, landlords may sell their property to a third party who must honor any current remaining lease agreements.

LO23-9 REGULATION OF COMMERCIAL LAND USE

State and local governments frequently pass statutes and ordinances that impose regulation on how a landowner may use a particular parcel of real estate. These regulations come in several forms, but the two types of regulations that are most crucial in business planning and operations are *zoning* ordinances and *environmental* regulation.

Zoning Ordinances

Zoning is generally done at the local level in the form of local ordinances passed by the county or municipal government. Counties, cities, boroughs, townships, villages, parishes, and the like are all forms of local government that pass ordinances. The power to pass zoning ordinances is well established in the law. Recall our discussion from Chapter 2, "Business and the Constitution," about the government's *police powers.* When a local government passes a zoning ordinance, it is exercising its police powers to advance legitimate objectives of the municipality as a whole. The Supreme Court has recognized this power,[14] but has also set limits on the government's control of private property.

Use Regulation   From a business perspective, one of the most important types of zoning regulation are ordinances that establish various districts for a particular use of the property. The municipality is typically divided into zones, in each of which only certain use of the land is permitted. These zones include areas for industrial, retail, and residential uses. Some municipalities divide up their land uses further, specifying such uses as light industrial, warehouse, and so on.

Enforcement and Appeals   A local administrative agent such as a zoning officer or building inspector employed by the municipality typically enforces local use ordinances. A zoning board or commission is often appointed by the local government to handle appeals from decisions of the zoning officer and to consider applications for parties that wish to have an exception to one of the zoning laws. These exceptions are known as *variances.* Local governments vary greatly in their guidelines for permitting a variance but, typically, if the variance does not harm the surrounding neighborhood or interfere with any local interests, the board will permit the variance.

---

[14]*Village of Euclid v. Ambler Realty Co.,* 272 U.S. 365 (1926).

Maximum Leverage in a Lease to Reach Business Objectives

PROBLEM *When considering leased space alternatives to locate its business, one important business objective is planning for expansion while minimizing risks.*

To achieve this objective, a business may lease space that is larger than their current needs, but will be needed to implement a ten-year expansion plan. However, the current cash flow of the business supports only a smaller leased area. For example, suppose that the management of Extreme Widget, Inc. (EWI), a manufacturer of high-performance widgets, locates a facility that is 10,000 square feet. Although EWI's current needs and financial ability supports only 5,000 square feet, the management team is anxious to secure the space because of its ideal location and competitive rental rate. EWI is also embarking on an expansion plan that will require at least another 5,000 square feet of space over the next five years. EWI's objectives are to (1) secure the 10,000 square foot parcel, (2) reduce the risk and liability of the added expenses by having alternatives for generating additional revenue to support the additional space until (or unless) it is needed, and (3) provide EWI with maximum flexibility in case expansion plans must be put on hold.

SOLUTION *Negotiate a subletting clause with an option for an assignment.*

One method of using the law to help achieve business objectives would be for EWI's management to approach the landlord of the facility and propose to include a *sublease and assignment clause* in a five-year lease. The clause could include the following provisions:

- EWI has the right to negotiate a sublease for up to 5,000 square feet of the facility with EWI remaining primarily liable to the landlord on the lease.
- EWI has the option of assigning all or part of the lease so long as the landlord has the opportunity to review the financial condition and creditworthiness of the proposed assignee. The landlord may accept or reject the candidate based on creditworthiness.
- If the landlord accepts the assignee, EWI remains primarily liable under the lease for a period of one year, and then is released from any obligations of the lease.

This solution achieves EWI's objectives by providing maximum flexibility to expand (or contract) while reducing the financial risks associated with leasing 10,000 square feet of property. The landlord also derives a benefit from the agreement because he now has a five-year lease in place for 10,000 square feet and the right to reject any proposed assignee.

Businesses in expansion mode may use subletting and assignment rights when leasing a property to maximize expansion opportunities while minimizing legal risk.

Limits on Zoning Regulations

Courts have ruled that the law sets limits on a local government's right to regulate private property usage through a variety of constitutional protections of property owners. First, if the zoning is so overreaching that it deprives the owner of all economic value of her property, the zoning will be categorized as a *taking* and the government is required to pay the owner the market value of the property as required in the Constitution's *Takings Clause*.[15] This is known as the power of *eminent domain* and is discussed in more detail in the next section. Second, under certain circumstances, those affected by a zoning ordinance are entitled to some procedural due process, such as a hearing by the local government.[16] Finally, a zoning law cannot discriminate because that violates the Equal Protection Clause of the Fourteenth Amendment. Courts in most states have also generally allowed zoning related to *aesthetics* so long as it is only one factor, not the sole factor, in a municipality's zoning decision.

Environmental Regulation

An increasing concern for business owners and managers is federal, state, and local regulation of land use based on the government's interest in advancing sound environmental policy. In general, governments may impose environmentally based land use regulations so long as they advance some substantial and legitimate state interest. For example, statutes aimed at preservation of open land areas have been found to be a legitimate government regulation of private property. Courts have generally held that wetlands and coastlands preservation ordinances that restrict the owner's right to develop, fill, or dredge the land are a legal use of the government's police powers. However, the Supreme Court curtailed this type of regulation by ruling that if the regulation completely depleted all economic value from the property, that act would constitute a government *taking* under the eminent domain power and trigger the government's obligation to pay compensation to the property owner. For example, suppose that Developer purchases 20 acres of Florida beachfront property with the intent to develop the acreage into a resort. In response to concerned environmental groups, the state of Florida then passes a statute that restricts the development along the coast running from the ocean to 1,000 yards inland. In Developer's case, this would amount to a loss of two prime acres of beachfront property, but Developer would have use of the remaining 18 acres. Developer sues for compensation because its partial loss of revenue was due to the state regulation. Most courts would rule against Developer because the government interest in preserving coastland has been held legitimate in the past and Developer lost only part of the revenue stream and additional revenue is too speculative. On the other hand, if the state's statute had been more overreaching and resulted in Developer losing all economic value of the property, Developer would be entitled to compensation from the government.[17]

Of course, apart from environmentally based land use regulations, business owners and managers must also be knowledgeable about a separate body of federal and state law aimed at broader environmental policies. These broad-based concerns, such as laws that regulate pollution, operation of factories, solid waste, and toxic chemicals are discussed in detail in Chapter 18, "Environmental Law."

LO23-10 EMINENT DOMAIN

It is important to understand the difference between a legitimate governmental land use *regulation* and a governmental *taking* of property that triggers a constitutional requirement to compensate the landowner. The authority of the state and federal government to take private property is called the power of *eminent domain,* which is derived from the Fifth Amendment that provides "[N]or shall private property be taken for public use without just compensation."

---

[15]U.S. Constitution, Fifth Amendment.

[16]U.S. Constitution, Fourteenth Amendment ("Due Process" clause).

[17]Based on the facts in *Nollan v. California,* 483 U.S. 825 (1987).

FACT SUMMARY   The City of New London ("City") devised an economic development plan that was projected to create more than 1,000 jobs and increase tax and other revenue. The plan called for a waterfront conference hotel; a marina; and various retail, commercial, and residential properties. The City's development authority designated a large area composed of adjacent parcels of real estate to be condemned in order to redevelop the property consistent with the redevelopment plan. The City's agent purchased the property from willing sellers and gave notice that they would institute condemnation proceedings via the power of eminent domain to acquire the remaining property from unwilling owners. The City purchased all but nine parcels of real estate and brought condemnations against nine property owners including Kelo, the name plaintiff. Although the City conceded that the condemned properties were not part of the blighted areas (in fact some had recently been renovated), they were condemned simply because of their location in the proposed development area. The lower courts' decisions were mixed, and the U.S. Supreme Court accepted the case on appeal to decide the question of whether the City's plan qualifies as a public use within the meaning of the Takings Clause of the Fifth Amendment to the U.S. Constitution.

SYNOPSIS OF DECISION AND OPINION   The Court ruled in favor of the City and articulated guideposts for appropriate use of the Takings Clause. The Court affirmed the principle that the government is not permitted take one party's private property for the sole purpose of transferring it to another private party and acknowledged that the City would not be able to take the property if they planned on bestowing it to a private development company or individual, or if any benefits from the plan would only be realized by private individuals. However, the City's development plan did not contemplate any direct bestowment of property rights upon private individuals or companies. Moreover, even though some of the uses would be private in nature, the Court ruled that

the standard to be used is the broader interpretation of the property being used for a *public purpose*. The Court found that the overall elimination of blight is a legitimate public purpose and held that the City's plan was a valid exercise of their eminent domain power.

WORDS OF THE COURT: Public Purpose   "[T]his 'Court long ago rejected any literal requirement that condemned property be put into use for the general public.' Indeed, while many state courts [. . .] endorsed 'use by the public' as the proper definition of public use that narrow view steadily eroded over time. Not only was the 'use by the public' test difficult to administer [. . .], but it proved to be impractical given the diverse and always evolving needs of society. Accordingly, when this Court began applying the Fifth Amendment to the States at the end of the 19th Century, it embraced the broader and more natural interpretation of public use as 'public purpose.' [. . .] Without exception, our cases have defined [this] concept broadly, reflecting our long-standing policy of deference to legislative judgments in this field. [. . .] Given the comprehensive character of the plan, the thorough deliberation that preceded its adoption [. . .] [it] unquestionably serves a public purpose."

Case Questions

1. In dissenting opinions, members of the Court argued that this decision makes all private property vulnerable to being taken and transferred to another private owner (against established principles the Court mentioned earlier), so long as the property is upgraded in some way. Moreover, they argued that this decision is advantageous to large corporations or individuals with political power or connections, while those with few resources are disadvantaged. Do you agree? Why or why not?

2. Would the case have been decided differently if the project built only a large industrial park? Why or why not?

Procedure

Eminent domain is traditionally invoked using a *condemnation proceeding*. Once a government has decided that certain real estate is necessary for public use, the government typically begins to negotiate sales agreements with the private property owners of the area(s) to be taken. If the negotiations fail, the government will formally institute a judicial proceeding to condemn the real estate. The court will be sure that procedural rights are being afforded to the property owner and will determine the fair market value of the real estate. Once the court has entered its order, the condemnation is complete and the government now holds title to the real estate.

Public Use

Note that the Constitution uses the phrase *public use* in the text. Typically, public use may mean the building of public highways, schools, public hospitals, and other traditional public governmental functions. However, the Supreme Court has construed the public use language very broadly for uses outside the traditional uses so long as the government can demonstrate that their actions were rationally related to some conceivable public purpose. This broad construction has been the source of controversy. For example, suppose that the government condemns a blighted area of a city in hopes of developing the condemned area into a thriving example of urban renewal that brings along new retail and office buildings. The plan calls for condemnation of some areas that are adjacent to the blight that have single family houses and thriving small, neighborhood businesses. Because the government does not intend to build any facilities for public use, is the taking unconstitutional? The Supreme Court took up that very issue in Case 23.3. It was perhaps the most important eminent domain decision since 1954.[18]

---

[18]The urban renewal interest was first sanctioned by the Supreme Court in *Berman v. Parker,* 348 U.S. 26 (1954).

KEY TERMS

Personal property p. 580   Any moveable or tangible object and includes everything except real property. Examples of personal property include computers, inventory, furniture, and jewelry.

Real property p. 580   Land, or anything growing on, attached to, or erected on the land. Examples of real property include parcels of land, homes, warehouses, stores, and crops.

Title p. 580   The legal term for ownership in property and the link between a person and property.

Actual owner p. 580   The individual that is recognized as having primary or residual title to the property and is, therefore, the ultimate owner of the property.

Ownership interests p. 583   The various rights that owners of real estate have. These interests are limited depending on the type of ownership.

Fee simple p. 584   The broadest property interest in land, which endures until the current holder dies without heirs.

Life estate p. 585   An ownership interest in real estate that lasts for the lifetime of a particular person.

Leasehold estate p. 586   The qualified right to use real estate in an exclusive manner for a limited period of time. The most common form of leasehold estate is a landlord-tenant agreement.

Easement p. 586   The privilege to use real estate owned by another.

Lease p. 588   An agreement between a landlord and a tenant for the rental of property.

Tenant remedies p. 589   The legal alternatives available to tenants as compensation in the event a landlord breaches a lease. Examples of common remedies include termination of the lease, suits for damages, and withholding of rent.

Assignment p. 591   A tenant transfer of its interest to a third party for the entire term remaining on a lease.

Sublease p. 591   A tenant transfer of its interest to a third party for anything less than the term remaining on a lease.

Restaurant Supply Inc. (RSI) is a wholesale supplier of food and nonfood kitchen products for restaurants and hotels. Last year, RSI signed up a large hotel chain as a new client. In order to fill the needs of their new client, the principals of RSI decided to expand by constructing a new warehouse in an industrially zoned section of the city. RSI also received a tax credit to install alternative energy sources in their new warehouse, so they invested $50,000 in a new solar panel system to be placed on the roof of the warehouse to serve as a source of power, with traditional gas and electric as a backup system. RSI eventually finished construction of the warehouse and the solar panels and immediately moved their food and nonfood inventory into the warehouse. A few months after RSI moved in to their new warehouse, the property adjacent to RSI's was sold to a glue factory.

1. Assume the glue factory ran 24 hours per day on a seven-day schedule and produced noxious fumes. Eventually, RSI began to suspect that the fumes were tainting the taste of the food that was being stored in RSI's warehouse. RSI then filed suit to stop the glue factory from discharging the noxious fumes. What is RSI's possible legal theory against the glue factory? What factors will a court use to analyze RSI's claim? Does the glue factory have any defenses?

2. Assume that the glue factory shuts down the factory in order to expand and upgrade its facilities to prevent the emission of the noxious fumes. In the process, the glue factory adds several stories to their facility. The additional stories resulted in a blockage of sun, which subsequently resulted in RSI's solar panels being rendered useless. RSI files suit against the glue factory for interference in RSI's property rights. What property right violation has RSI alleged? What case in the text gives you some guidance on this question? Is the RSI case distinguishable from that case? Who prevails in the RSI–glue factory case and why?

3. Assume that in preparation for the building renovation the glue factory conducted a survey and found that RSI's driveway was actually built 15 feet too wide and encroached on the glue factory's property. Since the time they built the warehouse, RSI has maintained the road and removed snow and so on. One day RSI gets a letter from the owner of the glue factory demanding that the driveway be ripped up and repaved consistent with the correct property line. Could RSI use the doctrine of adverse possession to refuse the demand? What are the standards that courts use to analyze ownership via adverse possession?

4. Suppose that RSI is owned by Abel and that his son, Abel Jr., is the top manager in charge of the business operations. When planning on how the business will pass from Abel to his son upon Abel's death, Abel wishes to have the ownership of the warehouse pass to his spouse for her lifetime, then to Abel Jr. What type of ownership interests could Abel use to accomplish this objective? What restrictions would his spouse have once she inherited the warehouse?

5. Assume that RSI wished to increase their solar panel usage by purchasing large "Brand A" panels and installing them on the rooftop of the warehouse. However, a city ordinance existed that banned the use of Brand A panels because they tend to make a building look less attractive. What is this type of ordinance called? Is this type of ordinance legal? Why or why not? Assuming that the ordinance is legal, are there any alternatives that RSI could pursue with local authorities?

Managers provide valuable input and analysis for business operation expansion planning efforts. We've seen how various legal issues related to ownership and use of property can impact those planning efforts. Assume that in Theory to Practice above, that you are part of a three-person management team for RSI and received the following e-mail from your senior manager:

> RSI is developing expansion plans that include new facilities in the southwestern United States. At this time, we are considering leasing office and operational space in several large cities, but are interested in a 25,000 square foot facility with an ideal location and rental rate. However, at this time, we only need 10,000 square feet. The landlord has said that she is willing to negotiate lease terms, but that we must lease the entire 25,000 square foot space. RSI wants to expand, but keep risk and financial exposure at a minimum.

Research alternatives for possible subleasing/assignment of the unused space to third parties, and develop a short presentation (no more than five PowerPoint slides) that could be presented to the landlord on proposed lease terms that would help RSI accomplish its objectives. Be sure to include a listing of advantages of this arrangement for the landlord and for RSI. A sample answer may be found on this textbook's Web site at www.mhhe.com/melvin.

BAILMENTS

Stoda Corporation operated a warehouse used by Singer to store 133 air-conditioner units. Upon storing their goods in the warehouse, officers and managers of Singer inspected the warehouse and observed that the warehouse had a network of sprinkler systems. A fire broke out at Stoda's warehouse, the sprinkler system failed to activate, and the fire destroyed all of the Singer goods. Singer sued, claiming Stoda's negligence in storing goods in a warehouse without adequate fire protection breached their bailment duties.

CASE QUESTIONS

1. Who prevails and why?
2. What is the standard that the bailee (Stoda) owes to the bailor (Singer)?

ADVERSE POSSESSION

In 1957, Hibbard decided to clear his land in order to open a trailer park. Because there was no clear boundary between Hibbard's property and the adjoining property to the east, Hibbard cleared the property up to a large drainage ditch and installed an access road to the left of the ditch to signify the property line. Hibbard opened a trailer park facility and later that year, McMurray, the owner of the eastern parcel, had a survey conducted. McMurray informed Hibbard that the access road encroached on his property by 20 feet. Subsequently, Hibbard sold the trailer park to Gilbert and noted in the sales contract that (1) the driveway encroached 20 feet on McMurray's property, (2) Gilbert agreed not to claim ownership of the property, and (3) Gilbert agreed he would remove the blacktop if ever requested to do so. From 1967 to 1976, the property changed ownership several times but no mention was made of the encroachment or contract provision from the Hibbard–Gilbert sale. In 1976, Sanders purchased the trailer park and was given notice of the encroachment and provision, but mistook the road to which the notice referred. Since the development of the trailer park, the road was continuously used and the area between the drainage ditch and road was maintained by the various trailer park property owners, including the planting of flowers, mowing the grass, and use by residents for picnics. Sanders also installed underground wiring and surface poles in the area. Two years later Chaplin purchased the eastern lot from McMurray, had a survey conducted, and had architects design buildings for development based on the true property line from the survey. Washington requires a 10-year period of use in order to establish adverse possession.

CASE QUESTIONS

1. Are all of the elements for adverse possession met so that Sanders now has title to the disputed parcel? Why or why not?
2. What is the appropriate starting time from which to measure qwnership in order to satisfy Washington's statutory requirement for 10-years of possession?

ASSIGNMENTS AND SUBLEASES

Dayenian entered into a two-year lease agreement for an apartment with Monticello Realty Corporation on July 14. On October 26 of that year she signed a portion of the lease headed "ASSIGNMENT," which stated that she assigned all her rights, title, and interest in the lease to Lambert from December 1 onward, but that she was not relieved of any liability under the lease. Lambert accepted this on November 8, by signing a section titled "ACCEPTANCE OF ASSIGNMENT," and that same day Monticello Realty executed a portion of the lease entitled "CONSENT TO ASSIGNMENT," which consented on the condition that Dayenian remain liable for payment of rent. In March of the following year, Lake Shore Drive Development Company mailed Lambert a notice of intent to convert the apartment building to a condominium and providing for a right of first refusal to purchase the apartment if he responded. Lambert never acted upon this notice, and in May the developer entered into a contract to sell the apartment to another party. Dayenian sued, claiming that she should have been given the right of first refusal because she was the tenant of the apartment at the time the notice to convert was sent and that the transfer to Lambert was a sublease.

CASE QUESTIONS

1. Is the transfer an assignment or a sublease? Why?
2. What do the courts look to in making this determination?

LANDLORD-TENANT AGREEMENTS

Jones operated a gas station, which he leased from Amoco Oil Company under a franchise agreement. The lease was a standard form signed by Jones in order to obtain the franchise. The lease required Jones to return the premises in substantially the same condition as received, less ordinary wear and tear, and also required him to perform necessary upkeep and maintenance on the premises, including clearing sidewalks. Although the lease did not indicate which party was responsible for fire insurance, it did note that Amoco could terminate the lease upon destruction of the premises. Early one morning a no-fault fire broke out gutting parts of the station and causing $118,850 in damage. After the fire, Amoco terminated the lease and leveled the station. They then sued Jones for not returning the station in substantially the same condition as he received it.

CASE QUESTIONS

1. Does a Jones have an obligation to rebuild the gas station? Why or why not?
2. Why would Amoco terminate the lease?

 Answers to SELF-CHECK

What is Swineburne's ownership interest?

1. Swineburne owns the property in fee simple absolute and is permitted to use the property for any lawful use including a luxury resort.

2. Swineburne's ownership was in fee simple defeasible (restricted by Carroll's "provided that" language in the agreement). When he violated the restriction the ownership rights reverted back to Carroll.

3. Swineburne's interest is in the form of a periodic (month-to-month) tenancy. Therefore, Carroll must give Swineburne at least one month's notice before terminating the lease.

4. Swineburne was a life tenant, so all ownership interests are extinguished upon his death. Carroll Jr. is then the owner in fee simple absolute and has the right to terminate Swineburne Jr.'s use of the real estate.

5. Swineburne has an express easement to use the driveway. Blago had reason to know of the easement at the time of purchase (via the easement statement recorded on the deed); therefore he must honor Swineburne's easement.

24 CHAPTER

Intellectual Property

learning outcomes **checklist**

After studying this chapter, students who have mastered the material will be able to:

24-1 Define a trade secret and other protectable business information and articulate the various legal implications for misappropriation of that information.

24-2 Classify trademarks marks based on their level of distinctiveness and give examples of trademarks, trade dress, and service marks.

24-3 Express how federal laws aimed at regulating trademarks in cyberspace apply to domain names.

24-4 Identify and understand the impact of trademark infringement and dilution.

24-5 Articulate the fundamental requirements for copyright protection, the legal ramifications of copyright infringement, and the impact of technology on copyright law.

24-6 Apply the fair use defense and give examples from case law.

24-7 Explain the process for obtaining and maintaining a patent and articulate the basic requirements for an invention to have patent protection.

24-8 Identify and understand the remedies for acts of patent infringement.

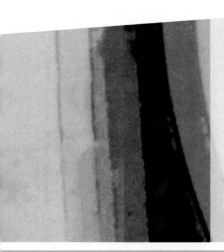

The formal protection of intellectual property has been a foundation of U.S. law since the ratification of the Constitution. In Article I, Section 8 of the U.S. Constitution, Congress is specifically authorized to protect intellectual property "by securing for limited Times to Authors and Inventors the exclusive Right to their respective Writings and Discoveries." A study published in the *Harvard Business Review* found that intellectual property represents approximately 70 percent of an average firm's value, and that number has nearly doubled in one decade.[1] This chapter discusses the increasingly important legal concepts of intellectual property protection that will help business owners and managers to make informed decisions on how best to protect their own intellectual property and prevent infringing upon the intellectual property rights of others. In this chapter, students will learn:

- Legal protections for trade secrets and other business information.

- Statutory and common law requirements for protection of trademarks, service marks, and trade dress.

- Requirements for protection under federal copyright laws, consequences of infringement, and application of the fair use test.

- Overview of protections for inventors through patent law and statutory requirements for obtaining a patent.

- International treaties and risks concerning intellectual property protection.

[1]K. Rivet and D. Kline, "Discovering New Value in Intellectual Property," *Harvard Business Review,* January 2000, p. 58.

TRADE SECRETS AND PROTECTION OF BUSINESS INFORMATION

One of the most valuable assets of any firm is their secret processes, formulas, methods, procedures, and lists that allow them a competitive advantage in their trade. It is important to understand that many of these types of trade secrets, business information, and business methods may *not* be protectable by patent or copyright laws. In fact, patent applicants generally rely on trade secret law to protect their inventions while patent applications are in progress. Businesses from across the spectrum of sectors turn to trade secret protection laws to protect some or all of their valuable creative ideas. Examples of technical and business information material that can be protected by trade secret law include customer lists, designs, instructional methods, manufacturing processes and product formulas, and document-tracking processes.

Courts use several factors under the common law of the majority of states to determine whether certain material constitutes a trade secret:

- The extent to which the information is known outside the claimant's (i.e., the firm claiming the information to be a trade secret) business.
- Measures taken by the claimant to guard the confidentiality of the information.
- The value of the information to competitors.
- The amount invested (in terms of time and money) in developing the information.
- The efforts to maintain trade secret confidentiality among the claimant's employees and third-party vendors (such as auditing firms).

TRADE SECRET PROTECTIONS

Trade secret protections are provided by state statutes and/or state common law. The Uniform Trade Secrets Act (UTSA)[2] defines trade secrets as information or articles that are to be kept secret because of its particular value. More formally, a trade secret is described as formula, pattern, compilation, program, device, method, technique, or process that meets the following criteria:

- Derives *independent economic value,* actual or potential, from not being generally known to, and not being readily ascertainable by proper means by other persons who can obtain economic value from its disclosure or use.
- Is the subject of efforts that are reasonable under the circumstances to maintain its secrecy. Economic value must be identified by the owner and secrecy must be kept.

Misappropriation

While the definition of **misappropriation** may cover a wide spectrum of illegal acts, most states use the fundamental definitions contained in the UTSA: acquisition of a trade secret of another by a person who knows or has reason to know that the trade secret was acquired by improper means, or any disclosure or use of a trade secret of another without express or implied consent.

Criminal Sanctions

While the UTSA does not contain any criminal sanctions, many states have added a separate set of statutes that make certain trade secret misappropriation a criminal offense. For example, in 1997, a district attorney in California prosecuted several executives and

---

[2]The UTSA is a model law drafted by the American Law Institute for use by state legislatures. For more information on the ALI and Model Laws, see Chapter 1, "Legal Foundations."

employees of Avant! Corporation, a firm that designed software related to semiconductor chips. The prosecutor was alerted to the case after a competitor of Avant! sued them in an action brought under California's Trade Secret Act, alleging that Avant! employees stole computer code from one of Avant!'s primary competitors.[3] Ultimately, Avant! accepted a plea bargain from the prosecutor that forced the company and seven individuals to pay $35 million in fines and resulted in incarceration for five of the defendants. The **Economic Espionage Act** is a federal statute passed in 1996 providing criminal penalties for domestic and foreign theft of trade secrets.

Exclusive Rights for Unlimited Duration

Perhaps the most significant advantage of trade secret protection over other forms of intellectual property (such as patents) is protection for trade secrets does not expire after a fixed period of time. A trade secret owner has the right to keep others from misappropriating and using the trade secret for the duration of the firm's existence. Although sometimes the misappropriation is a result of industrial espionage, most trade secret cases involve people who have taken their former employer's trade secrets for use in a new start-up business or for a new employer.

Trade secret protection endures so long as the requirements for protection continue to be met. The protection is lost if the owner fails to take reasonable steps to keep the information secret. For example, Sam discovers a new method for manipulating images in multimedia works. He demonstrates his new method to a number of other developers at a multimedia conference. Sam may have lost his trade secret protection for the image manipulation method because he failed to take appropriate steps to keep his method secret.

Trade secret owners have recourse only against misappropriation. Discovery of protected information through independent research or reverse engineering (taking a product apart to see how it works) is *not* misappropriation.

 SELF-CHECK   Trade Secrets

Which of the following may be protectable as a trade secret?

1. A list of customers compiled by a firm that included buying patterns, purchaser contact information, and preferred products of each customer.

2. A system used by a medical practice for scheduling patients for doctor's office visits.

3. The formula for a new brand of fruit drink for a beverage supply company.

4. The process used by an accounting firm to draft financial statements in accordance with Generally Accepted Accounting Procedures (GAAP).

5. New software that helps a manufacturer speed up the design process for new products.

   Answers to this Self-Check are provided at the end of the chapter.

TRADEMARKS, SERVICE MARKS, AND TRADE DRESS   LO24-2

A **trademark** is a word, symbol, or phrase used to identify a particular seller's products and distinguish them from other products. For example, the word *Nike* and the Nike "swoosh" symbol identify shoes made by Nike and distinguish them from shoes made by another company. Similarly, the Coca-Cola name and logo design distinguishes the brown-colored soda of one particular company from competing brown-colored sodas made by

---

[3]*Cadence Design Systems, Inc. v. Avant!,* 253 F.3d 1147 (9th Cir. 2002). The parties settled the civil suit for $265 million.

other companies. When such marks are used to identify services rather than products, they are known as **service marks.** *Visa,* for example, is a service mark related to the credit card services offered by Visa International Services Associated.

Trade Dress

Trademark protection also extends beyond words, symbols, and phrases to include other aspects of the product such as shape or the color scheme of its packaging. These features are known as **trade dress.** Increasingly, the U.S. Patent and Trademark Office (USPTO) and courts have granted trademark protection for such trade dress-related characteristics as product shapes, colors, and scents so long as a company can prove an exclusive link to the source product in the consumer's mind. For example, beginning in 2005, after having secured trademark registration for the two-dimensional iPod symbol and the cobranded "Made for iPod" symbol, Apple applied for trademark protection of the actual three-dimensional shape of their product. Apple provided the USPTO with evidence that (1) they had spent hundreds of millions of dollars in advertising targeted to building an association between iPod's shape and Apple, (2) there was a widespread consumer familiarity with the iPod's design, and (3) many consumers automatically linked the iPod's shape with Apple. In 2008, the USPTO granted Apple's application for trademark registration. Figure 24.1 shows the sketches submitted by Apple to the USPTO.

Trademarks as a Business Asset

Business owners often invest significant resources into their trademark design, advertisement, and protection because it is a valuable asset. Trademarks make it easier for consumers to quickly identify the sources of a given good. Trademark owners design and advertise their trademarks in hopes of helping to build brand loyalty, knowing that instead of reading the fine print on a product, consumers have instant recognition of their mark. Rather than having to ask a store clerk where to find a particular brand of sneaker, consumers are more likely to recognize a unique pattern of stripes or a "swoosh" symbol. Trademark protections are designed to ensure that competitors cannot have a free ride on a popular brand name. If a low-quality clothing manufacturer could freely use the name Aéropostale or the widely known trade dress associated with that mark, consumers might assume that they are buying authentic Aéropostale clothing. Sales and reputation may suffer as consumers now began to infer that the Aéropostale company had reduced *its* quality assurance standards.

FIGURE 24.1 Apple iPod Trademark Registration

Apple secured trademark protection for the iPod symbol (top left), its co-branded products symbol (bottom left), and for the shape of the iPod (right).

Trademarks also serve as an incentive for business owners to invest in the quality of their goods or services. If a consumer tries a brand of laundry detergent and finds the quality to be lacking, it will be easy for a consumer to avoid that brand in the future. Trademark law provides consumer protection by regulating the use of trademarks and prohibiting the use of a mark where consumer confusion may result.

SOURCE OF LAW

Trademark protections are a patchwork of federal and state law, but the major provisions and protections are found in a federal statute known as the Lanham Act. The statute prohibits the use in commerce, without the mark holder's consent, of any protected trademark in a way likely to cause consumer confusion. The act also prohibits the use of an unregistered common law trademark.[4]

Classifications of Trademarks

To qualify for protection as a trademark, the mark must be *distinctive*. That is, it must be capable of identifying the source of a particular good. In determining whether a mark is distinctive, marks can be grouped into three categories that are based on the mark's relationship to the underlying product. Because marks vary with respect to their distinctiveness, the requirements for, and degree of, legal protection afforded a particular trademark will depend upon which category it falls within.

Arbitrary or Fanciful A mark categorized as arbitrary or fanciful bears no logical relationship to the underlying product. For example, "Amazon.com" or "Kodak" bears no inherent relationship to their underlying products or services. Similarly, the Google name and symbol has no obvious connection to an Internet search engine. Arbitrary/fanciful marks are highly distinctive and are thus afforded a relatively high level of protection.

Suggestive A trademark is classified as suggestive if the mark itself evokes images of characteristics of the underlying product. Some exercise of imagination or knowledge of a particular field may be necessary to make this connection, but the mark itself suggests the underlying product. For example, Under Armour Clothing suggests some type of product to be used "under" something, but one needs a leap of imagination to understand the tied

Google is one of the strongest and most distinctive trademarks in the world.

[4]15 U.S.C. § 1114(1)(a).

FACT SUMMARY   Custom Vehicles registered the trademark "Work-N-Play" for one of their products. Work-N-Play vehicles were vans designed to be both a mobile office and, upon conversion that took the owner approximately one hour, a camper. Later, Forest River manufactured a van with a ramp door from the rear cargo section that had space fitted for a snowmobile, motorcycle, or ATV. They named the van Work and Play (without registering it as a trademark). Custom filed suit for trademark infringement, but the district court held that no infringement had taken place.

SYNOPSIS OF DECISION AND OPINION   The Seventh Circuit Court of Appeals affirmed the trial court's decision in favor of Forest, ruling that Custom's mark was *descriptive* but had not acquired a secondary meaning. Sales of Custom's product were relatively small, and there was no evidence that the mark would have any brand recognition. Thus, the mark was not sufficiently "famous" so as to be afforded trademark protection.

WORDS OF THE COURT: Secondary Meaning   "A trademark, like a patent, carries a presumption of validity. However, in the case of a registered descriptive mark, the presumption is that it has acquired secondary meaning. But the act of registration merely begins the process that leads to the presumption. Bare registration is not enough. Trademarks cannot be 'banked' or 'warehoused'—that is, an individual or entity cannot register thousands of names, unrelated to any product or service that it sells, in the hope of extracting a license fee from sellers of products or services for which one of the names might be apt. The register of a name must certify that the product is in use in commerce—defined as the bona fide use of a mark in the ordinary course of trade, and not made merely to reserve a right in a mark—within six months after the trademark is registered. Within those six months, the use of the trademark in one commercial sale is not enough to place the trademark in the ordinary course of trade, unless the sale is large enough to seize the attention of the relevant market."

Case Questions

1. Should Custom have waited until they sold more of this product before they registered Work-N-Play as a trademark?

2. Why must a descriptive mark acquire a secondary meaning in order to have protection?

product. Suggestive marks are similar to arbitrary marks in that they tend to be highly distinctive and are given a high level of protection.

Descriptive   A descriptive trademark is one in which the mark directly describes, rather than suggests, a characteristic of the underlying product or service in terms of color, function, and so forth. For example, "Pizza Hut" tells us something about the product they sell. Marks that indicate geographic ties, such as Vermont Maple Syrup, or marks that use a proper surname, such Ford Motor Company, are considered descriptive. However, unlike arbitrary marks, descriptive marks are *not* inherently distinct and may only gain trademark protection if they have acquired a **secondary meaning.** Descriptive marks must clear this additional hurdle precisely because these are frequently common terms that are connected to the product, but may also have alternate meanings in a different context.

Standards for Secondary Meaning   A secondary meaning is created when the consuming public primarily associates a mark with a *particular* product rather than any alternate meaning. For example, Microsoft attempted to protect the term *Windows* as a mark for its revolutionary operating system for many years. In order to attain that right, Microsoft was required to show that much of the consuming public more often associated that term with their operating system rather than panes of glass.

In Case 24.1, a federal court of appeals analyzes the requirements for a secondary meaning.

ACQUIRING RIGHTS FOR TRADEMARK PROTECTION

Assuming that a trademark qualifies for protection, rights to a trademark can be acquired in one of two ways: (1) by being the first to use the mark in commerce, or (2) by being the first to register the mark with the U.S. Patent and Trademark Office (USPTO or simply PTO). In the case of registration, one typically needs to put the product into use to obtain full protection. Remember, however, that descriptive marks qualify for protection (and can be registered) only after they have acquired secondary meaning. Thus, for descriptive marks, there is typically a period after the initial use of the mark in commerce before it acquires a secondary meaning, during which it is not entitled to trademark protection. Once it has achieved a secondary meaning, trademark protection attaches. The use of a mark in commerce generally means the actual sale of a product to the public with the mark attached or displayed.

The other way to acquire priority is to *register* the mark with the PTO with a bona fide intention to use the mark in commerce. Unlike use of a mark in commerce, registration of a mark with the PTO gives a party the right to use the mark nationwide, even if actual sales are only to a limited area. This right is limited, however, to the extent that others are already using the mark within a specific geographic area. If that is the case,

FACT SUMMARY   People for the Ethical Treatment of Animals (PETA) is the high-profile nonprofit organization devoted to educating the public at large and attempting to prevent the abuse of animals for corporate gain. Doughney registered PETA.org, claiming he was head of an organization called People Eating Tasty Animals and, thus, was entitled to use the name. Doughney's Web site contained links to furriers and others that would be in direct conflict with PETA's mission. PETA filed suit against Doughney alleging, among other things, his use of PETA.org violated the ACPA.

SYNOPSIS OF DECISION AND OPINION   The court ruled in favor of PETA, granted them summary judgment, and ordered Doughney to cease use of the PETA.org domain name. The court pointed out nine examples of bad faith action taken by Doughney and held that his actions violated the ACPA. The court rejected Doughney's claim that the Web site was merely a parody of the PETA organization because of the likelihood of confusion. In fact, Doughney admitted that "many people" would initially assume that they were accessing an authentic site sponsored by PETA.

WORDS OF THE COURT: Bad Faith   "[Under the ACPA], there are nine factors a court must consider in making a determination of whether the Defendant had a bad faith intent. Applying these factors, it appears that Doughney had the requisite bad faith intent.

First, Defendant possessed no intellectual property rights in 'PETA.ORG' when he registered the domain name in 1995. Second, the 'PETA.ORG' domain name is not the Defendant, Michael T. Doughney's legal name or any name that is otherwise used to identify the Defendant. Third, Defendant had not engaged in prior use of the 'PETA.ORG' domain name in connection with the bona fide offering of any goods or services prior to registering 'PETA.ORG.' Fourth, Defendant used the PETA mark in a commercial manner. Fifth, Defendant clearly intended to confuse, mislead and divert Internet users into accessing his website, which contained information antithetical, and therefore harmful to the goodwill represented by the PETA mark. Sixth, on Doughney's 'PETA.ORG' website, Doughney made reference to seeing what PETA would offer him if PETA did not like his website. Seventh, Defendant, when registering the domain name 'PETA.ORG,' falsely stated that 'People Eating Tasty Animals' was a non-profit educational organization and that this website did not infringe any trademark. Eighth, Defendant has registered other Internet domain names which are identical or similar to either marks or names of famous people or organizations he opposes. Ninth, the PETA mark used in the 'PETA.ORG' domain name is distinctive and famous and was so at the time Defendant registered this site in September 1995."

Case Questions

1. Was there any indication that Doughney was "cybersquatting"?

2. Could Doughney have avoided liability by making changes to his Web site or business model? What changes may help shield him from liability?

KEY POINT

In order for a plaintiff to recover under the ACPA, the defendant must have acted in *bad faith*.

webcheck   **uspto.gov/trademarks**
Have an idea for a trademark? Try a trademark registration search at the Web site above or link to it through this textbook's companion Web site at www.mhhe.com/melvin.

then the prior user of the mark retains the right to use that mark within that geographic area; the party registering the mark gets the right to use it everywhere else. In essence, different parties can have trademark protection simultaneously. For example, if Robert begins to use a trademark for a specialty coffee in his coffee shop in Boston, but does not use it in any other market, he has acquired the right to use it in *Boston only* because he was the first to put it into commerce. However, if National Brand Coffee (NBC) wants to use the very same trademark, they may register it with the PTO and be entitled to nationwide rights (except the right to use it in the

Advantages of Trademark Registration

PROBLEM *The common law and statutory law protections in the area of trademark protection result in too much uncertainty regarding a business's ability to use the mark.*

SOLUTION *Register your trademark as soon as possible with the USPTO.*

Although this may require attorneys' fees, the return on investment may well be worth it. The major advantages to registration are:

• Registration gives a party the right to use the mark nationwide, subject to any geographic exceptions.

• Registration constitutes nationwide constructive notice to the public of trademark ownership.

• Registration enables a party to bring an infringement suit in federal court.

• Registration allows a party to potentially recover treble (triple) damages, attorneys' fees, and other remedies.

• Registered trademarks may, after five years, become "incontestable," at which point the exclusive right to use the mark is conclusively established.

Registering a trademark with the USPTO provides maximum nationwide protection and gives the mark holder the right to enforce its rights in federal court.

same Boston geographic market). So both Robert and NBC have rights to the same trademark, but the rights only extend to the appropriate geographic area.

Applications and the PTO

Applications for registration are subject to approval by the PTO. The PTO may reject a registration on any number of grounds. For example, the PTO will refuse to register (1) any mark that is not inherently descriptive, (2) generic marks or descriptive marks that have not attained secondary meaning, (3) immoral or scandalous marks, (4) certain geographic marks, (5) marks that are primarily surnames, and (6) marks that are likely to cause confusion with existing marks. As noted above, rejection of the mark does not necessarily mean that it is not entitled to trademark protection. It means simply that the mark is not entitled to the statutory benefits provided by law (such as those listed in the preceding Solutions for Managers). Some famous rejections include:

- Twitter's 2009 application to trademark the term *tweet* because of insufficient evidence of secondary meaning.
- Chippendales' application to trademark their famous "cuffs-and-collar only" configuration worn by their waiters was rejected as not inherently distinctive. The USPTO was not sufficiently persuaded by the affidavit of an expert on American burlesque theatre that the Chippendales costumes are associated with "iconic characters" that makes the costume distinctive.

Preserving Trademark Protection

Legal Speak ›))

Prima Facie Literally "at first sight," prima facie cases are made when certain clear evidence exists as to a conclusion of law, but it is subject to further evidence or defense to rebut the original evidence.

The rights to a trademark can be lost through abandonment, improper licensing or assignment, or genericity. A trademark is abandoned when its use is discontinued with intent not to resume its use. Nonuse for three consecutive years is prima facie evidence of abandonment. The basic idea is that trademark law only protects marks that are being used, and parties are not entitled to warehouse potentially useful marks.

Trademark rights can also be lost through **genericity** (also known as *genericide*). Sometimes, a trademark that is originally distinctive can become generic over time, thereby losing its trademark protection. A word will be considered generic when, in the minds of a substantial majority of the public, the word denotes a broad genus or type of product and not a specific source or manufacturer. In a landmark genericity case, *Bayer v. United Drug Company*, decided in 1921, *aspirin* was held to be generic. Other examples include *zipper* and *elevator*, which were both formerly brand names. In deciding whether a term is generic, courts will often look to dictionary definitions, the use of the term in newspapers and magazines, and any evidence of attempts by the trademark owner to "police" its mark. Xerox Corporation, for example, runs full-page advertisements in national newspapers pointing out that it is incorrect to refer to the photocopying of a document as "Xeroxing" the document. Other companies working to police their mark to prevent genericity include Jeep, Google, and the makers of the Band-Aid brand of adhesive strip.

LO24-4 Trademark Infringement

If a party owns the rights to a particular trademark, that party can sue subsequent parties for trademark infringement. The standard is "likelihood of confusion." To be more specific, the use of a trademark in connection with the sale of a good constitutes infringement if it is likely to cause consumer confusion as to the source of that good or as to the sponsorship or approval of that good. In deciding whether consumers are likely to be confused, the courts will typically look to a number of factors. These factors, known as the Polaroid test, based on a landmark infringement case in *Polaroid Corp. v. Polarad Elecs. Corp.,*[5] include (1) the strength of the mark, (2) the proximity of the goods, (3) the similarity of the marks, (4) evidence of actual confusion, (5) the similarity of marketing channels used, (6) the degree of caution exercised by the typical purchaser, (7) the defendant's intent, and (8) the sophistication of the consumer.

The use of an identical mark on the same product would clearly constitute infringement. For example, suppose that Richard manufactures and sells personal computers from his home office that overlooks a dell meadow. He likes the dell meadow so much that he

---

[5]287 F.2d 492 (2d Cir. 1961).

uses the mark "Dell" on all of his computers. His use of that mark will likely cause confusion among consumers, because they may be misled into thinking that the computers are made by the more famous Dell, Inc. Using a very similar mark on the same product may also give rise to a claim of infringement if the marks are close enough in sound, appearance, or meaning so as to cause confusion to the consumer. Thus, while "Dell" may be off-limits for Richard's personal computer products (and perhaps also "Dell's Design"), use of Dell with an unrelated product will not give rise to an infringement claim. The famous Dell, Inc., and the local Dell's Deli can peacefully coexist, because consumers are not likely to think that the computers are being made by the deli, or vice versa. In an actual trademark case, Apple successfully blocked the importation of "Pineapple" computers from Taiwan because the marks were too similar and could cause consumer confusion.

Trademark Dilution

In addition to bringing an action for infringement, owners of trademarks may also bring an action for trademark dilution. In 1995, Congress passed the **Federal Trademark Dilution Act** that permits mark holders to recover damages and prevent another from "dilution" of distinctive trademarks. This is protection for the trademark owner who is *unable* to establish consumer confusion. Once the prerequisites for a dilution claim are satisfied, the owner of a mark can bring an action against any use of that mark that dilutes the distinctive quality of that mark, either through "blurring" or "tarnishment" of that mark; unlike an infringement claim, likelihood of confusion is not necessary. Blurring occurs when the power of the mark is weakened through its identification with dissimilar goods, for example, IBM brand bicycles or Xerox brand paint brushes Although neither example is likely to cause confusion among consumers, each dilutes the distinctive quality of the mark. Tarnishment occurs when the mark is cast in an unflattering light, typically through its association with inferior or unseemly products or services.

CONCEPT SUMMARY Trademarks

- A trademark is a word, symbol, or phrase used to identify a seller's product and distinguish it from other products.

- Businesses invest significant resources in trademark design; these marks are among a company's most valuable assets.

- Trademark protection is a combination of state law and a federal statute known as the Lanham Act.

- Trademark protection is obtained either through initial use in commerce or registration with the USPTO.

- Managers should focus special attention to policing their firm's mark, that is, having a policy in place and taking steps to prevent others from using the mark. Otherwise, the mark may be lost through abandonment or genericity

- In order to prove infringement, the mark owner must prove that use of the mark by another could cause consumer confusion or that the use of the mark dilutes or tarnishes the mark.

COPYRIGHT LAW: PROTECTIONS OF ORIGINAL EXPRESSIONS

Black's Law Dictionary defines a copyright as "the right of literary property as recognized and sanctioned by positive law." More precisely, copyright protection is an intangible right granted by the Copyright Act of 1976[6] (a federal statute) to the author or originator of an *original* literary or artistic production, where the artist is invested, for a specified period (see Table 24.1), with the sole and exclusive privilege of multiplying copies of the work along with the right to profit by publication and sale.

The Copyright Act allows creators to obtain a copyright by having an "original work of authorship fixed in any tangible medium of expression, not known or later developed, from which they can be perceived, reproduced, or otherwise communicated, either directly or with the aid of a machine or device."[7]

Protected works include literary works, musical works, dramatic works, choreographic works, motion pictures, sound recordings, and pictorial or graphical works. Works that *cannot* be protected include ideas, procedures, processes, systems, methods of operation, concepts, principles, or discoveries, no matter how it is explained, illustrated, or described.[8]

Fundamentally, in order to gain copyright protection, a work must meet a three-part test: (1) **originality,** (2) some degree of **creativity,** and (3) fixed in a **durable medium.**

TABLE 24.1 Copyright Protection Periods

Copyright Owner	Copyright Duration
Sole author or originator	70 years from death of the author or originator.
Publisher or other party (works for hire)	First of (1) 120 years from the date of creation, or (2) 95 years from the date of publication.
More than one author or originator	70 years from the death of the last surviving author or originator.

Originality and Creativity Requirements

The meaning of the word *original* has brought about the most controversy in interpreting the requirements of the Copyright Act. What is to be considered original, and what guidelines should be used to determine originality? The courts have ruled that an original work of authorship is a work that is original to the *author;* meaning, the author must use *her own creative capabilities* to create the work or medium. Does this mean that a compilation of noncopyrightable facts (such as names and telephone numbers) can be copyrighted as long as one author put the collaboration together first or in a creative way? In *Feist Publications, Inc. v. Rural Telephone Service,*[9] the landmark case on copyright originality and creativity,

---

[6]17 U.S.C. § 101, et seq.

[7]17 U.S.C. § 102(a).

[8]Note that ideas, procedures, systems, and the like may be covered by intellectual property protections other than copyright law.

[9]499 U.S. 340 (1991). This case was the beginning of the phone book battles. Once *Feist* was decided, several different publication companies began to compete with telephone companies for Yellow Pages advertising. This one decision spurred a new niche in the publishing industry.

the U.S. Supreme Court gave some guidance as to what level of creativity was necessary to meet the originality requirements. The Court ruled that, although compilations of facts could be copyrightable, there had to be some *creative* element used that made the compilation an original work. For example, the White Pages of a telephone directory do not meet the creativity requirement because they are simply arranged alphabetically. One federal appellate court has even held that the Yellow Pages listings of a telephone directory do not meet the originality requirement.[10]

Durable Medium

To be protected, a work must be fixed in a *durable medium.* This underscores the copyright law's requirement that the work must be more than just an idea or thought process. In fact, the work must be in a tangible form such as in writing, digital, video, and so forth. Copyright protections extend automatically to a work once created. Although there is no need to register the work with the United States Copyright Office to obtain protection, registration is a prerequisite to actually *enforcing* the holder's rights in court.

COPYRIGHT INFRINGEMENT

LO24-6

When a copyright holder pursues a party that it believes has infringed on its copyright, the aggrieved party will generally pursue one of three *theories of infringement.* These theories have been developed by the federal courts to sort out the various ways by which one could infringe upon a copyright. These theories are *direct, indirect* (also known as *contributory*), or *vicarious* infringement.

Direct Infringement

Direct infringement occurs when the copyright owner can prove legal ownership of the work in question and that the infringer copied the work without permission. While the first element is straightforward, the second element is more complex than appears at first glance. In the context of the copyright protections afforded by law, it is clear that the word *copied* must have an expansive definition rather than a narrow one (i.e., copy means more than an exact replica). At the same time, of course, the definition cannot be so expansive as to foreclose any works of the same category.

Courts have developed the *substantial similarity standard* to guide the definition of copy under copyright laws. Thus, a copyright holder need only prove that the infringer copied plots, structures, and/or organizations that made the infringing work substantially similar to the copyrighted work.

Indirect Infringement

Indirect infringement (also known as *contributory infringement*) involves three parties: the copyright owner, the direct infringer, and the *facilitator* of the infringement. The theory of indirect infringement is one that holds the facilitator liable for damages. Therefore, before pursuing a theory of indirect infringement, the copyright owner must identify the direct infringer. Normally, in order for the facilitator to be liable, the party must have knowledge (direct or imputed) of the infringement and/or contribute to the infringement in some material way. In the famous case of *A&M Records, Inc. v. Napster, Inc.,*[11] a federal appeals court held that Napster's business model of facilitating a peer-to-peer community for sharing of digital music files constituted contributory infringement because Napster had the ability to locate infringing material listed on its search

Legal Speak »))
Direct and Imputed Knowledge Direct knowledge implies a party has firsthand, actual knowledge of a fact. Imputed knowledge is gained from circumstances or a relationship with a third party where a diligent party "should have known" about the fact at issue.

---

[10]*BellSouth Advertising v. Donnelley Information Publishing,* 999 F.2d 1436 (11th Cir. 1993).
[11]239 F.3d 1004 (2001).

engines and the right to terminate users' access to the system. Digital file sharing is discussed more extensively later in this section (see Legal Implications in Cyberspace: Copyrights in the Digital Age).

Vicarious Infringement

The final copyright infringement theory, **vicarious infringement,** is similar to the indirect infringement theory in that they both involve third parties not involved in actual direct infringement. Vicarious liability is based on agency law (see Chapter 10, "Agency and Employment Relationships") and can be used as a theory of liability when the infringing party (the agent) is acting on behalf of or to the benefit of another party (the principal). In that case, the principal party is said to be vicariously liable. The copyright owner will be entitled to remedies against the principal to the same extent as the direct infringer. Vicarious liability most often occurs in an employer–employee circumstance where the employee is acting with authority from the employer and commits an act of infringement that benefits the employer.

The **No Electronic Theft Act**[12] (NET Act) of 1997 gave sharper teeth to the Copyright Act's previous criminal sanctions. The NET Act provides for criminal liability for anyone infringing on a copyright by making a reproduction or distribution, including by electronic means, of one or more copies of a copyrighted work with a total retail value of more $1,000. Penalties include maximum fines of $250,000 and potential incarceration.[13]

Defense to Infringement Claims: Fair Use

Copyright owners do not enjoy unlimited rights to their work. Rather, the law balances public interests with the property rights of copyright owners. The most common and powerful defense is **fair use.** A landmark case on the fair use defense is the U.S. Supreme Court's decision in *Universal Studios v. Sony,*[14] where the Court ruled that Sony's manufacturing and selling of Betamax (the first videocassette tape recording format used in a home videocassette recorder, or VCR, which was the precursor to digital video recording technology) was *not* **per se** infringement. The Court made clear that Congress did not give absolute control over all uses of copyrighted materials. Some uses were *permitted* and because the device could still be used for "substantial non-infringing uses" the Court held that Sony was not liable for contributory infringement. This *fair use exception,* known as the *Sony defense* or the *Betamax doctrine,* was used, unsuccessfully, as the basis for the defense in the *A&M Records v. Napster* case (discussed previously in this chapter) and was reexamined by the U.S. Supreme Court in the *MGM v. Grokster* case (discussed later in the chapter).[15] Fair use has also been extended to the use of a work for parody or satirical purposes.[16]

---

[12]17 U.S.C. § 506.

[13]A catalyst for this law was a criminal case brought against an MIT student that posted copyrighted software on the Web free of charge for anyone to download. The government could not obtain a conviction in the case because the existing law (prior to the NET Act) only imposed criminal liability when the infringement was undertaken for private *financial* gain. The NET Act eliminated the financial gain requirement for a criminal conviction. See *U.S. v. LaMacchia,* 871 F. Supp. 535 (D. Mass. 1994).

[14]464 U.S. 417. After Sony had started producing videotape recorders (sold under the brand name Betamax) in a price range that many consumers could afford, Universal saw the mass distribution of this product as a threat to its business and market share. They sued Sony on an infringement theory, claiming that consumers were using the Sony product to copy their copyrighted movies.

[15]See Legal Implications in Cyberspace: Copyrights in the Digital Age.

[16]*Campbell v. Acuff-Rose Music, Inc.,* 510 U.S. 569 (1994).

The term *fair use* has now been codified in the Copyright Act with four specific (though nonexclusive) guideposts: the *purpose* and *nature* of the use, the nature of the *work* itself, the *amount* and substantiality of the material used, and the *effect* of the use on the market.

Purpose and Nature of the Use   If the use of the work is to further education or scholarship, courts are more likely to be sympathetic to an assertion of fair use. This does not mean, however, that whole sections of textbooks or copied videotapes may be used with impunity. Also, if the use is for some commercially profitable purpose, this will weigh heavily against the infringer. This is not to say that commercial use is a complete bar to assertion of fair use.

Nature of the Work   If the copyrighted material has not yet been put into the public domain, fair use is a difficult defense. This is not to say that a complete bar to nonpublic works exists; newsworthy and factual information are still subject to fair use.

Amount and Substantiality Used   Courts essentially analyze the totality of the circumstances regarding the amount of copyrighted material used compared to the entire work at issue. Short phrases and limited use of the copyrighted work are often protected by the fair use defense.

Market Effect   Courts are reluctant to allow fair use as a defense (even if the use fits the other three categories) if a copyright holder demonstrates that the *value* of a copyrighted work will be diminished by allowing its use. Fair use cannot impair the marketability or economic success of the copyrighted work.

 Self-Check   Fair Use

Which of these situations would constitute fair use?

1. A manager photocopies an article of interest from *The Wall Street Journal* and distributes it to three co-workers who also may be interested.

2. A company buys one copy of a training manual from a publisher, and then distributes photocopies of entire chapters to its workforce.

3. An executive rents out a DVD on motivation from her local video/DVD store. The next day, she shows the DVD during work hours to her management team in order to inspire them to adopt certain leadership practices.

4. A firm that arranges corporate training sessions buys a DVD that features former General Electric CEO Jack Welch on problem-solving skills for executives. The firm shows 30 minutes of this DVD at the beginning of each of its eight-hour training sessions called "Solutions for Solving," for which they charge $500 per person for the entire session.

Answers to this Self-Check are provided at the end of the chapter.

RIAA Lawsuits

In addition to aggressively pursuing file-sharing services such as Napster and Grokster, the motion picture and music recording industry has filed thousands of infringement lawsuits against individuals engaged in file sharing. The Recording Industry Association of American (RIAA) has invested substantial resources in tracking down and recovering damages from individual infringers. In a 2009 case that garnered substantial media attention, a jury imposed damages of $1.92 million against Jammie Thomas-Rasset in a federal court in Minnesota. The award was the result of a lawsuit filed by RIAA against Thomas-Rasset that alleged she downloaded more than 1,700 copyrighted songs.

Legal Speak >))
Infringement The unlawful use of another's intellectual property.

Copyrights in the Digital Age

Technology has created new challenges for legislatures and courts struggling with applying copyright law in the digital age.

Computer Software   In order to settle uncertainty in the computer science field about the ability to copyright computer software, Congress amended the Copyright Act with the Computer Software Copyright Act.* This law, passed in 1980, specifically defined computer software programs as a literary work and, thus, entitled to protection. However, the nature of computer software brings with it a good deal of uncertainty in terms of copyright protection. In 1986, the landmark case of *Whelan v. Jaslow*[†] gave the first guidance by an appellate court on the issue of copyright protection for software and indicated that courts were willing to extend broad protection to computer programs, including both the "look and feel" of a program's displays and also the program's structure, sequence, and organization. More recently, courts have been carving back this broad protection and adopting a more sophisticated test. One appellate court also made clear that patents, not copyrights, would be the most suitable form of intellectual property protection to protect the dynamic aspects of writing computer software programs.[‡]

Evolution of Copyright Law and Technology

The revolutionary technological gains and the increasing popularity of the information superhighway has led to significant threats to copyright holders such as record labels and movie studios. In the past, copyright infringement of movies and music was limited because the technology that existed to copy these media was not capable of producing mass copies, except through a sophisticated criminal network. In short, the average consumer was limited in what he could copy and distribute and, thus, copyright holders had little fear that day-to-day consumer infringement would impact their revenue stream from sales of the original. However, when the digital age truly arrived, copyright holders responded by lobbying Congress for additional protections in the area of copyright laws.

*17 U.S.C.A. § 117.
[†]797 F.2d 1222 (3rd Cir. 1986).
[‡]*Computer Associates International v. Latai, Inc.*, 982 F.2d 693 (2nd Cir. 1992).

Audio Home Recording Act   The Audio Home Recording Act (AHRM), a 1992 amendment to the Copyright Act, was a response to the rapidly advancing technology of digital audio that emerged in the early 1990s. This new digital technology industry threatened the major record labels because it caused enforceability problems for the copyright protection of musical recordings. In the early 1990s, these digitally copied recordings became increasingly common because the recording device, a CD-Writer, became standard equipment with many computer packages. The AHRA forced manufacturers of CD-Writers to pay royalties (2 percent of their sales) to a fund administered by the Copyright Office, and eventually paid to copyright owners. It also required the producers of a digital audio recording device to include a Serial Copy Management System (SCMS) that, through computer software, prevents copies from copies to be made, but does not prevent copies from originals to be created.

Digital Millennium Copyright Act   Congress passed the Digital Millennium Copyright Act (DMCA) in 1998 in an attempt to modernize copyright law to deal with the new challenges that had emerged in the digital age. The DMCA was controversial because it added substantial protections to copyright holders of digital products and gave immunity to internet service providers (ISPs) for certain copyright liability. Some of the major provisions of the DMCA are:

- Civil and criminal penalties established for anyone who produces, sells, or distributes any product or service that circumvents antipiracy software or other antipiracy technology.

- Restriction of import or distribution of analog video recorders and camcorders that lack antipiracy features.

- ISPs have no liability for copyright infringement by their users (such as posting copyrighted software on an ISP's electronic bulletin board) so long as the ISP does not have actual knowledge of the infringing material.

File Sharing   Technology changed the status quo rapidly. The late 1990s saw the introduction of two very important technological advances: (1) the popular music file format known as MP3 (essentially compressed digital files), and (2) the increasing speed advancements

(continued)

of the Internet. These two additions changed the once hours-long process of transferring music and movies over the Internet to a process that took just a few minutes or less. The MP3 file popularity grew very quickly. This, in turn, brought about the ability to upload and download music and video files from one private personal computer to another. The ability to upload and download hundreds of files a day led to the establishment of peer-to-peer (P2P) networking and, of course, entrepreneurs who have leveraged this technology into profit. The pioneer of P2P file-sharing communities was Napster. As discussed, the Ninth Circuit Court of Appeals effectively shut down Napster after they ruled that Napster's business model was inherently illegal because Napster had imputed knowledge of copyright infringement. However, other Napster-like services were thriving under a business model whereby the P2P provider could not have any actual knowledge of copyright infringement. The motion picture and recording industries doggedly pursued each of these companies by suing them under a contributory infringement theory. Of course, Napster eventually reemerged as a pay for subscription service. Ultimately, the issue of what level of intent was necessary to constitute infringement was decided by the U.S. Supreme Court in Landmark Case 24.1.

CONCEPT SUMMARY   Copyrights

- Copyright protection is an intangible right granted by the Copyright Act to the author or originator of an original literary or artistic production.
- In order to obtain copyright protection, the work must be a result of some creative capability by the author/originator and it must be fixed in a durable medium (such as in writing).
- There are three theories of infringement: direct, indirect (also known as contributory), and vicarious.
- A powerful defense is "fair use" of copyrighted material where a court will examine the purpose and nature of the use, the nature of the work, the amount used, and the market effect of the use.

PATENTS: LEGAL PROTECTION OF INVENTIONS AND PROCESSES

A patent is a government-sanctioned monopoly right that allows an inventor the exclusive entitlement to make, use, license, and sell her invention for a limited period of time. Patent rights are important in the entire businesses community, but are particularly vital to the manufacturing, technology, and pharmaceutical sectors. Patents are often an important part of the planning for these firms because their business model depends on the benefits of obtaining a patent; that is, the full legal protection of their ideas, methods, and inventions. Once a patent is obtained, a competitor is barred from profiting off the patented device or process during the life of the patent. Thus, a patent can be a firm's most important and valuable asset.

Understanding the fundamentals and discarding the myths of patent laws are important for managers. The most common myth is an assumption that nearly any new idea or invention is "patentable" (able to obtain patent law protection). This assumption is *not* true

FACT SUMMARY After the Napster decision, a number of other P2P file-sharing communities emerged with a slightly different business model. One famous firm, Grokster, used a business model whereby it would be *impossible* for Grokster to know if the files being shared were an infringing use. Thus, Grokster argued, no Napster-like imputed liability could attach and no contributor infringement existed. According to Grokster (and many other such firms that were emerging), this is precisely the same business that Sony was in when selling the Betamax and they were entitled to the same type of fair use exception of "capable of substantial non-infringing uses" as the Supreme Court articulated in the *Sony* case. When MGM studios sued Grokster (and others including StreamCast, the distributor of Morpheus software) both the federal trial court and the federal court of appeals *agreed* with Grokster and allowed Grokster to use the *Sony* exception in their ruling against MGM.*

SYNOPSIS OF DECISION AND OPINION The Supreme Court unanimously held that Grokster *could* be liable for inducing copyright infringement and reversed the court of appeals ruling. The Court specifically ruled that anyone who distributes a device with the intent to promote its use to infringe copyright is liable for the resulting acts of infringement (contributory) by third parties. Although there was some disagreement among the Justices about the *Sony* defense, ultimately the Court held that the lower courts had misapplied the *Sony* exception because there was ample evidence that Grokster had acted with intent to cause copyright infringement via the use of their software.

WORDS OF THE COURT: Evidence of Intent "Three features of this evidence of intent are particularly notable. First, each company showed itself to be aiming to satisfy a known source of demand for copyright infringement, the market comprising former Napster users. StreamCast's internal documents made constant reference to Napster, it initially distributed its Morpheus software through an OpenNap program compatible with Napster, it advertised its OpenNap program to Napster users, and its Morpheus software functions as Napster did except that it could be used to distribute more kinds of files, including copyrighted movies and software programs. Grokster's name is apparently derived from Napster, it too initially offered an OpenNap program, its software's function is likewise comparable to Napster's, and it attempted to divert queries for Napster onto its own Web site. Grokster and StreamCast's efforts to supply services to former Napster users, deprived of a mechanism to copy and distribute what were overwhelmingly infringing files, indicate a principal, if not exclusive, intent on the part of each to bring about infringement."

Case Questions

1. Why was the Court so concerned about the Open Nap program offered by StreamCast and Grokster?

2. Why do your think the Court refused to apply the *Sony* exception in this case?

*Metro-Goldwyn-Mayer Studios v. Grokster, Ltd., 380 F.3d 1154 (9th Cir. 2004).

and may be an expensive lesson to learn. In fact, in order to obtain a patent, the idea or invention must meet stringent criteria set down in federal statutes. The patent application procedure is often very expensive because one must almost always obtain counsel that specializes in patent law. These law firms, known colloquially as intellectual property (or simply "IP") firms, are often more expensive than expert counsel in other areas of the law given the specialized nature of their services.

Even if one is successful in obtaining a patent, enforcing the patent via an infringement suit is an even more expensive undertaking. According to a study in *The New York Times,* the median cost for enforcing a patent (assuming an infringement suit is necessary) is around $1.2 million. This significant cost factor must be considered in a company's patent management strategy.

Avoiding Intellectual Property Liability: Landmines on the Web

PROBLEM *Managers that oversee an Internet-based marketing model are often barraged with conflicting information and advice about trademark and copyright law.*

By taking simple and inexpensive precautions, managers can help protect their company from infringement liability.

SOLUTION #1 *Limit your linking.*

Courts have allowed the use of a typical hypertext link so long as the use is reasonable under the circumstances. Inline imaging, framing, and even deep linking have all been given legal protection so long as the essence of the copyright and trademark laws are protected. However, an attempt to use a link to create confusion by the consumer that ultimately could result in the consumer being directed to a competing business would constitute infringement.

For example, let's suppose that MuseumTicketsRUs is a registered trademark of a company that sells tickets to museum exhibits in major cities and that it hosts a Web site, MuseumTicketsRUs.com. A second firm, Artists.com, hosts a Web site that provides links to all museum Web sites, all museum online stores, art supply stores, and the like. If Artists.com simply provides a link to MuseumTicketsRUs, then no copyright or trademark infringement has taken place. However, if Artists.com uses MusuemTicketsRUs's logo, similar name, or other similar identifying characteristic, and uses the link to direct a consumer-user to a competing site with which Artists.com has a commissioned-based agreement, this would clearly constitute infringement and expose Artists.com to significant legal liability. Thus, it is a good idea to take steps to avoid any consumer confusion such as displaying a disclaimer that the originating site with the link is *not* related to or a part of the linked site.

Deep linking (i.e., linking to an embedded site) may be cause for additional concerns if the embedded site skips through advertising that the Web page host has placed in the original site. It is a good practice to use links only to originating Web pages (home pages) or at the very least to offer links to *both* the originating home page and the deep-linked page in close proximity with labels for the user that describe the content of the page. Moreover, if the linked site has taken technical steps to prevent linking or given notice that they do not sanction deep linking, this should give a manager pause because they may be crossing the line of reasonableness into infringement.

The ultimate protection against infringement, of course, is obtaining express permission to deep link or image. The owner of the site will often give you permission so long as your site is not a competitor or a site that may tend to tarnish their image (such as adult-content sites). A simple form for this permission is shown.

Agreement and Permission to Use

This Agreement, made this ___ day of October, 2010, between Museum TicketsRUs (Owner) and Artists.com (User), acknowledging sufficient consideration, the parties agree as follows:

1. Owner permits User to link, deep link, inline image, or frame Owner's Web site (www.MuseumTicketsRUs.com) from User's Web site (www.Artists.com).

2. User shall be entitled to use this permission until such time as Owner gives User 48 hours' notice via e-mail to cease the use of the link. Owner has the absolute and unconditional power to revoke this permission at anytime and for any reason.

3. Upon such notice, User agrees to cease the use of any and all links to Owner's Web site as soon as possible.

4. Owner shall not be entitled to any compensation under this Agreement.

Signed: _____ (Owner)   Date:

_____ (User)   Date:

continued

Avoiding Intellectual Property Liability: Landmines on the Web

SOLUTION #2 *Make copyrighted images thumbnail size.*

A significant amount of litigation has ensued over the use of copyrighted photos in thumbnail size as a means to preview the content for a consumer using an Internet search engine or consumers who link to another page via the thumbnail image. The idea, of course, is to allow the consumer-user attempting to find a particular photograph or image to scan multiple images and choose, rather than having to actually link to the actual page to view, the photos, thus saving the consumer user time.

Copying the image of another is clearly infringement. For example, if Best Furniture, a large retailer of patio furniture, takes photographs of its products and displays them on their Web site, the use of those photos by a competing retailer on their own Web site (or in a catalog for that matter) is clearly illegal. However, let's suppose that a Web site that is hosted by Patio and Deck Contractors Inc. provides thumbnail images of Best Furniture's patio furniture photos on its Web site with a link to Best Furniture's site as a service to Patio and Deck Contractors' customers. In this instance, the uses of the images are legal under the fair use exception to the Copyright Act.

An overwhelming majority of courts have ruled that use of thumbnail photograph images by Internet Web sites has "transformed" the original photograph in such a way as to make the use of the images legal.

LO24-7

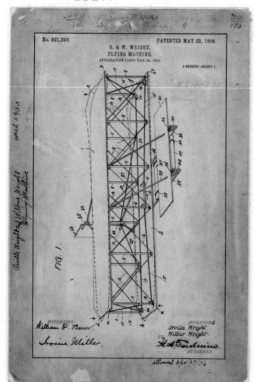

The patent issued to the Wright brothers in 1906 for their flying machine began a new era in global commerce.

FUNDAMENTALS OF PATENT LAW

Patent law in the United States dates back to 1790 and is governed by the Patent Act established by the very same Congress that ratified the U.S. Constitution. Of course, the law has been amended since then, but the basic standards have not changed much. A patent for inventions or processes (also known as "utility" and "business method patents," respectively) lasts for a period of 20 years from the date of filing the application with the USPTO. A "design" patent (discussed later) lasts for 14 years.

In order to obtain a patent, an invention must be *novel, nonobvious,* and a *proper subject matter* for protection under the patent law.

Novelty Standard

An invention or process must be unique and original, and a patent applicant must show that no other identical invention or process exists. The statute delineates the guidelines for this **novelty standard** based on a three-prong test. The first prong is the "public use" test, and requires that the invention or process *not already be* in public use. The second prong governs priority for inventors of the same invention or process. The American standard is known as the "first-to-invent" rule, which provides that the inventor who has been determined to *invent* first (not the inventor who has *filed* first) has priority over other inventors of the same product. The final prong requires a determination by the USPTO that the applicant

FACT SUMMARY DuPont chemical company produced a chemical known as Surlyn in 1964. Before DuPont found a commercial use for it, Butch Wagner, who was in the business of selling re-covered golf balls, began to experiment with Surlyn as a golf ball cover. In November 1964 he had developed the formula so that it was suitable to give unprecedented durability to a golf ball and began to sell the Surlyn covered balls that same year. Wagner never applied for a patent. Subsequently, Dunlop obtained a patent for Surlyn covered golf balls and when RAM began to produce the same type of golf balls, Dunlop sued RAM for infringement. RAM defended their use by challenging Dunlop's patent as invalid because Wagner made the invention public 10 years earlier via his sale of many Surlyn covered balls to a group of regular customers. Dunlop countered that Wagner had concealed an important ingredient and, thus, had concealed the actual invention from the public. The trial court agreed with RAM holding that Wagner's public use barred Dunlop from obtaining a patent.

SYNOPSIS OF DECISION AND OPINION The appellate court affirmed the ruling of the trial court against Dunlop. The court held Wagner's golf balls that were coated with the Surlyn-based invention were in public use because Wagner had marketed and sold the items as best he could as a sole proprietor. The court also ruled that the fact that Wagner did not reveal a key ingredient of the invention to the public was not relevant. Thus, Dunlop could not pass the first prong of the novelty standard (public use test) and is not entitled to a patent.

WORDS OF THE COURT: Public Use Test "The patent claims are broad enough to encompass any golf ball cover made principally of Surlyn, and there is no doubt that Wagner had made a large number of such golf balls and successfully placed them in public use. The only novel feature of this case arises from the fact that Wagner was careful not to disclose to the public the ingredient that made his golf ball so tough. [. . .] But in this case, although Wagner may have failed to act diligently to establish his own right to a patent, there was no lack of diligence in his attempt to make the benefits of his discovery available to the public. [. . .] [T]he evidence clearly demonstrates that Wagner endeavored to market his golf balls as promptly and effectively as possible. The balls themselves were in wide public use."

Case Questions
1. What factors did the court consider in ruling that Wagner's use was public?
2. What is Dunlop's theory as to why Wagner's conduct did not make the prior use public?

---

filed the patent within a reasonable time of the invention. Landmark Case 24.2 sets out the public use test of the novelty standard.

Nonobviousness Standard

The **nonobviousness standard** requires that an invention must be something more than that which would be obvious, in light of publicly available knowledge, to one who is skilled in the relevant field. In other words, a patent cannot be granted for minimal improvements that were relatively obvious to those in the field. For example, Joanna adds a small extender switch to her lawnmower (an existing patented invention) that will make it easier for taller people to kill the engine. Joanna is not entitled to a new patent because the invention is essentially a minimal (also called *de minimus*) improvement and relatively obvious.

Patentable Subject Matter Standard

Note that not all processes and inventions that are nonobvious and novel are patentable. The **patentable subject matter standard** bars laws of nature, natural phenomena, and abstract ideas from being patentable. Albert Einstein's theory of relativity was groundbreaking. It was new and nonobvious beyond question. But should this natural phenomenon be patentable? The patent system was not intended to cover every novel and nonobvious idea. The courts have held that some mathematical algorithms, materials common to nature (penicillin, for example), or unapplied ideas are not patentable. Ultimately, patent laws cover processes and ideas based on human ingenuity.

Business Method Patents   Because of the exclusion of certain subject matter from patent protection, courts have historically struggled with the notion of giving patent protection to a process developed by a business in the name of efficiency or some competitive advantage. Some courts rejected novel, useful, and commercially successful business methods as nonpatentable subject matter. However, in 1998, a federal appeals court helped settled many issues related to business method patents and provided guidance for other courts in the landmark case of *State Street Bank & Trust Co. v. Signature Financial Group.*[17] The *State Street* court articulated a cogent legal theory whereby business methods may be patentable so long as they accomplish something practically useful in a novel and nonobvious way. The case also provided a road map for the emerging Internet business community to plan Internet business models in such a way as to be eligible for patent protection. More recently, the U.S. Supreme Court upheld the notion that business methods, such as a system that institutions could use to hedge the seasonal risks of buying energy, were patentable.[18]

Design Patents   Patent laws also protect inventors of any new, original, and ornamental design for an article of manufacture. Design patents are subject to the same requirements as utility or business method patents (novelty and nonobvious) and the design must be primarily ornamental (not primarily functional). Design patents are mainly concerned with protecting the appearance of an article. The shape of the classic Coca-Cola bottle is a famous example of a design based primarily on appearance, not function.

LO24-8 INFRINGEMENT, NOTICE, AND REMEDIES

Infringement is defined in the Patent Act as "[W]hoever without authority makes, uses or sells any patented invention, within the United States during the term of the patent therefore, infringes the patent." Anyone who "actively induces infringement" of a patent is considered an infringer as well. Infringement occurs in one of two ways: *literal infringement* or through *equivalence.*

Literal Infringement

The courts have developed three rules for determining whether **literal patent infringement** has occurred. The **rule of exactness** applies when the infringer makes, uses, or sells an invention that is exactly the same as the claims made in the patent application, thus infringing on the patent. An infringement also occurs if the infringing device does *more* than is described in the patent application of the protected invention. This literal infringement is known as the **rule of addition.** Under the **rule of omission,** however, when the alleged infringing invention lacks an essential element of the patent holder's claims in the patent application, infringement has *not* occurred.

Equivalence

The rule of omission is subject to abuse because individuals may avoid infringement liability by omitting an element of the patented device and substituting another element that is substantially similar, but not exact. To prevent this abuse, the Supreme Court developed a

---

[17]149 F.3d 1368 (Fed. Cir. 1998). The case involved a challenge to a patent issued to Signature for a process that facilitated a method whereby several mutual funds pooled their investments into a single fund that achieved management cost savings over many other funds.
[18]*Bilsk: v. Kappos,* 561 U.S. ___ (2010)

Computer Software and Internet Business Methods

Computer Programs Of course, technology continues to give us new challenges as to what is and what is not patentable material. In the early 1970s, the Supreme Court took the view that computer programs and the machines that process them are nothing more than glorified algorithms and, therefore, not patentable. But in 1981, the Court decided *Diamond v. Diehr** and "clarified" (some would say reversed) its position, ruling that some computer programs *could* be patented. Eventually, the courts developed a test to determine whether algorithm-based computer programming was patentable. The test was designed to investigate whether the computer-related process was applied in some fashion to physical elements or processes. In other words, did the algorithm allow a certain physical transformation to take place? If the computer programs were accompanied by some physical transformation, then they were patentable.

Internet Business Method Patents After the court opened the door to business method patents in the 1998 *State Street* case (discussed earlier), many Internet-based businesses applied for patents. According to the USPTO, the number of patent applications for Internet business methods have increased nearly 800 percent. One of the most famous Internet business method patents was granted to Amazon for its "One-Click" ordering system that stores a customer's billing and shipping information so it does not have to be reentered on subsequent visits to the site. In a highly publicized case during the technology boom of the late 1990s, Amazon (still a relative newcomer in the bookselling business at the time) sued mega-bookseller Barnes and Noble over Barnes and Noble's use of an "Express Lane" option on its Web site that was similar to Amazon's patent in that the feature allowed consumers to "buy it now with just 1 click." Barnes and Noble defended on the basis that the patent should not have been issued because the invention was too obvious. After a preliminary defeat in the federal courts for Amazon,[†] the parties settled the dispute in March 2002. Although Amazon lost on what was essentially thought of as a procedural issue, one important victory was that they *did not* lose the patent on the basis of nonobviousness. Therefore, the court signaled that Internet business methods, so long as they fit the requirements for other utility and method patents, were protectible.

In some cases though, courts have been reluctant to enforce business method patents in the technology sector when the process described in the patent is too narrow due to the lack of technology at the time of the patent. In 2002, a California college professor sued Netscape, Microsoft, and AOL for infringing on a patent he obtained relating to efficiency in Web site interactivity. The federal appeals court affirmed the ruling of the trial court, which found that the professor's patents were invalid altogether and that the patent description was too generic to be enforceable.[‡]

---

*450 U.S. 175 (1981). The case involved a patent application for a computer program that facilitated molding uncured synthetic rubber into cured rubber. According to the patent application, the process differed from the previously employed method because of the use of specific mathematical formulas, which would allow for a more accurate measuring of material heating and feeding times. The patent was rejected by the USPTO because the patent examiner did not consider the process met the subject matter requirements of the Patent Act.
[†]*Amazon.com, Inc. v. Barnesandnoble.com, Inc.*, 239 F.3d 1343 (Fed. Cir. 2001).
[‡]*Netscape Corp. v. Konrad*, 295 F.3d 1315 (Fed. Cir. 2002).

---

doctrine that allowed courts to find infringement if the invention performs *substantially the same function* in substantially the same way to achieve the same result. The doctrine, known as the **doctrine of equivalence,** however, is limited to an evaluation of whether any of the key elements of the claim have been interchanged with known equivalents.

The Patent Act sets forth appropriate measures that must be taken to properly inform users that an article is patented. This is often done by placing the word *patent,* the symbol "pat.," or the patent number on the specific article. If no marking is identifiable, then the patentee is unable to collect damages from the infringers unless they were properly warned and still continued to infringe.

Patent infringers are subject to the following damages:

- *Actual damages.* Includes profit from lost sales and royalties for any sale made by the infringer, for example.
- *Prejudgment interest.* It is not uncommon for years to pass before an infringer is spotted; thus, revenue from possible sales may have been withheld from the patentee for a long period of time.
- *Attorney's fees.* The prevailing party may receive reasonable attorney's fees where the infringer has acted in bad faith (i.e., had received notice that the invention was patented and yet continued his infringing conduct).

CONCEPT SUMMARY Patents

- A patent is a government-sanctioned monopoly right that allows an inventor the exclusive rights over an invention or method for a limited period of time.
- In order to obtain a patent, the invention or method must be novel, nonobvious, and of proper subject matter (natural phenomena are not protected under patent laws).
- Some business methods are patentable so long as they accomplish something practically useful in a novel and nonobvious way.
- Infringement may occur through either literal means or through equivalence.

TABLE 24.2 Intellectual Property Protections

Type	Coverage	Source of Law	Example	Duration
Trade secrets	Secret processes, formulas, methods, procedures, and lists that provide the owner with economic advantage.	State statutes based on Uniform Trade Secret Act and/or state common law.	Customer lists with contact information, buying patterns, and credit histories.	Life of the entity/owner.
Trademarks/ Service marks/ Trade dress	Words, symbols, or phrases that identify a particular seller's product/service and distinguish them from other products/services. Trade dress extends trademark protection to shape or color scheme of a product.	Federal statute (Lanham Act) and some state and federal common law.	Google (Trademark) VISA (Service mark) iPod's shape (Trade dress)	Unlimited; so long as owner actively protects ("polices") the use of the mark.
Copyright	Authors and originators of literary or artistic production.	Federal statute (Copyright Act of 1976, as amended).	Rights of a recording artist and writer of a song.	Author: 70 years from death of the author. Work for hire: 120 years from date of creation or 95 years from publication.
Patents	Inventors for exclusive rights to make, use, license, or sell an invention.	Federal statute: Patent Act	Rights to a newly discovered pharmaceutical.	20 years from date of filing except for design patents (14 years).

Misappropriation p. 602 The acquisition of a trade secret of another by a person who knows or has reason to know that the trade secret was acquired by improper means, or disclosure of a trade secret to another without express or implied consent.

Economic Espionage Act p. 603 A federal statute passed in 1996 providing criminal penalties for domestic and foreign theft of trade secrets.

Trademark p. 603 A word, symbol, or phrase used to identify a particular seller's products and distinguish them from other products.

Service mark p. 604 A word, symbol, or phrase used to identify a particular seller's services and distinguish them from other services.

Trade dress p. 604 A product's distinctive design, packaging, color, or other appearance that makes it unique from other products or goods.

Secondary meaning p. 606 A requirement for a descriptive trademark to gain protection, acquired when the consuming public primarily associates the mark with a particular product rather than any alternate meaning.

Bad faith p. 607 A legal concept in which a malicious motive on the part of the defendant in a lawsuit is necessary in order for a plaintiff to recover. Under the Anticybersquatting Consumer Protection Act, the court looks to nine factors in making a determination of bad faith intent.

Genericity p. 610 Also known as genericide, the act or process of losing trademark protection occurring when, in the mind of a substantial majority of the public, the word denotes a broad genus or type of product and not a specific source or manufacturer.

Federal Trademark Dilution Act p. 611 A federal law enacted by Congress in 1995, which permits mark holders to recover damages and prevent another from diluting distinctive trademarks.

Originality p. 612 A requirement in order to gain copyright protection in which the author must use his or her own creative capabilities to create the work or medium.

Creativity p. 612 A requirement in order to gain copyright protection in which there must be some creative element used that made the compilation an original work.

Durable medium p. 612 A requirement in order to gain copyright protection in which the work must be in a tangible form such as in writing, digital, video, and so forth.

Direct infringement p. 613 A theory of copyright infringement occurring when the copyright owner can prove legal ownership of the work in question and that the infringer copied the work in a substantially similar manner without permission.

Indirect infringement p. 613 Also known as contributory infringement, a theory of copyright infringement holding a third-party facilitator liable for damages when it has knowledge of the infringement and/or contributes to the infringement in some material way.

Vicarious infringement p. 614 A theory of copyright infringement resulting when there has been a direct infringement and a third-party facilitator is in a position to control the direct infringement and benefits financially from the infringement.

No Electronic Theft Act p. 614 A federal law enacted in 1997 (also referred to as the NET Act), which provides for criminal liability for anyone who infringes on a copyright willfully for financial gain.

Fair use p. 614 A defense against copyright infringement where the court will examine the purpose and nature of the use, the nature of the work, the amount used, and the market effect of the use to determine whether the use is permitted.

Per se p. 614 A Latin term literally meaning "of, in, or by itself" without any additional facts needed to prove a point.

Novelty standard p. 620 A standard to obtain a patent requiring that an invention or process be unique and original and that a patent applicant show that no other identical invention or process exists.

Nonobviousness standard p. 621 A standard to obtain a patent requiring that an invention must be something more than that which would be obvious, in light of publicly available knowledge, to one who is skilled in the relevant field.

Patentable subject matter standard p. 621 A standard that bars laws of nature, natural phenomena, and abstract ideas from being patentable subject matter.

Literal patent infringement p. 622   One way in which patent infringement occurs, applying when the invention or process violates either the rule of exactness or the rule of addition.

Rule of exactness p. 622   A rule for determining whether literal patent infringement has occurred that applies when the infringer makes, uses, or sells an invention that is exactly the same as the claims made in the patent application.

Rule of addition p. 622   A rule for determining whether literal patent infringement has occurred that applies when the infringing device does more than is described in the patent application of the protected invention.

Rule of omission p. 622   A rule stating that when the alleged patent infringing invention lacks an essential element of the patent holder's claims in the patent application, infringement has not occurred.

Doctrine of equivalence p. 623   A doctrine that allows courts to find patent infringement if the invention performs substantially the same function in substantially the same way to achieve the same result.

THEORY TO PRACTICE

WidgetCo. is a manufacturer and wholesaler of a line of widget products with annual revenue of $50 million. Maurice, a mid-level manager at WidgetCo., supervises a work team responsible for assessing quality assurance for the widgets before they are shipped to various retailers around the United States. Maurice and his group have been highly successful in developing a quality assurance process, including the development of training manuals, a video series for new employees, and specific checklists and procedures to ensure that any defective or substandard widgets are detected and repaired prior to shipping.

1. Which forms of intellectual property protections are available to WidgetCo. to protect the quality assurance process and materials that Maurice's team have developed?

2. What are the major advantages and disadvantages to each protection?

3. Compare the facts of the hypothetical in this Theory to Practice with the standards for qualification of a trade secret. Could the process be considered a trade secret under these standards?

4. What steps could the company take to achieve its objective of having the process protected under trade secret laws and avoid misappropriation?

5. If WidgetCo. wanted copyright protection for its manuals and training video series, how would they obtain protection under the Copyright Act? If the manuals are simply a compilation of facts known in the industry, is that protectable?

MANAGER'S CHALLENGE

One major consideration in protecting a trade secret is the efforts by the company to keep the secret confidential. Develop a written policy for WidgetCo. (in Theory to Practice above) to help assure that these trade secrets and materials would be protected and kept confidential under the Uniform Trade Secrets Act. What considerations should management take into account when developing a policy on trade secrets? Be sure to think about primary stakeholders (such as employees who may depart with the trade secrets) and secondary stakeholders (such as third-party visitors or outside auditors that may be privy to the processes and materials). Note that this is not intended to be a legal document. Rather, the policy should be thought of as a draft statement of internal control on trade secrets, processes, and materials. A sample answer may be found on this textbook's Web site at www.mhhe.com/melvin.

TRADE SECRET

Harvey Bennett, Inc., is a company that developed a method designed to be taught to infants on how to survive in the water. The company developed a course in this technique called "swim-float-swim" and generated revenue by training and certifying instructors who then teach the technique to the public at large for a fee. The instructors are trained extensively on the nearly 2,000 procedures necessary to accomplish the technique. All instructors signed a nondisclosure form and an Agreement Not to Compete. When several of the instructors resigned and formed a venture called "Aquatic Survival," Bennett filed suit claiming, among other allegations, misappropriation of the swim-float-swim system.

CASE QUESTIONS

1. Does the swim-float-swim qualify as a trade secret?
2. What factors would the court use to assess whether the technique is a trade secret? Discuss.

TRADEMARKS/SERVICE MARKS

Reed Elsevier operated a Web site that allowed users to identify an attorney using a variety of criteria, including geographic location, practice expertise, and so forth. The Web site, www.lawyers.com, was first used in commerce by Reed in 1998. Later, Reed applied to have lawyers.com registered as a service mark.

CASE QUESTIONS

1. Is the mark too generic for protection?
2. If the court determines the mark is primarily descriptive, what further obstacle must Reed overcome in order to obtain protection for the mark?

PATENTS

KSR designs, manufactures, and sells parts to auto manufacturers (not consumers) and developed a pedal device for Ford vehicles. KSR received a patent on the pedal device. KSR also sold products to General Motors (GM) and, in order to make the pedal device compatible for GM cars, KSR added an electronic throttle control to the pedal device. Teleflex claimed to have a patent for the pedal device that could be connected to such a throttle and, therefore, sued KSR for patent infringement. KSR defended on the basis that the device produced for GM was simply a combination of two existing products and could not be patentable.

CASE QUESTIONS

1. What do you think Teleflex's specific theory of infringement was?
2. Which element of patentability does KSR claim Teleflex is missing in the combined device?

COPYRIGHT

Darden filed an application with the Copyright Office seeking to register his Web site, which he titled "APPRAISERSdotCOM." He described APPRAISERSdotCOM as a derivative work based on "US Census black and white outline maps" and "clip art." Darden's application identified "graphics, text, colors, and arrangement" as the material that he added to the preexisting work and in which he claimed copyright protection. Additionally, Darden filed a separate application for registration of the work "Maps for APPRAISERSdotCOM." Darden described his "maps" work as a derivative work that, similar to the "APPRAISERSdotCOM" work, was based on preexisting U.S. Census black and white outline maps.

CASE QUESTIONS

1. Determine whether Darden's compilation is protectable using the *Feist* doctrine.
2. Does Darden's idea contain the necessary elements for copyright protection? Discuss.

Self-Check **ANSWERS**

Trade Secrets

1. This type of customer data is protectable as a trade secret because of its potential value to a competitor.

2. Probably not protectable unless the system is something highly unique. But the basis of scheduling medical appointments is not typically protectable.

3. Formulas are protectable.

4. Unless the process is highly unique, it is not protectable because it is based on a public source.

5. Software source coding is protectable.

Fair Use

1. Covered by fair use. Limited amount used, noncommercial, and minimal market effect.

2. Not covered by fair use. Market effect and commercial nature of the use would exclude it from the fair use defense.

3. Probably not fair use. The market effect would determine this question, but the commercial nature and the fact that it is the entire DVD would weigh against fair use as a defense.

4. Not fair use. Commercial nature, profit motive, amount and substantiality used, and market effect would bar any use of fair use in this case.

25

CHAPTER

International Law and Global Commerce

learning outcomes checklist

After studying this chapter, students who have mastered the material will be able to:

25-1 Distinguish between international public law and international private law.

25-2 Give examples and explain the various sources that compose the body of international law.

25-3 Explain the role of the various international courts.

25-4 List the different categories of national legal systems used in the world and give an example of a country in each category.

25-5 Apply the standards of the Convention on the Recognition and Enforcement of Foreign Arbitral Awards.

25-6 Explain the various methods of alternate dispute resolution in an international context.

25-7 Articulate several specific laws that regulate international commercial law and understand when each law applies.

25-8 Identify the methods used to enforce the rights of intellectual property holders in foreign countries.

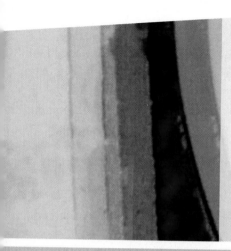

Rapid developments in technology, improvements in export logistics, and creation of additional transportation lines have all been catalysts that propelled our modern global economy. Although large multinational firms have had international business relationships and systems for decades, the new global marketplace has been expanded dramatically to include mid-sized and smaller firms who see international markets as an accessible vehicle for market share growth. Of course, while the potential return may be significant, the risks, especially legal risks, increase substantially in an international business transaction. A working knowledge of international law helps business owners and managers with global interests reduce risk and increase profits. In this chapter, students will learn:

- The definition and sources of international law.

- International dispute resolution methods.

- Commercial and intellectual property regulation in an international context.

DEFINITION, SOURCES, AND SYSTEMS OF INTERNATIONAL LAW

International law has traditionally been defined in very broad terms and not limited simply to rules that are applied to settle disputes in court. Rather, international law is influenced by a combination of law, religious tenets, and diplomatic relations between nations. This broad definition makes enforcement of international laws challenging, and adherence to international law is sometimes based on expectations of reciprocal behavior rather than legal sanctions.

Most legal sources define modern international law as a body of *rules* and *principles* of action binding on countries, international organizations, and individuals in their relations with one another.[1]

Public Law versus Private Law

One important distinction necessary to understanding international law is that it may be categorized as either **public international law,** which primarily addresses relations between individual countries and international organizations, and **private international law,** which focuses on regulation of private individuals and business entities.

Sources of International Law

In one sense, the primary source of international law is the body of law in each individual country. However, international law can also provide individual countries with some degree of harmonized standards that increases reliability and encourages fairness, due process, and barrier-free trade among nations. Therefore, treaties, customs, and judicial decisions are also considered to be sources of international law.

Treaties   A treaty is any agreement between two or more nations to cooperate in a certain manner. Treaties may be related to defense, trade, extradition, and other matters between two countries. Although treaties have been in use since before the Roman Empire, most existing modern day treaties were created after World War II. More recently, the **Vienna Convention on the Law of Treaties,** effective in 1980, has become one of the standards used by courts and other tribunals when interpreting treaty law.[2]

Customs   Along with treaty law, customary international law is a primary source of law affecting individuals and businesses engaged in international transactions. Customary law follows the basic principle of international law that individual conduct is permitted unless expressly forbidden. Therefore, prohibitions as well as affirmative practices must be proven by the state relying on them.

Judicial Decisions   Most treaties and national laws recognize both an international tribunal, such as the International Court of Justice (discussed later), or a ruling by a national court applying international law principles. One important concept related to judicial decisions as a source of international law is *comity.* **Comity** is the general notion that nations will defer to and give effect to the laws and court decisions of other nations. However, comity is not a legal doctrine that requires courts to accept the judgments of foreign courts. Rather, it is rooted in the idea that reciprocal treatment is a necessary element of international relations. In Case 25.1, a federal court considers the concept of comity when ruling on whether a foreign court's judgment is enforceable in the United States.

Legal Speak »)
Declaratory Judgment
A court order deciding the rights and status of litigants where there is doubt as to the legal rights of the parties.

KEY POINT

The three primary sources of international law are treaties, customs, and judicial decisions.

---

[1]*Restatement (Third) of the Foreign Relations Law of the United States* § 102.
[2]The U.S. has not yet ratified the Vienna Convention, but the U.S. government has recognized it as an authoritative source to guide tribunals in matters related to treaty law.

FACT SUMMARY   La Ligue Contre Le Racisme et L'Antisemitisme ("LICRA") and L'Union des Etudiants Juifs de France, citizens of France, are nonprofit organizations dedicated to eliminating anti-Semitism. Yahoo!, Inc. ("Yahoo!") operates various Internet Web sites and services that any computer user can access at the Uniform Resource Locator (URL) http://www. yahoo.com. Yahoo! subsidiary corporations operate regional Yahoo! sites and services in many other nations, including France.

Yahoo!'s auction site allows anyone to post an item for sale and solicit bids from any computer user from around the globe. Yahoo! monitors the transaction through limited regulation by prohibiting particular items from being sold (such as stolen goods, body parts, prescription and illegal drugs, weapons, and goods violating U.S. copyright laws or the embargos) Yahoo! informs auction sellers that they must comply with Yahoo!'s policies and may not offer items to buyers in jurisdictions in which the sale of such items violates the jurisdiction's applicable laws. Yahoo! does not actively regulate the content of each posting, and individuals are able to post, and have in fact posted, highly offensive memorabilia, including Nazi objects.

LICRA filed suit against Yahoo! in France based on a French law banning the sale of Nazi- and Third Reich-related goods through auction services. The French court concluded that the Yahoo.com auction site violated the French Criminal Code, which prohibits exhibition of Nazi propaganda and artifacts for sale. Yahoo! contends that such a ban would infringe impermissibly upon its rights under the First Amendment to the U.S. Constitution. Accordingly, Yahoo! filed a lawsuit in a U.S. federal district court seeking a declaratory judgment that the French court's orders are neither cognizable nor enforceable under the laws of the United States.

SYNOPSIS OF DECISION AND OPINION   The district court ruled in favor of Yahoo!, holding that U.S. courts were not bound by judgments of foreign courts when the judgment is inconsistent with the Constitution and laws of the United States. The court reasoned that because the display of Nazi memorabilia could not be prohibited in the United States because of First Amendment concerns, a U.S. court cannot honor a foreign judgment that would violate the Constitution were it to be applied in the United States. Moreover, although France has the sovereign right to regulate what speech is permissible in France, U.S. courts may not enforce a foreign order that violates the protections of the U.S. Constitution by regulating protected speech that occurs simultaneously within U.S. and French borders. The court based its authority on the concept of comity.

WORDS OF THE COURT: Comity   "[According to our federal law] [n]o legal judgment has any effect, of its own force, beyond the limits of the sovereignty from which its authority is derived. Although the United States Constitution and implementing legislation require that full faith and credit be given to judgments of sister states, territories, and possessions of the United States, the extent to which the United States, or any state, honors the judicial decrees of foreign nations is a matter of choice, governed by the comity of nations. Comity is neither a matter of absolute obligation, on the one hand, nor of mere courtesy and good will, upon the other."

Case Questions

1. Why did Yahoo! choose to obtain a declaratory judgment from a U.S. court rather than appeal the ruling in the French courts?

2. In effect, isn't the U.S. court ruling that the U.S. Constitution protects American companies even when they do business in a foreign country that does not recognize the concepts embodied by our First Amendment?

*It is important to note that an appellate court subsequently reversed the decision of this court on procedural grounds. The appellate court let stand the court's substantive reasoning regarding the concept of comity and ultimately agreed with much of the trial court's holding, but ruled that the case should be dismissed on grounds unrelated to the comity analysis. *Yahoo! v. La Ligue Contre Le Racisme et L'Antisemitisme*, 433 F.3d 1199 (7th Cir. 2006).

INTERNATIONAL ORGANIZATIONS

International organizations play a unique role in the development of international law. These organizations are typically structured through use of multinational representation and are created and regulated by treaty. Perhaps the most famous organization is the **United Nations (U.N.),** which was created after World War II to facilitate common international concerns on defense, trade, protection of human rights, and other matters. From a business perspective, the U.N. has made significant achievements in harmonizing laws related to the sale of goods between businesses in different countries and other international business transactions. The U.N. Commission on International Trade Law created the **Convention of Contracts for the International Sale of Goods (CISG),** which is used to set rules for certain business transactions. CISG is discussed in more detail later in this chapter.

Other important international organizations include:

- The World Trade Organization (WTO), which promotes and has certain authority over disputes involving trade barriers.
- The International Monetary Fund (IMF), which is intended to promote stability of world currencies and provide temporary assistance for countries to help prevent the collapse of their economies.
- The Organization for Economic Cooperation and Development (OEDC), which coordinates aid to developing countries and takes steps toward eliminating bribery and other corruption from developing economies.

LO25-3 INTERNATIONAL COURTS

International courts play a role in the development and interpretation of international law, but their power to enforce a ruling on sovereign nations can be tenuous and their jurisdiction may be limited.

The World Court, seen here in session in The Hague, Netherlands, is one of the principal international courts.

The **International Court of Justice** (also known as the *World Court*) is the judicial branch of the United Nations. It is based in the Netherlands and its main functions are to settle legal disputes submitted to it by member states and give advisory opinions on legal questions submitted to it by duly authorized international organs, agencies and the U.N. General Assembly. This court should not be confused with the International Criminal Court, which also potentially has global jurisdiction. Established in 1945 by the U.N. Charter, the World Court began work in 1946 as the successor to the Permanent Court of International Justice. The Statute of the International Court of Justice, similar to that of its predecessor, is the main constitutional document constituting and regulating the Court.

The Court's workload is characterized by a wide range of judicial activity. The Court has dealt with relatively few cases in its history, but there has clearly been an increased willingness to use the Court since the 1980s, especially among developing countries. The United States withdrew from compulsory jurisdiction in 1986, and so accepts the court's jurisdiction only on a case-to-case basis. The U.N. Charter authorizes the U.N. Security Council to enforce rulings, but such enforcement is subject to the veto power of the five permanent members of the Security Council.

The **European Court of Justice** sits in Luxembourg and is the final arbiter of the codes governing European Union (EU) member countries. The court is composed of judges from each EU member country and is structured in a civil law tradition, so that most of its procedures and decisions are based on treaties governing EU countries regarding commercial regulations, protections, and guarantees. National courts of EU members are obliged by treaty to honor the decisions of the court and are obligated to apply EU laws (known as *community laws*).

Sovereign Immunity

One of the oldest doctrines of international law is that of **sovereign immunity.** In general, this doctrine stands for the proposition that, with some exceptions, foreign nations are exempt from jurisdiction by U.S. courts (and vice versa). The **Foreign Sovereign Immunities Act (FSIA)** is a federal statute that incorporates this concept in explicitly prohibiting U.S. courts from rendering judicial actions against foreign nations or their government officials unless (1) the foreign nation has waived its immunity either explicitly or by implication, (2) the foreign nation is engaged in some commercial enterprise on U.S. soil, or (3) the foreign nation's actions have a direct effect on U.S. interests.

One implication of the FSIA for U.S. businesses is in the context of those companies that provide services to foreign governments. To what extent are they protected by federal law, such as employment discrimination protections, when they are carrying out their contractual obligations to the foreign government? A federal appeals court considers that question in Case 25.2.

LEGAL SYSTEMS OF NATIONS

LO25-4

Legal systems of the world may be thought of as falling into one of the following broad categories: civil law, common law, religious-based law (such Sharia law or Talmudic law), and mixed law systems (referring not to a single system but to a combination of systems).

Civil Law Systems

Countries using **civil law systems** have drawn their body of law largely from the Roman law heritage that uses written law as the highest source, and have opted for a systematic codification of their general law. They rely heavily on written codes to define their laws

FACT SUMMARY   Vance International (Vance) is a U.S. company that provides security services to corporations and foreign sovereigns, including the Kingdom of Saudi Arabia. Vance was hired to augment the security provided to a princess of the Saudi royal family while the princess underwent medical treatments in California. The Saudi military was responsible for protection and Saudi military officers supervised all security at the site.

Butters, a woman employed by Vance as a security officer, was assigned to the Saudi detail and, on several occasions, Butters temporarily worked as an acting supervisor in a security command post. Vance managers recommended to the Saudis that Butters be promoted to serving a full rotation in the command post, but the Saudi authorities rejected that recommendation. Their rejection was based on the Saudi military supervisor's contention that the appointment of a woman for that post was unacceptable under Islamic law, and Saudis would consider it inappropriate for their officers to spend long periods of time in a command post with a woman present.

Butters brought suit against Vance for gender discrimination in the loss of the promotion, and Vance asserted immunity under the Federal Sovereign Immunities Act because they were carrying out orders of the Saudi government. Butters argued that Vance fell under one of the exceptions to the FSIA because the company was engaged in a commercial activity.

SYNOPSIS OF DECISION AND OPINION   The Fourth Circuit Court of Appeals ruled in favor of Vance. The court reasoned that Vance was entitled to immunity from suit under the Foreign Sovereign Immunities Act because defendant's client, the Kingdom of Saudi Arabia, was responsible for plaintiff not being promoted. The court held the action here was not exempt from the FSIA as "commercial activities" because the relevant act was quintessentially an act peculiar to sovereigns and that Vance was entitled to derivative immunity under the FSIA because defendant was following Saudi Arabia's orders not to promote plaintiff.

WORDS OF THE COURT: Impact of Sovereign Immunity
"Any type of governmental immunity reflects a trade-off between the possibility that an official's wrongdoing will remain unpunished and the risk that government functions will be impaired. The resolution of immunity questions inherently requires a balance between the evils inevitable in any available alternative. FSIA immunity presupposes a tolerance for the sovereign decisions of other countries that may reflect legal norms and cultural values quite different from our own. Here Saudi Arabia made a decision to protect a member of its royal family in a manner consistent with Islamic law and custom. The Act requires not that we approve of the diverse cultural or political motivations that may underlie another sovereign's acts, but that we respect them."

Case Questions

1. How far does the FSIA immunity go? If one of Vance's employees were ordered by Saudi officials to physically detain Butters and she was injured, would Vance still be protected by the FSIA against any liability resulting from Butters's injury?

2. When the court states that the "FSIA immunity presupposes a tolerance for the sovereign decisions of other countries that may reflect legal norms and cultural values quite different from our own," what legal norms and cultural values is it referring to?

---

and do not favor the notion of courts filling in any gaps in the statutes. Rather, courts apply the code law to individual cases without the mandate of following cases that were decided by previous courts considering the same questions. Most European, Latin American, African, and Asian countries use civil law systems.

Common Law Systems

The common law system takes on a variety of cultural and legal forms throughout the world. Although there are differences from country to country, this category generally includes countries whose law, for the most part, is technically based on English common law concepts and legal organizational methods that strongly favor use of case law, as opposed to legislation, as the ordinary means of expressions of general law. If there is no case law to guide the court, common law systems allow courts to fill in the gaps not covered by statutes and may create new law consistent with public policy. Common law jurisdictions adhere to the concept of judicial review, whereby a court may strike down a law passed by the legislature if the law is found to violate some other overriding principle of law (such as the U.S. Constitution). As you may imagine, the common law tradition is used by countries that were once colonies or protectorates of Great Britain including the United States, Canada, and Australia.

Religious-Based Legal Systems

Religious-based legal systems are legal doctrines and guidelines directly based on certain religious tenets. For example, the Sharia, derived from the Qur'an (the scared text of Islam) regulates many aspects of life for Muslims including crime, politics, business transactions, family, sexuality, and hygiene. The Sharia is the centerpiece of Islamic law, which is now the most widely used religious-based legal system. Islamic law is interpreted by religious leaders and is carried out by a government body.

Mixed Legal Systems

Mixed legal systems (also known as *hybrid* or *composite legal systems*) include political entities where two or more systems apply cumulatively or interactively, but also entities where there is a combination of systems as a result of more or less clearly defined fields of application. For example, Saudi Arabia uses Islamic-based law to regulate personal conduct of its citizens and visitors, but a civil law system to regulate business transactions and other areas of the law.

INTERNATIONAL DISPUTE RESOLUTION

LO25-5, 25-6

The parties to an international dispute are typically corporations or government entities, rather than private individuals, while domestic dispute resolution can involve relatively small claims by individuals. Many countries, recognizing that different considerations apply to international disputes, have provided for a separate legal regime to govern international dispute resolution.

Arbitration

Arbitration is considered international if the parties to the arbitration are of different nationalities or the subject matter of the dispute involves a state other than the country in which the parties are nationals. An international arbitration usually has no connection with the country in which the arbitration is being held, other than the fact that it is taking place on its territory.

The major difference between international and domestic arbitrations is that international arbitration awards have very wide enforceability in many countries. This is largely attributable to the acceptance of international treaties such as the 1958 **Convention on the Recognition and Enforcement of Foreign Arbitral Awards** (Convention), which allows for the enforcement of arbitration awards in many major countries, provided that the arbitration is international. In Case 25.3, a federal court of appeals considers whether an arbitration clause that provides for disputing parties to arbitrate falls under the Convention rules.

FACT SUMMARY DiMercurio was a fisherman who was injured when a commercial shipping vessel owned by a Massachusetts company, Rosalie & Matteo Corporation, sank. DiMercurio prevailed in a personal injury suit against Rosalie & Matteo, but the company was without assets and could not pay the $350,000 judgment. Rosalie & Matteo subsequently assigned to DiMercurio all rights it had against their London-based insurance company, Sphere Drake, under an insurance policy issued to Rosalie & Matteo Corporation. DiMercurio then took his claim directly to Sphere Drake, demanding that the insurer pay the $350,000 judgment. Sphere Drake sought to invoke the arbitration process specified in the policy, which called for arbitration of all coverage disputes to be held in London under Convention rules. DiMercurio challenged the validity of the arbitration provision, contending that it was overly burdensome on the arbitrating parties given that he would have to travel to London.

SYNOPSIS OF DECISION AND OPINION The First Circuit Court of Appeals ruled in favor of Sphere Drake, holding that the arbitration clause was valid. The court reasoned when one party challenges the validity of an arbitration clause under the Convention, the court conducts a four-part analysis: (1) Is there a written agreement to arbitrate the subject of the dispute? (2) Does the agreement provide for arbitration in the territory of a signatory of the Convention? (3) Does the agreement arise out of a commercial relationship? (4) Is a party to the agreement not an American citizen, or does the commercial relationship have some reasonable relation with one or more foreign countries?

In this case, the court determined that the arbitration clause met the standards in the four-part analysis and, therefore, the clause was valid.

WORDS OF THE COURT: Burden of the Arbitration Clause "We adhere to our view that one-sided agreements to arbitrate are not favored. In this instance, however, both parties are required to arbitrate coverage disputes. The fact that the company may proceed in court to recover premiums or like fees—a proceeding that is likely to be much more confined than a coverage dispute—does not render the contract impermissibly unbalanced. Moreover, there is no evidence of undue power or deception on the part of the insurer in the negotiation of the policy. The particular coverage was selected by Rosalie & Matteo's broker, Marine Insurance Consultants International Limited, which was familiar with the Sphere Drake policy forms, including the arbitration provision. As Rosalie & Matteo's assignee, DiMercurio is bound by the terms and conditions to which the company agreed."

Case Questions

1. Recall that in the *Brower v. Gateway* case in Chapter 4 "Resolving Disputes: Litigation and Alternative Dispute Resolution Options" the court held that Gateway's inclusion of an arbitration clause in a terms and conditions agreement was invalid because of the choice of ICC as the arbitration forum. Why is this case distinguishable?

2. Given the court's language in this case, give an example of what types of agreements would be too one-sided to be valid.

International Arbitration Forums

Prominent bodies that administer arbitrations include the International Chamber of Commerce's (ICC) International Court of Arbitration in Paris, the London Court of International Arbitration (LCIA), and the American Arbitration Association (AAA). Each of these institutions has formulated its own arbitration rules; namely, the ICC Rules of Arbitration, the LCIA Rules, and the AAA International Arbitration Rules. Except for the AAA, which provides that its International Arbitration Rules apply only in the absence of any designated rules, the other two institutional rules are applied to the arbitrations administered by the arbitration bodies.

All the institutional rules govern the commencement of the arbitration, exchange of arbitration pleadings, appointment and removal of arbitrators, and hearing and interim measures of protection, among other rules. If parties have not agreed on the number of arbitrators, one arbitrator is appointed, although the arbitration institution may appoint three arbitrators if it appears that the dispute warrants it.

In terms of the choice of arbitrator, the LCIA Rules provide that it, alone, is empowered to appoint arbitrators, although arbitrators will be appointed with due regard to any criteria for selection agreed to by the parties in writing. The ICC Rules of Arbitration allow parties to nominate, by agreement, an arbitrator for the Court's confirmation; while the AAA International Arbitration Rules only require that parties notify it of any *designation* of an arbitrator.

Where the forum of the arbitration has not been agreed to, the LCIA generally determines it according to the parties' contentions and the circumstances of the arbitration. However, the LCIA Rules provide that in such situations, the seat of the arbitration will be London, unless on the basis of the parties' written comments, the LCIA Court deems another seat more appropriate in view of the circumstances.

Under the ICC Rules of Arbitration, a document known as the *Terms of Reference,* containing a summary of the parties' claims, list of issues to be determined, and applicable procedural rules, must be drafted and submitted to the arbitrator and the opposing party. Although time-consuming, discussion of agreed issues is designed to encourage settlement. Also, arbitration awards must be submitted to the ICC Court for approval. There are no similar requirements under the LCIA Rules and the AAA International Arbitration Rules.

Ad Hoc Arbitration Rules

Rules such as those set out in the U.N. Commission on International Trade Law (UNCITRAL) Arbitration Rules serve to bridge the gap for parties who are unwilling to fork out additional expense to use the services of an arbitration body, but who do not wish to spend time agreeing to the details of a procedure to govern their arbitration.

ALTERNATIVES TO THE ICC: THE WORLD INTELLECTUAL PROPERTY ORGANIZATION

There are arbitration institutions other than the ICC, some with regional specialization, and some with subject-matter specialization. The World International Property Organization (WIPO) in Geneva, Switzerland, created an arbitration center for arbitration related to intellectual property such as patents, trademarks, and copyrights. Some advantages of the WIPO center are:

- The WIPO lists best practices regarding nomination of arbitrators, including a list system, thus encouraging the parties to agree on people based on their *qualifications.*

- The WIPO explicitly states that, when nominating arbitrators, it will take into account any preferences expressed by the parties, *and* has created a mechanism to implement this in practice: a database of names and detailed qualifications.

- The WIPO rules explicitly cater to multiparty arbitrations.

INTERNATIONAL MEDIATION

The growing popularity of mediation and conciliation, both of which first took root in the United States but have gained increasing support in other jurisdictions, reflects a high degree of frustration with the cost and delays often associated with traditional dispute resolution procedures. Mediation and conciliation both involve a consensual (rather than adjudicative) process, often with the involvement of a neutral third party. Such forms of dispute resolution may loosely be described as "third-party-assisted negotiation."

Mediation and conciliation are now widely used in many countries, including the United States, Canada, Australia, Hong Kong, South Africa, New Zealand, Germany, Holland, and Switzerland. They are also gaining acceptance in the United Kingdom through the establishment of organizations dedicated to their promotion and use, such as the London-based Center for Dispute Resolution, although conciliation has long been practiced in the United Kingdom by the Advisory Conciliation and Arbitration Service in the field of employment-law disputes.

LO25-7 INTERNATIONAL COMMERCIAL LAW

Although the coverage of this chapter has been focused on the sources and processes for a broad-based category of international law disputes, *commercial transactions and trade practices* are also governed by various sources of international (and U.S.) law.

Foreign Corrupt Practices Act (FCPA)

The **Foreign Corrupt Practices Act (FCPA)**[3] of 1977 was enacted principally to prevent corporate bribery of foreign officials. This act had three major parts: (1) it requires the keeping by corporations of accurate books, records, and accounts; (2) it requires issuers registered with the Securities and Exchange Commission to maintain a responsible internal accounting control system; and (3) it prohibits bribery by American corporations of foreign officials.

The FCPA was amended by Congress in 1988 in response to numerous criticisms. One of the changes enacted a *knowing* standard in order to find violations of the act. A person's state of mind is knowing with respect to conduct, a circumstance, or a result if the person is aware of engaging in the conduct, that the circumstance exists, or that the result is substantially certain to occur or if the person has a firm belief that the circumstance exists or that the result is substantially certain to occur. The 1998 amendment to the FCPA brought it into compliance with the Organization for Economic Cooperation and Development's agreement on bribery.

The centerpiece of the FCPA is its antibribery provision. The law prohibits a company, its officers, employees, and agents from giving, offering, or promising anything of value to any foreign (non-U.S.) official, with the intent to obtain or retain business or any other advantage. This prohibition is interpreted broadly in that companies may be held liable for violating the antibribery provisions of the FCPA whether or not they took any action in the United States. Thus, a U.S. company can be liable for the conduct of its overseas employees or agents, even if no money was transferred from the United States and no American citizen participated in any way in the foreign bribery.

A foreign official means any officer or employee of a foreign government, regardless of rank; employees of government-owned or government-controlled businesses; foreign political parties and party officials; candidates for political office; and employees of public international organizations (such as the United Nations or the World Bank). This can include owner/employees as well. Even if the improper payment is not consummated, just offering it violates the FCPA. Likewise, instructing, authorizing, or allowing a third party to make a prohibited payment on a company's behalf, ratifying a payment after the fact, or making a payment to a third party knowing or having reason to know that it will likely be given to a government official constitute FCPA violations. This includes not only cash and cash equivalents, but also gifts, entertainment, travel expenses, accommodations, and anything else of tangible or intangible value.

---

[3]28 U.S.C. § 1602, et seq.

Does this proposed transaction violate the FCPA?

1. WidgetCo. applies for a permit to do business in Venezuela. The government official denies the permit, and a WidgetCo. executive pays for a lavish meal at a four-star restaurant while discussing the permit application with a government official.

2. WidgetCo. applies for a permit to do business in Venezuela. The government official denies the permit, so WidgetCo. hires a consultant in Venezuela who is the brother of the government official. WidgetCo. pays the consultant $100,000 to handle the permit process although the permit itself costs only $1,000.

3. WidgetCo. applies for a permit to do business in Venezuela. A government official denies the permit, so WidgetCo. hires a consultant in Venezuela who is the brother of the government official and pays a reasonable fee for services plus reimbursement of traveling expenses. The consultant submits a handwritten invoice for the reimbursements totaling $100,000.

4. WidgetCo. applies for a permit to do business in Venezuela. A government official denies the permit, so WidgetCo. hires a consultant in Venezuela who is the brother of the government official and pays a reasonable fee for services plus reasonable reimbursement of traveling expenses. When the permit is finally approved, WidgetCo. executives send the consultant a case of California wine as a thank-you gift.

The answers to this Self-Check are provided at the end of the chapter.

U.N. Convention on Contracts for the International Sale of Goods (UNCISG)

In 1988, the United States became a signatory nation to a U.N. treaty that attempts to establish an international commercial code. The **U.N. Convention on Contracts for the International Sale of Goods (UNCISG)** governs transactions between any of its

The Foreign Corrupt Practices Act provides for criminal penalties for business entities and employees that engage in any form of corruption with foreign officials.

63 member countries. Much like America's Uniform Commercial Code, the UNCISG exists to fill-in the terms of a sale of goods contract when the parties haven't otherwise agreed. Parties are free to negotiate the allocation of risk, insurance requirements, delivery, payment terms, choice of law, and the like to displace the UNCISG principles. It is particularly important for managers to understand *choice of law and forum* principles in international contracts, because risk and expense of enforcement become increasingly important factors that must be considered in arriving at appropriate pricing and delivery proposals. If one party will have to travel significant distances or hire special counsel to enforce an agreement or recover for damages suffered, adjusting the price or delivery terms accordingly may sometimes help to reduce the risks.

Coverage and Major Provisions of the UNCISG

The UNCISG operates on the same fundamental principle as many commercial codes around the world (including the Uniform Commercial Code[4] followed by most American states) in that the law favors the completion of a transaction as agreed upon, but also provides relief when one party has breached. The UNCISG covers parties that maintain a place of business in one of the signatory countries. Note that citizenship of shareholders, directors, or officers is not a factor under the UNCISG. Generally, the UNCISG covers contracts for the sale of goods between *merchants*. This is perhaps the biggest difference between the UCC and the UNCISG. The UNCISG provisions do *not* apply to transactions where one party is a nonmerchant. Other major important provisions include:

No Writing Required The UNCISG has no formal writing requirement (such as the UCC's Statute of Frauds) and specifically provides that contracts are not subject to requirements as to format. A totality of the circumstances, such as course of past dealing, evidence of oral or written negotiations between the parties, and industry practice, may be sufficient to prove that an enforceable contract exists.

Offer and Acceptance A contract for the sale of goods between businesses located in different UNCISG signatory countries begins with offer and acceptance. As with the UCC, the offer need not have complete terms in order to be valid. The offer requires only a brief description of the goods, quantity, and price. Beyond those three terms, so long as there is some evidence that the parties intended to form a contract, nothing more is needed for a valid offer. Acceptance may be made within a reasonable time and is effective only when it is received by the offeror (thus, the offer may be withdrawn at any point prior to that time).

Remedies The UNCISG provides for a party that has delivered nonconforming goods to be given an adequate opportunity to cure the problem. In general, the UNCISG gives sellers an absolute right and obligation to cure and buyers must allow the seller the opportunity to cure even if the time for performance is past due. Of course, a buyer must give notice of the nonconformance in a timely manner in order to trigger the seller's cure obligations. If the seller does not cure, the UNCISG provides a right for the buyer to pursue remedies.

INCO: International Chamber of Commerce Terms

With respect to title, risk of loss, and delivery terms, sometimes the language barrier can lead to confusion among the parties and to disputes regarding a loss. The International Chamber of Commerce provides international abbreviations, known as **INCO terms,** to designate many of the responsibilities. INCO terms are generally used in conjunction with the UNCISG. For example, in the absence of any agreement between the parties, the UNCISG provides that risk passes at the point at which the seller has delivered the goods to

---

[4]The Uniform Commercial Code was covered in Chapter 8, "Contracts for the Sale of Goods."

a carrier. If the goods are not to be delivered, the risk of loss passes in accordance with the INCO term, EXW (Ex Works). The INCO term EXW has the universal meaning that the parties understand the goods will not be delivered or transported by the seller. Rather, the seller need only make the goods available to the buyer at the seller's place of business and provide the buyer with appropriate documentation of title. There are 11 INCO terms in all. Some of the more common ones are:

- FCA: Free Carrier is where the seller provides transportation at seller expense only to the carrier named by the buyer.
- FOB: Free on Board is always accompanied by the name of a port (FOB New York) and applies only when transportation is via freighter ship. It means that seller's expense and risk of loss *end* when the seller delivers goods "over the ship's rail" to the freighter ship. The buyer is responsible for the freighter delivery charges and any losses occurring en route to delivery.

CONCEPT SUMMARY   Contracts for International Sales of Goods

- The UNCISG, the international counterpart to the UCC, is a treaty that governs sales contracts between businesses located in signatory countries.
- Four major differences between the UNCISG and the UCC are: it does not apply to nonmerchants, it has no writing requirement, offers can be withdrawn at any point prior the offeror receiving the acceptance, and the right to cure exists even after the performance period is over.
- INCO terms are standardized contractual terms and designations used in international sales contracts to avoid confusion due to language barriers and differing legal systems.

ENFORCING INTELLECTUAL PROPERTY RIGHTS ABROAD

LO25-8

While the laws of intellectual property protection are well settled in the United States, as U.S. companies become increasingly dependent on foreign sales and operations, global agreements have turned ever more important as well. This international law protection of intellectual property rights has primarily taken the form of multilateral agreements. However, as a practical matter, while many countries have improved intellectual property rights protection significantly over the past several decades, these agreements are still voluntary. Even when the government of a country agrees to abide by them (sometimes to avoid trade sanctions), these agreements are sometimes difficult to enforce in certain parts of the world. At the very least, enforcement of rights abroad significantly impacts the cost-benefit analysis of pursuing infringement claims in terms of additional fees and expenses related to foreign litigation.

Comprehensive Agreements

While U.S. firms are motivated to be committed to stronger intellectual property protection abroad, some countries' intellectual property trade agreements often lack a meaningful mechanism to ensure that signatory countries are actually fulfilling their obligations. Thus, the United States and other similarly situated countries backed the adoption of multinational minimal standards for intellectual property protection and an enforcement structure empowered with the ability to allow trade embargoes and other remedies designed to ensure that signatory countries comply with the agreement. As part of the **General Agreement on Tariffs and Trade (GATT),** administered by

The WTO (also called OMC, the abbreviation for its French language counterpart) plays an important role in protection of intellectual property in global commerce.

the multinational World Trade Organization (WTO), the agreement to set these standards is known as the **Agreement on Trade-Related Aspects of Intellectual Property (TRIPS).** TRIPS covers minimum requirements and standards for all areas of intellectual property protections and also provides an infrastructure for enforcement and dispute resolution.

Agreements on Trademarks

International trademark policy is governed primarily by two agreements: the *Paris Convention* and the *Madrid Protocol.* The Paris Convention was the first multinational agreement to establish minimum requirements for trademark protection and a general agreement by its signatories to establish protections against unfair competition. The **Madrid Protocol,** a 2003 agreement that was a descendent of the earlier Madrid Agreement, aims to help reduce the burden of multinational companies that desire multinational protection of their trademark by the use of a more uniform and single-sourced process. Although important, these international agreements are not so specific as to actually require fundamental enforcement from signatory countries and, thus, trademark protection may still be dubious and uneven in certain regions. Efforts to harmonize trademark laws on a regional level have been more successful.[5]

Agreement on Copyrights

Copyright protection in foreign countries is covered in the **Berne Convention** agreement. Fundamentally, this agreement requires that foreigners from signatory countries must be granted protection via reciprocity (known as "national treatment") under the copyright laws of any other member country. For example, if Samuel, an American, distributes his novel

---

[5]The European Union established a Community Trademark System to make trademark registration and protection more uniform in member states.

in Great Britain (or in any signatory country), British courts are bound by the Convention agreement to protect Samuel's rights under British law in the same way as if Samuel had been a citizen of Great Britain.

Agreement on Patents

The most important multilateral agreement on patents is the **Paris Convention** agreement. This agreement requires the approximately 160 member countries that signed the agreement to protect the same inventor rights under *any* member country's patent laws as those enjoyed by citizens of that member country. That is, each member agrees to extend national rights (or give full protection to) foreign inventors. However, risks still remain for the foreign inventor because the Paris Convention does not specify common standards for patentability and some jurisdictions may not allow certain inventions, which were patentable in the United States, to obtain patent protection in their own country due to noncompliance with its domestic law.

KEY TERMS

Public international law p. 632   Category of international law principles that primarily addresses relations between individual countries and international organizations.

Private international law p. 632   Category of international law principles that focuses on regulations of private individuals and business entities.

Vienna Convention on the Law of Treaties p. 632   One of the standards used by courts and other tribunals when interpreting treaty law.

Comity p. 632   The general notion that nations will defer to and give effect to the laws and court decisions of other nations.

United Nations (U.N.) p. 634   International organization created after World War II to facilitate common international concerns on defense, trade, protection of human rights, and other matters.

Convention of Contracts for the International Sale of Goods (CISG) p. 634   Created by the U.N. Commission on International Trade Law to establish uniform rules for drafting certain international sales contracts.

International Court of Justice p. 635   Also known as the *World Court,* the judicial branch of the United Nations charged with settling legal disputes submitted to it by member states and giving advisory opinions on legal questions submitted to it by duly authorized international organs, agencies, and the U.N. General Assembly.

European Court of Justice p. 635   The court functioning as the final arbiter of the codes governing European Union member states.

Sovereign immunity p. 635   Long-standing doctrine of international law that stands for the proposition that, with some exceptions, foreign nations are exempt from jurisdiction by U.S. courts and vice versa.

Foreign Sovereign Immunities Act (FSIA) p. 635   A federal statute that incorporates the concept of sovereign immunity in explicitly prohibiting U.S. courts from rendering judicial actions against foreign nations or their government officials unless the foreign nation has waived its immunity, is engaged in some commercial enterprise on U.S. soil, or when its actions have a direct effect on U.S. interests.

Civil law systems p. 635   Systems of law drawn largely from the Roman law heritage that use written law as the highest source and opt for a systematic codification of general law principles.

Convention on the Recognition and Enforcement of Foreign Arbitral Awards p. 637   An international treaty established in 1958 that allows for the enforcement of arbitration awards in many major countries, provided that the arbitration is international.

Foreign Corrupt Practices Act (FCPA) p. 640   Enacted in 1977 to prevent corporate bribery of foreign officials; require the keeping by corporations of accurate books, records, and accounts; and require issuers registered with the Securities and Exchange

Commission to maintain a responsible internal accounting control system.

U.N. Convention on Contracts for the International Sale of Goods (UNCISG) p. 641 A treaty that governs the international sales contracts among businesses located in member countries.

INCO terms p. 642 Standardized contractual terms and designation used in international sales contracts to avoid confusion due to language barriers and differing legal systems.

General Agreement on Tariffs and Trade (GATT) p. 643 A treaty organization administered by the World Trade Organization whose purpose is to facilitate international trade.

Agreement on Trade-Related Aspects of Intellectual Property (TRIPS) p. 644 A multinational agreement covering minimum requirements and standards for all areas of intellectual property protections as well as providing an infrastructure for enforcement and dispute resolution.

Madrid Protocol p. 644 A multinational agreement that aims to help reduce the burden of multinational companies that desire multinational protection of their trademark by the use of a more uniform and single-sourced process.

Berne Convention p. 644 A multinational agreement covering copyright protection, requiring that foreigners from signatory countries be granted protection via reciprocity under the copyright laws of any other member country.

Paris Convention p. 645 A multinational agreement covering patents, requiring signatory countries to protect the same inventor rights under any member country's patent laws as those enjoyed by citizens of that member country.

THEORY TO PRACTICE

Cold Call Company (CCC) is a cellular phone manufacturer and distributor based in Miami, Florida. The firm has a significant market share in the southeastern United States and began to expand into South America as a natural supplement to its existing market. CCC entered into a written distribution agreement with Telefonica, a Brazilian-based provider of cell phone service and retailer of cell phone units with stores throughout Latin America. Telefonica agreed to buy 25,000 units over 12 months at US$5 per unit. The agreement also contained a provision whereby the parties agreed to ICC dispute resolution in the event of a dispute arising out of the distribution agreement. After several months, a dispute developed and Telefonica filed suit against CCC in a federal district court in Miami.

1. What source(s) of international law(s) would generally govern this international business relationship?

2. When CCC asks the court to dismiss the case due to the ICC clause, Telefonica claims that the clause is invalid because they will have to travel to Europe to resolve the dispute and that is too burdensome. How will the federal court rule, and what case have you studied in this chapter that supports your answer?

Assume further that the CCC–Telefonica agreement provides that all shipments are "FOB Port of Rio de Janeiro, Brazil." During one shipment, a batch of 1,000 units was accidentally destroyed when being loaded on the freighter in Miami.

3. Under CISG, who bears the risk of this loss? When did title pass?

Assume that an executive at Telefonica arranges a golf outing with a politician in Argentina on behalf of the distribution manager of CCC. The Telefonica executive explained that it was customary in Argentina for business owners to entertain local politicians and that it was a necessary part of securing appropriate licenses for the CCC–Telefonica distribution relationship in Argentina. One day after the golf outing, the Telefonica executive sends a bill to CCC for the golf expenses, including equipment, food, and drinks ordered by the group.

4. If CCC pays the bill, would they potentially violate any U.S. laws? If so, does the law apply to these circumstances? Will CCC be at a competitive disadvantage if they follow the law?

Suppose that CCC refuses to pay the bill and that the Argentinean government prohibits CCC from importing any products into their country. CCC loses a significant portion of their investment with Telefonica as a result of the ban.

5. Does CCC have recourse against the Argentinean government in U.S. courts? Why or why not? What legal doctrine controls this question? Could this be an exception?

One important responsibility of a manager is to be vigilant about protecting his company from liability. One such liability in the international law context is a potential violation of the Foreign Corrupt Practices Act (FCPA). Individually or in small groups, take on the role of a CCC manager (from Theory to Practice above) and draft a two-page memorandum to your senior manager with a proposed policy for CCC employees to help them avoid any violations of the FCPA. The policy should contain at least 5 red-flag situations where CCC may be in danger of violating the act. For example, paying for entertainment of a government official when the official has some decision-making role is a red-flag situation where CCC employees must recognize potential FCPA violations and act with restraint. A sample answer may be found on this textbook's Web site at www.mhhe.com/melvin.

CASE SUMMARY 25.1 :: TermoRio v. Electricrificadora del Atlantico S.A., 2006 WL 695832 (D.D.C. 2006)

ARBITRATION ENFORCEMENT

Electranta is a power company owned by the Colombian government. Electranta became involved in a dispute with TermoRio, a U.S. company doing business in Colombia. The dispute was arbitrated consistent with International Chamber of Commerce rules and TermoRio was awarded US$60 million in damages. However, TermoRio could not convince the Colombian courts to enforce the award and the government of Colombia refused to pay. Electranta then filed suit in the U.S. attempting to have a federal court to declare the acts of the Colombia courts unlawful and recognize the arbitration award.

CASE QUESTIONS

1. Under the Convention on the Recognition and Enforcement of Arbitral Awards, would the U.S. courts have authority to decide this case?
2. What do the ICC rules provide?

CASE SUMMARY 25.2 :: Plaintiffs A, B, C v. Zemin, 224 F. Supp. 2d 52 (N.D. Ill. 2003)

SOVEREIGN IMMUNITY

Chinese ex-patriots now living in the United States are members of a religious movement, Falun Gong, which is outlawed in China, and brought suit against the Chinese government. Members of this movement are subject to arrest by Chinese government officials in the Falun Gong Control Office without any further charge, and the lawsuit maintained that they were subject to severe torture resulting in permanent physical damage. The suit named the former president of China and officials of the Control Office as defendants, but the defendants never responded to the lawsuit.

CASE QUESTIONS

1. May the federal court issue a default judgment against the defendants?
2. What role does the doctrine of sovereign immunity play in this case?

CONTRACTS FOR THE INTERNATIONAL SALE OF GOODS

Sabate, a France-based company, sold wine corks to Chateau, a Canadian winery, via Sabate's U.S. subsidiary. The parties made the agreement by telephone and no written contracts exist. After several transactions and the sale of over 1.2 million corks, Sabate began to send an invoice with each shipment that included a forum selection clause naming France as the agreed upon location to resolve disputes. Chateau sued Sabate in a U.S. court over the poor quality of the corks. Sabate moved to dismiss because the forum selection clause required the dispute to be litigated in France. Chateau claims that the forum selection clause was added after the terms were agreed upon and, thus, was invalid and not part of the original contract.

CASE QUESTIONS

1. Is Chateau's silence upon receiving the invoices binding on them under the Convention on Contracts for the International Sale of Goods (CISG)?
2. Would your answer be the same under the UCC?

FOREIGN SOVEREIGN IMMUNITIES ACT SCOPE

Altmann, a U.S. resident, filed suit in a federal district court against the Republic of Austria to recover a series of paintings that Altmann claims were wrongfully appropriated from her uncle just prior to WWII. The paintings had been held in her uncle's Vienna home until the German annexation of Austria in 1938. Altmann's uncle fled Austria fearing persecution and left half of his estate to Altmann in his will. The paintings were discovered by an Austrian journalist who alerted Altmann to the fact that her uncle's paintings were being held by the Austrian government in their art gallery archives. The Austrian government moved to dismiss the case based on the FSIA, but Altmann contended (among other arguments) that because the Austrian government's actions were taken *prior* to passage of the FSIA they were, therefore, outside the scope of the statute's immunity protection.

CASE QUESTIONS

1. Do sovereigns have immunity protection for actions prior to the FSIA's enactment?
2. Is it fair to allow Austria protection under these circumstances? Why or why not?

Self-Check ANSWERS

Foreign Corrupt Practices Act

1. Violates FCPA's prohibition of offering anything of value (meal at a four-star restaurant) with intent to obtain the permit.

2. Violates FCPA's prohibition of paying a third party to pay off the government official (a consultant).

3. Violates FCPA's prohibition of paying cash equivalents (travel) in connection with the permit.

4. Violates FCPA's prohibition of after the fact (ratification) payments related to the permit application.

BUSINESS LAW SIMULATION EXERCISE 3

Trademarks in Cyberspace: Cool Runnings v. BigBuy.com

learning outcomes **checklist**

After studying this simulation, students who have mastered the material will be able to:

1. Explain the legal doctrines that govern trademark protection and infringement.

2. Interpret and apply the rules set forth in current case law.

3. Articulate a cogent argument for each party/side in the dispute.

4. Negotiate a tenable solution as an alternative to a judicial forum.

This simulation is designed to help students understand how the various topics covered in Chapter 24, "Intellectual Property," connect together through use of a simulated legal dispute. The simulation is intended to provide students with as close as possible real-world experience in applying legal doctrines and use of analytical and critical thinking skills. This simulation is a sequential decision-making exercise structured around a model in which the participants assume a role in managing tasks and work toward a tenable solution.

The simulation is structured in three parts:

- Part 1 is a hypothetical fact pattern describing events leading up to a legal dispute in the hypothetical U.S. state of Longville.

- Part 2 is a set of two hypothetical case summaries from two federal trial courts, both situated in Longville, that provide a brief set of facts, several legal points, and short excerpts from the opinion itself. While these cases are hypothetical, they are based on actual cases from federal courts in various circuits.

- Part 3 is an assignment sheet handout that will be provided to you by your instructor to be used in conjunction with this simulation.

PART 1: STIPULATED FACTS

1. BigBuy.com Inc. is a company with a Web site that facilitates a Web-based discount wholesaler business model that target consumers wishing to buy products in bulk. In early 2008, BigBuy.com began developing a new marketing device that featured pop-up advertising. In October 2009, they launched "BargainNow" as integrated software for BigBuy users.

2. BigBuy.com made the BargainNow software available to computer users, at no charge, as part of a larger package of software that users downloaded from BigBuy's Web site. The BargainNow software uses an internal directory of Web site addresses, search terms, and keyword algorithms to generate pop-up advertisements in response to a user's Internet activity.

3. The advertisements generated are randomly drawn from a list of BigBuy's advertising clients. In essence, BigBuy's software operates behind the scenes monitoring a user's Internet activity and then responds according to keywords the software identifies as part of a user's activity such as words entered in an Internet search engine query or visited Web sites whose domain names match with information contained in the BigBuy internal directory.

4. The pop-ups occur only a few seconds after the user has reached a retail Web site and, thus, presents the user with a choice to close the pop-up and continue to navigate the Web site or click on the promotion and navigate away from the original retailer's Web site to a competitor's Web site.

5. Cool Runnings Corporation is a large retailer of skateboards and snowboards with a USPTO registered trademark for "Cool Runnings" and has sole and exclusive use of the mark. They sell their product both from a catalog system with a 1-800 number and via their Web site at www.coolrunnings.com.

6. In January 2010, BigBuy landed an advertising client that is a major competitor to Cool Runnings and, pursuant to their business model, BigBuy installed www.coolrunnings.com and key words such as "snowboards" and "skateboards" into their internal directory. Note they did *not* install the key words "Cool Runnings" in the directory.

This simulation exercise involves a trademark dispute between a snowboard retailer and an Internet advertising company.

PART 2: FEDERAL CASE LAW

1-800 Lenses, Inc., v. WhenU.com,
Federal District Court, Eastern District of Longville (2010)

Facts

- 1-800 Lenses, Inc. ("800-Lenses") sells and markets replacement lenses and related products through its Web site, located at www.1800Lenses.com, and also through telephone and mail orders. 800-Lenses obtained USPTO registration for the mark "1-800 LENSES" and the 1-800 LENSES logo.

- 800-Lenses has expended considerable sums on marketing these marks; in 2001, 800-Lenses spent $27,118,000 on marketing. Since the founding of 1-800 Lenses in 1995, Plaintiff has continuously used its service marks to promote and identify its products and services in the United States and abroad.

- 800-Lenses is the sole owner of the 1-800 Lenses.com Web site.

- WhenU.com is a software company that has developed and distributes, among other products, the "SaveNow" program, a proprietary software application.

- The SaveNow program is computer software that only operates on the Microsoft Windows operating system. The SaveNow software, when installed, resides on individual computer users' computer desktops. When a computer user who has installed the SaveNow software (a "SaveNow user") browses the Internet, the SaveNow software scans activity conducted within the SaveNow user's Internet browser, comparing URLs, Web site addresses, search terms, and Web page content accessed by the SaveNow user with a proprietary directory, using algorithms contained in the software.

- Entering a URL into the browser will trigger the SaveNow software to deliver a pop-up advertisement. When a user types in "1800lenses .com," the URL for 800-lenses' owned Web site, the SaveNow software recognizes that the user is interested in the eye-care category, and retrieves from an Internet server a pop-up advertisement from that category.

- 800-Lenses filed a trademark infringement claim after discovering that the SaveNow software produced pop-up advertising for Lenses Warehouse, a WhenU.com customer and competitor of 800-Lenses.

POINTS OF LAW AND OPINION EXCERPTS

Point (a)

The Lanham Act, a federal statute, prohibits the *use in commerce,* without consent, of any registered mark in connection with the sale, offering for sale, distribution, or advertising of any goods in a way that is likely to cause confusion.

Excerpt (a1)

"A trademark is 'used in commerce' for purposes of the Lanham Act when it is used or displayed in the sale or advertising of services and the services are rendered in commerce, or the services are rendered in more than one state or in the United States and a foreign country and the person rendering the services is engaged in commerce in connection with the services."

Excerpt (a2)

"WhenU (defendant) *uses* 1-800 Lenses (plaintiff) mark in commerce. First, in causing pop-up advertisements for a competitor to appear when SaveNow users have specifically attempted to access Plaintiff's website—on which Plaintiff's trademark appears—defendants are displaying plaintiff's mark in the advertising of a competitor's services. SaveNow users that type plaintiff's website address into their browsers are clearly attempting to access plaintiff's website because of prior knowledge of the website, knowledge that is dependent on plaintiff's reputation and goodwill. SaveNow users that type 1-800 Lenses into a search engine in an attempt to find the URL for plaintiff's website are exhibiting a similar knowledge of plaintiff's goods and services, and pop-up advertisements that capitalize on this are clearly using plaintiff's mark. Thus, by causing pop-up advertisements to appear when SaveNow users have specifically attempted to find or access plaintiff's website, defendants are 'using' plaintiff's marks that appear on plaintiff's website."

Excerpt (a3)

"WhenU.com also *uses* the mark by including Plaintiff's URL, www.1800Lenses.com, in the proprietary WhenU.com directory of terms that triggers pop-up advertisements on SaveNow users' computers. In so doing, WhenU.com 'uses' Plaintiff's mark by including a version of Plaintiff's 1-800 LENSES mark, to advertise and publicize companies that are in direct competition with the Plaintiff."

Point (b)

Confusion for purposes of the Lanham Act is shown where there is a likelihood that an appreciable number of ordinarily prudent purchasers are likely to be misled, or indeed simply confused, as to the source of the goods in question or where consumers are likely to believe that the challenged use of a trademark is somehow sponsored, endorsed, or authorized by its owner. Thus, "confusion" for purposes of the Lanham Act includes confusion of any kind, including confusion as to source, sponsorship, affiliation, connection, or identification.

Excerpt (b1)

"It is black letter law that actual confusion need not be shown to prevail under the Lanham Act, since actual confusion is very difficult to prove and the Act requires only a likelihood of confusion as to source. In order to support a claim of infringement, a plaintiff must show a probability, not just a possibility, of confusion; a likelihood of confusion is actionable even absent evidence of actual confusion."

Excerpt (b2)

"Confusion that occurs prior to a sale may be actionable under the Lanham Act. For example, *initial interest confusion* occurs when a consumer, seeking a particular trademark holder's product, is instead lured away to the product of a competitor because of the competitor's use of a similar mark, even though the consumer is not actually confused about the source of the products or services at the time of actual purchase."

Excerpt (b3)

"Federal courts assess the likelihood of consumer confusion by examining (1) the strength of plaintiff's mark, (2) the similarity between the plaintiff's and defendant's marks, (3) proximity of the parties' services, (4) the likelihood that one party will 'bridge the gap' into the other's product line, (5) the existence of actual confusion between the marks, (6) the good faith of the defendant in using the mark, (7) the quality of the defendant's services, and (8) the sophistication of the consumers."

Held

WhenU infringed the 1-800 Lenses trademark by using the 1-800 LENSES mark or confusingly similar terms as an element in the SaveNow proprietary directory. **Ruling in favor of 800-Lenses.**

Truck Rental International Inc. v. Web Marketing LLC, Federal District Court, Western District of Longville (2009)

Facts

- Truck Rental International Inc. (TRI) claimed that Web Marketing LLC's (Web Marketing) pop-up advertising model infringes upon TRI's trademark. TRI alleged that Web Marketing's pop-up advertisements, which crowd the computer user's screen and block out TRI's Web site display, in effect, infringe on TRI's registered trademark.

- The SuperSavings program is computer software that only operates on the Microsoft Windows operating system. The SuperSavings software, if installed, resides on individual computer users' computer desktops. When a computer user who has installed the SuperSavings software (a "SuperSavings user") browses the Internet, the SuperSavings software scans activity conducted within the SuperSavings user's Internet browser, comparing URLs, Web site addresses, search terms, and Web page content accessed by the SuperSavings user with a proprietary directory, using algorithms contained in the software.

- The average computer user who conducts a Web search for the TRI Web site would expect the TRI Web site to appear on her computer screen; however, in this case, the computer screen fills with the advertisement of a TRI competitor.

- The user must then click and close the pop-up advertisement window in order to get to his destination, the TRI Web site. While at first blush this detour in the user's Web search seems like a siphoning off of a business opportunity, the fact is that the computer user consented to this detour when the user downloaded Web Marketing's computer software from the Internet. In other words, the user deliberately or unwittingly downloaded the pop-up advertisement software.

POINTS OF LAW AND OPINION EXCERPTS

Point (a)

A fundamental prerequisite for claims of trademark infringement pursuant to unfair competition is proof that the defendant used one of the plaintiff's protected marks in commerce.

Excerpt (a1)

"Web Marketing's pop-up advertisement software resides in individual computers as a result of the invitation and consent of the individual computer user and, thus, the advertisements do not use, alter, or interfere with TRI's trademarks and copyrights. Alas, computer users must endure pop-up advertising along with her ugly brother unsolicited bulk e-mail, 'spam,' as a burden of using the Internet."

Excerpt (a2)

"Domain names, like trade names, do not act as trademarks when they are used to identify a business entity; in order to infringe they must be used to identify the source of goods or services' and 'where . . . the pure machine-linking function is the only use at issue, there is no trademark use and there can be no infringement.' Likewise in the instant case, Web Marketing's incorporation of TRI's URL and 'Truck Rental International' in the SuperSavings program is not a trademark use because Web Marketing merely uses the marks for the 'pure machine-linking function' and in no way advertises or promotes TRI's web address or any other TRI trademark."

Point b

In order to have a claim for trademark infringement under the Lanham Act, the mark owner must show that the defendant used the mark in a manner likely to confuse consumers.

Excerpt (b1)

"Consumer confusion is *not* established merely because trademarks are simultaneously visible to a consumer. Such comparative advertising does not violate trademark law, even when the advertising makes use of a competitor's trademark. A use of a rival's mark that does not engender confusion about origin or quality is permissible. For example, previous cases have held that the use of *'If You Like ESTEE LAUDER . . . You'll Love BEAUTY USA'* on product's packaging and point of sale advertising is lawful comparative advertising. Thus, the appearance of Web Marketing's ads on a user's computer screen at the same time as the TRI web page is a result of how applications operate in the Windows environment and not consistent with evidence of intent to confuse the consumer."

Excerpt (b2)

"The SuperSavings program does not hinder or impede Internet users from accessing TRI's website. The SuperSavings program resides within the user's computer and does not interact or communicate with TRI's website, its computer servers, or its computer systems. Further, the SuperSavings program does not change the underlying appearance of the TRI website. In addition, the SuperSavings program is installed by the computer user who can decline to accept the licensing agreement or decline to download the program. Thus, the user controls the computer display the moment the Web Marketing ad pops up, and the user may also have other programs with pop-up windows notifying the user of an event within the computer system. The SuperSavings program is, therefore, no different than an e-mail system that pops a window up when the registered user receives a new e-mail message."

Held

In favor of the *Web Marketing.com, Inc.* While pop-up advertisements seize the user's computer screen with a window of advertisement, blocking out the object of your search and your document, requiring you to click several times to clear your computer screen, these advertisements do not meet the use and consumer confusion requirements necessary to prove trademark infringement.

Overview and Objectives

In 1996, a deadly strain of bacteria broke out among residents of some West Coast states and eventually spread into western Canada. When the bacteria was traced to juice products made by the Odwalla Juice Company in California, the company's loyal customers and market analysts were shocked in disbelief. Odwalla had prided itself on being a socially responsible company that was passionate about producing the healthiest juice on the market.

The events that followed the outbreak provide an example of how vastly different areas of the law impact corporate strategy during a corporate crisis and how business ethics principles help drive the decision-making process. The objective of this case study[1] is to attempt to understand legal and ethical implications using a comprehensive and practical approach. In analyzing this case, students hone skills in constructing a business strategy for handing a crisis by (1) spotting the multifaceted legal and ethical challenges of the crisis, (2) recognizing the strengths and weaknesses in Odwalla's responses, and (3) using legal insight and ethical decision-making models to craft a response.

Review Legal Concepts

Prior to reading the case, briefly review the following legal concepts that were covered previously in this textbook: Food and drug safety (p. 535), Products liability (p. 226), Negligence (p. 217), Criminal law (p. 553), and Business ethics (p. 110). Think of these areas of the law as you read the case study facts and questions.

THE ODWALLA JUICE COMPANY'S ORIGINS

Odwalla Juice Company was started in 1986 by a group of health-conscious friends living together in the San Francisco Bay area. Starting with a hand juicer and organically grown fruit, the owners produced fresh juice in the back shed of one of the founder's homes and sold their juice by delivering it daily to area restaurants. Perhaps the most essential part of their business model was their claim that their juice was fresh from the fruit and without the pasteurization process that was used by other juice producers. In fact, Odwalla was one of the pioneers of a wider movement in the United States favoring more

organic food consumption. Odwalla's founders held the belief that pasteurization, the process of heating the juice to a certain temperature for purposes of killing any bacteria that had developed during growing, picking, or processing, affected the taste of the juice and was unnecessary. Instead, Odwalla used an acid-based rinsing process to kill bacteria. Producing fresh organic fruit juice as a central component of its business model, Odwalla developed a loyal following of consumers that desired the freshest juice possible and its sales grew exponentially. By the mid-1990s, Odwalla was selling nearly $90 million worth of juice per year.

"SOIL TO SOUL"

Odwalla's founders were at the forefront of the corporate social responsibility movement that can be traced to the mid-1980s. Indeed, as one of their founders was fond of saying, they embraced a "Zen-like philosophy" in all of their dealings, where community was an important factor in the equation. The company employed a *soil to soul* metaphor to describe its commitment to using fresh organic fruit (soil) to nurture the "body whole" (soul) of its consumer. Odwalla's reputation as a socially responsible, growth-oriented company flourished as they received awards from *Business Ethics* magazine in 1995 for Outstanding Corporate Environmentalism and from *Inc.* magazine in 1996 as Employer of the Year.

CRISIS ON THE COAST

In early October 1996, an outbreak of *E. coli*[2] struck several West Coast states, including California and Washington, and reached into western Canada as well. *E. coli* is a potentially deadly bacterium that develops as a result of contamination of food products or processing. On October 30, 1996, health officials in the state of Washington notified Odwalla that they were investigating a possible link between the *E. coli* outbreak and Odwalla apple and carrot juice. After learning of the potential link, Odwalla's executive management team had an emergency meeting to discuss their response. Although there was no demonstrable link at this

---

[1] A complete bibliography for this case study may be found on this textbook's Web site at www.mhhe.com/Melvin.

[2] For purposes of this case study *E. coli* is shorthand for *E. coli 0157:H7*, which is the name of a strain of bacteria that lives in the digestive tracts of humans and animals. *E. coli* has been found in uncooked meat, raw milk or dairy products, and in raw fruits and vegetables that have not been properly pasteurized or processed.

The Odwalla juice company faced a corporate crisis, which included legal issues and ethical questions, after their product was tied to an *E. coli* outbreak.

point, Odwalla's executive management team decided to mobilize a voluntary recall of products containing apple or carrot products. This was a major financial commitment involving the removal of Odwalla products from nearly 4,600 retail outlets in seven states in just 48 hours. Odwalla claimed that it spent $6.5 million on the recall effort.

Odwalla's corporate crisis took a tragic turn when in November 1996, a 16-month-old child died from *E. coli* after drinking Odwalla apple juice. As many as 60 other consumers were hospitalized with *E. coli*-related illnesses in a period of just one month. At the height of the outbreak, government investigators confirmed that the Odwalla products were in fact the source of the *E. coli* contamination. Odwalla implemented a media strategy including daily statements to the press, internal conference calls where managers were informed of updates, and setting up a Web site to disseminate information. Odwalla publicly promised to pay for all medical expenses of injured consumers and to reevaluate its manufacturing process immediately.

FALL OUT

Odwalla's brand name was decimated by the crisis. Immediately after the outbreak, Odwalla's stock price dropped 34 percent and sales of its juice products fell 90 percent in one month. The outbreak triggered numerous investigations by federal and state authorities. Customers filed negligence lawsuits claiming that Odwalla had known that the acid-rinse method was ineffective and that scientific studies had shown that the method was effective in killing bacteria that caused *E. coli* only 8 percent of the time. After it had been shown that pasteurization was a widely used practice in the industry (although not required by federal or state laws) and that Odwalla management had ignored its own head of quality assurance's warning about potential contamination sources in the factory, the Food and Drug Administration levied a $1.5 million fine, the largest in the agency's history at that time.

Immediately after the recall, Odwalla was widely praised by the media and commentators for its handling of the crisis. The company decided that, despite mounting financial pressures from lawsuits and fines, no employees would be laid off and that they would continue to donate to community charities. Odwalla hired a public relations firm that constructed a standard explanation that the contamination was unforeseeable and that all appropriate safety measures were in place. The public largely believed Odwalla's explanations because its reputation for social responsibility was iron-clad in its consumers' minds. Even the parents of the child whose *E. coli*-related death had ignited the crisis were quoted as saying that they didn't blame the company for her death and that Odwalla had done everything they could have under the circumstances.

However, during the discovery process in one of the lawsuits filed by an injured consumer, it was revealed that Odwalla had more knowledge of a potential health hazard prior to the outbreak than had been previously reported. A report surfaced that indicated that the U.S. Army had rejected Odwalla's proposal to sell their juice in U.S. Army commissaries after an Army inspector found uncommonly high levels of bacteria in a sample and concluded that the risk of contamination was extraordinarily high. The Army rejection had taken place four months prior to the *E. coli* outbreak. Responding to the Army's findings, Odwalla's head of quality assurance recommended that the company add an additional layer of contamination protection by employing a chlorine-based washing system for the fruit. His recommendations were rejected, however, due to management's concern that the chlorine wash would affect the taste of the juice. After the Army disclosures were made public, Odwalla settled several lawsuits despite its earlier resistance to a nonlitigation solution.

Soon after the settlement, *The Seattle Times* wrote a scathing editorial about Odwalla's course of action. The editorial predicted that Odwalla would forever be known as "the careless provider of poisoned fruit juice." Odwalla's stock was now trading at its lowest level ever, and the company was incurring massive debt to cover litigation costs and technology upgrades.

ODWALLA TODAY

After the fallout from the *E. coli* crisis, Odwalla invested heavily in quality assurance technology and eventually became an innovator of a "flash-pasteurization" process that killed all bacteria, but kept the fresh taste and quality of the juice intact. Just two years after the crisis began, the readers of *San Francisco Magazine* voted Odwalla "Best Brand." Although the company looked poised for a comeback, it had accrued substantial debt and was forced to begin exploring the possibility of merger opportunities. After a merger with East Coast juice maker Fresh Samantha in 2000, Odwalla ended up as part of a large acquisition by the Minute Maid division of The Coca-Cola Company in October 2001. Today, Odwalla remains a subsidiary of Coca-Cola and has over 650 employees. Their management continues to focus on its "soil to soul" model and now feature 25 organic products within eight product lines including smoothies, soy shakes, and food bars.

Connecting Legal and Ethical Concepts: Questions for Discussion

Chapter 5, Business Ethics

1. Is there a disconnect between Odwalla's corporate social responsibility model and its actions or course of conduct? In what ways did Odwalla's course of conduct differ from its stated social goals?
2. Because Odwalla was not specifically required to use the pasteurization process at the time, what ethical considerations factor into the decision on whether or not to use pasteurization?
3. Does the fact that the industry standards at the time were to subject the juice to pasteurization impact the ethical decision-making analysis?

Chapter 9, Product Liability

1. Did the manufacturing or *design process* of the juice render it an unreasonably dangerous product under the *Restatements?* Why or why not?
2. Are there any other ways in which the product could have been defective aside from manufacturing or design?

3. What defenses, if any, could Odwalla use to rebut a claim of a defective product?

Chapter 9, Negligence

1. Are there any incidents of negligence indicated in the case (either pre- or post-contamination)?
2. In the context of a negligence analysis, what legal duties did Odwalla owe to its consumers? Do they owe any special duty to consumers?
3. Does failing to comply with industry standards at the time of the contamination constitute a breach of duty?

Chapter 21, FDA Food Safety Regulation

1. What federal statute regulates Odwalla's processes and procedures?
2. Because the FDA required no specific pasteurization standards at the time, should Odwalla be fined for failing to use such a system?
3. If Odwalla had not voluntarily recalled the juice, what options did the FDA have in response to the outbreak?

Chapter 22, Criminal Law

1. Apply the Model Penal Code sections on criminal liability for business entities to the Odwalla case. Do the facts in the case indicate that Odwalla's action rose to the level of criminal culpability? If yes, what defense, if any, is available to Odwalla?
2. Odwalla's management consistently issued statements denying that they had any actual or constructive knowledge that Odwalla's processing systems were dangerous. Do any facts in the case study contradict those statements? Are these facts sufficient to establish the elements of criminal intent on the part of the executive that made the denials?

ASSIGNMENT: Devise Odwalla's Strategy

Odwalla ordered a voluntary recall that was expensive and potentially devastating to the company before an affirmative link was found. Assume you were one of the managers at the Odwalla emergency meeting held after the *E.coil* outbreak. What are Odwalla's options? Using the legal decisions in business analytical model in Chapter 1, "Legal Foundations," and the ethical decision-making paradigm in Chapter 5, "Business, Societal, and Ethical Contexts of Law," as a starting point, devise a strategy that includes the appropriate balance between (1) representing the best interests of the primary and secondary stakeholders, (2) protecting the company's future, (3) minimizing the risk of public harm, and (4) fulfilling the corporation's commitment to corporate social responsibility.

Overview and Objectives

In August 2001, the Federal Bureau of Investigation arrested eight individuals involved in a nationwide scheme to defraud the McDonald's Corporation and its customers by fraudulently manipulating McDonald's promotional prize contests over a period of five years. Although no McDonald's employees were implicated in the scam, the arrests sparked class-action litigation by customers and competitors against McDonald's under a variety of legal theories. The events that led up to the arrests and the legal and ethical implications of McDonald's response to the revelations of the fraud are examined in this case study.[1]

Review Legal Concepts

Prior to reading the case, briefly review the following legal concepts that were covered in the textbook: Standing (p. 79), Arbitration (p. 90), Consumer fraud (p. 524), Contracts-agreement (p. 130), Unjust enrichment (p. 126), Agency (p. 250), Criminal law (p. 553), and Business ethics (p. 110).

MCDONALD'S PROMOTIONAL GAMES

McDonald's is perhaps the most familiar fast-food restaurant name in the world. The business began in 1940 with a restaurant opened by brothers Richard and Maurice McDonald in San Bernardino, California. Their introduction of the "Speedee Service System" in 1948 established the principles of the modern fast-food restaurant. The present company dates it founding to the opening of one of the first McDonald's franchises by Ray Kroc. Eventually, Mr. Kroc purchased the McDonald brothers' shares and began a worldwide expansion. The company became listed on the public stock market in 1965 and there are now more than 32,000 McDonald's restaurants around the world.

Marketing Strategies
One of McDonald's most successful marketing strategies has been to use various cash games of chance based on themes from popular television shows such as *Who Wants to Be a Millionaire?* and another promotional cash game based on the popular board game *Monopoly*. McDonald's operates these games as part of a consolidated national and international advertising and marketing effort. Industry experts

have lauded McDonald's games as highly effective in attracting more customers and encouraging more visits by offering the opportunity to win instant prizes ranging from food to cash prizes of $1 million. Each of the promotional games has low-value, mid-value, and high-value prizes. In order to win a prize, a McDonald's customer obtains a game piece, which may be (1) handed out at a restaurant either attached to food paper products (such as french fry boxes and drink cups) or unattached and handed out separately, (2) found in an advertising insert of a newspaper, (3) received by direct mail, or (4) obtained by requesting a game piece via the mail. Customers have the opportunity to become instant winners or winners by collecting specific game pieces. Low-value prizes include food items and low-dollar cash prizes. High-value prizes include vehicles and cash prizes up to $1 million. Customers can either

The Department of Justice's announcement of arrests related to a fraud scheme involving game pieces from McDonald's *Monopoly* promotional game sparked legal and ethical challenges for the fast-food giant.

---

[1] A complete bibliography for this case study may be found on this textbook's Web site at www.mhhe.com/melvin.

win the cash prize by obtaining an instant $1 million winner game piece or by collecting a sufficient number of certain game pieces.

Simon Marketing

Simon Marketing, Inc. (Simon), an international marketing company headquartered in Los Angeles, was originally hired by McDonald's to develop its highly successful Happy Meals prize and promotional campaigns in the 1980s. Simon eventually became the exclusive company handling McDonald's promotional games including "Monopoly Game at McDonald's," "Hatch, Match and Win," "When the USA Wins, You Win," and "Who Wants to Be a Millionaire?" In order to claim a high-value prize, the winner was required to redeem the winning game piece through Simon's security procedures. After receiving a game piece claim, Simon confirmed the legitimacy of the game piece, and would notify McDonald's that the claim was legitimate. McDonald's then distributed the prize to the winner.

In addition to verification of winning game pieces, Simon was also responsible for printing and distribution of game pieces. As part of their agreement with McDonald's, Simon provided security measures to ensure the integrity of promotional games. Simon entrusted its security chief, retired police officer Jerome Jacobson, with the responsibility of ensuring the games' integrity and with disseminating the high-value pieces through legitimate channels.

Arrests and Indictments

In August 2001, the U.S. Attorney's Office filed criminal charges against eight people in Georgia, South Carolina, Florida, Texas, Indiana, and Wisconsin as part of a nationwide investigation into a plot to defraud the public by diverting winning game pieces from various McDonald's cash award giveaways. Dubbed "Operation Final Answer" by government investigators, the Department of Justice alleged that the group had been responsible for more than $20 million worth of winning game pieces that were diverted from proper delivery, then fraudulently claimed by winners pretending to be legitimate. The ringleader of the plot was 58-year-old Jerome Jacobson, the director of security at Simon Marketing. Jacobson devised a way to remove high-price game pieces prior to their distribution to retail McDonald's restaurants. Jacobson concocted a system of recruiters (none of whom were Simon or McDonald's employees) who solicited others willing to falsely claim that they were legitimate winners of the McDonald's games. Prosecutors alleged that Jacobson sold $1 million prize pieces from the games and charged the fake winner $50,000 in cash plus a commission for the recruiter. On mid-value

prizes and luxury vehicle prizes, the recruiters would sell the winning game pieces to other family members or friends. Among those arrested were a husband and wife whose son acted as one of Jacobson's recruiters.

After Jacobson agreed to cooperate with federal authorities in exchange for leniency, the government announced criminal indictments of 51 more individuals involved in the scam. Eventually, Jacobson pled guilty and was sentenced to 37 months in prison, assessed $750,000 in fines, and ordered to pay $13.4 million in restitution.

Civil Suits

Two weeks after the government announced the indictment, the first civil lawsuit was filed against McDonald's. By October 2001, so many civil suits had been filed against it that McDonald's asked the federal courts to consolidate all of the litigation into a single proceeding. Lawsuits alleged various claims, including violation of consumer fraud protection laws, unjust enrichment, and breach of contract. In many cases, the plaintiff sought class action[2] status.

In one case filed in an Illinois trial court, a customer sued McDonald's and Simon under the state consumer fraud statute and sought class action status. The plaintiffs alleged that McDonald's and Simon's actions constituted deceptive conduct and omissions of material terms from their promotional games. They pointed to evidence that McDonald's had been made aware of the fraud being conducted by Jacobson, but continued to market their promotional games, including publishing the odds of winning. for at least an additional 8 months. However, because of Jacobson's scheme, the plaintiffs alleged that their actual odds of winning a substantial prize were zero.

Other cases centered on a theory of unjust enrichment. In these cases, plaintiffs alleged that McDonald's promotional games were highly successful and resulted in increased revenue for McDonald's and Simon. The plaintiffs pointed to evidence that McDonald's had a spike in sales during certain promotions. They alleged that McDonald's continued to use the promotion even after they knew that the integrity of the game was compromised and, therefore, any profits made were caused by the fraud. Because customers were induced to purchase McDonald's products through the promotion, McDonald's was unjustly enriched by retaining the profits from the products.

---

[2]A class action lawsuit is a method for conducting a lawsuit in which a large group of persons with a well-defined common interest (class) has a representative of the group litigate the claim on behalf of the larger group, without the need to join every individual member of the class.

McDonald's was also sued by its competitors over the scandal. In *Phoenix of Broward, Inc. v. McDonald's Corporation*,[3] the owner of a Burger King franchise in Ft. Lauderdale, Florida, filed suit against McDonald's for false advertising and unfair competition. The owner alleged that McDonald's had enticed customers away from Burger King by employing the promotional game. Because the promotional materials represented that each customer had a fair chance to win the high-value prizes, Phoenix alleged that McDonald's actual knowledge that the game was rigged and their course of conduct after learning of the FBI investigation in continuing the promotion constituted unfair competition. Phoenix also claimed that the fraudulent games promotion yielded an unnatural spike in profits for McDonald's and that the Burger King franchise suffered damages as a result of McDonald's conduct.

MCDONALD'S STRATEGY

On the day the Justice Department announced the arrest of Jacobson and seven others, McDonald's announced that it was suspending the game entirely pending an internal investigation of the matter. They also announced a campaign to regain any lost public trust by launching an immediate $10 million promotional giveaway. The promotion allowed customers to win prizes of up to $1 million from promotional game pieces during a week-long period beginning in late August 2001.

Immediately after the arrests, McDonald's terminated its 25-year relationship with Simon by unilaterally cancelling its contract with the agency. The move was devastating to Simon because McDonald's represented two-thirds of the agency's annual revenue.[4] After the revelations of fraud, Simon's other major client, Philip Morris,[5] who contracted with Simon to run promotional campaigns for its Kraft and Marlboro brands, also terminated their relationship with Simon. In less than one week, the value of Simon's public shares plunged 78 percent and the company was facing dozens of lawsuits and a criminal investigation.

Aggressive Litigation McDonald's employed what can aptly be described as an aggressive litigation strategy by vigorously defending lawsuits while also pursuing Simon for reimbursement of the costs being incurred by McDonald's because of the fraudulent act of Simon's employee.

For each case that it defended that was related to the fraud, McDonald's either challenged the *standing* of the plaintiffs to bring an action against McDonald's based on the fraud, or they sought a court order to compel *arbitration* based on the published rules of the game.

Phoenix Case In the *Phoenix* case, McDonald's asserted that Phoenix did not have standing in a case alleging unfair competition because its actions were unrelated to any provable harm suffered by Phoenix's restaurant. Phoenix alleged that McDonald's misrepresented customers' chances to win high-value prizes, but also alleged that as a result of this false advertising, the fraudulent promotion induced customers who would have eaten at Phoenix's Burger King restaurants (and not any other fast-food restaurants). Ultimately the courts agreed with McDonald's and dismissed the lawsuit, holding that Phoenix's allegations of the link between the false advertising (McDonald's games) and the injury suffered by Phoenix (decrease in Burger King's sales) was too vague to have standing to sue.

Customer Lawsuits While McDonald's was successful at repelling suits by competitors, its attempts to halt lawsuits by its customers had mixed results. The stakes for customer lawsuits were becoming increasingly high as each plaintiff requested class action status. In each customer case, McDonald's argued that the plaintiff was bound by the terms of the Official Contest Rules (Rules) published by McDonald's in conjunction with each of its promotional cash giveaway games. The Rules included an arbitration clause whereby participants in the game promotion agreed to resolve any disputes by final and binding arbitration. The clause called for the arbitration to be held at the regional office of the American Arbitration Association (AAA) located closest to the participant.

In *Popovich v. McDonald's*,[6] a federal district court ruled that the arbitration clause included in the official rules was invalid because the arbitration costs were too prohibitive. Popovich argued that the fees associated with an arbitration proceeding rendered the arbitration agreement an ineffective way to enforce his statutory rights of recovery from McDonald's for their fraudulent conduct. Popovich submitted evidence that, under the AAA rules, his claim would have to be arbitrated using the high-fee *commercial* procedures instead of

---

[3]489 F.3d 1156 (11th Cir. 2007).

[4]In the year prior to the scandal, Simon's annual revenue was $768 million.

[5]Philip Morris changed its name in to Altria in 2003.

---

[6]189 F. Supp. 2d 772 (2002)

the much lower cost *consumer* procedures. In ruling in favor of Popovich, the court held that because Popovich sought $20 million in damages for his potential class action, the fees required by the AAA would be between $48,000 and $126,000. The court concluded that, in the context of this claim, the arbitration costs were prohibitive and the clause was thus unenforceable.

An alternate theory was advanced by the plaintiff in *James v. McDonald's Corp.*[7] In that case, James argued that she should not be forced to arbitrate her claims because she never entered into an agreement to arbitrate her dispute. The plaintiff claimed that she was not aware of the Rules, much less any rules that deprived her of a jury trial. She maintained that customers cannot be expected to read every container of food they purchase in order to know that they are entering into a contract. She also argued that, even if she was found to be bound by the Rules, the arbitration clause in the Rules was invalid because it was overly burdensome due to the high up-front costs required to pursue a claim through the AAA. However, the court ultimately ruled against James, found the arbitration clause to be valid, and refused to allow her lawsuit to go forward in the courts. In rejecting James's claim that the costs were too burdensome, the court pointed out that James had not submitted evidence that she considered applying for a fee waiver from the AAA that could have reduced the fees significantly.

SIMON LAWSUIT AND COUNTERSUIT

Two months after McDonald's terminated its relationship with Simon, its parent company filed a $1.9 billion lawsuit against McDonald's in which they alleged breach of contract, fraud, and defamation. Simon alleged that, after learning of the nearly year-long FBI investigation, McDonald's ran a fraudulent campaign to intentionally destroy Simon for its own public relations and financial benefit. The lawsuit also accused McDonald's of orchestrating a smear campaign through McDonald's representatives contacting other Simon clients and urging them to quit doing business with Simon. Simon alleged that McDonald's abrupt termination of their contract was unwarranted and unlawful and resulted in substantial losses.

McDonald's responded with a $105 million countersuit against Simon for negligence in failing to detect the fraud scheme and breach of contract. McDonald's contended that their contract with Simon required Simon to repay McDonald's for any losses it incurred as a result of Simon's conduct. Given the losses from the embezzlement and the subsequent giveaway that was required to restore public confidence, McDonald's argued that they were entitled to be reimbursed by Simon.

SETTLEMENTS AND AFTERMATH

After aggressively battling litigants in the courtroom for a year, McDonald's reevaluated its two-front litigation strategy. The company engaged in settlement negotiations with customer lawsuit plaintiffs and was able to structure an agreement with Simon's insurance carrier that ultimately helped settled the class action claims filed against it by various customers. One year later, McDonald's agreed to a final settlement with Simon.

Customer Class Actions The uncertainties surrounding the arbitration clause and expenses of litigating a class action case resulted in a change in McDonald's strategy. Beginning in April 2002, McDonald's and Simon began to settle the various class action complaints filed by consumers by tapping the proceeds from Simon's liability insurance policies. Eventually, McDonald's settled a similar class action consumer suit filed in Canada.

Simon Litigation In an August 2003 filing with the Securities and Exchange Commission, McDonald's reported that it had agreed to pay Simon $16.6 million to settle all claims that were raised in the lawsuit.[8] However, in the meantime, Simon had effectively eliminated a majority of its ongoing promotions business operations and was in the process of disposing of its assets and settling liabilities related to the fraud. During the second quarter of 2002, the company ceased operations altogether except for attempting to find a buyer for its remaining assets. A September 2009 filing indicated that the company had reduced its workforce to four employees (from 136 employees in 2001). Although the company was not successful in finding a buyer for many years, in December 2009, Simon's remaining directors issued public disclosures that they had formed a committee to investigate the potential of an acquisition or combination with another company.

---

[7]417 F.3d 672 (7th Cir. 2005).

[8]Simon also sued Philip Morris and Simon Marketing's auditing firms (KPMG, PricewaterhouseCoopers, and Ernst & Young). Each case was settled before trial with a favorable outcome for Simon.

Connecting Legal and Ethical Concepts: Questions for Discussion

Chapter 4, "Resolving Disputes: Litigation and Alternative Dispute Resolution Options"

1. In the *Phoenix* case, the court ruled that competitors didn't have standing to sue McDonald's for fraud in the promotional games. Compare the standards used to assess standing in *Alston v. Advance Brands and Importing Company* (Case 4.1) to the facts of this case study. Would competitors have standing to sue McDonald's using the *Alston* standard? Would customers have standing?

2. Could the arbitration clause used by McDonald's in their Rules fit into any of the four grounds for unenforceability under the Federal Arbitration Act? How does *Green Tree Financial Corporation v. Randolph* (Case 4.4) apply to this case study?

Chapter 5, "Business, Societal, and Ethical Contexts of Law"

1. Consider the ethical dilemma of McDonald's if they were approached by government authorities and informed that the promotion's integrity was suspect because of possible embezzlement. However, in order to gather additional evidence, investigators requested that McDonald's take no action until arrests were made. What was McDonald's ethical duty at this point? If they continue to run the game with knowledge of the fraud, no matter what their motives, doesn't that expose the company to significant liability?

2. Is there a conflict in this case between McDonald's duties to primary stakeholders and its duties to secondary shareholders?

3. Was McDonald's decision not to discontinue the promotion in the face of ongoing fraud more of a principles-based approach or a consequences-based approach to ethical decision-making?

4. Was the use of class action litigation ethically justified in this case? Were the civil suits an attempt to redress harm or a boon for law firms that specialize in class action litigation? Were the plaintiffs more interested in shaking down McDonald's or in justice?

Chapter 6, "Overview and Formation of Contracts"

1. Why did trial courts consider the Rules contractual language binding on participants of the games when it was obvious that most customers hadn't actually read them? Have the customers agreed to the terms of the Rules contract simply by purchasing a soft drink? Why or why not?

2. Assuming that offer and acceptance are satisfied, what consideration supports a customer–McDonald's contract?

3. Could the inclusion of an arbitration clause by McDonald's in an advertisement amid logos and trademarks be considered bad faith and held invalid as unconscionable?

Chapter 10, "Agency and Employment Relationships"

1. What is the agency status and relationship between McDonald's and Simon? Based on your answer, what duties did the parties owe each other? Were any duties breached?

2. To what extent is Simon liable for the embezzlement scheme of its employee Jacobson? Were Jacobson's actions within the scope of his employment? Why or why not?

Chapter 21, "Consumer Protection Law"

1. Could McDonald's conduct, specifically its continuing operations after being informed of possible fraud in its promotional games, constitute deceptive advertising and a deceptive sales practice under FTC regulations?

2. Suppose that one lawsuit that was brought against McDonald's was in New Jersey and the state court applied the New Jersey Consumer Fraud Act in the same way the appellate court applied it in *Vagias v. Woodmont Properties* (Case 21.1). Would McDonald's be liable under the state law? Why or why not?

3. Would the answer to your questions in 1 and 2 above be the same if McDonald's halted the promotion as soon as it learned of the FBI investigation?

Chapter 22, "Criminal Law and Procedure in Business"

1. Do Jacobson's actions amount to fraud? Embezzlement? Theft?

2. Ultimately, the government charged Jacobson and his co-conspirators with mail fraud and wire fraud. Why do you think the government did not charge them with embezzlement?

3. Could the executives of Simon be held criminally liable for the embezzlement perpetrated by Jacobson? Why or why not?

ASSIGNMENT: Devise a Strategy for McDonald's

Assume you are one of the managers called to a confidential meeting to discuss McDonald's strategy after notification by government authorities that its promotional games were being rigged by a Simon insider. What are McDonald's options? Using the legal decisions in business analytical model in Chapter 1, "Legal Foundations," and the ethical decision-making paradigm in Chapter 5, "Business, Societal, and Ethical Contexts of Law" as a starting point, devise a strategy that includes the appropriate balance between (1) representing the best interests of its primary and secondary stakeholders, (2) protecting the future of the company, (3) minimizing the risk of public harm, and (4) addressing factors related to corporate social responsibility. Memorialize your strategy in a two-page memorandum.

APPENDIX A

A Business Student's Guide to Understanding Cases and Finding the Law

This textbook emphasizes ways in which business owners and managers can add value to their companies by using legal insight for business planning and limiting risk. Using a basic system for understanding court case opinions improves one's ability to grasp the impact of the law on business. Because much of the law is composed of cases and statutes, learning the fundamentals of how and where to find the law allows business owners and managers to work more effectively with counsel and empowers them to become better decision makers by using legal considerations as a part of their strategic planning.

UNDERSTANDING CASE LAW: The SUR System

All of the legal cases in this textbook are reported in a unique format designed especially for business students. For each case, students are provided with a summary of the case facts and a synopsis of the court's decision and opinion. Students then read an actual excerpt from the case in the *words of the court* that is directly related to the legal point being covered in the text. All procedural language and parts of the opinion that are unrelated to the legal point have been edited out. This allows the reader to focus on one or two key points of law in the case. However, case law from other sources is likely to be a complete word-for-word reporting without any trustworthy explanation or summary. Understanding cases by reading the full text can be challenging even for attorneys. The *SUR system* provides business students with a systematic method for analyzing cases that will help draw out essential information without getting bogged down in legal details.

SUR stands for *Scan, Understand, Review.* Although this system is helpful for reading any complex or dense text, it is specifically tailored for reading legal cases. Not only will this method help students fully understand the cases contained in this text, it is also useful for comprehending full-length cases found in other sources.

Scan the case.   Read the *headings* and *first two sentences* of each section of the case until the end of the opinion. Then read the *last three* sentences of the case. While scanning, use a pencil or highlighter to note names of the parties, the court that decided the case, and the final decision of the court.

Understand the case.   After scanning, begin to read (and reread when necessary) the case from the beginning. Use a pencil to circle important facts and legal terms. At this stage, many students find it useful to draw flow charts and other summaries in order to understand a chain of facts more clearly. Look up legal terms using the online law dictionary provided in Table A.1 later in this appendix. Do your best to skip procedural language such as the standards of review for an appellate court or issues related to pretrial discovery or motions. While reading the fact summary in the beginning of the case, keep the following question in mind:

ISSUE: What legal *issues* are being created by the party's actions? That is, what legal *question* will the court have to answer?

Once you begin reading the court's ruling, continue with marking potentially important phrases with special attention to the court's statement of the current law. Look for wording such as "the statute provides for" or "the only relief available under the statute" to alert you to important language. As you read and mark the text, keep in mind the following questions and jot down any related thoughts:

RULE: What law *generally* applies to this situation and are there any exceptions? What statute, common law, or other legal doctrine is applicable in this situation? What

---

FIGURE A.1   Example of SUR System Using Case 1.1 Kaufman v. Kauffman

After the *Scan* step, the text would appear as follows:

> **CASE 1.1 Kauffman-Harmon v. Kauffman, 36 P. 3d 408 (Sup. Ct., Mont. 2001)**
>
> **FACT SUMMARY:** Kauffman created a corporation to hold certain assets in a manner intended to minimize tax liability. After creation of the corporation, a judgment was entered against Kauffman as a result of a lawsuit against him. In order to avoid paying the judgment, Kauffman transferred all of his stock into his spouse's name. His spouse eventually transferred ownership of the stock to several Kauffman children. Several years later, a dispute developed between the children concerning the stock and Kauffman intervened by filing a claim with the trial court requesting that all stock be transferred back to him on the basis that he was the rightful owner of the stock and that the transfer was nothing more than a temporary trust. The children contended that Kauffman is not the equitable owner of the stock and is not entitled to relief due to the clean hands doctrine.
>
> **SYNOPSIS OF DECISION AND OPINION:** The Supreme Court of Montana ruled in favor of the Kauffman children holding that Kauffman was not entitled to relief. Because Kauffman's transfer was in perpetrating an exchange of stock only to avoid paying the judgment legally entered against him, the transaction was a bad-faith action that bordered on a fraudulent transaction. The court reasoned that the rightful owner of the stock was the Kauffman children and that Kauffman's claims were barred by the clean hands doctrine. The court concluded that recognizing his claim would result in a gross wrong being done to the children and the shareholders of the corporation.
>
> **WORDS OF THE COURT: CLEAN HANDS DOCTRINE**
> "The doctrine of clean hands provides that parties must not expect relief in equity, unless they come into court with clean hands. [. . .] Thus, no one can take advantage of his own wrong. [. . .] Court['s] will not aid a party whose claim had its inception in the party's wrongdoing whether the victim of the wrongdoing is the other party or a third party."

precedent exists? Courts often start the legal analysis section of their opinion by stating what the law is or by quoting from the statute at issue.

ANALYSIS: How does the court apply the law to this set of facts? Are there any other factors that the court is considering when applying the law? Are there any legal exceptions or privileges that apply to these facts? Was it necessary to deviate from precedent?

CONCLUSION: What was the court's answer to the question posed in the issue phases of this analysis?

Review the case. Use a highlighter (some students may find it helpful to use a different color highlighter for reviewing than the color used for scanning) to go over the case one more time. Read the case at a reading speed that is halfway between scanning and

FIGURE A.2

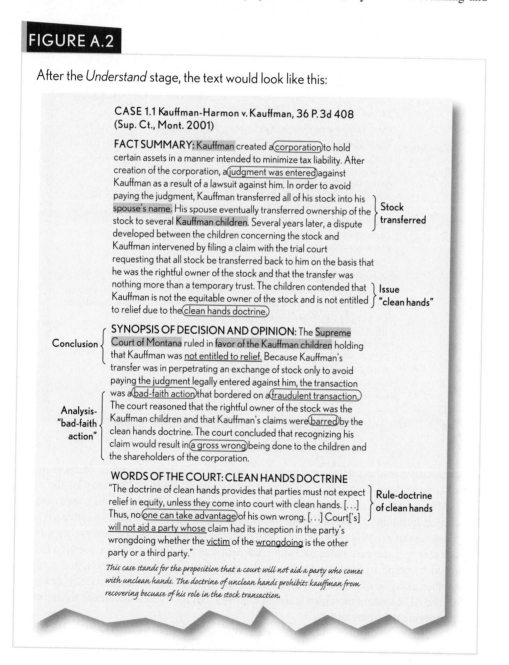

After the *Understand* stage, the text would look like this:

CASE 1.1 Kauffman-Harmon v. Kauffman, 36 P. 3d 408 (Sup. Ct., Mont. 2001)

FACT SUMMARY: Kauffman created a corporation to hold certain assets in a manner intended to minimize tax liability. After creation of the corporation, a judgment was entered against Kauffman as a result of a lawsuit against him. In order to avoid paying the judgment, Kauffman transferred all of his stock into his spouse's name. His spouse eventually transferred ownership of the stock to several Kauffman children. Several years later, a dispute developed between the children concerning the stock and Kauffman intervened by filing a claim with the trial court requesting that all stock be transferred back to him on the basis that he was the rightful owner of the stock and that the transfer was nothing more than a temporary trust. The children contended that Kauffman is not the equitable owner of the stock and is not entitled to relief due to the clean hands doctrine.

} Stock transferred

} Issue "clean hands"

Conclusion {

SYNOPSIS OF DECISION AND OPINION: The Supreme Court of Montana ruled in favor of the Kauffman children holding that Kauffman was not entitled to relief. Because Kauffman's transfer was in perpetrating an exchange of stock only to avoid paying the judgment legally entered against him, the transaction was a bad-faith action that bordered on a fraudulent transaction.

Analysis- "bad-faith action" {

The court reasoned that the rightful owner of the stock was the Kauffman children and that Kauffman's claims were barred by the clean hands doctrine. The court concluded that recognizing his claim would result in a gross wrong being done to the children and the shareholders of the corporation.

WORDS OF THE COURT: CLEAN HANDS DOCTRINE
"The doctrine of clean hands provides that parties must not expect relief in equity, unless they come into court with clean hands. [...] Thus, no one can take advantage of his own wrong. [...] Court['s] will not aid a party whose claim had its inception in the party's wrongdoing whether the victim of the wrongdoing is the other party or a third party."

} Rule-doctrine of clean hands

This case stands for the proposition that a court will not aid a party who comes with unclean hands. The doctrine of unclean hands prohibits kauffman from recovering becuase of his role in the stock transaction.

FIGURE A.3

After the *Review* stage, the text would look like this:

CASE 1.1 Kauffman-Harmon v. Kauffman, 36 P. 3d 408 (Sup. Ct., Mont. 2001)

FACT SUMMARY: Kauffman created a corporation to hold certain assets in a manner intended to minimize tax liability. After creation of the corporation, a judgment was entered against Kauffman as a result of a lawsuit against him. In order to avoid paying the judgment, Kauffman transferred all of his stock into his spouse's name. His spouse eventually transferred ownership of the stock to several Kauffman children. Several years later, a dispute developed between the children concerning the stock and Kauffman intervened by filing a claim with the trial court requesting that all stock be transferred back to him on the basis that he was the rightful owner of the stock and that the transfer was nothing more than a temporary trust. The children contended that Kauffman is not the equitable owner of the stock and is not entitled to relief due to the clean hands doctrine.

} Stock transferred

} Issue "clean hands"

SYNOPSIS OF DECISION AND OPINION: The Supreme Court of Montana ruled in favor of the Kauffman children holding that Kauffman was not entitled to relief. Because Kauffman's transfer was in perpetrating an exchange of stock only to avoid paying the judgment legally entered against him, the transaction was a bad-faith action that bordered on a fraudulent transaction. The court reasoned that the rightful owner of the stock was the Kauffman children and that Kauffman's claims were barred by the clean hands doctrine. The court concluded that recognizing his claim would result in a gross wrong being done to the children and the shareholders of the corporation.

Conclusion {

Analysis- "bad-faith action" {

WORDS OF THE COURT: CLEAN HANDS DOCTRINE

"The doctrine of clean hands provides that parties must not expect relief in equity, unless they come into court with clean hands. [...] Thus, no one can take advantage of his own wrong. [...] Court['s] will not aid a party whose claim had its inception in the party's wrongdoing whether the victim of the wrongdoing is the other party or a third party."

} Rule-doctrine of clean hands

This case stands for the proposition that a court will not aid a party who comes with unclean hands. The doctrine of unclean hands prohibits kauffman from recovering becuase of his role in the stock transaction.

---

comprehensive reading. Highlight sparingly and only what you found to be most important. Many students find it helpful to sketch out a flow chart or summary of the entire case. After reviewing the case, spot and note the answers to the issue, rule, analysis, and conclusion questions. Then put away the materials and consider a final question: *What is the fundamental premise of this case?* Write out the answer in two or three sentences and include that with the case notes for future use. Difficulty in answering that question may be remedied by going back to the *Understand* step and refining the issue, rule, and analysis. Remember that you may not look at the case again for several weeks or months before an exam. The SUR system increases learning intensity and provides a document ready for use when studying the material later.

For an example of the SUR system applied to a full length case, go to this textbook's Web site at www.mhhe.com/melvin.

FINDING THE LAW

The Internet has been the single most important force in providing unprecedented public access to the law. Cases, statutes, and topics on legal information are accessible online and largely free of charge. In addition to Internet services, several commercial services (such as Lexis/Nexus or Westlaw) provide special versions of case law that are enhanced with summaries, explanations, and a system that ties cases together based on legal topics. This four-step method provides a systematic way to find the law either through an Internet-based service or by using a commercial service.

Step 1: Identify a precise legal question.
The first step in finding the law is to clearly identify a legal question to answer. Using your knowledge of levels and sources of law covered in Chapter 1, try to determine whether the question is best answered by a statute or a case. For example, suppose that Adams is an employee of Coats and Hats Co. (CHC), a business with 45 employees. One morning he informs his manager, Icahn, that he has been subpoenaed for jury duty in a state court and will need the next day off with pay. Because the company was performing a crucial inventory count that week, Adams was needed in the warehouse or, alternatively, a replacement needed to be hired. Icahn wants to know if CHC is legally obligated to permit Adams the time off necessary to serve on jury duty. If so, is the company legally responsible for paying Adams while he is on jury duty? Because the issue is related to employer obligations to employees when called for jury duty to a state court, Icahn would likely find guidance in a *state statute*.

Step 2: Strategize based on resources.
Once you have determined the basic legal question and potential source of law, the strategy for tracking down the answer is necessarily based on resources. If commercial research services are available to you, it may be advantageous to use them in order to get the maximum amount of information in the least amount of time. However, such services are typically very expensive and, therefore, are usually limited to law firms, large companies, and academic institutions. Government, municipal, college, and law school libraries will also have federal and state statutes in book form. However, finding specific information on the law in books or through commercial services may be difficult without extensive training in legal research. Most legal research by nonlawyers is accomplished through the Internet. Pick the appropriate legal Web site (see Table A.1 for the best Web sites for finding the law) for your research. Depending on which you site you chose, try to find a general explanation on the topic. Alternatively, use the legal Web site's search engine to narrow your search in finding the source. In the CHC–Adams hypothetical above, Icahn may wish to use a Web site that gives a general explanation on rights of employees, but certain issues he seeks may be too narrow for a general explanation. In this case, Icahn will be best off simply using the Web site's search engine to find the statute in the state in which CHC employs Adams. For example, if CHC was located in Pennsylvania, Icahn would go to the Georgetown Law Center Web site and follow these steps: (1) select Statutes and Codes/State Codes from the Table of Contents on the left side to get to Pennsylvania resources, and (2) find the free electronic version of the statutes and use the search engine to find any relevant statute. Use of the words "jury duty" may be too general, so narrowing it down with modifiers such as "jury duty and employer" helps to hone in on the answer.

A word of caution about Internet sources.
While the Internet has made the law more accessible to the public, it has also created an environment where information goes unchecked and unverified. The best sources for legal research are typically those sites maintained by law school libraries. For more general legal information, Web sites should be evaluated based on sponsorship (Who maintains the Web site?), authority (Are

TABLE A.1 Reliable Sources for Legal Research on the Internet

Web Site Name	Source	Description	URL (Note: All Internet research Web sites may be accessed through this textbook's Web site at www.mhhe.com/melvin).
Free and low cost legal research	Georgetown University Law Center—Law Library	One of the very best tools for free and low cost online research. The Web site provides an excellent overview and links to different types of free materials and provides direct links to federal and state statutes and cases. It also summarizes the features and costs of less expensive databases.	www.ll.georgetown.edu/ guides/freelowcost.cfm
Free Internet legal sources	University of Washington School of Law	This Web site provides comprehensive offerings and easy to use layout for finding the law. It also provides an excellent brochure (in .pdf) called: "How to Research a Legal Problem: A Guide for non-Lawyers."	http://lib.law.washington.edu/ research/research.html#states
All Law: The Internet's premier law portal	Commercial Web site (primarily generates revenue through advertising).	Very simple layout and direct links make this Web site efficient for locating federal or state statutes and cases.	www.alllaw.com/law/
Free legal advice	Commercial Web site (primarily generates revenue through advertising).	Comprehensive topical information arranged by legal topic (also contains advice related to insurance). However, it is not useful for finding cases or specific statutes.	www.freeadvice.com/ all_topics.php
Online law dictionary	Commercial Web site (primarily generates revenue through advertising).	Comprehensive law dictionary with search engine.	http://dictionary.law.com

the authors of the information identified and are they attorneys?), and longevity (How long has the Web site been in existence?). The Web sites listed in Table A.1 are authoritative, have special features designed for non-attorneys, and are time-tested.

Step 3: Find an application.   Once you have located a statute, learn how the statute was applied in a case. Use the Web site's search engine that is designed to find cases by entering the name or citation of the statute. This allows the researcher to read how courts have applied the statute and whether any exceptions exist. For example, in the CHC–Adams case, Ichan would use the Georgetown Law Center Web site to find a case by selecting "Cases and Courts" from the Pennsylvania resources menu and entering terms in the search engine. This will allow him to read how courts have interpreted the statute, if necessary, and help him to understand how it applies to CHC.

TABLE A.2	Sample Research Strategy Using Internet Sources: CHC–Adams Example

Step 1	Identify precise legal question(s) and try to determine what source of law governs the issue(s).	**Questions:** 1. Is CHC required to permit Adams time off for jury duty in a state court? 2. If yes, is CHC obligated to pay Adams for the time he spends on jury duty? Sources: Look in the state statutes where CHC employs Adams.
Step 2	Strategize based on resources.	Use Georgetown's Web site 1. Table of Contents: Click on *Statutes and Codes: State Codes.* 2. Choose *State Research Guides*, then *Pennsylvania resources.* 3. Under "Electronic versions" choose *Free Web* and use the free search engine for the Pennsylvania code. 4. Use the search engine to find a statute by entering "Jury Duty and Employer." 5. Click on the first result and read the statute. Does it help resolve the question(s)?
Step 3	Find an application.	On the same Web page (Pennsylvania resources) click on *Cases and Courts* to use the search engine for any cases involving employers/employees and time off for jury duty.
Step 4	Consult with counsel.	Provide Adams with time off for jury duty, but without pay. Hire a temporary worker for the warehouse (not permitted to discipline or terminate Adams). Icahn checks his plan with his counsel before implementing.

Step 4: Consult with counsel.   It is dangerous to make any decision based on legal research by a nonattorney. Once a business owner or manager has a grasp of the issues, she should contact her counsel and discuss the issue and potential consequences of any decisions. The ability to find and understand the law in a business environment should be considered an *enhancement* to helping add value to a company through use of the law in business planning. It is not a substitute for working closely with an attorney. For example, in the CHC–Adams case, based on his research, Icahn is prepared to provide Adams with time off for jury duty (as required by statute), but does not intend to pay him. He will need to hire a temporary worker for the warehouse because he is not permitted to terminate Adams for missing work due to jury duty. However, before taking any actions he would consult with his counsel and make any adjustments necessary before implementing his plan.

Preamble

We the People of the United States, in Order to form a more perfect Union, establish Justice, insure domestic Tranquility, provide for the common defense, promote the general Welfare, and secure the Blessings of Liberty to ourselves and our Posterity, do ordain and establish this Constitution for the United States of America.

Article I

Section 1 All legislative Powers herein granted shall be vested in a Congress of the United States, which shall consist of a Senate and House of Representatives.

Section 2 The House of Representatives shall be composed of Members chosen every second Year by the People of the several States, and the Electors in each State shall have the Qualifications requisite for Electors of the most numerous Branch of the State Legislature.

No Person shall be a Representative who shall not have attained to the age of twenty five Years, and been seven Years a Citizen of the United States, and who shall not, when elected, be an Inhabitant of that State in which he shall be chosen.

Representatives and direct Taxes shall be apportioned among the several States which may be included within this Union, according to their respective Numbers, which shall be determined by adding to the whole Number of free Persons, including those bound to Service for a Term of Years, and excluding Indians not taxed, three fifths of all other Persons.[1] The actual Enumeration shall be made within three Years after the first Meeting of the Congress of the United States, and within every subsequent Term of ten Years, in such Manner as they shall by Law direct. The Number of Representatives shall not exceed one for every thirty Thousand, but each State shall have at Least one Representative, and until such enumeration shall be made, the State of New Hampshire shall be entitled to choose three, Massachusetts eight, Rhode-Island and Providence Plantations one, Connecticut five, New York six, New Jersey four, Pennsylvania eight, Delaware one, Maryland six, Virginia ten, North Carolina five, South Carolina five, and Georgia three.

When vacancies happen in the Representation from any State, the Executive Authority thereof shall issue Writs of Election to fill such Vacancies.

The House of Representatives shall chuse their Speaker and other Officers; and shall have the sole Power of Impeachment.

Section 3 The Senate of the United States shall be composed of two Senators from each State, chosen by the Legislature thereof,[2] for six Years; and each Senator shall have one Vote.

Immediately after they shall be assembled in Consequence of the first Election, they shall be divided as equally as may be into three Classes.

---

[1]Changed by the Fourteenth Amendment.

[2]Changed by the Seventeenth Amendment.

The Seats of the Senators of the first Class shall be vacated at the Expiration of the second Year, of the second Class at the Expiration of the fourth Year, and of the third Class at the Expiration of the sixth Year, so that one third may be chosen every second Year; and if Vacancies happen by Resignation, or otherwise, during the Recess of the Legislature of any State, the Executive thereof may make temporary Appointments until the next Meeting of the Legislature, which shall then fill such Vacancies.[3]

No Person shall be a Senator who shall not have attained to the Age of thirty Years, and been nine Years a Citizen of the United States, and who shall not, when elected, be an Inhabitant of that State for which he shall be chosen.

The Vice President of the United States shall be President of the Senate, but shall have no Vote, unless they be equally divided.

The Senate shall chuse their other Officers, and also a President pro tempore, in the Absence of the Vice President, or when he shall exercise the Office of President of the United States.

The Senate shall have the sole Power to try all Impeachments. When sitting for that Purpose, they shall be on Oath or Affirmation. When the President of the United States is tried, the Chief Justice shall preside: And no Person shall be convicted without the Concurrence of two thirds of the Members present.

Judgment in Cases of Impeachment shall not extend further than to removal from Office, and disqualification to hold and enjoy any Office of honor, Trust or Profit under the United States: but the Party convicted shall nevertheless be liable and subject to Indictment, Trial, Judgment and Punishment, according to Law.

Section 4 The Times, Places and Manner of holding Elections for Senators and Representatives, shall be prescribed in each State by the Legislature thereof; but the Congress may at any time by Law make or alter such Regulations, except as to the Places of chusing Senators.

The Congress shall assemble at least once in every Year, and such Meeting shall be on the first Monday in December, unless they shall by Law appoint a different Day.[4]

Section 5 Each House shall be the Judge of the Elections, Returns and Qualifications of its own Members, and a Majority of each shall constitute a Quorum to do Business; but a smaller Number may adjourn from day to day, and may be authorized to compel the Attendance of absent Members, in such Manner, and under such Penalties as each House may provide.

Each House may determine the Rules of its Proceedings, punish its Members for disorderly Behaviour, and with the Concurrence of two thirds, expel a Member.

Each House shall keep a Journal of its Proceedings, and from time to time publish the same, excepting such Parts as may in their Judgment require Secrecy; and the Yeas and Nays of the Members of either House on any question shall, at the Desire of one fifth of those Present, be entered on the Journal.

Neither House, during the Session of Congress, shall, without the Consent of the other, adjourn for more than three days, nor to any other Place than that in which the two Houses shall be sitting.

Section 6 The Senators and Representatives shall receive a Compensation for their Services, to be ascertained by Law, and paid out of the Treasury of the United States. They shall in all Cases, except Treason, Felony and Breach of the Peace, be privileged from Arrest during their Attendance at the Session of their respective Houses, and in going to and returning from the same; and for any Speech or Debate in either House, they shall not be questioned in any other Place.

No Senator or Representative shall, during the Time for which he was elected, be appointed to any civil Office under the Authority of the United States, which shall have been created, or the Emoluments whereof shall have been encreased during such time; and no Person holding any Office under the United States, shall be a Member of either House during his Continuance in Office.

Section 7 All Bills for raising Revenue shall originate in the House of Representatives; but the Senate may propose or concur with Amendments as on other Bills.

Every Bill which shall have passed the House of Representatives and the Senate, shall, before it becomes a Law, be presented to the President of the United States; If he approves he shall sign it, but if not he shall return it, with his Objections to that House in which it shall have originated, who shall enter the Objections at large on their Journal, and proceed to reconsider it. If after such Reconsideration two thirds of that House shall agree to pass the Bill, it shall be sent, together with the Objections, to the other House, by which it shall likewise be reconsidered, and if approved by two thirds of that House, it shall become a Law. But in all such Cases the Votes of both Houses shall be determined by Yeas and Nays, and the Names of the Persons voting for and against the Bill shall be entered on the Journal of each House respectively. If any Bill shall not

---

[3]Changed by the Seventeenth Amendment.

[4]Changed by the Twentieth Amendment.

be returned by the President within ten Days (Sundays excepted) after it shall have been presented to him, the Same shall be a Law, in like Manner as if he had signed it, unless the Congress by their Adjournment prevent its Return, in which Case it shall not be a Law.

Every Order, Resolution, or Vote to which the Concurrence of the Senate and House of Representatives may be necessary (except on a question of Adjournment) shall be presented to the President of the United States; and before the Same shall take Effect, shall be approved by him, or being disapproved by him, shall be repassed by two thirds of the Senate and House of Representatives, according to the Rules and Limitations prescribed in the Case of a Bill.

Section 8 The Congress shall have Power To lay and collect Taxes, Duties, Imposts and Excises, to pay the Debts and provide for the common Defence and general Welfare of the United States; but all Duties, Im-posts and Excises shall be uniform throughout the United States.

To borrow Money on the credit of the United States;

To regulate Commerce with foreign Nations, and among the several States, and with the Indian Tribes;

To establish an uniform Rule of Naturalization, and uniform Laws on the subject of Bankruptcies throughout the United States;

To coin Money, regulate the Value thereof, and of foreign Coin, and fix the Standard of Weights and Measures;

To provide for the Punishment of counterfeiting the Securities and current Coin of the United States;

To establish Post Offices and post Roads;

To promote the Progress of Science and useful Arts, by securing for limited Times to Authors and Inventors the exclusive Right to their respective Writings and Discoveries;

To constitute Tribunals inferior to the supreme Court;

To define and punish Piracies and Felonies committed on the high Seas, and Offences against the Law of Nations;

To declare War, grant Letters of Marque and Reprisal, and make Rules concerning Captures on Land and Water;

To raise and support Armies, but no Appropriation of Money to that Use shall be for a longer Term than two Years;

To provide and maintain a Navy;

To make Rules for the Government and Regulation of the land and naval Forces;

To provide for calling forth the Militia to execute the Laws of the Union, suppress Insurrections and repel Invasions;

To provide for organizing, arming, and disciplining, the Militia, and for governing such Part of them as may be employed in the Service of the United States, reserving to the States respectively, the Appointment of the Officers, and the Authority of training the Militia according to the discipline prescribed by Congress;

To exercise exclusive Legislation in all Cases whatsoever, over such District (not exceeding ten Miles square) as may, by Cession of particular States, and the Acceptance of Congress, become the Seat of the Government of the United States, and to exercise like Authority over all Places purchased by the Consent of the Legislature of the State in which the Same shall be, for the Erection of Forts, Magazines, Arsenals, dock-Yards, and other needful Buildings;—And

To make all Laws which shall be necessary and proper for carrying into Execution the foregoing Powers, and all other Powers vested by this Constitution in the Government of the United States, or in any Department or Officer thereof.

Section 9 The Migration or Importation of such Persons as any of the States now existing shall think proper to admit, shall not be prohibited by the Congress prior to the Year one thousand eight hundred and eight, but a Tax or duty may be imposed on such Importation, not exceeding ten dollars for each Person.

The Privilege of the Writ of Habeas Corpus shall not be suspended, unless when in Cases of Rebellion or Invasion the public Safety may require it.

No Bill of Attainder or ex post facto Law shall be passed.

No Capitation, or other direct, Tax shall be laid, unless in Proportion to the Census of Enumeration herein before directed to be taken.[5]

No Tax or Duty shall be laid on Articles exported from any State.

No Preference shall be given by any Regulation of Commerce or Revenue to the Ports of one State over those of another: nor shall Vessels bound to, or from, one State, be obliged to enter, clear, or pay Duties in another.

No Money shall be drawn from the Treasury, but in Consequence of Appropriations made by Law; and a regular Statement and Account of the Receipts and Expenditures of all public Money shall be published from time to time.

No Title of Nobility shall be granted by the United States: And no Person holding any Office of Profit or Trust under them, shall, without the Consent of the Congress, accept of any present, Emolument, Office,

[5]Changed by the Sixteenth Amendment.

or Title, of any kind whatever, from any King, Prince, or foreign State.

Section 10 No State shall enter into any Treaty, Alliance, or Confederation; grant Letters of Marque and Reprisal; coin Money; emit Bills of Credit; make any Thing but gold and silver coin a Tender in Payment of Debts; pass any Bill of Attainder, ex post facto Law, or Law impairing the Obligation of Contracts, or grant any Title of Nobility.

No State shall, without the Consent of the Congress, lay any Imposts or Duties on Imports or Exports, except what may be absolutely necessary for executing its inspection Laws: and the net Produce of all Duties and Imposts, laid by any State on Imports or Exports, shall be for the Use of the Treasury of the United States; and all such Laws shall be subject to the Revision and Controul of the Congress.

No State shall, without the consent of Congress, lay any Duty of Tonnage, keep Troops, or Ships of War in time of Peace, enter into any Agreement or Compact with another State, or with a foreign Power, or engage in War, unless actually invaded, or in such imminent Danger as will not admit of delay.

Article II

Section 1 The executive Power shall be vested in a President of the United States of America. He shall hold his Office during the Term of four Years, and, together with the Vice President, chosen for the same Term, be elected, as follows

Each state shall appoint, in such Manner as the Legislature thereof may direct, a Number of Electors, equal to the whole Number of Senators and Representatives to which the State may be entitled in Congress: but no Senator or Representative, or Person holding an Office of Trust or Profit under the United States, shall be appointed an Elector.

The Electors shall meet in their respective States, and vote by Ballot for two Persons, of whom one at least shall not be an inhabitant of the same State with themselves. And they shall make a List of all the Persons voted for, and of the Number of Votes for each; which List they shall sign and certify, and transmit sealed to the Seat of the Government of the United States, directed to the President of the Senate. The President of the Senate shall, in the Presence of the Senate and House of Representatives, open all the Certificates, and the Votes shall then be counted. The Person having the greatest Number of Votes shall be the President, if such Number be a Majority of the whole Number of Electors appointed; and if there be more than one who have such Majority, and have an equal Number of

Votes, then the House of Representatives shall immediately chuse by Ballot one of them for President; and if no Person have a Majority, then from the five highest on the List the said House shall in like Manner chuse the President. But in chusing the President, the Votes shall be taken by States, the Representation from each State having one Vote; A quorum for this purpose shall consist of a Member or Members from two thirds of the States, and a Majority of all the States shall be necessary to a Choice. In every Case, after the Choice of the President, the Person having the greatest Number of Votes of the Electors shall be the Vice President. But if there should remain two or more who have equal Votes, the Senate shall chuse from them by Ballot the Vice President.[6]

The Congress may determine the Time of chusing the Electors, and the Day on which they shall give their Votes; which Day shall be the same throughout the United States.

No Person except a natural born Citizen, or a Citizen of the United States, at the time of the Adoption of this Constitution, shall be eligible to the Office of President; neither shall any Person be eligible to that Office who shall not have attained to the Age of thirty five Years, and been fourteen Years a Resident within the United States.

In Case of the Removal of the President from Office, or of his Death, Resignation, or Inability to discharge the Powers and Duties of the said Office, the Same shall devolve on the Vice President, and the Congress may by Law provide for the Case of Removal, Death, Resignation or Inability, both of the President and Vice President, declaring what Officer shall then act as President, and such Officer shall act accordingly, until the Disability be removed, or a President shall be elected.[7]

The President shall, at stated Times, receive for his Services, a Compensation, which shall neither be increased nor diminished during the Period for which he shall have been elected, and he shall not receive within that Period any other Emolument from the United States, or any of them.

Before he enter on the Execution of his Office, he shall take the following Oath or Affirmation:—"I do solemnly swear (or affirm) that I will faithfully execute the Office of President of the United States, and will to the best of my Ability, preserve, protect, and defend the Constitution of the United States."

Section 2 The President shall be Commander in Chief of the Army and Navy of the United States, and of the

---

[6]Changed by the Twelfth Amendment.

[7]Changed by the Twenty-fifth Amendment.

Militia of the several States, when called into the actual Service of the United States; he may require the Opinion, in writing, of the principal Officer in each of the executive Departments, upon any Subject relating to the Duties of their respective Offices, and he shall have Power to grant Reprieves and Pardons for Offences against the United States, except in Cases of Impeachment.

He shall have Power, by and with the Advice and Consent of the Senate, to make Treaties, provided two thirds of the Senators present concur; and he shall nominate, and by and with the Advice and Consent of the Senate, shall appoint Ambassadors, other public Ministers and Consuls, Judges of the supreme Court, and all other Officers of the United States, whose Appointments are not herein otherwise provided for, and which shall be established by Law; but the Congress may by Law vest the Appointment of such inferior Officers, as they think proper, in the President alone, in the Courts of Law, or in the Heads of Departments.

The President shall have Power to fill up all Vacancies that may happen during the Recess of the Senate, by granting Commissions which shall expire at the End of their next Session.

Section 3 He shall from time to time give to the Congress Information of the State of the Union, and recommend to their Consideration such Measures as he shall judge necessary and expedient; he may, on extraordinary Occasions, convene both Houses, or either of them, and in Case of Disagreement between them, with Respect to the Time of Adjournment, he may adjourn them to such Time as he shall think proper; he shall receive Ambassadors and other public Ministers; he shall take Care that the Laws be faithfully executed, and shall Commission all the Officers of the United States.

Section 4 The President, Vice President and all civil Officers of the United States, shall be removed from Office on Impeachment for, and Conviction of, Treason, Bribery, or other high Crimes and Misdemeanors.

Article III

Section 1 The judicial Power of the United States, shall be vested in one supreme Court, and in such inferior Courts as the Congress may from time to time ordain and establish. The Judges, both of the supreme and inferior Courts, shall hold their Offices during good Behaviour, and shall, at stated Times, receive for their Services, a Compensation, which shall not be diminished during their Continuance in Office.

Section 2 The judicial Power shall extend to all Cases, in Law and Equity, arising under this Constitution, the Laws of the United States, and Treaties made, or which shall be made, under their Authority;—to all Cases affecting Ambassadors, other public Ministers and Consuls;—to all Cases of admiralty and maritime Jurisdiction;—to Controversies to which the United States shall be a party;—to Controversies between two or more States;—between a State and Citizens of another State;[8]—between Citizens of different States;—between Citizens of the same State claiming Lands under Grants of different States, and between a State, or the Citizens thereof, and foreign States, Citizens or Subjects.

In all Cases affecting Ambassadors, other public Ministers and Consuls, and those in which a State shall be Party, the supreme Court shall have original Jurisdiction. In all the other Cases before mentioned, the supreme Court shall have appellate Jurisdiction, both as to Law and Fact, with such Exceptions, and under such Regulations as the Congress shall make.

The Trial of all Crimes, except in Cases of Impeachment, shall be by Jury: and such Trial shall be held in the State where the said Crimes shall have been committed; but when not committed within any State, the Trial shall be at such Place or Places as the Congress may by Law have directed.

Section 3 Treason against the United States, shall consist only in levying War against them, or in adhering to their Enemies, giving them Aid and Comfort. No Person shall be convicted of Treason unless on the Testimony of two Witnesses to the same overt Act, or on Confession in open Court.

The Congress shall have Power to declare the Punishment of Treason, but no Attainder of Treason shall work Corruption of Blood, or Forfeiture except during the Life of the Person attainted.

Article IV

Section 1 Full Faith and Credit shall be given in each State to the public Acts, Records, and judicial Proceedings of every other State. And the Congress may by general Laws prescribe the Manner in which such Acts, Records and Proceedings shall be proved, and the Effect thereof.

Section 2 The Citizens of each State shall be entitled to all Privileges and Immunities of Citizens in the several States.

A Person charged in any State with Treason, Felony, or other Crime, who shall flee from Justice, and be found in another State, shall on Demand of the executive Authority of the State from which he fled,

---

[8]Changed by the Eleventh Amendment.

be delivered up, to be removed to the State having Jurisdiction of the Crime.

No Person held to Service or Labour in one State, under the Laws thereof, escaping into another, shall, in Consequence of any Law or Regulation therein, be discharged from such Service or Labour, but shall be delivered up on Claim of the Party to whom such Service or Labour may be due.[9]

Section 3 New States may be admitted by the Congress into this Union; but no new State shall be formed or erected within the Jurisdiction of any other State; nor any State be formed by the Junction of two or more States, or Parts of States, without the Consent of the Legislatures of the States concerned as well as of the Congress.

The Congress shall have Power to dispose of and make all needful Rules and Regulations respecting the Territory or other Property belonging to the United States; and nothing in this Constitution shall be so construed as to Prejudice any Claims of the United States, or of any particular State.

Section 4 The United States shall guarantee to every State in this Union a Republican Form of Government, and shall protect each of them against Invasion; and on Application of the Legislature, or of the Executive (when the Legislature cannot be convened) against domestic Violence.

Article V

The Congress, whenever two thirds of both Houses shall deem it necessary, shall propose Amendments to this Constitution, or, on the Application of the Legislatures of two thirds of the several States, shall call a Convention for proposing Amendments, which, in either Case, shall be valid to all Intents and Purposes, as Part of this Constitution, when ratified by the legislatures of three fourths of the several States, or by Conventions in three fourths thereof, as the one or the other Mode of Ratification may be proposed by the Congress; Provided that no Amendment which may be made prior to the Year One thousand eight hundred and eight shall in any Manner affect the first and fourth Clauses in the Ninth Section of the first Article; and that no State, without its Consent, shall be deprived of its equal Suffrage in the Senate.

Article VI

All Debts contracted and Engagements entered into, before the Adoption of this Constitution, shall be as

valid against the United States under this Constitution, as under the Confederation.

The Constitution, and the Laws of the United States which shall be made in Pursuance thereof; and all Treaties made, or which shall be made, under the Authority of the United States, shall be the supreme Law of the Land; and the Judges in every State shall be bound thereby, any Thing in the Constitution or Laws of any State to the Contrary notwithstanding.

The Senators and Representatives before mentioned, and the Members of the several State Legislatures, and all executive and judicial Officers, both of the United States and of the several States, shall be bound by Oath or Affirmation, to support this Constitution; but no religious Test shall ever be required as a Qualification to any Office or public Trust under the United States.

Article VII

The Ratification of the Conventions of nine States, shall be sufficient for the Establishment of this Constitution between the States so ratifying the Same.

Done in Convention by the Unanimous Consent of the States present the Seventeenth Day of September in the Year of our Lord one thousand seven hundred and eighty seven and of the Independance of the United States of America the Twelfth. In witness whereof We have hereunto subscribed our Names.

Amendments

(The first 10 amendments are known as the "Bill of Rights.")

Amendment I (Ratified 1791) Congress shall make no law respecting an establishment of religion, or prohibiting the free exercise thereof; or abridging the freedom of speech, or of the press; or the right of the people peaceably to assemble, and to petition the Government for a redress of grievances.

Amendment 2 (Ratified 1791) A well regulated Militia, being necessary to the security of a free State, the right of the people to keep and bear Arms, shall not be infringed.

Amendment 3 (Ratified 1791) No Soldier shall, in time of peace be quartered in any house, without the consent of the Owner, nor in time of war, but in a manner to be prescribed by law.

Amendment 4 (Ratified 1791) The right of the people to be secure in their persons, houses, papers, and effects, against unreasonable searches and seizures,

---

[9]Changed by the Thirteenth Amendment.

shall not be violated, and no Warrants shall issue, but upon probable cause, supported by Oath or affirmation, and particularly describing the place to be searched, and the persons or things to be seized.

Amendment 5 (Ratified 1791)   No person shall be held to answer for a capital, or otherwise infamous crime, unless on a presentment or indictment of a Grand Jury, except in cases arising in the land or naval forces, or in the Militia, when in actual service in time of War or public danger; nor shall any person be subject for the same of-fence to be twice put in jeopardy of life or limb; nor shall be compelled in any criminal case to be a witness against himself, nor be deprived of life, liberty, or property, without due process of law; nor shall private property be taken for public use, without just compensation.

Amendment 6 (Ratified 1791)   In all criminal prosecutions, the accused shall enjoy the right to a speedy and public trial, by an impartial jury of the State and district wherein the crime shall have been committed, which district shall have been previously ascertained by law, and to be informed of the nature and cause of the accusation; to be confronted with the witnesses against him; to have compulsory process for obtaining Witnesses in his favor, and to have assistance of counsel for his defence.

Amendment 7 (Ratified 1791)   In Suits at common law, where the value in controversy shall exceed twenty dollars, the right of trial by jury shall be preserved, and no fact tried by a jury, shall be otherwise re-examined in any Court of the United States, than according to the rules of the common law.

Amendment 8 (Ratified 1791)   Excessive bail shall not be required, nor excessive fines imposed, nor cruel and unusual punishments inflicted.

Amendment 9 (Ratified 1791)   The enumeration in the Constitution, of certain rights, shall not be construed to deny or disparage others retained by the people.

Amendment 10 (Ratified 1791)   The powers not delegated to the United States by the Constitution, nor prohibited by it to the States, are reserved to the States respectively, or to the people.

Amendment 11 (Ratified 1795)   The Judicial power of the United States shall not be construed to extend to any suit in law or equity, commenced or prosecuted against one of the United States by Citizens of another State, or by Citizens or Subjects of any Foreign State.

Amendment 12 (Ratified 1804)   The Electors shall meet in their respective states, and vote by ballot for President and Vice-President, one of whom, at least, shall not be an inhabitant of the same state with themselves; they shall name in their ballots the person voted for as President, and in distinct ballots the person voted for as Vice-President, and they shall make distinct lists of all persons voted for as President, and of all persons voted for as Vice-President, and of the number of votes for each, which lists they shall sign and certify, and transmit sealed to the seat of the government of the United States, directed to the President of the Senate;—The President of the Senate shall, in the presence of the Senate and House of Representatives, open all the certificates and the votes shall then be counted;—The person having the greatest number of votes for President, shall be the President, if such number be a majority of the whole number of Electors appointed; and if no person have such majority, then from the persons having the highest numbers not exceeding three on the list of those voted for as President, the House of Representatives shall choose immediately, by ballot, the President. But in choosing the President, the votes shall be taken by states, the representation from each state having one vote; a quorum for this purpose shall consist of a member or members from two-thirds of the states, and a majority of all the states shall be necessary to a choice. And if the House of Representatives shall not choose a President whenever the right of choice shall devolve upon them, before the fourth day of March next following, then the Vice-President shall act as president, as in the case of the death or other constitutional disability of the President.[10]—The person having the greatest number of votes as Vice-President, shall be the Vice-President, if such number be a majority of the whole number of Electors appointed, and if no person have a majority, then from the two highest numbers on the list, the Senate shall choose the Vice-President; a quorum for the purpose shall consist of two-thirds of the whole number of Senators, and a majority of the whole number shall be necessary to a choice. But no person constitutionally ineligible to the office of President shall be eligible to that of Vice-President of the United States.

Amendment 13 (Ratified 1865)   **Section 1** Neither slavery nor involuntary servitude, except as a

---

[10]Changed by the Twentieth Amendment.

punishment for crime whereof the party shall have been duly convicted, shall exist within the United States, or any place subject to their jurisdiction.

Section 2 Congress shall have power to enforce this article by appropriate legislation.

Amendment 14 (Ratified 1868) **Section 1** All persons born or naturalized in the United States, and subject to the jurisdiction thereof, are citizens of the United States and of the State wherein they reside. No State shall make or enforce any law which shall abridge the privileges or immunities of citizens of the United States; nor shall any State deprive any person of life, liberty, or property, without due process of law; nor deny to any person within its jurisdiction the equal protection of the laws.

Section 2 Representatives shall be apportioned among the several States according to their respective numbers, counting the whole number of persons in each State, excluding Indians not taxed. But when the right to vote at any election for the choice of electors for President and Vice President of the United States, Representatives in Congress, the Executive and Judicial officers of a State, or the members of the Legislature thereof, is denied to any of the male inhabitants of such State, being twenty-one[11] years of age, and citizens of the United States, or in any way abridged except for participation in rebellion, or other crime, the basis of representation therein shall be reduced in the proportion which the number of such male citizens shall bear to the whole number of male citizens twenty-one years of age in such State.

Section 3 No person shall be a Senator or Representative in Congress, or elector of President and Vice President, or hold any office, civil or military, under the United States, or under any State, who, having previously taken an oath, as a member of Congress, or as an officer of the United States, or as a member of any State legislature, or as an executive or judicial officer of any State, to support the Constitution of the United States, shall have engaged in insurrection or rebellion against the same, or given aid or comfort to the enemies thereof. But Congress may by a vote of two-thirds of each House, remove such disability.

Section 4 The validity of the public debt of the United States, authorized by law, including debts incurred for payment of pensions and bounties for services in suppressing insurrection or rebellion, shall not be questioned. But neither the United States nor any State shall assume or pay any debt or obligation incurred in aid of insurrection or rebellion against the United States, or any claim for the loss or emancipation of any slave; but all such debts, obligations and claims shall be held illegal and void.

Section 5 The Congress shall have power to enforce, by appropriate legislation, the provisions of this article.

Amendment 15 (Ratified 1870) **Section 1** The right of citizens of the United States to vote shall not be denied or abridged by the United States or by any State on account of race, color, or previous condition of servitude.

Section 2 The Congress shall have power to enforce this article by appropriate legislation.

Amendment 16 (Ratified 1913) The Congress shall have power to lay and collect taxes on incomes, from whatever source derived, without apportionment among the several States, and without regard to any census or enumeration.

Amendment 17 (Ratified 1913) The Senate of the United States shall be composed of two Senators from each State, elected by the people thereof, for six years; and each Senator shall have one vote. The electors in each State shall have the qualifications requisite for electors of the most numerous branch of the State legislatures.

When vacancies happen in the representation of any State in the Senate, the executive authority of such State shall issue writs of election to fill such vacancies: *Provided,* That the legislature of any State may empower the executive thereof to make temporary appointments until the people fill the vacancies by election as the legislature may direct.

This amendment shall not be so construed as to affect the election or term of any Senator chosen before it becomes valid as part of the Constitution.

Amendment 18 (Ratified 1919; Repealed 1933) **Section 1** After one year from the ratification of this article the manufacture, sale, or transportation of intoxicating liquors within, the importation thereof into, or the exportation thereof from the United States and all territory subject to the jurisdiction thereof for beverage purposes is hereby prohibited.

Section 2 The Congress and the several States shall have concurrent power to enforce this article by appropriate legislation.

Section 3 This article shall be inoperative unless it shall have been ratified as an amendment to the Constitution by the legislatures of the several States, as

---

[11]Changed by the Twenty-sixth Amendment.

provided in the Constitution, within seven years from the date of the submission hereof to the States by the Congress.[12]

Amendment 19 (Ratified 1920) The right of citizens of the United States to vote shall not be denied or abridged by the United States or by any State on account of sex.

Congress shall have power to enforce this article by ap propriate legislation.

Amendment 20 (Ratified 1933) **Section 1** The terms of the President and Vice President shall end at noon on the 20th day of January, and the terms of Senators and Representatives at noon on the 3d day of January, of the years in which such terms would have ended if this article had not been ratified; and the terms of their successors shall then begin.

Section 2 The Congress shall assemble at least once in every year, and such meeting shall begin at noon on the 3d day of January, unless they shall by law appoint a different day.

Section 3 If, at the time fixed for the beginning of the term of the President, the President elect shall have died, the Vice President elect shall become President. If a President shall not have been chosen before the time fixed for the beginning of his term, or if the President elect shall have failed to qualify, then the Vice President elect shall act as President until a President shall have qualified; and the Congress may by law provide for the case wherein neither a President elect nor a Vice President elect shall have qualified, declaring who shall then act as President, or the manner in which one who is to act shall be selected, and such person shall act accordingly until a President or Vice President shall have qualified.

Section 4 The Congress may by law provide for the case of the death of any of the persons from whom the House of Representatives may choose a President whenever the right of choice shall have devolved upon them, and for the case of the death of any of the persons from whom the Senate may choose a Vice President whenever the right of choice shall have devolved upon them.

Section 5 Sections 1 and 2 shall take effect on the 15th day of October following the ratification of this article.

Section 6 This article shall be inoperative unless it shall have been ratified as an amendment to the Constitution by the legislatures of three-fourths of the

several States within seven years from the date of its submission.

Amendment 21 (Ratified 1933) **Section 1** The eighteenth article of amendment to the Constitution of the United States is hereby repealed.

Section 2 The transportation or importation into any State, Territory, or possession of the United States for delivery or use therein of intoxicating liquors, in violation of the laws thereof, is hereby prohibited.

Section 3 This article shall be inoperative unless it shall have been ratified as an amendment to the Constitution by conventions in the several States, as provided in the Constitution, within seven years from the date of the submission hereof to the States by the Congress.

Amendment 22 (Ratified 1951) **Section 1** No person shall be elected to the office of the President more than twice, and no person who has held the office of President, or acted as President, for more than two years of a term to which some other person was elected President shall be elected to the office of the President more than once. But this Article shall not apply to any person holding the office of President when this Article was proposed by the Congress, and shall not prevent any person who may be holding the office of President, or acting as President, during the term within which this Article becomes operative from holding the office of President or acting as President during the remainder of such term.

Section 2 This Article shall be inoperative unless it shall have been ratified as an amendment to the Constitution by the legislatures of three-fourths of the several States within seven years from the date of its submission to the States by the Congress.

Amendment 23 (Ratified 1961) **Section 1** The District constituting the seat of Government of the United States shall appoint in such manner as the Congress may direct:

A number of electors of President and Vice President equal to the whole number of Senators and Representatives in Congress to which the District would be entitled if it were a State, but in no event more than the least populous State; they shall be in addition to those appointed by the States, but they shall be considered, for the purposes of the election of President and Vice President, to be electors appointed by a State; and they shall meet in the District and perform such duties as provided by the twelfth article of amendment.

Section 2 The Congress shall have power to enforce this article by appropriate legislation.

---

[12]Repealed by the Twenty-first Amendment.

Amendment 24 (Ratified 1964) **Section 1** The right of citizens of the United States to vote in any primary or other election for President or Vice President, for electors for President or Vice President, or for Senator or Representative in Congress, shall not be denied or abridged by the United States or any State by reason of failure to pay any poll tax or other tax.

Section 2 The Congress shall have power to enforce this article by appropriate legislation.

Amendment 25 (Ratified 1967) **Section 1** In case of the removal of the President from office or of his death or resignation, the Vice President shall become President.

Section 2 Whenever there is a vacancy in the office of the Vice President, the President shall nominate a Vice President who shall take office upon confirmation by a majority vote of both Houses of Congress.

Section 3 Whenever the President transmits to the President pro tempore of the Senate and the Speaker of the House of Representatives his written declaration that he is unable to discharge the powers and duties of his office, and until he transmits to them a written declaration to the contrary, such powers and duties shall be discharged by the Vice President as Acting President.

Section 4 Whenever the Vice President and a majority of either the principal officers of the executive departments or of such other body as Congress may by law provide, transmit to the President pro tempore of the Senate and the Speaker of the House of Representatives their written declaration that the President is unable to discharge the powers and duties of his office, the Vice President shall immediately assume the powers and duties of the office as Acting President.

Thereafter, when the President transmits to the President pro tempore of the Senate and the Speaker of the House of Representatives his written declaration that no inability exists, he shall resume the powers and duties of his office unless the Vice President and a majority of either the principal officers of the executive department or of such other body as Congress may by law provide, transmit within four days to the President pro tempore of the Senate and the Speaker of the House of Representatives their written declaration that the President is unable to discharge the powers and duties of his office. Thereupon Congress shall decide the issue, assembling within forty-eight hours for that purpose if not in session. If the Congress, within twenty-one days after receipt of the latter written declaration, or, if Congress is not in session, within twenty-one days after Congress is required to assemble, determines by two-thirds vote of both Houses that the President is unable to discharge the powers and duties of his office, the Vice President shall continue to discharge the same as Acting President; otherwise, the President shall resume the powers and duties of his office.

Amendment 26 (Ratified 1971) **Section 1** The right of citizens of the United States, who are eighteen years of age or older, to vote shall not be denied or abridged by the United States or by any State on account of age.

Section 2 The Congress shall have power to enforce this article by appropriate legislation.

Amendment 27 (Ratified 1992) No law, varying the compensation for the services of the Senators and Representatives, shall take effect, until an election of Representatives shall have intervened.

APPENDIX C

Uniform Commercial Code

ARTICLE 2—SALES

Part 1: Short Title, General Construction and Subject Matter

§ 2-101. Short Title.

This Article shall be known and may be cited as Uniform Commercial Code—Sales.

§ 2-102. Scope; Certain Security and Other Transactions Excluded from This Article.

Unless the context otherwise requires, this Article applies to transactions in goods; it does not apply to any transaction which although in the form of an unconditional contract to sell or present sale is intended to operate only as a security transaction nor does this Article impair or repeal any statute regulating sales to consumers, farmers or other specified classes of buyers.

§ 2-103. Definitions and Index of Definitions.

(1) In this Article unless the context otherwise requires
   (a) "Buyer" means a person who buys or contracts to buy goods.
   (b) "Good faith" in the case of a merchant means honesty in fact and the observance of reasonable commercial standards of fair dealing in the trade.
   (c) "Receipt" of goods means taking physical possession of them.
   (d) "Seller" means a person who sells or contracts to sell goods.
(2) Other definitions applying to this Article or to specified Parts thereof, and the sections in which they appear are:

"Acceptance"	Section 2-606.
"Banker's credit"	Section 2-325.
"Between merchants"	Section 2-104.
"Cancellation"	Section 2-106(4).
"Commercial unit"	Section 2-105.
"Confirmed credit"	Section 2-325.
"Conforming to contract".	Section 2-106.
"Contract for sale"	Section 2-106.
"Cover"	Section 2-712.
"Entrusting"	Section 2-403.
"Financing agency"	Section 2-104.
"Future goods"	Section 2-105.
"Goods"	Section 2-105.
"Identification"	Section 2-501.
"Installment contract"	Section 2-612.
"Letter of Credit"	Section 2-325.
"Lot"	Section 2-105.
"Merchant"	Section 2-104.

"Overseas"	Section 2-323.
"Person in position of seller"	Section 2-707.
"Present sale"	Section 2-106.
"Sale"	Section 2-106.
"Sale on approval"	Section 2-326.
"Sale or return"	Section 2-326.
"Termination"	Section 2-106.

(3) The following definitions in other Articles apply to this Article:

"Check"	Section 3-104.
"Consignee"	Section 7-102.
"Consignor"	Section 7-102.
"Consumer goods"	Section 9-109.
"Dishonor"	Section 3-502.
"Draft"	Section 3-104.

(4) In addition Article 1 contains general definitions and principles of construction and interpretation applicable throughout this Article.

As amended in 1994.

See Appendix XI for material relating to changes made in text in 1994.

§ 2-104. Definitions: "Merchant"; "Between Merchants"; "Financing Agency".

(1) "Merchant" means a person who deals in goods of the kind or otherwise by his occupation holds himself out as having knowledge or skill peculiar to the practices or goods involved in the transaction or to whom such knowledge or skill may be attributed by his employment of an agent or broker or other intermediary who by his occupation holds himself out as having such knowledge or skill.

(2) "Financing agency" means a bank, finance company or other person who in the ordinary course of business makes advances against goods or documents of title or who by arrangement with either the seller or the buyer intervenes in ordinary course to make or collect payment due or claimed under the contract for sale, as by purchasing or paying the seller's draft or making advances against it or by merely taking it for collection whether or not documents of title accompany the draft. "Financing agency" includes also a bank or other person who similarly intervenes between persons who are in the position of seller and buyer in respect to the goods (Section 2–707).

(3) "Between merchants" means in any transaction with respect to which both parties are chargeable with the knowledge or skill of merchants.

§ 2-105. Definitions: "Transferability"; "Goods"; "Future" Goods; "Lot"; "Commercial Unit".

(1) "Goods" means all things (including specially manufactured goods) which are movable at the time of identification to the contract for sale other than the money in which the price is to be paid, investment securities (Article 8) and things in action. "Goods" also includes the unborn young of animals and growing crops and other identified things attached to realty as described in the section on goods to be severed from realty (Section 2–107).

(2) Goods must be both existing and identified before any interest in them can pass. Goods which are not both existing and identified are "future" goods. A purported present sale of future goods or of any interest therein operates as a contract to sell.

(3) There may be a sale of a part interest in existing identified goods.

(4) An undivided share in an identified bulk of fungible goods is sufficiently identified to be sold although the quantity of the bulk is not determined. Any agreed proportion of such a bulk or any quantity thereof agreed upon by number, weight or other measure may to the extent of the seller's interest in the bulk be sold to the buyer who then becomes an owner in common.

(5) "Lot" means a parcel or a single article which is the subject matter of a separate sale or delivery, whether or not it is sufficient to perform the contract.

(6) "Commercial unit" means such a unit of goods as by commercial usage is a single whole for purposes of sale and division of which materially impairs its character or value on the market or in use. A commercial unit may be a single article (as a machine) or a set of articles (as a suite of furniture or an assortment of sizes) or a quantity (as a bale, gross, or carload) or any other unit treated in use or in the relevant market as a single whole.

§ 2-106. Definitions: "Contract"; "Agreement"; "Contract for Sales"; "Sale"; "Present Sale"; "Conforming" to Contract; "Termination"; "Cancellation".

(1) In this Article unless the context otherwise requires "contract" and "agreement" are limited to those relating to the present or future sale of goods. "Contract for sale" includes both a present sale of

goods and a contract to sell goods at a future time. A "sale" consists in the passing of title from the seller to the buyer for a price (Section 2–401). A "present sale" means a sale which is accomplished by the making of the contract.

(2) Goods or conduct including any part of a performance are "conforming" or conform to the contract when they are in accordance with the obligations under the contract.

(3) "Termination" occurs when either party pursuant to a power created by agreement or law puts an end to the contract otherwise than for its breach. On "termination" all obligations which are still executory on both sides are discharged but any right based on prior breach or performance survives.

(4) "Cancellation" occurs when either party puts an end to the contract for breach by the other and its effect is the same as that of "termination" except that the cancelling party also retains any remedy for breach of the whole contract or any unperformed balance.

§ 2-107. Goods to Be Severed from Realty: Recording.

(1) A contract for the sale of minerals or the like (including oil and gas) or a structure or its materials to be removed from realty is a contract for the sale of goods within this Article if they are to be severed by the seller but until severance a purported present sale thereof which is not effective as a transfer of an interest in land is effective only as a contract to sell.

(2) A contract for the sale apart from the land of growing crops or other things attached to realty and capable of severance without material harm thereto but not described in subsection (1) or of timber to be cut is a contract for the sale of goods within this Article whether the subject matter is to be severed by the buyer or by the seller even though it forms part of the realty at the time of contracting, and the parties can by identification effect a present sale before severance.

(3) The provisions of this section are subject to any third party rights provided by the law relating to realty records, and the contract for sale may be executed and recorded as a document transferring an interest in land and shall then constitute notice to third parties of the buyer's rights under the contract for sale. As amended in 1972.

Part 2: Form, Formation and Readjustment of Contract

§ 2-201. Formal Requirements; Statute of Frauds.

(1) Except as otherwise provided in this section a contract for the sale of goods for the price of $500 or more is not enforceable by way of action or defense unless there is some writing sufficient to indicate that a contract for sale has been made between the parties and signed by the party against whom enforcement is sought or by his authorized agent or broker. A writing is not insufficient because it omits or incorrectly states a term agreed upon but the contract is not enforceable under this paragraph beyond the quantity of goods shown in such writing.

(2) Between merchants if within a reasonable time a writing in confirmation of the contract and sufficient against the sender is received and the party receiving it has reason to know its contents, it satisfies the requirements of subsection (1) against such party unless written notice of objection to its contents is given within 10 days after it is received.

(3) A contract which does not satisfy the requirements of subsection (1) but which is valid in other respects is enforceable

(a) if the goods are to be specially manufactured for the buyer and are not suitable for sale to others in the ordinary course of the seller's business and the seller, before notice of repudiation is received and under circumstances which reasonably indicate that the goods are for the buyer, has made either a substantial beginning of their manufacture or commitments for their procurement; or

(b) if the party against whom enforcement is sought admits in his pleading, testimony or otherwise in court that a contract for sale was made, but the contract is not enforceable under this provision beyond the quantity of goods admitted; or

(c) with respect to goods for which payment has been made and accepted or which have been received and accepted (Sec. 2–606).

§ 2-202. Final Written Expression: Parol or Extrinsic Evidence.

Terms with respect to which the confirmatory memoranda of the parties agree or which are otherwise set forth in a writing intended by the parties as a final expression of their agreement with respect to such terms as are included therein may not be contradicted by evidence of any prior agreement or of a contemporaneous oral agreement but may be explained or supplemented

   (a) by course of dealing or usage of trade (Section 1–205) or by course of performance (Section 2–208); and

   (b) by evidence of consistent additional terms unless the court finds the writing to have been intended also as a complete and exclusive statement of the terms of the agreement.

§ 2-203. Seals Inoperative.

The affixing of a seal to a writing evidencing a contract for sale or an offer to buy or sell goods does not constitute the writing a sealed instrument and the law with respect to sealed instruments does not apply to such a contract or offer.

§ 2-204. Formation in General.

(1) A contract for sale of goods may be made in any manner sufficient to show agreement, including conduct by both parties which recognizes the existence of such a contract.

(2) An agreement sufficient to constitute a contract for sale may be found even though the moment of its making is undetermined.

(3) Even though one or more terms are left open a contract for sale does not fail for indefiniteness if the parties have intended to make a contract and there is a reasonably certain basis for giving an appropriate remedy.

§ 2-205. Firm Offers.

An offer by a merchant to buy or sell goods in a signed writing which by its terms gives assurance that it will be held open is not revocable, for lack of consideration, during the time stated or if no time is stated for a reasonable time, but in no event may such period of irrevocability exceed three months; but any such term of assurance on a form supplied by the offeree must be separately signed by the offeror.

§ 2-206. Offer and Acceptance in Formation of Contract.

(1) Unless otherwise unambiguously indicated by the language or circumstances

   (a) an offer to make a contract shall be construed as inviting acceptance in any manner and by any medium reasonable in the circumstances;

   (b) an order or other offer to buy goods for prompt or current shipment shall be construed as inviting acceptance either by a prompt promise to ship or by the prompt or current shipment of conforming or non-conforming goods, but such a shipment of non-conforming goods does not constitute an acceptance if the seller seasonably notifies the buyer that the shipment is offered only as an accommodation to the buyer.

(2) Where the beginning of a requested performance is a reasonable mode of acceptance an offeror who is not notified of acceptance within a reasonable time may treat the offer as having lapsed before acceptance.

§ 2-207. Additional Terms in Acceptance or Confirmation.

(1) A definite and seasonable expression of acceptance or a written confirmation which is sent within a reasonable time operates as an acceptance even though it states terms additional to or different from those offered or agreed upon, unless acceptance is expressly made conditional on assent to the additional or different terms.

(2) The additional terms are to be construed as proposals for addition to the contract. Between merchants such terms become part of the contract unless:

   (a) the offer expressly limits acceptance to the terms of the offer;

   (b) they materially alter it; or

   (c) notification of objection to them has already been given or is given within a reasonable time after notice of them is received.

(3) Conduct by both parties which recognizes the existence of a contract is sufficient to establish a contract for sale although the writings of the parties do not otherwise establish a contract. In such case the terms of the particular contract consist of those terms on which the writings of the parties agree, together with any supplementary terms incorporated under any other provisions of this Act.

§ 2-208. Course of Performance or Practical Construction.

(1) Where the contract for sale involves repeated occasions for performance by either party with knowledge of the nature of the performance and opportunity for objection to it by the other, any course of performance accepted or acquiesced in

without objection shall be relevant to determine the meaning of the agreement.

(2) The express terms of the agreement and any such course of performance, as well as any course of dealing and usage of trade, shall be construed whenever reasonable as consistent with each other; but when such construction is unreasonable, express terms shall control course of performance and course of performance shall control both course of dealing and usage of trade (Section 1–205).

(3) Subject to the provisions of the next section on modification and waiver, such course of performance shall be relevant to show a waiver or modification of any term inconsistent with such course of performance.

§ 2-209. Modification, Recission and Waiver.

(1) An agreement modifying a contract within this Article needs no consideration to be binding.

(2) A signed agreement which excludes modification or rescission except by a signed writing cannot be otherwise modified or rescinded, but except as between merchants such a requirement on a form supplied by the merchant must be separately signed by the other party.

(3) The requirements of the statute of frauds section of this Article (Section 2–201) must be satisfied if the contract as modified is within its provisions.

(4) Although an attempt at modification or rescission does not satisfy the requirements of subsection (2) or (3) it can operate as a waiver.

(5) A party who has made a waiver affecting an executory portion of the contract may retract the waiver by reasonable notification received by the other party that strict performance will be required of any term waived, unless the retraction would be unjust in view of a material change of position in reliance on the waiver.

§ 2-210. Delegation of Performance; Assignment of Rights.

(1) A party may perform his duty through a delegate unless otherwise agreed or unless the other party has a substantial interest in having his original promisor perform or control the acts required by the contract. No delegation of performance relieves the party delegating of any duty to perform or any liability for breach.

(2) Unless otherwise agreed all rights of either seller or buyer can be assigned except where the assignment would materially change the duty of the other party, or increase materially the burden or risk imposed on him by his contract, or impair materially his chance of obtaining return performance. A right to damages for breach of the whole contract or a right arising out of the assignor's due performance of his entire obligation can be assigned despite agreement otherwise.

(3) Unless the circumstances indicate the contrary a prohibition of assignment of "the contract" is to be construed as barring only the delegation to the assignee of the assignor's performance.

(4) An assignment of "the contract" or of "all my rights under the contract" or an assignment in similar general terms is an assignment of rights and unless the language or the circumstances (as in an assignment for security) indicate the contrary, it is a delegation of performance of the duties of the assignor and its acceptance by the assignee constitutes a promise by him to perform those duties. This promise is enforceable by either the assignor or the other party to the original contract.

(5) The other party may treat any assignment which delegates performance as creating reasonable grounds for insecurity and may without prejudice to his rights against the assignor demand assurances from the assignee (Section 2–609).

Part 3: General Obligation and Construction of Contract

§ 2-301. General Obligations of Parties.

The obligation of the seller is to transfer and deliver and that of the buyer is to accept and pay in accordance with the contract.

§ 2-302. Unconscionable Contract or Clause.

(1) If the court as a matter of law finds the contract or any clause of the contract to have been unconscionable at the time it was made the court may refuse to enforce the contract, or it may enforce the remainder of the contract without the unconscionable clause, or it may so limit the application of any unconscionable clause as to avoid any unconscionable result.

(2) When it is claimed or appears to the court that the contract or any clause thereof may be unconscionable the parties shall be afforded a reasonable opportunity to present evidence as to its commercial setting, purpose and effect to aid the court in making the determination.

§ 2-303. Allocation or Division of Risks.

Where this Article allocates a risk or a burden as between the parties "unless otherwise agreed", the agreement may not only shift the allocation but may also divide the risk or burden.

§ 2-304. Price Payable in Money, Goods, Realty, or Otherwise.

(1) The price can be made payable in money or otherwise. If it is payable in whole or in part in goods each party is a seller of the goods which he is to transfer.

(2) Even though all or part of the price is payable in an interest in realty the transfer of the goods and the seller's obligations with reference to them are subject to this Article, but not the transfer of the interest in realty or the transferor's obligations in connection therewith.

§ 2-305. Open Price Term.

(1) The parties if they so intend can conclude a contract for sale even though the price is not settled. In such a case the price is a reasonable price at the time for delivery if
   (a) nothing is said as to price; or
   (b) the price is left to be agreed by the parties and they fail to agree; or
   (c) the price is to be fixed in terms of some agreed market or other standard as set or recorded by a third person or agency and it is not so set or recorded.

(2) A price to be fixed by the seller or by the buyer means a price for him to fix in good faith.

(3) When a price left to be fixed otherwise than by agreement of the parties fails to be fixed through fault of one party the other may at his option treat the contract as cancelled or himself fix a reasonable price.

(4) Where, however, the parties intend not to be bound unless the price be fixed or agreed and it is not fixed or agreed there is no contract. In such a case the buyer must return any goods already received or if unable so to do must pay their reasonable value at the time of delivery and the seller must return any portion of the price paid on account.

§ 2-306. Output, Requirements and Exclusive Dealings.

(1) A term which measures the quantity by the output of the seller or the requirements of the buyer means such actual output or requirements as may occur in good faith, except that no quantity unreasonably disproportionate to any stated estimate or in the absence of a stated estimate to any normal or otherwise comparable prior output or requirements may be tendered or demanded.

(2) A lawful agreement by either the seller or the buyer for exclusive dealing in the kind of goods concerned imposes unless otherwise agreed an obligation by the seller to use best efforts to supply the goods and by the buyer to use best efforts to promote their sale.

§ 2-307. Delivery in Single Lot or Several Lots.

Unless otherwise agreed all goods called for by a contract for sale must be tendered in a single delivery and payment is due only on such tender but where the circumstances give either party the right to make or demand delivery in lots the price if it can be apportioned may be demanded for each lot.

§ 2-308. Absence of Specified Place for Delivery.

Unless otherwise agreed
   (a) the place for delivery of goods is the seller's place of business or if he has none his residence; but
   (b) in a contract for sale of identified goods which to the knowledge of the parties at the time of contracting are in some other place, that place is the place for their delivery; and
   (c) documents of title may be delivered through customary banking channels.

§ 2-309. Absence of Specific Time Provisions; Notice of Termination.

(1) The time for shipment or delivery or any other action under a contract if not provided in this Article or agreed upon shall be a reasonable time.

(2) Where the contract provides for successive performances but is indefinite in duration it is valid for a reasonable time but unless otherwise agreed may be terminated at any time by either party.

(3) Termination of a contract by one party except on the happening of an agreed event requires that reasonable notification be received by the other party and an agreement dispensing with notification is invalid if its operation would be unconscionable.

§ 2-310. Open Time for Payment or Running of Credit; Authority to Ship Under Reservation.

Unless otherwise agreed
   (a) payment is due at the time and place at which the buyer is to receive the goods even though

the place of shipment is the place of delivery; and

(b) if the seller is authorized to send the goods he may ship them under reservation, and may tender the documents of title, but the buyer may inspect the goods after their arrival before payment is due unless such inspection is inconsistent with the terms of the contract (Section 2–513); and

(c) if delivery is authorized and made by way of documents of title otherwise than by subsection (b) then payment is due at the time and place at which the buyer is to receive the documents regardless of where the goods are to be received; and

(d) where the seller is required or authorized to ship the goods on credit the credit period runs from the time of shipment but postdating the invoice or delaying its dispatch will correspondingly delay the starting of the credit period.

§ 2-311. Options and Cooperation Respecting Performance.

(1) An agreement for sale which is otherwise sufficiently definite (subsection (3) of Section 2–204) to be a contract is not made invalid by the fact that it leaves particulars of performance to be specified by one of the parties. Any such specification must be made in good faith and within limits set by commercial reasonableness.

(2) Unless otherwise agreed specifications relating to assortment of the goods are at the buyer's option and except as otherwise provided in subsections (1)(c) and (3) of Section 2–319 specifications or arrangements relating to shipment are at the seller's option.

(3) Where such specification would materially affect the other party's performance but is not seasonably made or where one party's cooperation is necessary to the agreed performance of the other but is not seasonably forthcoming, the other party in addition to all other remedies

(a) is excused for any resulting delay in his own performance; and

(b) may also either proceed to perform in any reasonable manner or after the time for a material part of his own performance treat the failure to specify or to cooperate as a breach by failure to deliver or accept the goods.

§ 2-312. Warranty of Title and Against Infringement; Buyer's Obligation Against Infringement.

(1) Subject to subsection (2) there is in a contract for sale a warranty by the seller that

(a) the title conveyed shall be good, and its transfer rightful; and

(b) the goods shall be delivered free from any security interest or other lien or encumbrance of which the buyer at the time of contracting has no knowledge.

(2) A warranty under subsection (1) will be excluded or modified only by specific language or by circumstances which give the buyer reason to know that the person selling does not claim title in himself or that he is purporting to sell only such right or title as he or a third person may have.

(3) Unless otherwise agreed a seller who is a merchant regularly dealing in goods of the kind warrants that the goods shall be delivered free of the rightful claim of any third person by way of infringement or the like but a buyer who furnishes specifications to the seller must hold the seller harmless against any such claim which arises out of compliance with the specifications.

§ 2-313. Express Warranties by Affirmation, Promise, Description, Sample.

(1) Express warranties by the seller are created as follows:

(a) Any affirmation of fact or promise made by the seller to the buyer which relates to the goods and becomes part of the basis of the bargain creates an express warranty that the goods shall conform to the affirmation or promise.

(b) Any description of the goods which is made part of the basis of the bargain creates an express warranty that the goods shall conform to the description.

(c) Any sample or model which is made part of the basis of the bargain creates an express warranty that the whole of the goods shall conform to the sample or model.

(2) It is not necessary to the creation of an express warranty that the seller use formal words such as "warrant" or "guarantee" or that he have a specific intention to make a warranty, but an affirmation merely of the value of the goods or a statement purporting to be merely the seller's opinion or commendation of the goods does not create a warranty.

§ 2-314. Implied Warranty: Merchantability; Usage of Trade.

(1) Unless excluded or modified (Section 2–316), a warranty that the goods shall be merchantable is implied in a contract for their sale if the seller is a merchant with respect to goods of that kind. Under this section the serving for value of food or drink to be consumed either on the premises or elsewhere is a sale.

(2) Goods to be merchantable must be at least such as

   (a) pass without objection in the trade under the contract description; and

   (b) in the case of fungible goods, are of fair average quality within the description; and

   (c) are fit for the ordinary purposes for which such goods are used; and

   (d) run, within the variations permitted by the agreement, of even kind, quality and quantity within each unit and among all units involved; and

   (e) are adequately contained, packaged, and labeled as the agreement may require; and

   (f) conform to the promise or affirmations of fact made on the container or label if any.

(3) Unless excluded or modified (Section 2–316) other implied warranties may arise from course of dealing or usage of trade.

§ 2-315. Implied Warranty: Fitness for Particular Purpose.

Where the seller at the time of contracting has reason to know any particular purpose for which the goods are required and that the buyer is relying on the seller's skill or judgment to select or furnish suitable goods, there is unless excluded or modified under the next section an implied warranty that the goods shall be fit for such purpose.

§ 2-316. Exclusion or Modification of Warranties.

(1) Words or conduct relevant to the creation of an express warranty and words or conduct tending to negate or limit warranty shall be construed wherever reasonable as consistent with each other; but subject to the provisions of this Article on parol or extrinsic evidence (Section 2–202) negation or limitation is inoperative to the extent that such construction is unreasonable.

(2) Subject to subsection (3), to exclude or modify the implied warranty of merchantability or any part of it the language must mention merchantability and in case of a writing must be conspicuous, and to exclude or modify any implied warranty of fitness the exclusion must be by a writing and conspicuous. Language to exclude all implied warranties of fitness is sufficient if it states, for example, that "There are no warranties which extend beyond the description on the face hereof."

(3) Notwithstanding subsection (2)

   (a) unless the circumstances indicate otherwise, all implied warranties are excluded by expressions like "as is", "with all faults" or other language which in common understanding calls the buyer's attention to the exclusion of warranties and makes plain that there is no implied warranty; and

   (b) when the buyer before entering into the contract has examined the goods or the sample or model as fully as he desired or has refused to examine the goods there is no implied warranty with regard to defects which an examination ought in the circumstances to have revealed to him; and

   (c) an implied warranty can also be excluded or modified by course of dealing or course of performance or usage of trade.

(4) Remedies for breach of warranty can be limited in accordance with the provisions of this Article on liquidation or limitation of damages and on contractual modification of remedy (Sections 2–718 and 2–719).

§ 2-317. Cumulation and Conflict of Warranties Express or Implied.

Warranties whether express or implied shall be construed as consistent with each other and as cumulative, but if such construction is unreasonable the intention of the parties shall determine which warranty is dominant. In ascertaining that intention the following rules apply:

   (a) Exact or technical specifications displace an inconsistent sample or model or general language of description.

   (b) A sample from an existing bulk displaces inconsistent general language of description.

   (c) Express warranties displace inconsistent implied warranties other than an implied warranty of fitness for a particular purpose.

§ 2-318. Third Party Beneficiaries of Warranties Express or Implied. Note:

If this Act is introduced in the Congress of the United States this section should be omitted. (States to select one alternative.)

Alternative A

A seller's warranty whether express or implied extends to any natural person who is in the family or household of his buyer or who is a guest in his home if it is reasonable to expect that such person may use, consume or be affected by the goods and who is injured in person by breach of the warranty. A seller may not exclude or limit the operation of this section.

Alternative B

A seller's warranty whether express or implied extends to any natural person who may reasonably be expected to use, consume or be affected by the goods and who is injured in person by breach of the warranty. A seller may not exclude or limit the operation of this section.

Alternative C

A seller's warranty whether express or implied extends to any person who may reasonably be expected to use, consume or be affected by the goods and who is injured by breach of the warranty. A seller may not exclude or limit the operation of this section with respect to injury to the person of an individual to whom the warranty extends.

§ 2-319. F.O.B. and F.A.S. Terms.

(1) Unless otherwise agreed the term F.O.B. (which means "free on board") at a named place, even though used only in connection with the stated price, is a delivery term under which

   (a) when the term is F.O.B. the place of shipment, the seller must at that place ship the goods in the manner provided in this Article (Section 2–504) and bear the expense and risk of putting them into the possession of the carrier; or

   (b) when the term is F.O.B. the place of destination, the seller must at his own expense and risk transport the goods to that place and there tender delivery of them in the manner provided in this Article (Section 2–503);

   (c) when under either (a) or (b) the term is also F.O.B. vessel, car or other vehicle, the seller must in addition at his own expense and risk load the goods on board. If the term is F.O.B. vessel the buyer must name the vessel and in an appropriate case the seller must comply with the provisions of this Article on the form of bill of lading (Section 2–323).

(2) Unless otherwise agreed the term F.A.S. vessel (which means "free alongside") at a named port, even though used only in connection with the stated price, is a delivery term under which the seller must

   (a) at his own expense and risk deliver the goods alongside the vessel in the manner usual in that port or on a dock designated and provided by the buyer; and

   (b) obtain and tender a receipt for the goods in exchange for which the carrier is under a duty to issue a bill of lading.

(3) Unless otherwise agreed in any case falling within subsection (1)(a) or (c) or subsection (2) the buyer must seasonably give any needed instructions for making delivery, including when the term is F.A.S. or F.O.B. the loading berth of the vessel and in an appropriate case its name and sailing date. The seller may treat the failure of needed instructions as a failure of cooperation under this Article (Section 2–311). He may also at his option move the goods in any reasonable manner preparatory to delivery or shipment.

(4) Under the term F.O.B. vessel or F.A.S. unless otherwise agreed the buyer must make payment against tender of the required documents and the seller may not tender nor the buyer demand delivery of the goods in substitution for the documents.

§ 2-320. C.I.F. and C. & F. Terms.

(1) The term C.I.F. means that the price includes in a lump sum the cost of the goods and the insurance and freight to the named destination. The term C. & F. or C.F. means that the price so includes cost and freight to the named destination.

(2) Unless otherwise agreed and even though used only in connection with the stated price and destination, the term C.I.F. destination or its equivalent requires the seller at his own expense and risk to

   (a) put the goods into the possession of a carrier at the port for shipment and obtain a negotiable bill or bills of lading covering the entire transportation to the named destination; and

   (b) load the goods and obtain a receipt from the carrier (which may be contained in the bill of lading) showing that the freight has been paid or provided for; and

   (c) obtain a policy or certificate of insurance, including any war risk insurance, of a kind and on terms then current at the port of shipment in the usual amount, in the currency of the contract, shown to cover the same goods covered by the bill of lading and providing for payment of loss to the order of the buyer or for the account of whom it may concern; but the seller may add to the price the amount of the premium for any such war risk insurance; and

(d) prepare an invoice of the goods and procure any other documents required to effect shipment or to comply with the contract; and

(e) forward and tender with commercial promptness all the documents in due form and with any indorsement necessary to perfect the buyer's rights.

(3) Unless otherwise agreed the term C. & F. or its equivalent has the same effect and imposes upon the seller the same obligations and risks as a C.I.F. term except the obligation as to insurance.

(4) Under the term C.I.F. or C. & F. unless otherwise agreed the buyer must make payment against tender of the required documents and the seller may not tender nor the buyer demand delivery of the goods in substitution for the documents.

§ 2-321. C.I.F. or C. & F.: "Net Landed Weights"; "Payment on Arrival"; Warranty of Condition on Arrival.

Under a contract containing a term C.I.F. or C. & F.

(1) Where the price is based on or is to be adjusted according to "net landed weights", "delivered weights", "out turn" quantity or quality or the like, unless otherwise agreed the seller must reasonably estimate the price. The payment due on tender of the documents called for by the contract is the amount so estimated, but after final adjustment of the price a settlement must be made with commercial promptness.

(2) An agreement described in subsection (1) or any warranty of quality or condition of the goods on arrival places upon the seller the risk of ordinary deterioration, shrinkage and the like in transportation but has no effect on the place or time of identification to the contract for sale or delivery or on the passing of the risk of loss.

(3) Unless otherwise agreed where the contract provides for payment on or after arrival of the goods the seller must before payment allow such preliminary inspection as is feasible; but if the goods are lost delivery of the documents and payment are due when the goods should have arrived.

§ 2-322. Delivery "Ex-Ship".

(1) Unless otherwise agreed a term for delivery of goods "ex-ship" (which means from the carrying vessel) or in equivalent language is not restricted to a particular ship and requires delivery from a ship which has reached a place at the named port of destination where goods of the kind are usually discharged.

(2) Under such a term unless otherwise agreed

(a) the seller must discharge all liens arising out of the carriage and furnish the buyer with a direction which puts the carrier under a duty to deliver the goods; and

(b) the risk of loss does not pass to the buyer until the goods leave the ship's tackle or are otherwise properly unloaded.

§ 2-323. Form of Bill of Lading Required in Overseas Shipment; "Overseas".

(1) Where the contract contemplates overseas shipment and contains a term C.I.F. or C. & F. or F.O.B. vessel, the seller unless otherwise agreed must obtain a negotiable bill of lading stating that the goods have been loaded in board or, in the case of a term C.I.F. or C. & F., received for shipment.

(2) Where in a case within subsection (1) a bill of lading has been issued in a set of parts, unless otherwise agreed if the documents are not to be sent from abroad the buyer may demand tender of the full set; otherwise only one part of the bill of lading need be tendered. Even if the agreement expressly requires a full set

(a) due tender of a single part is acceptable within the provisions of this Article on cure of improper delivery (subsection (1) of Section 2–508); and

(b) even though the full set is demanded, if the documents are sent from abroad the person tendering an incomplete set may nevertheless require payment upon furnishing an indemnity which the buyer in good faith deems adequate.

(3) A shipment by water or by air or a contract contemplating such shipment is "overseas" insofar as by usage of trade or agreement it is subject to the commercial, financing or shipping practices characteristic of international deep water commerce.

§ 2-324. "No Arrival, No Sale" Term.

Under a term "no arrival, no sale" or terms of like meaning, unless otherwise agreed,

(a) the seller must properly ship conforming goods and if they arrive by any means he must tender them on arrival but he assumes no obligation that the goods will arrive unless he has caused the non-arrival; and

(b) where without fault of the seller the goods are in part lost or have so deteriorated as no longer to conform to the contract or arrive after the contract time, the buyer may proceed as if there had been casualty to identified goods (Section 2–613).

§ 2-325. "Letter of Credit" Term; "Confirmed Credit".

(1) Failure of the buyer seasonably to furnish an agreed letter of credit is a breach of the contract for sale.

(2) The delivery to seller of a proper letter of credit suspends the buyer's obligation to pay. If the letter of credit is dishonored, the seller may on seasonable notification to the buyer require payment directly from him.

(3) Unless otherwise agreed the term "letter of credit" or "banker's credit" in a contract for sale means an irrevocable credit issued by a financing agency of good repute and, where the shipment is overseas, of good international repute. The term "confirmed credit" means that the credit must also carry the direct obligation of such an agency which does business in the seller's financial market.

§ 2-326. Sale on Approval and Sale or Return; Consignment Sales and Rights of Creditors.

(1) Unless otherwise agreed, if delivered goods may be returned by the buyer even though they conform to the contract, the transaction is
(a) a "sale on approval" if the goods are delivered primarily for use, and
(b) a "sale or return" if the goods are delivered primarily for resale.

(2) Except as provided in subsection (3), goods held on approval are not subject to the claims of the buyer's creditors until acceptance; goods held on sale or return are subject to such claims while in the buyer's possession.

(3) Where goods are delivered to a person for sale and such person maintains a place of business at which he deals in goods of the kind involved, under a name other than the name of the person making delivery, then with respect to claims of creditors

of the person conducting the business the goods are deemed to be on sale or return. The provisions of this subsection are applicable even though an agreement purports to reserve title to the person making delivery until payment or resale or uses such words as "on consignment" or "on memorandum". However, this subsection is not applicable if the person making delivery

(a) complies with an applicable law providing for a consignor's interest or the like to be evidenced by a sign, or

(b) establishes that the person conducting the business is generally known by his creditors to be substantially engaged in selling the goods of others, or

(c) complies with the filing provisions of the Article on Secured Transactions (Article 9).

(4) Any "or return" term of a contract for sale is to be treated as a separate contract for sale within the statute of frauds section of this Article (Section 2–201) and as contradicting the sale aspect of the contract within the provisions of this Article on parol or extrinsic evidence (Section 2–202).

§ 2-327. Special Incidents of Sale on Approval and Sale or Return.

(1) Under a sale on approval unless otherwise agreed
(a) although the goods are identified to the contract the risk of loss and the title do not pass to the buyer until acceptance; and
(b) use of the goods consistent with the purpose of trial is not acceptance but failure seasonably to notify the seller of election to return the goods is acceptance, and if the goods conform to the contract acceptance of any part is acceptance of the whole; and
(c) after due notification of election to return, the return is at the seller's risk and expense but a merchant buyer must follow any reasonable instructions.

(2) Under a sale or return unless otherwise agreed
(a) the option to return extends to the whole or any commercial unit of the goods while in substantially their original condition, but must be exercised seasonably; and
(b) the return is at the buyer's risk and expense.

§ 2-328. Sale. by Auction.

(1) In a sale by auction if goods are put up in lots each lot is the subject of a separate sale.

(2) A sale by auction is complete when the auctioneer so announces by the fall of the hammer or in other customary manner. Where a bid is made while the hammer is falling in acceptance of a prior bid the auctioneer may in his discretion reopen the bidding or declare the goods sold under the bid on which the hammer was falling.

(3) Such a sale is with reserve unless the goods are in explicit terms put up without reserve. In an auction with reserve the auctioneer may withdraw the goods at any time until he announces completion of the sale. In an auction without reserve, after the auctioneer calls for bids on an article or lot, that article or lot cannot be withdrawn unless no bid is made within a reasonable time. In either case a bidder may retract his bid until the auctioneer's announcement of completion of the sale, but a bidder's retraction does not revive any previous bid.

(4) If the auctioneer knowingly receives a bid on the seller's behalf or the seller makes or procures such a bid, and notice has not been given that liberty for such bidding is reserved, the buyer may at his option avoid the sale or take the goods at the price of the last good faith bid prior to the completion of the sale. This subsection shall not apply to any bid at a forced sale.

Part 4: Title, Creditors and Good Faith Purchasers

§ 2-401. Passing of Title; Reservation for Security; Limited Application of This Section.

Each provision of this Article with regard to the rights, obligations and remedies of the seller, the buyer, purchasers or other third parties applies irrespective of title to the goods except where the provision refers to such title. Insofar as situations are not covered by the other provisions of this Article and matters concerning title become material the following rules apply:

(1) Title to goods cannot pass under a contract for sale prior to their identification to the contract (Section 2–501), and unless otherwise explicitly agreed the buyer acquires by their identification a special property as limited by this Act. Any retention or reservation by the seller of the title (property) in goods shipped or delivered to the buyer is limited in effect to a reservation of a security interest. Subject to these provisions and to the provisions of the Article on Secured Transactions (Article 9), title to goods passes from the seller to the buyer in any manner and on any conditions explicitly agreed on by the parties.

(2) Unless otherwise explicitly agreed title passes to the buyer at the time and place at which the seller completes his performance with reference to the physical delivery of the goods, despite any reservation of a security interest and even though a document of title is to be delivered at a different time or place; and in particular and despite any reservation of a security interest by the bill of lading

    (a) if the contract requires or authorizes the seller to send the goods to the buyer but does not require him to deliver them at destination, title passes to the buyer at the time and place of shipment; but

    (b) if the contract requires delivery at destination, title passes on tender there.

(3) Unless otherwise explicitly agreed where delivery is to be made without moving the goods,

    (a) if the seller is to deliver a document of title, title passes at the time when and the place where he delivers such documents; or

    (b) if the goods are at the time of contracting already identified and no documents are to be delivered, title passes at the time and place of contracting.

(4) A rejection or other refusal by the buyer to receive or retain the goods, whether or not justified, or a justified revocation of acceptance revests title to the goods in the seller. Such revesting occurs by operation of law and is not a "sale".

§ 2-402. Rights of Seller's Creditors Against Sold Goods.

(1) Except as provided in subsections (2) and (3), rights of unsecured creditors of the seller with respect to goods which have been identified to a contract for sale are subject to the buyer's rights to recover the goods under this Article (Sections 2–502 and 2–716).

(2) A creditor of the seller may treat a sale or an identification of goods to a contract for sale as void if as against him a retention of possession by the seller is fraudulent under any rule of law of the state where the goods are situated, except that retention of possession in good faith and current course of trade by a merchant-seller for a commercially reasonable time after a sale or identification is not fraudulent.

(3) Nothing in this Article shall be deemed to impair the rights of creditors of the seller

    (a) under the provisions of the Article on Secured Transactions (Article 9); or

    (b) where identification to the contract or delivery is made not in current course of trade but in satisfaction of or as security for a pre-existing claim for money, security or the like and is made under circumstances which under any rule of law of the state where the goods are situated would apart from this Article constitute the transaction a fraudulent transfer or voidable preference.

§ 2-403. Power to Transfer; Good Faith Purchase of Goods; "Entrusting".

(1) A purchaser of goods acquires all title which his transferor had or had power to transfer except that a purchaser of a limited interest acquires rights only to the extent of the interest purchased. A person with voidable title has power to transfer a good title to a good faith purchaser for value. When goods have been delivered under a transaction of purchase the purchaser has such power even though

    (a) the transferor was deceived as to the identity of the purchaser, or

    (b) the delivery was in exchange for a check which is later dishonored, or

    (c) it was agreed that the transaction was to be a "cash sale", or

    (d) the delivery was procured through fraud punishable as larcenous under the criminal law.

(2) Any entrusting of possession of goods to a merchant who deals in goods of that kind gives him power to transfer all rights of the entruster to a buyer in ordinary course of business.

(3) "Entrusting" includes any delivery and any acquiescence in retention of possession regardless of any condition expressed between the parties to the delivery or acquiescence and regardless of whether the procurement of the entrusting or the possessor's disposition of the goods have been such as to be larcenous under the criminal law. [*Publisher's Editorial Note: If a state adopts the repealer of Article 6—Bulk Transfers (Alternative A), subsec. (4) should read as follows:*]

(4) The rights of other purchasers of goods and of lien creditors are governed by the Articles on Secured Transactions (Article 9) and Documents of Title

(Article 7). [*Publisher's Editorial Note: If a state adopts Revised Article 6—Bulk Sales (Alternative B), subsec. (4) should read as follows:*]

(4) The rights of other purchasers of goods and of lien creditors are governed by the Articles on Secured Transactions (Article 9), Bulk Sales (Article 6) and Documents of Title (Article 7).

As amended in 1988.

For material relating to the changes made in text in 1988, see section 3 of Alternative A (Repealer of Article 6—Bulk Transfers) and Conforming Amendment to Section 2–403 following end of Alternative B (Revised Article 6—Bulk Sales).

Part 5: Performance

§ 2-501. Insurable Interest in Goods; Manner of Identification of Goods.

(1) The buyer obtains a special property and an insurable interest in goods by identification of existing goods as goods to which the contract refers even though the goods so identified are non-conforming and he has an option to return or reject them. Such identification can be made at any time and in any manner explicitly agreed to by the parties. In the absence of explicit agreement identification occurs

    (a) when the contract is made if it is for the sale of goods already existing and identified;

    (b) if the contract is for the sale of future goods other than those described in paragraph (c), when goods are shipped, marked or otherwise designated by the seller as goods to which the contract refers;

    (c) when the crops are planted or otherwise become growing crops or the young are conceived if the contract is for the sale of unborn young to be born within twelve months after contracting or for the sale of crops to be harvested within twelve months or the next normal harvest season after contracting whichever is longer.

(2) The seller retains an insurable interest in goods so long as title to or any security interest in the goods remains in him and where the identification is by the seller alone he may until default or insolvency or notification to the buyer that the identification is final substitute other goods for those identified.

(3) Nothing in this section impairs any insurable interest recognized under any other statute or rule of law.

§ 2-502. Buyer's Right to Goods on Seller's Insolvency.

(1) Subject to subsection (2) and even though the goods have not been shipped a buyer who has paid a part or all of the price of goods in which he has a special property under the provisions of the immediately preceding section may on making and keeping good a tender of any unpaid portion of their price recover them from the seller if the seller becomes insolvent within ten days after receipt of the first installment on their price.

(2) If the identification creating his special property has been made by the buyer he acquires the right to recover the goods only if they conform to the contract for sale.

§ 2-503. Manner of Seller's Tender of Delivery.

(1) Tender of delivery requires that the seller put and hold conforming goods at the buyer's disposition and give the buyer any notification reasonably necessary to enable him to take delivery. The manner, time and place for tender are determined by the agreement and this Article, and in particular

  (a) tender must be at a reasonable hour, and if it is of goods they must be kept available for the period reasonably necessary to enable the buyer to take possession; but

  (b) unless otherwise agreed the buyer must furnish facilities reasonably suited to the receipt of the goods.

(2) Where the case is within the next section respecting shipment tender requires that the seller comply with its provisions.

(3) Where the seller is required to deliver at a particular destination tender requires that he comply with subsection (1) and also in any appropriate case tender documents as described in subsections (4) and (5) of this section.

(4) Where goods are in the possession of a bailee and are to be delivered without being moved

  (a) tender requires that the seller either tender a negotiable document of title covering such goods or procure acknowledgment by the bailee of the buyer's right to possession of the goods; but

  (b) tender to the buyer of a non-negotiable document of title or of a written direction to the bailee to deliver is sufficient tender unless the buyer seasonably objects, and receipt by the bailee of notification of the buyer's rights fixes those rights as against the bailee and all third persons; but risk of loss of the goods and of any failure by the bailee to honor the non-negotiable document of title or to obey the direction remains on the seller until the buyer has had a reasonable time to present the document or direction, and a refusal by the bailee to honor the document or to obey the direction defeats the tender.

(5) Where the contract requires the seller to deliver documents

  (a) he must tender all such documents in correct form, except as provided in this Article with respect to bills of lading in a set (subsection (2) of Section 2–323); and

  (b) tender through customary banking channels is sufficient and dishonor of a draft accompanying the documents constitutes non-acceptance or rejection.

§ 2-504. Shipment by Seller.

Where the seller is required or authorized to send the goods to the buyer and the contract does not require him to deliver them at a particular destination, then unless otherwise agreed he must

  (a) put the goods in the possession of such a carrier and make such a contract for their transportation as may be reasonable having regard to the nature of the goods and other circumstances of the case; and

  (b) obtain and promptly deliver or tender in due form any document necessary to enable the buyer to obtain possession of the goods or otherwise required by the agreement or by usage of trade; and

  (c) promptly notify the buyer of the shipment. Failure to notify the buyer under paragraph (c) or to make a proper contract under paragraph (a) is a ground for rejection only if material delay or loss ensues.

§ 2-505. Seller's Shipment Under Reservation.

(1) Where the seller has identified goods to the contract by or before shipment:

  (a) his procurement of a negotiable bill of lading to his own order or otherwise reserves in him a security interest in the goods. His procurement of the bill to the order of a financing agency or of the buyer indicates in addition only the seller's expectation of transferring that interest to the person named.

(b) a non-negotiable bill of lading to himself or his nominee reserves possession of the goods as security but except in a case of conditional delivery (subsection (2) of Section 2–507) a non-negotiable bill of lading naming the buyer as consignee reserves no security interest even though the seller retains possession of the bill of lading.

(2) When shipment by the seller with reservation of a security interest is in violation of the contract for sale it constitutes an improper contract for transportation within the preceding section but impairs neither the rights given to the buyer by shipment and identification of the goods to the contract nor the seller's powers as a holder of a negotiable document.

§ 2-506. Rights of Financing Agency.

(1) A financing agency by paying or purchasing for value a draft which relates to a shipment of goods acquires to the extent of the payment or purchase and in addition to its own rights under the draft and any document of title securing it any rights of the shipper in the goods including the right to stop delivery and the shipper's right to have the draft honored by the buyer.

(2) The right to reimbursement of a financing agency which has in good faith honored or purchased the draft under commitment to or authority from the buyer is not impaired by subsequent discovery of defects with reference to any relevant document which was apparently regular on its face.

§ 2-507. Effect of Seller's Tender; Delivery on Condition.

(1) Tender of delivery is a condition to the buyer's duty to accept the goods and, unless otherwise agreed, to his duty to pay for them. Tender entitles the seller to acceptance of the goods and to payment according to the contract.

(2) Where payment is due and demanded on the delivery to the buyer of goods or documents of title, his right as against the seller to retain or dispose of them is conditional upon his making the payment due.

§ 2-508. Cure by Seller of Improper Tender or Delivery; Replacement.

(1) Where any tender or delivery by the seller is rejected because non-conforming and the time for performance has not yet expired, the seller may seasonably notify the buyer of his intention to cure and may then within the contract time make a conforming delivery.

(2) Where the buyer rejects a non-conforming tender which the seller had reasonable grounds to believe would be acceptable with or without money allowance the seller may if he seasonably notifies the buyer have a further reasonable time to substitute a conforming tender.

§ 2-509. Risk of Loss in the Absence of Breach.

(1) Where the contract requires or authorizes the seller to ship the goods by carrier

    (a) if it does not require him to deliver them at a particular destination, the risk of loss passes to the buyer when the goods are duly delivered to the carrier even though the shipment is under reservation (Section 2–505); but

    (b) if it does require him to deliver them at a particular destination and the goods are there duly tendered while in the possession of the carrier, the risk of loss passes to the buyer when the goods are there duly so tendered as to enable the buyer to take delivery.

(2) Where the goods are held by a bailee to be delivered without being moved, the risk of loss passes to the buyer

    (a) on his receipt of a negotiable document of title covering the goods; or

    (b) on acknowledgment by the bailee of the buyer's right to possession of the goods; or

    (c) after his receipt of a non-negotiable document of title or other written direction to deliver, as provided in subsection (4)(b) of Section 2–503.

(3) In any case not within subsection (1) or (2), the risk of loss passes to the buyer on his receipt of the goods if the seller is a merchant; otherwise the risk passes to the buyer on tender of delivery.

(4) The provisions of this section are subject to contrary agreement of the parties and to the provisions of this Article on sale on approval (Section 2–327) and on effect of breach on risk of loss (Section 2–510).

§ 2-510. Effect of Breach on Risk of Loss.

(1) Where a tender or delivery of goods so fails to conform to the contract as to give a right of rejection the risk of their loss remains on the seller until cure or acceptance.

(2) Where the buyer rightfully revokes acceptance he may to the extent of any deficiency in his effective insurance coverage treat the risk of loss as having rested on the seller from the beginning.

(3) Where the buyer as to conforming goods already identified to the contract for sale repudiates or is otherwise in breach before risk of their loss has passed to him, the seller may to the extent of any deficiency in his effective insurance coverage treat the risk of loss as resting on the buyer for a commercially reasonable time.

§ 2-511. Tender of Payment by Buyer; Payment by Check.

(1) Unless otherwise agreed tender of payment is a condition to the seller's duty to tender and complete any delivery.

(2) Tender of payment is sufficient when made by any means or in any manner current in the ordinary course of business unless the seller demands payment in legal tender and gives any extension of time reasonably necessary to procure it.

(3) Subject to the provisions of this Act on the effect of an instrument on an obligation (Section 3–310), payment by check is conditional and is defeated as between the parties by dishonor of the check on due presentment.

As amended in 1994.

See Appendix XI for material relating to changes made in text in 1994.

§ 2-512. Payment by Buyer Before Inspection.

(1) Where the contract requires payment before inspection non-conformity of the goods does not excuse the buyer from so making payment unless

(a) the non-conformity appears without inspection; or

(b) despite tender of the required documents the circumstances would justify injunction against honor under this Act (Section 5–109(b)).

(2) Payment pursuant to subsection (1) does not constitute an acceptance of goods or impair the buyer's right to inspect or any of his remedies.

As amended in 1995.

See Appendix XIV for material relating to changes made in text in 1995.

§ 2-513. Buyer's Right to Inspection of Goods.

(1) Unless otherwise agreed and subject to subsection (3), where goods are tendered or delivered or identified to the contract for sale, the buyer has a right before payment or acceptance to inspect them at any reasonable place and time and in any reasonable manner. When the seller is required or authorized to send the goods to the buyer, the inspection may be after their arrival.

(2) Expenses of inspection must be borne by the buyer but may be recovered from the seller if the goods do not conform and are rejected.

(3) Unless otherwise agreed and subject to the provisions of this Article on C.I.F. contracts (subsection (3) of Section 2–321), the buyer is not entitled to inspect the goods before payment of the price when the contract provides

(a) for delivery "C.O.D." or on other like terms; or

(b) for payment against documents of title, except where such payment is due only after the goods are to become available for inspection.

(4) A place or method of inspection fixed by the parties is presumed to be exclusive but unless otherwise expressly agreed it does not postpone identification or shift the place for delivery or for passing the risk of loss. If compliance becomes impossible, inspection shall be as provided in this section unless the place or method fixed was clearly intended as an indispensable condition failure of which avoids the contract.

§ 2-514. When Documents Deliverable on Acceptance; When on Payment.

Unless otherwise agreed documents against which a draft is drawn are to be delivered to the drawee on acceptance of the draft if it is payable more than three days after presentment; otherwise, only on payment.

§ 2-515. Preserving Evidence of Goods in Dispute.

In furtherance of the adjustment of any claim or dispute

(a) either party on reasonable notification to the other and for the purpose of ascertaining the facts and preserving evidence has the right to inspect, test and sample the goods including such of them as may be in the possession or control of the other; and

(b) the parties may agree to a third party inspection or survey to determine the conformity or condition of the goods and may agree that the findings shall be binding upon them in any subsequent litigation or adjustment.

Part 6: Breach, Repudiation and Excuse

§ 2-601. Buyer's Rights on Improper Delivery.

Subject to the provisions of this Article on breach in installment contracts (Section 2–612) and unless otherwise agreed under the sections on contractual limitations of remedy (Sections 2–718 and 2–719), if the goods or the tender of delivery fail in any respect to conform to the contract, the buyer may

    (a) reject the whole; or

    (b) accept the whole; or

    (c) accept any commercial unit or units and reject the rest.

§ 2-602. Manner and Effect of Rightful Rejection.

(1) Rejection of goods must be within a reasonable time after their delivery or tender. It is ineffective unless the buyer seasonably notifies the seller.

(2) Subject to the provisions of the two following sections on rejected goods (Sections 2–603 and 2–604),

    (a) after rejection any exercise of ownership by the buyer with respect to any commercial unit is wrongful as against the seller; and

    (b) if the buyer has before rejection taken physical possession of goods in which he does not have a security interest under the provisions of this Article (subsection (3) of Section 2–711), he is under a duty after rejection to hold them with reasonable care at the seller's disposition for a time sufficient to permit the seller to remove them; but

    (c) the buyer has no further obligations with regard to goods rightfully rejected.

(3) The seller's rights with respect to goods wrongfully rejected are governed by the provisions of this Article on Seller's remedies in general (Section 2–703).

§ 2-603. Merchant Buyer's Duties as to Rightfully Rejected Goods.

(1) Subject to any security interest in the buyer (subsection (3) of Section 2–711), when the seller has no agent or place of business at the market of rejection a merchant buyer is under a duty after rejection of goods in his possession or control to follow any reasonable instructions received from the seller with respect to the goods and in the absence of such instructions to make reasonable efforts to sell them for the seller's account if they are perishable or threaten to decline in value speedily. Instructions are not reasonable if on demand indemnity for expenses is not forthcoming.

(2) When the buyer sells goods under subsection (1), he is entitled to reimbursement from the seller or out of the proceeds for reasonable expenses of caring for and selling them, and if the expenses include no selling commission then to such commission as is usual in the trade or if there is none to a reasonable sum not exceeding ten per cent on the gross proceeds.

(3) In complying with this section the buyer is held only to good faith and good faith conduct hereunder is neither acceptance nor conversion nor the basis of an action for damages.

§ 2-604. Buyer's Options as to Salvage of Rightfully Rejected Goods.

Subject to the provisions of the immediately preceding section on perishables if the seller gives no instructions within a reasonable time after notification of rejection the buyer may store the rejected goods for the seller's account or reship them to him or resell them for the seller's account with reimbursement as provided in the preceding section. Such action is not acceptance or conversion.

§ 2-605. Waiver of Buyer's Objections by Failure to Particularize.

(1) The buyer's failure to state in connection with rejection a particular defect which is ascertainable by reasonable inspection precludes him from relying on the unstated defect to justify rejection or to establish breach

    (a) where the seller could have cured it if stated seasonably; or

    (b) between merchants when the seller has after rejection made a request in writing for a full and final written statement of all defects on which the buyer proposes to rely.

(2) Payment against documents made without reservation of rights precludes recovery of the payment for defects apparent on the face of the documents.

§ 2-606. What Constitutes Acceptance of Goods.

(1) Acceptance of goods occurs when the buyer

    (a) after a reasonable opportunity to inspect the goods signifies to the seller that the goods are conforming or that he will take or retain them in spite of their non-conformity; or

(b) fails to make an effective rejection (subsection (1) of Section 2–602), but such acceptance does not occur until the buyer has had a reasonable opportunity to inspect them; or

(c) does any act inconsistent with the seller's ownership; but if such act is wrongful as against the seller it is an acceptance only if ratified by him.

(2) Acceptance of a part of any commercial unit is acceptance of that entire unit.

§ 2-607. Effect of Acceptance; Notice of Breach; Burden of Establishing Breach After Acceptance; Notice of Claim or Litigation to Person Answerable Over.

(1) The buyer must pay at the contract rate for any goods accepted.

(2) Acceptance of goods by the buyer precludes rejection of the goods accepted and if made with knowledge of a non-conformity cannot be revoked because of it unless the acceptance was on the reasonable assumption that the non-conformity would be seasonably cured but acceptance does not of itself impair any other remedy provided by this Article for non-conformity.

(3) Where a tender has been accepted

(a) the buyer must within a reasonable time after he discovers or should have discovered any breach notify the seller of breach or be barred from any remedy; and

(b) if the claim is one for infringement or the like (subsection (3) of Section 2–312) and the buyer is sued as a result of such a breach he must so notify the seller within a reasonable time after he receives notice of the litigation or be barred from any remedy over for liability established by the litigation.

(4) The burden is on the buyer to establish any breach with respect to the goods accepted.

(5) Where the buyer is sued for breach of a warranty or other obligation for which his seller is answerable over

(a) he may give his seller written notice of the litigation. If the notice states that the seller may come in and defend and that if the seller does not do so he will be bound in any action against him by his buyer by any determination of fact common to the two litigations, then unless the seller after seasonable receipt of the notice does come in and defend he is so bound.

(b) if the claim is one for infringement or the like (subsection (3) of Section 2–312) the original seller may demand in writing that his buyer turn over to him control of the litigation including settlement or else be barred from any remedy over and if he also agrees to bear all expense and to satisfy any adverse judgment, then unless the buyer after seasonable receipt of the demand does turn over control the buyer is so barred.

(6) The provisions of subsections (3), (4) and (5) apply to any obligation of a buyer to hold the seller harmless against infringement or the like (subsection (3) of Section 2–312).

§ 2-608. Revocation of Acceptance in Whole or in Part.

(1) The buyer may revoke his acceptance of a lot or commercial unit whose non-conformity substantially impairs its value to him if he has accepted it

(a) on the reasonable assumption that its non-conformity would be cured and it has not been seasonably cured; or

(b) without discovery of such non-conformity if his acceptance was reasonably induced either by the difficulty of discovery before acceptance or by the seller's assurances.

(2) Revocation of acceptance must occur within a reasonable time after the buyer discovers or should have discovered the ground for it and before any substantial change in condition of the goods which is not caused by their own defects. It is not effective until the buyer notifies the seller of it.

(3) A buyer who so revokes has the same rights and duties with regard to the goods involved as if he had rejected them.

§ 2-609. Right to Adequate Assurance of Performance.

(1) A contract for sale imposes an obligation on each party that the other's expectation of receiving due performance will not be impaired. When reasonable grounds for insecurity arise with respect to the performance of either party the other may in writing demand adequate assurance of due performance and until he receives such assurance may if commercially reasonable suspend any performance for which he has not already received the agreed return.

(2) Between merchants the reasonableness of grounds for insecurity and the adequacy of any assurance offered shall be determined according to commercial standards.

(3) Acceptance of any improper delivery or payment does not prejudice the aggrieved party's right to demand adequate assurance of future performance.

(4) After receipt of a justified demand failure to provide within a reasonable time not exceeding thirty days such assurance of due performance as is adequate under the circumstances of the particular case is a repudiation of the contract.

§ 2-610. Anticipatory Repudiation.

When either party repudiates the contract with respect to a performance not yet due the loss of which will substantially impair the value of the contract to the other, the aggrieved party may

(a) for a commercially reasonable time await performance by the repudiating party; or

(b) resort to any remedy for breach (Section 2–703 or Section 2–711), even though he has notified the repudiating party that he would await the latter's performance and has urged retraction; and

(c) in either case suspend his own performance or proceed in accordance with the provisions of this Article on the seller's right to identify goods to the contract notwithstanding breach or to salvage unfinished goods (Section 2–704).

§ 2-611. Retraction of Anticipatory Repudiation.

(1) Until the repudiating party's next performance is due he can retract his repudiation unless the aggrieved party has since the repudiation cancelled or materially changed his position or otherwise indicated that he considers the repudiation final.

(2) Retraction may be by any method which clearly indicates to the aggrieved party that the repudiating party intends to perform, but must include any assurance justifiably demanded under the provisions of this Article (Section 2–609).

(3) Retraction reinstates the repudiating party's rights under the contract with due excuse and allowance to the aggrieved party for any delay occasioned by the repudiation.

§ 2-612. "Installment Contract"; Breach.

(1) An "installment contract" is one which requires or authorizes the delivery of goods in separate lots to be separately accepted, even though the contract contains a clause "each delivery is a separate contract" or its equivalent.

(2) The buyer may reject any installment which is non-conforming if the non-conformity substantially impairs the value of that installment and cannot be cured or if the non-conformity is a defect in the required documents; but if the non-conformity does not fall within subsection (3) and the seller gives adequate assurance of its cure the buyer must accept that installment.

(3) Whenever non-conformity or default with respect to one or more installments substantially impairs the value of the whole contract there is a breach of the whole. But the aggrieved party reinstates the contract if he accepts a non-conforming installment without seasonably notifying of cancellation or if he brings an action with respect only to past installments or demands performance as to future installments.

§ 2-613. Casualty to Identified Goods.

Where the contract requires for its performance goods identified when the contract is made, and the goods suffer casualty without fault of either party before the risk of loss passes to the buyer, or in a proper case under a "no arrival, no sale" term (Section 2–324) then

(a) if the loss is total the contract is avoided; and

(b) if the loss is partial or the goods have so deteriorated as no longer to conform to the contract the buyer may nevertheless demand inspection and at his option either treat the contract as avoided or accept the goods with due allowance from the contract price for the deterioration or the deficiency in quantity but without further right against the seller.

§ 2-614. Substituted Performance.

(1) Where without fault of either party the agreed berthing, loading, or unloading facilities fail or an agreed type of carrier becomes unavailable or the agreed manner of delivery otherwise becomes commercially impracticable but a commercially reasonable substitute is available, such substitute performance must be tendered and accepted.

(2) If the agreed means or manner of payment fails because of domestic or foreign governmental regulation, the seller may withhold or stop delivery unless the buyer provides a means or manner of payment which is commercially a substantial equivalent. If delivery has already been taken, payment by the means or in the manner provided by the regulation discharges the buyer's obligation unless the regulation is discriminatory, oppressive or predatory.

§ 2-615. Excuse by Failure of Presupposed Conditions.

Except so far as a seller may have assumed a greater obligation and subject to the preceding section on substituted performance:

(a) Delay in delivery or non-delivery in whole or in part by a seller who complies with paragraphs (b) and (c) is not a breach of his duty under a contract for sale if performance as agreed has been made impracticable by the occurrence of a contingency the non-occurrence of which was a basic assumption on which the contract was made or by compliance in good faith with any applicable foreign or domestic governmental regulation or order whether or not it later proves to be invalid.

(b) Where the causes mentioned in paragraph (a) affect only a part of the seller's capacity to perform, he must allocate production and deliveries among his customers but may at his option include regular customers not then under contract as well as his own requirements for further manufacture. He may so allocate in any manner which is fair and reasonable.

(c) The seller must notify the buyer seasonably that there will be delay or non-delivery and, when allocation is required under paragraph (b), of the estimated quota thus made available for the buyer.

§ 2-616. Procedure on Notice Claiming Excuse.

(1) Where the buyer receives notification of a material or indefinite delay or an allocation justified under the preceding section he may by written notification to the seller as to any delivery concerned, and where the prospective deficiency substantially impairs the value of the whole contract under the provisions of this Article relating to breach of installment contracts (Section 2–612), then also as to the whole,

(a) terminate and thereby discharge any unexecuted portion of the contract; or

(b) modify the contract by agreeing to take his available quota in substitution.

(2) If after receipt of such notification from the seller the buyer fails so to modify the contract within a reasonable time not exceeding thirty days the contract lapses with respect to any deliveries affected.

(3) The provisions of this section may not be negated by agreement except in so far as the seller has assumed a greater obligation under the preceding section.

Part 7: Remedies

§ 2-701. Remedies for Breach of Collateral Contracts Not Impaired.

Remedies for breach of any obligation or promise collateral or ancillary to a contract for sale are not impaired by the provisions of this Article.

§ 2-702. Seller's Remedies on Discovery of Buyer's Insolvency.

(1) Where the seller discovers the buyer to be insolvent he may refuse delivery except for cash including payment for all goods theretofore delivered under the contract, and stop delivery under this Article (Section 2–705).

(2) Where the seller discovers that the buyer has received goods on credit while insolvent he may reclaim the goods upon demand made within ten days after the receipt, but if misrepresentation of solvency has been made to the particular seller in writing within three months before delivery the ten day limitation does not apply. Except as provided in this subsection the seller may not base a right to reclaim goods on the buyer's fraudulent or innocent misrepresentation of solvency or of intent to pay.

(3) The seller's right to reclaim under subsection (2) is subject to the rights of a buyer in ordinary course or other good faith purchaser under this Article (Section 2–403). Successful reclamation of goods excludes all other remedies with respect to them.

As amended in 1966.

§ 2-703. Seller's Remedies in General.

Where the buyer wrongfully rejects or revokes acceptance of goods or fails to make a payment due on or before delivery or repudiates with respect to a part or the whole, then with respect to any goods directly affected and, if the breach is of the whole contract (Section 2–612), then also with respect to the whole undelivered balance, the aggrieved seller may

(a) withhold delivery of such goods;

(b) stop delivery by any bailee as hereafter provided (Section 2–705);

(c) proceed under the next section respecting goods still unidentified to the contract;

(d) resell and recover damages as hereafter provided (Section 2–706);

(e) recover damages for non-acceptance (Section 2–708) or in a proper case the price (Section 2–709);

(f) cancel.

§ 2-704. Seller's Right to Identify Goods to the Contract Notwithstanding Breach or to Salvage Unfinished Goods.

(1) An aggrieved seller under the preceding section may
   (a) identify to the contract conforming goods not already identified if at the time he learned of the breach they are in his possession or control;
   (b) treat as the subject of resale goods which have demonstrably been intended for the particular contract even though those goods are unfinished.

(2) Where the goods are unfinished an aggrieved seller may in the exercise of reasonable commercial judgment for the purposes of avoiding loss and of effective realization either complete the manufacture and wholly identify the goods to the contract or cease manufacture and resell for scrap or salvage value or proceed in any other reasonable manner.

§ 2-705. Seller's Stoppage of Delivery in Transit or Otherwise.

(1) The seller may stop delivery of goods in the possession of a carrier or other bailee when he discovers the buyer to be insolvent (Section 2–702) and may stop delivery of carload, truckload, planeload or larger shipments of express or freight when the buyer repudiates or fails to make a payment due before delivery or if for any other reason the seller has a right to withhold or reclaim the goods.

(2) As against such buyer the seller may stop delivery until
   (a) receipt of the goods by the buyer; or
   (b) acknowledgment to the buyer by any bailee of the goods except a carrier that the bailee holds the goods for the buyer; or
   (c) such acknowledgment to the buyer by a carrier by reshipment or as warehouseman; or
   (d) negotiation to the buyer of any negotiable document of title covering the goods.

(3) (a) To stop delivery the seller must so notify as to enable the bailee by reasonable diligence to prevent delivery of the goods.
   (b) After such notification the bailee must hold and deliver the goods according to the directions of the seller but the seller is liable to the bailee for any ensuing charges or damages.
   (c) If a negotiable document of title has been issued for goods the bailee is not obliged to obey a notification to stop until surrender of the document.

(d) A carrier who has issued a non-negotiable bill of lading is not obliged to obey a notification to stop received from a person other than the consignor.

§ 2-706. Seller's Resale Including Contract for Resale.

(1) Under the conditions stated in Section 2–703 on seller's remedies, the seller may resell the goods concerned or the undelivered balance thereof. Where the resale is made in good faith and in a commercially reasonable manner the seller may recover the difference between the resale price and the contract price together with any incidental damages allowed under the provisions of this Article (Section 2–710), but less expenses saved in consequence of the buyer's breach.

(2) Except as otherwise provided in subsection (3) or unless otherwise agreed resale may be at public or private sale including sale by way of one or more contracts to sell or of identification to an existing contract of the seller. Sale may be as a unit or in parcels and at any time and place and on any terms but every aspect of the sale including the method, manner, time, place and terms must be commercially reasonable. The resale must be reasonably identified as referring to the broken contract, but it is not necessary that the goods be in existence or that any or all of them have been identified to the contract before the breach.

(3) Where the resale is at private sale the seller must give the buyer reasonable notification of his intention to resell.

(4) Where the resale is at public sale
   (a) only identified goods can be sold except where there is a recognized market for a public sale of futures in goods of the kind; and
   (b) it must be made at a usual place or market for public sale if one is reasonably available and except in the case of goods which are perishable or threaten to decline in value speedily the seller must give the buyer reasonable notice of the time and place of the resale; and
   (c) if the goods are not to be within the view of those attending the sale the notification of sale must state the place where the goods are located and provide for their reasonable inspection by prospective bidders; and
   (d) the seller may buy.

(5) A purchaser who buys in good faith at a resale takes the goods free of any rights of the original

buyer even though the seller fails to comply with one or more of the requirements of this section.

(6) The seller is not accountable to the buyer for any profit made on any resale. A person in the position of a seller (Section 2–707) or a buyer who has rightfully rejected or justifiably revoked acceptance must account for any excess over the amount of his security interest, as hereinafter defined (subsection (3) of Section 2–711).

§ 2-707. "Person in the Position of a Seller".

(1) A "person in the position of a seller" includes as against a principal an agent who has paid or become responsible for the price of goods on behalf of his principal or anyone who otherwise holds a security interest or other right in goods similar to that of a seller.

(2) A person in the position of a seller may as provided in this Article withhold or stop delivery (Section 2–705) and resell (Section 2–706) and recover incidental damages (Section 2–710).

§ 2-708. Seller's Damages for Non-acceptance or Repudiation.

(1) Subject to subsection (2) and to the provisions of this Article with respect to proof of market price (Section 2–723), the measure of damages for non-acceptance or repudiation by the buyer is the difference between the market price at the time and place for tender and the unpaid contract price together with any incidental damages provided in this Article (Section 2–710), but less expenses saved in consequence of the buyer's breach.

(2) If the measure of damages provided in subsection (1) is inadequate to put the seller in as good a position as performance would have done then the measure of damages is the profit (including reasonable overhead) which the seller would have made from full performance by the buyer, together with any incidental damages provided in this Article (Section 2–710), due allowance for costs reasonably incurred and due credit for payments or proceeds of resale.

§ 2-709. Action for the Price.

(1) When the buyer fails to pay the price as it becomes due the seller may recover, together with any incidental damages under the next section, the price

(a) of goods accepted or of conforming goods lost or damaged within a commercially reasonable time after risk of their loss has passed to the buyer; and

(b) of goods identified to the contract if the seller is unable after reasonable effort to resell them at a reasonable price or the circumstances reasonably indicate that such effort will be unavailing.

(2) Where the seller sues for the price he must hold for the buyer any goods which have been identified to the contract and are still in his control except that if resale becomes possible he may resell them at any time prior to the collection of the judgment. The net proceeds of any such resale must be credited to the buyer and payment of the judgment entitles him to any goods not resold.

(3) After the buyer has wrongfully rejected or revoked acceptance of the goods or has failed to make a payment due or has repudiated (Section 2–610), a seller who is held not entitled to the price under this section shall nevertheless be awarded damages for non-acceptance under the preceding section.

§ 2-710. Seller's Incidental Damages.

Incidental damages to an aggrieved seller include any commercially reasonable charges, expenses or commissions incurred in stopping delivery, in the transportation, care and custody of goods after the buyer's breach, in connection with return or resale of the goods or otherwise resulting from the breach.

§ 2-711. Buyer's Remedies in General; Buyer's Security Interest in Rejected Goods.

(1) Where the seller fails to make delivery or repudiates or the buyer rightfully rejects or justifiably revokes acceptance then with respect to any goods involved, and with respect to the whole if the breach goes to the whole contract (Section 2–612), the buyer may cancel and whether or not he has done so may in addition to recovering so much of the price as has been paid

(a) "cover" and have damages under the next section as to all the goods affected whether or not they have been identified to the contract; or

(b) recover damages for non-delivery as provided in this Article (Section 2–713).

(2) Where the seller fails to deliver or repudiates the buyer may also

(a) if the goods have been identified recover them as provided in this Article (Section 2–502); or

(b) in a proper case obtain specific performance or replevy the goods as provided in this Article (Section 2–716).

(3) On rightful rejection or justifiable revocation of acceptance a buyer has a security interest in goods

in his possession or control for any payments made on their price and any expenses reasonably incurred in their inspection, receipt, transportation, care and custody and may hold such goods and resell them in like manner as an aggrieved seller (Section 2–706).

§ 2-712. "Cover"; Buyer's Procurement of Substitute Goods.

(1) After a breach within the preceding section the buyer may "cover" by making in good faith and without unreasonable delay any reasonable purchase of or contract to purchase goods in substitution for those due from the seller.

(2) The buyer may recover from the seller as damages the difference between the cost of cover and the contract price together with any incidental or consequential damages as hereinafter defined (Section 2–715), but less expenses saved in consequence of the seller's breach.

(3) Failure of the buyer to effect cover within this section does not bar him from any other remedy.

§ 2-713. Buyer's Damages for Non-delivery or Repudiation.

(1) Subject to the provisions of this Article with respect to proof of market price (Section 2–723), the measure of damages for non-delivery or repudiation by the seller is the difference between the market price at the time when the buyer learned of the breach and the contract price together with any incidental and consequential damages provided in this Article (Section 2–715), but less expenses saved in consequence of the seller's breach.

(2) Market price is to be determined as of the place for tender or, in cases of rejection after arrival or revocation of acceptance, as of the place of arrival.

§ 2-714. Buyer's Damages for Breach in Regard to Accepted Goods.

(1) Where the buyer has accepted goods and given notification (subsection (3) of Section 2–607) he may recover as damages for any non-conformity of tender the loss resulting in the ordinary course of events from the seller's breach as determined in any manner which is reasonable.

(2) The measure of damages for breach of warranty is the difference at the time and place of acceptance between the value of the goods accepted and the value they would have had if they had been as warranted, unless special circumstances show proximate damages of a different amount.

(3) In a proper case any incidental and consequential damages under the next section may also be recovered.

§ 2-715. Buyer's Incidental and Consequential Damages.

(1) Incidental damages resulting from the seller's breach include expenses reasonably incurred in inspection, receipt, transportation and care and custody of goods rightfully rejected, any commercially reasonable charges, expenses or commissions in connection with effecting cover and any other reasonable expense incident to the delay or other breach.

(2) Consequential damages resulting from the seller's breach include

(a) any loss resulting from general or particular requirements and needs of which the seller at the time of contracting had reason to know and which could not reasonably be prevented by cover or otherwise; and

(b) injury to person or property proximately resulting from any breach of warranty.

§ 2-716. Buyer's Right to Specific Performance or Replevin.

(1) Specific performance may be decreed where the goods are unique or in other proper circumstances.

(2) The decree for specific performance may include such terms and conditions as to payment of the price, damages, or other relief as the court may deem just.

(3) The buyer has a right of replevin for goods identified to the contract if after reasonable effort he is unable to effect cover for such goods or the circumstances reasonably indicate that such effort will be unavailing or if the goods have been shipped under reservation and satisfaction of the security interest in them has been made or tendered.

§ 2-717. Deduction of Damages from the Price.

The buyer on notifying the seller of his intention to do so may deduct all or any part of the damages resulting from any breach of the contract from any part of the price still due under the same contract.

§ 2-718. Liquidation or Limitation of Damages; Deposits.

(1) Damages for breach by either party may be liquidated in the agreement but only at an amount

which is reasonable in the light of the anticipated or actual harm caused by the breach, the difficulties of proof of loss, and the inconvenience or nonfeasibility of otherwise obtaining an adequate remedy. A term fixing unreasonably large liquidated damages is void as a penalty.

(2) Where the seller justifiably withholds delivery of goods because of the buyer's breach, the buyer is entitled to restitution of any amount by which the sum of his payments exceeds

    (a) the amount to which the seller is entitled by virtue of terms liquidating the seller's damages in accordance with subsection (1), or

    (b) in the absence of such terms, twenty per cent of the value of the total performance for which the buyer is obligated under the contract or $500, whichever is smaller.

(3) The buyer's right to restitution under subsection (2) is subject to offset to the extent that the seller establishes

    (a) a right to recover damages under the provisions of this Article other than subsection (1), and

    (b) the amount or value of any benefits received by the buyer directly or indirectly by reason of the contract.

(4) Where a seller has received payment in goods their reasonable value or the proceeds of their resale shall be treated as payments for the purposes of subsection (2); but if the seller has notice of the buyer's breach before reselling goods received in part performance, his resale is subject to the conditions laid down in this Article on resale by an aggrieved seller (Section 2–706).

§ 2–719. Contractual Modification or Limitation of Remedy.

(1) Subject to the provisions of subsections (2) and (3) of this section and of the preceding section on liquidation and limitation of damages,

    (a) the agreement may provide for remedies in addition to or in substitution for those provided in this Article and may limit or alter the measure of damages recoverable under this Article, as by limiting the buyer's remedies to return of the goods and repayment of the price or to repair and replacement of non-conforming goods or parts; and

    (b) resort to a remedy as provided is optional unless the remedy is expressly agreed to be exclusive, in which case it is the sole remedy.

(2) Where circumstances cause an exclusive or limited remedy to fail of its essential purpose, remedy may be had as provided in this Act.

(3) Consequential damages may be limited or excluded unless the limitation or exclusion is unconscionable. Limitation of consequential damages for injury to the person in the case of consumer goods is prima facie unconscionable but limitation of damages where the loss is commercial is not.

§ 2–720. Effect of "Cancellation" or "Rescission" on Claims for Antecedent Breach.

Unless the contrary intention clearly appears, expressions of "cancellation" or "rescission" of the contract or the like shall not be construed as a renunciation or discharge of any claim in damages for an antecedent breach.

§ 2–721. Remedies for Fraud.

Remedies for material misrepresentation or fraud include all remedies available under this Article for non-fraudulent breach. Neither rescission or a claim for rescission of the contract for sale nor rejection or return of the goods shall bar or be deemed inconsistent with a claim for damages or other remedy.

§ 2–722. Who Can Sue Third Parties for Injury to Goods.

Where a third party so deals with goods which have been identified to a contract for sale as to cause actionable injury to a party to that contract

    (a) a right of action against the third party is in either party to the contract for sale who has title to or a security interest or a special property or an insurable interest in the goods; and if the goods have been destroyed or converted a right of action is also in the party who either bore the risk of loss under the contract for sale or has since the injury assumed that risk as against the other;

    (b) if at the time of the injury the party plaintiff did not bear the risk of loss as against the other party to the contract for sale and there is no arrangement between them for disposition of the recovery, his suit or settlement is, subject to his own interest, as a fiduciary for the other party to the contract;

    (c) either party may with the consent of the other sue for the benefit of whom it may concern.

§ 2-723. Proof of Market Price: Time and Place.

(1) If an action based on anticipatory repudiation comes to trial before the time for performance with respect to some or all of the goods, any damages based on market price (Section 2–708 or Section 2–713) shall be determined according to the price of such goods prevailing at the time when the aggrieved party learned of the repudiation.

(2) If evidence of a price prevailing at the times or places described in this Article is not readily available the price prevailing within any reasonable time before or after the time described or at any other place which in commercial judgment or under usage of trade would serve as a reasonable substitute for the one described may be used, making any proper allowance for the cost of transporting the goods to or from such other place.

(3) Evidence of a relevant price prevailing at a time or place other than the one described in this Article offered by one party is not admissible unless and until he has given the other party such notice as the court finds sufficient to prevent unfair surprise.

§ 2-724. Admissibility of Market Quotations.

Whenever the prevailing price or value of any goods regularly bought and sold in any established commodity market is in issue, reports in official publications or trade journals or in newspapers or periodicals of general circulation published as the reports of such market shall be admissible in evidence. The circumstances of the preparation of such a report may be shown to affect its weight but not its admissibility.

§ 2-725. Statute of Limitations in Contracts for Sale.

(1) An action for breach of any contract for sale must be commenced within four years after the cause of action has accrued. By the original agreement the parties may reduce the period of limitation to not less than one year but may not extend it.

(2) A cause of action accrues when the breach occurs, regardless of the aggrieved party's lack of knowledge of the breach. A breach of warranty occurs when tender of delivery is made, except that where a warranty explicitly extends to future performance of the goods and discovery of the breach must await the time of such performance the cause of action accrues when the breach is or should have been discovered.

(3) Where an action commenced within the time limited by subsection (1) is so terminated as to leave available a remedy by another action for the same breach such other action may be commenced after the expiration of the time limited and within six months after the termination of the first action unless the termination resulted from voluntary discontinuance or from dismissal for failure or neglect to prosecute.

(4) This section does not alter the law on tolling of the statute of limitations nor does it apply to causes of action which have accrued before this Act becomes effective.

Excerpts from the Sarbanes-Oxley Act of 2002

15 U.S.C. § 7241. Corporate Responsibility for Financial Reports

(a) Regulations required

The Commission shall, by rule, require, for each company filing periodic reports under section 78m (a) or 78o (d) of this title, that the principal executive officer or officers and the principal financial officer or officers, or persons performing similar functions, certify in each annual or quarterly report filed or submitted under either such section of this title that—

(1) the signing officer has reviewed the report;

(2) based on the officer's knowledge, the report does not contain any untrue statement of a material fact or omit to state a material fact necessary in order to make the statements made, in light of the circumstances under which such statements were made, not misleading;

(3) based on such officer's knowledge, the financial statements, and other financial information included in the report, fairly present in all material respects the financial condition and results of operations of the issuer as of, and for, the periods presented in the report;

(4) the signing officers—

(A) are responsible for establishing and maintaining internal controls;

(B) have designed such internal controls to ensure that material information relating to the issuer and its consolidated subsidiaries is made known to such officers by others within those entities, particularly during the period in which the periodic reports are being prepared;

(C) have evaluated the effectiveness of the issuer's internal controls as of a date within 90 days prior to the report; and

(D) have presented in the report their conclusions about the effectiveness of their internal controls based on their evaluation as of that date;

(5) the signing officers have disclosed to the issuer's auditors and the audit committee of the board of directors (or persons fulfilling the equivalent function)—

(A) all significant deficiencies in the design or operation of internal controls which could adversely affect the issuer's ability to record, process, summarize, and report financial data and have identified for the issuer's auditors any material weaknesses in internal controls; and

(B) any fraud, whether or not material, that involves management or other employees who have a significant role in the issuer's internal controls; and

(6) the signing officers have indicated in the report whether or not there were significant changes in internal controls or in other factors that could significantly affect internal controls subsequent to the date of their evaluation, including any corrective actions with regard to significant deficiencies and material weaknesses.

(b) Foreign reincorporations have no effect

Nothing in this section shall be interpreted or applied in any way to allow any issuer to lessen the legal force of the statement required under this section, by an issuer having reincorporated or having engaged in any other transaction that resulted in the transfer of the corporate domicile or offices of the issuer from inside the United States to outside of the United States.

(c) Deadline

The rules required by subsection (a) of this section shall be effective not later than 30 days after July 30, 2002.

15 U.S.C. § 7262. Management Assessment of Internal Controls

(a) Rules required

The Commission shall prescribe rules requiring each annual report required by section 78m (a) or 78o (d) of this title to contain an internal control report, which shall—

(1) state the responsibility of management for establishing and maintaining an adequate internal control structure and procedures for financial reporting; and

(2) contain an assessment, as of the end of the most recent fiscal year of the issuer, of the effectiveness of the internal control structure and procedures of the issuer for financial reporting.

(b) Internal control evaluation and reporting

With respect to the internal control assessment required by subsection (a) of this section, each registered public accounting firm that prepares or issues the audit report for the issuer shall attest to, and report on, the assessment made by the management of the issuer. An attestation made under this subsection shall be made in accordance with standards for attestation engagements issued or adopted by the Board. Any such attestation shall not be the subject of a separate engagement.

15 U.S.C. § 1519. Destruction, Alteration, or Falsification of Records in Federal Investigations and Bankruptcy

Whoever knowingly alters, destroys, mutilates, conceals, covers up, falsifies, or makes a false entry in any record, document, or tangible object with the intent to impede, obstruct, or influence the investigation or proper administration of any matter within the jurisdiction of any department or agency of the United States or any case filed under title 11, or in relation to or contemplation of any such matter or case, shall be fined under this title, imprisoned not more than 20 years, or both.

Absolute privilege A defense to a defamation claim provided to government officials, judicial officers and proceedings, and state legislatures, where the defendants need not proffer any further evidence to assert the defense.

Acceptance The offeree's expression of agreement to the terms of the offer. The power of acceptance is created by a valid offer.

Accord and satisfaction A doctrine that allows one party to create an agreement, or *accord,* with the other party to accept a substitute performance in order to *satisfy* the original performance; the completion of the new duty discharges the old one.

Account A subduty of fiduciary duty in which the agent is required to keep records such as a written list of transactions, noting money owed and money paid and other detailed statements of mutual demands.

Acknowledgement form A form commonly used in sales contracts as an acceptance from the seller, responding to a purchase order that contains preprinted provisions and has blanks to accommodate the specifics of that transaction.

Act requirement Also called by its Latin name, *actus reus,* requires the government to prove that a defendant's actions objectively satisfied the elements of a particular offense.

Actual authority A source of the agent's authority occurring when the parties either expressly agree to create an agency relationship or where the authority is implied based on custom or the course of past dealings.

Actual damages A fundamental element to recover a lawsuit against a tortfeasor for negligence where the injured party must prove that it suffered some physical harm that resulted in identifiable losses.

Actual owner The individual that is recognized as having primary or residual title to the property and is, therefore, the ultimate owner of the property.

Adjudication (Administrative law) The judicial function preformed by administrative agencies, whereby the agencies make policy. This function is performed by administrative law judges who hear cases brought before the specific agency.

Adjudication (Criminal law) A phase of the criminal justice system in which the prosecutor elects to proceed with the charges following an investigation.

Administrative agencies Governmental bodies with the authority to implement and administer particular legislation. Administrative agencies include department, nondepartment, and independent agencies.

Administrative law A body of law and regulations that governs the organization and operation of administrative agencies.

Administrative law judge An attorney employed by an agency to adjudicate disputes.

Age Discrimination in Employment Act of 1967 (ADEA) A statute prohibiting employers from discriminating against employees on the basis of their age once an employee has reached age 40.

Agency law Laws that govern the relationships created when one party hires another party to act on the hiring party's behalf.

Agent One who agrees and is authorized to act on behalf of another, a *principal,* to legally bind an individual in particular business transactions with third parties pursuant to an agency relationship.

Agreement Any meeting of the minds resulting in mutual assent to do or refrain from doing something.

Agreement on Trade-Related Aspects of Intellectual Property (TRIPS) A multinational agreement covering minimum requirements and standards for all areas of intellectual property protections as well as providing an infrastructure for enforcement and dispute resolution.

Ambiguous terms Contract terms that are vague and indefinite. In contract law, these terms are construed by the court against the interest of the side that drafted the agreement.

Amendments Changes made to the Constitution since its ratification.

American Recovery and Reinvestment Act of 2009 Created a loan program and underlying mandates for corporations most acutely impacted by the financial crisis beginning in 1998 and established the Troubled Assets Relief Program (TARP) to administer the loans.

Americans with Disabilities Act of 1990 (ADA) A statute that seeks to eliminate discriminatory employment practices against disabled persons. The ADA requires that employers with 15 or more employees offer reasonable accommodations for a disabled employee in the workplace so long as the accommodation does not cause the employer to suffer an undue hardship.

Answer Defendant's formal response to each paragraph of the complaint.

Anticipatory repudiation When one party makes clear that he has no intention to perform as agreed, the nonbreaching party is entitled to recover damages in anticipation of the breach rather than waiting until performance is due.

Apparent authority A source of the agent's authority occurring when there is an appearance of legitimate authority to a third party rather than express authorization by the principal.

Appellate courts Courts that review the decision of trial courts and have the authority to overturn decisions if they are inconsistent with the current state of the law.

Arbitrary and capricious Failure to exercise honest judgment instead of reasoned consideration of all relevant factors.

Arbitrary and capricious standard The broad judicial benchmark used to determine if an agency's actions are lawful. Under the standard, the agency must show that a reasoned decision-making process was used rather than actions that are arbitrary and capricious. Decisions are considered to be arbitrary and capricious if they are not based on a consideration of relevant factors or are the result of a clear error in judgment.

Arbitration Method of alternative dispute resolution where the parties present their side of the dispute to one or more neutral parties who then render a decision. Arbitration often involves a set of rules designed to move from dispute to decision quickly.

Articles The main provisions of the Constitution that set out the government's structure, power, and procedures.

Articles of incorporation The document filed with a state authority that sets in motion the incorporation process, including the corporation's name, purpose, number of shares issued, and address of the corporation's headquarters.

Articles of organization (also called certificates of organization) Document used to create an LLC. Most states require only basic information such as the name of the entity, the location of its principal place of business, and the names of its members.

Assent A conscious approval or confirmation of facts. In contract law, assent is the knowing, voluntary, and mutual approval of the terms of a contract by each party.

Assignment (Agency) The transfer of one party's current rights under a contract to a third party such that the original party's rights are extinguished.

Assignment (Real estate) A tenant transfer of its interest to a third party for the entire term remaining on a lease.

Assumption of the risk A defense to claims of negligence where the injured party knows that a substantial and apparent risk was associated with certain conduct, and the party went ahead with the dangerous activity anyway.

Assurances A pledge or guarantee that gives confidence to one party that the other party is able to complete performance under a contract.

Authorization cards Signed statements by employees indicating that they wish to unionize and/or are electing to be represented by an existing union.

Automatic stay A legal prohibition from creditors either initiating or continuing any debt collection action against the debtor or her property.

Bad faith A legal concept in which a malicious motive on the part of the defendant in a lawsuit is necessary in order for a plaintiff to recover. Under the Anticybersquatting Consumer Protection Act, the court looks to nine factors in making a determination of bad faith intent.

Bail The security, in the form or cash or a bond, given to the court to assure the appearance of a defendant in court at a later date. If the defendant appears in court, the bail is returned. If he flees, the bail is forfeited.

Ballot proposition A question put to the voters during a state election to decide (usually controversial) issues such as imposing a new income tax or whether the state should allow marijuana to be used for medicinal purposes. In some states, this is known as a ballot *initiative* or a *referendum*.

Bankruptcy A procedure by which a debtor's assets are reorganized and liquidated by a court in order to pay off creditors and free the debtor from obligations under existing contracts.

Bankruptcy estate The debtor's available assets in a bankruptcy proceeding.

Bankruptcy trustee Often an attorney highly skilled in bankruptcy law, appointed in Chapter 7 or Chapter 13 cases and charged with the duty to take control of the bankruptcy estate and reduce it to cash for distribution, preserving the interests of both the debtor and the creditors.

Bargained for exchange Aspect of consideration differentiating contracts from gifts by holding that a performance or return promise is bargained for only if it was exchanged for another promise.

Battle of the forms The conflict between the terms written into standardized purchase (offer) and acknowledgment (acceptance) forms, which differ in that one form favors the buyer and the other the seller. The Uniform Commercial Code attempts to broker a truce in this battle while keeping the contract of sale intact.

Bench trial Trial without a jury where the judge is both the finder of law and the finder of fact.

Berne Convention A multinational agreement covering copyright protection, requiring that foreigners from signatory countries be granted protection via reciprocity under the copyright laws of any other member country.

Beyond a reasonable doubt Heightened burden of proof used in criminal cases in which a fact finder must be convinced that the defendant's criminal liability is not in doubt to a reasonable person.

Bilateral contract A contract involving two promises and two performances.

Bill of Rights The first ten amendments to the Constitution that preserve the rights of the people from unlawful acts of government officials, freedom of speech and religion, and so on.

Black's Law Dictionary The leading legal dictionary.

Blue-sky laws State securities laws intended to cover purely intrastate securities offerings and serve as an additional safeguard for investors when the federal government declines to exercise their jurisdiction over a particular securities offering.

Borrower The individual to whom credit is extended and who owes the debt.

Breach The failure to meet a contractual obligation.

Breach of duty A fundamental element to recover a lawsuit against a tortfeasor for negligence where the injured party must prove that the tortfeasor failed to exercise reasonable care in fulfilling its obligations.

Breach of warranty Legal violation that occurs when a product fails to perform as promised by the seller.

Burden of proof The responsibility of producing sufficient evidence necessary in support of a fact or issue and favorably convincing the fact finder of that fact or issue.

Business Corporation Law Often the title for a specific state law that covers such matters as the structure of the corporation, oversight of the activity of the corporation's managers, rights of the principals in the case of the sale of assets or ownership interests, annual reporting requirements, and other issues that affect the internal rules of the business venture.

Business judgment rule A protection for corporation officers and directors from their fiduciary duties when they have acted in good faith, have no private financial self-interest, and used diligence to acquire the best information related to a proposed decision, but still made an unwise decision that resulted in some loss to the corporation.

Business trust Nonstatutory form of entity used in specialized circumstances where a certain type of flexibility is important to the principals.

Capacity Requirement for a valid contract necessitating that both parties have the power to contract. Certain classes of persons have only limited powers to contract, including minors and those with mental incapacity.

Case precedent The opinion of an appellate court, which is binding on all trial courts from that point in time onward so that any similar case would be decided according to the precedent.

Cause in fact A fundamental element to recover a lawsuit against a tortfeasor for negligence where the injured party must prove that except for the breach of duty by the tortfeasor, they would not have suffered damages.

Celler-Kefauver Antimerger Act A federal antitrust law enacted in 1950 amending the Clayton Act provisions by severely restricting anticompetitive mergers resulting from the acquisition of assets.

Certificate of limited partnership The document filed with the state government authority by the general partner to form a limited partnership, requiring routine information such as the names, addresses, and capital contribution of each partner.

Certify The process in which a collective bargaining unit is recognized as a union, occurring when a legally sound election reveals a simple majority of pro-union votes.

Charging of the jury Instructions given from judge to jury on how to work through the process of coming to a factual decision in the case.

Choice of law and forum clauses Actual terms of a contract that predetermine which nation's laws and court system will be used in a potential lawsuit under that contract.

Citation The special format used by the legal community to express where a statutory law can be found.

Citizen suits Lawsuits brought by members of the public, who are directly affected by an agency action, against either violators of the regulation or the administrative agency itself for failing to fulfill a duty imposed upon it.

Citizen suits provisions Laws that authorize private individuals or watchdog groups to file environmental enforcement lawsuits.

Civil law systems Systems of law drawn largely from the Roman law heritage that use written law as the highest source and opt for a systematic codification of general law principles.

Civil laws Laws designed to compensate parties for money lost as a result of another's conduct.

Civil litigation The term used to describe a dispute resolution process where the parties and their counsel argue their view of a civil controversy in a court of law.

Class action Method for conducting a lawsuit in which a large group of persons with a well-defined common interest (class) has a representative of the group litigate the claim on behalf of the larger group, without the need to join every individual member of the class. A class action must meet certain criteria in order to be certified by a trial court to proceed as a class.

Clayton Act A federal antitrust law first enacted in 1914 as a preventative statute that deals with specific types of restraints, including exclusive dealing arrangements, tie-in sales, price discrimination, mergers and acquisitions, and interlocking directorates.

Clean Air Act (CAA) First enacted in 1963 to improve, strengthen, and accelerate programs for the prevention and abatement of air pollution, focusing on stationary and mobile sources in the United States.

Clean Water Act (CWA) A federal statute that is implemented and enforced by the EPA to regulate water quality standards.

Closing arguments Attorneys' summation of the case with the objective of convincing the jury of what theory to decide the case upon, occurring after testimony is completed and evidence has been submitted.

Codified A common law doctrine that was previously not expressed in a code, but has now been arranged into an ordered, written code is referred to as being *codified.*

Collateral Property or land that a debtor promises to her creditor in case she fails to repay her debt.

Collective bargaining The process of negotiating terms and conditions of employment for employees in the collective bargaining unit.

Collective bargaining agreements Written agreements or contracts that are the result of negotiations between an employer and a union.

Collective bargaining unit An employee group that, on the basis of a mutuality of interests, is an appropriate unit for collective bargaining.

Comity The general notion that nations will defer to and give effect to the laws and court decisions of other nations.

Commerce Clause The constitutional clause giving congress the power to regulate commerce.

Commercially impracticable Rule adopted by the Uniform Commercial Code when a delay in delivery or nondelivery has been made impracticable by the occurrence of an unanticipated event, so long as the event directly affected a basic assumption of the contract.

Common law Law that has not been passed by the legislature, but rather is made by the courts and is based on the fundamentals of previous cases with similar facts.

Common stock (common shares) A form of equity instrument in which the equity owner is entitled to payments based on the current profitability of the company.

Communications Decency Act of 1996 Enacted by Congress to extend immunity to the ISP's by protecting them from any defamation liability as a "publisher or speaker of any information provided by another information content provider."

Comparative negligence A defense to claims of negligence where the injured party's conduct has played a factor in the harm suffered and, thus, the proportion of negligence should be divided.

Compensatory damages Compensatory damages are meant to make the injured person whole again. In contract law, they seek to place the nonbreaching party in the position he would have been in had the contract been executed as agreed.

Complaint The first formal document filed with the local clerk of courts when the plaintiff initiates a lawsuit claiming legal rights against another.

Comprehensive Environmental Response Compensation and Liability Act (CERCLA) A statute enacted by Congress in 1980 to create a tax on the chemical and petroleum industries and provide broad federal authority to respond directly to releases or threatened releases of hazardous substances that may endanger public health or the environment.

Computer Fraud and Abuse Act A law prohibiting unauthorized use of computers to commit seven different crimes: (1) espionage; (2) accessing unauthorized information; (3) accessing a nonpublic government computer; (4) fraud by computer; (5) damage to a computer; (6) trafficking in passwords; and (7) extortionate threats to damage a computer.

Conciliation negotiations The required attempts by the EEOC to settle a discrimination case instead of filing a lawsuit.

Condition A term or requirement stated in a contract, which must be met for the other party to have the duty to fulfill her obligations in order to allocate the risk that some part of a contract may not be completed.

Confirmation memorandum A written verification of an agreement. Under the statute of frauds section of the Uniform Commercial Code, a merchant who receives a signed confirmation memorandum from another merchant will be bound by the memorandum just as if she had signed it, unless she promptly objects.

Consent When an agent agrees to act for the principal; in the context of agency law, courts apply an objective standard to determine if the agent did in fact agree to the agency relationship.

Consent order An agreement between the government and a party that spells out detailed conditions and compliance measures that the party agrees to take in exchange for the government not pursuing a court action.

Consequential damages Consequential damages repay the injured party for any foreseeable but indirect losses that flow from the breach of contract.

Consequential damages under the UCC Such damage, loss, or injury as does not flow directly and immediately from the act of the party, but only from some consequences or results of such act.

Consideration Requirement for an enforceable contract in addition to agreement in which there is a benefit that must be bargained for between the parties. Generally, a promise is supported by consideration if the promisee suffers a legal detriment by giving up something of value or some legal right and the promisor makes her promise as part of a bargained for exchange.

Constitutional law The body of law interpreting state and federal constitutions.

Consumer Credit Protection Act The centerpiece of federal statutory regulation of credit transactions, which regulates credit transactions between a creditor and a borrower in the areas of disclosure of credit terms, credit reporting, antidiscrimination laws, and collection of debts from consumers.

Consumer law The statutory and administrative body of law that protects consumers engaging in transactions with merchants and creditors.

Consumer Leasing Act A statute that regulates lessors engaged in leasing or arranging leases for consumers in the ordinary course of business.

Consumer Product Safety Act The statute that created the Consumer Product Safety Commission, with the aim of making consumer products safer.

Controlling the Assault of Non-Solicited Pornography and Marketing Act of 2003 Often called the CAN-SPAM Act, this statute regulates the sending of unsolicited e-mail (spam) by prohibiting certain practices such as falsifying the "from" name and information in the subject line and requires the sender to provide a physical address of the producer of the e-mail.

Convention of Contracts for the International Sale of Goods (CISG) Created by the U.N. Commission on International Trade Law to establish uniform rules for drafting certain international sales contracts.

Convention on the Recognition and Enforcement of Foreign Arbitral Awards An international treaty established in 1958 that allows for the enforcement of arbitration awards in many major countries, provided that the arbitration is international.

Corporate governance The procedure and system used by the officers and directors to establish lines of responsibility, approval, and oversight among key stakeholders, and set out rules for making corporate decisions.

Corporate veil The liability protection shareholders, directors, and officers of a corporation have from personal liability in case the corporation runs up large debts or suffers some liability.

Corporation A fictitious legal entity that exists as an independent "person" separate from its principals.

Counsel Another name for an attorney.

Counterclaim Filed when the defendant believes that the plaintiff has caused her damages arising out of the very same set of facts as articulated in the complaint.

Counteroffer An action terminating an offer whereby the offeree rejects the original offer and proposes a new offer with different terms.

Country of origin principle General agreement between the United States, Canada, and the European Union governments to apply the law of the country where the defendant's servers are located.

Court A judicial tribunal duly constituted for the hearing and determination of cases.

Covenants not to compete Type of contract where one party agrees not to compete with another party for a specified period of time.

Cover A nonbreaching buyer's right to purchase substitute goods on the open market after a delivery of nonconforming goods from the original seller and to sue for the difference.

Cram down provision A term used in bankruptcy law to refer to the Chapter 11 provision that allows the debtor to request that the court force the creditors to accept a plan that is fair, equitable, and feasible.

Creativity A requirement in order to gain copyright protection in which there must be some creative element used that made the compilation an original work.

Credit Card Accountability Responsibility and Disclosure Act of 2009 Known as the CARD Act, this law protects consumers from unreasonable interest rate increases and credit card fees and requires card issuers to give a 45-day advance notice of any impending rate increase.

Creditor Any party regularly extending credit and to whom a debt becomes owed.

Criminal law The body of law that defines the boundaries of behavior and sanctions for violating those boundaries for the purposes of preventing harm to society.

Criminal procedure Refers to constitutional protections afforded to individuals or business entities during criminal investigations, arrests, trials, and sentencing.

Cross-claim Filed when the defendant believes that a third party is either partially or fully liable for the damages that the plaintiff has suffered and, therefore, should be involved as an indispensable party in the trial.

Cross-examination The opportunity for the attorney to ask questions in court, limited to issues that were brought out on direct examination, of a witness who has testified in a trial on behalf of the opposing party.

Culpability The quality of being blameworthy in criminal law; it is used to assess the accused's guilt and determine whether he committed the crime purposefully, knowingly, recklessly, or negligently.

Damages Money lost as a result of another's conduct.

De facto Existing in fact; having effect even though not formally recognized.

De jure Existing in or by right of law.

Debt A common tool for raising capital including promissory notes, bonds, and debentures that represent a fixed rate of return regardless of the profitability of the corporation with repayment expected after a certain period of years. Debt is senior in priority to equity instruments.

Debtor The borrower in a secured transaction.

Debtor in possession (DIP) A Chapter 11 bankruptcy proceeding where the debtor generally remains in control of assets and business operations in an attempt to rehabilitate the business entity.

Declaratory judgment A remedy used to determine the rights of the parties in a set of circumstances (such as the enforceability of a contract) and is binding on the litigants even though no damages were awarded.

Defamation An intentional act of making an untrue public statement about a party that caused some loss to be suffered by the defamed party.

Defeasible Capable of being canceled.

Defendant The party sued in a civil lawsuit or the party charged with a crime in a criminal prosecution. In some types of cases (such as divorce), a defendant may be called a *respondent.*

Delegation One party's appointment of a third party to perform her duties under a contract, while still holding the original party liable for any breach.

Deliberations The process in which a jury in a trial discusses in private the findings of the court and decides by vote with which argument to agree of either opposing side.

Depositions Method of discovery where a witness gives sworn testimony to provide evidence prior to trial.

Destination contract A contract in which the seller is required to deliver the goods to a chosen destination and not just to the carrier; and only after the goods have been tendered at the destination has the seller fulfilled his duty and the buyer takes title and risk of loss.

Detour Term used to describe conduct classified as a small-scale deviation that is normally expected in the workday and, therefore, within the ambit of respondeat superior.

Detrimental reliance When the offeree makes preparations prior to acceptance based on a reasonable reliance on the offer.

Direct examination The first questioning of a witness during a trial in which the plaintiff's attorney first asks questions of the witnesses on the plaintiff's list.

Direct infringement A theory of copyright infringement occurring when the copyright owner can prove legal ownership of the work in question and that the infringer copied the work in a substantially similar manner without permission.

Directors Those responsible for oversight and management of the corporation's course of direction.

Disability A physical or mental impairment that substantially limits a person's ability to participate in major life activities.

Discharge In contract law, discharge is the removal of all legal obligations under the agreement and occurs only after full performance of the party.

Disclaim The act of renouncing ones legal right or claim.

Disclosure The underlying premise of all securities regulation in which companies are to release all information, positive or negative, that might bear on an investment decision, as required by the Securities and Exchange Commission to protect investors and assure public confidence in the integrity of the securities market.

Discovery Process for the orderly exchange of information and evidence between the parties involved in litigation (or in some cases arbitration) prior to trial.

Disparate impact Theory of employment discrimination where employee evaluation techniques that are not themselves discriminatory have a different, adverse, impact on members of a protected class.

Disparate treatment Theory of employment discrimination predicated on overt and intentional discrimination. This includes being treated differently because of one's membership in a protected class.

Dissociation (Partnership) Term used by RUPA to describe the act of separation of one partner from the partnership.

Dissociation (LLC) Individual members of an LLC exercise the right to withdraw from the partnership.

Dissolution In the context of an LLC, a liquidation process triggered by an event that is specified in the operating agreement (such as the death of a key member) or the majority of membership interests (or the percentage called for in the operating agreement) deciding to dissolve the company.

Diversity of citizenship When opposing parties in a lawsuit are citizens of different states or if one party is a citizen of a foreign country, the case is placed under federal court jurisdiction if the amount in controversy exceeds $75,000.

Doctrine of equivalence A doctrine that allows courts to find patent infringement if the invention performs substantially the same function in substantially the same way to achieve the same result.

Doctrine of stare decisis The principle that similar cases with similar facts under similar circumstances should have a similar outcome.

Double jeopardy The Fifth Amendment guarantee providing that a defendant cannot be subject to prosecution twice for the same offense.

Due care A subduty of fiduciary duty in which the agent is required to act in the same careful manner when conducting the principal's affairs as a reasonable person would use in conducting her own personal affairs.

Due process Principle that the government must respect all of the legal rights that are owed to a person according to the law.

Due Process Clause The constitutional clause protecting individuals from being deprived of "life, liberty, or property" without due process of law.

Durable medium A requirement in order to gain copyright protection in which the work must be in a tangible form such as in writing, digital, video, and so forth.

Duress Basis for avoiding a contract when one party uses any form of unfair coercion to induce another party to enter into or modify a contract.

Duty A fundamental element to recover a lawsuit against a tortfeasor for negligence where the injured party must prove that the tortfeasor owed them a duty of care.

Duty of care A fiduciary duty owed to shareholders in which officers and directors must exercise that degree of skill, diligence, and care that a reasonably prudent person would exercise under the same circumstances, acting in good faith and in a manner that is reasonably calculated to advance the best interests of the corporation.

Duty of loyalty A fiduciary duty owed to shareholders in which officers and directors must not engage in self-dealing or conflicts of interests, requiring fiduciaries to put the corporation's interests ahead of their own.

Easement The privilege to use real estate owned by another.

Economic Espionage Act A federal statute passed in 1996 providing criminal penalties for domestic and foreign theft of trade secrets.

Election A vote to elect or reject unionization by the entire bargaining unit.

Electronic Communications Privacy Act (ECPA) A federal law enacted in 1986, extending legal protection against wiretapping and other forms of unauthorized interception and explicitly allowing employers to monitor communications by employees using the employers' equipment so long as it is in the ordinary course of business or if the employee consents to the monitoring.

Employee agents One of three broad categories in classifying agents; generally, anyone who performs services for a principal is considered an employee if the principal can control what will be done and how it will be done.

Employee Polygraph Protection Act An act that prohibits most private sector employers from requiring a polygraph test as a condition of employment.

Employee Retirement Income Security Act (ERISA) A federal law enacted in 1974, creating a comprehensive set of laws and regulations that requires employers to make certain disclosures related to investment risk, providing transparency for plan beneficiaries.

Employment-at-will Deep-seated common law rule that stands for the proposition that employers have the right to terminate an employee with or without advance notice and with or without just cause, subject to certain exceptions.

Employment discrimination A broad term that includes workplace-related discrimination in the hiring process and treatment of employees. Employment discrimination encompasses everything from promotions or demotions to scheduling, working conditions, and disciplinary measures.

Enabling statute A law passed when Congress establishes an administrative agency, which is the source of an agency's authority and describes the agency's scope and jurisdiction over certain matters.

Endangered Species Act (ESA) An environmental law passed in 1973 that lays out a procedure for identification and preservation from extinction of imperiled species.

Energy bank Business model adopted by Enron Corporation in which they purchased energy from one source at a discount rate and sold it to markets where demand was greatest for energy following deregulation of the energy markets.

Enforceability A term used to determine whether a properly formed contract can be imposed by examining whether it is a product of genuine assent and is in writing (under certain circumstances).

Enforcement Administrative agencies have prosecutorial discretion in deciding when and whom to regulate, and this discretion is unreviewable by the judiciary. Administrative agencies generally carry out their enforcement responsibilities though their Office of General Counsel.

Enumerated powers Those powers that are explicitly granted to the three branches of government in the Constitution.

Equal Credit Opportunity Act Passed in 1974, this statute prohibits discrimination of a credit applicant based on the applicant's race, religion, national origin, color, gender, age, or marital status.

Equal Employment Opportunity Commission (EEOC) A five-member federal administrative agency that enacts congressional mandates that assure victims of discrimination adequate protection. The EEOC accepts and investigates worker complaints and, in certain cases, will sue on behalf of employees.

Equal Pay Act of 1963 Makes it illegal for employers to pay unequal wages to men and women who perform substantially equal work.

Equitable maxims Common laws rules that guide courts in deciding cases and controversies and are intended to be broad statements of rules based on notions of fairness and justice.

Equitable relief A type of remedy, including injunctions and restraining orders, that is designed to compensate a party when money alone will not do, but instead forces the other party to do (or not do) something.

Equity Ownership interest in a corporation where financial return on the investment is based primarily on the performance of the venture.

Escrow In a lease context, escrow is an amount of money delivered by the tenant to a third party (such as an attorney) to be held by the third party until the dispute between landlord and tenant is resolved.

Escrow agent A neutral third party designated to hold a sum of money while the parties fulfill conditions in a contract.

Estate In addition to land, assets, and personal property, a person's *estate* also consists of legal rights and entitlements after death. This includes the right to sue for the tortious conduct that caused the death.

Ethics Term used to describe having a conscious system in use for deciding moral dilemmas.

European Court of Justice The court functioning as the final arbiter of the codes governing European Union member states.

Exculpatory evidence Evidence that tends to prove innocence or nonliability.

Execute the judgment If a winning plaintiff has obtained a court order for the defendant to pay the amount of the judgment, the plaintiff may take certain steps to collect the money owed from the defendant. In extreme cases, this may take the form of seizing the defendant's personal property for sale by the sheriff or garnishing the wages of the defendant.

Executive branch Established under Article II of the Constitution and consists of the president and vice president.

Exempt assets The bankruptcy code (and some state laws) allow the debtor to keep certain assets even if he has filed for bankruptcy protection. These are known as *exempt assets.* An example is the *homestead exemption,* which allows a debtor to keep all or at least part of the equity in his home.

Exempt employees Classification of employees that are not included in FLSA protection, generally consisting of employees whose responsibilities are primarily executive, administrative, or professional.

Exemptions Types of securities or transactions that an issuer may use to sell a security that are not subject to certain Securities and Exchange Commission regulations pertaining to registering securities, in order to assist business ventures seeking smaller amounts of capital from the public investment community.

Expert evaluation Method of alternative dispute resolution where an independent expert acts as the neutral fact-finder; particularly useful for parties involved in a business dispute where the issues are somewhat complex and related to the intricacies of a certain industry or profession.

Expert evaluator The neutral fact-finder in expert evaluation who reviews documents and evidence provided by each party and draws on her range of experience and expertise in the industry to offer an opinion on the merits and value of the claim and recommend a settlement amount.

Expiration Method in which an agency relationship is terminated by the parties agreeing to a fixed term for the representation.

Express acts Acts in which an agency relationship is terminated through either simply communicating the desire to terminate the relationship, the expiration of a fixed term, or satisfaction of purpose.

Express contract A contract created when the parties have specifically agreed on the promises and performances.

Express partnerships Partnerships where the parties have agreed to conduct a partnership on certain terms and conditions.

Express warranty A warranty that occurs when a seller makes a representation of fact about a product.

Fair and Accurate Credit Transactions Act Often referred to as the FACT Act, this statute requires credit bureaus to stop reporting any fraudulent account information once a consumer alleges identity theft until an investigation is conducted.

Fair Credit Reporting Act A statute that sets privacy rights for consumer credit reports and requires that the credit bureaus give individual consumers complete and timely access to their own credit reports.

Fair Debt Collection Practices Act A statute that regulates agents of the debtor involved in debt collection for consumer debts and that requires the collection agency to make known certain rights of the debtor.

Fair Labor Standards Act (FLSA) A federal law enacted in 1938 and intended to cover all employers engaged in interstate commerce in providing payment of a minimum wage, a maximum 40-hour workweek, overtime pay, and restrictions on children working in certain occupations and during certain hours.

Fair use A defense against copyright infringement where the court will examine the purpose and nature of the use, the nature of the work, the amount used, and the market effect of the use to determine whether the use is permitted.

Family Medical Leave Act (FMLA) A federal law enacted in 1993 that requires certain employers to give time off to employees to take care of their own or a family member's illness, or to care for a newborn or adopted child.

Federal cause of action A statutorily created right to sue a violator in federal court. Such statutes typically give federal courts specific subject matter jurisdiction over violations of a statute.

Federal courts Adjudicate matters dealing primarily with national laws, federal constitutional issues, and other cases that are outside the purview of state courts.

Federal Odometer Act A law making it criminal to change vehicle odometers and requires that any faulty odometer be plainly disclosed in writing to potential buyers.

Federal question Some issue arising from the constitution, federal statute or regulation, or federal common law.

Federal Register A daily publication distributed by the federal government (found in major libraries) primarily for announcing proposed agency rules, final agency regulations, and other administrative agency or executive branch announcements such as executive orders.

Federal system System in which a national government coexists with the government of each state.

Federal Trade Commission An agency charged with the broad mandate of preventing unfair and deceptive acts or practices in commercial transactions.

Federal Trade Commission Act (Antitrust) Enacted in 1914, establishing the Federal Trade Commission to administer the Act, intended as a catch-all enactment that has been construed to include the prohibitions of the other antitrust laws.

Federal Trade Commission Act (Consumer protection) A statute that created the Federal Trade Commission and prohibited deceptive trade practices.

Federal Trademark Dilution Act A federal law enacted by Congress in 1995, which permits mark holders to recover damages and prevent another from diluting distinctive trademarks.

Federal Unemployment Tax Act (FUTA) A federal law enacted in 1935 to provide limited payments, funded through employment taxes used to fund state workforce agencies, to workers who had been temporarily or permanently terminated from employment through no fault of their own.

Fee simple The broadest property interest in land, which endures until the current holder dies without heirs.

Felonies Classification of crimes that generally carry one year or more of incarceration as the penalty.

Fiduciary duties Under the Revised Uniform Partnership Act, general partners have the duties of loyalty, care, and good faith to ensure they are acting in the best interest of the partnership.

Fiduciary relationship A broad term embracing the notion that two parties may agree that one will act for another party's benefit with a high level of integrity and good faith in carrying out the best interests of the represented party.

Fifth Amendment Provides that no person "shall be compelled in any criminal case to be a witness against himself," guaranteeing individuals the right to remain silent both during the investigation and during any subsequent judicial proceedings.

Food, Drug and Cosmetic Act The statute that created the Food and Drug Administration.

Foreign Corrupt Practices Act (FCPA) A criminal statute that was enacted in 1977 principally to prevent corporate bribery of foreign officials in business transactions.

Foreign Sovereign Immunities Act (FSIA) A federal statute that incorporates the concept of sovereign immunity in explicitly prohibiting U.S. courts from rendering judicial actions against foreign nations or their government officials unless the foreign nation has waived its immunity, is engaged in some commercial enterprise on U.S. soil, or when its actions have a direct effect on U.S. interests.

Fourth Amendment Protects individual citizens' rights to be secure in their "persons, houses, papers and effects."

Franchise A business arrangement (not a form of business entity) of continuing commercial relationship for the right to operate a business pursuant to the franchisor's trade name or to sell the seller's branded goods.

Franchisee Individual or business with the legal right to operate a franchised business and use the business's trademarks and trade secrets.

Franchisor A business entity that has a proven track record of success and ability to franchise its products.

Fraudulent misrepresentation When one party has engaged in conduct that meets the standards for misrepresentation, but that party has actual knowledge that the representation is not true.

Frolic An exception to the respondeat superior doctrine occurring when an agent, during a normal workday, does something purely for her own reasons that are unrelated to his or her employment.

Frustration of purpose A party is excused from performance if, before a breach, a state of things that was the basis for forming the contract no longer exists, by no fault of either party.

Fully disclosed agency A type of agency relationship created where the third party entering into the contract is aware of the identity of the principal and knows the agent is acting on behalf of the principal in the transaction.

General Agreement on Tariffs and Trade (GATT) A treaty organization administered by the World Trade Organization whose purpose is to facilitate international trade.

Genericity Also known as *genericide,* the act or process of losing trademark protection occurring when, in the mind of a substantial majority of the public, the word denotes a broad genus or type of product and not a specific source or manufacturer.

Genuine assent Requirement for a contract to be enforceable necessitating the knowing, voluntary, and mutual approval of the terms of a contract by each party.

Good faith The obligation to act in good faith is the duty to honestly adhere to the contract's common purpose. Under this obligation neither party can do anything to prevent the other party from enjoying the "fruits of the contract." Instead, both must try and make the deal work as written.

Goods In contract law, goods are defined by the Uniform Commercial Code as that which is tangible and moveable from place to place.

Goodwill Intangible assets that represent value to the business such as its reputation for quality and/or service.

Gratuitous agents One of three broad categories in classifying agents; generally, anyone who acts on behalf of a principal without receiving any compensation.

Grievances In labor law, a complaint filed with or by a union to challenge an employer's treatment of one or more union members.

Guarantor A third party that agrees *only* to be liable to pay a loan *if* the debtor actually defaults.

Heirs Individuals who are legally entitled to inherit a decedent's property.

Horizontal restraints Per se violations of the Sherman Act in which the restraining of trade involves agreements between competitors to take action resulting in the elimination or reduction of competition from other competitors.

Hung jury Term used to describe a jury that cannot come to a consensus decision on which party should prevail in a case.

Hybrid contracts Contracts that involve terms for both goods and services, where the source of law is established by determining the predominant thrust of the subject matter.

Implied contract A contract in which the agreement is reached by the parties' actions rather than their words.

Implied partnerships Partnerships where the parties have acted like general partners even if the parties did not agree or intend to form a partnership.

Implied warranty A warranty protecting consumers even when the seller does not make a specific representation about the product.

Impossibility Impossibility excuses performance when an essential part of the contract has become impossible because a crucial, irreplaceable thing has been destroyed; a crucial person has died; a crucial means of performance no longer exists; or a crucial action has become illegal.

Impracticability Impracticability excuses performance when an extreme circumstance occurs or reveals itself that destroys the value of the performance to the party, when that circumstance was the fault of either party and was not reasonably foreseeable.

Incidental damages under the UCC Any commercially reasonable charges, expenses, or commissions incurred in stopping delivery, or in transportation, care, and custody of goods after a buyer's breach.

INCO terms Standardized contractual terms and designations used in international and some domestic sales contracts to avoid confusion due to language barriers and differing legal systems.

Inculpatory evidence Evidence that tends to prove a wrong.

Indemnification Right of reimbursement from another for a loss suffered due to a third party's act or default.

Independent contractor agents One of three broad categories in classifying agents; generally, anyone who performs services for a principal is considered an independent contractor if the principal has the right to control or direct only the result of the work and not the means and methods of accomplishing the result.

Indirect infringement Also known as *contributory infringement,* a theory of copyright infringement holding a third-party facilitator liable for damages when it has knowledge of the infringement and/or contributes to the infringement in some material way.

Induce To establish a cause and effect relationship between the tortfeasor's misstatement and the victim's detrimental action. Liability only occurs when the wrongdoing induces the harmful action.

Infringement The unlawful use of another's intellectual property.

Injunctive relief A court order to refrain from performing a particular act.

Insider trading When a corporate insider has access to certain information not available to the general investor public and the insider trades in their company's stock on the basis of the inside information.

Insider trading laws Federal securities statutes that prohibit corporate insiders who have access to certain information that is not available to the general investment public from trading their company's stock based on the insider knowledge.

Insider Trading and Securities Fraud Enforcement Act Passed by Congress in 1988 to raise the criminal and civil penalties for insider trading, increase the liability of brokerage firms for wrongful acts of their employees, and give the Securities and Exchange Commission more power to pursue violations of insider trading.

Insolvent When a business venture no longer has adequate assets to maintain its operations and can no longer pay its bills as they become due in the usual course of trade and business.

Inspections: The act of monitoring a business's compliance with administrative regulations whereby an administrative agency secures a warrant and then enters and inspects the business's premises.

Installment contract A contract allowing delivery of goods or payments for goods at separate times, to be accepted or rejected separately.

Intentional torts A category of torts where the tortfeasor was willful in bringing about a particular event that caused harm to another party.

Intermediate-level scrutiny The middle level of scrutiny applied by courts deciding constitutional issues through judicial review, upheld if the government shows that a regulation involves an important governmental objective that is furthered by substantially related means.

International Court of Justice Also known as the *World Court,* the judicial branch of the United Nations charged with settling legal disputes submitted to it by member states and giving advisory opinions on legal questions submitted to it by duly authorized international organs, agencies, and the U.N. General Assembly.

Interrogatories Method of discovery where one party submits written questions to the opposing party attempting to gather evidence prior to trial.

Investigation The initial phase of the criminal justice system in which authorities become aware of an alleged criminal act and begin gathering physical evidence and interviewing witnesses and potential suspects.

Involuntary bankruptcy petition A petition filed in the bankruptcy court against a debtor by a group of three or more creditors with an unsecured aggregate claim of at least $11,625 who claim that the debtor is failing to pay the debt as it comes due.

Irrevocable offers Classification of offers that cannot be withdrawn by the offeror. These include offers in the form of an option contract, offers where the offeree partly performed or detrimentally relied on the offer, and firm offers by a merchant under the Uniform Commercial Code.

Joint and several liability The legal principle that makes two or more parties liable for an entire debt either individually or jointly in any proportional combination.

Joint venture Business relationship between two or more parties for a limited-in-time venture.

Jointly and severally liable Legal principle that imposes liability on partners both together (jointly) and separately (severally) for debts and liabilities of the partnership.

Judicial branch Established under Article III of the Constitution and consists of the Supreme Court and other federal courts.

Judiciary A collection of federal and state courts existing primarily to adjudicate disputes and charged with the responsibility of judicial review.

Jurisdiction An English word derived through the combination of two Latin words combining *juris* (of law or of right) and *dictio* (speaking). Thus, the combination of the words refers to a specific court's right to *speak the law* or render a decision in a legal dispute.

Jurisprudence The science and philosophy of law that defines various approaches to the appropriate function of law and how legal doctrines should be developed and applied.

Jury selection The process of asking potential jurors questions to reveal any prejudices that may affect their judgment of the facts.

Labor Management Relations Act A federal law enacted in 1947 as an amendment to the NLRA, prohibiting the forcing of employees to join or continue membership in a union as a condition of employment (also known as the *Taft-Hartley Act*).

Labor-Management Reporting and Disclosure Act A federal law enacted in 1959 to establish a system of reporting and checks intended to uncover and prevent fraud and corruption among union officials through regulating internal operating procedures and union matters (also known as the *Landrum-Griffin Act*).

Lapse of time Term used to describe an event covered under operation of law in which a contract may be terminated once either the offeror's expressed time limit has expired or reasonable time has passed.

Law A body of rules of action or conduct prescribed by controlling authority, and having legal binding force.

Lease An agreement between a landlord and a tenant for the rental of property.

Leasehold estate The qualified right to use real estate in an exclusive manner for a limited period of time. The most common form of leasehold estate is a landlord-tenant agreement.

Legality (Contracts) Requirement for an enforceable contract necessitating that both the subject matter and performance of the contract must be legal.

Legality (Criminal law) A principle of criminal law that protects individuals from being charged with some unspecified general offense by requiring that crimes be specifically proscribed by law in advance of the conduct sought to be punished.

Legislative branch Established under Article I of the Constitution and consists of the House of Representatives and the Senate.

Legislative history The records kept by the legislature including the debates, committee and conference reports, and legislative findings of fact used when creating a law, which can be used to show the legislature's intent.

Libel Written defamation, in which publishing in print (including pictures), writing, or broadcast through radio, television, or film, an untruth about another that will do harm to that person's reputation or honesty or subject a party to hate, contempt, or ridicule.

Licensing The task of issuing a license authorizing a business or industry to do something.

Life estate An ownership interest in real estate that lasts for the lifetime of a particular person.

Limited liability company (LLC) A multiperson form of business entity that offers liability protection for its principals with various tax options.

Limited liability partnership (LLP) Form of business entity that provides the same level of liability protection to a general partner in an LLP as is provided to a limited partner in a limited partnership form of entity.

Liquidated damages Liquidated damages are reasonable estimates of the actual damages resulting if the contract is breached, which is agreed to by the parties ahead of time.

Literal patent infringement One way in which patent infringement occurs, applying when the invention or process violates either the rule of exactness or the rule of addition.

Lockout The shutdown of a business by the employer to prevent employees from working, thus depriving them of their employment and putting economic pressure on the union's members before the union can do the same to the employer through a strike.

Madrid Protocol A multinational agreement that aims to help reduce the burden of multinational companies that desire multinational protection of their trademark by the use of a more uniform and single-sourced process.

Mail Fraud Act Enacted by Congress in 1990 as a comprehensive approach to criminalizing any fraud where the defrauding party uses the mail or any wire, radio, or television in perpetrating fraud.

Mailbox rule Governs common law contracts and provides a rule for when a contract is considered to be deemed accepted by the offeree, thus depriving the offeror of the right to revoke the offer. Generally, the mailbox rule provides that the acceptance of an offer is effective upon dispatch and not when the acceptance is received by the offeree.

Malice Typically defined as intentional doing of a wrongful act with intent to harm. However, in *New York Times v. Sullivan,* the U.S. Supreme Court used the somewhat confusing phrase *actual malice* to describe (1) actual knowledge of a false statement or (2) a reckless disregard for the truth. It is clear from subsequent case law that evidence of ill will is not required for the plaintiff to prevail in a defamation claim.

Manager-managed LLC LLC members name a manager (or managers) who generally has the day-to-day operational responsibilities while the nonmanaging members are typically investors with little input on the course of business taken by the entity except for major decisions.

Manifest Apparent and evident to the senses; in the context of agency law, courts apply an objective standard to determine if the principal intended for an agency to be created.

Market-based approach Instituted by the 1990 Clean Air Act amendments to give businesses a choice of methods embracing an economic incentive in complying with pollution standards.

Med-Arb Method of alternative dispute resolution whereby the parties begin with mediation and if mediation fails in a fixed time period, the parties agree to submit to arbitration.

Mediation Method of alternative dispute resolution where a mediator attempts to settle a dispute by learning the facts of a dispute and then negotiating a settlement between two adverse parties.

Member-managed LLC LLC management structure similar to a general partnership with all the members having the authority to bind the business.

Mental incapacity (Contracts) Category of individuals who have limited capacity to contract, covering those who are unable to understand the nature and consequences of the contract, or are unable to act in a reasonable manner in relation to the transaction and the other party has reason to know of her condition.

Mental incapacity (Criminal law) A defense to avoid criminal liability whereby the defendant's actions are related to some type of mental disease or defect.

Merchant Someone that is regularly engaged in the sale of a particular good.

Merchant's firm offer An offer in writing between merchants to buy or sell goods along with a promise without consideration to keep that offer for a stated amount of time, or if unstated no longer than three months.

Merchant's privilege A narrow privilege provided for under the *Restatements* to shield a merchant from liability for temporarily detaining a party who is reasonably suspected of stealing merchandise.

Minimum contacts A defendant's activities within or affecting the state in which a lawsuit is brought that are considered legally sufficient to support jurisdiction in that state's courts.

Minors Category of individuals who have limited capacity to contract, covering those younger than the majority age of 18. Until a person reaches her majority age, any contract that she may enter into is voidable at the minor's option.

Mirror image rule Principle stating that the offeree's response operates as an acceptance only if it is the precise mirror image of the offer.

Misappropriation The acquisition of a trade secret of another by a person who knows or has reason to know that the trade secret was acquired by improper means, or disclosure of a trade secret to another without express or implied consent.

Misdemeanors Classification of crimes that carry up to one year of incarceration as the penalty.

Misfeasance Some act by one party that harms or endangers another party.

Misrepresentation When one party to an agreement makes a promise or representation about a material fact that is not true.

Mistake In contract law, an erroneous belief that is not in accord with the existing facts.

Mitigating circumstances A fact that does not excuse a crime but may lessen the punishment. For example, mitigating circumstances that might lessen the sentence for murder from death to life imprisonment include no prior criminal history, minor participation in the killing, mental illness, or young age at the time of the killing.

Mixed motives Theory of employment discrimination where the cause of employment action was motivated by both legitimate and discriminatory motives.

Mobile sources of air pollution Nonstationary sources of air pollutants, such as automobiles, buses, trucks, ships, trains, aircraft, and various other vehicles.

Model Business Corporation Act (MBCA) Model act drafted by the American Law Institute and adopted by over half of the states as a template for compiling their own statutes governing corporations.

Model Penal Code (MPC) A statutory text adopted by the American Law Institute in 1962 in an effort to bring greater uniformity to the state laws by proffering certain legal standards and reforms.

Model state statutes Statutes drafted by legal experts to be used as a model for state legislatures to adopt in their individual jurisdictions in order to increase the level of uniformity and fairness across courts in all states.

Money damages Money damages are sums levied on the breaching party(ies) and awarded to the nonbreaching party(ies) to remedy a loss from breach of contract.

Morals Term referring to generally accepted standards of right and wrong in a given society.

Mortgage A written document specifying the parties and the real estate that is filed with a state and/or local government agency when real estate is being used to collateralize a loan.

Mortgage foreclosure When a creditor declares the loan in default and takes title and possession of the collateralized real estate in hopes of selling the property to pay off the debt owed.

Mortgagee The creditor when real estate is being used to collateralize a loan.

Mortgagor The borrower when real estate is being used to collateralize a loan.

Motions A request by one party to the court asking it to issue a certain order (such as a "motion for summary judgment"). Motions may be made by either party before, during, and after the trial.

Mutual assent The broad underlying requirement to form an enforceable contract necessitating that the parties must reach an agreement using a combination of offer and acceptance and that the assent must be genuine.

Mutual consent Circumstance under which contracting parties may be discharged from obligation where neither party has fully performed and they agree to cancel the contract.

Mutual mistake When both parties hold an erroneous belief concerning a basic assumption on which a contract was made.

National Environmental Policy Act (NEPA) Enacted in 1969 to serve as a national charter for environmental regulation by establishing a process that must be followed by federal agencies in making decisions that have the potential to have a significant impact on the environment.

National Labor Relations Act (NLRA) A federal law enacted in 1935 providing general protections to the rights of workers to organize, engage in collective bargaining, and take part in strikes and other forms of concerted activity in support of their demands (also known as the *Wagner Act*).

National Labor Relations Board (NLRB) An independent federal agency created by the NLRA, charged with administering, implementing and enforcing NLRA provisions, as well as monitoring union elections for fraud and setting guidelines for employers and unions with respect to fair labor practices.

Necessary and Proper Clause The constitutional clause giving Congress the general implied authority to make laws necessary to carry out its other enumerated powers.

Negligence A category of torts where the tortfeasor was absent of willful intent in bringing about a particular event that caused harm to another party.

Negligent hiring doctrine A tort-based theory of liability for employers for negligent or intentional torts of employees when the employer had reason to know that the employee may cause harm within his scope of employment.

No Electronic Theft Act A federal law enacted in 1997 (also referred to as the NET Act), which provides for criminal liability for anyone who infringes on a copyright willfully for financial gain, but also by reproducing or distributing, including by electronic means, one or more copies of a copyrighted work with a total retail value of more than $1,000.

Nominal consideration Consideration that is stated in a written contract even though it is not actually exchanged.

Nonfeasance The failure to act or intervene in certain situations.

Nonobviousness standard A standard to obtain a patent requiring that an invention must be something more than that which would be obvious, in light of publicly available knowledge, to one who is skilled in the relevant field.

Nonvoting stock Shares in a corporation that entitle the shareholder to very little or no vote on corporate matters.

Novation Novation occurs when the duties of the contract remain the same but a new third party assumes the duties of an original party, discharging the original party from further obligations. (Note that many courts use *novation* for new parties and new terms or substitute agreements).

Novelty standard A standard to obtain a patent requiring that an invention or process be unique and original and that a patent applicant show that no other identical invention or process exists.

Nuisance A common law legal action to redress harm arising from the use of one's property based on the aggrieved party's right to enjoy his/her property without interference from a third party.

Objective intent Requirement for an offer to have legal effect necessitating that generally, the offeror must have a serious intention to become bound by the offer and the terms of the offer must be reasonably certain.

Occupational Safety and Health Act (OSHA) A federal law enacted in 1970, setting forth workplace rules and regulations to promote safety of workers and prevent workplace injuries.

Offer A promise or commitment to do (or refrain from doing) a specified activity. In contract law, the expression of a willingness to enter into a contract by the offeror promising an offeree that she will perform certain obligations in exchange for the offeree's counter-promise to perform.

Officers Those appointed by the board of directors to carry out the directors' set course of direction through management of the day-to-day operation of the business.

Oil Pollution Act (OPA) A statute enacted in 1990 to streamline and strengthen the Environmental Protection Agency's ability to prevent and respond to catastrophic oil spills in water sources.

Omitted terms Contract terms that are left out or absent. In contract law, courts may supply a reasonable term in a situation where the contract is silent.

Open terms Unspecified terms in a sales contract that do not detract from the validity of the contract so long as the parties intended to make the contract and other specified terms give a basis for remedy in case of breach.

Opening statements Attorneys' presentation of their theory of the case and what they hope to prove to the jury at the onset of the trial.

Operating agreements Used in an LLC to set out the structure and internal rules for operation of the entity.

Operating permits Licenses issued by authorities to existing stationary sources that permit pollution emission at certain levels.

Operation of law (Contracts) Another way in which an offer may be terminated by certain happenings or events. Generally, these include lapse of time, death or incapacity of the offeror or offeree, and destruction of the subject matter of the contract prior to acceptance.

Operation of law (Sales) Circumstances in which contract obligations may be discharged where fairness demands it through the doctrines of impossibility, impracticability, and frustration of purpose.

Operation of law (Agency) Method in which an agency relationship is terminated as provided for a statute or through certain common law doctrines covering the destruction of an essential subject matter, or death, bankruptcy, or lack of requisite mental capacity.

Ordinances Local statutes passed by local legislatures.

Originality A requirement in order to gain copyright protection in which the author must use his or her own creative capabilities to create the work or medium.

Output contract A contract in which the buyer agrees to buy all the goods that the seller produces for a set time and at a set price, and the seller may sell only to that one buyer. The quantity for the contract is the seller's output.

Overtime compensation A higher rate of pay, calculated at one and one-half times the employee's hourly base rate, for the hours nonexempt employees work in excess of 40 hours in one seven-day workweek.

Ownership interests The various rights that owners of real estate have. These interests are limited depending on the type of ownership.

Paris Convention A multinational agreement covering patents, requiring signatory countries to protect the same inventor rights under any member country's patent laws as those enjoyed by citizens of that member country.

Parole evidence rule Provides that any writing intended by the parties to be the final expression of their agreement may not be contradicted by any oral or written agreements made prior to the writing.

Partially disclosed agency A type of agency relationship created where the third party knows that the agent is representing a principal, but does not know the actual identity of the principal.

Partnership Multiple-person business entity where the partners conduct an ongoing business relationship in which profits and losses are shared.

Party A person or entity making or responding to a claim in a court.

Pass-through entity Business entity that does not pay corporate taxes, such as a partnership. Rather, any profits are taxed at individual rates when distributed to the partners.

Past consideration Type of contract that is not considered to meet the bargained for exchange requirement when the promise is made in return for a detriment previously made by the promisee.

Patentable subject matter standard A standard that bars laws of nature, natural phenomena, and abstract ideas from being patentable subject matter.

Pecuniary harm Lost revenue or profits, both actual and potential.

Pension A retirement benefit in which the employer promises to pay a monthly sum, ordinarily based on the length of service and the employee's final salary rate, to employees who retire from the company after a certain number of years of service.

Per se A Latin term literally meaning "of, in, or by itself," without any additional facts needed to prove a point.

Per se standard A Latin term literally meaning "of, in, or by itself," without any additional facts needed to prove a point, this is one standard used by federal courts in deciding whether or not a certain transaction or action violates the Sherman Act, occurring when concerted activities are blatantly anticompetitive.

Perfect tender rule This rule requires the seller to deliver her goods precisely as the contract requires in quantity, quality, and all other respects or risk the buyer's lawful rejection of the goods.

Perfecting Procedure for the secured party to establish priority in the collateral over other creditors as provided by Article 9 of the Uniform Commercial Code.

Personal guarantee An agreement that allows a creditor to obtain a judgment against the personal assets of one or more shareholders in the event of a default by the corporation.

Personal guaranty Safeguard for creditors in a business loan where the principals of a business have pledged their personal assets if the assets of the business are insufficient to repay the loan in the event of a default by the business entity/debtor.

Personal jurisdiction The court's authority over the parties involved in the dispute.

Personal property Any moveable or tangible object and includes everything except real property. Examples of personal property include computers, inventory, furniture, and jewelry.

Picketing A union's patrolling alongside the premises of a business to organize the workers, to gain recognition as a bargaining agent, or to publicize a labor dispute with the owner or with whomever the owner deals.

Piercing the corporate veil When the court discards the corporate veil and holds some or all of the shareholders personally liable because fairness demands it in certain cases of inadequate capitalization, fraud, and failing to follow corporate formalities.

Plain view doctrine A doctrine stating that authorities generally do not commit a Fourth Amendment violation where they obtain evidence by virtue of seeing an object that is in plain view of a government agent who has the right to be in the position to have that view.

Plaintiff The party who initiates a lawsuit by filing a complaint with the clerk of the court against the defendant(s) demanding damages, performance, and/or court determination of rights.

Preamble The introductory part of the Constitution that states its broad objectives.

Precedent When courts apply the law of a previous case to current cases with similar facts.

Preempt A federal law preempts a state law when it addresses what a state law is trying to do.

Preemption The power to override state law that is granted by the Supremacy Clause.

Preexisting duty A duty that one is already legally obligated to do and, thus, generally not recognized as a legal detriment.

Preferred stock A form of equity instrument that has less risk than common stock because it has certain quasi-debt features and whose holders have preference rights over common stockholders in receiving dividends from the corporation.

Preliminary adjudication A hearing where the prosecutor presents evidence of the defendant's guilt and the decision maker (either the grand jurors or a magistrate) determines whether sufficient probable cause exists to hold the defendant over for trial.

Preponderance of the evidence A standard used to decide a civil case whereby the jury is to favor one party when the evidence is of greater weight and more convincing than the evidence that is offered in opposition to it (i.e., more likely than not). It is a substantially lower standard of proof than that used in a criminal case.

Preponderance of the evidence More likely than not. A lower standard of proof as compared to "clear and convincing evidence."

Preponderance of the evidence Burden of proof used in civil cases in which the fact finder need only be convinced that the defendant's liability was more likely than not.

Pretext A false reason offered to justify an action.

Pretrial conference A meeting between the attorneys for the parties and the judge in the case several weeks prior to trial, with the objectives of encouraging settlement and resolving any outstanding motions or procedural issues that arose during the pleadings or discovery stages.

Prima facie Literally "at first sight," prima facie cases are made when certain clear evidence exists as to a conclusion of law, but it is subject to further evidence or information to rebut the original evidence.

Prima facie case Establishing certain evidence that is sufficient to prevail in a discrimination claim without proving additional facts, unless disproved or rebutted by the opposing party.

Principal (Business entity) The term used to denote those persons with ownership interest in a business venture.

Principal (Agency) An agent's master; the person from whom an agent has received instruction and authorization and to whose benefit the agent is expected to perform and make decisions pursuant to an agency relationship.

Principals Owners of a business entity.

Private international law Category of international law principles that focuses on regulations of private individuals and business entities.

Private laws Laws recognized as binding between two parties even though no specific statute or regulation provides for the rights of the parties.

Private placement A securities law provision exempting an issuer from registration where the issuer only accepts investments from those who meet the standards for accredited investors.

Private Securities Litigation Reform Act of 1995 (PSLRA) An act passed by Congress to protect publicly held companies from frivolous litigation by making it more difficult to pursue litigation under the securities laws based solely on commentary by the company executives.

Privately held corporation A corporation that does not sell ownership interests through sales via a broker to the general public or to financial institutions or investors.

Probable cause A reasonable amount of suspicion supported by circumstances sufficiently strong to justify a belief that a person has committed a crime.

Procedural laws Laws that provide a structure and set out rules for pursuing substantive rights.

Product disparagement statutes Statutes intended to protect the interest of a state's major industries such as agriculture, dairy, or beef.

Promissory estoppel Theory allowing for the recovery of damages by the relying party if the promisee actually relied on the promise and the promisee's reliance was reasonably foreseeable to the promisor.

Promissory note A contract whereby the borrower promises to pay back the creditor at a certain rate of interest over a specified period of years.

Promoter An individual who begins to carry out a business venture's activity before the articles of incorporation are filed, often responsible for raising capital or funds for the new undertaking.

Prospectus The first part of the registration statement of a security prescribed by Securities and Exchange Commission regulations, which is intended to give investors a realistic view of the issuer's business, risk factors, financial position, financial statements, and disclosures concerning directors, officers, and controlling shareholders.

Protected classes The classes of individuals laid out in Title VII including color, race, national origin, religion, gender, or pregnancy.

Proximate (legal) cause A fundamental element to recover a lawsuit against a tortfeasor for negligence where the injured party must prove a legally recognized and close-in-proximity link between the breach of duty and the damages it suffered.

Public international law Category of international law principles that primarily addresses relations between individual countries and international organizations.

Public laws Laws derived from some government entity.

Public policy Requirement for an enforceable contract necessitating that the terms are consistent with public policy objectives.

Punishment A principle of criminal law imposing a hardship in response to misconduct based on the concepts that criminal law acts as a deterrent, removes dangerous criminals from the population, and that rehabilitation is an important part of the criminal justice system.

Punitive damages Money awarded in addition to actual damages of an injured party that is intended to punish the wrongdoer and deter unlawful conduct in the future.

Purchase order A form commonly used in sales contracts as an offer from the buyer that contains preprinted clauses along with blanks to accommodate the specifics of that transaction.

Qualified privilege A defense to a defamation claim provided for the media and employers, where the defendants must offer evidence of good faith and be absent of malice to be shielded from liability.

Quasi-contract A classification that permits a contract to be enforceable in cases where no express or implied contract exists, where one party suffers losses as a result of another party's unjust enrichment.

Ratification A retroactive source of the agent's authority occurring when the principal affirms a previously unauthorized act by either (1) expressly ratifying the transactions, or (2) not repudiating the act via retaining the benefits while knowing that the benefits resulted from an unauthorized act by the agent.

Rational basis The lowest level of scrutiny applied by courts deciding constitutional issues through judicial review, upheld if the government shows that the law has a reasonable connection to achieving a legitimate and constitutional objective.

Real property Land, or anything growing on, attached to, or erected on the land. Examples of real property include parcels of land, homes, warehouses, stores, and crops.

Reasonable accommodations Accommodations, required under the Americans with Disabilities Act, which allow disabled individuals to adequately perform essential job functions.

Reformation Rewritten contract by the court to conform to the parties' actual intentions when the parties have imperfectly expressed their agreement and this imperfection results in a dispute.

Regulation A rule that is effective and was published in the Code of Federal Regulations and now has legal force.

Regulation D A securities law provision exempting an issuer from registration where the issuer is selling the security for limited offers of a relatively small amount of money or offers made in a limited manner.

Regulation Z A part of the Truth in Lending Act requiring that certain written disclosures be made prior to the time that a credit transaction is consummated.

Rejection An action terminating an offer whereby the offeree rejects the offer outright prior to acceptance.

Remand To send a case back to the lower court from which it came for further action consistent with the opinion and instructions of the higher court.

Remedial Requires the Environmental Protection Agency to identify the most hazardous waste sites and generate a National Priorities List as established by the Superfund law.

Remedies Either monetary, performance, or injunctive, the court-ordered means of enforcing rights and redressing wrongs after a breaches.

Removal Authorizes actions to be taken to address releases or imminent releases of hazardous materials as established by the Superfund law.

Reorganization plan The keystone to a Chapter 11 case, generally filed by the debtor, which articulates a specific strategy and financial plan for emerging from financial distress.

Replacement workers A term that refers to nonunion employees hired in order to continue operations during a strike.

Request for admissions A set of statements sent from one litigant to an adversary, for the purpose of determining what facts are in dispute and which facts both parties accept as true.

Requests for production Requests aimed at producing specific items to help one party discover some important fact in the case.

Requirements contract A contract in which the buyer agrees to buy whatever he needs from the seller during a set period, and the buyer may buy only from that one seller. The quantity for the contract is what the buyer requires.

Rescission A contract is rescinded when both parties agree to discharge each other from all duties under that contract and end the agreement, no matter what has been done or left undone.

Resource Conservation and Recovery Act (RCRA) A federal law enacted in 1976 to regulate active and future facilities that produce solid waste and/or hazardous materials.

Respondeat superior [Latin for "let the master answer."] A common law doctrine that makes a principal (employer) liable for the actions of the servant/agent's (employee) tort when that act resulted in some physical harm or injury and occurred within the agent's scope of employment.

Restatement of Torts An influential document issued by the American Law Institute (ALI) summarizing the general principles of U.S. tort law and recognized by the courts as widely applied principles of law. Note that ALI amended the *Restatements* twice and therefore these sources of law are called the *Restatement (Second) of Torts* and the *Restatement (Third) of Torts*.

Restatements (Second) of Agency A set of principles, issued by the American Law Institute, intended to clarify the prevailing opinion of how the law of agency stands.

Restatements of the Law A collection of uniform legal principles focused in a particular area of the law, which contains statements of common law legal principles and rules in a given area of law.

Restitution Restitution restores to the plaintiff the value of the performance that he has already rendered to the breaching party, and by which the breaching party has been unjustly enriched.

Restoring American Financial Stability Act of 2009 Legislation with sweeping reforms proposing to overhaul the regulation of U.S. financial services and markets.

Revocation An action terminating an offer whereby the offeror decides to withdraw the offer by expressly communicating the revocation to the offeree prior to acceptance.

Revoking acceptance Even after accepting the goods, a buyer can still revoke acceptance if the goods are nonconforming in a way that substantially affects their value and he notifies the seller of the revocation in a timely fashion.

Rightful rejection The justified refusal to accept nonconforming goods under a sales contract.

Risk of loss The risk of one party having to bear the loss due to damage, destruction, or loss of goods bargained for under a sales contract.

Robinson-Patman Act A federal antitrust law enacted in 1936 amending the Clayton Act provisions to provide for a broader regulatory authority to curb price discrimination.

Rule of addition A rule for determining whether literal patent infringement has occurred that applies when the infringing device does more than is described in the patent application of the protected invention.

Rule of exactness A rule for determining whether literal patent infringement has occurred that applies when the infringer makes, uses, or sells an invention that is exactly the same as the claims made in the patent application.

Rule of omission A rule stating that when the alleged patent infringing invention lacks an essential element of the patent holder's claims in the patent application, infringement has not occurred.

Rule of reason standard A second standard used by federal courts in deciding whether or not a certain transaction or action violates the Sherman Act, contemplating a scale in which the court weighs any anticompetitive harm suffered against marketwide benefits of their actions.

Rulemaking The legislative function charged to administrative agencies, whereby they create legally enforceable rules in order to fill in the details of a statute.

Safe Drinking Water Act (SDWA) A federal statute that sets minimum quality and safety standards for every public water system and every source of drinking water in the United States.

Sales contracts Agreements to transfer title to real property or tangible assets at a given price.

Sarbanes-Oxley Act (SOX Act) of 2002 Amendments to the '33 and '34 Securities Acts intended to impose stricter regulation and controls on how corporations do business, through regulation of auditing, financial reporting, and internal corporate governance.

Scienter Evidence of specific intent to deceive, manipulate, or defraud.

Seasonable notice Notification to the other party either within an agreed upon time or a reasonable amount of time given the nature and goals of the contract.

Secondary meaning A requirement for a descriptive trademark to gain protection, acquired when the consuming public primarily associates the mark with a particular product rather than any alternate meaning.

Secondary sources Sources of law that have no independent authority or legally binding effect, but can be used to illustrate a point or clarify a legal issue.

Section 16 Provision of the Securities Act of 1934 that imposes restrictions and reporting requirements on ownership positions and stock trades made by certain corporate insiders named in the statute.

Secured creditor Title given to a creditor when the borrower has pledged collateral in order to obtain credit.

Secured party The creditor in a secured transaction.

Securities Act of 1933 The act that covers the process of issuing or reissuing securities to the public. The law requires registration and certain disclosures and authorizes the Securities and Exchange Commission to oversee the transactions.

Securities Act of 1934 The act that regulates the sale of securities between investors after an investor purchased it from a business entity issuer.

Securities and Exchange Commission (SEC) The independent federal administrative agency charged with rulemaking, enforcement, and adjudication of federal securities laws.

Securities law The body of federal and state laws governing the issuance and trading of equity and debt instruments to public investors.

Securities Litigation Uniform Standards Act of 1998 An amendment to the Securities Act of 1934, intended to prevent a private party from instituting certain lawsuits in federal or state court based on the statutory or common law of any state that punishes "a misrepresentation or omission of a material fact" or the use of "any manipulative device or contrivance" concerning the purchase or sale of a covered security.

Security interest The rights of the secured party in a transaction.

Self-defense A defense to avoid criminal liability whereby the law recognizes that certain cases require the use of deadly force to repel an attack in which the defendant reasonably feared that death or substantial harm was about to occur either to the defendant or to a third party.

Senior in priority When a business must liquidate assets because a venture fails and either dissolves or files for bankruptcy protection, payments to creditors and shareholders are made according to priority. Thus, those that are "senior" in priority get paid first.

Sentencing guidelines Statutorily prescribed standards for determining the punishment that a convicted criminal should receive based on the nature of the crime and the offender's criminal history.

Separation of powers The system of checks and balances created by the Constitution whereby the three branches have unique powers that allow them to resolve conflicts among themselves, thus ensuring no one branch exceeds its constitutional authority.

Service mark A word, symbol, or phrase used to identify a particular seller's services and distinguish them from other services.

Shareholders The owners of a corporation who act principally through electing and removing directors and approving or withholding approval of major corporate decisions.

Sherman Act (1890) The centerpiece of the statutory scheme of federal antitrust law, prohibiting contracts, combinations, conspiracies in restraint of trade, and monopolization.

Shipment contract A contract in which the seller is required to send the goods to the buyer via a carrier; when the carrier receives the goods the seller has fulfilled his duty and the buyer now has title and bears the risk of loss.

Slander Oral defamation, in which someone tells one or more persons an untruth about another that will harm the reputation or honesty of the person defamed or subject a party to hate, contempt, or ridicule.

Social Security Act of 1935 (SSA) A federal law providing for a broad set of benefits for workers that are funded by mandatory employment taxes paid by both employer and employee into a trust fund administered by the federal government.

Soft per se analysis Developed by the courts for determining the legality of a tying arrangement. Under this analysis, sellers that tie a second product to the first product are illegal per se if the seller possesses sufficient market power as to render the tie-in as coercive.

Sole proprietorship One-person business entity with minimal filing requirements.

Sovereign immunity Long-standing doctrine of international law that stands for the proposition that, with some exceptions, foreign nations are exempt from jurisdiction by U.S. courts and vice versa.

Special relationship In tort law, a heightened duty created between a common carrier to its passengers, innkeepers to guests, employers to employees, businesses to patrons, a school to students, and a landlord to tenants and landowners.

Specific performance A remedy whereby a court orders the breaching party to render the promised performance by ordering the party to take a specific action.

Speedy Trial Act A federal statute that sets out specific time periods in which an accused must be brought to trial.

Stakeholder An expansive term that includes a business entity's owners, investors, employees, customers, suppliers, and the wider community.

Standing Requirement for any party to maintain a lawsuit against another party, necessitating that the party asserting the claim must have suffered an injury in fact and that harm must be direct, concrete, and individualized.

State appellate courts State-level courts of precedent, concerned primarily with reviewing the decisions of trial courts.

State common law The governing body of law of contracts for services or real estate.

State courts Adjudicate matters dealing primarily with cases arising from state statutory, state common, or state constitutional law.

State Implementation Plan (SIP) A mandated state plan for complying with the federal Clean Air Act, administered by the Environmental Protection Agency, which consists of a collection of regulations that help to achieve a reduction in pollution.

State long-arm statutes State statutes intended to allow a court to reach into another state and exercise jurisdiction over a nonresident defendant due to the defendant's conduct or other circumstances.

State statutory law The governing body of law of contracts for goods or products based on the Uniform Commercial Code.

State trial courts The first courts at the state level before which the facts of a case are decided.

Statement of qualification Document used to form a limited liability partnership by converting a general partnership.

Stationary sources of air pollution Fixed-site emitters of air pollutants, such as fossil-fueled power plants, petroleum refineries, petrochemical plants, food processing plants, and other industrial sources.

Statute of frauds The law governing which contracts must be in writing in order to be enforceable.

Statute of limitations A statute that places a time limit on the enforcement of certain contracts in order to ensure diligent enforcement.

Statutory law The body of law created by the legislature and approved by the executive branch of state and federal governments.

Statutory scheme The structure of a statute and the format of its mandates.

Strict liability In tort law, where a tortfeasor may be held liable for an act regardless of intent or willfulness, applying primarily to cases of defective products and abnormally dangerous activities.

Strict scrutiny The most stringent standard of scrutiny applied by courts deciding constitutional issues through judicial review when the government action is related to a fundamental right or is based on a suspect classification, upheld if the government shows a compelling need that justifies the law being enacted and no less restrictive alternatives existed.

Strike A concerted and sustained refusal by workers to perform some or all of the services for which they were hired in order to induce the employer to concede certain contract terms during collective bargaining or to engage in fair labor practices.

Strong-arm clause Provision of the bankruptcy code that allows the debtor in possession to avoid any obligation or transfer of property that the debtor would otherwise be obligated to perform.

Structural offenses Antitrust laws designed to combat the problem of monopolization by outlawing affirmative action toward monopolizing or attempting to monopolize a part of trade or commerce.

Subchapter S A form of corporation, subject to certain restrictions set out by the Internal Revenue Service, for most companies with 100 or fewer shareholders, which allows the protection of limited liability with direct flow-through tax treatment.

Subject matter jurisdiction The court's authority over the dispute between the parties.

Sublease A tenant transfer of its interest to a third party for anything less than the term remaining on a lease.

Subordinate In the context of stock ownership rights, a subordinate position is a lower or secondary position in terms of being entitled to profits or assets. For example, common stockholders are subordinate to preferred stockholders.

Substantial performance Performance of the essential terms of the contract such that performance can be considered complete less damages for anything still unperformed.

Substantive laws Laws that provide individuals with rights and create certain duties.

Substitute agreement (Modification) A modification occurs when two parties agree to different duties under the contract; these new duties then replace and dissolve the original obligations of that agreement.

Summons Formal notification to the defendant that she has been named in the lawsuit and informs her that an answer must be filed within a certain period of time.

Superfund Another name for the CERCLA derived from its main provisions on the notion that cleanup operations for abandoned toxic waste sites were to be funded by a self-sustaining quasi-escrow fund to be administered by the federal government.

Superfund Amendments and Reauthorization Act (SARA) An amendment to the CERCLA in 1986 containing a new requirement for states to establish emergency response commissions to draft and implement emergency procedures in the event of a hazardous chemical accident; for businesses to disclose the presence of certain chemicals within a community; and to impose an affirmative obligation on businesses to notify authorities of any spills or discharges of hazardous materials.

Supremacy Clause The constitutional clause that makes clear that federal law is always supreme to any state law that is in direct conflict.

Surety A third party that agrees to be primarily liable to pay a loan.

Tax-deferred retirement savings account A retirement savings plan where the employee commits to saving a certain percentage in an account that is controlled directly by the employee, and the funds grow tax-free until they are withdrawn.

Telephone Consumer Protection Act and Telemarketing and Consumer Fraud and Abuse Prevention Act Two statutes that regulate telemarketing firms and practices, including allowing consumers to opt out of unwanted calls from telemarketers, banning the use of unsolicited recorded calls and faxes, and prohibiting telemarketers from making false representations.

Tenant remedies The legal alternatives available to tenants as compensation in the event a landlord breaches a lease. Examples of common remedies include: termination of the lease, suits for damages, and withholding of rent.

Tender An unconditional performance of the seller by delivering or making the purchased goods available to the buyer.

Tender of delivery For delivery of goods, tender occurs when the seller produces goods conforming to the contract and provides adequate notice of their delivery to the buyer.

Termination Method in which either the principal (revocation) or the agent (renunciation) can end the agency relationship by simply communicating the desire to dissolve the relationship.

Third-party beneficiary Someone who, while not party to a contract, stands to benefits from the existence of that contract.

Threshold requirement A requirement that must be met by the plaintiff prior to the court engaging in further legal analysis to determine the rights of the parties.

Title Title is the legal right to ownership in a good and all the privileges and responsibilities it entails.

Title VII The centerpiece of antidiscrimination law. This section of the Civil Rights Act of 1964 applies to any private sector employer with 15 or more full-time employees, as well as unions, employment agencies, state and local governments, and most federal government employers. The law covers a comprehensive set of job-related transactions and is most known for its prohibition on discrimination in the workplace on the basis of an employee's race, color, national origin, gender or religion.

Tort A civil wrong where one party has acted, or in some cases failed to act, and that action or inaction causes a loss to be suffered by another party.

Tortfeasor One who commits a civil wrong against another resulting in injury to person or property.

Tortious conduct The wrongful action or inaction of a tortfeasor.

Toxic Substances Control Act (TSCA) A federal statute that gives the Environmental Protection Agency jurisdiction to control risks that may be posed by the manufacturing, processing, use, and disposal of chemical compounds.

Trade dress A product's distinctive design, packaging, color, or other appearance that makes it unique from other products or goods.

Trade libel A tort used to sue where a competitor has made a false statement that disparaged a competing product.

Trademark A word, symbol, or phrase used to identify a particular seller's products and distinguish them from other products.

Trial Stage of litigation occurring when the case cannot be settled, generally taking place in front of a judge as the finder of law and with a jury as a finder of fact.

Troubled Assets Relief Program (TARP) A program established by the American Recovery and Reinvestment Act of 2009 to purchase assets and equity from financial institutions to strengthen the U.S. financial sector.

Truth in Lending Act A part of the Consumer Protection Act that requires lenders to disclose to borrower applicants certain information about the loan or terms of credit and mandates uniform methods of computation and explanation of the terms of the loan or credit arrangements.

U.N. Convention on Contracts for the International Sale of Goods (UNCISG) A treaty that governs the international sales contracts among businesses located in U.N. member countries.

U.S. courts of appeal The intermediate appellate courts in the federal system frequently referred to as the *circuit courts of appeal,* consisting of thirteen courts, each of which reviews the decisions of federal district courts in the state or several states within its circuit.

U.S. district courts Serve the same primary trial function as state trial courts, but for issues involving federal matters.

U.S. Food and Drug Administration The federal agency that regulates the testing, manufacture, and distribution of foods, medications, and medical devices and requires the makers of certain food ingredients, additives, drugs, or medical devices to obtain formal FDA approval before selling the product to the general public.

U.S. Supreme Court The ultimate arbiter of federal law that reviews not only decisions of the federal courts but also reviews decisions of state courts that involve some issue of federal law.

Unconscionability A defense that may allow a party to potentially avoid a contract on the grounds that they suffered a grossly unfair burden that shocks the objective conscience.

Undisclosed agency A type of agency relationship created where a third party is completely unaware that an agency relationship exists and believes that the agent is acting on her own behalf in entering a contract.

Undue influence A defense that gives legal relief to a party that was induced to enter into a contract through the improper pressure of a trusted relationship.

Unenforceable contract A contract that meets the elements required by law for an otherwise binding agreement, but is subject to a legal defense.

Unilateral contract A contract involving one promise, followed by one performance, which then triggers a second performance from the offeror.

Unilateral mistake When only one party had an erroneous belief about a basic assumption in the terms of an agreement.

Unilaterally altered A contract is unilaterally altered when one party changes a term of the offer or acceptance after the contract has been made and without the consent of the other party, who is then discharged from performing.

United Nations (U.N.) International organization created after World War II to facilitate common international concerns on defense, trade, protection of human rights, and other matters.

Unsecured Credit that is not collateralized.

Usurp In the context of the corporate opportunity doctrine, usurp is to seize a particular opportunity for oneself when the opportunity rightfully belongs to the corporation.

Utilitarian Model of moral philosophy stating that an action is ethically sound if it produces positive results for the most people.

Valid contract A contract that has the necessary elements and, thus, can be enforceable.

Validation disclosure A Fair Debt Collection Practices Act requirement that, when making initial contact with a debtor, a collection agency must make known certain rights of the debtor, including the fact that he has 30 days to dispute the debt.

Values management The prioritizing of moral values for an organization and ensuring behaviors are aligned with those values.

Venture capital Private equity funding provided by a group of professional investors for use in developing a business.

Venue A determination of the most appropriate court location for litigating a dispute.

Verdict The final decision of a jury in a case.

Vertical price-fixing When a seller attempts to control the resale price of a product at a lower level in the supply chain.

Vertical restraints Per se violations of the Sherman Act in which the restraining of trade involves agreements between noncompetitors acting in concert with another party on a different distributional level in the chain of commercial supply.

Vesting An ERISA guideline stipulating that employees are entitled to their benefits from various employer-contributed benefit plans, within a certain period of time, even if they no longer work for their employer.

Vicarious infringement A theory of copyright infringement resulting when there has been a direct infringement and a third-party facilitator is in a position to control the direct infringement and benefits financially from the infringement.

Vicarious liability Liability that a supervisory party (typically an employer) bears for the actionable conduct of a subordinate or associate (such as an employee).

Vienna Convention on the Law of Treaties Effective in 1980, one of the standards used by courts and other tribunals when interpreting treaty law.

Void contract A contract where the agreements have not been formed in conformance with the law from the outset of the agreement and, thus, cannot be enforced by either party.

Voidable contract A contract where one party may, at its option, either disaffirm the contract or enforce it.

Voidable transfers Certain transfers that are considered an unfair advantage of one creditor over another.

Voluntary bankruptcy petition A petition filed in the bankruptcy court by the debtor that includes the names of creditors; list of debts; and a list of the debtor's assets, income, and expenses.

Voting stock Shares in a corporation that entitle the shareholder to voting and proxy rights.

Warrant A court order authorizing an official to do something she would otherwise be prohibited from; the most common are warrants for arrest, search, or seizure.

Warranty A seller's (or lessor's) legally enforceable promise to a consumer concerning the quality and/or functionality of a product.

Whistle-blower An employee or agent who reports some legal misconduct or statutory violation of their employer to the authorities.

Willful conduct Intentional behavior directed by the "will" but not necessarily with intent to harm.

Winding up Period after dissolution where debts of the partnership are paid and remaining assets are liquidated/distributed.

Withdrawal Term used by RULPA to describe the act of separation of one partner from the partnership.

Worker Adjustment and Retraining Notification Act (WARN Act) A federal law enacted in 1989 to protect employees by requiring most employers with 100 or more employees to provide at least a 60-day written notification of facility closings and mass layoffs of employees.

Workers' compensation Statutes that provide an employee, injured in the course of employment, with a partial payment funded through employer-paid insurance policies, in exchange for mandatory relinquishment of the employee's right to sue his or her employer for the tort of negligence.

Workout The process of a debtor meeting a loan commitment by satisfying altered repayment terms to turn around a business when the principles wish to continue operations of a business that is under performing and in poor financial condition.

Writ of certiorari A discretionary order issued by the Supreme Court (and federal appellate courts) granting a request to argue an appeal. A party filing for an appeal must file a petition for a writ of certiorari.

Written express warranty A warranty whose terms are put into writing for the consumer.

***Zippo* standard** The legal framework used by trial courts in determining personal jurisdiction when one party is asserting minimum contacts based on a certain level of Internet activity by the defendant.

Chapter 22

© AP Photo/Kathy Willens, 560; © Stockbyte/Getty Images/DAL, 565; © Brand X Pictures/DAL, 570.

Chapter 23

© PhotoLink/Getty Images/DAL, 582; © AP Photo, 585; © AP Photo/Paul Sakuma, 593

Chapter 24

© AP Photo/Paul Sakuma, 605; © Paul J. Richards/AFP/Getty Images, 609; © AP Photo/U.S. National Archives Records Administration, 620.

Chapter 25

© AP Photo/Peter Dejong, 634; © 2007 Getty Images, Inc./DAL, 641; © KEYSTONE/Fabrice Coffrini, 644.

Business Law Simulation Exercise 3

© Doug Berry/Corbis/DAL, 651.

Capstone Case Study 1

© Jeff Greenberg/Alamy, 657.

Capstone Case Study 2

© Tim Boyle/Getty Images, 659.

Page numbers followed by n refer to notes.

Page numbers followed by n refer to notes.

subject index

Audio Home Recording Act, 616
Audit reforms (SOX Act), 424
Authority, in agency, 250–251

B

Bad faith, 607, 625
Bail, 563
Bailments, 581, 598
Ballot propositions, 34, 41
Bankruptcy
  alimony, 516
  automatic stay
    basic provisions, 510
    case summary, 520
    Chapter 7, 511
    definition, 518
  Bankruptcy Abuse Prevention and
    Consumer Protection Act
    (BAPCPA), 514–516
  case summaries
    automatic stay, 520
    nondischargeable debts, 520
    reorganization (Chapter 11), 521
    voidable transfers, 520
  Chapter 7: liquidation and
    discharge, 511–512
  Chapter 11: reorganization, 521
    basic provisions, 513–514
    case summary, 521
    definition, 518
  child support, 516
  contract performance, 168, 177
  cram down provision
    (Chapter 11), 514, 518
  credit counseling, 516
  debtor in possession
    (Chapter 11), 514, 518
  debtor's options, 511–514
  distribution and discharge
    (Chapter 7), 511–512
  estate, 510, 518
  fraudulent transfer, 510
  income, proof of, 516
  involuntary bankruptcy petition,
    511, 518
  liquidation and discharge
    (Chapter 7), 511–512
  means test, 516
  meeting of creditors
    (Chapter 7), 511–512
  nondischargeable debts
    (case summary), 520
  overview, 509
  preferential transfer, 510
  reorganization (Chapter 11)

basic provisions, 513–514
case summary, 521
definition, 518
repayment plan (Chapter 13), 514
strong-arm clause, 514, 518
trustee, 510, 518
voidable transfers
  basic provisions, 510
  case summary, 520
  definition, 518
voluntary bankruptcy petition,
  511, 518
Bankruptcy Abuse Prevention and
  Consumer Protection Act,
  514–516
Battle of the forms, 185, 201
Bench trials, 87, 97
Bender, H. H., 149n, 175n
Bentham, Jeremy, 105n
Berne Convention, 644–645, 646
"Beyond a reasonable doubt" standard,
  551, 573
Bilateral contracts, 126, 153
Bill of Rights
  background, 28–29
  business, implications for, 38–42
  definition, 47
  states, applicability to, 43
Bills, 9
Binding rulings, 53
Bipartisan Campaign Reform Act, 41
Black's Law Dictionary, 8, 22
Blue sky laws, 423, 430
Bonds, 410
Bonusgate scandal (AIG), 115–117
Boycotts, 294–295
Branches of government, 28
Breach of contract, 12, 168–170, 177
Breach of warranty, 91
Bribery, 561
Briefs, 53
British common law, 10–11
British Petroleum (BP), 472–473
Burden of proof (criminal law), 551, 573
Business and law
  best management practices, 5
  Bill of Rights, 38–42
  congressional powers, 29
  counsel's role, 7
  criminal law, 553–554, 576
  dispute resolution, 78
  environmental law, 464
  intentional torts, 209–217
  jurisdiction, 59
  laws that impact business, 15
  legal decisions by managers, 19–20

model laws, 16
overview, 5
stare decisis, 14–15
strategic planning, 6–7
Business Corporation Law, 380, 400
Business entities
  business trusts, 374, 375
  choice of, 340–341
  criminal law, 553–554, 576
  franchises; *see* Franchise
  joint ventures, 343, 355
  limited liability company;
    see Limited liability
    company (LLC)
  limited liability partnership;
    see Limited liability
    partnership (LLP)
  partnerships; *see* Partnerships
  sole proprietorships, 341–342, 355
  summary of types, 340–341
  trusts, 488
Business judgment rule
  case summary, 403
  definition, 382, 400
  duty of care, 394–395
Business lawyers, 7
Business records, production of,
  568–569

C

Calamari, J. D., 149n
CAN-SPAM Act, 527
Capacity, in contracts, 144–145, 153
Care, duty of
  agency law, 257–258, 269
  corporations, 392–395, 400–401
Case law, SUR system for
  understanding, 665–668
Case precedents.; *see* Precedents
Causey, Rick, 112
Celler-Kefauver Antimerger Act, 498
Certiorari, writ of, 56
Child labor laws, 279–280
Child Online Protection Act, 572
Child Protection and Toy Safety
  Act, 534
Child support (bankruptcy), 516
Christie's International, 491
Circuit courts of appeal, 54–55
Citations, 10, 22
Civil law, 11, 18, 22
Civil litigation
  admission, requests for, 85, 97
  answer, 81, 96
  appeals, 88